THE
OLYMPICS
FACTBOOK

THE
OLYMPICS FACTBOOK

A SPECTATOR'S GUIDE TO THE WINTER AND SUMMER GAMES

Martin Connors   **Diane L. Dupuis**   **Brad Morgan**

WITHDRAWN

VISIBLE™
I N K
PRESS

DETROIT   CHICAGO   WASHINGTON D.C.   LONDON

The Olympics Factbook

Published by Visible Ink Press™
a division of Gale Research Inc.
835 Penobscot Building
Detroit, MI 48226-4094

Visible Ink Press is a trademark of Gale Research Inc.

ISBN 0-8301-9417-0

Art Director: Arthur Chartow
Design Supervisor: Cynthia Baldwin
Interior Design: Mary Krzewinski
Cover Design: Pangborn Design, Ltd.

CONTENTS

WINTER GAMES

A Lifetime Ago:
1980's Team USA
105

LUGE

SKIING—ALPINE

Alberto Tomba
121

Marc Giardelli
122
Vreni Schneider
124
Petra Kronberger
125
Anton "Toni" Sailor
128
Jean-Claude Killy
130
Franz Klammer
131
Ingemar Stenmark
132
Phil and Steve Mahre
133
Pirmin Zurbriggen
134
Hanni Wenzel
138
First U.S. Medalists
129 & 137

SKIING—FREESTYLE

SKIING—NORDIC CROSS-COUNTRY

SKIING—NORDIC SKI JUMPING AND NORDIC COMBINED

SPEEDSKATING

SUMMER GAMES

On the Road to Barcelona
George Cantor
183

DIVING

China's Diving Team
266
Greg Louganis
269
*The Diving
McCormicks*
272

EQUESTRIAN

FENCING

FIELD HOCKEY

GYMNASTICS

*Tracking the 1984
USA Men's Team*
331
*Olga, Nadia, and
Mary Lou*
341

JUDO

MODERN PENTATHLON

ROWING

SHOOTING

SOCCER

SWIMMING

SYNCHRONIZED SWIMMING

TABLE TENNIS

TEAM HANDBALL

TENNIS

Steffi Graf
470

TRACK AND FIELD (ATHLETICS)—JUMPING

VOLLEYBALL

Karch Kiraly
562

WATER POLO

Terry Schroeder
569

WEIGHTLIFTING

WRESTLING

John Smith
587

Dennis Conner
609

INTRODUCTION

E very four years (and after 1992, every two), the Olympics capture our attention like no other sporting event. Front page of the news, splashy magazine covers, prime-time television. It's an international festival, celebrating a gathering of the finest athletes from around the world. Thousands compete in some forty sports and more than three hundred separate events, a smorgasbord of athletic delight for both the ardent and casual spectator. Three hundred hours of television cast today's version of the modern Games as a televiewer's paradise, providing high drama, tragedy, and glory at the touch of your basic remote control. More than four weeks—morning, noon, and night—of televised Olympic spectacle await.

fact: Also-rans outnumber medalists by a ratio of 17 to 1.

Thousands of amateur athletes with names unfamiliar are competing in sports you rarely see, their images captured by hundreds of zig-zagging broadcast and cable network cameras. The Olympics are the candy store of sports, with something for everyone's taste and aisle after aisle of impulse items. Yet where do you turn for information on *hopefuls in the luge competition?* Rules for badminton? *Synchronized swimming roots?* Winner of the long jump in 1952? *Scoring a ski jump?* Where do you turn for the facts?

The *Olympics Factbook* is designed to be your companion to the Games, counterpointing the commentary, fleshing out the images on the television screen, guiding you to points past and present on the Olympic map. The background information will help you fully enjoy individual events, providing context and detail. We call it a *Spectator's Guide* because it truly is; the *Factbook* is designed to answer questions you may have as you watch the Olympics on television or on-site in Albertville and Barcelona.

xix

fact: IOC rules forbid the host city from staging any
sporting events not officially authorized for the Games.

The *Factbook* is *the* convenient reference source on rules and
procedures, history and highlights, hopefuls and legends. Traditional
Olympic sports are covered, as are the many new and relatively new events,
such as badminton, baseball, women's judo, and freestyle skiing.

Finding Your Way Through the Factbook

The *Factbook* presents information in three parts: **Opening Ceremonies,
Winter Games,** and **Summer Games.** **Opening Ceremonies** is, as you
might guess, concerned with the preliminaries. It begins with an insightful
examination of what draws us to the Olympics, written by award-winning
journalist Roger Rosenblatt, editor-at-large for *LIFE Magazine* and formerly a
senior writer and essayist with *TIME.* Next, **Opening Ceremonies** presents
a chronology of the Olympics ranging from the Games of ancient Greece to
the Games of Albertville, Barcelona, and beyond. The man behind the
Olympics, International Olympics Committee President Juan Antonio
Samaranch, is profiled here. Then *New York Times* sports reporter Joe
Lapointe takes an in-depth look at the relationship between television and the
Olympics. The CBS and NBC television schedules follow.

The **Winter Games** and **Summer Games** sections are organized
alphabetically by sport and are identical in format. Each sport section
includes:

➤ The **Warm-Up:** How and where did the sport begin, and who invented
it? Many of the sports on the Olympic program trace their origins to
ancient civilizations flourishing thousands of years ago. Some started
with surrogate clubs and rocks (tennis, hockey); others developed as
means of defense (archery, fencing, shooting); and then there are the
basic transportation modes: running, jumping, swimming, horseback
riding, skating, skiing, boating. We'll tell you about those very first
games, who played them, and how the games came to be played the
way they are today.

➤ **Spectators' Guide:** How do you play the game? How do you win? The
Olympics feature many sports the average fan may not follow on a
regular basis (luge, for instance), including some with very unique
scoring procedures. The scoring for several events—boxing,
gymnastics, and figure skating among them—approaches a sort of
mystical mathematics. The **Spectators' Guide** clears up the confusion
fast, enabling you to grasp the essentials and get on with the most
enjoyable part of Olympic viewing—watching the athletes perform. Our

overview of the important rules, procedures, equipment, terminology, and technical demands of each sport enables you to better appreciate the spectacle at hand, and more accurately predict the medal winners.

➤ **Hopefuls**: For each event, who has the best chance of bringing home a medal? Based on pre-Olympic competitions held worldwide, our preview supplies the names of the favorites.

➤ **Schedule**: In which we answer the question, "When do they play?" The **Schedule** lists a full event calendar for each sport.

➤ **Highlights**: The Olympics have always invited a walk through history. Every time a medalist takes the stand, he or she is compared to the greats of past Olympics. From 1896 to the present, the **Highlights** trip back through the history of the event, relating notable wins, ignoble defeats, famous victors, favorite losers.

➤ **Medalists**: Who's won the event in the past, and by what margin? We provide a complete list of all gold, silver, and bronze winners, along with sponsoring country, winning times, and point totals or other scoring data.

Sprinkled throughout the regular features on these pages you'll find the odd fact, the tantalizing tidbit of lore that makes you want to accost your friends and co-workers with, "Did you know ..." You'll recognize these time-out morsels because they announce themselves like this:

fact: At the alternative Games held in boycotting Eastern bloc countries in 1984, more than 20 athletes posted better marks than those in the Los Angeles Olympics, and at least seven set new world records.

And like this:

fact: A large proportion of China's winter sports stars come from Manchuria.

They're part of the fun of appreciating the Games in a broader context, with a perspective on all the momentous and trivial threads woven into the fabric of the Olympic flag.

And finally, the *Olympic Factbook* is about people.

The *Factbook* reports on dozens of past, present, and future Olympic stars, from American swimmer (and Tarzan) Johnny Weismuller to German ice skating queen Katarina Witt to Soviet high jumper Sergei Bubka. The *Factbook* also answers numerous "whatever happened to" questions, including:

➤ Stars of the 1980 gold-medal hockey team

➤ Legendary speedskater Eric Heiden and sister Beth

➤ The teen gymnasts who changed the sport—Olga Korbut, Nadia Comaneci, and Mary Lou Retton.

As you treat yourself to Olympics action with this *Factbook* in hand, you may read while you watch, watch while you read, or read, then watch (or just watch—and look it up later). No matter what your personal style, you'll have scored a perfectly enriching Olympic experience, and possibly set a record for amateur sports enjoyment.

You can look it up.

Acknowledgments

Our thanks to:

Mike Boyd, for his tireless typesetting efforts; Christa Brelin, for jumping on board and lending an energetic, professional hand; Mary Krzewinski, for peerless design; the crew of Micki Nowinski, Mary Beth Trimper, Dorothy Maki, and Evi Seoud for their production expertise; Zander Hollander and Associated Features for lending advice and material; Beth Dempsey for making vital contacts; Keith Reed for his efforts in securing photographs; Sandra Davis for text permissions; Jeanne Gough for her permissions overview; Michael Harris for his legal expertise; Jody Delavern, Kelly Krust, Gary Iott, and MaryAlice Rattenbury for vital logistical support; Amy Lucas and Kathi Gruber for their help in coordinating the project; Lucy Schoener for her flexibility; Dedria Bryfonski, Rod Gauvin, and Barbara Eschner for pushing the pedal to the metal; Keith Lassner for the hat and the glasses; and to all the contributors, for writing well and meeting their deadlines.

We would also like to thank the following organizations and, in particular, their media and communications people, for so cordially accommodating our pursuit of the facts:

United States Olympic Committee

National Archery Association of the United States

The Athletics Congress of the United States

United States Badminton Association

United States Baseball Federation
USA Basketball
United States Bobsled and Skeleton
  Federation
USA Amateur Boxing Federation
United States Canoe and Kayak
  Team
United States Cycling Federation
United States Diving
American Horse Shows Association
United States Equestrian Team
United States Fencing Association
Field Hockey Association of America
United States Field Hockey
  Association
United States Figure Skating
  Association
United States Gymnastics Federation
Amateur Hockey Association of the
  United States
United States Luge Association
United States Modern Pentathlon
  Association
United States Rowing Association
National Rifle Association
United States Ski Association
United States Soccer Federation
United States International
  Speedskating Association
United States Swimming
United States Synchronized
  Swimming
United States Table Tennis
  Association
United States Team Handball
  Federation
United States Tennis Association
United States Volleyball Association
United States Water Polo
United States Weightlifting
  Federation
USA Wrestling
United States Yacht Racing Union
Olson Travelworld, Ltd.

CONTRIBUTORS

David Bianco: Currently a freelance writer, Dave is author of several books on pop music, including *Heatwave: The Motown Fact Book.*

George Cantor: One of the deans of Detroit sports writing (yet, he hastens to add, a man still in his prime), George Cantor is a *Detroit News* sports columnist and host of a syndicated radio show. George began his career with the *Detroit Free Press* in 1963, where he worked the baseball beat and served as travel editor. Prior to assuming the sports columnist position at the *News*, he wrote a daily features column for that paper. Cantor is the author of *Historic Black Landmarks: A Traveler's Guide, The Great Lakes Guidebook,* and *Where the Old Roads Go.*

Steven Carey: Steve is a freelance designer and writer with an avid interest in boats with paddles, boats with oars, and boats with sails. He claims to be inspired by Phil Bolger (who designs and writes about boats) and composed most of the boating pieces while at anchor.

David Collins: Dave is a freelance writer whose work has appeared in numerous reference works and on the sports page of the *Ann Arbor News*. He's occupied the rarified airtime of public radio with sports commentaries and professes to be interested in any type of competition, particularly if it involves winning and losing. Dave quarterbacks his currently undefeated (and untied) touch football team.

Kay Courneya: The *Factbook's* equestrian correspondent has been riding horses for more than 18 years (though not continuously). Kay and her two horses compete throughout the Midwest at hunter/jumper shows and in training-level dressage. In her spare time she holds down a full-time job in the marketing department of a major Detroit publisher.

Harvey Dickson: Harvey has been a reporter for the *Boston Herald* since 1986. He's covered the opening of the Berlin Wall, the reunification of Germany, and the Persian Gulf War, but admits that working on the *Factbook* is probably the highlight of his career. Prior to covering the world for the *Herald*, Harvey worked for newspapers in Florida and Michigan.

Paul Green: A former sports reporter with the *Bennington* (Vermont) *Eagle*, the *San Antonio* (Texas) *Herald Tribune*, and the *Yuma* (Arizona) *Times-Summit*, Paul is now a freelance writer working out of Dayton, Ohio. Throughout his career, Paul has maintained an enthusiastic interest in fencing. He was a standout on his college team, although a freak accident with a sabre cut short (literally) his competitive career, forcing him into journalism.

Eric Kinkopf: Eric is a former sports writer for the *Detroit Free Press* and, most recently, a sports columnist for the *St. Paul* (Minnesota) *Pioneer Press*. In 1990, Eric took first place in the Minnesota AP competition for human interest reporting and was nominated by the *Pioneer Press* for the Pulitzer Prize in feature writing (in 1986, he was nominated for a Pulitzer by the *Free Press*). A resident of Shaker Heights, Ohio, Eric currently makes his living as a freelance writer.

Mark Kram: Currently sports feature writer at the *Philadelphia Daily News*, Mark has written pieces that have appeared in the *Sporting News* as well as in the 1988, 1989, and 1990 *SN* anthologies, *Best Sports Stories*. From 1983 to 1987, he wrote sports features for the *Detroit Free Press*.

Joe Lapointe: Joe is a sports reporter for *The New York Times*. Prior to joining the *Times*, he was a long-time sportswriter for the *Detroit Free Press*, where he was known for his occasional essays on the foul state of obstructed view seats at Tiger Stadium. Joe started in the journalism biz at the *Chicago Sun-Times*.

Brian Lysaught: Brian is a veteran reporter, world traveler, and avid Olympics watcher who is currently working as a freelance writer. He lists Shane MacGowan as one of his major influences.

Marie MacNee: An avid cyclist and ski instructor, Marie is a freelance writer/editor/caterer. She has contributed to numerous publications, including *VideoHound's Golden Movie Retriever.*

Roger Rosenblatt: Roger writes a monthly column for *LIFE*, where he is editor-at-large. Prior to joining that magazine, he served as editor of *U.S. News & World Report*, senior writer and essayist for *TIME Magazine* (where he originally wrote the **Factbook** piece), columnist for *The Washington Post*, and literary editor of *The New Republic*. In 1992, Random House will publish a collection of his writings as well as his book on abortion in America.

Pat Schutte: The *Factbook* ski correspondent was born and raised in Rochester, Michigan and is currently employed as a sportswriter with the *Ann Arbor News*. Due to nagging knee injuries, Pat no longer skis, but has become an enthusiastic snowboarder, racing on the Midwest circuit for the K2 Corporation. In the off-season (which is frequent), Pat enjoys putt-putt golf, rope swings, and barbecue.

OPENING CEREMONIES

▼

Why We Watch These Games

▼

ROGER ROSENBLATT

ost of us now, even athletes awaiting their turn in the Olympic Village, experience the Olympics as a televised event. Billions of people all around this great trembling world lay down their washing and watch these Games. Why?

Does one watch the Olympics to see a spectacle of individuals? A festival of nerve? Perhaps something collective as well. *Something.*

They said boycotts would kill the Games, but no boycott has done real damage. They said commercialism would kill the Games. Hardly. Even war rarely gets in the way; it takes a World War to interrupt the flow. The Irelands even unite North and South for a moment to create a single team.

They matter, these Games: to Botswana's yachtsman, Belgium's cyclists, Lebanon's trapshooters, Argentina's single sculler, Holland's swimmers, the boxers from the Seychelles, Pakistan's and India's field hockey teams. Cheers for the Chadians. Hail to the Swazis. Where else would these people come together so eagerly? Not the UN.

Is this the center, then: An international Woodstock? "The Olympic flame is the only hope for brotherhood, understanding and dialogue," says Juan Antonio Samaranch, president of the International Olympic Committee. What else would he say? "The Olympics are the only times in the history of the world when so many nations come together in one spot in an association of friendship," says Charles Palmer, former president of the British Olympic Association. Vested interest. According to Kurthan Fisek, a professor of public management from the University of Ankara, "No single institution in the entire history of mankind has been able to equate itself with world peace as effectively and consistently." Let's not get carried away.

Yet not all of this is cant. A figure skater, gliding strong and solid on the ice, pushes off an edge of steel and flies twirling through the air, then lands and is suddenly transformed by a joyous smile that gains incandescence. When the music

3

stops, that smile illuminates even the far back rows of the arena, stretching all the way to us. Why are we pleased?

Heroes must be part of the answer. There are those like Carl Lewis who enter the Olympics with greatness already thrust upon them; one will test their performances against their reputations. Better still, sudden heroes always seem to emerge and establish themselves, often in sports one has dismissed as boring or has paid no attention to before. Olga Korbut and Nadia Comaneci created gymnastics for most Americans, not because Americans never heard of gymnastics, but because they had not seen the sport performed by virtuosos. A subtle surprise of the Olympics is how individuals can transform the events in which they participate. Boxing enrages you and disgusts you. Then Sugar Ray Leonard skips into the ring, and the sport is God and country.

Much of the appeal of the Olympics centers on individual heroes, yet heroism in the Games is lightweight; it bears none of the mythic armor of professional sports. With professional athletes, allegories develop with the records; Mantle was pain, Unitas skill, Ali poetry and power. The Olympic Games are too brief for spectators to construct a folklore. Personalities like Nadia float to the top for a few days, but only as they are attached to performances. The hero and the act are one. If an allegorical hero is to be found in the Games, it is youth in general. A time of life is held still. For two weeks nothing ages; at least that is the illusion. The Olympics make the illusion grand. All the world agrees to it.

Individuals compete with one another; that accounts for the Games' appeal as well. Some athletes claim to be oblivious of the competition, but the audience never is. One need not argue the merits of winning or playing the game. The fact is that the sight of someone winning is a pleasurable thing. A rarity of the times, it is clean and unambiguous. So is losing. In any Olympic event there is at least one athlete who does not expect to lose. Not *she*. She has never lost. Yet she will lose today. She will pit her enormous will against her battered body, and come in second, third or ninth. One looks for the shock on her face, beneath the fatigue or despair. The shock is everyone's.

Individuals also compete against themselves, and the selves are complicated. "More than an athlete, I'm a human being," said runner John Carlos, 1968's bronze medalist in the 200 meters. The image of Carlos that remains with most Olympic fans is on a podium in Mexico City, standing in the grainy evening light rigid as an exclamation point. The black-power salute; an antique of the '60s. In 1984 Carlos worked at the headquarters of the Los Angeles Olympic Organizing Committee. "I have emotions, needs, wants," he continued. "I got the whole shot." In every volleyball game, in every foot race one sees the whole shot: mind over matter, mind over mind. John Landy turns his head; Roger Bannister shoots by. On the field it often seems more than a struggle for victory; it seems a struggle for a place in the world, self-assertion through combat. Sometimes it looks sublime—in a dive off the 10-meter platform, on the parallel bars. Sometimes it looks dispassionately cruel. Either way the struggle wins the

4

affection of the crowd, which sees in the exercise of discipline a morality play not necessarily related to sports. Throats go dry merely because a fellow human being is doing all that is remotely possible.

Whatever else, these displays of individual worth are simply beautiful. In a way, the Games extend definitions of beauty. Why is synchronized swimming no more beautiful than the bulging grimace of a weightlifter? Art rarely pins these things down. Painters miss it. Writers do worse, with exceptions such as Mailer on boxing, Updike on golf, Hemingway on a bobsled run: "a bob shot past, all the crew moving in time, and as it rushed at express train speed for the first turn, the crew all cried 'Ga-a-a-a-r!' and the bob roared in an icy smother around the curve and dropped off down the glassy run below." The *ands* do it. Everything must keep moving. Housman celebrated an "athlete dying young" because the boy would never have to learn that eventually things slow down, grow old, stop.

The beauty is motion, and motion does not last. Most things ephemeral have limited appeal, but the heart of the Olympics is that things shine for a moment and no more. Did Dwight Stones really clear that bar at 7 ft 8 in? One saw it happen a second ago. One saw it again on instant replay. Yet the jump no longer exists, nor can it return. Billy Mills, who won the 10,000-meter run in Tokyo, said, "For one fleeting moment an athlete will know he or she is the best in the world. Then the moment is gone." Bill Russell, pro basketball's philosopher, likes the short-term nature of sports because it bespeaks a world of reasonable expectations. "Sports not only claims smaller bits of time," says Russell, "it also claims smaller bits of truth.... The only truth [sports] claims is the score." Since nothing lasts, pleasure relies on memory. It is not the feats that are preserved but the joy.

Beauty also seems inseparable from excellence. Often the Games provide more than excellence, since mere proficiency presumes existing standards of performance, and some athletes set wholly new standards. "I began to run slowly," Jesse Owens recalled. "Then faster, gaining speed with each step. My legs were moving at top speed now. I came closer and closer to the takeoff board with a pounding right foot. I felt my body rise in the air, and I scissors-kicked at the peak of it, flying 15, then 20, then 25 ft. through the air—straining closer and closer to the towel. And then I landed—past it!"

Reasons to do with individuals, reasons to do with nations. Every time a bloc of nations decides to boycott the Olympics, there is talk of holding a nationless Olympics, individuals competing as individuals alone. Such a plan is unlikely to work; people would identify athletes by nationality no matter what colors they wore. In fact, nationalism seems an attraction, not an impediment to the Games. People belong to nations as to families. The Baltic nations, breaking free of the USSR after decades, immediately explore the possibility of competing in the Olympics under their new/old flags. Things only sour when nationalism brings intentions outside sports. When the Soviets bloodied the Hungarians in a water-polo match in 1956, one was not witnessing nationalism but war.

So much importance is given to mere participation. Governments spend a great deal of money and effort for no purpose but showing up, for taking a place in a community of nations. Many African nations see the Games as a chance to become part of international sports. Carlos Giron, a diver from Mexico at the 1984 Games, views it wider: "You feel like a citizen of the world." Mohammed Abdel Meguid Mohyeldin, one-time secretary-general of the Egyptian Olympic Committee, believes that "participation shows you are interested in humanity, not merely sports."

Such interest creates not one spectacle but two: the spectacle of the Games and that of those watching them. If television cameras had a "reverse gear" that could be applied from country to country, one might see quite a show of Peruvians, Thais and Iowans privately gasping and clapping as they watch the action. Excessive communications are said to work against human feelings, but here the effect is the opposite. Not a show of world peace, perhaps, but something valuable, nonetheless, in a shared set of relatively benign emotions on so vast a scale.

Yet the feelings are not entirely formless, either. There are very few historical experiences that the world holds in common. The Olympic Games are one. "A tradition," says George Liveris, former president of the Greek Shooting Federation, and once an Olympic participant. "They are the longest lasting social activity that exists." Maybe that accounts for the remarkable success of the torch relays. On the roads, the cheers for the torchbearers come out sounding like old-fashioned patriotism, but the impulse seems to go both broader and deeper, to a connection with Greece, with the past, with everyone's past.

Perhaps this connection is tied to the dreams of peaceful coexistence that the Games seem to promote. "The ideological differences between the Greeks of Sparta and Athens were fully as profound as those between the Soviet Union and the United States [during the Cold War]," wrote historian and journalist I. F. Stone. "Nevertheless the Games provided the chief Pan Hellenic festival at which all Hellenic peoples came together under a kind of truce on war and politics." No sports fan, by his own admission, and no cockeyed optimist either, Stone nonetheless saw the early Games as "a symbol of badly needed unity among the peoples, just as the Olympic Games today could be a symbol of unity among all members of the human race." The question is what power such a symbol has, and how long its effects survive. It is easy to point to the 1,503-year hiatus between Emperor Theodosius' suspension and Baron De Coubertin's resuscitation of the Games and conclude that the world did not need them, but the world only painted itself into a deadly corner in the last half of this century. If, as Stone said, the Games really are a symbol of the "human fraternity," who these days would remove such a symbol?

Or is the appeal of the Games simpler than all this? What one has here, after all, are simple contests, simple consequences, the simple delight of observers at basic human activities. Remove the banners, the fencing, and the scene is pastoral. Someone jumps or throws a discus. Someone swims. People play ball.

Close out the noise, remove the fancy equipment, and one could feel that the Games show the world rediscovering itself in absolute serenity and innocence. Nothing is supposed to be innocent any more, of course, but it is hard to read corruption in the 400-meter freestyle.

Henry David Thoreau (second cousin three times removed) was the Olympic commissioner of track and field in 1984. Is track and field the center of the Olympics, Mr. Thoreau? Definitely. "Everyone can understand it."

His second cousin three times removed was all for things readily understood. "Simplify the problem of life, distinguish the necessary and the real. Probe the earth and see where your main roots run." The motto of the Games: CITIUS, ALTIUS, FORTIUS—faster, higher, stronger. Simplify the problem. Now workers are washing down an Olympic track. A light breeze swirls in the arena's vast cone. Suds fill the lanes where the kids will run.

When US track and field legend Al Oerter won his fourth gold medal in the discus at the 1968 Games, he was the first athlete to win four gold medals in four consecutive Olympiads.

WREATHS AND MEDALS: THREE THOUSAND YEARS IN FIFTEEN MINUTES

▼

The Ancient Games

T he Games begin as a tribute to the gods—believed to gift mortals with fleet-footedness and long-windedness—at various religious locations across Greece. Part of a circuit of sports festivals, the games at Olympia honor Zeus, taking place every four years, without interruption. Not that life outside the Games is without strife: the "call to the Games" enacts a "sacred truce" to protect Games-goers from assault for as long as three months.

Athletes, sworn to be freemen guilty of no crime or sacrilege, vow not to attempt to win by unfair means, a promise policed by purple-robed judges who submit to ten months' training. Only the chariot events—because of the expense of keeping horses—discriminate against poor competitors: the first winner on the Olympic rolls is a cook.

Were there a creed for the ancient Games, it might read, "The important thing in the Games is winning. The essential thing in life is conquering." Much of the value of physical training is considered to be preparation for warfare, and events such as the pentathlon test the mettle of warrior-athletes. Boxing and wrestling don't discriminate among weight classes, and the pankration—a pre-Hulk Hogan form of wrestling—condones kicking, strangling and arm-twisting. No biting or eye-gouging allowed.

Athletes compete nude from 720 BC on, and spectators express their approval—depending on where they're from—by snorting and smacking their lips. Only the early Games are straightforward paeans to the gods. By the 4th Century BC, the athletes (from the Greek word for "prize seeker") and their respective homelands are the primary recipients of Olympic kudos; and the Games don't prohibit professional athletes from competing.

Although a wreath of olive leaves is the Games' sole reward, city-states offer cash and gifts, free room and board, and various and sundry other perks to ease the burden of the athlete's life. Not to mention fame: poets and sculptors the

9

likes of Pindar and Praxiteles earnestly endeavor to transmute fifteen minutes of fame into eternity. But the Games themselves are not immortal: commercialism and corruption are ultimately faulted as the cause of their demise (why does this sound familiar?). That, and Emperor Theodosius's interdiction of pagan games.

A number of names of victors survive through history, but information about athletes' feats is less than reliable, at best (reports of a 50-foot long jump, even with the requisite hand weights, seem greatly exaggerated).

Between the Games

With the Games banned by imperial edict, the city of Olympus is soon—and soundly—looted. Olympus is further routed when Theodosius II orders the destruction of pagan temples—including those at Olympus—and, if that weren't enough, an earthquake rounds out the damage.

Richard Chandler first discovers the ruins in 1766; in 1820, the French government starts but soon abandons excavations, and the German government continues the project in 1876, discovering, after six years' labor, 50 structures and 130 statues.

Five-foot-three Baron de Coubertin, a Parisian sometime-fencer, is inspired by the Olympian discoveries. Enamored with the idea of the Games and convinced that physical culture and competition build moral fiber, Coubertin proposes a modern Olympics to a meeting of the Athletic Sports Union in Paris in 1892. Two years of indefatigable PR woos enough public support so that the 1894 International Athletic Congress approves an Olympics to be held in Athens in April of 1896. (The original stadium in Olympia is beyond repair.) The Olympic motto is created—"The important thing in the Games is not winning but taking part. The essential thing is not conquering but fighting well" (sound like an ad for running shoes?)—and misattributed to Coubertin. At any rate, though modeled after the ancient Games, the modern Games don't entirely—in theory—share the ethos of their predecessors.

1896

Athens

To Parisians' dismay—and Athenians' delight—the first Games are held in Athens, funded by a gift from architect Georgios Averoff and the sale of Olympic stamps and medals. 311 athletes from 13 countries compete in a stadium with room for 50,000 spectators, with the USS *San Francisco* anchored just offshore. Although Greek and American college athletes dominate the events, performances are mediocre and athletes benefit from next to no athletic organization. The new cinder track (based on the ancient design of two straightaways with two hairpin turns) has too much cinder and too little clay, making it a slow surface; 1896 records are soon broken.

- Expecting to train for twelve days before the Games, American athletes find they have to compete the day after their arrival: no one had taken into account the difference between the Greek and American calendars.

- Harvard student exchanges Ivy League for crown of laurels: refused a leave of absence from school, James Connolly hops, steps, and jumps to the first Olympic victory in 1500 years, as track and field events inaugurate the Modern Olympics.

- Greek shepherd Spiridon Louis runs 42km to victory on the course first run by the Greek courier Pheidippides from the battlefield of Marathon.

- Greek shooter Georgios Orphanidis is 1896's eldest medalist, at the ripe old age of 37; Hungarian swimmer Alfred Hajos, a mere 18-year-old, is the youngest.

1900

Paris

The 1900 Games—held in Coubertin's native Paris—are marked by studious insouciance: more athletes than spectators (fewer than 1000) attend the five-day carnival, thanks to the unfortunate coincidence of the Paris exposition. No cinder tracks or pits are provided for the track and field athletes, a grassy field is the venue for the field events, and surrounding trees catch the hammer and discus throwers' shots. Nonetheless, records are set in all track and field events—which isn't saying much after the 1896 performances—and Americans win 17 of 23 events (still without national uniforms). "Valuable artifacts," rather than wreaths or medals, are awarded to the Games winners.

- Archery becomes an official event—the original Games having been founded by well-known archer Hercules. Without standardized rules, the 1904, 1908, and 1920 Games feature various rounds and rules; archery goes on hiatus from 1924 until 1972.

- Marathon-winning bakery deliveryman Michel Theato (France) is accused of taking a shortcut to victory.

- Margaret Abbott scores US's first female Olympic championship in the nine-hole women's golf event.

- Alvin Kraenzlein sets a never-surpassed record of four indi-

11

vidual golds in track and field in a single Olympics, and introduces the leg-extended hurdling style.

• Live pigeon-shooting event makes its only Olympic appearance; after a Belgian sharpshooter slays 21 birds, the event is barred from future Games.

• Australia's Frederick Lane beats a circuitous path to the gold in the never-repeated swimming obstacle race.

• Cricket and croquet make their only Olympic appearance.

St. Louis

Originally slated for the Windy City; President Roosevelt sides with St. Louis to hold the Games in conjunction with the Louisiana Purchase exhibition. Upstaged again, the Games take a backseat to the St. Louis World's Fair: a Hungarian Olympic official describes the 1904 Games as "a fair where there are also sports." European participation is negligible—no athletes from England, France, or Sweden attend—and even Coubertin stays home. 84 of the medals go to the US, which represents 85 of the competitors.

• American George Sheldon's 10m platform dive victory is contested by the Germans, who argue that final entry should not be figured into the diver's score.

• George Poage, the first black to compete in the Games, hurdles to the bronze in the 400m event.

• American J. Scott Leary is declared the winner of the 50m freestyle after finishing one foot behind Hungarian Zoltan Halmay, who strokes to gold in the rematch.

• The US dominates the team title in the second and last appearance of golf at the Games. Reason for its omission: lack of general appeal.

• Roque, a form of croquet, enjoys its moment in the sun in its singular Olympic appearance. American Charles Jacobus hits gold.

• Two teams enter official lacrosse in 1904 and 1908; lacrosse reappears as a demo sport in 1928, 1932, and 1948.

Athens

Dismayed by the waning enthusiasm for the Games, Coubertin proposes a new four-year cycle to be held in Athens beginning in 1906. Record crowds attend and the first official Olympic teams participate in the second Games at Athens, but political strife causes officials to cancel further intercalated Games. The IOC does not recognize the 1906 results as official.

London

Forced to give up the Games for financial reasons, Rome sits out another 52 years before becoming an Olympic host city. Reassigned to London, the Games are held in newly constructed Shepherd's Bush stadium (68,000 capacity), complete with cycling and running tracks, soccer field, pool, and a platform for wrestling and gymnastics. Only entries by nations—rather than individuals—are permitted in competition lasting from April to October, with events in 21 sports. Run entirely by Brits, the 1908 Games are rife with conflicts: other nations protest the prejudicial British rules, the erstwhile redcoats and colonists are at each others' throats, the English attempt to prevent the Irish flag from flying, and the Russians attempt to ground the Finnish colors.

- The Olympic committee decides to award medals to the top three winners, and the first official report is compiled.

- Figure skating makes its first Olympic appearance, with four events. Swedish skater Ulrich Salchow claims the first title, lending his name to a much-performed jump.

- Forest Smithson protests Sunday competition by leaping, Bible in hand to high hurdles victory.

- The standard marathon distance is established when the 25-mile distance is revised to start the race at the royal nursery on Windsor Castle grounds. The 26-mile, 385-yard distance remains a worldwide standard.

- *Jeu de paume* enjoys official status in one Games, reappearing in 1928 as a demo sport, and rackets and motor boating appear in their one-and-only Games.

- John Taylor, the second black to compete in the Games, runs a 1600m relay to fame as a gold medalist.

Stockholm

The Games come of age in Stockholm, on the eve of World War I. Counted among the two or three best-ever Olympics, these Games initiate the modern age of Olympic competition. The Stockholm Organizing Committee prepares a comprehensive list of official events, officials are thoroughly trained, and modern paraphernalia—electric timing devices, a public address system, and photo finishes for track events—are introduced. A 22,000-spectator stadium and a new swimming pool are built, as is housing for athletes and officials; the 400m dash is run in lanes for the first time in the Games. Jim Thorpe, lauded by King Gustave as "the greatest living athlete," becomes the Games' first real individual star, although his victory is soon eclipsed.

- IOC issues rule limiting power of local organizing committees after Swedes refuse to hold boxing matches.

- Japan enters the Games for the first time, sending 14 athletes. Japanese athletes first enter the Winter Games in 1928.

- A West Point lieutenant—the only American to enter the Military Pentathlon—outscores much of his competition in four events, but drops to fifth overall with poor shooting scores. Thus ends George S. Patton's Olympic career.

- In a blazing 10 3/4 hours, South African Rudolph Lewis pedals to the medal in the Games' longest road race ever: the 320km event.

- University of Michigan sprinter Ralph Craig dashes to double victory in the 100m and 200m sprints, and returns 36 years later to compete in a yachting event.

- King Gustav proclaims Native American pentathlon and decathlon gold medalist Jim Thorpe the "greatest living athlete." Thorpe's medals are stripped and his name erased from the records in 1913 when the IOC discovers he had accepted a token sum for summer baseball. His medals are eventually reinstated.

Canceled

The ancient Games, held every four years for almost 1200 years during what ultimately developed into the Peloponnesian War, protected antagonistic participants with the "Truce of God," violators of which were severely penalized. The modern Games have no such truces; World War I cancels all performances.

1920

Antwerp

Eighteen months after the armistice is signed, the Games resume under a new flag—five interlocked colored rings on a white background—symbolizing the fraternity of nations. Austria, Germany, Hungary, and Turkey are not invited, but the number of participating countries nevertheless reaches a record high. Crowds, however, are at a near-record low, and performances suffer from the lack of preparation and impromptu nature of the Antwerp Games ... the inevitable result of the Games' eight-year hiatus.

- Brit Albert Hill double-golds in the 800m and 1500m ... a feat not repeated for 44 years.

- Hockey makes its first Olympic appearance.

- The States medal for the first time in fencing, in the third team foil.

- The US Olympic rugby team—the only rugby team in the US—trounces France in a surprise victory.

1924

WINTER
Chamonix
The First Winter Games

The International Sports Week—later dubbed the Winter Games—is at first not supported by the Scandinavian countries, whose Nordic Games are thought to be in conflict with the Winter Games. The Games nonetheless receive a go-ahead. Norway and Finland own the Chamonix Games, which include figure skating, ice hockey, bobsledding, speedskating, nordic skiing, and curling. The IOC—which also had opposed the introduction of Winter Games—approves the official addition of a winter cycle at the Congress of Prague in 1925, and Chamonix is retroactively given the title of the 1st Olympic Winter Games.

- Nordic skiing, speedskating, and bobsledding are added to the Games, which are dominated by Norway and Finland.

15

Alpine skiing is not yet part of the Games.

- Charles Jewtraw (US) speeds to the first gold of the Winter Games, out-muscling his speedskating competition despite lukewarm national sentiment for the sport.

- The golden era of American bobsledding continues from the 1920s through the 1940s;

US teams medal 14 times, including five golds, until the American bobsled hegemony ends in 1956.

- Two days before the closing ceremony, The International Ski Federation (FIS) is formed.

- Military patrol—the grandfather of the biathlon—is demonstrated for the first time, with repeat exhibitions in 1928, 1936, and 1948.

SUMMER
Paris

Convinced that practice makes perfect, Paris claims the thirtieth anniversary Games (after a successful lobbying attempt by Coubertin to transfer the Games from Amsterdam), this time taking care to overcome the ennui that marked the 1900 Games. The Colombes Stadium is enlarged to accommodate 60,000 rapt spectators, and record-breaking abounds in track and field—where runner Paavo Nurmi strains the limits of endurance—and in the pool, as soon-to-be-Tarzan Johnny Weismuller swims record-breaking laps. The Games are becoming more organized: the IOC prohibits host countries from adding events at will (could it have been the 1900 pigeon shoot?), Juries of Appeal are introduced, and all sports are organized by their international governing bodies. Germany, no bosom buddy to France, is still absent from the Games.

- America's Carl Osburn nails 11 medals in three Olympics: 1912–1924 ... more than any rifleman in the history of the Games.

- Finnish runner Paavo Nurmi finishes with the first five-gold performance in Games' history, winning the 1500m and 5000m within 1 1/2 hours of each other.

- DeHart Hubbard (US) long-jumps to fame as the first black to win an individual gold.

- Helen Wills, one of history's greatest female tennis players, adds two golds to her volley of victories. The US medals 15 times from 1896 until 1924, when the sport is sidelined from the Games until Seoul.

- Near riot follows another American upset rugby victory;

rugby is dismissed from the Games. (Only two countries competed in 1920, three in 1924.)

- Johnny Weismuller—a.k.a. Tarzan—makes a splash in Paris, claiming three golds in freestyle swimming and a bronze in water polo.

1928

WINTER
St. Moritz

Not for the last time, weather wreaks havoc on the Winter Games: two of the four bobsled runs and a speedskating event are canceled due to unseasonable weather. Norway continues its Winter Games hegemony, taking six golds, four silver, and five bronzes back to the land of the Midnight Sun. The definition of "amateur"—an issue at the Congress of Prague in 1925—continues to plague organizers.

- Comely Sonja Henie—the youngest member of the class of '28—wins her first gold for her "Dying Swan" routine, kicking off a new era in figure skating.

- Norway's Jacob Tullin-Thams proves he'd do anything to defend his ski jumping gold, crashing at the end of a 73m jump. Tullin-Thams's jump far exceeds jump course designers' expectations.

- Five-man bobsled teams make their first—and only—appearance. America's team bobs to victory, making the 16-year-old driver the youngest gold medalist at St. Moritz.

SUMMER
Amsterdam

Although unable to provide appropriate facilities for the Winter Games, the Dutch—after three unsuccessful applications—finally host the Summer Games. Record participation and superlative competition mark the Amsterdam Games, held in a newly built 40,000-spectator stadium. The Dutch Games introduce an easily read results board, a soon-to-be-standard 400m running track, and flocks of pigeons symbolizing peace. Germany, after a 16-year absence, returns to compete.

17

- The Olympic flame is introduced and continues to burn from start to finish of Games thereafter.

- The first Indian field hockey team to enter the Olympics captures the gold, a trend in the making.

- Algerian marathon winner Mohamed El Ouafi—although running for France—is the first of the great distance runners from Africa.

- Not without great consternation, women are allowed to compete in five track and field events. The 800m, held first in 1928; is subsequently omitted until 1964.

1932

WINTER
Lake Placid

Lake Placid hosts 17 gaming nations, despite a spate of warm weather. Along with snow brought over from Canada, a last-minute chill provides favorable conditions, although the four-man bobsled event is postponed until after the closing ceremony. New York State Governor Franklin D. Roosevelt opens the ceremony. First Lady Eleanor bobs down the sled run.

- 1920's golden pugilist Eddie Eagen medals on the 1932 bobsled team, the first summer-winter medalist of the Games.

- 52-year-old pairs skater Joseph Savage (US) slides into the geriatric hall of fame as the oldest contestant ever in the Winter Games.

- Blond bombshell Sonja Henie—once again the youngest competitor of the Games—charms her second figure skating gold at Lake Placid.

- Figure skating moves indoors, and women's speedskating is introduced as a demonstration sport. It must wait 28 years, though, to become official. Unaccustomed to mass,—or pack,—starts, the European speedskating men are decidedly disadvantaged under the American rules.

- A dozen seven-canine power sled teams pull dog sled racing—as a demo sport—into the public eye.

SUMMER
Los Angeles

Despite worldwide depression, the Los Angeles Olympic Committee—with nine years to prepare for the fun and Games—is well financed and organized. Transportation and room and board subsidies woo athletes from abroad, persuading them to overcome an apparent European phobia concerning the California climate. LA leaves a lasting mark on the Games: ring-inside referees for boxing bouts, tri-level winners' stands, and photo-finish paraphernalia debut in 1932, not to mention the first Olympic Village (albeit for men only). Crowds are sizeable, if not always manageable; announcer Bill Henry admonishes unruly American spectators, "Remember please, these people are our guests."

- 20-year-old Argentinean Juan Zabala is the youngest athlete ever to run away with the marathon gold.

- Mildred (Babe) Didriksen medals in high-jumping, hurdle-running, and javelin-tossing, the only athlete ever to medal in all three events. (Babe is said to have been miffed that she was allowed to enter only three events.)

- American track athletes Louise Stokes and Tydia Pickett are the first black women to compete in the Games.

- Two US teams bump shoulders in an exhibition game of American football.

1936

WINTER
Garmisch-Partenkirchen

Weather again troubles the Winter Games, this time due to blizzard conditions in southern Germany. A record 27 countries participate, while record crowds attend ... despite rumors of boycott in protest of the German government's racist policies. The Games are not the sole attraction: Adolf Hitler draws quite a crowd, swelling the daily population of Garmisch-Partenkirchen to nearly 75,000.

- Norwegian Birger Ruud successfully defends his ski jumping title—the first such Olympic success—and finds more gold on the slopes in the men's combined Alpine event.

- Europeans dominate the victory stand when speedskaters return to the continental style of racing against the clock.

- Thrice-gilded Sonja Henie

19

skates to her final gold as she pirouettes off to Sun Valley.

- Rudi Ball—one of two Jewish athletes recalled from France by Germany—laces up for the German ice hockey team.

- Puckish Brits surprise all with an ice hockey win ... though most of the team was born under the Maple Leaf.

SUMMER
Berlin

Not for the last time, the Games are highly politicized: the Olympic village is rife with swastikas and goose-stepping uniformed soldiers, and Hitler attends daily. Five thousand athletes from 53 countries compete in front of more than one million spectators in what the Nazi party intends as a paean to the blond'n blue Aryan superman. In the ranks, however, is American track athlete Jessie Owens, who the previous year had—over the course of 45 minutes—broken three world records and tied a fourth. Superman appears at the Games, but he doesn't have blond hair and he's not from Germany.

- The torch relay—to bring the Olympic flame from the Temple of Zeus—is run for the first time: 3000 runners trek over seven countries.

- Jesse Owens owns the 1936 Games, picking up four golds as he ties the 100m world record and sets records in the 200m dash, the broad (long) jump, and the 400m relay. Tuesday, August 4, is affectionately dubbed "Black Tuesday."

- Mathew (Mack) Robinson— Jackie Robinson's brother— earns silver in the 200m, three yards behind Owens.

- Germany's hopes for fencing gold are foiled when Helene Mayer—Germany's only Jewish competitor (and promised "Aryan" classification so she would return from America)— crosses swords with Hungarian Ilona Elek—also Jewish.

- The Games are televised for the first time, albeit on closed-circuit.

- Athletes paddle and shoot hoops for the first time at the Games: basketball and canoeing gain official status.

Canceled

Games scheduled for Sapporo and Tokyo are canceled when Japan invades China. Winter Games are rescheduled for Garmisch-Partenkirchen (the 1936 site), but are canceled upon Germany's invasion of Poland, less than five months before the Games' scheduled starting date. The summer Games, rescheduled for Helsinki, are canceled again when Finland is invaded by Soviet troops. The ancient "Truce of God" is again disregarded.

WINTER
St. Moritz

After much shuffling and voting, the IOC determines to hold the Games on neutral slopes, in Switzerland. Nearly 1000 athletes from 28 countries participate, while the Japanese and German teams are invited to stay home. Postwar woes dampen the public's enthusiasm, and poor weather cooperates not at all with the spirit of fair play. Debates over amateurism take on hockey-brawlish proportions, and Sunday competition is again hotly contested.

- Birger Ruud—now a concentration camp veteran—ends his ski-jumping career, at the age of 37, with a silver.

- American John Heaton slides to victory two times in two decades in the skeleton toboggan—an event held only when St. Moritz hosts the Games.

- Iconoclastic American figure skaters open judges eyes: Dick Button—the year's youngest champion—ices the competition in the men's division.

- Swedes prove themselves gluttons for punishment in 3500m winter pentathlon exhibition.

SUMMER
London

Housed in RAF and Army camps, athletes from a record 59 countries inhabit a post-war Olympic Village modeled—in form—after the Berlin Village of 1936.

Radio coverage makes itself heard for the second time at the Olympics: 250 broadcasters narrate the Games in 40 languages. Germany and Japan sit home again, but the IOC determines—with less-than-unanimous support—not to rescind their records.

• China sends its last team to the Summer Games ... until 1984.

• Communist nations participate in the Games for the first time; athletes defect in the Olympic venue, not for the last time.

• Holland's 30-year-old "Fanny" Blankers-Koen quadruples her gold in athletics, setting a women's record.

• At 17, London's youngest individual athletics golden boy, (and later-to-be-US Congress-

man) Bob Mathias dominates the decathlon.

• American fencer Janice Lee Romary enters her first Games on her way to compete in more Olympics than any woman in history. Her career ends in 1968, sans a single medal.

• Audrey (Mickey) Patterson finishes third in the 200m run, the first black woman to medal. Later in the Games, Alice Coachman high-jumps to an Olympic record, for the first gold awarded to a black woman.

1952

WINTER
Oslo

700,000 spectators attend the first—and only—Winter Games to be hosted by a Nordic country ... a slightly ironic circumstance since the preponderance of cold-weather medals are gathered by the high countries. Up to 150,000 ski-jump groupies line the slopes of Holmenkollen Hill, a record for an Olympic event—summer or winter. Germany and Japan are invited back into the Olympic fold, the Soviets demure, and the British sport black armbands out of respect for King George VI's funeral. The Oslo Games are touted as the best Winter Games to date.

• Dick Button sews up another gold, astonishing the judges with jumps in his figure skating routine.

• Norwegian Stein Eriksen—lat-

er the archetypal debonair Nordic ski instructor—mines the slopes for gold in the giant slalom.

• Silver-skiing Martin Stokken—

also from the host country—is one of the few athletes to compete in the Winter and Summer Games ... in the same year.

* Women kick and glide into their first Winter Olympics when women's nordic ski races are added to the program.

* Andrea Mead Lawrence shreds the competition in Oslo to become the first US skier in Olympic history to slide to two gold medals in Alpine events.

SUMMER
Helsinki

A state-of-the-art Olympic complex on the outskirts of Helsinki houses athletes from 69 countries: yet another attendance record-breaker. The Soviet Union enters its first Games, historically having sat them out because Lenin believed the Games to be decadent. A second Olympic Village, with high fences and low profile, is constructed for the Soviet bloc athletes.

* Nina Romaschkova captures the first Soviet gold, out-hurling her discus competition by 14 feet.

* Czech Emil Zatopek runs away with triple gold in the 5000m, 10,000m, and marathon. 60 minutes after Zatopek's 5000m finish, his wife Dana throws the javelin for gold.

* Barbara Jones runs on the winning US relay team. At 15 years of age, Jones is the youngest track and field gold medalist.

* Luxemburger Josy Barthel upsets the competition—and the band—finishing the 1500m first. No one had foreseen the need to provide the music for Luxembourg's national anthem. Maybe just hum something.

1956

WINTER
Cortina d'Ampezzo

For the first time, the Winter Games hit the silver screen. Sunshine melts snow imported to the spanking-new ski runs, causing practice runs to be canceled. A stadium built to hold 10,000 spectators—in a town of 6000 or so—showcases

23

the skating and hockey events. Crown Prince Olav, Prince Harald, and some 32,000 of the hoi polloi attend, and many of the teams from the 32 participating nations go on to Oslo for the World Championship Winter Games the following month.

- Soviets enter the Winter Games for the first time since 1908, sweeping the medals not for the last time.

- 47-year-old Italian Giacomo Conti bobsleds to victory and his place on the geriatric rolls, as the Winter Games' oldest gold medalist.

- Speedskaters set chilling records on the fastest Olympic ice ever—at an altitude of 1755m.

- Finns soar to victory with a new ski jump technique, shutting out erstwhile Norwegian champs in the first six events.

SUMMER
Melbourne

The 1956 Summer Games—the first to be held in the Southern hemisphere—run from November 22 to December 8, because seasons are reversed Down Under. The international scene is rife with bad karma: the Soviets invade Hungary and there's trouble with a capital "T" in the Suez. A number of no-shows protest Soviet acceptance, and Communist China sits home because Nationalist China participates. Nonetheless, 67 countries attend.

- American diver Pat McCormick double-dips for gold ... for the second time.

- Perennial contender Laszlo Papp punches out his third boxing victory for Hungary.

- Soviet water polo players pummel Hungarian competition, forcing Swedish referee to intervene in "boxing match under water."

- Al Oerter tosses the discus a record distance, earning his first of four golds.

- Amateur Aussie teams play exhibition game of Australian rules football.

WINTER
Squaw Valley

Following on the heels of the 1959 Pan-American Games in Chicago, the climate is right for the 1960 Winter Games. Except for the blizzard. The Disney-directed opening ceremonies start off in cartoon-catastrophe fashion: driving snow delays the festival, prop-laden trucks sit in traffic in some faraway place, the Master of Opening Ceremonies is called to stay an execution, and the Vice President (Richard Nixon) acts as his stand-in. Awarded to Squaw Valley over Innsbruck by a less-than-landslide IOC vote (32–30), the Olympics host 740 athletes from 30 nations who boldly go where no athlete has gone before. Thanks to landowner Alexander Cushing—and nearly $9 million in IOC funds—Squaw Valley is the first Winter Games venue to be constructed on demand ... in what had been a town of 300 inhabitants.

- Women's speedskating is made official ... at last.

- Metal Alpine skis debut at the Games, and no skier medals twice.

- East and West Germany compete as one. The national anthem? Beethoven's Ninth.

- Soviet speedskater Yevgeny Grishin stumbles and skids in the final stretch, but still manages the gold by one second.

- The underdog US ice hockey team cleans up on the ice, winning every one of its games; the final match between the US and the Soviets concludes with the 8500 spectators delivering a standing ovation.

- Squaw Valley becomes the first Olympic venue for gunsmoke on boards: the Biathlon is added to the Winter Games. Bobsledding is 86'd from the Games due to the prohibitive cost of erecting a bob run.

SUMMER
Rome

Planning for the Games since 1908, the Italians make an Olympic venue of something old and something new. Ancient ruins and brand-new stadia, not to mention an Olympic Village complete with banks and post office, entice 7000 athletes from 84 nations to compete in Rome. The temperature is scorching, the competition fervid: records fall daily, and standards are so high that previous Games medalists don't always qualify in the finals.

- Hungarian Aladar Gerevich medals in his sixth consecutive Games—taking his sixth gold in the team sabre—an Olympic record.

- Lance Larson (US) places second to Aussie John Devitt in the 100m in the pool ... even though timed as 1/10 second faster. Full electronic timing is used in subsequent Games.

- Wilma Rudolph basks in Roman gold for both the 100m and 200m dash, as well as the 400m relay.

- Cassius Clay stings the competition to earn gold in the Light Heavyweight category; later he claims to have thrown his gold medal off an Ohio River bridge; Later still, becomes The Geatest, Muhammad Ali.

- Denmark's cyclist Knut Jensen collapses and dies—not from sunstroke, but from a drug overdose.

- South Africa competes in its last Olympics until 1992; ten years later, the IOC bans South Africa because of its racial apartheid laws.

WINTER
Innsbruck

The Games come of computer age: microchips assist in the judging and timing of events. Having missed hosting the 1960 Games by the seat of their lederhosen, the Austrians are primed for the event. Over one million spectators attend, with a new record of 36 competing countries. The weather demurs to cooperate once again, and 3000 soldiers from the home country haul snow by the ton to the Olympic venue.

- The first Winter Games torch relay is run, and the luge is added to the program.

- India enters its first Winter Games.

- Soviet skaters Ludmila Belovsova and Oleg Protopopov introduce classical ballet to pairs skating.

- Italian bobsledder Eugenio Monti earns the Pierre de Coubertin Fair Play Trophy for supplying the replacement bolt that allows Brits to bob to victory.

SUMMER
Tokyo

The IOC awards the 1964 Summer Olympics to Tokyo—the world's largest city—in 1959. Five years and $2 billion later, Tokyo convinces skeptics that it has sufficiently recovered from the war to be a good host. The Summer of '64 is a runner-up in the best-ever Games contest, with a seventeen-story hotel, a new expressway for the occasion, and a precision-built Olympic Village. Originally slated to host the 1940 Olympics, Tokyo is the first Asian Games site: Emperor Hirohito opens the ceremonies, and a 19-year-old, born near Hiroshima the day the bomb dropped, carries the Olympic flame.

- Joe Frazier socks his way to Tokyo gold and heavyweight fame.

- Soon-to-be Dallas Cowboy Bob Hayes—the aureate 100m sprinter—spurs his team to the gold in the 400m relay.

- Italy's Klaus Dibiasi, a.k.a. *angelo biondo* (blond angel), takes a dive for silver in 1964 and later rips for gold in three more Games.

- Gargantuan Dutchman Anton Geesink floors Tokyo by taking the open class judo title.

- Ethiopian marathoner Abebe Bikila is the first man to defend the marathon title successfully; he wears shoes only for his second victory.

- Budo—Japanese wrestling, fencing, and archery—is demonstrated.

1968

WINTER
Grenoble

Charles de Gaulle opens the 1968 Winter Games, which, for the first time, recognize the East-West rift in Germany. A mere 70,000 spectators weather the snowy Games—whose organizers are criticized for lack of logistical acumen— while another 500 million watch a celluloid spectacle from the comfort of home. 200 athletes from 17 countries compete (Germany gets two this time), and no new sports are added to the program.

- Nineteen-year-old American figure skater Peggy Fleming shimmers in gold, while the women's speedskating silver splits three ways among US women.

- French heartthrob Jean-

Claude Killey storms the men's downhill competition, taking three golds.

• Italy's Eugenio Monti—the previous Games' good sport—gets his just desserts with the bobsled gold.

• Sex is tested at the Games: female competitors undergo sex tests for the first—and not the last—time.

SUMMER
Mexico City

The first Games to be held in Latin America bring the Olympics to a new high ... 7573 feet above sea level, to be exact (658 feet is the highest elevation to date). Reports of possible deaths turn out to be greatly exaggerated, although exhaustion is a problem among athletes who train low at sea-level. The political climate is again torrid: Czechoslovakia is fraught with turmoil, student riots in Mexico City are soundly squelched just before the Games' start, and the IOC's initial readmission of South Africa meets with the promise of boycott by some African nations (the IOC repents). A victory-stand photo opportunity turns controversial: two black-socked American track medalists raise gloved-and-clenched fists in support of Black Power, earning suspension and expulsion from the Olympic Village.

• Al Oerter throws his fourth consecutive discus gold, the only athlete to win the same track and field event four times running.

• Heavyweight pugilist George Foreman proves there's gold in them there gloves.

• Bob Beamon astonishes the world by soaring to a record-breaking 29 feet, 2 1/2 inches in the long jump, while teammate Dick Fosbury sets an Olympic record for the running high jump.

• Fosbury's flop is a winner: American athlete scores gold and revolutionizes high jump with unique "flop" style.

• The US dominates the Summer Games for the last time until 1984.

• Pelota Basque is demonstrated for the first time since 1924.

WINTER
Sapporo

The first Winter Games to be held in Asia (originally scheduled for 1940), the 1972 Winter Olympics become the Sapporo inquisition. The argument over the definition of amateurism reaches new heights in semantic gymnastics, and Austrian ski-god Karl Schranz is DQ'd for the indiscretion of openly endorsing a ski manufacturer. The paparazzi flock to the event in record droves, outnumbering the athletes two to one, and some 54,000 spectators attend the $55 million hoopla.

• Canada fuels the debate over professionalism, refusing to play hockey in protest of state-sponsored Eastern bloc teams.

• American Barbara Cochran gets the edge on her slalom competition by the closest-ever margin: 0.02 seconds, winning the first US Alpine gold in 20 years.

• Austrian Trixie Schuba figures for gold in spite of mediocre free skating performance. Scoring is soon revised to weight free skating more heavily than compulsories.

• Diane Holum muscles her way to a 1500m Olympic record and the first American gold in women's speedskating.

SUMMER
Munich

The television age officially arrives, as millions and millions of people—1000 million, to be precise—watch the opening ceremonies via satellite, a new record in Olympic voyeurism. One week before the Games start, the IOC rescinds its invitation to Rhodesia to prevent a boycott, and the Munich Games are beset by false starts and *faux pas*. Athletes now have 195 chances to medal, thanks to the addition of new sports and events, and the edge-cutting gutter design of the Munich pool sets the stage for piscine history. But, but . . . Black September, an Arab terrorist group, kills eleven Israeli athletes held captive in the Olympic Village. The Games are suspended the following morning for a memorial service, after which, with the approval of the Israelis, they reconvene.

• Pool shark Mark Spitz swims in gold—medals, that is, gold medals—setting an Olympic

29

record for the most medals at a single Games.

- Soviet gymnast Olga Korbut tumbles into the limelight to take the gold for the balance beam and combined team exercises.

- 400m freestyle winner Rick DeMont (US) is DQ'd for a positive drug test—because team officials failed to inform the IOC of his asthma treatment.

- Archery—now with standardized rules set by the FITA—reappears as an Olympic sport.

- Valery Borzov reels in the first Soviet golds in the 100m and 200m dash.

- Soviets score gold when a court-long pass nets the winning points in the final three seconds of a basketball face-off with the US. Twice the final three seconds are played, permitting the Soviets to capitalize on second chance.

- 36 competitors don boards in water skiing exhibition, while 11 countries go to the net in badminton demonstration.

1976

WINTER
Innsbruck

Athletes are again outnumbered almost two to one, this time not by the paparazzi but by the Austrian police. The Olympics are awarded to the Tyrolean venue in 1973 after the state of Colorado vetoes financing the Games in Denver; Innsbruck uses many of the facilities from the 1964 Olympics, constructing a new bob run for the 1976 Games. 1.5 million spectators attend, and 1040 athletes from 37 countries participate, while $4 million of television equipment telecasts the couch-potato version to millions of international viewers. Interviews, background vignettes, and expert commentary bring the Games to new heights of infotainment.

- 25 of the 1976 Olympians succumb to the flu ... a drug testing nightmare.

- Dorothy Hamill—singlehandedly changing the hairstyle of American girl-teens—pirouettes to the women's gold in figure skating.

- Champion cyclist Sheila Young thrice medals—in speedskating—to become the first American woman to medal three times in a single Games, and the only person to be a world sprint champion in cycling and skating in the same year.

- Smashing Olympic records at 102.828 km/h, Austrian skier Franz Klammer nails the men's downhill gold.

- Hanni Wenzel brings home Liechtenstein's first medal, a bronze in the women's slalom, while West German Rosi Mittermaier misses becoming history's first grand dame of all three alpine races by twelve-hundredths of a second.

- With a less-than-enthusiastic reception by the IOC, ice dancing takes its place in the Games.

SUMMER
Montréal

The Soviets and the States bid for the 1976 Summer Games, but, in a compromising decision, the IOC awards the Games to Montréal. A slight miscalculation underestimates the cost of financing the Games ... to the tune of $1090 million more than the initial $310 million estimate. Security continues to be a major concern: 16,000 military and police patrol the Games, not for free (but for $100 million). Taiwan refuses to participate because Canada won't recognize them as the Republic of China, and at the eleventh hour, 20 Third World nations boycott the Games in protest of New Zealand's participation (because their rugby team had been to South Africa).

- Edwin Moses hurdles to victory, winning the gold for 400m hurdles (and again in 1984).

- America KO's the competition with the best US boxing team in history, including Leo Randolph, Howard Davis, Sugar Ray Leonard, and the brothers Spinks. Middleweight Michael Spinks knocks the wind out of Soviet Rufat Riskiev's bid for the gold with a blow to the stomach.

- A record 18,000 spectators watch as Romanian gymnast Nadia Comaneci scores perfect 10s seven times.

- Cuban Alberto Juantorena, a.k.a. *El Caballo* (the horse), trots to the rare victory of double gold in the 400m and the 800m.

WINTER
Lake Placid

Following on the heels of mega-bucks media-blitz Winter Games, the Lake Placid Games are touted as "an Olympics in perspective"—that is, an event for the participants, not the entertainment seekers. But Lake Placid is entertainment, although not always intentionally, and the 1980 Winter Games are rife with gaffes and imbroglios of Olympic proportions. So much so that the New York State governor is forced, a week into the Games, to declare a limited state of emergency: the Adirondack hamlet is virtually frozen in state by a paralyzed bus system, leaving scores of spectators shivering out in the cold. Rebuilt from the 1932 Games, the Village becomes a post-Games, tundra-like penal institution.

- Soviet cross country ski racer Nikolai Zimyatov three times poles to gold (and again in 1984 in the 30km).

- Eric Heiden shuts out the speedskating competition—the first to take all five golds.

- Willie Davenport and Jeff Gadley (US), and Bob Wilson (Canada), all bobsledders, are—as far as records indicate—the Winter Games' first black athletes.

- The US hockey team does a zamboni on the 16-year Soviet winning streak en route to victory against the Finns.

- A work stoppage among bus drivers hired for the Games spawns an omnilingual outdoor cursing record.

- American skating pair Tai Babilonia and Randy Gardner—dubbed the "star-crossed lovers" by the press—figure to medal but are sidelined by injury.

SUMMER
Moscow

The Soviets—who had staged alternate games, a.k.a. "Workers Olympics," for the socialist world during Lenin's tenure—argue that their participation and performance in the Games since 1952 earns them the right to their turn as Olympic host. Refused for the previous Games, Moscow's approval in 1974 for the summer of 1980 is met with little disapproval. But the 1979 invasion of Afghanistan turns the tide, and the Games, again politicized, are boycotted by the United States and as many as 62 other non-communist countries, including Japan and the Federal Republic of Germany.

- Britain's Daley Thompson goes gold in "nine Mickey Mouse events and a 1500m"; he wins every decathlon he enters from 1977 to 1984.

- Swimmers from East Germany net 26 of the 35 women's swimming medals.

- Brit Allan Wells dashes the competition in the 100m in the closest finish in 28 years; countrymen Sebastian Coe and Steve Ovett confuse the crowds by winning each oth-er's events (the 1500m and 800m, respectively).

- Pentathlon silver medalist Olga Rukavishnikova finishes first in the last 800m, making her world record holder—for 0.4 seconds, the shortest tenure ever.

- Soviet gymnast Aleksandr Ditiatin earns a record eight golds and the first maximum score given to a male gymnast.

1984

WINTER
Sarajevo

At the Games' start, Yuri Andropov is dead, there is chaos in Beirut, and the Olympic venue is best known for having been the site of the assassination that led to World War I. Two years' work, with the assistance of the military, readies the Yugoslavian village with TV cables, new bobsled and luge runs, and ski lifts and trails. Succumbing to the perennial Winter Games' fear of snowlessness, the Sarajevans invest in enough Swiss snow-making equipment to cover the cross-country loop, but not the downhill race courses. The US arrives with no squad of greenhorns: the stars 'n stripes team includes seven current or recent world title holders. A record 49 countries participate in the first Winter Games to be held in Eastern Europe. Accused again of verbal backflips, the IOC disqualifies two skiers because of "professionalism."

- Dubbed "the GDR's Brooke Shields," Katarina Witt figure skates to gold by a narrow margin.

- All-American boy Scott Hamilton handily skates away with the men's gold, with Canadian Brian Orser following in his tracks to take silver.

- East German speed skater Karin Enke—a.k.a. "monster woman"—muscles her second gold, for the 1000m, in Olympic record time.

- Finn Marja-Liisa Hamalainen is 1984's first double gold medalist, winning the women's 5km and 10km cross-country ski races.

- Jayne Torvill and Christopher Dean's innovative Bolero routine points ice dancing in a new direction.

SUMMER
Los Angeles

A number of countries refuse to make the Olympian pilgrimage to the showbiz mecca of the western world. The Soviet Union and 16 sympathizers boycott the Games, as do two independent prefer-not-to's. Officially, the Soviets decline for reasons of "fear," while skeptics are more specific: fear of drug testing. Libya withdraws from the Games at the last minute when two Libyan journalists are refused entry to the US on suspicion of terrorism. Still and all, LA 1984 is the biggest bash in the history of the Games, with 7800 athletes from 140 nations. Northern and the Republic of Ireland compete as one, and the two Koreas consider—briefly—doing the same. Despite cries of medal inflation due to Soviet-et-al absenteeism, the 630 US athletes are hailed as the best American team in Olympic history. Many are first-crop beneficiaries of the 1978 Amateur Sports Act, which is responsible for an Olympic job program, the Olympic Training Center in Colorado Springs, and biomechanical technology improvements.

- Communist China enters its first Games, with 353 competitors. Japan and Australia send their biggest, most expensive teams ever.

- Carl Lewis strikes gold four times—in the 100m, 200m, long jump, and 4 x 100m relays—the first such haul since Jesse Owens'.

- Hard-luck American trackster Mary Decker, hoping to medal, tumbles to the agony of defeat.

- With no competition from the "Leningrad tomboy" Elena Shushunova, Mary Lou Retton's gymnastic pixiehood is unchallenged, earning her precious medals (gold, silver, and bronze), and Wheaties box fame.

- Greg Louganis dives for gold in both the platform and the springboard, becoming the first Olympian to win both since 1928.

- Cyclist Connie Carpenter-Phinney sprints to the gold in the first Olympic women's road race. Having speedskated in Sapporo in 1972, she's the only woman to have competed in both the Summer and Winter Games.

- 11 athletes are inducted into

the Olympic Hall of Shame for positive drug tests.

WINTER
Calgary

Weather again proves the perennial foe of the Winter Games: wind gusts up to 70 mph ruthlessly blow snow off the slopes, forcing the cancellation of numerous refrigerated sports events. And logistics are again the source of much grumbling, with the Alpine and Nordic events at some 90km distance from other venues. The commercial value of the Games reaches yet another summit: ABC pays $309 million for television rights, three times the Sarajevo tag.

- France's World Cup-less Franck Piccard underdogs the competition—who fall and fly off the icy downhill course—to pick up the gold for the men's super-G and bronze for the downhill.

- Italian Stallion Alberto Tomba—seasoned already with seven World Cup victories—finds gold in the gates, capturing the men's slalom and giant slalom titles.

- American speedskater Bonnie Blair takes back the world record from East German Christa Rothenburger—whose tenure lasted 2 months—crossing the 500m finish a skate's length ahead.

- US hopes for a men's speedskating medal are shattered when sprinter Dan Jansen—who receives the news of his sister's death during the Games—catches an edge and slides on hands-and-knees into the wall.

- Short-track speedskating—dubbed "kung fu war on ice"—debuts as an exhibition sport.

- The men's figure skating competition is christened "dueling Brians." American Brian Boitano—the "technical one"—goes gold, while Canadian Brian Orser silvers.

- American Debi Thomas' disappointing third-place finish allows Canadian figure skater Elizabeth Manley a surprise silver.

- Actress-aspiring Katarina Witt is the first to twice don the gold necklace in figure skating since Sonja Henie.

- The US hockey team, skating on thin ice, finishes seventh and is jeered by the IOC President.

35

- Three-time Soviet ice-dancing champions Natalie Bestemianova and Andrei Bukin— a.k.a. "B and B"—scored perfect 6s, despite whispers of "vulgarity."

SUMMER
Seoul

The 1988 why-do-you-think-they-call-it-dope Summer Games begin with the IOC president's claim that "doping equals death"; the list of banned substances now numbers in the hundreds. The lengthening list of suspected drug abusers is the talk of the town. Though scarred by the drug-test debacle, Seoul nevertheless stages a spectacular show, primarily using facilities already in place for the 1986 Asian Games. Threats of boycott precede the Games, but only North Korea—and their unfathomable ally Cuba—follow through on the threat; North Korea insists, without IOC support, that it has the right to host half of the Games. Fears of terrorism at the Games prove unjustified, but rah-rah Yankee nationalism sometimes strains the host country's hospitality. The number of medal events climbs to 237, to be dominated again by the Soviets, followed by East Germany and the US. Amateurism is again the talk of the town, and governments and Olympic committees promise for the first time—publicly, at least—to award cash prizes for medals.

- 1936's marathon winner, Japanese team member Sohn Kee Chung, carries the torch into the Olympic stadium ... this time under the aegis of his own country, South Korea.

- Aussie surfer-swimmer Duncan Armstrong—ranking 46th in the World at the Games' start—strongarms Biondi et al in the men's 200m freestyle.

- American Arlene Limas blocks South Korea's sweep of Taekwondo medals, winning the demonstration sport's welterweight title.

- Greg Louganis dives for gold again, becoming the first man to repeat double springboard and platform wins.

- Diminutive Janet Evans (US) performs swimmingly in the pool: three golds, one world record, and one Olympic record.

- Ben Johnson blazes past Carl Lewis et al to win the 100m; unfortunately, his victory is short-lived as he tests positive for steroids. He trades his gold medal for a place in the Hall of Shame. Besides Johnson, two other gold medalists, one silver, and one bronze are stripped of their wins.

- Daley Thompson's hopes of

thrice gold-medaling in the decathlon splinter as his pole-vault breaks in half, causing an old injury to flare.

• Tennis returns to the Games after a 64-year hiatus, while China and South Korea horde the gold when table tennis makes its first Olympic appearance.

1992 will be the last Games to be held in a single year; after the 1992 Games the Olympics will shift to a staggered two-year schedule to avoid the quadrennial down-time. Next Olympic stop is 1994 in Lillehammer, Norway, for the Winter Games. Adding women's fastpitch softball and women's modern pentathlon to the program, the 1996 Summer Games will be held in Atlanta, Georgia, USA, commemorating the 100th anniversary of the modern Games; some sort of joint ceremony with the Greek Olympic Committee is desired but not probable, since Greece lost out on hosting this Olympiad (so did Melbourne, Australia). The 1998 Winter Games—receiving bids from Salt Lake City, Utah; Oestersund, Sweden; Jaca, Spain; and Aosta, Italy—will be held in Nagano, Japan, a return of the Winter Games to Asia for the first time since 1972. The 2000 Summer Games' site will be decided in 1993, with Sidney, Australia, and Milan, Italy, putting in bids. The 2002 Winter Games' site will be chosen in 1995; Salt Lake City, which bid for the 1972, 1976, and 1998 Games, may bid again.

The debate over amateurism is far from settled, although the IOC is moving progressively toward a more "open" Olympics (never mind that the ancient Games made no distinction about professionalism).

Some radical global changes have been taking place since the 1988 Games, and the 1992 Games promise to be a departure from the past in a number of respects. South Africa, banned from international sports competitions since 1970 because of its refusal to abandon apartheid, has been returned to the fold by the IOC. In an effort to permit the country to catch up competitively, the IOC awarded South Africa $2 million for coaching, training, and scholarships. But three decades of competitive isolation have undoubtedly affected South Africa.

The two Germanies, now one, are also poised to become a big Olympic story. East Germany excels in swimming, track, figure skating, rowing, and diving; the West in skiing, tennis, soccer, and wrestling. Comparative data: In Seoul, the US won 94 medals, the Soviets 132, East Germany 102, and West Germany 40.

As the world turns, climax: The Eastern bloc countries are smack in the midst of an identity crisis—not to mention a profound financial crisis. The Soviet Union is no more, although a unified team is proposed for the Olympics. And how will future Soviet teams train and be supported in a society chasing democracy and capitalism? Tune in soon for the answers...

37

Juan Antonio Samaranch was elected president of the International Olympic Committee in 1980, and has been a member of the IOC since 1966, after serving a dozen years on the Spanish Olympic Committee.

Juan Antonio Samaranch

▼

B oycotts, bans, drugs, professionalism, commercialism. These are just some of the issues that face Juan Antonio Samaranch, president of the International Olympic Committee (IOC), the governing body of worldwide Olympic competition. Rather than dealing strictly with rules and record books, the IOC in recent years has found itself increasingly embroiled in political, sociological, and medical controversy. Yet through it all, Samaranch insists that "the Olympic movement has grown stronger" than ever.

Born July 17, 1920, in Barcelona, Spain, Samaranch was encouraged in his early interest in sports by his parents, Francisco and Juana. He inherited his father's upholstery business, and later tried his hand at banking, but it was his love of athletics that determined the course of his life. He became a member of the Spanish Olympic Committee in 1954 and was appointed to the IOC in 1966, serving as president of the Spanish Committee. In 1976, he became Spain's ambassador to the Soviet Union—the first the Spanish ambassador to that country since 1939. And in 1980, Samaranch was elected president of the IOC.

That was the year in which the United States led a boycott of the Moscow Olympics to protest the Soviet presence in Afghanistan. It was hoped that Samaranch, with his ties to Eastern Europe, could serve as a bridge between the two factions within the IOC. Although greatly respected by both sides, he was unable to prevent a subsequent Soviet boycott of the 1984 Los Angeles Olympics. Sadly, Samaranch stated, "As always, the athletes were the losers, just as they were when the U.S. and several other nations boycotted the Moscow games."

Another political issue that has plagued Samaranch is the banning of South Africa from participation in the Olympics because of its apartheid system of racial discrimination. With the relaxation of some of these policies by the South African government, the IOC voted in the summer of 1991 to reinstate that country for the 1992 Games in Barcelona. The decision has been a controversial one, which could result in further protests at the Games.

The use of performance-enhancing drugs, particularly anabolic steroids, by athletes is another ongoing problem for Samaranch and the IOC. Steroids— synthetic hormones that increase muscle size and density dramatically—are banned from all Olympic events and from most other amateur athletic competitions. In order to ensure compliance, the IOC has instituted regular, mandatory drug testing for Olympic athletes. In the 1988 Olympics it was determined that gold-medal winning Canadian sprinter Ben Johnson had used steroids, and the IOC immediately stripped him of his medal.

Other questions are under consideration: Should professional athletes be allowed to compete in the Games? If not, what is the definition of "amateur"? (Can an athlete take endorsement money and still be an amateur? What about accepting gifts? Free room and board while training?) And what about the commercial nature of the Games themselves? (Questions have been raised concerning profits from Olympic competitions.) These and many other challenges lie ahead for the IOC, and Samaranch will need to continue to employ his considerable diplomatic skills to ensure that the Games themselves remain the focus of international competition.

The Olympics on Television

▼

JOE LAPOINTE

he modern Olympic era began in 1896 in Greece, but the modern Olympic television era began in 1972, in what then was known as West Germany. The pivotal events of that summer didn't involve Americans, but their impact profoundly affected both television viewers in the United States and the broadcasting businesses that package sports programming.

The major moment involved sports just peripherally. Armed Palestinian terrorists captured and later executed 11 athletes representing Israel. TV cameras, at a safe distance and with long-range lenses, showed the activity from the outside looking in.

The hooded men, the weapons and the scurrying forces of law provided TV with what it craves and exploits well: strong images, blended with tension and action, leading to a dramatic conclusion—in this case, a tragic one.

Another memorable development that summer was the performance of Olga Korbut, a teenage gymnast from the Soviet Union who won medals and admirers with a display that was as effervescent as it was technically correct. Once again, TV got images, tension and action—this time with a happy ending.

But violent politics and heroic sports performances date back to Ancient Greece and before. What made all this different? Two things: instantaneous coverage of a news event and starmaking decided by TV producers.

Until this particular summer in Munich, the main entrees of the American sports menu existed much as they had for most of the 20th century. Defined by sports editors of big newspapers, they were baseball's World Series, boxing's major title fights, and the championships and bowl games of football's professional and college leagues. Everything else, including the Olympics, fell into line in lessening importance.

Even in what is known as "hard news," the television networks generally followed the agenda set by major papers. TV could provide better images, especially in fixed settings (including a man walking on the moon in 1969), but transportation and editing of film made the turnaround to air time less-than-instantaneous for day-to-day, breaking stories.

The Munich Olympics—and the ABC television network—brought into sharp focus the technical advancements that had been gradually evolving in both

41

sportscasting and newscasting in the previous decade. After Munich, Olympics on American TV would never be the same.

By 1972, satellite technology and videotape capabilities allowed networks to cover breaking, action-oriented news stories with greater speed and better apparent clarity than had previously been possible with print or TV.

During athletic competition, these satellites and tape machines allowed producers and directors to bend, shape, and mold the "story line" to fit the constraints of network programming schedules.

Of course the massacre of the athletes was out of TV's control, but its technical ability to show even fragments of the whole episode gave viewers a sense of the event they never could or would get from a printed page.

The Korbut phenomenon had more profound implications for sports reporting. Few American newspaper sports departments knew about her until that summer, but they sure had to catch up quickly because, suddenly, their readers knew as much about her as ABC had told them.

From then on, for sports events and sports personalities, TV would call the tune, especially during the Olympic Games. Driven by the Olympic model, sports in the United States have become a lucrative and expensive television commodity.

All of this isn't necessarily all good. Abuses of TV power have proliferated over the years. Television, because it "created" the Olympics in the modern sense of entertainment for the global village, distorts reality and doesn't always level with the viewer in reporting the news of an Olympic event.

The classic example came in February of 1980, when the United States hockey team upset the Soviet Union and went on to win the gold medal with a victory over Finland two days later in the Winter Games of Lake Placid.

Many Americans remember the game with the Soviet Union as one of the most thrilling moments in Olympic history: the tension, the action, the images. They recall the flags waving, the players skating, the fans chanting—"USA! USA!"—and, finally, the victory as the athletes dressed in red, white, and blue fell shouting and laughing into each others arms and rolled on the cold ice in celebration.

"Do you believe in miracles?" yelped Al Michaels, ABC's play-by-play announcer. "Yes!"

What many Americans didn't fully realize at that time was that the event had taken place several hours before. The game had started at 5 p.m., Eastern time. ABC wanted to show the game live, in prime time, at 8 p.m., and it lobbied with Olympic officials to change the starting time.

When the officials refused, ABC simply taped the game to show when it suited ABC, when the audience would be largest. Of course, ABC refused to report the result, which was known when it went on the air, until the end of the tape. Viewers in Canada and the Soviet Union saw the telecast live. In the U.S., where the host nation won its biggest victory, the home fans had to wait until the host network was good and ready to package it for them. Action, images, drama,

42

and tension, even false tension, created a growing audience that stuck with a program through prime time commercials.

Would any network have dared to treat the World Series or Super Bowl with such manipulation? Of course not. But the Olympics had become a different sort of American sport show, not exactly made *for* TV but made *by* TV. The trend toward manipulation continues, usually in subtle ways.

In 1984, when Carl Lewis of the United States tried for a fifth gold medal in the Summer Games of Los Angeles, his attempt in the long jump was scheduled for just before prime time in the East. Instead of showing it live, ABC taped it and held it for viewing just a few minutes later, after the start of prime time.

In 1988, when NBC carried the Summer Games from Seoul, South Korea, it wanted to show big events involving Americans on live TV in prime time. In order to do this, many events had to begin in the early morning, Korean time, to satisfy American TV. Even then, some that could have been shown live were taped and held to fit a schedule littered with commercials and unpredicted news developments.

All of this doesn't mean that TV never reports the Olympics as a news event or never reports the results as they happen. But, more so than with most major sports, TV molds the drama to suit the needs of TV.

When watching the Olympics on TV in 1992, it is best to ask the occasional question: Is this event taking place as we watch it? Do the announcers or the programmers behind the scenes already know who won and lost? Has its natural rhythm been edited to increase the dramatic tension?

What events have they chosen *not* to show? Which story angles are being stressed and which ones are being played down? What did we miss while the cameras were showing something else? And, how much of a network's "live" coverage of the Olympics is really a taped feature about a participant or merely a "live" conversation between anchor men and women at a desk in a studio?

The Games take on a new television dimension in 1992 with the Winter Games from Albertville, France, and the Summer Games from Barcelona, Spain.

As usual, one network will have exclusive rights to over-the-air coverage. CBS has the Winter Games and NBC the Summer Games.

What is different this year is the entry of cable companies. Growing since the late 1970s, cable is now ready to bite off a large slice of the Olympic pie. So much will still appear on the "free" TV of over-the-air networks that most viewers won't realize a major change. For the first time, however, some viewers will have to pay to see some of the events.

Winter Games: CBS and TNT

CBS will be carrying its first Olympics since covering both the Summer and Winter Games of 1960. In the Winter Games of Squaw Valley, California, in 1960, CBS broadcast 15 hours of coverage and was the first network to pay for the Olympic rights. The fee was $50,000. In 1992, CBS will telecast 116 hours over 17 days. Like the number of hours, the fee has escalated somewhat, to $243 million. CBS also paid $300 million for the 1994 Winter Olympics.

The amount of air time is greater than the previous high for a Winter Olympics set in 1988 when ABC carried 94.5 hours from Calgary. CBS says 52 of its hours in 1992 will be in prime time.

The new wrinkle for winter is the presence of the Turner Broadcasting System, which will provide supplemental coverage on its TNT channel. In most cable systems, TNT is part of what is called "basic service," which is included at the lowest tier of cable prices.

Turner is paying CBS $50 million to carry an estimated 50 hours of original cable broadcasting. Most of it will be seen on weekday afternoons from 1 p.m. until 6 p.m. Because of the six-hour time difference between France and the eastern United States, TNT cable will have access to major events that are taking place in the evening in France.

For instance: men's figure skating is scheduled for 7:30 p.m., French time, in France on Thursday, Feb. 13. If TNT chooses, it can carry the event live that afternoon.

Despite the scheduling break, viewers must depend on the whims of TNT producers, who will choose what viewers see and when they see it. When TNT covered the World Cup soccer tournament from Italy in the summer of 1990, it irked many viewers by cutting away to commercials and missing goals.

Among the CBS announcers will be Scott Hamilton, Tracy Wilson, Katarina Witt, and Verne Lundquist for figure skating, John Davidson, Mike Emrick, and Mike Eruzione for hockey, and Mary Carillo for skiing.

Anchoring the coverage as hosts from studio desks will be Tim McCarver and Paula Zahn for prime time; Andrea Joyce and Jim Nantz for weekend daytime; Greg Gumbel and Harry Smith for weekday mornings; James Brown for weekday midday and Pat O'Brien for the half-hour show at 11:30 p.m., Eastern time, each night.

The key person will be McCarver, a former baseball player who has spent most of his broadcasting career covering that sport.

His role will be similar to that of Jim McKay, who hosted ABC's Olympic coverage in the 1970s and 1980s, when that network used sports to move from a poor third place to a strong first.

The studio anchor holds the show together and narrates the "story line," making many unrelated events somehow seem like small, linked portions of a long, large tale. Others who have tried it, including Bryant Gumbel (Greg's brother) of NBC, have yet to match McKay's success. As a baseball announcer, McCarver tends to bombard the viewer with so much inside expertise that he can become tedious.

In relating stories about sports with which he is less familiar, will McCarver seem uninformed and lacking for telling details or will he bring fresh questions and insights to the ears of the viewers?

TNT will mix the CBS production with that of the host broadcaster that provides the "world feed." Some CBS announcers will appear on TNT, but TNT announcers such as Skip Caray and Ernie Johnson are likely to be assigned.

As of late 1991, TNT said it appeared in 55 million homes, about 60 percent of American homes with television.

Summer Games: NBC and Cablevision

NBC, which carried the Summer Games from Korea, is back again in 1992, having paid $401 million this time around.

Pulling out all the stops, NBC plans to show 161 hours of Olympic programming, including a weekday morning telecast from 7 a.m. to 10 a.m., a prime-time show each night from 7 p.m. to midnight, and a late-night show from 12:30 a.m. until 2 a.m.

The radical change in the Summer telecasts will be the introduction of pay-per-view cable television that will coincide with much of NBC's programming.

The pay channels are being offered by NBC Cable and the Cablevision Systems Corporation, which paid NBC $75 million for the rights. Each channel will show 12 hours of original programming, followed by 12 hours of replay. The cable packagers promise no commercial interruptions and no switching away from the event in progress.

Although the delivery system for this programming—pay-per-view—is relatively new to American television, such extensive programming is hardly revolutionary. In recent Olympiads, it has been the host broadcaster who provides a "world feed" that covers almost every minute of every competition. Broadcasters from other nations who have paid for the programming rights have had the right to pick and choose from any or all of the world feed.

In the Calgary Games of 1988, the world feed was available throughout the Olympic Villages and in the venues of competition on a system of closed-circuit television. Anyone with access to a monitor could flip the channels and watch all the events as they happened. In many European countries, where Olympic sports have more popularity in non-Olympic years than they do in the United States, such extensive Olympic television programming has long been available. It is usually just basic, raw material, uncluttered by commercials and story lines and nationalistic points of view.

Essentially what the cable packagers are doing for the American television audience in 1992 is taking this feed, dressing it up with a few of its own production touches, and marketing it for a large sum of money through pay-per-view subscriptions. On the surface, the idea seems brilliant.

Depending on how much they wish to watch, viewers can choose among *gold, silver,* and *bronze* packages with suggested retail prices of $95, $125, and $170, respectively. The channels will be called *red, white,* and *blue.* If three million homes buy some of the programming, Cablevision believes it will break even. As of late 1991, about 20 million homes were capable of receiving some kind of pay-per-view programming.

The pay-per-view package will be available on all three channels simultaneously, around the clock. Once again, for emphasis: The existence of such Olympic coverage has long been in place. It is the pay-per-view technology—and the fee—that is new. Promoters of major American sports—baseball, football, basketball, hockey—will be watching closely.

If people will pay a large sum for three weeks of Olympic programming that appears once every four years, how much will they play for a regular stream of games that occur every year in seasons that last from six to nine months? Occasional pay-per-view telecasts of big boxing events have been profitable. Many in the sports industry think pay-per-view is the cash cow of the 21st century. Olympic viewers will be among the first to decide.

As for NBC, its prime-time host will be Bob Costas, who, like McCarver, has a background strong in baseball. Dick Enberg and Katherine Couric will anchor the morning shows. Other Summer Games commentators include Kathleen Sullivan and John Tesh. Costas, also the host of the NBC's pre-game show for pro football, is versatile and inoffensive, with a glib tongue and an effective interviewing style.

NBC's weekday coverage will air for three hours in the morning, from 7 a.m. until 10 a.m; and in the evening, from 7:30 p.m. until midnight. A late-night show will air at 12:30 a.m. until 2 a.m. Weekend coverage will be more extensive.

After Barcelona, what about the future? How much will Olympics rights fees continue to rise? How much can the marketplace stand? To mix animal metaphors, will Olympic TV continue to be a cash cow or is a doomed goose laying golden (or silver and bronze) eggs? How much Olympic programming can Americans stand before they lose interest and begin again to wander the malls?

"The International Olympic Committee can no longer expect to extract every last dollar from the major American networks," wrote Jim Spence, the former senior vice-president of ABC Sports, in a 1988 article for *The New York Times*. "As the costs of television rights have risen dramatically, the total hours of broadcast have been increased, so that additional commercial units (are sold) at ever increasing prices (to) help the networks recover the costs."

The pattern, Spence argued, results in the dilution of the impact of the games. Recent bidding for the rights, he stressed, has included only one or two American networks.

"It is clearly not in the IOC's best interest for an American broadcaster to drop out of the Olympic television rights process," Spence wrote.

"The Olympics are the world's greatest sporting event, but, unless there is a realistic approach based on the United States marketplace, the IOC certainly is in danger of killing that goose that has laid those golden eggs, ironically, as the modern Olympic movement approaches its 100th anniversary in 1996."

For the ardent Olympic viewer, the Olympics on television can be a cornucopia of delights, as wave after wave of tense, live drama, sublime victory, and crushing defeat emit from the tube. The commonality and mass appeal of the Olympics focuses a large segment of the viewing public, providing plenty of ammunition around the office coffee machine the following morning. New stars are born, television stars, with athletic pedigrees. Soon afterward, they'll be endorsing running shoes and breakfast cereals, again on the telly. Their faces we'll know almost as well as our own.

And we owe it all to television's most astonishing live miniseries, The Olympics.

OLYMPICS TELEVISION SCHEDULE

CBS OLYMPICS BROADCAST SCHEDULE
Albertville, France
February 6-February 23, 1992
Note that all times are Eastern Standard

Thursday, February 6
8-10 p.m.—Olympic Preview

Saturday, February 8
4-6 p.m.
8-11 p.m.—Opening Ceremony
11:30 p.m.-12 midnight

Sunday, February 9
9 a.m.-12 noon
2-6 p.m.
8-11 p.m.
11:30 p.m.-12 midnight

Monday, February 10
7-9 a.m.
12:15-12:30 p.m.*
8-11 p.m.
11:30 p.m.-12 midnight

Tuesday, February 11
7-9 a.m.
12:15-12:30 p.m.*
8-11 p.m.
11:30 p.m.-12 midnight

Wednesday, February 12
7-9 a.m.
12:15-12:30 p.m.*
8-11 p.m.
11:30 p.m.-12 midnight

Friday, February 14
7-9 a.m.
12:15-12:30 p.m.*
8-11 p.m.
11:30 p.m.-12 midnight

Saturday, February 15
1-6 p.m.
7-11 p.m.
11:30 p.m.-12 midnight

Sunday, February 16
9 a.m.-12 noon
3:30 p.m.-6 p.m.
8-11 p.m.
11:30 p.m.-12 midnight

Monday, February 17
7-9 a.m.
12:15-12:30 p.m.*
8-11 p.m.
11:30 p.m.-12 midnight

Tuesday, February 18
7-9 a.m.
12:15-12:30 p.m.*
8-11 p.m.
11:30 p.m.-12 midnight

Wednesday, February 19
7-9 a.m.
12:15-12:30 p.m.*
8-11 p.m.

*Optional

49

11:30 p.m.-12 midnight

Thursday, February 20
7-9 a.m.
12:15-12:30 p.m.*
8-11 p.m.
11:30 p.m.-12 midnight

Friday, February 21
7-9 a.m.
12:15-12:30 p.m.*
8-11 p.m.

11:30 p.m.-12 midnight

Saturday, February 22
1-6 p.m.
7-11 p.m.
11:30 p.m.-12 midnight

Sunday, February 23
9 a.m.-12 noon—Hockey Gold
Medal Game
4:30-6 p.m.
8-11 p.m.—Closing Ceremony

NBC OLYMPICS BROADCAST SCHEDULE
Barcelona, Spain
July 24-August 9, 1992

Friday, July 24
9-11 p.m.—Olympic Preview

Saturday, July 25
8 p.m.-12 midnight—Opening
Ceremony

Sunday, July 26
12 noon-6 p.m.
7 p.m.-12 midnight
12:30-2 a.m.

Monday, July 27
7-10 a.m.
7:30 p.m.-12 midnight
12:30-2 a.m.

Tuesday, July 28
7-10 a.m.
7:30 p.m.-12 midnight
12:30-2 a.m.

Wednesday, July 29
7-10 a.m.
7:30 p.m.-12 midnight
12:30-2 a.m.

Thursday, July 30
7-10 a.m.
7:30 p.m.-12 midnight
12:30-2 a.m.

Friday, July 31
7-10 a.m.
7:30 p.m.-12 midnight
12:30-2 a.m.

Saturday, August 1
12 noon-6 p.m.
7:30 p.m.-12 midnight
12:30-2 a.m.

Sunday, August 2
8-11 a.m.
12 noon-6 p.m.
7 p.m.-12 midnight
12:30-2 a.m.

Monday, August 3
7-10 a.m.
7:30 p.m.-12 midnight
12:30-2 a.m.

Tuesday, August 4
7-10 a.m.
7:30 p.m.-12 midnight
12:30-2 a.m.

Wednesday, August 5
7-10 a.m.
7:30 p.m.-12 midnight
12:30-2 a.m.

Thursday, August 6
7-10 a.m.
7:30 p.m.-12 midnight
12:30-2 a.m.

Friday, August 7
7-10 a.m.
7:30 p.m.-12 midnight
12:30-2 a.m.

*Optional

50

Saturday, August 8
12 noon-6 p.m.
7:30 p.m.-12 midnight
12:30-2 a.m.

Sunday, August 9
8-11 a.m.
12 noon-6 p.m.
7-11 p.m.—Closing Ceremony

WINTER
GAMES

Cruising Albertville

▼

GEORGE CANTOR

When the International Olympics Committee announced that the 1992 Winter Games would be awarded to Albertville, France, the response was fairly standard around the world.

It was: "Huh?"

When it comes to name recognition among the top winter resorts, Albertville has almost none. Chamonix and Grenoble, the two previous French venues for the Winter Games, are immediately identifiable. But Albertville?

Well, France has a plan. This area is speckled with some of the best-known ski resorts in Europe—Courchevel, Val d'Isere, Meribel. None of them, however, has the size or the facilities to host the entire range of events and the massive crowds associated with the Olympics.

So the Games will be spread out over 10 of them, across 600 square miles of Alps, and be used as a vehicle for economic development in the province of Savoie.

Albertville is the rail station that serves these resorts. It is a major junction on the route of the TGV, the 185-mile-an-hour supertrain that makes the run from Paris' Gare de Lyon in about four hours. It is also the connecting point for trains from Geneva and Lyon.

So while it has none of the glamour or cachet of the famed resorts in the adjacent mountains, little Albertville, population 18,000, is being transformed by the Games into the transportation and communications hub for the entire area.

The opening and closing ceremonies will be held here, as well as the skating events. A new stadium, with a seating capacity exactly twice the size of the town's population, has been built, as well as two skating arenas, one for the speed events and another for figure skating and ice dancing.

Beyond Albertville, however, the Games will be entering unknown terrain. Never before has a Winter Olympics been spread out over such a wide area. Experienced travelers in this area say that even on clear days it can take up to three hours on mountain roads to drive from one end of it to the other. With the sort of bus and car traffic the Olympics will draw, they fear the time may easily double.

Nonsense, say the organizers. The logistics are under control. Sophisticated traffic management, the incredible system of inter-connecting lifts that run among the ski villages and the fact that many of the athletes and spectators will already be situated in the immediate area, will ease the crunch. But even they admit that it will be impossible to see it all. They suggest you concentrate on the events you find most interesting and base yourself as close as possible to where they will be held.

The skill of the organizers will be determined from February 8 to 23, when the Games are held. But because of the location of these Games, it is essential to nail down room reservations as far in advance as possible. There will be few backup lodging facilities for emergencies. Best bet is to contact the reservation office of each resort.

While many Americans equate great European skiing with Switzerland and Austria, the cognoscenti know that for sheer breadth of choice, nothing in the world compares to the Tarentaise Valley of the French Alps. For range of difficulty, types of snow, sheer number of runs available, it is the nonpareil. But each of the resorts exudes a slightly different ambience—from super chic to family-style simplicity, and from traditional to an architectural style that looks as if it had just arrived crated up in a starship.

A very limited number of rooms are available in Albertville itself and most of them have already been assigned to Olympics officials, sponsors, and media. This is not a resort, per se, and accommodations are far more basic than at the other sites. But if you'd like to try, the Tourist Bureau is the agency for assigning rooms. Telephone: (33) 79 32 04 22. Telex: 309634. Fax: 79 37 07 50.

This is how the 10 Olympic sites line up:

Val d'Isere
(Men's alpine skiing)

This is the resort for serious skiers; for those who are indifferent to the subsidiary attractions of the sport and live for the challenges of the slopes. Basic and uncluttered, it counts as its most celebrated resident Jean-Claude Killy. The three-time gold medalist of the 1968 Games at Grenoble was raised in this area. The ski range is called l'Espace Killy, and his signature is embossed, particularly, on the Bellevarde run, upon which the alpine events will be held.

This course scares even world-class skiers. It was designed by Killy and Bernhard Russi, gold medalist at the 1972 Games, and is intended to take the most challenging skiable way down the mountain, with most of the natural contours left in. Killy insists that the last three Olympics were run over downhill courses so wide and so flat that they amounted to "big highways." "Here, we will guarantee that the best skier on that given day will win," he says.

Perhaps the most gifted skier of all time, Killy has been the force behind the 1992 Winter Olympics. The theme of the Games is "Returning the Olympics to the Mountains" and at Bellevarde he has done that with a vengeance. Experts predict that the course should provide the most exciting downhill events in the recent history of the Games. So if skiing, and skiing alone, is what you want to see, Val d'Isere is the place to locate. Because it is at the farthest end of the Olympics area, however, connections to the other sites, except for the neighboring town of Tignes, will be difficult.

Val d'Isere is regarded as the birthplace of the sport in the Savoie. The first lifts were installed in 1934 and since then it has burnished its reputation for powder and off-course skiing, priding itself on being a shrine for real skiers. Its motto is "Total Skiing."

But it has managed to retain the feel of its origin as a tiny mountain village, too, with an 11th century church standing in the central square. From here, you have access to 100 square miles of skiing, 130 lifts (including the Funival, sort of a vertical TGV that takes skiers up 6,344 feet to the top of the mountain in four minutes) and 200 miles of trails. And if that isn't enough, you can board a helicopter for a short flight across the Italian border, and ski in another country. Val d'Isere's three ski schools are regarded as the best in France and its Club des Sports boasts that 20 Olympic medalists are among the members.

As in most places in this area, private apartments will be the best bet for those who do not already have a hotel reservation. With 23,000 beds, however, it is one of the smallest of the major sites in terms of accommodations. Reservation Office—Telephone: (33) 79 06 18 90. Telex: 980077. Fax: (33) 79 41 12 06.

Tignes
(Freestyle skiing—ballet, moguls, and aerials)

Situated right across the mountain slope, this is Val d'Isere's companion resort. Tignes is easily accessible by lifts and trails from its neighbor. Located at the foot of La Grande Motte glacier, Tignes offers skiing all year round and is part of the Espace Killy complex.

Tignes is named after an old town that was submerged in a hydroelectric power project in the 1950s. The new resort just borrowed its name and moved it further up the slopes. Tignes now consists of a series of small, modern, built-for-skiing resort clusters situated at various altitudes along the mountain. The main village, and the most attractive, is Tignes Lac, which is located on the shores of a natural lake. A branch of Harry's Bar is nestled in the town, but Tignes is primarily regarded as a private party place, where most people entertain in their own apartments.

The skiing is rated as not quite as difficult as Val d'Isere but with easier access to the slopes and a wider range of runs suited for the intermediate level. The ski events here will be held in the new Lognan Stadium.

30,000 beds are available at Tignes. Reservation Office—Telephone: (33) 79 06 35 60. Telex: 980030. Fax: (33) 79 06 45 44.

Les Arcs
(Speed skiing—demonstration sport)

This is another of the purpose-built resorts, with apartment clusters situated at three different altitude levels. While rather isolated in itself, Les Arcs is connected by funicular railroad with the town below, Bourg-St. Maurice, which sits at the rail and highway hub of the mountain area. So for easiest access to all the other sites, this may actually be the best spot in which to locate.

Les Arcs has long been associated with speed skiing competition, and has organized the World Cup events in the sport for a number of years. The area is somewhat better known as a summer resort, though. Les Arcs has some of the best tennis facilities in the area and Bourg-St. Maurice is famed for its orchards and as a base for scenic drives over the high mountain passes, all of which are closed in the winter months.

26,000 beds are available in the Les Arcs area. Reservation Office—Telephone: (33) 79 07 26 00. Telex: 980347. Fax: (33) 79 07 43 36.

Les Saisies
(Men's and women's cross country skiing and biathlon)

This is one of the smallest and most remote of the resorts participating in the Olympics. Les Saisies directly faces Mont Blanc, highest peak in the Alps, and gets heavier snow than any other location in this vicinity. It is accessible by valley roads from Bourg-St. Maurice and Albertville.

When all else fails, this could be the best bet for accommodations because of its isolated location and relative obscurity. Unless you are really into cross country and biathlon, however, commuting problems could be formidable.

There are 8,500 beds available in Les Saisies. Reservation Office—Telephone: (33) 79 38 90 30 Telex: 980857. Fax: (33) 79 38 95 67.

La Plagne
(Bobsled and luge)

Another of the purpose-built resorts, this consists of a set of six independent apartment villages, each with its own center. La Plagne offers an exceptional variety of winter sports. The skiing is first rate, with more than 100 lifts, including the longest cable car in Europe, leading to more than 120 miles of trails, ranging from forests to glaciers to wide valleys.

But La Plagne also accommodates the less intent, with a wide assortment of restaurants and other sporting pastimes. It was chosen for the sled events because of its artificial run, at the La Roche village cluster, which affords an especially large viewing area. The resort can be reached by cab from the TGV depot at Moutiers, about halfway between Albertville and Bourg-St. Maurice.

La Plagne has 30,000 beds available. Reservation Office—Telephone: (33) 79 09 79 79. Telex: 980973. Fax: (33) 79 09 70 10.

Courchevel
(Ski jumping)

This has been called "Rodeo Drive in the snow." Or, better yet, "the Aspen of France." It sometimes refers to itself as "The Star," or a place "for those who lead exceptional lives." Well, you get the idea. This is the most exclusive of the resorts in the area, where shipping magnates could be on the next lift and movie stars at the next table in the two-star restaurant. Courchevel's nightlife is all-encompassing. And it is all extremely expensive.

Among the first of the purpose-made resorts, Courchevel was founded in 1947. It now consists of four separate chalet and apartment villages, and the higher you go the higher the prices ascend. Courchevel 1850 is the summit in both categories, while the 1650 and 1550 villages (the numbers reflect their altitudes in meters above sea level) are a bit less exalted. The higher prices are also a function of convenience, because the ski trails wind right past the front door of the apartments. The base village, Le Praz, is a bit more traditional in appearance and it is here that the jumping events will take place in a new stadium.

This is also the point of entry to The Three Valleys, a skiing area that dwarfs even l'Espace Killy. With 200 lifts and 300 miles of slopes, Three Valleys is almost like a skiing supermarket. You can take your choice as to what sort of skiing experience you prefer and be whisked there in a matter of minutes by the highly sophisticated system of inter-connected lifts. While line-ups are common, travelers say that rarely does anyone have to wait more than 15 minutes to board.

The best shopping, best dining, best people-watching, even the best hang gliding in the area is located here. But it will also be the toughest room to find.

Courchevel has 33,000 beds. Reservation Office—Telephone: (33) 79 08 00 29. Telex: 980083. Fax: (33) 79 08 33 54.

Meribel
(Hockey and women's alpine skiing)

This may be ground zero for the entire region when it comes to the interests and convenience of Americans. It is located right in the middle of the massive Three Valleys ski area, largest in Europe. It has the most traditional feel to it, since Meribel started out as a real village and has made every effort to maintain a visual unity in all new construction. The resort was established by British skiers and almost everyone speaks English, which is not true at many of the smaller sites.

Finally, the events hosted by Meribel are those that most engage Americans. Hockey has always been the most widely covered of the Winter Olympics sports and a new 7,000-seat arena has been built to accommodate it. The women's alpine events also should be stirring. Bernhard Russi, who teamed with Killy to design the controversial men's run at Val d'Isere, has applied the same principles to the women's course at Meribel.

His run down the Roc de Fer features a 2,717-foot vertical drop. This was 420 feet longer than the maximum allowed by international rules. But the Olympic Committee decided to ignore the rules and certified it anyhow. All the alpine events will finish in a common area, which is just a short walk from the hockey arena. All things considered, if you can wangle a room in Meribel, do it.

There are 27,000 beds available in the Meribel area. Reservation Office— Telephone: (33) 79 00 50 00. Telex: 980001. Fax: 79 00 59 61.

Les Menuires
(Men's slalom)

The most controversial element in this place is its architecture. Traditionalists and environmentalists have attacked its massive, ultra-modern look as being insensitive to its surroundings and reflecting a "brutalism" in appearance. On the other hand, Les Menuires is one of the most succesful of the newer resorts and is a thriving part of the Three Valleys complex.

It is also connected by a stunningly beautiful lift ride to Val Thorens, the highest alpine resort in Europe, with a maximum altitude of 11,545 feet. It is regarded as a cold and gloomy sort of place, but offers incredible challenges on its 3,000-foot descent from the peak to the village itself. It has become very popular with German and Scandinavian skiers.

The combined resorts of Les Menuires and Val Thorens has 39,000 beds. Reservation Office—Telephone: (33) 79 00 79 79. Telex: 980084. Fax: (33) 79 00 75 06.

Pralognan la Vanoise
(Curling—demonstration sport)

This is another of the more remote venues for the Games, although it is just over the slope from Courchevel. The village is situated in a breathtakingly beautiful area, a valley surrounded by waterfalls, glaciers, and untouched forests. Some of the best cross-country skiing in the French Alps is found here and the emphasis is decidedly on nature and simple joys.

Curling, a demonstration sport at Calgary in 1988, is again being played on a demonstration basis, this time at Pralognan la Vanoise's sports complex, which also includes facilities for bowling, swimming, and billiards.

There are just 8,220 beds at Pralognan la Vanoise. Reservation Office— Telephone: (33) 79 08 73 22. Telex: 980240. No fax.

BIATHLON

WARM-UP

Although not a Winter Olympic sport until 1960, biathlon, a grueling sport that combines furious cross-country skiing with expert marksmanship, has its origins in ancient Scandinavian society. Early Scandinavians, after inventing skis for transportation across the snowy terrain, soon discovered that stalking prey was easier on skis than afoot.

Later, when survival became less of a day-to-day struggle, the combination of skiing and shooting was included in the training of infantry soldiers, particularly in Finland. This led to the military ski patrol race, which began early this century among European armies.

In 1958, the first world biathlon championship was held in Austria. The 20-kilometer biathlon was added to the Olympics program in 1960; in 1968, the 30-kilometer relay was added. The 10-kilometer race made its Olympic debut in 1980. Olympic biathlon had been an all-male preserve, but in 1992 women will ski and shoot in three events: the 7.5km, 15km, and a relay (3 x 7.5km).

SPECTATORS' GUIDE

Combine cross-country skiing with riflery and what do you get? A sport that few in the US seem to understand. Biathlon is something of an unknown competition in America, with fewer than 1,000 Americans participating. It is as much a test of composure as it is a race against the clock. While much of the skiing occurs out of sight of the spectators (and the television audience as well), the start, finish, shooting range, and penalty loops are within the stadium and camera range.

At the start of the race, biathletes leave from a starting gate just in front of the stands, one at a time, one minute apart. Each competitor skis a set distance along the course, the .22 caliber rifle (which weighs as much as 11 pounds) slung over a shoulder. Then, with heart racing at 160 to 180 beats per minute, heaving breath, and no time to spare, the racer comes to a complete stop, aims, and shoots, from alternating prone and standing positions, at a configuration of five black dots 50 meters away. If a competitor skis too quickly, he or she will be unable to slow his breathing and heartbeat as he approaches the range. The best biathletes are able to come down from 180 to 120 beats when they're shooting, squeezing the trigger in that millisecond of relative stillness between heartbeats.

Concentration is, of course, essential. Those dots they're aiming at have diameters of 115 millimeters (4.76 inches) for the more difficult standing shots, 45 millimeters (1.76 inches) for prone shots. Each miss in the men's 20km and women's 15km race adds one minute to the competitor's final time; each miss in the men's 10km and women's 7.5km and both relay events means the competitor must ski a 150-meter penalty loop.

In the men's 20km, which covers about 12.5 miles, the competitors return four times to shoot five shots at five targets 50 meters away. The women's 15km follows similar rules. The 10km and 7.5km sprints require only two shooting stops.

The men's relay team comprises four racers, while the women's team has three members, each skiing 7.5 kilometers (4.5 miles). Each member stops twice to shoot up to eight rounds at five metal targets. The three extra rounds are loaded as single shots, meaning the competitor must open the bolt of the rifle for each extra shot required, take out a round, and insert a round. About 10 seconds are needed for reloading, and a penalty loops tags on some 40 seconds to a contestant's time, depending on snow conditions.

Unlike the individual races, the relays feature a mass start. They do not feature a baton exchange. The passover zone in the relay is a 20-meter length of track wherein the person completing his or her leg must physically touch a teammate's body with his or her hand. A hand-to-hand tag is not permitted.

▼

HOPEFULS

The Scandinavians, Germans, and Soviets will probably continue winning the biathlon medals in the 1992 Olympics. The Soviets, in particular, have their sights set on a sixth straight gold in the men's relay, along with another remarkable performance from relay team member Sergei Tchepikov, who won the 10km bronze at Calgary. Spectators should watch Italy, though—a newcomer to the biathletic elite—whose relay team members, including Johann Passler and Andreas Zingerle, won their country's first medal (a bronze) at Calgary. In addition, Passler earned another bronze in the 20km event, and Zingerle was a top contender in the 1991 World Cup games.

The USA's best shot at a medal will probably come in the newly added women's events. Several US women finished among the top ten in 1991 World Cup competitions, including Anna Sonnerup. With a silver medal in one 1990

World Cup race and two bronze finishes in that year's Polar Cup, Sonnerup looks promising if she improves her shooting, which harmed her performance in 1991 international events. Eight-time national champion Josh Thompson, who finished 25th (a record, though still a disappointment) for the United States in the 20km race at Calgary, will compete again at Albertville. Duncan Douglas, too, set a US record in 1991 by placing 19th in a World Cup race, and he'll shoot for an Olympic medal in 1992.

Schedule

The tentative biathlon schedule is as follows:

Tuesday, February 11
7.5km, women

Wednesday, February 12
10km, men

Friday, February 14
3 x 7.5km relay, women

Sunday, February 16
4 x 7.5km relay, men

Wednesday, February 19
15km, women

Thursday, February 20
20km, men

▼

HIGHLIGHTS

Biathlon competition was not part of the Winter Games until 1960, when the 20km event made its appearance. The 4 x 7.5km relay event debuted at the 1968 Games in Grenoble, and the 10km event was inaugurated in 1980 at Lake Placid. The Scandinavians, East Germans and Soviets have long dominated the sport.

Soviet biathlete Alexandr Privalov captured the bronze in the 20km race in 1960 and a silver in 1964, while contenders from Sweden, Finland, Norway, and the Soviet Union rounded out the medalists those first two years. A French biathlete, Victor Arbez, was the fastest skier in 1960, but proved to be a dismal marksman, missing 18 of his 20 targets. Norway's Magnar Solberg took the gold in the 20km with a perfect shooting score in 1968 and captured the gold again in 1972, at the age of 35. Finland's Heikki Ikola was favored to win the 20km in 1976, but had to settle for silver behind Nikolai Kruglov, a Russian Army lieutenant. The Scandinavians were completely shut out at Lake Placid, where West Germany managed to capture a bronze in the relay, the only medal not won by East Germany or the USSR. The 1980 champion in the 20km event was Russian Anatoli Aljabiev, the only man to hit all his targets; he also took the bronze in the 10km event. East German Frank Ullrich won two medals in 1980.

Alexander Tikhonov won his record fourth gold in Lake Placid as a member of the Soviet relay team.

US biathlete Lyle Nelson was 34 when he competed in his third Olympics at Sarajevo in 1984. That year Eirik Kvalfoss of Norway took the gold in the 10km ahead of West German Peter Angerer and East German Matthias Jacob. Angerer captured the 20km gold ahead of 19-year-old East German Frank-Peter Roetsch and bronze medalist Kvalfoss. The relay was again won by the Soviet Union, with Norway claiming the silver and East Germany the bronze; the US team placed eighth.

For the 1988 Games Josh Thompson, the first US medal contender in biathlon, toted a new, lighter but stronger rifle stock designed by US biathlete Glen Eberle. But the Calgary Games belonged to East German biathlete Frank-Peter Roetsch, the first ever to capture both the 10km and the 20km biathlons; he had been silver medalist in the 20km event in 1984. Three Soviets also medaled in the 10km and 20km events in 1988, while Italian Johann Passler took the bronze in the 20km. In Calgary the Soviet Union continued its stranglehold on the relay, winning its sixth gold out of six times this event has been held at the Winter Games. Italy took a surprise bronze in the relay, behind West Germany.

Medalists

Biathlon — 10 Kilometers

1988
1. Frank-Peter Roetsch, East Germany, 25:08.1
2. Valeri Medvedtsev, Soviet Union, 25:23.7
3. Sergei Tchepikov, Soviet Union, 25:29.4

1984
1. Eirik Kvalfoss, Norway, 30:53.8
2. Peter Angerer, West Germany, 31:02.4
3. Matthias Jacob, East Germany, 31:10.5

1980
1. Frank Ullrich, East Germany, 32:10.69
2. Vladimir Alikin, Soviet Union, 32:53.10
3. Anatoli Alyabiev, Soviet Union, 33:09.16

Biathlon — 20 Kilometers

1988
1. Frank Peter Roetsch, East Germany, 56:33.3
2. Valeri Medvedtsev, Soviet Union, 56:54.6
3. Johann Passler, Italy, 57:10.1

1984
1. Peter Angerer, West Germany, 1:11:52.7
2. Frank-Peter Roetsch, East Germany, 1:13:21.4
3. Eirik Kvalfoss, Norway, 1:14:02.4

1980
1. Anatoli Alyabiev, Soviet Union, 1:08:16.31

2. Frank Ullrich, East Germany, 1:08:27.79
3. Eberhard Rosch, East Germany, 1:11:11.73

1976
1. Nikolai Kruglov, Soviet Union, 1:14:12.26
2. Heikki Ikola, Finland, 1:15:54.10
3. Aleksandr Elizarov, Soviet Union, 1:16:05.57

1972
1. Magnar Solberg, Norway, 1:15:55.50
2. Hans-Jorg Knauthe, East Germany, 1:16:07.60
3. Lars-Goran Arwidson, Sweden, 1:16:27.03

1968
1. Magnar Solberg, Norway, 1:13:45.9
2. Aleksandr Tikhonov, Soviet Union, 1:14:40.4
3. Vladimir Gundartsev, Soviet Union, 1:18:27.4

1964
1. Vladimir Melanin, Soviet Union, 1:20:26.8
2. Aleksandr Privalov, Soviet Union, 1:23:42.5
3. Olav Jordet, Norway, 1:24:38.8

1960
1. Klas Lestander, Sweden, 1:33:21.6
2. Antti Tyrvainen, Finland, 1:33:57.7
3. Aleksandr Privalov, Soviet Union, 1:34:54.2

1924-1956 Not held

64

Biathlon — 4x7.5-Kilometer Relay

1988
1. Soviet Union, 1:22:30.0, Dmitri Vassiliev, Sergei Tchepikov, Alexandre Popov, Valeri Medvedtsev
2. West Germany, 1:23:37.4, Ernst Reiter, Stefan Hoeck, Peter Angerer, Friderich Fischer
3. Italy, 1:23:51.5, Werner Kiem, Gottlieb Taschler, Johann Passler, Andreas Zingerle

1984
1. Soviet Union, 1:38:51.7, Dmitri Vassiliev, Yuri Kachkarov, Alguimantas Shalna, Serguey Bouliguin
2. Norway, 1:39:03.9, Odd Lirhus, Eirik Kvalfoss, Rolf Storsveen, Kjell Soebak
3. West Germany, 1:39:05.1, Ernst Reiter, Walter Pichler, Peter Angerer, Fritz Fischer

1980
1. Soviet Union, 1:34:03.27, Vladimir Alikin, Aleksandr Tikhonov, Vladimir Barnashov, Anatoli Alyabiev
2. East Germany, 1:34:56.99, Mathias Jung, Klaus Siebert, Frank Ullrich, Eberhard Roesch
3. West Germany, 1:37:30.26, Franz Bernreiter, Hans Estner, Peter Angerer, Gerd Winkler

1976
1. Soviet Union, 1:57:55.64, Ivan Biakov, Aleksandr Elizarov, Nikolai Kruglov, Aleksandr Tikhonov
2. Finland, 2:01:45.58, Hendrik Flojt, Esko Saira, Juhani Suutarinen, Heikki Ikola
3. East Germany, 2:04:08.61, Karl-Heinz Menz, Frank Ullrich, Manfred Beer, Manfred Geyer

1972
1. Soviet Union, 1:51:44.92, Aleksandr Tikhonov, Rinnat Safine, Ivan Biakov, Viktor Mamatov
2. Finland, 1:54:37.25, Esko Saira, Juhani Suutarinen, Heikki Ikola, Mauri Roppanen
3. East Germany, 1:54:57.67, Hans-Jorg Knauthe, Joachim Meischner, Dieter Speer, Horst Koschka

1968
1. Soviet Union, 2:13:02.4, Aleksandr Tikhonov, Nikolai Pusanov, Viktor Mamatov, Vladimir Gundartsev
2. Norway, 2:14:50.2, Ola Waerhaug, Olav Jordet, Magnar Solberg, Jon Istad
3. Sweden, 2:17:26.3, Lars-Goran Arwidson, Tore Eriksson, Olle Petrusson, Holmfrid Olsson

1924-1964 Not held

BOBSLEDDING

WARM-UP

Using a strip of animal skin stretched between pieces of wood, humans first started sledding some 15,000 years ago as a means of transportation. During the heyday of the Roman Empire, one-man handsleds were used to carry supplies and mail, a practice that was also common among Native North American tribes. A giant step in winter navigation occurred when the Eskimos hitched dogs to their sleds.

During the 1870s, tobogganing became popular in Canada. Racing officially began in 1877 in Davos, Switzerland. In 1883, the British staged the first Davos international race. A year later the Grand National Toboggan Race attracted a field of 20 at St. Moritz.

fact: The first structured toboggan run was built in 1884 in St. Moritz, Switzerland.

St. Moritz and Davos both profess to be the birthplace of bobsledding. The first bobsled used for sport was brought to Davos in the winter of 1888–89 by Stephen Whitney, a tourist from New York. The bobsled consisted of two low "American" sleds bolted together.

The American sleds had made their debut in 1887 and had proven their superiority over the local Davos sleds. To create the longer bobsled, the sleds were bolted together with a board. The front sled, used for steering, was connected to the long board by a round bolt so that it would be free to turn. It had a thick wooden rod running crossways through the front sled and extending 20 centimeters on either side to form handles. This new model was tested on the run, where it reached a considerable speed and was described as "a very dangerous machine to drive."

According to legend, the earliest of the sleds had no brakes, so the driver used a garden rake to stop. Primitive rope steering often permitted the sledders to veer successfully off course and into harm's way. Whitney and his bruised followers steered their one-man sleds lying down, head first, the better with which to run into snowbanks and trees. The problem of the erratic steering was solved to an extent by introducing heavier sleds; the first steel bobsled was a two-seater or multi-seater, used in the winter of 1889–90. The sleds were shortly thereafter named Bob, inspired by the "bobbing" of crew members on straightaways to increase speed. In 1896, the St. Moritz Bobsleigh Club was formed, and the sport began to grow. Other winter resorts took up the daredevil sport. By 1911, some sixty runs served sledders in Switzerland, although only a very few were more than ordinary streets with snow-reinforced curves. The first artificial bobsled run was built at St. Moritz in 1904.

fact: The East Germans are responsible for the sport's big innovations, including the two-part rear axle, the independent suspension system, and a better steering mechanism.

Austria was the site of the first national championship in 1908, followed two years later by Germany. The first European championships were staged in 1914. During the early racing years, when the sleds carried five people, the rules stipulated that two members of each team be women. But as bobsleds became slicker and faster and the danger increased, men were allowed to replace the women.

Until the 1920s, no equipment rules existed. Sporting attire for men consisted of thick woolen caps pulled down to expose only the eyes and nose to the cold, sweaters, elbow-length gloves, cuffs or leggings made of sailcloth or leather, and high hiking boots. At the outset, women always wore long winter coats over long skirts, high-topped boots, hoods, or the ever-present broad-brimmed hats tied by scarves; otherwise, the clothing was the same as that for skiing.

Safety was first addressed by simple protective devices, starting with seat cushions, runners with iron struts, and hand and belt loops that offered a grip. Between 1920 and 1930, bobsledders started wearing protective helmets made of compressed cardboard, leather, plywood, and other materials; they became regulation items in the early 1930s.

fact: The official organizing body for bobsled has one of the best names in all the Olympics: Fédération Internationale de Bobsleigh et de Tobogganing.

In 1923, the International Federation of Bobsled and Tobogganing was organized, just in time to permit bobsledding to be included in the 1924 Winter Olympics, the sport's first recognized international race. In 1927, the first world championship was held at St. Moritz.

SPECTATORS' GUIDE

The Olympic program includes two bobsled races, the two-man and four-man. Four-man racing was part of the 1924 Olympic schedule, while two-man was added in 1932. Although among the pioneers of the sport, women have never competed in the Olympics.

The chief attractions of bobsledding are the speed of the sleds (approaching 90 miles per hour) and the danger to the crew (resting on a sled less than a foot above the ground while flying down a mile-long course containing a series of curves designed to control speed as well as increase it).

Bobsled speed is affected by three main factors: weight, air resistance, and friction. All things being equal, the heaviest sled/crew combination will run the fastest. Therefore, a maximum weight is set for each sled and crew combination. A four-man sled cannot exceed 630 kilograms (approximately 1,338 pounds), while two-man sleds cannot exceed 390 kilograms (859 pounds). Lighter crews can add weight to their sleds before a race. But heavier sleds can prove more difficult to start, a critical element to racers. Explosive starts result in fast finish times. Racers who beat a competitor's time by a second at the beginning of the race can finish up to three seconds faster at the bottom. Considering this, adding weight to a sled for competition can be more detrimental than helpful to a lighter bobsled team.

fact: Push time is the crucial factor— how long it takes the sledders to propel their craft and leap into it over the 50-meter starting run; a tenth of a second of shaved off push time can translate into a third of a second off the run time.

Steering and the downhill line of the bobsled are also very critical elements. The sled's steering component is a rope pulley system. Drivers barely have to move the ropes to affect the direction of the sled. Therefore, less steering minimizes movement of the sled. Best results are when the crew stays as still as possible and the driver lets the sled do the work for him.

The downhill line of the sled should be as close to a straight line as possible. Sleds can lose tremendous amounts of speed at the top of the race by merely bumping into a wall. This translates into slower down times for the entire race. Drivers try to keep the sleds from rocking side to side when exiting curves, maintaining the straightest possible line down the course. A sled appearing to slingshot cleanly out of a curve is the sled that will post the faster finish time.

fact: The hardest part of launching a bobsled is jumping into it without scratching your teammates with the hundreds of needles projecting from the soles of your sledding shoes; the needles grip the ice during push time.

The brakeman must be strong, and, since he is the last man to jump on the sled, must be the best pusher. He also is responsible for stopping the sled smoothly at the end of the run, using a lever attached to a saw-toothed brake bar that digs into the ice. The other two men on the four-man team follow the instructions of the brakeman, and the three of them will bob on signal from almost a lying position to a sitting position on the straightaways to help the sled jump forward. If the brake is applied before the finish line, the sled is disqualified.

For each event four heats are run, and the results are based on total time.

Each country is allowed a squad of 12, and competitors can be entered in both events. A country is permitted to enter two teams in each event. The starting lineups don't have to be selected until shortly before each event, and the draw to determine the starting order can be critical, since the early starters are likely to have a slower track.

The technical side of the bobsled is very specific. For example, the maximum distance from the front tip of the front runners to the rear tip of the rear runners is 270 centimeters for the two-man sled, 335 centimeters for the four-man sled.

▼

HOPEFULS

Though Switzerland and Germany will probably continue their reign over the bobsledding events, the US is inspired by its near-miss (two-hundredths of a second) at the four-man bronze medal in 1988. With ace driver Chuck Leonowicz leading the four-man team and professional football player Herschel Walker adding some critical push speed, the US hopes to gain enough momentum to capture its first bobsledding medal since 1956.

Schedule

The tentative bobsled schedule is as follows:

Saturday, February 15
Two man

Sunday, February 16
Two man

Friday, February 21
Four man

Saturday, February 22
Four man

▼

HIGHLIGHTS

Bobsledding was one of the original sports at the first Winter Games in 1924. The US won five bobsledding gold medals during the 1920s, 1930s, and 1940s, garnering in all 14 Olympic medals by 1956, including five gold, four silver, and five bronze. Since then the East Germans and Swiss have dominated the sport. Of 24 total medals awarded in the Olympics from 1976 to 1988, East Germany won 13 and Switzerland 6.

Switzerland won the first four-man gold awarded in the 1924 Games, with England taking the silver and Belgium the bronze; the Swiss sled carried two brothers, Alfred and Heinrich Schläppi. In 1928 the competition was plagued by a heavy thaw; the US took the gold and the silver in the five-man event, the only Games in which that event was held. US pilot William Fiske was only 16 when he won the gold in the five-man, making him the youngest male Winter Games gold medalist ever; his teammate in the second-place sled, Thomas Doe, Jr., was only 15 years old.

The weather was so bad in 1932 that the bobsled competitions were held after the official closing of the Games. Again in 1932 the US teams took the gold and silver in an event, this time the four-man; the US also captured the gold in the two-man event, with a sled carrying brothers Hubert and Curtis Stevens. Heavy rains threatened to disrupt the competition in 1936, but the course eventually smoothed out. The US maintained its streak in 1936, winning the gold and bronze in the two-man event, but Switzerland won its second gold in the four-man that year.

At the next Games, in 1948, the US recaptured the four-man gold, and for the first time a non-US team won the gold in the two-man, earned by a Swiss team; a burst waterpipe flooded the course and halted competition in the middle of the second run. In 1952 German pilot Andreas Ostler became the first man to drive two gold medal winning sleds in the same Olympics. That year the US took the two silvers, and Switzerland the two bronzes.

71

fact: Spying on rival teams' equipment is a revered tradition among aficionados of bobsled technology.

Italy helped confirm the end of American bobsledding dominance in 1956, taking the gold and silver in the two-man event and the silver in the four-man; Switzerland won the two-man bronze and the four-man gold; the US had to settle for a bronze in the four-man. One of Italy's sledders in the two-man, Giocomo Conti, was 47 years old, the oldest gold medalist in the history of the Winter Games; Switzerland's gold medal winning pilot in the four-man, Franz Kapus, was 46 years old.

No bobsledding events were held in 1960, due to a lack of facilities at Squaw Valley; bobsled runs are expensive to construct and often see little use after the Olympic Games. In 1964 Canada won its first gold in the four-man, four bachelors from Montréal pulling off what was considered to be the biggest upset in bobsledding history; Britain took the two-man.

One of the most popular victories in the sport's history occurred in 1968, under threats of a dangerous thaw, when the fabled red-haired Italian, Eugenio Monti, led his country to a double victory in the two-man and four-man. In two previous Olympics, Monti had earned two silver medals and two bronze and, at the age of 40, he finally got his gold. West Germany garnered top honors in 1972, placing first and second in the two-man and taking the bronze in the four-man behind first-place Switzerland and second-place Italy; Switzerland also took the four-man bronze. That year the US failed for the first time to place a sled in the top ten.

The 1976 East German team came to Innsbruck with superb sleds and well-conditioned athletes; at these Games East German driver Meinhard Nehmer won the gold in the two-man and four-man bob. In so doing, he joined Ostler and Monti as the only drivers to pilot two sleds to the gold in the same Olympics. West Germany and Switzerland each took a silver and bronze at Innsbruck. In 1980 at Lake Placid East Germany took the gold and bronze in the four-man, with Nehmer again piloting the gold medal team, and silver and bronze—again with Nehmer medalling—in the two-man. Switzerland won the gold in the two-man and the four-man silver at Lake Placid.

fact: A common—though illegal—practice among bobsledders is to coat their runners with silicone.

In 1980 US team member Willie Davenport was attempting to equal the feat of Eddie Eagan, who became the first man to earn gold medals in both the Summer and Winter Games when he won a gold in the 1932 four-man bobsled to add to the boxing gold medal he'd won as a light heavyweight in 1920. Davenport competed in the 110m hurdles four times from 1964 to 1976, and was gold

Winter

medalist in 1968 and bronze medalist in 1976. In 1980 Davenport and bobsled teammate Jeffrey Gadley were the first African-Americans to compete in the Winter Games. A controversy between Davenport and his coach, Gary Sheffield, erupted over a racially inflected remark attributed to Davenport; shaken, the four-man sleds came in twelfth and thirteenth. The US team failed to garner a medal at Lake Placid, though placing fifth and sixth in the two-man was the team's best performance since 1956.

East German driver Wolfgang Hoppe earned the gold in both the two-man and four-man competitions in 1984, and two silvers in those events in 1988. With his 1984 victories he became the fourth driver to win two bobsled golds in the same Olympics.

The US team brought sleek new sleds to the 1988 Games, competing against the likes of the Puerto Rican team, made up of two New Yorkers, and Prince Albert Alexandre Louis Pierre of Monaco, the Marquis de Baux, who in 1988 was the youngest member of the IOC. Prince Albert's grandfather and uncle, the two Jack Kellys of Philadelphia, had also competed in the Games, the senior winning three gold medals in single and double sculls in 1920 and 1924, the junior winning a bronze in the single sculls in 1956. And then there was the underdog favorite, the 1988 Jamaican team, with only four months training behind them; they included a helicopter pilot, a reggae singer, and a sprint champion. Their team sponsor, a US business consultant, got the idea for a Jamaican bobsled team while watching the annual pushcart derby in Kingston in the summer of 1987.

Medalists

Bobsled — Two-Man

1988
1. Soviet Union (I), 3:53.48, Ianis Kipours, Vladimir Kozlov
2. East Germany (I), 3:54.19, Wolfgang Hoppe, Bogdan Musiol
3. East Germany (II), 3:54.64, Bernhard Lehmann, Mario Hoyer

1984
1. East Germany (II), 3:25.56, Wolfgang Hoppe, Dietmar Schauerhammer
2. East Germany (I), 3:26.04, Bernhard Lehmann, Bogdan Musiol
3. Soviet Union (II), 3:26.16, Zintis Ekmanis, Vladimir Aleksandrov

1980
1. Switzerland (II), 4:09.36, Erich Schaerer, Josef Benz
2. East Germany (II), 4:10.93 Bernhard Germeshausen, Hans Jurgen Gerhardt
3. East Germany (I), 4:11.08, Meinhard Nehmer, Bogdan Musiol

1976
1. East Germany (I), 3:44.42, Meinhard Nehmer, Bernhard Germeshausen
2. West Germany (I), 3:44.99, Wolfgang Zimmerer, Manfred Schumann

3. Switzerland (I), 3:45.70, Erich Schaerer, Josef Benz

1972
1. West Germany (II), 4:57.07, Wolfgang Zimmerer, Peter Utzschneider
2. West Germany (I), 4:58.84, Horst Floth, Pepi Bader
3. Switzerland (I), 4:59.33, Jean Wicki, Edy Hubacher

1968
1. Italy (I), 4:41.54, Eugenio Monti, Luciano De Paolis
2. West Germany (I), 4:41.54, Horst Floth, Pepi Bader
3. Romania (I), 4:44.46, Ion Panturu, Nicolae Neagoe

1964
1. Great Britain (I), 4:21.90, Anthony Nash, Robin Dixon
2. Italy (II), 4:22.02, Sergio Zardini, Romano Bonagura
3. Italy (I), 4:22.63, Eugenio Monti, Sergio Siorpaes

1960 Not held

1956
1. Italy (I), 5:30.14, Lamberto Dalla Costa, Giacomo Conti
2. Italy (II), 5:31.45, Eugenio Monti, Renzo Alvera

3. Switzerland (I), 5:37.46, Max Angst, Harry Warburton

1952 1. Germany (I), 5:24.54, Andreas Ostler, Lorenz Nieberl
2. USA (I), 5:26.89, Stanley Benham, Patrick Martin
3. Switzerland (I), 5:27.71, Fritz Feierabend, Stephan Waser

1948 1. Switzerland (II), 5:29.2, Felix Endrich, Friedrich Waller
2. Switzerland (I), 5:30.4, Fritz Feierabend, Paul Eberhard
3. USA (II), 5:35.3, Fred Fortune, Schuyler Carron

1936 1. USA (I), 5:29.29, Ivan Brown, Alan Washbound
2. Switzerland (II), 5:30.64, Fritz Feierabend, Joseph Beerli
3. USA(II), 5:33.96, Gilbert Colgate, Richard Lawrence

1932 1. USA (I), 8:14.74, Hubert Stevens, Curtis Stevens
2. Switzerland (II), 8:16.28, Reto Capadrutt, Oscar Geier
3. USA (II), 8:29.15, John R. Heaton, Robert Minton

1924-1928 **Not held**

Bobsled — Four-Man

1988 1. Switzerland (I), 3:47.51, Ekkehard Fasser, Kurt Meier, Marcel Faessler, Werner Stocker
2. East Germany (I), 3:47.58, Wolfgang Hoppe, Dietmar Schauerhammer, Bogdan Musiol, and Ingo Voge
3. Soviet Union (II), 3:48.26, Ianis Kipours, Gountis Ossis, Iouri Tone, Vladimir Kozlov

1984 1. East Germany (I), 3:20.22, Wolfgang Hoppe, Roland Wetzig, Dietmar Schauerhammer, Andreas Kirchner
2. East Germany (II), 3:20.78, Bernhard Lehmann, Bogdan Musiol, Ingo Voge, Eberhard Weise
3. Switzerland (I), 3:21.39, Silvio Giobellina, Heinz Stettler, Urs Salzmann, Rico Freiermuth

1980 1. East Germany (I), 3:59.92, Meinhard Nehmer, Bogdan Musiol, Bernhard Germeshausen, Hans Jurgen Gerhardt
2. Switzerland (I), 4:00.87, Erich Schaerer, Ulrich Baechli, Rudolf Marti, Josef Benz
3. East Germany (II), 4:00.97, Horst Schoenau, Roland Wetzig, Detlef Richter, Andreas Kirchner

1976 1. East Germany (I), 3:40.43, Meinhard Nehmer, Jochen Babcok, Bernhard Germeshausen, Bernhard Lehmann
2. Switzerland (II), 3:40.89, Erich Schaerer, Ulrich Baechli, Rudolf Marti, Josef Benz
3. West Germany (I), 3:41.37, Wolfgang Zimmerer, Peter Utzschneider, Bodo Bittner, Manfred Schumann

1972 1. Switzerland (I), 4:43.07, Jean Wicki, Hans Leutenegger, Werner Camichel, Edy Hubacher

2. Italy (I), 4:43.83, Nevio De Zordo, Adriano Frassinelli, Corrado Dal Fabbro, Gianni Bonichon
3. West Germany (I), 4:43.92, Wolfgang Zimmerer, Stefan Gaisreiter, Walter Steinbauer, Peter Utzschneider

1968 1. Italy (I), 2:17.39, Eugenio Monti, Luciano De Paolis, Roberto Zandonella, Mario Armano
2. Austria (I), 2:17.48, Erwin Thaler, Reinhold Durnthaler, Herbert Gruber, Josef Eder
3. Switzerland (I), 2:18.04, Jean Wicki, Hans Candrian, Willi Hofmann, Walter Graf

1964 1. Canada (I), 4:14.46, Victor Emery, Peter Kirby, Douglas Anakin, John Emery
2. Austria (I), 4:15.48, Erwin Thaler, Adolf Koxeder, Josef Nairz, Reinhold Durnthaler
3. Italy (II), 4:15.60, Eugenio Monti, Sergio Siorpaes, Benito Rigoni, Gildo Siorpaes

1960 **Not held**

1956 1. Switzerland (I), 5:10.44, Franz Kapus, Gottfried Diener, Robert Alt, Heinrich Angst
2. Italy (II), 5:12.10, Eugenio Monti, Ulrico Girardi, Renzo Alvera, Renato Mocellini
3. USA (I), 5:12.39, Arthur Tyler, William Dodge, Charles Butler, James Lamy

1952 1. Germany (I), 5:07.84, Andreas Ostler, Friedrich Kuhn Lorenz Nieberl, Franz Kemser
2. USA (I), 5:10.48, Stanley Benham, Patrick Martin, Howard Crossett, James Atkinson
3. Switzerland (I), 5:11.70, Fritz Feierabend, Albert Madorin, Andre Filippini, Stephan Waser

1948 1. USA(II), 5:20.1, Francis Tyler, Patrick Martin, Edward Rimkus, William D'Amico
2. Belgium (I), 5:21.3, Max Houben, Freddy Mansveld, Louis-George Niels, Jacques Mouvet
3. USA (I), 5:21.5, James Bickford, Thomas Hicks, Donald Dupree, William Dupree

1936 1. Switzerland (II), 5:19.85, Pierre Musy, Arnold Gartmann, Charles Bouvier, Joseph Beerli
2. Switzerland (I), 5:22.73, Reto Capadrutt, Hans Aichele, Fritz Feierabend, Hans Butikofer
3. Great Britain (I), 5:23.41, Frederick McEvoy, James Cardno, Guy Dugdale, Charles Green

1932 1. USA (I), 7:53.68, William Fiske, Edward Eagan, Clifford Gray, Jay O'Brien
2. USA (II), 7:55.70, Henry Homburger, Percy Bryant, Paul Stevens, Edmund Horton
3. Germany (I), 8:00.04, Hanns Kilian, Max Ludwig, Dr. Hans Melhorn, Sebastian Huber

1928 1. USA (II), 3:20.5, William Fiske, Nion Tocker, Charles Mason, Clifford Gray, Richard Parke

2. USA (I), 3:21.0, Jennison Heaton, David Granger, Lyman Hine, Thomas Doe, Jay O'Brien
3. Germany (III), 3:21.9, Hanns Kilian, Valentin Krempl, Hans Hess, Sebastian Huber, Hans Nagle

1924 1. Switzerland (I), 5:45.54, Eduard Scherrer, Alfred Neveu, Alfred Schlappi, Heinrich Schlappi

2. Great Britain (II), 5:48.83, Ralph H. Broome, T. A. Arnold, H. A. W. Richardson, Rodney E. Soher
3. Belgium (I), 6:02.29, Charles Mulder, Rene Mortiaux, Paul van den Broeck, Victor Verschueren, Henri Willems

Norway's Sonja Henie was a dominant force in ladies' figure skating, capturing the Olympic gold in 1928, 1932, and 1936, and later skating her way to a highly lucrative film career.

FIGURE SKATING

WARM-UP

The first known skates were carved out of rib or shank bones of elk and reindeer. Early northern Europeans tied the skates to their feet and propelled themselves across the ice with poles. The word "skate" probably is derived from the very old Low German word "schake," meaning a shank or leg bone, as well as from the Dutch "schaats," Danish "skoite," English "scatch," and Scottish "sketcher."

Although skating was born in Europe, figure skating as we know it traces its origins directly back to an American—Jackson Haines—who was born in New York in 1840 and died in Finland in 1875, a victim of pneumonia, infected during a raging blizzard while traveling by sled from St. Petersburg to Stockholm.

Prior to that rather cold but romantic demise, Haines enjoyed his 15 minutes of fame and glory. Just before the Civil War, a skating craze, accompanied by a dancing craze, swept the country, inspiring ballet master Haines to combine virtuoso skating skills with expressive dance movements. At that time, figure skating was a stiff and rigid exhibition, a favorite with European aristocrats who dabbled in "artistic skating" for the amusement of friends and family. Haines won figure skating's Championships of America (now called the US Championships). But continued cool reception in the US prompted him to leave for Europe, where he was, of course, warmly received. He made his home in Vienna, creating the "International Style of Figure Skating." Haines translated ballet steps to skates, and the ensuing craze that swept Europe inspired composers to create special waltzes for dancers on skates.

But it was not until the first decade of the 20th century that this style was fully accepted in America. Haines, however, became known as the "American Ice Master" in Europe, opening skating schools in several countries.

One of the men influenced by Haines was Canadian Louis Rubinstein, who formed the Amateur Skating Association of Canada in 1878. Nine years later the Skating Club of the United States was established in Philadelphia. Rubinstein, who won the Canadian figure skating championship every year from 1878 to 1889, was the US champion in 1888 and 1889, and in 1890 he won the world championship in Russia.

Figure skating was added to the 1908 Olympic Games, 16 years prior to the start of the Winter Olympic Games. However, the sport continued to function

77

informally in the US through local skating clubs until 1921, when the United States Figure Skating Association (USFSA) was formed.

But figure skating did not become widely popular in America until a 13-year-old Norwegian girl by the name of Sonja Henie created a figure-skating stir in the 1920s. At the mere age of 10 in 1924, Henie won the Norwegian figure skating championship. Starting in 1927 (at the more mature age of 13), she took the world championship 10 straight years, fitting in three Olympic gold medals during the same period (the first in 1928 and the last in 1936). It was Henie who made figure skating the most popular of the Olympic events and professionalized the sport as a lucrative career.

In 1961, with the US reigning supreme as the world's premier figure skating team, tragedy struck. In February, a plane carrying the American team to the world championship in Prague crashed near Brussels, killing all 73 people aboard, including 18 team members, five coaches, the team manager, and friends and relatives. The team was shattered; though they'd won gold medals in the men's and ladies' singles during the 1956 and 1960 Games, the US did not take the gold again in either of these events until 1968, when Peggy Fleming won the ladies' singles. In the men's singles competition, the US did not win a gold medal until 1984, when Scott Hamilton triumphed.

Ice dancing was added to the Winter Olympic program in 1976, joining men's and ladies' singles and pairs skating. As its name implies, ice dancing is based on different aspects of dance, with the emphasis on rhythm and steps. The beauty of ice dancing lies in its precise footwork, coordination, and creative flair. Another change in figure skating competition is in store for the 1992 Winter Games, where for the first time the compulsory figures, those 42 enticing variations on the figure eight, will not figure into the men's and ladies' singles competitions.

▼

SPECTATORS' GUIDE

Figure skaters actually skate on water; as the steel blade cuts through the ice, the friction causes the ice to momentarily melt; it immediately refreezes after the blade passes.

Rather than a flat blade with a single edge, the figure skate blade is concave, creating two sharp edges that must be continually sharpened to maintain an even speed for cutting through the ice. The skates have an outside edge, on the outside of the foot, and an inside edge toward the body. Each edge has a front and a back, so that the skate has four pressure points. Different moves and jumps are done from specific edges of the skate blade. Figure skating blades also feature little spikes on the toes called "picks." These toe picks are used to perform certain maneuvers, jumps, and spins.

Two basic types of jumps are attempted: edge jumps and toe-assisted jumps. In toe-assisted jumps, the picks on one skate are pushed into the ice to help propel the skater into the air. On edge jumps, a skater presses into the ice with a certain edge of the skate and swings into the air with the force of the arms and other leg (the free leg). The majority of skaters spin to the left (counterclockwise).

Olympic figure skating competition includes four separate disciplines: men's singles, ladies' singles, pairs, and ice dancing. Each draws on similar basic skills and techniques, but adheres to different rules and guidelines. Judges award marks to each skater ranging from 0.0 (did not skate) to 6.0 (perfect). Decimal points are used for exact placements, such as 4.8 or 5.3. In skating, the low and high marks *are not dropped*, and all of the points *are not added together*. Each judge's mark is converted into places—1st, 2nd, 3rd, etc. The skater winning the majority of first placements wins that event.

When you see the judge's marks posted in the arena, you are seeing them "horizontally" for one skater. You must look at all of the marks "vertically" to see the judges' marks for the skaters in relation to one another. Following each event, the placement that a skater earns is multiplied by a percentage, which is determined according to the value of the event.

Whew!

Scoring in figure skating is often the cause of controversy, and political influence is frequently suspected. Judging observes no binding guidelines on which to base marks, and occasionally a wide disparity in marks for a skater will result. With nine judges, however, excessively high or low marks can usually be balanced.

The rules are similar for both **men's and ladies' singles**. Each competition is composed of two separate events: an original program and a long program. The combined placement from all the events makes up a competitor's total score. A third event, the **compulsory figures** (also known as "school figures"), was eliminated from international competition in 1990 but may be skated as a separate medal in some competitions.

In the **original program**, also called the short program, the skater must execute, in two minutes and 40 seconds, eight required moves within a choreographed program using music. The required moves can be performed in any sequence of the skater's choice. The elements include a double axel; a double jump (men are permitted to do a triple jump); a jump combination (two jumps following each other without a step in between); a flying jump spin; a spin with at least two changes of foot for men and a layback spin for women; a spin with at least one change of foot and at least two changes of position; two sequences of steps or footwork done in either a straight line, serpentine, or circular shape (one step sequence must be done in a spiral position for women).

Each skater receives two marks from each judge for the original program. The first mark is for technical merit—how well each of the required moves is done and how difficult they are. The second mark is for presentation and style (sometimes called artistic impression), which evaluates the overall presentation of the program.

The **long program** (also called the freestyle) is skated free of required elements. Four and a half minutes in length for men and four minutes for women, the long program is the most demanding part of the singles competition, requiring extreme stamina and concentration. Skaters select their own music and choreography, blending many different jumps, spins, and interpretive moves in a program designed to best display their technical and artistic skills.

As in the original program, two sets of marks are given. The first is for technical merit, the second for presentation and style of the overall program. While spectators may find that the grace, strength, and expression in a performance is pleasing, the judges are looking for technical and artistic excellence. An error, such as a fall, does not mean that the skater will lose the competition. Difficulty of moves and jumps, how they are executed, and the overall presentation are all considered.

If two skaters are tied at the end of the competition, the winner is determined first by the one who received the highest placement in the long program. If they are still tied, then the one with the highest presentation and style marks in the long program is declared the winner.

Pairs skating is essentially skating performed in unison by partners, with the addition of daring and often dangerous lifts and throw jumps.

The key to pairs skating is exact timing and togetherness. Whether the partners skate in physical contact or apart, their movements should be synchronized with matching body lines, spins, gestures, and footwork.

In pairs skating, you will see "shadow skating," in which the couple skates in unison without touching, as well as "mirror skating," in which each skates identical moves in different directions, giving the illusion of a mirror. You will also see a variety of lifts and throws.

The pairs skating competition involves two parts—the original program and the long program. Each event is skated to the couple's own choice of music and choreography and includes scores for technical merit as well as style and presentation.

The **original program**, at two minutes, 40 seconds and 33.3% of the final score, includes eight required elements. These are: an overhead lift; a double twist lift; side-by-side solo double jumps; a solo spin in unison; a pair spin with at least one change of position and one change of foot; a death spiral; a spiral sequence; a step or footwork sequence of the skaters' choice. The required moves may be performed in any order.

The **long program** consists of technical and artistic moves choreographed to best display the skaters' individual strengths and abilities. Four and a half minutes long and 66.7% of the final score, the long program involves double and

80

triple throw jumps, different overhead lifts and spins, variations on standard moves, and many original moves. Creativity, strength, endurance, and technical skills are all important.

When watching **ice dancing**, watch for the flow of the program, the apparent ease with which difficult technical steps and moves are performed, and how well the music is interpreted. Ice dancers skate extremely close to each other and must remain in unison and contact during the program. They cannot separate for more than a few seconds. The strong, athletic moves seen in pair skating, such as overhead lifts and jumps, are prohibited in dance.

Ice dancing is comprised of three events: two compulsory dances, amounting to 20% of the final score; an original set pattern dance that is 30% of the final tally; and a four-minute free dance that counts for 50% of the total score.

Compulsory dances—such as the foxtrot, tango, blues, rhumba, Viennese waltz, and Yankee polka—are international dances frequently performed by ice dancers worldwide. From this list of dances, the couple selects two dances at random. To prescribed rhythms the skaters execute specific steps in an exact manner. The skaters receive one score for each dance. The marks are added together to determine placements, and the couple scoring the highest mark finishes first.

The **original set pattern dance** is an original dance created by the couple to a previously announced rhythm, such as a waltz, tango, or polka. While the rhythm is preselected by skating officials, the music and choreography are chosen by the individual dancers. A definite dance pattern is created by the skaters, using the full surface of the ice. The skaters are judged on how well they interpret the rhythm and create an appropriate dance. Two marks are given: one for composition, which includes originality, difficulty of steps, variety, and the placement of steps in the pattern, the second mark is given for presentation, which reflects such components as timing, harmony of movements to the rhythm, and the interpretive style of the couple.

The **free dance** is performed to musical selections and choreography selected by the skaters. You may see different popular dances and rhythms used, such as graceful waltzes or fast jitterbugs, or you may see classical presentations. Although certain types of small lifts and original moves are used, free dance is differentiated from pairs skating by restrictions on the execution and number of these moves. Judges look for style and interpretation, expression of the music, difficulty of standard and original steps, and an overall harmonious blending of the couple's performances throughout the program. Two sets of marks are awarded, one for technical merit and the other for style and presentation.

Figure Skating

Quick Skating Glossary

AXEL is the easiest jump to recognize because it is the only jump taken from a forward position. The skater glides forward on one foot, takes off from a forward outside edge, rotates (1.5 revolutions for a single, 2.5 for a double, and 3.5 for a triple axel), and lands on the opposite foot skating backward.

DEATH SPIRAL is a required move in pairs skating in which the man spins in a pivot position while holding one hand of the lady, who is spinning in a horizonal position on one edge of the skate with her body parallel to the ice.

FLIP is a toe-assisted jump, taken off from the left foot going backward and landed on the right foot.

LOOP is taken off and landed on the same foot and edge. At the point of takeoff, the skater's feet may look as if they are together. The free leg is then thrown sideways and upward in the direction of the jump.

LUTZ is one of the few jumps that takes off counter to the natural rotation of the edge. The skater usually approaches in a long curve, takes off from the left back outside edge with assistance from the right toe, and turns counter-clockwise, landing on the outside back edge of the right foot.

SALCHOW is a jump with a wide leg swing. At the moment before takeoff, the back inside edge of the skating foot curves sharply and the free leg is brought forward to initiate rotation. The skater lands on the back outside edge of the opposite foot of takeoff.

SPIN is the rotation of the body in one spot on one foot. Many different kinds of spins exist; if a skater leaps into the air before coming down into the spin, it is usually called a jump or flying spin.

SPLIT JUMP is a flashy move seen in single skating, in which the skater jumps into the air and performs a split in mid-air with the hands touching the ankles or toes. Also called a "Russian split," the move is referred to as a split flip when a half-revolution is added after touching the toes.

THREE TURN is a turn on one foot from forward to backward or backward to forward (from outside to inside edge or inside to outside edge).

THROW JUMPS are seen in pair skating, when the male partner assists the lady in the air into a jump.

TOE LOOP is rarely performed as a single jump but is very popular as a double and triple. The skater takes off from the back outside edge, strikes the toe of the free foot into the ice, turns in the air, and lands on the original back outside edge. The free leg stretches along the line of travel before takeoff.

HOPEFULS

Men's Singles: A dazzling array of talent awaits figure skating fans in 1992. The Soviet Union's Viktor Petrenko, who won the Olympic bronze medal in the 1988 men's singles competition, will compete again, having won a gold medal in the 1991 European Championships and a silver in that year's World Championships. Canadian Kurt Browning, who received his third gold medal in the 1991 World competition, promises to be an impressive contender. And Todd Eldredge, twice winner of the US National Championships and bronze medalist in the 1991 Worlds, also hopes to make Olympic history in 1992. Other strong singles contenders include Czechoslovakia's Petr Barna, the United States' Christopher Bowman, and the Soviet Union's Viacheslav Zagorodniuk.

Ladies' Singles: The ladies' singles performances will display a wealth of young talent, much of it from the United States, whose skaters garnered the top three places in the 1991 World Championships. Gold medalist Kristi Yamaguchi intends to add to her repertoire a triple axel, which silver medalist Tonya Harding has already perfected. Nancy Kerrigan's performance in her first World competition gave her the bronze medal. Japan's Midori Ito—who was the first woman to land a triple axel in competition and may attempt a quadruple—is also expected to place well. Though she only placed fourth in the 1991 Worlds because of injuries from a fall, Ito had placed first and second in the two previous competitions. And the United States' Jill Trenary, named 1990 Athlete of the Year by the US Olympic Committee and past winner of the US National competition, missed both the 1991 US National and World Championships because of an ankle injury but still hopes to compete in the 1992 Olympic Games. France's Surya Bonaly, Canada's Josée Chouinard, and Germany's Evelyn Grossman and Marina Kielmann round out the list of singles hopefuls.

Pairs: The Soviet Union may dominate the pairs competition with the three couples who won the 1991 European Championships. Natalia Mishkutinok and Artur Dmitriev earned gold medals in both the 1991 European and World competitions. European silver medalists Elena Bechke and Denis Petrov, and bronze medalists Evgenia Shishkova and Vadim Naumov, also placed highly in the World games that year. These couples will be challenged, though, by the World Championships' silver and bronze medalists: Isabelle Brasseur and Lloyd Eisler of Canada, and Natasha Kuchiki and Todd Sand of the United States.

Ice Dancing: Longtime Soviet contenders Marina Klimova and Sergei Ponomarenko, who won the Olympic bronze medal in 1984 and the silver in 1988, will return to the ice dancing competition in 1992, hoping this time for the gold. Their closest competitors will probably be France's beloved sister-brother team of Isabelle and Paul Duchesnay (though raised in Canada, they skate for France), who placed first in the 1991 World Championships and second in the European Championships. (Klimova and Ponomarenko had placed second in that year's Worlds and first in the European games.) Also competing will be the Soviet Union's Maia Usova and Alexandr Zhulin, who received bronze medals in the 1991 World and European games, and the United States' April Sargent and Russ Witherby.

Midori Ito

Technically, Midori Ito is a flawless figure skater, the first woman ever to perform a triple axel in a major international competition. A native of Nagoya, Japan, Ito will certainly be a dominant force in the 1992 Olympics, but recent throat surgery and injuries have loosened the grip she seemed to have on a gold medal.

Ito thrilled audiences at the 1988 Winter Olympics in Calgary both with her daredevil jumping and her infectious exuberance. Had she not performed relatively poorly in the compulsory figures, she might have been one of the medal winners. Instead, she finished fifth overall and was seen as a promising contender who could win international titles if she improved the artistic content of her program.

Little is known about the day-to-day life of Midori Ito. The 4-foot-9, 97-pound Ito was born in Nagoya, a city of two million. She began skating almost as soon as she could walk, and by the age of four she was being trained by Machiko Yamada, a well-known Japanese skating coach.

When Ito was six her parents divorced. She went to live with Yamada's family, and has stayed with them since. "At that time, she accepted me as one of her children," Ito told the *Los Angeles Times* of her coach. "So I didn't feel that I was a hardship for her."

The youngster showed amazing prowess. As an eleven-year-old in the World Junior Championships, she completed three triple jumps. In 1983 she won the World Juniors Championship. Ito told the *Los Angeles Times:* "As a child, I felt I could master some of the jumps quicker than the other children. Jumps that would take them three hours to learn took me an hour and a half." Ito did find herself at a disadvantage in international competition, however. She often experienced trouble with her compulsory figures, and judges faulted her highly athletic performances for lack of artistic merit.

At least one of those drawbacks will no longer haunt her. Compulsories have been eliminated from senior singles skating, giving Ito an edge over her American counterparts Jill Trenary and Kristi Yamaguchi. Ito has also been studying ballet in an effort to improve the artistic element of her program. Her long and short programs now are often choreographed by ballet teachers rather than skating coaches—but they still feature the magnificent jumping that has made a name for the Japanese star.

Ito's finest moment to date came in 1989, when she won the Women's World Figure Skating Championship in Paris. Her long routine—including the dazzling triple axel—earned five perfect marks for technical merit. Ito was the first Japanese woman ever to win a World Championship in figure skating, and

Japan's Midori Ito, a technically brilliant skater, is the first woman ever to perform a triple axel in a major international competition.

France's beloved sister-brother ice dancing team, Isabelle and Paul Duchesnay, have turned their sport in a new direction.

she became a national heroine in her native land. She was even invited to meet with Emperor Akihito in his palace.

Since then injuries and complications from surgery have dogged Ito. She is determined to be ready for the 1992 Olympics, even though she finished poorly in the 1991 World Championships. The qualified American skaters are watching her with trepidation, honing their own jumping abilities in order to compete with her.

Los Angeles Times correspondent Randy Harvey perhaps offered the most apt description of Ito when he called her "a smile attached to wings." —*M.K.*

Schedule

The tentative figure skating schedule is as follows:

Sunday, February 9
Originals, pair

Tuesday February 11
Freestyle, pair

Thursday, February 13
Originals, men

Friday, February 14
Compulsories, ice dancing

Saturday, February 15
Freestyle, men

Sunday, February 16
Originals, ice dancing

Monday, February 17
Freestyle, ice dancing

Wednesday, February 19
Originals, women

Friday, February 21
Freestyle, women

Saturday, February 22
Exhibitions

MEN'S SINGLES
▼

HIGHLIGHTS

Ulrich Salchow of Sweden, a world champion ten times between 1901 and 1911, was the first Olympic gold medalist in the men's singles, leading two other Swedes into the medals. Russian Nikolai Panin, who withdrew from illness or in protest, is the record holder in perpetuity of the special figures title, a discontinued event that required elaborate patterns cut into the ice. His real name was Nilolai Kolomenkin, and in 1912 he competed in Stockholm as a member of the fourth-place Russian pistol team. Beginning in 1920 Sweden's Gillis Grafström won three consecutive gold medals in the men's competitions; he was among the first to embrace the artistic advantage of interpreting music on the ice. The bronze medalist in 1920, Norway's Martin Stixrud, was 44 years old when he garnered his medal. Grafström's elegant reign ended when he took second place to Karl Schäfer of Austria in 1932—but Grafström remains the only skater to win medals in four Games. Ernst Baier of Germany was silver medalist behind Schäfer in 1936 and also won the gold in the pairs with his future wife Maxi Herber; Baier thus became the only figure-skating competitor to have won a gold and silver in two different events.

US skater Dick Button, a superlative jumper, captured Olympic golds in 1948 and 1952. He had only mastered the double axel two days before he performed it in his 1948 free-skating program, and brought a newly developed triple loop to the 1952 Games. Button was followed by countryman Hayes Alan Jenkins, gold medalist in 1956, whose brother, David Jenkins, won the bronze that year; silver medalist Ronald Robertson came between the brothers to effect an American sweep of the event. Hayes Jenkins later married 1960 ladies' gold medalist Carol Heiss. David Jenkins came back in 1960 to win the gold with some spectacular triple jumps. West German Manfred Schnelldörfer, a former roller-skating champion, captured the gold in 1964, besting Alain Calmat of France and an exuberant Scot Allen of the US; Allan was two days short of his 15th birthday when he won the bronze, becoming the youngest person to medal in the Winter Games. Austrian Wolfgang Schwartz, gold medalist in 1968, narrowly took the field over Tim Wood of the US and third-place Patrick Pera of France. Pera was back as bronze medalist in 1972, behind Ondrej Nepela of Czechoslovakia (who won on his school figures and fell trying a triple-toe loop) and silver medalist Sergei Chetveroukhin of the USSR. Ken Shelley, the US national champion, took fourth place in the men's singles and also placed fourth along with partner JoJo Starbuck in the pairs.

US skater Terry Kubicka is famous for being the first and last skater to perform a backflip in the Olympics, part of his program at Innsbruck in 1976. The move was later banned as too dangerous. That year John Curry of Britain, a magnificent stylist known as the "Nureyev of the Ice" for his ballet-like movements, won the gold, followed by Vladimir Kovalev of the USSR and Canadian Toller Cranston. US skater David Santee placed sixth. In 1980 British skater Robin Cousins got off to a disappointing start at Lake Placid when he stood only fourth after the compulsories. But Cousins, then the finest freeskater in the world, moved into second place in the short program, then skated past his competitors in the final to bring Britain its second consecutive men's champion. Silver medalist Jan Hoffman of East Germany was competing in his fourth Olympics. US skater Charles Tickner claimed the bronze. Santee moved up to fourth in this Olympiad, while US skater Scott Hamilton took fifth place. Hamilton's turn came in 1984, when he edged out Canada's Brian Orser for the gold, mostly based on their scores for the school figures. Czechoslovakia's Jozef Sabovtchik took the bronze.

In 1988 the "battle of the Brians" matched the 1984 silver medalist from Canada, Brian Orser, against Brian Boitano of the US. Boitano was best known for the quadruple toe loop, which he did not attempt for the Calgary competition. In 1982 he was the first skater to land a triple axel in the Nationals, and the following year he was the first skater to land all six triple jumps in the world championships: the salchow, lutz, axel, toe loop, loop, and flip. He also developed a trademark 'Tano triple, which adds to a triple lutz the gravitational challenge of one arm upstretched overhead while the other is cupped away from the body, cradled in front. The arm position slows down rotation, and so requires towering height on the jump. Orser, who had to settle for the silver medal in 1984 because of a seventh place finish in the figures, boasted a trademark triple axel jump in his 1988 Olympic repertoire. Orser won the competition's only perfect 6.0 score, but bobbled in his long program and simplified a jump at the end. Boitano skated at his peak to claim the gold. Canadian Kurt Browning performed the only quadruple jump of the 1988 Games, but fell in the process.

Salchow and Button

Instruction performing doing a Salchow: 1. Jump up from the back inside edge of either skate. 2. Complete a full turn in the air. 3. Land on the back outside edge of the second skate. Repeat as necessary. Ulrich Salchow, the legendary Swede, was the first to do what is now a compulsory jump in any figure skating program. Then, a single Salchow was revolutionary. Contemporary programs now require two or three revolutions in the air.

By the 1908 London Olympics—the debut of figure skating as an Olympic event—Salchow was already a seven-time world champion. However, he had lost earlier that year to Russian Nicolai Panin. In London, though, Salchow won three first place votes for his compulsory figures to Panin's two. The Russian, complaining of bias, dropped out, setting the stage for a Swedish sweep of all three medals, led by Salchow.

Until separate Winter Games began in 1924, figure skating events were held only if there happened to be a convenient skating rink. Salchow's next chance to defend his Olympic title came in Antwerp in 1920. Salchow, then 43, lost to countryman Gillis Grafström.

The American Richard Button first executed salchows, winning two gold medals in 1948 an 1952, and then talked about them as a network television commentator for the Olympics. At both Games, Button tossed new and exciting jumps into his freestyle program, including the first triple (a loop) in the 1952 Games. Over the two Games he earned 17 of 18 first place votes from judges. Button, born July 18, 1929 in Englewood, New Jersey, is author of the autobiography *Dick Button on Skates*. After the 1952 Games, Button turned professional, touring with the Ice Capades as well as earning a law degree. —H.D.

The Battling Brians: Boitano and Orser

It was billed as the "Battle of the Brians"—the showdown between American Brian Boitano and Canadian Brian Orser at the 1988 Winter Olympics in Calgary, Canada. Boitano and Orser had been friends off the ice for a number of years, but their tense rivalry in several World Championships set the stage for an exciting Olympic encounter.

As Randy Harvey of the *Los Angeles Times* put it, the 1988 Winter Games would stand as the ultimate test for the two young skaters. Harvey wrote: "Veteran figure skating observers ... said they had never seen a closer competition between two men who were so near the edge of their considerable abilities."

Orser and Boitano came to Calgary with different training methods and philosophies, but they did agree on one matter: they thought the press overplayed the significance of their "battle." Orser was the defending World Champion, having won in 1987, but Boitano had finished first in the two world championships prior to that. No one was sure which man would win in 1988, but most observers—including Boitano—agreed that the skaters had long been aware of each other's talents.

"We push each other; that's what's good," Boitano told the *Chicago Tribune.* "We're all better skaters because of it."

Boitano was born in 1963 in Sunnyvale, California. He began skating just for the fun of it when he was eight, after dazzling his neighbors with his prowess on roller skates. His ice skating coach, Linda Leaver, was an unknown group teacher who detected the seeds of excellence in Boitano. He learned quickly and was fearless and graceful on the ice. Leaver—who had been teaching skating only to generate income while her husband earned his PhD—had always dreamed of coaching an Olympic-calibre athlete. She persuaded her spouse to put his own career on hold while she worked with Boitano.

The skating community encouraged Boitano time and again to abandon Leaver for a more experienced coach, but the two remained together sixteen years. Boitano did seek extra advice elsewhere—from veterans such as John Nicks, Frank Carroll, and Barbara Roles Williams—but he did the greatest part of his work with Leaver.

At eighteen he was the first in the United States nationals to land the triple axel cleanly in competition, but to his frustration he found himself often playing second fiddle to World Champion Scott Hamilton. In the 1984 Winter Olympics, for instance, he finished fifth.

Boitano began winning American and World Championships after Hamilton retired. He was United States Champion every year between 1985 and 1988, finished third in the 1985 World Championships, and finished first in the 1986 World Championship. Somehow, both he and the judges remained dissatisfied with his performance. In retrospect, he told the *Chicago Tribune,* he looked like "a robot on springs." He added: "If I hadn't been criticized like I was then, I wouldn't be where I am now. I used to be unable to look at [old] tapes because all I saw was good jumps. Now I can smile at them and see the progression."

Enter Brian Orser, perhaps a bit less technically perfect but far more artistic on the ice. Orser was born in 1961 in Penetanguishene, Ontario, Canada. He was raised in Midland, Ontario, and was introduced to the sport of skating at the age of five by his mother, a skating teacher. He began working with a professional coach, Doug Leigh, when he was nine. By the time he turned seventeen, he had perfected the triple axel to the point that his friends erected a sign—"You're in Triple Axel Country"—at the arena where he practiced.

Orser was Canadian Champion every year from 1981 until 1988. He earned a silver medal in the 1984 Olympics, winning both the short and long programs but performing poorly in the compulsories. Observers expected Orser to step into the World Championship shoes of Scott Hamilton when the latter retired in 1984, but Orser seemed jinxed by a series of second-place finishes. The skater told the *Los Angeles Times* that the pressures of competition began to weigh him down. After finishing second in two World Championships, he was favored to win in 1986.

Instead, he became so nervous prior to his long program that he stumbled on two triple axels and settled for second place yet again—behind Brian Boitano.

At that point Orser hired a sports psychologist, Peter Jensen, to help him overcome his fears. Orser also hired a masseuse, a new choreographer, a costume designer, a nutritionist, a financial manager, and a public relations agent. The costs were underwritten by the Canadian Figure Skating Association. Apparently, this ploy worked. Orser won the 1987 World Championships, beating Boitano for the first time, and came into the Olympics as the favorite.

Boitano took the 1987 defeat seriously himself. Long known as more of an athletic than aesthetic skater, he decided to hire a new choreographer. Ironically, he looked to Canada, hiring Sandra Bezic. It was Bezic who designed the cocky, showy "Napoleon" number that ultimately won Boitano the gold medal at Calgary in an extremely close competition. Boitano had gained only a slim lead over Orser in the compulsories and the short program when he skated onto the ice for his "Napoleon" routine. That program he performed nearly flawlessly, cleanly hitting seven of his eight planned triple jumps and making an almost imperceptible error on one triple axel.

Orser might still have won the gold for Canada with his own dramatic long program, "The Bolt," but he stumbled slightly after one of his triple jumps and substituted a double axel for a planned triple axel near the end of the performance. He was given a standing ovation by the partisan Canadian crowd, and he was surprised when he learned that he had finished second.

"I felt I had done it," he told the *Los Angeles Times.*

Boitano, on the other hand, was less interested in winning the gold medal than in skating his very best. "I had done what I had come to do," he told the *Los Angeles Times* after his long program. "It really didn't matter which color medal I won, a gold, a silver, or a bronze. I just wanted to skate my best. I skated the best that I've ever skated in my life." When he was presented with the gold medal, however, he admitted: "I consider this victory a medal for all America."

Both Orser and Boitano have retired from amateur figure skating. Orser was awarded his country's highest civilian honor, the Order of Canada. Boitano has enjoyed a lucrative career in ice shows, sometimes performing with both

Orser and former Olympian Katarina Witt. Asked about the "Battle of the Brians" in the *Los Angeles Times,* Boitano said that the media hype never affected the close friendship he had formed with Orser. "We just laugh about it," he said. "This big rivalry has been pushed on us. A lot of people are trying to pull us apart and make us enemies. We really are not. On the ice, we have our own jobs to do, and we both want to win, but we're very good friends off the ice."

That mutual respect has carried into retirement, where the two Brians no longer face the glare of the media or the expectations of their prospective nations. —*M.K.*

Winter

Figure Skating — Men's Singles

1988	1. Brian Boitano, USA, 3.0
	2. Brian Orser, Canada, 4.2
	3. Viktor Petrenko, Soviet Union, 7.8
1984	1. Scott Hamilton, USA, 3.4
	2. Brian Orser, Canada, 5.6
	3. Jozef Sabovtchik, Czechoslovakia, 7.4
1980	1. Robin Cousins, Great Britain, 189.48
	2. Jan Hoffman, East Germany, 189.72
	3. Charles Tickner, USA, 187.06
1976	1. John Curry, Great Britain, 192.74
	2. Vladimir Kovalev, Soviet Union, 187.64
	3. Toller Cranston, Canada, 187.34
1972	1. Ondrej Nepela, Czechoslovakia, 2,739.1
	2. Sergei Chetveroukhin, Soviet Union, 2,672.4
	3. Patrick Pera, France, 2,653.1
1968	1. Wolfgang Schwarz, Austria, 1,904.1
	2. Tim Wood, USA, 1,891.6
	3. Patrick Pera, France, 1,864.5
1964	1. Manfred Schnelldorfer, West Germany, 1,916.9
	2. Alain Calmat, France, 1,876.5
	3. Scott Allen, USA, 1,873.6
1960	1. David Jenkins, USA, 1,440.2
	2. Karol Divin, Czechoslovakia, 1,414.3
	3. Donald Jackson, Canada, 1,401.0
1956	1. Hayes Alan Jenkins, USA, 1,497.95

	2. Ronald Robertson, USA, 1,492.15
	3. David Jenkins, USA, 1,465.41
1952	1. Richard Button, USA, 1,730.3
	2. Helmut Seibt, Austria, 1,621.3
	3. James Grogan, USA, 1,627.4
1948	1. Richard Button, USA, 1,720.6
	2. Hans Gerschwiler, Switzerland, 1,630.1
	3. Edi Rada, Austria, 1,603.2
1936	1. Karl Schafer, Austria, 2,959.0
	2. Ernst Baier, Germany, 2,805.3
	3. Felix Kaspar, Austria, 2,801.0
1932	1. Karl Schafer, Austria, 2,602.0
	2. Gillis Grafstrom, Sweden, 2,514.5
	3. Montgomery Wilson, Canada, 2,448.3
1928	1. Gillis Grafstrom, Sweden, 2,698.25
	2. Willy Bockl, Austria, 2,682.50
	3. Robert van Zeebroeck, Belgium, 2,578.75
1924	1. Gillis Grafstrom, Sweden, 2,575.25
	2. Willy Bockl, Austria, 2,518.75
	3. Georges Gautschi, Switzerland, 2,233.50
1920	1. Gillis Grafstrom, Sweden, 2,838.50
	2. Andreas Krogh, Norway, 2,634.00
	3. Martin Stixrud, Norway, 2,561.50
1912	**Not held**
1908	1. Ulrich Salchow, Sweden, 1,886.5
	2. Richard Johansson, Sweden, 1,826.0
	3. Per Thoren, Sweden, 1,787.0

US figure skater Dick Button won gold medals at the 1948 and 1952 Games and followed his sport to further fame as a network television skating commentator.

Canadian figure skater Brian Orser, who won silver medals at the 1984 and 1988 Games, earned the only perfect 6.0 score awarded in his event at Calgary.

Silver medalist in 1952, US figure skater Tenley Albright overcame injury to skate away with the ladies' gold in 1956.

Dorothy Hamill's sparkling free skating brought the US another ladies' gold in 1976, and another fad hairstyle, the wedge.

LADIES' SINGLES

▼

HIGHLIGHTS

British skater Madge Syers had finished second to Sweden's Ulrich Salchow in the 1902 world championships, which was then open to both genders. Syers came out of retirement to win the first ladies' Olympic gold in 1908; she also took a bronze in the pairs. In 1920 Sweden had a champion in Magda Julin; that year the bronze medalist from the US, Theresa Weld, was reprimanded by the judges for making the unfeminine mistake of including a salchow in her program. Weld also placed fourth in the pairs competition with Nathaniel Niles. Austria's Herma Planck-Szabó took the gold in 1924, with US skater Beatrix Loughran earning a silver. Loughran came back to win a bronze in 1928, and in 1932 came back for a silver in the pairs with Sherwin Badger.

Skating's first mega-star, Sonja Henie of Norway, competed in the 1924 Games at age 11, then took the gold in 1928, 1932, and 1936, leading skating to new areas of athleticism. Henie was influential in popularizing figure skating, first as an Olympic event and later as an entertainment vehicle, when she performed in ice shows and motion pictures. Her skating eventually earned her a fortune estimated at nearly 50 million dollars. US skater Maribel Vinson won the bronze in 1932; as the mother of two promising skaters on the US team she perished along with them in the 1961 Brussels plane crash that killed 73 people, including 18 team members, five coaches, the team manager, and friends and relatives. Canadian Barbara Ann Scott earned the gold in 1948, followed by British skater Jeannette Altwegg in 1952. Shunning the ice capades route, Altwegg retired to work at the Pestalozzi Children's Village in Trogen, Switzerland.

American women have periodically captured the singles gold, including Tenley Albright in 1956 (silver medalist in 1952) and Carol Heiss in 1960 (silver medalist in 1956). Albright had been stricken with nonparalytic polio when she was 11 years old; after retiring from skating she followed her father's career path and became a surgeon. Heiss married men's 1956 champion Hayes Alan Jenkins. The silver medalist in 1960, Sjoukje Dijkstra of the Netherlands, earned the gold in 1964. US skater Peggy Fleming was champion in 1968, skating in costumes sewn by her mother. Fleming won the only US gold medal of the Grenoble Games. Austrian Beatrix Schuba won the gold in 1972 on her compulsory figures, while the real dazzler in the free-skating program that year was US skater Janet Lynn, who took the bronze behind Canada's Karen Magnussen. The compulsory figures were subsequently reduced in overall importance, and US skater Dorothy Hamill turned in a sparkling free program for the gold in 1976. Dianne de Leeuw, an American citizen who competed for the Netherlands, was the silver medalist and Christine Errath of East Germany took the bronze. US skater Linda Fratianne, hurt by her compulsory figures, earned a silver medal in 1980 behind

East German Anett Pötzsch, in the closest competition in 60 years. Rosalynn Sumners won another silver for the US in 1984, behind East Germany's glamorous ice queen, Katarina Witt.

The American contender in 1988, Debi Thomas, was famous for a triple salchow double toe loop combination, a treacherous maneuver. She faced off in 1988 against Witt, the reigning Olympic queen. They both skated their long program to music from Bizet's *Carmen*. When it was all over, Thomas had to settle for the bronze—thereby becoming the first black athlete to win a medal in the Winter Games. Canada's Elizabeth Manley turned in an exciting and lively routine in front of a hometown crowd for the silver medal, and Witt, claiming the gold for the second time, became the first woman figure-skating champion to repeat at the Olympics since Sonja Henie. Especially charming was Japan's Midori Ito, who finished fifth with a triple lutz and a standing ovation from the crowd.

Henie and Other Greats

Sonja Henie of Norway became the most famous figure skater of all time, and possibly the best. Henie skated in four Olympics, beginning with the 1924 Games in Chamonix when she was just 11 years old, then winning gold medals at the next three.

Henie, born in Oslo on April 8, 1912, won her first major title at the 1927 World Championships held, for Henie, on familar ice in Oslo. Of the five judges, three were Norwegian, all of whom voted for Henie. The Austrian and German judges voted for Austrian Herma Planck-Szabó. After that competition, only one judge from any one country was included on the panel. Henie won her first gold at the St. Moritz Games in 1928 when she was still 15. Her style combined grace with a solid athleticism.

Henie dominated the first two Olympics in which she participated, although by 1932 in Lake Placid she was already facing Sonja Henie imitators. At St. Moritz she won six of seven first-place votes in the freestyle portion of the competition, and four years later she was the unanimous selection in Lake Placid.

But the 1936 Games at Garmish-Partenkirchen saw the first chink in her armor—and perhaps helped Henie decide on retirement from amateur competition: Following compulsory figures, the young Brit Cecilia Colledge, who skated in the Henie school, was just 3.6 points behind her role model. Henie barely edged her in the freestyle portion of the competition, but was able to take the gold.

By the time she retired, Henie had won 10 straight world championships (only Swede Ulrich Salchow won more) and more than 1,400 prizes in all. When Henie turned professional, 20th Century Fox handed her a film contract, and she made 11 movies between 1938 and 1960. In 1941, Henie became a US citizen. She married, then divorced, two Americans (to attendant Liz Taylor-style publicity) before wedding her childhood boyfriend, a fellow Norwegian. Henie, who developed cancer, died on October 12, 1969, in a plane carrying her from Paris to Oslo for medical treatment.

America has also produced a long string of female figure skaters who set new standards for the sport. Tenley Albright of Newton Center, Massachusetts, who had suffered from a mild form of polio as a child, fell during training two weeks before the 1956 Cortina Olympics and badly cut her right ankle. Her surgeon father stitched her up and she won the gold. Peggy Fleming easily captured the gold at the 1968 Grenoble Games—wearing costumes sewn by her mother. In 1976, Dorothy Hamill claimed a unanimous victory and ushered in a new hairstyle, the wedge, to a waiting America. —*H.D.*

Katarina Witt

Katarina Witt dominated ladies' figure skating throughout the 1980s. Not only did she win four World Championships, she also became the first woman since Sonja Henie to win a gold medal at consecutive Winter Olympic Games. As a skater, Witt seemed to have it all—arresting beauty, a flair for the dramatic, technical brilliance, and grace under pressure. *Chicago Tribune* correspondent Phil Hersh wrote of Witt: "She is the improbable—a sex symbol from a frigid land."

Witt gave up her amateur status in 1988, after winning her second gold medal at the Winter Games in Calgary and her fourth World Championship. The ensuing years have not been easy ones for her, because the political climate under which she was nurtured as a pampered athlete has since fallen right along with the Iron Curtain.

Hersh writes: "For nearly a decade, Witt assumed, with good reason, that East Germans worshipped her and the other athletes whose Olympic successes were held up as examples of communist rightness." In the wake of a reunited Germany, and the fall of communism, "East Germans were calling their elite athletes privileged parasites who lived off a system that preached social equality and, at even the highest governmental levels, practiced self-indulgent abuse of position. That athletes could travel and immediately get cars and apartments for which others waited decades had become a sin."

Witt told the *Chicago Tribune* that her new, less exalted status in her home country "hurts" because she performed not only for herself and her government but for "the people who loved to watch skating." Still, she hastened to admit, "If you wanted to be something special in East Germany, you did it with sports."

Katarina Witt began skating after her kindergarten class visited Karl Marx Stadt, East Germany's leading Olympic training ground. Soon she was begging her parents for lessons, which were free under government-subsidized programs. Her parents relented, and before long her special talents drew the attention of Jutta Mueller, Olympic coach at the Stadt. Witt was only a child, but Mueller singled her out for the most intensive training.

That training included four to six hours a day of skating, plus running, hurdling, working on a trampoline, dance lessons, and a full courseload of schoolwork. After six years of this regimen, Witt finished second at the 1982 World Championships. The East German government rewarded their budding young star with her own apartment and a Soviet-made Lada automobile, luxuries that most East German adults could only dream about.

Between 1983 and 1986, the only time Witt *lost* the World Championships was in 1986, when she finished second to American Debi Thomas in Switzerland. Otherwise, the engaging skater completely dominated her sport through two Olympic Games and four World Championships. Hersh notes that the East German state "never missed a chance to exploit her sex appeal," allowing her stylish American clothes and free travel to America and elsewhere. The ploy worked: The *Chicago Tribune* quotes a *Sports Illustrated* commentator who described Witt as "fresh-faced, ... blue-eyed, ... ruby-lipped, ... 12-car pileup gorgeous."

None of this detracts from Witt's accomplishments on the ice. Never brilliant in her compulsory work, she usually garnered the most points for her technical skill and artistic interpretations in her long and short programs. She made good use of both modern, Western music and classical works, and her cool presence in both practice and performance situations intimidated her rivals for years. Her decision to "retire" came just as she began to lose the slightest edge in her technical ability.

Witt's professional future almost certainly lies in the United States, where she has been offered starring roles in ice shows and movies. She may also find work as a cosmetics and hair model, something her former government did not allow her to do. She also starred in "Carmen on Ice" with Brians Orser and Boitano.

"I'm still thankful for everything my country gave me, but they used me, too," Witt told the *Chicago Tribune.* "I understand now that's why they gave athletes so much support and money, because the sports system presented the socialist system. They put too much attention on this and missed a lot of other things, like the economy." *—M.K.*

Medalists

Figure Skating — Ladies' Singles

1988 1. Katarina Witt, East Germany, 4.2
2. Elizabeth Manley, Canada, 4.6
3. Debi Thomas, USA, 6.0

1984 1. Katarina Witt, East Germany, 3.2
2. Rosalynn Sumners, USA, 4.6
3. Kira Ivanova, Soviet Union, 9.2

1980 1. Anett Potzsch, East Germany, 189.00
2. Linda Fratianne, USA, 188.30
3. Dagmar Lurz, West Germany, 188.04

1976 1. Dorothy Hamill, USA, 193.80
2. Dianne de Leuuw, Netherlands, 190.24
3. Christine Errath, East Germany, 188.16

1972 1. Beatrix Schuba, Austria, 2,751.5

2. Karen Magnussen, Canada, 2,673.2
3. Janet Lynn, USA, 2,663.1

1968 1. Peggy Fleming, USA, 1,970.5
2. Gabriele Seyfert, East Germany, 1,882.3
3. Hana Maskova, Czechoslovakia, 1,828.8

1964 1. Sjoukje Dijkstra, Netherlands, 2,018.5
2. Regine Heitzer, Austria, 1,945.5
3. Petra Burka, Canada, 1,940.0

1960 1. Carol Heiss, USA, 1,490.1
2. Sjoukje Dijkstra, Netherlands, 1,424.8
3. Barbara Roles, USA, 1,414.9

1956 1. Tenley Albright, USA, 1,866.39
2. Carol Heiss, USA, 1,848.24
3. Ingrid Wendl, Austria, 1,753.91

Dubbed "the Brooke Shields of East Germany," glamorous figure skater Katarina Witt captured her first ladies' gold in 1984 and successfully defended her title in 1988, displaying her characteristic combination of seductive dramatic flair and technical brilliance.

At the 1980 Games US pairs skaters Tai Babilonia and Randy Gardner were poised to repeat their 1979 world championship triumph over the top Soviet figure skating pair, thus breaking a Soviet gold streak in their Olympic event; partway through the competition injury forced the US couple to withdraw, leaving fans stunned.

1952	1. Jeannette Altwegg, Great Britain, 1,455.8
	2. Tenley Albright, USA, 1,432.2
	3. Jacqueline du Bief, France, 1,422.0
1948	1. Barbara Ann Scott, Canada, 1,467.7
	2. Eva Pawlik, Austria, 1,418.3
	3. Jeannette Altwegg, Great Britain, 1,405.5
1936	1. Sonja Henie, Norway, 2,971.4
	2. Cecilia Colledge, Great Britain, 2,926,8
	3. Vivi-Anne Hulten, Sweden, 2,763.2
1932	1. Sonja Henie, Norway, 2,302.5
	2. Fritzi Burger, Austria, 2,167.1
	3. Maribel Y. Vinson, USA, 2,158.50
1928	1. Sonja Henie, Norway, 2,452.25
	2. Fritzi Burger, Austria, 2,248.50
	3. Beatrix Loughran, USA, 2,254.50
1924	1. Herma Planck-Szabo, Austria, 2,094.25
	2. Beatrix Loughran, USA, 1,959.00
	3. Ethel Muckelt, Great Britain, 1,750.50
1920	1. Magda Julin-Mauroy, Sweden, 913.50
	2. Svea Noren, Sweden, 887.75
	3. Theresa Weld, USA, 898.00
1912	Not held
1908	1. Madge Syers, Great Britain, 1,262.5
	2. Elsa Rendschmidt, Germany, 1,055.0
	3. Dorothy Greenhough-Smith, Great Britain, 960.5

PAIRS

▼

HIGHLIGHTS

Germans Heinrich Burger and Anna Hubler won the first pairs gold in 1908; that year the ladies' singles gold medalist, British skater Madge Syers, won a bronze in the pairs with her partner, Edgar Syers. In 1920 the ladies' singles bronze medalist, US skater Theresa Weld, took fourth place in the pairs with her partner Nathaniel Niles; that year Finland won its first skating gold with the husband-and-wife team of Walter and Ludovika Jakobsson; Walter was 38 when they won their gold and Ludovika 35. The Jakobssons were edged out of the gold in 1924 by Austrian pair Alfred Berger and Helene Engelmann. Andrée Joly and Pierre Brunet of France, bronze medalists in 1924, came back to claim the gold in 1928 and 1932; they earned their second gold as Monsieur & Madame Brunet. The 1932 silver medalists were US skater Sherwin Badger paired with Beatrix Loughran, the ladies' singles silver medalist in 1924 and bronze medalist in 1928.

The men's singles silver medalist in 1932, German Ernst Baier, also won a gold in the pairs with Maxi Herber, who later became his wife; Baier is the only figure-skating competitor to have won gold and silver in two different events. Herber was only 15 when they won their gold. They were known for pioneering "shadow skating," in which both skaters perform the same moves without touching.

In 1952 West Germans Ria and Paul Faulk took the gold; the US had silver medalists in Karol and Michael Kennedy. The 1956 competition was marred by dubious judging; the disgruntled crowd in Cortina pelted the officiators with oranges, requiring the ice to be cleared repeatedly. That year Austrian skaters Elisabeth Schwarz and Kurt Oppelt claimed the gold, closely contended by Canadian silver medalists Frances Dafoe and Norris Bowden. The 1960 gold went to Canadians Barbara Wagner and Robert Paul, with US skaters Nancy and Ronald Ludington capturing the bronze. Paul became choreographer for future skating champions Peggy Fleming, Dorothy Hamill, and Linda Fratianne—as well as for entertainers Donny and Marie Osmond.

The Soviet Union has dominated pairs skating for the past three decades, claiming every Olympic pairs gold medal since 1964. The Soviet pair Lyudmilla Belousova and Oleg Protopopov skated to gold in 1964 and, as a married couple, in 1968; the legendary couple was known for their balleticism and almost oblivious passion on ice. The Protopopovs invented the haunting death spiral, now a mainstay of pairs programs. They were followed to the gold in the next three Games by Irina Rodnina and her two partners, Alexei Ulilov (in 1972) and Aleksandr Zaitsev (in 1976 and 1980), who skated a more powerful and technical style. The silver medalists in 1972 were also a Soviet pair, Lyudmila Smirnova and Andrei Suraikin. Rodnina's partner Ulilov developed a romance with Smirnnova that broke up the top Soviet pair. Smirnova and Ulilov married, and Rodnina trained for the gold with a new partner, Zaitsev; the latter couple was married in 1975.

US pair Randy Gardner and Tai Babilonia had upset the Soviets in the 1979 world championships and had been expected to break the Soviet gold streak at Lake Placid in 1980. They stunned American fans when their bid for the medal was shattered by a serious groin injury that Gardner sustained just before heading to Lake Placid. Warming up on the ice before the Olympic short program Gardner, shot with painkillers, fell four times; the pair was forced to withdraw. Rodnina and Zaitsev took their second gold, less than a year after the birth of their son. Marina Cherkasova, half of the Soviet pair that placed second in 1980, turned 15 just three days before medalling.

In 1984 US pair Kitty and Peter Carruthers won a tight competition for the silver, the first silver for the US in pairs skating since the 1952 Olympics in Oslo. The 1984 gold medalists, Elena Valova and Oleg Vassiliev, skated to the silver in Calgary. The new Soviet pair appearing in 1988, Ekaterina Gordeeva and Sergei Grinkov, brought a trademark quadruple twist lift to the Games. This appealing couple skated with a lively and youthful simplicity and came away with a gold and spectators' hearts worldwide. US pair Peter Oppegard and Jill Watson won a bronze in Calgary, demonstrating their trademark swoop, in which Oppegard swung Watson's face just inches from the ice.

Medalists

Figure Skating — Pairs

1988
1. Ekaterina Gordeeva, Sergei Grinkov, Soviet Union, 1.4
2. Elena Valova, Oleg Vassiliev, Soviet Union, 2.8
3. Jill Watson, Peter Oppegard, USA, 4.2

1984
1. Elena Valova, Oleg Vassiliev, Soviet Union, 1.4
2. Kitty Carruthers, Peter Carruthers, USA, 2.8
3. Larissa Selezneva, Oleg Makorov, Soviet Union, 3.8

1980
1. Irina Rodnina, Aleksandr Zaitsev, Soviet Union, 147.26

96

2. Marina Cherkosova, Sergei Shakrai,
Soviet Union, 143.80
3. Manuela Mager, Uwe Bewersdorff,
East Germany, 140.52
1976 1. Irina Rodnina, Aleksandr Zaitsev,
Soviet Union, 140.54
2. Romy Kermer, Rolf Oesterreich, East
Germany, 136.35
3. Manuela Gross, Uwe Kagelmann, East
Germany, 134.57
1972 1. Irina Rodnina, Aleksei Ulanov, Soviet
Union, 420.4
2. Lyudmila Smirnova, Andrei Suraikin,
Soviet Union, 419.4
3. Manuela Gross, Uwe Kagelmann, East
Germany, 411.8
1968 1. Lyudmila Belousova, Oleg Protopopov,
Soviet Union, 315.2
2. Tatiana Zhuk, Aleksandr Gorelik,
Soviet Union, 312.3
3. Margot Glockshuber, Wolfgang
Danne, West Germany, 304.4
1964 1. Lyudmila Belousova, Oleg Protopopov,
Soviet Union, 104.4
2. Marika Kilius, Hans-Jurgen Baumler,
West Germany, 103.6
3. Debbi Wilkes, Guy Revell, Canada,
98.5
1960 1. Barbara Wagner, Robert Paul,
Canada, 80.4
2. Marika Kilius, Hans-Jurgen Baumler,
West Germany, 76.8
3. Nancy Ludington, Ronald Ludington,
USA, 76.2
1956 1. Elisabeth Schwarz, Kurt Oppelt,
Austria, 101.8
2. Frances Dafoe, Norris Bowden,
Canada, 101.9
3. Marianna Nagy, Laszlo Nagy,
Hungary, 99.3
1952 1. Ria Falk, Paul Falk, West Germany,
102.6
2. Karol Kennedy, Michael Kennedy,
USA, 100.6

3. Marianna Nagy, Laszlo Nagy,
Hungary, 97.4
1948 1. Micheline Lannoy, Pierre Baugniet,
Belgium, 123.5
2. Andrea Kekessy, Ede Kiraly, Hungary,
122.2
3. Suzanne Morrow, Wallace
Diestelmeyer, Canada, 121.0
1936 1. Maxi Herber, Ernst Baier, Germany,
103.3
2. Ilse Pausin, Erik Pausin, Austria, 102.7
3. Emilie Rotter, Laszlo Szollas, Hungary,
97.6
1932 1. Andree Brunet-Joly, Pierre Brunet,
France, 76.7
2. Beatrix Loughran, Sherwin C. Badger,
USA, 77.5
3. Emilie Rotter, Laszlo Szollas, Hungary,
76.4
1928 1. Andree Joly, Pierre Brunet, France,
100.50
2. Lilly Scholz, Otto Kaiser, Austria,
99.25
3. Melitta Brunner, Ludwig Wrede,
Austria, 93.25
1924 1. Helene Engelmann, Alfred Berger,
Austria, 74.50
2. Ludovika Jakobsson-Eilers, Walter
Jakobsson, Finland, 71.75
3. Andree Joly, Pierre Brunet, France,
69.25
1920 1. Ludovika Jakobsson-Eilers, Walter
Jakobsson, Finland, 80.75
2. Alexia Bryn, Yngvar Bryn, Norway,
72.75
3. Phyllis Johnson, Basil Williams, Great
Britain, 66,25
1912 Not held
1908 1. Anna Hubler, Heinrich Burger,
Germany, 56.0
2. Phyllis Johnson, James Johnson, Great
Britain, 51.5
3. Madge Syers, Edgar Syers, Great
Britain, 48.0

ICE DANCING

▼

HIGHLIGHTS

Ice dancing became an Olympic sport in 1976, and the Soviet Union captured the first two places. Ludmilla Pakhomova and Aleksandr Gorshkov edged out Irina Moiseeva and Andrei Minenkov; the surprise bronze medalists were US skaters Colleen O'Connor and Jim Millins. The 1980 gold went to Soviets Natalia Linichuk and Gennadi Karponosov; Hungary got the silver and another Soviet couple won the bronze. Gold medalists Jayne Torvill and Christopher Dean of Britain were awarded a maximum nine 6.0 scores for artistic impression in their 1984 program, and three 6.0 scores for technical merit. In 1988 Soviet ice

97

dancers Natalia Bestemianova and Andrei Bukin claimed the gold with three perfect 6.0 scores. Another Soviet pair, Sergei Ponomarenko and Marina Klimova, won the silver, while Canadians Tracy Wilson and Robert McCall took the bronze. But it was a non-medalling performance that stirred the crowd: Isabelle and Paul Duchesnay, siblings raised in Québec but skating for France, who finished eighth but pushed the sport in a new direction with their innovative style and technique.

Medalists

Figure Skating — Ice Dancing

1988
1. Natalia Bestemianova, Andrei Boukine, Soviet Union, 2.0
2. Marina Klimova, Sergei Ponomarenko, Soviet Union, 4.0
3. Tracy Wilson, Robert McCall, Canada, 6.0

1984
1. Jayne Torvill, Christopher Dean, Great Britain, 2.0
2. Natalia Bestemyanova, Andrei Boukin, Soviet Union, 4.0
3. Marina Klimova, Sergei Ponomarenko, Soviet Union, 7.0

1980
1. Natalia Linichuk, Gennadi Karponosov, Soviet Union, 205.48
2. Krisztina Regoeczy, Andras Sallay, Hungary, 204.52
3. Irina Moiseeva, Andrei Minenkov, Soviet Union, 201.86

1976
1. Ljudmila Pakhomova, Alexandr Gorshkov, Soviet Union, 209.92
2. Irina Moiseeva, Andrei Minenkov, Soviet Union, 204.88
3. Colleen O'Connor, Jimmy Millins, USA, 202.64

British ice dancers Jayne Torvill and Christopher Dean performed a routine to Ravel's "Bolero" that took top honors at the 1984 Games.

The 1980 US Olympic hockey team, the "Miracle on Ice," captured the gold medal by defeating first the Soviet Union, then Finland.

ICE HOCKEY

WARM-UP

An electric Olympic moment: 1980, Lake Placid, the US hockey team erupts on the ice, having defeated Finland for their first gold medal since 1960 and only the second since the Olympics began. Against the odds. The miracle on ice. In the stands, they begin to chant. "USA! USA! USA!" Goose bump time. Sports columns overflow with emotion, the public joyously celebrates, the country beams with pride, the young men on the American hockey team are canonized as national heros.

And hockey was temporarily embraced as the national American sport. Never mind that it has been the national sport of Canada for most of this century.

But hockey actually began hundreds of centuries before that shining American moment at Lake Placid. Hockey is the oldest known game played on ice. The ancient Greeks and Romans played a form of field hockey and the principle of knocking an object with a stick into a designated area was adopted by the French, who called the game "hocquet," or curved shepherd's crook. A monk in the 12th century described a scene near the walls of London:

> When it is frozen, many young men run over the ice. Some of them have bones tied to their feet and use a stick with a sharp end. They slide as quickly as a bird flying in the air or the arrow from a bow. Sometimes from two opposite points, at a large distance, two young men race towards each other and one of them, or perhaps both, falls to the ground after beating each other with their sticks. Many of them incur head wounds, and most of them break an arm or a leg; but in our day and age young is forever seeking glory and these mock fights make them more courageous when it comes to real fighting.

Sounds somewhat like a typical National Hockey League game.

In the 19th century, the game made its way across the Channel from France to Britain, then was brought over by Scottish settlers to Canada, where it was known as "shinty." The long Canadian winter provided plenty of ice, so it was that children adapted the sport to their environment, playing with broomsticks and stones on the frozen ponds. Groups of up to fifty a side would gather in the harbor at Halifax and go at each other all afternoon.

Even today, many of the players in the National Hockey League have their first taste of hockey on an outdoor sheet of ice, often playing in subzero temperatures.

The cities of Montréal, Québec, and Halifax all lay claim to having staged the earliest ice hockey game (or near ice hockey game), but the first documented game was played in 1855 at Kingston, Ontario, involving soldiers of the Royal Canadian Rifles. The first organized league was formed in Kingston soon thereafter, while the first set of rules are credited to John George Alwyn Creighton, an engineer from Halifax who was working in Montréal. A rugby and lacrosse player, Creighton embraced hockey apparently because he and his friends were searching for a new game that would allow them to stay in shape during the long Canadian winters. On March 3, 1875, Creighton and 17 others appeared at the Victoria Skating Rink in Montréal, armed with bandy sticks, skates, and a lacrosse ball.

In 1893, ice hockey was introduced to two US universities, Yale and Johns Hopkins. The Amateur Hockey Association of the United States was formed in 1894. Two years later a four-team league was started in New York, and soon after that, the Baltimore Hockey League was founded.

fact: North Americans skate with short, chopping strides, pushing off the inside edge of skates placed widely apart, with the power generated by thigh and groin muscles; Swedish and Czechoslovakian skaters use the more powerful quadriceps and buttock muscles to thrust skates that start closer together, pushing straight back and gliding on the outside edge of the front skate—results are faster and smoother skating.

The sport continued to grow in the northern climes of the US and Canada. In 1893 (hockey's watershed year?), Lord Stanley, the Governor of Canada, donated a $50 trophy cup that still bears his name (and has presumedly appreciated), to be awarded to the world's best amateur ice hockey team. The first recipients of the trophy were the Montréal Wheelers of the Amateur Hockey Association of Canada. In 1908, the Ontario Professional Hockey League was organized, with the Cup as the championship prize. Since 1910, the Stanley Cup has been emblematic of professional hockey supremacy, and is now awarded to the National Hockey League's champion.

The first US team to win the Stanley Cup was the Seattle Metropolitans in 1917, the same year that the NHL was formed. Strictly a Canadian circuit until Boston joined the league in 1924, the NHL added Chicago, Detroit, and New York in 1926. Montréal and Toronto completed the "original six." In 1967, the league doubled to 12 teams and in the next few years expanded to 21.

Worldwide, hockey has continued to grow. In 1908, the International Ice Hockey Federation (IIHF) was formed in London, with Great Britain, France, Belgium, Switzerland, and Bohemia as founding members.

fact: The first gold-medal team was not a Canadian national team; it was the Winnipeg Falcons.

Today the sport is very popular in several European countries, particularly Sweden, Finland, Czechoslovakia, Switzerland, Poland, Germany, and, of course, Russia. Their chief incentive for playing, apart from sheer recreation, is the Olympics. The international style of play, popularized by the superb Soviet teams, has changed hockey throughout the world in the last decade. Typified by speed and razor-sharp passing, the new style of hockey relies less on muscle and reaction and more on play-planning.

▼

SPECTATORS' GUIDE

Hockey is a high-speed game where much of the action occurs away from the puck, that hard rubber disc the players swat with such abandon and is so hard to see on a television screen. During three 20-minute periods, the teams furiously battle up and down the ice with one basic goal in mind: scoring more goals than their opponents. Preventing the other team from knocking the puck past your goalie (the one wearing the mask) is also admirable and highly desired.

The route to a goal is often a rough-and-tumble path. Hockey combines the grace of figure skating with the brawn of boxing, offering intricate teamwork as well; nothing is quite as exciting as two teams playing full-out, dashing from "end-to-end," creating continuous action. Everything is fast about hockey; forward line changes are made every 60 seconds or so, the puck is just a blur as it is passed about the ice, changing hands moment by moment, and even the referees must move quickly as they try to keep up with the flow of the play.

The cardinal rule for an attacking team is that the puck must precede the first player across the offensive blueline. Otherwise, and this is a frequent violation, an offside is called, resulting in a faceoff. The puck cannot be sent from one end of the ice to the other without being touched or carried by members of the offensive team, unless that team is playing shorthanded. Such an infraction is called icing, and the puck is brought back for a faceoff deep in the offending team's zone. A shorthanded team is permitted to clear the puck from one end to the other; this is considered very good defense in these situations.

A team at full strength consists of a goaltender and five skaters: the forward line, consisting of a center and two wings, plus two defensemen. Numerous infractions of the rules may prevent a team from playing at full strength much of the time; players are sent to the penalty box, where they serve two minutes, for such rule violations as tripping, slashing (using the stick as a weapon), high sticking (ditto), and cross-checking. If the opposing team scores during the penalty period, the player in the box is released. Up to two players may serve these "minor" penalties at a time, so a team may play two men short. A five-minute major penalty for fighting or other more serious offenses may be called as well; a player receiving a major will serve his full penalty, regardless of how many goals the opponent scores during this time period.

When a team gains an advantage in the number of men on the ice because of a penalty situation, it is said to be on its "power play," and usually puts forth its best shooters on the ice. The team on the power play will try to maintain the puck in the opponent's zone and pepper the goalie (the guy wearing the mask) with as many shots as possible.

Olympic hockey rules differ in several respects from those of the National Hockey League. An offside pass crossing the center, or red line, would be called immediately in the NHL, and play would stop. In the Olympics, extenuating circumstances may permit play to continue at the referee's discretion. Similarly, play is stopped in the NHL for any offside or when a player enters the faceoff circle at the time of a faceoff. But in the Olympics, no whistle is blown if the non-offending team gains possession of the puck.

fact: Olympic ice hockey consists of patient weaving and passing, vastly different from the NHL brawls that North American fans are used to.

In Olympic hockey, a second major penalty carries an automatic game misconduct and a trip to the locker room. Any Olympian starting a fight is assessed a match penalty.

For the Winter Olympics, twelve countries are eligible, based on their finish in the previous year's world championships. The defending Olympic champion (in this case, the Soviet Union) is given an automatic berth, as is the host nation.

The countries will be split into two groups, with each group engaging in a five-game round-robin series. The two teams with the best records from each division will advance to the semifinals, where the winner of each group meets the second place team of the other. The two survivors then will play for the championship.

▼

HOPEFULS

The Soviet Union has ruled the Olympic ice for more than two decades, having captured gold medals since 1956 in all but two Olympic competitions—and its team won medals during those years, too. Despite the loss of five Soviet players who left the 1988 team to join the National Hockey League, the Soviets expect to retain their championship status under the guidance of returning coach Viktor Tokhonov. As always, fierce competition will come from the Swedes, who earned bronze medals in the past three Olympic Games, and the Czechs, who earned their fourth consecutive medal in 1984. Finland, whose team garnered the country's first hockey medal by placing second at Calgary, may also provide a tough rally. And Team USA, helped by returning coach Dave Peterson and a rigorous pre-Olympic training and exhibition schedule (but not much by the new eligibility of NHL players, who will be in the midst of their professional season and thus largely unavailable for Olympic competition), hopes to repeat its 1980 victory.

Schedule

The tentative ice hockey schedule is as follows:

Saturday, February 8
Canada vs. France

Saturday, February 8
Czechoslovakia vs. Norway

Saturday, February 8
USSR vs. Switzerland

Sunday, February 9
Sweden vs. Poland

Sunday, February 9
Finland vs. Germany

Sunday, February 9
USA vs. Italy

Monday, February 10
USSR vs. Norway

Monday, February 10
Czechoslovakia vs. France

Monday, February 10
Canada vs. Switzerland

Tuesday, February 11
Finland vs. Poland

Tuesday, February 11
USA vs. Germany

Tuesday, February 11
Sweden vs. Italy

Wednesday, February 12
Canada vs. Norway

Wednesday, February 12
Switzerland vs. France

Wednesday, February 12
USSR vs. Czechoslovakia

Thursday, February 13
Italy vs. Poland

Thursday, February 13
Sweden vs. Germany

Thursday, February 13
USA vs. Finland

Friday, February 14
USSR vs. France

Friday, February 14
Switzerland vs. Norway

103

Friday, February 14 Canada vs. Czechoslovakia	**Monday, February 17** Finland vs. Italy
Saturday, February 15 USA vs. Poland	**Monday, February 17** Sweden vs. USA
Saturday, February 15 Sweden vs. Finland	**Tuesday, February 18** Three Medal Round Games
Saturday, February 15 Italy vs. Germany	**Wednesday, February 19** Three Medal Round Games
Sunday, February 16 Norway vs. France	**Thursday, February 20** Three Medal Round Games
Sunday, February 16 Czechoslovakia vs. Switzerland	**Friday, February 21** Three Medal Round Games
Sunday, February 16 Canada vs. USSR	**Saturday, February 22** Three Medal Round Games
Monday, February 17 Germany vs. Poland	**Sunday, February 23** Final

▼

HIGHLIGHTS

Ice hockey first appeared at the Summer Games at Amsterdam in 1920. Canada took the first four gold medals, ceding to Great Britain (whose team included some renegade Canadians) in 1936, then captured the last two golds before the USSR entered the arena. Between 1920 and 1952, Canadian teams played 41 Olympic games in which they scored 403 goals and allowed only 34. The Soviets were late in coming to the sport; it is thought that they might never have taken up hockey at all if it had not been an Olympic sport. Since the Soviets appeared in the Winter Olympics in 1956, they have won the gold in hockey seven times, losing only to the US, in 1960 at Squaw Valley and in 1980 at Lake Placid. The US has won six silver medals and one bronze to add to their two golds, including a surprise silver at the 1972 Games in Sapporo. Canada has earned two silver and two bronze medals to add to their pile of gold, while Sweden has won two silver medals and four bronze. The diverse definitions of the amateur versus professional status accorded their teams by different nations has caused such controversy that even Canada chose to boycott its national sport in the 1972 and 1976 Games.

fact: In 1948 two teams showed up to represent the United States.

104

The 1980 competition was overlain with political tensions between the USSR and the US. When the heavily favored Soviet team was upset by an inexperienced US team, the crowd at Lake Placid was jubilant, as were television audiences across the nation. But the US squad still had to beat Finland in the final to capture the gold. In typical fashion, fighting from behind for the sixth time in seven games, the gallant Americans behind coach Herb Brooks produced a 4–2 victory with three goals in the final period.

fact: Swiss hockey player Richard "Bibi" Torriani won a bronze medal in 1928 and another in 1948.

The 1980 Games were the third Olympics for the great Soviet goaltender Vladislav Tretiak. His countrymen recaptured the gold in 1984, ahead of Czechoslovakia. The medal round of the hockey competition was expanded from four teams to six in 1988. That year Canada's team made it to the medal round, but the gold was captured once again by the Soviet team, the silver going to Finland. In 1980, 1984, and 1988 Sweden maintained a lock on the hockey bronze.

A Lifetime Ago

For many fans—and certainly for the players—it was, and will remain, the most memorable sporting event of their lifetime. There has been little—could there ever be *anything?*—to match the excitement, emotion and pride generated by the 1980 US hockey team's Cinderella story at the Lake Placid Winter Games. The US team, 20 hockey players in their early to mid-20s, defeated the superb Soviets, 4–3, in one heart-stopping game, then rallied to beat spunky Finland, 4–2, in the gold medal game.

During one incredible weekend in February, "USA! ... USA! ... USA!," and "Do you believe in miracles?" gave a discouraged America, a country besieged by high prime-lending and inflation rates, unnerved by the Soviet invasion of Afghanistan, and frustrated by the plight of 52 hostages held by Iran, something to really cheer about.

"For a lot of people, it was more than just a hockey game," team captain Mike Eruzione told the *St. Paul Pioneer Press.*

"It was a case," said Eruzione, who scored the game-winning goal against the Soviets with 10 minutes to play, "of a country not feeling as powerful as we once did, going up against a power at their own game and beating them with a bunch of kids."

The US hadn't defeated the Soviets since winning the gold medal at the 1960 Games and had been outscored 28–7 by the men in red in subsequent Olympic matchups. Less than a week before the 1980 Games, the Soviets had clobbered the US team, 10–3, in an exhibition at Madison Square Garden.

And after winning the gold medal?

"Here we (were)," Rob McClanahan told the *Pioneer Press*, "a team that was together 10 months and had just done something incredible, and the next day it was over. We're still a team in a sense, but we would never play together again. We didn't get a chance to celebrate as a team. It's kind of sad."

Indeed, life went on, even for these immortalized Boys of Winter.

Ten years later, in 1990, on the anniversary of their triumph, while many recapped their Olympian feats for reporters, the players had far different stories to tell each other.

In the intervening years, Coach Herb Brooks went on to coach the New York Rangers and Minnesota North Stars in the NHL, then provided color commentary on SportsChannel NHL cable telecasts. He was later inducted into the US Hockey Hall of Fame and then signed to coach the New Jersey Devils farm team in Utica, New York.

Twelve players had NHL tales to tell, some better than others. The most notable pro careers belonged to Neal Broten, Mark Johnson, Dave Christian, Mike Ramsey and Ken Morrow. Broten became the first American-born player to score 100 points in an NHL season (105 in 1985–86); Morrow was the only player from the 1980 team to win a Stanley Cup ring, winning four with the New York Islanders. Retiring in 1990, he went on to become a professional coach.

Off the ice, Mike Eruzione seemed to capitalize the most on the team's success, parlaying his involvement into a TV-commentating and motivational-speaker career. And we'll all be able to catch up with him as he provides hockey color commentary at the 1992 Games in Albertville. Goalie Jim Craig had a brief and disappointing stint in the NHL and was involved in a traffic accident that resulted in the death of a 29-year-old woman. He became a salesman for a newspaper advertising-insert company.

McClanahan became a trader at a Chicago brokerage house; Phil Verchota played on the 1984 Olympic team, then turned to commercial banking; Eric Strobel was selling AT&T equipment; Buzz Schnieder was a supervisor with a moving company; Steve Christoff became a Northwest Airlines pilot; Bill Baker, graduating second in his dentistry class, was well on his way to becoming an oral surgeon and serving as the dentist for the University of Minnesota hockey team.

John Harrington played on the 1984 Olympic hockey team and became an assistant coach at the University of Denver, later moving on to St. Cloud (Minnesota) State; Steve Janaszak, the back-up goalie to Craig, was a Long Island real estate developer; Jack O'Callahan was a stock broker in Chicago; Mark Pavelich was a businessman in Eveleth, Minnesota; Dave Silk was playing in West Germany, where he was the MVP of his league; Bob Suter was running a sporting goods store in Madison, Wisconsin, and Mark Wells was managing a family restaurant in suburban Detroit.

Times had, indeed, changed.

"I work 70 to 75 hours a week," Wells told the *Detroit Free Press.* "I only have time to go home and do the laundry."

106

He tried to explain the 1980 miracle from the inside. "In '80 we were all placed at a village . . . (and) all we did in '80 was go from the ice arena to the village and back. Everything was kind of blurry to me; a lot of guys felt the same way. Everything was too fast. That's because all we did was focus on our event." Said Verchota, in the *Pioneer Press:* "It's almost like someone else's life, to be honest with you."

"Sometimes," Craig said, "it seems like a another lifetime ago."

Said Wells: "What we're doing today doesn't really matter. What it comes down to is lasting friendship."

And a lasting memory. —*E.K.*

Ice Hockey

![Medalists]

Ice Hockey

1988 1. Soviet Union, Ilia Biakin, Igor Stelnov, Vyacheslav Fetisov, Alexei Gusarov, Alexei Kasatonov, Sergei Starikov, Vyacheslav Bykov, Sergei Yachin, Valeri Kamensky, Sergei Svetlov, Alexander Tchernykh, Andrei Khomutov, Vladimir Krutov, Igor Larionov, Andrei Lomakin, Sergei Makarov, Alexandre Nogilny, Anatoli Semyonov, Alexander Kozhevnikov, Igor Kravchuk

2. Finland, Timo Blomqvist, Kari Eloranta, Raimo Helminen, Iiro Jaervi, Esa Keskinen, Erkki Laine, Kari Laitinen, Erkki Lehtonen, Sakari Lindfors, Jyrki Lumme, Reijo Mikkolainen, Jarmo Myllys, Teppo Numminen, Janne Ojanen, Arto Ruotanen, Reijo Ruotsalainen, Simo Saarinen, Kai Suikkanen, Timo Susi, Jukka Tammi, Jari Torkki, Pekka Toumisto, Jukka Virtanen

3. Sweden, Anders Bergman, Peter Lindmark, Peter Aslin, Peter Andersson, Anders Eldebrink, Tomas Eriksson, Lars Ivarsson, Lars Karlsson, Mats Kihlstroem, Tommy Samuelson, Mikael Andersson, Bo Berglund, Jonas Bergovist, Thom Eklund, Peter Eriksson, Michael Hjaelm, Mikael Johansson, Lars Molin, Lars-Gunnar Pettersson, Thomas Lundqvist, Ulf Sandstroem, Hakan Soedergren, Jens Oehling

1984 1. Soviet Union, Viatcheslav Fetissov, Aleksei Kassatonov, Sergei Makarov, Igor Larionov, Vladimir Kroutov, Vassili Pervoukhin, Zenetoula Biliatletdinov, Sergei Chepelev, Alexandre Guerassimov, Andrei Khomoutov, Igor Stelnov, Sergei Starikov, Nikolay Drozdetskiy, Victor Tumenev, Alexandre Kozhevnikov, Alexandre Skvortsov, Vladimir Kovin, Mikhail Vasilev, Vladimir Zoubkov

2. Czechoslovakia, Milan Chalupa, Jaroslav Benak, Jiri Lala, Vladimir Kyhos, Frantischek Tchernik, Arnold Kadlec, Miloslav Horava, Igor Liba, Darius Rusnak, Vincent Lukatch, Radoslav Svoboda, Eduard Uvira, Pavel Richter, Vladimir Ruzsitchka, Vladimir Cladr, Jiri Hrdina, Duschan Paschek, Jaroslav Korbela

3. Sweden, Arne Michael Thelven, Bo Ericsson, Jens Erik Ohling, Per-Erik Eklung, Peter Olog Gradin, Thomas Valter Ahlen, Mats Gunnar Thelin, Karl Hakan Soedergren, Mats Stefan Waltin, Tommy Jan Motrh, Goeran Folke Lindblom, Leif Hakan Nordin, Thomas Sandstroem, Lars Hakan Eriksson, Thom Lennart Eklund, Peter Michael Hjalm, Thomas Per Rundquist, Mats Gunnar Hessel

1980 1. USA, James Craig, Kenneth Morrow, Michael Ramsey, William Baker, John O'Callahan, Bob Suter, David Silk, Neal Broten, Mark Johnson, Steven Christoff, Mark Wells, Mark Pavelich, Eric Strobel, Michael Eruzione, David Christian, Robert McClanahan, William "Buzz" Schneider, Philip Verchota, John Harrington

2. Soviet Union, Vladimir Myshkin, Vladislav Tretiak, Vyacheslav Fetisov, Vasily Pervukhin, Varery Vasiliev, Aleksei Kasatonov, Sergei Starikov, Zinetulla Bilyaletdinov, Vladimir Krutov, Aleksandr Maltsev, Yuri Lebedev, Boris Mikhailov, Vladimir Petrov, Valery Kharlamov, Helmut Balderis, Viktor Zlukov, Aleksandr Golikov, Sergei Makarov, Vladimir Golikov, Aleksandr Skvortsov

107

3. Sweden, Per-Eric "Pelle" Lindbergh, William Lofqvist, Tomas Jonsson, Sture Andersson, Ulf Weinstock, Jan Eriksson, Tommy Samuelsson, Mats Waltin, Thomas Eriksson, Per Lundqvist, Mats Ahlberg, Hakan Eriksson, Mats Naslund, Lennart Norberg, Bengt Lundholm, Leif Holmgren, Dan Soderstrom, Harald Luckner, Lars Mohlin, Bo Berglund

1976
1. Soviet Union, Vladislav Tretiak, Aleksandr Sidelnikov, Boris Aleksandrov, Sergei Babinov, Aleksandr Gusiev, Valeri Kharlamov, Aleksandr Yakushev, Viktor Zlukov, Sergei Kapustin, Vladimir Lutchenko, Yuri Lyapkin, Aleksandr Maltsev, Boris Mikhailov, Vladimir Petrov, Vladimir Chadrin, Viktor Szalimov, Gennady Tsygankov, Valeri Vasiliev

2. Czechoslovakia, Jiri Holecek, Jiri Crha, Oldrich Machac, Milan Chalupa, Frantisek Pospisil, Miroslav Dvorak, Milan Kajkl, Jiri Bubla, Milan Novy, Vladimir Martinec, Jiri Novak, Bohuslav Stastny, Jiri Holik, Ivan Hlinka, Eduard Novak, Jaroslav Pouzar, Bohuslav Ebermann, Josef Augusta

3. West Germany, Erich Weishaupt, Anton Kehle, Rudolf Thanner, Josef Volk, Udo Keissling, Stefan Metz, Klaus Auhuber, Ignaz Berndaner, Rainer Phillip, Lorenz Funk, Wolfgang Boos, Ernst Kopf, Ferenc Vozar, Walter Koberle, Erich Kuhnhacki, Alois Schloder, Martin Hinterstocker, Franz Reindl

1972
1. Soviet Union, Vladislav Tretiak, Aleksandr Pachkov, Vitali Davydov, Vladimir Lutshenko, Alexsandr Ragulin, Viktor Kuzkin, Gennady Tsygankov, Valeri Vasiliev, Valeri Kharlamov, Yuri Blinov, Vladimir Petrov, Anatoli Firsov, Aleksandr Maltsev, Vladimir Chadrin, Boris Mikhailov, Vladimir Vikulov, Aleksandr Yakushev

2. USA, Michael Curran, Peter Sears, Walter Olds, Thomas Mellor, Frank Sanders, James McElmury, Charles Brown, Richard McGlynn, Ronald Naslund, Robbie Ftorek, Stuart Irving, Kevin Ahearn, Henry Boucha, Craig Sarner, Timothy Sheehy, Keith Christiansen, Mark Howe

3. Czechoslovakia, Vladimir Dzurilla, Jiri Holecek, Vladimir Bednar, Rudolf Tajcnar, Oldrich Machac, Frantisek Pospisil, Josef Horesovksy, Karel Vohralik, Vaclav Nedomansky, Jiri Holik, Jaroslav Holik, Jiri Kochta, Eduard Novak, Richard Farda, Josef Cerny, Vladimir Martinec, Ivan Hlinka, Bohuslav Stastny

1968
1. Soviet Union, Viktor Konovalenko, Viktor Zinger, Viktor Blinov, Aleksandr Ragulin, Viktor Kuzkin, Oleg Zaitsev, Igor Romichevsky, Vitali Davydov, Yevgeny Zymin, Vyacheslav Starshinov, Boris Mayorov, Viktor Polupanov, Anatoly Firsov, Yuri Moiseyev, Anatoli Ionov, Yevgeny Michakov, Veniamin Aleksandrov, Vladimir Vikulov

2. Czechoslovakia, Vladimir Nadrchal, Vladimir Dzurilla, Oldrich Machac, Josef Horesovsky, Jan Suchy, Frantisek Pospisil, Karel Masopust, Frantisek Sevcik, Josef Golonka, Jaroslav Jirik, Jan Havel, Petr Hejma, Jiri Holik, Jan Hrbaty, Jiri Kochta, Josef Cerny, Vaclav Nedomansky, Jan Klapac

3. Canada, Kenneth Broderick, Wayne Stephenson, Marshall Johnston, Barry MacKenzie, Brian Glennie, Paul Conlin, Terrence O'Malley, Ted Hargreaves, Raymond Cadieux, Francis Huck, Morris Mott, Stephen Monteith, Gary Dineen, Herbert Pinder, William MacMillan, Danny O'Shea, Roger Bourbonnais, Gerry Pinder

1964
1. Soviet Union, Venianin Aleksandrov, Aleksandr Alyimetov, Vitaly Davidov, Anatoli Firsov, Eduard Ivanou, Viktor Konovalenko, Viktor Kuzkin, Konstantin Loktev, Boris Mayorov, Yevgeny Mairov, Stanislaus Petuchov, Aleksandr Ragulin, Vyacheslav Starshinov, Leonid Volkov, Viktor Yakushev, Boris Zaitsev

2. Sweden, Kjell Svensson, Lennart Haggroth, Gert Blome, Nils Johansson, Roland Stoltz, Bert-Ola Nordlander, Nils Nilsson, Ronald Pettersson, Lars-Erik Lundvall, Eilert Maatta, Anders Andersson, Ulf Sterner, Carl-Goran Oberg, Sven Johansson, Uno Ohrlund, Hans Mild, Lennart Johansson

3. Czechoslovakia, Vladimir Dzurilla, Vladimir Nadrchal, Rudolf Potsch, Frantisek Tikal, Frantisek Gregor, Stanislav Sventek, Ladislav Smid, Vlastimil Bubik, Jaroslav Walter, Miroslav Vlach, Jiri Dolana, Jiri Holik, Josef Cerny, Stanislav Pryl, Josef Golonka, Jaroslav Jirik, Jan Klapac

1960
1. USA, John McCartan, Laurence Palmer, Robert Owen, John Kirrane, John Mayasich, Rodney Paavola, Richard Rodenheiser, Paul Johnson, Weldon Olson, Roger Christian, William Christian, Thomas Williams, Eugene Grazia, Richard Meredith, William Cleary, Robert Cleary, Robert McVey

2. Canada, Harold Hurley, Donald Head, Harry Sinden, John Douglas, Darryl Sly, Maurice Benoit, George Samolenko, Robert Attersely, Fred Etcher, Clifford Pennington, Robert Forhan, Robert McKnight, Floyd Martin, Kenneth Laufman, Donald Rope, James Connelly, Robert Rousseau

3. Soviet Union, Veniamin Aleksandrov, Aleksandr Alyimetov, Yuri Baulin, Mikhail Bychkov, Vladmir Grebennikov, Yevgeny Groshev, Viktor Yakushev, Yevgeny Yerkin, Nikolai Karpov, Alfred Kuchevsky, Konstantin Loktev, Stanislav Petuchov, Viktor Prjazhnikov, Nikolai Puchkov, Genrich Sidorenkov, Nikolai Sologubov, Yuri Tsitsinov

1956 1. Soviet Union, Yevgeny Babich, Usevolod Bobrov, Nikolai Chlystov, Aleksey Guryshev, Yuri Krylov, Alfred Kuchevsky, Valentin Kusin, Grigory Mkrtchan, Viktor Nikiforov, Yuri Pantyuchov, Nikolai Puchkov, Viktor Shuvalov, Genrich Sidorenkov, Nikolai Sologubov, Ivan Tregubov, Dmitri Ukolov, Aleksandr Uvarov
2. USA, Willard Ikola, Donald Rigazio, Richard Rodenheiser, Daniel McKinnon, Edward Sampson, John Matchefts, Richard Meredith, Richard Dougherty, Kenneth Purpur, John Mayasich, William Cleary, Wellington Burnett, Wendell Anderson, Eugene Campbell, Gordon Christian, Weldon Olson, John Petroske
3. Canada, Denis Brodeur, Keith Woodall, Floyd Martin, Howard Lee, Arthur Hurst, John McKenzie, James Logan, Paul Knox, Donald Rope, Byrle Klinck, William Colvin, Gerald Theberge, Alfred Horne, Charles Brooker, George Scholes, Robert White, Kenneth Laufman

1952 1. Canada, Eric Paterson, Ralph Hansch, John Davies, Robert Meyers, Allen Purvis, William Dawe, Donald Gauf, Robert Watt, George Abel, Bruce Dickson, David Miller, Francis Sullivan, Louis Secco, William Gibson, Gordon Robertson, Thomas Pollock
2. USA, Richard Desmond, Donald Whiston, Allen Van, Joseph Czarnota, Robert Rompre, Gerald Kilmartin, Kenneth Yackel, Leonard Ceglarski, Ruben Bjorkman, John Noah, Andre Gambucci, James Sedin, Clifford Harrison, Arnold Oss, John Mulhern
3. Sweden, Thord Flodqvist, Lars Svensson, Ake Andersson, Rune Johansson, Sven Thunman, Gote Almqvist, Lars Bjorn, Ake Lassas, Gote Blomqvist, Gosta Johansson, Erik Johansson, Stig Tvilling, Hans Tvilling, Lars Pettersson, Hans Oberg, Sven Johansson, Holger Nurmela

1948 1. Canada, Murray Dowey, Bernard Dunster, John Lecompte, Henri-Andre Laperriere, Walter Halder, George Mara, Reginald Schroeter, Thomas Hibberd, Albert Renaud, Jean Orval Gravelle, Patrick Guzzo, Irving Taylor
2. Czechoslovakia, Bohumil Modry, Zdenek Jarkovsky, Dr. Miroslav Slama, Josef Trousilek, Premysl Hajny, Vilibald Stovik, Oldrich Zabrodsky, Miloslav Pokorny, Ladislav Trojak, Vladimir Zabrodsky, Stanislav Konopasek, Vaclav Rozinak, Jaroslav Drobny, Karel Stibor, Gustav Bubnik, Vladimir Bouzek, Vladimir Kobranov
3. Switzerland, Hand Banninger, Reto Perl, Emil Handschin, Ferdinand Cattini, Hans Cattini, Heinrich Boller, Hans Durst, Walter Durst, Richard Torriani, Gebhard Poltera, Ulrich Poltera, Hans Trepp, Beat Ruedi, Alfred Bieler, Heini Lohrer, Werner Lohrer, Otto Schubiger

1936 1. Great Britain, James Foster, Carl Erhardt, Gordon Dailley, Archibald Stinchcombe, Edgar Brenchley, John Coward, James Chappell, Alexander Archer, Gerry Davey, James Borland, Robert Wyman, John Kilpatrick
2. Canada, Francis Moore, Arthur Nash, Herman Murray, Walter Kitchen, Raymond Milton, David Neville, Kenneth Farmer-Horn, Hugh Farquharson, Maxwell Deacon, Alexander Sinclair, William Thomson, James Haggarty, Ralph Saint Germain
3. USA, Thomas Moone, Francis Shaugnessy, Philip LaBatte, Frank Stubbs, John Garrison, Paul Rowe, John Lax, Gordon Smith, Elbridge Ross, Francis Spain, August Kammer

1932 1. Canada, William Cockburn, Hugh Sutherland, Roy Hinkel, Walter Monson, Victor Lindquist, Romeo Rivers, Harold Simpson, Norman Malloy, Aliston Wise, Clifford Crowley, Albert Duncanson, George Garbutt, Kenneth Moore, Stanley Wagner
2. USA, Franklin Farrell, John Garrison, Osborn Anderson, John Chase, Douglas Everett, Winthrop Palmer, John Bent, John Cookman, Joseph Fitzgerald, Edward Frazier, Gerard Hallock, Robert Livingston, Francis Nelson, Gordon Smith
3. Germany, Walter Leinweber, Alfred Heinrich, Erich Romer, Rudi Ball, Martin Schrottle, Gustav Jaenecke, Erich Herker, Werner Korff, Marquardt Slevogt, Georg Strobl

1928 1. Canada, Dr. Joseph Sullivan, Ross Taylor, John Porter, Dr. Louis Hudson, David Trottier, Norbert Mueller, Hugh Plaxton, Frank Sullivan, Frank Fisher, Herbert Plaxton, Roger Plaxton, Charles Delahay
2. Sweden, Nils Johansson, Kurt Sucksdorff, Carl Abrahamsson, Henry Johansson, Emil Bergman, Wilhelm Petersen, Gustaf Johansson, Birger Holmqvist, Sigurd Oberg, Ernst Karlberg, Bertil Linde, Erik Larsson
3. Switzerland, Arnold Martignoni, Charles Fasel, Mezzi Andreossi, Giannin Andreossi, Robert Breiter, Richard Torriani, Dr. Luzius Ruedi, Albert Geromini, Fritz Kraatz, Heini Meng, Anton Morosani, Louis Dufour

1924 1. Canada, Duncan Munro, W. Beattie Ramsay, Harry Watson, Reginald Smith, Albert McCaffery, Cyril Sig. Slater, Harold McMunn, Jack Cameron, Ernest Collett
2. USA, Alphonse Lacroix, Irving Small, Clarence Abel, Herbert Drury, Justin McCarthy, Willard Rice, John Lyons, Frank Synott, John A. Langley
3. Great Britain, Colin Carruthers, Eric Carruthers, Ross Cuthbert, Edward Pitblado, Hamilton Jukes, W. H. Anderson, Lorne Carr-Harris, Blane Sexton, George Holmes, Guy Clarkson

109

1920 **1.** Canada, Walter "Wally" Byron,
Konrad Johannessen, Robert Benson,
Allan "Huck" Woodman, Haldor
"Slim" Halderson, Frank Fredrickson,
Mike Goodman, Chris Fridfinnson

2. USA, Raymond Bonney, Cyril
Weidenborner, George Geran, J.
Edward Fitzgerald, Frank Goheen,
Leon Tuck, Anthony Conroy, Herbert
Drury, Joseph McCormick, Lawrence
McCormick, Frank Synott

3. Czechoslovakia, Jan Peka, Karel
Walzer, Jan Palous, Otakar Vindys,
Dr. Karel Hartman, Vilem Loos, Josef
Sroubek, Dr. Karel Pesek

LUGE

WARM-UP

L uge probably has the distinction of being considered by American viewers as the strangest Winter Olympic sport. Although it has roots in prehistoric sledding and bears a close resemblance to the familiar childhood sport of "belly-whomping" on a winter hill, luge has yet to catch on in a big way in the USA. This may be because the US has not yet come close to winning a medal, and Americans are a success-oriented people. And though Americans love daredevils, riding down a bending track at 70 miles per hour while on your back with no particular way to steer may be a stretch for the average sledder.

Historians have found evidence that sleds resembling the modern-day luge were used in Norway more than 1,000 years ago. Luge, the French word for sleigh, had practical origins several centuries ago as a means of travel in the mountainous regions of Austria, Poland, Germany, northern Italy, and Russia. The first international luge race took place in Switzerland in 1883, sponsored by a group of Swiss hotel owners. Seven countries took part, including the US. In 1914, the first European championship was held in Austria. But it was not until 1953 that luge formally separated itself from bobsledding with the formation of the International Luge Federation. And in 1964, luge was added to the Winter Olympic program.

fact: Luge sliders minimize wind resistance by keeping their limbs aligned and body flat.

At that time, critics protested that the sport was too dangerous for the Olympics. Their fears were well founded; two weeks before the first Olympic event in Innsbruck, Austria, a member of the British team died after a crash during a trial run. Stricter safety regulations have eliminated fatalities in recent years, but for the luger, fear is still the co-pilot. 1984 men's singles gold medal winner Paul Hildgartner of Italy, who broke his back on a bumpy natural ice run in 1981, says, "Certainly I know fear. After a heavy injury, I am scared to go down the chute again."

Until the Olympic run was completed on Mt. Van Hoevenberg for the 1980 Games, not a single "bahn" (course or road) suitable for international competition

111

was located in the Western Hemisphere. Before Lake Placid, the only available bahn in the Western Hemisphere was a 750-foot practice track in Toronto. This meant that American lugers had to use the bobrun at Mt. Van Hoevenberg when it was available, or train in Europe. Consequently, the US has yet to win a medal in an Olympic contest, while East Germany (now Germany) has dominated the medal awards, particularly in the women's singles.

▼

SPECTATORS' GUIDE

Luge has been described as the most dangerous of Olympic sports, with the sleds careening downhill at speeds of more than 120 kilometers per hour, the riders flat on their back, feet extending beyond the runners. For roughly 40 seconds the pressure that flattens them against the sled could be up to seven times the force of gravity, or twice that exerted on an astronaut during a shuttle launch. From a spectator's point of view, it looks like a mighty uncomfortable ride. One hand grips the reins and the other the sled. A luge is so flexible that even a slight repositioning of the head can cause the sled to veer into a wall or off the track altogether.

"If you start to veer out of control, you can't let yourself panic," former US champion Frank Masley once noted. "If you let up your concentration for a split second, you'll crash into the wall."

That wall always in mind, the luger lies on his or her back with shoulders resting on the seat in the rear, head up and feet forward. Except for a steering strap, no panels or straps hold the competitor on the sled. A luge cannot contain any mechanical steering or braking devices. The driver steers the luge by exerting foot and leg pressure, downward and sideways, on the forward extensions of the runners and by shifting his or her body.

fact: Each time a luger raises her head to check her path she loses precious time; she may only look up two or three times during a run that takes about 50 seconds.

So luge has its exciting moments. Olympic luge consists of men's and women's singles and men's doubles. Singles competition consists of four heats, while doubles has only two. In doubles competition, one luger lies flat on top of his teammate. The rider on top is the driver, while his partner assists with body positioning and acts as ballast.

The bahn must be between 1,000 and 1,200 meters long and between 1.35 and 1.5 meters wide, with an incline measuring between 9 and 12%. Included among the curves must be one hairpin, one left and one right, one "S" and one labyrinth. The start platforms must be between three and 10 meters high. The length of the run is 20% shorter for men's doubles and the women's singles.

fact: If a luger loses a tenth of a second in the pretimed part of the race, when he's pushing the sled down a steep incline toward the starting line, he's probably blown his chances entirely.

The highly customized luge can weigh a maximum of 22 kilograms (48.4 pounds) for a one-person sled, and 24 kilograms (52.8 pounds) for a two-person sled. The maximum width between runners is about 18 inches. Most sleds are about four feet long, although length is not restricted.

For the one-person sleds, the maximum weight total for men is 242 pounds and for women, 220. The heavier driver has an advantage on the straightaway while the lighter driver is quicker on the curves. If a luger is under the weight limit, he or she may carry half the weight that is missing. Thus, if a man weighs 200 pounds, he may carry an additional 21 pounds.

▼

HOPEFULS

Germany will undoubtedly continue its domination of the luge event. Possible stars include Jens Mueller and Georg Hackl, who won the men's singles gold and silver medals, respectively, in 1988. Two-time gold medalist Steffi Walter-Martin, silver medalist Ute Oberhofner, and bronze medalist Cerstin Schmidt may again vie for their places in the 1992 women's event. Nearing its goal of someday winning an Olympic medal in a luge event, the US places high hopes on Bonny Warner, who finished sixth at the Calgary women's event and tenth in the 1991 World Championships, and Cammy Myler, who placed ninth at the World. Duncan Kennedy looks promising for the men's singles race, having reached a higher rank (seventh) at the 1991 World than any previous American man.

Winter

The tentative luge schedule is as follows:

Sunday, February 9
Single, men

Monday, February 10
Single, men

Tuesday, February 11
Single, women

Wednesday, February 12
Single, women

Friday, February 14
Double, men

▼

HIGHLIGHTS

Luge competition was not part of the Winter Games until the Innsbruck Games in 1964. Since then, East Germany has won 34 of the 63 Olympic medals awarded in luge. Bad weather shortened the competition in 1968, but not before three East German women were disqualified for heating the metal runners on their sleds—a practice that had been legal in 1964. Manfred Schmid, taking the Olympic gold in singles in 1968, is the only Austrian to have done so. A problem with the starting gate canceled the results of the first run in the two-man event in 1972; a disputed tie was finally resolved by the awarding of a double gold, to East Germany and Italy.

fact: Many lugers draw their knees up at the start of the race to delay by a fraction of a second triggering the electric beam of the timer, which is placed three inches above the ice and begins recording the time elapsed during the run; at the end of the race the lugers extend their toes as far in front of the sled as possible, to trigger the timer beam at the bottom of the run a fraction of a second sooner.

While East German Ute Rührold was capturing her second straight silver medal at age 21 at the 1976 Olympics, the US team took pride in the fact that the whole team finished all their runs in the three events. East Germans Hans Rinn and Norbert Hahn became the first repeat gold medalists in luge when they

114

won the 1980 two-man event. That year the USSR picked up a rare gold, and Italy clinched two silvers. One of Italy's 1980 silver medalists, Paul Hilgartner, was 31 when he took the 1984 gold in men's singles; another 1984 gold medal winner, Hans Stangassinger of the West German two-man team, weighed 244 pounds. In 1988 the East German women swept the medals in luge singles. That year East German men and women won six of the nine luge medals, and all the gold. US luger Bonny Warner came in sixth, the best US finish ever.

Medalists

Luge — Men's Singles

1988 1. Jens Mueller, East Germany, 3:05.548
2. Georg Hackl, West Germany, 3:05.916
3. Iouri Kharchenko, Soviet Union, 3:06.274

1984 1. Paul Hildgartner, Italy, 3:4.258
2. Serguev Danilin, Soviet Union, 3:4.962
3. Valeri Doudin, Soviet Union, 3:5.012

1980 1. Bernhard Glass, East Germany, 2:54.796
2. Paul Hildgartner, Italy, 2:55.372
3. Anton Winkler, West Germany, 2:56.545

1976 1. Detlef Guenther, East Germany, 3:27.688
2. Josef Fendt, West Germany, 3:28.196
3. Hans Rinn, East Germany, 3:28.574

1972 1. Wolfgang Scheidl, East Germany, 3:27.58
2. Harald Ehrig, East Germany, 3:28.39
3. Wolfram Fiedler, East Germany, 3:28.73

1968 1. Manfred Schmid, Austria, 2:42.48
2. Thomas Kohler, East Germany, 2:52.66
3. Klaus-Michael Bonsack, East Germany, 2:53.33

1964 1. Thomas Kohler, East Germany, 3:26.77
2. Klaus-Michael Bonsack, East Germany, 3:27.04
3. Hans Plenk, West Germany, 3:30.15

1924-1960 Not held

Luge — Men's Doubles

1988 1. East Germany, 1:31.940, Joerg Hoffmann, Jochen Pietzsch
2. East Germany, 1:32.039, Stefan Krausse, Jan Behrendt
3. West Germany, 1:32.274, Thomas Schwab, Wolfgang Staudinger

1984 1. West Germany, 1:23.620, Hans Stangassinger, Franz Wembacher
2. Soviet Union, 1:23.660, Yevgeny Belooussov, Alexandar Belyakov
3. East Germany, 1:23.887, Joerg Hoffmann, Jochen Pietzsch

1980 1. East Germany, 1:19.331, Hans Rinn, Norbert Hahn
2. Italy, 1:19.606, Peter Schnitzer, Karl Brunner
3. Austria, 1:19.795, George Fluckinger, Karl Schrott

1976 1. East Germany 1:25.604, Hans Rinn, Norbert Hahn
2. West Germany, 1:25.899, Hans Brner, Balthasar Schwarm
3. Austria, 1:25.919, Manfred Schmid, Franz Schachner

1972 1. Italy, 1:28.35, Paul Hildgartner, Walter Plaikner
1. East Germany, 1:28.35, Horst Hornlein, Reinhard Bredow
3. East Germany, 1:29.16, Klaus-M. Bonsack, Wolfram Fiedler

1968 1. East Germany, 1:35.85, Klaus-M. Bonsack, Thomas Kohler
2. Austria, 1:36.34, Manfred Schmid, Ewald Walch
3. West Germany, 1:37.29, Wolfgang Winkler, Fritz Nachmann

1964 1. Austria, 1:41.62, Josef Feistmantl, Manfred Stengl
2. Austria, 1:41.91, Reinhold Senn, Helmut Thaler
3. Italy, 1:42.87, Walter Aussendorfer, Sigisfredo Mair

1924-1960 Not held

Luge — Women's Singles

1988 1. Steffi Walter-Martin, East Germany, 3:03.973
2. Ute Oberhofner, East Germany, 3:04.105
3. Cerstin Schmidt, East Germany, 3:04.181

1984 1. Steffi Martin, East Germany, 2:46.570
2. Bettina Schmidt, East Germany, 2:46.873
3. Ute Weiss, East Germany, 2:47.248

1980 1. Vera Zozulia, Soviet Union, 2:36.537
2. Melitta Sollmann, East Germany, 2:37.657
3. Ingrida Amantova, Soviet Union, 2:37.817

115

Winter

1976	**1.** Margit Schumann, East Germany, 2:50.621
	2. Ute Ruehrold, East Germany, 2:50.846
	3. Elisabeth Demleitner, West Germany, 2:51.056
1972	**1.** Anna-Maria Muller, East Germany, 2:59.18
	2. Ute Ruehrold, East Germany, 2:59.49
	3. Margit Schumann, East Germany, 2:59.54
1968	**1.** Erica Lechner, Italy, 2:28.66

2. Christa Schmuck, West Germany, 2:29.37
3. Angelika Dunhaupt, West Germany, 2:29.56

1964 **1.** Ortrun Enderlein, East Germany, 3:24.67
2. Ilse Geisler, East Germany, 3:27.42
3. Helene Thurner, Austria, 3:29.06

1924-
1960 **Not held**

SKIING—ALPINE

WARM-UP

Skiing, once the province (or at least the hill) of the rich in the US, became a sport popular with the masses after World War II, with former members of the famed 10th Mountain Division (the "hallowed ski troops") invigorating the ski industry. Other returning servicemen, who had been given a chance to ski in Europe after or even during the war, also contributed to the growing popularity of the sport. Everyone wanted to forget the hard times of the war; silently traversing the winter landscape on skis proved a tonic for some.

Although the American interest in skiing is relatively new, skiing has been practiced in northern Europe for centuries. The oldest known ski, found in a peat bog at Umea, Sweden, goes back nearly 45 centuries to 2500 BC. However, a Stone Age petroglyph in Rodoy, Norway showing a skier has been dated at 5000 BC, a sure sign that someone, now very old, was on skis more than 7,000 years ago. A sled runner about 10 feet long was pulled out of a Finnish bog and carbon-dated to 7000 BC, or 9,000 years ago. As Ted Bates notes in his book, *Nine Thousand Years of Skis,* "Where there were sled runners, there were probably skis." But thousands of years of relying on skis for transportation did not naturally give way to sport; only in the last century has it become a recreational and competitive sport.

In the early days, skiing invariably meant nordic: ski jumping and cross-country. When the British began to popularize skiing in central Europe during the late 19th century, the Alps gave their name to alpine skiing.

fact: Downhillers are considered by other skiers to be insane.

Henry Lunn of Great Britain, a travel agent, founded the Public Schools Alpine Sports Club and promoted alpine skiing to lure elite Britons to Switzerland and the Alps. In 1911, Lunn organized the first downhill race, the Roberts of Kandahar Challenge (so named because the trophy was put up by Lord Kandahar), held in what is now Crans-Montana, Switzerland. His son, Arnold Lunn, staged the first modern slalom in 1922 in Murren, Switzerland.

For the first three Olympics, only nordic events were staged, and were only held for men. In 1948, alpine events were fully integrated into the Olympic

117

program. The inaugural alpine event, the combined, which was introduced in 1936 and included women, was dropped as an Olympic event after 1948, not to reappear until 1988. The 1948 Olympics saw the introduction of men's and women's downhill and slalom events. Men's and women's giant slalom was added to the Olympic lineup in 1952, and super giant (super-G) slalom and combined events placed on the program in 1988.

▼

SPECTATORS' GUIDE

Downhill and super giant slalom are generally grouped together as speed events, while slalom and giant slalom are considered technical events. Generally, skiers compete in either the speed or the technical events, since each involves unique skills and equipment and requires different strategies to be successful.

The top 15 skiers are seeded and unless course conditions are poor, this group has the advantage of going down first on a fresh course. When conditions are poor, lower-ranked skiers are sent off first to create a firmer trail. If two heats are involved, the top 15 reverses its order for the second run. Virtually all of the medalists will come from the top-seeded group, although an unseeded skier will occasionally surprise and grab a medal.

Alpine skis are more durable and wider than those used for cross country. The slalom ski has a more defined side cut and is a little narrower at the center. The giant slalom side cut isn't as defined while the downhill model is almost straight. Built for speed, the downhill ski is the longest of the racing models, measuring approximately seven feet. Slalom racers tend to favor shorter skis for greater maneuverability, while the length of the giant slalom ski falls between the downhill and slalom.

Slalom is an event requiring the execution of many short, quick turns through two heats on two different courses. The times for the two heats are added together to determine the final finish order.

A slalom course is required to have 55–75 gates for men and 40–60 gates for women. The competitors are required to pass between all the gates (alternate red/blue pairs of flag poles) in sequence down the course. The course is composed of various gate combinations designed to test a skier's skill and strategy. As long as a racer's feet pass between the markers, no penalty is charged for knocking down the flags with arms or shoulders. But if a gate is missed, the racer will be disqualified unless he or she returns to the gate and passes through it. The vertical drop on slalom courses is between 140–220 meters for men and 120–180 meters for women.

Giant Slalom is characterized as the discipline that requires the most technical skill; skiers race down the mountain through a faster, longer, and more open course than in slalom. The number of gates on the course is determined by the vertical drop of the course. The FIS requires that all giant slalom races be run on courses with vertical drops of 250–400 meters for men and 250–350 meters for women. The minimum distance between gates is 13 feet. Competitors stay low between gates and straighten up for turns.

Speed and drama go hand and hand during the **downhill**, run in one cutthroat heat with the fastest time winning. And it's all over in less than two minutes. Skiers tear down the course at speeds of 60 to 80 miles per hour between a series of red poles set at about the same distance as in the giant slalom. To make conditions safer and inhibit the reckless nature of the skiers, a minimum number of control and direction flags are set up along the course. The men's course has at least an 800-meter vertical drop, while the women's course is between 500 and 700 meters.

Super giant slalom, or super-G, is a hybrid of downhill and giant slalom. Like downhill, the winner is decided in one run. Long, sweeping, high-speed turns make this event popular with spectators.

▼

HOPEFULS

A little bit about the Olympic mountain range: Val d'Isere, the most consistent (in snow coverage) and longest-running stop on the World Cup circuit, will give way to a "new and improved" series of courses cut into the adjacent Bellevarde Mountain. The latest in Olympic-caliber courses (everything but slalom, which will be held at the far western end of the Olympic mountain range), the runs on Bellevarde were partially designed by Switzerland's Bernhard Russi, an Olympic medalist.

The "improved" portion of the "new" course will not necessarily benefit or hamper the racers as much as it will benefit the spectators. Virtually all of the super giant slalom and giant slalom will be visible to the 20,000 alpine fans expected at the base of the mountain. Also, 80% of the downhill (which winds down the mountain for some two miles) will be visible as well. This should aid CBS and sub-contractor TNT in their coverage of the racing.

One interesting note is that skiers have not been able to test Bellevarde in a race situation. Last winter's test was canceled due to too much snow. So the first actual world-class racing done at Bellevarde will be in the Albertville Games.

The Speed Events—Men

Downhill: Last season welcomed a host of newcomers to the World Cup downhill scene, including 1991 super-G overall points runner-up Stefan Eberharter of Austria and downhill points runner-up Atle Skaardal of Norway. Both skiers were runners-up to the same competitor, the veteran Swiss sensation Franz Heinzer. Heinzer, 29, fourth in the 1991 World Cup overall standings, won four downhills on the season—including the prestigious Hahnenkamm in Kitzbuehel, Austria. Other medal candidates are Switzerland's Daniel Mahrer and Austrian Helmut Hoeflehner, ranking third and fourth, respectively, in the 1991 World Cup downhill standings.

US Outlook: Is there another Bill Johnson (1984 Sarajevo Games downhill gold) waiting to bust loose and set the skiing world on its ear with a rip-roaring ride to Olympic victory? Alaskan Tommy Moe, tied for 29th in the 1991 World Cup downhill point standings, and New York's A. J. Kitt, America's top seed in downhill the last two years, have an outside shot at best.

Super-G: Again, Heinzer, Eberharter, and Skaardal have to be the favorites coming into the second speed event, though the betting man's pick might be homeboy Franck Piccard, who grew up on the mountains surrounding Albertville. Add to that his gold medal in the super-G in Calgary and a crowd that may cause an avalanche with all of the noises they'll make when he reaches the finish line, and Piccard becomes one of the real favorites.

US Outlook: Tommy Moe was the 1989 world junior champion in super-G, but youth may tend to hurt more than help the US team in the speed events. Most of the top downhillers are 25 years and older and veterans of 10 or more World Cup seasons.

The Technical Events—Men

Slalom: Last year Luxembourg's Marc Giardelli won the overall World Cup slalom title on, as his coach/father puts it, "one leg." Whether or not he can hold up during the 1991 season and save enough for the 1992 Olympics remains to be seen. If he's healthy, he's got to be the favorite. Though Giardelli has never won an Olympic medal (just four overall World Cup titles), one of his chief competitors has: Italy's Alberto Tomba, the defending Olympic slalom champion. Also add to the hunt for gold Norway's Ole Kristian Furuseth, Sweden's Tomas Fogdoe, and Austrian Thomas Stangassinger. Austrian great Rudolf Nierlich, third in slalom, second in giant slalom, and third overall in the 1991 World Cup, was killed in the spring of 1991 in a car accident.

US Outlook: Once a dominant force on the World Cup circuit, it's now AM (after Mahre) for the US in the World Cup slalom standings. Felix McGrath, ranked sixth in the 1990 overall slalom standings, retired in 1991 at age 28. Americans didn't score a single World Cup slalom point in 1990–91; slalom represents their slimmest chance for a medal in Albertville.

Giant Slalom: Alberto Tomba rules the giant slalom event. With five wins in giant slalom alone on the 1991 circuit, Tomba has the best chance at gold— and repeat gold at that. The other not-as-precious medals will be sought by Giardelli (if healthy), Switzerland's Urs Kaelin, Sweden's Fredrik Nyberg, Furuseth, and Eberharter. And don't count out Piccard on his home snow.

US Outlook: This may be the men's best chance at a medal. Park City, Utah's Jeremy Nobis, 21, turned in two top-15 finishes in the World Cup last year and was the leading point US scorer on the World Cup circuit last year. "We're ready," says alpine program director Dennis Agee, "for some breakthroughs here."

Downhill/Slalom Combined: The two extremes in racing, the high speed downhill and the tightly turning slalom, are combined in this event in hopes of finding the best overall skier. Added to the program during the Calgary Olympics, the combined event is a real tester for the world's greatest skiers. Giardelli won the 1991 World Cup combined title. If he's hurting at the Olympics, he may forgo this event to concentrate on the other ones. If he does decide to run it, he'll most likely win. Other favorites include: Norway's future champion, 20-year-old Lasse Kjus, and Austrian veteran Guenther Mader.

US Outlook: A. J. Kitt was the only American with a World Cup combined score last year.

Alberto Tomba

At the post-race press conference following the final alpine skiing event in the 1988 Calgary Winter Olympics, a handsome, muscular 21-year-old Italian skier met with the press. There he propositioned the 1988 Olympics' other darling, East Germany's figure skater Katarina Witt, for a date. "If she doesn't win one she can have one of mine," Alberto Tomba boldly told the media, referring to his two gold medals (slalom and giant slalom). Witt won her gold medal that night and Tomba never got his date.

One of the top-ranked technical skiers (slalom and giant slalom) on the World Cup circuit over the last several years, Tomba did receive a compliment from another skiing great that may not have been as nice as dating Witt, but when he decides to finally garage his skis, it should make him awfully proud. "Tomba may be the greatest slalom skier ever," said the legendary Ingemar Stenmark, dual gold medal winner at the 1980 Lake Placid Games and 85-time World Cup giant slalom and slalom winner.

Tomba thoroughly dominated the 1990–91 World Cup giant slalom, topping the second place finisher Austria's Rudolf Nierlich (who died in an auto accident at season's end) by 51 points and placing him second behind Marc Giardelli for the overall title.

An interesting footnote to Tomba's skiing is that he really only concentrates on the technical events (slalom and giant slalom) and doesn't get involved too much in the speed events (downhill and super giant slalom). The reason for this is not just due to the danger factor, but mostly out of respect for his parents, with whom he still lives in a mansion on the outskirts of Bologna.

Forgoing the speed events may have cost Tomba the overall World Cup title last season, so in an effort to be more competitive with Giardelli (who beat Tomba by 20 points for the overall title, scoring 23 points in downhill and super-G to Tomba's 0 points), Tomba plans on racing some of the super-Gs.

If so, before he leaves his home he may want to don the helmet that he uses to smash through giant slalom gates at over 40 mph and take out his parents' TV. —*P.S.*

Marc Giardelli

Some athletes deal with pain much better than others. And in a sport like skiing, where athletes are frequently on the brink of disaster at 60 mph-plus, a slight miscalculation can lead to an abrupt and painful stop. In December of 1989, skier Marc Giardelli was at highway-type speed on a super-G course in Sestriere, Italy, when he lost control. Flying completely off the course, Giardelli crashed not into fresh snow (due to the dry season) but into dirt—frozen like rock.

The results were hideous. A concussion, a lacerated kidney, and enough internal bleeding to rob him of two and a half quarts of blood within two hours of the crash. And it wasn't until a month later that doctors found a hole (ripped by his pelvic bone) in his hip muscle that had also been bleeding since the crash.

When the 1990 World Cup season came around, Giardelli, and his father/coach Helmut, convinced Giardelli's doctors that he could race in the upcoming World Cup. After a 71st place finish in the opening race, Giardelli went on to an amazing 13 top-four finishes and his fourth overall World Cup title.

"I've had constant pain since 1989," said Giardelli, who damaged his knee so badly in a crash in 1983 that it led his orthopedic surgeon Dr. Richard Steadman to say that "in no sport that I'm aware of has anyone come back from an injury like that to become the best in the world."

Giardelli began skiing on the World Cup circuit at the age of 16. At 18, he finished sixth in the overall title hunt. Within three years he won his first World Cup. But in taking over the reins from Switzerland's Pirmin Zurbriggen as the most successful overall World Cup skier, Giardelli has yet to win an Olympic medal; he was 9th in the downhill, 20th in the giant slalom at the Calgary Games, during an injury-plagued season in which he finished 5th overall in the World Cup.

And at the 1984 Winter Olympics, the Austrian-born Giardelli (who refused to join the Austrian Ski Federation because he wanted to be coached by his father) declared himself a citizen of Luxembourg (a Rhode Island-sized country next to Belgium), but was disallowed entrance into the Sarajevo Games.

Though a gold medal at Albertville would look nice next to Giardelli's four crystal World Cup trophies, the skier who has been referred to as a "robot" has his sights set on yet another overall title. "A fifth one would make me number one in history, the best ever," he said. —*P.S.*

The Speed Events—Women

Downhill: Petra Kronberger—remember that name. The odds of Austrian Kronberger winning five gold medals at Albertville are listed as better than Pirmin Zurbriggen's shot at the same feat during the Calgary Games. As you read on, her name will come up as a favorite for each of the five events. Most likely to be somewhere on the winner's stand with Kronberger will be her teammate Sabine Ginther and Switzerland's Chantal Bournissen, the 1991 World Cup downhill overall winner.

US Outlook: First off, the US women's team has a much better chance at medals than the men do. A breakthrough in the downhill may come from Alaska's Hilary Lindh, the 1986 world junior downhill champion and strongest finisher in recent years for the Americans. Dianne Roffe, coming off a back injury, will be ready for the 1992 season, along with newcomer Megan Gerety.

Super-G: Does the name Kronberger ring a bell? She swept the women's super-G and downhill at Meribel, France last year. The 22-year-old, two-time World Cup overall champion finished second in the 1991 World Cup super-G standings . . . even with a late-season knee injury that forced her out of several races. France's Carole Merle, the top-ranked super-G skier last year, will be backed by an enthusiastic home crowd as she duels the world's most successful skier.

US Outlook: Edith Thys, America's top super-G finisher in Calgary (ninth) and on the 1991 World Cup (13th) leads a war-torn women's team that also features giant slalom specialists Eva Twardokens (fourth 1991 overall giant slalom) and Julie Parisien, winner of the first US World Cup victory in four years, the giant slalom at Waterville Valley, New Hampshire.

The Technical Events—Women

Slalom: Kronberger edged out Sweden's super-soph Pernilla Wilberg and Spain's Blanca Fernandez-Ochoa to capture the 1991 overall slalom title, Kronberger's strongest event. And we should add to the medal hunt Switzerland's Vreni Schneider (1988 Calgary slalom gold, 35 World Cup wins—a record 14 in the 1989 season, and World Cup slalom titles in 1989–90) and Kronberger's teammate Ingrid Salvenmoser.

US Outlook: Twardokens and Parisien look to have the best chance at a medal. World Cup veterans Roffe and Kristi Terzian (coming back from off-season surgery, as are several on the women's team) also have an outside chance. Slalom will probably be the toughest medal for the women.

Giant Slalom: If Kronberger's sweep is broken, and probably it will be, the giant slalom may be the culprit. Schneider (defending Olympic giant slalom champion) is the reigning queen of giant slalom. Also ahead of Kronberger is teammate Anita Wachter (second to Schneider in the 1991 World Cup) and Wilberg (third overall).

US Outlook: Giant slalom is the USA's best chance at a medal. Led by Twardokens (fourth overall in the 1991 World Cup giant slalom standings) and Parisien (10th overall), nearly half of America's 1991 World Cup points came in giant slalom.

Combined: Austrian Sabine Ginther and France's Florance Masnada tied for the 1991 combined title. You could give the home-mountain edge to Masnada

123

except for one thing: Kronberger. Masnada is better in the speed event, but Kronberger's dominance in slalom should more than make up the difference.

US Outlook: Twardokens was the only American to score in the women's combined. Parisien and Roffe may also have an slight chance at a medal.

Vreni Schneider

Switzerland's Vreni Schneider rode into the 1988 Calgary Games in the wake of two of the more popular Swiss skiers of the times.

Michela Figini, the youngest skier ever to win a gold medal (17 when she won the downhill at Sarajevo) and 1988 World Cup downhill points leader, and Maria Walliser, who after her two Calgary bronzes (combined and super-G), told a tabloid newspaper that "I'm going to Hollywood."

Funny how things can change.

The low-key Schneider, a technical specialist who just may be the greatest female giant slalom skier of all time, torched the rest of the field in slalom and giant slalom and led the 1988 Games (along with Italy's Alberto Tomba) with two gold medals. In the opening technical event, the giant slalom, Schneider was sitting in fifth place after the first run. On her second run she showed the greatest skiers in the world why she owns the giant slalom event—winning by a whole second.

In slalom, though she wasn't favored to medal, Schneider again put down a second run that was nothing short of breathtaking. Leading by only a couple hundredths of a second over the second- and third-place racers after the first run, Schneider's chance to sweep the Calgary technical events looked to be in place.

Sweden's Camilla Nilsson (who was in second place after the first run) fell on what turned out to be a very demanding new course. Yugoslavia's Mateja Svet then let go with a very fast second run to take the lead. Out of the starting gate, Schneider, in what's been called "the most brilliant single effort of the alpine in women's Olympic history," floored those in attendance by clocking a run that gave her the gold by an amazing 1.68 seconds.

Along with Walliser's two bronze medals, the heavily favored Figini managed only a silver in the super-G.

Near the end of the Olympic festivities, Yugoslavia's Svet asked Schneider if "she (Verni) might be the second Tomba?" Schneider replied "Oh, no, I am not like Tomba ... I want to remain Vreni like I have always been."

The following ski season, the Olympic great from the small Swiss village known simple as "Elm," had her best year ever, winning the World Cup overall title and in the process setting a record with 14 wins. Still skiing giant slalom as strongly as ever, Schneider will be the biggest challenge for the next Olympic great, Austria's Petra Kronberger, in Kronberger's quest for much gold at Albertville. —P.S.

Petra Kronberger

It used to be a guy named Clark Kent who wore a big "S" on his chest, flew around, and did things that no other human could do.

Not any more.

In Albertville, though she won't be wearing a big "S" on her chest, she will be flying ... and doing things no other human can do. Petra Kronberger, Austria's "wunderkind," will be the most talked-about athlete to don the alpine planks and bomb down the French mountainside.

She has a legitimate chance, even more so than that of Switzerland's Pirmin Zurbriggen in 1988, of becoming the first Olympic five-gold medal winner in alpine events. The 22-year-old's 1991 World Cup record is legendary.

On a team that nearly tripled the second-place team, Switzerland, in the Nations Cup scoring race, Krongerger out-scored 10 other nations ... singlehandedly. And she basically had the overall points championship wrapped up by New Year's.

In the three weeks following her first win in the World Cup tour opener in Val Zoldana, Italy, Kronberger scored a win in every discipline—in essence hitting for skiing's equivalent of baseball's cycle faster than anyone in history.

One month later, at the World Championship break, Kronberger had accumulated 276 points (at season's end, the second-place finisher had totaled only 195 points) and was leading in the standings in every event but giant slalom and combined. But, starting in January, 1991, at the World Championships, she was slowed by a knee injury and missed a number of races in the second half of the season. By season's end, though, she was back, winning a late-season race and finishing first overall, first in slalom, second in super-G, and third in downhill and accumulating an amazing 312 points.

In Olympic history, the most successful performances have come in recent years. At the 1976 Games in Innsbruck, West Germany's Rosi Mittermaier captured gold in the slalom and giant slalom to go with a silver in the downhill. Then, in the 1980 Games in Lake Placid, Liechtenstein's Hanni Wenzel pulled off the same feat on Whiteface Mountain.

A healthy Kronberger will be one of the most exciting athletes to watch at the 1992 Winter Games, and she may ski rings around Rosi and Hanni's record. —*P.S.*

Schedule

The tentative alpine skiing schedule is as follows:

Sunday, February 9
Downhill, men

Monday, February 10
Combined downhill, men

Tuesday, February 11
Combined, slalom, men

Sunday, February 16
Super-G, men

125

Tuesday, February 18
Giant slalom, men

Wednesday, February 12
Combined downhill, women

Thursday, February 13
Combined slalom, women

Saturday, February 15
Downhill, women

Monday, February 17
Super-G, women

Wednesday, February 19
Giant slalom, women

Thursday, February 20
Slalom, women

Saturday, February 22
Slalom, men

MEN'S ALPINE EVENTS

▼

HIGHLIGHTS

Norwegian Birger Ruud won both the downhill and the jumping events when alpine skiing was in its infancy in 1936. At the 1948 Games Henri Oreiller of France was a double gold medal winner, taking the downhill and combined (an event subsequently discontinued until 1988), and earned a bronze in the slalom. James Couttet of France and Karl Molitor of Switzerland also landed two medals apiece.

In the 1952 Games at Olso, Norwegian Stein Eriksen captured the giant slalom gold and won the silver in the slalom; he later became a legendary ski instructor who seemed to be straight from Central Casting. At age 33 Zeno Colò of Italy took a gold in the downhill despite his unorthodox style, finishing fourth in the other two events. Othmar Schneider of Austria, silver medalist in the downhill, took a gold in the slalom.

Austria's legendary Toni Sailer swept all three alpine events held in 1956; he took the downhill using a ski strap supplied at the last minute by the trainer for the Italian team. French skiers introduced waxless metal skis for the 1960 Games, and came away from Squaw Valley with three medals; in the downhill Jean Vuarnet captured the gold and Guy Périllat the bronze. Périllat took the downhill silver eight years later. In the slalom at Squaw Valley it was Ernst Hinterseer of Austria for the gold, and Swiss skier Roger Staub won an upset gold in the giant slalom.

Prince Karim, the Aga Kahn, skied the downhill and slalom for Iran at the 1964 Games, which were conducted under the shadow of tragedy; 19-year-old Australian Ross Milne was killed practicing on the downhill course just days before the final competition. That year the US men finally earned alpine medals when Billy Kidd and Jimmy Heuga placed second and third behind 26-year-old Austrian ski veteran Josef "Pepi" Stiegler in the slalom; Stiegler also won the bronze in the giant slalom. Austrian Egon Zimmerman took the downhill gold, and

126

French skier François Bonlieu defied his coaches all the way to the gold in the giant slalom, with Austrian Karl Schranz taking the silver.

fact: The ideal downhiller is pearshaped, heavily muscled in the thighs and buttocks—for better absorption of the shocks encountered skiing at high speeds on bumpy slopes—and slight in the shoulders and upper arms, for the least wind resistance.

Twelve years after Toni Sailer swept the alpine events, French skier Jean-Claude Killy duplicated his feat at the Grenoble Games. Controversy over Killy's amateur status threatened to disqualify the handsome customs inspector, but Killy was eventually allowed to compete. Suspense mounted when Austrian legend Karl Schranz was allowed to restart his second run in the slalom due to spectator interference, and turned in a better time than Killy's; it was later determined, but not unanimously, that Schranz had missed a gate before the spectator interfered with him on his aborted run, and he was disqualified, giving the sweep to Killy.

Schranz was a great all-around skier, but never won an Olympic gold; he was barred from the 1972 Games for allowing "use of his name and pictures in commercial advertisements." The Austrian team felt Schranz had been scapegoated and threatened to pull out of the Games in sympathy, but Schranz insisted they continue. Spain claimed its first ever alpine medal in 1972 when Francisco "Paquito" Fernandez-Ochoa took the gold in slalom. Gustavo Thöni of Italy won the very steep giant slalom and added a silver medal in the slalom. Bernhard Russi and Roland Collombin gave Switzerland a 1-2 finish in the downhill. Russi came back to take the downhill silver four years later, and recently he helped design some of the ski runs for the Albertville Games.

fact: Downhill racers crouch with their chests to their knees to cut wind resistance.

But at Innsbruck in 1976, hometown favorite Franz Klammer of Austria took the downhill gold from the defending Russi by one-third of a second. Italy's Thöni was back for a silver in the slalom, edged out for the gold by his teammate and protegé, Piero Gros. By 0.20 seconds over teammate Ernst Good, Swiss skier Heini Hemmi won the giant slalom, where defending champion Thöni placed fourth behind Swedish come-from-behind legend Ingemar Stenmark. US skiers Phil and Steve Mahre competed in their first Games at Innsbruck.

Phil Mahre was medalist caliber in 1980, winning a silver in the slalom. Despite a serious injury in September 1979, Sweden's Ingemar Stenmark won both the slalom and the giant slalom at Lake Placid, with Andreas Wenzel, half of Liechtenstein's brother-sister ski team, claiming the giant slalom silver. The men's downhill delighted Austrian hearts, with Leonhard Stock and Peter Wirnsberger placing 1-2. Canada's Steve Podborski won a bronze at Lake Placid, the first medal ever won by a non-European in the downhill. He was the youngest of the so-called Crazy Canucks, a group of Canadian daredevils that in the late 1970s began to break the European stranglehold on the downhill.

Franz Klammer, skiing star of the 1970s and 1976 gold winner in the downhill, failed to make Austria's 1980 team but was back for a sentimental showing in the 1984 Games. But 1984 saw European skiing dominance shaken. That year the men's downhill gold was won by US skier Bill Johnson, and brothers Phil and Steve Mahre took a gold and silver, respectively, in the slalom, confirming North American emergence in the skiing arena. At the 1984 Games, champion skier Ingemar Stenmark was ruled out of Olympic competition for technicalities relating to his amateur status, and thus could not defend his 1980 Olympic golds.

fact: When Bill Johnson ran the downhill in 1984 his average speed was clocked at over 64 mph.

Stenmark was back in competition for the 1988 Games, a sentimental favorite at nearly 32 years of age without much hope to medal. Marc Giardelli of Luxembourg was barred from the 1980 and 1984 Games over a citizenship snafu; in 1988 he competed but did not medal. In a curious sidenote, Prince Hubertus von Hohenlohe skied the Alpine events for Mexico in 1988. Pirmin Zurbriggen of Switzerland was favored to win as many as five gold medals going into the 1988 Games in Calgary, but he managed only one gold, in the downhill, and a bronze in the giant slalom. Behind Zurbriggen, Swiss teammate Peter Müller won his second Olympic downhill silver. But 1988 was the year for Italy's Alberto Tomba, who took a gold in the giant slalom and another in the slalom. And France's Franck Piccard, after taking a bronze in the downhill, won the first Olympic gold awarded for the super-G, a race in which 33 of the 94 starters failed to finish. Piccard is a native of Albertville, France, a detail that was not lost on those looking to the 1992 Winter Games.

Anton "Toni" Sailer

Perhaps he's not as well known as Jean-Claude Killy to today's Olympic spectator, but his performance at the 1956 Olympics in Cortina, Italy, may have even been more dominating than Killy's three-gold performance in the Olympics.

Austrian Anton "Toni" Sailer, affectionately known at the "Blitz from Kitz" (after his hometown of Kitzbuhel, Austria), so thoroughly dominated the Winter Games that year that his performance may never be equalled.

In the giant slalom, Sailer won by over six seconds. Amazingly, he did this with only one run—not with combined times.

The giant slalom course set at Cortina was to be a very demanding one at that. It began on an extreme steep near the summit of Tondi di Faloria and wound down the mountainside, sometimes cutting through ridges and valleys that made for quite a rollercoaster ride on skis of that era, which amounted to not much more than planks of wood with boots nailed into them.

When the first Austrian, Anderl Molterer (starting sixth) raced down through the course, he was mobbed by Austrian fans at the finish line.

Molterer waved them away.

"Toni hasn't come yet," said Molterer, who knew he was destined for the silver medal with a time of 3:06.3.

Starting from the 18th position, Sailer, who claimed that the Cortina giant slalom course was "the toughest I'd ever seen," kept the flats of his skis on the snow as much as possible and absorbed the worst of the depressions and bumps en route to a 3:00.1 finish—6.2 seconds ahead of teammate Molterer. And fellow Austrian Walter Schuster rounded out the Austrian sweep of the event with a 3:07.2.

Sailer went on to capture the downhill and slalom in similar fashion. In the seventh Winter Olympic Games, he pulled off what the Europeans back then called "The Olympic Hat Trick."

But it was probably Japan's Chiharu "Chick" Igaya (silver medal in the slalom) who put it best after he crashed in the downhill while chasing Sailer: "I made the mistake of trying to beat Sailer in the downhill," he said. —P.S.

The First US Men to Win Alpine Medals

By 1964 the US men had yet to win a medal in alpine skiing in four Winter Olympics. This changed on a snowy Saturday in February on the out-run of the mighty Birgitskopfl peak in Innsbruck, Austria. There, Americans Billy Kidd, from Stowe, Vermont, and Jimmy Heuga, of Lake Tahoe, California, upset the heavily favored Europeans for the silver and bronze medals.

The demanding course quieted a number of the favorites right from the start. France's Jean-Claude Killy torqued his binding right out of his ski after 20 gates and his teammate Guy Périllat hooked the last gate, spun around, and put himself into 27th position going into the second run.

This set the stage for Kidd and Heuga.

Kidd had already logged a time putting him right up there with the leaders, when Heuga, racing out of the 24th slot, put forth a masterful run and found himself in third place. On their second runs (Heuga again raced from the back of the pack due to his first run placement), the Americans skied the 71-gate course to near-perfection and captured the silver and bronze medals behind Austria's

Josef Stiegler. And to this day, no Olympic racer has started from a position similar to Heuga's and gone on to win a medal.

Billy Kidd went on to finish seventh in the giant slalom, which gave him a third place finish in the alpine combined category, although no medal was awarded for the combined finish that year. —*P.S.*

Jean-Claude Killy

A skier who had just arrived at the pearly gates noticed a skier who greatly resembled the legendary Jean-Claude Killy on the slopes, and who was in the process of signing autographs at the base of Heaven's ski area.

"Is that Jean-Claude Killy?," said the skier to St. Peter, pointing him out.

"Oh him," St. Peter laughed. "No that's not Killy. That's God. He only thinks He's Jean-Claude Killy."

In 1968, it had been 12 years since Austrian Toni Sailer completed the almost unthinkable—sweeping three gold medals in the three disciplines of alpine skiing. To this day, with one exception, no one has ever come close to duplicating Sailer's achievement.

That exception took place in the 1968 Olympics in Grenoble, France. There, coming off of the 1967 World Cup season in which he won all three categories (slalom, giant slalom, and downhill) and scored a maximum 225 points (a record that has yet to be equalled), Killy was thought to have a chance of matching Sailer's "Olympic Hat Trick."

"It wouldn't surprise anyone if Jean-Claude Killy were to repeat Toni Sailer's Olympic feat of 1956—sweeping all three gold medals," read an article in the February, 1968, Olympic preview issue of *Skiing* magazine.

"At the start of the Olympic season I wasn't skiing too well," recalls Killy, contesting that forecast.

And it was actually a second-place finish in the Hahnenkamm (Kitzbuhlen, Austria) downhill, which is the Indy 500 of the European downhill races, that gave Killy the confidence he needed heading into the Olympics. "I had made a serious error on a section of the course that forced me to lose a great deal of speed," explained Killy. "I knew that if I hadn't made that error I would have won, which told me I was back in shape, my skis were fast and I was skiing very well."

At the Olympics, Killy readied himself for a bout with history. A half-hour before his run in the downhill, he inadvertently skied over a patch of ice and stripped a good portion of the wax off of the base of his skis. This almost cost him his first gold medal. When he found his coach and explained to him what had happened, his coach had the right words. He replied simply, "Don't worry. Get a good start and you'll win anyway."

His confidence intact, Killy negotiated a rolling portion of the course better than anyone in the field, and although he almost lost the race near the finish in the warmer snow (where the wax he lost would have enabled him to glide better), Killy held on to win by 8/100ths of a second.

"Winning the downhill gave me confidence and took some of the pressure off," said Killy. "So, in the giant slalom, I hardly had the feeling that I was racing in the Olympics at all."

Killy went on to capture the giant slalom by over two seconds and edged Austrian Herbert Huber by 9/110ths of a second in the slalom.

An interesting note concerning the giant slalom was what happened to Killy the night before the race. It seems that the heater in the room he shared with Alain Penz (a former French alpine team member) was not working properly. The room became so cold that the two skiers were shaken out of their sleep by what they thought was a gun shot—but what actually turned out to be a bottle of champagne (that Killy intended to drink after his victory the next day) exploding.

After Penz left for another, warmer room, Killy swiped his blankets and went back to bed. Still freezing, he began to put on more clothes ... his long johns, warmup pants, ski coat, socks, gloves and a hat. "When it was time to get up I was all dressed to go skiing," he said.

Killy hung up his skis for some five years after his three-gold performance at Grenoble. Then, at 30 years of age, he joined the International Ski Racers Association circuit.

Since 1986, Killy has represented France as the co-president of the Albertville organizing committee, sharing the post with national assembly representative Michel Barnier. In the early going, the position gave Killy more headaches than he could handle, to the point that he actually left the post in early 1987 for a year. International Olympic Committee president Juan Antonio Samaranch, understanding the impact of a Killy-less French Olympics, finally convinced Killy to get back aboard. Killy returned and applied the level of determination that once made him the world's most successful skier. The stamp of Killy will be very evident on the Albertville Games. —P.S.

Franz Klammer

It's tough to agree on the greatest moment of a given sport. Was it Hank Aaron's 715th home run, or Don Larsen's perfect game in the World Series? Was it Wilt Chamberlain's 100-point performance? Or five-foot, seven-inch Spud Webb winning the NBA's Slam Dunk contest?

Skiing has its share of great moments as well. But one performance seems to stand out among all of the others.

Many within the inner ski racing circle believe that the greatest single run of all time was Austrian Franz Klammer's come-from-behind performance on the Patscherkofel downhill course at the 1976 Innsbruck Games.

World Cup champion and Olympic favorite Bernhard Russi, 27, of Switzerland, seemed to have a lock on the gold medal when the young Klammer—as his country's last hope for the gold—entered the starting gate.

The bright yellow suit, that would later become synonymous with his famous run, was shredded in spots after a high-speed tumble he'd taken at Val d'Isere, France, prior to the Games; it was the same portion of the course that took the life of top French downhiller Michel Dujon during the same race.

"I've won wearing it and I've lost wearing it, too," Klammer would later comment.

As he exploded out of the start, the crowd—tens of thousands—that lined the course and the finish line erupted as well. As Klammer gained speed down the 10,379-foot course, he was followed by ABC cameras that had put together the most comprehensive top-to-bottom downhill coverage in Olympic history.

Gaining speed through the course, comprising a virtual minefield of gullies and unpredictable changes in terrain and bumps, Klammer, not known for his stellar technique, was all over the course. At midpoint he had only clocked the third fastest time.

The crowd got thicker toward the bottom of the course. The customary cowbells rang out. "Hup, up, up, up, up," the Austrians yodeled as he streaked by, still gaining speed.

As Klammer reached speeds of up to 80 mph, the bright yellow suit, tipped with a blazing red helmet, now looked liked a meteorite raging down the mountainside. At times he was airborne, looking as if he'd never pull out of it. Then, as if he could slow things down at 80 mph, evaluate the situation, and correct it, he'd regain control—in a split second.

Winning by four-tenths of a second, and already a European hero, the 1976 Olympics gave Franz Klammer to the world. —*P.S.*

Ingemar Stenmark

If you were to ask skiers who have competed at the last several Winter Olympics—"Who is the greatest skier of all time?"—they would probably come up with several different answers.

"Toni Sailer or Jean-Claude Killy," because of their three gold medal Olympic performances.

"Franz Klammer," for his strength and bravery in the downhill.

Or "Marc Giardelli," for his ability to succeed after injury.

But ask the same skiers who is the closest to technical perfection on a pair of skis and you'll inevitably receive just one answer.

"Ingemar Stenmark."

Growing up in the Arctic, some 1,000 miles north of Stockholm, Sweden, Stenmark began skiing on mountains. Much of his skiing plummeted through the dusk, for during certain days of the year in that area the sun only shines for some 30 minutes.

If he'd have grown up on Mt. Olympus with Zeus, he might have been dubbed "Stenmarkus, the God of Skiing."

The longest reigning and most consistent slalom and giant slalom specialist on the World Cup circuit, Stenmark achieved his Olympic highlight in the 1980 Lake Placid Games. There, he swept gold in those two events.

French skier Jean-Claude Killy swept the men's alpine events at Grenoble in 1968, winning three gold medals. He's back in the Olympic arena in the 1990s, as co-president of the Albertville organizing committee and designer of some of the competitive ski runs slated for the Winter Games.

In a come-from-behind victory, Austrian skier Franz Klammer showed exceptional tenacity in the downhill run that won him the gold in 1976.

Sweden's King Carl Gustav, left, was on hand at Lake Placid when Swedish skier Ingemar Stenmark, right, won gold medals in slalom giant slalom.

Phil Mahre skied to a silver medal in the 1980 slalom event, then out-skied his twin brother, Steve, to capture the slalom gold in 1984, becoming the most successful American alpine skier to date.

Stenmark fell behind after his first runs at the giant slalom and slalom courses, almost falling moments from the finish line in his giant slalom run. He found himself starting his second run from the third position.

On his second run, Stenmark carved through the course with surgeon-like precision and took the gold by almost a second—which in recent Olympics would be like the USA basketball team beating the Soviets by 60 points. It's just not supposed to happen.

In the slalom, Stenmark let go with another one of his patented second runs, clipping American leader Phil Mahre (silver medal) by a more realistic half second.

An interesting footnote to Stenmark's 1980 dual-gold Olympic performance was that several months before the Olympics, Stenmark was concentrating on some serious downhill training above Val Senales in the Italian Alps when he took a brutal tumble that didn't come to a halt until some 200 yards later.

Helicoptered to Bolzano, Italy, Stenmark—from his hospital bed (predating Schwarzenegger by some 10 years)—stated, "I'll be back." —*P.S.*

Mahres on Skis

Phil Mahre, without a doubt, is the most successful American alpine skier to date.

With two Olympic medals, a gold in slalom from the 1984 Olympics in Sarajevo (twin brother Steve won the silver), and a silver in the 1980 Lake Placid Games, Mahre is the only American male alpine skier to have medaled twice in the Olympics.

But more impressive than his Olympic performances, to Mahre at least, are his World Cup overall titles in 1981, 1982, and 1983.

"This, to me, is just another victory," said Mahre after his gold medal slalom run in Sarajevo.

Mahre's comments, though painfully honest and seeming ungracious, stood very true at Sarajevo. First off, the two top World Cup slalom specialists that year, Luxembourg's Marc Giardelli (1985, 1986, 1989, and 1991 World Cup champion) and the legendary Ingemar Stenmark (who had won six World Cup slalom races heading into the 1984 Olympics) were both absent from the race.

And second, the Sarajevo slalom course took its toll on the world's top skiers like no other course in the history of the Olympics. Close to half (seven, to be exact) of the top 15 seeded racers were disqualified due to crashes or missed gates.

Still, Marhe, the second American male to win an Olympic gold medal at those Games (Bill Johnson won the downhill three days earlier) remains as our country's most successful amateur skier.

Born in 1957, Phil four minutes before Steve, the Mahre brothers grew up in White Pass, Washington, at the foot of the Dairy Queen peaks of the Cascade Mountain range. And if it wasn't for Phil's accomplishments, Steve would have very well been one of our country's greatest amateur skiers.

133

Besides his three World Cup overall titles and two Olympic medals, Phil also won the United States Championships seven times. After hanging up the skis for several years, Mahre returned to the professional skiing scene where he's finished second overall in two of the last three years on the US Pro Tour. —*P.S.*

Pirmin Zurbriggen

Of the 1,793 athletes heading into the 1988 Calgary Winter Olympics, one had a "realistic" chance of winning five gold medals. Pirmin Zurbriggen, then 25, was Switzerland's hope to repeat Frenchman Jean-Claude Killy's sweep of alpine gold at the 1968 Grenoble Winter Games. By 1988 a sweep involved five medals rather than Killy's three, with super giant slalom and the downhill/slalom combined medal added to the program post-Killy.

Going into the Games, Zurbriggen was one of only two skiers ever to win four World Cup overall titles. Italian Gustavo Thoeni did it first and now Luxembourg's Marc Giardelli has done it since. In the World Cup season leading into the 1988 Games, Zurbriggen was plagued with a respiratory problem and won only two of 16 races he entered. But one of the two victories came in the pre-Olympic downhill at Schladming, Austria, which moved him into first place in the World Cup standings, ahead of Italy's Alberto Tomba.

The downhill was the opening event at Calgary. Zurbriggen's chief competitor and fellow countryman, Peter Mueller, drew the No. 1 starting position. Coincidentally, Zurbriggen drew No. 14—the same number Killy had worn at Grenoble. Zurbriggen rode the turny downhill to near perfection, edging teammate Mueller for the gold. France's Franck Piccard took the bronze.

The following day, in the downhill/slalom combined event—an event that Zurbriggen had the best chance of winning out of all of them—he took a half-second lead after the first run. Needing just to ski an easy, clean run to lock up his second gold medal, Zurbriggen hooked a tip on a gate two-thirds of the way through his slalom run, slammed, and was disqualified from the race.

After a respectable fifth in the super-G, in which 33 of the 94 racers blew out of the course, Zurbriggen captured the bronze medal in giant slalom, two seconds behind Tomba.

Zurbriggen skied for two more years on the World Cup circuit, retiring before the 1990–91 season. Although he didn't come through the Calgary Games laden with gold, his place in skiing history is assured, given his World Cup and Olympic successes. —*P.S.*

Medalists

Skiing, Alpine — Men's Downhill

1988   1. Pirmin Zurbriggen, Switzerland, 1:59.63

2. Peter Mueller, Switzerland, 2:00.14
3. Franck Piccard, France, 2:01.24

1984   1. William Johnson, USA, 1:45.59
2. Peter Mueller, Switzerland, 1:45.86

3. Anton Steiner, Austria, 1:45.95
1980 **1.** Leonhard Stock, Austria, 1:45.50
2. Peter Wirnsberger, Austria, 1:46.12
3. Steve Podborski, Canada, 1:46.62
1976 **1.** Franz Klammer, Austria, 1:45.73
2. Bernhard Russi, Switzerland, 1:46.06
3. Herbert Plank, Italy, 1:46.59
1972 **1.** Bernhard Russi, Switzerland, 1:51.43
2. Roland Collombin, Switzerland, 1:52.07
3. Heini Messner, Austria, 1:52.40
1968 **1.** Jean-Claude Killy, France, 1:59.85
2. Guy Perillat, France, 1:59.93
3. Jean-Daniel Datwyler, Switzerland, 2:00.32
1964 **1.** Egon Zimmermann, Austria, 2:18.16
2. Leo Lacroix, France, 2:18.90
3. Wolfgang Bartels, West Germany, 2:19.48
1960 **1.** Jean Vuarnet, France, 2:06.0
2. Hans-Peter Lanig, West Germany, 2:06.5
3. Guy Perillat, France, 2:06.9
1956 **1.** Toni Sailer, Austria, 2:52.2
2. Raymond Fellay, Switzerland, 2:55.7
3. Andreas Molterer, Austria, 2:56.2
1952 **1.** Zeno Colo, Italy, 2:30.8
2. Othmar Schneider, Austria, 2:32.0
3. Christian Pravda, Austria, 2:32.4
1948 **1.** Henri Oreiller, France, 2:55.0
2. Franz Gabl, Austria, 2:59.1
3. Karl Molitor, Switzerland, 3:00.3
3. Ralph Olinger, Switzerland, 3:00.3
1924-
1936 **Not held**

Skiing, Alpine — Men's Slalom

1988 **1.** Alberto Tomba, Italy, 1:39.47
2. Frank Woerndl, West Germany, 1:39.53
3. Paul Frommelt, Liechtenstein, 1:39.84
1984 **1.** Phil Mahre, USA, 1:39.41
2. Steven Mahre, USA, 1:39.62
3. Didier Bouvet, France, 1:40.20
1980 **1.** Ingemar Stenmark, Sweden, 1:44.26
2. Phil Mahre, USA, 1:44.76
3. Jacques Luethy, Switzerland, 1:45.06
1976 **1.** Piero Gros, Italy, 2:03.29
2. Gustav Thoni, Italy, 2:03.73
3. Willy Frommelt, Liechtenstein, 2:04.28
1972 **1.** Francisco Fernandez Ochoa, Spain, 109.27
2. Gustav Thoni, Italy, 110.28
3. Roland Thoni, Italy, 110.30
1968 **1.** Jean-Claude Killy, France, 99.73
2. Herbert Huber, Austria, 99.82
3. Alfred Matt, Austria, 100.09
1964 **1.** Pepi Stiegler, Austria, 131.13
2. Bill Kidd, USA, 131.27
3. James Heuga, USA, 131.52
1960 **1.** Ernst Hinterseer, Austria, 128.9
2. Hias Leitner, Austria, 130.3
3. Charles Bozon, France, 130.4
1956 **1.** Toni Sailer, Austria, 194.7
2. Chiharu Igaya, Japan, 198.7
3. Stig Sollander, Sweden, 200.2
1952 **1.** Othmar Schneider, Austria, 120.0
2. Stein Eriksen, Norway, 121.2
3. Guttorm Berge, Norway, 121.7
1948 **1.** Edi Reinalter, Switzerland, 130.3

2. James Couttet, France, 130.8
3. Henri Oreiller, France, 132.8
1924-
1936 **Not held**

Skiing, Alpine — Men's Giant Slalom

1988 **1.** Alberto Tomba, Italy, 2:06.37
2. Hubert Strolz, Austria, 2:07.41
3. Pirmin Zurbriggen, Switzerland, 2:08.39
1984 **1.** Max Julen, Switzerland, 2:41.18
2. Jurij Franko, Yugoslavia, 2:41.41
3. Andreas Wenzel, Liechtenstein, 2:41.75
1980 **1.** Ingemar Stenmark, Sweden, 2:40.74
2. Andreas Wenzel, Liechtenstein, 2:41.49
3. Hans Enn, Austria, 2:42.51
1976 **1.** Heini Hemmi, Switzerland, 3:26.97
2. Ernst Good, Switzerland, 3:27.17
3. Ingemar Stenmark, Sweden, 3:27.41
1972 **1.** Gustav Thoni, Italy, 3:09.62
2. Edmund Bruggmann, Switzerland, 3:10.75
3. Werner Mattle, Switzerland, 3:10.99
1968 **1.** Jean-Claude Killy, France, 3:29.28
2. Willy Favre, Switzerland, 3:31.50
3. Heini Messner, Austria, 3:31.83
1964 **1.** Francois Bonlieu, France, 1:46.71
2. Karl Schranz, Austria, 1:47.09
3. Pepi Stiegler, Austria, 1:48.05
1960 **1.** Roger Staub, Switzerland, 1:48.3
2. Pepi Stiegler, Austria, 1:48.7
3. Ernst Hinterseer, Austria, 1:49.1
1956 **1.** Toni Sailer, Austria, 3:00.1
2. Andreas Molterer, Austria. 3:06.3
3. Walter Schuster, Austria, 3:07.2
1952 **1.** Stein Eriksen, Norway, 2:25.0
2. Christian Pravda, Austria, 2:26.9
3. Toni Spiss, Austria, 2:28.8
1924-
1948 **Not held**

Skiing, Alpine — Men's Super Giant Slalom

1988 **1.** Franck Piccard, France, 1:39.66
2. Helmut Mayer, Austria, 1:40.96
3. Lars-Boerje Eriksson, Sweden, 1:41.08

Skiing, Alpine — Men's Combined (Downhill and Slalom)

1988 **1.** Hubert Strolz, Austria, 36.55
2. Bernhard Gstrein, Austria, 43.45
3. Paul Accola, Switzerland, 48.24
1952-
1984 **Not held**
1948 **1.** Henri Oreiller, France, 3.27
2. Karl Molitor, Switzerland, 6.44
3. James Couttet, France, 6.95
1940-
1944 **Not held**
1936 **1.** Franz Pfnur, Germany, 99.25
2. Gustav Lantschner, Germany, 96.26
3. Emile Allais, France, 94.69

WOMEN'S ALPINE EVENTS

▼

HIGHLIGHTS

Winter

In 1948 US skier Gretchen Fraser won the giant slalom and took a silver in the combined (an event discontinued afterward until 1988) behind Austrian Trude Jochum-Beiser, who also took a silver in the downhill. The downhill gold medalist that year was Hedy Schlunegger of Switzerland. Four years later US skier Andrea Mead Lawrence won some rare gold when she placed first in the slalom and giant slalom, despite a lack of snow. Jochum-Beiser was back for a gold in the downhill. Austria's 1952 silver medalist in the giant slalom, Dagmar Rom, was a film actress.

Canada's Lucille Wheeler captured a bronze in the downhill in 1956, behind gold medalist Madeleine Berthod of Switzerland. A Swiss pharmacy student, Renée Colliard, won the gold in the slalom and German Ossi Reichert captured top honors in the giant slalom.

Another Canadian, Anne Heggtveit, took the slalom in 1960, while US skier Penny Pitou came away with silvers in the downhill and giant slalom and her teammate Betsy Snite brought the US a third silver in the slalom. Heidi Biebl of Germany took the downhill gold and Yvonne Rüegg of Switzerland triumphed in the giant slalom by 0.1 seconds.

fact: A skier tries to avoid being airborne in the downhill because time spent in the air increases the distance she must travel. To keep from being pitched skyward by bumps, she prejumps them by pulling her skis off the snow just before they hit the bumps.

At the 1964 Games, Austria swept the women's downhill at Innsbruck, pleasing the home crowd. US skier Jean Saubert tied France's Christine Goitschel for the giant slalom silver behind Goitschel's sister Marielle; Saubert also picked up the bronze in the slalom behind the Goitschel sisters, with Christine taking the gold. Marielle Goitschel returned in 1968 to capture the slalom gold in Grenoble. That year Canada's Nancy Greene skied to the gold in giant slalom, by a huge margin of 2.64 seconds, and took a silver in the slalom. The downhill gold went to Olga Pall of Austria.

At Sapporo in 1972 US skier Barbara Cochran was a surprise gold in the slalom by 0.02 seconds, while teammate Susan Corrock snatched a bronze in the downhill. That year Annemarie Moser-Pröll of Austria settled for silvers in the

136

In 1948 US skier Gretchen Fraser won the USA's first medal in alpine skiing, a gold medal in the giant slalom, and took a silver in the slalom/downhill combined as well.

Andrea Mead Lawrence competed with teammate Fraser in 1948, but turned in her best performance at the Oslo Games in 1952, skiing to gold medals in the slalom and giant slalom events.

Skier Hanni Wenzel brought three medals home to Liechtenstein in 1980, taking gold in the slalom and giant slalom events, and silver in the downhill.

downhill and giant slalom, due to upset victories by Swiss newcomer Marie Theres Nadig. Moser-Pröll retired from skiing before the 1976 Olympics, but eventually went back on the circuit to claim the downhill gold in Lake Placid.

At Innsbruck in 1976 West German Rosi Mittermaier took golds in the downhill and the slalom, earning a chance to be the first female skier to achieve an Olympic slam. But Kathy Kriner captured the giant slalom for Canada by a slim margin of 0.12 seconds. The only skiing medal won by the US at Innsbruck was Cindy Nelson's bronze in the downhill. Liechtenstein's Hanni Wenzel came away with a bronze in the slalom. Four years later, in Lake Placid, Wenzel took the gold in slalom and giant slalom, and the silver in the downhill behind Moser-Pröll. Wenzel's haul of two golds and a silver equalled the feat of Rosi Mittermaier in the previous Olympics. Wenzel's brother brought their tiny principality a silver medal in 1980 as well.

fact: When skiers Hanni and Andreas Wenzel between them earned four medals at the 1980 Games, the wins brought the principality of Liechtenstein one medal for every 6000-some people (a comparable ratio for the US would yield 36,000 medals).

Wenzel was ruled out of Olympic competition in 1984 for technicalities relating to her amateur status. At Sarajevo American Debbie Armstrong took a gold in women's giant slalom from the Europeans. 1984 also smiled on some newcomers, Italy's Paoletta Magoni, gold medalist in the women's slalom, and Switzerland's Michela Figini, who won the women's downhill in 0.05 seconds, becoming the youngest skier ever to take a gold.

Four years later Figini earned a silver in the super-G. Also in 1988, Canada's Karen Percy took a bronze in the super-G and another bronze in the downhill, while Swiss skier Brigitte Oertli captured two silvers. Her teammate, Vreni Schneider, won two golds in 1988, the fifth woman alpine skier to have won two golds in the same Games. West German Marina Kiehl won a surprise gold in the downhill that year. Sentimental favorite Christa Kinshofer-Güthlein of West Germany took a silver in giant slalom, to add to the slalom silver she won at Lake Placid in 1980. Also competing in 1988 was Spain's Blanca Fernandez-Ochoa, a member of the family that produced the men's slalom gold medalist in 1972.

Fraser and Mead: The USA's First Alpine Medals

Back in 1948 at St. Moritz, Switzerland, the year alpine skiing was fully introduced to the Winter Olympics, American Gretchen Fraser raced to a gold medal in the slalom, the USA's first medal in alpine skiing. On a gorgeous Swiss afternoon in the Alps, Fraser (who drew the No. 1 starting position) skied to near perfection, leading a pack of European skiers—four of whom were within one-tenth of a second of the American's lead.

"We in the grandstands watched the girl racers slowly climbing up the long, steep slope in the beautiful setting of Survretta for the last ordeal to decide who would win the gold medal," wrote the US women's team manager Alice Kiaer in her 1948 Olympic report. As Fraser stood at the starting gate, communication between the start and finish line failed for 17 minutes—which can seem like hours to a racer concentrating on their run. When finally given the green light, Fraser skied flawlessly, edging Switzerland's Antoinette Meyer and Austria's Erika Mahringer for the gold. Fraser also went on to win a silver medal in the slalom/downhill combined event.

Along with Fraser on that 1948 Olympic team was 15-year-old Andrea Mead.

There are other, more recognizable names in the history of American women's skiing (like Suzy "Chapstick" Chaffee). And other skiers have put forth better numbers on the World Cup circuit. But you'd be hard pressed to find a better performance by any American skier than that of Andrea Mead Lawrence's showing in the 1952 Winter Olympics in Oslo.

On snow hauled in from other areas of Norway (what amounted to about 100 train cars of it) and packed down by hundreds of soldiers and volunteers, the 19-year-old Mead Lawrence skied to a two-gold performance in the slalom and giant slalom events. Said Gretchen Fraser, the team manager that year, "As captain of the team she [Mead Lawrence] was a great help to me and an inspiration to the rest of the team. She is the finest type of sportswoman we could have to represent this country." —P.S.

Hanni Wenzel

When people talk of alpine skiing powerhouses, their attention naturally wanders to places like Austria, Switzerland, Sweden, and Norway. So it was no wonder that in 1980 at the Lake Placid Games people had a hard time pronouncing Liechtenstein (lick-ten-shtine). What they didn't have a hard time pronouncing, though, was the tiny country's most famous athlete—Hanni Wenzel.

Bottom line, at the 1980 Games, Wenzel matched the greatest Olympic skiing performance ever put forth by a woman. Her gold medal sweep in slalom and giant slalom, coupled with her silver in downhill, duplicated West German Rosi Mittermaier's 1976 Innsbruck Games first near-perfect alpine sweep.

The giant slalom, in which the strong German team of Maria Epple (1980 World Cup giant slalom champ) and teammate, 19-year-old Christa Kinshofer (who won five World Cup giant slalom's leading up to the Olympics), were the heavy favorites, was not supposed to be Wenzel's strongest event. Although she had finished in the top 10 in every giant slalom that season, Wenzel did not seem to have what it would take to put together a medal-winning performance. That was, until, she won the last World Cup giant slalom before the Olympics by over five seconds!

The next technical event, slalom, was dominated during the year by the Austrians. They had finished 1–2–3 in the previous World Cup season. In the 1980 season, no fewer than six skiers had won in the eight races. An Austrian 20-year-old was to be on the Olympic victory stand twice, and so was Wenzel. The bronze medalist at Innsbruck in the slalom, Wenzel tore through the tough course at Lake Placid to win by a second-and-a-half.

The big race of the 1980 Games was Wenzel's weakest event, the downhill. None of the pre-Olympic publications counted her even near medal contention. So when the times were put into the books, James Major, former World Cup Editor for *Skiing* magazine put it this way: "Anne-Marie Moser's (Austria) gold was the victory of the favorite, Wenzel's silver the upset, and Marie-Theres Nadig's (Switzerland) bronze a defeat."

That Olympic year was a very special one for Wenzel. Not only did she match the greatest Olympic skiing achievement ever by a woman, she also won the World Cup overall title. And she got to share in the celebration with her brother Andreas, who also medaled at the 1980 Games (silver in giant slalom) and won the men's World Cup overall title. —*P.S.*

Medalists

Skiing, Alpine — Women's Downhill

1988
1. Marina Kiehl, West Germany, 1:25.86
2. Brigitte Oertli, Switzerland, 1:26.61
3. Karen Percy, Canada, 1:26.62

1984
1. Michela Figini, Switzerland, 1:13.36
2. Maria Walliser, Switzerland, 1:13.41
3. Olga Charvatova, Czechoslovakia, 1:13.53

1980
1. Annemarie Moser-Proell, Austria, 1:37.52
2. Hanni Wenzel, Liechtenstein, 1:38.22
3. Marie-Theres Nadig, Switzerland, 1:38.36

1976
1. Rosi Mittermaier, West Germany, 1:46.16
2. Brigitte Totschnig, Austria, 1:46.68
3. Cynthia Nelson, USA, 1:47.50

1972
1. Marie-Theres Nadig, Switzerland, 1:36.68
2. Annemarie Proell, Austria, 1:37.00
3. Susan Corrock, USA, 1:37.68

1968
1. Olga Pall, Austria, 1:40.87
2. Isabelle Mir, France, 1:41.33
3. Christl Haas, Austria, 1:41.41

1964
1. Christl Haas, Austria, 1:55.39
2. Edith Zimmermann, Austria, 1:56.42
3. Traudl Hecher, Austria, 1:56.66

1960
1. Heidi Biebl, West Germany, 1:37.6
2. Penny Pitou, USA, 1:38.6

3. Traudl Hecher, Austria, 1:38.9

1956
1. Madeleine Berthod, Switzerland, 1:40.7
2. Frieda Danzer, Switzerland, 1:45.4
3. Lucile Wheeler, Canada, 1:45.9

1952
1. Trude Jochum-Beiser, Austria, 1:47.1
2. Annemarie Buchner, West Germany, 1:48.0
3. Giuliana Minuzzo, Italy, 1:49.0

1948
1. Hedy Schlunegger, Switzerland, 2:28.3
2. Trude Beiser, Austria, 2:29.1
3. Resi Hammerer, Austria, 2:30.2

1924-1936 Not held

Skiing, Alpine — Women's Slalom

1988
1. Vreni Schneider, Switzerland, 1:36.69
2. Mateja Svet, Yugoslavia, 1:38.37
3. Christa Kinshofer-Guetlein, West Germany, 1:38.40

1984
1. Paoletta Magoni, Italy, 1:36.47
2. Perrine Pelen, France, 1:37.38
3. Ursula Konzett, Liechtenstein, 1:37.50

1980
1. Hanni Wenzel, Liechtenstein, 1:25.09
2. Christa Kinshofer, West Germany, 1:26.50
3. Erika Hess, Switzerland, 1:27.89

1976
1. Rosi Mittermaier, West Germany, 1:30.54

139

2. Claudia Giordani, Italy, 1:30.87
3. Hanni Wenzel, Liechtenstein, 1:32.20

1972
1. Barbara Cochran, USA, 91.24
2. Daniele Debenard, France, 91.26
3. Florence Steurer, France, 92.69

1968
1. Marielle Goitschel, France, 85.86
2. Nancy Greene, Canada, 86.15
3. Annie Famose, France, 87.89

1964
1. Christine Goitschel, France, 89.86
2. Marielle Goitschel, France, 90.77
3. Jean Saubert, USA, 91.36

1960
1. Anne Heggtveit, Canada, 109.6
2. Betsy Snite, USA, 112.9
3. Barbi Henneberger, West Germany, 116.6

1956
1. Renee Colliard, Switzerland, 112.3
2. Regina Schopf, Austria, 115.4
3. Yevgenia Sidorova, Soviet Union, 116.7

1952
1. Andrea Mead Lawrence, USA, 130.6
2. Ossi Reichert, Germany, 131.4
3. Annemarie Buchner, Germany, 133.3

1948
1. Gretchen Fraser, USA, 117.2
2. Antoinette Meyer, Switzerland, 117.7
3. Erika Mahringer, Austria, 118.0

1924-
1936 Not held

Skiing, Alpine — Women's Giant Slalom

1988
1. Vreni Schneider, Switzerland, 2:06.49
2. Christa Kinshofer-Guetlein, West Germany, 2:07.42
3. Maria Walliser, Switzerland, 2:07.72

1984
1. Debbie Armstrong, USA, 2:20.98
2. Christin Cooper, USA, 2:21.38
3. Perrine Pelen, France, 2:21.40

1980
1. Hanni Wenzel, Liechtenstein, 2:41.66
2. Irene Epple, West Germany, 2:42.12
3. Perrine Pelen, France, 2:42.41

1976
1. Kathy Kreiner, Canada, 1:29.13
2. Rosi Mittermaier, West Germany, 1:29.25
3. Daniele Debernard, France, 1:29.95

1972
1. Marie-Theres Nadig, Switzerland, 1:29.90

2. Annemarie Proell, Austria, 1:30.75
3. Wiltrud Drexel, Austria, 1:32.35

1968
1. Nancy Greene, Canada, 1:51.97
2. Annie Famose, France, 1:54.61
3. Fernande Bochatay, Switzerland, 1:54.74

1964
1. Marielle Goitschel, France, 1:52.24
2. Christine Goitschel, France, 1:53.11
2. Jean Saubert, USA, 1:53.11

1960
1. Yvonne Ruegg, Switzerland, 1:39.9
2. Penny Pitou, USA, 1:40.0
3. Giuliana Chenal-Minuzzo, Italy, 1:40.2

1956
1. Ossi Reichert, West Germany, 1:56.5
2. Josefine Frandl, Austria, 1:57.8
3. Dorothea Hochleitner, Austria, 1:58.2

1952
1. Andrea Mead Lawrence, USA, 2:06.8
2. Dagmar Rom, Austria, 2:09.0
3. Annemarie Buchner, Germany, 2:10.0

1924-
1948 Not held

Skiing, Alpine — Women's Super Giant Slalom

1988
1. Sigrid Wolf, Austria, 1:19.03
2. Michela Figini, Switzerland, 1:20.03
3. Karen Percy, Canada, 1:20.29

Skiing, Alpine — Women's Combined (Downhill and Slalom)

1988
1. Anita Wachter, Austria, 29.25
2. Brigitte Oertli, Switzerland, 29.48
3. Maria Walliser, Switzerland, 51.28

1952-
1986 Not held

1948
1. Trude Beiser, Austria, 6.58
2. Gretchen Fraser, USA, 6.95
3. Erika Mahringer, Austria, 7.04

1940-
1944 Not held

1936
1. Christl Cranz, Germany, 97.06
2. Kathe Grasegger, Germany, 95.26
3. Laila Schou Nilsen, Norway, 93.48

---▼---

SKIING—FREESTYLE

WARM-UP

Americans first popularized freestyle skiing back in the late 1960s and early 1970s. Called "hot-dogging," it was a free-form exhibition that threw caution to the wind—and rules out the door. Throughout the 1970s and into the early 1980s, the sport received harsh press due to the danger and injuries involved. Competitions, once prevalent in the early days of the sport, became numbered due to escalating insurance premiums.

fact: Inverted aerials—backflips on skis done off small, steep ramps—were banned from freestyle contests in the late 1970s.

Those closely involved with the sport, understanding its incredibly high excitement level and ability to draw spectators whose numbers are rivaled by only those of the alpine World Cup, sought official recognition for the sport, receiving it in 1979 from the International Ski Federation.

A demonstration sport in Calgary, freestyle skiing—comprising moguls, aerials, and ballet, plus a combined event—is now a full-medal sport in Albertville, even though medals are awarded only for the mogul events.

fact: Freestyle skiers use shorter skis and longer, stronger poles than Alpine skiers.

In recent years, the US has dominated the world, capturing its sixth straight Nations Cup title following the 1991 season and winning seven medals at the 1991 World Freestyle Ski Championships in Lake Placid, New York. International Olympic Committee approval is still pending on awarding medals for the other events at the 1994 Winter Olympics.

141

SPECTATORS' GUIDE

The mogul freestyle event makes its full-medal debut during the 1992 Olympics. The event consists of carefully calculated high-speed turns on a heavily moguled slope (a slope pestered with snow bumps).

In the first round, all skiers will run down the course. Judges rate the competitors on their speed and on the quality and technique of their turns and aerials. Of the seven judges' scores, the high and low are discarded. The top 16 men and the top eight women then move to the finals. The finals will either be a one-run or a dual-format competition. During a dual-mogul event, athletes compete directly against one another. The winner of the run advances to the next round in the competition.

Also on the program at Albertville is speed skiing. The angle to the sport (run straight down a 70-degree slope) allows for speeds in excess of 130 mph . . . the fastest speeds humans can attain on land without the use of mechanical propulsion.

A demonstration event in Albertville, speed skiing actually pre-dates most other forms of competitive skiing, with events held as early as the 1870s. In 1988, speed skiers came under the jurisdiction of the International Ski Federation and now compete on their own World Cup circuit.

HOPEFULS

The mogul event is the sole freestyle full-medal competition. New Jersey's Donna Weinbrecht has won the World Cup title the last two seasons (15 wins in 21 starts), including the World Championships in 1991. She will be the favorite going into Albertville. Once there, she will receive stiff competition from France's Raphaelle Monod, Norway's Stine Lise Hattestad, and Canadian Lee Morrisson.

fact: Some freestyle moves have names like the Rudy, the Post Toastie, the Thumper, and the Bucher spin.

The mogul men are led by 1988 and 1989 World Cup winner Colorado's Nelson Carmichael and Vermont's Chuck Martin. Keep an eye on France's two-time World Cup champion Edgar Grospiron, whose bionic skiing and boastful behavior will make him one of the more interesting personalities at Albertville.

In the ballet competition (non-medal), where skiers gracefully spin down the mountain on skis that barely come up past their knees and use poles that rise up to their ears, American's Ellen Breen (1991 World Cup ballet champion) and Lane Spina, winner of the 1991 World Championships, will be the US and overall favorites.

fact: Freestyle ballet skiing resembles both figure skating and alpine skiing.

Twisting, twirling, flipping, and sometimes flopping will be the Olympic aerialists, led by the Canadian Air Force's defending World Cup champion Phillippe LaRoche, the "Human Corkscrew" Lloyd Langlois, and John Ross. These Canadians should spin the air portion of the team title in Canada's direction.

fact: In the gut flip, the skier plants her pole tips in the snow and the other ends against her abdomen and then launches herself into a forward full flip.

Also flying high above the French countryside will be France's Didier Meda (runner-up to LaRoche last year) and Jean-Marc Bacquin. Kris Feddersen and Trace Worthington will be the American men's best hopes, while Sue Michalski, Stacey Blumer, and Kriste Porter will challenge for yet another nonexistent medal.

France and Finland will field the strongest teams in the speed skiing demonstration event. US men are led by C. J. Mueller, who finished second in the 1990 World Cup standings and eighth last season. The US women's Kristin Culver, fifth overall in the 1991 World Cup standings, also looks good for a strong showing.

Schedule

The tentative freestyle skiing schedule is as follows:

Sunday, February 9
Ballet, heat, men and women

Monday, February 10
Ballet, final, men and women

Wednesday, February 12
Moguls, heat, men and women

Thursday, February 13
Moguls, final, men and women

Saturday, February 15
Aerials, heat, men and women

Sunday, February 16
Aerials, final, men and women

The tentative speed skiing schedule is as follows:

Tuesday, February 18
Group 1

Wednesday, February 19
Group 2

Friday, February 21
Semifinals

Saturday, February 22
Final

Winter

SKIING—NORDIC CROSS-COUNTRY

WARM-UP

S kiing has been practiced in northern Europe for centuries. The oldest known ski, found in a peat bog at Umea, Sweden, goes back nearly 45 centuries to 2500 BC. However, a Stone Age petroglyph in Rodoy, Norway, showing a skier has been dated at 5000 BC, a sure sign that someone, now very old, was on skis more than 7,000 years ago. A sled runner about 10 feet long was pulled out of a Finnish bog and carbon-dated to 7000 BC, or 9,000 years ago. As Ted Bates notes in his book, *Nine Thousand Years of Skis*, "Where there were sled runners, there were probably skis." But thousands of years of relying on skis for transportation did not naturally give way to sport; only in the last century has it become a recreational and competitive sport.

Norwegian soldiers patrolled on skis as early as 960 AD, before the Vikings came to North America. Within two centuries of that time, Sweden maintained its own skiborne troops. In 1767, the Norwegian military began to stage races, while the first civilian race was held in 1843. As Scandinavians immigrated to the United States, they brought their ski heritage with them. The records of the early US ski competitions appear to have been taken from the Oslo or Stockholm telephone book, though, of course, telephones had not yet been invented.

Norwegians introduced skiing to northern New England and the upper Midwest. In southern Wisconsin, Scandinavians are reported to have been skiing before 1840. Scandinavians also played a key role in importing skiing to the West, with competitions being held in California during the 1850s. The Scandinavians also brought their tradition of village sports clubs to the US, which encouraged recreational skiing.

In the US, competitive skiing began in earnest at the turn of the century. The first official national championship was held in 1904 in Ishpeming, Michigan, and the National Ski Association (NSA) was formed a year later. (The NSA evolved into the US Ski Association, which became part of US Skiing in 1990.) In the early days, skiing invariably meant nordic: ski jumping and cross-country.

The Norwegian Ski Federation organized the first international ski congress in 1910, and annual meetings were held until World War I. In 1921, meetings resumed and rules for international events—only cross-country and jumping were recognized—were formulated. The NSA joined the congress in 1922.

145

In 1924, the group reorganized as the International Ski Federation, or Fédération Internationale de Ski (FIS), in time for the first Olympic Winter Games held at Chamonix, France. For the first three Olympics, only nordic events were staged, and those were only for men. Although women were part of the inaugural alpine event (the combined) in 1936, they did not compete in cross-country until 1952. In the US, the females did not participate in a national cross-country championship until 1967, when 13-year-old Alison Owen competed in a junior boys' race.

US skier Bill Koch revolutionized the sport in 1982 when he spread the word about a crisscross technique in which the skier actually skates on the skis, pushing off the inside edge of the weight-bearing ski.

The technique is thought to have first been used in 1971 by East German Gerhard Grimmer, racing in Holmenkollen, Norway. The snow conditions that day were strange, and skiers using the traditional parallel—or classic—technique had to continually rewax or change skis to maintain their kick. Grimmer won the race by a huge margin.

Skiers began experimenting with variations on Grimmer's technique, and Koch perfected and popularized it. Purists tried to ban this swifter style, but it was finally allowed in half the cross-country events held in 1988 at the Calgary Games. The men's 15km and 30km races and the women's 5km and 10km races were skied using the classic technique; the men's 50km and 4 x 10km relay races and the women's 20km and 4 x 5km relay races permitted any style, and the style of choice for both winners and contenders was skating.

Cross-country skiing produces the best-conditioned athletes in terms of overall fitness. Sweden's Sven-Ake Lundbäck, a 1972 gold medalist, was once tested as having an oxygen consumption rate as high as 94.6 milliliters per kilogram of body weight per minute; the best runners are in the low 80s. In 1988, Soviet cross-country skiers won eight of twelve medals, amid charges that they engaged in illegal blood-doping. This practice involves removing and storing a quantity of an athlete's blood prior to competition, then reinjecting it—or just the red blood cells—shortly before the event. The extra red blood cells increase endurance by carrying more oxygen to the muscles. It is an undetectable means of performance enhancement.

▼

SPECTATORS' GUIDE

In **cross-country** skiing, ski technique is combined with strength and endurance required to ski long distances over demanding terrain. Races for men are held over 15, 30, and 50 kilometers (9.3, 18.6, and 31.2 miles), plus a 40-kilometer relay. Women compete in 5, 10, and 20 kilometer (added in 1984) events, as well as a 20-kilometer relay.

The courses are laid out with a challenging mixture of uphill, downhill, and rolling terrain. The machine-prepared trails are 12–18 feet wide; grooves are set into them on most downhill sections. During the individual races, skiers are usually sent off at 30-second intervals in the individual races, although if there is a large field they could be started two at a time on parallel tracks.

fact: Cross-country events require great upper-body strength to double-pole across level terrain.

Cross-country skiers use two techniques: the classical, which requires the conventional form of parallel stride (the basic kick, pole, and glide technique), and skating (pushing off diagonally from the inside edge of the weight-bearing ski). In freestyle races, which place no restrictions on technique, competitors take advantage of skating, the faster technique. For each technique, specialized boots, skis, and poles have been developed.

The skis used for cross-country are very light and about half the width of those used in alpine, making them more flexible and better suited for the narrow nordic track. They are often referred to as "skinny skis."

fact: No one comes close to cross-country skiers in physiological tests of fitness.

The **nordic relay** races feature a uniform start, enabling the viewer to follow the race more easily. Since the races are run on relatively short courses, with each woman racing five kilometers and each man 10, the event is better followed by television than the longer events. The racers employ strategies common to bicycling and track and field, such as drafting off of one another, taking turns leading, and sprinting for the finish.

▼

HOPEFULS

The Olympic nordic events will again be ruled by the Scandinavian and Soviet countries. "Norwegians, Swedes, and Soviets ... men and women," says US cross-country program director Alan Ashley on the favorites at Albertville.

Not before or since Bill Koch's 30km silver medal in the 1976 Innsbruck Games has an American come close to medaling in a World Cup or Olympic nordic event. So a top-15 place finish would be the equivalent to gold for the US men or women.

According to Ashley, fans of the skinny skis should keep their eye on the Soviet Union's Vladimir Smirvon at Albertville. Smirvon, along with Sweden's Torgny Mogren and Gunde Svan, were the long multiple-event medalists at the 1991 World Championships. And as for the most dominant athlete in cross-country skiing in the 1980s—the Wayne Gretzky of nordic skiing—Sweden's Svan is taking the year, and the Albertville Games, off due to what he calls a lack of "motivation and incentive." Svan has won nearly everything there is to win in the sport.

The top women to watch will be Norway's Trude Dybendhal and Soviet Elena Viabe, both of whom won multiple medals in the last World Championships.

US Outlook: California's Nancy Fiddler, who Ashley says "is clearly our best performer over the last two years," has a good shot at a top-15 finish in the 5km and 15km races.

Schedule

The tentative cross-country skiing schedule is as follows:

Sunday, February 9
15km, women

Monday, February 10
30km, men

Thursday, February 13
10km, men
5km, women

Saturday, February 15
15km, men

10km, women

Monday, February 17
4x5km, women

Tuesday, February 18
4x10km, men

Friday, February 21
30km, women

Saturday, February 22
50km, men

MEN'S CROSS-COUNTRY EVENTS

▼

HIGHLIGHTS

Norway's Thorlief Haug garnered three golds in 1924, taking the 15km, the 50km, and the combined. His countryman, Johan Gröttumsbråten, claimed bronze medals in the 50km and the Nordic combined and a silver medal in the 15km. He then captured the gold in the combined and the 15km in 1928, and returned for the combined gold in 1932. Another Norwegian, Hallgeir Brenden, captured the

148

gold in the 15km in 1952 and 1956. Brenden was a lumberjack and farmer who was also Norway's steeplechase champion.

Finland's Veikko Hakulinen won seven Olympic medals beginning in 1952 with the 50km gold; he won silvers in that event during the next two Games, a gold in the 30km in 1956, a bronze in the 15km in 1960, and two relay medals, the silver in 1956 and the gold in 1960. The 1960 relay featured an exciting anchor leg by Hakulinen, in which he overtook the Norwegian skier in the final strides to win by three feet.

Sweden's legendary "king of the skis," Sixten Jernberg, won the 50km gold in 1956 and 1964. He also competed in the 15km for silver medals in 1956 and 1960 and a bronze in 1964. But Jernberg wasn't finished yet. In the 30km event, he skied for silver in 1956 and the gold in 1960, and helped Sweden to a bronze in 1956 and a gold in 1964 in the 4 x 10km relay. Jernberg won his final Olympic gold at Innsbruck on the day before his 35th birthday.

Finn Ero Mäntyranta and Norwegian Harald Grönningen finished 1–2 in both the 15km and the 10km in 1964; they traded places in the 15km in 1968, and Mäntyranta took a bronze in the 30km at the Grenoble Games. In the relay Mäntyranta also won a gold in 1960, a silver in 1964, and a bronze in 1968. Grönningen claimed a relay silver in 1960 and a gold in 1968.

Sven-Ake Lundbäck of Sweden won the 15km gold at Sapporo in 1972, while the first Soviet to take an individual gold, Vyacheslav Vedinine, captured the 30km event. The 50m event was won in a very closely contested race by Pål Tyldum of Norway. In 1976 the Soviet skiers Nikolai Bayukoy and Evgeny Beliaev negotiated a 1–2 sweep of the 15km event, confirming the Soviet threat.

The Swedish team long benefitted from the leadership of Thomas Wassberg; he won a gold medal in 1980 in the 15km event a scant one one-hundredth of a second ahead of Finland's Juha Mieto. Bulgaria received its first Winter Games medal in Lake Placid when Ivan Lebanov won a bronze in the 30km.

Sweden's Gunde Svan medaled in all four cross-country events in 1984 at the age of 22, and the Swedish men's team captured three golds that year. Finland's Harri Kirvesniemi took a bronze in the 15km in 1984, but by the 1980s the Soviet Union and East Germany had stepped in to redirect the medal flow. Soviet cross-country skier Nikolai Zimyatov skied for three gold medals at Lake Placid and added another in 1984. Soviet men captured four gold medals in 1988.

Bill Koch

The United States is not known as a nordic (cross-country) skiing powerhouse. The great majority of Americans do not use cross-country skis during the snowy months for transportation, preferring the freeway instead. The top American nordic skiers are not the athletes of choice for product promotion on TV and other media, as they are in the northern European countries. After all, the US has Michael Jordan and Bo Jackson.

In short, it's hard to be a cross-country star in the USA.

149

Before the 1976 Olympics in Innsbruck, no American cross-country skier had ever been evenly remotely close to capturing an Olympic medal. America's best Olympic finish, a 15th, came in the 1932 Olympics in Lake Placid.

In 1976, with all the Olympic spectator and media attention on either Franz Klammer in the men's downhill or on the men's speedskating events, American Bill Koch, 20 years old at the time, from Guilford, Vermont, pulled off one of the most unexpected performances in Olympic history: a silver medal in the grueling 30km race (about 18 miles).

Koch, who actually led the 30km race at one point, had only competed in a few world-class races leading up to the Olympics and had only skied the 30km race twice.

The pre-race favorite, Thomas Magnusson, had left the Olympics to be with his family, following the death of his father the day before the race. This left two Soviet skiers, Serge Saveliev, a Russian soldier, and countryman Ivan Garanin, the veteran on the Soviet nordic team, as the picks for medals.

After Saveliev caught and passed Koch (he eventually went on to capture the gold and set an Olympic record time in the process), Koch put together a furious finishing kick that enabled him to keep pace ahead of Garanin and to trail the gold medal winner by little more than 28 seconds, which is equivalent to a few ski lengths in nordic racing.

Koch, who believed that he could pull off the best finish ever by an American, was nonetheless pleased with his historic effort. "To finish in the first ten was my goal," he said. "Of course, I'm even happier with the medal."

Headlines read "KOCH'S THE REAL THING," and "A SECOND FOR KOCH, A FIRST FOR THE USA." When asked about the lack of coverage at the finish line for his silver medal performance—none of the American press or ABC television reporters were on hand for the finish—Koch paused for a moment. "They'll be there next time," he said. —P.S.

Medalists

Skiing, Nordic — Men's 15-Kilometer Cross Country

1988
1. Mikhail Deviatyarov, Soviet Union, 41:18.9
2. Pal Mikkelsplass, Norway, 41:33.4
3. Vladimir Smirnov, Soviet Union, 41:48.5

1984
1. Gunde Anders Swan, Sweden, 41:25.6
2. Aki Karvonen, Finland, 41:34.9
3. Harri Kirvesniemi, Finland, 41:45.6

1980
1. Thomas Wassberg, Sweden, 41:57.63
2. Juha Mieto, Finland, 41:57.64
3. Ove Aunli, Norway, 42:28.62

1976
1. Nikolai Bazhukov, Soviet Union, 43:58.47

2. Yevgeny Beliaev, Soviet Union, 44:01.10
3. Arto Koivisto, Finland, 44:19.25

1972
1. Sven-Ake Lundback, Sweden, 45:28.24
2. Fedor Simashov, Soviet Union, 46:00.84
3. Ivar Formo, Norway, 46:02.68

1968
1. Harald Gronningen, Norway, 47:54.2
2. Eero Mantyranta, Finland, 47:56.1
3. Gunnar Larsson, Sweden, 48:33.7

1964
1. Eero Mantyranta, Finland, 50:54.1
2. Harald Gronningen, Norway, 51:34.8
3. Sixten Jernberg, Sweden, 51:42.2

1960
1. Haakon Brusveen, Norway, 51:55.5
2. Sixten Jernberg, Sweden, 51:58.6
3. Veikko Hakulinen, Finland, 52:03.0

1956
1. Hallgeir Brenden, Norway, 49:39.0

150

2. Sixten Jernberg, Sweden, 50:14.0
3. Pavel Kolchin, Soviet Union, 50:17.0
1952 1. Hallgeir Brenden, Norway, 1:01:34.0
2. Tapio Makela, Finland, 1:02:09.0
3. Paavo Lonkila, Finland, 1:02:20.0
1948 1. Martin Lundstrom, Sweden, 1:13:50.0
2. Nils Ostensson, Sweden, 1:14:22.0
3. Gunnar Eriksson, Sweden, 1:16:06.0
1936 1. Erik-August Larsson, Sweden,
1:14:38.0
2. Oddbjorn Hagen, Norway, 1:15:33.0
3. Pekka Niemi, Finland, 1:16:59.0
1932 1. Sven Utterstrom, Sweden, 1:23:07.0
2. Axel T. Wikstrom, Sweden, 1:25:07.0
3. Veli Saarinen, Finland, 1:25:24.0
1928 1. Johan Grottumsbraaten, Norway,
1:37:01.0
2. Ole Hegge, Norway, 1:39:01.0
3. Reidar Odegaard, Norway, 1:40:11.0
1924 1. Thorleif Haug, Norway, 1:14:31.0
2. Johan Grottumsbraaten, Norway,
1:15:51.0
3. Tapani Niku, Finland, 1:26:26.0

Skiing, Nordic — Men's 30-Kilometer Cross Country

1988 1. Alexei Prokurorov, Soviet Union,
1:24:26.3
2. Vladimir Smirnov, Soviet Union,
1:24:35.1
3. Vegard Ulvang, Norway, 1:25:11.6
1984 1. Nikolai Zimiatov, Soviet Union,
1:28:56.3
2. Alexandr Zavyalov, Soviet Union,
1:29:23.3
3. Gunde Anders Swan, Sweden,
1:29:35.7
1980 1. Nikolai Zimiatov, Soviet Union,
1:17:02.80
2. Vassily Rochev, Soviet Union,
1:27:34.22
3. Ivan Levanov, Bulgaria, 1:28:03.87
1976 1. Sergei Saveliev, Soviet Union,
1:30:29.38
2. Bill Koch, USA, 1:30:57.84
3. Ivan Garanin, Soviet Union,
1:31:09.29
1972 1. Vyacheslav Vedenine, Soviet Union,
1:36:31.15
2. Pal Tyldum, Norway, 1:37:25.30
3. Johs Harviken, Norway, 1:37:32.44
1968 1. Franco Nones, Italian, 1:35:39.2
2. Odd Martinsen, Norway, 1:36:28.9
3. Eero Mantyranta, Finland, 1:36:55.3
1964 1. Eero Mantyranta, Finland, 1:30:50.7
2. Harald Gronningen, Norway,
1:32:02.3
3. Igor Voronchikin, Soviet Union,
1:32:15.8
1960 1. Sixten Jernberg, Sweden, 1:51:03.9
2. Rolf Ramgard, Sweden, 1:51:16.9
3. Nikolai Anikin, Soviet Union, 1:52:28.2
1956 1. Veikko Hakulinen, Finland, 1:44:06.0
2. Sixten Jernberg, Sweden, 1:44:30.0
3. Pavel Kolchin, Soviet Union, 1:45:45.0
**1924-
1952** **Not held**

Skiing, Nordic — Men's 50-Kilometer Cross Country

1988 1. Gunde Anders Svan, Sweden,
2:04:30.9
2. Maurilio DeZolt, Italy, 2:05:36.4
3. Andy Gruenenfelder, Switzerland,
2:06:01.9
1984 1. Thomas Wassberg, Sweden, 2:15:55.8
2. Gunde Anders Swan, Sweden,
2:16:00.7
3. Aki Karvonen, Finland, 2:17:04.7
1980 1. Nikolai Zimiatov, Soviet Union,
2:27:24.60
2. Juha Mieto, Finland, 2:30:20.52
3. Alexandr Zavyalov, Soviet Union,
2:30:51.52
1976 1. Ivar Formo, Norway, 2:37:30.05
2. Gert-Dietmar Klause, East Germany,
2:38:13.21
3. Ben Soedergren, Sweden, 2:39:39.21
1972 1. Pal Tyldum, Norway, 2:43:14.75
2. Magne Myrmo, Norway, 2:43:29.45
3. Vyacheslav Vedenine, Soviet Union,
2:44:00.19
1968 1. Ole Ellefsaeter, Norway, 2:28:45.8
2. Vyacheslav Vedenine, Soviet Union,
2:29:02.5
3. Josef Haas, Switzerland, 2:29:14.8
1964 1. Sixten Jernberg, Sweden, 2:43:52.6
2. Assar Ronnlund, Sweden, 2:44:58.2
3. Arto Tiainen, Finland, 2:45:30.4
1960 1. Kalevi Hamalainen, Finland, 2:59:06.3
2. Veikko Hakulinen, Finland, 2:59:26.7
3. Rolf Ramgard, Sweden, 3:02:46.7
1956 1. Sixten Jernberg, Sweden, 2:50:27.0
2. Veikko Hakulinen, Finland, 2:51:45.0
3. Fedor Terentyev, Soviet Union,
2:53:32.0
1952 1. Veikko Hakulinen, Finland, 3:33:33.0
2. Eero Kolehmainen, Finland, 3:38:11.0
3. Magnar Estenstad, Norway, 3:38:28.0
1948 1. Nils Karlsson, Sweden, 3:47:48.0
2. Harald Eriksson, Sweden, 3:52:20.0
3. Benjamin Vanninen, Finland, 3:57:28.0
1936 1. Elis Wiklund, Sweden, 3:30:11.0
2. Axel T. Wikstrom, Sweden, 3:33:20.0
3. Nils-Joel Englund, Sweden, 3:34:10.0
1932 1. Veli Saarinen, Finland, 4:28:00.0
2. Vaino Liikkanen, Finland, 4:28:20.0
3. Arne Rustadstuen, Norway, 4:31:53.0
1928 1. Per-Erik Hedlund, Sweden, 4:52:03.0
2. Gustaf Jonsson, Sweden, 5:05:30.0
3. Volger Andersson, Sweden, 5:05:46.0
1924 1. Thorleif Haug, Norway, 3:44:32.0
2. Thoralf Stromstad, Norway, 3:46:23.0
3. Johan Grottumsbraaten, Norway,
3:47:46.0

Skiing, Nordic — Men's 4x10-Kilometer Relay

1988 1. Sweden, 1:43:58.6, Jan Ottosson,
Thomas Wassberg, Gunde Anders
Svan, Torgny Morgen
2. Soviet Union, 1:44:11.3, Vladimir
Smirnov, Vladimir Sakhnov, Mikhail
Deviatyarov, Alexei Prokurorov

Skiing—Nordic Cross-Country

151

3. Czechoslovakia, 1:45:22.7, Radim Nyc, Vaclav Korunka, Pavel Benc, Ladislav Svanda

1984 1. Sweden, 1:55:06.30, Thomas Wassberg, Benny Tord Kohlberg, Jan Bo Otto Ottosson, Gunde Anders Swan

2. Soviet Union, 1:55:16.50, Alexandre Batuk, Alexandr Zavyalov, Vladimir Nikitin, Nikolai Zimiatov

3. Finland, 1:56:31.40, Kari Ristanen, Juha Mieto, Harri Kirvesniemi, Aki Karvonen

1980 1. Soviet Union, 1:57:08.46, Vassily Rochev, Nikolai Bazhukov, Yevgeny Beliaev, Nikolai Zimiatov

2. Norway, 1:58:45.77 Lars Erik Eriksen, Per Knut Aaland, Ove Aunli, Oddvar Bra

3. Finland, 2:00:00.18 Harri Kirvesniemi, Pertti Teurajarvi, Matti Pitkanen, Juha Mieto

1976 1. Finland, 2:07:59.72, Matti Pitkanen, Juha Mieto, Pertti Teurajarvi, Arto Koivisto

2. Norway, 2:09:58.36 Pal Tyldum, Einar Sagstuen, Ivar Formo, Odd Martinsen

3. Soviet Union, 2:10:51.46 Yevgeny Beliaev, Nikolai Bazhukov, Sergei Saveliev, Ivan Garanin

1972 1. Soviet Union, 2:04:47.94, Vladimir Voronkov, Yuri Skobov, Fedor Simashov, Vyacheslav Vedenine

2. Norway, 2:04:57.06, Oddvar Bra, Pal Tyldum, Ivar Formo, Johs Harviken

3. Switzerland, 2:07:00.6, Alfred Kalin, Albert Giger, Alois Kalin, Eduard Hauser

1968 1. Norway, 2:08:33.5, Odd Martinsen, Pal Tyldum, Harald Gronningen, Ole Ellefsaeter

2. Sweden, 2:10:13.2, Jan Halvarsson, Bjarne Andersson, Gunnar Larsson, Assar Ronnlund

3. Finland, 2:10:56.7, Kalevi Oikarainen, Hannu Taipale, Kalevi Laurila, Eero Mantyranta

1964 1. Sweden, 2:18:34.6, Karl-Ake Asph, Sixten Jernberg, Janne Stefansson, Assar Ronnlund

2. Finland, 2:18:42.4, Vaino Huhtala, Arto Tiainen, Kalevi Laurila, Eero Mantyranta

3. Soviet Union, 2:18:46.9, Ivan Utrobin, Gennady Vaganov, Igor Voronchikin, Pavel Kolchin

1960 1. Finland, 2:18:45.6, Toimi Alatalo, Eero Mantyranta, Vaino Huhtala, Veikko Hakulinen

2. Norway, 2:18:46.4, Harald Gronningen, Hallgeir Brenden, Einar Ostby, Haakon Brusveen

3. Soviet Union, 2:21:21.6, Anatoli Shelyushki, Gennady Vaganov, Aleksei Kuznetsov, Nikolai Anikin

1956 1. Soviet Union, 2:15:30.0, Fedor Terentyev, Pavel Kolchin, Nikolai Anikin, Vladimir Kuzin

2. Finland, 2:16:31.0, August Kiuru, Jorma Kortalainen, Arvo Viitanen, Veikko Hakulinen

3. Sweden, 2:17:42.0, Lennart Larsson, Gunnar Samuelsson, Per-Erik Larsson, Sixten Jernberg

1952 1. Finland, 2:20:16.0, Heikki Hasu, Paavo Lonkila, Urpo Korhonen, Tapio Makela

2. Norway, 2:23:13.0, Magnar Estenstad, Mikal Kirkholt, Martin Stokken, Hallgeir Brenden

3. Sweden, 2:24:13.0, Nils Tapp, Sigurd Andersson, Enar Josefsson, Martin Lundstrom

1948 1. Sweden, 2:32:08.0, Nils Ostensson, Nils Tapp, Gunnar Eriksson, Martin Lundstrom

2. Finland, 2:41:06.0, Lauri Silvennoinen, Teuvo Laukkanen, Sauli Rytky, August Kiuru

3. Norway, 2:44:33.0, Erling Evensen, Olav Okern, Reidar Nyborg, Olav Hagen

1936 1. Finland, 2:41:33.0, Sulo Nurmela, Klaes Karppinen, Matti Lahde, Kalle Jalkanen

2. Norway, 2:41:39.0, Oddbjorn Hagen, Olaf Hoffsbakken, Sverre Brodahl, Bjarne Iversen

3. Sweden, 2:43:03.0, John Berger, Erik A. Larson, Artur Haggblad, Martin Matsbo

1924-1932 Not held

WOMEN'S CROSS-COUNTRY EVENTS

▼

HIGHLIGHTS

Claudia Boyarskikh of the USSR swept all three women's nordic events in 1964. In 1968 Swedish skier Toini Gustafsson took the 5km and 10km gold and earned a silver with the fastest leg in the relay. Skiing for the USSR, Galina Kulakova claimed four gold, two silver, and two bronze medals from 1968 to 1980; she was 37 when she was awarded her last medal. Not to be outdone, her teammate, Raisa Smetanina, totalled up three gold medals (in the 10km in 1976 and the 5km and relay in 1980), five silver medals (in the 5km in 1976, the relay in 1980, the 10km and 20km in 1984, and the 10km in 1988), and one bronze (in the 20km in 1988). She thus tied for the most decorated competitor in the history of the Winter Games.

Finland's Marja-Liisa Hämäläinen competed in the 1976 and 1980 Olympics without medaling, but finally skied for three gold medals in 1984, in the 5km, 10km, and 20km races. That made her the first woman ever to win three individual gold medals in cross-country. She also took a bronze in the relay. In 1988 her 19-year-old countrywoman, Marjo Matikainen, who had also won a relay bronze in 1984, was the only non-Soviet skier to finish in the top five in the 10km race, taking a bronze; her strong third leg in the 4 x 5km relay brought Finland another bronze.

Medalists

Skiing, Nordic — Women's 5-Kilometer Cross Country

1924-1960 Not held

1988
1. Marjo Matikainen, Finland, 15:04.0
2. Tamara Tikhonova, Soviet Union, 15:05.3
3. Vida Ventsene, Soviet Union, 15:11.1

1984
1. Marja-L. Haemaelainen, Finland, 17:04.0
2. Berit Aunli, Norway, 17:14.1
3. Kvetoslava Jeriova, Czechoslovakia, 17:18.3

1980
1. Raisa Smetanina, Soviet Union, 15:06.92
2. Hilkka Riihivuori, Finland, 15:11.96
3. Kvetoslava Jeriova, Czechoslovakia, 15:23.44

1976
1. Helena Takalo, Finland, 15:48.69
2. Raisa Smetanina, Soviet Union, 15:49.73
3. Nina Baldycheva, Soviet Union, 16:12.82

1972
1. Galina Kulakova, Soviet Union, 17:00.50
2. Marjatta Kajosmaa, Finland, 17:05.50
3. Helena Sikolova, Czechoslovakia, 17:07.32

1968
1. Toini Gustafsson, Sweden, 16:45:2
2. Galina Kulakova, Soviet Union, 16:48.4
3. Alevtina Kolchina, Soviet Union, 16:51.6

1964
1. Claudia Boyarskikh, Soviet Union, 17:50.5
2. Mirja Lehtonen, Finland, 17:52.9
3. Alevtina Kolchina, Soviet Union, 18:08.4

Skiing, Nordic — Women's 10-Kilometer Cross Country

1988
1. Vida Ventsene, Soviet Union, 30:08.3
2. Raisa Smetanina, Soviet Union, 30:17.0
3. Marjo Matikainen, Finland, 30:20.5

1984
1. Marja-L. Haemaelainen, Finland, 31:44.2
2. Raisa Smetanina, Soviet Union, 32:02.9
3. Brit Pettersen, Norway, 32:12.7

1980
1. Barbara Petzold, East Germany, 30:31.54
2. Hilkka Riihivuori, Finland, 30:35.05
3. Helena Takalo, Finland, 30:45.25

1976
1. Raisa Smetanina, Soviet Union, 30:13.41
2. Helena Takalo, Finland, 30:14.28
3. Galina Kulakova, Soviet Union, 30:38.61

1972
1. Galina Kulakova, Soviet Union, 34:17.82
2. Alevtina Olunina, Soviet Union, 34:54.11
3. Marjatta Kajosmaa, Finland, 34:56.48

1968
1. Toini Gustafsson, Sweden, 36:46.5
2. Berit Mordre, Norway, 37:54.6
3. Inger Aufles, Norway, 37:59.9

1964
1. Claudia Boyarskikh, Soviet Union, 40:24.3
2. Eudokia Mekshilo, Soviet Union, 40:26.6

153

3. Maria Gusakova, Soviet Union, 40:46.6
1960 1. Maria Gusakova, Soviet Union, 39:46.6
2. Lyubov Baranova-Kosyreva, Soviet Union, 40:04.2
3. Radya Eroshina, Soviet Union, 40:06.0
1956 1. Lyubov Kosyreva, Soviet Union, 38:11.0
2. Radya Eroshina, Soviet Union, 38:16.0
3. Sonja Edstrom, Sweden, 38:23.0
1952 1. Lydia Wideman, Finland, 41:40.0
2. Mirja Hietamies, Finland, 42:39.0
3. Siiri Rantanen, Finland, 42:50.0
1924-
1948 Not held

Skiing, Nordic — Women's 20-Kilometer Cross Country

1988 1. Tamara Tikhonova, Soviet Union, 55:53.6
2. Anfisa Reztsova, Soviet Union, 56:12.8
3. Raisa Smetanina, Soviet Union, 57:22.1
1984 1. Marja-L. Haemaelainen, Finland, 1:01:45.0
2. Raisa Smetanina, Soviet Union, 1:02:26.7
3. Anne Jahren, Norway, 1:03:13.6

Skiing, Nordic — Women's 4x5-Kilometer Relay

1988 1. Soviet Union, 59:51.1, Svetlana Nagueikina, Nina Gavriliuk, Tamara Tikhonova, Anfisa Reztsova
2. Norway, 1:01:22.0, Trude Dybendahl, Marit Wold, Anne Jahren, Marianne Dahlmo
3. Finland, 1:01:53.8, Pirkko Maatta, Marja Liisa Kirvesniemi, Marjo Matikainen, Jaana Savolainen
1984 1. Norway, 1:06:49.70, Inger Helene Nybraaten, Anne Jahren, Brit Pettersen, Berit Aunli
2. Czechoslovakia, 1:07:34.70, Dagmar Schvubova, Blanka Paulu, Gabriela Svobodova, Kvetoslava Jeriova
3. Finland, 1:07:36.70, Pirkko Maatta, Eija Hyytiainen, Marjo Matikainen, Marja-L. Haemaelainen

1980 1. East Germany, 1:02:11.10, Marlies Rostock, Carol Anding, Veronica Hesse-Schmidt, Barbara Petzold
2. Soviet Union, 1:03:18.30, Nina Badlycheva, Nina Rocheva, Galina Kulakova, Raisa Smetanina
3. Norway, 1:04:13.50, Brit Pettersen, Anette Boe, Marit Myrmael, Berit Aunli
1976 1. Soviet Union, 1:07:49.75, Nina Baldycheva, Zinaida Amosova, Raisa Smetanina, Galina Kulacova
2. Finland, 1:08:36.57, Liisa Suihkonen, Marjatta Kajosmaa, Hilkka Kuntola, Helena Takalo
3. East Germany, 1:09:57.95, Monika Debertshauser, Sigrun Krause, Barbara Petzold, Veronika Schmidt
1972 1. Soviet Union, 48:16.15, Lyubov Mukhatcheva, Alevtina Oljunina, Galina Kulakova
2. Finland, 49:19.37, Helena Takalo, Hilkka Kuntola, Marjatta Kajosmaa
3. Norway, 49:51.49, Inger Aufles, Aslaug Dahl, Berit Lammedal-Mordre
1968 1. Norway, 57:30.0, Inger Aufles, Babben Enger-Damon, Berit Mordre
2. Sweden, 57:51.0, Britt Strandberg, Toini Gustafsson, Barbro Martinsson
3. Soviet Union, 58:13.6, Alevtina Kolchina, Rita Aschkina, Galina Kulakova
1964 1. Soviet Union, 59:20.2, Alevtina Kolchina, Eudokia Mekshilo, and Claudia Bojarskikh
2. Sweden, 1:01:27.0, Barbro Martinsson, Britt Strandberg, Toini Gustafsson
3. Finland, 1:02:45.1, Senja Pusula, Toini Poysti, Mirja Lehtonen
1960 1. Sweden, 1:04:21.4, Irma Johansson, Britt Strandberg, Sonja Ruthstrom-Edstrom
2. Soviet Union, 1:05:02.6, Radja Eroshina, Maria Gusakova, and Lyubov Baranova-Kosyreva
3. Finland, 1:06:27.5, Siiri Rantanen, Eeva Ruoppa, Toini Poysti
1956 1. Finland, 1:09:01.0, Sirkka Polkunen, Mirja Hietamies, Siiri Rantanen
2. Soviet Union, 1:09:28.0, Lyubov Kosyreva, Alevtina Kolchina, Radya Eroshina
3. Sweden, 1:09:48.0, Irma Johansson, Anna-Lisa Eriksson, Sonja Edstrom
1924-
1952 Not held

154

Bill Koch pulled off a stunning performance at the Innsbruck Games in 1976, winning a silver medal in the 30km nordic event, the first cross-country skiing medal ever for the US. He competed in 1980 as well, but could not defend his medal.

▼

SKIING—NORDIC SKI JUMPING AND NORDIC COMBINED

WARM-UP

I n 1882, Norwegian immigrants built a ski jump in Berlin, New Hampshire, not far from the Canadian border. When explorer Fridtjof Nansen of Norway visited Berlin in 1890, the club became very excited, and, in his honor, renamed itself. The Nansen Ski Club staged jumping meets into the 1970s and remains the oldest continuously operating club in the nation. In Minnesota, the St. Paul club began in 1885; a year later the Red Wing Ski Club was formed. In 1887, the Ishpeming (Michigan) Ski Club met for the first time.

During this period, skis became more functional. Ranging up to 14 feet in length and made from ash, pine, hickory, and oak, some boards weighed up to 25 pounds. Bindings usually were simply a loop over the front part of the foot. Heel bindings were unheard of until Norwegian jumper Sondre Norheim, a poor sharecropper from the district of Telemark, designed an effective binding made from twisted birch root, officially displaying them at a jumping meet in 1866. The new bindings revolutionized alpine and nordic skiing.

fact: Ski manufacture is so quirky that no ski factory can produce two pairs of skis that are identical.

Norheim's contributions to skiing extended beyond bindings. In 1850, Norheim became the first person to make a parallel turn. In 1860, he made the first officially measured jump. And Norheim is also credited with developing the telemark turn, named for his home county. Used by jumpers as a means of stopping after landing, the telemark is taken in a kneeling position with one ski moving forward until the tip of the other ski is touching the boot.

The first major jumping meet was held at Husebybakken in Oslo in 1879, and produced a winning jump of 66 feet. Within 20 years, that distance had nearly doubled, to 117 feet. In 1917 a Norwegian immigrant, Henry Hall, jumped 203 feet at Steamboat Springs, Colorado. As with the other nordic sports, skiing came to the US via Scandinavian immigrants, and two former students of Norheim were among the early champions. Mikkel Hennm set an American record of 102 feet at Redwing, Minnesota, in 1891, and two years later, his brother Jorjus extended that mark by a foot.

When the Winter Olympics began in 1924, skiing events were classified as "special" (as if a specialist competed) and "combined." Competitions included one "special" jumping event, two "special" cross-country races, and the "combined" event, consisting of a separate 18-kilometer ski race and jumping competition. Six Americans participated, with US jumper Anders Haugen winning the bronze medal in the 70-meter jump. Unfortunately for Haugen, the medal was awarded erroneously to Thorleif Haug of Norway. A scoring miscalculation wasn't discovered until a half-century later when Jakob Vaage, long-time curator of the Norwegian Ski Museum, and Norwegian Toralf Stroemstad, who had been silver medalist in nordic combined in 1924, were computing the various distance and style points. They found Haugen actually had finished third ahead of Haug. In 1974, Haugen accepted the bronze medal from Haug's daughter in a special ceremony held in Oslo, under the heading, "better late than never."

One of the most honored US ski jumpers was Torger Tokle, a Norwegian who adopted the US in 1939. Tokle won 42 of the 48 meets he entered. In 1945, he was killed in action while serving with the 10th Mountain Division in Italy.

During the 1950s, large hill jumping became the hot trend in the sport. At the 1964 Olympics, the large hill (90 meters) was added to the program, joining the small hill (70 meter) leap, which had been part of the Winter Games since their inception.

▼

SPECTATORS' GUIDE

A great crowd pleaser, ski jumping is one of the most spectacular of all Winter Olympic sports, employing speed and power in conjunction with the application of basic flight principles. Aerodynamics has become such a factor in ski jumping that, on the larger hills, jumpers actually speak of floating or gliding. Longer and heavier than alpine skis, jumping skis are made of wood, fiberglass, and epoxy. The skis are one-and-a-half times as wide and weigh up to 16 pounds each.

Ski jumps consist of an inrun (the approach), where virtually everyone has their own style and points are not deducted for form; the critical takeoff, occurring at the end of the inrun, the jumper timing his flight precisely, ski tips rising; the flight, with the jumper extending himself almost parallel to his skis, riding the air; the landing, when the jumper assumes the telemark position to allow the knees and hips to absorb the shock; and the outrun, the flat area where the skier decelerates and stops.

fact: In ski jumping, the competitor lands with one ski in front of the other, knees flexed, hips bent and arms straight out at the sides; this is the telemark position, named after a region in Norway where the sport originated.

Wind and velocity must be watched carefully to ensure that competitors are not blown off the landing or turned over in the air. When conditions are right, ski jumping is a very safe sport with a low incidence of injury. Contrary to how it appears on television, jumpers are usually not more than 10 feet in the air at any one time as their flight curve follows that of the hill. In the event of a fall, the athlete normally slides along the landing hills and harmlessly onto the flat.

Aside from the nordic combined, two individual jumping events are on the Olympic program, the 70-meter ("normal hills") and 90-meter ("large hills"). In 1988 a men's 90-meter team ski jumping competition was added. No jumping events for women are held. In the team jumping competition, each team is composed of four jumpers; the top three scores in each of two rounds are combined to give the total team score.

In the individual competitions, each competitor makes two jumps, earning points based on distance and form. These two elements are roughly equal in value in the scoring of the jump. While it is conceivable that the longest jump will not win, great distances are unusual without great form. But long jumps with bumpy landings can bring a score down.

fact: The length of a ski jumper's leap is still measured by the naked eye. Officials stand on either side of the hill, at one-meter intervals, watching the skiers feet as he lands; the official closest to the touchdown point raises his hand to indicate the distance of the jump.

The size of any jump is determined by the distance along the ground from the point of takeoff to a spot on the landing known as the norm point, which lies approximately two-thirds of the way to the point where the landing begins to pull out. Each of the five judges can award up to 20 points for a jump. High and low marks are thrown out, and the remaining scores added together to determine each jumper's final score. A perfect jump would be awarded a score of 60.

The jumpers are judged on the quality of their takeoffs, the smoothness of their air flights, and whether their landings are clean and safe. When a jump is executed correctly, the skier is in a complete forward lean position with a slight bend at the hips and with arms feathered at his side to minimize drag. Skis should be parallel, with no extraneous movement, and this position is held until the point of landing. Points are deducted during the flight for such items as bent knees, hips, or back, poor body position, and improper positioning of skis.

fact: To capitalize on aerodynamics, ski jumpers hold their arms at their sides to form an airfoil, getting as much updraft as possible after takeoff from the slope.

An unsteady landing, or premature preparation to land, will also result in point deductions. Once the skier has landed, the judges watch for such infractions as touching the snow or skis or any other sign of an rocky landing.

The nordic combined is an exceedingly demanding test, requiring endurance for the cross-country and speed and power for the jumping. The nordic combined events include an individual 70-meter jump and 15-kilometer cross-country race as well as a team combined (three men to a team) featuring a 70-meter jump with a 30-kilometer relay race. Unlike the regular jumping competition, nordic combined permits each competitor to jump three times, with only the two best jumps counting toward the score. In the cross-country part of the race, times are converted to points based on a set of tables, and these points are added to the jumping points to determine the combined score.

▼

HOPEFULS

Europeans will again sweep the medals in the ski jumping events. The only difference between this year and any other Olympic year in ski jumping will be the writing on the back of the medals. The Austrians, led by World Cup champion Andi Felder and teammate Stefan Horngacher, will be the favorites to capture the team title on the large (90m) hill.

Switzerland's Stefan Zuend, Finland's Ari-Pekka Nikkola (1990 World Cup champion), and Germany's Gens Weissflog (1984 Sarajevo Games gold medal winner) and Dieter Thoma will press Felder for the Albertville jumping golds.

The nordic combined event will again be dominated by the Europeans. The young US team, featuring a 17-year-old from Colorado named Ryan Heckman, also received a boost when two-time defending national champion Joe Holland rejoined the team after taking two years off to complete his schooling at the University of Vermont. At the end of last season, Holland scored the first World Cup combined points in six seasons for the US.

US Outlook: In the not-too-distant future Heckman may surprise some people in the World Cup, as well as being a legitimate chance for a top-ten jumping finish in the 1996 Games.

Schedule

The tentative ski jumping schedule is as follows:

Sunday, February 9
70m

Friday, February 14
90m, team

Sunday, February 16
90m

The tentative nordic combined schedule is as follows:

Tuesday, February 11
90m ski jumping

Wednesday, February 12
15km cross country

Monday, February 17
90m ski jumping, team

Tuesday, February 18
3x10km cross country, team

HIGHLIGHTS

From 1924 to 1952 Norwegians won all six gold medals awarded in jumping. Norwegian Birger Ruud won two golds and a silver medal from 1932 to 1948; he was 36 when he won his last medal. He also won the downhill segment of the Alpine combined event in 1936. His brother Sigmund won a silver in 1928, and a third brother, Asbjorn, competed in 1948.

Finns, Germans, and Austrians began to practice on larger hills and rose to dominance after 1952. After trying to discourage jumping on large hills, the Norwegians finally joined the sport's trend and recaptured their medal prowess in 1964, when Toralf Engan won a gold and a silver in jumping and Torgeir Brandtzäg took two bronzes. 1972 produced the oldest and youngest gold medalists: 28-year-old Yukio Kasaya of Japan in the 70m and 19-year-old Wojciech Fortuna of Poland in the 90m, which he won on the strength of his spectacular first jump.

fact: Ski jumpers attain speeds of about 60 mph; as much as 10% of drag while the jumper is airborne is caused by air molecules coming into contact with the surface of the body.

A pair of Austrian jumpers, Karl Schnabl and Toni Innauer, won the gold and silver medals, respectively, in the 90m event at Innsbruck in 1976; Toni was only 17 at the time. In 1980 it was Austrian Innauer for the gold in the 70m event while Jouko Törmänen of Finland captured the 90m gold. Finland's Matti Nykänen was already a legendary ski jumper when he competed in the 1984 Games—legendary for his temper tantrums and off-skis antics. But in 1984 he jumped for the gold at 90m and the silver at 70m, the first in Olympic history to do so. East German Jens Weissflog earned the 70m gold and the 90m silver. Back for more in 1988, Nykänen won another gold in the 70m, making him the first jumper in some 50 years to finish first in more than one Olympics, then captured the 90m gold to further his triumphant making of Olympic history.

Matti Nykänen

Big air. Real big air.

Finland's Matti Nykänen, ski jumping's phenom of the last two Olympics, still stands out as one of the greatest to ever ride the sheet of air. His dual gold performance in the 70- and 90-meter events at the 1988 Calgary Olympics was the first ever Olympic jumping sweep. In the 70-meter jump, "Nukes" distanced himself from the silver medal by 17 points—which was a greater margin than between second and 10th place.

In a sport where all of the athletes are very close in size (Nykänen is actually on the larger end of the height curve at 5' 10", but stretches that out at only 132 pounds), the domination by Nykänen leaves even the experts wondering. His inrun speed is well below average (54 mph for Nukes vs. the 58 mph average at Calgary), leading experts to believe he has the quickest takeoff reaction time, clocked at 0.12, in the sport. Nykänen also developed a style in which he throws himself slightly sideways in the air, grasping for more wind resistance, which allows him to get more "float" out of his jumps. Some folks even joke that the secret of his success is that he has bird bones, i.e., they're hollow.

Nykänen, on the other hand, sees his success in his attitude. "The secret is that I can trust myself so much on every jump," he said. "I think I can judge better than the others."

As attitude helped him rise to the pinnacle of his sport, attitude also forced him to crash—off the hill. Despite his four Olympic medals (he also took the 90m gold and 70m silver in Sarajevo) and numerous World Cup victories, Nykänen displayed a brash attitude that got him kicked off the Finland's national team on more than one occasion.

As Mike Tyson is to American papers today, Nykänen was the topic of many Finnish tabloid headlines. "We sell a lot of magazines when we feature Matti," said gossip magazine *Seura* editor Isto Lysma.

Out of the World Cup scene in 1990–91, it will be interesting to see if Nykänen will appear at the Albertville Games. At 28, does the sometimes tarnished Finnish golden boy have any golden jumps left in him? Stay tuned. —*P.S.*

Medalists

Skiing, Nordic — Men's 70-Meter Ski Jumping

1988
1. Matti Nykanen, Finland, 229.1
2. Pavel Ploc, Czechoslovakia, 212.1
3. Jiri Malec, Czechoslovakia, 211.8

1984
1. Jens Weissflog, East Germany, 90.0-87.0, 215.2
2. Matti Nykanen, Finland, 91.0-84.0, 214.0
3. Jari Puikkonen, Finland, 81.5-91.5, 212.8

1980
1. Anton Innauer, Austria, 87.2-87.7, 266.30
2. Manfred Deckert, East Germany, 88.2-88.2, 249.20
2. Hirokazu Yagi, Japan, 87.2-87.1, 249.20

1976
1. Hans-Georg Aschenbach, East Germany , 84.5-82.0, 252.0
2. Jochen Dannenberg, East Germany, 83.5-82.5, 246.2
3. Karl Schnabl, Austria, 82.5-81.5, 242.0

1972
1. Yukio Kasaya, Japan, 84.0-79.0, 244.2
2. Akitsugu Konno, Japan, 82.5-79.0, 234.8
3. Seiji Aochi, Japan, 83.5-77.5, 229.5

1968
1. Jiri Raska, Czechoslovakia, 79.0-72.5, 216.5
2. Reinhold Bachler, Austria, 77.5-76.0, 214.2
3. Baldur Preiml, Austria, 80.0-72.5, 212.6

1964
1. Veikko Kankkonen, Finland, 80.0-79.0, 229.9
2. Toralf Engan, Norway, 78.5-79.0, 226.3
3. Torgeir Brandtzaeg, Norway, 79.0-78.0, 222.9

1960
1. Helmut Recknagel, East Germany, 93.5-84.5, 227.2
2. Niilo Halonen, Finland, 92.5-83.5, 222.6
3. Otto Leodolter, Austria, 88.5-83.5, 219.4

1956
1. Antti Hyvarinen, Finland, 81.0-84.0, 227.0
2. Aulis Kallakorpi, Finland, 83.5-80.5, 225.0
3. Harry Glass, East Germany, 83.5-80.5, 224.5

1952
1. Arnfinn Bergmann, Norway, 67.5-68.0, 226.0
2. Torbjorn Falkanger, Norway, 68.0-64.0, 221.5
3. Karl Holmstrom, Sweden, 67.0-65.5, 219.5

1948
1. Petter Hugsted, Norway, 65.0-70.0, 228.1
2. Birger Ruud, Norway, 64.0-67.0, 226.6
3. Thorleif Schjelderup, Norway, 64.0-67.0, 225.1

1936
1. Birger Ruud, Norway, 75.0-74.5, 232.0
2. Sven Eriksson, Sweden, 76.0-76.0, 230.5
3. Reidar Andersen, Norway, 74.0-75.0, 228.9

1932
1. Birger Ruud, Norway, 66.5-69.0, 228.1
2. Hans Beck, Norway, 71.5-63.5, 227.0
3. Kaare Wahlberg, Norway, 62.5-64.0, 219.5

1928
1. Alf Andersen, Norway, 60.0-64.0, 19,208
2. Sigmund Ruud, Norway, 57.5-62.5, 18,542
3. Rudolf Burkert, Czechoslovakia, 57.0-59.5, 17,937

1924
1. Jacob Tullin Thams, Norway, 49.0-49.0, 18,960
2. Narve Bonna, Norway, 47.5-49.0, 18,689
3. Anders Haugen, Norway, 44.0-44.5, 18,000 (Thorlief Haug was awarded the medal. However, 50 years later, a mathematical error was discovered and Anders Haugen was declared the winner.)

161

Skiing, Nordic — Men's 90-Meter Ski Jumping

1988 1. Matti Nykanen, Finland, 118.5-107.0, 224.0
2. Erik Johnsen, Norway, 114.5-102.0, 207.9
3. Matjaz Debelak, Yugoslavia, 113.08-108.00, 207.7
1984 1. Matti Nykanen, Finland, 116.0-111.0, 231.2
2. Jens Weissflog, East Germany, 107.0-107.5, 213.7
3. Pavel Ploc, Czechoslovakia, 103.5-109.0, 202.9
1980 1. Jouko Tormanen, Finland, 96.7-96.4, 271
2. Hubert Neuper, Austria, 97.1-97, 262.40
3. Jari Puikkonen, Finland, 96.5-96.5, 248.50
1976 1. Karl Schnabl, Austria, 97.5-97.0, 234.8
2. Anton Innauer, Austria, 102.5-91.0, 232.9
3. Henry Glass, East Germany, 91.0-97.0, 221.7
1972 1. Wojciech Fortuna, Poland, 111.0-87.5, 219.9
2. Walter Steiner, Switzerland, 94.0-103.0, 219.8
3. Rainer Schmidt, East Germany, 98.5-101.5, 219.3
1968 1. Vladimir Beloussov, Soviet Union, 101.5-98.5, 231.3
2. Jiri Raska, Czechoslovakia, 101.0-98.0, 229.4
3. Lars Grini, Norway, 99.0-93.5, 214.3
1964 1. Toralf Engan, Norway, 93.5-90.5, 230.7
2. Veikko Kankkonen, Finland, 95.5-90.5, 228.9
3. Torgeir Brandtzaeg, Norway, 90.0-87.0, 227.2
1924-1960 Not held

Skiing, Nordic — Men's 90-Meter Team Ski Jumping

1988 1. Finland, 634.4, Ari Pekka Nikkola, Matti Nykanen, Tuomo Ylipulli, and Jari Puikkonen
2. Yugoslavia, 625.5, Primoz Ulaga, Matjaz Zupan, Matjaz Debelak, and Miran Tepes
3. Norway, 596.1, Ole Eidhammer, Jon Kjorum, Ole Fidjestol, and Erik Johnsen

Skiing, Nordic — Men's Combined (70-Meter Jump, 15 Kilometers)

1988 1. Hippolyt Kempf, Switzerland, 217.9; 38:16.8
2. Klaus Sulzenbacher, Austria, 228.5; 39:46.5

3. Allar Levandi, Soviet Union, 216.6; 39:12.4
1984 1. Tom Sandberg, Norway, 422.595
2. Jouko Karjalainen, Finland, 416.900
3. Jukka Ylipulli, Finland, 410.825
1980 1. Ulrich Wehling, East Germany, 432.200
2. Jouko Karjalainen, Finland, 429.500
3. Konrad Winkler, East Germany, 425.320
1976 1. Ulrich Wehling, East Germany, 423.390
2. Urban Hettich, West Germany, 418.900
3. Konrad Winkler, East Germany, 417.470
1972 1. Ulrich Wehling, East Germany, 413.340
2. Rauno Miettinen, Finland, 405.505
3. Karl-Heinz Luck, East Germany, 398.800
1968 1. Franz Keller, West Germany, 449.040
2. Alois Kalin, Switzerland, 447.990
3. Andreas Kunz, East Germany, 444.100
1964 1. Tormod Knutsen, Norway, 469.280
2. Nikolai Kiselev, Soviet Union, 453.040
3. Georg Thoma, West Germany, 452.880
1960 1. Georg Thoma, West Germany, 457.952
2. Tormod Knutsen, Norway, 453.000
3. Nikolai Gusakov, Soviet Union, 452.000
1956 1. Sverre Stenersen, Norway, 455.00
2. Bengt Eriksson, Sweden, 437.400
3. Franciszek Gron-Gasienica, Poland, 436.800
1952 1. Simon Slattvik, Norway, 451.621
2. Heikki Hasu, Finland, 447.500
3. Sverre Stenersen, Norway, 436.335
1948 1. Heikki Hasu, Finland, 448.800
2. Martti Huhtala, Finland, 433.650
3. Sven Israelsson, Sweden, 433.400
1936 1. Oddbjorn Hagen, Norway, 430.300
2. Olaf Hoffsbakken, Norway, 419.800
3. Sverre Brodahl, Norway, 408.100
1932 1. Johan Grottumsbraaten, Norway, 446.00
2. Ole Stenen, Norway, 436.050
3. Hans Vinjarengen, Norway, 434.600
1928 1. Johan Grottumsbraaten, Norway, 17.833
2. Hans Vinjarengen, Norway, 15.303
3. John Snersrud, Norway, 15.021
1924 1. Thorleif Haug, Norway, 18.906
2. Thoralf Stromstad, Norway, 18.219
3. Johan Grottumsbraaten, Norway, 17.854

Skiing, Nordic — Men's Team Combined (70-Meter Jump, 3x10-Kilometer Relay)

1988 1. West Germany, Thomas Mueller, Hans Pohl, and Hubert Schwarz, 629.8; 1:20:46.0
2. Switzerland, Fredy Glanzmann, Hippolyt Kempf, and Andreas Schaad, 571.4; 1:15:57.4

162

3. Austria, Hansjoerg Aschenwald,
Guenther Csar, and Klaus
Sulzenbacher, 626.6; 1:21:00.9

Skiing—Nordic Ski Jumping and Nordic Combined

SPEEDSKATING

WARM-UP

Skating is one of many sports (including running, horse racing, conoeing, swimming, and cycling) inspired by basic means of transportation. Of the three forms of skating—speedskating, ice hockey, and figure skating—speedskating was the first to develop as a sport.

The Vikings, Norsemen with a penchant for wandering and pirating, had much to do with the development of both skiing and its predecessor, skating. In England, Germany, Switzerland, and other countries with Viking settlements, archaeologists have found numerous ice skates of Viking manufacture. Early Scandinavian literature is full of allusions to skating on iron skates as early as 200 AD.

For centuries before this, the people of northern countries—Such as Sweden, Finland, Norway, Russia, Holland, and Scotland—used skates made of polished animal bones for transportation over frozen lakes, rivers, canals, and icy fields. During the 14th century, people began to make skates with runners of highly waxed wood instead of bones. As there was no sharp edge on bone or wood runners, a long pole was pushed against the ice to propel the skater across the surface.

fact: Speedskating is a national passion in the Netherlands.

More than 500 years ago, a form of speedskating gained popularity in the Netherlands, as racing down the frozen canals of Holland à la Hans Brinker became a public passion. But racing on ice wasn't a practical affair until all-iron skates were invented in Scotland in the 16th century, lending growing popularity to the sport and leading to the eventual formation of the Skating Club of Edinburgh in 1742, the world's first such club. In 1850, the skates dramatically improved when all-steel blades were introduced. Unlike the iron blades, they were light and strong, maintaining their sharp edge for months.

During the 18th century, speedskating developed into a national sport in Britain and the Netherlands. The first recorded speedskating competition took place on the Fens in England over a distance of 15 miles on February 4, 1763. Soon, skating clubs and tournaments spread throughout northern Europe.

(Skating was exclusively an outdoor, winter sport until the invention of an artificial ice surface in 1876 by an Englishman, W. A. Parker.) Participants in the tournaments were usually laborers, while the aristocrats tended to favor figure skating and placing bets on the speed racers. In 1879, the National Skating Association of Great Britain was founded, with the objective of protecting speedskating from the more unscrupulous promoters.

In 1879, the first American competitors raced over courses of 10 and 20 miles. Canada held its first national championship in 1887, and the US staged a championship four years later.

In 1885, rules were adopted to stage all international races on a double track, with pairs racing over short, medium, and long distances. Seven years later, the International Skating Union was formed in the Netherlands and the following year the first world championship was held in Amsterdam. At that time a skater had to win at least three of the four races (500, 1500, 5000, and 10,000 meters) to win the world championship. Jaap Eden of Holland was the first "Champion of the World," a title that was known to win him a pint or two at the local pub. A point system was adopted in 1908, changing to its current format in 1928.

fact: Speedskate blades are half as long again as a hockey or figure skate; the shoe is less stiff, to increase balance as the racer stays weighted over one foot much longer than a hockey skater.

Men's speedskating began as a Winter Olympic sport in 1924. Long track speedskating now features five events: 500, 1000, 1500, 5000, and 10,000 meters. The 1000m race is the newest addition for men, having been added in 1976. In 1960, women's speedskating was added as a full medal sport, with 500, 1000, 1500, and 3000 meter races. The 5000m race for women was added in 1988 to the Olympic schedule.

Short track speedskating, which was in exhibition event at the 1988 Calgary Games, is a full medal sport at Albertville.

▼

SPECTATORS' GUIDE

With racers in their aerodynamic finery flying around the track at nearly 40 miles per hour, speedskating is the fastest an individual can move under his or her own power. Two distinct competitions are held in the Olympics, the long track and short track events.

Held on an outdoor 400m track, **long track competition** is conducted in pairs, rather than the "pack style" or "track style" racing common to short track racing. Two skaters at a time go head-to-head against the clock, and the ultimate winner is the fastest competitor at the end of the day. Speedskaters usually prefer to skate with the fastest skating partner possible. The faster the other person in the pair, the faster both times are likely to be.

The track features two separate lanes, with the inside lane being shorter than the outside lane. So that the competitors in each race skate the same distance, they must change lanes once each lap. A flagman stands at the crossover point with a red and green flag and directs the leading skater to cross over first.

Short track speedskating (call by some the "roller derby on ice") is held on a 111-meter indoor track and features pack races, with four to six skaters competing at the same time. When the finalists line up, the spectators know that the first person to reach the finish line will be the winner. The skaters compete in elimination heats, quarterfinals, semifinals, and a final. Skaters use strategies from track and cycling, including breakaways, drafting, and sprinting. You will undoubtedly see a competitor go quickly into a lead in an attempt to "burn out" the other skaters. You may also see races in which a slow pace is set, with the skaters jockeying for position in anticipation of a sprint for the finish line during the last three or four laps.

Passing on a short track must be done cleanly and without body contact, calling for split-second timing and excellent judgment. If the pass is executed poorly, it can cause disqualification as well as costly falls. If the lead skater strays too far from the track markers, he or she can be passed on the inside by an alert skater. If the track is skated tightly, passing must be done on the outside.

The men's competitions are a 1000m individual race and a 5000m relay (the US did not qualify for the men's relay), while the women race in a 500m individual and a 3000m relay (the US women will be in the relay). In the relay, the four-person teams can alternate skaters any time they want, except that one person must skate the final two laps. The figurative relay baton is passed when one skater pushes—or shoves—a teammate into action.

Equipment is important to the sport. Racing skates have extra-long blades to allow for a longer glide without loss of speed. The skintight and highly stretchable speedskating uniforms, covering the skater from head to toe in one piece, are designed to avoid air resistance, saving precious tenths of a second for a racer.

HOPEFULS

Men's Long Track: The men's long track events will showcase the persistence of US skater Dan Jansen, who, for the third time, will sprint for an Olympic medal. After finishing fourth in the 1984 500m race and becoming the 1988 World Sprint Champion, Jansen was expected to secure gold medals in the 1988 Calgary Olympics. The death of his sister from leukemia hours before his first race, however, shattered Jansen's concentration, and he fell in both the 500m and 1000m races. The United States has watched its favorite skater regain his momentum recently, though, as he placed fourth for three years at the World Sprint Championships, won two gold medals and a silver at the 1990–91 World Cup final, and placed first in the 1990 and 1991 US International Speedskating Association competitions.

Also skating for the United States will be Eric Flaim, whose silver medal in 1988 made him the first man to win a speedskating medal for the US since another Eric, gold medalist Eric Heiden, swept all five events in 1980. In addition to his silver in the 1500m race, Flaim reached three fourth-place finishes and, despite recent knee surgery, hopes to place well again in 1992. Nick Thometz—unofficially the fastest 500m and 1000m skater in the world—Dave Besteman, and Nathaniel Mills also promise fine performances for the United States. Like Jansen, Thometz is on the comeback trail for this Olympics, having suffered from a blood disorder that made him susceptible to illness during the 1988 Games, where he finished only eighth and 18th.

Germany boasts an especially strong contender in the sprint events, four-time World Cup 500 Champion Jens-Uwe Mey, who skated for a gold and a silver medal at Calgary. The Soviet Union's Igor Schelesovski (whom you may have to identify under various other spellings, such as Zhelezovski or Gelezovsky), a four-time World Sprint Champion and 1988 Olympic bronze medalist, also looks promising in the shorter distances. Norway's Johann Olav Koss, the current World All-Around Champion, tends to perform especially well in the longer-distance events.

Women's Long Track: The German team may be formidable (although its performance of late has been subpar): sprinter Christa Ludig (formerly Rothenburger) won the 1000m gold medal and 500m silver at Calgary, and the 500m gold in 1984; current World Sprint Champion Monique Garbrecht; current World All-Around Champion Gunda Kleeman; and World All-Around runner-up Heike Warnicke. The United States' Bonnie Blair, though—a former World Sprint Champion—managed to out-skate Ludwig by two-hundredths of a second for the gold medal at Calgary, where she also won the 1000m bronze and a fourth place finish in the 1500m race. Another speedy contender is triple gold medal winner Yvonne van Gennip of the Netherlands, who dominated the longer-distance events in 1988 and holds the world record for the 5000m race.

Men's and Women's Short Track: Results for the short track competitions, which had previously been only demonstration events, are wide-open to speculation. Current World Champion Wilfred O'Reilly of Great Britain looks promising for the men's events, and five-time World Champion Sylvia Daigle should place highly for Canada in the women's events.

The Heartbreak Kid

Dan Jansen became an Olympic star and media *cause célèbre* by not winning at the 1988 Winter Games in Calgary. Jansen went into the Games as a gold medal contender in the two shortest speed skating events, the 500 and 1000 meter races. He had placed fourth in the 500 meter race four years earlier in Sarajevo, just 0.16 seconds out of the medals. But three hours before his first race in Calgary, his sister, Jane Beres, died of leukemia. Jansen fell in both his races—an insurmountable obstacle at those distances.

One of the indelible images from 1988: Jansen skating aimlessly, head down, around and around the rink after his fall in the 500; his coach finally coming on the ice to put an arm on Jansen's shoulders and skate with him. Jansen was later given the Olympic Spirit Award.

Born June 17, 1965, in Milwaukee, Jansen was the youngest child in a family of nine. His brother, Mike, is a former world-class speed skater. In 1987, Jansen suffered from mononucleosis, but still finished third in the World Cup 500 and 1000 meter races. Because of that illness, too, it was decided that Jansen could not be a bone marrow donor for his sister, something Jansen had been willing to sacrifice his career for.

In 1988, though, separate from his Olympic spills, Jansen had already become World Sprint Champion, which he won in Milwaukee. But the next three years brought a string of fourth-place finishes at the World Sprint Championships. He won the overall men's title at the 1990 US International Speedskating Association, even though he skated with frostbitten toes.

Now gearing up for Albertville, Jansen seems to be on steadier ground then he's been in some time. Always a contender, he is expected to lead, with Bonnie Blair, the USA team's effort to assert its speedskating superiority once again.
—*H.D.*

Bonnie Blair

Sprint champion Bonnie Blair sustains high hopes for the 1992 Olympic Games. In addition to defending the gold medal she earned in the 500m women's speedskating event at Calgary, she intends to reach one of the top two places in the 1000m event (for which she'd won a bronze in 1988) and medal in the 1500m, in which she'd previously placed fourth.

A bout with bronchitis early in 1991 did slow her performance at the 1990–91 World Sprint Championships, where she placed fifth, and that season's World Cup, where she placed third in the 500m and 1000m after falling in the

500m finale. Still, Blair's training and experience will carry her well at Albertville.

Since placing 8th in the 500m event in the 1984 Olympics, Blair has maintained two American speed records and one world record (39.10 seconds in the 500m race), which she set during her gold medal performance at Calgary. In 1989 she won the World Sprint Championships, and at the following year's World Cup tournaments she tied for first in the 500m event, won a silver in the 1000m, and placed fourth in the 1500m. For seven straight years Blair has led the US Sprint Championships, and she's won a medal in nearly every international race she entered in 1991, including golds in about half her 500m races.

Blair, who began skating at age two, says she'd also like to break the 39-second barrier—and thus her own world record—in the 500m, her top event.

Schedule

The tentative speed skating schedule is as follows:

Sunday, February 9
3000m, women

Monday, February 10
500m, women

Wednesday, February 12
1500m, women

Thursday, February 13
5000m, men

Friday, February 14
1000m, women

Saturday, February 15
500m, men

Sunday, February 16
1500m, men

Monday, February 17
5000m, women

Tuesday, February 18
1000, men

Thursday, February 20
. 10,000m, men

The tentative short track schedule is as follows:

Tuesday, February 18
Heats, women and men

Thursday, February 20
1000m, men

3000m relay, women

Saturday, February 22
500m, women
5000m relay, men

170

MEN'S SPEEDSKATING EVENTS

▼

HIGHLIGHTS

Speedskating was one of the original sports at the first Winter Games in 1924. The first gold medal in speedskating was won by American Charles Jewtraw in the 500m race. Finland collected the other three speedskating gold medals in 1924 as Clas Thunberg won both the 1500m and the 5000m and earned a silver behind compatriot Julien Skutnabb in the 10,000m; Skutnabb took a silver in the 5000m in 1924 and 1928. A 35-year-old Thunberg came back in 1928 to capture two more golds, tying with Norwegian Bernt Evensen in the 500m and successfully defending his title in the 1500m. Another Norwegian, Ivar Ballangrud, won the 5000m gold and the 1500m silver.

The 1932 Lake Placid Games was the only Olympics in which the American system of pack racing was allowed, and this factor obviously played a major role, disorienting the Europeans. The US squad made a clean sweep on the home ice; Irving Jaffee won the 5000m and the 10,000m, John Shea took the 500m and the 1500m, and Edward Murphy earned a silver in the 5000m. Frank Stack of Canada experienced his personal Olympic highlight in 1932, winning the bronze in the 10,000m; he continued to compete in Olympic speedskating for the next 20 years, finishing 12th in the 500m in 1952 at age 46.

Norwegian Ivar Ballangrud, one of the great skaters of all time, had to settle for a single silver in the 10,000 in 1932, but came back strong in 1936, his third Olympics, to become the first triple crown winner. He took the gold in the 500m, the 5000m, and the 10,000m, missing his bid for a Grand Slam when he placed second to compatriot Charles Mathisen in the 1500m. Either Norway or Sweden won the next six consecutive 10,000m events. In 1948 the speedskating golds went to three Norwegians and one Swede. Norwegian truck driver Hjalmar Andersen became the second triple crown winner in 1952, taking the gold in the 1500m, 5000m, and 10,000m. US skaters Kenneth Henry and Donald McDermott placed 1–2 in the 500m event.

Powerful skaters from the Soviet Union arrived in 1956, as Yevgeny Grishin won the 500m and tied with compatriot Uri Mikhailov in the 1500m, and Boris Shilkov took the 5000m. The 10,000m went to Sigvard Ericsson of Sweden, just ahead of Norway's Knut Johannesen. Soviet skaters came back in full force in 1960: Grisin successfully defended his 500m crown and tied with Norway's Roald Aas in the 1500m; Viktor Kosichkin took the 5000m. Norwegian Knut Johannesen captured the 10,000m, an event he'd silvered in at Cortina. Four years later Johannesen led a surprise 1–2–3 sweep for his country in the 5000m, but Sweden's Jonny Nilsson defeated Johannesen in the 10,000m at Innsbruck.

fact: On ice that's too cold, gliding is impeded because the skateblade's friction can't create enough of that thin layer of water that makes skating possible; ice that's too warm allows too much water to form, and the resulting water resistance cuts down speed.

US men won a gold in 1964 when Richard "Terry" McDermott scored an upset over veteran defending champion Grishin in the 500m. McDermott added a silver in 1968, losing his 500m title to Erhard Keller of West Germany, having drawn a poor position on rapidly deteriorating ice. Keller felt McDermott would have won the event if he'd skated earlier when the ice was still good, but the German retained his title in the 500m in 1972.

Sapporo's 1972 Games really belonged to Ard Schenk of the Netherlands, who became another triple gold winner with victories in the 1500m, the 5000m, and the 10,000m; Schenk's win in the latter event ended the Scandinavian hold on the 10,000m gold. At the 1976 Games a new men's distance was added, the 1000m, and US skater Peter Mueller (now coach of the US team) took the event's first gold; his teammate Dan Immerfall was a surprise bronze medalist in the 500m. Norway claimed two gold medals in 1976, in the 1500m and the 5000m, while the 500m was a Soviet victory and the 10,000m again went to the Netherlands.

When US speedskater Eric Heiden—coached by former US champion Dianne Holum—swept all five men's events in 1980, he was the only competitor ever to win five individual golds at a single Olympics (swimmer Mark Spitz's seven golds in 1972 included three relay medals). He started off by winning his weakest event, the 500m, then added the 5000m, then the 1000m, then the 1500m, which he won by almost a second and a half even though he lost his balance at one point. Finally, the grueling 10,000m race, 25 laps around the track, brought Heiden his fifth gold. Canada's Gaétan Boucher won a silver in 1980, then added two golds and a bronze in 1984, making him the most bemedaled Canadian Winter Olympian ever. Igor Malkov was only 19 in 1984 when he won the 10,000m event.

fact: The US Long Track Speedskating Team still reigns among the world's elite, as evidenced by its 26 Olympic medals in the last six Winter Games; 21 individual World Champions the past two decades; and 11 World Cup champions the past six years.

US sprint skater Dan Jansen competed against tragedy in 1988 and was overcome. He's considered a contender for the speedskating medals in 1992.

Speedskating legend Eric Heiden swept all five men's events in 1980, becoming the only competitor ever to win five individual golds at single Olympics. The American was unique in his sport, triumphing in sprints and endurance events.

At Innsbruck in 1976 speedskater Sheila Young became the first American ever to win three medals in one Winter Olympics, taking home a gold in the 500m, a silver in the 1500m, and a bronze in the 1000m.

In 1980 Beth Heiden was the world's best overall women's speedskater, and she confirmed that rating at the Lake Placid Games, turning in the best performance of any woman over the four events held that year; she captured a bronze medal in the 3000m.

The US cherished high hopes for its men's speedskating team in 1988, but tragedy and illness took out favorites Dan Jansen and Nick Thometz. Only Eric Flaim was able to medal, taking a silver in the 1500m race. East German Jens-Uwe Mey took the gold in the 500m and silver in the 1000m. His gold was the first that the East German men's speedskating team had ever won. Swedish skater Sven Tomas Gustafson captured the gold in the 5000m and the 10,000m.

The Heidens

Asked to name the most memorable incident of the 1980 Winter Olympics in Lake Placid, most Americans would probably recall the thrilling Soviet-toppling gold medal performance by the young US hockey team. Coming in a close second, however, would be the performance of a quietly determined young speedskater from West Allis, Wisconsin, by the name of Eric Heiden.

But while the hockey victory was certainly dramatic, sports historians now agree that Heiden's performance was one of the greatest individual feats in Olympics history. "Perhaps the most vivid single image of the 1980 Winter Games," declared *Time* magazine, "was the sight of Eric Heiden's heroically muscled thighs molded in a skating skin of gold as he stroked his way to five Olympic golds, five Olympic records and one world record."

fact: When he was competing, Eric Heiden boasted a 32-inch waist and 29-inch thighs.

Such tributes were common for Heiden that winter's fortnight, but the jubilation he felt must have been tempered somewhat by the fate of his feisty speedskating sister, Beth, whose seventh, fifth, seventh, and third-place finishes in four events that same Olympiad were treated as a failure by an overzealous press, which had unreasonably projected her as a gold medal winner as well. Still, Beth skated away from Lake Placid with one bronze medal, and by the mid-1980s this determined, multi-talented athlete had added a 1980 world bicycling championship and an NCAA cross-country skiing championship to her impressive trophy case.

Surely, the Heiden siblings are a duo who have always enjoyed new challenges. While they were growing up, Eric maintains, it was in fact Beth who provided the impetus to get him involved in speedskating. "There was many a time when Beth wanted to hit the ice, and I'd say, 'Aw, let's forget it today,'" Eric recalls. "But her tenacity would get the better of me—and that's what made the difference between success and failure." Like most kids from the northern Midwest, Eric played hockey as a boy and Beth was a figure skater, but by the time they reached adolescence both began to concentrate fully on speedskating.

Also arriving on the scene around that time was Dianne Holum, a 1972 gold medal winner-turned-University of Wisconsin student, who took a job coaching at the local speedskating club where the Heidens practiced. Quickly determining

Speedskating

that Beth and Eric were serious about the sport, Holum put them on a rigorous training program that included bicycling, weightlifting, duck-walking for miles, and, of course, hours on the ice. While the regimen added a strong upper body and tree-like thighs to Eric's perfectly suited 6'1", 185-pound frame, the pint-sized Beth soon reached her physical limitations and so began to concentrate doubly hard on her technique and determination. In a sport dominated by Soviets and Europeans, the Heidens were an instant curiosity when they began competing in—and winning—international events, especially when Eric captured his first world championship at the age of 18.

"Americans had never thought they had the ability to win a world [speedskating] title," Holum said, "but Eric has shown them the way." In 1979, skating against women far bigger and stronger, Beth followed with her first world championship by adding an equal dose of guts to her flawlessly executed striding technique.

Thus, when the Heidens prepared to skate before their countrymen at the 1980 Winter Games, expectations were high that both would skate away with pockets full of gold. Eric by that time had been dominating men's speedskating for three years, rarely losing a race, and Beth was fresh from her world title a year previous. But what skating insiders knew at the time—and the press did not bother to understand—was that Beth's world championship had been based on *overall* performance in four events. At the Olympics, each event is awarded separately, and while Beth was excellent in all four, she was not particularly dominant in any. At Lake Placid she did take third in the 3000 meter race, and indeed her overall performance was the best at the Games.

But when some members of the press chided her for not keeping pace with Eric, Beth, who was also skating on an injured ankle she told no one about, broke down. "I'm happiest when I skate for myself," she said, "but this year I have to skate for the press. The hell with you guys."

But expectations were surely not lost on Eric, who skated whole seconds off of world and Olympic record times in a sport where hundredths of a second can mean the difference between a champion and an also-ran. From the shortest sprints to the longest endurance races, at 500m, 1000m, 1500m, 5000m and 10,000m, Heiden dominated other racers, many of whom had prepared solely for one of the events. Comparing his feat to running helps to put Heiden's performance in perspective—it would be like the world's best sprinter turning around in two days and winning the marathon.

"In Norway, we say that if you can be good in the 5000 and 10,000, you can't do the 500," said Norwegian coach Sten Stenson at the time. "But Eric can do it. We have no idea how to train to take him. We just hope he retires."

Shortly after Heiden's gold-medal haul, Stenson received his wish. A private, intelligent 21-year-old, Heiden looked forward to eschewing the media spotlight and returning to his original dream of becoming an orthopedic surgeon like his father. Beth, too, moved on to new challenges. Having trained extensively on a bicycle to complement her skating, Beth won a world championship in the sport in 1980. After becoming an honors physics student at the University of Vermont in the early 1980s, Beth took up cross-country skiing on a whim and soon found herself winning the NCAA championship in the 7.5km event. She later helped to develop extensive cross-country facilities in Michigan's Upper Peninsula.

Eric also took up competitive cycling after Lake Placid, but he found the going much rougher in his new sport. Although he was teased as being too big and clumsy to handle the fleet, lightweight cycles, Heiden did manage to muscle out a victory in the United States pro cycling championship in 1985. In 1986 he participated in the Tour de France, cycling's most prestigious event, and between semesters of pre-med study Heiden found time to provide television commentary for Olympic speedskating coverage.

But for a man who could easily have turned his Lake Placid gold medals into hard endorsement cash, Heiden has remained true to the spirit of amateur sport and not exploited his incredible 1980 accomplishments. He passed on movie deals and an offer to record a song, and at age 28 entered Stanford Medical School. In 1991 Heiden graduated and began his residency as an orthopedic surgeon.

Throughout their stellar athletic and academic careers, both Eric and Beth Heiden have remained happy because they have never rested on their laurels. "We're not looking for money," Eric told a fawning media, as he said goodbye to that magical Lake Placid winter. "For me, next year will be a time to try things I've never done. I don't just skate and turn left. Sports aren't everything."
—D.C.

Medalists

Speedskating — Men's 500 Meters

1988
1. Jens-Uwe Mey, East Germany, 36.45 (WR,OR)
2. Jan Ykema, Netherlands, 36.76
3. Akira Kuroiwa, Japan, 36.77

1984
1. Sergei Fokitchev, Soviet Union, 38.19
2. Yoshihiro Kitazawa, Japan, 38.30
3. Gaetan Boucher, Canada, 38.39

1980
1. Eric Heiden, USA, 38.03 (OR)
2. Yevgeny Kulikov, Soviet Union, 38.37
3. Lieuwe De Boer, Holland, 38.48

1976
1. Yevgeny Kulikov, Soviet Union, 39.17 (OR)
2. Valery Muratov, Soviet Union, 39.25
3. Dan Immerfall, USA, 39.54

1972
1. Erhard Keller, West Germany, 39.44 (OR)
2. Hasse Borjes, Sweden, 39.69
3. Valery Muratov, Soviet Union, 39.80

1968
1. Erhard Keller, West Germany, 40.3
2. Richard McDermott, USA, 40.5
3. Magne Thomassen, Norway, 40.5

1964
1. Richard McDermott, USA, 40.1 (OR)

2. Alv Gjestvang, Norway, 40.6
2. Yevgeny Grishin, Soviet Union, 40.6
2. Vladimir Orlov, Soviet Union, 40.6

1960
1. Yevgeny Grishin, Soviet Union, 40.2 (EWR)
2. William Disney, USA, 40.3
3. Rafael Gratch, Soviet Union, 40.4

1956
1. Yevgeny Grishin, Soviet Union, 40.2 (EWR)
2. Rafael Gratch, Soviet Union, 40.8
3. Alv Gjestvang, Norway, 41.0

1952
1. Kenneth Henry, USA, 43.2
2. Donald McDermott, USA, 43.9
3. Gordon Audley, Canada, 44.0
3. Arne Johansen, Norway, 44.0

1948
1. Finn Helgesen, Norway, 43.1 (OR)
2. Kenneth Bartholomew, USA, 43.2
2. Thomas Byberg, Norway, 43.2
2. Robert Fitzgerald, USA, 43.2

1936
1. Ivar Ballangrud, Norway, 43.4 (EOR)
2. Georg Krog, Norway, 43.5
3. Leo Freisinger, USA, 44.0

1932
1. John A. Shea, USA, 43.4
2. Bernt Evensen, Norway
3. Alexander Hurt, Canada

1928
1. Bernt Evensen, Norway, 43.4 (OR)

175

1. Clas Thunberg, Finland, 43.4 (OR)
3. John O'Neil Farrell, USA, 43.6
3. Jaakko Friman, Finland, 43.6
3. Roald Larsen, Norway, 43.6
1924 **1.** Charles Jewtraw, USA, 44.0
2. Oskar Olsen, Norway, 44.2
3. Roald Larsen, Norway, 44.8
3. Clas Thunberg, Finland, 44.8

Speedskating — Men's 1,000 Meters

1988 **1.** Nikolai Gouliaev, Soviet Union, 1:13.03 (OR)
2. Jens-Uwe Mey, East Germany, 1:13.11
3. Igor Ghelezovsky, Soviet Union, 1:13.19
1984 **1.** Gaetan Boucher, Canada, 1:15.80
2. Sergei Khlebnikov, Soviet Union, 1:16.63
3. Kai Arne Engelstad, Norway, 1:16.75
1980 **1.** Eric Heiden, USA, 1:15.18 (OR)
2. Gaetan Boucher, Canada, 1:16.68
3. Vladimir Lobanov, Soviet Union, 1:16.91
3. Frode Roenning, Norway, 1:16.91
1976 **1.** Peter Mueller, USA, 1:19.32 (OR)
2. Jorn Didriksen, Norway, 1:20.45
3. Valery Muratov, Soviet Union, 1:20.57

Speedskating — Men's 1,500 Meters

1988 **1.** Andre Hoffmann, East Germany, 1:52.06 (WR,OR)
2. Eric Flaim, USA, 1:52.12
3. Michael Hadschieff, Austria, 1:52.31
1984 **1.** Gaetan Boucher, Canada, 1:58.36
2. Sergei Khlebnikov, Soviet Union, 1:58.83
3. Oleg Bogiev, Soviet Union, 1:58.89
1980 **1.** Eric Heiden, USA, 1:55.44 (OR)
2. Kai Arne Stenshjemmet, Norway, 1:56.81
3. Terje Andersen, Norway, 1:56.92
1976 **1.** Jan-Egil Storholt, Norway, 1:59.38 (OR)
2. Yuri Kondakov, Soviet Union, 1:59.97
3. Hans Van Helden, Netherlands, 2:00.87
1972 **1.** Ard Schenk, Netherlands, 2:02.96 (OR)
2. Roar Gronvold, Norway, 2:04.26
3. Goran Claeson, Sweden, 2:05.89
1968 **1.** Cornelis Verkerk, Netherlands, 2:03.4 (OR)
2. Ivar Eriksen, Norway, 2:05.0
2. Ard Schenk, Netherlands, 2:05.0
1964 **1.** Ants Antson, Soviet Union, 2:10.3
2. Cornelis Verkerk, Netherlands, 2:10.6
3. Villy Haugen, Norway, 2:11.2
1960 **1.** Roald Aas, Norway, 2:10.4
1. Yevgeny Grishin, Soviet Union, 2:10.4
3. Boris Stenin, Soviet Union, 2:11.5
1956 **1.** Yevgeny Grishin, Soviet Union, 2:08.6 (WR)
1. Yuri Mikailov, Soviet Union, 2:08.6 (WR)

3. Toivo Salonen, Finland, 2:09.4
1952 **1.** Hjalmar Andersen, Norway, 2:20.4
2. Willem van der Voort, Netherlands, 2:20.6
3. Roald Aas, Norway, 2:21.6
1948 **1.** Sverre Farstad, Norway, 2:17.6 (OR)
2. Ake Seyffarth, Sweden, 2:18.1
3. Odd Lundberg, Norway, 2:18.9
1936 **1.** Charles Mathiesen, Norway, 2:19.2 (OR)
2. Ivar Ballangrud, Norway, 2:20.2
3. Birger Wasenius, Finland, 2:20.9
1932 **1.** John A. Shea, USA, 2:57.5
2. Alexander Hurd, Canada
3. William F. Logan, Canada
1928 **1.** Clas Thunberg, Finland, 2:21.1
2. Bernt Evensen, Norway, 2:21.9
3. Ivar Ballangrud, Norway, 2:22.6
1924 **1.** Clas Thunberg, Finland, 2:20.8
2. Roald Larsen, Norway, 2:22.0
3. Sigurd Moen, Norway, 2:25.6

Speedskating — Men's 5,000 Meters

1988 **1.** Tomas Gustafson, Sweden, 6:44.63 (WR,OR)
2. Leo Visser, Netherlands, 6:44.98
3. Gerard Kemkers, Netherlands, 6:45.92
1984 **1.** Sven Tomas Gustafson, Sweden, 7:12.38
2. Igor Malkov, Soviet Union, 7:12.30
3. Rene Schoefisch, East Germany, 7:17.49
1980 **1.** Eric Heiden, USA, 7:02.29 (OR)
2. Kai Arne Stenshjemmet, Norway, 7:03.28
3. Tom Erik Oxholm, Norway, 7:05.59
1976 **1.** Sten Stensen, Norway, 7:24.48
2. Piet Klein, Netherlands, 7:26.47
3. Hans Van Helden, Netherlands, 7:26.54
1972 **1.** Ard Schenk, Netherlands, 7:23.61
2. Roar Gronvold, Norway, 7:28.18
3. Sten Stensen, Norway, 7:33.39
1968 **1.** Fred Anton Maier, Norway, 7:22.4 (WR)
2. Cornelis Verkerk, Netherlands, 7:23.2
3. Petrus Nottet, Netherlands, 7:25.5
1964 **1.** Knut Johannesen, Norway, 7:38.4 (OR)
2. Per Ivar Moe, Norway, 7:38.6
3. Fred Anton Maier, Norway, 7:42.0
1960 **1.** Viktor Kosichkin, Soviet Union, 7:51.3
2. Knut Johannesen, Norway, 8:00.8
3. Jan Pesman, Netherlands, 8:05.1
1956 **1.** Boris Shilkov, Soviet Union, 7:48.7 (OR)
2. Sigvard Ericsson, Sweden, 7:56.7
3. Oleg Goncharenko, Soviet Union, 7:57.5
1952 **1.** Hjalmar Andersen, Norway, 8:10.6 (OR)
2. Kees Broekman, Netherlands, 8:21.6
3. Sverre Haugli, Norway, 8:22.4
1948 **1.** Reidar Liaklev, Norway, 8:29.4
2. Odd Lundberg, Norway, 8:32.7
3. Gothe Hedlund, Sweden, 8:34.8
1936 **1.** Ivar Ballangrud, Norway, 8:19.6 (OR)
2. Birger Wasenius, Finland, 8:23.3

3. Antero Ojala, Finland, 8:30.1
1932 1. Irving Jafee, USA, 9:40.8
2. Edward S. Murphy, USA
3. William F. Logan, Canada
1928 1. Ivar Ballangrud, Norway, 8:50.5
2. Julius Skutnabb, Finland, 8:59.1
3. Bernt Evensen, Norway, 9:01.1
1924 1. Clas Thunberg, Finland, 8:39.0
2. Julius Skutnabb, Finland, 8:48.4
3. Roald Larsen, Norway, 8:50.2

Speedskating — Men's 10,000 Meters

1988 1. Sven Tomas Gustafson, Sweden, 13:48.20 (WR,OR)
2. Michael Hadschieff, Austria, 13:56.11
3. Leo Visser, Netherlands, 14:00.55
1984 1. Igor Malkov, Soviet Union, 14:39.90
2. Sven Tomas Gustafson, Sweden, 14:39.95
3. Rene Schoefisch, East Germany, 14:46.91
1980 1. Eric Heiden, USA, 14:28.13 (OR,WR)
2. Piet Kleine, Netherlands, 14:36.03
3. Tom Erik Oxholm, Norway, 14:36.60
1976 1. Piet Kleine, Netherlands, 14:50.59 (OR)
2. Sten Stensen, Norway, 14:53.30
3. Hans Van Helden, Netherlands, 15:02.02
1972 1. Ard Schenk, Netherlands, 15:01.35 (OR)
2. Cornelis Verkerk, Netherlands, 15:04.70

3. Sten Stensen, Norway, 15:07.08
1968 1. Johnny Hoglin, Sweden, 15:23.6 (OR)
2. Fred Anton Maier, Norway, 15:23.9
3. Orjan Sandler, Sweden, 15:31.8
1964 1. Jonny Nilsson, Sweden, 15:50.1
2. Fred Anton Maier, Norway, 16:06.0
3. Knut Johannesen, Norway, 16:06.3
1960 1. Knut Johannesen, Norway, 15:46.6 (WR)
2. Viktor Kosichkin, Soviet Union, 15:49.2
3. Kjell Backman, Sweden, 16:14.2
1956 1. Sigvard Ericsson, Sweden, 16:35.9 (OR)
2. Knut Johannesen, Norway, 16:36.9
3. Oleg Goncharenko, Soviet Union, 16:42.3
1952 1. Hjalmar Andersen, Norway, 16:45.8 (OR)
2. Kees Broekman, Netherlands, 17:10.6
3. Carl-Erik Asplund, Sweden, 17:16.6
1948 1. Ake Seyffarth, Sweden, 17:26.3
2. Lauri Parkkinen, Finland, 17:36.0
3. Pentti Lammio, Finland, 17:42.7
1936 1. Ivar Ballangrud, Norway, 17:24.3 (OR)
2. Birger Wasenius, Finland, 17:28.2
3. Max Stiepl, Austria, 17:30.0
1932 1. Irving Jaffee, USA, 19:13.6
2. Ivar Ballangrud, Norway
3. Frank Stack, Canada
1928 Event called off in the fifth race because of the bad condition of the ice.
1924 1. Julius Skutnabb, Finland, 18:04.8
2. Clas Thunberg, Finland, 18:07.8
3. Roald Larsen, Norway, 18:12.2

WOMEN'S SPEEDSKATING EVENTS

▼

HIGHLIGHTS

Women's events were added to the Olympic speedskating calendar in 1960. That year Lydia Skoblikova of the Soviet Union took gold in the 1500m and the 3000m, with teammate Klara Guseva taking the 1000m. Helga Haase of Germany reigned in the 500m. Skoblikova returned in 1964 and turned in an incredible performance. The 24-year-old Siberian schoolteacher captured all four races in four successive days, the first four-gold medal performance ever in the Winter Games. Along the way she set Olympic records in the 500m, the 1000m, and the 1500m. Melting ice made her six-tenths of a second slower than her own record in the 3000m; that event produced a surprise silver for North Korean skater Pil-Hwa Han, who also skated on bad ice.

The 500m event in 1968 concluded in an unusual way, as the three American entries tied for second place behind Russia's Ludmila Titova. As a result, Dianne Holum, Jennifer Fish, and Mary Meyers were each awarded a

177

silver medal. Holum also picked a bronze in the 1000m. She was honored at Sapporo in 1972 when she became the first woman to bear the American flag during the opening ceremonies of a Winter Games, and she enjoyed another moment of glory when she won her country's first gold medal of the Games, capturing the 1500m. Holum padded her Olympic treasury to four medals with a silver in the 3000m, won by 33-year-old Christina Baas-Kaiser of the Netherlands. US skater Anne Henning was also a double medal winner, setting an Olympic record in the 500m and placing third behind Monika Pflug of West Germany in the 1000m. Holum was back in the Olympic arena as coach of the US speedskating team.

At Innsbruck in 1976, US skater Sheila Young became the first American ever to win three medals in one Winter Olympics, taking home a gold in the 500m, a silver in the 1500m and a bronze in the 1000m. Young was also a world champion cyclist. Her speedskating teammate, Leah Poulos, captured a 1000m silver in 1976, behind Tatiana Averina of the Soviet Union, who also took the gold in the 3000m and bronzed in the 500m and the 1500m.

In 1980 Leah Poulos Mueller earned two silver medals for the US, in the 500m and the 1000m, while teammate Beth Heiden picked up a bronze in the 3000m. Canada's Cathy Priestner brought home a silver in the 500m. Women from the Netherlands completed a 1–2 sweep of the 1500 in 1980. Soviet skater Natalia Petruseva took the 1000m, and Bjorg Eva Jensen of Norway won the 3000m.

fact: Speedskaters develop slowly; they need the stamina and musculature of a mature athlete to excel.

East German women began to dominate the skating scene in 1980. Karin Enke won a 500m gold at Lake Placid in 1980, and two golds and two silvers at the 1984 Games. Skating as Karin Kania at Calgary, she took a bronze in the 500m and silvers in the 1000m and 1500m races. Andrea Mitscherlich had taken a silver medal in the women's 3000m in 1976 at age 15; skating as Andrea Schoene in 1984, she sped to a gold in the 3000m and two silvers in the 1000m and 1500m. At the Calgary Games in 1988, this time as Andrea Ehrig, she captured silvers in the 3000m and 5000m races, and a bronze in the 1500m race. At Sarajevo, East German Christa Rothenburger took the gold in the women's 500m but had to settle for a silver in that event in 1988, when she captured gold in the 1000m. Her countrywoman Gabi Zange emerged in 1988 to capture the bronze in the 3000m and the 5000m.

The Netherlands enjoyed a good showing in women's speedskating at the 1988 Games when Yvonne van Gennip skated away with the gold in the 1500m, the 3000m, and the 5000m races. For the US in 1988, Bonnie Blair won a gold in the 500m race—by about the length of a speedskating blade—and a bronze in the 1000m.

178

Speedskating — Women's 500 Meters

1988 **1.** Bonnie Blair, USA, 39.10 (WR,OR)
2. Christa Rothenburger, East Germany, 39.12
3. Karin Kania-Enke, East Germany, 39.24
1984 **1.** Christa Rothenburger, East Germany 41.02 (OR)
2. Karin Kania-Enke, East Germany, 41.28
3. Natalia Chive, Soviet Union, 41.50
1980 **1.** Karin Enke, East Germany, 41.78 (OR)
2. Leah Poulos Mueller, USA, 42.26
3. Natalia Petruseva, Soviet Union, 42.42
1976 **1.** Sheila Young, USA, 42.76 (OR)
2. Cathy Priestner, Canada, 43.12
3. Tatiana Averina, Soviet Union, 43.17
1972 **1.** Anne Henning, USA, 43.33 (OR)
2. Vera Krasnova, Soviet Union, 44.01
3. Lyudmila Titova, Soviet Union, 44.45
1968 **1.** Lyudmila Titova, Soviet Union, 46.1
2. Jennifer Fish, USA, 46.3
2. Dianne Holum, USA, 46.3
2. Mary Meyers, USA, 46.3
1964 **1.** Lydia Skoblikova, Soviet Union, 45.0 (OR)
2. Irina Yegorova, Soviet Union, 45.4
3. Tatiana Sidorova, Soviet Union, 45.5
1960 **1.** Helga Haase, East Germany, 45.9
2. Natalia Donchenko, Soviet Union, 46.0
3. Jeanne Ashworth, USA, 46.1
1936-
1956 **Not held**
1932 **1.** Jean Wilson, Canada, 58.0
2. Elizabeth Dubois, USA
3. Kit Klein, USA
1924-
1928 **Not held**

Speedskating — Women's 1,000 Meters

1988 **1.** Christa Rothenburger, East Germany , 1:17.65 (WR,OR)
2. Karin Kania-Enke, East Germany, 1:17.70
3. Bonnie Blair, USA, 1:18.31
1984 **1.** Karin Kania-Enke, East Germany, 1:21.61 (OR)
2. Andrea Schoene, East Germany, 1:22.83
3. Natalia Petruseva, Soviet Union, 1:23.21
1980 **1.** Natalia Petruseva, Soviet Union, 1:24.10 (OR)
2. Leah Poulos Mueller, USA, 1:25.41
3. Sylvia Albrecht, East Germany, 1:26.46
1976 **1.** Tatiana Averina, Soviet Union, 1:28.43 (OR)
2. Leah Poulos, USA, 1:28.57
3. Sheila Young, USA, 1:29.14
1972 **1.** Monika Pflug, West Germany, 1:31.40 (OR)

2. Atje Keulen-Deelstra, Netherlands, 1:31.61
3. Anne Henning, USA, 1:31.62
1968 **1.** Carolina Geijssen, Netherlands, 1:32.6 (OR)
2. Lyudmila Titova, Soviet Union, 1:32.9
3. Dianne Holum, USA 1:33.4
1964 **1.** Lydia Skoblikova, Soviet Union, 1:33.2 (OR)
2. Irina Yegorova, Soviet Union, 1:34.3
3. Kaija Mustonen, Finland, 1:34.8
1960 **1.** Klara Guseva, Soviet Union, 1:34.1
2. Helga Haase, East Germany, 1:34.3
3. Tamara Rylova, Soviet Union, 1:34.8
1936-
1956 **Not held**
1932 **1.** Elizabeth Dubois, USA, 2:04.0
2. Hattie Donaldson, Canada
3. Dorothy Franey, USA
1924-
1928 **Not held**

Speedskating — Women's 1,500 Meters

1988 **1.** Yvonne van Gennip, Netherlands, 2:00.68 (OR)
2. Karin Kania-Enke, East Germany, 2:00.82
3. Andrea Ehrig, East Germany, 2:01.49
1984 **1.** Karin Kania-Enke, East Germany, 2:03.42 (OR)
2. Andrea Schoene, East Germany, 2:05.29
3. Natalia Petruseva, Soviet Union, 2:05.78
1980 **1.** Annie Borckink, Netherlands, 2:10.95 (OR)
2. Ria Visser, Netherlands, 2:12.24
3. Sabine Becker, East Germany, 2:12.38
1976 **1.** Galina Stepanskaya, Soviet Union, 2:16.58 (OR)
2. Sheila Young, USA, 2:17.06
3. Tatiana Averina, Soviet Union, 2:17.96
1972 **1.** Dianne Holum, USA, 2:20.85 (OR)
2. Christina Baas-Kaiser, Netherlands, 2:21.05
3. Atje Keulen-Deelstra, Netherlands, 2:22.05
1968 **1.** Kaija Mustonen, Finland, 2:22.4 (OR)
2. Carolina Geijssen, Netherlands, 2:22.7
3. Christina Kaiser, Netherlands, 2:24.5
1964 **1.** Lydia Skoblikova, Soviet Union, 2:22.6 (OR)
2. Kaija Mustonen, Finland, 2:25.5
3. Berta Kolokoltseva, Soviet Union, 2:27.1
1960 **1.** Lydia Skoblikova, Soviet Union, 2:25.2 (WR)
2. Elvira Seroczynska, Poland, 2:25.7
3. Helena Pilejczyk, Poland, 2:27.1
1936-
1956 **Not held**
1932 **1.** Kit Klein, USA, 3:00.6
2. Jean Wilson, Canada
3. Helen Bina, USA

179

Speedskating — Women's 3,000 Meters

1988 1. Yvonne van Gennip, Netherlands, 4:11.94 (WR,OR)
2. Andrea Ehrig, East Germany, 4:12.09
3. Gabi Zange, East Germany, 4:16.92

1984 1. Andrea Schoene, East Germany, 4:24.79 (OR)
2. Karin Kania-Enke, East Germany, 4:26.33
3. Gabie Schoenbrunn, East Germany, 4:33.13

1980 1. Bjoerg-Eva Jensen, Norway, 4:32.13 (OR)
2. Sabine Becker, East Germany, 4:32.79
3. Beth Heiden, USA, 4:33.77

1976 1. Tatiana Averina, Soviet Union, 4:45.19 (OR)
2. Andrea Mitscherlich, East Germany, 4:45.23
3. Lisbeth Korsmo, Norway, 4:45.24

1972 1. Christina Baas-Kaiser, Netherlands, 4:52.14 (OR)

2. Dianne Holum, USA, 4:58.67
3. Atje Keulen-Deelstra, Netherlands, 4:59.91

1968 1. Johanna Schut, Netherlands, 4:56.2 (OR)
2. Kaija Mustonen, Finland, 5:01.0
3. Christina Kaiser, Netherlands, 5:01.3

1964 1. Lydia Skoblikova, Soviet Union, 5:14.9
2. Pil-Hwa Han, Democratic People's Republic of Korea, 5:18.5
2. Valentina Stenina, Soviet Union, 5:18.5

1960 1. Lydia Skoblikova, Soviet Union, 5:14.3
2. Valentina Stenina, Soviet Union, 5:16.9
3. Eevi Huttunen, Finland, 5:21.0

1924- 1956 Not held

Speedskating — Women's 5,000 Meters

1988 1. Yvonne van Gennip, Netherlands, 7:14.13 (WR)
2. Andrea Ehrig, East Germany, 7:17.12
3. Gabi Zange, East Germany, 7:21.61

SUMMER GAMES

▼

On the Road to Barcelona

▼

GEORGE CANTOR

The traveler was on his way to the railroad station in Barcelona when his cab driver asked where he was headed.
"Madrid," said the traveler.
"Oh," said the cabbie. "So you're going to Spain."
Although the map clearly shows Barcelona situated within the Spanish border, there is a strong difference of opinion about that in the city. The people of this Mediterranean seaport consider themselves Catalan, bearers of a different culture and language than Spain and attached to the larger country only through a series of historical accidents.

So the significance of the 1992 Summer Olympics, which will run from July 25 to August 9, means different things to different people in the same country.

Spanish scholars regard the Games as the symbolic recognition of Spain's rejoining the rest of Europe. After decades, some would say centuries, of isolation, the newly prosperous and firmly democratic Spain wants 1992 to be marked as the year that its destiny was inextricably linked with that of progressive Europe.

Barcelona feels no such impulse. It has always regarded itself as looking more towards the rest of Europe than to Spain anyhow and regards the Games as a showcase by which it can demonstrate its own independent turn of mind to the world.

No wonder that one of the major concerns of these games is the possibility of terrorism by Catalan extremists and that security precautions will be fully as rigorous as they were in Korea in 1988.

Even the setting of the main events of the Games, the stadium on Montjuic (Hill of Jews), is a symbol of Catalan resistance. The stadium was built in 1929 in an effort to convince the International Olympics Committee to schedule the 1936 games here. But they went to Berlin, instead.

This outraged the strongly anti-Fascist Catalan government headed by Lluis Companys. It went ahead and planned a People's Olympiad for the same summer. Three days before its scheduled start, however, the Spanish Civil War broke out. For the next two and a half years, Barcelona was a focus of resistance to the Fascist forces of General Francisco Franco. Companys, regarded as one of

183

Catalonia's greatest heroes, fled to France in 1939. But when the Nazis took over he was returned to Spain, court martialed at Montjuic Castle and executed in 1940. His last request was that he be executed with his shoes off so that his bare feet would touch Catalan soil. A plaque in the north gate of the stadium marks the spot of his death.

Franco's government tried to suppress the Catalan language and government. But after the dictator's death, in 1975, Catalan was officially reinstated in Barcelona. The city's street signs were even changed to that language. Catalan also is one of the four official languages of these Olympics.

The city is old, dating back to the dawn of European history. According to one legend, it was founded by Hercules, who was shipwrecked nearby on his way to the Trojan War. Others say that it is Carthaginian, settled by ancestors of Hannibal, and that its name derives from that of his family, Barca. It was a major outpost of Roman Spain and by the late 15th Century was the most prosperous port of the western Mediterranean.

But then another traveler passed through town, heading for Spain, and history changed its course. Christopher Columbus came to Barcelona seeking support for his voyage to the western seas. But the city had no particular interest in developing a route that could deprive it of its accustomed Mediterranean trade, so Columbus sailed under the flag of Castile. His discoveries turned Spain into a world power and shifted the routes of commerce away from Barcelona. The city forgave him, though, and a statue of Columbus stands on the waterfront today, pointing out to sea. While 1992 marks the 500th anniversary of his voyage, with a major world's fair in Seville to celebrate it, Barcelona regards all that as Spain's business.

The Olympics are Barcelona's business and quite a business it is. An estimated $7.5 billion is being spent to prepare for the Games. Most of this is being packaged under the name "Barcelona '93," as a way of convincing the city's residents that the improvements being made will be of permanent benefit to them. Political leaders say that only about one-sixth of the amount will go into actual athletic facilities. The rest is being placed in long overdue transportation, communication, and housing projects.

The Olympic Village, developed along the seacoast in a formerly rundown area of factories and warehouses, will become a permanent community after the games. It already has a name, Poblenu, and will include a new harbor, 2000 housing units, two 44-story office towers, shopping malls, parks and four kilometers of new beach, providing Barcelona with a much needed recreational outlet to the sea. Along with this comes a sewage modernization program that will make the new beaches usable. Pollution of the beaches along the Costa Brava is regarded as a national scandal.

Part of the money will also go into a system of ring roads that, theoretically, will ease traffic congestion in this city, which is wedged tightly between mountains and sea. New telecommunications facilities, installed for the international media, also will remain behind to benefit Barcelona.

While this is a city that sees its share of tourists in a normal year, it has not experienced anything like the crush of visitors anticipated for the Olympics. Almost all hotel rooms within the city already are reserved (going for about $450 a night in the mid-range and twice that in some deluxe hotels). Visitors making reservations now should expect to be housed in nearby communities, up to two hours by car or bus from the site of the Games.

The city also has turned to an expedient it used 104 years ago, when the World's Fair of 1888 took all its hotel rooms. It brought in passenger ships to the harbor and lodged visitors aboard them. Eight such vessels will port in Barcelona for the Olympics, but most of the berths will go to games sponsors and officials. Because of their proximity to the action, they will also be among the most expensive. The city originally had planned to build nine new hotels to house visitors. But travel surveys indicated that most of them would fail after the Olympics were history. So the number was reduced to four and the ships were summoned.

The American agent for tickets and accommodations at the Games is Olson-Travelworld (800-874-1992.) They arrange several packages, and while other tour operators offer Olympics deals, they all must go through Olson for their tickets.

Barcelona predicts that travelers will not have a difficult time getting to the various venues, because they are situated within a relatively small area. Barcelona occupies a tiny amount of land compared to Los Angeles, site of the 1988 Games, and no great travel inconveniences were experienced there. Still, the main stadium is on a hilltop, not served by the city's excellent subway system nor easy to reach on foot or by car (although a funicular railway does make the ascent.) The pressure on buses and cabs will be enormous.

Conditions at Montjuic Stadium have also raised concerns. The field is used by the Barcelona Dragons of the World League of American Football and the damage the gridiron performers inflict upon the turf is enormous. A test of the track in June, 1991, prompted complaints from most of the athletes. One of them said it was "unthinkable" for the Olympics to be staged on a field in that condition. There are also concerns that the Dragons' home schedule in 1992 might push a scheduled 10,000-seat stadium expansion back to the eve of the Games. But a 17,000-seat basketball arena has been completed adjacent to Montjuic Stadium and there are absolutely no complaints about that.

Other new facilities and refurbishing of older ones, such as the cycling vélodrome, are proceeding on schedule.

Of even greater concern are the plans of ETA, a Basque terrorist organization that has shown chilling efficiency and a flair for maximum media exposure in the past. It assassinated Franco's hand-picked successor in 1973, and just this year staged bombing attacks on two cities that will host subsidiary Olympic events, Vic and Valencia. Barcelona officials insist that it would be "counter productive" for the group to disrupt the Olympics, in terms of international support for its cause. But other threatening forces include two

Catalan separatist groups that have threatened action during the Games, as well as the general run of terrorist organizations that have shadowed every Olympics since 1972 in Munich. Security will be tight.

Walking Barcelona

Barcelona prefers to concentrate on Cobi. This friendly, surrealistic pooch, designed by Javier Mariscal, is the symbol of the Barcelona Games and a reminder of the city's long connection with the avant-garde in European art. Some thought it might be a little too strong a reminder. One local paper criticized the Cobi design for being so stylized that it didn't carry a universal appeal. But Barcelona toy stores have a hard time keeping the mutt in stock as local children have made him an instant classic.

Pablo Picasso regarded Barcelona as his adopted hometown and it was also where Salvador Dali and Joan Miró started out. The favorite son among local artists, however, is Antoni Gaudi and it is he who has left his mark most indelibly on the city. His Church of the Holy Family (Sagrada Familia) is Barcelona's identifying landmark, no less impressive for being unfinished after 108 years.

Gaudi was obsessed with creating buildings that expressed natural forms. His concrete structures twist and weave like visions from a fairy tale, incorporating sinuous lines and almost plantlike adornments. No straight lines, no right angles in his works. Instead, they seem to grow right out of the soil.

He began work on the Church of the Holy Family in 1884, at the age of 32, and was still puttering away at it in 1926 when he was run over by a streetcar and killed. Work halted for 14 years before being resumed by the government. But since Gaudi left no plans and the building was wholly a product of his inner vision, it was difficult to figure out just how to proceed. So the scaffolding remains in the center of the unroofed church, while the undulating Gaudi style stamps the stones around it.

It is not to everyone's taste. George Orwell, in his "Homage to Catalonia," suggests that with all the damage caused by the Spanish Civil War it was a terrible shame that the church didn't get blown up, too. Some businessmen have suggested that with modern computer technology the church could probably be completed within a year. Barcelona will have none of that. One gets the idea that the city prefers it the way it is, unfinished, as a statement of its own Catalan vision.

The subway stops right at the back of the church, on the Carrer de Provenca. A walk starting from this point is a good way to get to know a bit of Barcelona. Start heading back towards the middle of town along Provenca, past the crosstown boulevard called The Diagonal, to the Passeig de Gracia. This magnificent, geometrically paved boulevard is the city's most distinguished address, the Fifth Avenue of Barcelona. At the corner, you'll see another Gaudi building, the Casa Mila apartment, dating from 1905, with its wavy facade and fantastically decorated wrought iron balconies. Turn left and a few blocks ahead on the Gracia is the Casa Bottlo, yet another Gaudi masterwork.

Most of what you will see on this street dates from the late 19th century, when Barcelona recovered its prosperity on a wave of foreign trade. Wealthy merchants sent their children to study in Paris. When they returned, they started tearing down the old medieval walls of the city and replacing them with broad Parisian boulevards, such as this one.

The Gracia ends at the massive Placa de Catalunya. At the far end of the huge square is the start of the city's most famous thoroughfare, the Ramblas. This tree-lined walkway to the harbor is the lifeline of Barcelona. This is where the city comes to stroll in the warm evening. Open markets, kiosks, and vendors line its length and people walk by to shop for trinkets or to watch each other walk by.

After a few blocks, cut to the left on the Carrer Porteferrisa, which leads to the Gothic Quarter. This is the core of the ancient city and traces of Roman construction can be seen in the streets around the cathedral, which is the center of the quarter. When pirates destroyed the town in the fourth century, a fortified rectangle was built and within its walls was contained this Barcelona of the Middle Ages. The cathedral dates from the late 13th century and you'll find houses of equal age as you stroll the narrow streets that surround it.

After exploring the area, head back to the Ramblas along the Carrer de Ferran. Just where it rejoins the Ramblas is the Plaza Real, the most magnificent square of the old city, with its colonnades and unified appearance. Then continue along the Ramblas to the waterfront, with its great statue of Columbus. Nearby, is the Maritime Museum, housed in the 14th-century royal dockyard. The building itself is regarded as the most perfectly preserved medieval shipyard in the world and it also contains lifesize models of many of the craft made here.

Catch a cab and take it up to Montjuic, the locale of the Olympics. This is where Barcelona first raised the banner of revolt from Castile in 1640, and allied itself with France for the next 14 years before the rebellion was crushed. During the Olympics, you'll often see the Catalan flag under which they fought. Its four distinctive red bars symbolize of the blood of those who died fighting for Catalonia. From the terrace of the castle that once stood here, you could savor wonderful views over the waterfront and harbor, to the distant coast.

Also on Montjuic is the home of Miró, now the Center for Contemporary Art Studies, which displays many of the artist's works and possessions. But the chief attraction of Montjuic, besides the Olympic Stadium, is the Palacio Nacional. Built for an international exhibition in 1929, it was supposed to be knocked down when the show ended. But the building was so popular that it was preserved instead and now houses the Museum of Catalonian Art.

Its collection of Romanesque and Gothic items—murals, altarpieces and carved statues—gathered here from dozens of churches across Catalonia, is the expression of a nation's genius. So only a few hundred yards from where Barcelona will show off its face to the world at the Olympics, you will find a vision of its soul.

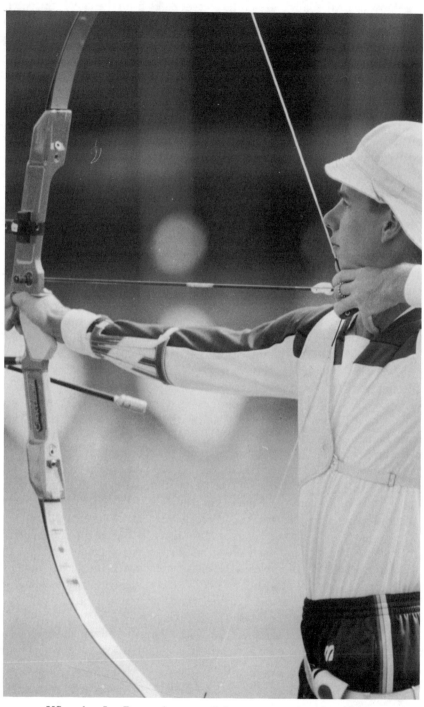

US archer Jay Barrs aims to nail down a second gold medal in Barcelona.

ARCHERY

WARM-UP

William Tell's aim was true, his arrow piercing the apple atop his son's head. Cupid does his romantic work with bow in hand, arrow at the ready. One of history's most popular legends, Robin Hood, was an archer, as Kevin Costner will attest. In fact, a "Robin Hood" is part of the archery jargon: it occurs when an archer drives the tip and shaft of one arrow deep into the end of another arrow already in the bullseye; this is the archery equivalent of a hole-in-one.

Invented some 100,000 years ago, archery has been called one of the four most important inventions in human history, next to fire, language, and microwave ovens. For prehistoric humans, archery was a means toward an end, that end being survival. Legend has it that the ancient Olympic Games, held from 776 BC to 395 AD, were founded by Hercules, an archer. Back then, the games featured tethered doves as the targets. During the heat of the compete, ancient broadcasters were fond of saying, "Now the feathers are really flying," thus giving birth to a valuable cliché.

But several thousand years before the Olympics, Egyptians were using bows as tall as themselves and arrows with flint arrowheads, later replaced by bronze. In 1800 BC, the Assyrians developed the shorter recurve bow, which provided more power and easier handling. The skill of shooting from moving chariots, so popular in cinematic tales, was developed by the Hittites around 1200 BC. In 500 AD, the Romans, known as second-rate archers, began drawing the arrow to the face rather than the chest, improving their accuracy dramatically.

Archery as a sport traces its heritage back to 17th-century England, as part of community festivals. In the US, the National Archery Association was founded in 1879 by two brothers, J. Maurice and William H. Thompson. The brothers Thompson, like other Confederate soldiers, were not allowed firearms after the Civil War. Naturally, they took to bow and arrow instead. The National Archery Association belongs to FITA (Fédération Internationale de Tir à Arc), the international governing federation for archery.

In 1900, the sport became an official event in the modern Olympics, and was featured in the 1904, 1908, and 1920 games. For lack of interest, the sport was dropped for nearly 50 years, returning in 1972. That year, John Williams and Doreen Wilber won the men's and women's gold medals for the US. In 1988, Jay

Barrs of the US won the men's individual championship, while the women's individual gold was taken by Soo-Nyung Kim of South Korea. And men's and women's team competition, just added to the Olympic menu in 1988, were also won by South Koreans.

Summer

SPECTATORS' GUIDE

Imagine standing on the goal line of a football field and hitting an apple with an arrow under the opposite goalpost. At 90 meters, the archer is aiming at a 10-ring target face that is 4.8 inches in diameter. The entire target at 90 meters compares in size to the head of a thumbtack held at arm's length. And if there's a wind...

Olympic archery competition uses the recurve bow, featuring limbs that curve away from the archer to increase power. The lever effect created can propel arrows in excess of 150 miles per hour. The average draw weight of a man's bow is 50 pounds. In an typical tournament, the bow is lifted and drawn more than 312 times for a total of 15,500 pounds, or nearly eight tons, pulled over four days. Women pull more than five tons with their 34-pound bows.

The bows are generally constructed of wood, fiberglass, and graphite or carbon composites. Most strings are made of Fast Flight, a hydrocarbon product, while some still are made of kevlar, the material used to make bullet-proof vests. The arrows are either of aluminum, which are more uniform in weight and shape, or carbon graphite, which flies faster.

Olympic-style target archery includes two formats: the Single FITA round and the Grand FITA round. A single FITA round consists of 36 arrows shot from four distances for a total of 144 arrows. The distances are 90, 70, 50, and 30 meters for men; 70, 60, 50, and 30 meters for women. Scoring ranges from 10 in the center gold circle to 1 in the outer white ring. The maximum possible score for a single FITA round is 144 "10s," or 1,440.

Stanislav Zabrodsky, URS, established the current men's record of 1,342 points in 1989. The women's world record of 1368 was set by Soo-Nyung Kim of Korea in 1989.

The Grand Fita round, adopted in 1985, was used for the first time in the Olympics at Seoul. The Grand FITA, designed to increase spectator interest in "the quiet sport," makes archery more competitive through eliminations. Besides having to make each cut, archers must adjust to different distances every nine arrows, which makes establishing a rhythm just a bit more challenging.

The FITA/Grand FITA round starts with a two-day Single FITA of 144 arrows. On the third day, the top 24 male and top 24 female archers' scores start at zero. Four elimination rounds of nine arrows at each distance then take place,

190

with scores starting at zero to begin each new round. This eliminates the chance to take a big lead into the finals, a situation providing hope for the underdogs.

Six archers are eliminated after the morning round, plus six more in the afternoon. The semi-final round reduces the competitors to the top eight, and the final round determines the medal winners.

Team competition involves a Grand FITA round, with scoring and eliminations just like the individual round. Each team fields three archers.

▼

HOPEFULS

Having taken seven medals in the 1988 Summer Olympics, including all three women's individual medals and the women's team gold, the Koreans will aim to meet or beat their performance in 1992. But with a talented women's team, including US champion Denise Parker, who helped win the team's 1988 Olympic bronze medal at age 14, the USA hopes to make its mark in the women's events. Olympic gold medal-winner Jay Barrs will compete again with the US men, along with US Olympic Festival champion Ed Edliason and World Indoor champion Joe Asay, each of whom has an excellent shot at a medal.

Jay Barrs

Bring up the subject of archery and the average sports fan will picture calm, reserved, middle-aged men with steely nerves taking aim at a colorful, distant target in an a country setting. But American Jay Barrs may be the world's first heavy-metal champion.

The 29-year-old Barrs did much to knock down misconceptions about this little-known sport with his gold-medal performance at the 1988 Summer Olympics in Seoul. With his quiver slung low around his hips like an Old West gunfighter, Barrs was a picture of American bravado as he narrowly outpointed South Korea's own Park Sung Soo 338–336 to win the finals of the men's individual competition at Seoul. His performance went a long way to securing another medal, this one the silver, for his fellow US Archery Team members.

"I have been waiting for this moment for the past eight years," said the Mesa, Arizona, resident, who also coaches at Arizona State University. Awarded the target used to catch his gold medal arrows, Barrs proclaimed, "I'm going to give it to my mother."

Perhaps as noteworthy as Barrs's accomplishment was the style he displayed in reaching it. Between each set of three arrows he fired (archers shoot a total of nine arrows from distances of 30, 50, 70, and 90 meters), Barrs would return to his seat, strap on his headphones, and pump up his adrenaline with the ear-splitting music of such hard rock bands as Sammy Hagar and Mötley Crüe, sometimes recreating the flailing gestures of the musicians. "I play all the air instruments real well, air guitar, air drums," Barrs said. When his turn came to shoot again, Barrs would confidently fire his three arrows in rapid succession, then return to his seat. If there were such a thing as an archery shoe, Barrs would be just the man to endorse it on television, à la Bo Jackson.

All of which cannot take away from the Jacksonville, Florida, native's proficiency in his sport. In addition to his two Olympic medals, Barrs set an Olympic record in 1988 in the 90-meter double event and was a member of America's world record-holding team at the 1987 Pan Am Games. He also holds six US National records and was the Male Archery Athlete of the Year in 1987, 1988, and 1990.

Serious competition has brought about at least one major change in this free-spirited athlete's life-style—mainly regarding his eating habits. "I used to eat from the three basic food groups," Barrs quipped. "McDonalds, Wendy's, and Burger King." —D.C.

Schedule

The tentative archery schedule is as follows:

Friday, July 31
70m women
90m men
60m women
70m men

Saturday, August 1
50m women
50m men
30m women
30m men

Sunday, August 2
70, 60, 50, 30m women
90, 70, 50, 30m men
Quarterfinal, men & women

Monday, August 3
Semifinal, men & women
Final, men & women

Tuesday, August 4
Team semifinal, men & women
Team final, men & women

▼

HIGHLIGHTS

Archery was absent from the Summer Games for more than fifty years. In the early going, from 1900 through 1920, competing archers came mostly from the host countries, and the event was not considered to be of world champion calibre. US archers cleaned up all the medals in St. Louis in 1904, led by Will Thompson and Lyda Scott Howell, both long-time national champions. The British dominated in London in 1908, led by William Dod and Charlotte Dod; the latter was 36 when she took a silver in 1908. And the Belgians just happened to triumph in Antwerp in 1920, counting among their competitors Hubert van Innis, 54 years old in 1920, who added four gold and two silver medals to the two golds and one silver he'd won in 1900. None of the archery events held between 1904 and 1920 carried over to the present Olympic program.

When archery returned to the Olympics in 1972, the US was ready: John Williams and Doreen Wilber won the men's and women's golds that year, when Wilber was 42 years old and Williams was 18. In 1976 US archer Darrell Pace took the men's gold, while Luann Ryon won the women's gold for the US in Montréal; Ryon had never before competed at the international level. Tomi Poikolainen of Finland took the men's gold at the Moscow Games, with Keto Losaberidze of the Soviet Union capturing the women's gold. Pace repeated his gold-medal performance in 1984, while teammate Rick McKinney earned a silver medal. A 17-year-old North Korean archer, Hyang-Soon Seo, captured the women's title in 1984. Fourteen-year-old Denise Parker made her debut on the US women's team in 1988, but was met with a South Korean sweep of the women's event. The men's gold in Seoul went to US archer Jay Barrs, also competing in 1992, ahead of two South Korean archers. 1984's silver medalist, Rick McKinney, will lead the 1992 US men's team, and Parker will again compete in 1992 as leader of the US women's team.

Archery

Medalists

Archery — Men's Individual

1988 1. Jay Barrs, U.S.A., 338
2. Sung-soo Park, South Korea, 336
3. Vladimir Echeev, South Korea, 335
1984 1. Darrell Pace, U.S.A., 2616 (OR)
2. Richard McKinney, U.S.A. 2564
3. Hiroshi Yamamoto, Japan, 2563
1980 1. Tomi Poikolainen, Finland, 2455
2. Boris Isachenko, Soviet Union, 2452
3. Giancarlo Ferrari, Italy, 2449
1976 1. Darrell Pace, U.S.A., 2571 (OR, WR)
2. Hiroshi Michinaga, Japan, 2502
3. Carlo Ferrari, Italy, 2495
1972 1. John Williams, U.S.A., 2528 (WR)
2. Gunnar Jervill, Sweden, 2481
3. Kyosti Laasonen, Finland, 2467
1924-
1968 Not held

Archery — Men's Team

1988 1. South Korea, 986, In-Soo Chun, Han-Sup Lee and Sung-Soo Park
2. U.S.A., 972, Jay Barrs, Rick McKinney and Darrell Pace
3. Great Britain, 968, Steven Hallard, Richard Priestman and Leroy Watson

Archery — Women's Individual

1988 1. Soo-nyung Kim, South Korea, 344
2. Hee-kyung Wang, South Korea, 332
3. Young-sook Yun, South Korea, 327
1984 1. Hyang-Soon Seo, Republic of Korea, 2568 (OR)
2. Lingjuan Li, People's Republic of China, 2559
3. Jin-Ho Kim, Republic of Korea, 2555
1980 1. Keto Losaberidze, Soviet Union, 2491
2. Natalia Butuzova, Soviet Union, 2477
3. Paivi Meriluoto, Finland, 2449
1976 1. Luann Ryon, U.S.A., 2499 (OR, WR)
2. Valentina Kovpan, Soviet Union, 2460
3. Zebiniso Rustamova, Soviet Union, 2407
1972 1. Doreen Wilber, U.S.A., 2424 (WR)
2. Irena Szydlowska, Poland, 2407
3. Emma Gapchenko, Soviet Union, 2403
1912-
1968 Not held

Archery — Women's Team

1988 1. South Korea, 982, Soo-Nyung Kim, Hee-Kyung Wang and Young- Sook Yun

2. Indonesia, 952, Lilies Handayani,
Nirfitriyana Saiman and Kusuma
Wardhani

3. U.S.A., 952, Debra Ochs, Denise
Parker and Melanie Skillman

BADMINTON

WARM-UP

I n 1992 badminton makes its Olympic medal debut, a promotion from exhibition status in 1988 (in its other Olympic appearance in 1972, badminton was a demo sport). Second in world sport popularity only to soccer, badminton began on the Asian continent, although the exact circumstances are unknown. It may have began as *Ti Jian Zi*, or shuttlecock kicking, in China of the 5th-century BC. The modern version of badminton can be traced to India, where *poona* matches were contested during the 1800s.

British military officers stationed in the country during that time became interested in *poona* due to its similarities to lawn tennis. When they returned to their homeland, the Brits brought the game with them. In particular, the game became a popular pastime on the Gloucestershire estate of the Duke of Beauforts, where the sport was officially launched at a party given in 1873. The estate's name was "Badminton" and participants were given to referring to the sport as "that game at Badminton." The name, as they say, stuck.

Until 1887, the sport was played in England under the *poona* rules, which, from the English point of view, were often contradictory and confusing. The first organized badminton association in England, the Bath Badminton Club, anglicized and standardized the rules. In 1895, the rules were further refined by the Badminton Association (of England), which assumed authority of the sport from the Bath club.

Badminton soon spread to the US, Canada, Australia, and New Zealand. Badminton was established in the US in 1878, when the first club formed in New York City. At the turn of the century, badminton was the trendy little sport in the Big Apple, especially among the élite. Players like Rockefeller, Astor, Roosevelt, and Vanderbilt helped popularize the game in the States.

Although the game was first played by men, women became early enthusiasts. The first All-England Championships (the "Wembley") for men were held in 1899, and in 1900 the inaugural tournament for women was arranged. These, however, were regarded as unofficial. 1904 marks the beginning of the official All-England matches.

It was not until 1939 that international play almost began, following the spread of national championships to Australia, Denmark, India, Malaya, Norway, Sweden, Mexico, the Netherlands, and the United States. Named after Sir

George A. Thomas, president of the International Badminton Federation, the Thomas Cup Matches were delayed until the 1948–49 season by the war and by postwar shortages of shuttlecocks.

Since that time, the game of badminton has continually grown to become one of the most popular participation sports in the world. Currently, more than two million competitive players tangle about the nets in Great Britain and more than five million compete in China. The United States Badminton Association, with some 3000 members, hopes to number more than 10,000 after the 1992 Olympics.

▼

SPECTATORS' GUIDE

Although the backyard version of badminton and the Olympic event both involve hitting a shuttlecock (the bird) over a net with a racket, the similarity ends there. Competitive badminton play is ranked as the world's fastest racket sport, featuring shuttlecocks zooming off the surface of the lightweight rackets at speeds approaching 200 miles per hour. Players require lightening-like reflexes and dexterity and the game is seldom delayed due to the bird becoming stuck in a tree or a gutter or floating in the birdbath or pond.

At its competitive level, the sport is a physically demanding contest of strategy and stamina. It has been noted in the world badminton press, never one given to hyperbole, that to excel at the highest levels of badminton, a player must have "the agility of an acrobat, the killer instinct of a panther, the accuracy of a marksman, the power of a racehorse, the speed of a sprinter, and the stamina of a marathon runner." Not to mention the wingspan of a crane, the determination of an ant, and the net play of a Jimmy Connors.

The speed is generated in part by the equipment. The shuttlecock weighs less than two ounces and is just under three inches in length. The bird is constructed of 16 goose feathers, taken from the identical wing of four different geese to ensure that the shuttle flies "true." The base from which the shuttle is struck is cork wrapped in kid leather. The accuracy and speed of the bird is paramount—hidden inside is a small metal screw that may be adjusted for weight and altitude considerations.

The racket typically weighs three to four ounces(!) and is composed of high-tech composites such as boron, fiberglass, carbon, graphite, and ceramic.

The Olympics features four badminton events: men's and ladies' singles and doubles. Courts measure 13.4 meters (44 feet) in length and 6.10 meters (20 feet) in width. For singles play, the width is narrowed to 17 feet. For doubles play, the "long" serve boundary is brought in 2.5 feet on either side. The net is 1.55 meters high (five feet in the middle, one inch higher at the posts).

All matches are played to the best two out of three games. The game is won by the player or side (doubles) first reaching 15 points, scored one at a time (with the exception of ladies' singles, in which the game is 11 points). Only the serving player or side can score; if a rally is lost by the serving player or side, it brings no change in the score but a loss of the right to serve. If the score reaches 13-all, the side having made 13 points first has the privilege of deciding whether the game shall remain at 15 or be "set" at 18; at 14-all the alternative is 15 or 17. In ladies' singles it is 11 or 12 from either 9-all or 10-all.

Serving is an important aspect of the game. During the delivery of a serve, all players must have both feet in contact with the floor. The server must not hit the shuttle from above his or her waist, and no part of the racket head may be above the hand holding it at the moment of contact. Service is diagonal, right service court to right service court (even serves) and left service court to left service court (odd serves).

Badminton strategy is similar to that of tennis. In singles, the idea is to move the opponent primarily up and back and to minimize errors. In doubles play, the game becomes a flurry of frantic energy as teams constantly reposition to either attack the opposition or repel an attack. The offensive formation places one player at the net, the other smashing from the back court. In the defensive position both players play side-by-side, each defending his or her side of the court.

▼

HOPEFULS

Guesses about who will place in the badminton events, which make their competitive Olympic debut in 1992, are flying like finely feathered shuttlecocks. The US team hopes to make an impression with 1991 National Team leaders Benny Lee and Meiling Okuno, both of whom won gold medals in singles at the 1990 US Olympic Festival. Other possible players include 1991 US Olympic gold medalists Chris Jogis for the men's team, and Linda French for the women's team.

Schedule

The tentative badminton schedule is as follows:

Tuesday, July 28
24 classification round games

Wednesday, July 29
24 classification round games

Thursday, July 30
24 classification round games

Friday, July 31
16 classification round games

Saturday, August 1
16 classification round games

Sunday, August 2
16 quarterfinal games

Monday, August 3
8 semifinal games

Tuesday, August 4
4 final games

HIGHLIGHTS

Badminton was a demonstration sport at the 1972 Games in Munich and an exhibition sport at the 1988 Games in Seoul. It makes its first appearance as a full medal sport in Barcelona.

BASEBALL

WARM-UP

After almost 90 years, baseball, a game played by an estimated 20 million people in approximately 60 countries, including the former USSR, is finally an official full-medal sport.

Baseball had been a demonstration sport in 1904 in St. Louis; in 1912 in Stockholm (where a makeshift team of US track and field athletes banded together and bombed a Swedish team, 13–3); in 1936 in Berlin (where 125,000 watched a game between two US teams); in 1952 in Helsinki; in 1956 in Melbourne; 1964 in Tokyo; 1984 in Los Angeles; and 1988 in Seoul.

Certainly, baseball has always been a gold-medal sport in the hearts of Americans, who consider it *their* game.

Though some historians give credit to Egyptians and succeeding cultures for developing some sort of precursor to what is played today, it was in America that the English game of "rounders" evolved into baseball.

The game we know—or some reasonable facsimile thereof—began in Hoboken, New Jersey, in 1846. There, umpire Alexander J. Cartwright, acting under the authority of rules he designed, supervised a game between the Knickerbockers and the New York Nine, which was won by the Nine, 23–1.

Thereon, in dribs and drabs, lurches and sprints, the game developed. Leagues sprang up, teams evolved—in Cleveland, for example, the franchise was known variously as the Forest Citys, Spiders, the Blues, Bronchos, the Naps (for Hall of Famer Napoleon Lajoie), and now, the Indians (for Native American Louis Sockalexis, a former player)—and stars were born: Babe Ruth, Mickey Mantle, Jackie Robinson, Henry Aaron ... Sadaharu Oh.

Oh? Exactly. The Japanese slugger—in the Far East a Ruth and Aaron rolled into one—played in the Japanese majors 22 years and is considered in some parts of the globe as the greatest home-run hitter ever. Aaron hit 755 home runs; Ruth hit 714; Oh had 868. It wasn't long before Oh was more than an expression of surprise to US baseball fans, who were slowly—and often reluctantly—learning that baseball wasn't just an American sport anymore.

Baseball has been played in countries such as Italy and France since World War II, when the sport was introduced by American GIs. But it wasn't until Asian Little League teams became consistent winners of the Little League World Series

199

in Williamsport, Pennsylvania, that Americans really began to take notice of the foreign participation—and competition.

Now Canadian franchises compete in the US majors. And US professionals come from hockey provinces like Saskatchewan (Terry Puhl, longtime Astros outfielder), from Nicaragua (Expos pitcher Dennis Martinez), and even from Down Under (Padres infielder Craig Shipley). Japanese pros came to America and American pros went to Japan—and then returned. (Most notably among the latter are Detroit Tigers slugger Cecil Fielder, who has played professionally in three countries: for the Toronto Blue Jays in Canada; in Japan; and now in the US for Detroit.)

Slowly but surely, with the College World Series growing into our national consciousness (mainly through ESPN telecasts) and the inclusion of baseball as a demonstration sport in the 1984 Olympics (on US turf, no less), fans also grew more aware of amateur baseball—and the dominance of the Cuban teams, peppered with older, experienced players, many of whom would have enjoyed professional careers if Cuba had allowed them to play in the US.

Even the Soviets got into the act.

"We are in kindergarten now," retired Colonel Vikton Planek, one of the five Soviet national team baseball coaches, told journalist Steve Goldstein in 1987, while watching his charges fielding some "rollings" on a hard-bitten diamond forged on a soccer field in Kiev. Western observers, Goldstein wrote, rated the team, which had been together for about a year, at "about high school level."

But progress has been made. Although the Soviet team that competed in the Intercontinental Cup in Barcelona in July, 1991, was a mish-mosh of converted wrestlers, javelin throwers, and team handball players and was terribly outclassed by teams from Cuba, Mexico, and South Korea, it had already become good enough to win the European B Cup in 1990.

The US has never excelled in international competition. It has won the Pan Am gold medal only once—in 1967—and has taken one bronze, in 1983. It won a gold medal in Seoul in 1988, but only, most agree, because Cuba boycotted the games in solidarity with North Korea, which was not awarded co-sponsorship of the Olympics with South Korea.

Still, Americans expect their teams to dominate at *their* game.

Not likely.

"What would it look like," 1992 Team USA coach Ron Fraser said before the 1991 Pan Am Game in Havana, "if we had the Olympics and baseball was a gold-medal sport for the first time and we didn't have a team?"

The US needed to finish in the top four at the Pan Am Games to qualify for the Olympics. Well, the US finished third. But Fraser's legitimate concern goes to show just how much of an international game America's pastime has become. What next?

A true *World* Series?

SPECTATORS' GUIDE

The Olympic field consists of eight teams in two four-team divisions. The tournament format is expected to be similar, if not exactly like, that at the 1984 and 1988 Games. Each division will play a round-robin, with the top two teams in each division advancing to the medal round. The first-place teams will play the second-place teams in the opposite division, with the winners playing for the gold medal. The losers will play for the bronze.

The eight-team field comprises Spain, which gets an automatic berth as the host team; the top four teams from the 1991 Pan Am Games—Cuba, Puerto Rico, the US, and the Dominican Republic; the top two teams from the Asian Games; and Italy, the winner of the European championships.

The games will be played under International Baseball Association rules, which are the same as professional rules, except that aluminum bats are allowed. The teams are limited to 20 players.

HOPEFULS

Despite being the defending gold-medal team, the US is not expected to repeat in Barcelona. Cuba, an established powerhouse in international baseball, will be the favorite.

Cuba, winner of the 1991 Pan Am medal—and winner of eight of the 11 Pan Am Games baseball gold medals—won the gold medal at the 1989 Intercontinental Cup in San Juan, Puerto Rico; the gold medal at the 1991 Goodwill Games in Seattle, Washington; and the gold medal at the 1990 World Championships in Edmonton, Alberta, Canada.

US teams finished sixth in San Juan, third in Seattle, and seventh in Edmonton.

The Cuban team, made up of players in their mid- to late-20s (with a few thirtysomethings) is led by third baseman Omar Linares, who has been playing for the Cuban national team for about six years—since he was 17. According to professional scouts, Linares would surely be playing in the major leagues if Cuba allowed its players to participate professionally.

Although many of the Team USA players will be unfamiliar to most sports fans, the team should provide a glimpse of future professionals. Eleven of the 20 players on the 1984 team were among the first 17 players selected in that year's major league draft.

Team USA coach Fraser is the coach at the University of Miami and enjoys the best win record among active college coaches.

Ninety players were invited to tryouts in November, 1991, at the Homestead, Florida, Sports Complex. The number will be trimmed to 40 for additional tryouts in Millington, Tennessee, in June, 1992. From those, a team of 25 will be selected, later to be trimmed to 20.

Some names to watch: Chris Roberts, 20, an outfielder/pitcher from Florida State; Jeffrey Hammonds, 20, an outfielder from Stanford; and Charles Johnson, 20, a catcher from the University of Miami.

Schedule

The tentative baseball schedule is as follows:

Sunday, July 26
4 games, preliminaries

Monday, July 27
4 games, preliminaries

Tuesday, July 28
4 games, preliminaries

Wednesday, July 29
4 games, preliminaries

Friday, July 31
4 games, preliminaries

Saturday, August 1
4 games, preliminaries

Sunday, August 2
4 games, preliminaries

Tuesday, August 4
2 games, semifinals

Wednesday, August 5
1 game, semifinals (3rd & 4th places)
1 game, final

▼

HIGHLIGHTS

Ex-Olympians who have gone on to the majors include Will "The Thrill" Clark, first baseman for the San Francisco Giants; Andy Benes, starting pitcher for the San Diego Padres; Cincinnati Reds shortstop Barry Larkin; Minnesota Twins outfielder Shane Mack; Cleveland Indians pitcher Greg Swindell; and California Angels lefty Jim Abbott, who won the gold-medal game against Japan for Team USA in Seoul.

Jim Abbott

The Olympics aren't just about sports. Equally important are such things as desire and politics and national pride and individuals struggling to overcome impossible odds. And those are the things that came together at Seoul in 1988 for an extraordinary young man named Jim Abbott.

National pride was on the line. The American baseball team had been defeated by Japan at the 1984 Games in Los Angeles—a shocking, almost unbelievable upset. The 1988 Olympics provided the perfect showcase for revenge: the US would meet Japan once again for the gold medal, the final game to be pitched by Abbott.

The game was dramatic and filled with suspense. Abbott pitched the full nine innings and made a spectacular fielding play in the bottom of the eighth inning to kill a rally by Japan. The Americans came away with a 5–3 victory and Abbott was the hero of the day, swarmed by his team in an exuberant post-game celebration. He was awarded the 1988 Sullivan Award as the outstanding amateur athlete in the United States.

The Olympics capped an impressive amateur baseball career for the then 21-year-old Flint, Michigan, native. He was a Little League standout who threw a no-hitter in his first game, led his high school baseball, basketball, and football teams, and starred as a pitcher for the University of Michigan. While in college, he was selected for Team USA and became the first US pitcher to beat the Cuban team in Cuba in 25 years, helping the team win a silver medal in 1987.

After his gold-medal performance in the Olympics, Abbott was drafted in the first round by the California Angels in 1988. He has been a steady performer with the Angels, sporting a very creditable 14–8 record toward the end of the 1991 season (sixth in the American League), with an impressive 2.95 earned run average.

Just one of the amazing things about Abbott is the fact that he was born with no right hand. He refers to this as a "situation" but never a handicap. As he says: "Growing up, I always pictured myself as a baseball player, but I can't remember how many hands I had in my dreams."

Abbott was born September 19, 1967, the son of Mike (a beer distributor sales manager) and Laura (an attorney) Abbott. From the beginning his parents stressed that Jim could do anything he wanted to do. What he wanted to do was play baseball.

He spent countless hours throwing a ball against a brick wall perfecting the move that allows him to field his position: he balances his glove on his right wrist, throws left-handed, slips on the glove in his follow-through, and is ready to field. It works so well that, watching him from a distance, it's practically impossible to tell he's one-handed; and, as many batters have found out, it's nearly impossible to bunt your way on base with Jim Abbott on the mound.

As former California Angels manager Doug Rader puts it: "Jim is the most unhandicapped person I know. He's a singular human being." —E.K.

BASKETBALL

WARM-UP

The legend of Dr. James A. Naismith and his two peach baskets is fairly well known. In 1891, Naismith was given an assignment to devise an indoor game for a group of students at the International YMCA Training College (now Springfield College) in Springfield, Massachusetts.

After some brainstorming, Naismith derived the concept for a game that would not involve physical contact (basketball irony). After drawing up 13 rules—many of which are still in effect—he organized the first game on January 20, 1892. He nailed two peach baskets on opposite ends of the YMCA balcony, 10 feet high, and divided up the 18 students into two teams of nine each. With the aid of a soccer ball, the first basketball game was played.

And sports history was made.

Although Naismith was born and educated in Canada, basketball is the only major game created in the US without roots deriving from another sport. At the turn of the century, basketball was well on its way to becoming a popular sport. The Organizing Committee for the 1904 St. Louis Games made it a demonstration sport, as did the Olympic committees in Paris (1924) and Amsterdam (1928). But Los Angeles, site of the 1932 Olympics, ignored basketball. The rejection of basketball on the sport's native turf galvanized basketball's proponents (which included the NCAA) into pushing for a 1936 Olympic berth in Berlin.

In 1936, playing outdoors due to a lack of indoor facilities, the US prevailed and won the gold, beginning a 50-year stretch of Olympic game dominance. The first Olympic tournament was an interesting one: due to disqualifications and controversy resulting from the semi-professionalism of many US players, the US actually sent two teams: one from Universal movie studio and another known as the McPherson Globe Oilers. Universal played in games one and three and was to play the championship game, but a prior game was canceled, allowing McPherson to represent the US in the finals. McPherson/US defeated Canada, 19–8 in a driving rainstorm that filled the court with water and made dribbling impossible. Only two baskets were scored for each team in the last half on the gravel court.

Although the USA men have captured the gold in nine of 11 Olympics, in recent years the pickings have been slimmer. The USA missed the gold at the 1987 Pan Am Games, the 1988 Seoul Olympics, the 1990 Goodwill Games, and the 1991 Havana Pan Am Games. All of these defeats were sustained by a group of college players against older international athletes. To offset this advantage, US professional players will be allowed to participate (along with top collegiate stars) in 1992. This, by the way, is not the first US basketball squad to include professionals, but will be the first in which the team has to qualify to play in the Olympics. A cast of Magic Johnson, Michael Jordan, and other NBA greats should be fun to watch as they take on the world.

Women's basketball was added as a medal sport in 1976, and the US team has dominated, grabbing the gold in the last two Olympics.

▼

SPECTATORS' GUIDE

For the men's tournament, 12 teams qualify, evenly divided into two groups of six teams. Automatic berths are awarded to the first and second place finisher from the last Olympics (the Soviet Union and Yugoslavia) as well as the host country.

In the preliminary round robin, each country will play the other five teams in its bracket, with the top four clubs of each group advancing to the next round.

In the quarterfinals, each division winner will be matched against the fourth-place finisher of the other division, and the two second-place teams will cross over to face the third-place finishers.

The four survivors qualify for the semifinals, with the winners of the games involving the two divisional leaders from the preliminaries being paired against the winners of the second-third place showdowns.

The two countries winning these games meet for the championship and the two losers play for the bronze.

In the women's tournament, six countries compete in a straight round robin (five games for each team). The gold-medal winner from the last Olympics and the host country are assured berths. Should the top two teams of the tournament wind up with the same won-lost records, the gold medal is awarded to the winner of their head-to-head meeting.

International rules vary somewhat from National Basketball Association regulations:

Time: A 30-second time clock (rather than a 24-second) is in effect, during which span an offensive team must attempt a shot. Generally, in international play a game consists of two 20-minute periods. Each team receives two one-minute timeouts per half. In the event of a tie at the end of regulation, the game resumes with a five-minute overtime following a two-minute break. Each team receives one time-out during an overtime period.

Throw-ins: A recent rule change requires the official to handle the ball for all sideline throw-ins that are made from the backcourt. Formerly, the official didn't handle the ball on backcourt violations, such as traveling.

Fouling: The eighth team foul in each half, and all succeeding ones, will result in two free throws for the other team. The individual foul limit is five. No shots are awarded on offensive fouls.

Substitution: Substitution rules are somewhat different from the pro and college game. On a possession after a violation, the offense may substitute, and the defense may substitute only if the offense substitutes. After successful free throws, the shooter may be replaced if requested prior to the first free throw. The opponent is allowed on substitute if requested before the last free throw.

Lanes: The lanes on an international court flare out more deeply and are not box-like as in the US, creating more opportunities for three-second violations and driving lay-ups, since the lane is less congested.

Three-point play: Olympic marksmen shoot from a distance roughly midway between those of the college and professional sports. The three-point distance in the international game is a little over 20.5 feet, or 6.25 meters, compared to 23 feet, nine inches in the NBA (at the top of the key) and the NCAA's 19 feet, nine inches.

▼

HOPEFULS

Men's Basketball: The battle between the American and Soviet world powers is sure to be fierce at Barcelona this summer. The Soviet men, who won the Olympic gold the only two years the Americans didn't, will fight to keep their Olympic title in 1992. And the American men, fortified by the addition of professional basketball players to their Olympic roster, plan to win back the gold and their honor.

America has been humiliated in recent years by the performance of their national amateur team, which must compete in world competitions against teams generally comprised of professional-calibre players. The country's embarrassment is largely exaggerated; although the USA hasn't won a major event since the 1986 World Championships, they've still won medals, including the 1988 Olympic silver, the 1990 Goodwill Games silver, and the 1991 Pan Am bronze. But with a 12-man Olympic team composed of at least 10 professional players, led by Chuck Daly—coach of the two-time NBA championship Detroit Pistons—the USA fully expects to regain its status in 1992 as the greatest basketball playing nation in the world.

Such an expectation may be a bit overzealous, since a collection of star players does not necessarily yield a stellar team, but the results will be riveting when several of America's best hit the court. In September, 1991, 10 of the 12 Olympic players were named, including superstar Michael Jordan, who led the Bulls to their 1991 NBA championship and is a veteran of the USA's 1983 gold-medal Pan Am team and 1984 gold-medal Olympic team.

The USA's other guards are Los Angeles Laker Magic Johnson, Chris Mullin of the Golden State Warriors, and John Stockton of the Utah Jazz. (Notably missing—amid controversy—is Detroit Piston Isiah Thomas, considered one of the best point guards in professional basketball; reasons for the omission range from his rocky relationship with Jordan to a simple lack of space for all the great and deserving pros.) Centers will be Patrick Ewing of the New York Knicks and David Robinson of the San Antonio Spurs. Philadelphia 76er Charles Barkley, Boston Celtic Larry Bird, Utah Jazz player Karl Malone, and Chicago's Scottie Pippen will be the team's forwards. Two players remained unnamed in September, leaving space for at least one amateur player and possibly another professional player (perhaps Thomas?).

Women's Basketball: The US women's basketball team, considered the best in the world, is expected to retain its two-time Olympic championship status at Barcelona. The USA has dominated women's basketball during the 1980s, with a 42-game winning streak in international competition that began after the Americans' last loss in 1982—to the Soviets in the finals of the World Championships—and ended in 1991 when they lost to Puerto Rico in a Pan Am showdown, settling for a bronze. Olympic success seems certain with veteran coach Theresa Grentz of Rutgers University, who coached the team as they swept undefeated through the 1990 World Championships and Goodwill Games, and a mixture of enthusiastic new talent and seasoned veterans, including two-time Olympians Teresa Edwards and Lynette Woodard and 1988 Olympian Katrina McClain.

Chuck Daly

He is known in Detroit as the Prince of Pessimism. The slogan that instructs his life is: "Don't trust happiness." And yet Chuck Daly, coach of the US Olympic basketball team, says flatly, "I expect to come back from Barcelona with the gold medal."

Daly was named to the position after guiding the Detroit Pistons to consecutive National Basketball Association championships. The selection committee said he was picked because he had demonstrated an ability to win at all levels of competition. But he may find that pessimism is the reasonable frame of mind to carry into the task ahead of him.

For the first time, the professional superstars of the NBA are eligible for the games. So Daly is faced with the job of melding some of the largest egos in athletics into a cohesive team.

Moreover, he is not the only one who anticipates gold at Barcelona. Americans always expect their basketball team to carry off the Olympic gold. When they fail, it is regarded as a national embarrassment, if not a scandal.

Since 1936, when basketball was admitted to the Olympics, American teams have lost a total of two games, both of them to the Soviet Union. In the 1972 finals, the actions of the officials, who seemingly made blatantly favorable calls for the Soviets in the last few seconds, caused an international furor. And in 1988, a decisive loss in the semifinals sustained by an American team that lacked consistent outside scoring, brought down a torrent of criticism on coach John Thompson's selection process.

Now it is Daly's turn in the fire. It is recognized that America's success in the games is no longer a matter of course. European teams have achieved tremendous advances in basketball. Professional leagues thrive in several countries and the game is followed avidly. But with the players at his disposal, Daly is not only expected to win but to win easily.

"Losing is not going to enter my mind," he says. "There will be pressure to win and I can accept the fact. Every one of the guys we play will not only have super physical ability but superior intelligence as far as basketball is concerned. I have every confidence that these guys can handle any challenge."

"There is going to be a lot more to this than playing the games. I'm looking forward to all phases of it. There's going to be a selling job. I'm going to have to ask some of the greatest players in the world to give up playing time to somebody else. But that's nothing new for an NBA coach. I have no doubts regarding the commitment of the players. Many of them told me that the thought of playing for their country is still something they get excited about."

That's what Daly says publicly. What he really thinks may be far less upbeat.

The clash of personalities, the fragile balancing of a dozen huge talents, the adjustment of men who make millions of dollars a year—and live like it—to the comfort level of amateur athletes is not going to be anybody's cakewalk.

Some of his players behave as if they believe their own commercials. Some of them absolutely detest each other. Yet their talents are regarded as so superior to any other country's collection of players that losing is inconceivable. If they do lose, it will be humiliating for both Daly and the NBA. That's a load to live with.

Daly calls himself "a lifer" in basketball.

"I'm very happy that I'll be representing all the coaches in this country who are lifers. This game has been a way of life for me. It is what I always wanted to do."

He has done very well at it, too. Starting as a high school coach in Kane, Pennsylvania, he worked his way up through seven years at the University of Pennsylvania, a brief and unsuccesful stint with Cleveland and an assistant's job with Philadelphia before landing in Detroit as head coach in 1983. The Pistons had never experienced two consecutive winning seasons in Detroit. But Daly took them to the division finals in four years, the championship round in five and the NBA title in six.

209

His emphasis on grinding defense has not been universally popular in the NBA. His Pistons teams were known as the "Bad Boys" and some of their members among the most hated individuals in the game's history. Eventually, however, his defensive style was copied by other successful teams and Daly was credited with changing the face of professional basketball.

He is known as a man with a wry, self-deprecating sense of humor and a wardrobe out of *Gentleman's Quarterly*. The players call him "Daddy Rich" and his clothes closet reputedly extends beyond the county line. But his defining genius with the Pistons is generally recognized as being in the same area that will test him with the Olympic team—handling disparate personalities and making them work as a team.

Even his players in Detroit feel that he is up to the job.

"He is definitely a players' coach and whoever goes with that team, they are going to like playing for him," says Piston Mark Aguirre.

"He will bring an easy atmosphere and just go out there and let you do your job," echoes teammate Dennis Rodman. "He lets us be men, and he doesn't try to break us down and say: 'You do this and you do that.' With the Olympic team, he will let the guys be men and let the players play."

That sort of review would make any coach happy. But it's unlikely that Chuck Daly will put his trust in that particular emotion until the medals are handed out in Barcelona. —*G.C.*

Schedule

The tentative basketball schedule is as follows:

Sunday, July 26
6 games, preliminaries, men

Monday, July 27
6 games, preliminaries, men

Wednesday, July 29
6 games, preliminaries, men

Thursday, July 30
4 games, preliminaries, women

Friday, July 31
6 games, preliminaries, men

Saturday, August 1
4 games, preliminaries, women

Sunday, August 2
6 games, preliminaries, men

Monday, August 3
4 games, preliminaries, women

Tuesday, August 4
2 games, classification, men
4 games, quarterfinals, men

Wednesday, August 5
2 games, classification
2 games, semifinals, women

Thursday, August 6
2 games, placing matches (9th-12th places), men
2 games, classification
2 games, semifinals, men

Friday, August 7
2 games, final matches (3rd-6th places), women
1 game, final match (7th & 8th places)
1 game, final, women

Emphasizing defense, Chuck Daly expects to coach the US Olympic basketball team back to a gold medal in Barcelona. When not an Olympian, he coaches the NBA's Detroit Pistons.

An All-American basketball player at Princeton, Bill Bradley was a member of the 1964 US Olympic team that earned a gold medal in Tokyo. He later joined the NBA's New York Knicks, and is currently a US senator and possible presidential hopeful.

1 game, final match (7th & 8th
places)
1 game, final, men

▼

HIGHLIGHTS

For years the US men's basketball team has dominated Olympic competition, ever since its introduction to the Games in 1936. The exception was in Munich, in 1972, when dubious officiating gave the gold to the Soviet team. The USA refused the silver, and Cuba took the bronze. The first women's games were played at the Montréal Olympics in 1976; the US took a silver medal behind the Soviet women that year, with Bulgaria claiming the bronze medal. In the 1980 games—boycotted by the US and other Western nations—Yugoslavia, always a contender, captured the men's gold, and the Soviet team had to settle for a bronze behind Italy. Soviet women were able to bring in the gold in 1980 ahead of Bulgaria and Yugoslavia.

At the Los Angeles Games in 1984 basketball was a monotonous string of victories for the American teams. Spain played to the men's silver, led by Juan Antonio San Epifanio. Yugoslavia took the 1984 men's bronze. In 1984 the American men beat their opponents by an average margin of 32; the women by 33. American women Cheryl Miller and Lynette Woodard stood out among the women's teams; the Republic of Korea took the silver medal and Canada the bronze. In 1988 the Central African Republic fielded a team for the first time, and were jubilant when they beat South Korea. The Soviet men's team again captured the gold in 1988, Yugoslavia the silver, and the US settled for bronze. For the women, USA took the 1988 gold ahead of Yugoslavia and the Soviet Union.

Congressional Olympians

Two of the three former Olympians currently serving in Congress are pretty well known.

Senator Bill Bradley (D–New Jersey), elected to Congress in 1978, played on the 1964 gold-medal basketball team in Tokyo. Bradley, 48, a three-time All-American at Princeton and a Rhodes scholar, went on to play for the NBA New York Knicks. He averaged 10.1 points per game for the US team in 1964.

Bradley serves on the Energy and Natural Resources, Finance, Intelligence, and Aging committees in Washington and has been mentioned as a future presidential candidate. In fact, as early as 1964, when Bradley was still at Princeton, Leonard Shecter of the *New York Post* began a column this way: "In twenty-five years or so our presidents are going to have to be better than ever. It's nice to know that Bill Bradley will be available."

Representative Tom McMillen (D–Maryland), elected in 1986, boasts some of the same credentials. McMillen, 39, averaged 7.6 points and 4.3 rebounds for the 1972 silver-medal team that suffered that crushing, controversial last-second defeat to the Soviets, 51–50, in Munich. He played collegiately at Maryland, was a Rhodes scholar, and played an 11-year NBA career with Buffalo, New York, Atlanta, and Washington. He serves on the Energy and Commerce and Science, Space and Technology committees. He, like Bradley, has been outspoken on athletic reforms for college sports.

The third ex-Olympian on Capitol Hill—and the least famous—is Representative Ben Nighthorse Campbell (D–Colorado), also elected in 1986.

Campbell, a member of the Black Belt Hall of Fame in Burbank, California, and the only Native American in Congress, captained the 1964—and first—US Olympic judo team.

And he's been quite the newsmaker recently.

Campbell, who serves on the Agriculture and Interior and Insular Affairs committees and whose great-grandfather fought at the Battle of the Little Bighorn—Custer's last stand—has led the charge to rename the Custer Battlefield National Monument in Montana, the site of the battle, its new designation would be renamed the Little Bighorn Battlefield National Monument. It's an effort aimed at honoring the Native American warriors as well as the soldiers. "It's now time to tell the world that we made a mistake in denying American Indians equal and fair honor on the battlefield," Campbell says.

Campbell, 58, also made the news in March, 1991, when he fought off a mugger while returning to his Capitol Hill apartment from a nearby grocery store. When the mugger warned he was wielding a .45, Campbell answered, "Let's see it." When the thug came up empty, Campbell dusted off his chops—the martial arts variety.

Sort of.

"I found out in one fell swoop that I wasn't a 28-year-old judo champ anymore," said Campbell, who chased off, and after, the mugger, tearing some ankle ligaments in the process. "I found out I'm a 58-year-old out-of-shape congressman. But he didn't get my peanut butter and jelly."

Then, in May, 1991, Campbell finally received his high school diploma—40 years after his class had graduated. The teenage Campbell dropped out of Placer High in Auburn, California, his hometown, joined the Air Force, passed a high school equivalency test, and went on to earn a bachelor's degree at San Jose State University.

"There's been something missing," Campbell said.

He wasn't talking about a gold medal. *E.K.*

Basketball — Men's Team

1988 1. Soviet Union, A. Belostennyi, Valeri
Goborov, V. Khomitchious, R.
Kourtinaitis, R-CMartchioulenis, Igor
Migliniex, V. Pankrachkine, A. Sabonis,
Tilt Sokk, S. Tarakanov, V.
Tikhonenko, A. Volkov
2. Yugoslavia, Franjo Arapovic, Zoran
Cutura, D. Cvjeticanin, Vlade Divac,
Toni Kukoc, Z. Obradovic, Zarko
Paspalj, Drazen Petrovic, Dino Radja,
Z. Radulovic, S. Vrankovic, Jurij Zdovc
3. U.S.A., Willie Anderson, Stacey
Augmon, Vernell Coles, Jeffrey
Grayer, Hersey Hawkins, Dan Majerle,
Danny Manning, Herman "J.R." Reid,
Mitch Richmond, David Robinson,
Charles D. Smith, Charles E. Smith IV

1984 1. U.S.A., Steve Alford, Leon Wood,
Patrick Ewing, Vern Fleming, Alvin
Robertson, Michael Jordan, Joseph
Kleine, Jon Koncak, Wayman Tisdale,
Chris Mullin, Samuel Perkins, Jeffrey
Turner
2. Spain, Jose Manuel Beiran, Jose Luis
Llorente, Fernando Arcega, Jose
Maria Margall, Andres Jimenez, Juan
Antonio San Epifanio, Fernando
Romay, Fernando Martin, Juan Antonio
Corbalan, Ignacio Solozabal, Juan
Domingo de la Cruz, Juan Maria
Lopez I
3. Yugoslavia, Drazan Petrovic, Aleksandr
Petrovic, Nibojsa Zorkic, Rajko Zizic,
Ivan Sunara, Emir Mitapcic, Sabit
Hadzic, Andro Knego, RAtko
Radovanovic, Mihovil Nakic-Vojnovic,
Drazen Dalipagic, Branko Vukicevic

1980 1. Yugoslavia, Andro Knego, Dragan
Kicanovic, Rajko Zizic, Mihoril Nakic,
Zeljko Jerkov, Branko Skroce, Zoran
Slavnic, Kresimir Cosic, Ratko
Radovanovic, Duje Krstulovic, Drazen
Dalipagic, Mirza Delibasic
2. Italy, Romeo Sachetti, Roberto
Brunamonti, Michael Silvester, Enrico
Gilardi, Fabrizio DellaFiori, Marco
Solfrini, Marco Bonamico, Dino
Meneghin, Renato Villalta, Renzo
Vecchiato, Pierluigi Marzorati, Pietro
Generali
3. Soviet Union, Stanislav Eremin, Valeri
Miloserdov, Sergei Tarakanov,
Aleksandr Salinikov, Andrey Lopatov,
Nikolai Deruguin, Sergei Belov,
Vladimir Tkachenko, Anatoli Myshkin,
Sergei Yovaysha, Aleksandr
Belostenny, Vladimir Zhiguily

1976 1. U.S.A., Phil Ford, Steven Sheppard,
Adrian Dantley, Walter Davis, Quinn
Buckner, Mitchell Kupchak, Ernie
Grunfeld, Kenneth Carr, Scott May,
Mike Armstrong, Thomas LaGarde,
Philip Hubbard

2. Yugoslavia, Blagoje Georgijevski,
Dragan Kicanovic, Vinko Jelovac,
Rajko Zizic, Zeljko Jerkov, Andro
Knego, Zoran Slavnic, Kresimir Cosic,
Damir Solman, Zarko Varajic, Drazen
Dalipagic, Mirza Delibasic
3. Soviet Union, Vladimir Arzamaskov,
Aleksandr Salnikov, Valery Miloserdov,
Alshan Sharmukhamedov, Andrei
Makeev, Ivan Edeshko, Sergei Belov,
Vladimir Tkachenko, Anatoly Myshkin,
Mikhail Korkiya, Aleksandr Belov,
Vladimir Zhigily

1972 1. Soviet Union, Anatoli Polivoda,
Modestas Paulauskas, Zurab
Sakandelidze, Alshan
Sharmukhamedov, Aleksandr Boloshev,
Ivan Edeshko, Sergei Belov, Mishako
Korkia, Ivan Dvorni, Gennady Volnov,
Aleksandr Belov, Sergei Kovalenko
2. U.S.A., Kenneth Davis, Douglas Collins,
Thomas Henderson, Michael Bantom,
Robert Jones, Dwight Jones, James
Forbes, James Brewer, Tommy
Burleson, Thomas McMillen, Kevin
Joyce, Ed Ratleff
3. Cuba, Juan Domecq, Ruperto Herrera,
Juan Roca, Pedro Chappe, Jose M.
Alvarez Pozo, Rafael Canizares,
Conrado Perez, Miguel Calderon,
Tomas Herrera, Oscar Varona,
Alejandro Urgelles, Franklin Standard

1968 1. U.S.A., John Clawson, Ken Spain,
Joseph White, Michael Barrett,
Spencer Haywood, Charles Scott, Bill
Hoskett, Calvin Fowler, Michael
Silliman, Glynn Saulters, James King,
Donald Dee
2. Yugoslavia, Aljosa Zorga, Radivoje
Korac, Zoran Maroevic, Trajko
Rajkovic, Vladimir Cvetkovic, Dragoslav
Raznatovic, Ivo Daneu, Kresmir Cosic,
Damir Solman, Nikola Plecas, Dragutin
Cermak, Peter Skansi
3. Soviet Union, Anatoli Krikun, Modestas
Paulauskas, Zurab Sakandelidze,
Vadim Kapranov, Yuri Selikhov,
Anatoli Polivoda, Sergei Belov, Priit
Tomson, Sergei Kovalenko, Gennady
Volnov, Yaak Lipso, Vladimir Andreyev

1964 1. U.S.A., Jim Barnes, William Bradley,
Lawrence Brown, Joe Caldwell, Mel
Counts, Richard Davies, Walter
Hazzard, Lucius Jackson, John
McCaffrey, Jeffry Mullins, Jerry Ship,
George Wilson
2. Soviet Union, Valdis Muischnieks,
Nikolai Bagley, Armenak Alachachyan,
Aleksandr Travin, Vyacheslav Khrynin,
Yanis Kruminsch, Levan Mosechvili,
Yuri Korneyev, Aleksandr Petrov,
Gennady Voinov, Yaak Lipso, Yuris
Kaininsch

Basketball

213

3. Brazil, Amaury A. Pasos, Wlamir Marques, Ubiratan Pereira Maciel, Carlos Domingos Massoni, Friedrich Wilhelm Braun, Carmo de Souza, Jatyr Eduardo Schall, Edson Bispo dos Santos, Antonio Salvador Sucar, Victor Mirshawka, Sergio de Toledo Machado, Jose Edvar Simoes

1960 1. U.S.A., Jay Arnette, Walter Bellamy, Robert Boozer, Terry Dischinger, Burdette Haldorson, Darall Imhoff, Allen Kelley, Lester Lane, Jerry Lucas, Oscar Robertson, Adrian Smith, Jerry West

2. Soviet Union, Yuri Korneyev, Yanis Kruminsch, Guram Minaschvill, Valdis Muischnieks, Cesar Ozers, Aleksandr Petrov, Mikhail Semyonov, Vladimir Ugrekhelidze, Maigonis Valdmanis, Albert Valtin, Gennady Volnov, Viktor Zubkov

3. Brazil, Edson Bispo Dos Santos, Moyses Blas, Waldemar Blatkauskas, Zenny De Azevedo, Carmo De Souza, Carlos Domingos Massoni, Waldyr Geraldo Boccardo, Wlamir Marques, Amaury Antonio Pasos, Fernando Pereira De Freitas, Antonio Salvador Sucar, Jatyr Eduardo Schall

1956 1. U.S.A., Carl C. Cain, William Hougland, K.C. Jones, William Russell, James P. Walsh, William Evans, Burdette Haldorson, Ronald Tomsic, Richard J. Boushka, Gilbert Ford, Robert E. Jeangerard, Charles F. Darling

2. Soviet Union, Valdis Muischnieks, Maigonis Valdmanis, Vladimir Torban, Stassis Stonkus, Kazis Petkyavichus, Arkady Bochkaryov, Yanis Kruminsch, Mikhail Semyonov, Algirdas Lauritenas, Yuri Ozerov, Viktor Zubkov, Mikhail Studenetsky

3. Uruguay, Carlos Blixen, Ramiro Cortes, Hector Costa, Nelson Chelle, Nelson Demarco, Hector Garcia Otero, Carlos Gonzalez, Sergio Matto, Oscar Moglia, Raul Mera, Ariel Olascoaga, Milton Scaron

1952 1. U.S.A., Charles Hoag, William Hougland, Melvin D. Kelley, Robert Kenney, Clyde Lovellette, Marcus Frieberger, Victor W. Glasgow, Frank McCabe, Daniel Pippin, Howard Williams, Ronald Bontemps, Robert Kurland, William Lienhard, John Keller

2. Soviet Union, Viktor Vlassov, Styapas Butautas, Yvan Lysov, Kazis Petkyavichus, Nodar Dshordshikiya, Anatoli Konyev, Otar Korkiya, Ilmar Kullam, Yuri Ozerov, Aleksandr Moiseyev, Heino Kruus, Yustinas Lagunavichus, Maigonis Vladmanis, Stassis Stonkus

3. Uruguay, Martin Acosta y Lara, Enrique Balino, Victorio Cieslinskas, Hector Costa, Nelson Demarco, Hector Garcia Otero, Roberto Lovera, Adesio Lombardo, Tabare Larre, Borges, Sergio Matto, Wilfredo Pelaez, Carlos Rossello

1948 1. U.S.A., Clifford Barker, Donald Barksdale, Ralph Beard, Lewis Beck, Vincent Boryla, Gordon Carpenter, Alex Groza, Wallace Jones, Robert Kurland, Raymond Lumpp, Robert Pitts, Jesse Renick, Robert Robinson, Kenneth Rollins

2. France, Andre Barrais, Michel Bonnevie, Andre Buffiere, Rene Chocat, Rene Derency, Maurice Desaymonnet, Andre Even, Maurice Girardot, Fernand Guillou, Raymond Offner, Jacques Perrier, Yvan Quenin, Lucien Rebuffie, Pierre Thiolon

3. Brazil, Zenny De Azevedo, Joao Francisco Braz, Marcus Vinicius Dias, Affonso Azevedo Evora, Ruy De Freitas, Alexandre Gemignani, Alberto Marson, Alfredo Rodrigues Da Motta, Nilton Pacheco De Oliveira, Massinet Sorcinelli

1936 1. U.S.A., Ralph Bishop, Joe Fortenberry, Carl S. Knowles, Jack W. Ragland, Carl Shy, William Wheatly, Francis Johnson, Sam Balter, John H. Gibbons, Frank J. Lubin, Arthur O. Mollner, Donald A. Piper, Duane A. Swanson, Willard Schmidt

2. Canada, Gordon Aitchison, Jan Allison, Arthur Chapman, Charles Chapman, Douglas Peden, James Stewart, Malcolm Wiseman, Edward J. Dawson, Irving Meretsky

3. Mexico, Carlos Borja Morca, Victor H. Borja Morca, Raul Fernandez Robert, Francisco Martinez Cordero, Dr. Jesus Olmos Moreno, Greer Skousen Spilsbury, Luis I. de la Vega Leija, Rodolfo Choperena Irizarri, Jose Pamplona Lecuanda, Andres Gomez Dominguez, Silvio Hermandez del Valle

1904 1. U.S.A., A. W. Manweiler, A. A. Heerdt, G. L. Redlein, William Rhode, Ed Miller, Charles Monahan

2. U.S.A., J. A. Jardine, Axel Berggien, John Schominer, M. B. Indarius, Carl Watson, W. K. Armstrong, W. A. Williams, Seth Collins

3. U.S.A., James Donovan, C. B. Cleveland, James Kenny, J. S. Smith, J. Leitz, Frnak Craven, E. J. Koche, W. Herschel

1896-
1900 **Not held**

Basketball — Women's Team

1988 1. U.S.A., Teresa Edwards, Mary "Kamie" Ethridge, Cynthia Brown, Anne Donovan, Teresa Weatherspoon, Bridgette Gordon, Vicky Bullett, Andrea Lloyd, Katrina McClain, Jennifer Gillom, Cynthia Cooper, Suzie McConnell

2. Yugoslavia, A. Arbutina, Vesna Bajkusa, Polona Dornik, Sladjana Golic, K. Kvesic, Mara Lakic, Zana Lelas, B. Milosevic, R. Mujanovic, Danira Nakic, S. Vangelovska, Eleonora Wild

214

3. Soviet Union, Olessia Barel, Olga Bouriakina, Olga Evkova, Irina Guerlits, Olga Lakovleva, E. Khoudachova, A. Leonova, Irina Minkh, G. Savitskaia, I. Soumnikova, V. Touomaite, N. Zassoulskaia

1984 1. U.S.A., Teresa Edwards, Lea Henry, Lynette Woodard, Anne Donovan, Cathy Boswell, Cheryl Miller, Janice Lawrence, Cindy Noble, Kim Mulkey, Denise Curry, Pamela McGee, Carol Menken-Schaudt
2. Republic of Korea, Aei-Young Choi, Yang-Gae Park, Eun-Sook Kim, Kyung-Sook Lee, Kyung-Hee Choi, Mi-Ja Lee, Kyung-Ja Moon, Hwa-Soon Kim, Myung-Hee Jeong, Young-Hee Kim, Jung-A Sung, Chan-Sook Park
3. Canada, Lynn Poison, Tracie McAra, Anna Pendergast, Debbie Huband, Carol Jane Sealey, Alison Lang, Bev Smith, Sylvia Sweeney, Candi Clarkson-Lohr, Toni Kordic, Andrea Blackwell, Misty Thomas, Don McCrae

1980 1. Soviet Union, Angele Rupshene, Lyubov Sharmay, Vida Besselene, Olga Korosteleva, Tatiana Ovevhkina, Nadezhda Olkhova, Iuliyana Semenova, Lyudmila Rogozina, Nelly Feriabnikova, Olga Sukharnova, Tatiana Nadyrova, Tatiana Ivinskaya

2. Bulgaria, Nadka Golcheva, Penka Metodieva, Petkana Makaveeva, Snezhana Mihailova, Vania Dermandzhieva, Krassimira Bogdanova, Angelina Mihailova, Diana Brainova, Evladia Zakatanova, Kostadinka Radkova, Silvia Germanova, Penka Stoyanova
3. Yugoslavia, Vera Djuraskovic, Mersada Becirspahic, Jelica Komnenovic, Mira Bjedov, Vukica Mitic, Sanja Ozegovic, Sofija Pekic, Marija Tonkovic, Zorica Djurkovic, Vesna Despotovic, Biljana Majstorovic, Jasmina Perazic

1976 1. Soviet Union, Angele Rupshene, Tatyana Zakharova, Raisa Kurvyakova, Olga Barisheva, Tatyana Ovechkina, Nadezhda Shubaeva, Iuliyana Semenova, Nadezhda Zakharova, Nelly Feriabnikova, Olga Sukharnova, Tamara Daunene, Natalya Klimova
2. U.S.A., Cindy Brogdon, Susan Rojcewicz, Ann Meyers, Luisa Harris, Nancy Dunkle, Charlotte Lewis, Nancy Liebermann, Gail Marquis, Patricia Roberts, Mary Anne O'Connor, Patricia Head, Julienne Simpson
3. Bulgaria, Nadka Golcheva, Penka Metodieva, Petkana Makaveeva, Snezhana Mihailova, Krassima Gyurova, Krassimira Bogdanova, Todorka Yordanova, Diania Dilova, Margarita Shturkelova, Maria Stoyanova, Girgina Skerlatova, Penka Stoyanova

BOXING

WARM-UP

As long as people have held sway on the planet, they've employed fighting and fisticuffs as a means of settling debates. Boxing as an Olympic sport was introduced in 688 BC, during the 23rd Ancient Olympiad (the event in 776 BC is considered the first). The boxers wore headgear and wrapped their fists with long leather thongs known as *caestus* to protect their hands and increase the power of their punches. The fights were not divided into rounds; the boxers fought until one combatant dropped or conceded by raising a fist in the air.

Hard leather gloves, with cutting edges, later replaced the thongs. The Romans introduced a more brutal aspect to the sweet science, as boxers used gloves studded with spikes, knots, nails, and/or bits of metal. A fight often ended with a death, which is how many Roman events ended.

Famous boxers of the very distant past include Theagenes from Thassos, who won the boxing event during the 75th Olympiad in 480 BC, the boxing and pancratium (a combination of boxing and wrestling) events during the 76th and 77th Olympiads, and the boxing, pancratium, and wrestling events in the 78th games. Cleitomachus from Thebes, a famous boxer and pancratist, won both events during the 141st Olympiad in 216 BC. Another boxer of the period, Melagomas from Caria, Asia Minor, forced his opponents to admit their defeat without blows being exchanged, because, he said, "to hit, to wound and be wounded was not bravery." Mentally intimidated, his opponents would admit defeat and withdraw. Current ring psychology still draws on Melagomas's strategy; hence the stare-down contest during the prefight introductions.

With the fall of the Roman Empire, boxing's recorded history disappeared until the 17th century in England. James Figg was an early champion, using a mixture of bare knuckles and fencing tactics. A former fencer, Figg would hit, thrust, and parry, or float like a butterfly and sting like a bee. His style came to dominate the sport, as kicking, gouging, and wrestling were discouraged.

In the 1800s, the Marquis of Queensberry introduced a set of rules to further diminish the brutality of the sport. These rules remain the core of the sport: the use of gloves; three-minute rounds with a 60-second rest between rounds; a 24-foot square ring; and a 10-second count after each knockdown.

At the first modern Olympics in 1896, boxing was omitted from the program because it was considered too dangerous and ungentlemanly by the

Athens committee. It was not until the third Olympic Games in St. Louis that boxing was included, due to its popularity in America. Women's boxing was also featured on the program as a demonstration event. The host of the 1912 Olympics, pacifistic Sweden, decided not to stage a boxing event in their Olympiad, since it was against national law. Following the war, boxing was added back to the program in 1920, and some 25 countries competed for the gold. From that point on, boxing took hold as an international amateur sport and one of the more popular Olympic pursuits.

In the US, an Olympic medal remains a passport to professional success, graduating fighters such as Floyd Patterson (1952, middleweight gold), Muhammad Ali, then known as Cassius Clay (1960, light heavyweight gold), Joe Frazier (1964, heavyweight gold), Sugar Ray Leonard (1976, light welterweight gold), Michael Spinks (1976, middleweight gold), brother Leon Spinks (1976, light heavyweight gold), Pernell Whitaker (1984, lightweight gold), Mark Breland (1984, welterweight gold), Virgil Hill (1984, middleweight silver), Evander Holyfield (1984, light heavyweight bronze), and Riddick Bowe (1988, super heavyweight silver).

▼

SPECTATORS' GUIDE

Olympic boxing features 12 weight classes: light flyweight (up to 48 kg/106 lbs); flyweight (48 kg to 51 kg/112 lbs); bantamweight (51 kg to 54 kg/119 lbs); featherweight (54 kg to 57 kg/125 lbs); lightweight (57 kg to 60 kg/132 lbs); light welterweight (60 kg to 63.5 kg/139 lbs); welterweight (63.5 kg to 67 kg/147 lbs); light middleweight (67 kg to 71 kg/156 lbs); middleweight (71 kg to 75 kg/165 lbs); light heavyweight (75 kg to 81 kg/178 lbs); heavyweight (81 kg to 91 kg/201 lbs); and super heavyweight (more than 91 kg/201 lbs).

The boxing competition is a single elimination tournament, with the survivors of each match proceeding to the next level of competition. A bout consists of three, three-minute rounds, with a one-minute interval between rounds. The referee is the sole authority in the ring, needing only three words to maintain control: stop (boxing), box (begin again), and break (step back, used to break up clinches). Any boxer who does not obey immediately may be disqualified on the spot.

The bouts are judged by three to five judges, who award points to the fighters for legal blows landed. Three scoring blows are counted as one point; for example, a boxer landing 15 scoring punches would be awarded five points. A scoring blow must be clean, fair, unguarded, land on the front of the face or body, and carry the proper weight. Basically, the white part of the glove, covering the knuckles, must make contact to be a scoring blow. All legal blows are scored equally, including knockdown blows.

During each round, each judge will add up the scoring blows delivered by each boxer, awarding 20 points to the round's winner and a lesser number to the loser.

The judges award points after each round. When the bout is over, the scores are added to determine the winner. Fouls enter into the scoring, resulting in a point deduction. Fighters are usually cautioned before a point deduction occurs. Common fouls include hitting below the belt, kicking or head butting, lying against the ropes or using them unfairly, offensive language, not breaking on command, and behaving aggressively against the referee.

The referee can stop a bout if he thinks a boxer is totally outclassed or if a boxer is injured. The match is also stopped if one of the boxers receives an eight-count three times in one round or four times in a bout. Unlike in professional boxing, the bell cannot save a boxer from a stopped contest. The count continues to completion, regardless of when the bell rings, *except in the finals of the tournament.*

A boxer is considered "down" if he touches the floor with anything other than his feet (chin, knee, forehead, etc.). He is also down if he is dangling on the ropes or is wholly or partially outside the ropes as a result of a blow. A boxer can be considered down while standing up in dazed condition. And, of course, the boxer's corner can literally "throw in the towel" and retire from the match.

For safety, thumbless gloves are used. Boxers from 106 through 147 pounds use eight-ounce gloves, while 10-ounce gloves are used for the heavier categories. Headgear is mandatory.

A feature unique to boxing (and judo) among Olympic events is the awarding of two bronze medals, since the Olympic boxing elimination tournament dispenses with a consolation bout of the two semifinal losers.

▼

HOPEFULS

The US expects prize-winning fights from its boxing team. Two-time US Champion Oscar de la Hoya is the most convincing lightweight hopeful, and two-time World Cup winner, US Olympic Cup winner, and 1990 US Athlete of the Year Eric Griffin looks especially promising in the light flyweight category. Also impressive are US Olympic gold-medal heavyweight John Bray, super heavyweight Larry Donald, and light welterweight Steve Johnston—the only non-Cuban boxer to win a gold in the 1991 Pan American events.

Cuban fighters to watch for include World Champions Julio Gonzales and Felix Savon.

The Koreans, who took two Olympic gold medals and a silver in 1988, and the Soviets, who won four medals overall, will be fighting for more at Barcelona as well.

Schedule

The tentative boxing schedule is as follows:

Sunday, July 26
Preliminary bouts

Monday, July 27
Preliminary bouts

Tuesday, July 28
Preliminary bouts

Wednesday, July 29
Preliminary bouts

Thursday, July 30
Preliminary bouts

Friday, July 31
Preliminary bouts

Saturday, August 1
Preliminary bouts

Sunday, August 2
Preliminary bouts

Monday, August 3
Quarterfinal

Tuesday, August 4
Quarterfinal

Thursday, August 6
Semifinals

Friday, August 7
Semifinals

Saturday, August 8
Finals

Sunday, August 9
Finals

▼

HIGHLIGHTS

Perhaps not surprisingly, boxing has been the most contentious sport on the Olympic program. Throughout the years the sport has been riddled with questionable officiating, resulting in protests, grievances, dubious disqualifications, and reversed decisions.

It wasn't until the 1904 Games in St. Louis that boxing found its way onto the Olympic program. All of the gold medal winners that year were Americans, including Oliver L. Kirk, who won gold medals in two weight divisions (featherweight and bantamweight), back when the rules allowed such things. That year the program even included a demonstration of women boxing. Again in 1908 all the weight divisions were won by host-country boxers, including 37-year-old featherweight Richard Gunn, who had been Britain's amateur champion from 1894 to 1896 and came out of retirement for the Games. Also medalling in

220

London were John Douglas, a renowned cricketer, and Reginald Baker, who also competed as a springboard diver at the 1908 Games.

Boxing was not part of the program in 1912, but after World War I the sport returned to the Olympic arena at the 1920 Games in Antwerp, with 25 nations competing. England and the US dominated, but gold medalists hailed from South Africa, France, and Canada as well. Some of the first protested decisions and grievances emerged from these Games. Controversy again surfaced at the 1924 Games, over the match between Britain's Harry Mallin and France's Roger Brousse; Brousse initially got the decision, but Mallin demonstrated that he had been bitten vigorously several times on the chest. Brousse claimed the teeth marks were administered inadvertently, even though his previous opponent had also accused Brousse of biting; the decision was eventually reversed. In another bout, a US boxer knocked out his Swedish opponent and was then declared the loser for a supposed infraction.

At the 1928 Games debatable decisions again arose; Argentinean fans fought Dutch police, the US boxing team threatened to withdraw in protest over a decision in the flyweight category, and Czech fans accosted the judges. In 1932 no disputes emerged, and the US, South Africa, and Argentina claimed two titles apiece.

The Americans were shut out at the 1936 Games, where once again decisions were contested. At the 1948 Games, the Jury of Appeals was physically assaulted twice by outraged contingents protesting decisions. That year South African light heavyweight George Hunter was the outstanding contender; Argentina's flyweight champion, Pascual Perez, went on to win a professional title. The US came back with five champions in 1952, including 17-year-old Floyd Patterson. At the Helsinki Games, Ireland won its first Olympic boxing medal with bantamweight silver medalist John McNally.

In 1956 Britain gained its first gold since 1924, winning two weight classes, and Soviet boxers scored their first gold in 1956, winning three weight classes, but boxing at the Melbourne Games is most remembered for the performance of László Papp of Hungary. The left-handed Papp had won the middleweight gold in 1948, came back for the light middleweight gold in 1952, and successfully defended the light middleweight title in 1956.

Italy came up with three champions in 1960, the year US boxer Cassius Clay (later Muhammad Ali) claimed the light heavyweight gold. Half of the Olympic judges and referees were dismissed at the Rome Games.

The USSR and Poland each won three titles in 1964, and Nigeria gleaned its first Olympic medal, a bronze in the light middleweight category. That year an incensed Korean flyweight, Don-Kih Choh, protested his disqualification during a quarterfinal bout by remaining in the ring for almost an hour. In another weight class, Spanish featherweight Valentin Loren punched a referee in the face and was banned from boxing for life. Argentinean light middleweight Jose Chirino also punched a referee at the Tokyo Games.

In 1968 Soviet light middleweight Boris Lagutin and Polish light welter-weight Jerzy Kulej repeated their gold-medal performances of four years before. Eye injuries were down in 1968 due to the introduction of a new leather glove from Germany that was soft and seamless. That year more than a dozen referees and judges were dismissed for incompetence, and two officials had to follow British middleweight Christopher Finnegan to a restaurant to obtain a urine sample.

In 1972 the match between Soviet featherweight Boris Kusnetsov and Kenya's Philip Waruinge was widely disputed. That year Cuba brought three gold medalists to the Games, including Teofilo Stevenson, who won the heavyweight title from 1972 through 1980.

The 1976 US team was rich with champions, including "Sugar" Ray Leonard, the Spinks brothers, and Howard Davis. A Thai boxer, Payao Pooltarat, took third place in the light flyweight class that year, winning his country's first Olympic medal. Cuban boxer Angel Herrera took the featherweight gold in 1976 and the lightweight gold in 1980; his countryman, Andrés Aldama was light welterweight silver medalist in 1976 and won the welterweight gold in 1980.

A record-setting American team won eleven medals in 1984, including a bronze for Evander Holyfield in the light heavyweight class. The competitions were once again shrouded in judging controversies that alienated almost every team competing. That year two Canadians entered the spotlight, light middle-weight Shawn O'Sullivan and heavyweight Willie deWit. Protective headgear was introduced at the 1984 Games as well.

In Seoul boxing was again marred by ugly incidents. A US boxer had to forfeit a match due to a mix-up in times, venues, and transportation; many felt the competitive South Koreans had deliberately led the American boxer astray. Then Keith Walker, a referee from New Zealand, was physically assaulted in the ring by angry South Korean boxing officials, including at least two coaches. A fellow referee tried to shield Walker from the attack, while South Korean security police moved slowly in to break up the melee. Residents of Seoul expressed embarrassment over the behavior of their countrymen.

Many US boxers have used the Olympics as a springboard into professional boxing. One of the most intriguing Olympic champions in history was destined never to fight professionally. Cuba's Teofilo Stevenson, heavyweight gold medalist in 1972, 1976, and 1980, swore by his country's "amateur" system, which only added to his mystic presence, as boxing fans continue to speculate on how far his wondrous boxing skills would have taken him in the professional ring.

Sugar Ray Leonard

Born May 17, 1956, Ray Charles Leonard (he was named after the singer) was raised in the Washington suburb of Palmer Park, Maryland. Initially his parents, Cicero and Getha, were concerned that the quiet, introspective Ray enjoyed few interests outside of school work and the church choir, but then, at the age of fourteen, Ray discovered boxing.

As an amateur, Leonard amassed an impressive 145–5 record. He participated in the 1975 Pan American Games, where he won a gold medal, and then went on to capture the light welterweight gold at the 1976 Olympics in Montréal. In post-match interviews, the handsome and personable Leonard charmed the press, and a celebrity was born. He called himself "Sugar Ray" after the great Sugar Ray Robinson and started working with Muhammad Ali's former trainer, Angelo Dundee.

Leonard's first title fight took place in 1979, when he beat welterweight Wilfredo Benitez in the 15th round with a technical knock-out (TKO). To defend that title, Leonard entered the ring in 1980 with Panamanian Roberto Duran, who unseated Leonard in a brutal slugfest. Their famous rematch five months later showcased Leonard's speed and agility, rather than Duran's brute strength, and resulted in Duran's withdrawal ("no mas") in the eighth round.

Shortly thereafter, Leonard faced then-undefeated Thomas "Hit Man" Hearns, in what was one of the great fights of the decade. A battered and exhausted Leonard, behind on all the judges' cards, found something extra in the 14th round and flailed at Hearns along the ropes until the referee stepped in and ended the fight, giving Leonard the decision in a TKO.

During a training match in 1982, Leonard suffered a potentially blinding detached retina. He subsequently announced his retirement from the ring. But in 1984 he returned to boxing, intending to prepare for a long-awaited bout with "Marvelous" Marvin Hagler. Before that battle came about, though, Leonard retired again. In 1986 he returned to serious training, and challenged Hagler to a match. The match finally took place in 1987, and, miraculously, Leonard emerged victorious, dispatching the brutal Hagler in twelve rounds. He then went on to a rematch with Hearns in 1989, which ended in a draw (most in the fight community believe that Hearns won), and another fight with Duran that same year, which Leonard won.

In February, 1991, Leonard, for the fourth time in his career, announced his retirement from the ring. On the heels of a bloody defeat at the hands of 23-year-old Terry Norris, Leonard declared: "I had a great career. It took this fight to show me it is no longer my time.... Now I am going to learn how to play golf." —P.G.

Boxing

Medalists

Boxing — 106 lbs./48 kg (Light Flyweight)

1988
1. Ivalio Hristov, Bulgaria
2. Michael Carbajal, USA
3. Robert Isaszegi, Hungary
3. Leopoldo Serantes, Philippines

1984
1. Paul Gonzales, USA
2. Salvatore Todisco, Italy

3. Jose Marcelino Bolivar, Venezuela
3. Keith Mwila, Zambia

1980
1. Shamil Sabyrov, Soviet Union
2. Hipolito Ramos, Cuba
3. Byong-Uk Li, Democratic People's Republic of Korea
3. Ismail Mustafov, Bulgaria

1976
1. Jorge Hernandez, Cuba

223

2. Byong-Uk Li, Democratic People's
Republic of Korea
3. Orlando Maldonado, Puerto Rico
3. Payao Pooltarat, Thailand
1972   1. Gyorgy Gedo, Hungary
2. U Gil Kim, Democratic People's
Republic of Korea
3. Ralph Evans, Great Britain
3. Enrique Rodriguez, Spain
1968   1. Francisco Rodriguez, Venezuela
2. Yong-ju Chi, Republic of Korea
3. Harlan Marbley, USA
3. Hubert Skrzypczak, Poland
1886-
1964   **Not held**

Boxing — 112 lbs./51 kg (Flyweight)

1988   1. Kwang-Sun Kim, South Korea
2. Andreas Tews, East Germany
3. Mario Gonzalez, Mexico
3. Timofel Skriabin, Soviet Union
1984   1. Steven McCrory, USA
2. Redzep Redzepovski, Yugoslavia
3. Ibrahim Bilali, Kenya
3. Eyup Can, Turkey
1980   1. Petr Lesov, Bulgaria
2. Viktor Miroshnichenko, Soviet Union
3. Hugh Russell, Ireland
3. Janos Varadi, Hungary
1976   1. Leo Randolph, USA
2. Ramon Duvalon, Cuba
3. Leszek Blazynski, Poland
3. David Torozyan, Soviet Union
1972   1. Georgi Kostadinov, Bulgaria
2. Leo Rwabwogo, Uganda
3. Leszek Blazynski, Poland
3. Douglas Rodriguez, Cuba
1968   1. Ricardo Delgado, Mexico
2. Artur Olech, Poland
3. Servilio Oliveira, Brazil
3. Leo Rwabwogo, Uganda
1964   1. Fernando Atzori, Italy
2. Artur Olech, Poland
3. Robert Carmody, USA
3. Stanislav Sorokin, Soviet Union
1960   1. Gyula Torok, Hungary
2. Sergei Sivko, Soviet Union
3. Abdelmoneim Elguindi, United Arab
Republic
3. Kiyoshi Tanabe, Japan
1956   1. Terence Spinks, Great Britain
2. Mircea Dobrescu, Romania
3. John Caldwell, Ireland
3. Rene Libeer, France
1952   1. Nathan Brooks, USA
2. Edgar Basel, West Germany
3. Anatoli Bulakov, Soviet Union
3. William Toweel, South Africa
1948   1. Pascual Perez, Argentina
2. Spartaco Bandinelli, Italy
3. Su-an Han, Republic of Korea
1936   1. Willy Kaiser, West Germany
2. Gavino Matta, Italy
3. Louis Daniel Lauria, USA
1932   1. Istvan Enekes, Hungary
2. Francisco Cabanas, Mexico
3. Louis Salica, USA
1928   1. Antal Kocsis, Hungary

2. Armand Apell, France
3. Carlo Cavagnoli, Italy
1924   1. Fidel LaBarba, USA
2. James McKenzie, Great Britain
3. Raymond Fee, USA
1920   1. Frank Genaro, USA
2. Anders Petersen, Denmark
3. William Cuthbertson, Great Britain
1906-
1912   **Not held**
1904   1. George Finnegan, USA
2. Miles Burke, USA
1896-
1900   **Not held**

Boxing — 119 lbs./54 kg (Bantamweight)

1988   1. Kennedy McKinney, USA
2. Alexandar Hristov, Bulgaria
3. Jorge Julio Rocha, Colombia
3. Phajol Moolsan, Thailand
1984   1. Maurizio Stecca, Italy
2. Hector Lopez, Mexico
3. Pedro J. Nolasco, Dominican Republic
3. Dale Walters, Canada
1980   1. Juan Hernandez, Cuba
2. Bernardo Jose Pinango, Venezuela
3. Michael Anthony, Guyana
3. Dumitru Cipere, Romania
1976   1. Yong-Jo Gu, Democratic People's
Republic of Korea
2. Charles Mooney, USA
3. Patrick Cowdell, Great Britain
3. Viktor Rybakov, Soviet Union
1972   1. Orlando Martinez, Cuba
2. Alfonso Zamora, Mexico
3. Ricardo Carreras, USA
3. George Turpin, Great Britain
1968   1. Valeri Sokolov, Soviet Union
2. Eridari Mukwanga, Uganda
3. Kyu-chu Chang, Republic of Korea
3. Eiji Morioka, Japan
1964   1. Takao Sakurai, Japan
2. Sin-jo Chong, Republic of Korea
3. Juan Fabila Mendoza, Mexico
3. Washington Rodriguez, Uruguay
1960   1. Oleg Grigoryev, Soviet Union
2. Primo Zamparini, Italy
3. Brunon Bendig, Poland
3. Oliver Taylor, Australia
1956   1. Wolfgang Behrendt, East Germany
2. Sun-chun Song, Republic of Korea
3. Claudio Barrientos, Chile
3. Frederick Gilroy, Ireland
1952   1. Pentti Hamalainen, Finland
2. John McNally, Ireland
3. Gennady Garbusov, Soviet Union
3. Jun-ho Kang, Republic of Korea
1948   1. Tibor Csik, Hungary
2. Giovanni Battista Zuddas, Italy
3. Juan Venegas, Puerto Rico
1936   1. Ulderico Sergo, Italy
2. Jack Wilson, USA
3. Fidel Ortiz, Mexico
1932   1. Horace Gwynne, Canada
2. Hans Ziglarski, Germany
3. Jose Villanueva, Philippines
1928   1. Vittorio Tamagnini, Italy
2. John Daley, USA

224

3. Harry Isaacs, South Africa
1924 1. William Smith, South Africa
2. Salvatore Tripoli, USA
3. Jean Ces, France
1920 1. Clarence Walker, South Africa
2. Chris J. Graham, Canada
3. James McKenzie, Great Britain
1912 **Not held**
1908 1. A. Henry Thomas, Great Britain
2. John Condon, Great Britain
3. W. Webb, Great Britain
1906 **Not held**
1904 1. Oliver Kirk, USA
2. George Finnegan, USA
1896-
1900 **Not held**

Boxing — 125 lbs./57 kg (Featherweight)

1988 1. Giovanni Parisi, Italy
2. Daniel Dumitrescu, Romania
3. Abdulahak Achik, Morocco
3. Jae-Hyunk Lee, South Korea
1984 1. Meldrick Taylor, USA
2. Peter Konyegwache, Nigeria
3. Turgut Aykac, Turkey
3. Omar Catari Paraza, Venezuela
1980 1. Rudi Fink, East Germany
2. Adolfo Horta, Cuba
3. Krzysztof Kosedowski, Poland
3. Viktor Rybakov, Soviet Union
1976 1. Angel Herrera, Cuba
2. Richard Nowakowski, East Germany
3. Leszek Kosedowski, Poland
3. Juan Paredes, Mexico
1972 1. Boris Kuznetsov, Soviet Union
2. Philip Waruinge, Kenya
3. Andras Botos, Hungary
3. Clemente Rojas, Columbia
1968 1. Antonio Roldan, Mexico
2. Albert Robinson, USA
3. Ivan Mihailov, Bulgaria
3. Philip Waruinge, Kenya
1964 1. Stanislav Stepashkin, Soviet Union
2. Anthony Villanueva, Philippines
3. Charles Brown, USA
3. Heinz Schulz, East Germany
1960 1. Francesco Musso, Italy
2. Jerzy Adamski, Poland
3. Jormal Limmonen, Finland
3. William Meyers, South Africa
1956 1. Valdimir Safronov, Soviet Union
2. Thomas Nicholls, Great Britain
3. Pentti Hamalainen, Finland
3. Henryk Niedzwiedzki, Poland
1952 1. Jan Zachara, Czechoslovakia
2. Sergio Caprari, Italy
3. Leonard Leisching, South Africa
3. Joseph Ventaja, France
1948 1. Ernesto Formenti, Italy
2. Dennis Shepherd, South Africa
3. Aleksy Antkiewicz, Poland
1936 1. Oscar Casanovas, Argentina
2. Charles Catterall, South Africa
3. Josef Miner, Germany
1932 1. Carmelo Robledo, Argentina
2. Josef Schleinkofer, Germany
3. Allan Carlsson, Sweden

1928 1. Lambertus "Bep" van Klaveren, Netherlands
2. Victor Peralta, Argentina
3. Harold Devine, USA
1924 1. John "Jackie" Fields, USA
2. Joseph Salas, USA
3. Pedro Quartucci, Argentina
1920 1. Paul Fritsch, France
2. Jean Gachet, France
3. Edoardo Garzena, Italy
1912 **Not held**
1908 1. Richard Gunn, Great Britain
2. C. W. Morris, Great Britain
3. Hugh Roddin, Great Britain
1906 **Not held**
1904 1. Oliver Kirk, USA
2. Frank Haller, USA
1896-
1900 **Not held**

Boxing — 132 lbs./60 kg (Lightweight)

1988 1. Andreas Zuelow, East Germany
2. George Cramne, Sweden
3. Romallis Ellis, USA
3. Nerguy Enkhbat, Mongolia
1984 1. Pernell Whitaker, USA
2. Luis F. Ortiz, Puerto Rico
3. Chil-Sung Chun, Republic of Korea
3. Martin Ndongo Ebanga, Cameroon
1980 1. Angel Herrera, Cuba
2. Viktor Demianenko, Soviet Union
3. Kazimierz Adach, Poland
3. Richard Nowakowski, East Germany
1976 1. Howard Davis, USA
2. Simion Cutov, Romania
3. Ace Rusevski, Yugoslavia
3. Vasili Solomin, Soviet Union
1972 1. Jan Szczepanski, Poland
2. Lazzlo Orban, Hungary
3. Samuel Mbugua, Kenya
3. Alfonso Perez, Colombia
1968 1. Ronald Harris, USA
2. Jozef Grudzien, Poland
3. Calistrat Cutov, Romania
3. Zvonimir Vujin, Yugoslavia
1964 1. Jozef Grudzien, Poland
2. Velikton Barannikov, Soviet Union
3. Ronald Harris, USA
3. James McCourt, Ireland
1960 1. Kazimierz Pazdzior, Poland
2. Sandro Lopopolo, Italy
3. Abel Laudonio, Argentina
3. Richard McTaggart, Great Britain
1956 1. Richard McTaggart, Great Britain
2. Harry Kurschat, Great Britain
3. Anthony Byrne, Ireland
3. Anatoli Lagetko, Soviet Union
1952 1. Aureliano Bolognesi, Italy
2. Aleksy Antkiewicz, Poland
3. Gheorghe Fiat, Romania
3. Erkki Pakkanen, Finland
1948 1. Gerald Dreyer, South Africa
2. Joseph Vissers, Belgium
3. Svend Wad, Denmark
1936 1. Imre Harangi, Hungary
2. Nikolai Stepulov, Estonia
3. Erik Agren, Sweden
1932 1. Lawrence Stevens, South Africa

2. Thure Ahlqvist, Sweden
3. Nathan Bor, USA
1928　1. Carlo Orlandi, Italy
2. Stephen Halaiko, USA
3. Gunnar Berggren, Sweden
1924　1. Hans Nielsen, Denmark
2. Alfredo Copello, Argentina
3. Frederick Boylstein, USA
1920　1. Samuel Mosberg, USA
2. Gotfred Johansen, Denmark
3. Clarence "Chris" Newton, Canada
1912　Not held
1908　1. Frederick Grace, Great Britain
2. Frederick Spiller, Great Britain
3. H. H. Johnson, Great Britain
1906　Not held
1904　1. Harry Spanger, USA
2. James Eagan, USA
3. Russell Van Horn, USA
1896-
1900　Not held

Boxing — 139 lbs./63.5 kg (Light Welterweight)

1988　1. Viatcheslav Janovski, Soviet Union
2. Grahame Cheney, Australia
3. Reiner Gies, West Germany
3. Lars Myrberg, Sweden
1984　1. Jerry Page, USA
2. Dhawee Umponmaha, Thailand
3. Mircea Fulger, Romania
3. Mirko Puzovic, Yugoslavia
1980　1. Patrizio Oliva, Italy
2. Serik Konakbaev, Soviet Union
3. Jose Aguilar, Cuba
3. Anthony Willis, Great Britain
1976　1. "Sugar" Ray Leonard, USA
2. Andres Aldama, Cuba
3. Vladimir Kolev, Bulgaria
3. Kazimierz Szczerba, Poland
1972　1. Ray Seales, USA
2. Angel Angelow, Bulgaria
3. Issaka Daborg, Niger
3. Zvonimir Vujin, Yugoslavia
1968　1. Jerzy Kulej, Poland
2. Enrique Regueiferos, Cuba
3. Arto Nilsson, Finland
3. James Wallington, USA
1964　1. Jerzy Kulej, Poland
2. Yevgeny Frolov, Soviet Union
3. Eddie Blay, Ghana
3. Habib Galhia, Tunisia
1960　1. Bohumil Nemecek, Czechoslovakia
2. Clement Quartey, Ghana
3. Quincelon Daniels, USA
3. Marian Kasprzyk, Poland
1956　1. Vladimir Yengibaryan, Soviet Union
2. Franco Nenci, Italy
3. Constantin Dumitrescu, Romania
3. Henry Loubscher, South Africa
1952　1. Charles Adkins, USA
2. Viktor Mednov, Soviet Union
3. Erkki Mallenius, Finland
3. Bruno Visintin, Italy
1896-
1948　Not held

Boxing — 147 lbs./67 kg (Welterweight)

1988　1. Robert Wangila, Kenya
2. Laurent Boudouani, France
3. Jan Dydak, Poland
3. Kenneth Gould, USA
1984　1. Mark Breland, USA
2. Young-Su An, Republic of Korea
3. Luciano Bruno, Italy
3. Joni Nyman, Finland
1980　1. Andres Aldama, Cuba
2. John Mugabi, Uganda
3. Karl-Heinz Kruger, East Germany
3. Kazimierz Szczerba, Poland
1976　1. Jochen Bachfeld, East Germany
2. Pedro Gamarro, Venezuela
3. Reinhard Skricek, West Germany
3. Victor Zilberman, Romania
1972　1. Emilio Correa, Cuba
2. Janos Kajdi, Hungary
3. Dick Tiger Murunga, Kenya
3. Jesse Valdez, USA
1968　1. Manfred Wolke, East Germany
2. Joseph Bessala, Cameroon
3. Mario Guilloti, Argentina
3. Vladimir Mussalimov, Soviet Union
1964　1. Marian Kasprzyk, Poland
2. Richardas Tamulis, Soviet Union
3. Silvano Bertini, Italy
3. Pertti Purhonen, Finland
1960　1. Giovanni Benvenuti, Italy
2. Yuri Radonyak, Soviet Union
3. Leszek Drogosz, Poland
3. James Lloyd, Great Britain
1956　1. Nicolae Linca, Romania
2. Frederick Tiedt, Ireland
3. Nicholas Gargano, Great Britain
3. Kevin Hogarth, Australia
1952　1. Zygmunt Chychla, Poland
2. Sergei Scherbakov, Soviet Union
3. Gunther Heidemann, Germany
3. Victor Jorgensen, Denmark
1948　1. Julius Torma, Czechoslovakia
2. Horace Herring, USA
3. Alessandro D'Ottavio, Italy
1936　1. Sten Suvio, Finland
2. Michael Murach, Germany
3. Gerhard Petersen, Denmark
1932　1. Edward Flynn, USA
2. Erich Campe, Germany
3. Bruno Ahlberg, Finland
1928　1. Edward Morgan, New Zealand
2. Raul Landini, Argentina
3. Raymond Smillie, Canada
1924　1. Jean Delarge, Belgium
2. Hector Mendez, Argentina
3. Douglas Lewis, Canada
1920　1. Albert "Bert" Schneider, Canada
2. Alexander Ireland, Great Britain
3. Frederick Colberg, USA
1906-
1912　Not held
1904　1. Albert Young, USA
2. Harry Spanger, USA
3. Jack Eagan, USA
3. Joseph Lydon, USA
1896-
1900　Not held

226

Boxing — 156 lbs./71 kg (Light Middleweight)

1988
1. Si-Hun Park, South Korea
2. Roy Jones, USA
3. Raymond Downey, Canada
3. Richard Woodhall, Great Britain

1984
1. Frank Tate, USA
2. Shawn O'Sullivan, Canada
3. Christophe Tiozzo, France
3. Manfred Zielonka, West Germany

1980
1. Armando Martinez, Cuba
2. Aleksandr Koshkin, Soviet Union
3. Jan Franek, Czechoslovakia
3. Detlef Kastner, East Germany

1976
1. Jerzy Rybicki, Poland
2. Tadija Kacar, Yugoslavia
3. Rolando Garbey, Cuba
3. Viktor Savchenko, Soviet Union

1972
1. Dieter Kottysch, West Germany
2. Wieslaw Rudkowski, Poland
3. Alan Minter, Great Britain
3. Peter Tiepold, East Germany

1968
1. Boris Lagutin, Soviet Union
2. Rolando Garbey, Cuba
3. John Baldwin, USA
3. Gunther Meier, West Germany

1964
1. Boris Lagutin, Soviet Union
2. Joseph Gonzales, France
3. Jozef Grzesiak, Poland
3. Nojim Maiyegun, Nigeria

1960
1. Wilbert McClure, USA
2. Carmelo Bossi, Italy
3. William Fisher, Great Britain
3. Boris Lagutin, Soviet Union

1956
1. Laszlo Papp, Hungary
2. Jose Torres, USA
3. John McCormack, Great Britain
3. Zbigniew Pietrzykowski, Poland

1952
1. Laszlo Papp, Hungary
2. Theunis van Schalkwyk, South Africa
3. Eladio Herrera, Argentina
3. Boris Tischin, Soviet Union

1896-1948 Not held

Boxing — 165 lbs./75 kg (Middleweight)

1988
1. Henry Maske, East Germany
2. Egerton Marcus, Canada
3. Chris Sande, Kenya
3. Hussain Shah Syed, Pakistan

1984
1. Joon-Sup Shin, Republic of Korea
2. Virgil Hill, USA
3. Aristides Gonzales, Puerto Rico
3. Mohamed Zaoui, Algeria

1980
1. Jose Gomez, Cuba
2. Viktor Savchenko, Soviet Union
3. Jerzy Rybicki, Poland
3. Valentin Silaghi, Romania

1976
1. Michael Spinks, USA
2. Rufat Riskiev, Soviet Union
3. Luis Martinez, Cuba
3. Alec Nastac, Romania

1972
1. Vyacheslav Lemeschev, Soviet Union
2. Reima Virtanen, Finland
3. Prince Amartey, Ghana
3. Marvin Johnson, USA

1968
1. Christopher Finnegan, Great Britain
2. Aleksei Kisselyov, Soviet Union
3. Alfred Jones, USA
3. Agustin Zaragoza, Mexico

1964
1. Valeri Popenchenko, Soviet Union
2. Emil Schulz, Great Britain
3. Franco Valle, Italy
3. Tadeusz Walasek, Poland

1960
1. Edward Crook, USA
2. Tadeusz Walasek, Poland
3. Yevgeny Feofanov, Soviet Union
3. Ion Monea, Romania

1956
1. Gennady Schatkov, Soviet Union
2. Ramon Tapia, Chile
3. Gilbert Chapron, France
3. Victor Zalazar, Argentina

1952
1. Floyd Patterson, USA
2. Vasile Tita, Romania
3. Boris Nikilow, Bulgaria
3. Stig Sjolin, Sweden

1948
1. Laszlo Papp, Hungary
2. John Wright, Great Britain
3. Ivano Fontana, Italy

1936
1. Jean Despeaux, France
2. Henry Tiller, Norway
3. Raul Villareal, Argentina

1932
1. Carmen Barth, USA
2. Amado Azar, Argentina
3. Ernest Pierce, South Africa

1928
1. Piero Toscani, Italy
2. Jan Hermanek, Czechoslovakia
3. Leonard Steyaert, Belgium

1924
1. Harry Mallin, Great Britain
2. John Elliott, Great Britain
3. Joseph Beecken, Belgium

1920
1. Harry Mallin, Great Britain
2. Georges A. Prud-Homme, Canada
3. Moe H. Herscovitch, Canada

1912 Not held

1908
1. John Douglas, Great Britain
2. Reginald Baker, Australia
3. W. Philo, Great Britain

1906 Not held

1904
1. Charles Mayer, USA
2. Benjamin Spradley, USA

1896-1900 Not held

Boxing — 178 lbs./81 kg (Light Heavyweight)

1988
1. Andrew Maynard, USA
2. Nourmagomed Chanavazov, Soviet Union
3. Henryk Petrich, Poland
3. Damir Skaro, Yugoslavia

1984
1. Anton Josipovic, Yugoslavia
2. Kevin Barry, New Zealand
3. Evander Holyfield, USA
3. Mustapha Moussa, Algeria

1980
1. Slobodan Kacar, Yugoslavia
2. Pawel Skrzecz, Poland
3. Herbert Bauch, East Germany
3. Ricardo Rojas, Cuba

1976
1. Leon Spinks, USA
2. Sixto Soria, Cuba
3. Costica Dafinoiu, Romania
3. Janusz Gortat, Poland

1972
1. Mate Parlov, Yugoslavia
2. Gilberto Carrillo, Cuba

Summer

	3. Janusz Gortat, Poland
	3. Isaac Ikhouria, Nigeria
1968	**1.** Dan Posnyak, Soviet Union
	2. Ion Monea, Romania
	3. Stanislaw Dragan, Poland
	3. Georgi Stankov, Bulgaria
1964	**1.** Cosimo Pinto, Italy
	2. Aleksei Kisselyov, Soviet Union
	3. Aleksandar Nikolov, Bulgaria
	3. Zbigniew Pietrzykowski, Poland
1960	**1.** Cassius Clay, USA
	2. Zbigniew Pietrzykowski, Poland
	3. Anthony Madigan, Australia
	3. Giulio Saraudi, Italy
1956	**1.** James Boyd, USA
	2. Gheorghe Negrea, Romania
	3. Carlos Lucas, Chile
	3. Romualdas Murauskas, Soviet Union
1952	**1.** Norvel Lee, USA
	2. Antonio Pacenza, Argentina
	3. Anatoli Perov, Soviet Union
	3. Harri Siljander, Finland
1948	**1.** George Hunter, South Africa
	2. Donald Scott, Great Britain
	3. Maurio Cia, Argentina
1936	**1.** Roger Michelot, France
	2. Richard Vogt, Germany
	3. Francisco Risiglione, Argentina
1932	**1.** David Carstens, South Africa
	2. Gino Rossi, Italy
	3. Peter Jorgensen, Denmark
1928	**1.** Victor Avendano, Argentina
	2. Ernst Pistulla, Germany
	3. Karel L. Miljon, Netherlands
1924	**1.** Harry Mitchell, Great Britain
	2. Thyge Petersen, Denmark
	3. Sverre Sorsdal, Norway
1920	**1.** Edward Eagan, USA
	2. Sverre Sorsdal, Norway
	3. H. Franks, Great Britain
1896-1912	**Not held**

Boxing — 201 lbs./91 kg (Heavyweight)

1988	**1.** Ray Mercer, USA
	2. Hyun-Man Baik, South Korea
	3. Andrzej Golota, Poland
	3. Arnold Vanderlidje, Netherlands
1984	**1.** Henry Tillman, USA
	2. Willie Dewitt, Canada
	3. Angelo Musone, Italy
	3. Arnold Vanderlidje, Netherlands
1980	**1.** Teofilo Stevenson, Cuba
	2. Pyotr Zaev, Soviet Union
	3. Jurgen Fanghanel, East Germany
	3. Istvan Levai, Hungary
1976	**1.** Teofilo Stevenson, Cuba
	2. Mircea Simon, Romania
	3. Clarence Hill, Bermuda
	3. Johnny Tate, USA
1972	**1.** Teofilo Stevenson, Cuba
	2. Ion Alexe, Romania
	3. Peter Hussing, West Germany

	3. Hasse Thomsen, Sweden
1968	**1.** George Foreman, USA
	2. Ionas Chepulis, Soviet Union
	3. Giorgio Bambini, Italy
	3. Joaquin Rocha, Mexico
1964	**1.** Joe Frazier, USA
	2. Hans Huber, West Germany
	3. Giuseppe Ros, Italy
	3. Vadim Yemelyanov, Soviet Union
1960	**1.** Franco De Piccolo, Italy
	2. Daniel Bekker, South Africa
	3. Josef Nemec, Czechoslovakia
	3. Gunter Siegmund, West Germany
1956	**1.** Peter Rademacher, USA
	2. Lev Mukhin, Soviet Union
	3. Daniel Bekker, South Africa
	3. Giacomo Bozzano, Italy
1952	**1.** H. Edward Sanders, USA
	2. Ingemar Johansson, Sweden (was disqualified)
	3. Ilkka Koski, Finland
	3. Andries Nieman, South Africa
1948	**1.** Rafael Iglesias, Argentina
	2. Gunnar Nilsson, Sweden
	3. John Arthur, South Africa
1936	**1.** Herbert Runge, Germany
	2. Guillermo Lovell, Argentina
	3. Erling Nilsen, Norway
1932	**1.** Santiago Lovell, Argentina
	2. Luigi Rovati, Italy
	3. Frederick Feary, USA
1928	**1.** Arturo Rodriguez Jurado, Argentina
	2. Nils Ramm, Sweden
	3. M. Jacob Michaelsen, Denmark
1924	**1.** Otto von Porat, Norway
	2. Soren Petersen, Denmark
	3. Alfredo Porzio, Argentina
1920	**1.** Ronald Rawson, Great Britain
	2. Soren Petersen, Denmark
	3. Xavier Eluere, France
1912	**Not held**
1908	**1.** A. L. Oldham, Great Britain
	2. S. C. H. Evans, Great Britain
	3. Frederick Parks, Great Britain
1906	**Not held**
1904	**1.** Samuel Berger, USA
	2. Charles Mayer, USA
	3. William M. Michaels, USA
1896-1900	**Not held**

Boxing — over 201 lbs./over 91 kg (Super Heavyweight)

1988	**1.** Lennox Lewis, Canada
	2. Riddick Bowe, USA
	3. Alexandre Mirochnitchenko, Soviet Union
	3. Janusz Zarenkiewicz, Poland
1984	**1.** Tyrell Biggs, USA
	2. Francesco Damiani, Italy
	3. Azis Salihu, Yugoslavia
	3. Robert Wells, Great Britain
1896-1980	**Not held**

228

▼

CANOE/KAYAK

WARM-UP

The most primitive form of boat, the canoe is found in some form or other in most cultures with a yen for aquatic transportation. The form these boats assumed in various parts of the world stemmed from the type of materials available locally and what the intended function of the canoe was to be.

In the Pacific Northwest of the United States, where large trees were plentiful, the Tlinget and Haida peoples carved dugout canoes out of whole trees. These sturdy craft could reach impressive proportions, sometimes carrying as many as 30 to 50 people, and with many paddlers the boats were swift and seaworthy. The boats were used for a wide spectrum of activities, including transportation, fishing, hunting of marine mammals, and, of course, waging war.

Farther north, tree populations dwindle, so the Aleuts and other Arctic peoples resorted to other methods of boat construction. Their skin-on-frame kayaks (along with those of Greenland natives) represent a highly developed boatbuilding tradition. The Eskimo's kayak was composed of a framework of whalebone and driftwood, lashed together to support a sea lion skin stretched taut and treated with whale fat for waterproofing. Extremely agile and seaworthy in the hands of a skilled paddler, the boats were used for fishing and for hunting everything from seals and sea otters to whales.

Facing an entirely different set of circumstances imposed upon them by their noncoastal environment, native peoples in the interior of North America invented a unique solution to water transportation. As with the dugout builders of the Pacific Northwest, wood was available as a building material. But their type of river travel forced them to have to carry their canoes overland; thus, lightness was an essential trait. The bark canoe, a wooden framework covered with the bark of a birch or other tree, was a nimble rivercraft that could navigate tricky river currents, carry large loads, and yet portage (be carried) easily. This canoe was used by European explorers of North America and was the standard mode of transportation for native and non-native fur traders, and so played an important role in the history of North America.

fact: Kayaks were often tailored to an individual paddler's dimensions and skills.

Other variations on the canoe are found throughout the world. Polynesian cultures built their version of the dugout canoe with outriggers for stability and sails to power the boats on extended ocean crossings between islands. Dugouts are also found in rainforest cultures such as those of the Amazon.

Credit for the birth of canoeing as a recreational sport is given to an English barrister, John MacGregor, who designed a boat based on the Eskimo kayak that he called *Rob Roy*. Between 1845 and 1869 he took the boat on extended journeys on the rivers and lakes of Europe. During this period he wrote a popular series of books and delivered lectures detailing his canoeing adventures. People were captivated by his tales of paddling a small boat in the wilderness, and soon many similar craft were being built by Englishmen. That particular type of canoe is still known as a Rob Roy.

In 1866, MacGregor founded the Royal Canoe Club to encourage interest in the new sport. The Prince of Wales became the first Commodore of the club and remained in that office until 1901, when he stepped down to assume another post (king of England). In 1867 the club held its first regatta and was busy codifying a set of rules to govern competitive canoe racing. By 1868, the group had swelled to 300 enthusiastic paddlers, who traveled the waterways of Europe and North America, exposing the local populations to the thrills of canoeing. As the popularity of canoeing grew, clubs sprang up in Europe and North America; the New York Canoe Club was founded in 1871.

During this time the open birchbark type of canoe was gaining favor among canoeists. Earlier boatbuilders of the Penobscot, or Oldtown, tribe had substituted canvas for the birchbark covering material, and European settlers copied the design in an all-wood construction. These so-called "Canadian canoes," having been designed for river travel, were better suited to that medium than the Rob Roys, which were based on open-water Eskimo kayaks, and gradually replaced the Rob Roy in recreational paddling. During the 1880s, Canadian canoe builders found a ready market for their boat in Europe.

The rise in popularity of canoeing led to the proliferation of organizations. In 1880 the American Canoe Association was launched to establish racing rules for both sail- and paddle-propelled craft. In 1887 the British Canoe Association was founded, primarily as a cruising-oriented group. Regattas were held in North America and many countries, and by 1921 national associations had been established in Sweden, Bohemia, Germany, Austria, and Denmark. In 1924 delegates from the European paddling community met in Copenhagen and created the Internationella Representantskapet för Kanotidrott (IRK), an international body to formulate rules for competitive racing worldwide.

Another development in the sport occurred during the 1920s: the invention by German Alfred Heurich of the *falboot*, or folding boat. This type of kayak was a skin-on-frame boat like those of the Eskimos. Its fabric skin, however, could be removed and its framework dismantled, enabling a canoeist to pack her boat into one or two duffle bags and transport it as she would baggage. This facilitated making trips to far-away destinations and further widened the appeal of the sport. It also added a category of boats to the list of events in organized racing.

fact: Folding kayaks performed effectively for Allied Special Forces missions during World War II.

In 1924, the same year that the IRK was formed, an international regatta was mounted in Paris as an exhibition to coincide with the Olympic Games. The regatta was a success, and the IRK began setting its sights on acceptance by the IOC of canoeing as an official Olympic event. Their efforts, however, were not immediately rewarded. The IOC rejected their suit for the Amsterdam and Los Angeles Games of 1928 and 1932.

In order to gain legitimacy, the IRK staged a European championship in Prague in 1933. They redoubled their efforts to persuade the IOC to include canoeing in the 1936 Games in Berlin. With the IRK headquartered in Munich and a strong national German canoeing organization lobbying as well, enthusiasts were optimistic that the German-hosted Games would include the paddle sports. Disappointed they were when, once again, the IOC rejected the application. However, the IRK appealed the ruling and canoe racing was finally admitted as an Olympic sport for the Berlin Games.

The 1936 program for canoe/kayak consisted of flatwater courses of 1000 and 10,000 meter lengths, to be raced by single and pairs kayaks, single and pairs folding canoes; and single and pairs Canadian canoes. The event was a great success, with 19 nations participating and the 27 medals divided between 8 countries. Hopes were high for the future of Olympic canoeing.

But as luck would have it, World War II intervened, disrupting (among other pursuits) canoeing as an international sport. The situation for canoeing at the end of the war was made worse by the Munich location of the IRK headquarters. The organization was in a shambles politically, as was the building that housed it, the target of Allied bombing during the war.

In 1946, Jonas Asschier, the pre-war vice president of the IRK, convened a meeting of the representatives of the worldwide paddling community to rebuild an international organization and prepare for the upcoming 1948 Olympics. The new organization was called the International Canoe Federation (ICF). The 1948 Olympics saw the sport of canoeing somewhat diminished, with only 17 countries participating. The program had changed also: folding boat events were eliminated and a women's event, the 500-meter kayak singles, was added.

fact: Some canoes are now made of kevlar, a light and extremely tough fabric originally developed for its bullet-proofing character.

With each Olympiad, the number of entrants has increased, and over the years the program has been tinkered with. In Rome in 1956, the 10,000m races were eliminated and a relay race (4 x 500m) for kayak singles was added. That year the practice of repêchage was instituted, allowing an entrant a second chance before elimination from competition. At the 1964 Tokyo Games, the relay race was replaced by a 1000m event for four-man kayaks.

A major innovation to the program occurred in 1972 when canoe slalom was introduced. This event is based on the kind of canoeing done on "whitewater"—torrential rivers coursing along in rapids and falls—making it fundamentally different from the flatwater events. Participants in kayak singles (and Canadian canoe singles and pairs) race down a course on the turbulent water, navigating through gates such as those found on a slalom ski course.

SPECTATORS' GUIDE

A canoe is a long, narrow watercraft usually sharp at both ends and typically propelled by handheld paddles. The fact that the paddler sits facing forward and the paddle is unsupported distinguishes the sports of canoeing and kayaking from the rowing sports, where an *oar* pivots on a fixed fulcrum and the rower "pulls" the oar from a seated position facing backward.

The distinction between the terms *canoe* and *kayak* is somewhat hazy. The larger category of canoes includes the kayak (that is, all kayaks are canoes, but only some canoes are kayaks). The main thing that distinguishes kayaks from other canoes is the position of the paddler(s). In a kayak the paddler sits with her legs outstretched in front of her, whereas other canoeists paddle from a kneeling position. Also, a kayak is typically a decked or covered boat and is paddled with a double-bladed paddle, while a canoe is more often an open boat powered by a single-bladed paddle.

The 16 events on the Olympic program for canoe/kayak are classified first by the type of water paddled (flatwater or whitewater) and, second, by the type of boat (Canadian canoe or kayak, and number of paddlers). A shorthand system of nomenclature makes it easier to keep all the types of boats straight: the letter C for Canadian canoe and the letter K for kayak are followed by a digit representing the number of crew on board. For example, K-4 is a four-man/woman kayak, C-1 a single Canadian canoe.

The biggest distinction between any of the canoe events is whitewater versus flatwater. The two environments result in boat designs and paddling techniques that are vastly different. In flatwater sprint racing, the essential ingredient is flat-out straight-line speed. The boats, whether Canadian canoe or kayak, are long and narrow for high hull speed, and low in profile to reduce wind resistance. In profile the keel, or bottom edge of the hull, of a flatwater boat appears very straight. This straight keel-line enables the boat to track a straight course easily through flatwater. A whitewater boat, by contrast, is shorter, with a more curved keel profile, to enable it to turn quickly as it is maneuvered around gates. The whitewater boat's sides are higher, to keep the turbulent water at bay. In either type of whitewater boat the crew wears spray skirts, which attach around the cockpit and seal the paddler into the boat to prevent water from entering. The spray skirt is unnecessary in the calm conditions of the flatwater events.

Flatwater events: Twelve of the 16 events in the program are flatwater sprints. The men compete at 500m and 1000m in singles and doubles kayaks (K-1 and K-2) and singles and doubles Canadian canoes (C-1 and C-2). A 1000m race in fours kayaks (K-4) is also run as a men's event. Women compete at 500m in the three kayak types (K-1, K-2, and K-4). In the kayak events, racers sit in the traditional kayak posture, with legs forward, and use a double-bladed paddle. In the Canadian canoe events, a single-bladed paddle is wielded from a kneeling position.

Each boat paddles a straight course within a marked 9-meter-wide lane. Leaving one's lane or coming within 5 meters of a neighboring boat results in disqualification. The races, as the label indicates, are essentially sprints, in which paddlers go all-out from start to finish. Boat design is constrained by specifications set forth by the ICF, and so each boat will perform, to a large degree, the same, leaving it up to the strength and stamina of the athletes to make the winning difference.

To determine which competitors make it to the finals, a system of heats, repêchages (or second chances; in French, literally, "fishing again"), and semi-finals is used. The first eight finishers of the heats move on to the semi-final races, while the others go to a repêchage. Through the repêchage stage four crews can get back into the semi-finals. The top six finishers in the semi-finals move on to the finals, where the medalists and fourth through sixth places are determined, while the bottom six finishers of the semifinals go to a petit final, or "little" final, that determines 7th through 12th places.

Whitewater slalom events: The four events in the whitewater slalom portion of the Olympic program are men's single kayak (K-1), men's single and pairs Canadian canoe (C-1 and C-2) and women's kayak (K-1W). In the whitewater events, boats are raced downstream on a course of rapidly moving water that can range in length from 400 to 1200 meters. Although patterned after a stretch of wilderness "wild water," the Olympic course is usually a man-made structure featuring particular hazards that are specially designed into the course. The specific path of the course to be run is marked off by a series of "gates" suspended above the waterway and reaching down to just above the water's surface.

Scoring is based on elapsed time to run the course, corrected for navigation errors. Touching a gate adds five seconds to a paddler's time, while missing a gate altogether tacks on 50 seconds. The gates themselves fall into two categories: upstream or downstream gates, depending on which direction the boat must pass through. Green-and-white striped gates are to be passed through in a downstream direction, while red-and-white striped gates are negotiated against the stream.

Canoe/Kayak Speak

BEAM: The widest part of the canoe.

BLADE: The wide part of the paddle; it is the part of the paddle that passes through the water.

BOW (rhymes with *plow*): The front of the boat.

DOWNSTREAM GATE: A slalom gate that is negotiated in the same direction as the flow of the water; distinguished from an upstream gate by its green and white stripes.

DRAW: A stroke pulling in toward the paddler at 90 degrees to the direction of travel; when executed by the bowman, the bow of the canoe will turn in the direction of the drawing side.

GUNWALE (pronounced *gun'l*): The upper edge of the canoe's side.

"J" STROKE: A paddle stroke that ends in a rudder maneuver (see below).

KEEL: The ridge running the length of the canoe on the bottom.

PETIT-FINAL: Literally, in French, "small final"; used to determine final placement of athletes who do not earn a starting position in the finals of a sprint event.

REPÊCHAGE: French for "second chance," literally, fishing again; this stage of a sprint racing event permits athletes a second chance to earn a spot in the next round of competition (semi-finals).

RIVER LEFT: The left side of the waterway as it would appear to a paddler facing downstream.

RIVER RIGHT: The right side of the waterway as it would appear to a paddler facing downstream.

RUDDER: Dragging the paddle to create resistance; when executed by the sternsman the stern of the canoe turns in the direction of the rudder side.

SHAFT: The narrow part of the paddle, gripped by the paddler.

STERN: The back of the boat.

SWEEP: A stroke made in a broad curve; when executed by the sternsman, the canoe turns in the direction opposite the sweeping side.

THWART: A supporting member of a canoe's structure, extending across the canoe from side to side between the gunwales.

UPSTREAM GATE: A slalom gate that must be negotiated against the flow of the water; distinguished from a downstream gate by its red and white stripes.

---▼---

HOPEFULS

The German men and women will undoubtedly paddle swiftly toward the medals in Barcelona, followed closely by Hungarians, Bulgarians, and the Soviet men's team. With their rise since 1984 from a 13th-place ranking to one among the top five, though, the US men's and women's teams hope to catch up to—and perhaps surpass—the world's top paddlers.

On the men's side, the US team faces competition from the aforementioned Germans, Bulgarians, and Hungarians, along with the Soviets. The US team boasts exceptional depth, and it includes five-time World Champion Jon Lugbill, who may be the best competitive whitewater paddler ever, as well as Olympian Greg Barton. Barton, you'll recall, won the men's 1000m singles gold at Seoul and, less than 90 minutes later, began his gold-medal-winning 1000m pair race with Norm Bellingham, thus becoming the first Olympic kayaker to win two gold medals.

Jamie McEwan, who gave the US its first Olympic whitewater medal in 1972, still paddles on the US team, along with Jim Terrell and Mike Herbert. Terrell finished fourth in the 500m semifinals at Seoul and holds the record for the number of medals won (27) at US Olympic Festivals. Herbert took two silvers at the 1990 World Championships and the USA's only gold medal at the 1991 Pan American games.

Dana Chladek, the daughter of two-time Czechoslovakian World Champion kayakers Stan and Ema Chladek, is the US women's team's most promising whitewater racer. Chladek, the World Cup Champion in 1988, placed first in the 1990 Champion International Whitewater Series and fifth—having fallen in the last event from a second-place ranking—in that year's World Cup tournament. 1988 Olympians Traci Phillips, who won three National Championship titles in 1989, and Cathy Marino, who has won 10 National Championship titles and took three golds at the 1991 US Olympic Festival, will lead the women's flatwater sprint team.

Greg Barton

Greg "Buck" Barton says his upbringing helped him become the first American to win an Olympic gold medal in kayaking.

Barton was raised on a pig farm in the southern Michigan town of Homer. He says farm chores—early in the morning before work and late in the evenings after—developed the discipline necessary to succeed.

"I do the sport because I enjoy it, not because there is a lot of payoff," he told the *Detroit Free Press* at the 1988 Games in Seoul. "You don't see kayakers get rich or famous. It's a personal goal for myself to see if I can be the best in the world."

Barton is an engineering graduate of the University of Michigan. He learned to paddle on the streams, lakes, and rivers of his native state. His parents introduced him to the sport when he was young.

"It's always fun to be outside and to pull on the paddle and feel the boat accelerate under your body," he says.

As a youth Barton, who now lives in Bellingham, Washington, and works for a kayak design firm, wasn't solely a paddler. Despite being born with club feet, he wrestled and ran cross country in high school.

"I was born with this problem," he told *Olympian* magazine in the summer of 1989. "Ten years ago, I had some surgery, but instead of helping, my feet ended up a lot worse. The doctor fused the bones together—so I lost a lot of motion in my ankles; mostly my ankles and calves are messed up and one leg ended up shorter then the other. I'm in no hurry for surgery."

He knows, then, what it is to work and overcome obstacles—in life and in kayak racing.

"Towards the end of a race," he says, "your whole body is numb, in agony."

Barton was world champion in one kayaking event in 1985—the first American to win a world title in the sport—and champ in two events in 1987.

"To people who know the sport and really compete in it, the world championships are just as important as the Olympics," said Barton, whose bronze medal at the 1984 Games in Los Angeles is considered by most to be the catalyst for the development of competitive kayaking in the US. "But with the Olympics, there is so much more attention."

The bronze medal he won in LA was the first Olympic bronze won by a US kayaker in more than 20 years.

Barton, who also was a member of the 1980 team that did not compete in Moscow, topped off his ascension by beating Australia's Grant Davies—3:55.27 to 3:55.28—in the singles 1000m event at Seoul.

The win didn't come without some extra, well, numbness. To Barton's amazement, Davies was proclaimed the winner on the venue's electronic scoreboard, even though it appeared as though Barton had eked across the finish line first.

Said Barton: "I looked up at the scoreboard and I said, 'Oh, man, I hope someone is up in the photo-finish room.'"

The judges were. Barton already had signed the finish sheet as the runner-up when the panel, after studying a freeze-frame film for 10 minutes, reversed the decision.

Charles Dambach, chairman of the US team, said the finish might have been closer then 0.01 of a second.

"It was five 1,000ths of a second," he said. "But the official results don't go that far."

And just how close is that?

"They actually considered awarding two gold medals," Dambach said.

Barton said he felt happy, but "kind of bad for Grant."

"They must have slowed down the tape and studied it," Davies said. "It's pretty disappointing, but Greg won fair and square. If that's my biggest disappointment in life, I can handle that. It's an honor to be that close to Greg."

Before the event, Barton had said, "Two medals is a real possibility, but it's tough doing two in a day. It's a rare combination." But less than 90 minutes later, Barton competed in the 1000m pairs event with teammate Norman Bellingham, of Cambridge, Massachusetts, and finished ahead of New Zealand. Australia took the bronze.

Afterward, he said: "I've been kayaking for 18 years. I've worked a long time for this. Winning two golds is just the icing on the cake. I'm kind of basking in the glory."

Indeed.

Barton took a year off after the Seoul Games and returned to competition in 1990. Most recently, he finished third in the 1000m singles in the 1991 World Championships at Paris, and first in the non-Olympic 10,000m singles. He finished second in the 1000m singles in the Pre-Olympic Regatta in Barcelona.

He will be a favorite to repeat at the Barcelona Games. —*E.K.*

Canoe/Kayak

Schedule

The tentative canoe/kayak schedule is as follows:

Friday, July 31
Preliminary sessions, whitewater

Saturday, August 1
Final, whitewater

Sunday, August 2
Finals, men, whitewater

Monday, August 3
500m, heats men & women, flatwater

500m, repêchages men & women, flatwater

Tuesday, August 4
1000m, heats
1000m, repêchages, men
500m, repêchages, women

Wednesday, August 5
500m, semifinals men & women

237

Thursday, August 6
1000m, semifinals men
500m, semifinals, women

Friday, August 7
500m, finals, men

500m, finals, women

Saturday, August 8
1000m, finals, men
500m, finals, women

▼

HIGHLIGHTS

Americans and Canadians dominated in the early days of canoe/kayak before it was an official Olympic sport. At the Olympic debut of the sport in 1936, the medals clustered around Austrian, Dutch, German, Czech, and Swedish competitors, though Canada captured one gold, one silver, and one bronze. The US team went home with a bronze medal.

After the war, Scandinavian, Czech, and French paddlers triumphed; Canada paddled to a silver and a bronze in 1948. That year the US won a gold and two silver medals, on a team that included Frank Havens; Havens competed in 1952 for a gold in the C-1 10,000m event, and placed 8th in the same event four years later. Standout athletes in these years included Czech paddler Jan Brzák-Felix and Sweden's Gert Fredriksson, who ultimately won six gold medals, one silver, and one bronze, and went on to coach the 1964 Swedish team.

Europeans continued to dominate in the 1950s and 1960s, especially the USSR, Hungary, and Romania in the single-blade events. In 1964 the US women captured additional medals for the US, taking a silver in the K-2 and a bronze in the K-1; that team featured the efforts of Marcia Jones Smoke. At the Tokyo Games, the three medalist crews in the men's K-4 event finished within one second of each other.

Altitude in Mexico City affected many of the crews in 1968, making the performances there something of a disappointment. In the late 1960s and early 1970s Hungary's Mihály Hesz and Aleksandr Shaparenko of the USSR made marks for themselves in the men's events, as did Soviet paddler Lyudmila Pinayeva-Khvedosyuk in the women's contests. Jamie McEwan earned the first US whitewater Olympic medal with a bronze in C-1 slalom competition in 1972; the two Germanies dominated the slalom in Munich, while the Soviets practically swept the flatwater events. Canada was nosed out of a gold in the C-1 500m at Montréal in 1976, where Soviets and East Germans again showed strongly, including East German Rüdiger Helm, the youngest competitor in 1976. At the Moscow Games, Eastern-bloc countries again triumphed, with Vladimir Parfenovich picking up three gold medals.

In 1984 New Zealand burst on the scene for four gold medals—three for Ian Ferguson alone—to Canada's two gold, two silver, and two bronze medals.

238

The four-person kayak competition was added to the Olympics and US kayaker Greg Barton won the bronze in the K-1 1000m event.

Barton was back in 1988 for a 0.005-second victory in the K-1 1000m event, then took a second gold with teammate Norman Bellingham in the K-2 1000m event, thus becoming the first athlete to win two Olympic kayaking golds at the same Games. In Seoul, New Zealand again showed strong, capturing one gold and two silver medals; Soviet paddlers claimed three gold, three silver, and one bronze medal.

Medalists

Canoe/Kayak — Men's Canadian Singles, 500 Meters

1988
1. Olaf Heukrodt, East Germany, 1:56.42
2. Mikhail Slivinski, Soviet Union, 1:57.26
3. Martin Marinov, Bulgaria, 1:57.27

1984
1. Larry Cain, Canada, 1:57.01
2. Henning L. Jakobsen, Denmark, 1:58.45
3. Costica Olaru, Romania, 1:59.86

1980
1. Sergei Postrekhin, Soviet Union, 1:53.37
2. Liubomir Liubenov, Bulgaria, 1:53.49
3. Olaf Heukrodt, East Germany, 1:54.38

1976
1. Aleksandr Rogov, Soviet Union, 1:59.23
2. John Wood, Canada, 1:59.58
3. Matija Ljubek, Yugoslavia, 1:59.60

Canoe/Kayak — Men's Canadian Singles, 1,000 Meters

1988
1. Ivan Klementiev, Soviet Union, 4:12.78
2. Joerg Schmidt, East Germany, 4:15.83
3. Nikolai Boukhalov, Bulgaria, 4:18.94

1984
1. Ulrich Eicke, West Germany, 4:06.32
2. Larry Cain, Canada, 4:08.67
3. Henning L. Jakobsen, Denmark, 4:09.51

1980
1. Liubomir Liubenov, Bulgaria, 4:12.38
2. Sergei Postrekhin, Soviet Union, 4:13.53
3. Eckhard Leue, East Germany, 4:15.02

1976
1. Matija Ljubek, Yugoslavia, 4:09.51
2. Vassili Urchenko, Soviet Union, 4:12.57
3. Tamas Wichmann, Hungary, 4:14.11

1972
1. Ivan Patzaichin, Romania, 4:08.94
2. Tamas Wichmann, Hungary, 4:12.42
3. Detlef Lewe, West Germany, 4:13.63

1968
1. Tibor Tatai, Hungary, 4:36.14
2. Detlef Lewe, West Germany, 4:38.31
3. Vitali Galkov, Soviet Union, 4:40.42

1964
1. Jurgen Eschert, East Germany, 4:35.14
2. Andrei Igorov, Romania, 4:37.89
3. Yevgeny Penyayev, Soviet Union, 4:38.31

1960
1. Janos Parti, Hungary, 4:33.93

2. Aleksandr Silayev, Soviet Union, 4:34.41
3. Leon Rotman, Romania, 4:35.87

1956
1. Leon Rotman, Romania, 5:05.3
2. Istvan Hernek, Hungary, 5:06.2
3. Gennady Bukharin, Soviet Union, 5:12.7

1952
1. Josef Holecek, Czechosolavakia, 4:56.3
2. Janos Parti, Hungary, 5:03.6
3. Olavi Ojanpera, Finland, 5:08.5

1948
1. Josef Holecek, Czechoslovakia, 5:42.0
2. Douglas Bennett, Canada, 5:53.3
3. Robert Boutigny, France, 5:55.9

1936
1. Francis Amyot, Canada, 5:32.1
2. Bohuslav Karlik, Czechoslovakia, 5:36.9
3. Erich Koschik, Germany, 5:39.0

1896-1932 Not held

Canoe/Kayak — Men's Canadian Pairs, 500 Meters

1988
1. Soviet Union, 1:41.77. Victor Reneiski, Nikolai Jouravski
2. Poland, 1:43.61, Marek Dopierala, Marek Lbik
3. France, 1:43.81, Phillipe Renaud, Joel Bettin

1984
1. Yugoslavia, 1:43.67, Matija Ljub, Mirko Nisovic
2. Romania, 1:45.68, Ivan Potzaichin, Toma Simionov
3. Spain, 1:47.71, Enrique Miguez, Narcisco Suarez

1980
1. Hungary, 1:43.39, Laszlo Fultan, Istvan Vaskuti
2. Romania, 1:44.12, Ivan Patzaichin, Petre Capusta
3. Bulgaria, 1:44.83, Borislav Ananiev, Nikolai Ilkov

1976
1. Soviet Union, 1:45.81 Sergei Petrenko, Aleksandr Vonogradov
2. Poland, 1:47.77, Jerzy Opara, Andrzej Gronowicz
3. Hungary, 1:48.35, Tamas Buday, Oszkar Frey

Canoe/Kayak — Men's Canadian Pairs, 1,000 Meters

1988 1. Soviet Union, 3:48.36, Victor Reneiski, Nikolai Jouravski
2. East Germany, 3:51.44, Olaf Heukrodt, Ingo Spelly
3. Poland, 3:54.33, Marek Dopierala, Marek Lbik

1984 1. Romania, 3:40.60, Ivan Potzaichin, Toma Simionov
2. Yugoslavia, 3:41.56, Matija Ljubek, Mirko Nisovic
3. France, 3:48.01, Didier Hoyer, Eric Renaud

1980 1. Romania, 3:47.65, Ivan Patzaichin, Toma Simionov
2. East Germany, 3:49.93, Olaf Heukrodt, Uwe Madeja
3. Soviet Union, 3:51.28, Vassili Yurchenko, Yuri Lobanov

1976 1. Soviet Union, 3:52.76, Sergei Petrenko, Aleksandr Vinogradov
2. Romania, 3:54.28, Gheorghe Danilov, Gheorghe Simionov
3. Hungary, 3:55.66, Tamas Buday, Oszkar Frey

1972 1. Soviet Union, 3:52.60, Vladas Chessyunas, Yuri Lobanov
2. Romania, 3:52.63, Ivan Patzaichin, Serghei Covaliov
3. Bulgaria, 3:58.10, Fredja Damjanow, Iwan Burtschin

1968 1. Romania, 4:07.18, Ivan Patzaichin, Serghei Covaliov
2. Hungary, 4:08.77, Tamas Wichmann, Gyula Petrikovics
3. Soviet Union, 4:11.30, Naum Prokupets, Mikhail Zamotin

1964 1. Soviet Union, 4:04.64, Andrei Khimich, Stepan Oschepkov
2. France, 4:06.52, Jean Boudehen, Michel Chapuis
3. Denmark, 4:07.48, Peer Norrbohm Nielsen, John R. Sorensen

1960 1. Soviet Union, 4:17.94, Leonid Geischtor, Sergei Makarenko
2. Italy, 4:20.77, Aldo Dezi, Francesco La Macchia
3. Hungary, 4:20.89, Imre Farkas, Andras Toro

1956 1. Romania, 4:47.4, Alexe Dumitru, Simion Ismailciuc
2. Soviet Union, 4:48.6, Pavel Kharin, Gratsian Botev
3. Hungary, 4:54.3, Karoly Wieland, Ferenc Mohacsi

1952 1. Denmark, 4:38.3, Bent Peder Rasch, Finn Haunstoft
2. Czechoslovakia, 4:42.9, Jan-Felix Brzak, Bohumil Kudrna
3. Germany, 4:48.3, Egon Drews, Wilfried Soltau

1948 1. Czechoslovakia, 5:07.1, Jan-Felix Brzak, Bohumil Kudrna
2. USA, 5:08.2, Stephen Lysak, Stephen Macknowski
3. France, 5:15.2, Georges Dransart, Georges Gandil

1936 1. Czechoslovakia, 4:50.1, Vladimir Syrovatka, Jan-Felix Brzak
2. Austria, 4:53.8, Rupert Weinstabl, Karl Proisl
3. Canada, 4:56.7, Frank Saker, Harvey Charters

1896-1932 Not held

Canoe/Kayak — Men's Kayak Singles, 500 Meters

1988 1. Zsolt Gyulay, Hungary, 1:44.82
2. Andreas Staehle, East Germany, 1:46.38
3. Paul MacDonald, New Zealand, 1:46.46

1984 1. Ian Ferguson, New Zealand, 1:47.84
2. Lars-Erik Moberg, Sweden, 1:48.18
3. Bernard Bregeon, France, 1:48.41

1980 1. Vladimir Parfenovich, Soviet Union, 1:43.43
2. John Sumegi, Australia, 1:44.12
3. Vasile Diba, Romania, 1:44.90

1976 1. Vasile Diba, Romania, 1:46.41
2. Zoltan Sztanity, Hungary, 1:46.96
3. Rudiger Helm, East Germany, 1:48.30

Canoe/Kayak — Men's Kayak Singles, 1,000 Meters

1988 1. Greg Barton, USA, 3:55.27
2. Grant Davies, Australia, 3:55.28
3. Andre Wohllebe, East Germany, 3:55.55

1984 1. Alan Thompson, New Zealand, 3:45.73
2. Milan Janic, Yugoslavia, 3:46.88
3. Greg Barton, USA, 3:47.38

1980 1. Rudiger Helm, East Germany, 3:48.77
2. Alain Lebas, France, 3:50.20
3. Ion Birladeanu, Romania, 3:50.49

1976 1. Rudiger Helm, East Germany, 3:48.20
2. Geza Csapo, Hungary, 3:48.84
3. Vasile Diba, Romania, 3:49.65

1972 1. Aleksandr Shaparenko, Soviet Union, 3:48.06
2. Rolf Peterson, Sweden, 3:48.35
3. Geza Csapo, Hungary, 3:49.38

1968 1. Mihaly Hesz, Hungary, 4:02.63
2. Aleksandr Shaparenko, Soviet Union, 4:03.58
3. Erik Hansen, Denmark, 4:04.39

1964 1. Rolf Peterson, Sweden, 3:57.13
2. Mihaly Hesz, Hungary, 3:57.28
3. Aurel Vernescu, Romania, 4:00.77

1960 1. Erik Hansen, Denmark, 3:53.00
2. Imre Szollosi, Hungary, 3:54.02
3. Gert Fredriksson, Sweden, 3:55.89

1956 1. Gert Fredriksson, Sweden, 4:12.8
2. Igor Pissaryev, Soviet Union, 4:15.3
3. Lajos Kiss, Hungary, 4:16.2

1952 1. Gert Fredriksson, Sweden, 4:07.9
2. Thorvald Stromberg, Finland, 4:09.7
3. Louis Gantois, France, 4:20.1

1948 1. Gert Fredriksson, Sweden, 4:33.2
2. Johann F. Kobberup, Denmark, 4:39.9
3. Henri Eberhardt, France 4:41.4

1936 1. Gregor Hradetzky, Austria, 4:22.9

240

2. Helmut Cammarer, Germany, 4:25.6
3. Jacob Kraaier, Netherlands, 4:35.1

**1896-
1932   Not held**

Canoe/Kayak — Men's Kayak Pairs, 500 Meters

1988
1. New Zealand, 1:33.98, Ian Ferguson, Paul MacDonald
2. Soviet Union, 1:34.15, Igor Nagaev, Victor Denissov
3. Hungary, 1:34.32, Attila Abraham, Ferenc Csipes

1984
1. New Zealand, 1:34.21, Ian Ferguson, Paul McDonald
2. Sweden, 1:35.26, Per-Inge Bengtsson, Lars-Erik Moberg
3. Canada, 1:35.41, Hugh Fisher, Alwyn Morris

1980
1. Soviet Union, 1:32.38, Vladimir Parfenovich, Sergei Chukhrai
2. Spain, 1:33.65, Herminio Menendez, Guillermo del Riego
3. East Germany, 1:34.00, Rudiger Helm, Bernd Olbricht

1976
1. East Germany, 1:35.87, Bernd Olbricht, Joachim Mattern, 1:35.87
2. Soviet Union, 1:36.81, Vladimir Romanovsky, Sergei Nagorny
3. Romania, 1:37.43, Laria Serghei, Policarp Malihin

**37.43,
Larion
Serghei,
Policarp
Malihin**

Canoe/Kayak — Men's Kayak Pairs, 1,000 Meters

1988
1. USA, 3:32.42, Greg Barton, Norman Bellingham
2. New Zealand, 3:32.71, Ian Ferguson, Paul MacDonald
3. Australia, 3:33.76, Peter Foster, Kelvin Graham

1984
1. Canada, 3:24.22, Hugh Fisher, Alwyn Morris
2. France, 3:25.97, Bernard Bregeon, Patrick Lefoulon
3. Australia, 3:26.80, Barry Kelly, Grant Kenny

1980
1. Soviet Union, 3:26.72, Vladimir Parfenovich, Sergei Chukhrai
2. Hungary, 3:28.49, Istvan Szabo, Istvan Joos
3. Spain, 3:28.66, Luis Ramos-Misione, Herminio Menendez

1976
1. Soviet Union, 3:29.01, Sergei Nagorny, Vladimir Romanovsky
2. East Germany, 3:29.33, Bernd Olbricht, Joachim Mattern
3. Hungary, 3:30.36, Istvan Szabo, Zoltan Balko

1972
1. Soviet Union, 3:31.23, Nikolai Gorbachev, Viktor Kratassyuk
2. Hungary, 3:32.00, Jozsef Deme, Janos Ratkai

3. Poland, 3:33.83, Wladyslaw Szuszkiewicz, Rafal Piszcz

1968
1. Soviet Union, 3:37.54, Aleksandr Shaparenko, Vladimir Morozov
2. Hungary, 3:38.44, Csaba Giczi, Istvan Timar
3. Austria, 3:40.71, Gerhard Seibold, Gunther Pfaff

1964
1. Sweden, 3:38.54, Sven-Olov Sjodelius, Gunnar Utterberg
2. Netherlands, 3:39.30, Antonius Geurts, Paul Hoekstra
3. West Germany, 3:40.69, Heinz Buker, Holger Zander

1960
1. Sweden, 3:34.73, Gert Fredriksson, Sven-Olov Sjodelius
2. Hungary, 3:34.91, Gyorgy Meszaros, Andras Szente
3. Poland, 3:37.34, Stefan Kaplaniak, Wladyslaw Zielinski

1956
1. West Germany, 3:49.6, Michel Scheuer, Meinrad Miltenberger
2. Soviet Union, 3:51.4, Mikhail Kaaleste, Anatoli Demitkov
3. Austria, 3:55.8, Max Raub, Herbert Wiedermann

1952
1. Finland, 3:51.1, Kurt Wires, Yrjo Hietanen
2. Sweden, 3:51.1, Lars Glasser, Ingemar Hedberg
3. Austria, 3:51.4, Max Raub, Herbert Wiedermann

1948
1. Sweden, 4:07.3, Hans Berglund, Lennart Klingstrom
2. Denmark, 4:07.5, Ejvind Hansen, Bernhard Jensen
3. Finland, 4:08.7, Thor Axelsson, Nils Bjorklof

1936
1. Austria, 4:03.8, Adolf Kainz, Alfons Dorfner
2. Germany, 4:08.9, Ewald Tilker, Fritz Bondroit
3. Netherlands, 4:12.2, Nicolaas Tates, Willem F. van der Kroft

**1896-
1932   Not held**

Canoe/Kayak — Men's Kayak Fours, 1,000 Meters

1988
1. Hungary, 3:00.20, Zsolt Gyulag, Ferenc Csipes, Sandor Hodosi, Attila Abraham
2. Soviet Union, 3:01.40, Alexandre Motouzenko, Sergei Kirsanov, Igor Nagaev, Victor Denissov
3. East Germany, 3:02.37, Kay Bluhm, Andre Wohllebe, Andreas Staehle, Hans-Joerg Bliesener

1984
1. New Zealand, 3:02.28, Grant Bramwell, Ian Ferguson, Paul McDonald, Alan Thompson
2. Sweden, 3:02.81, Per-Inge Bengtsson, Tommy Karls, Lars- Erik Moberg, Thomas Ohisson
3. France, 3:03.94, Francois Barouh, Philippe Boccara, Pascal Boucherit, Didier Vavasseur

1980
1. East Germany, 3:13.76, Rudiger Helm, Bernd Olbricht, Harold Marg, Bernd Duvigneau

Canoe/Kayak

2. Romania, 3:15.35, Mihai Zafiu, Vasile Diba, Ion Geanta, Nicusor Eseanu
3. Bulgaria, 3:15.46, Borislav Borisov, Bozhidar Milenkov, Lazar Khristov, Ivan Manev

1976 1. Soviet Union, 3:06.69, Sergei Chukhrai, Aleksandr Degtiarev, Yuri Filatov, Vladimir Morozov
2. Spain, 3:08.95, Jose M. Esteban, Jose R. Lopez, Herminio Menendez, Luis G. Ramos
3. East Germany, 3:10.76 Rudiger Helm, Frank-Peter Bischof, Juergen Lehnert, Bernd Duvigneau

1972 1. Soviet Union, 3:14.02, Yuri Filatov, Yuri Stezenko, Vladimir Morozov, Valeri Didenko
2. Romania, 3:15.07, Aurel Vernescu, Mihai Zafiu, Roman Vartolomeu, Atanase Sciotnic
3. Norway, 3:15.27, Egil Soby, Steinar Amundsen, Tore Berger, Jan Johansen

1968 1. Norway, 3:14.38, Steinar Amundsen, Egil Soby, Tore Berger, Jan Johansen
2. Romania, 3:14.81, Anton Calenic, Dimitrie Ivanov, Haralambie Ivanov, Mihai Turcas
3. Hungary, 3:15.10, Csaba Giczi, Istvan Timar, Imre Szollosi, Istvan Csizmadia

1964 1. Soviet Union, 3:14.67, Nikolai Tschuschikow, Anatoli Grischin, Vyacheslav Ionovw, Vladimir Morozov
2. West Germany, 3:15.39, Gunther Perleberg, Bernhard Schulze, Friedhelm Wentzke, Holger Zander
3. Romania, 3:15.51, Simion Cuciuc, Atanase Sciotnic, Mihai Turcas, Aurel Vernescu

1896-1960 Not held

Canoe/Kayak — Women's Kayak Singles, 500 Meters

1988 1. Vania Guecheva, Bulgaria, 1:55.19
2. Birgit Schmidt, East Germany, 1:55.31
3. Izabela Dylewska, Poland, 1:57.38
1984 1. Agneta Andersson, Sweden, 1:58.72
2. Barbara Schuttpelz, West Germany, 1:59.93
3. Annemiek Derckx, Netherlands, 2:00.11
1980 1. Birgit Fischer, East Germany, 1:57.96
2. Vania Gecheva, Bulgaria, 1:59.48
3. Antonina Melnikova, Soviet Union, 1:59.66
1976 1. Carola Drechsler-Zirzow, East Germany, 2:01.05
2. Tatiana Korshunova, Soviet Union, 2:03.07
3. Klara Rajnai, Hungary, 2:05.01
1972 1. Yulia Ryabchinskaya, Soviet Union, 2:03.17
2. Mieke Jaapies, Netherlands, 2:04.03
3. Anna Pfeffer, Hungary, 2:05.50
1968 1. Lyudmila Pinayeva-Khvedosyuk, Soviet Union, 2:11.09
2. Renate Breuer, West Germany, 2:12.71
3. Viorica Dumitru, Romania, 2:13.22

1964 1. Lyudmila Khvedosyuk, Soviet Union, 2:12.87
2. Hilde Lauer, Romania, 2:15.35
3. Marcia Jones, USA, 2:15.68
1960 1. Antonina Seredina, Soviet Union, 2:08.08
2. Therese Zenz, West Germany, 2:08.22
3. Daniela Walkowiak, Poland, 2:10.46
1956 1. Yelisaveta Dementyeva, Soviet Union, 2:18.9
2. Therese Zenz, West Germany, 2:19.6
3. Tove Soby, Denmark, 2:22.3
1952 1. Sylvi Saimo, Finland, 2:18.4
2. Gertrude Liebhart, Austria, 2:18.8
3. Nina Savina, Soviet Union, 2:21.6
1948 1. Karen Hoff, Denmark, 2:31.9
2. Alida van der AnkerDoekans, Netherlands, 2:32.8
3. Fritzi Schwingl, Austria, 2:32.9
1896-1936 Not held

Canoe/Kayak — Women's Kayak Pairs, 500 Meters

1988 1. East Germany, 1:43.46, Birgit Schmidt, Anke Nothnagel
2. Bulgaria, 1:44.06, Vania Guecheva, Diana Paliiska
3. Netherlands, 1:46.00, Annemiek Derckx, Annemarie Cox
1984 1. Sweden, 1:45.25, Agneta Anderson, Anna Olsson
2. Canada, 1:47.13, Alexandra Barre, Sue Holloway
3. West Germany, 1:47.32. Josefa Idem, Barbara Schuttpelz
1980 1. East Germany, 1:43.88, Carsta Genauss, Martina Bischof
2. Soviet Union, 1:46.91, Galina Alekseyeva, Nina Trofimova
3. Hungary, 1:47.95, Eva Rakusz, Maria Zakarias
1976 1. Soviet Union, 1:51.15, Nina Popova, Galina Kreft
2. Hungary, 1:51.69, Anna Pfeffer, Klara Rajnai
3. East Germany, 1:51.81, Barbel Madhaus-Koester, Carola Drechsler-Zirzow
1972 1. Soviet Union, 1:53.50, Lyudmila Pinayeva-Khvedosyuk, Jekaterina Kuryshko
2. East Germany, 1:54.30, Ilse Kaschube, Petra Grabowski
3. Romania, 1:55.01, Maria Nichiforov, Viorica Dumitru
1968 1. West Germany, 1:56.44, Roswitha Esser, Annemarie Zimmermann
2. Hungary, 1:58.60, Anna Pfeffer, Katalin Rozsnyoi
3. Soviet Union, 1:58.61, Lyudmila Pinayeva-Khvedosyuk, Antonina Seredina
1964 1. West Germany, 1:56.95, Roswitha Esser, Annemarie Zimmermann
2. USA, 1:59.16, Francine Fox, Gloriane Perrier

3. Romania, 2:00.25, Hilde Lauer,
   Cornelia Sideri

1960 1. Soviet Union, 1:54.76, Maria Chubina,
   Antonina Seredina
2. West Germany, 1:56.66 Therese
   Zenz, Ingrid Hartmann
3. Hungary, 1:58.22, Klara Fried-
   Banfalvi, Vilma Egresi

**1896–
1956 Not held**

Canoe/Kayak — Women's
Kayak Fours, 500 Meters

1988 1. East Germany, 1:40.78, Birgit Schmidt,
   Anke Nothnagel, Ramona Portwich,
   Heike Singer

2. Hungary, 1:41.88, Erika Geczi, Erika
   Meszaros, Eva Rakuscz, Rita Koban
3. Bulgaria, 1:42.63, Vania Guecheva,
   Diana Paliiska, Ogniana Petkova.
   Borislava Ivanova

1984 1. Romania, 1:38.34, Agafia Constantin,
   Nastasia Ionescu, Tecia Marinescu,
   Maria Stefan
2. Sweden, 1:38.87, Agneta Andersson,
   Anna Olsson, Eva Karlsson, Susanne
   Wiberg
3. Canada, 1:39.40, Alexandra Barre,
   Lucie Guay, Sue Holloway, Barb
   Olmsted

Connie Paraskevin-Young was a member of the 1980 and 1984 US
Olympic speedskating teams, and as a cyclist captured a bronze in
Seoul in the match sprints. She'll be pedalling for gold in Barcelona.

Soviet cyclist Erika Salumiae, who sometimes trains with
Paraskevin-Young, will defend her match sprint gold medal in
Barcelona, but under which flag?

CYCLING

WARM-UP

Bicycling is so familiar that we take it for granted. Bicyclists, unlike lugers, are nearly everywhere. The bike is a supreme form of cheap two-wheel transportation and recreation. But though the wheel and human history are long intertwined, the bicycle is a relative newcomer.

One of the earliest bicycles—if you can call it that—was demonstrated by one Comte de Sivrac in the gardens of the Palais Royal in Paris in 1791. More of a caricature of the modern two-wheeler, the *célérifère*, as it was called, consisted of a wooden bar, with padded saddle, supported by two rather large wheels; what it didn't have is pedals. These hobby horses, resembling an overgrown children's toy, moved when riders thrust their feet on the ground from side to side, while at the same time holding tightly to their dignity. The same sort of centaur-like creation is said to be pictured on a stained-glass window in Stoke Poges Church, near Windsor, England.

Despite the less-than-desirable control of direction—since the front wheel, directly affixed to the frame and fork, could not swivel—the riders of these contraptions formed a club and raced along the Champs Élysées. Straightaways were considered a blessing.

A more serious mode of transportation came in 1817 when Karl, Baron von Drais de Sauerbrun, of Mannheim, added the luxury of steering to his two-wheeler. After its public debut in the Luxembourg Gardens in 1818, the new-improved "dandy horse" or *"Draisienne"* made quite an impression, and later became the preferred mode of transportation for some French rural postmen.

Later attempts included the tricycle and the high-wheeler, so called because the rear wheel outsized the front wheel five times over. Finally, in 1834, a Scottish blacksmith named Kirkpatrick McMillan invented pedals with connecting rods, producing a vehicle recognizable as the previous incarnation of the modern bicycle.

The first bicycle, made entirely of wood except for the iron-covered tires, was brought to the United States in 1866, where it received a lukewarm welcome. In 1868, rubber tires replaced wood and iron ones, and the inaugural bicycle race took place at Parc de Saint Cloud in France. An Englishman, James Moore, pedaled to the first official bicycle racing victory.

With the advent of the edge-cutting pneumatic tire in 1888, long-distance cycling—in these pre-automobile halcyon days—became the rage. It wasn't uncommon for bikers to trek from country to country on their trusty steeds. By the turn of the century, bicycling was a popular sport with an enthusiastic following, not least of all in the States. Racing was popular in the US from the 1880s on, and grueling six-day races, held indoors at Madison Square Garden, became a national obsession in the 1920s and 1930s.

The first World Championships were held in Chicago in 1893, and cycling events have been featured in the Olympics since the first Games in 1896 ... one of a half-dozen sports to lay claim to regular Olympic presence. In 1903, the first Tour de France was held and soon became one of the most prestigious cycling events then and now. Founded by Henri Desgranges, who set the first hour record in 1893, "Le Tour" turned bicycle racing in a new direction; no one had ever thought to stage races in sequence.

Desgranges, a Parisian sports paper editor, made a sports marketing coup of the event. To this day, the Tour, dubbed "the ultimate bike race," is among the most revered cycling events.

Cycling's popularity continued to mount in Europe: France, Belgium, Italy, Switzerland, the Netherlands, Britain, and Luxembourg, in particular, took the sport to heart. Races of all sorts proliferated (and continue to thrive): the Tour of Italy tested rider's mettle in the hills, the Paris-Roubaix—christened the "tour d'enfer" or "tour of hell"—pushed the limits of the cyclists who rode over cobblestoned streets.

In the States, however, the sport took a backseat to another wheeled vehicle: in the 1930s, enamored with the newly introduced automobile, America turned its back on cycling. While the sport became a national passion for a number of countries on the European continent, cycling in the US finally hit its all-time low-point in the 1970s, when only a few thousand licensed racers competed. Six-day races—which had enjoyed such celebrity in the first decades of the century—ended in 1961.

In the 1980s, for a variety of reasons, the sport enjoyed an about-face. Speedskating phenomenon Eric Heiden turned a few heads when he turned to cycling, a number of major corporations—such as 7 Eleven, Mohawk Carpets, and Lowenbrau Beer—sponsored cycling teams, and the energy crunch caused a lot of average Joes to turn to the bike, for transportation if not for health. Add to this the success of Greg LeMond, the first American ever to win the Tour de France (he did so three times), and suddenly cycling as a competitive sport was enjoying a resurgence. By the end of the 1980s, more than 85 million cyclists were peddling in the US—200,000 of whom raced their bikes—making cycling the fourth most popular weekend activity (with 21 million weekend warriors). Not to mention the 2.7-odd million commuters who share the road.

As you might have guessed, a demographic shift has taken place: for the first time this century, adult riders outnumber younger cyclists. As a matter of fact, the average adult cyclist in the US is between 25 and 34 years old; 55% are male, 45% are female, and the largest occupation category is profession-al/managerial.

SPECTATORS' GUIDE

Until fairly recently, the shape of the bicycle has not changed much; even now, despite ultra high-tech materials and "radical" innovations, the bike still consists of a frame, two wheels, moving contact points (the crank arms and pedals) and components for the transmission of motion (chain rings and chain).

Fundamental design aside, secondary characteristics of the bike have been modified more significantly. Frame material, wheel design, and handlebar configuration (and consequently riding position) have undergone more than a few changes in recent years.

Aerodynamics—the motion of air acting on bodies in motion—is a major factor in bike racing; the less wind resistance a rider encounters, the less effort it takes to go fast.

Aerodynamic "funny bikes" debuted at the 1984 Olympic Games. With frames that often weigh as little as seven pounds, they are usually constructed of fiberglass and a synthetic composite called kevlar. Best suited to the pursuit and time-trial events, "funny bikes" lack the maneuverability required in pack-riding situations.

fact: How much is that bicycle in the window? Kevlar—also used in air-planes, bulletproof clothing, ca-noes, and other high-tech ob-jects—is a pricey material: the 1988 Olympic bicycles each carried a $45,000 price tag.

Disc wheels add to the aerodynamic efficiency of track and time-trial bikes. The wheels, which lessen the amount of wind resistance the bike encounters as it rolls, are usually made of fiberglass or kevlar, and are laminated. Usually heavier than standard wheels, discs are normally not desirable for events in which it is important to make sudden jumps, or increases in speed.

"Bullhorn" handlebars, another aerodynamic innovation, originated when a track racer turned his standard Maes-bend bars upside down and cut off the "drops," or what is normally the lowest part of the handlebar. Various "aero" bars, widely used among triathletes at first, later were accepted within the conservative bike ranks. With this new configuration, the rider can lower the stem (the part that holds the handlebars intact with the bike frame) to ride leaning closer to the front wheel; this position decreases the amount of wind resistance created by the rider's body.

And speaking of wind resistance created by the rider's body, high-tech cycling clothing is more than a fashion statement. In 1976, the West German team was not allowed to wear their one-piece silk bodysuits, but 1981 marked a new fashion era when so-called Darth Vader helmets and rubberized skin suits were allowed in competition. And do riders shave their legs for that aerodynamic advantage? Not really ... it's just that shaved legs are easier to massage, and in the event of a crash, are more easily cleaned.

The Events

Cycling consists of two distinct categories of racing: track and road. Bikes used in track events are single-geared, with no brakes. Road bikes vary among events, and are highly specialized; they can have up to 14 gears, and are built with aerodynamic qualities. While track events take place on banked tracks called vélodromes, road races—as you might have guessed—take place on paved roadways.

Bike racing is a strategic sport, and the winner is not always the fastest. A smart rider knows his or her own strengths and weaknesses, as well as the strengths and weaknesses of the competition, and rides a race based on a script that takes these elements into account.

Match Sprint: Riders are seeded based on 200m time trials: each cyclist is given a lap to gain momentum, and is then timed for the final "flying 200." A fast time is important because it keeps the rider from competing against the top-seeded opponents until later in the game.

In the match sprint itself, riders meet in a best-of-three competition. With no lane markings, riders use the entire width of the track, often diving from the top of the embankment to gain momentum. Often called a cat-and-mouse game, the race usually starts out at a slow pace (though it must be at least a walking pace). One rider is required to lead the first lap. A drawing takes place prior to the first sprint to determine which rider will take the inside position during the first lap, and riders switch position each race thereafter. Riders constantly jockey for position during the second lap, attempting to position themselves in front of or behind their competitors, depending on their preference and how they've read the competition. Sometimes the riders use a "track stand"—where both remain motionless and balanced on the track—to attempt to force another rider into the lead. The third and final lap, the "bell lap," is a sprint to the finish; the final 200 meters of the race is timed.

Individual Pursuit: Two riders, positioned exactly opposite to each other on the track, chase each other in circles ... sort of. A rider can win the race in one of two ways: by passing the other rider, or by recording the fastest time. Times are posted when the rider reaches each half lap: each rider may have one—and only one—person announce his (and this year her) times. If both riders post the same time at the finish, they are placed according to the better time at the end of the previous lap.

Both endurance and speed are important in the individual pursuit, and riders' strategies vary. Some start out slow, lulling the competition into a false sense of security, to come on strong at the end; others go out fast, to rattle the opponent's confidence.

Team Pursuit: The team pursuit follows the same guidelines as the individual, except that a team of four rides as a unit. The winner of the race is determined when the third member of the fastest team crosses the finish line, at which point the time is recorded. A team is considered caught when the third rider of one team draws even with the third member of the team that has been overtaken. If both teams post the same time at the finish, they will be placed according to the faster time at the end of the previous lap.

The racers ride in a single file, known as a pace line, taking turns leading the team around the track. At each turn the lead rider moves up the embankment, allowing the other three riders to proceed, and then moves to the back of the pace line. The lead rider is responsible for maintaining the pace, while the other cyclists work with the draft to keep their speed. Precision and cooperation among team members are essential in the team pursuit.

Points Race: One of the most difficult races to understand, the points race can be a lot of fun to watch. It's unusual to see this one on TV because the race is long, and conveying the action to viewers is difficult.

In a nutshell, riders cover a distance of 40 kilometers, or 100 laps, and the rider who accumulates the most points, or the rider who laps the field—regardless of his total points—wins the race. Points are awarded during lap sprints, which occur every fifth lap. Five points are awarded to the sprint winner, three to the second, two to the third, and one to the fourth. The fiftieth lap and the final lap are bonus laps, and the points awarded are doubled. When a rider laps the field, he must maintain this advantage throughout the race in order to be awarded the victory without having the highest point total. If more than one rider laps the field the one with the most points is declared the winner.

Kilometer Time Trial: The "kilo" or "killermeter" is perhaps one of the most demanding track events. An all-out race, the cyclist rides as fast as possible for 1000 meters. It's easy to call this one: the fastest time wins.

Alone on the track, riders compete *contre la montre*—against the clock in this so-called race of truth. The rider's greatest challenge is to pace throughout the race, going fast enough to turn in a best-possible time, but not so fast as to "hit the wall" and burn out before the end of the race. Some cyclists use a technique called "floating," which incorporates a soft-pedaled stroke at intervals in order to prevent muscular burnout.

The best riders ride a tight line on the inside of the track—particularly in the turns—shaving those hundredths of seconds that make or break the finish.

Individual Road Race: Mass-start events, road races can be point-to-point races or long loops of five to 25 miles in length. Although teamwork is

249

essential in the Olympic road race, riders are nonetheless seeking individual victory. Again, the concept is simple: first across the finish wins.

What goes on in the pack, however, is not so simple. Because of the staying power required in a long road race, drafting—riding close behind another rider— is important. A rider who "grabs a wheel" saves about 25% of his or her effort. Riders who break away most often take turns drafting in order to stay away from the pack.

Strong, aggressive riders often attempt solo breaks. The solo rider risks being caught by the field, allowing a sprinter who has been "sitting in"—riding protected to conserve energy—to jump to the finish line.

Watch for teammates taking turns setting the pace, allowing others to rest by drafting. Most teams feature strong sprinters, and may work together to protect the sprinter and position him or her for the final sprint to the finish. Behind a breakaway, you may also see riders in the front of the main pack blocking—that is, deliberately slowing down the pace of the pack to prevent them from chasing the breakaway riders.

Team Time Trial: In this race against the clock, team members work together to cover a designated distance in as short a time as possible. Similar to riding in the team pursuit, cyclists rotate position throughout the race, resting in the paceline and "pulling"—or bearing the aerodynamic brunt of being the lead rider—at the front.

VeloTalk

BREAK/BREAKAWAY: A rider or group of riders that leaves the main group behind.

BRIDGE: To leave one group of riders to join another group that is farther ahead.

CONTRE LA MONTRE: French term for time trial—against the clock.

DRAFTING: Riding in a slipstream—a pocket of moving air—created by the rider in front, in order for the drafting rider to maintain speed with less effort. You might hear a number of expressions that refer to drafting; "grab a wheel," "jump on a wheel," and "get a wheel" all refer to drafting.

ECHELON: A staggered line of riders in a paceline, each downwind of the rider ahead. This formation is often used in cross-winds.

FIELD: The main group of riders, also known as the "pack" or "peloton."

FIELD SPRINT: To sprint to the finish among the main group of riders.

FORCE THE PACE: When one rider presses harder than the pack to increase the tempo.

GAP: The distance between individuals or groups of riders. Not a clothing store.

HAMMERING: An all-out, go-for-broke effort.

JAM: An extended chase.

JUMP: A quick acceleration that usually develops into a sprint.

MASS START: Any race in which all riders start at the same time.

PACE LINE: A string of riders who take turns at the front and sitting in.

POLE LINE: The innermost line on the vélodrome, used to measure the length of the track (usually 333.33 meters).

PULL: To take a turn at the front of the group, maintaining a constant speed.

SITTING IN: To ride protected, in the draft of other riders.

TAKE A FLYER: To ride off the front suddenly.

WIND-UP/WIND-OUT: A gradual acceleration that develops into a sprint. Usually initiated with more than a lap to go.

HOPEFULS

The scope of international cycling has changed tremendously with the loosening of restrictions in the Eastern bloc. Many of the more well-known men have turned professional, and support for the amateur programs has decreased. The Soviet Union still maintains one of the strongest cycling programs in the world, but the US is rapidly gaining, ranking second on the eve of the 1992 Games. Other recent European powers include Italy, France, and Czechoslovakia. Both East and West German teams have been formidable powers in the past, and a united Germany—competing for the first time as a united team in an international championship in the 1991 Junior World Championships—could prove to be a heavyweight contender at Barcelona. Elsewhere in the world, Australia and Canada, whose teams typically excel in track events, continue to maintain strong programs.

Changes to the US team, motivated by the Seoul-searching that took place after the 1988 Games, will be put to the test in Barcelona. The US Cycling Team enters the Games with the momentum gained from one of its most successful international seasons ever. US cyclists took home five medals from the World Cycling Championships in Tokyo, Japan three from the Junior World Cycling Championships in Cleveland, England, and seven at the Goodwill Games in

Seattle, Washington, including four gold. The International Cycling Union (UCI) recently ranked the US second among cycling countries. The current US national team is a good mix of young athletes and seasoned veterans.

The US women enjoy the most depth of talent in the world. A number of other competing countries boast an outstanding woman—or two—in selected events, but, overall, the US harbors the most formidable range of talent.

Many of the best riders in the world are lured away from Olympic eligibility: professional riders can earn $3 million yearly if they ride for a top team. No doubt Greg LeMond's three-year, $5.7 million contract with the Z Team is some consolation for not being allowed to compete in the Games.

A good deal of speculation centered on the inclusion of professional cyclists in the 1992 Olympics, but it was ultimately decided to continue to disallow them from the Games. A very good chance exists, according to the USCF, that the pros will be allowed to compete in the Atlanta Games. In the meantime, however, to sustain their amateur or "eligible" status, cyclists can earn up to $2500 per day of racing in prize money. Any prize money over that amount goes to the various cycling clubs. The USCF has instituted a bonus pool for the top eight finishers in the world championships, the Olympics, and the Pan Am Games, and it's reported that an Olympic gold could be worth $5000 to $6000.

Lance Armstrong

At one time in his career, Lance Armstrong was assessed by a coach this way: "He's got the legs of a champion but not the experience." Now, experience—as much as one born in 1971 can have—is fast demonstrating results in Armstrong's cycling résumé.

At the 1990 World Championships—his first year as a senior rider—Armstrong finished eleventh in the individual road race, the best American finish since 1976. Not to mention a number of other impressive results: eighth place in the 1990 Tour of Sweden, fifth place in the 1990 USCF time trial championship, and second in the 1990 USCF team time trial championship. In 1991, the Texas-bred Armstrong pedaled to a stage-race victory in Italy against an elite field and also grabbed first place in the US Senior National Championships.

First competing (for six years) as a professional triathlete, Armstrong won the 1989 and 1990 National Sprint Triathlon Championships. With an eye to competing in the Olympics—in which triathlon has sought but never received acceptance—Armstrong concentrated on cycling, pumped up with plenty of muscle from competitive swimming and cross-training.

As Armstrong gains the tactical savvy that comes with having some more experience under his belt, chances become slim that the press in Barcelona won't be well acquainted with his name. National men's road coach Chris Carmichael claims, "Lance is not only a fantastic road racer, but he is a strong team time-trial rider. His strongest assets are his aggressiveness and his natural athletic ability."

Frank about his aspirations, Armstrong has been heard to say, "I want to become a cycling star—one of the greats in the sport." He eventually aspires to turn pro and compete on the European circuit. Touted by some as the next Greg LeMond, Armstrong has turned down six-figure contracts from the professional teams who are knocking at his door. Why? Because walking into the Olympic Stadium "has to be an incredible rush."

With the erstwhile Texan triathlete in their arsenal, the US men are looking to improve their international standings in road events.—*M.M.*

Connie Pareskevin-Young

When women's cycling was added to the 1984 Olympic roster, Connie Pareskevin-Young—who held the World Match Sprint title for 1982, 1983 and 1984—was forced to sit on the sidelines: only a women's road race had been added to the cycling events, leaving women track specialists with no place in the LA Games.

Not that Pareskevin-Young was a stranger to the Olympics; she was a member of the 1980 and 1984 Olympic speedskating teams (not to mention that she double-bronzed in the 1978 World Speed Skating Championships). Her cycling record is no less impressive: six-time national champion, 1988 USCF Cyclist of the Year, Pan American Games gold medalist, former world record holder for the 200m time-trial ... she's got a lot of hardware to her name.

Not least of which is the only cycling medal that the US team captured in 1988, a bronze in the first-ever Olympic women's match sprints.

Most people would be pretty happy with an Olympic bronze, but not if you're shooting for gold. The acknowledged queen of North American sprinting, Pareskevin-Young had qualified with her fourth best time—not, however, the fastest, as she was in the 1986 Worlds. Easily besting the other riders in the first-round three-up, she encountered no problem accelerating away from her quarter-final competitor. But her attempt to shorten the sprint in the final bout left her outmuscled by Soviet Erika Salumiae.

"I went out there and did what I had to do tactically, but I didn't have it," Pareskevin-Young said, later attributing her difficulty with Salumiae to under-gearing. Choice of gear—which affects the distance the bike travels with one complete crank revolution—is of paramount importance on the track, where you live or die by the gear you've chosen.

Of the match sprint, she says, "You have to outsmart the other rider. I have to play up my strengths and use them to put my opponent at a disadvantage." 1988 was a learning experience, and Pareskevin-Young banks on not being predictable. A firm believer that the only way to improve is against top competition, she has chosen top competition to train with: her sometime-nemesis, Erika Salumiae, has been a part of her Barcelona-bound strategy. Further setting herself apart from other US team riders, Pareskevin-Young resides in Indianapolis and trains with her coach-husband, Roger Young.

Born in Detroit, on July 4, 1961, the once-and-future gold medalist took up cycling way back when Nixon was president, and a women's cycling program was not so much as a glint in anybody's eye. Women's cycling has come a long way

Cycling

since those days, and with the addition of the women's individual pursuit in Barcelona, the women's field should continue to gain depth.

As for Pareskevin-Young's chances at the Barcelona Games, Craig Griffin, the national pursuit coach, asserts, "There's no doubt that Connie is one of the best woman sprinters of all-time. She is one of the best candidates the US has for a gold medal at the 1992 Barcelona Olympics."—*M.M.*

Schedule

The tentative cycling schedule is as follows:

Sunday, July 26
100km team time trial, final men
Individual road race final, women

Monday, July 27
4000m individual pursuit, men
1000m time trial, final, men

Tuesday, July 28
Sprint qualifications, men & women
4000m individual pursuit, men
Individual points race, qualifications, men

Wednesday, July 29
Sprint, quarterfinals, men & women
4000m individual pursuit, semifinals, men
Individual points race,

qualifications, men
Sprint, quarterfinals, men
4000m individual pursuit, final, men
3000 individual pursuit, women

Thursday, July 30
4000m team pursuit, qualifications & quarterfinal, men & women
Sprint, semifinals, men & women

Friday, July 31
4000m team pursuit, semifinals & finals, men
3000 individual pursuit, semi-finals & finals, women
Sprint, finals, men & women
Individual points race, final, men

Sunday, August 2
Individual road race, final, men

▼

HIGHLIGHTS

The Games have seen a lot of jockeying among nations leading the cycling competition. The first Olympic cyclist to win the gold, Leon Flameng, circled a 333.33m cement track 300 times to out-pedal his weary competitors. Flameng was the first of a host of Frenchmen to turn cycling into a golden opportunity: to date, France has taken a total of 62 medals—27 of them gold. (Italy, in second place, has taken 46 medals, of which 26 were gold, while the US has dipped four of 12 medals in gold.) In the 1960s, a number of new arrivals started to turn heads at the Games: the traditional European dominance was challenged by

254

competitors from Poland, the German Democratic Republic, Romania, and the USSR.

Although cycling has been an Olympic constant, a number of events have come and gone: the 12-hour race, oddly, was never held again after the 1896 Games, a one-lap (603.49) race appeared in 1908 only, the 5000m, the 10km, 20km, 50km, and 100km track races have all bitten the dust, and the last 2000m tandem race was held in 1972.

Four years later, some cycling events went indoors for the first time at the Games, a year that also marked the Czechoslovakian team's unfortunate loss of the team wheels to a garbage compressor. The US, which hadn't medalled in cycling in the Olympics since 1912, dusted the competition in LA at the 1984 Games, where four golds, three silvers, and a bronze were awarded to riders wearing the stars and stripes. Women, long ignored by the Games, first competed in 1984 when a women's road race was added to the program; Americans Connie Carpenter-Phinney and Rebecca Twigg took the gold and silver.

In 1988, a track event was added, allowing Connie Pareskevin-Young to earn the only medal the US took in cycling in Seoul.

fact: What kind of effort does it entail for a cyclist to go faster? To increase from 18 kph to 25 kph, a rider must double her strength; to reach 40 kph, six times the effort is required. The faster you go, the harder it gets.

The individual road race, which has missed only three Games, has given rise to its share of memorable—and sometimes forgettable— trivia. The 1896 course ran from Athens to Marathon, where riders had to sign their names and turn around. The winner, Aristidis Konstantintidis, from Greece, rode three bikes in the race, although not all at the same time.

Three Games later, an imbroglio developed over the race results: the course was intersected at six points by railway crossings that produced a number of delays, and guards posted at the crossings recorded the delays. The first cyclist into the stadium, Henry Kaltenbrun, was greeted as the winner. A little arithmetic, however, revealed that Harry Stenquist, who had waited four minutes at a railway crossing, was the first-place finisher.

And then there's the story of meals on wheels during the 1932 Games. According to the press, Italian first-place winner Attilio Pavesi carried a bucket of water, soup, spaghetti, sweet rolls, cheese sandwiches, jam—and two spare tires.

Just how fast do these guys go, anyway? The fastest-ever Olympic ride took place in the altitudinous vélodrome in Mexico City. Daniel Morelson and Pierre Trentin, from France, blazed through the final 200 meters of the tandem race in 9.83 seconds; that's 73.24km/h or 45.51 mph. At the 1980 Moscow Games,

Soviet rider Sergey Kopylov clocked the last 200 meters of the 1000m time-trial at 10.47 seconds, setting the fastest individual speed record at 68.76km/h or 42.73 mph.

Lore has it that drugs were an integral part of grueling stage races, such as the Tour de France, in the early days of the sport. The 1960 Rome Games produced tragic results for the Danish team. When two Danish teammates collapsed during the arduous 100km road race, everyone believed that they had been struck by sunstroke in the 93-degree Roman Summer. One of the two Danes, Knut Enemark Jensen, fractured his skull in the fall, and died en route to the hospital; he became the first athlete to die in Olympic competition since the 1912 marathon. Later, a postmortem revealed that Jensen had taken a large overdose of the blood circulation stimulant Ronicol.

Spurred by Jensen's death, the International Cycling Federation (UCI) became the first to institute drug control, well before the International Medical Commission issued mandatory drug testing for all sports in 1968. In 1989, the USCF established a stringent drug policy, stiffening the penalties for athletes who fail the test. Anyone testing positive—subject to random testing—suffers a two-year suspension for the first offence, and four years for the second. Riders refusing to be tested are automatically suspended for one year.

Nevertheless, despite international dope policing, cycling has contributed its share of inductees to the Hall of Shame. In the 1972 Games, Spain's third-place medalist in the individual road race and Holland's third-place medalist in the team road race were both disqualified for ergogenic cheating.

Eddy Merckx

Better known for his total domination of the Tour de France (five wins), and for having set the hour record (later smashed by Francesco Moser), Eddy Merckx—one of the most famous cyclists in the world—competed in the 1964 Olympics.

A mere 19 in Tokyo in 1964, Merckx stayed at the front throughout the road race, until just several hundred meters from the finish. There, a crash left him behind the pack, but the Belgian die-hard jammed to the finish, a mere 11/100 seconds behind Mario Zanin, the Italian winner. Sounds close, but he finished twelfth.

Merckx retired at the age of 33 to much fame and fortune, the attainment of an Olympic medal out of reach. Wonder if he knew the oldest Olympic cycling gold medalist was 38? —*M.M.*

Cycling — Men's Cycling

Cycling — Men's 100-Kilometer Team Time Trial

1988 1. East Germany, 1:57:44.7, Uwe Ampler, Mario Kummer, Maik Landsmann, Jan Schur
2. Poland, 1:57:47.3, Joachim Halupczok, Zenon Jaskula, Marek Lesniewski, Andrzej Sypytkowski
3. Sweden, 1:59:47.3, Bjorn Johansson, Jan Karlsson, Michel Lafis, Anders Jarl

1984 1. Italy, 1:58:28, Marcello Bartalini, Marco Giovannetti, Eros Polis, Claudio Vandelli
2. Switzerland, 2:02:38, Alfred Acherman, Richard Trinkler, Laurent P. Vial, Benno Wiss
3. USA, 2:02:46, Ronald Kiefel, Roy Knickman, Davis Phinney, Andrew Weaver

1980 1. Soviet Union, 2:01:21.7, Yuri Kashirin, Oleg Logvin, Sergei Shelpakov, Anatoli Yarkin
2. East Germany, 2:02:53.2, Falk Boden, Bernd Drogan, Olaf Ludwig, Hans-Joachim Hartnick
3. Czechoslovakia, 2:02:53.9, Michal Klasa, Vlastibor Konecny, Alipi Kostadinov, Jiri Skoda

1976 1. Soviet Union, 2:08:53.0, Anatoli Chukanov, Valeri Chaplygin, Vladimir Kaminsky, Aavo Pikkuus
2. Poland, 2:09:13.0, Tadeusz Mytnik, Myeczyslaw Nowicki, Stanislaw Szozda, Ryszard Szurkowski
3. Denmark, 2:12:20.0, Verner Blaudzin, Gert Frank, Jorgen Emil Hansen, Jorn Lund, Niels Fredborg

1972 1. Soviet Union, 2:11:17.8, Boris Chuchov, Valeri Iardi, Gennady Komnatov, Valeri Likhachov
2. Poland, 2:11:47.5, Lucjan Lis, Edward Barcik, Stanislaw Szozda, Ryszard Szurkowski
3. 3rd place team was Netherlands, but disqualified due to drug use.

1968 1. Netherlands, 2:07:49.06, Fedor den Hertog, Jan Krekels, Marinus Pijnen, Henk Zoetemelk
2. Sweden, 2:09:26.60, Erik Pettersson, Gosta Pettersson, Sture Pettersson, Tomas Pettersson
3. Italy, 2:10:18.74, Giovanni Bramucci, Vittorio Marcelli, Mauro Simonetti, Pierfranco Vianelli

1964 1. Netherlands, 2:26:31.19, Evert G. Dolman, Gerben Karstens, Johannes Pieterse, Hubertus Zoet
2. Italy, 2:26:55.39, Sverino Andreoli, Luciano Dalla Bona, Pietro Guerra, Ferrucio Manza
3. Sweden, 2:27:11.52, Sven Hamrin, Erik Pettersson, Gosta Pettersson, Sture Pettersson

1960 1. Italy, 2:14:33.53, Antonio Bailetti, Ottavio Cogliati, Giacomo Fornoni, Livio Trape

2. East Germany, 2:16:56.31, Gustav-Adolf Schur, Egon Adler, Erich Hagen, Gunter Lorke
3. Soviet Union, 2:18:41.67, Viktor Kapitonov, Yevgeni Klevzov, Yuri Melichov, Aleksei Petrov

1896-1956 Not held

Cycling — Men's One-Kilometer Time Trial

1988 1. Alexander Kirichenko, Soviet Union, 1:04.499
2. Martin Vinnicombe, Australia, 1:04.784
3. Robert Lechner, West Germany, 1:05.114

1984 1. Fredy Schmidtke, West Germany, 1:06.104
2. Curtis Harnett, Canada, 1:06.436
3. Fabrice Colas, France, 1:06.649

1980 1. Lothar Thoms, East Germany, 1:02.955 (WR)
2. Aleksandr Panfilov, Soviet Union, 1:04.845
3. David Weller, Jamaica, 1:05.241

1976 1. Klaus Juergen Gruenke, East Germany, 1:05.927
2. Michel Vaarten, Belgium, 1:07.516
3. Niels Fredborg, Denmark, 1:07.617

1972 1. Niels Fredborg, Denmark, 1:06.44
2. Daniel Clark, Australia, 1:06.87
3. Jurgen Schutze, East Germany, 1:07.02

1968 1. Pierre Trentin, France, 1:03.91 (WR)
2. Niels Fredborg, Denmark, 1:04.61
3. Janusz Kierzkowski, Poland, 1:04.63

1964 1. Patrick Sercu, Belgium, 1:09.59
2. Giovanni Pettenella, Italy, 1:10.09
3. Pierre Trentin, France, 1:10.42

1960 1. Sante Gaiardoni, Italy, 1:07.27 (WR)
2. Dieter Gieseler, West Germany, 1:08.75
3. Rostislav Vargashkin, Soviet Union, 1:08.86

1956 1. Leandro Faggin, Italy, 1:09.8 (OR)
2. Ladislav Foucek, Czechoslovakia, 1:11.4
3. Alfred J. Swift, South Africa, 1:11.6

1952 1. Russell Mockridge, Australia, 1:11.1 (OR)
2. Marino Morettini, Italy, 1:12.7
3. Raymond Robinson, South Africa, 1:13.0

1948 1. Jacques Dupont, France, 1:13.5
2. Pierre Nihant, Belgium, 1:14.5
3. Thomas Godwin, Great Britain, 1:15.0

1936 1. Arie van Vliet, Netherlands, 1:12.0 (OR)
2. Pierre Georget, France, 1:12.8
3. Rudolf Karsch, Germany, 1:13.2

1932 1. Edgar Gray, Australia, 1:13.0
2. Jacobus van Egmond, Netherlands, 1:13.3
3. Charles Rampelberg, France, 1:13.4

1928 1. Willy Falck Hansen, Denmark, 1:14.4

2. Gerard Bosch van Drakestein,
   Netherlands, 1:15.2
3. Edgar Gray, Australia, 1:15.6

1908-
1924   **Not held**
1906   1. Francesco Verri, Italy, 22.8
        2. H. Crowther, Great Britain, 22.8
        3. Menjou, France, 23.2
1900-
1904   **Not held**
1896   1. Paul Masson, France, 24.0
        2. Stamatios Nikolopoulos, Greece, 25.4
        3. Adolf Schmal, Austria, 26.6

Cycling — Men's 4,000-Meter Individual Pursuit

1988   1. Gintaoutas Umaras, Soviet Union,
           4:32.00
        2. Dean Woods, Australia, 4:35.00
        3. Bernd Dittert, East Germany, 4:34.17
1984   1. Steve Hegg, USA, 4:39.35
        2. Rolf Golz, West Germany, 4:43.83
        3. Leonard Nitz, USA, 4:44.03
1980   1. Robert Dill-Bundi, Switzerland, 4:35.66
        2. Alain Bondue, France, 4:42.96
        3. Hans-Henrik Orsted, Denmark, 4:36.54
1976   1. Gregor Braun, West Germany,
           4:47.61
        2. Hermann Ponsteen, Netherlands,
           4:49.72
        3. Thomas Huschke, East Germany,
           4:52.71
1972   1. Knut Knudsen, Norway, 4:45.74
        2. Xavier Kurmann, Switzerland, 4:51.96
        3. Hans Lutz, West Germany, 4:50.80
1968   1. Daniel Rebillard, France, 4:41.71
        2. Mogens Frey Jensen, Denmark,
           4:42.43
        3. Xavier Kurmann, Switzerland, 4:39.42
1964   1. Jiri Daler, Czechoslovakia, 5:04.75
        2. Giorgio Ursi, Italy, 5:05.96
        3. Preben Isaksson, Denmark, 5:01.90
1896-
1960   **Not held**

Cycling — Men's 4,000-Meter Team Pursuit

1988   1. Soviet Union, 4:13.31, Viatcheslav
           Ekimov, Artouras Kaspoutis, Dmitri
           Nelubine, Gintaoutas Umaras
        2. East Germany, 4:14.09, Steffen
           Blochwitz, Roland Hennig, Dirk Meier,
           Carsten Wolf
        3. Australia, 4:16.02, Brett Dutton,
           Wayne McCarney, Stephen McGlede,
           Dean Woods
1984   1. Australia, 4:25.99, Michael Grenca,
           Kevin Nichols, Michael Turtur, Dean
           Woods
        2. USA, 4:29.85, David Grylls, Steve
           Hegg, R. Patrick McDonough, Leonard
           Nitz
        3. West Germany, 4:25.60, Reinhard
           Alber, Rolf Golz, Roland Gunther,
           Michael Marx

1980   1. Soviet Union, 4:15.70, Viktor
           Manakov, Valeri Movchan, Vladimir
           Osokin, Vitali Petrakov
        2. East Germany, 4:19.67, Gerald
           Mortag, Matthias Wiegand, Volker
           Winkler, Uwe Unterwalder
        3. Czechoslovakia, 4:32.68, Teodor
           Cerny, Martin Penc, Jiri Pokorny, Igor
           Slama
1976   1. West Germany, 4:21.06, Gregor
           Braun, Hans Lutz, Gunther
           Schumacher, Peter Vonhof
        2. Soviet Union, 4:27.15, Vladimir
           Osokin, Aleksandr Perov, Vitali
           Petrakov, Viktor Sokolov
        3. Great Britain, 4:22.41, Ian Banbury,
           Michael Bennett, Robin Croker, Ian
           Hallam
1972   1. West Germany, 4:22.14, Jurgen
           Colombo, Gunther Haritz, Udo
           Hempel, Gunther Schumacher
        2. East Germany, 4:25.25, Thomas
           Huschke, Heinz Richter, Herbert
           Richter, Uwe Unterwalder
        3. Great Britain, 4:23.78, Michael
           Bennett, Ian Hallam, Ronald Keeble,
           William Moore
1968   1. Denmark, 4:22.44, Gunnar Asmussen,
           Per Lyngemark, Reno B. Olsen,
           Mogens Frey Jensen
        2. West Germany, 4:18.94, Udo Hempel,
           Karl Link, Karlheinz Henrichs, Jurgen
           Kissner
        3. Italy, 4:18.35, Lorenzo Bosisio,
           Cipriano Chemello, Luigi Roncaglia,
           Giorgio Moribiato
1964   1. West Germany, 4:35.67, Lothar
           Claesges, Karlheinz Henrichs, Karl
           Link, Ernst Streng
        2. Italy, 4:35.74, Luigi Roncaglia,
           Vincenzo Mantovani, Carlo Rancati,
           Franco Testa
        3. Netherlands, 4:38.99, Gerard Koel,
           Hendrik Cornelisse, Jacob Oudkerk,
           Cornelis Schurring
1960   1. Italy, 4:30.90, Luigi Arienti, Franco
           Testa, Mario Vallotto, Marino Vigna
        2. East Germany, 4:35.78, Siegfried
           Kohler, Peter Groning, Manfred
           Klieme, Bernd Barleben
        3. Soviet Union, 4:34.05, Stanislav
           Moskvin, Viktor Romanov, Leonid
           Kolumbet, Arnold Belgardt
1956   1. Italy, 4:37.4, Leandro Faggin,
           Valentino Gasparella, Antonio
           Domenicali, Franco Gandini
        2. France, 4:39.4, Michel Vermeulin,
           Jean-Claude Lecante, Rene Bianchi,
           Jean Graczyk
        3. Great Britain, 4:42.2, Donald Burgess,
           Michael Gambrill, John Geddes,
           Thomas Simpson
1952   1. Italy, 4:46.1, Marino Morettini, Guido
           Messina, Mino De Rossi, Loris
           Campana
        2. South Africa, 4:53.6, Thomas F.
           Shardelow, Alfred J. Swift, Robert G.
           Fowler, George Estman
        3. Great Britain, 4:51.5, Ronald C.
           Stretton, Alan Newton, George A.
           Newberry, Donald C. Burgess

1948 1. France, 4:57.8, Charles Coste, Serge
Blusson, Ferdinand Decanali, Pierre
Adam
2. Italy, 5:36.7, Arnaldo Benfenati,
Guido Bernardi, Anselm Citterio, Rino
Pucci
3. Great Britain, 4:55.8, Alan Geldard,
Thomas Godwin, David Ricketts,
Wilfred Waters
1936 1. France, 4:45.0, Robert Charpentier,
Jean Goujon, Guy Lapebie, Roger Le
Nizerhy
2. Italy, 4:51.0, Bianco Bianchi, Mario
Gentili, Armando Severino Rigoni
3. Great Britain, 4:53.6, Harry Hill,
Ernest A. Johnson, Charles King,
Ernest Mills
1932 1. Italy, 4:53.0, Marco Cimatti, Paolo
Pedretti, Alberto Ghilardi, Nino Borsari
2. France, 4:55.7, Amede Fournier, Rene
Legreves, Henri Mouillefarine, Paul
Chocque
3. Great Britain, 4:56.0, Ernest A.
Johnson, William Harvell, Frank W.
Southall, Charles Holland
1928 1. Italy, 5:01.8, Luigi Tasselli, Giacomo
Gaioni, Cesare Facciani, Mario Lusiani
2. Netherlands, 5:06.2, Adriaan
Braspenninx, Jan Maas, Johannes
Pijnenburg, Piet van der Horst
3. Great Britain, Frank Wyld, Leonard
Wyld, Percy Wyld, M. George
Southall
1924 1. Italy, 5:15.0, Angelo De Martino,
Alfredo Dinale, Aleardo Menegazzi,
Francesco Zucchetti
2. Poland, Jozef Lange, Jan Lazarski,
Tomasz Stankiewicz, Franciszek
Szymczyk
3. Belgium, Leonard Daghelinckx, Henri
Hoevenaers, Fernand Saive, Jean van
den Bosch
1920 1. Italy, 5:20.0, Franco Giorgetti,
Ruggero Ferrario, Arnaldo Carli, Primo
Magnani
2. Great Britain, Albert White, Horace
Thomas Johnson, William Stewart,
Cyril A. Alden
3. South Africa, James Walker, William
Smith, Henry J. Kaltenbrun, Harry W.
Goosen
1912 **Not held**
1908 1. Great Britain, 2:18.6, Leon Meredith,
Benjamin Jones, Ernest Payne, Charles
Kingsbury
2. Germany, 2:28.6, Hermann Martens,
Max Gotze, Karl Neumer, Rudolf
Katzer
3. Canada, 2:29.6, William Morton,
Walter Andrews, Frederick McCarthy,
William Anderson
1896-
1906 **Not held**

Cycling — Men's Match Sprint

1988 1. Lutz Hesslich, East Germany
2. Nikolai Kovche, Soviet Union
3. Gary Neiwand, Australia
3. Gary Niewand, Australia
1984 1. Mark Gorski, USA, 10.49

2. Nelson Vails, USA, 10.95
3. Tsutomu Sakamoto, Japan, 11.03
1980 1. Lutz Hesslich, East Germany
2. Yave Cahard, France
3. Sergei Kopylov, Soviet Union
1976 1. Anton Tkac, Czechoslovakia
2. Daniel Morelon, France
3. Hans-Juergen Geschke, East Germany
1972 1. Daniel Morelon, France, 11.25
2. John M. Nicholson, Australia
3. Omar Pchakadse, Soviet Union
1968 1. Daniel Morelon, France, 10.68
2. Giordano Turrini, Italy
3. Pierre Trentin, France
1964 1. Giovanni Pettenella, Italy, 13.69
2. Sergio Bianchetto, Italy
3. Daniel Morelon, France
1960 1. Sante Gaiardoni, Italy, 11.1
2. Leo Sterckx, Belgium
3. Valentino Gasparella, Italy
1956 1. Michel Rousseau, France, 11.4
2. Guglielmo Pesenti, Italy
3. Richard Ploog, Austria
1952 1. Enzo Sacchi, Italy, 12.0
2. Lionel Cox, Australia
3. Werner Potzernheim, Germany
1948 1. Mario Ghella, Italy, 12.0
2. Reginald Harris, Great Britain
3. Axel Schandorff, Denmark
1936 1. Toni Merkens, Germany, 11.8
2. Arie van Vliet, Netherlands
3. Louis Chaillot, France
1932 1. Jacobus van Egmond, Netherlands,
12.6
2. Louis Chaillot, France
3. Bruno Pellizzari, Italy
1928 1. Roger Beaufrand, France, 13.2
2. Antoine Mazairac, Netherlands
3. Willy Falck Hansen, Denmark
1924 1. Lucien Michard, France, 12.8 (last 200
m)
2. Jacob Meijer, Netherlands
3. Jean Cugnot, France
1920 1. Maurice Peeters, Netherlands, 1:38.3
2. Horace Thomas Johnson, Great Britain
3. Harry Ryan, Great Britain
1912 **Not held**
1908 Final was declared void owing to the
time limit being exceeded
1906 1. Francesco Verri, Italy, 1:42.2
2. H. C. Bouffler, Great Britain
3. Eugene Debongnie, Belgium
1904 **Not held**
1900 1. Georges Taillandier, France, 2:52.0
(last 200 m 13.0)
2. Fernand Sanz, France
3. John Henry Lake, USA
1896 1. Paul Masson, France, 4:56.0
2. Stamatios Nikolopoulos, Greece,
5:00.2
3. Leon Flameng, France

Cycling — Men's Individual Points Race

1988 1. Dan Frost, Denmark, 38
2. Leo Peelen, Netherlands, 26
3. Maral Ganeev, Soviet Union, 46 (one
lap down)
1984 1. Rogers Ilegems, Belgium, 37

259

2. Uwe Messerschmidt, West Germany, 35
3. Jose Manuel Youshimatz, Mexico, 29

Cycling — Men's Individual Road Race

1988
1. Olaf Ludwig, East Germany, 4:32.22
2. Bernd Groene, West Germany, 4:32.25
3. Christian Henn, West Germany, 4:32.46

1984
1. Alexi Grewal, USA, 4:59:57
2. Steve Bauer, Canada, 4:59:57
3. Dag Otto Lauritzen, Norway, 5:00:18

1980
1. Sergei Sukhoruchenkov, Soviet Union, 4:48:28.9
2. Czeslaw Lang, Poland, 4:51:26.9
3. Yuri Barinov, Soviet Union, 4:51:29.9

1976
1. Bernt Johansson, Sweden, 4:46:52.0
2. Giuseppe Martinelli, Italy, 4:47:23.0
3. Mieczyl Nowicki, Poland, 4:47:23.0

1972
1. Hennie Kuiper, Netherlands, 4:14:37.0
2. Kevin C. Sefton, Australia, 4:15:04.0

1968
1. Pierfranco Vianelli, Italy, 4:41:25.24
2. Leif Mortensen, Denmark, 4:42:49.71
3. Gosta Pettersson, Sweden, 4:43:15.24

1964
1. Mario Zanin, Italy, 4:39:51.63
2. Kjeld Rodian, Denmark, 4:39:51.65
3. Walter Godefroot, Belgium, 4:39:51.74

1960
1. Viktor Kapitonov, Soviet Union, 4:20:37.0
2. Livio Trape, Italy, 4:20:37.0
3. Willy van den Berghen, Belgium, 4:20:57.0

1956
1. Ercole Baldini, Italy, 5:21:17.0
2. Arnaud Geyre, France, 5:23:16:0
3. Alan Jackson, Great Britain, 5:23:16.0

1952
1. Andre Noyelle, Belgium, 5:06:03.4
2. Robert Grondelaers, Belgium, 5:06:51.2
3. Edi Ziegler, West Germany, 5:07:47.5

1948
1. Jose Beyaert, France, 5:18:12.6
2. Gerardus P. Voorting, Netherlands, 5:18:16.2
3. Lode Wouters, Belgium, 5:18:16.2

1936
1. Robert Charpentier, France, 2:33:05:0
2. Guy Lapebie, France, 2:33:05.2
3. Ernst Nievergelt, Switzerland, 2:33:05.8

1932
1. Attilio Pavesi, Italy, 2:28:05.6
2. Guglielmo Segato, Italy, 2:29:21.4

3. Bernhard Britz, Sweden, 2:29:45.2

1928
1. Henry Hansen, Denmark, 4:47:18.0
2. Frank W. Southall, Great Britain, 4:55:06.0
3. Gosta Carlsson, Sweden, 5:00:17.0

1924
1. Armand Blanchonnet, France, 6:20:48.0
2. Henri Hoevenaers, Belgium, 6:30:27.0
3. Rene Hamel, France, 6:30:51.6

1920
1. Harry Stenqvist, Sweden, 4:40:01.8
2. Henry J. Kaltenbrun, South Africa, 4:41:26.6
3. Fernand Canteloube, France, 4:42:54.4

1912
1. Rudolph Lewis, South Africa, 10:42:39.0
2. Frederick Grubb, Great Britain, 10:51:24.2
3. Carl Schutte, USA, 10:52:38.8

1908 Not held

1906
1. B. Vast, France, 2:41:28.0
2. M. Bardonneau, France, 2:41:28.4
3. Luguet, France, 2:41:28.6

1900-1904 Not held

1896
1. Aristidis Konstantinidis, Greece, 3:22.31
2. August Goedrich, Germany, 3:42.18
3. F. Battel, Great Britain

Cycling — Women's Match Sprint

1988
1. Erika Saloumiae, Soviet Union
2. Christa Rothenburger-Luding, East Germany
3. Connie Paraskevin-Young, USA

Cycling — Women's Individual Road Race

1988
1. Monique Knol, Netherlands, 2:00.52
2. Jutta Niehaus, West Germany, 2:00.52
3. Laima Zilporitee, Soviet Union, 2:00.52

1984
1. Connie Carpenter-Phinney, USA, 2:11.14
2. Rebecca Twigg, USA, 2:11.14
3. Sandra Schumacher, West Germany, 2:11.14

DIVING

WARM-UP

F lying through the air with the greatest of ease, spiraling downward before slipping into the water with barely a splash, divers participate in one of the more elegant and breathtaking Olympic events. Few would disagree that the grace, beauty, and form inherent in a near flawless dive is unmatched in competitive athletics.

Diving dates back to the 17th century when gymnasts in Sweden and Germany would practice their sport over water on equipment set up on the beaches during the summer months. The activity became popular, eventually branching away from gymnastics in the late 19th century to form the new acrobatic sport of diving. As late as the 1920s, however, it was often included in gymnastic competitions.

fact: A background in gymnastics, trampoline, or dance can be beneficial for aspiring divers.

Diving was first introduced in England in 1893 with a plunging championship, and two years later the Royal Life Saving Society of Great Britain initiated a nationwide graceful diving competition, which continued in various forms until 1961.

Diving was included in the Olympic program at the 1904 Games in St. Louis, when a men's springboard competition was held. Men's 10-meter platform was added for the 1908 Games in London, while women's platform began at the following Olympics. Women's springboard was added in 1920.

Since the introduction of diving to the Olympic Games, the US divers have enjoyed extraordinary success. The American team has won 45 of 70 gold medals and 121 of 210 total medals, including 15 of 19 gold medals in men's and 11 of 16 in women's three-meter springboard. In the platform, US divers have taken 11 of 18 gold medals in the men's competition and eight of 16 in the women's event.

SPECTATORS' GUIDE

The Olympic diving competition consists of the men's and women's platform (10 meters or 33 feet high—about equal in height to a three-story building) and springboard (3 meters or almost 10 feet) events. The springboard is an adjustable diving board that regulates "springiness." The platform is a stationary, nonbending board that is at least 20 feet long and six and a half feet wide.

In each of the four events, a preliminary round is held to bring the number of divers down to 12 finalists. In the springboard preliminary, the men perform a series of 11 dives and the women 10, a sequence that is repeated in the finals. In the platform events, the men perform 10 dives and the women eight in each round.

fact: From the ten-meter platform a diver is travelling about 35 mph when she enters the water.

The springboard event requires that the men perform five voluntary dives with a total degree of difficulty not exceeding 9.5, and six voluntary dives without limit. The women's springboard is similar except they execute five voluntary dives without limit.

On the platform, both men and women perform four voluntary dives with a total degree of difficulty not exceeding 7.6, while the men execute six voluntary without limit and the women four.

Olympic diving contests are judged by a crew of seven. After each dive, each judge determines the point total for the dive on a scale of 0 (lowest) to 10 (highest), in half or whole point increments.

The seven point scores are displayed, with the highest and lowest eliminated. The remaining scores are added and then multiplied by the degree of difficulty. The **degree of difficulty** is a rating for executing a specific dive, ranging from 1.1 to 3.5. The result is then reduced by 3/5 (0.6), in keeping with the tradition that a diver's score comes from three judges.

For example: a dive earns scores of 6-5-5-5-5-5-4. The sum, after high (6) and low (4) scores are eliminated, is 25. Let's say the degree of difficulty is 2.0, so 25 multiplied by 2 is 50. 50 multiplied by 0.6 comes to 30, the score for the dive.

Compared to figure skating, the diving scoring system is simplicity itself.

At the beginning of a dive, the diver's body should be straight, head erect, heels together and arms straight to the sides. Once the diver stands on the front end of the board to perform a standing dive, the judges assume the dive has begun. In judging a dive, certain parts of each dive must be analyzed and evaluated, and an overall award obtained.

Parts of a Dive

Approach: In forward dives, the starting position is assumed when the diver is ready to take the first step. The forward approach must be smooth, straight, and forceful. It should be comprised of no fewer than three steps before the **hurdle** (the jump to the end of the board in which both feet contact the end of the board simultaneously). If a diver takes fewer than three steps, the referee deducts two points off the award of each judge.

Takeoff: The takeoff should be forceful and confident, show control and balance, and proceed without delay. In running dives, the takeoff from the springboard must be from both feet simultaneously. The final segment of a diver's approach to the takeoff is called the **hurdle**, and consists of a spring to the end of the board, taking off from one foot, and landing on two feet at the end of the board.

In **back takeoffs**, the diver is not allowed to lift his feet from the board before actual takeoff, but may use his own method of arm swings. During a back dive, a diver is not allowed to excessively rock the board before taking off. A violation costs two points from each judge's score. Divers also use armstand takeoffs in platform diving.

Elevation: The amount of spring or lift a diver receives from the takeoff greatly affects the appearance of the dive. Since more height means more time, a higher dive generally permits greater accuracy and smoothness of movement. If, on any dive, the diver touches the end of the board or dives to the side of the direct line of flight, the judges may deduct points at their discretion.

Execution: As important as the dive itself. A judge watches for proper mechanical performance, technique, form, and grace.

Entry: The entry is very significant because it is the last element of the dive the judges see, and is probably the one they will remember best. The two criteria to be evaluated on entry are the angle, which should be near vertical with toes pointed, and the amount of splash, which should be as little as possible. In a head-first entry, arms should be stretched above the head in line with the body and hands close together. In feet-first entries, the arms should be held close to the body, without bending the elbows.

From the 10-meter platform, a diver is traveling about 35 miles per hour at entry. A **rip** is an entry into the water that makes a "ripping" sound and leaves little splash.

Types of Dives

For the springboard event, one dive from each of the first five groups listed below is required. The platform event requires four of the six to be performed (including the armstand).

Forward: The diver faces the front of the board and rotates toward the water. Dives in this group vary from the simple front dive to the extremely difficult forward four and one-half somersault.

Back: At the beginning of the dive, the diver is at the end of the board with his or her back toward the water. The direction of rotation is away from the board.

Reverse: These dives (formerly called "gainers") begin with the diver facing the front of the board (using a forward approach) and rotating toward the board.

Inward: The diver stands on the end of the board, back toward the water, and rotates toward the board (opposite of back dives). Formerly called "cutaways."

Twisting: Includes any forward, back, inward, or reverse dive with a twist. This group includes the greatest number of dives because of all the possible combinations.

Armstand: Used only in platform diving, these dives begin with the diver assuming a handstand position on the edge of the platform before executing the dive.

Body Positions

The official dive chart lists 87 basic dives. With body positions of straight, pike, tuck, or free, 338 dive variations exist.

Straight: No bending at the waist or the knees. The arm placement is either by the diver's choice or defined by the dive performed.

Pike: Legs are straight with the body bent at the waist. Again, arm position is either decided by the diver or dictated by the dive.

Tuck: The body is bent at both the waist and the knees. The thighs are drawn to the chest while the heels are kept close to the buttocks.

Free: This is the diver's option of using a combination of the other three positions, with the most common combination being straight and pike. The free position is only used in dives that include twists.

▼

HOPEFULS

A showdown between diving champions from China and the USA will be in store for Olympic fans again in 1992. China showed its prowess during the 1991 World Aquatic Championships in Perth, Australia, by taking four of the six gold medals. For the **Chinese men's team,** platform diver Sun Shuwei took the country's only men's title, ahead of 1988 Olympic silver medalist Xiong Ni (the diver who had nearly beaten Greg Louganis out of his fourth Olympic gold medal at Seoul). Other strong Chinese veterans of the men's team include two-time Olympic silver medalist Tan Liangde, who placed second in the 3-meter dive at the World

Championships, and 1988 Olympic bronze medalist Li Deliang, who placed fourth in the 3-meter dive.

For the **Chinese women,** Olympic springboard champion Gao Min won the 1-meter and 3-meter springboard events at the Worlds (the 1-meter is not an Olympic event), and Fu Mingxia took the platform gold. A fourth-place finish in the women's platform dive was achieved by 1988 Olympic platform champion Xu Yanmei. And 1984 Olympic gold medalist Zhou Jihong has also been diving with finesse, winning the platform gold at the 1991 Alamo Challenge in Moscow.

Although the US team lost its best divers when two-time Olympian Kelly McCormick and four-time Olympic champion Greg Louganis retired, it enjoys a deep pool of talent from which to draw for the 1992 Summer Games. Five-time US Champion Kent Ferguson, a 3-meter springboard diver, leads the **US men's team** with numerous international and national medals, including two world titles and a gold at the 1991 HTH Classic. 1988 Olympian and three-time US Springboard Champion Mark Bradshaw hopes for another chance at a medal, and newcomer Mark Lenzi—a high school wrestler who began diving in 1986, inspired by watching Louganis—has made undeniably striking progress. In 1991 he became the first to score more than 100 points on a single dive, breaking Louganis's 99-point record, and he was the first springboard diver to complete a 4.5 somersault in competition. His medals include a 3-meter World Cup gold, a 1-meter silver at the 1991 World Aquatic Championships, and 1-meter golds at the 1991 Pan American Games and HTH Classic.

The US men's platform team may rely on four-time National Champ Matt Scoggin, whose 1991 medals include a gold at the HTH Classic and silvers at the Alamo Challenge and the Pan American Games. Two men have proven themselves in both springboard and platform events: 1988 Olympian Patrick Jeffrey and five-time US Champion Pat Evans, who won three of his national titles in 1-meter diving and two in the platform event.

1988 Olympic finalist Wendy Lucero—a nine-time National Springboard Champion—hopes to lead the **US women's team** to a springboard medal in 1992. Karen LaFace also shows great talent on the springboard, having won three gold medals in the 3-meter event in 1991. In the platform event watch for veteran diver Cokey Smith, recent winner of two US Olympic Festival titles. Several US women dive equally well in the springboard and platform events, including Mary Ellen Clark, who won the 3-meter silver at the 1991 HTH Classic and the platform silver at the 1991 Phillips 66 Indoor Championships, and Allison Maisch, who took the 1-meter silver at the 1991 Pan American Games and the platform gold at the HTH Classic. And A. Jill Schlabach, whose springboard diving shows exceptional promise, has managed to work three 12-hour overnight nursing shifts a week at the University of Michigan Medical Center's surgical intensive care unit, practice and sleep for five hours (each) a day, and also win 1-meter gold medals in 1991 at the Pan American Games and the HTH Classic.

The Chinese Divers—Beneath the Surface

"The depth on China's diving team," *Miami Herald* sports writer Jim Martz wrote in May 1991, "seems deeper than the Atlantic Ocean."

That was no news for former US Olympian Michele Mitchell. Three years earlier, she told the *New York Times*: "Every meet we go to they send different teams."

Why such a tidal wave of talent from a country that lost a generation of athletes to the Great Revolution and the Gang of Four's anti-sports competition philosophy (sports competition was deemed capitalistic, individualistic and bad) and didn't begin diving internationally until 1982?

"Diving people in China know advanced knowledge," three-meter diver Lan Wei told Martz.

Well, they've got something down pat, anyway.

At the 1988 Seoul Games, the Chinese divers won a pair of silver medals in the mens' events and a gold in the women's platform and a gold and a silver in women's springboard.

In three major international diving competitions since the 1988 Olympics—the 1989 FINA World Diving Cup, the 1990 Goodwill Games, and the 1991 World Aquatic Championships—Chinese divers have won 12 of 18 gold medals. The US has won five.

And in 1990, platform diver Fu Mingxia, then 11, became the youngest world titlist in the history of any aquatic event. (FINA, the sport's governing body, later announced it was limiting future world championships, Olympics, and World Cup events to divers 14 and older, though a loophole will allow Fu to compete as a 13-year-old in Barcelona. The law is supposed to prevent injuries. Ironically, Fu was kicked out of a school gymnastics program in China because officials thought she was getting too old to become world class.)

"The reason for our success," a Chinese coach said in *McLean's* magazine in 1983, "comes from long, strenuous practice days, much patience, devotion of the heart and soul to the task and a close harmonious relationship with themselves, each other and the coach."

There's also this: In China, some of the divers who are recruited have never seen a swimming pool, but are selected on strength and flexibility alone. Trip Gabriel wrote in the *New York Times* in 1988 that Chinese coaches also look for specific athletes, those who are "short, compact, perhaps with hyperextended elbows, that is, elbows that touch when the arms are raised above the head, making for a less splashy entry into the water."

Dr. Gao Chongxuan, of the National Research Institute of Sports Science in Bejing, told Gabriel: "In the West, your primary schools have pools, a gymnasium, even their own tennis courts. We don't have enough facilities, so we have to select athletes who've never played sports before."

The system designed by head national diving coach Xu Yiming accentuates fast spinning and clean entries.

Wrote Gabriel: "The Chinese are masters of the ripped entry, an almost splashless finale that sounds like fabric being torn, which is created when a diver locks his wrists and hits the water with hands flat, drilling a hole through which the entire body flows."

Male Chinese divers to watch in Barcelona are: 1988 silver medalist Tan Liangde and Li Deliang in the springboard; and silver medalist Xiong Ni and 1991 World champion Sun Shuwei in the platform.

Women to watch include: Gao Min, the 1988 Olympic gold medalist in the springboard; and on the platform, 1988 gold medal winner Xu Yanmei and Fu, the 1991 World Champion.

"I aim to be an Olympic champion," Fu told Martz. Don't bet against her. —E.K.

Schedule

The tentative diving schedule is as follows:

Sunday, July 26
Platform preliminaries, women

Monday, July 27
Platform final, women

Tuesday, July 28
Springboard preliminaries, men

Wednesday, July 29
Springboard final, men

Saturday, August 1
Springboard preliminaries, women

Sunday, August 2
Platform preliminaries, men

Monday, August 3
Springboard final, women

Tuesday, August 4
Platform final, men

MEN'S DIVING EVENTS

▼

HIGHLIGHTS

USA's own G.E. Sheldon won the first Olympic diving event in 1904. Sweden's Hjalmar Johansson was 34 when he took the gold in 1908, and captured a silver four years later. From 1920 the US had mounted the most consistent diving performances. The long string of US gold medals in the men's springboard event that began in 1920 has only been broken in 1972 and 1980; US men also captured the springboard silver every Olympiad from 1920 to 1968. In that period, in fact, the US swept the springboard event at every Games except four. Platform divers Richmond Eve of Australia in 1924, and Joaquin Capilla Pérez of

Mexico in 1956, were among those divers who broke the American stranglehold on diving titles.

The first two men to win two gold medals in diving in the same Games were both Americans, Albert White in 1924 and Peter Desjardins—a native Canadian—in 1928. Michael Galitzen of the US won a springboard silver and a platform bronze in 1928 and a springboard gold and platform silver in 1932; he later married diver Georgia Coleman. Richard Degener headed the US sweep of the springboard in 1936.

fact: Like slalom ski racing, springboard diving requires both agility and timing as the diver uses the flex of the board, timing the dive to catch maximum spring.

US diver Dr. Sammy Lee won golds in platform diving in 1948 and 1952; he continued his diving career as coach to the phenomenal American diver Greg Louganis from 1974 to 1977. Bob Clotworthy won a springboard bronze in 1952, claiming the gold in that event four years later. Bob Webster of the US was a double gold winner in the platform event in 1960 and 1964. Italy's *angelo biondo* (blond angel), Klaus Dibiasi, was a master of the rip entry. He won a platform silver medal in the 1964 Olympics, a springboard silver in 1968, and platform golds in 1968, 1972, and 1976. Soviet diver Vladimir Vasin took the springboard gold from the Americans in 1972, claiming the first diving medal for the USSR.

A protegé of Sammy Lee, US diver Greg Louganis took up the diving mantle from Dibiasi, winning a silver in 1976, then, after missing the 1980 Games due to the boycott, pulling in two golds in 1984, the first two-gold male since 1928. Louganis had won by record-setting margins over the silver medalists. His teammate Bruce Kimball won the platform silver, ahead of China's Kongzheng Li. On the springboard in 1984, Louganis's teammate Ronald Merriott captured the bronze behind China's Liangde Tan. Some thought Louganis would retire after 1984, but he continued to refine his sport, gaining eight pounds of muscle in the four years between Olympiads.

fact: Platform diving is like downhill ski racing, a dangerous, breathless plunge that seems like folly to spectators and sometimes to divers.

Louganis seemed a shoo-in to double-gold in the 1988 Games as well. But in the springboard preliminaries Louganis cracked his head on the board performing a reverse 2 1/2 in the pike position.

With four temporary sutures in place he finished the preliminaries, then sported five mattress stitches and a waterproof patch in the finals. He faced creditable competition from veteran Chinese diver and 1984 silver medalist Tan Liangde, but by round seven had opened up a 20-point lead. When it came time for Louganis to execute the reverse 2 1/2, the crowd was hushed, then roared when the dive was performed to scores between 8.0 and 9.0. He aced his final and most difficult dive to claim the gold. Tan Liangde settled for silver once more, ahead of his compatriot, Li Deliang. In the platform event Louganis took the title ahead of Chinese silver medalist Xiong Ni and Mexican bronze medalist Jesus Mena, clinching the second double-gold performance of his Olympic career.

Greg Louganis

His record-breaking two gold medals in each of two successive Olympic diving competitions, his unprecedented platform score of more than 700 points, and his gold-medal success in every major national and international diving event he entered during the 1980s—not to mention his classically good looks and charming, modest personality—have made Gregory Louganis, the world's best diver, an American legend.

Louganis, of Samoan and European ancestry, was adopted a few months after his birth in 1960 by American parents who recognized early his athletic ability. He took dance classes with his sister, gymnastics to combat childhood asthma, and—after his family noticed him performing acrobatic leaps into the backyard pool—diving lessons. By the time he arrived at a Junior Olympics competition in 1971, where he scored a "perfect ten," he was well known by coaches nationwide and attracted the attention of Olympic gold-medal diver Dr. Sammy Lee. When Louganis was fifteen, Lee volunteered to be his personal coach, charging the family nothing for his services except that Louganis clean Lee's pool. A year after that, Louganis won a silver medal at Montréal in his first Olympic diving competition.

Though he couldn't compete in the 1980 Olympics in Moscow, which the United States and other Western nations boycotted to protest the Soviet invasion of Afghanistan, he had already begun building his reputation as the greatest diver in the world. Having won twenty-six US championships, four Pan American events, and three world championships, Louganis was clearly favored to win the platform and springboard diving events in the 1984 Olympic Games.

Not only did Louganis win gold medals in both events (becoming the first .nan to do so in fifty-six years), he won the springboard competition by more than ninety points over the silver medalist, and he set a record for points scored in the platform event.

Four years later, at the Summer Olympics in Seoul, Louganis's competitive edge was complicated by physical problems, including an injured wrist, a fever, and a three-inch head wound he'd sustained by striking the springboard during a preliminary competition dive. Nonetheless, Louganis finished the springboard event and won the gold, and he performed a superior final platform dive, which ensured him that gold medal, too. For his gutsy performance at the 1988 Olympics, Louganis was also granted the Olympic Spirit Award.

269

Since retiring from competitive diving, Louganis has pursued an acting career and is involved with Earth's Communications Office, an association of entertainers promoting environmental causes.

Medalists

Diving — Men's Platform

1988 1. Gregory Louganis, USA, 638.61
2. Xiong Ni, People's Republic of China, 637.47
3. Jesus Mena, Mexico, 594.39
1984 1. Gregory Louganis, USA, 710.91
2. Bruce Kimball, USA, 643.50
3. Kongzheng Li, China, 638.28
1980 1. Falk Hoffmann, East Germany, 835.650
2. Vladimir Aleynik, Soviet Union, 819.705
3. David Ambartsumyan, Soviet Union, 817.440
1976 1. Klaus Dibiasi, Italy, 600.51
2. Gregory Louganis, USA, 576.99
3. Vladimir Aleynik, Soviet Union, 548.61
1972 1. Klaus Dibiasi, Italy, 504.12
2. Richard Rydze, USA, 480.75
3. Franco Cagnotto, Italy, 475.83
1968 1. Klaus Dibiasi, Italy, 164.18
2. Alvaro Gaxiola, Mexico, 154.49
3. Edwin Young, USA, 153.93
1964 1. Robert Webster, USA, 148.58
2. Klaus Dibiasi, Italy, 147.54
3. Thomas Gompf, USA, 146.57
1960 1. Robert Webster, USA, 165.56
2. Gary Tobian, USA, 165.25
3. Brian Phelps, Great Britain, 157.13
1956 1. Joaquin Capilla Perez, Mexico, 152.44
2. Gary Tobian, USA, 152.41
3. Richard Connor, USA, 149.79
1952 1. Dr. Samuel Lee, USA, 156.28
2. Joaquin Capilla Perez, Mexico, 145.21
3. Gunther Haase, West Germany, 141.31
1948 1. Dr. Samuel Lee, USA, 130.05
2. Bruce Harlan, USA, 122.30
3. Joaquin Capilla Perez, Mexico, 113.52
1936 1. Marshall Wayne, USA, 113.58
2. Elbert Root, USA, 110.60
3. Hermann Stork, Germany, 110.31
1932 1. Harold Smith, USA, 124.80
2. Michael Galitzen, USA, 124.28
3. Frank Kurtz, USA, 121.98
1928 1. Peter Desjardins, USA, 98.74
2. Farid Simaika, Egypt, 99.58
3. Michael Galitzen, USA, 92.34
1924 1. Albert White, USA, 97.46
2. David Fall, USA, 97.30
3. Clarence Pinkston, USA, 94.60
1920 1. Clarence Pinkston, USA, 100.67
2. Erik Adlerz, Sweden, 99.08
3. Harry Prieste, USA, 93.73
1912 1. Erik Adlerz, Sweden, 73.94
2. Albert Zurner, Germany, 72.60

1908 3. Gustaf Blomgren, Sweden, 69.56
1. Hjalmar Johansson, Sweden, 83.75
2. Karl Malmstrom, Sweden, 78.73
3. Arvid Spangberg, Sweden, 74.00
1906 1. Gottlob Walz, Germany, 156.00
2. Georg Hoffmann, Germany, 150.20
3. Otto Satzinger, Austria, 147.40
1904 1. Dr. George Sheldon, USA, 12.66
2. Georg Hoffmann, Germany, 11.66
3. Alfred Braunschweiger, Germany, 11.33
3. Frank Kehoe, USA, 11.33
1896-
1900 Not held

Diving — Men's Springboard

1988 1. Gregory Louganis, USA, 730.80
2. Liangde Tan, People's Republic of China, 704.88
3. Li Deliang, People's Republic of China, 665.28
1984 1. Gregory Louganis, USA, 754.41
2. Liangde Tan, China, 662.31
3. Ronald Merriott, USA, 661.32
1980 1. Aleksandr Portnov, Soviet Union, 905.025
2. Carlos Giron, Mexico, 892.140
3. Franco Cagnotto, Italy, 871.500
1976 1. Philip G. Boggs, USA, 619.05
2. Franco Cagnotto, Italy, 570.48
3. Aleksandr Kosenkov, Soviet Union, 567.24
1972 1. Vladimir Vasin, Soviet Union, 594.09
2. Franco Cagnotto, Italy, 591.63
3. Craig Lincoln, USA, 577.29
1968 1. Bernie Wrightson, USA, 170.15
2. Klaus Dibiasi, Italy, 159.74
3. James Henry, USA, 158.09
1964 1. Kenneth Sitzberger, USA, 159.90
2. Francis Gorman, USA, 157.63
3. Larry Andreasen, USA, 143. 77
1960 1. Gary Tobian, USA, 170.00
2. Samuel Hall, USA, 167.08
3. Juan Botella, Mexico, 162.30
1956 1. Robert Clotworthy, USA, 159.56
2. Donald Harper, USA, 156.23
3. Joaquin Capilla Perez, Mexico, 150.69
1952 1. David Browning, USA, 205.29
2. Miller Anderson, USA, 199.84
3. Robert Clotworthy, USA, 184.92
1948 1. Bruce Harlan, USA, 163.64
2. Miller Anderson, USA, 157.29
3. Dr. Samuel Lee, USA, 145.52
1936 1. Richard Degener, USA, 163.57
2. Marshall Wayne, USA, 159.56
3. Al Greene, USA, 146.29

270

Considered the best diver of all time, Greg Louganis shows the precise and graceful form that earned the US platform and springboard gold medals in the 1984 and 1988 Games.

Pat McCormick was described as a California housewife when she swept the women's platform and springboard gold medals at the 1952 and 1956 Games. Her achievement is matched only by Greg Louganis.

1932	1. Michael Galitzen, USA, 161.38
	2. Harold Smith, USA, 158.54
	3. Richard Degener, USA, 151.82
1928	1. Peter Desjardins, USA, 185.04
	2. Michael Galitzen, USA, 174.06
	3. Farid Simaika, Egypt, 172.46
1924	1. Albert White, USA, 696.4
	2. Peter Desjardins, USA, 693.2
	3. Clarence Pinkston, USA, 653.0
1920	1. Louis Kuehn, USA, 675.4
	2. Clarence Pinkston, USA, 655.3

	3. Louis Balbach, USA, 649.5
1912	1. Paul Gunther, Germany, 79.23
	2. Hanns Luber, Germany, 76.78
	3. Kurt Behrens, Germany, 73.73
1908	1. Albert Zurner, Germany, 85.5
	2. Kurt Behrens, Germany, 85.3
	3. George Gaidzik, USA, 80.8
	3. Gottlob Walz, Germany, 80.8
1896-
1906	Not held

WOMEN'S DIVING EVENTS

▼

HIGHLIGHTS

Diving events for women commenced with the 1912 Games in Stockholm. Aileen Riggin won a springboard gold for the US in 1920 and a springboard silver in 1924; she also captured a bronze in the backstroke at the 1924 Games. US diver Elizabeth Becker was the first woman to win two diving titles, capturing the springboard gold in 1924 and, after marrying men's diving champion Clarence Pinkston, adding a platform gold in 1928.

Georgia Coleman of the US won a platform silver and a springboard bronze in 1928 and a springboard gold and platform silver in 1932; later married to diver Michael Galitzen, she was the first woman to perform a 2 1/2 forward somersault. Her teammate, Katherine Rawls, took silvers in the springboard event in 1932 and 1936, and added a bronze as a member of the US freestyle relay team. Dorothy Poynton brought the US two golds, capturing the platform in both 1932 and, as Dorothy Poynton Hill, 1936; she had won a springboard silver in 1928 at age 13, and took the springboard bronze eight years later. Marjorie Gestring of the US was also only 13 when she took the springboard gold in 1936. Another US diver, Vickie Draves, swept both events in 1948, the first woman to do so.

fact: Divers aiming for a clean entry into the water are encouraged to think of aiming for the bottom of the pool instead of the surface of the water.

French diver Madeleine Moreau was the first woman to prevent US divers from sweeping the springboard event; she captured the silver medal in 1952. Pat McCormick was a four-time Olympic champion for the US, sweeping springboard and platform golds in 1952 and 1956. Her compatriot, Paula Myers-Pope, won a platform silver in 1952 and 1960, a platform bronze in 1956, and a springboard silver in 1960.

Until 1980, the only non-American to win the women's springboard event was East German diver Ingrid Krämer, who triumphed in springboard and platform in 1960 and repeated for the springboard gold in 1964 as Ingrid Engel-Krämer. She also competed in Mexico City as Ingrid Gulbin.

fact: The most difficult dives are the forward 4 1/2 somersault tuck from the 3-meter springboard or platform, and the reverse 3 1/2 somersault tuck from the 3-meter springboard.

The springboard title came back to the US in 1968, with a victory by Sue Gossick. US diver Micki King broke her arm when she hit the board in Mexico City at the 1968 Games, but returned in 1972 to capture the springboard gold; as Micki Hogue she was team manager for the US divers in 1988. Czech diver Milena Duchková enjoyed the crowd's support in Mexico City when she bested Soviet Natalya Lobanova (Kuznetsova) for the platform gold; Duchková took the silver in the platform event in Munich. Jennifer Chandler claimed the springboard gold in 1976, the last time a US woman triumphed in the event. The women's platform event has eluded American women since 1964, although Michele Mitchell took silvers in the event in 1984 and 1988, behind divers from China.

Kelly McCormick, daughter of US champion Pat McCormick, earned a springboard silver in 1984, ceding to the Canadian gold medalist, Sylvie Bernier, and a bronze in 1988, behind Chinese divers Gao Min and Li Quing.

The Diving McCormicks

If diving fans feel any disappointment prior to the 1992 Games, it is that America will probably have to wait at least a generation for another McCormick diver.

That will be too long—though probably well worth the wait.

Pat McCormick was 22 when she won the springboard and platform gold medals at the 1952 Helsinki Games. In 1956, just months after giving birth to her first child, a son, she won the same pair at Melbourne.

Twenty-eight years later, her daughter, Kelly, then 24, won the silver medal in the springboard competition at the Los Angeles Games; four years later, she won the bronze medal in Seoul.

Pat McCormick was years ahead of her time. She perfected dives seldom attempted by men—dives outlawed by the Olympic committee before her appearance at the Helsinki Games as too dangerous for women. An oft-told tale features McCormick visiting a doctor. After examining her accumulation of cracked bones and scars from practicing 100 dives a day six days a week, he remarked, "I've seen worse casualty cases, but only where a building caved in."

It has also been said that if Pat McCormick had competed in front of today's amassed media, America would have done a half-gainer over her. As it was, when McCormick returned home from the Helsinki Games, a puzzled neighbor asked her if she had been away on vacation.

It's not that Pat McCormick didn't receive her due from her peers. She was named AP Athlete of the Year and Sullivan Award winner in 1956 and was the first woman inducted into the International Swimming Hall of Fame. It was just that Pat didn't really enjoy the spotlight until Kelly came along.

It helped, of course, that Kelly had a good portion of the free spirit her mother had—pumping herself up with a boom box in rooms between dives during competitions and once evaluating her performance this way: "If you land on your head 10 times, you should be happy."

My mother "showed me her medal when I was a little girl," Kelly told *Sports Illustrated* before the 1984 Games. "I made a bet with her that someday I'd make an Olympic team and win [a gold medal]. The bet's for a Porsche and either an ocelot or a cheetah."

Kelly got the car—but not the cat. She finished three points shy of the gold at the LA Games.

After the those Games and after surviving the intense pressure to match her mother's performances, Kelly said: "It's a relief to me it's over. But [my mother] told me that she's really proud of me and that she loves me."

Kelly's style, which emphasized her gymnastic ability—she studied as a gymnast for 8 years, then gave it up, saying she just couldn't stand being cooped up indoors—was described as "eerily similar" to her mother's. She showed the same stunning grace and strength, though was hounded by a lack of consistency.

She is remembered by others for more than her diving.

When a teammate clinched an Olympic berth then cried, wishing that her father, who had died a few months earlier, had been there to see her, Kelly stopped her interview with a reporter, turned away and assured her friend. "He's here," Kelly whispered. "You know that."

Kelly McCormick is retired from competitive diving and currently is assistant coach of the Emerald City Divers in Federal Way, Washington. She continues to train protegés—while we wait for the next generation's McCormick.—*E.K.*

Diving (side tab)

Medalists

Diving — Women's Platform

1988 1. Yanmei Xu, People's Republic of China, 445.20
2. Michele Mitchell, USA, 436.95
3. Wendy Williams, USA, 400.44

1984 1. Jihong Zhou, China, 435.51
2. Michele Mitchell, USA, 431.19

3. Wendy Wyland, USA, 422.07

1980 1. Martina Jaschke, East Germany, 596.250
2. Servard Emirzyan, Soviet Union, 576.465
3. Liana Tsotadze, Soviet Union, 575.925

1976 1. Elena Vaytsekhovskaya, Soviet Union, 406.59

2. Ulrika Knape, Sweden, 402.60
3. Deborah Wilson, USA, 401.07
1972 1. Ulrika Knape, Sweden, 390.00
2. Milena Duchkova, Czechoslovakia, 370.92
3. Marina Janicke, East Germany, 360.54
1968 1. Milena Duchkova, Czechoslovakia, 109.59
2. Natalia Lobanova, Soviet Union, 105.14
3. Ann Peterson, USA, 101.11
1964 1. Lesley Bush, USA, 99.80
2. Ingrid Engel-Kramer, East Germany, 98.45
3. Galina Alekseyeva, Soviet Union, 97.60
1960 1. Ingrid Kramer, East Germany, 91.28
2. Paula Jean Pope-Myers, USA, 88.94
3. Ninel Krutova, Soviet Union, 86.99
1956 1. Patricia McCormick, USA, 84.85
2. Juno Irwin-Stover, USA, 81.64
3. Paula Jean Myers, USA, 81.58
1952 1. Patricia McCormick, USA, 79.37
2. Paula Jean Myers, USA, 71.63
3. Juno Irwin-Stover, USA, 70.49
1948 1. Victoria Draves, USA, 68.87
2. Patricia Elsener, USA, 66.28
3. Birte Christoffersen, Denmark, 66.04
1936 1. Dorothy Hill-Poynton, USA, 33.93
2. Velma Dunn, USAn, 33.63
3. Kathe Kohler, West Germany, 33.43
1932 1. Dorothy Poynton, USA, 40.26
2. Georgia Coleman, USA, 35.56
3. Marion Roper, USA, 35.22
1928 1. Elizabeth Pinkston-Becker, USA, 31.60
2. Georgia Coleman, USA, 30.60
3. Lala Sjoquist, Sweden, 29.20
1924 1. Caroline Smith, USA, 33.2
2. Elizabeth Becker, USA, 33.4
3. Hjordis Topel, Sweden, 32.8
1920 1. Stefani Fryland-Clausen, Denmark, 34.6
2. Eileen Armstrong, Great Britain, 33.3
3. Eva Ollivier, Sweden, 33.3
1912 1. Greta Johanson, Sweden, 39.9
2. Lisa Regnell, Sweden, 36.0
3. Isabelle White, Great Britain, 34.0
1896-1908 Not held

Diving — Woman's Springboard

1988 1. Min Gao, People's Republic of China, 580.23

2. Qing Li, People's Republic of China, 534.33
3. Kelly McCormick, USA, 533.19
1984 1. Sylvie Bernier, Canada, 530.70
2. Kelly McCormick, USA, 527.46
3. Christina Seufert, USA, 517.62
1980 1. Irina Kalinina, Soviet Union, 725.910
2. Martina Proeber, East Germany, 698.895
3. Karin Guthke, East Germany, 685.245
1976 1. Jennifer Chandler, USA, 506.19
2. Christa Koehler, East Germany, 469.41
3. Cynthia McIngvale, USA, 466.83
1972 1. Micki King, USA, 450.03
2. Ulrika Knape, Sweden, 434.19
3. Marina Janicke, East Germany, 430.92
1968 1. Sue Gossick, USA, 150.77
2. Tamara Pogoscheva, Soviet Union, 145.30
3. Keala O'Sullivan, USA, 145.23
1964 1. Ingrid Engel-Kramer, East Germany, 145.00
2. Jeanne Collier, USA, 138.36
3. Mary Willard, USA, 138.18
1960 1. Ingrid Kramer, East Germany, 155.81
2. Paula Jean Pope-Myers, USA, 141.24
3. Elizabeth Ferris, Great Britain, 139.09
1956 1. Patricia McCormick, USA, 142.36
2. Jeanne Stunyo, USA, 125.89
3. Irene MacDonald, Canada, 121.40
1952 1. Patricia McCormick, USA, 147.30
2. Mady Moreau, France, 139.34
3. Zoe Ann Jensen-Olsen, USA, 127.57
1948 1. Victoria Draves, USA, 108.74
2. Zoe Ann Olsen, USA, 108.23
3. Patricia Elsener, USA, 101.30
1936 1. Marjorie Gestring, USA, 89.27
2. Katherine Rawls, USA, 88.35
3. Dorothy Hill-Poynton, USA, 82.36
1932 1. Georgia Coleman, USA, 87.52
2. Katherine Rawls, USA, 82.56
3. Jane Fauntz, USA, 82.12
1928 1. Helen Meany, USA, 78.62
2. Dorothy Poynton, USA, 75.62
3. Georgia Coleman, USA, 73.38
1924 1. Elizabeth Becker, USA, 474.5
2. Aileen Riggin, USA, 460.4
3. Caroline Fletcher, USA, 436.4
1920 1. Aileen Riggin, USA, 539.9
2. Helen Wainwright, USA, 534.8
3. Thelma Payne, USA, 534.1
1896-1912 Not held

274

EQUESTRIAN

WARM-UP

The first known use of the horse as a domesticated animal in prehistoric times was for pulling or dragging loads (before that maybe eohippus was just dinner). Horseback riding evolved through the centuries as the horse did, because the prehistoric equine were dramatically smaller than the animal we are familiar with today. The Scythians, residents of what is now south-central Russia, are believed to be the earliest innovators in horseback riding, developing types of equipment still in use today.

Writings and artwork from around 365 BC document some of the Greek methods of selecting and training horses based on their education by the Scythians. Records of the ancient Olympic Games of 688 BC show that competitions for four-horse chariot racing were included, and horseback riding competitions were included in the following Olympiad of 648 BC.

Modern equestrian competition began developing in the 16th century when classical riding schools opened in Naples, Italy Vienna, Austria, and Saumer, France. The training, movements, and equipment used have changed little since those days. Yet as recently as the 1900s seemingly rudimentary changes in horseback riding *techniques* have been made. For example, the elementary development of the "forward seat," that is to say, leaning forward (not backwards) with the body when the horse is jumping, came about in 1902, introduced by Federico Caprilli of Italy.

With the mechanization of transportation, equestrian pursuits fell to sporting events, wagering, and the military. Prior to World War II most international equestrian competitions were the exclusive showplace of cavalry officers and their mounts. Though civilians participated on occasion, from their first inclusion in 1912 (Stockholm) until the 1952 Helsinki Games—when the forty-year monopoly in show jumping competitions was broken by Frenchman Pierre Jonqueres d'Oriola—the military dominated the majority of international competitions. In fact, it is because of the strong influence of the cavalry in equestrian sports that three-day eventing was developed. And even today, some of the top show jumpers hail from their nation's cavalry.

The real origins of show jumping can be traced back to the 1800s when "leaping" contests were held over a single high fence. Though not included in

275

modern Olympics until 1912, international show jumping competitions were held before the turn of the century.

With the formation of the FEI (Fédération Equestre Internationale) in 1921, the rules and standards of international and Olympic show jumping and other equestrian disciplines became regulated. Military as well as male domination prevailed in Olympic show jumping until the 1956 Stockholm Games when women were first allowed to compete.

Olympic dressage was, like the other equestrian events, dominated by the military from 1912 until 1952.

Emerging as a sport only after World War II, three-day eventing was considered training for the cavalry before that. Competitions are based on and descended from the French Championship for Military Horses. Eventing appeared along with the other equestrian disciplines in the 1912 Olympics as a competition for military officers to demonstrate their preparedness and as a comparison of breeds and cavalry training techniques.

▼

SPECTATORS' GUIDE

Show Jumping: Of all the Olympic equestrian events, show jumping is the most televised, the easiest to understand and score by armchair judges, and arguably the most thrilling. Horse and rider teams set out to tackle an imposing course of 12–15 obstacles at breakneck speed. The courses are designed with colorful jumps intended to blend in with the background or to draw the horses' attention away from the top rail—which is set over five feet high (often over the head of the horse) and lightly balanced in a slight cup. Courses are designed to challenge both the technical ability of the rider to control the horse, regulate its speed, and, at the same time calculate the best as well as the quickest approach to each fence. Traversing the course sight-unseen, the horse demonstrates his sheer athletic power, confidence, and complete trust in the rider.

The team competition, also called the Nations' Cup, is run in two rounds over the same course, with only the best of three scores of the four-person national team counting in each round. Faults are incurred for each rail a horse knocks down with either its front or back feet, putting a foot in the water or on the tape that marks the edge of a water jump, refusing a fence, and finally, for exceeding the time allowed to navigate the course. Time is a crucial factor in show jumping because if horses/riders go around faultless, the fastest times determine the placings. The times are calculated in thousandths of a second, and decisions often come down to this increment. After the two rounds, if there is a tie in faults, a jump-off over a shortened course is held, with an increase in faults as well (just to up the ante).

The individual medal competition is open only to the four individuals with the best scores from the team competition. Their standings are tallied during the team competition and the four then proceed to the two-round individual Grand Prix with a clean slate. Competition between fellow teammates is not uncommon here, as demonstrated in 1984 when the US made a clean sweep of the individual medals in addition to the team gold.

Dressage: This event is often regarded as the stuffy stepsister of other equestrian events. One non-devotee even called it "as exciting as watching mold grow," as horses and riders perform in silence executing the exact same movements (called a "test") one after another. To many viewers, dressage lacks the thrills that show jumping or the three day event provide, but the beauty and exacting perfection of Grand Prix dressage at the Olympics is winning over more and more viewers each year.

Olympic dressage competitions showcase a series of 36 movements natural to the horse. Unlike the popular Lipizzaners from the Spanish Riding School in Vienna, Olympic dressage riders perform none of the exciting "airs above the ground," or unnatural circus-like movements designed with military usage in mind (a foot soldier's nightmare: to have a horse leap in the air and kick him one). The goal is to perform a test that showcases the horse's training as well as its calmness, submissiveness, flexibility, athletic power, the rider's position, and the use of often invisible prompts known in the horse business as "aids."

fact: In dressage, warmbloods and warmblood crosses are favored for their even temperament and big, expressive, fluid gaits. Event riders can be seen competing on thoroughbred/warmblood crossed horses. This combination seems to offer the best of the thoroughbred speed and agility with the warmbloods temperament and endurance capabilities. Show jumpers ride a wide variety of cross-bred horses, but the most popular are again the warmblood/thoroughbred crosses.

Two different tests are used in for the Olympic Games. The first is the FEI Grand Prix team competition followed by the Grand Prix Special individual medal competition (using the same movements in a different order). The seven to seven-and-a-half minute tests are ridden from memory in an arena marked with letters around the outside (as well as imaginary ones down the center). Each movement is performed at or in between these letters for five judges that are seated at three vantage points. Scoring in both competitions ranges from 0 (a movement not executed) to 10 (excellent), with movements that are especially difficult counting double.

Watch for advanced movements like passage (elegant, bouncy suspended trot), half pass (sideways trot or canter where legs completely cross), flying or tempi changes (skips in midair at the canter to switch legs every 2 steps and every other step), canter pirouette (hind legs stay almost in place while front move around small circle), and piaffe (trot completely in place).

Three-Day Event: Logistically, three-day eventing is a difficult sport to televise as well as watch. It is the "combined" event in the equestrian, a test of endurance and versatility for both the horse and rider in three distinct competitions. Though the cross-country phase is the heart (and heart-stopper) of the competition, horse and rider must be competitive in the other phases to contend for a medal. Team placings are tabulated by adding the highest three scores of four competitors in each phase. Using a ratio of 3:12:1 for individual scores in the three events, medals are awarded to both individuals and teams.

Each day's competition holds a vastly different challenge, beginning with the dressage competition. Though still called three-day eventing, the dressage phase actually takes two days to run. The "test," or series of movements performed from memory, consists of 20 movements executed for three judges to demonstrate the versatility, general obedience, flexibility, and training of the horse and the ability of the rider. The scoring is the same as for Olympic dressage; however, after the score is handed out it is subtracted from the optimum, multiplied by 0.6 and multiplied again by a factor depending on the course and condition of the endurance competition.

Why, you ask? All this is done to make the scores consistent with the scoring of the other phases (based on penalties) and to give the dressage phase enough weight to influence the outcome. In previous Olympic competitions this phase was treated rather lightly, especially as it is difficult to find a horse versatile enough to obey in dressage yet function as a powerhouse in the last two competitions. Riders and coaches relied on the fact that they could make up ground on the endurance course. Not so today.

The endurance competition is the real heart of three-day eventing, and falls second in popularity only to the flash and spectacle of show jumping. The competition is run in four consecutive phases denoted by the letters A through D. Phases A and C, both called Roads and Tracks, consist of trot (A) or slow canter (C) over a marked course and are timed with one penalty point given for each second over or under the time allotted. They serve the basic function of warming (in A) or cooling down (in C) the horses as well as moving them from the start to phase B and on to phase D.

Phase B is a steeplechase over ten fences placed around a turf track. Like phases A and C, it is little televised or paid attention to, as it is fairly straightforward. Scoring for phases B and D take place within a 33-yard penalty zone around fences, with a refusal or runout counting 20 points (second refusal =

40 and third = elimination) and a fall of horse and/or rider counting 60 points (second fall in phase B or a third in phase D = elimination).

Phase D—cross-country jumping—is the real excitement of the event. Imposing (up to 3'11") and immobile fences are constructed over varying terrain designed to test the skill and athletic ability of the pair. Each fence is constructed with two options for the horse/rider to take, a longer, safer (albeit slower) route or a harder and faster (and riskier) route. Keep in mind that the course is jumped no matter what the condition of the footing and that these fences, when hit by a 1500-plus pound horse, do not give way. Riders are started over the same course at intervals throughout the day, and are required to stop for veterinary checks (for the horses, not the riders). Jumps include ditches, banks, drops, and (scariest for the horse) water. Watch for the water obstacle, since it tends to claim the most victims. The horses (as in show jumping) have not seen the course before and cannot tell how deep the water they are being asked to jump into is, an uncomfortable, to say the least, situation for the horse.

The ultimate trust between the horse and rider is put to the test here and at almost every obstacle around the course. It is not unusual to lose a quarter of the competitors at this phase, and mandatory veterinary check points are set up to insure no competitor is in distress. The challenge often becomes keeping the horse fit enough simply to complete the last day of competition.

The final day of competition for those who survived consists of a modified show jumping. Though not a standard jumping competition, considering the challenges of the previous day, the ten to twelve fences are nonetheless challenging. Show jumping faults or penalties are given for knocking down rails (5 faults each) and for a horse refusing (10 faults first time). The final placings, as in show jumping, often come down to split-second timing and surefooted execution.

Horse Sense (A Glossary)

AHSA: American Horse Show Association; membership organization founded in 1917 that determines, regulates and enforces uniform rules and procedures, official licenses and standings, recognizing shows and events.

AIDS: Prompts given to the horse by a rider using body weight, legs, hands, or voice.

CANTER: Gait in which the legs move in vertical pairs.

COURSE: Series of fences to be negotiated by horse/rider; riders are allowed to view the course prior to each event to plan a strategy.

DRESSAGE: French word that means training.

DISTANCE: Refers to the space between or in front of a fence or obstacle, usually stated in the number of strides.

FAULT: Penalty point incurred for a fall, knockdown, or disobedience; the amount depends on the equestrian event.

FEI: Fédération Equestre Internationale; Swiss-based organization formed in 1921 to regulate the standards, rules, and judging of international equestrian competitions.

FENCE: In **show jumping**, an obstacle some five feet high and some breadth (usually not to exceed height), typically constructed of colorful poles, planks, flowers, hedges, fake stone/brick, water, and other materials designed to test the skill of team. In **three-day eventing**, cross-country phase, a fixed obstacle (no more than 3' 11'') designed in conjunction with the surrounding terrain, usually of natural materials, which tests the skill of the team; two approaches are available (safer/slow or harder/fast).

GRAND PRIX DRESSAGE: The highest level of dressage competition.

GRAND PRIX JUMPING: Highest level, two-round show jumping event that awards the most prize money in non-Olympic contests.

HAZARD: In combined driving, a maze-like obstacle of fixed construction with two options of approach (easy/slow or hard/fast) that the team must negotiate within an allotted time.

ON THE FLAT (or flat work): Term referring to riding, training or performance done at the walk, trot, canter, gallop without obstacles.

STRIDE: The natural distance each horse covers with each step. Riders must be able to regulate this distance to negotiate obstacles without knockdown or falling, or to exhibit a horse's obedience and athletic ability on the flat.

TEST: In dressage, the execution of a series of movements, performed from memory in all higher-level competitions.

TROT: Gait in which legs move in diagonal pairs (faster than walk, slower than canter).

USET: United States Equestrian Team; a nonprofit membership organization who officially represents the United States in FEI and international equestrian competition. The USET is responsible for the selection, training, equipping, and financing of the representative equestrian teams that compete in the Olympic Games.

WALK: Gait in which legs move individually in diagonal pattern.

WALKING THE COURSE: Only chance for riders to view and pace out the distance between fences or obstacles and plan an approach prior to negotiating it.

HOPEFULS

All sporting events involve some measure of unpredictability. However, in equestrian sports, that measure is quickly multiplied by two. Each horse/rider may perform the exact same movement, or travel the exact same course, and yet the outcome is entirely different. "Good days" or "bad days" and the ability of the pair to perform under a great deal of pressure factor heavily in competitions.

Dressage: The volatility of equestrian sports makes it difficult to forecast who will have the honor of representing each nation. In dressage, a sport dominated by West Germany and Switzerland in the recent past, watch for the former Olympians Nicole Uphoff of Germany, Margit Otto-Crepin of France, Christine Stueckelberger of Switzerland, as well as strong US hopefuls Carol Lavell, Michael Poulin, Carlotte Bredhal, and Jane Savoie.

Show Jumping: Show jumping talent will be represented from many countries, including medal favorites from the dominant countries of France, Germany, and the USA. Some of the familiar names we might see include US riders Lisa Jacquin, Anne Kursinski, Conrad Homfeld, Greg Best, Joe Fargis, and Leslie Burr. Other riders to look for include Pierre Durand, of France and Karsten Huck of Germany.

Three-Day Event: Teams from Great Britain, New Zealand, the USA, and Germany are expected to be strong finishers in 1992. Great riders like two-time individual gold medalist and team bronze medalist Mark Todd of New Zealand, individual silver and two-time team silver medalist Ian Stark of Great Britain, as well as Britons Virginia Leng (two-time individual bronze, team bronze and silver) and Lucindia Green (team silver) are expected to contend. Other names we are likely to hear again in Olympic competition include the USA's Karen Stives (individual silver, team gold), Mike Plump (team gold), Torrance Fleischmann (team gold) and Bruce Davidson (team gold).

fact: Squads in each of the four disciplines are chosen both for the Games and the World Championships by the USET Selection Committee based on evaluation of the competitive results from designated events. Unlike many other sporting events, today both male and female equestrians compete on an even basis.

US Olympic equestrian contenders today face the same restrictions experienced by most US Olympic hopefuls in that they must retain an amateur status to be eligible for US competitions as well as for the Games. Due to the inequality between countries subsidizing their teams and those that do not, the International Olympic Committee relaxed its rules in 1986 to allow professional riders to regain their amateur status prior to and for one Olympics. Riders may apply winnings to or obtain grants and sponsorship from equestrian organizations such as the AHSA and USET (United States Equestrian Team), as well as receiving funding from corporations, private sources for training and the purchase of mounts.

fact: Horses for the American riders are selected by the USET and its coaching staff based on their soundness and talent in each discipline. They are loaned to the team for use, but are owned by individuals such as their rider, by a syndicate, or by nonriding team supporters.

Schedule

The tentative equestrian events schedule is as follows:

Monday, July 27
Three-day event, dressage test

Tuesday, July 28
Three-day event, dressage test

Wednesday, July 29
Training
Circuit d'hipica

Thursday, July 30
Three-day event, jumping test,
  finals

Sunday, August 2
Team dressage competition
Team dressage competition, final

Monday, August 3
Team dressage

Team dressage, final

Tuesday, August 4
Team jumping,
1st qualification
Team jumping finals

Wednesday, August 5
Individual dressage, final

Friday, August 7
Individual jumping competition,
2nd qualification

Sunday, August 9
Individual jumping competition,
final

DRESSAGE

▼

HIGHLIGHTS

Olympic dressage competition was not only exclusively military from 1912 to 1952, it was also strictly an enforced competition for commissioned officers. (In 1948 the Swedes, who would have taken home the team gold and had earned an additional individual sixth, were disqualified after it was discovered that team member Gehnall Persson was ineligible to compete based on his lack of rank. France was awarded the gold instead.) The rules in this equestrian event underwent some radical changes before the competition reached today's level. Most notably, team competitions were not even included until 1928, and were not held at the Rome Games of 1960.

As in all equestrian events, 1952 was a landmark year, as the Games were opened to women and civilians in all levels of equestrian competition. Four women represented their countries in this event, and the silver medal was won by Lis Hartel of Denmark, though her legs from the knee down remained paralyzed from polio.

In the 1956 Games Henri Saint Cyr of Sweden became the only person to win the individual gold twice when he took the last of his four gold medals. Cyr won individual and team golds in both 1952 and 1956, and had also been a member of the disqualified gold medalist 1948 team.

After 1956 the Swedish and Dutch domination swayed in favor of the German teams. Beginning in 1964, Dr. Reiner Klimke of West Germany began an incredible Olympic career that includes team golds in 1964, 1968, 1976, 1984, and 1988, the individual bronze in 1968 and 1976, and the individual gold in 1984. In 1972, the only time in a 24-year span Dr. Klimke was not an Olympic medalist, countrywoman Liselott Linsenhoff became the first female individual gold medalist (also 1956 bronze individual medalist behind Denmark's Lis Hartel and Sweden's Cyr, as well as 1956 team silver, 1968 team gold, and 1972 team silver).

The US team has won medals in dressage competition on only four occasions. In 1932 and 1976 it won the team bronze and in 1948 the team silver. The lone individual medal (the bronze) was taken by Hiram Tuttle in 1932.

Summer

Equestrian — Individual Dressage

1988
1. Nicole Uphoff, West Germany, Rembrandt 24, 1,521
2. Margitt Otto-Crepin, France, Corlandus, 1,462
3. Christine Stueckelberger, Switzerland, Gauguin de Lully Ch., 1,417

1984
1. Dr. Reiner Klimke, West Germany, Ahlerich, 1,504
2. Anne Grethe, Denmark, Marzog, 1,442
3. Otto J. Hofer, Switzerland, Limandus, 1,364

1980
1. Elisabeth Theurer, Austria, Mon Cherie, 1,370
2. Yuri Kovshov, Soviet Union, Igrok, 1,300
3. Viktor Ugriumov, Soviet Union, Shkval, 1,234

1976
1. Christine Stueckelberger, Switzerland, Granat, 1,486.0
2. Harry Boldt, West Germany, Woycek, 1,435.0
3. Reiner Klimke, West Germany, Mehmet, 1,395.0

1972
1. Liselott Linsenhoff, West Germany, Piaff, 1,229
2. Yelena Petushkova, Soviet Union, Pepel, 1,185
3. Josef Neckermann, West Germany, Venetia, 1,177

1968
1. Ivan Kisimov, Soviet Union, Ichor, 1,572
2. Josef Neckermann, West Germany, Mariano, 1,546
3. Dr. Reiner Klimke, West Germany, Dux, 1,537

1964
1. Henri Chammartin, Switzerland, Woermann, 1,504
2. Harry Boldt, West Germany, Remus, 1,503
3. Sergei Filatov, Soviet Union, Absent, 1,486

1960
1. Sergei Filatov, Soviet Union, Absent, 2,144.0
2. Gustav Fischer, Switzerland, Wald, 2,087.0
3. Josef Neckermann, West Germany, Asbach, 2,082.0

1956
1. Henri St. Cyr, Sweden, Juli, 860.0
2. Lis Hartel, Denmark, Jubilee, 850.0
3. Liselott Linsenhoff, West Germany, Adular, 832.0

1952
1. Henri St. Cyr, Sweden, Master Rufus, 561.0
2. Lis Hartel, Denmark, Jubilee, 541.5
3. Andre Jousseaume, France, Harpagon, 541.0

1948
1. Hans Moser, Switzerland, Hummer, 492.5
2. Andre Jousseaume, France, Harpagon, 480.0
3. Gustav-Adolf Boltenstern, Jr., Sweden, Trumf, 477.5

1936
1. Heinz Pollay, Germany, Kronos, 1,760.0
2. Freidrich Gerhard, Germany, Absinth, 1,745.5
3. Alois Podhajsky, Austria, Nero, 1,721.5

1932
1. Xavier Lesage, France, Taine, 343.75
2. Charles Marion, France, Linon, 305.42
3. Hiram Tuttle, USA, Olympic, 300.50

1928
1. Carl Friedrich Freiherr von Langen, Germany, Draufganger, 237.42
2. Charles Marion, France, Linon, 231.00
3. Ragnar Olson, Sweden, Gunstling, 229.78

1924
1. Ernst Linder, Sweden, Piccolomini, 276.4
2. Bertil Sandstrom, Sweden, Sabel, 275.8
3. Xavier Lesage, France, Plumard, 265.8

1920
1. Janne Lundblad, Sweden, Uno, 27.937
2. Bertil Sandstrom, Sweden, Sabel, 26.312
3. Hans von Rosen, Sweden, Running Sister, 25.125

1912
1. Carl Bonde, Sweden, Emperor, 15
2. Gustav-Adolf Boltenstern, Sr., Sweden, Neptun, 21
3. Hans von Blixen-Finecke, Sr., Sweden, Maggie, 32

**1896-
1908** Not held

Equestrian — Team Dressage

1988
1. West Germany, 4,302, Reiner Klimke, Ann Kathrin Linsenhoff, Monica Theodorescu, Nicole Uphoff
2. Switzerland, 4,164, Otto J. Hofer, Christine Stueckelberger, Daniel Ramseier, Samuel Schatzmann
3. Canada, 3,969, Cynthia Ishoy, Eva Maria Pracht, Gina Smith, Ashley Nicoll

1984
1. West Germany, 4,955, Reiner Klimke, Uwe Sauer, Herbert Krug
2. Switzerland, 4,673, Otto J. Hofer, Christine Stueckelberger, Amy Catherine De Bary
3. Sweden, 4,630, Ulla Hakansson, Ingamay Bylund, Louise Nathhorst

1980
1. Soviet Union, 4,383, Yuri Kovshov, Viktor Ugriumov, Vera Misevich
2. Bulgaria, 3,580, Petr Mandadzhiev, Svetoslav Ivanov, Georgi Gadzhev
3. Romania, 3,346, Anghelache Donescu, Dumitru Veliku, Petre Rosca

1976
1. West Germany, 5,155.0, Harry Boldt, Reiner Klimke, Gabriela Grillo
2. Switzerland, 4,684, Christine Stueckelberger, Ulrich Lehmann, Doris Ramseier
3. USA, 4,647, Hilda Gurney, Dorothy Morkis, Edith Master

1972
1. Soviet Union, 5,095, Yelena Petushkova, Ivan Kisimov, Ivan Kalita

2. West Germany, 5,083, Liselott Linsenhoff, Josef Neckermann, Karin Schluter
3. Sweden, 4,849, Ulla Hakansson, Ninna Swaab, Maud von Rosen

1968 1. West Germany, 2,699, Josef Neckermann, Dr. Reiner Klimke, Liselott Linsenhoff
2. Soviet Union, 2,657, Ivan Kisimov, Ivan Kalita, Yelena Petushkova
3. Switzerland, 2,547, Gustav Fischer, Henri Chammartin, Marianne Gossweiler

1964 1. West Germany, 2,558, Harry Boldt, Reiner Klimke, Josef Neckermann
2. Switzerland, 2,526, Henri Chammartin, Gustav Fischer, Marianne Gossweiler
3. Soviet Union, 2,311, Sergei Filatov, Ivan Kisimov, Ivan Kalita

1960 Not held

1956 1. Sweden, 2,475, Henri St. Cyr, Gehnall Persson, Gustav-Adolf Boltenstern, Jr.
2. West Germany, 2,346, Liselott Linsenhoff, Hannelore Weygand, Anneliese Kuppers
3. Switzerland, 2,346, Gottfried Trachsel, Henri Chammartin, Gustav Fischer

1952 1. Sweden, 1,597.5, Henri St. Cyr, Gustav-Adolf Boltenstern, Jr., Gehnall Persson
2. Switzerland, 1,579.0, Gottfried Trachsel, Henri Chammartin, Gustav Fischer

3. Germany, 1,501.0, Heinz Pollay, Ida von Nagel, Fritz Thiedemann

1948 1. France, 1,269.0, Andre Jousseaume, Jean Saint-Fort Paillard, Maurice Buret
2. USA, 1,256.0, Robert Borg, Earl Thomson, Frank Henry
3. Portugal, 1,182.0, Fernando Pais, Francisco Valadas, Luiz Mena e Silva

1936 1. Germany, 5,074.0, Heinz Pollay, Freidrich Gerhard, Hermann von Oppeln-Bronikowski
2. France, 4,846.0, Andre Jousseaume, Gerrard de Ballore, Daniel Gillois
3. Sweden, 4,660.5, Gregor Adlercreutz, Sven Colliander, Folke Sandstrom

1932 1. France, 2,818.75, Xavier Lesage, Charles Marion, Andre Jousseaume
2. Sweden, 2,678.00, Thomas Bystrom, Gustav-Adolf Boltenstern, Jr., Bertil Sandstrom
3. USA, 2,576.65, Hiram Tuttle, Isaac Kitts, Alvin Moore

1928 1. Germany, 669.72, Carl Friedrich Freiherr von Langen, Hermann Linkenbach, Eugen Freiherr von Lotzbeck
2. Sweden, 650.86, Ragnar Olson, Janne Lundblad, Carl Bonde
3. Netherlands, 642.96, Jan H. van Reede, Pierre M. R. Versteegh, Gerard W. Le Heux

**1896-
1924** Not held

SHOW JUMPING

▼

HIGHLIGHTS

At the first individual show jumping competition in 1912, the gold medal went to French military officer Jean Cariou and his mount Mignon, a hard-fought win considering that they competed in all three equestrian events. Cariou also helped his team to the silver in show jumping, took home a bronze in the individual three-day event, and, with his teammates, just missed collecting the team three-day bronze.

For the next forty years military riders dominated Olympic competition and medal placings. A civilian first captured a medal in 1952, when Frenchman Pierre Jonqueres d'Oriola took the individual gold. He returned to recapture the individual gold and helped his team win the silver in Tokyo in 1964 and then remained an Olympic competitor through 1968.

1956 proved to be an interesting year for the Olympic equestrian events. A restrictive six-month quarantine on horses made it financially impossible to hold the equestrian events at the Melbourne, Australia, site. Olympic equestrians competed instead in Stockholm, Sweden. In Stockholm, not only were civilians and women allowed to compete for the first time, but the show jumping team bronze went to Great Britain, whose team included Patricia Smythe. Other women competitors soon were distinguishing themselves and their teams. In 1968, Great Britain's Marion Coakes and her incredible mount, a 14.2-hand (that's only 57 inches tall) pony named Stroller, took the individual silver medal.

From 1956 to 1968 the German team dominated show jumping with famous riders like Hans Gunter Winkler, who earned the distinction of winning the most gold medals in Olympic equestrian history. His incredible career includes five gold medals: individual gold in 1956, team gold in 1956, 1960, 1964, and 1972, as well as the team bronze in 1968, and the team silver in 1976.

After 1952 the United States began to stake its own claim on show jumping medals, but only Bill Steinkraus has matched Winkler's impressive twenty-year medal winning span with the 1952 team bronze, 1960 team silver, the individual gold in 1968 (on the famous jumper Snowbound), and the 1972 team silver.

After the boycotted 1980 Moscow Olympics (where, not surprisingly, five gold medals went to the Russian team) the 1984 show jumping events proved to be a US-dominated competition. The individual gold and silver medals as well as the first-ever team gold were taken home to Gladstone, New Jersey, home of the USET. The strong finish by individual silver medalist Greg Best and his mount Gem Twist helped the USET take home the team silver in 1988.

Medalists

Equestrian — Individual Show Jumping

1988
1. Pierre Durand, France, Jappeloup, 1.25
2. Greg Best, USA, Gem Twist, 4.00 (won jump-off)
3. Karsten Huck, West Germany, Nepomuk 8, 4.00

1984
1. Joe Fargis, USA, Touch of Class, 4.00
2. Conrad Homfeld, USA, Abdullah, 4.00
3. Heidi Robbiani, Switzerland, Jessica V, 8.00

1980
1. Jan Kowalczyk, Poland, Artemor, 8.00
2. Nikolai Korolkov, Soviet Union, Espadron, 9.50
3. Oswaldo Mendez Herbruger, Guatemala, Pampa, 12.00
3. Joaquin Perez de la Heras, Mexico, Alymony, 12.00

1976
1. Alwin Schockemoehle, West Germany, Warwick Rex, 0.00
2. Michel Vaillancourt, Canada, Branch County, 12.00
3. Francois Mathy, Belgium, Gai Luron, 12.00

1972
1. Graziano Mancinelli, Italy, Ambassador, 8/0

1968
2. Ann Moore, Great Britain, Psalm, 8/3
3. Neal Shapiro, USA, Sloopy, 8/8
1. William Steinkraus, USA, Snowbound, 4
2. Marion Coakes, Great Britain, Stroller, 8
3. David Broome, Great Britain, Mister Softee, 12

1964
1. Pierre Jonqueres d'Oriola, France, Lutteur, 9
2. Hermann Schridde, West Germany, Dozent, 13.75
3. Peter Robeson, Great Britain, Firecrest, 16

1960
1. Raimondo D'Inzeo, Italy, Posillipo, 12
2. Piero D'Inzeo, Italy, The Rock, 16
3. David Broome, Great Britain, Sunsalve, 23

1956
1. Hans-Gunter Winkler, West Germany, Halla, 4
2. Raimondo D'Inzeo, Italy, Merano, 8
3. Piero D'Inzeo, Italy, Uruguay, 11

1952
1. Pierre Jonqueres d'Oriola, France, Ali Baba, 8/0
2. Oscar Cristi, Chile, Bambi, 8/4
3. Fritz Thiedemann, Germany, Meteor, 8/8

1948
1. Humberto Mariles Cortes, Mexico, Arete, 6.25

2. Ruben Uriza, Mexico, Harvey, 8/0
3. Jean F. d'Orgeix, France, Sucre de Pomme, 8/4

1936 **1.** Kurt Hasse, Germany, Tora, 4/4/59.2
2. Henri Rang, Romania, Delfis, 4/4/72.8
3. Jozsef von Platthy, Hungary, Sello, 8/0/62.6

1932 **1.** Takeichi Nishi, Japan, Uranus, 8
2. Harry Chamberlin, USA, Show Girl, 12
3. Clarence von Rosen, Sweden, Empire, 16

1928 **1.** Frantisek Ventura, Czechoslovakia, Eliot, 0/0/0
2. Pierre Bertran de Balanda, France, Papillon, 0/0/2
3. Chasimir Kuhn, Switzerland, Pepita, 0/0/4

1924 **1.** Alphonse Gemuseus, Switzerland, Lucette, 6
2. Tommaso Lequio, Italy, Trebecco, 8.75
3. Adam Krolikiewicz, Poland, Picador, 10

1920 **1.** Tommaso Lequio, Italy, Trebecco, 2
2. Alessandro Valerio, Italy, Cento, 3
3. Gustaf Lewenhaupt, Sweden, Mon Coeur, 4

1912 **1.** Jean Cariou, France, Mignon, 186
2. Rabod W. von Krocher, Germany, Dohna, 186
3. Emanuel de Blommaert de Soye, Belgium, Clonmore, 185

1904-
1908 **Not held**
1900 **1.** Aime Haegeman, Belgium, Benton II, 2:16.0
2. Georges van de Poele, Belgium, Windsor Squire, 2:17.6
3. de Champsavin, France, Terpischore, 2:26.0

1896 **Not held**

Equestrian — Team Show Jumping

1988 **1.** West Germany, 17.25, Ludger Beerbaum, Wolfgang Brinkmann, Dirk Hafemeister, Franke Sloothaak
2. USA, 20.50, Greg Best, Lisa Jacquin, Anne Kursinski, Joe Fargis
3. France, 27.50, Bourdy Hubert, Frederic Cottier, Michel Robert, Pierre Durand

1984 **1.** USA, 12.00, Joe Fargis, Conrad Homfeld, Leslie Burr, Melanie Smith
2. Great Britain, 36.75, Michael Whitaker, John Whitaker, Steven Smith, Timothy Grubb
3. West Germany, 39.25, Paul Schockemohle, Peter Luther, Franke Sloothaak, Fritz Ligges

1980 **1.** Soviet Union, 20.25, Viacheslav Chukanov, Viktor Poganovski, Viktor Asmaev, Nikolai Korolkov
2. Poland, 56.00, Marion Kozicki, Jan Kowalczyk, Wieslaw Hartman, Janusz Bobik
3. Mexico, 59.75, Joaquin Perez de la Heras, Jesus Gomez Portugal, Gerardo Tazzer Valencia, Alberto Valdes Lacarra

1976 **1.** France, 40.00, Hubert Parot, Marc Roguet, Marcel Rozier, Michel Roche
2. West Germany, 44.00, Alwin Schockemoehle, Hans-Gunter Winkler, Sonke Soenksen, Paul Schockemoehle
3. Belgium, 63.00, Francois Mathy, Eric Wauters, Edgar-Henri Cuepper, Stanny Van Paeschen

1972 **1.** West Germany, 32, Fritz Ligges, Gerhard Wiltfang, Hartwig Steenken, Hans-Gunter Winkler
2. USA, 32.25, William Steinkraus, Neal Shapiro, Kathy Kusner, Frank Chapot
3. Italy, 48, Vittorio Orlandi, Raimondo D'Inzeo, Graziano Mancinelli, Piero D'Inzeo

1968 **1.** Canada, 102.75, Jim Elder, Jim Day, Tom Gayford
2. France, 110.50, Janou Lefebvre, Marcel Rozier, Pierre Jonqueres d'Oriola
3. West Germany, 117.25, Alwin Schockemoehle, Hans-Gunter Winkler, Hermann Schridde

1964 **1.** West Germany, 68.50, Hermann Schridde, Kurt Jarasinski, Hans-Gunter Winkler
2. France, 77.75, Pierre Jonqueres d'Oriola, Janou Lefebvre, Guy Lefrant
3. Italy, 88.50, Piero D'Inzeo, Raimondo D'Inzeo, Graziano Mancinelli

1960 **1.** West Germany, 46.50, Hans-Gunter Winkler, Fritz Thiedemann, Alwin Schockemoehle
2. USA, 66.00, Frank Chapot, William Steinkraus, George Morris
3. Italy, 80.5, Raimondo D'Inzeo, Piero D'Inzeo, Antonio Oppes

1956 **1.** West Germany, 40, Hans-Gunter Winkler, Fritz Thiedemann, Alfons Lutke-Westhues
2. Italy, 66, Raimondo D'Inzeo, Piero D'Inzeo, Salvatore Oppes
3. Great Britain, 69, Wilfred H. White, Patricia Smythe, Peter Robeson

1952 **1.** Great Britain, 40.75, Wilfred H. White, Douglas Stewart, Harry M. Llewellyn
2. Chile, 45.75, Oscar Cristi, Cesar Mendoza, Ricardo Echeverria
3. USA, 52.25, William Steinkraus, Arthur J. McCashin, John Russel

1948 **1.** Mexico, 34.25, Humberto Mariles Cortes, Ruben Uriza, Alberto Valdes Lacarra
2. Spain, 56.50, Jaime Garcia Cruz, Jose Navarro Morenes, Marcelino Gavilan y Ponce de Leon
3. Great Britain, 67, Harry M. Llewellyn, Henry M. V. Nicoll, Arthur Carr

1936 **1.** Germany, 44, Kurt Hasse, Martin von Branekow, Heinz Brandt
2. Netherlands, 51.5, Johan J. Greter, Jan A. de Bruine, Henri L. M. van Schaik
3. Portugal, 56, Jose Beltrao, Luiz Marques do Funchal, Luiz Mena e Silva

1932 No nation completed the course with three riders.

1928 1. Spain, 4, Jose Navarro Morenes, Jose
         Alvarez de los Trujillos, Julio Garcia
         Fernandez
      2. Poland, 8, Kazimierz Gzowski,
         Kazimierz Szosland, Michal
         Antoniewicz
      3. Sweden, 10, Karl Hansen, Carl
         Bjornstjerna, Ernst Hallberg
1924 1. Sweden, 42.25, Ake Thelning, Axel
         Stahle, Age Lundstrom
      2. Switzerland, 50, Alphonse Gemuseus,
         Werner Stuber, Hans Buhler
      3. Portugal, 53, Antonio Borges de
         Almeida, Helder de Souza Martins,
         Jose Mousinho de Albuquerque

1920 1. Sweden, 14, Hans von Rosen, Claes
         Konig, Daniel Norling
      2. Belgium, 16.25, Henri Lamme, Andre
         Coumans, Herman de Gaiffier
         d'Hestroy
      3. Italy, 18.75, Ettore Caffaratti, Giulio
         Cacciandra, Alessandro Alvisi
1912 1. Sweden, 25, Gustaf Lewenhaupt,
         Gustaf Kilman, Hans von Rosen
      2. France, 32, Michel d'Astafort, Jean
         Cariou, Bernard Meyer
      3. Germany, 40, Sigismund Freyer,
         Wilhelm Graf von Hohenau, Ernst-
         Hubertus Deloch
1896-
1908 Not held

THREE-DAY EVENT

▼

HIGHLIGHTS

The US squad has fared best in the three-day event. Though no member has yet to capture an individual gold, Americans have earned a total of four silver and two bronze individual medals. In the team competition the US has won three gold, four silver (including a three time/twelve year streak—1964 through 1972—of silver medals) as well as the initial bronze medal in 1912. The original powerhouse dressage team, Sweden, began fading in the 1950s. Sweden has won seven individual medals (including three gold in 1912, 1920 and 1956) and five team medals (gold in 1912, 1920 and 1952; silver in 1924 and 1948).

fact: In 1988, possibly for the first time in the history of the Olympic Games, a winner's wife presented him with his medal; England's Princess Anne, who is also the president of the Fédération Equestre Internationale, bestowed the team silver on Mark Phillips, who was part of the British team and is married to HRH Anne.

The Netherlands also were a dominant force in three-day eventing in the 1920s and early 1930s, taking seven medals: three individual golds in 1924, 1928, and 1932, as well as team gold in 1924 and 1928. Great Britain and New Zealand have remained competitive, with the British capturing the team silver in 1988 and 1984, as well as the individual bronze in 1988 (Virginia Leng) and 1984

288

(Virginia Holgate). New Zealand's Mark Todd captured the gold on Charisma in the 1988 and 1984 individual events and also helped his team to the 1988 bronze.

Equestrian — Individual Three-Day Event

1988
1. Mark Todd, New Zealand, Charisma, 42.60
2. Ian Stark, Great Britain, Sir Wattie, 52.80
3. Virginia Leng, Great Britain, Master Craftsman, 62.00

1984
1. Mark Todd, New Zealand, Charisma, 51.60
2. Karen Stives, USA, Ben Arthur, 54.20
3. Virginia Holgate, Great Britain, Priceless, 56.80

1980
1. Federico Euro Roman, Italy, Rossinan, 108.60
2. Aleksandr Blinov, Soviet Union, Galzun, 120.80
3. Yuri Salnikov, Soviet Union, Pintset, 151.60

1976
1. Edmund Coffin, USA, Bally-Cor, 114.99
2. J. Michael Plumb, USA, Better and Better, 125.85
3. Karl Schultz, West Germany, Madrigal, 129.45

1972
1. Richard Meade, Great Britain, Laurieston, 57.73
2. Alessandro Argenton, Italy, Woodland, 43.33
3. Jan Jonsson, Sweden, Sarajevo, 39.67

1968
1. Jean-Jacques Guyon, France, Pitou, 38.86
2. Derek Allhusen, Great Britain, Lochinvar, 41.61
3. Michael Page, USA, Foster, 52.31

1964
1. Mauro Checcoli, Italy, Surbean, 64.40
2. Carlos Moratorio, Argentina, Chalan, 56.40
3. Fritz Ligges, West Germany, Donkosak, 49.20

1960
1. Lawrence Morgan, Australia, Salad Days, 7.15
2. Neale Lavis, Australia, Mirrabooka, 16.50
3. Anton Buhler, Switzerland, Gay Spark, 51.21

1956
1. Petrus Kastenman, Sweden, Illuster, 66.53
2. August Lutke-Westhues, West Germany, Trux v. Kamax, 84.87
3. Frank Weldon, Great Britain, Kilbarry, 85.48

1952
1. Hans von Blixen-Finecke, Jr., Sweden, Jubal, 28.33
2. Guy Lefrant, France, Verdun, 54.50
3. Wilhelm Busing, Germany, Hubertus, 55.50

1948
1. Bernard Chevallier, France, Aiglonne, 4
2. Frank Henry, USA, Swing low, 21
3. Robert Selfelt, Sweden, Claque, 25

1936
1. Ludwig Stubbendorf, Germany, Nurmi, 37.70
2. Earl Thomson, USA, Jenny Camp, 99.90
3. Hans Mathiesen-Lunding, Denmark, Jason, 102.20

1932
1. Charles F. Pahud de Mortanges, Netherlands, Marcroix, 1,813.83
2. Earl Thomson, USA, Jenny Camp, 1,811.00
3. Clarence von Rosen, Jr., Sweden, Sunnyside Maid, 1,809.42

1928
1. Charles F. Pahud de Mortanges, Netherlands, Marcroix, 1,969.82
2. Gerard de Kruijff, Netherlands, Va-t-en, 1,967.26
3. Bruno Neumann, Germany, Ilja, 1,944.42

1924
1. Adolph van der Voort van Zijp, Netherlands, Silver piece, 1,976.00
2. Frode Kirkebjerg, Denmark, Meteor, 1,853.50
3. Sloan Doak, USA, Pathfinder, 1,845.50

1920
1. Helmer Morner, Sweden, Germany, 1,775.00
2. Age Lundstrom, Sweden, Yrsa, 1,738.75
3. Ettore Caffaratti, Italy, Traditore, 1,733.75

1912
1. Axel Nordlander, Sweden, Lady Artist, 46.59
2. Friedrich von Rochow, Germany, Idealist, 46.42
3. Jean Cariou, France, Cocotte, 46.32

1896–1908
Not held

Equestrian — Team Three-Day Event

1988
1. West Germany, 225.95, Claus Erhon, Matthias Baumann, Thies Kaspareit, Ralf Ehrenbrink
2. Great Britain, 265,80, Mark Phillips, Karen Straker, Virginia Leng, Ian Stark
3. New Zealand, 271.20, Mark Todd, Marges Knighton, Andrew Bennie, Tinks Pottinger

1984
1. USA, 186.00, J. Michael Plumb, Karen Stives, Torrance Fleischmann, Bruce Davidson
2. Great Britain, 189.20, Virginia Holgate, Ian Stark, Diana Clapham, Lucinda Green

289

3. West Germany, 234.00, Dietmar Hogrete, Bettina Overesch, Burkhard Tesdorpf, Claus Erhom

1980 1. Soviet Union, 457.00, Aleksandr Blinov, Yuri Salnikov, Valeri Volkov, Sergei Rogozhin
2. Italy, 656.20, Federico Euro Roman, Anna Casagrande, Mauro Roman, Marina Sciocchetti
3. Mexico, 1,172.85, Manuel Mendivil, David Barcena, Soto Jose Luis Perez, Fabian Vazquez

1976 1. USA, 441.00, Edmund Coffin, J. Michael Plumb, Bruce Davidson, Mary Anne Tauskey
2. West Germany, 584.60, Karl Schulz, Herbert Bloecker, Helmut Rethemeier, Otto Ammerman
3. Australia, 599.54, Mervyn Bennett, William Roycroft, Denis Piggott

1972 1. Great Britain, 95.53, Richard Meade, Mary Gordon-Watson, Bridget Parker, Mark Phillips
2. USA, 10.81, Kevin Freeman, Bruce Davidson, J. Michael Plumb, James Wofford
3. West Germany, 18.00, Harry Klugmann, Ludwig Gossing, Karl Schultz, Horst Karsten

1968 1. Great Britain, 175.93, Derek Allhusen, Richard Meade, Reuben Jones
2. USA, 245.87, Michael Page, James Wofford, J. Michael Plumb
3. Australia, 331.26, Wayne Roycroft, Brian Cobcroft, William Roycroft

1964 1. Italy, 85.80, Mauro Checcoli, Paolo Angioni, Giuseppe Ravano
2. USA, 65.86, Michael Page, Kevin Freeman, J. Michael Plumb
3. West Germany, 56.73, Fritz Ligges, Horst Karsten, Gerhard Schulz

1960 1. Australia, 128.18, Lawrence Morgan, Neale Lavis, William Roycroft
2. Switzerland, 386.02, Anton Buhler, Hans Schwarzenbach, Rudolf Gunthardt
3. France, 515.71, Jack Louis Le Goff, Guy Lefrant, Jean R. Le Roy

1956 1. Great Britain, 355.48, Frank Weldon, Arthur L. Rock, Albert E. Hill
2. West Germany, 475.91, August Lutke-Westhues, Otto Rothe, Klaus Wagner
3. Canada, 572.72, John Rumble, James Elder, Brian Herbinson

1952 1. Sweden, 221.94, Hans von Blixen-Finecke, Jr., Olof Stahre, Folke Frolen

2. Germany, 235.49, Wilhelm Busing, Klaus Wagner, Otto Rothe
3. USA, 587.16, Charles Hough, Walter Staley, John Wofford

1948 1. USA, 161.50, Frank Henry, Charles Anderson, Earl Thomson
2. Sweden, 165.00, Robert Selfelt, Olof Stahre, Sigurd Svensson
3. Mexico, 305.25, Humberto Mariles Cortes, Raul Campero, Joaquin Solano Chagoya

1936 1. Germany, 676.65, Ludwig Stubbendorf, Rudolf Lippert, Konrad Van. Wangenheim
2. Poland, 991.70, Henryk Rojcewicz, Zdzislaw Kawecki, Serweryn Kulesza
3. Great Britain, 9,195.50, Alec Scott, Edward Howard-Vyse, Richard Fanshawe

1932 1. USA, 5,083.083, Earl Thomson, Harry Chamberlin, Edwin Argo
2. Netherlands, 4,689.083, Charles F. Pahud de Mortanges, Karel J. Schummelketel, Aernout v. Lennep

1928 1. Netherlands, 5,865.68, Charles F. Pahud de Mortanges, Gerard de Kruijff, Adolph van der Voort van Zijp
2. Norway, 5,395.68, Bjart Ording, Arthur Quist, Eugen Johansen
3. Poland, 5,067.92, Michal Antoniewicz, Jozef Trenkwald, Karol de Rommel

1924 1. Netherlands, 5,297.5, Adolph van der Voort van Zijp, Charles F. Pahud de Mortanges, Gerard de Kruijff
2. Sweden, 4,743.5, Claes Konig, Torsten Sylvan, Gustaf Hagelin
3. Italy, 4,512.5, Alberto Lombardi, Alessandro Alvisi, Emanuele Di Pralorma

1920 1. Sweden, 5,057.50, Helmer Morner, Age Lundstrom, Georg von Braun
2. Italy, 4,735.00, Ettore Caffaratti, Garibaldi Spighi, Giulio Cacciandra
3. Belgium, 4,560.00, Roger Moeremans d'Emaus, Oswald Lints, Jules Bonvalet

1912 1. Sweden, 139.06, Axel Nordlander, Nils Adlercreutz, Ernst Casparsson
2. Germany, 138.48, Friedrich von Rochow, Richard Graf von Schaesberg-Tannheim, Eduard v. Lutcken
3. USA, 137.33, Benjamin Lear, John Montgomery, Guy Henry

1896-
1908 **Not held**

290

New Zealand's Mark Todd, center, captured the 1988 gold in three-day eventing ahead of silver medalist Ian Stark and bronze medalist Virginia Leng, both of Great Britain. They're likely to contend for Barcelona's equestrian medals as well.

FENCING

WARM-UP

Like several other Olympic sports—archery and javelin, to name two of the most obvious—fencing traces its roots to armed combat. At one point in prehistory, some bright fellow must have come to the conclusion that, rather than smiting his fellow humans with a blunt object, like a rock or club, it might be more efficient to poke them vigorously with a sharply pointed stick. This would allow an individual, with a mere jab, to render an opponent incapacitated or dead, a real improvement over the relatively high amount of energy needed to achieve the same result bashing around with a heavier object. As an incremental benefit, the sharp stick undoubtedly also proved handy for dispatching game animals and other food items.

As warfare became better organized, with tribes mounting campaigns against each other, some sort of formal training probably became necessary. And at that point it must have dawned on our early ancestors, even with their somewhat inferior brain capacity, that practicing on your tribal compatriots with real weapons was rather impractical, having the effect, as it would, of reducing the number of available warriors for your side. So someone hit upon the idea of practicing with blunted, or "foiled," sticks. (This will tie in neatly a bit later.) Thus was noncombative swordplay invented. Or, rather, noncombative poking with sticks. It couldn't really be called swordplay until much later, when actual swords were invented.

The making of bladed weapons requires metal of some sort, and there's quite a gap between the sharp-stick scenario and the time when civilization had evolved to the point of being able to produce real swords. But it's generally agreed that when the age of metals finally arrived, one of the first things people did was fashion weapons out of the new materials. Swords evolved out of the daggers that were first made during the Bronze Age (4000 to 3000 BC), although nothing really practical for fighting turned up until the early Iron Age (some time prior to 1000 BC).

A decorative relief depicting practice swordplay with knobs on the ends of the weapons, dating back at least to 1190 BC, has been found in Egypt, so clearly people at this time also saw the value of training with blunted swords. The relief shows the fencers wearing face protection and earflaps, and it also includes umpires, tournament organizers, and spectators, so presumably this was not just a military exercise but an actual sporting event. And, in fact, fencing was one of the earliest sports to be regulated by theoretical and practical rules—necessary to ensure safety as well as to make the sport follow as closely as possible the pattern of a real sword fight.

Although the sword was the main weapon of battle from these early times until the introduction of gunpowder, little is known about the technique of swordsmanship prior to 1400. The Romans and Greeks favored a short, wide sword that would seem to capitalize on speed and agility. During the age of chivalry, the long, heavy two-handed broadsword used by the knights to crack heavy armor would suggest slower action, large movements, and the need for a great deal of strength on the part of the combattant.

With the advent of firearms in the fifteenth century, armor became obsolete, and the sword was permanently replaced as the primary weapon of the military (although it certainly remained for several centuries as an important secondary battle weapon). Lighter and better-balanced swords came into vogue, and they became the standard sidearm for the European gentleman. Cutting an opponent with the honed edge of the weapon, which was considered the most effective technique until about 1500, gradually diminished as the width of the blade decreased. The rapier, a very narrow, straight, two-edged sword, became popular, and with it came the style of fighting familiar to fans of swashbuckling movies, in which thrusting with the point of the weapon is favored. The rapier was primarily an offensive sword, defense being the province of a dagger held in the other hand.

The next major advance in technique was the use of the same weapon for both offense and defense, which resulted in the development of the smallsword in about 1650. This period heralded the arrival of modern fencing technique with a single, light, highly maneuverable weapon being held in one hand.

The Italians, Spanish, and French all claim to have created modern fencing, with plenty of available evidence supporting each country. Throughout Europe, swordplay took on the aura of a mystical high art, and fencing masters jealously guarded their secret techniques, conducting instruction behind locked doors and charging obscene fees for their wisdom. This changed in the sixteenth century when the publication of several illustrated fencing books allowed comparison of the techniques of the various masters. It quickly became apparent that the differences between them were minimal: all stressed concentration, economy of movement, surprise, and timing—in other words, the basic elements that are still the key to success in a fencing bout.

The sport of fencing as we know it, with its distinctive rules and scoring system, can be traced back to the eighteenth century with the publication of treatises on the subject by G. Danet and D. Angelo. The equipment they describe includes the foil, originally designed as a practice weapon for the smallsword, a metal mask with a horizontal eye slit, and a protective vest or jacket. The rules they set up were intended to simulate real combat and ensure the safety of the combatants. A "convention" was adopted that limited the target to the trunk of the body, a safety factor but also probably a throwback to the time when a killing thrust to this area by a rapier or smallsword would be highly desirable (to the attacker, of course).

Another convention provided for an orderly and realistic alternation of play by stating that an attack had the "right of way" until it was parried, or neutralized; then the defender's counterattack had the right of way until it was parried, and so forth. This convention served two obvious purposes: first, it had the practical use of allowing an official to determine, clearly, which fencer had scored a legal touch, rather than trying to ascertain split-second timing; and, second, it provided for realistic sword-fighting action (in a real fight a defender would never leave himself exposed to a sharp blade while cutting into an attack; he would always parry his opponent's thrust first, then counterattack).

No discussion of fencing history would be complete without some mention of dueling. After the sword was rendered obsolete as a combat weapon by the introduction of firearms, it remained for many centuries a favored method by which gentlemen settled differences of opinion. Dueling to the death, although practiced widely even until very recently, proved to be a fairly drastic way of resolving disputes. After all, not every point of honor is actually worth dying for. Instead, many relatively minor differences of opinion were settled by seeing who could draw first blood in a sword fight. Under some circumstances, a poke in the arm or shoulder could just as easily end the argument—with the added advantage that the two opponents might be able to have a glass of wine together after the duel was finished. The modern épée, the second of fencing's three weapons, had its origins with swords that were specifically developed for dueling purposes. (Its name comes from the French term for dueling sword, *épée de terrain.*)

The third modern fencing weapon, the sabre, is a direct descendant of the cavalry sabre used for centuries by mounted troops, although clearly its origins go back even further to ancient times, to the first flat-bladed swords with a honed edge. It is the only one of the three that may be used with a cutting motion in addition to the thrusting moves of the foil and épée.

At the time of the first modern Olympics, in 1896, fencing was a clear choice to be included in the program. For one thing, the sword was still an important military weapon, with students at all respectable military academies taking instruction in the art of swordsmanship. And, of course, sword fighting was by that time a well established European tradition with centuries of history behind it. Also, French Baron Pierre de Coubertin, who initiated the Modern Games, was himself a fencer. Since that time, fencing has been one of only six sports to have been featured in every modern Olympic Games.

Needless to say, Europeans dominated the sport from the beginning, with champions in the thrusting weapons emerging from a variety of countries, including France, Italy, Spain, Great Britain, the Soviet Union, and the Netherlands; Hungary became the traditional leader in the sabre competition. Following World War II, however, state support of athletes in the socialist countries allowed them to make remarkable strides in Olympic fencing competition, and the Eastern European nations became the leaders for many years. The 1960 Olympics in Rome marked the end of an era: for the first time in 48 years neither a French nor an Italian fencer won the foil event, the gold medal being taken that year by the USSR.

In the last twenty years, a considerable realignment has taken place in international fencing. The Poles broke the Hungarian stronghold in the sabre, while the Hungarians asserted themselves in the thrusting weapons, especially épée. Then came several years of Soviet domination. Today, Hungary, Italy, and the Soviet Union are considered roughly equal, with the Hungarians still favoring the épée events.

▼

SPECTATORS' GUIDE

On the surface, fencing may appear to be a fairly simple and straightforward proposition: fencing is swordfighting, and whomever gets hit with the pointy end loses. But, of course, it's more complicated than that. Fencing has, in fact, been called "chess with muscles," an indication of the complicated strategy, the moves, counter-moves, and counter-counter-moves, that make up a fencing bout. Even such a simple thing as determining when a hit has taken place (at one time merely a matter of seeing who was bleeding, or, later, relying on an honorable opponent to mention a hit scored against himself by acknowledging, "I was touched," or "touché") is complicated by the flashing blades and lightning-quick movements of the competitors. The sport of modern fencing, with its emphasis on agility, quickness, and subtlety of movement, can be difficult to follow without at least a brief explanation of its fundamentals.

The key to fencing is distance and timing. The whole point is to deliver the business end of the weapon on target by getting close enough to your opponent to score the touch at a time when he or she is out of position to block the attack. The basic attack move is the **lunge**, in which the body is propelled forward by straightening the back leg while the front leg is advanced and the blade is extended toward the target. This may be countered by a recovery from a lunge on the part of the opponent (if he or she is already in a lunge position) or by a retreat, in which the defender moves backward several paces.

Occasionally, an attacker will choose to employ the **flèche,** or running attack. This is a very dramatic and flamboyant movement (especially when employed in a sabre bout), in which the fencer actually runs at his or her opponent. It is also incredibly risky, as it sacrifices balance, limits the types of recoveries available, and generally exposes the fencer to a variety of counterattacks. Nevertheless, the flèche can be an effective strategy, and it never fails to impress onlookers.

Eight fencing events are held at the Olympics, six for men (individual and team events in each of the three weapons) and two for women (individual and team foil, only). Through the years, other fencing events have come and gone, some of them rather strange—for example, outdoor fencing—and some a bit less bizarre—such as three-weapon events (in which entrants competed in all three weapons, although not at the same time, which would put it in the category of the truly bizarre). One other Olympic event, the modern pentathlon, features fencing, along with running, swimming, riding, and shooting.

The Weapons

The foil is the sword of choice for the majority of fencers. Designed as a training weapon, the foil still serves as the introductory weapon for virtually all fencers. That does not mean, however, that it should be regarded only as a beginner's weapon. On the contrary, the foil is often said to be the most difficult of the three to master.

A foil may be up to 1100 millimeters (43.307 inches) in total length and up to 500 grams (17.637 ounces) in weight, although with the modern emphasis on quickness, they are often much lighter. Foils feature four-sided blades, rectangular in cross-section, a circular hand guard, and a handle that can vary according to the preference of the individual fencer. Traditionally, the French preferred a relatively straight grip, about eight inches in length, while the Italian version added a cross bar about two inches behind the guard. Today, however, rather oddly shaped orthopedic grips, specially designed for comfort and precise control, have become commonplace.

Although the foil is, of course, blunted, it is in theory a pointed sword capable of inflicting a puncture wound only; the blade is not presumed to be honed along its edge. A touch (note that this is not pronounced "too-*shay*"; not even a club fencer would use this term, normally heard on Saturday morning cartoon shows, when scoring a touch) in a foil event is scored only when the point of the blade hits a valid target area. And the valid foil target is the torso only, from the collar to the groin lines in front, and from the collar to the hips in back. Since this is, historically, a training event for combat, only those hits that would inflict potentially fatal wounds are counted. (Notice, however, that the head is not a valid target, a holdover from the days before masks, when even a blunted weapon could cause severe damage to the face.)

Off-target hits don't count against a fencer but result in the bout being temporarily stopped, then re-started. The bout is also stopped if either competitor steps off the fencing "strip," a narrow rectangle 2 meters wide by 14 meters long on which matches in all three weapons take place; a fencer who goes off the side of the strip is penalized by the loss of ground, and one who retreats more than a limited distance is penalized by having a touch scored against him or her. A match is ended when a fencer has been touched five times in a men's bout or four times in a women's event.

Foil fencing is characterized by a group of "conventions," rules that have evolved from the desire to make the sport resemble as closely as possible a real sword fight. Once an attack has been started, the defender must neutralize, or "parry" the thrust before beginning a counterattack. If a defender attacks into an attack (a very dangerous and foolhardy move that could, in a real duel, result in the death of both opponents), that defender does not score a legal touch. The determination of "right of way" is made by a tournament official called the president or director.

To assist the director in making these judgments, electrical scoring was introduced to foil fencing in 1955. (It had been in use in épée events since 1935.) Lights come on to signal hits—usually a colored light for a touch on a valid target, white on an invalid target. Before electricity, fencers were expected to do the sportsmanlike thing and acknowledge valid hits scored upon themselves by saying "touché," French for "I was touched." Competitors wear metallic vests that delineate the valid target area; a wire running up the back and down the sleeve connects to a button at the tip of the weapon; simply pushing in the button against any surface other than the vest results in signalling an invalid hit, while the button's contact with the metal in the vest signals a good touch. But in watching a foil bout, bear in mind that the timing of the hits is crucial, and even though lights may go on simultaneously, the official may award a point to one fencer based on the right-of-way convention.

The **épée** (pronounced *eh*-pay in English, or eh-*pay*, if you insist on proper French) is similar to the foil in that it is a thrusting weapon only and is the same length as the foil. But the épée is considerably heavier, weighing up to 770 grams (27.16 ounces). The blade of an épée is triangular in cross section, making it quite a bit stiffer than a foil, and its hand guard is significantly larger.

Since the épée evolved from dueling weapons, and since the object of many duels was to draw first blood and not necessarily deliver a fatal thrust, the épée has no invalid target. Hits from head to toe count as touches. It is, therefore, the simplest of the three weapons to follow in a bout. And it was the first of the three to be electrified in the 1930s; all that was required was a rudimentary plunger on the end of the blade.

The only thing remotely sophisticated about electric épée equipment is its ability to "lock out" a second light within a split second, thus eliminating constant simultaneous touches and, incidentally, making this the easiest type of fencing for the novice viewer to understand: The light signals a point.

The **sabre** is the only weapon that can score points by cutting, or slicing, in addition to thrusting. Its blade is V-shaped and narrow, fairly stiff when used with a cutting motion but quite flexible in the flat plane (that is, when moved side to side). The maximum overall length of the sabre is 1050 millimeters (41.338 inches), and it has the same maximum weight as the foil. While in the *enguard*, or "ready," position, a foil or épée fencer's arm is generally in line with the blade, while the sabre is held roughly perpendicular to the arm. As a result, the sabre's handguard sweeps around the back of the hand to the pommel, so that it protects the fencer's knuckles against cuts.

Evolving, as it did, from the cavalry sabre, the fencing sabre takes as its target area the entire body above the waist, the most logical targets for a mounted warrior. As in foil competition, sabre bouts are regulated by conventions, with the same right-of-way rule in effect. Unlike foil and épée bouts, however, sabre matches until very recently were officiated manually, since this weapon proved to be the most complicated to electrify. The director presided over the bout with four judges watching for touches. But new advances in technology have finally allowed the sabre to catch up with the other weapons, and in 1992 (for the first time), Olympic sabre matches will be officiated with the aid of electrical equipment.

Sabre fencing is often considered the most exciting of the three weapons to watch. Since the sabre offers a wider variety of targets than the foil, as well as cutting attacks not possible with either the foil or the épée, sabre movements tend to be noisier and more flamboyant. The movements are also larger than the tiny, quick maneuvers of the other weapons, making sabre bouts easier for casual fans to enjoy.

No matter which weapon is being used, some movements are common to all fencing bouts. The action begins at the center of the strip with the opponents facing each other, masks in hand. They salute the director first, then each other, by raising their weapons, guard level with the chin, then snapping them down smartly.

At the command *"en guard"* from the director, the competitors put on their masks and assume the ready position, standing sideways to each other (to present the smallest possible target), the weapon held out in front of the body, the empty hand raised behind the body to help provide balance (except in sabre fencing, in which the empty hand is rested on the hip), with the weight evenly distributed, ready to move either backward or forward. At the command "fence," they are free to engage each other, trying to touch and avoid being touched.

Although, ultimately, a time limit is imposed on all fencing bouts, the action generally continues until a hit is made, either valid or invalid, or until one of the contestants steps off the strip. If a legal touch is scored, the fencers return to the center of the strip to begin the next point. If an invalid hit occurs, the action picks up at that point. And if a fencer leaves the strip, the director may assess a penalty against the violator by resuming the action closer to that competitor's end of the strip, causing him or her to "lose ground," or give up maneuvering room.

A few final points on viewing fencing matches: Do not expect to hear competitors screaming "Touché" after scoring points; as noted previously, this would be considered extremely gauche, even for beginners. However, traditionally, before the advent of electrical scoring, the competitor upon whom a touch was scored was expected to acknowledge the touch by uttering a "touché," to avoid any unseemly argument that would mar the battle. Disarming an opponent with a large circular motion that sends his or her weapon flying across the room counts for nothing, even if you shout "Hah–*HAH!*" while doing it. (If a fencer should lose his or her weapon, the director stops the bout until both competitors are ready to resume.) No fencer in any match will ever be wearing a red heart on his or her chest. No one, not even a sabre fencer, will draw a "Z" on any part of an opponent's body. At no time are competitors allowed to leap onto tables and continue fencing from there. Likewise, stairways.

Finally, never, under any circumstances, will any Olympic fencer swing from a chandelier during a bout, as entertaining as that might be to watch.

Glossaire d'Escrime

ADVANCE: A short step forward.

ATTACK: A series of movements by which a fencer tries to score a touch.

BEAT: A sharp tap made on the opponent's blade to deflect it.

CLOSING IN (or *corps à corps*): Occurs when blade guards or fencers' bodies come in contact with each other; results in a penalty in foil or sabre.

COMPOSITE ATTACK: An attack in more than one movement.

COUNTERATTACK: An attack by a fencer who has just defeated—or "parried'—an attack by an opponent.

COUNTER-PARRY (or circular parry): A defensive movement executed by making a small circle with the point of the weapon around the opponent's blade.

COUNTER-RIPOSTE: A riposte that follows the parry of an opponent's riposte.

COUPÉ: An attack made by passing the blade over an opponent's blade.

DIRECTOR: The primary (or, in most cases, the only) official presiding over a fencing bout.

DISENGAGE: Any break of contact between blades; term commonly used to indicate any avoidance of contact.

DOUBLE TOUCH: Both fencers being hit at the same time; if one has the right of way, in foil or sabre, a touch is counted against the other; in épée, both fencers have a touch scored against them.

ENGAGEMENT: Contact of blades.

EN GUARD (or on guard): The position taken before the fencers begin a bout; also, a command given by the director to warn the fencers that the bout is about to begin.

ENVELOPPEMENT: A continuous binding movement so that the opponent's blade is carried for at least one complete circle.

FEINT: A false attack, intended to cause the opponent to move his or her guard, thus opening a new line for attack.

FLÈCHE: A running attack; literally, "arrow" or "dart."

GLIDE: A gentle forward action in contact with the opponent's blade.

GUARD: The part of the weapon that protects the hand.

JUMP: An advance in which both feet move at the same time.

LUNGE: The most common and basic attack, characterized by a straightening of the back leg and the advancing of the front leg as the weapon is thrust forward.

PARRY: A defensive action that blocks an attacking blade to keep it off target.

PISTE: The French term (meaning "path") for the fencing strip.

POMMEL: A nut at the butt-end of the weapon that holds it together.

PRESIDENT: Another name for the director.

RECOVER: Return to the *en guard* position after lunging.

REMISE (or replacement): Immediately attacking again after an initial attack.

RIPOSTE: The defender's counterattack after a parry.

SIMPLE: An action completed in one movement (as opposed to a composite).

STOP THRUST: A counterattack against an opponent's attack or riposte, intended to land with sufficient time advantage over an opponent's action to score a touch.

STRIP: The fencing area, 2 meters wide by 14 meters in length.

TAKING: Controlling an opponent's blade.

THRUST: Extending the arm and threatening the target with the tip of the weapon.

▼

HOPEFULS

The USSR should once again field a very strong fencing squad in 1992. The Soviets have a number of talented young hopefuls, as well as several formidable veterans, including the 1988 gold-medal winning men's team foil champions. Meanwhile, Germany would like to see a repeat performance by 1988 gold medalists Arnd Schmitt in épée and Anja Fichtel in foil (as well as its other women's foilists, Sabine Bau and Zita Funkenhauser, who took the silver and bronze, completing a sweep of that event).

France took the gold in team épée in the 1988 Olympics, where Jean-François Lamour won the individual sabre competition. Italy was well represented in 1988, with Stefano Cerioni taking the gold in the men's individual event. Another country to keep an eye on in 1992 is Cuba, considered to be a fencing "sleeper."

Although the United States has not traditionally been a major force in fencing, a number of Americans could make a strong showing in Barcelona. In men's foil, three-time Olympian Michael Marx, seven-time national champion and currently the top-ranked foilist in the country, could make a bid for a medal. Also expected to compete are Jack Tichacek, ranked second in this weapon and member of the silver-medal winning US team at the 1987 Pan American Games; Marty Yu, a member of the 1990 World Championships team, ranked fourth in the country; and Al Carter, the youngest member of the 1990 World Championships team.

Women's foil contenders include Caitlin Bilodeaux, ranked number one in the United States, who finished eleventh in the 1980 Olympics; she is a three-time national champion and six-time member of the World Championships team. Molly Sullivan was the 1985 national champion and a member of the gold-medal winning team at the 1987 Pan American Games. Another member of that 1987 Pan Am team, Sharon Monplaisir finished 35th at the Seoul Olympics and is ranked third in the country. Mary Jane O'Neill and Jennifer Yu are tied for the fourth-place national ranking; O'Neill finished just behind Monplaisir in Seoul and is a four-time member of the US World Championships team, while Yu is the 1990 national champion.

The top-ranked US épée fencer is Robert Marx (older brother of foilist Michael). He has competed in two Olympics, 1984 and 1988, and is a six-time member of the World Championships team. Another strong épée contender is Jon Normile, ranked number two, who was an alternate for the 1988 Olympic team. Chris O'Loughlin, ranked fourth, was a member of the 1990 World Championships team; and Rob Strull, a member of the 1984 Modern Pentathlon team, won the gold medal in that event and the silver in épée at the 1987 Pan Am Games.

The most likely US medal bid should be in the sabre competition. This team is led by four-time Olympian Peter Westbrook, twelve-time national champion who became the first American in 24 years to take a medal in fencing, capturing the bronze at the 1984 Olympics. He finished twelfth in 1988 and also competed in the 1976 and 1980 Olympics. Another member of the 1988 Olympic sabre team expected to make a strong showing in 1992 is Robert Cottingham, a four-time member of the World Championships team.

Also watch for John Friedberg, another member of the 1990 World Championships team, and Michael Lofton, who competed in the 1984 and 1988 Olympics and won a silver medal in men's team sabre at the 1987 Pan Am Games.

Schedule

The tentative fencing schedule is as follows:

Thursday, July 30
Foil—individual preliminaries, women
Foil—individual finals, women

Friday, July 31
Foil—individual preliminaries, men
Foil—individual finals, men

Saturday, August 1
Épée—individual preliminaries, men
Épée—individual finals, men

Sunday, August 2
Sabre—individual preliminaries, men
Sabre—individual finals, men

Monday, August 3
Foil—team preliminaries, women

Tuesday, August 4
Foil—team preliminaries, women
Foil—team finals, women

Wednesday, August 5
Épée—team preliminaries, men
Foil—team preliminaries, men
Foil—team finals, men

Thursday, August 6
Sabre—team preliminaries, men
Épée—team preliminaries, men
Épée—team finals, men

Friday, August 7
Sabre—team preliminaries, men
Sabre—team finals, men

▼

HIGHLIGHTS

Fencing has been a part of every modern Olympics, one of only six sports able to make this claim. Men's events have been featured since the first modern Games in 1896, while women began competing in Olympic competition in 1924.

Interestingly (and, perhaps, fittingly), Jean Georgiadis of Greece took the gold medal in the sabre competition at the 1896 games, the last time the Greeks ever won that event. In the early years, amateur and professional fencers (fencing masters) competed against each other. In 1900, in a joint foil-épée contest, professional Albert Ayat of France came in first, defeating Cuban champion Ramon Fonst. Fonst was Ayat's pupil. And one of the greatest masters of the time, Italo Santelli, competed along with the amateurs. A generation of Santelli-trained Hungarian sabre fencers began a period of Hungarian domination of that weapon that started with the London Olympics in 1908 and lasted for sixty years.

fact: Many of West Germany's numerous fencing medals won in 1976, 1984, and 1988 could be traced to the Tauberbischofsheim fencing club, situated in a town of 12,000 residents.

The United States won its first fencing medal in Antwerp in 1920, a bronze in team foil. (American Albertson Van Zo Post won a gold in team foil in 1904, the only American ever to receive a gold medal in Olympic fencing, but he was teamed with Cubans Fonst and Manuel Diaz at the time.) The first American individual medalist was George C. Calnan, a Navy lieutenant who took the bronze in épée at the 1928 Olympics. In the first post-World War II Olympics, held in London in 1948, the US sabre team took the bronze, and the foil team finished fourth; Maria Cerra Tishman finished fourth in women's foil, while George V. Worth was the best male finisher with a fifth place in sabre.

At the 1960 Rome Olympics, Albert Axelrod took third place in individual foil, and the US sabre team finished fourth. Peter Westbrook's bronze medal in individual sabre capped the 1984 Olympics. The best overall US Olympic performance ever was probably 1932 in Los Angeles, when the American fencers took third place in team foil, third in team épée, and fourth in team sabre, while George Calnan finished sixth in sabre, Norman Armitage was ninth in sabre, and Marion Lloyd Vince took ninth place in women's foil.

Medalists

Fencing — Men's Individual Épée

1988
1. Arnd Schmitt, West Germany
2. Philippe Riboud, France
3. Andrei Chouvalov, Soviet Union

1984
1. Philippe Boisse, France
2. Bjorne Vaggo, Sweden
3. Philippe Riboud, France

1980
1. Johan Harmenberg, Sweden
2. Erno Kolczonay, Hungary
3. Philippe Riboud, France

1976
1. Alexander Pusch, West Germany
2. Juergen Hehn, Great Britain
3. Gyozo Kulcsar, Hunary

1972
1. Dr. Csaba Fenyvesi, Hungary
2. Jacques Ladegaillerie, France
3. Gyozo Kulcsar, Hungary

1968
1. Gyozo Kulcsar, Hungary
2. Grigori Kriss, Soviet Union

1964
3. Gianluigi Saccaro, Italy
1. Grigori Kriss, Soviet Union
2. Henry Hoskyns, Great Britain
3. Guram Kostava, Soviet Union

1960
1. Giuseppe Delfino, Italy
2. Allan Jay, Great Britain
3. Bruno Khabarov, Soviet Union

1956
1. Carlo Pavesi, Italy
2. Giuseppe Delfino, Italy
3. Edoardo Mangiarotti, Italy

1952
1. Edoardo Mangiarotti, Italy
2. Dario Mangiarotti, Italy
3. Oswald Zappelli, Switzerland

1948
1. Luigi Cantone, Italy
2. Oswald Zappelli, Switzerland
3. Edoardo Mangiarotti, Italy

1936
1. Franco Riccardi, Italy
2. Saverio Ragno, Italy
3. Giancarlo Cornaggia-Medici, Italy

1932
1. Giancarlo Cornaggia-Medici, Italy
2. Georges Buchard, France

3. Carlo Agostoni, Italy
1928 1. Lucien Gaudin, France
2. Georges Buchard, France
3. George Calnan, USA
1924 1. Charles Delporte, Belgium
2. Roger Ducret, France
3. Nils Hellsten, Sweden
1920 1. Armand Massard, France
2. Alexandre Lippmann, France
3. Gustave Buchard, France
1912 1. Paul Anspach, Belgium
2. Ivan Osiier, Denmark
3. Philippe Le Hardy de Beaulieu,
Belgium
1908 1. Gaston Alibert, France
2. Alexandre Lippmann, France
3. Eugene Olivier, France
1906 1. Georges de la Falaise, France
2. Georges Dillon-Kavanagh, France
3. Alexander van Blijenburgh,
Netherlands
1904 1. Ramon Fonst, Cuba
2. Charles Tatham, Cuba
3. Albertson Van Zo Post, Cuba
1900 1. Ramon Fonst, Cuba
2. Louis Perree, France
3. Leon See, France
1896 **Not held**

Fencing — Men's Team Épée

1988 1. France, Frederic Delpla, Jean Michel
Henry, Olivier Lenglet, Philippe
Riboud, Eric Srecki
2. West Germany, Elmer Borrmann,
Volker Fischer, Thomas Gerull,
Alexander Pusch, Arnd Schmitt
3. Soviet Union, Andrei Chouvalov, Pavel
Kolobkov, Vladimir Reznitchenko,
Mikhail Tichko, Igor Tikhomirov
1984 1. West Germany, Elmer Borrmann,
Volker Fischer, Gerhard Heer, Rafael
Nickel, Alexander Pusch
2. France, Philippe Boisse, Jean-Michel
Henry, Olivier Lenglet, Philippe
Riboud, Michel Salesse
3. Italy, Stefano Bellone, Sandro Cuomo,
Cosimo Ferro, Roberto Manzi, Angelo
Mazzoni
1980 1. France, Philippe Riboud, Patrick Picot,
Hubert Gardas, Philippe Boisse,
Michel Salesse
2. Poland, Piotr Jabikowski, Andrzej Lis,
Leszek Swornowski, Ludomir
Chronowski, Mariusz Strzalka
3. Soviet Union, Ashot Karagian, Boris
Lukomski, Aleksandr Abushakhmetov,
Aleksandr Mozhaev
1976 1. Sweden, Carl von Essen, Hans
Jacobson, Rolf Edling, Orvar Jonsson,
Goran Flodstrom
2. West Germany, Alexander Pusch,
Juergen Hehn, Hanns Jana, Rheinhold
Behr, Volker Fischer
3. Switzerland, Jean-Blaise Evequoz,
Michel Poffet, Daniel Giger, Christian
Kauter, Francois Suchanecki
1972 1. Hungary, Sandor Erdos, Gyozo
Kulcsar, Dr. Csaba Fenyvesi, Pal
Schmitt, Istvan Osztrics

2. Switzerland, Guy Evequoz, Peter
Lotscher, Daniel Giger, Christian
Kauter, Francois Suchanecki
3. Soviet Union, Viktor Modsalevsky,
Georgi Saschitski, Sergei Paramonov,
Igor Valetov, Grigori Kriss
1968 1. Hungary, Csaba Fenyvesi, Zoltan
Nemere, Pal Schmitt, Gyozo Kulcsar,
Pal Nagy
2. Soviet Union, Grigori Kriss, Yosif
Vitebsky, Aleksei Nikanchikov, Yuri
Smoliakov, Viktor Modzelevsky
3. Poland, Bogdan Andrzejewski, Michal
Butkiewicz, Bogdan Gonsior, Henryk
Nielaba, Kazimierz Barburski
1964 1. Hungary, Gyozo Kulcsar, Zoltan
Nemere, Tamas Gabor, Dr. Istvan
Kausz, Arpad Barany
2. Italy, Gianluigi Saccaro, Giovanni
Battista Breda, Gianfranco Paolucci,
Giuseppe Delfino, Alberto Pellegrino
3. France, Claude Brodin, Yves Dreyfus,
Claude Bourquard, Jack Guittet,
Jacques Brodin
1960 1. Italy, Giuseppe Delfino, Alberto
Pellegrino, Carlo Pavesi, Edoardo
Mangiarotti, Fiorenzo Marini, GianLuigi
Saccaro
2. Great Britain, Allan Jay, Michael
Howard, John Pelling, Henry Hoskyns,
Raymond Harrison, Michael Alexander
3. Soviet Union, Guram Kostava, Bruno
Khabarov, Arnold Chernushevich,
Valentin Chernikov, Aleksandr
Pavlovsky
1956 1. Italy, Giuseppe Delfino, Alberto
Pellegrino, Edoardo Mangiarotti, Carlo
Pavesi, Giorgio Anglesio, Franco
Bertinetti
2. Hungary, Jozsef Sakovics, Bela
Rerrich, Lajos Balthazar, Ambrus
Nagy, Jozsef Marosi, Barnabas
Berzsenyi
3. France, Armand Mouyal, Claude
Nigon, Daniel Dagallier, Yves Dreyfus,
Rene Queyroux
1952 1. Italy, Dario Mangiarotti, Edoardo
Mangiarotti, Franco Bertinetti, Carlo
Pavesi, Giuseppe Delfino, Roberto
Battaglia
2. Sweden, Bengt Ljungquist, Berndt-Otto
Rehbinder, Sven Fahlman, Per
Carleson, Carl Forssell, Lennart
Magnusson
3. Switzerland, Otto Rufenacht, Paul
Meister, Oswald Zappelli, Paul Barth,
Willy Fitting, Mario Valota
1948 1. France, Henri Guerin, Henri Lepage,
Marcel Desprets, Michel Pecheux,
Edouard Artigas, Maurice Huet
2. Italy, Luigi Cantone, Antonio
Mandruzzato, Dario Mangiarotti,
Edoardo Mangiarotti, Fiorenzo Marini,
Carlo Agostoni
3. Sweden, Per Carleson, Frank Cervell,
Carl Forssell, Bengt Ljungquist, Sven
Thofelt, Arne Tollbom
1936 1. Italy, Saverio Ragno, Alfredo Pezzana,
Giancarlo Cornaggia-Medici, Edoardo
Mangiarotti, Franco Riccardi, Giancarlo
Brusati

303

2. Sweden, Hans Granfelt, Sven Thofelt, Gosta Almgren, Gustaf Dyrssen, Hans Drakenberg, Birger Cederin
3. France, Michel Pecheux, Bernard Schmetz, Georges Buchard, Henri Dulieux, Paul Wormser, Philippe Cattiau

1932
1. France, Philippe Cattiau, Georges Buchard, Bernard Schmetz, Jean Piot, Fernand Jourdant, Georges Tainturier
2. Italy, Carlo Agostoni, Giancarlo Cornaggia-Medici, Renzo Minoli, Franco Riccardi, Saverio Ragno
3. USA, George Calnan, Gustave Heiss, Frank Righeimer, Tracy Jaeckel, Curtis Shears, Miguel De Capriles

1928
1. Italy, Carlo Agostoni, Marcello Bertinetti, Giancarlo Cornaggia-Medici, Renzo Minoli, Giulio Basletta, Franco Riccardi
2. France, Armand Massard, Georges Buchard, Gaston Amson, Emile Cornic, Bernard Schmetz, Rene Barbier
3. Portugal, Paulo d'Eca Leal, Mario de Noronha, Jorge Paiva, Frederico Paredes, Joao Sassetti, Henrique da Silveira

1924
1. France, Lucien Gaudin, Georges Buchard, Roger Ducret, Andre Labatut, Lionel Liottel, Alexandre Lippmann, Georges Tainturier
2. Belgium, Paul Anspach, Joseph De Craecker, Charles Delporte, Fernand de Montigny, Ernest Gevers, Leon Tom
3. Italy, Giulio Basletta, Marcello Bertinetti, Giovanni Canova, Vincenzo Cuccia, Virgilio Mantegazza, Oreste Moricca

1920
1. Italy, Nedo Nadi, Aldo Nadi, Abelardo Olivier, Tullio Bozza, Giovanni Canova, Andrea Marrazzi, Dino Urbani, Antonio Allocchio, Tommaso Costantino, Paolo Thaon de Revel
2. Belgium, Ernest Gevers, Paul Anspach, Felix Goblet d'Alviella, Victor Boin, Joseph De Craecker, Leon Tom, Maurice De Wee, Philippe Le Hardy de Beaulieu
3. France, Armand Massard, Alexandre Lippmann, Gustave Buchard, Georges Trombert, S. Casanova, Gaston Amson, E. Moreau

1912
1. Belgium, Paul Anspach, Henri Anspach, Robert Hennet, Fernand de Montigny, Jacques Ochs, Francis Rom, Gaston Salmon, Victor Willems
2. Great Britain, Edgar Seligman, Edward Amphlett, Robert Montgomery, John Blake, Percy Davson, Arthur Everitt, Sydney Martineau, Martin Holt
3. Netherlands, Adrianus E. W. de Jong, Willem P. Hubert van Blijenburgh, Jetze Doorman, Leo Nardus, George van Rossem

1908
1. France, Gaston Alibert, Bernard Gravier, Alexandre Lippmann, Eugene Olivier, Henri-Georges Berger, Charles Collignon, Jean Stern

2. Great Britain, Edward Amphlett, C. Leaf Daniell, Cecil Haig, Robert Montgomerie, Martin Holt, Edgar Seligman
3. Belgium, Paul Anspach, Fernand Bosmans, Fernand de Montigny, Francis Rom, Victor Willems, Desire Beaurain, Ferdinand Feyerick

1906
1. France, Pierre d'Hugues, Georges Dillon-Kavanagh, Mohr, Georges de la Falaise
2. Great Britain, William H. Desborough, Cosmo E. Duff-Gordon, Charles N. Robinson, Edgar Seligman
3. Belgium, Constant Cloquet, Fernand de Montigny, Edmond Crahay, Philippe Le Hardy de Beaulieu

1896–1904 Not held

Fencing — Men's Individual Foil

1988
1. Stefano Cerioni, Italy
2. Udo Wagner, East Germany
3. Aleksandr Romankov, Soviet Union

1984
1. Mauro Numa, Italy
2. Matthias Behr, West Germany
3. Stefano Cerioni, Italy

1980
1. Vladimir Smirnov, Soviet Union
2. Aleksandr Romankov, Soviet Union
3. Pascal Jolyot, France

1976
1. Fabio dal Zotto, Italy
2. Aleksandr Romankov, Soviet Union
3. Bernard Talvard, France

1972
1. Witold Woyda, Poland
2. Dr. Jeno Kamuti, Hungary
3. Christian Noel, France

1968
1. Ion Drimba, Romania
2. Dr. Jeno Kamuti, Hungary
3. Daniel Revenu, France

1964
1. Egon Franke, Poland
2. Jean-Claude Magnan, France
3. Daniel Revenu, France

1960
1. Viktor Zhdanovich, Soviet Union
2. Yuri Sissikin, Soviet Union
3. Albert Axelrod, USA

1956
1. Christian d'Oriola, France
2. Giancarlo Bergamini, Italy
3. Antonio Spallino, Italy

1952
1. Christian d'Oriola, France
2. Edoardo Mangiarotti, Italy
3. Manlio Di Rosa, Italy

1948
1. Jehan Buhan, France
2. Christian d'Oriola, France
3. Lajos Maszlay, Hungary

1936
1. Giulio Gaudini, Italy
2. Edward Gardere, France
3. Giorgio Bocchino, Italy

1932
1. Gustavo Marzi, Italy
2. Joseph Levis, USA
3. Giulio Gaudini, Italy

1928
1. Lucien Gaudin, France
2. Erwin Casmir, Germany
3. Giulio Gaudini, Italy

1924
1. Roger Ducret, France
2. Philippe Cattiau, France
3. Maurice van Damme, Belgium

1920
1. Nedo Nadi, Italy
2. Philippe Cattiau, France
3. Roger Ducret, France

1912
1. Nedo Nadi, Italy

2. Pietro Speciale, Italy
3. Richard Verderber, Austria
1906 1. Georges Dillon-Kavanagh, France
2. Gustav Casmir, Germany
3. Pierre d'Hugues, France
1904 1. Ramon Fonst, Cuba
2. Albertson Van Zo Post, Cuba
3. Charles Tatham, Cuba
1900 1. Emile Coste, France
2. Henri Masson, France
3. Jacques Boulenger, France
1896 1. Emile Gravelotte, France
2. Henri Callot, France
3. Perikles Mavromichalis-Pierrakos,
Greece

Fencing — Men's Team Foil

1988 1. Soviet Union, Aleksandr Romankov,
Ilgar Mamedov, Vladimir Aptsiaouri,
Anvar Ibraguimov, Boris Koretski
2. West Germany, Mathias Gey,
Thorsten Weidner, Matthias Behr,
Ulrich Schreck, Thomas Endres
3. Hungary, Zsolt Ersek, Pal Szekeres,
Istvan Szelei, Istvan Busa, Robert
Gatai
1984 1. Italy, Mauro Numa, Andrea Borella,
Stefano Cerioni, Angelo Scuri
2. West Germany, Matthias Behr,
Mathias Gey, Harald Hein, Frank Beck
3. France, Philippe Omnes, Patrick Groc,
Frederic Pietruszka, Pascal Jolyot
1980 1. France, Didier Flament, Pascal Jolyot,
Bruno Boscherie, Philippe Bonin,
Frederic Pietruszka
2. Soviet Union, Aleksandr Romankov,
Vladimir Smirnov, Sabirzhan Ruziev,
Ashot Karagian, Vladimir Lapitsky
3. Poland, Adam Robak, Boguslaw Zych,
Lech Koziejowski, Marian Sypniewski
1976 1. West Germany, Matthias Behr,
Thomas Bach, Harald Hein, Klaus
Reichert, Erk Sens-Gorius
2. Italy, Fabio Dal Zotto, Attilio
Calatroni, Carlo Montano, Stefano
Simoncelli, Giovan Battista Coletti
3. France, Daniel Revenu, Christian Noel,
Didier Flament, Bernard Talvard,
Frederic Pietruszka
1972 1. Poland, Witold Woyda, Lech
Koziejowski, Jerzy Kaczmarek, Marek
Dabrowski, Arkadiusz Godel
2. Soviet Union, Vassili Stankovitsch,
Anatoli Kotescev, Vladimir Denissov,
Leonid Romanov, Viktor Putyatin
3. France, Daniel Revenu, Christian Noel,
Bernard Talvard, Jean-Claude
Magnan, Gilles Berolatti
1968 1. France, Daniel Revenu, Gilles Berolatti,
Christian Noel, Jean-Claude Magnan,
Jacques Dimont
2. Soviet Union, German Sveshnikov, Yuri
Scharov, Vassili Stankovitsch, Viktor
Putyatin, Yuri Sissikin
3. Poland, Witold Woyda, Ryszard
Parulski, Egon Franke, Zbigniew
Skrudlik, Adam Lisewski
1964 1. Soviet Union, German Sveshnikov, Yuri
Sissikin, Mark Midler, Viktor
Zhdanovich, Yuri Scharov

2. Poland, Zbigniew Skrudlik, Witold
Woyda, Egon Franke, Ryszard
Parulski, Janusz Rozycki
3. France, Daniel Revenu, Jacky
Courtillat, Pierre Rodocanachi,
Christian Noel, Jean-Claude Magnan
1960 1. Soviet Union, Viktor Zhdanovich, Mark
Midler, Yuri Sissikin, German
Sveshnikov, Yuri Rudov
2. Italy, Alberto Pellegrino, Luigi
Carpaneda, Mario Curletto, Aldo
Aureggi, Edoardo Mangiarotti
3. West Germany, Jurgen Brecht, Tim
Gerrescheim, Eberhard Mehl, Jurgen
Theuerkauff
1956 1. Italy, Edoardo Mangiarotti, Giancarlo
Bergamini, Antonio Spallino, Luigi
Carpaneda, Manlio Di Rosa, Vittorio
Lucarelli
2. France, Christian d'Oriola, Bernard
Baudoux, Claude Netter, Jacques
Lataste, Roger Closset, Rene Coicaud
3. Hungary, Jozsef Gyuricza, Jozsef
Sakovics, Mihaly Fulop, Endre Tilli,
Lajos Somodi, Jozsef Marosi
1952 1. France, Jehan Buhan, Christian
d'Oriola, Adrien Rommel, Claude
Netter, Jacques Noel, Jacques Lataste
2. Italy, Giancarlo Bergamini, Antonio
Spallino, Manlio Di Rosa, Giorgio
Pellini, Renzo Nostini, Edoardo
Mangiarotti
3. Hungary, Endre Tilli, Aladar Gerevich,
Endre Palocz, Lajos Maszlay, Tibor
Berczelly, Jozsef Sakovics
1948 1. France, Andre Bonin, Rene Bougnol,
Jehan Buhan, Jacques Lataste,
Christian d'Oriola, Adrien Rommel
2. Italy, Renzo Nostini, Manlio Di Rosa,
Edoardo Mangiarotti, Giuliano Nastini,
Giorgio Pellini, Saverio Ragno
3. Belgium, Georges DeBourguignon,
Henri Paternoster, Edouard Yves,
Raymond Bru, Andre van de Werwe
de Vorsselaer, Paul Valcke
1936 1. Italy, Giulio Gaudini, Gioacchino
Guaragna, Gustavo Marzi, Giorgio
Bocchino, Manlio Di Rosa, Ciro
Verratti
2. France, Jacques Coutrot, Andre
Gardere, Rene Lemoine, Rene
Bougnol, Edward Gardere, Rene
Bondoux
3. Germany, Siegfried Lerdon, August
Heim, Julius Eisenecker, Erwin Casmir,
Stefan Rosenbauer, Otto Adam
1932 1. France, Philippe Cattiau, Edward
Gardere, Rene Lemoine, Rene
Bondoux, Jean Piot, Rene Bougnol
2. Italy, Giulio Gaudini, Gustavo Marzi,
Ugo Pignotti, Giorgio Pessina,
Gioacchino Guaragna, Rodolfo Terlizzi
3. USA, George Calnan, Joseph Levis,
Hugh Allesandroni, Dernell Every,
Richard Steere, Frank Righeimer
1928 1. Italy, Ugo Pignotti, Oreste Puliti, Giulio
Gaudini, Giorgio Pessina, Giorgio
Chiavacci, Gioacchino Guaragna
2. France, Lucien Gaudin, Philippe
Cattiau, Roger Ducret, Andre Labatut,
Raymond Flacher, Andre Gaboriaud

305

3. Argentina, Roberto Larraz, Raul Anganuzzi, Luis Lucchetti, Hector Lucchetti, Carmelo Camet

1924 1. France, Lucien Gaudin, Philippe Cattiau, Jacques Coutrot, Roger Ducret, Henri Jobier, Andre Labatut, Guy de Luget, Joseph Peroteaux
2. Beligum, Desire Beaurain, Charles Crahay, Fernand de Montigny, Maurice Van Damme, Marcel Berre, Albert De Roocker
3. Hungary, Laszlo Berti, Sandor Posta, Zoltan Schenker, Odon Terstyanszky, Istvan Lichteneckert

1920 1. Italy, Baldo Baldi, Tommaso Costantino, Aldo Nadi, Nedo Nadi, Abelardo Olivier, Oreste Puliti, Pietro Speciale, Rodolfo Terlizzi
2. France, Lionel Bony de Castellane, Gaston Amson, Philippe Cattiau, Roger Ducret, Andre Labatut, Georges Trombert, Marcel Perrot, Lucien Gaudin
3. USA, Henry Breckinridge, Francis Honeycutt, Arthur Lyon, Harold Rayner, Robert Sears

1906–1912 **Not held**

1904 1. Cuba, Ramon Fonst, Albertson Van Zo Post, Manuel Diaz
2. International Team Charles Tatham, Cuba; Charles Townsend, USA; Arthur Fox, USA

1896–1900 **Not held**

Fencing — Men's Individual Sabre

1988 1. Jean-Francois Lamour, France
2. Janusz Olech, Poland
3. Giovanni Scalzo, Italy
1984 1. Jean-Francois Lamour, France
2. Marco Marin, Italy
3. Peter Westbrook, USA
1980 1. Viktor Krovopuskov, Soviet Union
1. Viktor Krovopuskov, Soviet Union
2. Mikhail Burtsev, Soviet Union
2. Mikhail Burtsev, Soviet Union
3. Imre Gedovari, Hungary
3. Imre Gedovari, Hungary
1976 1. Viktor Krovopuskov, Soviet Union
2. Vladimir Nazlymov, Soviet Union
3. Viktor Sidiak, Soviet Union
1972 1. Viktor Sidiak, Soviet Union
2. Peter Maroth, Hungary
3. Vladimir Nazlymov, Soviet Union
1968 1. Jerzy Pawlowski, Poland
2. Mark Rakita, Soviet Union
3. Tibor Pezsa, Hungary
1964 1. Tibor Pezsa, Hungary
2. Claude Arabo, France
3. Umar Mavlikhanov, Soviet Union
1960 1. Rudolf Karpati, Hungary
2. Zoltan Horvath, Hungary
3. Wladimiro Calarese, Italy
1956 1. Rudolf Karpati, Hungary
2. Jerzy Pawlowski, Poland
3. Lev Kuznyetsov, Soviet Union
1952 1. Pal Kovacs, Hungary

2. Aladar Gerevich, Hungary
3. Tibor Berczelly, Hungary
1948 1. Aladar Gerevich, Hungary
2. Vincenzo Pinton, Italy
3. Pal Kovacs, Hungary
1936 1. Endre Kabos, Hungary
2. Gustavo Marzi, Italy
3. Aladar Gerevich, Hungary
1932 1. Gyorgy Piller, Hungary
2. Giulio Gaudini, Italy
3. Endre Kabos, Hungary
1928 1. Odon Terstyanszky, Hungary
2. Attila Petschauer, Hungary
3. Bino Bini, Italy
1924 1. Dr. Sandor Posta, Hungary
2. Roger Ducret, France
3. Janos Garay, Hungary
1920 1. Nedo Nadi, Italy
2. Aldo Nadi, Italy
3. Adrianus E. W de Jong, Netherlands
1912 1. Dr. Jeno Fuchs, Hungary
2. Bela Bekessy, Hungary
3. Ervin Meszaros, Hungary
1908 1. Dr. Jeno Fuchs, Hungary
2. Bela Zulavszky, Hungary
3. Vilem Goppold von Lobsdorf, Bohemia
1906 1. Jean Georgiadis, Greece
2. Gustav Casmir, West Germany
3. Federico Cesarano, Italy
1904 1. Manuel Diaz, Cuba
2. William Grebe, USA
3. Albertson Van Zo Post, Cuba
1900 1. Georges de la Falaise, France
2. Leon Thiebaut, France
3. Fritz Flesch, Austria
1896 1. Jean Georgiadis, Greece
2. Telemachos Karakalos, Greece
3. Holger Nielsen, Denmark

Fencing — Men's Team Sabre

1988 1. Hungary, Gyorgy Nebald, Bence Szabo, Laszlo Csongradi, Imre Bujdoso, Imre Gedovari
2. Soviet Union, Serguei Mindirgassov, Mikhail Bourtsev, Gueorgui Pogossov, Andre Alchan, Serguei Koriajkine
3. Italy, Giovanni Scalzo, Marco Marin, Gianfranco Dalla Barba, Ferdinando Meglio, Massimo Cavaliere
1984 1. Italy, Marco Marin, Gianfranco Dalla Barba, Giovanni Scalzo, Ferdinando Meglio, Angelo Arcidiacono
2. France, Jean-Francois Lamour, Pierre Guichot, Herve Granger-Veyron, Philippe Deirieu, Franck Ducheix
3. Romania, Marin Mustata, Ioan Pop, Alexandru Chiculita, Corneliu Marin
1980 1. Soviet Union, Mikhail Burtsev, Viktor Krovopuskov, Viktor Sidiak, Vladimir Nazlymov, Nikolai Alekhin
2. Italy, Michele Maffei, Mario Aldo Montano, Marco Romano, Ferdinando Meglio, Giovanni Scalzo
3. Hungary, Imre Gedovari, Rudolf Nebald, Pal Gerevich, Ferenc Hammang, Gyorgy Nebald
1976 1. Soviet Union, Eduard Vinokurov, Viktor Krovopuskov, Mikhail Burtsev, Viktor Sidiak, Vladimir Nazlymov

306

2. Italy, Mario Aldo Montano, Michele Maffei, Angelo Arcidiacono, Tommaso Montano, Mario Tullio Montano

3. Romania, Dan Irimiciuc, Ioan Pop, Marin Mustata, Corneliu Marin, Alexandru Nilca

1972 1. Italy, Michele Maffei, Aldo Montano, Rolando Rigoli, Tullio Montano, Cesare Salvadori

2. Soviet Union, Vladimir Nazlymov, Eduard Vinokurov, Viktor Sidiak, Viktor Bajenov, Mark Rakita

3. Hungary, Pal Gerevich, Tamas Kovacs, Peter Maroth, Tibor Pezsa, Dr. Peter Bakonyi

1968 1. Soviet Union, Vladimir Nazlymov, Eduard Vinokurov, Viktor Sidyak, Mark Rakita, Umar Mavlikhanov

2. Italy, Wladimiro Calarese, Cesare Salvadori, Michele Maffei, Pier-Luigi Chicca, Rolando Rigoli

3. Hungary, Tamas Kovacs, Miklos Meszena, Dr. Janos Kalmar, Peter Bakonyi, Tibor Pezsa

1964 1. Soviet Union, Yakov Rylsky, Nugsar Asatiani, Mark Rakita, Umar Mavlikhanov, Boris Melnikov

2. Italy, Wladimiro Calarese, Cesare Salvadori, Giampaolo Calanchini, Pier-Luigi Chicca, Mario Ravagnan

3. Poland, Emil Ochyra, Jerzy Pawlowski, Ryszard Zub, Andrzej Piatkowski, Wojciech Zablocki

1960 1. Hungary, Zoltan Horvath, Rudolf Karpati, Tamas Mendelenyi, Pal Kovacs, Gabor Delneky, Aladar Gerevich

2. Poland, Andrzej Piatkowski, Emil Ochyra, Wojciech Zablocki, Jerzy Pawlowski, Ryszard Zub, Marek Kuszewski

3. Italy, Wladimiro Calarese, Giampaolo Calanchini, Pier-Luigi Chicca, Mario Ravagnan, Roberto Ferrari

1956 1. Hungary, Rudolf Karpati, Aladar Gerevich, Pal Kovacs, Attila Keresztes, Jeno Hamori, Daniel Magay

2. Poland, Jerzy Pawlowski, Wojciech Zablocki, Marek Kuszewski, Zygmunt Pawlas, Ryszard Zub, Andrzej Piatkowski

3. Soviet Union, Lev Kuznyetsov, Yakov Rylsky, Yevgeny Cherepovski, David Tyschler, Leonid Bogdanov

1952 1. Hungary, Pal Kovacs, Aladar Gerevich, Tibor Berczelly, Rudolf Karpati, Laszlo Rajcsanyi, Bertalan Papp

2. Italy, Vincenzo Pinton, Mauro Racca, Roberto Ferrari, Gastone Dare, Renzo Nostini, Giorgio Pellini

3. France, Jacques Lefevre, Jean Laroyenne, Maurice Piot, Jean Levavasseur, Bernard Morel, Jean-Francois Tournon

1948 1. Hungary, Aladar Gerevich, Rudolf Karpati, Pal Kovacs, Tibor Berczelly, Laszlo Rajcsanyi, Bertalan Papp

2. Italy, Gastone Dare, Carlo Turcato, Vincenzo Pinton, Mauro Racca, Aldo Montano, Renzo Nostini

3. USA, Norman Armitage, George Worth, Tibor Nyilas, Dean Cetrulo, Miguel De Capriles, James Flynn

1936 1. Hungary, Endre Kabos, Aladar Gerevich, Tibor Berczelly, Pal Kovacs, Laszlo Rajcsanyi, Imre Rajczy

2. Italy, Vincenzo Pinton, Giulio Gaudini, Aldo Masciotta, Gustavo Marzi, Aldo Montano, Athos Tanzini

3. Greece, Richard Wahl, Julius Eisenecker, Erwin Casmir, August Heim, Hans Esser, Hans Jorger

1932 1. Hungary, Gyorgy Piller, Endre Kabos, Attila Petschauer, Erno Nagy, Gyula Glykais, Aladar Gerevich

2. Italy, Renato Anselmi, Arturo De Vecchi, Emilio Salafia, Ugo Pignotti, Gustavo Marzi, Giulio Gaudini

3. Poland, Adam Papee, Tadeusz Friedrich, Wladyslaw Segda, Leszek Lubicz-Nycz, Wladyslaw Dobrowolski, Marian Suski

1928 1. Hungary, Odon Terstyanszky, Dr. Sandor Gombos, Attila Petschauer, Janos Garay, Jozsef Rady, Gyula Glykais

2. Italy, Bino Bini, Renato Anselmi, Gustavo Marzi, Oreste Puliti, Emilio Salafia, Giulio Sarrocchi

3. Poland, Adam Papee, Tadeusz Friedrich, Kazimierz Laskowski, Wladyslaw Segda, Aleksander Malecki, Jerzy Zabielski

1924 1. Italy, Renato Anselmi, Guido Balzarini, Marcello Bertinetti, Bino Bini, Vincenzo Cuccia, Oreste Moricca, Oreste Puliti, Giulio Sarrocchi

2. Hungary, Laszlo Berti, Janos Garay, Sandor Posta, Jozsef Rady, Zoltan Schenker, Laszlo Szechy, Odon Terstyanszky, Jeno Uhlyarik

3. Netherlands, Adrianus E. W. de Jong, Jetze Doorman, Hendrik D. Scherpenhuizen, Jan van der Wiel, Maarten H. van Dulm, Henri J. M. Wijnoldij-Daniels

1920 1. Italy, Nedo Nadi, Aldo Nadi, Oreste Puliti, Baldo Baldi, Francesco Gargano, Giorgio Santelli, Dino Urbani

2. France, Georges Trombert, J. Margraff, Marc Perrodon, Henri de Saint Germain

3. Netherlands, Jan van der Wiel, Adrianus E. W. de Jong, Jetze Doorman, Willem P. Hubert van Blijenburgh, Louis A. Delaunoij, Salomon Zeldenrust, Henri J. M. Wijnoldij-Daniels

1912 1. Hungary, Dr. Jeno Fuchs, Laszlo Berti, Ervin Meszaros, Dr. Dezso Foldes, Dr. Oszkar Gerde, Zoltan Schenker, Dr. Peter Toth, Lajos Werkner

2. Austria, Richard Verderber, Dr. Otto Herschmann, Rudolf Cvetko, Friedrich Golling, Andreas Suttner, Albert Bogen, Reinhold Trampler

3. Netherlands, Willem P. Hubert vanBlijenburgh, George van Rossem, Adrianus E. W. de Jong, Jetze Doorman, Dirk Scalongne, Hendrik de Jongh

1908 1. Hungary, Dr. Jeno Fuchs, Oszkar Gerde, Peter Toth, Lajos Werkner, Dezso Foldes
2. Italy, Riccardo Nowak, Alessandro Pirzio-Biroli, Abelardo Olivier, Marcello Bertinetti, Santi Ceccherini
3. Bohemia, Vilem Goppold von Lobsdorf, Jaroslav Tucek, Vlastimil Lada-Sazavsky, Otakar Lada, Bedrich Schejbal

1906 1. West Germany, Gustav Casmir, Jacob Erckrath de Bary, August Petri, Emil Schon
2. Greece, Jean Georgiadis, Menelaos Sakorraphos, Ch Zorbas, Triantaphylos Kordogiannis
3. Netherlands, James Melvill van Carnbee, Johannes F. Osten, George van Rossem, Maurits J. van Loben Sels

1896-1904 **Not held**

Fencing — Women's Individual Foil

1988 1. Anja Fichtel, West Germany
2. Sabine Bau, West Germany
3. Zita Funkenhauser, West Germany
1984 1. Jujie Luan, China
2. Cornelia Hanisch, West Germany
3. Dorina Vaccaroni, Italy
1980 1. Pascale Trinquet-Hachin, France
2. Magdolina Maros, Hungary
3. Barbara Wysoczanska, Poland
1976 1. Ildiko Schwarzenberger-Tordasi, Hungary
2. Marta C. Collino, Italy
3. Yelena Belova-Novikova, Soviet Union
1972 1. Antonella Lonzi-Ragno, Italy
2. Ildiko Bobis, Hungary
3. Galina Gorokhova, Soviet Union
1968 1. Yelena Novikova, Soviet Union
2. Pilar Roldan, Mexico
3. Ildiko Ujlaki-Rejto, Hungary
1964 1. Ildiko Ujlaki-Rejto, Hungary
2. Helga Mees, West Germany
3. Antonella Ragno, Italy
1960 1. Heidi Schmid, West Germany
2. Valentina Rastvorova, Soviet Union
2. Maria Vicol, Romania
1956 1. Gillian Sheen, Great Britain
2. Olga Orban, Romania
3. Renee Garilhe, France
1952 1. Irene Camber, Italy
2. Ilona Elek, Hungary
3. Karen Lachmann, Denmark
1948 1. Ilona Elek, Hungary
2. Karen Lachmann, Denmark
3. Ellen Muller-Preis, Austria
1936 1. Ilona Elek, Hungary
2. Helene Mayer, Germany
3. Ellen Preis, Austria
1932 1. Ellen Preis, Austria
2. J. Heather Guinness, Great Britain
3. Erna Bogen, Hungary
1928 1. Helene Mayer, Germany
2. Muriel Freeman, Great Britain
3. Olga Oelkers, Germany
1924 1. Ellen Osiier, Denmark

2. Gladys Davis, Great Britain
3. Grete Heckscher, Denmark
1896-1920 **Not held**

Fencing — Women's Team Foil

1988 1. West Germany, Anja Fichtel, Sabine Bau, Zita Funkenhauser, Annette Klug, Christiane Weber
2. Italy, Margherita Zalaffi, Dorina Vaccaroni, Annapia Gandolfi, Francesca Bortolozzi, Lucia Traversa
3. Hungary, Zsuzsanna Janosi, Gertrud Stefanek, Zsuz Sanna Szocs, Katalin Tuschak, Edit Kovacs
1984 1. West Germany, Christiane Weber, Cornelia Hanisch, Sabine Bischoff, Zita Funkenhauser
2. Romania, Aurora Dan, Koszto Veber, Rozalia Oros, Marcela Zsak, Elisabeta Guzganu
3. France, Laurence Modaine, Pascale Trinquet-Hachin, Brigitte Gaudin, Veronique Brouquier
1980 1. France, Brigitte, Latrille-Gaudin, Pascale Trinquet-Hachin, Isabelle Regard, Veronique Brouquier, Christine Muzio
2. Soviet Union, Valentina Sidorova, Nailia Giliazova, Yelena Belova-Novikova, Irina Ushakova, Larisa Tsagaraeva
3. Hungary, Ildiko Bobis-Schwarczenberger, Magdolna Maros, Gertrud Stefanek, Zsuz Sanna Szocs, Edit Kovacs
1976 1. Soviet Union, Yelena Belova-Novikova, Olga Kniazeva, Valentina Sidorova, Nailia Guiliazova, Valentina Nikonova
2. France, Brigitte Latrille, Brigitte Dumont-Gapais, Christine Muzio, Veronique Trinquet, Claudie Josland
3. Hungary, Ildiko Schwarczenberger-Tordasi, Edit Kovacs, Maga Magdolna Maros, Ildiko Sagi-Ujlaki-Rejto, Ildiko Bobis
1972 1. Soviet Union, Yelena Belova-Novikova, Aleksandra Zabelina, Galina Gorokhova, Tatiane Samusenko, Svetlana Chirkova
2. Hungary, Ildiko Sagi-Ujlaki-Rejto, Ildiko Tordasi, Maria Szolnoki, Ildiko Bobis, Ildiko Matuscsak
3. Romania, Olga Szabo, Ileana Gyulai-Drimba, Ana Passcu-Ene, Ecaterina Stahl
1968 1. Soviet Union, Aleksandra Zebelina, Yelena Novikova, Galina Gorokhova, Tatiane Samusenko, Svetlana Chirkova
2. Hungary, Ildiko Bobis, Lidia Sakovics, Ildiko Ujlaki-Rejto, Maria Gulacsy, Paula Marosi
3. Romania, Clara Iencic, Ileana Drimba, Olga Szabo, Maria Vicol, Ana Ene-Dersidan
1964 1. Hungary, Ildiko Ujlaki-Rejto, Katalin Juhasz-Nagy, Lidia Sakovics-Domolky, Judit Mendelenyi-Agoston, Paula Marosi

308

2. Soviet Union, Galina Gorokhova, Valentina Prudskova, Tatiane Samusenko-Petrenko, Ljudmila Schishova, Valentina Rastvorova
3. West Germany, Heidi Schmid, Helga Mees, Rosemarie Scherberger, Gudrun Theuerkauff

1960 1. Soviet Union, Tatiane Petrenko, Valentina Rastvorova, Ljudmila Schishova, Valentina Prudskova, Aleksandra Zabelina, Galina Gorokhova

2. Hungary, Gyorgyi Szekely, Ildiko Rejto, Magdolna Kovacs-Nyari, Katalin Iuhasz-Nagy, Lidia Domolky
3. Italy, Irene Camber, Welleda Cesari, Antonella Ragno, Bruna Colombetti, Claudia Pasini

1896–1956 **Not held**

FIELD HOCKEY

WARM-UP

Always a game of the upper classes, field hockey is now one of the most popular team sports in the world, with more than 100 national associations claiming membership in the Fédération Internationale de Hockey (FIH), the world governing body for the sport. When played by the experts, the game is a blend of power, speed, and agility. When play by you or me, the game involves a lot of "Hey, watch it with that stick!" and heavy breathing.

The earliest record of field hockey is a drawing dated more than 4000 years ago decorating a tomb at Beni-Hasen in Egypt's Nile Valley. The mural shows two men holding sticks with curved ends that are similar to those used by early 20th-century field hockey players. As if in a faceoff (or, as they say in field hockey, a push back), the men stand over a small hoop or ball, obviously immersed in strategic thinking.

Historians believe that in addition to the Egyptians, ancient Greeks and Persians were also adept at field hockey. During the Middle Ages, the Araucano Indians of Argentina invented a game similar to hockey, called **cheuca**. The Araucanos believed that the game, played with sticks curved at one end, would make them better warriors. Needless to say, high sticking was fairly common.

Evidence also suggests that Native American tribes played a vigorous form of field hockey for several thousand years, although the game was somewhat different from today's. For instance, the goals were several miles apart, the game lasted from sunrise to sunset (no doubt in order to negotiate the distance), and a team might consist of 1000 players or so. Halftime was more a state of mind and Gatorade had not yet been invented.

Modern field hockey evolved in the British Isles. No doubt the ancient Irish game of hurling is the granddaddy of several related games, including field hockey, shinty in Scotland, and bandy in Wales. In the Canterbury Cathedral, the colored glass in a 600-year-old window shows a boy striking a round ball with a crooked stick. The oldest hockey club still in existence is Blackheath, England, with records dating back to 1860. The game grew in popularity throughout the British Empire, particularly in India and Pakistan, where field hockey is considered a national pastime. In 1886, the Hockey Association was formed in Britain and shortly thereafter, the rules were standardized.

Women started playing the game during the second half of the 19th century. For a time, field hockey was considered the only proper team sport for women. The first women's club started in Surrey, England, in 1887, and the first national association, the Irish Ladies Hockey Union, sprang up in Dublin seven years later. By the end of the 19th century, women's field hockey had spread to New Zealand, South Africa, the Netherlands, Germany, Switzerland, and elsewhere. In 1927, the International Federation of Women's Hockey Associations (IFWHA) was formed.

The game was introduced in the US by Constance M.K. Applebee, a British physical education teacher who staged an exhibition of the sport at Harvard in the summer of 1901. During the next two years, Applebee taught the game to women at Smith, Wellesley, Mt. Holyoke, and other colleges in the region.

Although the sport has long welcomed active female participation, as an Olympic event women's field hockey did not debut until more than 70 years after the initial men's competition. Men's field hockey was added to the Olympic Games in 1908, but it wasn't until 1980 that womens teams were invited as well.

England, ever the stronghold for the sport, won that first Olympics handily, beating Ireland in the finals. In 1920, when hockey was next included on the Olympic program, Great Britain again won. The Fédération Internationale de Hockey was formed in 1924, without British participation, since those in the British field hockey community opposed competitions involving medals and prizes. This controversy affected the Olympics, as again in 1924 the Games did not feature field hockey.

In 1932, the US fielded its first men's team, losing to gold medalist India, then the dominant team in the world, by a score of 24–1, followed by a 9–2 defeat at the hands of silver medalist Japan. As luck would have it, however, the US managed to win the bronze, being the third team in a three-team field. It was to be the first and last medal ever collected by the US men's team, as the game continues to be dominated by India, Pakistan, Great Britain, and Germany.

▼

SPECTATORS' GUIDE

Although the objective of the game is to score more goals than your opponent, defensive strategy is the key to field hockey. Similar to soccer, the game features a fast pace and demands individual coordinated skills, team play, fitness, and finesse.

Field hockey consists of two 35-minute halves; two teams of 11 players each (during an Olympic game, no substitutions are allowed) armed with hardwood sticks that resemble ice hockey sticks, though slightly smaller; a field roughly the size of a football field; two umpires; one timekeeper; and a smooth, seamless ball, slightly larger than a baseball and weighing about 5.5 ounces. The head of the stick is flat on one side and rounded on the other, and only the flat side (which is always on the left) may be used to hit the ball. With a proper whack, the ball travels around the field at up to 100 miles per hour. Players wear shin guards to protect against the occasional wicked stick slapped at the knees and the more frequent accidental pitch to the turf.

The goals are 12 feet wide and seven feet high. The front of the goal posts touches the outer edge of the goal line, across which the attacker must propel the ball in order for a point to be gained. A **shooting circle** is placed 16 yards from the goal.

Only within this circle may an attacker shoot for a goal. It is not uncommon for a team to pull its forwards back until an almost impenetrable wall of bodies is formed in front of the goal. Quick, accurate passing is the most efficient method for evading the defense and scoring a goal. While teams such as India have favored short, crisp passes, the continental style has been to try and hit the open person with a long pass.

The goalkeeper is allowed to use any part of his or her body to stop the ball. The goalkeeper can kick the ball, the only person on the field who may do so. Unlike ice hockey, the goalie's stick is the same as the other players', although the goalie is allowed to wear additional protective clothing.

Instant Field Hockey Jargon

At the start of each half and after each goal, play begins with a **push back.**

Within the 25-yard line, an attacking player must either have the ball or at least two opponents (one may be the goalkeeper) between him or her and the goal line. Otherwise, **offside** is called.

When you watch a field hockey match, you may notice the umpire whistling a foul called **"obstruction."** In every other team sport, shielding the ball or puck with one's body is an integral part of the game's strategy. But not in field hockey. A player may not use his or her body to prevent an opponent from playing the ball. All players have an equal chance to gain control of the ball as it is dribbled and passed down the field.

For any breach of the rules, an umpire may award a free hit, a penalty corner, or a penalty stroke. The **free hit** must be taken at the site of the foul. At a free hit, no player may stand within five yards of the player with the ball; any stroke, except a scoop or a flick into the air (which may lead to dangerous play), is permissible.

If a player puts the ball over the sideline, a free hit is awarded to the opposing team and is taken on the line where the ball went out. If the ball deflects off a defender's stick and goes over the end line, the attacking team is awarded a **corner hit.** The corner hit may be taken from the sideline or from the end line within five yards of the corner.

If the ball is hit over the end line by the attacking team, the defenders are given a free hit within 16 yards of the end line and in line with the point where it went out.

If the ball is hit over the end line by the defenders, the attacking team is awarded a penalty corner.

Since goals may only be scored from within the shooting circle, penalties are more severe for fouls committed in that area. Penalty corners are generally awarded for infractions that occur within the shooting circle as well as deliberate fouls within 25 yards of the end line. A **penalty corner** is essentially a free hit by the attackers from a point on the goal line that is at least ten yards from the goal. To begin the penalty corner, no attacking players may be within the circle. Six defenders are behind the end line and five behind the midfield. As an attacking player puts the ball into play from a point ten yards from the goal, both attackers and defenders may enter the circle to play the ball.

If an intentional foul is committed by a defender within the circle or a defender stops a sure goal by committing a foul, a **penalty stroke** is awarded. A push or flick shot from seven yards out is taken by one attacking player with only the goalkeeper in the goal to defend.

HOPEFULS

Since no one country has emerged as a leader in the sport of field hockey, all those who qualify for Olympic competition stand a good chance of capturing a medal. The British men will be defending their title at Barcelona, as will the Australian women. Although Germany hasn't won a gold medal since 1972, they have fielded consistently good teams: in 1984 both the men and women brought home silver medals, and in 1988 the men repeated their performance.

The Netherlands, likewise, are consistently strong, having won bronze medals in 1988 and the women's gold in 1984. A US field hockey team most recently earned an Olympic medal in 1984, when the women's team won the bronze—although in 1988 that team finished eighth out of eight. The American players showed improvement, however, during the 1991 Pan American games, where both teams placed third behind Argentina, the gold medalists, and Canada.

The tentative field hockey schedule is as follows:

Sunday, July 26
6 games, preliminaries, men

Monday, July 27
4 games, preliminaries, women

Tuesday, July 28
6 games, preliminaries, men

Wednesday, July 29
4 games, preliminaries, women

Thursday, July 30
6 games, preliminaries, men

Saturday, August 1
6 games, preliminaries, men

Sunday, August 2
4 games, preliminaries, women

Monday, August 3
6 games, preliminaries, men

Tuesday, August 4
2 games, classifications, women
2 games, semifinals, women

Wednesday, August 5
4 games, classifications, men
2 games, semifinals, men

Thursday, August 6
Finals, men (5th-8th places)
Finals, women (5th-8th places)

Friday, August 7
8 games, finals, men (5th-12th places)
Finals, women, (3rd-4th places)
1 game, final, women

Saturday, August 8
1 game, final, men (3rd & 4th places)
1 game, finals, men

HIGHLIGHTS

Field hockey first appeared in the Games in 1908, when only the British Isles competed: England beat Ireland, followed by Scotland and Wales. The sport was next included in the Games in 1920, when Great Britain, this time with competition from other countries—two, to be exact—again took first place; Denmark and Belgium finished second and third. Omitted from the 1924 Olympics, field hockey permanently returned to the program in 1928, the year that marked the beginning of India's participation in the sport in the Olympic arena—and, consequently, the beginning of India's nearly 30-year spate of gold medals. India won its first of six consecutive gold medals in 1928.

During India's tenure as the Olympic field hockey "masters," the US team entered its first Games in 1932, fortuitously winning its first and only medal. They also enjoyed the dubious honor of having lost to the highest-ever score in an international match. India was accompanied by a number of other countries on the victory stand during its six-Games reign: in 1928, the Netherlands took silver, Germany gold; in 1932, Japan took silver; in 1936, Germany stood above the Netherlands; in 1948 Great Britain placed before the Netherlands—and vice

315

versa in 1952. Interestingly, 1948 was the year that marked India's independence from Britain, and their first-ever competition together at the Olympics.

In 1956, Pakistan took silver, while the Federal Republic of Germany took bronze, a year that ended a chapter in Olympic field hockey history. India's hegemony ended in Rome in 1960, when Pakistan became heir to the gold in the final match, winning 1–0. The India-Pakistan rivalry continued through the next couple of Games: India reappropriated the gold in 1964 only to lose it again in 1968, when the Indian team placed third behind Australia. India's bronze medal lacked some of its luster since the Indian team had gained their place by forfeit: during a preliminary match with India, the Japanese team, in protest of a penalty stroke awarded to their opponents, walked off the field, forfeiting the match.

At the Munich Games, the West German team stunned the public and its competitors with its emergence as a major contender, and managed to keep the gold at home. The Indian team settled for bronze, but the silver-medalling Pakistani team and its fans were less than pleased at the host country's upset victory; they so thoroughly misbehaved, they were suspended from the Games for four years. Eleven of the Pakistani players were permanently barred from the Olympics.

At the Montréal Games in 1976, yet another contender emerged: New Zealand took the gold while Australia took silver in a closely contested 1–0 final. Pakistan, the heavy favorite after its four-year absence, won only bronze. In 1980—for the first time since 1964—India returned to victory, followed this time by Spain and the Soviet Union. Also in 1980, women competed in field hockey for the first time in the Games; Zimbabwe placed first, followed by Czechoslovakia and the Soviet Union.

At the 1984 Games, the once-victorious British team returned to the victory stand, this time to accept a bronze medal. Rematched again with a German team in the final, Pakistan turned the tables on the Federal Republic of Germany's team, to take the gold it had so ungraciously lost in Munich. In the women's field, the Netherlands placed first, followed by the Federal Republic of Germany, and the US women's team brought home the bronze.

In 1988, Great Britain fully realized its comeback, winning a gold medal in a final against the Federal Republic of Germany. The Netherlands, a sometime runner-up, won the bronze. The Australians placed first among the women, followed by South Korea and the Netherlands.

Field Hockey — Men's Team

1988
1. Great Britain, Paul Barber, S. Batchelor, Dulbir Bhaura, Robert Clift, Richard Dodds, David Faulkner, Russell Garcia, Martyn Grimley, Sean Kerly, James Kirkwood, Richard Leman, Stephen Martin, Veryan Pappin, Jon Potter, Imran Sherwani, Ian Taylor
2. West Germany, Stefan Bloecher, Dirk Brinkmann, T. Brankman, Heiner Dopp, H. Fastrich, Carsten Fischer, Tobias Frank, Volker Fried, Ulrich Haenel, Michael Hilgers, Andreas Keller, Michael Metz, A. Mollandin, Thomas Reck, C. Schiliemann, E. Schmidt-Opper
3. Netherlands, Marc Benninga, F. Bove Lander, J. Brinkman, Maurits Crugg, Marc Delissen, C. Diepeveen, Patrick Faber, Ronald Jansen, Rene Klaassen, H. Kooijman, J. Kruize, Prank Leistra, Erik Parlevliet G. Schlatmann, Tim Steens, Van Den Honert

1984
1. Pakistan, G. Moinuddin, Qasim Zia, Nasir Ali, A. Rashid, Ayaz Mehmood, Naeem Akhtar, Kaleemullah, Manzoor Hussain, Hasan Sardar, Hanir Khan, Khlid Hameed, Shahid Ali Khan, Tauqeer Dar, Ishtiaq Ahmen, Salleem Sherwani, Mushtaq Ahmad
2. West Germany, Christian Bassemir, Yobias Frank, Ulrich Hanel, Carsten Fischer, Joachim Hurter, Ekkhard Schmidt-Oppet, Reinhard Krull, Michael Peter, Stefan Blocher, Andreas Keller, Thomas Reck, Maekku Slawyk, Thomas Gunst, Heiner Dopp, Volker Fried, Dirk Brinkmann
3. Great Britain, Ian Taylor, Veryan Pappin, Stephen Martin, Paul Barber, Robert Cattrall, Jonathan Potter, Richard Dodds, William McConnell, Norman Hughes, David Westcott, Richard Leman, Stephen Batchelor, Sean Kerly, James Duthie, Kulbir Bhaura, Mark Precious

1980
1. India, Allan Schofield, Chettri Bir Bhadur, Dung Dung Sylvanus, Rajinder Singh, Davinder Singh, Gurmail Singh, Ravinder Pal Singh, Vasudevan Baskaran, Somaya Maneypanda, Marahaj Krishon Kaushik, Charanjit Kumar, Mervyn Fernandis, Amarjit Rana Singh, Shahid Mohamed, Zafar Iqbal, Surinder Singh
2. Spain, Jose Garcia, Juan Amat, Santiago Malgosa, Rafael Garralda, Francisco Fabregas, Juan Luis Coghen, Ricardo Cabot, Jaimes Arbos, Carlos Roca, Juan Pellon, Miguel de Paz, Miguel Chavez, Juan Arbos, Javier Cabot, Paulino Monsalve, Jaime, Zumalacarregui

3. Soviet Union, Vladimir Pleshakov, Vyacheslav Lampeev, Leonid Pavlovsky, Sos Airapetyan, Farit Zigangirov, Valeri Belyakov, Sergei Klevtsov, Oleg Zagoroonev, Aleksandr Gusev, Sergei Pleshakov, Mikhail Nichepurenko, Minneula Azizov, Aleksandr Sytchev, Aleksandr Myasnikov, Viktor Deputatov, Aleksandr Goncharov

1976
1. New Zealand, Paul Ackerley, Jeff Archibald, Thur Borren, Alan Chesney, John Christensen, Greg Dayman, Tony Ineson, Alan McIntyre, Neil McLeod, Barry Maister, Selwyn Maister, Trevor Manning, Arthur Parkin, Mohan Patel, Ramesh Patel, Les Wilson
2. Australia, Robert Haigh, Richard Charlesworth, David Bell, Gregory Browning, Ian Cooke, Barry Dancer, Douglas Golder, Wayne Hammond, James Irvine, Malcolm Poole, Robert Proctor, Graham Reid, Ronald Riley, Trevor Smith, Terry Walsh
3. Pakistan, Saleem Sherwani, Manzoor Hassan, Munawaruz Zaman, Saleem Nazim, Rasool Akhtar, Iftikhar Syed, Islah Islahuddin, Manzoor Hussain, Abdul Rashid, Shanaz Skeikh, Samiulah Khan, Qamar Zia, Arshad Mahmood, Arshad Ali Chaudry, Mudassar Asghar, Haneef Khan

1972
1. West Germany, Peter Kraus, Michael Peter, Dieter Freise, Michael Krause, Eduard THelen, Horst Drose, Carsten Keller, Ulrich Klaes, Wolfgang Baumgart, Uli Vos, Peter Trump, Wolfgang Rott, Detlef Kittstein, Werner Kaessmann, Fritz Schmidt, Wolfgang Strodter, Edkart Suhl, and Rainer Siefert
2. Pakistan, Saleem Sherwani, Akhtarul Islam, Manawarux Zaman, Saeed Anwar, Riaz Ahmed, Fazalur Rehman, Islahud Din, Mudassar Asghar, Abdul Rashid, Mohammad Asad Malik, Mohammad Shahnaz, Jahangir Ahmad Butt, Rasool Akhtar, Iftikhar Ahmed, Mohammad Zahid
3. India, Cornelius Charles, Mukhbain Singh, Kindo Michael, Krishnamurty Perumal, Ajitpal Singh, Harmik Singh, Ganesh Mollerapoovayya, Harbinder Singh, Govin Billimogaputtaswamy, Ashok Kumar, Harcharan Singh, Manuel Frederick, Kulwant Singh, Virinder Singh

1968
1. Pakistan, Zakir Hussain, Tanvir Ahmad Dar, Tariq Aziz, Saeed Anwar, Riaz Ahmed, Gulrez Akhtar, Khalid Mahmood Hussain, Mohammad Ashfaq, Abdul Rashid, Mohammad Asad Malik, Jahangir Ahmad Butt, Riaz-ud-Din, Tariq Niazi

317

2. Australia, Paul Dearing, James Mason, Brian Glencross, Gordon Pearce, Julian Pearce, Robert Haigh, Donald Martin, Raymond Evans, Ronald Riley, Patrick Nilan, Donald Smart, Desmond Piper, Eric Pearce, Frederick Quinn
3. India, Rajendra A. Christy, Gurbux Singh, Prithipal Singh, Balbir Singh II, Ajitpal Singh, Krishnamurty Perumal, Balbir Singh III, Balbir Singh I, Harbinder Singh, Inamur Rehman, Inder Singh, Munir Sait, Harmik Singh, Jagjit Singh, John V. Peter, Tarsem Singh

1964 1. India, Shankar Laxman, Prithipal Singh, Dharam Singh, Mohinder Lal, Charanjit Singh, Gurbux Singh, Joginder Singh, John V. Peter, Harbinder Singh, Kaushik Haripal, Darshan Singh, Jagjit Singh, Bandu Patil, Udham Singh, Ali Sayeed
2. Pakistan, Abdul Hamid, Munir Ahmad Dar, Manzur Hussain Atif, Saeed Anwar, Anwar Ahmad Khan, Muhammad Rashid, Khalid Mahmood, Zaka-ud-Din, Muhammad Afzal Manna, Mohammad Asad Malik, Mutih Ullah, Tariq Niazi, Zafar Hayat, Khurshid Azam, Khizar Nawaz, Tariq Aziz
3. Australia, Paul Dearing, Donald McWatters, Brian Glencross, John McBryde, Julian Pearce, Graham Wood, Robin Hodder, Raymond Evans, Eric Pearce, Patrick Nilan, Donald Smart, Antony Waters, Mervyn Crossman, Desmond Piper

1960 1. Pakistan, Abdul Rashid, Bashir Ahmad, Manzur Hussain Atif, Ghulam Rasul, Anwar Ahmad Khan, Habib Ali Kiddi, Noor Alam, Abdul Hamid, Abdul Waheed, Nasir Ahmad, Mutih Ullah, Mushtaq Ahmad, Munir Ahmad Dar, Kurshid Aslam
2. India, Shankar Laxman, Prithipal Singh, Jaman Lal Sharma, Leslie W. Claudius, Joseph Antic, Mohinder Lal, Joginder Singh, John V. Peter, Jaswant Singh, Udham Singh, Raghbir Singh Bhola, Charanjit Singh, Govind Savant
3. Spain, Pedro Amat Fontanals, Francisco Caballer Soteras, Juan Angel Calzado de Castro, Jose Colomer Rivas, Carlos Del Coso Iglesias, Jose Antonio Dinares Massague, Eduardo Dualde Santos de Lamadrid, Joaquin Dualde Santos de Lamadrid, Rafael Egusquiza Basterra, Ignacio Macaya Santos de Lamadrid, Pedro Murua Leguizamon, Pedro Roig Juyent, Luis Maria Usoz Qintana, Narciso Ventallo Surralles

1956 1. India, Shankar Laxman, Bakshish Singh, Randhir Singh Gentle, Leslie W. Claudius, Amir Kumar, Govind Perumal, Raghbir Lal, Gurdev Singh, Balbir Singh, Udham Singh, Raghbir Singh Bhola, Charles Stephen, Ranganandhan Francis, Balkishan Singh, Amit Singh Bakshi, Kaushik Haripal, Hardyal Singh

2. Pakistan, Zakir Hussain, Munir Ahmad Dar, Manzur Hussain Atif, Ghulam Rasul, Answar Ahmad Khan, Hussain Mussarat, Noor Alam, Abdul Hamid, Habibur Rehman, Nasir Ahmad, Mutih Ullah, Latifur Rehman, Husein Akhtar, Habib Ali Kiddi
3. West Germany, Alfred Lucker, Helmut Nonn, Gunther Ullerich, Gunther Brennecke, Werner Delmes, Eberhard Ferstl, Hugo Dollheriser, Heinz Radzikowski, Wolfgang Nonn, Hugo Budinger, Werner Rosenbaum

1952 1. India, Ranganandhan Francis, Dharam Singh, Randhir Singh Gentle, Leslie Claudius, Keshava Datt, Govind Perumal, Raghbir Lal, Kunwar Digvijai Singh, Balbir Singh, Udham Singh, Muniswamy Rajgopal, Chinadorai Deshmutu, Meldric St. Clair Daluz, Grahanandan Singh
2. Netherlands, Laurentz S. Mulder, Henri J. J. Derckx, Johan F. Drijver, Julius T. Ancion, Hermanus P. Loggere, Edouard H. Tiel, Willem van Heel, Rius T. Esser, Jan H. Kruize, Andries C. Boerstra, Leonard H. Wery
3. Great Britain, Graham B. Dadds, Roger K. Midgley, Denys J. Carnill, John A. Cockett, Dennis M. R. Eagan, Anthony J. B. Robinson, Anthony S. Nunn, Robin A. Fletcher, Richard O. A. Norris, John V. Conroy, John P. Taylor, Derek M. Day, Neil A. Nugent

1948 1. India, Leo Pinto, Trilochan Singh, Randhir Singh Gentle, Keshava Datt, Amir Kumar, Maxie Vaz, Kishan Lal, Kunwar Digvijai Singh, Grahanandan Singh, Patrick Jansen, Lawrie Fernandes, Ranganandhan Francis, Akhtar Hussain, Leslie Claudius, Jaswant Rajput, Reginald Rodrigues, Latifur Rehman, Balbir Singh, Walter D'Souza, Gerry Glacken
2. Great Britain, David L. S. Brodie, George B. Sime, William L. C. Lindsay, Michael Walford, Frank Reynolds, Robin Lindsay, John M. Peake, Neil White, Robert E. Adlard, Norman Borrett, William S. Griffiths, Ronald Davies
3. Netherlands, Antonius M. Richter, Henri J. J. Derckx, Johan F. Drijver, Jenne Langhout, Hermanus P. Loggere, Edouard H. Tiel, Willem van Heel, Andries C. Boerstra, Pieter M. J. Bromberg, Jan H. Kruize, Ruis Theo Esser, Henricus N. Bouwman

1936 1. India, Richard J. Allen, Carlyle C. Tapsell, Mohomed Hussain, Baboo Narsoo Nimal, Earnest J. Cullen, Joseph Galibardy, Shabban Shahab ud Din, Dara Singh, Dhyan Chand, Roop Singh, Sayed M. Jaffar, Cyril J. Michie, Fernandes P. Peter, Joseph Phillip, Garewal Gurcharan Singh, Ahsan Mohomed Khan, Ahmed Sher Kahn, Lionel C. Emmett, Mirza Nasir ud Din Masood

318

2. Germany, Karl Drose, Herbert Kemmer, Dr. Erich Zander, Alfred Gerdes, Erwin Keller, Heinz Schmalix, Harald Huffmann, Werner Hamel, Kurt Weiss, Hans Scherbart, Fritz Messner, Tito Warnholtz, Detlef Okrent, Hermann Auf der Heide, Heinrich Peter, Carl Menke, Heinz Raack, Paul Mehlitz, Ludwig Beisiegel, Karl Ruck, Erich Cuntz, Werner Kubitzki
3. Netherlands, Jan de Looper, Reindert B. J. de Waal, Max Westerkamp, Hendrik C. de Looper, Rudolf J. van der Haar, Antoine R. van Lierop, Pieter A. Gunning, Henri C. W. Schnitger, Ernst W. van den Berg, Agathon de Roos, Rene Sparenberg, Carl E. Heybroek

1932 1. India, Arthur C. Hind, Carlyle C. Tapsell, Leslie C. Hammond, Masud Minhas, Broome E. Pinniger, Lal Shah Bokhari, Richard J. Carr, Gurmit Singh, Dhyan Chand, Roop Singh, Sayed M. Jaffar
2. Japan, Shumkichi Hamada, Akio Sohda, Sadayoshi Kobayashi, Katsumi Shibata, Yoshio Sakai, Eiichi Nakamura, Haruhiko Kon, Hiroshi Nagata, Kenichi Konishi, Toshio Usami, Junzo Inohara
3. USA, Harold Brewster, Samuel Ewing, Leonard O'Brien, Henry Greer, James Gentle, Horace Disston, Lawrence Knapp, Charles Shaeffer, Amos Deacon, William Boddington, David McMullin, Frederick Wolters

1928 1. India, Richard J. Allen, Leslie C. Hammond, Michael E. Rocque, Sayed M. Yusuf, Broome E. Pinniger, Rex A. Norris, William J. Cullen, Frederic S. Seaman, Dhyan Chand, George E. Marthins, Maurice A. Gateley, Jaipal Singh, Shaukat Ali, Feroze Khan
2. Netherlands, Adriaan J. L. Katte, Reindert B. J. de Waal, Albert W. Tresling, Jan G. Ankerman, Emil P. J. Duson, Johannes W. Brand, August J. Kop, Gerrit J. A. Jannink, Paulus van de Rovaert, Robert van der Veen, Hendrik P. Visser t'Hooft
3. Germany, Georg Brunner, Heinz Woltje, Werner Proft, Erich Zander, Theo Haag, Werner Freyberg, Herbert Kemmer, Herbert Hobein, Bruno Boche, Herbert Muller, Friedrich Horn, Erwin Franzkowiak, Hans Haussmann, Karl Heinz Irmer, Aribert Heymann, Kurt Haverbeck, Rolf Wollner, Gerd Strantzen, Heinz Forstendorf

1924 Not held
1920 1. Great Britain, Harry Haslam, John Bennett, Charles Atkin, Harold Cooke, Eric Crockford, Cyril Wilkinson, William Smith, George McGrath, John McBryan, Stanley Shoveller, Rex Crummack, Arthur Leighton, Harold K. Cassels, Colin Campbell, Charles Marcom

2. Denmark, Andreas Rasmussen, Hans C. Herlak, Frans Faber, Erik Husted, Henning Holst, Hans J. Hansen, Hans A. Bjerrum, Thorvald Eigenbrod, Svend Blach, Steen Due, Ejvind Blach
3. Belgium, Charles Delelienne, Maurice van den Bempt, Raoul Daufresne de la Chevalerie, Rene Strauwen, Fernand de Montigny, Adolphe Goemaere, Pierre Chibert, Andre Becquet, Raymond Keppens, Pierre Valcke, Jean van Nerom, Robert Gevers, Louis Diercxsens

1912 Not held
1908 1. Great Britain (England), H. I. Wood, Harry S. Freeman, L. C. Baillon, John Robinson, Edgar Page, Alan Noble, Percy Rees, Gerald Logan, Stanley Shoveller, Reginald Pridmore, Eric Green
2. Great Britain (Ireland), E. P. C. Holmes, Henry Brown, Walter Peterson, William Graham, Walter Campbell, Henry Murphy, C. F. Power, G. S. Gregg, Eric Allman-Smith, Frank Robinson, Robert L. Kennedy, W. G. McCormick
3. Great Britain (Wales), Bruce Turnbull, E. W. G. Richards, Llewellyn Evans, C. W. Shephard, R. Lyne, F. Connah, F. Gordon Phillips, A. A. Law, P. B. Turnbull, J. Ralph Williams, W. J. Pallott
3. Great Britain (Scotland), John Burt, Hugh Neilson, Charles H. Foulkes, Hew Fraser, AlexanderBurt, Andrew Dennistoun, Norman Stevenson, Ivan Laing, John Harper-Orr, Hugh Walker, William Orchardson

1896-
1906 Not held

Field Hockey — Women's Team

1988 1. Australia, Tracey Belbin, Deborah Bowman, Lee Capes, Michelle Capes, Sally Carbon, Elspeth Clement, Loretta Dorman, Maree Fish, Rechelle Hawkes, Lorraine Hillas, K. Partridge, Sharon Patmore, I. Pereira, Sandra Pisani, Kim Small, Liane Tooth
2. South Korea, Eun-Jung Chang, Ki-Hyang Cho, Choon-Ok Choi, Eun-Kyung Chung, Sang-Hyun Chung, Keum-Sil Han, Ok-Kyung Han, Keum-Sook Hwang, Won-Sim Jin, Mi-Sun Kim, Soon-Duk Kim, Young-Sook Kim, Kye-Sook Lim, Soon-ja Park, Hyo-Sun Seo, Kwang-Mi Seo
3. Netherlands, W. Aardenburg, Carina Benninga, M. Bolhuis, Yvonne Buter, B. De Beus, Annemieke Fokke, Noor Holsboer, I. Lejeune, A. Nieuwenhuizen, Martine Ohr, H. Van Der Ben, M. Van Doorn, A. Van Manen, S. Von Weiler, L. Willemse, Ingrid Wolff

1984
1. Netherlands, Bernadette De Beus, Alette Pos, Margnet Zegers, Laurien Willemse, Marjolein Eysvogel, Josephine Boekhorst, Carina Benninga, Alexandra Le Poole, Francisca Hillen, Marieke Van Doom, Sophie Von Weiler, Arlette Van Manen, Irene Hendriks, Elisabeth Sevens, Martine Ohr, Anneloes Nieuwenhuizen
2. West Germany Ursula Thielemann, Elke Drull, Beate Deininger, Christina Moser, Hella Roth, Dagmar Breiken, Birgit Hagen, Birgit Hahn, Gabriele Appel, Andrea Weiermann-Lietz, Corinna Lingnau, Martina Koch, Gabriele Schley, Patricia Ott, Susanne Schmid, Sigrid Landgraf
3. USA, Gwen Cheeseman, Beth Anders, Kathleen McGahey, Anita Miller, Regina Buggy, Christine Larson-Mason, Beth Beglin, Marcella Place, Julie Staver, Diane Moyer, Sheryl Johnson, Charlene Morett, Karen Shelton, Brenda Stauffer, Leslie Milne, Judy Strong

1980
1. Zimbabwe, Sarah English, Ann Mary Grant, Brenda Phillips, Patricia McKillop, Sonia Robertson, Patricia Davies, Maureen George, Linda Watson, Susan Huggett, Gillian Cowley, Elizabeth Chase, Sandra Chick, Helen Volk, Christine Prinsloo, Arlene Boxall, Anthea Stewart
2. Czechoslovakia, Jamila Krachckova, Berta Hruba, Iveta Srankova, Lenda Vymazalova, Jirina Krizova, Jirina Kadlecova, Jirina Cermakova, Marta Urbanova, Kveta Petrickova, Marie Sykorova, Ida Hubackova, Milada Blazkova, Jana Lahodova, Alena Kyselicova, Jirina Hajkova, Viera Podhanyiova
3. Soviet Union, Galina Inzhuvatova, Nelli Gorbatkova, Valentina Zazdravnykh, Nadezhda Ovechkina, Natella Krasnikova, Natalya Bykova, Lydia Glubokova, Galina Vyuzhanina, Natalya Buzunova, Lyailya Akhmerova, Nadezhda Filippova, Yelena Gureva, Tatiana Yembakhtova, Tatiana Shvyganova, Alina Kham, Ljudmila Frolova

GYMNASTICS

WARM-UP

I n recent years, gymnastics has become an Olympic favorite in the US, bolstered by the televised drama of photogenic teenagers such as Olga Korbut, Nadia Comaneci, and Mary Lou Retton ascending to championships. And who can forget watching the great (or at least the over-achieving) 1984 American men's team led by veteran Bart Conner? Gymnastics is truly an event made for television, the athletes commanding the screen as they tumble, twist, leap, and vault within camera range. But the history of gymnastics stretches back beyond television, past ancient Greece, to our earliest acrobatic ancestors.

Swinging from trees being one of humankind's prerequisites (notwithstanding the opposable thumb thing), gymnastics perhaps owes its origins to early primate behavior. The art was further developed by ancient Chinese, Persians, Indians, and Greeks, who all practiced a form of gymnastics as a means of readying young men for battle. The word gymnastics derives from the Greek word *gymnos*, meaning naked. The exercises were performed in the nude at *gymnasia*, which were public exercise facilities.

fact: At the ancient all-male Olympic Games, athletes competed nude.

Although gymnastics were included in the ancient Olympics, and the wooden horse used in vaulting and the pommel horse both date back to the glory days of Rome, gymnastics was largely a forgotten sport for many centuries. Acrobats of all sorts continued to use gymnastics techniques, but the modern resurrection of gymnastics began in Germany during the 18th century.

John Basedow introduced the sport to schools in that country, while Johann Guts Muth published the first major tome on the sport, called *Gymnastics for Youth*, in which he encouraged the use of climbing poles, ropes, balance beams, and ladders. Yet another German of that period, Friederich Jahn, introduced the parallel bars and rings along with routines for the horizontal bars.

Toward the end of the 19th century, gymnastic clubs sprang up in Germany and elsewhere in Europe. In 1881, the International Gymnastics Federation/Fédération Internationale de Gymnastique (FIG) was formed (then called the Bureau of the European Gymnastics Federation), opening the way for international competition. The first large-scale meeting of gymnasts was the 1896 Olympics, where Germany virtually swept the medal parade. Seventy-five gymnasts from five countries competed in the men's horizontal bar, parallel bars, pommel horse, still rings, and horse vault events.

At the 1900 Games in Paris, only one gymnastic event was held, an individual combined exercise. The first international gymnastics competition outside of the Olympics was held in 1903 in Antwerp, Belgium, and gymnasts from Belgium, France, Luxembourg, and the Netherlands competed in what is now considered the first world championship. At St. Louis in 1904, the men's team combined competition was added to the Olympic program.

An interesting side note to the world championships is that in 1922, swimming and track and field events were added to the competition in Antwerp. Soon after this experiment, the sport's leaders agreed that swimming had no business in a gymnastics competition. But at the ninth world championship in 1930 at Luxembourg, the competition included the pole vault, broad jump, shot put, rope climb, and a 100-meter sprint. Track and field did not fully disappear from the world championship gymnastics circuit until the 1954 competition.

At the 1924 Games in Paris, the basis of modern Olympic gymnastic competition was firmly established. The athletes (men) began to compete for individual Olympic titles on apparatus, as well as in combined individual and team exercises. The 1928 Games witnessed the debut of the first women's event, the team combined exercise, won by the Netherlands. A quarter of a century after that breakthrough, five individual events for women were added in 1952: the combined, balance beam, floor exercise, uneven bars, and horse vault. The women's rhythmic individual all-around was added in 1984.

Through 1960, the Olympics (and world championships) were dominated by European teams, with the Italians (and in the 1950s, the Soviets) reigning supreme. In the 1960s and 1970s, the Japanese ruled as the number-one men's team, while the Soviets held forth as the women's team to beat. With the exception of the US men's team stunning upset in the Eastern-bloc boycotted 1984 Games, the Soviets continue to produce the world's best men's and women's gymnastics teams.

SPECTATORS' GUIDE

Two types of gymnastics are performed at the Olympics: artistic and rhythmic. The men compete in eight artistic events, while the women vie for medals in six artistic events and one rhythmic event. The events for men include: team competition, individual all-around, floor exercise, pommel horse, still rings, vault, parallel bars, and horizontal bars. Women's events include team competition, individual all-around, vault, uneven bars, balance beam, floor exercise, and the rhythmic individual all-around.

The chief difference between artistic and rhythmic gymnastics is that while artistic events are performed *on an apparatus*, such as balance beams, parallel bars, and vaults, rhythmics are performed *with apparatus*, such as 20-foot ribbons, hoops, and ropes. The rhythmic props are rolled along the ground, jumped through, and wound around the body, with emphasis placed on grace, beauty, and coordination of movement between prop and athlete. The event, a combination of gymnastics and ballet, is performed to music.

Artistic gymnastics competition is divided into compulsory and optional movements. Four judges give grades following each individual's exercise. The highest and lowest scores are discarded, with the average of the middle two scores standing as the final grade. The highest possible score is a 10. In awarding their scores, judges take into consideration the degree of difficulty of a gymnast's program, along with aesthetic appeal. Points are deducted for such faults as poor execution, lack of control, falling, or exceeding the time limit.

fact: The "perfect 10.00" score was first awarded in world-class competition to Nadia Comaneci at the 1976 Olympic Games.

The individual all-around (combined) champions for men and women are determined by totaling scores on all the apparatus. For the men's and women's team combined, the total of the top six scores on each apparatus is the team's score.

What to Look for on Each Apparatus

Floor Exercise: Today's floor exercise routines for men consist of dynamic tumbling skills that only a few years ago were performed solely on the trampoline. Multiple saltos (flips or somersaults) and twists are increasingly common. The best will incorporate three or four tumbling passes of substantial difficulty, performing twisting double saltos on the second or third passes. Unlike the women's competition, the men's floor exercise is not performed to music.

Always a crowd favorite, women's floor exercise is best identified with Nadia Comaneci's perfect precision and Mary Lou Retton's powerful tumbling. The most important aspect to the floor exercise is grace. Look for dancer-like command of music, rhythm, and space. The gymnastics elements should flow freely into each other—the leaps covering impressive distances; the pirouettes and turns adding excitement to the music; the displays of strength, flexibility and balance all complementing each other. Difficult tumbling, ranging from triple twists to double-back somersaults with a full twist, are expected.

Vault: Men's and women's vault competition begins with a strong, accelerated run. The best vaulters explode off the board, getting their feet up over their head with tremendous quickness during the first flight phase of the vault from the springboard to contact with the horse. The judges are looking for proper body, shoulder, and hand position and instantaneous repulsion. The second flight phase and the landing are critical. Watch for height and distance of travel, as well as the number of saltos and twists—usually the more of each, the higher the difficulty value of the vault. The sudden impact of a no-step, "stuck" landing creates a favorable impression. Note that male gymnasts are not allowed to perform the round-off vault, or Yurchenko, named after the Soviet woman who invented the maneuver.

fact: Men vault onto the horse set vertically out from the launching board, while the women's horse is set perpendicular to the approach.

Pommel Horse (men only): Considered by many to be the most difficult of all men's gymnastics events, the pommel horse is also the most subtle. Each move is defined by complex hand placements and body positions. The difficulty stems from two factors. First, the gymnast is performing moves that differ from the swinging and tumbling skills of the other five events. Second, he spends most of each routine on only one arm, as the free hand reaches for another part of the horse to begin the next move. Look for a long series of moves in which the gymnast reaches his hands behind his back, or places both hands on a single pommel. The hand placements should be quick, quiet, and rhythmic.

Rings (men only): The rings are the least stable of the men's apparatus. Stillness is paramount and those with the best command of the event will display extraordinary skill in arriving at all holds with absolute precision. The rings should not wobble or swing, the body should not sag or twist, and the arms should not waver or shake.

Parallel Bars (men only): Although not a requirement, some of the better gymnasts move outside the two rails, performing handstands, presses, kips and hip circles on only one bar. The most difficult skills require the gymnast to lose sight of the bars for a moment, as in front and back saltos.

Horizontal Bar (men only): Watch for blind releases, in which the gymnast loses sight of the bar while executing a salto or twist. One-arm giants are extremely difficult, and if the gymnast performs several in succession as he changes directions, or if he performs a blind release out of one-arm giants, he has performed admirably.

Uneven Bars (women only): The most spectacular of the women's events. Watch for the big swings that begin in handstands on the high bar—two, three, or four in succession, incorporating multiple hand changes, pirouettes, and release/flight elements.

fact: The beam is sixteen feet, three inches long, four inches wide, and almost four feet off the floor; it is the great winnower of women gymnasts.

Balance Beam (women only): The overall execution should give the impression that the gymnast is performing on a floor, not on a strip four inches wide. Watch for variations in rhythm, changes in level (from sitting on the beam to sailing head-height above it) and the harmonious blend of gymnastics and acrobatic elements.

Jumping Gymnastics: A Glossary

AERIAL: A stunt in which the gymnast turns completely over in the air without touching the apparatus with his or her hands.

FLIP-FLOP: A back handspring; a jump backward from the feet through handstand position and back to the feet again.

GIANT: A swing in which the body is fully extended and moving through a 360-degree rotation around the bar.

HALF-IN, HALF-OUT: A double salto with a full twist—the complete twist performed during the first salto.

KIP: Movement from a position below the equipment to a position above.

KOVAC: Performed on men's horizontal bar; involves a swing forward with a back salto traveling backward over the bar to recatch the bar.

PIKE POSITION: Body bent forward more than 90 degrees at the hips while the legs are kept straight out.

PIROUETTES: When the gymnast changes direction while being supported by the hands and arms; twists while in the handstand position.

PLANCHE: A balance position on the hands in which the body is held at an angle with shoulders forward of hands.

SALTO: Flip or somersault, with the feet coming up over the head and the body rotating around the waist.

TKATCHEV: Giant circle backward to a straddle release backward over the bar to a hang on the bar.

TSUKAHARA: Vault with a one-half turn onto the horse followed by a backward one and one-half salto; named for its innovator, Japanese gymnast Mitsuo Tsukahara.

Gymnastics

THOMAS FLAIRS: Straddle leg circles on pommel horse in similar fashion as "helicopter swings"; named for its innovator, US gymnast Kurt Thomas.

TUCK: A position in which the knees and hips are bent and drawn into the chest, the body folded at the waist.

VALDEZ: Backward walkover with alternate hand placement originating from a seated position.

YURCHENKO: A vault that is preceded by a round-off onto the board, a flip-flop onto the horse, and a back one and one-half salto off; named for its innovator, Soviet gymnast Natalia Yurchenko.

▼

HOPEFULS

Men's Gymnastics

The **Soviet** men are undoubtedly the world's best gymnasts. They swept the all-around at the 1988 Olympic Games and won the gold and silver medals at the 1989 and 1991 World Championships, 1990 Goodwill Games, and 1990 World Cup. Top Soviet Olympians could include 1988 Olympic alternate Igor Korobchinsky, who won the all-around title and floor exercise gold at both the 1989 World and European Championships; 1990 all-around world champion Valeri Belenky, who garnered six medals at the 1990 Goodwill Games; and Vitali Scherbo, whose recent medals include three golds from the 1990 European Championships and five medals from 1990 Goodwill Games.

East Germany's team ranked second at the 1988 Olympic Games and the following year's World Championships, but a unified **Germany** placed only third at the 1991 World games. Their best gymnasts are probably 1988 Olympic team silver medalist Sylvio Kroll, who tied for 10th all-around at both the Seoul Olympics and 1989 World Championships, then reached sixth at the 1990 Goodwill Games, and 1988 Olympian Andreas Wecker, who tied for fourth place at the 1989 World Championships and, at the 1990 World Cup, finished sixth all-around and won a bronze medal on the pommel horse.

China's team is becoming a major force with its bronze- and silver-medal showings at the 1989 and 1991 World Championships and strong performances by Li Jing, who performs a rare round-off entry vault with a layout double twist. At the 1989 World Championships Li Jing tied for the gold on parallel bars and won two bronze medals, and the next year he won World Cup gold and bronze medals.

326

After finishing eighth at the 1989 World Championships, the US men have improved with a second place finish at the 1990 Goodwill Games and other strong international showings. 1988 Olympian Lance Ringnald took three medals—the all-around and high bar titles and the parallel bars bronze—at the 1990 Goodwill Games. Chris Waller shows Olympic promise as the USA's 1991 all-around and pommel horse champion.

And doubtful—but nonetheless possible—is a comeback by Kurt Thomas, once the best US gymnast and pioneer of the "Thomas flair" pommel horse move. The most decorated gymnast in 1970 and the second-best in the world by 1979, Thomas was a victim of the 1980 Olympic boycott and did not compete that year or in 1984. Five years later, though, in his mid-30s, Thomas began training again with the intention of earning the only world medal—an Olympic medal—that his career hadn't provided. Hindered by shoulder and ankle injuries, though, Thomas faces an uncertain Olympic future.

fact: As gymnastics routines become more complex and difficult, the maximum score of 10 does not mean perfection so much as it means a better and harder performance than the previous competitor's. For that reason, the order in which gymnasts compete is crucial: coaches send out their lineups of six team members in inverse order of accomplishment. The weakest competitor in an event goes first, and her score becomes the base against which the rest are compared. If the first scores well and the second a bit better, the judges' scores escalate until, finally, the top performer goes out last in hopes of building on a base now escalated to 9.90 or 9.95.

Women's Gymnastics

The **Soviet** women, world team champions and winners of every Olympic team title for which they've competed, remain the team to beat. Most notable among them is Svetlana Boguinskaia, four-time medalist and vaulting champion at the 1988 Olympic Games. Also the 1989 all-around world champion (losing in 1991 to American Kim Zmeskal), Boguinskaia won or tied every event at the 1990 European Championships, scoring a perfect 10.00 on the floor exercise and balance beam. Natalia Kalinina, all-around champion of the 1990 Goodwill Games, finished right behind Boguinskaia at the European competition, tying her for first place on the bars and beam. Also among the Soviets' top gymnasts is Tatiana Lisenko, who defeated the reigning World Cup champion—Boguinskaia—in 1990 to take the all-around title, along with a gold for her performance on the uneven bars.

By winning the team bronze at the 1989 World Championships, **China** has emerged as a strong contender. Look for 1990 World Cup gold medalist Yang Bo's steady performance on the balance beam, and World Cup silver medalist Li Li's expertise on the beam and uneven bars.

The East German team fell from a third-place Olympic finish in 1988 to a fifth-place World Championship finish in 1989, leaving the gymnastic community wondering what a unified **Germany** will bring. **Romania** may make a showing with Cristina Bontas, whose World Championship winnings include two medals at the 1989 games and a tie for the gold in the floor exercise in 1991.

The **US** team improved upon its fourth-place Olympic and 1989 World Championship finishes with a silver at the 1991 World Championships. Also at the World games, two-time national champion Kim Zmeskal became the country's first woman to win an all-around world gymnastics championship, in addition to her bronze in the floor exercise. 1990's all-around runner-up and national balance beam champion, Betty Okino, took a bronze in that event at the World competition. America's smallest gymnast, four-foot, three-inch Shannon Miller, tied for second place on the uneven bars.

Schedule

The tentative gymnastics schedule is as follows:

Sunday, July 26
Compulsory exercises, team, women

Monday, July 27
Compulsory exercises, team, men

Tuesday, July 28
Optional exercises, team, women
Optional exercises, team, final, women

Wednesday, July 29
Optional exercises, team, men
Optional exercises, team, final, men

Thursday, July 30
All-around individual final, women

Friday, July 31
All-around individual final, men

Saturday, August 1
Apparatus, final, women

Sunday, August 2
Apparatus, final, men

Thursday, August 6
Rhythmic preliminaries

Friday, August 7
Rhythmic preliminaries

Saturday, August 8
Rhythmic final

MEN'S GYMNASTICS EVENTS

▼

HIGHLIGHTS

Long dominated by Europeans, especially the Soviets, gymnastics until the 1980s stressed grace and style as much as athletic power. Japanese gymnasts began to make their mark in the 1960s with exceptional smoothness and elegance. In the 1980s innovations in the sport's equipment allowed gymnasts to emphasize physical power; for instance, instead of functioning as padding, the tumbling mats are now mounted on springs, affording athletes extra hang time for aerial maneuvers.

US men won gold medals in 1904 and 1932, including golds at the 1932 Los Angeles Games for rope climb, Indian clubs, and tumbling. Among notable medal winners, Japan's Akinori Nakayama earned six gold medals, two silver, and two bronze in the late 1960s; he was followed by his countryman Sawao Kato, who captured six gold, two silver, and one bronze. The male record for individual gymnastics gold medals is six each for Boris Shakhlin, competing in the 1960s, and Nikolai Andrianov, competing in 1976 and 1980, both of the USSR. Shakhlin also won a team gold medal, and four silver and two bronze. Andrianov set a record for the most medals by a male competitor in any sport, winning a total of 15.

At the Moscow Games in 1980 Aleksandr Ditiatin was the first male gymnast to gain medals in all eight categories open to him at a single Games. The US's first black Olympic gymnast, Charles Lakes, competed in 1988.

Individual All-Around Combined Exercises: This competition was not held for men in 1896 but has been part of every Olympiad since 1900. Men's combined exercises include the horse vault, the side (pommel) horse, the horizontal bar, parallel bars, flying rings, and floor exercises.

Gustave Sandras of France was the first men's all-around champion, leading a French sweep of the competition at the Paris Games. In 1904 the title was won by Julius Lenhardt, competing for the US team. France's Pierre Payssé won two individuals (a five- and a six-event competition) in the unofficial Olympics of 1906, both times besting Italy's Alberto Braglia. Braglia was the first gymnast to win two consecutive Olympic medals in the individual combined exercises, in 1908 and 1912.

More than four decades later the Soviet Union's Victor Chukarin achieved the same feat when he won his second medal in this event in 1956, defeating Japan's Takashi Ono by only 0.05 points. Ono was again beaten by a Soviet in 1960, again by only 0.05 points. Behind Ono both times was Soviet gymnast Yuriy Titov.

In 1972 Japan's Sawao Kato became the third man to win the all-round gold medal twice, leading the Japanese to a sweep of this event. Japan's Akinori

Nakayama took the bronze in 1968 and 1972. At the Montréal Games Kato came back for a silver in the all-around, behind Soviet Nikolai Andrianov and ahead of Japan's Mitsuo Tsukahara. Andrianov settled for silver behind teammate Aleksandr Ditiatin in 1980.

The USA's Peter Vidmar was silver medalist in this competition in 1984, ceding gold by a mere 0.025 of a point to Japan's Koji Gushiken, the smallest men's margin of victory. In 1988 this event was swept by the Soviets.

Team Combined Exercises: The Swedish team captured the gold in 1908, then Italy won the men's team championships four times between 1912 and 1932. After Germany and Finland each won once, the USSR captured the team gold in 1952 and 1956. Finland's bronze medal-winning team in 1952 included 44-year-old Haikki Savolainen, who set a record by competing in five Games from 1928 to 1952. Starting in 1960, Japan claimed the team title five times in a row. The 1960 Japanese team included 40-year-old Masao Takemoto, the oldest gold-medaling gymnast. In 1976 the Japanese team won on the strength of Mitsuo Tsukahara's performance on the horizontal bar.

The Soviet team captured the gold in the boycott year of 1980. Going into the 1984 Games, needless to say, American men had endured a long drought in gymnastics. In fact, before 1984, no American gymnast had won a gold since the 1932 Games, when male gymnasts also climbed ropes and juggled Indian clubs. But in 1984, albeit with the Eastern bloc countries absent, the US men's team took the gold, winning a close contest against China, to Japan's bronze. In 1988 the Soviet men, led by all-around champion Vladimir Artemov, won the team gold medal ahead of East Germany, with Japan again claiming the bronze.

Floor Exercise: Swiss competitor Georges Miez enthralled the Berlin crowd in 1936, when he placed first in this event. Miez had won the all-around gold in 1928, and by 1936 his Olympic medal total came to four gold, three silver, and one bronze. K. William Thoresson of Sweden captured the floor exercise gold in 1952 and was part of a unique three-way tie for the silver in 1956, sharing the medal with Viktor Chukarin of the Soviet Union and Japan's Nobuyuki Aihara, who returned in 1960 to claim the gold.

Italy's Franco Menichelli took a bronze before the home crowd at the 1960 Rome Games and four years later was awarded the gold. Akinori Nakayama of Japan silver medaled in 1968 and 1972. A surprise bronze came for US gymnast Peter Kormann in this event in 1976. Chinese gymnasts captured the two top spots in 1984, and the Soviets did likewise in Seoul.

Horizontal Bar: Yugoslavia's Leon Stukelj struck gold in 1924, the year that Swiss competitor Georges Miez placed fourth; four years later, Miez was good as gold. Heikki Savolainen, competing for Finland, took a silver on the horizontal bar in 1932 and, twenty years later, placed fifth.

Another elder gymnast, Japan's Masao Takemoto, earned a silver medal on the horizontal bar in 1960 at the age of 40. Mitsuo Tsukahara won the gold in 1972 and 1976. Japanese gymnasts claimed the gold and bronze in 1984, while two Soviets tied for gold four years later.

Parallel Bars: US gymnast George Eyser took the gold in 1904, aided (or at least not hampered) by a wooden leg. He ultimately won another gold, two silver, and a bronze at the St. Louis Games. The next American to capture the gold in the parallel bars was Bart Conner, in 1984; his teammate, Mitch Gaylord, claimed the bronze. In 1988 Soviet gymnasts took the top two spots.

Pommel Horse (or Sidehorse): This event was not held from 1908 to 1920. Heikki Savolainen of Finland captured the bronze in the pommel horse in 1928 and twenty years later, in 1948. Zoltán Magyar of Hungary claimed the gold twice, in 1976 and 1980. In 1984 US gymnast Peter Vidmar tied with China's Li Ning for the gold, and Timothy Daggett of the US brought in the bronze. A three-way tie for the gold resulted in 1988, with Dimitri Bilozertchev of the Soviet Union, Hungary's Zsolt Borkai, and Lyubomir Gueraskov of Bulgaria sharing the top honor.

Still Rings: Ioannis Mitropolos won the gold in 1896, the modern Olympics' first announced Greek champion. Yugoslavia's Leon Stukelj took fourth place in 1924, then moved up for the gold in 1928; he was 37 when he won the silver on the rings in 1936, adding to the three gold and two bronze medals he'd won at previous games over a dozen years, including the all-around gold in 1924.

Japan's Akinori Nakayama repeated for the gold on the rings in 1968 and 1972. Aleksandr Dityatin of the USSR followed his silver in this event in 1976 with a gold in 1980. In 1984 Mitch Gaylord of the US captured a bronze, behind Li Ning of China and Koji Gushiken of Japan, who tied for the gold. Holger Behrendt of East Germany and Dmitri Bilozertchev of the Soviet Union also shared the gold at Seoul.

Horse (or Longhorse) Vault: The event's first gold medalist was German Carl Schuhmann in 1896. In 1964 Haruhiro Yamashita of Japan won the gold with a handspring in a pike position, and the maneuver was subsequently named the Yamashita. In 1972, East Germany's Klaus Köste won the title with a Yamashita and a forward somersault, claiming the first gold for his country in men's gymnastics. The USSR's Aleksandr Dityatin was the first male gymnast to receive a 10.0 score from judges in Olympic competition, accorded for a horse vault in 1980. Four years later US gymnast Mitch Gaylord settled for a quarter share of the silver, as he tied with Koji Gushiken and Shninji Morisue of Japan and China's Li Ning. Alone at the top was Yun Lou of China.

Tracking the 1984 USA Men's Gymnastic Team

"Say hello to the 1984 equivalent of the 1980 U.S. hockey team," *Miami Herald* sports columnist Edwin Pope wrote from the Los Angeles Olympic Games. The US men's gymnastic team had just won its first gold medal in eight decades of competition—and its first team medal of *any* kind since a silver in 1932.

"Winning a gold as a team—it's a miracle," US gymnast Scott Johnson affirmed.

Gymnastics

"It's pretty amazing," teammate Bart Conner acknowledged then. "If you'd taken a poll of the world gymnastic community on our chances, we wouldn't have gotten very many votes a week ago."

But voting had nothing to do with anything in LA. What won the gold—an untarnished medal (though the Soviets and many Eastern bloc countries boycotted the games, the US defeated the reigning world champion Chinese)—were incredible performances by all members of the team: Conner, Tim Daggett, Peter Vidmar, Mitch Gaylord, James Hartung, and Scott Johnson.

"We got 'em on depth," Conner explained.

Indeed. The US earned a passel of perfect 10s, from performances by team captain Vidmar, as well as Daggett, Gaylord, and Conner, and strong ninth and 16th overall finishes from Hartung and Johnson respectively.

"Those 'lows'" Pope wrote of Hartung and Johnson's finishes, "actually were remarkably high in overall competition."

And the highs didn't end there, though after sweating and straining in relative obscurity for years, the gymnasts found their newfound celebrity could be something more difficult to balance. Vidmar complained of the apparent arrogance of having to wear sunglasses in public to avoid recognition.

"I'm just uncomfortable with it," he revealed a few months after the Games. "You walk by and people look at you and their mouths hit the floor and it scares you, almost. You back up not knowing what to do."

Things had truly changed.

Before the 1984 triumph, the US gymnastic team would go to the Olympics to "meet Dwight Stones and to see Harvey Glance run and to talk with the security guards in the Olympic Village," Conner recalled. "When you swim for the United States, you go to the Games with the idea that you can win a medal. That wasn't the case in gymnastics."

Wasn't. Past tense.

But their popularity—matinee-idol status, in many instances—turned out to be a catapult, too.

Vidmar, born on June 30, 1961, completed a Mormon missionary assignment in the Los Angeles area after the Games. He has developed a TV analyst–motivational speaking career.

Mitch Gaylord, born on March 10, 1961, appeared in *SuperTeen* magazine, gave his name to a gymnastic maneuver (the *Gaylord II*, a one-and-one-half flip on the high bar), and competed in the 1988 Games. He has not yet become a marquee movie star, but has appeared in numerous TV shows and some films: a 1986 production, *American Anthem*, and a 1990 film, *American Tiger*, a supernatural thriller about a college student who is drawn into a web of intrigue after taking a part-time job as a rickshaw puller in Miami.

Conner, born on March 28, 1958, is a three-time Olympian from the University of Oklahoma. He parlayed his increased visibility into further development of his career as a TV analyst. Conner signed to appear in some TV series and movies; has competed in celebrity road-racing events; was chosen one of the top-10 best-dressed short men in 1990 (in company with actor Michael J. Fox and novelist Tom Wolfe); and has been romantically linked with former Romanian Olympic gymnast Nadia Comaneci, who defected to the US in 1989. Daggett runs a gym in Massachusetts and provides some analysis for network TV.

Only Hartung, who is on the board of the US Gymnastics Federation and also coaches, and Scott Johnson, who works in management for McDonald's Hamburgers in Florida, have pretty much been overlooked by—or have dodged—that ever-searching spotlight. —*E.K.*

Medalists

Gymnastics, Artistic — Men's Individual All-Around (Combined Exercises)

1988 1. Vladimir Artemov, Soviet Union, 119.125
2. Valeri Lioukine, Soviet Union, 119.025
3. Dmitri Bilozertchev, Soviet Union, 118.975

1984 1. Koji Gushiken, Japan, 118.700
2. Peter Vidmar, USA, 118.675
3. Li Ning, China, 118.575

1980 1. Aleksandr Dityatin, Soviet Union, 118.650
2. Nikolai Andrianov, Soviet Union, 118.225
3. Stoian Delchev, Bulgaria, 118.000

1976 1. Nikolai Andrianov, Soviet Union, 116.650
2. Sawao Kato, Japan, 115.650
3. Mitsuo Tsukahara, Japan, 115.575

1972 1. Sawao Kato, Japan, 114.650
2. Eizo Kenmotsu, Japan, 114.575
3. Akinori Nakayama, Japan, 114.325

1968 1. Sawao Kato, Japan, 115.90
2. Mikhail Voronin, Soviet Union, 115.85
3. Akinori Nakayama, Japan, 115.65

1964 1. Yukio Endo, Japan, 115.95
2. Viktor Lisitski, Soviet Union, 115.40
2. Boris Shakhlin, Soviet Union, 115.40
2. Shuji Tsurumi, Japan, 115.40

1960 1. Boris Shakhlin, Soviet Union, 115.95
2. Takashi Ono, Japan, 115.90
3. Yuri Titov, Soviet Union, 115.60

1956 1. Viktor Chukarin, Soviet Union, 114.25
2. Takashi Ono, Japan, 114.20
3. Yuri Titov, Soviet Union, 113.80

1952 1. Viktor Chukarin, Soviet Union, 115.70
2. Grant Shaginyan, Soviet Union, 114.95
3. Josef Stalder, Switzerland, 114.75

1948 1. Veikko Huhtanen, Finland, 229.70
2. Walter Lehmann, Switzerland, 229.00
3. Paavo Aaltonen, Finland, 228.80

1936 1. Alfred Schwarzmann, Germany, 113.100
2. Eugen Mack, Switzerland, 112.334

3. Konrad Frey, Germany, 111.532

1932 1. Romeo Neri, Italy, 140.625
2. Istvan Pelle, Hungary, 134.925
3. Heikki Savolainen, Finland, 134.575

1928 1. Georges Miez, Switzerland, 247.500
2. Hermann Hanggi, Switzerland, 246.625
3. Leon Stukelj, Yugoslavia, 244.875

1924 1. Leon Stukelj, Yugoslavia, 110.340
2. Robert Prazak, Czechoslovakia, 110.323
3. Bedrich Supcik, Czechoslovakia, 106.930

1920 1. Giorgio Zampori, Italy, 88.35
2. Marco Torres, France, 87.62
3. Jean Gounot, France, 87.45

1912 1. Alberto Braglia, Italy, 135.0
2. Louis Segura, France, 132.5
3. Serafino Mazzarochi, Italy, 131.5

1908 1. Alberto Braglia, Italy, 317.0
2. S. W. Tysal, Great Britain, 312.0
3. Louis Segura, France, 297.0

1906 1. Pierre Paysse, France, 116 (five apparatuses)
1. Pierre Paysse, France, 97 (six apparatuses)
2. Alberto Braglia, Italy, 115 (five apparatuses)
2. Alberto Braglia, Italy, 95 (six apparatuses)
3. Georges Charmoille, France, 113 (five apparatuses)
3. Georges Charmoille, France, 94 (six apparatuses)

1904 1. Julius Lenhart, Austria, 69.80
2. Wilhelm Weber, Germany, 69.10
3. Adolf Spinnler, Switzerland, 67.99

1900 1. Gustave Sandras, France, 302
2. Noel Bas, France, 295
3. Lucien Demanet, France, 293

1896 **Not held**

333

Gymnastics, Artistic — Men's Team (Combined Exercises)

1988 1. Soviet Union, 593.350, Vladimir Gogoladze, Vladimir Novikov, Serguei Kharikov, Dmitri Bilozertchev, Vladimir Artemov, Valeri Lioukine
2. East Germany, 588.450, Ulf Hoffman, Andreas Wecker, Sven Tippelt, Ralf Buechner, Holger Behrendt, Sylvio Kroll
3. Japan, 585.600, Hiroyuki Konishi, Takahiro Yamada, Toshiharu Sato, Daisuke Nishikawa, Koichi Mizushima, Yukio Iketani

1984 1. USA, 591.40, Scott Johnson, James Hartung, Timothy Daggett, Bart Conner, Peter Vidmar, Mitchell Gaylor
2. China, 590.80, Yuejiu Li, Xiaoping Li, Yun Lou, Zhigiang Xu, Fei Tong, Ning Li
3. Japan, 586.70, Shinji Morisue, Noritoshi Hirata, Nobuyuki Kajitani, Kyoji Yamawaki, Koji Sotomura, Koji Gushiken

1980 1. Soviet Union, 589.60, Nikolai Andrianov, Eduard Azaryan, Bogdan Makuts, Vladimir Markelov, Aleksandr Dityatin, Aleksandr Tkachov
2. East Germany, 581.15, Lutz Mack, Ralf-Peter Hemman, Lutz Hoffmann, Michael Nikolay, Andreas Bronst, Roland Brueckner
3. Hungary, 575.00, Ferenc Donath, Gyorgy Guczoghy, Zoltan Keleman, Peter Kovacs, Istvan Vamos, Dr. Zoltan Magyar

1976 1. Japan, 576.85, Sawao Kato, Hiroshi Kajiyama, Eizo Kenmotsu, Hisato Igarashi, Shun Fujimoto, Mitsuo Tukahara
2. Soviet Union, 576.45, Nikolai Andrianov, Vladimir Markelov, Aleksandr Dityatin, Gennady Kryssin, Vladimir Marchenko, Vladimir Tikhonov
3. East Germany, 564.65, Lutz Mack, Bernd Jaeger, Michael Nikolay, Roland Brueckner, Wolfgang Klotz, Rainer Hanschke

1972 1. Japan, 571.25, Sawao Kato, Eizo Kenmotsu, Shigeru Kasamatsu, Akinori Nakayama, Mitsuo Tsukahara, Teruichi Okamura
2. Soviet Union, 564.05, Nikolai Andrianov, Mickail Voronin, Viktor Klimenko, Edvard Mikhaelyan, Aleksandr Maleyev, Vladimir Shukin
3. East Germany, 559.70, Klaus Koste, Matthias Brehme, Wolfgang Thune, Wolfgang Klotz, Reinhard Rychly, Jurgen Paeke

1968 1. Japan, 575.90, Sawao Kato, Akinori Nakayama, Eizo Kenmotsu, Takeshi Kato, Yukio Endo, Mitsuo Tsukahara
2. Soviet Union, 571.10, Mikhail Voronin, Sergei Diomidov, Viktor Klimenko, Valeri Karassev, Viktor Lisitski, Valeri Ilyinykh

3. East Germany, 557.15, Matthias Brehme, Klaus Koste, Siegfried Fulle, Peter Weber, Gerhard Dietrich, Gunter Beier

1964 1. Japan, 577.95, Yukio Endo, Shuji Tsurumi, Haruhiro Yamashita, Takuji Hayata, Takashi Mitsukuri, Takashi Ono
2. Soviet Union, 575.45, Boris Shakhlin, Viktor Lisitsky, Viktor Leontyer, Yuri Tsapenko, Yuri Titov, Sergei Diomidov
3. West Germany, 565.10, Siegfried Fulle, Klaus Koste, Erwin Koppe, Peter Weber, Philipp Furst, Gunter Lyhs

1960 1. Japan, 575.20, Takashi Ono, Shuji Tsurumi, Yukio Endo, Masao Takemoto, Nobuyuki Aihara, Takashi Mitsukuri
2. Soviet Union, 572.70, Boris Shakhlin, Yuri Titov, Albert Azaryan, Vladimir Portnoi, Nikolai Miligulo, Valeri Kerdemelidi
3. Italy, 559.05, Franco Menichelli, Giovanni Carminucci, Angelo Vicardi, Pasquale Carminucci, Orlando Polmonari, Gianfranco Marzolla

1956 1. Soviet Union, 568.25, Viktor Chukarin, Yuri Titov, Valentin Muratov, Albert Azaryan, Boris Shakhlin, Pavel Stolbov
2. Japan, 566.40, Takashi Ono, Masao Takemoto, Masami Kubota, Nobuyuki Aihara, Shinsaku Tsukawaki, Akira Kono
3. Finland, 555.95, Kalevi Suoniemi, Berndt Lindfors, Martti Mansikka, Onni Lappalainen, Olavi Leimuvirta, Raimo Heinonen

1952 1. Soviet Union, 574.40, Viktor Chukarin, Grant Shaginyan, Valentin Muratov, Yergeny Korolkov, Vladimir Belyakov, Josif Berdijev, Mikhail Perelman, Dmitri Leonkin
2. Switzerland, 567.50, Josef Stalder, Hans Eugster, Jean Tschabold, Jack Gunthard, Melchior Thalmann, Ernst Gebendinger, Hans Schwarzentruber, Ernst Fivian
3. Finland, 564.20, Onni Lappalainen, Berndt Lindfors, Paavo Aaltonen, Kaino Lempinen, Heikki Savolainen, Kalevi Laitinen, Kalevi Viskari, Olavi Rove

1948 1. Finland, 1358.30, Veikko Huhtanen, Paavo Aaltonen, Kalevi Laitinen, Olavi Rove, Einari Terasvirta, Heikki Savolainen
2. Switzerland, 1356.70, Walter Lehmann, Josef Stalder, Christian Kipfer, Emil Studer, Robert Lucy, Michael Reusch
3. Hungary, 1330.85, Lajos Toth, Dr. Lajos Santha, Laszlo Baranyai, Ferenc Pataki, Janos Mogyorosi-Klencs, Ferenc Varkoi

1936 1. Germany, 657.430, Alfred Schwarzmann, Konrad Frey, Matthias Volz, Willi Stadel, Franz Beckert, Walter Steffens
2. Switzerland, 654.802, Eugen Mack, Michael Reusch, Edi Steinemann, Walter Bach, Albert Bachmann, Georges Miez

334

3. Finland, 638.468, Martti Uosikkinen, Heikki Savolainen, Mauri Noroma-Nyberg, Aleksanteri Saarvala, Esa Seeste, Veikko Pakarinen

1932 1. Italy, 541.850, Romeo Neri, Mario Lertora, Savino Guglielmetti, Oreste Capuzzo

2. USA, 522.275, Frank Haubold, Frederick Meyer, Alfred Jochim, Frank Cumiskey

3. Finland, 509.995, Heikki Savolainen, Mauri Noroma-Nyberg, Veikko Pakarinen, Einari Terasvirta

1928 1. Switzerland, 1718.625, Georges Miez, Hermann Hanggi, Eugen Mack, Melchior Wetzel, Edi Steinemann, August Guttinger, Hans Grieder, Otto Pfister

2. Czechoslovakia, 1712.250, Ladislav Vacha, Emanuel Loffler, Jan Gajdos, Josef Effenberger, Bedrich Supcik, Vaclav Vesely, Jan Koutny, Ladislav Tikal

3. Yugoslavia, 1648.750, Leon Stukelj, Josip Primozic, Anton Malej, Eduard Antosiewicz, Boris Gregorka, Ivan Porenta, Stane Derganc, Dragutin Ciotti

1924 1. Italy, 839.058, Ferdinando Mandrini, Mario Lertora, Vittorio Lucchetti, Francesco Martino, Luigi Cambiaso, Giuseppe Paris, Giorgio Zampori, Luigi Maiocco

2. France, 820.528, Jean Gounot, Leon Delsarte, Albert Seguin, Eugene Cordonnier, Francois Gangloff, Arthur Hermann, Andre Higelin, Joseph Huber

3. Switzerland, 816.661, August Guttinger, Jean Gutweniger, Hans Grieder, Georges Miez, Josef Wilhelm, Otto Pfister, Carl Widmer, Antoine Rebetez

1920 1. Italy, 359.855, Arnaldo Andreoli, Pietro Bianchi, Ettore Bellotto, Luigi Cambiaso, Luigi Contessi, Carlo Costigliolo, Luigi Costigliolo, Fernando Bonatti, Giuseppe Domenichelli, Roberto Ferrari, Carlo Fregosi, Romualdo Ghiglione, Ambrogio Levati, Francesco Loy, Vittorio Lucchetti, Luigi Maiocco, Fernando Mandrini, Gianni Mangiante, Renzo Mangiante, Antonio Marovelli, Michele Mastromarino, Giuseppe Paris, Manlio Pastorini, Ezio Roselli, Paolo Salvi, Giovan Battista Tubino, Giorgio Zampori, Angelo Zorzi

2. Belgium, 346.785, Eugenius Auwerkerken, Theophile Bauer, Francois Claessens, Auguste Cootmans, Frans Gibens, Jean Van Guysse, Albert Haepers, Dominique Jacobs, Felicien Kempeneers, Jules Labeeu, Hubert Lafortune, Auguste Landrieu, Charles Lannie, Constant Loriot, Alphonse Van Mele, Ferdinand Minnaert, Nicolas Moerloos, Louis Stoop, Francois Verboven, Jean Verboven, Julien Verdonck, Joseph Verstraeten, Georges Vivex, Julianus Wagemans

3. France, 340.100, Emile Bouches, Paul J. Durin, Paulin A. Lemaire, Georges Berger, Leon Delsarte, Georges Duvant, Louis Kempe, Lucien Demanet, Auguste Hoel, Rene Boulanger, Fernand Fauconnier, Albert Hersoy, Georges Lagouge, Ernest Lespinasse, Jules Pirard, Julien Wartelle, Paul Wartelle, Emile Martel, Georges Thurnherr, Alfred Buyenne, Eugene Cordonnier, Arthur Hermann, Andre Higelin, Eugene Pollet

1912 1. Italy, 265.75, Guido Boni, Giuseppe Domenichelli, Luciano Savorini, Guido Romano, Angelo Zorzi, Giorgio Zampori, Gianni Mangiante, Renzo Mangiante, Adolfo Tunesi, Pietro Bianchi, Paolo Salvi, Alberto Braglia, Alfredo Gollini, Serafino Mazzarocchi, Francesco Loy, Carlo Fregosi

2. Hungary, 227.25, Jozsef Bittenbinder, Imre Erdoby, Samu Foti, Imre Gellert, Gyozo Haberfeld, Otto Hellmich, Istvan Herezeg, Jozsef Keresztessy, Lajos Kmetyko, Janos Krizmanich, Elemer Paszty, Arpad Pedery, Jeno Rittich, Ferene Szuts, Odon Tery, Geza Tuli

3. Great Britain, 184.50, Albert E. Betts, Harry Dickason, Samuel Hodgetts, Alfred W. Messenger, Edward E. Pepper, Charles A. Vigurs, Samuel John Walker, John Whitaker, Sidney Cross, Bernard W. Franklin, Edward W. Potts, Reginald H. Potts, George J. Ross, Henry A. Oberholzer, Charles Simmons, Arthur George Southern, Ronald G. McLean, Charles James Luck, Herbert J. Drury, William MacKune, William Titt, William Cowhig, Leonard Hanson

1908 1. Sweden, 438, Gosta Asbrink, Carl Bertilsson, Andreas Cervin, Hjalmar Cedercrona, Rudolf Degermark, Carl W. Folcker, Sven Forssman, Erik G. Granfelt, Carl Harleman, Nils E. Hellsten, Gunnar Hojer, Arvid Holmberg, Carl Holmberg, Osvald Holmberg, Hugo Jahnke, John Jarlen, Harald Jonsson, Rolf Jonsson, Nils G. Kantzow, Sven Landberg, Olle Lanner, Axel Ljung, Ossvald Moberg, Carl M. Norberg, Erik Norberg, Thor Norberg, Axel Norling, Daniel Norling, Gosta Olsson, Leonhard Peterson, Sven Rosen, Gustaf Rosenquist, Axel Sjoblom, Birger Sorvik, Haakon Sorvik, Karl-Johan Svensson, Karl-Gustaf Vingqvist, Nils Widforss

2. Norway, 425, Arthur Amundsen, Carl A. Andersen, Otto Authen, Hermann Bohne, Trygve Boysen, Oskar W. Bye, Conrad Carlsrud, Sverre Groner, Harald Halvorsen, Harald Hansen, Petter Hol, Eugen Ingebretsen, Ole Iversen, Mathias Jespersen, Sigge Johannesen, Nicolai Kior, Karl Klaeth, Thor Larsen, Rolf Lefdahl, Hans Lem, Anders Moen, Fridtjof Olsen, Carl A. Pedersen, Paul Pedersen, John Skrataas, Harald Smedvik, Sigvard Sivertsen, Andreas Strand, Olaf Syvertsen, Thomas Thorstensen

3. Finland, 405, Eino Forsstrom, Otto Granstrom, Johan Kemp, Jivari Kyykoski, Heikki Lehmusto, John Lindroth, Yrjo Linko, Edvard Linna, Matti Markanen, Kalle Mikkolainen, Veli Nieminen, Kalle K. Paasia, Arvi Pohjanpaa, Aarne Pohjonen, Eino Railio, Heikki Riipinen, Arno Saarinen, Einari V. Sahlstein, Arne Salovaara, Kaarlo Sandelin, Elias Sipila, Viktor Smeds, Kaarlo Soinio, Kurt E. Stenberg, Vaino Tiiri, Magnus Wegelius

1906   1. Norway, 19.00, Carl A. Andersen, Oskar W. Bye, Conrad Carlsrud, Harald A. Eriksen, Osvald Falch, Christian Fjeringen, Yngvar Fredriksen, Karl J. Haagensen, Harald Halvorsen, Petter Hol, Andreas Hagelund, Eugen Ingebretsen, Mathias Jespersen, Finn Munster, Fridtjof Olsen, Carl A. Pedersen, Rasmus Pettersen, Thorleif Pettersen, Thorleif Rehn, Johan Stumpf

2. Denmark, 18.00, Carl Andersen, Halvor Birch, H. Bukdahl, K. Gnudtzmann, Knud Holm, Erik Klem, Harald Klem, R. Kraft, Edvard Larsen, J. Lorentzen, Robert Madsen, C. Manicus-Hansen, Oluf Olsen, Christian Petersen, Hans Pedersen, Niels Petersen, Viktor Rasmussen, M. K. Skram-Jensen, Marius Thuesen

3. Italy, 16.71, Manlio Pastorini, Spartaco Nerozzi, Federico Bertinotti, Vitaliano Masotti, Raffaello Giannoni, Quintillo Mazzoncini, Azeglio Innocenti, Filiberto Innocenti, Ciro Civinini, Maurizio Masetti

1904   1. Philadelphia, 374.43, Julius Lenhart, Philipp Kassel, Anton Heida, Max Hess, Ernst Reckeweg, John Grieb

2. New York, 356.37, Otto Steffen, John Bissinger, Emil Beyer, Max Wolf, Julian Schmitz, Arthur Rosenkampf

3. Chicago, 349.69, George Mayer, John Duha, Edward Siegler, Phillip Schuster, Robert Mayack, Charles Krause

1896-
1900   Not held

Gymnastics, Artistic — Men's Floor Exercise

1988   1. Serguei Kharihov, Soviet Union, 19.925

2. Vladimir Artemov, Soviet Union, 19.900
3. Yukio Iketani, Japan, 19.850
3. Yun Lou, People's Republic of China, 19.850

1984   1. Ning Li, China, 19.925
2. Yun Lou, China, 19.775
3. Koji Sotomura, Japan, 19.700
3. Philippe Vatuone, France, 19.700

1980   1. Roland Bruckner, East Germany, 19.750
2. Nikolai Andrianov, Soviet Union, 19.725
3. Aleksandr Dityatin, Soviet Union, 19.700

1976   1. Nikolai Andrianov, Soviet Union, 19.450
2. Vladimir Marchenko, Soviet Union, 19.425
3. Peter Kormann, USA, 19.300

1972   1. Nikolai Andrianov, Soviet Union, 19.175
2. Akinori Nakayama, Japan, 19.125
3. Shigeru Kasamatsu, Japan, 19.025

1968   1. Sawao Kato, Japan, 19.475
2. Akinori Nakayama, Japan, 19.400
3. Takeshi Kato, Japan, 19.275

1964   1. Franco Menichelli, Italy, 19.450
2. Yukio Endo, Japan, 19.350

1960   2. Viktor Lisitski, Soviet Union, 19.350
1. Nobuyuki Aihara, Japan, 19.450
2. Yuri Titov, Soviet Union, 19.325
3. Franco Menichelli, Italy, 19.275

1956   1. Valentin Muratov, Soviet Union, 19.20
2. Nobuyuki Aihara, Japan, 19.10
2. Viktor Chukarin, Soviet Union, 19.10
2. William Thoresson, Sweden, 19.10

1952   1. William Thoresson, Sweden, 19.25
2. Tadao Uesako, Japan, 19.15
3. Jerzy Jokiel, Poland, 19.15

1948   1. Ferenc Pataki, Hungary, 38.70
2. Janos Magyorosi-Klencs, Hungary, 38.40
3. Zdenek Ruzicka, Czechoslovakia, 38.10

1936   1. Georges Miez, Switzerland, 18.666
2. Josef Walter, Switzerland, 18.500
3. Konrad Frey, Germany, 18.466
3. Eugen Mack, Switzerland, 18.466

1932   1. Istvan Pelle, Hungary, 9.60
2. Georges Miez, Switzerland, 9.47
3. Mario Lertora, Italy, 9.23

1896-
1928   Not held

Gymnastics, Artistic — Men's Horizontal Bar

1988   1. Vladimir Artemov, Soviet Union, 19.90
1. Valeri Lioukine, Soviet Union, 19.90
2. No award
3. Holger Behrendt, East Germany, 19.800
3. Marius Gherman, Romania, 19.800

1984   1. Shinji Morisue, Japan, 20.000
2. Tong Fei, China, 19.975
3. Koji Gushiken, Japan, 19.950

1980   1. Stoian Delchev, Bulgaria, 19.825
2. Aleksandr Dityatin, Soviet Union, 19.750

336

3. Nikolai Andrianov, Soviet Union, 19.675
1976 1. Mitsuo Tsukahara, Japan, 19.675
2. Eizo Kenmotsu, Japan, 19.500
3. Henri Boerio, France, 19.475
3. Eberhard Gienger, West Germany, 19.475
1972 1. Mitsuo Tsukahara, Japan, 19.725
2. Sawao Kato, Japan, 19.525
3. Shigeru Kasamatsu, Japan, 19.450
1968 1. Akinori Nakayama, Japan, 19.550
1. Mikhail Voronin, Soviet Union, 19.550
3. Eizo Kenmotsu, Japan, 19.375
1964 1. Boris Shakhlin, Soviet Union, 19.625
2. Yuri Titov, Soviet Uhion, 19.550
3. Miroslav Cerar, Yugoslavia, 19.500
1960 1. Takashi Ono, Japan, 19.600
2. Masao Takemoto, Japan, 19.525
3. Boris Shakhlin, Soviet Union, 19.475
1956 1. Takashi Ono, Japan, 19.60
2. Yuri Titov, Soviet Union, 19.40
3. Masao Takemoto, Japan, 19.30
1952 1. Jack Gunthard, Switzerland, 19.55
2. Alfred Schwarzmann, Germany, 19.50
2. Josef Stalder, Switzerland, 19.50
1948 1. Josef Stalder, Switzerland, 39.70
2. Walter Lehmann, Switzerland, 39.40
3. Veikko Huhtanen, Finland, 39.20
1936 1. Aleksanteri Saarvala, Finland, 19.367
2. Konrad Frey, Germany, 19.267
3. Alfred Schwarzmann, Germany, 19.233
1932 1. Dallas Bixler, USA, 18.33
2. Heikki Savolainen, Finland, 18.07
3. Einari Terasvirta, Finland, 18.07
1928 1. Georges Miez, Switzerland, 19.17
2. Romeo Neri, Italy, 19.00
3. Eugen Mack, Switzerland, 18.92
1924 1. Leon Stukelj, Yugoslavia, 19.730
2. Jean Gutweniger, Switzerland, 19.236
3. Andre Higelin, France, 19.163
1906-
1920 **Not held**
1904 1. Anton Heida, USA, 40
1. Edward Hennig, USA, 40
3. George Eyser, USA, 39
1900 **Not held**
1896 1. Hermann Weingartner, Germany
2. Alfred Flatow, Germany

Gymnastics, Artistic — Men's Parallel Bars

1988 1. Vladimir Artemov, Soviet Union, 19.925
2. Valeri Lioukine, Soviet Union, 19.900
3. Sven Tippelt, East Germany, 19.750
1984 1. Bart Conner, USA, 19.950
2. Nobuyuki Kajitani, Japan, 19.925
3. Mitchell Gaylord, USA, 19.850
1980 1. Aleksandr Tkachyov, Soviet Union, 19.775
2. Aleksandr Dityatin, Soviet Union, 19.750
3. Roland Bruckner, German Democratic Repubilc, 19.650
1976 1. Sawao Kato, Japan, 19.675
2. Nikolai Andrianov, Soviet Union, 19.500
3. Mitsuo Tsukahara, Japan, 19.475

1972 1. Sawao Kato, Japan, 19.475
2. Shigeru Kasamatsu, Japan, 19.375
3. Eizo Kenmotsu, Japan, 19.250
1968 1. Akinori Nakayama, Japan, 19.475
2. Mikhail Voronin, Soviet Union, 19.425
3. Vladimir Klimenko, Soviet Union, 19.225
1964 1. Yukio Endo, Japan, 19.675
2. Shuji Tsurumi, Japan, 19.450
3. Franco Menichelli, Italy, 19.350
1960 1. Boris Shakhlin, Soviet Union, 19.400
2. Giovanni Carminucci, Italy, 19.375
3. Takashi Ono, Japan, 19.350
1956 1. Viktor Chukarin, Soviet Union, 19.20
2. Masami Kubota, Japan, 19.15
3. Takashi Ono, Japan, 19.10
3. Masao Takemoto, Japan, 19.10
1952 1. Hans Eugster, Switzerland, 19.65
2. Viktor Chukarin, Soviet Union, 19.60
3. Josef Stalder, Switzerland, 19.50
1948 1. Michael Reusch, Switzerland, 19.75
2. Veikko Huhtanen, Finland, 19.65
3. Christian Kipfer, Switzerland, 19.55
3. Josef Stalder, Switzerland, 19.55
1936 1. Konrad Frey, Germany, 19.067
2. Michael Reusch, Switzerland, 19.034
3. Alfred Schwarzmann, Germany, 18.967
1932 1. Romeo Neri, Italy, 18.97
2. Istvan Pelle, Hungary, 18.60
3. Heikki Savolainen, Finland, 18.27
1928 1. Ladislav Vacha, Czechoslovakia, 18.83
2. Josip Primozic, Yugoslavia, 18.50
3. Hermann Hanggi, Switzerland, 18.08
1924 1. August Guttinger, Switzerland, 21.63
2. Robert Prazak, Czechoslovakia, 21.61
3. Giorgio Zampori, Italy, 21.45
1908-
1920 **Not held**
1904 1. George Eyser, USA, 44
2. Anton Heida, USA, 43
3. John Duha, USA, 40
1900 **Not held**
1896 1. Alfred Flatow, Germany
2. Louis Zutter, Germany
3. Hermann Weingartner, Germany

Gymnastics, Artistic — Men's Pommel Horse

1988 1. Dmitri Bilozertchev, Soviet Union, 19.950
1. Zsolt Borkai, Hungary, 19.950
1. Lyubomir Gueraskov, Bulgaria 19.950
2. No award
3. No award
1984 1. Ning Li, China, 19.950
1. Peter Vidmar, USA, 19.950
3. Timothy Daggett, USA, 19.825
1980 1. Zoltan Magyar, Hungary, 19.925
2. Aleksandr Dityatin, Soviet Union, 19.800
3. Michael Nikolay, East Germany, 19.775
1976 1. Zoltan Magyar, Hungary, 19.700
2. Eizo Kenmotsu, Japan, 19.575
3. Nikolai Andrianov, Soviet Union, 19.525
3. Michael Nikolay, East Germany, 19.525

337

1972 1. Viktor Klimenko, Soviet Union, 19.125	**1968** 1. Akinori Nakayama, Japan, 19.450

1972 1. Viktor Klimenko, Soviet Union, 19.125
     2. Sawao Kato, Japan, 19.000
     3. Eizo Kenmotsu, Japan, 18.950
1968 1. Miroslav Cerar, Yugoslavia, 19.325
     2. Olli E. Laiho, Finland, 19.225
     3. Mikhail Voronin, Soviet Union, 19.200
1964 1. Miroslav Cerar, Yugoslavia, 19,525
     2. Shuji Tsurumi, Japan, 19.325
     3. Yuri Tsapenko, Soviet Union, 19.200
1960 1. Eugen Ekman, Finland, 19.375
     1. Boris Shakhlin, Soviet Union, 19.375
     3. Shuji Tsurumi, Japan, 19.150
1956 1. Boris Shakhlin, Soviet Union, 19.25
     2. Takashi Ono, Japan, 19.20
     3. Viktor Chukarin, Soviet Union, 19.10
1952 1. Viktor Chukarin, Soviet Union, 19.50
     2. Yevgeny Korolkov, Soviet Union, 19.40
     3. Grant Shaginyan, Soviet Union, 19.40
1948 1. Paavo Aaltonen, Finland, 38.70
     1. Veikko Huhtanen, Finland, 38.70
     1. Heikki Savolainen, Finland, 38.70
     2. Luigi Zanetti, Italy, 38.30
     3. Guido Figone, Italy, 38.20
1936 1. Konrad Frey, Germany, 19.333
     2. Eugen Mack, Switzerland, 19.167
     3. Albert Bachmann, Switzerland, 19.067
1932 1. Istvan Pelle, Hungary, 19.07
     2. Omero Bonoli, Italy, 18.87
     3. Frank Haubold, USA, 18.57
1928 1. Hermann Hanggi, Switzerland, 19.75
     2. Georges Miez, Switzerland, 19.25
     3. Heikki Savolainen, Finland, 18.83
1924 1. Josef Wilhelm, Switzerland, 21.23
     2. Jean Gutweniger, Switzerland, 21.13
     3. Antoine Rebetez, Switzerland, 20.73
1906-
1920 **Not held**
1904 1. Anton Heida, USA, 42
     2. George Eyser, USA, 33
     3. William Merz, USA, 29
1900 **Not held**
1896 1. Louis Zutter, Switzerland
     2. Hermann Weingartner, Germany

1968 1. Akinori Nakayama, Japan, 19.450
     2. Mikhail Voronin, Soviet Union, 19.325
     3. Sawao Kato, Japan, 19.225
1964 1. Takuji Hayata, Japan, 19.475
     2. Franco Menichelli, Italy, 19.425
     3. Boris Shacklin, Soviet Union, 19.400
1960 1. Albert Azaryan, Soviet Union, 19.725
     2. Boris Shakhlin, Soviet Union, 19.500
     3. Welik Kapsazow, Bulgaria, 19.425
     3. Takashi Ono, Japan, 19.425
1956 1. Albert Azaryan, Soviet Union, 19.35
     2. Valentin Muratov, Soviet Union, 19.15
     3. Masami Kubota, Japan, 19.10
     3. Masao Takemoto, Japan, 19.10
1952 1. Grant Shaginyan, Soviet Union, 19.75
     2. Viktor Chukarin, Soviet Union, 19.55
     3. Hans Eugster, Switzerland, 19.40
     3. Dmitri Leonkin, Soviet Union, 19.40
1948 1. Karl Frei, Switzerland, 39.60
     2. Michael Reusch, Switzerland, 39.10
     3. Zdenek Ruzicka, Czechoslovakia, 38.50
1936 1. Alois Hudec, Czechoslovakia, 19.433
     2. Leon Stukelj, Yugoslavia, 18.867
     3. Matthias Volz, Germany, 18.667
1932 1. George Gulack, USA, 18.97
     2. William Denton, USA, 18.60
     3. Giovanni Lattuada, Italy, 18.50
1928 1. Leon Stukelj, Yugoslavia, 19.25
     2. Ladislav Vacha, Czechoslovakia, 19.17
     3. Emanuel Loffler, Czechoslovakia, 18.83
1924 1. Francesco Martino, Italy, 21.553
     2. Robert Prazak, Czechoslovakia, 21.483
     3. Ladislav Vacha, Czechoslovakia, 21.430
1906-
1920 **Not held**
1904 1. Hermann Glass, USA, 45
     2. William Merz, USA, 35
     3. Emil Voigt, USA, 32
1900 **Not held**
1896 1. Ioannis Metropoulos, Greece
     2. Hermann Weingartner, Germany
     3. Petros Persakis, Greece

Gymnastics, Artistic — Men's Still Rings

1988 1. Holger Behrendt, East Germany, 19.925
     1. Dmitri Bilozertchev, Soviet Union, 19.925
     2. No award
     3. Sven Tippelt, East Germany, 19.875
1984 1. Koji Gushiken, Japan, 19.850
     1. Li Ning, China, 19.850
     3. Mitchell Gaylord, USA, 19.825
1980 1. Aleksandr Dityatin, Soviet Union, 19.875
     2. Aleksandr Tkachyov, Soviet Union, 19.725
     3. Jiri Tabak, Czechoslovakia, 19.600
1976 1. Nikolai Andrianov, Soviet Union, 19.650
     2. Aleksandr Dityatin, Soviet Union, 19.550
     3. Danut Grecu, Romania, 19.500
1972 1. Akinori Nakayama, Japan, 19.350
     2. Mikhail Voronin, Soviet Union, 19.275
     3. Mitsuo Tsukahara, Japan, 19.225

Gymnastics, Artistic — Men's Horse Vault

1988 1. Yun Lou, People's Republic of China, 19.875
     2. Sylvio Kroll, East Germany, 19.862
     3. Jong-hoon Park, South Korea, 19.775
1984 1. Yun Lou, China, 19.950
     2. Mitchell Gaylord, USA, 19.825
     2. Koji Gushiken, Japan, 19.825
     2. Shinji Morisue, Japan, 19.825
     2. Li Ning, China, 19.825
1980 1. Nikolai Andrianov, Soviet Union, 19.825
     2. Aleksandr Dityatin, Soviet Union, 19.800
     3. Roland Bruckner, East Germany, 19.775
1976 1. Nikolai Andrianov, Soviet Union, 19.450
     2. Mitsuo Tsukahara, Japan, 19.375
     3. Hiroshi Kajiyama, Japan, 19.275
1972 1. Klaus Koste, East Germany, 18.850
     2. Viktor Klimenko, Soviet Union, 18.825

Italy's Alberto Braglia was the first gymnast to win two consecutive Olympic gold medals in the individual combined exercises, in 1908 and 1912. He also collected a team gold in 1912.

Scoring the first perfect 10.0 in Olympic gymnastics history for her performance on the uneven bars, Romanian gymnast Nadia Comaneci also captured the individual all-around gold in 1976.

3. Nikolai Andrianov, Soviet Union, 18.800
1968 1. Mikhail Voronin, Soviet Union, 19.000
2. Yukio Endo, Japan, 18.950
3. Sergei Diomidov, Soviet Union, 18.925
1964 1. Haruhiro Yamashita, Japan, 19.600
2. Viktor Lisitski, Soviet Union, 19.325
3. Hannu Rantakari, Finland, 19.300
1960 1. Takashi Ono, Japan, 19.350
1. Boris Shakhlin, Soviet Union, 19.350
3. Vladimir Portnoi, Soviet Union, 19.225
1956 1. Helmut Bantz, West Germany, 18.85
1. Valentin Muratov, Soviet Union, 18.85
3. Yuri Titov, Soviet Union, 18.75
1952 1. Viktor Chukarin, Soviet Union, 19.20
2. Masao Takemoto, Japan, 19.15
3. Takashi Ono, Japan, 19.10
3. Tadao Uesako, Japan, 19.10
1948 1. Paavo Aaltonen, Finland, 39.10
2. Olavi Rove, Finland, 39.00
3. Janos Mogyorosi-Klencs, Hungary, 38.50
3. Ferenc Pataki, Hungary, 38.50

3. Leo Sotornik, Czechoslovakia, 38.50
1936 1. Alfred Schwarzmann, Germany, 19,200
2. Eugen Mack, Switzerland, 18.967
3. Matthias Volz, Germany, 18.467
1932 1. Savino Guglielmetti, Italy, 18.03
2. Alfred Jochim, USA, 17.77
3. Edward Carmichael, USA, 17.53
1928 1. Eugen Mack, Switzerland, 9.58
2. Emanuel Loffler, Czechoslovakia, 9.50
3. Stane Derganc, Yugoslavia, 9.46
1924 1. Frank Kriz, USA, 9.98
2. Jan Koutny, Czechoslovakia, 9.97
3. Bohumil Morkovsky, Czechoslovakia, 9.93
1906-1920 Not held
1904 1. George Eyser, USA, 36
1. Anton Heida, USA, 36
3. William Merz, USA, 31
1900 Not held
1896 1. Carl Schuhmann, Germany
2. Louis Zutter, Switzerland

WOMEN'S GYMNASTICS EVENTS
▼

HIGHLIGHTS

Gymnastics competition for women was introduced in 1928, but awards were only presented for the team combined exercises. The individual events, added in 1952, were soon dominated by Eastern Europeans, especially the Soviets. Until the 1980s, women's (and men's) gymnastics stressed grace and style as much as athletic power, which is now the trend in the sport.

Larissa Latynina of the Soviet Union won a record-setting 18 medals between 1956 and 1964, including nine golds (a female Olympics record), five silvers, and four bronzes. She was followed by Czech gymnast Vera Cáslavská, who won seven individual golds in 1964 and 1968 (also a record) to add to four silver medals. Hungary's Ágnes Keleti won ten Olympic medals from 1948 through 1956, including five gold, four silver, and one bronze.

Individual All-Around Combined Exercises, Artistic: For women the individual all-around (combined exercises) event was first held in 1952. Women's combined exercises include the balance beam, the horse vault, uneven bars, and floor exercises. In 1960 the Soviet Union's Larissa Latynina won her second medal for individual combined exercises.

Czechoslovakia's Vera Cáslavská dominated the women's competitions in 1964 and again in 1968. Four years later Soviet gymnast Olga Korbut won fans around the world without placing in this event; her teammate Ludmila Tourischeva captured the 1972 gold, settling for bronze four years later behind her teammate, silver-medalist Nelli Kim. By 1976 Romania's Nadia Comaneci had become the new darling, taking a gold in this event; she came back, missing the gold by 0.075 points, to tie for the silver in 1980.

Continuing the tradition of pixie-like television favorites, Mary Lou Retton became the first American to win this event in 1984. Retton beat Romanian rival Ecaterina Szabo by only 0.05 points for the individual gold, the closest women's margin. Part of what helped her win that score was her unique (among women) mastery of the full-twisting layout double Tsukahara on the vault, a maneuver only a few men in the world could manage in 1984. Retton also defied gender in the type of floor exercises she could pull off, including a layout double back somersault.

Elena Shushunova edged Romanian Daniela Silivas for the all-around title in 1988. The decision came down to the final vault, in which Shushunova performed her trademark full-twisting Yurchenko.

Team Combined Exercises: The American women's best results in Olympic gymnastics before 1984 was a team bronze in 1948, when the judging was held to be highly questionable. That year the Czech team lost one of its members to infantile paralysis while in London and still managed to win the gold. Soviet women dominated this competition beginning in 1952, retaining the title until the 1984 boycott. That year Romania claimed the gold by one point over the US team, with China earning a bronze.

In 1988 Elena Shushunova led the Soviet women's team to the team gold ahead of the Romananians. A questionable ruling cost the US women's team the bronze medal, when East German official Ellen Berger assessed a harsh penalty of 0.5 point for an arguable infraction; the US lost their medal to East Germany by 0.3 point. Two days after the decision, gymnastics rules were changed to prevent similar actions in the future.

Balance Beam: Eva Bosáková of the Soviet Union took the silver in 1956 and returned four years later for the gold in Rome, where Czech Vera Cáslavská placed sixth. The Czech was back for the gold in 1964 and the silver in 1968. The darling of the 1972 Games, Soviet gymnast Olga Korbut, was the first Olympic competitor ever to perform a backflip on the balance beam, as her daring earned her the gold. In Montréal she settled for silver behind the next sensation, Romania's Comaneci, who again captured the gold in 1980.

The US recorded a medal in 1984, as Kathy Johnson took a bronze. She trailed two Romananians, Simona Pauca and Ecaterina Szabo. US gymnast Phoebe Mills was her country's only medalist in 1988, claiming a bronze on the beam behind silver medalist Elena Shoushounova of the Soviet Union and gold keeper Daniela Silivas of Romania.

Floor Exercise: Agnes Keleti of Hungary swept the first two golds in 1952 and 1956, followed by back-to-back golds in 1960 and 1964 for the Soviet Union's Larissa Latynina. Czech gymnast Vera Cáslavská tied for the gold in 1968 with Soviet gymnast Larissa Petrik.

Olga Korbut of the USSR captured the floor exercise gold in 1972, ahead of Lyudmila Tourischeva of the USSR. Tourischeva took second again in 1976, behind teammate Nelli Kim. Kim captured the floor exercise gold that year with a perfect 10.0 score, then silver medaled in 1980 behind Romania's Comaneci. Kim was officiating gymnastics at the Seoul Games in 1988.

In 1984 Ecaterina Szabo of Romania triumphed in the floor exercise, ahead of US gymnast Julianne McNamara and her teammate, Mary Lou Retton. Daniela Silivas of Romania reigned in Seoul.

Uneven Bars: 35-year-old Hungarian Agnes Keleti defied age and won the gold in 1956. A younger Polina Astakhova of the Soviet Union captured the gold in 1960 and 1964. East German Karin Janz warmed up with the silver in 1968 before taking the gold in 1972. She placed ahead of silver medalist Olga Korbut of the USSR, who captured the world's hearts instead.

In 1976 Romananian Nadia Comaneci on the uneven bars posted the first perfect 10.0 scores ever in Olympic competition, becoming the story of the Games; she was only 14 years old when she captured the gold in this event.

Three tied for bronze at the Moscow Games, as Maria Filatova of the Soviet Union, Steffi Kraeker of East Germany, and Melita Ruhn of Romania settled for thirds. In 1984 Yanhong Ma of China tied with Julianne McNamara of the US for the gold, ahead of bronze medalist Mary Lou Retton. In Seoul, Romanian Silivas struck gold again and Soviet Elena Shoushounova nabbed the bronze behind East German Dagmar Kersten.

Horse Vault: Czech gymnast Vera Cáslavská grabbed the gold in 1964 and 1968. Nelli Kim of the USSR earned perfect 10.0 scores vaulting the horse in 1976. In 1983 Soviet Natalia Yurchenko displayed the round-off vault, now called the Yurchenko, a highly risky move that paralyzed US gymnast Juliss Gomez in 1988. Men are not allowed to perform this maneuver. Mary Lou Retton of the US brought a full-twisting layout double Tsukahara to the vault in 1984, a maneuver only a few men in the world could manage at the time; it earned her a silver behind Romania's Ecatarina Szabo. Soviet vaulter Svetlana Boguinskaia triumphed in Seoul.

Individual All-Around Combined Exercises, Rhythmic: This event was introduced in 1984, when Lori Fung earned a rare gold for Canada. Marina Lobatch of the Soviet Union captured the gold in 1988.

Olga, Nadia, and Mary Lou

Together they transformed the entire philosophy of Olympic gymnastics—Olga Korbut, the teenaged Soviet pixie who wept on the sidelines after a crucial mistake; poker-faced Nadia Comaneci, a Romanian and the first gymnast to score a perfect 10.0; and bouncy Mary Lou Retton, a native of West Virginia who braved injury and pressure to win a gold medal in 1984. Before these talented teenagers happened into the sport, gymnastics was the province of older women who performed less like athletes than like ballerinas.

Korbut changed all of that in 1972, when she injected new daring and dash into the sport. Comaneci followed suit with her flawless work on the uneven parallel bars and the balance beam. Retton, watching these performances on television as a child, vowed to do the very same thing.

Olga Korbut was perhaps the first notable example of a changing trend in women's gymnastics. As international competitions intensified during the 1960s, coaches began to look for younger and younger children who could be trained to perform daring stunts before natural fear processes set in. Korbut, born in 1955, was nine when she began to work out at a gymnastics club in Grodno, near the Polish border. A mere five years later she was a national star, the first athlete ever to perform a back flip on the balance beam. She became the entire world's darling at the 1972 Olympics, earning gold medals for Soviet team victory, balance beam, and floor exercises, and a silver medal for her performance on the uneven bars.

Korbut's return to the 1976 Games was overshadowed by a powerhouse from Romania, fourteen-year-old Nadia Comaneci. Comaneci had literally *lived* gymnastics for years, having been plucked from a classroom by coach Bela Karolyi for his fledgling National Institute of Gymnastics. As a resident of Karolyi's institute, Comaneci received an education, free meals and lodging, training, equipment, and coaching, all paid for by the Romanian government. She developed slowly but showed a willingness to try moves no one had done before.

It was this daring that led her to the Olympics in 1976, where her work on the uneven bars and balance beam made history with the first perfect scores ever awarded. Comaneci left Montréal that year with two gold medals, a silver for team finish, and a bronze for floor exercise. As Walter Bingham put it in *Sports Illustrated,* the youngster compiled routines "that had the audience first gasping, then roaring with applause."

From the sidelines in Montréal, Olga Korbut viewed Comaneci's commanding performance. Mary Lou Retton watched it on television at her home in Fairmont, West Virginia. Born in 1968, Retton was a natural athlete who was galvanized into action by the 1976 Olympics. She began gymnastics classes in nearby Morgantown, but as she progressed she realized that the training facilities in West Virginia simply were not adequate. She had formulated decisive goals, as she told *Sports Illustrated:* "I had it timed perfectly in my head. I'd be 16 [in 1984] and in my prime."

Reluctantly, Retton decided that, in order to develop into a medal-calibre athlete, she would have to leave home. Taking her high school courses by correspondence, she moved to Houston and placed herself under the tutelage of none other than Bela Karolyi, Comaneci's former coach. Karolyi had defected to the United States and was working at a private gym called Sundance. There Retton reduced her weight from 100 pounds to 92 and completely re-vamped her technique. She recalled: "I'd do a routine I thought was good ... and he'd say 'no, no, no.' It felt good to me but it just wasn't good enough for him."

Retton's showdown in the 1984 Olympics was one of the closest ever. With her scores hovering within .10 of opponent Ecaterina Szabo—and coming off knee and wrist injuries—Retton earned her own medals. She won the all-around

Olga Korbut of the Soviet Union won fans around the world and
three gold medals at the 1972 Games, including one for the balance
beam, on which she was the first gymnast to perform a backflip.

The individual all-around gold medal winner in 1984, US gymnast
Mary Lou Retton vaulted to the top with a full-twisting layout
double Tsukahara on the horse.

gold, silver in team and vault, and bronze in uneven bars and floor exercise, earning a place in the record books next to the champions who had inspired her.

Youth is an absolute premium now in gymnastics, thanks to the exploits of Korbut, Comaneci, Retton, and their peers. It is no coincidence that each of the three champions retired before the age that most people go to work. As Retton declared in 1989: "I just can't do it [anymore]. My body's strong enough, but I don't have the discipline. The girl who won those medals was a machine. Gymnastics was her life. I've found other things now—that you actually can go to a movie on a Thursday night, and it can be very nice. Just go to a movie."

Retton's life these days is relatively normal. She attends college part time and speaks to groups about her experiences in the Olympics. In 1989 she and Korbut performed in a tour of eight American cities, but otherwise she has been satisfied to enjoy the fruits of her product endorsements and live a quiet life away from the media glare.

Recent years have not been so kind to Korbut and Comaneci. Korbut married a well-known Soviet rock star and had a son who is now in his early teens. The family visited America in 1991, not to discuss gymnastics, but to have themselves tested for exposure to radiation from the 1986 Chernobyl nuclear disaster. Fortunately, tests at a cancer research center in Seattle show no immediate signs that the nuclear accident has caused Korbut, her son, or her husband any health problems. Korbut has accepted a position teaching gymnastics in Hammonton, New Jersey, but she plans to return to Russia soon.

Comaneci's life since the Olympics has been rife with melodrama. In the spring of 1990 she escaped Romania with the help of an American, Constantin Panait. The tabloids jumped on the story, especially when reporters discovered that Panait was married and the father of four. Her reputation tarnished by allegations of a romantic attachment to Panait, Comaneci retreated to Montréal, where she is living near the Olympic Stadium. A movie based on her adventures is forthcoming, and perhaps a book as well. "I want to let the time prove that I am the same person that America knew when I was a gold winner at the Olympic Games," she told the *Chicago Tribune.*

Their offstage exploits notwithstanding, Korbut, Comaneci, and Retton have pioneered a new style of Olympic woman gymnast—one who is physically daring and agile as well as graceful and balletic. Future generations of Olympians will remember these three women as the first crest of a wave that will take gymnastics in a different direction as the new century dawns. —*M.K.*

Gymnastics

Gymnastics, Artistic — Women's Individual All-Around (Combined Exercises)

1988 1. Elena Shoushounova, Soviet Union, 79.662
2. Daniela Silivas, Romania, 79.637
3. Svetlana Boguinskaia, Soviet Union, 79.400

1984 1. Mary Lou Retton, USA, 79.175
2. Ecaterina Szabo, Romania, 79.125
3. Simona Pauca, Romania, 78.675

1980 1. Yelena Davydova, Soviet Union, 79.150
2. Maxi Gnauck, East Germany, 79.075
3. Nadia Comaneci, Romania, 79.075

1976 1. Nadia Comaneci, Romania, 79.275
2. Nelli Kim, Soviet Union, 78.675
3. Lyudmila Tourischeva, Soviet Union, 78.625

1972 1. Lyudmila Tourischeva, Soviet Union, 77.025
2. Karin Janz, East Germany, 76.875
3. Tamara Lakakovitch, Soviet Union, 76.850

1968 1. Vera Caslavska, Czechoslovakia, 78.25
2. Zinaida Voronina, Soviet Union, 76.85
3. Natalia Kuchinskaya, Soviet Union, 76.75

1964 1. Vera Caslavska, Czechoslovakia, 77.564
2. Larissa Latynina, Soviet Union, 76.998
3. Polina Astakhova, Soviet Union, 76.965

1960 1. Larissa Latynina, Soviet Union, 77.031
2. Sofia Muratova, Soviet Union, 76.696
3. Polina Astakhova, Soviet Union, 76,164

1956 1. Larissa Latynina, Soviet Union, 74.933
2. Agnes Keleti, Hungary, 74.633
3. Sofia Muratova, Soviet Union, 74.466

1952 1. Maria Gorokhovskaya, Soviet Union, 76.78
2. Nina Bocharova, Soviet Union, 75.94
3. Margit Korondi, Hungary, 75.82

1896-1948 Not held

Gymnastics, Artistic — Women's Team (Combined Exercises)

1988 1. Soviet Union, 395.475, Svetlana Baitova, Elena Chevtchenko, Olga Strajeva, Svetlana Boguinskaia, Natalia Lachtchenova, Elena Schoushounova
2. Romania, 394.125, Camelia Voinea, Eugenia Golea, Celestina Popa, Gabriela Potorac, Daniela Silivas, Aurelia Dobre
3. East Germany, 390.875, Martina Jentsch, Gabriele Faehnrich, Ulrike Klotz, Bettina Schieferdecker, Doerte Thuemmler, Dagmar Kersten

1984 1. Romania, 392.20, Simona Pauca, Mihaela Stanulet, Cristina Grigoras, Laura Cutina, Lavinia Agache, Escaterina Szabo
2. USA, 391.20, Michelle Dusserre, Pamela Bileck, Kathy Johnson, Julianne MacNamara, Tracee Talavera, Mary Lou Retton
3. People's Republic of China, 388.60, Qun Huang, Qiuri Zhou, Yanhong Ma, Yongyan Chen, Ping Yhou, Jiani Wu

1980 1. Soviet Union, 394.90, Yelena Davydova, Marija Filatova, Nelli Kim, Yelena Naimuschina, Natalia Shaposhnikova, Stella Zakharova
2. Romania, 393.50, Nadia Comenici, Rodica Dunca, Emilia Eberle, Melita Ruhn, Dumitrita Turner, Cristina Elena Grigoras
3. East Germany, 392.55, Maxi Gnauck, Silvia Hindorff, Katharina Rensch, Karola Sube, Steffi Kraeker, Birgit Suess

1976 1. Soviet Union, 390.35, Svetlana Grozdova, Elvira Saadi, Marija Filatova, Olga Korbut, Ljudmila Tourischeva, Nelli Kim
2. Romania, 387.15, Nadia Comaneci, Teodora Ungureanu, Mariana Constantin, Anca Grigoras, Gabriela Trusca, Georgeta Gabor
3. East Germany, 382.10, Gitta Sommer-Escher, Marion Kische, Kerstin Kurrat-Gerschau, Angelica Keilig-Hellman, Steffi Kraeker, Carola Dombeck

1972 1. Soviet Union, 380.50, Ljudmila Tourischeva, Olga Korbut, Tamara Lazakovitsch, Lyubow Burda, Elvira Saadi, Antonina Koshel
2. East Germany, 376.55, Karin Janz, Erika Zuchold, Angelika Hellmann, Irene Abel, Christine Schmitt, Richarda Schmeisser
3. Hungary, 368.25, Ilona Bekesi, Monika Csaszar, Krisztina Medveczky, Aniko Kery, Marta Kelemen, Zsuzsa Nagy

1968 1. Soviet Union, 382.85, Sinaida Voronina, Natalia Kuchinskaya, Larissa Petrik, Olga Karasseva, Ljudmila Tourischeva, Lyubow Burda
2. Czechoslovakia, 382.20, Vera Caslavska, Bohumila Rimnacova, Miroslava Sklenickova, Maria Krajcirova, Hana Liskova, Jana Kubickova
3. East Germany, 379.10, Erika Zuchold, Karin Janz, Maritta Bauerschmidt, Ute Starke, Marianne Noack, Magdalena Schmidt

1964 1. Soviet Union, 380.890, Larissa Latynina, Polina Astakhova, Yelena Volchetskaya, Tamara Zamotailova-Lyukhina, Tamara Manina, Ljudmila Gromova

344

2. Czechoslovakia, 379.989, Vera Caslavska, Hana Ruzickova, Jaroslava Sedlackova, Adolfina Tkacikova, Maria Krajcirova, Jana Posnerova
3. Japan, 377.889, Keiko Ikeda-Tanaka, Toshiko Aihara-Shirasu, Kiyoko Ono, Taniko Nakamura, Ginko Chiba-Abukawa, Hiroko Tsuji

1960
1. Soviet Union, 382.320, Larissa Latynina, Sofia Muratova, Polina Astakhova, Margarita Nikolayeva, Lydia Ivanova-Kalinina, Tamara Lyukhina
2. Czechoslovakia, 373.323, Vera Caslavska, Eva Bosakova, Ludmila Svedova, Adolfina Tacova, Matylda Matouskova-Sinova, Hana Ruzickova
3. Romania, 372.053, Sonia Iovan, Elena Leustean, Emilia Lita, Atanasia Ionesia, Uta Poreceanu, Elena Niculescu

1956
1. Soviet Union, 444.80, Larissa Latynina, Sofia Muratova, Tamara Manina, Ljudmila Yegorova, Polina Astakhova, Lydia Kalinina
2. Hungary, 443.50, Agnes Keleti, Olga Tass, Margit Korondi, Andrea Molnar-Bodo, Erzsebet Gulyas-Koteles, Aliz Kertesz
3. Romania, 438.20, Elena Leustean, Sonia Iovan, Georgeta Hurmuzachi, Emilia Vatasoiu, Elena Margarit, Elena Sacalici

1952
1. Soviet Union, 527.03, Maria Gorokhovskaya, Nina Bocharova, Galina Minaicheva, Galina Urbanowich, Pelageya Danilova, Galina Schamrai, Medeja Dzugeli, Yekaterina Kalinchuk
2. Hungary, 520.96, Margit Korondi, Agnes Keleti, Edit Perenyi-Vasarhelyi, Olga Tass, Erzsebet Gulyas-Koteles, Maria Zalai-Kovi, Andrea Bodo, Iren Daruhazi-Karpati
3. Czechoslovakia, 503.32, Eva Vechtova, Alena Chadimova, Jana Rabasova, Bozena Srncova, Hana Bobkova, Matylda Sinova, Vera Vancurova, Alena Reichova

1948
1. Czechoslovakia, 445.45, Zdenka Honsova, Miloslava Misakova, Vera Ruzickova, Bozena Srncova, Milena Mullerova, Zdenka Vermirovska, Olga Silhanova, Marie Kovarova
2. Hungary, 440.55, Edit Vasarhelyi, Maria Kovi, Iren Karpati-Karcsics, Erzsebet Gulyas, Erzsebet Balazs, Olga Tass, Anna Feher, Maria Sandor
3. USA, 422.63, Helen Schifano, Clara Schroth, Meta Elste, Marian Berone, Ladislava Bakanic, Consetta Lenz, Anita Simonis, Dorothy Dalton

1936
1. Germany, 506.50, Trudi Meyer, Erna Burger, Kathe Sohnemann, Isolde Frolian, Anita Barwirth, Paula Pohlsen, Friedl Iby, Julie Schmitt
2. Czechoslovakia, 503.60, Vlasta Foltova, Vlasta Dekanova, Zdenka Vermirovska, Matylda Palfyova, Anna Hrebrinova, Bozena Dobesova, Marie Vetrovska, Jaroslava Bajerova

3. Hungary, 499.00, Margit Csillik, Judit Toth, Margit Nagy, Gabriella Meszaros, Eszter Voit, Olga Toros, Ilona Madary, Margit Kalocsai

1932 Not held
1928
1. Netherlands, 316.75, Petronella P.J. Van Randwijk, Jacomina E.S. Van Den Berg, Ans Polak, Helena Nordheim, Alida J. Van Den Bos, Hendrika A. Van Rumt, Anna M. Van Der Vegt, Elly De Levie, Jacoba C. Stelma, Estella Agsteribbe, Petronella Burgerhof, Jud Simons
2. Italy, 289.00, Bianca Ambrosetti, Lavinia Gianoni, Luigina Perversi, Diana Pizzavini, Luigina Giavotti, Anna Tanzini, Carolina Tronconi, Ines Vercesi, Rita Vittadini, Virginia Giorgi, Germana Malabarba, Clara Marangoni
3. Great Britain, 258.25, Margaret Hartley, E. Carrie Pickles, Annie Broadbent, Amy C. Jagger, Ada Smith, Lucy Desmond, Doris Woods, Jessie T. Kite, Queenie Judd, Midge Moreman, Ethel Seymour, Hilda Smith

1896-1924 Not held

Gymnastics, Artistic — Women's Balance Beam

1988
1. Daniela Silivas, Romania, 19.924
2. Elena Shoushounova, Soviet Union, 19.875
3. Phoebe Mills, USA, 19.837
3. Gabriela Potorac, Romania, 19.837

1984
1. Simona Pauca, Romania, 19.800
1. Ecaterina Szabo, Romania, 19.800
3. Kathy Johnson, USA, 19.650

1980
1. Nadia Comaneci, Romania, 19.800
2. Yelena Davydova, Soviet Union, 19.750
3. Natalia Shaposhnikova, Soviet Union, 19.725

1976
1. Nadia Comaneci, Romania, 19.950
2. Olga Korbut, Soviet Union, 19.725
3. Teodora Ungureanu, Romania, 19.700

1972
1. Olga Korbut, Soviet Union, 19.400
2. Tamara Lazakovitch, Soviet Union, 19.375
3. Karin Janz, East Germany, 18.975

1968
1. Natalia Kutschinskaya, Soviet Union, 19.650
2. Vera Caslavska, Czechoslovakia, 19.575
3. Larissa Petrik, Soviet Union, 19.250

1964
1. Vera Caslavska, Czechoslovakia, 19.449
2. Tamara Manina, Soviet Union, 19.399
3. Larissa Latynina, Soviet Union, 19.382

1960
1. Eva Bosakova, Czechoslovakia, 19.283
2. Larissa Latynina, Soviet Union, 19.233
3. Sofia Muratova, Soviet Union, 19.232

1956
1. Agnes Keleti, Hungary, 18.800
2. Eva Bosakova, Czechoslovakia, 18.633
2. Tamara Manina, Soviet Union, 18.633

1952
1. Nina Bocharova, Soviet Union, 19.22

345

2. Maria Gorokhovskaya, Soviet Union, 19.13

3. Margit Korondi, Hungary, 19.02

1896-
1948 Not held

Gymnastics, Artistic — Women's Floor Exercise

1988 **1.** Daniela Silivas, Romania, 19.937
2. Svetlana Boguinskaia, Soviet Union, 19.887
3. Diana Doudeva, Bulgaria, 19.850
1984 **1.** Ecaterina Szabo, Romania, 19.975
2. Julianne McNamara, USA, 19.950
3. Mary Lou Retton, USA, 19.775
1980 **1.** Nelli Kim, Soviet Union, 19.875
2. Nadia Comaneci, Romania, 19.875
3. Maxi Gnauck, East Germany, 19.825
3. Natalia Shaposhnikova, Soviet Union, 19.825
1976 **1.** Nelli Kim, Soviet Union, 19.850
2. Lyudmila Tourischeva, Soviet Union, 19.825
3. Nadia Comaneci, Romania, 19.750
1972 **1.** Olga Korbut, Soviet Union, 19.575
2. Lyudmila Tourischeva, Soviet Union, 19.550
3. Tamara Lazakovitch, Soviet Union, 19.450
1968 **1.** Vera Caslavska, Czechoslovakia, 19.675
1. Larissa Petrik, Soviet Union, 19.675
3. Natalia Kuchinskaya, Soviet Union, 19.650
1964 **1.** Larissa Latynina, Soviet Union, 19.599
2. Polina Astakhova, Soviet Union, 19.500
3. Aniko Janosi, Hungary, 19.300
1960 **1.** Larissa Latynina, Soviet Union, 19.583
2. Polina Astakhova, Soviet Union, 19.532
3. Tamara Lyukhina, Soviet Union, 19.449
1956 **1.** Agnes Keleti, Hungary, 18.733
1. Laarissa Latynina, Soviet Union, 18.733
3. Elena Leustean, Romania, 18.700
1952 **1.** Agnes Keleti, Hungary, 19.36
2. Maria Gorokhovskaya, Soviet Union, 19.20
3. Margit Korondi, Hungary, 19.00
1896-
1948 Not held

Gymnastics, Artistic — Women's Uneven Bars

1988 **1.** Daniela Silivas, Romania, 20.000
2. Dagmar Kersten, East Germany, 19.987
3. Elena Shoushounova, Soviet Union, 19.962
1984 **1.** Yanhong Ma, China, 19.950
1. Julianne McNamara, USA, 19.950
3. Mary Lou Retton, USA, 19.800
1980 **1.** Maxi Gnauck, East Germany, 19.875
2. Emilia Eberle, Romania, 19.850
3. Maria Filatova, Soviet Union, 19.775

3. Steffi Kraeker, East Germany, 19.775
3. Melita Ruhn, Romania, 19.775
1976 **1.** Nadia Comaneci, Romania, 20.000
2. Teodora Ungureanu, Romania, 19.800
3. Marta Egervari, Hungary, 19.775
1972 **1.** Karin Janz, East Germany, 19.675
2. Olga Korbut, Soviet Union, 19.450
3. Erika Zuchold, East Germany, 19.450
1968 **1.** Vera Caslavska, Czechoslovakia, 19.650
2. Karin Janz, East Germany, 19.500
3. Zinaida Voronina, Soviet Union, 19.425
1964 **1.** Polina Astakhova, Soviet Union, 19.332
2. Katalin Makray, Hungary, 19.216
3. Larissa Latynina, Soviet Union, 19.199
1960 **1.** Polina Astakhova, Soviet Union, 19.616
2. Larissa Latynina, Soviet Union, 19.416
3. Tamara Lyukhina, Soviet Union, 19.399
1956 **1.** Agnes Keleti, Hungary, 18.966
2. Larissa Latynina, Soviet Union, 18.833
3. Sofia Muratova, Soviet Union, 18.800
1952 **1.** Margit Korondi, Hungary, 19.40
2. Maria Gorokhovskaya, Soviet Union, 19.26
3. Agnes Keleti, Hungary, 19.16
1896-
1948 Not held

Gymnastics, Artistic — Women's Horse Vault

1988 **1.** Svetlana Boguinskaia, Soviet Union, 19.905
2. Gabriela Potorac, Romania, 19.830
3. Daniela Silivas, Romania, 19.818
1984 **1.** Ecaterina Szabo, Romania, 19.875
2. Mary Lou Retton, USA, 19.850
3. Lavinia Agache, Romania, 19.750
1980 **1.** Natalia Shaposhnikova, Soviet Union, 19.725
2. Steffi Kraeker, East Germany, 19.675
3. Melita Ruhn, Romania, 19.650
1976 **1.** Nelli Kim, Soviet Union, 19.800
2. Lyudmila Tourischeva, Soviet Union, 19.650
3. Carola Dombeck, East Germany, 19.650
1972 **1.** Karin Janz, East Germany, 19.525
2. Erika Zuchold, East Germany, 19.275
3. Lyudmila Tourischeva, Soviet Union, 19.250
1968 **1.** Vera Caslavska, Czechoslovakia, 19.775
2. Erika Zuchold, East Germany, 19.625
3. Zinaida Voronina, Soviet Union, 19.500
1964 **1.** Vera Caslavska, Czechoslovakia, 19.483
2. Larissa Latynina, Soviet Union, 19.283
2. Birgit Radochla, East Germany, 19.283
1960 **1.** Margarita Nikolayeva, Soviet Union, 19.316
2. Sofia Muratova, Soviet Union, 19.049
3. Larissa Latynina, Soviet Union, 19.016
1956 **1.** Larissa Latynina, Soviet Union, 18.833
2. Tamara Manina, Soviet Union, 18.800

3. Ann-Sofi Colling, Sweden, 18.733
3. Olga Tass, Hungary, 18.733

1952 1. Yekaterina Kalinchuk, Soviet Union, 19.20
2. Maria Gorokhovskaya, Soviet Union, 19.19
3. Galina Minaicheva, Soviet Union, 19.16

1896-
1948 **Not held**

Gymnastics, Rhythmic —
Women's Individual All-Around

1988 1. Marina Lobatch, Soviet Union, 60.00
2. Adriana Dounavska, Bulgaria, 59.950
3. Alexandra Timochenko, Soviet Union, 59.875

1984 1. Lori Fung, Canada, 57.950
2. Doina Staiculescu, Romania, 57.900
3. Regina Weber, West Germany, 57.700

JUDO

WARM-UP

Derived from *jiu-jitsu*, a hand-to-hand combat technique favored by the *samurai* warriors of ancient Japan, judo (literally, "soft way") was developed by Dr. Jigoro Kano in the 1880s. Many of the *samurai* elements, designed to subdue an enemy fighter, survive in the modern sport: a contest is still won after a fighter either throws an opponent forcibly on his back, strangles or arm locks him into submission, or holds him immobile on his back for thirty seconds.

Seeking to develop a sport not quite as dangerous as *jiu-jitsu*, Dr. Kano studied *jiu-jitsu* and other martial arts. Kano's objective was a sport/self defense technique in which the opponent's own moves were used to pull the opponent off balance and into a throw. Kano selected various elements of jiu-jitsu, combining them with self-defense techniques of his own, and called his new sport Kodokan judo. In 1882 he opened the Kodokan School of Judo, and popularized the sport in Japan by winning a series of matches against proponents of other martial arts techniques.

fact: The philosophy of judo proposes that training should produce a mind and body in a state of harmony and balance.

During the next 50 years, disciples of Kano began judo schools in countries around the world. In 1902, the first US school opened, and three years later, the Paris police were taught judo. The first club in Europe, The Budokwai, was founded by Gunji Koizumi in 1918, and became a mecca for the sport on that continent. Shinzo Takagaki took judo to Australia in 1928 and Africa in 1931.

Although Japan instituted its All-Japan Championships in 1930, it was not until after World War II that international competition flourished. In 1948, the European Judo Union was founded in London and the first European Championships were held three years later. The International Judo Federation was established in 1951 and organized the first world championships in Tokyo in 1956.

Weight classes became part of the sport with the arrival of Antonius Geesink, who placed third in the first world championship. Proponents of the sport had always claimed that it was possible for a big skilled fighter to be beaten by an equally skillful smaller man, since the key ingredients are leverage and timing. Hence, one competition for everyone was the rule of the sport through the 1950s. But the success of Geesink, a 6 1/2-foot, 253-pound Dutchman, against smaller opponents helped hasten the arrival of weight classes. In 1961 during one of the last open-weight competitions, Geesink won the world championship, beating three Japanese in consecutive rounds.

Back to Kano for a moment. In 1909, Kano became the first Oriental member of the International Olympic Committee, becoming known as the "Father of Japanese Olympics." More than 50 years later, as a tribute to Kano, judo was added to the 1964 Olympic program at the insistence of the host country, Japan. For the Tokyo Olympic Games, four divisions were established: lightweight, middleweight, heavyweight, and open class. Japan took three of the categories, with big Geesink reigning as king of the open category.

In the 1968 Olympics at Mexico City, judo was not included on the program, although a year later Mexico City hosted the world championships. Since the 1972 Games at Munich, judo has been a regular part of the Olympic program, with seven weight classifications. In 1988, the open category, which often drew the best athletes, was discontinued. Women's events have been added for Barcelona: in 1992, seven full-medal competitions (by weight class) for women will be held for the first time.

▼

SPECTATORS' GUIDE

Judo contestants are called *judokas* and compete wearing traditional baggy white pants and wrap-around coats tied by a belt that signifies their rank, white being the lowest and black the highest. They compete on a 30-foot-square mat.

After a ceremonial bow, the contestants await the referee's command of *"hajme,"* which means "begin fighting." Olympic matches last 10 minutes and are won by a single point, which may be scored if one contestant throws his opponent to the mat so that his back strikes the canvas. If the throw is executed with perfect form, a point is awarded and the match is over. If the form is not perfect, half a point may be awarded; another half can be gained by holding the opponent on the mat 20 seconds. Thirty seconds of holding is worth a full point as well.

If no point is scored in the full 10 minutes, the decision is up to the referee and judges. An extra three minutes of competition may be held at the judges'

350

Summer

request. As with boxing, two bronze medals are awarded, one to each losing semifinalist.

Events for men include: extra lightweight (up to 60 kg); half lightweight (60 kg to 65 kg); lightweight (65 kg to 71 kg); half middleweight (71 kg up to 78 kg); middleweight (78 kg to 86 kg); half heavyweight (86 kg to 95 kg); and heavyweight (over 96 kg).

Women's events include extra lightweight (up to 48 kg); half lightweight (48 kg to 52 kg); lightweight (52 kg to 56 kg); half middleweight (56 kg to 61 kg); middleweight (61 kg to 66 kg); half heavyweight (66 kg 72 kg); and heavyweight (over 72 kg).

The Five Forms of Throwing an Opponent

TEWAZA, or hand technique.

KOSHIWAZA, or hip method.

ASHIWAZA, or foot-and-leg system.

MASUTEMI WAZA, or throwing with one's back on the mat.

YOKOSUTEMI WAZA, or throwing with one's side on the mat.

▼

HOPEFULS

Japan and Korea, traditional leaders in judo, should again offer the toughest competition in the men's events. Expect a unified Germany, though, to field an especially talented team featuring the best of the East and West. Three-time Olympian Michael Swain, who won the USA's only medal (a bronze in the lightweight category) in 1988, is hungry for a gold this time. And US national champion Eddie Liddie, who has won a medal in all 11 US Olympic Festivals, is determined to take an Olympic medal at Barcelona.

The US women's team looks strong with 106-pound Tammie Liddie (Eddie's wife), who placed third in the 1991 US Olympic Festival; 99-pound Hillary Wolf (the actress who played the bratty sister in *Home Alone*) and 114-pound Valerie Ann Lafon, both Festival gold medalists; and Lynn Roethke, whose career medals include a silver in the 1988 Olympic exhibition games, a World Championship silver, a Pan Am gold, five US Olympic Festival medals, and eight consecutive national championships.

The tentative judo schedule is as follows:

Summer

Monday, July 27
Extra lightweight, men & women

Tuesday, July 28
Half lightweight, men & women

Wednesday, July 29
Lightweight, men & women

Thursday, July 30
Half middleweight, men & women

Friday, July 31
Middleweight, men & women

Saturday, August 1
Half heavyweight, men & women

Sunday, August 2
Heavyweight, men & women

▼

HIGHLIGHTS

1964 was the year Tokyo hosted the Olympics; under the IOC's rules, the host country was permitted to select a sport of its choosing to be added to that year's program. Japan chose judo, and four weight divisions were established: lightweight, middleweight, heavyweight, and an open class.

Japan's Takehide Nakatani won the first gold medal, in the lightweight class, and two other golds remained in the host country. However, a 6' 6" Dutchman, Anton Geesink, created quite an upset in the open class, in which the Japanese were again heavily favored. In Nippon Budokan Hall—with 15,000 witnesses—Geesink defeated Akio Kaminaga, the three-time All-Japan champion. And he did so twice. The Soviet Union, another surprise contender, earned four bronze medals. James Bregman of the US won the bronze in the middleweight category. It was clear from the start that judo would attract an international cast of medalists in the Games.

Omitted from the Mexico City Games, judo reappeared on the program in Munich, thanks to the 1966 IOC ruling to include three new sports in 1972. Each country was allowed one competitor in each of the six divisions. Although the Japanese were favored in most of the categories, other countries proved their mettle in the sport.

Willem Ruska, another Dutchman, won the first category on the program, the heavyweight division, devastating Japan's hopes of an opening-day medal. In the light-heavyweight division, Japanese favorite Fumio Sasahara—the two-time world champion—was soundly beaten by Soviet Shota Khokhoshvili, who went on to defeat Britain's Dave Starbrook in the final. Although Japan earned gold medals in the lightweight, half-middleweight and middleweight categories, not a single medal went to them in the open category; Ruska, the sport's first double

352

gold-medalist, placed first, followed by Soviet Viatli Kuznetsov. Ruska is the sport's oldest gold medalist (he was 32).

fact: After Japan's performance in the 1972 judo events, all the team's trainers were fired.

Third place was shared between Jean-Claude Brondani of France, and nineteen-year-old Angelo Parisi, who entered for Britain. Parisi went on to win three more medals in the Games: next representing France, Parisi won a gold and two silvers in 1980 and 1984. Also in 1972, Mongolian Bakhaavaa Buidaa, the lightweight silver medalist, was the first competitor to be disqualified for failing a drug test in any international competition in the sport.

In Montréal, Japan took three of the six gold medals, while the Soviets earned two and Cuba—taking its first medal in the sport—captured one gold. Fifteen countries won medals at Moscow in 1980, when Japan was absent from the Games: the Soviet Union and France claimed two golds apiece, while the gold rush continued with East Germany, Italy, Hungary, Switzerland, and Belgium. Mongolia won a silver and a bronze (half of the medals it won in Moscow). Cuba, West Germany, the Netherlands, Bulgaria, Czechoslovakia, Yugoslavia, and Great Britain also medaled in Moscow.

In 1984—even with Japan competing—judo again featured an international array of medalists. Medals went to traditional and surprise victors: Japan, West Germany, Korea, Great Britain, Italy, France, Brazil, Romania, Iceland, Canada, and Egypt all medaled. Robert Berland became the first American silver medalist and his country's second medalist overall.

The Seoul Games were unusual in a number of respects: Japan captured only one gold medal, the open category was not included on the program, and women's judo was introduced as a demonstration sport. Gold medals went to Poland, Austria, Brazil, France and South Korea. The US medaled twice: Michael Swain earned a bronze in the lightweight division, while Kevin Asana finessed his way to the silver as an extra lightweight.

Judo

Medalists

Judo — Men's Extra Lightweight (Up to 60 kg)

1988
1. Jae-Yup Kim, Republic of Korea
2. Kevin Asano, USA
3. Shinji Hosokawa, Japan
3. Amiran Totikachvili, Soviet Union

1984
1. Shinji Hosokawa, Japan
2. Jae-Yup Kim, Republic of Korea
3. Neil Eckersley, Great Britain

1980
3. Felice Mariani, Italy
1. Thierry Rey, France
2. Rafael Rodriguez, Cuba
3. Aramby Emizh, Soviet Union
3. Tibor Kincses, Hungary

1896-1976 Not held

Judo — Men's Half Lightweight (Up to 65 kg)

1988	1. Kyung-Keun Lee, South Korea
	2. Janusz Pawlowski, Poland
	3. Bruno Carabetta, France
	3. Yosuke Yamamoto, Japan
1984	1. Yoshiyuki Matsuoka, Japan
	2. Jung-Oh Hwang, Republic of Korea
	3. Marc Alexandre, France
	3. Josef Reiter, Austria
1980	1. Nikolai Solodukhin, Soviet Union
	2. Tsendying Damdin, Mongolia
	3. Ilian Nedkov, Bulgaria
	3. Janusz Pawlowski, Poland
1896-1976	Not held

Judo — Men's Lightweight (Up to 71 kg)

1988	1. Marc Alexandre, France
	2. Sven Loll, East Germany
	3. Michael Swain, USA
	3. Gueorgui Tenadze, Soviet Union
1984	1. Byeng-Keun Ahn, Korea
	2. Ezio Gamba, Italy
	3. Kerrith Brown, Great Britain
	3. Luis Onmura, Brazil
1980	1. Ezio Gamba, Italy
	2. Neil Adams, Great Britain
	3. Ravdan Davaadalai, Mongolia
	3. Karl-Heinz Lehmann, East Germany
1976	1. Hector Rodriguez, Cuba
	2. Eunkung Chang, Republic of Korea
	3. Felice Mariani, Italy
	3. Marian Standowicz, Poland
1972	1. Takao Kawaguchi, Japan
	3. Yong-ik Kim, Democratic People's Republic of Korea
	3. Jean-Jacques Mounier, France
1968	Not held
1964	1. Takehide Nakatani, Japan
	2. Eric Hanni, Switzerland
	3. Aron Bogolyubov, Soviet Union
	3. Oleg Stepanov, Soviet Union
1896-1960	Not held

Judo — Men's Half Middleweight (Up to 78 kg)

1988	1. Waldemar Legien, Poland
	2. Frank Wieneke, West Germany
	3. Torsten Brechot, East Germany
	3. Bachir Varaev, Soviet Union
1984	1. Frank Wieneke, West Germany
	2. Neil Adams, Great Britain
	3. Mireca Fratica, Romania
	3. Michel Nowak, France
1980	1. Shota Khabareli, Soviet Union
	2. Juan Ferrer, Cuba
	3. Harald Heinke, East Germany
	3. Bernard Tchoullauyan, France
1976	1. Vladimir Nevzorov, Soviet Union
	2. Koji Kuramoto, Japan
	3. Marion Talaj, Poland
	3. Patrick Vial, France
1972	1. Toyokazu Nomura, Japan

	2. Antoni Zajkowski, Poland
	3. Dietmar Hotger, East Germany
	3. Antoli Novikov, Soviet Union
1896-1968	Not held

Judo — Men's Middleweight (Up to 86 kg)

1988	1. Peter Seisenbacher, Austria
	2. Vladimir Chestakov, Soviet Union
	3. Akinobu Osako, Japan
	3. Ben Spijkers, Netherlands
1984	1. Peter Seigenbacher, Austria
	2. Robert Berland, USA
	3. Walter Carmona, Brazil
	3. Seiki Nose, Japan
1980	1. Jurg Rothlisberger, Switzerland
	2. Isaac Azcuy, Cuba
	3. Detlef Ultsch, East Germany
	3. Aleksandr Yatskevich, Soviet Union
1976	1. Isamu Sonoda, Japan
	2. Valery Dvoinikov, Soviet Union
	3. Slavko Obadov, Yugoslavia
	3. Youngchul Park, Republic of Korea
1972	1. Shinobu Sekine, Japan
	2. Seung-lip Oh, Republic of Korea
	3. Jean-Paul Coche, France
	3. Brian Jacks, Great Britain
1968	Not held
1964	1. Isao Okano, Japan
	2. Wolfgang Hofmann, West Germany
	3. James Bregman, USA
	3. Ui-tae Kim, Republic of Korea
1896-1960	Not held

Judo — Men's Half Heavyweight (Up to 95 kg)

1988	1. Aurelio Miguel, Brazil
	2. Marc Meiling, West Germany
	3. Dennis Stewart, Great Britain
	3. Robert van de Walle, Belgium
1984	1. Hyoung-Zoo Ha, Korea
	2. Douglas Vieira, Brazil
	3. Bjarni Fridriksson, Iceland
	3. Gunter Neureuther, West Germany
1980	1. Robert van de Walle, Belgium
	2. Tengiz Khubuluri, Soviet Union
	3. Dietmar Lorenz, East Germany
	3. Henk Numan, Netherlands
1976	1. Kazuhiro Ninomiya, Japan
	2. Ramaz Harshiladze, Soviet Union
	3. Jurg Rothlisberger, Switzerland
	3. David Starbrook, Great Britain
1972	1. Schota Chochoshvili, Soviet Union
	2. David Starbrook, Great Britain
	3. Paul Barth, West Germany
	3. Chiak Ishii, Brazil
1896-1968	Not held

Judo — Men's Heavyweight (Over 95 kg)

1988	1. Hitoshi Saito, Japan
	2. Henry Stoehr, East Germany
	3. Yong-Chul Cho, South Korea

3. Grigori Veritchev, Soviet Union
1984   1. Hitoshi Saito, Japan
        2. Angelo Parisi, France
        3. Mark Berger, Canada
        3. Yong-Chul Cho, Republic of Korea
1980   1. Angelo Parisi, France
        2. Dimitr Zaprianov, Bulgaria
        3. Vladimir Kocman, Czechoslovakia
        3. Radomir Kovacevic, Yugoslavia
1976   1. Sergei Novikov, Soviet Union
        2. Gunter Neureuther, West Germany
        3. Allen Coage, USA
        3. Sumio Endo, Japan
1972   1. Wim Ruska, Netherlands
        2. Klaus Glahn, West Germany
        3. Motoki Nishimura, Japan
        3. Givi Onashvili, Soviet Union
1968   Not held
1964   1. Isao Inokuma, Japan
        2. Alfred Rogers, Canada
        3. Parnaoz Chikviladze, Soviet Union
        3. Ansor Kiknadse, Soviet Union
1896-
1960   Not held

Judo — Men's Open Category

1988   Not held
1984   1. Yasuhiro Yamashita, Japan
        2. Mohamed Rashwan, Egypt
        3. Mihai Cioc, Romania
        3. Arthur Schnabel, West Germany
1980   4. Andras Ozsvar, Hungary
        1. Dietmar Lorenz, East Germany
        2. Angelo Parisi, France
        3. Arthur Mapp, Great Britain
1976   1. Haruko Uemura, Japan
        2. Keith Remfry, Great Britain
        3. Jeaki Cho, Republic of Korea
        3. Jean Luc Rouge, France
1972   1. Wim Ruska, Netherlands
        2. Vitali Kuznetsov, Soviet Union
        3. Jean-Claude Brondani, France
        3. Angelo Parisi, Great Britain
1968   Not held
1964   1. Antonius Geesink, Netherlands
        2. Akio Kaminaga, Japan
        3. Theodore Boronovskis, Australia
        3. Klaus Glahn, West Germany
1896-
1960   Not held

Judo

MODERN PENTATHLON

WARM-UP

Modern pentathlon is one of the older Olympic sports, having been introduced at the 1912 games in Stockholm. The Swedish Olympic Committee devised the five events for this competition, which may account for the Swedish pentathletes placing in six of the seven top places.

The fifth-place finisher, the lone non-Swede, was a US Army lieutenant by the name of George S. Patton, Jr., who went on to greater fame in his military career. Patton would have finished much higher had he been able to shoot straighter; he finished sixth in riding, fourth in fencing, seventh in swimming, and third in the run. But he could only manage 21st in the pistol shoot, ironic considering the mythic portrait of Patton during World War II, two pearl-handled revolvers slung on his hips. Just watch where you aim those things, General.

Pentathlon was introduced in ancient Olympic competition at the 18th Olympic Games in 708 BC, as officials catered to the whims of whining Spartans. The Spartans, known for their war-mongering demeanor and eschewing of the normal materialistic possessions, complained that the Games were all slanted toward wimpy civilian competition, with nothing of interest or help to bold warriors.

The pentathlon was therefore designed for the soldier athlete and included discus, spear or javelin throwing, broad jumping, running, and wrestling. Unlike modern pentathlon, in which every person competes to the end, the original pentathlon was an elimination contest. All participants took part in the broad jumping contest. Those who jumped a certain distance entered the second event, spear or javelin throwing. The four best in that event qualified for the sprint. The top three in the sprint entered the discus throw, and the two surviving athletes wound up the grueling competition in a grunt and groan session—wrestling each other to a finish. The exhausted winner was crowned the Olympic pentathlon champion.

When the Modern Olympics were introduced in 1896, the pentathlon was not included because of the crowded program, but in 1912, it was felt that a modern pentathlon event—one with a military background—should be added to attract soldier-athletes. Baron Pierre de Courbertin, the Frenchman who revived the modern-day Olympics, was personally responsible for the return of pentathlon in 1912. He felt that better world relations and peace might occur if soldiers of the world's armies could meet in friendly competition, rather than the battlefield. And he wanted to attract top athletes by creating a sport combining some of the most difficult competitions of the Olympic Games.

True to its warrior spirit, modern pentathlon is based upon the duties of an unlucky 19th-century military courier assigned to deliver a message to his commander across enemy lines. First, the courier mounts a strange horse (they've never met before), riding over uneven terrain and varied obstacles, the direct predecessor to modern pizza delivery. He is challenged by an enemy soldier who draws a sword. Winning the duel, the messenger remounts his horse, only to have it shot out from under him by another enemy soldier. The messenger fires one shot from his pistol and kills the enemy. Unfortunately, his horse is now dead as well. Undeterred, the messenger runs great distances, swims rivers and streams, shoots his way through enemy ranks, and repels any remaining opposition with his sword. Arriving at his destination, soggy message hanging limply from his hand, he collapses at the feet of his commander, who mumbles a brief, "What took you?"

Thus, five events comprise the modern pentathlon: pistol shooting, equestrian, fencing, swimming, and cross-country running. The only event of the five that has changed significantly from the 1912 format is the equestrian, which went from a 5000-meter cross-country course to a 600-meter stadium-jumping course. The scoring system has been completely revised to produce a points award for each individual performance, so that the highest point total after five events is the winner. Both individual and team competitions are held.

Women's pentathlon was officially introduced in 1977, when the first major competition was conducted in San Antonio, Texas, in conjunction with the World Championships. Although not a part of the 1992 Olympics, the women's pentathlon will be part of the 1996 Summer Olympics in Atlanta. Lori Norwood, 1989 world champion, is pleased.

"I'm incredibly excited," says Norwood, who'll be 30 in 1996. "I've achieved most of my goals, but without the Olympics, there wouldn't have been that much more to fight for."

SPECTATORS' GUIDE

In Barcelona, 66 athletes from 25 countries are expected to participate in the modern pentathlon. The Olympic competition will take place over four days. The order of events in the modern pentathlon is fencing, swimming, shooting, cross-country running, and riding. Each competition is held on a separate day, except for swimming and shooting, which are both contested on the second day.

Individual and team classifications are based on points awarded for each competitor's performances in each of the five disciplines. Teams field three members, and retain one substitute. With the exception of the fencing contest, all of the competitions pit the athlete against the clock.

Modern Pentathlon Event-o-rama Guide

FENCING: Each competitor faces all others one at a time on a fencing strip in a duel with épées, which are similar to dueling swords. Each match continues until one of the fencers scores a hit or touch. A bout cannot last for more than two minutes. If no touch has been made within the time allotment, both fencers receive a defeat. Scoring is determined by percentage of wins. An athlete winning 70 of the 30 total bouts will receive 1,000 pentathlon points.

SWIMMING: 300-meter freestyle against the clock; 1000 points are awarded for a time of three minutes, 54 seconds, with four points added or subtracted for each half-second faster or slower.

SHOOTING: Competitors fire .22-caliber pistols. The targets, 25 meters away, face the shooter for three seconds, then rotate away for seven seconds. During the three seconds, the contestant must raise the pistol, aim, and fire one shot. After four rounds of five shots each, the scores are totaled. Each bullet is worth up to 10 points, with the highest possible target score being 200 points. Only twice in Olympic history has a perfect score been achieved. A target score of 182 earns 1000 pentathlon points, with 15 being added or subtracted for each target score above or below 182. An added complication is that the competitors may suffer from limp muscles, since the late-afternoon shooting contest follows the early-afternoon swimming event.

RUNNING: A 4000-meter cross-country course must be run in 14 minutes, 15 seconds for 1000 points, with three points added or subtracted for each second faster or slower. Scores in excess of 1200 (or 13 minutes) are considered excellent. Athletes are started separately at 30-second intervals according to the overall competition standings.

RIDING: This contest concludes the pentathlon. On horses selected by random draw immediately before the competition, the riders are allowed a maximum of 20 minutes to practice with their mount. Horse and rider take on a 600-meter course with 15 jumps, including a double and a triple. Points are taken off for refusals, falls, knockdowns, and for riding too slowly. A "clean" ride under one minute, 43 seconds earns a maximum 1100 points. Horse and rider are eliminated if they fail to finish the course in three minutes and 26 seconds.

Modern Pentathlon

359

HOPEFULS

Sixty-six athletes from 25 countries will vie for individual and team medals at Barcelona. The Soviet Union and Hungary are considered the world powers of the team competition—each has won four of the ten Olympiads since 1952—while Italy, France, Great Britain, and the USA will be contending for the bronze.

1980 Olympic gold medalist Anatoli Starostin of the **Soviet Union,** who won the World Championships in 1983, retired from competition for three years but has come back strong. In 1990 he placed second at the Worlds, and he's been a member of four World Championship gold medal teams. Another Soviet hopeful is Eduard Zenovka, 1989 Junior World Champion and a member of the 1990 Senior Championship team, whose youth and abundant talent have already earned him worldwide respect.

1989 world champ Laszlo Fabian was a member of **Hungary**'s 1988 Olympic gold medal team and is one of the few pentathletes in the world to gain both junior and senior world champion titles. An especially strong fencer, Fabian was a member of the Hungarian National and Olympic Épée Teams in 1988 and won both the Hungarian Modern Pentathlon and Épée Fencing Nationals in 1990. Fabian, along with 1988 Olympic champion Janos Martinek and 1985 world champ Attila Mizser, won three consecutive team world championships for Hungary, their reign ending when the Soviet team won the 1990 World competitions.

Italy's brightest star, 1990 world champ Gianluca Tiberti, broke his collarbone in a riding accident early in 1991, but by the 1992 Olympic Games he should be ready to defend his team's 1988 Olympic silver. 1986 world champ Calro Massullo may also compete for Italy, 1987 world champ Joel Bouzou will probably represent **France,** two-time Olympian Richard Phelps could help defend **Great Britain**'s 1988 team bronze, and 1990 World Cup Champion Peter Steinmann will probably compete in his third Olympic Games for **Switzerland.**

The **USA**'s strongest hope at Barcelona will be Robert Stull, two-time US national champion in modern pentathlon and, in 1988, national champion in épée fencing. Stull was an alternate for the 1984 Olympic silver medal team and captain of the 1988 Olympic team, and he hopes to lead the US to a medal in 1992. Mike Gostigian, also a 1988 Olympian, won the US Olympic Festival gold and boasts the fastest run/swim combination in US pentathlon. Other possible US Olympians include 1990 US Olympic Festival winner Conrad Adams and 1989 Festival winner Douglass Stull, one of the top challengers to his older brother Robert's position as the nation's leading pentathlete.

The tentative modern pentathlon schedule is as follows:

Sunday, July 26
Fencing (Palau de la Metal-lurgia, Montjuic)

Monday, July 27
Swimming (Piscines Bernat Picornell, Montjuic)
Shooting (Camp de Tir Olimoic de Mollet)

Tuesday, July 28
Cross Country (Cross Country Course, Montjuic)

Wednesday, July 29
Riding (Miniestadi)

▼

HIGHLIGHTS

Modern Pentathlon was dominated by Sweden during its first decade at the Games; the first non-Swedish modern pentathlon medalist came in 1928, when Germany's Helmuth Kahl won a bronze medal. Although the Swedes swept the 1912 competition, the sport's most famous participant—George S. Patton, Jr.—came in fifth. Then a twenty-six-year-old army lieutenant, Patton was in the running for the gold until the shooting competition; insisting that he use a non-standard issue pistol, he shot his way to 21st place (with 150 target points) in a field of 32, putting him out of the running for the gold, or any medal, for that matter. Patton's results are interesting to look at: he received 0 time faults and 0 riding faults, with a 10:42 riding time, to give him 100 points, or 6th place in the riding event; 20 victories in fencing put him in 4th place; a 5:55 time put him in 7th place in the swimming event, and a 20:01 running time put him in his best standing, third, in running. Patton never competed again in the Olympics, but gained not a little fame as a general during WWII.

The Swede who actually won the 1912 competition—Gosta Lilliehook—totalled only 27 points on individual finishes of 4th, 5th, 3rd, 10th and 5th, in the order of the events. Interestingly, each of the competitors placing in the final four spots behind Lilliehook actually finished better than the gold medalist in three of the five events, but Lilliehook's consistency created the crucial margin for victory.

The sports's first non-military medalist came in 1952, when Lars Hall, a twenty-five-year-old Swede, won the gold. Hall's medal, it turns out, resulted from a couple of fortuitous events: when the horse he was assigned was discovered to be lame, he was reassigned a horse considered to be the best mount in Norway, and later in the event, he escaped being disqualified for arriving twenty minutes late to the pistol-shooting event, thanks to a Soviet protest that

Modern Pentathlon

was still in progress. 1952 also marked the introduction of the team event, in which the Swedes placed second behind the first-place Hungarian team; the Finnish team took third place.

The assignment of a horse has affected the outcome of more than one pentathlete's scores. In 1968 in Mexico City, Hans-Jürgen Todt was allotted an intransigent—albeit handsome—horse named Ranchero, who three times balked at one of the obstacles. Dismayed at the horse's contribution to his poor score, Todt attacked the animal, and had to be restrained by his teammates.

Drugs and alcohol have a couple of times been an issue in Olympic pentathlon competition. In the 1972 Games, drug tests caused quite a scandal, but no disqualifications, when at least fourteen pentathletes were revealed to have taken tranquilizers prior to the shooting event—apparently a fairly common practice, to steady the athlete's aim. Since the drugs—valium and lithium—were then banned by the International Pentathlon Union but not by the IOC, the athletes were spared disqualification. The previous Games' would-be bronze medalist hadn't been so lucky, though: traces of alcohol in his blood after the shooting event left Swede Hans-Gunnar Liljenvall—who claimed to have imbibed only two beers—disqualified from the team event. The entire Swedish team, with a total of 14,188 points, was disqualified, allowing the French team, with 13,289 points, to take the bronze.

fact: Some consider modern pentathlon to be the supreme test of the all-around athlete.

Scandals haven't been limited to drug and alcohol abuse, either. Perhaps the most infamous event occurred in 1976, when the Soviet team was disqualified because one of its members—1972's individual silver medalist, Boris Onischenko—was discovered to have tampered with the electrical parts of his épée so that he could, at will, register a hit without actually touching his opponent. Onischenko's épée scores prior to the 1976 Games (which had begun an upward climb beginning in 1970) have since been viewed with not a little suspicion.

The US has never earned a gold medal in the individual or the team event, and hasn't medaled in the individual since Robert Beck won a bronze medal in 1960; his medal was preceded by a US bronze in 1932, a silver in 1936, and a silver in 1948. The US team took a bronze medal home from the 1960 Games (with Robert Beck on their team), and three times placed second, most recently in the 1984 Games. Italy finished first, and France third in the team event in 1984. The US failed to place in either the individual or the team event in 1988, while Italy this time took second place to Hungary; Great Britain took home the bronze medal.

Modern Pentathlon, Individual

1988	1. Janos Martinek, Hungary, 5,404
	2. Carlo Massullo, Italy, 5,379
	3. Vakhtang Iagorachvili, Soviet Union, 5,367
1984	1. Daniele Masala, Italy, 5,469
	2. Svante Rasmuson, Sweden, 5,456
	3. Carlo Massullo, Italy, 5,406
1980	1. Anatoli Starostin, Soviet Union, 5,568
	2. Tamas Szombathelyi, Hungary, 5,502
	3. Pavel Lednev, Soviet Union, 5,382
1976	1. Janusz Pyciak-Peciak, Poland, 5,520
	2. Pavel Lednev, Soviet Union, 5,485
	3. Jan Bartu, Czechoslovakia, 5,466
1972	1. Andras Balczo, Hungary, 5,412
	2. Boris Onischenko, Soviet Union, 5,335
	3. Pavel Lednev, Soviet Union, 5,328
1968	1. Bjorn Ferm, Sweden, 4,964
	2. Andras Balczo, Hungary, 4,953
	3. Pavel Lednev, Soviet Union, 4,795
1964	1. Ferenc Torok, Hungary, 5,116
	2. Igor Novikov, Soviet Union, 5,067
	3. Albert Mokeyev, Soviet Union, 5,039
1960	1. Ferenc Nemeth, Hungary, 5,024
	2. Imre Nagy, Hungary, 4,988
	3. Robert Beck, USA, 4,981
1956	1. Lars Hall, Sweden, 4,843
	2. Olavi Mannonen, Finland, 4,774.5
	3. Vaino Korhonen, Finland, 4,750
1952	1. Lars Hall, Sweden, 32
	2. Gabor Benedek, Hungary, 39
	3. Istvan Szondy, Hungary, 41
1948	1. William Grut, Sweden, 16
	2. George Moore, USA, 47
	3. Gosta Gardin, Sweden, 49
1936	1. Gotthard Handrick, Germany, 31.5
	2. Charles Leonard, USA, 39.5
	3. Silvano Abba, Italy, 45.5
1932	1. Johan Oxenstierna, Sweden 32
	2. Bo Lindman, Sweden, 35.5
	3. Richard Mayo, USA, 38.5
1928	1. Sven Thofelt, Sweden, 47
	2. Bo Lindman, Sweden, 50
	3. Helmuth Kahl, Germany, 52
1924	1. Bo Lindman, Sweden, 18
	2. Gustaf Dyrssen, Sweden, 39.5
	3. Bertil Uggla, Sweden, 45
1920	1. Gustaf Dyrssen, Sweden, 18
	2. Erik de Laval, Sweden, 23
	3. Gosta Runo, Sweden, 27
1912	1. Gosta Lilliehook, Sweden, 27
	2. Gosta Asbrink, Sweden, 28
	3. Georg de Laval, Sweden, 30
1896-1908	**Not held**

Modern Pentathlon, Team

1988	1. Hungary, 15,886, Janos Martinek, Attila Mizser, Laszlo Fabian

	2. Italy, 15,571, Carlo Massullo, Daniele Masala, Gianluca Tiberti
	3. Great Britain, 15,276, Richard Phelps, Dominic Mahony, Graham Brookhouse
1984	1. Italy, 16,060, Daniele Masala, Carlo Massullo, Pierpaolo Cristofori
	2. USA, 15,568, Michael Storm, Robert Gregory Losey, Dean Glenesk
	3. France, 15,565, Paul Four, Didier Boube, Joel Bouzou
1980	1. Soviet Union, 16,126, Anatoli Starostin, Pavel Lednev, Yevgeny Lipeev
	2. Hungary, 15,912, Tamas Szombathelyi, Tibor Maracsko, Laszlo Horvath
	3. Sweden, 15,845, Svante Rasmuson, Lennart Pettersson, George Horvath
1976	1. Great Britain, 15,559, Adrian Parker, Robert Nightingale, Jeremy Fox
	2. Czechoslovakia, 15,451, Jan Bartu, Bohumil Starnovsky, Jiri Adam
	3. Hungary, 15,395, Tamas Kancsa, Tibor Maracsko, Svetiszlar Sasics
1972	1. Soviet Union, 15,968, Boris Onischenko, Pavel Lednev, Vladimir Schmelyov
	2. Hungary, 15,348, Andras Balczo, Zsigmond Villanyi, Pal Bako
	3. Finland, 14,812, Risto Hurme, Veikko Salminen, Martti Ketela
1968	1. Hungary, 14,325, Andras Balczo, Istvan Mona, Ferenc Torok
	2. Soviet Union, 14,248, Pavel Lednev, Boris Onischenko, Stasis Schaparnis
	3. France, 13,289, Raoul Gueguen, Lucien Guiguet, Jean Pierre Giudicelli
1964	1. Soviet Union, 14,961, Igor Novikov, Albert Mokeyev, Viktor Mineyev
	2. USA, 14,189, James Moore, David Kirkwood,Paul Pesthy
	3. Hungary, 14,173, Ferenc Torok, Imre Nagy, Otto Torok
1960	1. Hungary, 14,863, Ferenc Nemeth, Imre Nagy, Andras Balczo
	2. Soviet Union, 14,309, Igor Novikov, Nikolai Tatarinov, Hanno Selg
	3. USA, 14,192, Robert Beck, Jack Daniels, George Lambert
1956	1. Soviet Union, 13,690.5, Igor Novikov, Aleksandr Tarassov, Ivan Derjugin
	2. USA, 13,482, George Lambert, William Andre, Jack Daniels
	3. Finland, 13,185.5, Olavi Mannonen, Vaino Korhonen, Berndt Katter
1952	1. Hungary, 166, Gabor Benedek, Istvan Sandy, Aladar Kovacsi
	2. Sweden, 182, Lars Hall, Torsten Lindqvist, Claes Egnell
	3. Finland, 213 Olavi Mannonen, Lauri Vilkko, Olavi Rokka
1896-1948	**Not held**

Modern Pentathlon

363

ROWING

WARM-UP

Rowing became an Olympic event at the 1900 Paris Games, introducing five events. By the second Olympic regatta in Stockholm, the modern 2000m (about 1 1/2 mile) course had been established. Other wrinkles needed smoothing in Stockholm, however, such as a hazard in the form of a midstream "bathing shed" that had to be negotiated around in mid-race.

The sport of rowing, however, precedes its Olympic debut by several thousand years. The earliest boats were propelled by paddles held entirely in the boatmans' hands. About two thousand years ago the Greeks decided to try mounting their paddles to the side of their boat at a fulcrum point, to increase the efficiency of their stroke: the rowboat resulted. Earlier evidence suggests that the Egyptians were rowboat enthusiasts. The rowing prowess of King Amenophis II is illuminated in an inscription on his tomb dating from 1430 BC.

Throughout history, all kinds of boats have been rowed, from small workboats and fishing boats to large ships of commerce and war. The galleys of the Roman Empire could be as long as 150 feet and were driven by the efforts of 50 or more captive oarsmen (usually slaves, convicts, prisoners of war, or other unfortunates who got on the wrong side of the guys with whips).

fact: The Roman poet Virgil includes an account of a rowing race in his epic *Aeneid*.

Racing has been a part of rowing from the start. Evidence indicates that racing of longboats was a pastime in prehistoric China and Southeast Asia, and oared barges competed on the Nile as early as 2500 BC. In modern times, rowboat racing has been embraced wherever rowboats plied the waters commercially. One of the longest-running continuous sporting events in the world began in 1715 among boatmen on the Thames in England. Thomas Doggett, a popular Irish actor, offered a prize to the winner of a race from the London Bridge to Chelsea. The event is known today by the quaint, if puzzling, name of the Doggett's Coat and Badge rowing race.

In the US, boatmen in New York Harbor in the 1880s could row for fun and profit in professional racing. At that time it was possible to sustain a handsome livelihood as a professional rower, vying for prizes up to $6000. But the *really* big earnings were going to the gamblers whose shady behavior, such as rigging races and sabotaging boats, sullied the reputation of the sport and caused the popularity of professional rowing to fade.

The amateur branch of the sport, however, flourished in America and England. In the United States, rowing became popular among Ivy League colleges and universities. The country's first inter-collegiate athletic event, the Harvard/Yale boat race, was held for the first time in 1852. The body governing amateur rowing, the International Federation of Rowing Societies (Fédération Internationale des Sociétés d'Aviron, or FISA) was formed in 1892.

fact: Whalers in Tasmania pioneered competitive rowing Down Under.

Technologically, the development of the rowing shell, as the boat is called, underwent many refinements and a couple of quantum leaps in the mid-nineteenth century. The first major change came with the invention of the outrigger by Britain's Henry Clasper. Prior to this development, the oarlock, which is the fulcrum point of the oar, was mounted on the gunwale of the boat. (The gunwale is the upper edge of the side of the boat. If you inverted a rowboat and placed it on sawhorses, it would be resting on its gunwales.) The width of the boat was necessarily constrained by considerations of oarlock location. To make a fast hull design, a narrow beam (beam: the boat's width at its widest part) is desired. But as the beam becomes narrower, the span between the oarlocks on the gunwales becomes smaller, until the oarlocks are too far inboard to function properly. The solution offered by the outrigger, or "rigger," was to suspend the oarlocks by means of rigid metal frameworks *outboard* of the boat's gunwales. By using riggers, a boat designer could craft as narrow a boat as was desired for speed's sake. Indeed, modern shells can be as narrow as 10 inches at the beam.

Boat designs evolved into longer and narrower dimensions, and into these longer boats rowers began putting longer seats. Rowers could slide forward and back on these broad seats, thus somewhat lengthening their stroke and adding leg power to the rowing motion. The oarsmen at Harvard, putting their superior educations to good purpose, realized that greasing their leather rowing pants would facilitate this sliding motion. Yale's contribution to the burgeoning technology was to try oatmeal as a lubricant; they sure earned their sheepskin in those days. Finally someone did it right when in 1857 J.C. Babcock of New York invented a seat on rollers, which maximized the sliding motion and allowed the rower to use as many muscle groups as possible to propel the boat.

Once the outriggers and sliding seats were incorporated, further developments consisted of gradual fine-tuning: smoothing the hull, lightening it, and adjusting hull design. Interestingly, even though FISA, the governing body of the sport, imposes very few limitations on boat design for competition, today's racing shells show very little variation from one boat to another. The design's evolution has arrived at the point of seeming near-perfection for rowing fast in flat water.

▼
_____

SPECTATORS' GUIDE

The Boats

Simply keeping the terminology straight in the world of rowing should be considered an athletic pursuit. Many terms are obscure, and some items are called by more than one name, depending on who's doing the calling. First, there's the matter of rowing itself. Rowing is not paddling. The paddler of a canoe or kayak sits or kneels facing forward and uses an unsupported paddle. A person rowing a boat wields an oar—not a paddle—and sits facing the rear of the boat. The oar pivots in an oarlock, which acts as a fulcrum, for mechanical advantage. The boats in competitive rowing are called shells. Within that main group is the subclassification of sculls. All sculls are shells, but all shells are not sculls.

fact: Some shells are constructed with hulls only 1/16-inch thick.

Whether a shell is a scull or not depends on the arrangement of the oars. In a scull, each crew member rows with two oars—one on either side—called sculling oars. Competitive sculls can be made for a single rower, two rowers, or four. A shell that is *not* a scull is set up with one oar—a sweep oar—per crew member. The sweep rower pulls his oar with both hands as he rows on one side of the boat; the rower next in line rows on the opposite side. This keeps the boat's propulsion balanced so that the shell can track a straight line. This sweep-oar type of shell comes in versions for crews of two, four, or eight rowers.

To confuse matters more, certain crew configurations may or may not include an extra member, called a coxswain (pronounced *cox'n*), who does not row but who steers by means of a rudder and coaches the rowers. The coxswain observes the progress from his vantage point, usually in the back of the boat, and directs the crew in matters of cadence, form, etc. Altogether, eight different boat arrangements result, and each goes by at least a couple of different names.

The Sculls (people who row sculls are **scullers** and they use **sculling oars**—which makes sense, oddly enough):

Single scull (1x), or "the single," rowed by one person

Double scull (2x), or "the double," rowed by two people

367

Quadruple scull (4x), or "the quad," rowed by four people

Not too bad so far, but it gets dicier with the next group.

The Shells That Are Not Sculls (the rowers of these boats each pull one oar, a sweep oar):

A pair without coxswain (2-), or a "straight pair," or a "pair without," or a "coxless pair," crewed by two rowers only

A pair with coxswain (2+), or a "pair with," or a "coxed pair," crewed by two rowers plus a coxswain

A four without coxswain (4-), or a "straight four," or a "four without," or a "coxless four," crewed by four rowers only

A four with coxswain (4+), or a "coxed four," or a "four with," crewed by four rowers plus a coxswain

An eight (8+)—that's the only name!—crewed by eight rowers plus a coxswain; all eights carry a coxswain

The shells themselves range in length from 26 feet for a single scull to about 58 feet for an eight. They can be built of high-tech materials such as kevlar and graphite fiber, but some of the most competitive boats are still mate of ultrathin plywood.

The Races

Olympic races, like other international competition in rowing, are run on a 2000m course (about 1 1/2 miles). A system of heats, semifinals, and repêchages is used to determine who will be in the finals. The top finishers in each heat go to the semifinals while the remaining crews go into a repêchage, or "second chance," round to try to get back into the semifinals. The top three crews of each of the two semifinal races then go on to the final, where medalists and final 4th, 5th, and 6th place are determined. Meanwhile the 4th, 5th, and 6th place finishers of each semifinal go into a petit final to determine final rankings of 7th through 12th place finishers.

The Times

Speeds attained by the various classes of shells can range from about 10 1/2 miles per hour for a single scull to more than 13 miles per hour for an eight. That kind of speed may not seem too impressive to someone living in the age of internal combustion, but for a human-powered watercraft it's truly remarkable.

HOPEFULS

Germany's unification will bring together probably the best rowers in the world, thus assuring the Germans top finishes in many events. But Barcelona offers room for other teams to place. The USA will hope to challenge the consistently well-organized Europeans with 1990 World Champion double scull team Robert Dreher and Steve Peterson. Attempting to edge out Romania's traditionally strong women will be USA's Katie Young, who set the pace for the 1990 World silver medalist women's-eight team; the 1991 National Championship doubles team Kris Karlson and Alison Townley, who also won two World Championship bronze medals; and single sculler Anne Marden, who has earned two Olympic silver medals and hopes this time for a gold.

Schedule

The tentative rowing schedule is as follows:

Monday, July 27
Elimination heats, men & women

Tuesday, July 28
Elimination heats, men & women

Wednesday, July 29
Repechages, men & women

Thursday, July 30
Semifinals, men & women

Friday, July 31
Semifinals, repechages, men & women

Saturday, August 1
Finals, men & women

Sunday, August 2
Finals, men & women

MEN'S ROWING EVENTS

HIGHLIGHTS

America's John Kelly may be best known as the father of film star Grace Kelly, the late Princess Grace of Monaco, but he also has the distinction of having won three Olympic gold medals in rowing. His victory in single sculls at Antwerp was one of 126 consecutive races he won during 1919 and 1920. He also teamed with his cousin, Paul Costello, to win the double sculls in both 1920 and 1924. Costello's Olympic golds also totalled three, the last in 1928 with partner Charles McIlvaine; Costello's son Bernard won a double sculls silver in 1956.

Kelly's son, John Jr., was also an Olympic competitor in single sculls. At the 1948 Games in London he failed to make the finals, and four years later at Helsinki he was overtaken in the stretch and finished fourth. Shortly before his last Olympics, at Melbourne, he promised to bring back a medal as a wedding gift to his sister, who was about to marry Prince Rainier of Monaco. Kelly didn't say which medal he would bring, but he did deliver, and Princess Grace wound up with some bronze of tremendous sentimental value for the royal coffers.

Rowing was first included in the Olympics at Paris in 1900, although Greek crews had given several demonstrations at Athens four years earlier. The German crew in the coxed fours event in 1900 included three brothers, Oskar, Gustav, and Carl Gossler (Carl as coxswain). At Paris the US won the first of many gold medals in the eights event. British rowers dominated at the 1908 Games in London and again in Stockholm, where Germany also picked up a medal.

Among the British medalists in 1908 was Guy Nickalls, Sr., who won an eights gold at the age of 42; Guy Nickalls, Jr., won eights silvers in 1920 and 1928. Another gold medalist on Britain's eights team in 1908, Charles Burnell, sired a rowing son, Richard, who triumphed in the double sculls with B. Herbert Bushnell in 1948. On the team for Britain in 1912 was Julius Beresford, who took a silver in the coxed fours event; his son Jack was also a successful Olympic rower, capturing three gold medals between 1920 and 1936, as well as two silvers.

After World War I the US came to the fore in rowing. A US crew from Yale that included medical student Benjamin Spock won the eights event in 1924. Between 1920 and 1956 crews from different American universities and clubs won the eights event eight straight times. In the single sculls, US rowers William Garrett Gilmore, Ken Myers, and Bill Miller won three consecutive silvers between 1924 and 1932. Canada, Britain, Australia, and Germany also floated strong rowers in those years.

Standouts into the 1950s included Britons Jack Beresford (son of Julius), W.G. "Ran" Laurie, and Jack Wilson and Australians Bob (Henry Robert) Pearce and Mervyn Wood. Pearce was known for letting a family of ducks pass before finishing his gold-medal performance in the single sculls in 1928; he relocated to Canada but still rowed for Australia in 1932.

The Soviet Union and East Germany dominated rowing beginning in the 1950s. Soviet rower Yuri Tyukalov grabbed the single sculls in 1952, and his countryman, Vyacheslav Ivanov, stroked to an unprecedented three straight gold medals in the single sculls from 1956 to 1964. Ivanov was a master of the come-from-behind finish.

fact: An oar with a wider blade is easier to grip the water with, but feels heavier to the oarsman, especially at the beginning of the stroke.

Robert Zimonyi was 46 when he coxed the US eights to a gold in 1964; in 1948, competing for Hungary, he had coxed a pair to a bronze medal. Canada also captured some rare gold, in 1956 in the coxless fours, and in 1964, in the coxless pairs, to go with an eights silver won in Rome.

At the Mexico City Games in 1968 the two Germanies captured three gold and two silver medals, including an eights gold for East Germany in a much lighter boat, while US rowers claimed a silver and a bronze. At Munich the US managed only a silver in the eights event behind New Zealand's eight (who were funded by a series of bingo games and a "dream kitchen" raffle), and otherwise in 1972 the two Germanies were dominant. The double sculls race in 1972 featured a spectacularly close finish in which a Soviet crew barely bested a Norwegian crew.

East German Siegfried Brietzke captured three gold medals from 1972 to 1980, in the coxless pairs and coxless fours events. Norwegian brothers Frank and Alf Hansen won the double sculls event in 1976, and US coxless pairs Calvin Coffey and Michael Staines drew a silver medal. But the real powerhouse at the Montréal Games was East Germany, taking four of the eight men's gold medals awarded. In 1980 at the Moscow Games East Germans made off with seven men's gold medals. In the coxless pairs event in 1980 the East German Landvoight twins outstroked the Soviet Pimenov twins. Canada took the gold from a favored US crew in the men's eights in 1984. That year Rumanian rower Ivan Patzaichin competed in his fifth Olympics.

Finnish single-sculler Pertti Karppinen, a fireman, won the gold in 1976, 1980, and 1984. Karppinen had developed a long-standing rivalry with West German Peter-Michael Kolbe, who took a silver behind Karppinen in 1976 and 1984 (having boycotted the Moscow Games). Karppinen didn't make the finals in 1988, however, and Kolbe settled for silver once again, almost 5 seconds behind East German Thomas Lange, eleven years Kolbe's junior.

Andrew Sudduth was a member of the American eight that took a silver medal in 1984, and competed as a single sculler in 1988. In Seoul US men stroked to a silver in the men's four without coxswain and a bronze in the men's eight.

Medalists

Rowing — Men's Single Sculls

1988
1. Thomas Lange, East Germany, 6:49.86
2. Peter Michael Kolbe, West Germany, 6:54.77
3. Eric Verdonk, New Zealand, 6:58.66

1984
1. Pertti Karppinen, Finland, 7:00.24
2. Peter-Michael Kolbe, West Germany, 7:02.19
3. Robert Mills, Canada, 7:10.38

1980
1. Pertti Karppinen, Finland, 7:09.61
2. Vassili Yakusha, Soviet Union, 7:11.66
3. Peter Kersten, East Germany, 7:14.88

1976
1. Pertti Karppinen, Finland, 7:29.03
2. Peter-Michael Kolbe, West Germany, 7:31.67
3. Joachim Dreifke, East Germany, 7:38.03

1972
1. Yuri Malishev, Soviet Union, 7:10.12
2. Alberto Demiddi, Argentina, 7:11.53
3. Wolfgang Guldenpfennig, East Germany, 7:14.45

1968	1. Henri Jan Wienese, Netherlands, 7:47.80
	2. Jochen Meissner, West Germany, 7:52.00
	3. Alberto Demiddi, Argentina, 7:57.19
1964	1. Vyacheslav Ivanov, Soviet Union, 8:22.51
	2. Achim Hill, East Germany, 8:26.24
	3. Gottfried Kottmann, Switzerland, 8:29.68
1960	1. Vyacheslav Ivanov, Soviet Union, 7:13.96
	2. Achim Hill, East Germany, 7:20.21
	3. Teodor Kocerka, Poland, 7:21.26
1956	1. Vyacheslav Ivanov, Soviet Union, 8:02.5
	2. Stuart Mackenzie, Australia, 8:07.7
	3. John Kelly, Jr., USA, 8:11.8
1952	1. Yuri Tyukalov, Soviet Union, 8:12.8
	2. Mervyn Wood, Australia, 8:14.5
	3. Teodor Kocerka, Poland, 8:19.4
1948	1. Mervyn Wood. Australia, 7:24.4
	2. Eduardo Risso, Uruguay, 7:38.2
	3. Romolo Catasta, Italy, 7:51.4
1936	1. Gustav Schafer, Germany, 8:21.5
	2. Josef Hasenohrl, Austria, 8:25.8
	3. Daniel Barrow, USA, 8:28.0
1932	1. Henry Pearce, Australia, 7:44.4
	2. William Miller, USA, 7:45.2
	3. Guillermo Douglas. Uruguay, 8:13.6
1928	1. Henry Pearce, Australia, 7:11.0
	2. Kenneth Myers, USA, 7:20.8
	3. T. David Collet, Great Britain, 7:19.8
1924	1. Jack Beresford, Jr., Great Britain, 7:49.2
	2. William E. Garrett Gilmore, USA, 7:54.0
	3. Josef Schneider, Switzerland, 8:01.1
1920	1. John Kelly Sr., USA, 7:35.0
	2. Jack Beresford, Jr., Great Britain, 7:36.0
	3. D. Clarence Hadfield d'Arcy, New Zealand, 7:48.0
1912	1. William Kinnear, Great Britain, 7:47.6
	2. Polydore Veirman, Belgium
	3. Everard B. Butler, Canada
	3. Maximilian Kusik, Soviet Union
1908	1. Harry Blackstaffe, Great Britain, 9:26.0
	2. Alexander McCulloch, Great Britain
	3. Karoly Levitzkty, Hungary
	3. Bernhard von Gaza, Germany
1906	1. Gaston Delaplane, 5:53.4
	2. Joseph Larran, France, 6:07.2
1904	1. Frank Greer, USA, 10:08.5
	2. James Juvenal, USA
	3. Constance Titus USA
1900	1. Henri Barrelet, France, 7:35.6
	2. Andre Gaudin, France, 7:41.6
	3. George St. Ashe, Great Britain, 8:15.6
1896	**Not held**

Rowing — Men's Double Sculls

1988	1. Netherlands, 6:21.13, Ronald Florijn, Nicolaas Rienks
	2. Switzerland, 6:22.59, Beat Schwerzmann, Ueli Bodenmann
	3. Soviet Union, 6:22.87, Alexandre Martchenko, Vassily Iakoucha

1984	1. USA, 6:36.87, Bradley Lewis, Paul Enquist
	2. Belgium, 6:38.19, Pierre-Marie Deloof, Dirk Crois
	3. Yugoslavia, 6:39.59, Zoran Pancic, Milorad Stanulov
1980	1. East Germany, 6:24.33, Joachim Dreifke, Kroppelien Klaus
	2. Yugoslavia, 6:26.34, Zoran Pancic, Milorad Stanulov
	3. Czechoslovakia, 6:29.07, Zdenek Pecka, Vaclav Vochoska
1976	1. Norway, 7:13.20, Frank Hansen, Alf Hansen
	2. Great Britain, 7:15.26, Christopher Baillieu, Michael Hart
	3. East Germany, 7:17.45, Hans-Ulrich Schmied, Jurgen Bertow
1972	1. Soviet Union, 7:01.77, Aleksandr Timoshinin, Gennady Korshikikov
	2. Norway, 7:02.58, Frank Hansen, Svein Thogersen
	3. East Germany, 7:05.55, Joachim Bohmer, Hans- Ulrich Schmied
1968	1. Soviet Union, 6:51.82, Anatoli Sass, Aleksandr Timoschinin
	2. Netherlands, 6:52.80, Leendert F. van Dis, Henricus A. Droog
	3. USA, 6:54.21, William Maher, John Nunn
1964	1. Soviet Union, 7:10.66, Oleg Tyurin, Boris Dubrovski
	2. USA, 7:13.16, Seymour Cromwell, James Storm
	3. Czechoslovakia, 7:14.23, Vladimir Andrs, Pavel Hofman
1960	1. Czechoslovakia, 6:47.50, Vaclav Kozak, Pavel Schmidt
	2. Soviet Union, 6:50.49, Aleksandr Berkutov, Yuri Tyukalov
	3. Switzerland, 6:50.59, Ernst Hurlimann, Rolf Larcher
1956	1. Soviet Union, 7:24.0, Aleksandr Berkutov, Yuri Tyukalov
	2. USA, 7:32.2, Bernard Costello Jr., James Gardiner
	3. Australia, 7:37.4, Murray Riley, Mervyn Wood
1952	1. Argentina, 7:32.2, Tranquilo Cappozzo, Eduardo Guerrero
	2. Soviet Union, 7:38.3, Georgi Zhilin, Igor Yemchuk
	3. Uruguay, 7:43.7, Miguel Seijas, Juan Rodriguez
1948	1. Great Britain, 6:51.3, Richard Burnell, B. Herbert Bushnell
	2. Denmark, 6:55.3, Ebbe Parsner, Aage Ernst Larsen
	3. Uruguay, 7:12.4, William Jones, Juan Rodriguez
1936	1. Great Britain, 7:20.8, Jack Beresford, Jr., Leslie Southwood
	2. Germany, 7:26.2, Willy Kaidel, Joachim Pirsch
	3. Poland, 7:36.2, Roger Verey, Jerzy Ustupski
1932	1. USA, 7:17.4, Kenneth Myers, William E. Garrett Gilmore
	2. Germany, 7:22.8, Herbert Buhtz, Gerhard Boetzelen
	3. Canada, 7:27.6, Charles Pratt, Noel de Mille

1928 1. USA, 6:41.4, Paul Costello, Charles
McIlvaine
2. Canada, 6:51.0, Joseph Wright, John
Guest
3. Austria, 6:48.8, Leo Losert, Viktor
Flessl
1924 1. USA, 6:34.0, Paul Costello, John Kelly,
Sr.
2. France, 6:38.0, Marc Detton, Jean-
Piere Stock
3. Switzerland, Rudolf Bosshard, Heini
Thoma
1920 1. USA, 7:09.0, John Kelly, Sr., Paul
Costello
2. Italy, 7:19.0, Erminio Dones, Pietro
Annoni
3. France, 7:21.0, Alfred Ple, Gaston
Giran
1906-
1912 **Not held**
1904 1. USA, 10:03.2, John Mulcahy, William
Varley
2. USA, James McLoughlin, John Hoben
3. USA, Joseph Ravanack, John Wells
1896-
1900 **Not held**

Rowing — Men's Coxless Pair

1988 1. Great Britain, 6:36.84, Andrew
Holmes, Steven Redgrave
2. Romania, 6:38.06, Dragos Neagu,
Danut Dobre
3. Yugoslavia, 6:41.01, Bojan Presern,
Sadik Mujkic
1984 1. Romania, 6:45.39, Petru Iosub, Valer
Toma
2. Spain, 6:48.44, Fernando Climent, Luis
Lasurtegui
3. Norway, 6:51.81, Hans Magnus
Grepperud, Sverre Loken
1980 1. East Germany, 6:48.01, Bernd
Landvoigt, Jurgen Landvoigt
2. Soviet Union, 6:50.50, Yuri Pimenov,
Nikolai Pimenov
3. Great Britain, 6:51.47, Charles
Wiggin, Malcom Carmichael
1976 1. East Germany, 7:23.31, Jurgen
Landvoigt, Bernd Landvoigt
2. USA, 7:26.73, Calvin Coffey, Michael
Staines
3. West Germany, 7:30.03, Peter Van
Roye, Thomas Straub
1972 1. East Germany, 6:53.16, Siegfried
Brietzke, Wolfgang Meyer
2. Switzerland, 6:57.06, Heinrich Fischer,
Alfred Bachmann
3. Netherlands, 6:58.70, Roelof
Luynenburg, Ruud Stokvis
1968 1. East Germany, 7:26.56, Jorg Lucke,
Heinz-Jurgen Bothe
2. USA, 7:26.71, Lawrence Hough, Philip
Johnson
3. Denmark, 7:31.84, Peter Fich
Christiansen, Ib Ivan Larsen
1964 1. Canada, 7:32.94, George Hungerford,
Roger Ch. Jackson
2. Netherlands, 7:33.40, Steven Blaisse,
Ernst W. Veenemans
3. West Germany, 7:38.63, Michael
Schwan, Wolfgang Hottenrott

1960 1. Soviet Union, 7:02.01, Valentin
Boreiko, Oleg Golovanov
2. Austria, 7:03.69, Alfred Sageder,
Josef Kloimstein
3. Finland, 7:03.80, Veli Lehtela, Toimi
Pitkanen
1956 1. USA, 7:55.4, James Fifer, Duvall Hecht
2. Soviet Union, 8:03.9, Igor Buldakov,
Viktor Ivanov
3. Austria, 8:11.8, Alfred Sageder, Josef
Kloimstein
1952 1. USA, 8:20.7, Charles Logg, Thomas
Price
2. Belgium, 8:23.5, Michel Knuysen,
Robert Baetens
3. Switzerland, 8:32.7, Kurt Schmid, Hans
Kalt
1948 1. Great Britain, 7:21.1, John Wilson, W.
George Laurie
2. Switzerland, 7:23.9, Hans Kalt, Josef
Kalt
3. Italy, 7:31.5, Felice Fanetti, Bruno Boni
1936 1. Germany, 8:16.1, Willi Eichhorn, Hugo
Strauss
2. Denmark, 8:19.2, Richard Olsen,
Harry Julius Larsen
3. Argentina, 8:23.0, Horacio Podesta,
Julio Curatella
1932 1. Great Britain, 8:00.0, H.R. Arthur
Edwards, Lewis Clive
2. New Zealand, 8:02.4, Cyril Stiles,
Frederick Thompson
3. Poland, 8:08.2, Henryk Budzynski,
Janusz Mikolajczyk
1928 1. Germany, 7:06.4, Bruno Muller, Kurt
Moeschter
2. Great Britain, 7:08.8, Terence O'Brien,
R. Archibald Nisbet
3. USA, 7:20.4, Paul McDowell, John
Schmitt
1924 1. Netherlands, 8:19.4, Antonie C.
Beijnen, Wilhelm H. Rosingh
2. France, 8:21.6, Maurice Bouton,
Georges Piot
1912-
1920 **Not held**
1908 1. Great Britain, 9:41.0, J. R. K. Fenning,
Gordon Thomson
2. Great Britain, 2.5 Lengths, George
Fairbairn, Philip Verdon
1896-
1906 **Not held**

Rowing — Men's Coxed Pair

1988 1. Italy, 6:58.79, Carmine Abbagnale,
Giuseppe Abbagnale, Giuseppe
DiCapua
2. East Germany, 7:00.63, Mario Streit,
Detlef Kirchhoff, Rene Rensch
3. Great Britain, 7:01.95, Andrew
Holmes, Steven Redgrave, Patrick
Sweeney
1984 1. Italy, 7:05.99, Carmine Abbagnale,
Giuseppe Abbagnale, Giuseppe Di
Capua
2. Romania, 7:11.21, Dimitrie Popescu,
Vasile Tomoiaga, Dumitru Raducanu
3. USA, 7:12.81, Kevin Still, Robert
Espeseth, Douglas Herland

1980 1. East Germany, 7:02.54, Harald
Jahrling, Friedrich-Wilhelm Ulrich,
Georg Spohr
2. Soviet Union, 7:03.35, Viktor
Pereverzev, Gennady Kriuchkin,
Aleksandr Lukianov
3. Yugoslavia, 7:04.92, Dusko Mrduljas,
Zlatko Celent, Josip Reic

1976 1. East Germany, 7:58.99, Harald
Jahrling, Friedrich-Wilhelm Ulrich,
Georg Spohr
2. Soviet Union, 8:01.82, Dimitri
Bekhterev, Yuri Shurkalov, Yuri
Lorentsson
3. Czechoslovakia, 8:03.28, Oldrich
Svojanovsky, Pavel Svojanovsky,
Ladislav Vebr

1972 1. East Germany, 7:17.25, Wolfgang
Gunkel, Jorg Lucke, Klaus-Dieter
Neubert
2. Czechoslovakia, 7:19.57, Oldrich
Svojanovsky, Pavel Svojanovsky,
Vladimir Petricek
3. Romania, 7:21.36, Stefan Tudor, Petre
Ceapura, Ladislau Lowrenschi

1968 1. Italy, 8:04.81, Primo Baran, Renzo
Sambo, Bruno Cipolla
2. Netherlands, 8:06.80, Herman J.
Suselbeek, Hadriaan van Nees,
Roderick Rijnders
3. Denmark, 8:08.07, Jorn Krab, Harry
Jorgensen, Preben Krab

1964 1. USA, 8:21.23, Edward Ferry, Conn
Findlay, Henry K. Mitchell
2. France, 8:23.15, Jacques Morel,
Georges Morel, Jean- Claude Darouy
3. Netherlands, 8:32.42, Jan Jaspers
Bos, Herman J. Rouwe, Frederik
Hartsuiker

1960 1. West Germany, 7:29.14, Bernhard
Knubel, Heinz Renneberg, Klaus Zerta
2. Soviet Union, 7:30.17, Antanas
Bogdanavichus, Sigmas Yukna, Igor
Rudakov
3. USA, 7:34.58, Richard Draeger, Conn
Findlay, Henry K. Mitchell

1956 1. USA, 8:26.1, Arthur Ayrault, Conn
Findlay, Armin K. Seifert
2. West Germany, 8:29.2, Karl-Heinrich
von Groddeck, Horst Arndt, Rainer
Borkowsky
3. Soviet Union, 8:31.0, Igor Yemtshuk,
Georgi Schilin, Vladimir Petrov

1952 1. France, 8:28.6, Raymond Salles,
Gaston Mercier, Bernard Malivoire
2. Germany, 8:32.1, Heinz Manchen,
Helmut Heinhold, Helmut Noll
3. Denmark, 8:34.9, Svend Pedersen,
Poul Svendsen, Jorgen Frandsen

1948 1. Denmark, 8:00.5, Finn Pedersen, Tage
Henriksen, Carl Ebbe Andersen
2. Italy, 8:12.2, Giovanni Steffe, Aldo
Tarlao, Alberto Radi
3. Hungary, 8:25.2, Antal Szendey, Bela
Zsitnik, Robert Zimonyi

1936 1. Germany, 8:36.9, Gerhard Gustmann,
Herbert Adamski, Dieter Arend
2. Italy, 8:49.7, Almiro Bergamo, Guido
Santin, Luciano Negrini
3. France, 8:54.0, Georges Tapie,
Marceau Fourcade, Noel Vandernotte

1932 1. USA, 8:25.8, Joseph Schauers, Charles
Kieffer, Edward Jennings
2. Poland, 8:31.2, Jerzy Braun, Janusz
Slazak, Jerzy Skolimowski
3. France, 8:41.2, Anselme Brusa, Andre
Giriat, Pierre Brunet

1928 1. Switzerland, 7:42.6, Hans Schochlin,
Karl Schochlin, Hans Bourquin
2. France, 7:48.4, Armand Marcelle,
Edouard Marcelle, Henri Preaux
3. Belgium, 7:59.4, Leon Flament,
Francois De Coninck, Georges
Anthony

1924 1. Switzerland, 8:39.0, Edouard
Candeveau, Alfred Felber, Emile
Lachapelle
2. Italy, 8: 39.1, Ercole Olgeni, Giovanni
Scatturin, Gino Sopracordevole
3. USA, 3 Lengths, Leon Butler, Harold
Wilson, Edward Jennings

1920 1. Italy, 7:56.0, Ercole Olgeni, Giovanni
Scatturin, Guido De Filip
2. France, 7:57.0, Gabriel Poix, Maurice
Bouton, Ernest Barberolle
3. Switzerland, Edouard Candeveau,
Alfred Felber, Paul Piaget

1908-
1912 **Not held**

1906 1. Italy, 7:32.4, Enrico Bruna, Emilio
Fontanella, Giorgio Cesana
1. Italy, 4:23.0, Enrico Bruna, Emilio
Fontanella, Giorgio Cesana
2. Italy, 4:30.0, Luigi Diana, Francesco
Civera, Emilio Cesarana
2. Belgium, 8:03.0, Max Orban, Remy
Orban, Th. Psiliakos
3. France, 8:08.6, Adolphe Bernard,
Joseph Halcet, Jean-Baptiste Mathieu
3. France, Gaston Delaplane, Charles
Delaporte, Marcel Freibourg

1904 **Not held**
1900 1. Netherlands, 7:34.2, Francois A.
Brandt, Roelof Klein, Dr. Hermanus
Brockmann
2. France, 7:34.4, Louis Martinet, Waleff
3. France, 7:57.2, Carlos Deltour,
Antoine Vedrenne, Paoli

1896 **Not held**

Rowing — Men's Quadruple Sculls

1988 1. Italy, 5:53.37, Piero Poli, Gianluca
Farina, Davide Tizzano, Agostino
Abbagnale
2. Norway, 5:55.08, Lars Bjonness, Vetle
Vinje, Rolf Bernt Thorsen, Alf Hansen
3. East Germany, 5:56.13, Steffan Bogs,
Steffan Zuehlke, Heiko Habermann,
Jens Koeppen

1984 1. West Germany, 5:57.55, Albert
Hedderich, Raimund Hormann, Dieter
Wiedenmann, Michael Dursch
2. Australia, 5:57.98, Paul Reedy, Gary
Gullock, Timothy Mclaren, Anthony
Lovrich
3. Canada, 5:59.07, Doug Hamilton,
Mike Hughes, Phil Monckton, Bruce
Ford

1980 1. East Germany, 5:49.81, Frank Dundr, Karsten Bunk, Uwe Heppner, Martin Winter
2. Soviet Union, 5:51.47, Yuri Shapochka, Yevgeny Barbakov, Valeri Kleshnev, Nikolai Dovgan
3. Bulgaria, 5:52.38, Mincho Nikolov, Liubomir Petrov, Ivo Rusev, Bogdan Dobrev

1976 1. East Germany, 6:18.65, Wolfgang Gueldenpfennig, Rudiger Reiche, Michael Wolfgramm, Karl-Heinz Bussert
2. Soviet Union, 6:19.89, Yevgeny Duleyev, Yuri Yakimov, Aivar Lazdenieks, Vatautas Butkus
3. Czechoslovakia, 6:21.77, Jaroslav Helebrand, Vaclav Vochoska, Zdenek Pecks, Vladek Lacina

Rowing — Men's Coxless Four

1988 1. East Germany, 6:03.11, Roland Schroeder, Thomas Greiner, Ralf Brudel, Olaf Foerster
2. USA, 6:05.53, Raoul Rodriguez, Thomas Bohrer, David Krmpotich, Richard Kennelly, Jr.
3. West Germany, 6:06.22, Norbert Kesslau, Volker Grabow, Jorg Puttliz, Guido Grabow

1984 1. New Zealand, 6:03.48, Leslie O'Connell, Shane O'Brien, Conrad Robertson, Keith Trask
2. USA, 6:06.10, David Clark, Jonathan Smith, Philip Stekl, Alan Forney
3. Denmark, 6:07.72, Michael Jessen, Lars Nielsen, Per H. S. Rasmussen, Erik Christiansen

1980 1. East Germany, 6:08.17, Jurgen Thiele, Andreas Decker, Stefan Semmler, Siegfried Brietzke
2. Soviet Union, 6:11.81, Aleksei Kamkin, Valeri Dolinin, Aleksandr Kulagin, Vitali Yeliseyev
3. Great Britain, 6:16.58, John Beattie, Ian McNuff, David Townsend, Martin Cross

1976 1. East Germany, 6:37.42, Siegfried Brietzke, Stefan Semmler, Andreas Decker, Wolfgang Mager
2. Norway, 6:41.22, Ole Nafstad, Arne Bergodd, Finn Tveter, Rolf Andreasson
3. Soviet Union, 6:42.52, Raul Arnemann, Nikolai Kuznetsov, Valeri Dolinin, Anushavan Gasan-Dzhalolov

1972 1. East Germany, 6:24.27, Frank Forberger, Frank Ruhle, Dieter Grahn, Dieter Schubert
2. New Zealand, 6:25.64, Dick Tonks, Dudley Storey, Ross Collinge, Noel Mills
3. West Germany, 6:28.41, Joachim Ehrig, Peter Funnekotter, Franz Held, Wolfgang Plottke

1968 1. East Germany, 6:39.18, Frank Forberger, Dieter Grahn, Frank Ruhle, Dieter Schubert
2. Hungary, 6:41.18, Zoltan Melis, Gyorgy Sarlos, Jozsef Csermely, Antal Melis

3. Italy, 6:44.01, Renato Bosatta, Tullio Baraglia, Pier Angelo Conti Manzini, Abramo Albini

1964 1. Denmark, 6:59.30, John O. Hansen, Bjorn Haslov, Erik Petersen, Kurt Helmudt
2. Great Britain, 7:00.47, John M. Russell, Hugh Wardell- Yerburgh, William Barry, John James
3. USA, 7:01.37, Geoffrey Picard, Richard Lyon, Theodore Mittet, Ted Nash

1960 1. USA, 6:26.26, Arthur Ayrault, Ted Nash, John Sayre, Richard Wailes
2. Italy, 6:28.78, Tullio Baraglia, Renato Bosatta, Giancarlo Crosta, Giuseppe Galante
3. Soviet Union, 6:29.62, Igor Akhremchik, Yuri Bachurov, Valentin Morkovkin, Anatoli Tarabrin

1956 1. Canada, 7:08.8, Archibald McKinnon, Lorne Loomer, I. Walter D'Hondt, Donald Arnold
2. USA, 7:18.4, John Welchli, John McKinlay, Arthur McKinlay, James McIntosh
3. France, 7:20.9, Rene Guissart, Yves Delacour, Gaston Mercier, Guy Guillabert

1952 1. Yugoslavia, 7:16.0, Duje Bonacic, Velimir Valenta, Mate Trojanovic, Petar Segvic
2. France, 7:18.9, Pierre Blondiaux, Jacques Guissart, Marc Bouissou, Roger Gautier
3. Finland, 7:23.3, Veikko Lommi, Kauko Wahlsten, Oiva Lommi, Lauri Nevalainen

1948 1. Italy, 6:39.0, Giuseppe Moioli, Elio Morille, Giovanni Invernizzi, Franco Faggi
2. Denmark, 6:43.5, Helge Halkjaer, Askel B. Hansen, Helge Schroder, Ib Storm Larsen
3. USA, 6:47.7, Frederick J. Kingsbury, Stuart Griffing, Gregory Gates, Robert Perew

1936 1. Germany, 7:01.8, Rudolf Eckstein, Anton Rom, Martin Karl, Wilhelm Menne
2. Great Britain, 7:06.5, Thomas Bristow, Alan Barrett, Peter Jackson, John D. Sturrock
3. Switzerland, 7:10.6, Hermann Betschart, Hans Homberger, Alex Homberger, Karl Schmid

1932 1. Great Britain, 6:58.2, John C. Badcock, Hugh R.A. Edwards, Jack Beresford, Rowland D. George
2. Germany, 7:03.0, Karl Aletter, Ernst Gaber, Walter Flinsch, Hans Maier
3. Italy, 7:04.0, Antonio Ghiardello, Francesco Cossu, Giliante D'Este, Antonio Provenzani

1928 1. Great Britain, 6:36.0, John G. H. Lander, Michael H. Warriner, Richard Beesly, Edward V. Bevan
2. USA, 6:37.0, Charles Karle, William Miller, George Heales, Ernest Bayer
3. Italy, 6:31.6, Cesare Rossi, Pietro Freschi, Umberto Bonade, Paolo Gennari

1924 1. Great Britain, 7:08.6, Charles R. M. Eley, James A. MacNabb, Robert E. Morrison, Terrence R.B. Sanders
2. Canada, 1 Length, Colin H. B. Finlayson, Archibald C. Black, George F. Mackay, William Wood
3. Switzerland, 2 Lengths, Emile Albrecht, Alfred Probst, Eugen Sigg, Hans Walter

1912-1920 Not held

1908 1. Great Britain, 8:34.0, C. Robert Cudmore, James A. Gillan, Duncan McKinnon, Robert Somers-Smith
2. Great Britain, 1.5 Lengths, Philip R. Filleul, Harold R. Barker, J. R. K. Fenning, Gordon L. Thomson

1906 Not held

1904 1. USA, 9:53.8, George Dietz, August Erker, Albert Nasse, Arthur Stockhoff
2. USA, Charles Aman, Michael Begley, Martin Fromanack, Frederick Suerig

1896-1900 Not held

Rowing — Men's Coxed Four

1988 1. East Germany, 6:10.74, Frank Klawonn, Bernd Eichwurzel, Bernd Niesecke, Karsten Schmeing, Hendrick Reiher
2. Romania, 6:13.58, Dimitrie Popescu, Ioan Snep, Valentin Robu, Vasile Tomoiaga, Ladislau Lovrenski
3. New Zealand, 6:15.78, George Keys, Ian Wright, Gregory Johnston, Christopher White, Andrew Bird

1984 1. Great Britain, 6:18.64, Martin Cross, Richard Budgett, Andrew Holmes, Steven Redgrave, Adrian Ellison
2. USA, 6:20.28, Thomas Kiefer, Gregory Springer, Michael Bach, Edward Ives, John Stillings
3. New Zealand, 6:23.68, Kevin Lawton, Donald Symon, Barrie Vlabbott, Ross Tong, Brett Hollister

1980 1. East Germany, 6:14.51, Dieter Wendisch, Ullrich Diessner, Walter Diessner, Gottfried Dohn, Andreas Gregor
2. Soviet Union, 6:19.05, Artur Garonskis, Dimant Krishianis, Dzintars Krishianis, Zhorzh Tikmers, Yuris Berzynsh
3. Poland, 6:22.52, Grzegorz Stellak, Adam Tomasiak, Grzegorz Nowak, Ryszard Stadniuk, Ryszard Kubiak

1976 1. Soviet Union, 6:40.22, Vladimir Yeshino, Nikolai Ivanov, Mikhail Kuznetsov, Aleksandre Klepikov, Aleksandr Lukianov
2. East Germany, 6:42.70, Rudiger Kunze, Walter Diessner, Ullrich Diessner, Johannes Thomas
3. West Germany, 6:46.96, Ralph Kubail, Hans-Johann Faerber, Siegfried Fricke, Peter Niehusen, Hartmut Wenzel

1972 1. West Germany, 6:31.85, Peter Berger, Hans-Johann Farber, Gerhard Auer, Alois Bierl, Uwe Benter

2. East Germany, 6:33.30, Dietrich Zander, Reinhard Gust, Eckhard Martens, Rolf Jobst, Klaus-Dieter Ludwig
3. Czechoslovakia, 6:35.64, Otakar Marecek, Karel Neffe, Vladimir Janos, Frantisek Provaznik, Vladimir Petricek

1968 1. New Zealand, 6:45.62, Richard J. Joyce, Dudley L. Storey, Ross H. Collinge, Warren J. Cole, Simon Ch. Dickie
2. East Germany, 6:48.20, Peter Kremtz, Roland Gohler, Manfred Gelpke, Klaus Jacob, Dieter Semetzky
3. Switzerland, 6:49.04, Denis Oswald, Hugo Waser, Peter Bolliger, Jakob Grob, Gottlieb Frohlich

1964 1. West Germany, 7:00.44, Peter Neusel, Bernhard Britting, Joachim Werner, Egbert Hirschfelder, Jurgen Oelke
2. Italy, 7:02.84, Renato Bosatta, Emilio Trivini, Giuseppe Galante, Franco De Pedrina, Giovanni Spinola
3. Netherlands, 7:06.46, Alex Mullink, Jan van de Graaf, Frederick R. van de Graaf, Robert van de Graaf, Marius Klumperbeek

1960 1. West Germany, 6:39.12, Gerd Cintl, Horst Effertz, Klaus Riekemann, Jurgen Litz, Michael Obst
2. France, 6:41.62, Robert Dumontois, Claude Martin, Jacques Morel, Guy Nosbaum, Jean Klein
3. Italy, 6:43.72, Fulvio Balatti, Romano Sgheiz, Franco Trincavelli, Giovanni Zucchi, Ivo Stefanoni

1956 1. Italy, 7:19.4, Alberto Winkler, Romano Sgheiz, Angelo Vanzin, Franco Trincavelli, Ivo Stefanoni
2. Sweden, 7:22.4, Olof Larsson, Gosta Eriksson, Ivar Aronsson, Sven E. Gunnarsson, Bertil Goransson
3. Finland, 7:30.9, Kauko Hanninen, Reino Poutanen, Veli Lehtela, Toimi Pitkanen, Matti Niemi

1952 1. Czechoslovakia, 7:33.4, Karle Mejta, Jiri Havlis, Jan Jindra, Stanislav Lusk, Miroslav Koranda
2. Switzerland, 7:36.5, Enrico Bianchi, Karl Weidmann, Heinrich Scheller, Emile Ess, Walter Leiser
3. USA, 7:37.0, Carl Lovested, Alvin Ulbrickson, Richard Wahlstrom, Matthew Leanderson, Albert Rossi

1948 1. USA, 6:50.3, Warren Westlund, Robert Martin, Robert Will, Gordon Giovanelli, Allen Morgan
2. Switzerland, 6:53.3, Rudolf Reichling, Erich Schriever, Emile Knecht, Pierre Stebler, Andre Moccand
3. Denmark, 6:58.6, Erik Ch. Larsen, Borge R. Nielsen, Henry C. Larsen, Harry M. Knudsen, Jorgen Ib Olsen

1936 1. Germany, 7:16.2, Hans Maier, Walter Volle, Ernst Gaber, Paul Sollner, Fritz Bauer
2. Switzerland, 7:24.3, Hermann Betschart, Hans Homberger, Alex Homberger, Karl Schmid, Rolf Spring
3. France, 7:33.3, Fernand Vandernotte, Marcel Vandernotte, Marcel Cosmat, Marcel Chauvigne, Noel Vandernotte

1932 1. Germany, 7:19.0, Hans Eller, Horst Hoeck, Walter Meyer, Joachim Spremberg, Karlheinz Neumann
2. Italy, 7:19.2, Bruno Vattovaz, Giovanni Plazzer, Riccardo Divora, Bruno Parovel, Giovanni Scherl
3. Poland, 7:26.8, Jerzy Braun, Janusz Slazak, Stanislaw Urban, Edward Kobylinski, Jerzy Skolimovski

1928 1. Italy, 6:47.8, Valerio Perentin, Giliante D'Este, Nicolo Vittori, Giovanni Delise, Renato Petronio
2. Switzerland, 7:03.4, Ernst Haas, Joseph Meyer, Dr. Otto Bucher, Karl Schwegler, Fritz Bosch
3. Poland, 7:12.8, Franciszek Bronikowski, Edmund Jankowski, Leon Birkholc, Bernard Ormanowski, Bronislaw Drewek

1924 1. Switzerland, 7:18.4, Emile Albrecht, Alfred Probst, Eugen Sigg, Hans Walter, Emile Lachapelle
2. France, 7:21.6, Eugene Constant, Louis Gressier, Georges Lecointe, Raymond Talleux, Marcel Lepan
3. USA, Robert Gerhardt, Sidney Jelinek, Edward Mitchell, Henry Welsford, John Kennedy

1920 1. Switzerland, 6:54.0, Willy Bruderlin, Max Rudolf, Paul Rudolf, Hans Walter, Paul Staub
2. USA, 6:58.0, Kenneth Meyers, Carl Otto Klose, Franz Federschmidt, Erich Federschmidt, Sherman Clark
3. Norway, 7:02.0, Birger Var, Theodor Klem, Henry Larsen, Per Gulbrandsen, Thoralf Hagen

1912 1. Germany, 6:59.4, (Ludwigshafener R.V.), Albert Arnheiter, Otto Fickeisen, Rudolf Fickeisen, Hermann Wilker, Otto Maier
2. Great Britain, (Thames R.C.), Julius Beresford sen., Charles G. Vernon, Charles Rought, Bruce Logan, Geoffrey Carr
3. Denmark, (Polyteknic R.C.), Erik Bisgaard, Rasmus P. Frandsen, Magnus Simonsen, Paul Thymann, Eigil Clemmensen

1908 Not held
1906 1. Italy, 8:13.0, (Bucintoro), Enrico Bruna, Emilio Fontanella, Riccardo Zardinoni, Giuseppe Poli, Giorgio Cesana
2. France, (Societe Nautique de la Basse Seine), Gaston Delaplane, Charles Delaporte, Leon Delignieres, Paul Echard, Marcel Frebourg
3. France, (Societe Nautique de Bayonne), Adolphe Bernard, Joseph Halcet, Jean-Baptiste Laporte, Jean-Baptiste Mathieu, Pierre Sourbe

1904 Not held
1900 1. France, 7:11.0, (Cercle de l'Aviron de Roubaix) Emile Delchambre, Jean Cau, Henri Boukaert, Henri Hazebroucq, ... Charlot
1. Germany, 5:59.0, (Germania R.C. Hamburg), Oskar Gossler, Walter Kartzenstein, Waldemar Tietgens, Gustav L. Gossler, Carl Heinrich Gossler

2. France, 7:18.0, (Club Nautique de Lyon) Charles Perrin, Daniel Soubeyran, Emile Wegelin, Georges Lumpp
2. Netherlands, 6:33.0, (Minerva Amsterdam), Gerhard O. Lotsy, Gerhard Hiebendaal, Paulus J. Lotsy, Johannes H. Terwogt, Dr. Hermanus Brockmann
3. Germany, 6:35.0, (Ludwigshafener R.V.), Carl Lehle, Ernst Felle, Herman Wilker, Otto Fickeisen, Franz Krowerath
3. Germany, 7:18.2, (R.C. Favorite Hammonia, Hamburg), Hugo Ruster, Wilhelm Carstens, Julius Korner, Adolf Moller, Max Ammermann

1896 Not held

Rowing — Men's Eight Oars

1988 1. West Germany, 5:46.05, Thomas Moellenkamp, Matthias Mellinghaus, Eckhardt Schultz, Ansgar Wessling, Armin Eichholz, Thomas Domian, Wolfgang Maennig, Bahne Rabe, Manfred Klein
2. Soviet Union, 5:48.01, Vinea Mine Bout, Nikolai Komarov, Vassili Tikhanov, Alexandre Doumtchev, Pavel Gourkovsky, Victor Didouk, Victor Omelianovitch, Andrei Vassiliev, Alexandre Loukianov
3. USA, 5:48.26, Doug Burden, Jeff McLaughlin, Peter Nordell, Edward Patton, John Pescatore, John Rusher, John Smith, Michael Teti

1984 1. Canada, 5:41.32, Pat Turner, Kevin Neufield, Mark Evans, Grant Main, Paul Steele, Mike Evans, Dean Crawford, Blair Horm, Brian McMahon
2. USA, 5:41.74, Walter Lubsen, Jr., Andrew Sudduth, John Terwillinger, Christopher Penny, Thomas Darling, Earl Borchelt, Charles Clapp III, Bruce Ibbetson, Robert Jaugstetter
3. Australia, 5:43.40, Craig Muller, Clyde Hefer, Sam Patten, Timothy Willoughby, Ian Edmunds, James Battersby, Ion Popa, Steve Evans, Gavin Thredgold

1980 1. East Germany, 5:49.05, Bernd Krauss, Hans-Peter Koppe, Ulrich Kons, Jorg Friedrich, Jens Doberscheutz, Ulrich Karnatz, Uwe Duehring, Bernd Hoing, Klaus-Dieter Ludwig
2. Great Britain, 5:51.92, Duncan McDougall, Allan Whitwell, Henry Clay, Chris Mahoney, Andrew Justice, John Pritchard, Malcolm McGowan, Richard Stanhope, Colin Moynihan
3. Soviet Union, 5:52.66, Viktor Kakoschin, Andrei Tishchenko, Alexandr Tkatschenko, Jonas Pinskus, Jonas Narmontas, Andrei Lugin, Aleksandr Mantsewitsch, Igor Maistrenko, Grigori Dmitrenko

1976 1. East Germany, 5:58.29, Bernd Baumgart, Gottfried Doehn, Werner Kalatt, Hans-Joachim Lueck, Dieter Wendisch, Roland Kostulski, Ulrich Karnatz, Karl-Heinz Prudoehl, Karl-Heinz Danielowski
2. Great Britain, 6:00.82, Richard Lester, John Yallop, Timothy Crooks, Hugh Matheson, David Maxwell, James Clark, Frederick Smallbone, Leonard Robertson, Patrick Sweeney
3. New Zealand, 6:03.51, Ivan Sutherland, Lindsay Wilson, Athol Earl, Trevor Coker, Dave Roger, Alex McLean, Peter Dignan, Tony Hurt, Simon Ch. Dickie

1972 1. New Zealand, 6:08.94, Tony Hurt, Wybo Veldman, Richard "Dick" Joyce, John Hunter, Lindsay Wilson, Athol Earl, Trevor Coker, Gary Robertson, Simon Dickie
2. USA, 6:11.61, Lawrence Terry, Fritz Hobbs, Peter Raymond, Timothy Mickelson, Eugene Clapp, William Hobbs, Cleve Livingston, Michael Livingston, Paul Hoffman
3. East Germany, 6:11.67, Hans-Joachim Borzym, Jorg Landvoigt, Harold Dimke, Manfred Schneider, Hartmut Schreiber, Manfred Schmorde, Bernd Landvoigt, Heinrich Mederow, Dietmar Schwarz

1968 1. West Germany, 6:07.00, Horst Meyer, Dirk Schreyer, Rudiger Henning, Wolfgang Hottenrott, Lutz Ulbricht, Egbert Hirschfelder, Jorg Siebert, Nico Ott, Gunther Tiersch
2. Australia, 6:07.98, Alfred Duval, Michael Morgan, Joseph Fazio, Peter Dickson, David Douglas, John Ranch, Gary Pearce, Robert Shirlaw, Alan Grover
3. Soviet Union, 6:09.11, Zigmas Yukna, Antanas Bogdanavichus, Vladimir Sterlik, Yosanas Yagelavichus, Aleksandr Martyschkin, Vitautas Briedis, Valentin Kravchuk, Viktor Suslin, Yuri Lorentsson

1964 1. USA, 6:18.23, Joseph Amlong, Thomas Amlong, Harold Budd, Emory Clark, Stanley Cwiklinski, Hugh Foley, William Knecht, William Stowe, Robert Zimonyi
2. West Germany, 6:23.29, Klaus Aeffke, Klaus Bittner, Karl-Heinrich von Groddeck, Hans-Jurgen Wallbrecht, Klaus Behrens, Jurgen Schroder, Jurgen Plagemann, Horst Meyer, Thomas Ahrens
3. Czechoslovakia, 6:25.11, Petr Cermak, Jiri Lundak, Jan Mrvik, Julius Tocek, Josef Ventus, Ludek Pojezny, Bohumil Janousek, Richard Novy, Miroslav Konicek

1960 1. West Germany, 5:57.18, Manfred Rulffs, Walter Schroder, Frank Schepke, Kraft Schepke, Karl-Heinrich von Groddeck, Karl-Heinz Hopp, Klaus Bittner, Hans Lenk, Willi Padge

2. Canada, 6:01.52, Donald Arnold, Walter D'Hondt, Nelson Kuhn, John Lecky, Lorne Loomer, Archibald McKinnon, William McKerlich, Glen Mervyn, Sohen Biln
3. Czechoslovakia, 6:04.84, Bohumil Janousek, Jan Jindra, Jiri Lundak, Stanislav Lusk, Vaclav Pavkovic, Ludek Pojezny, Jan Sveda, Josef Ventus, Miroslav Konicek

1956 1. USA, 6:35.2, Thomas Charlton, David Wight, John Cooke, Donald Beer, Caldwell Esselstyn, Charles Grimes, Richard Wailes, Robert Morey, William Becklean
2. Canada, 6:37.1, Philip Kueber, Richard McClure, Robert Wilson, David Helliwell, Donald Pretty, William McKerlich, Douglas McDonald, Lawrence West, Carlton Ogawa
3. Australia, 6:39.2, Michael Aikman, David Boykett, Angus Benfield, James Howden, Garth Manton, Walter Howell, Adrian Monger, Bryan Doyle, Harold Hewitt

1952 1. USA, 6:25.9, Franklin Shakespeare, William Fields, James Dunbar, Richard Murphy, Robert Detweiler, Henry Proctor, Wayne Frye, Edward Stevens, Charles Manring
2. Soviet Union, 6:31.2, Yevgeny Brago, Vladimir Rodimuskin, Aleksei Komarov, Igor Borisov, Slava Amiragov, Leonid Gissen, Yevgeny Samsonov, Vladimir Krukov, Igor Polyakov
3. Australia, 6:33.1, Robert Tinning, Ernest Chapman, Nimrod Greenwood, Mervyn Finlay, Edward Pain, Phiip Cayzer, Thomas Chessel, David Anderson, Geoffrey Williamson

1948 1. USA, 5:56.7, Ian Turner, David Turner, James Hardy, George Ahlgren, Lloyd Butler, David Brown, Justus Smith, John Stack, Ralph Purchase
2. Great Britain, 6:06.9, Christopher Barton, Maurice Lapage, Guy Richardson, Paul Bircher, Paul Massey, Charles B. Lloyd, David Meyrick, Andrew Mellows, Jack Dearlove
3. Norway, 6:10.3, Kristoffer Lepsoe, Torstein Krakenes, Hans E. Hansen, Halfdan Gran Olsen, Harald Krakenes, Leif Naess, Thor Pedersen, Carl H. Monssen, Sigurd Monssen

1936 1. USA, 6:25.4, Herbert Morris, Charles Day, Gordon Adam, John White, James McMillin, George Hunt, Joseph Rantz, Donald Hume, Robert Moch
2. Italy, 6:26.0, Guglielmo Del Bimbo, Dino Barsotti, Oreste Grossi, Enzo Bartolini, Mario Checcacci, Dante Secchi, Ottorino Quaglierini, Enrico Garzelli, Cesare Milani
3. Germany, 6:26.4, Alfred Rieck, Helmut Radach, Hans Kuschke, Heinz Kaufmann, Gerd Vols, Werner Lockle, Hans-Joachim Hannemann, Herbert Schmidt, Wilhelm Mahlow

1932 1. USA, 6:37.6, Edwin Salisbury, James Blair, Duncan Gregg, David Dunlap, Burton Jastram, Charles Chandler, Harold Tower, Winslow Hall, Norris Graham

2. Italy, 6:37.8, Vittorio Cioni, Mario Balleri, Renato Bracci, Dino Barsotti, Roberto Vestrini, Guglielmo Del Bimbo, Enrico Garzelli, Renato Barbieri, Cesare Milani

3. Canada, 6:40.4, Earl Eastwood, Joseph Harris, Stanley Stanyar, Harry Fry, Cedric Liddell, William Thoburn, Donald Boal, Albert Taylor, George MacDonald

1928 1. USA, 6:03.2, Marvin Stalder, John Brinck, Francis Frederick, William Thompson, William Dally, James Workman, Hubert Caldwell, Peter Donlon, Donald Blessing

2. Great Britain, 6:05.6, James Hamilton, Guy O. Nickalls, John Badcock, Donald Gollan, Harold Lane, Gordon Killick, Jack Beresford, Harold West, Arthur Sulley

3. Canada, 6:03.8, Frederick Hedges, Frank Fiddes, John Hand, Herbert Richardson, Jack Murdock, Athol Meech, Edgar Norris , William Ross, John Donnelly

1924 1. USA, 6:33.4, Leonard Carpenter, Howard Kingsbury, Daniel Lindley, John Miller, James Rockefeller, Frederick Sheffield, Benjamin Spock, Alfred Wilson, Laurence Stoddard

2. Canada, 6:49.0, Arthur Bell, Robert Hunter, William Langford, Harold Little, John Smith, Warren Snyder, Norman Taylor, William Wallace, Ivor Campbell

3. Italy, Antonio Cattalinich, Francesco Cattalinich, Simeone Cattalinich, Giuseppe Crivelli, Latino Galasso, Pietro Ivanov, Bruno Sorich, Carlo Toniatti, Vittorio Gliubich

1920 1. USA, 6:02.6, Virgil Jacomini, Edwin Graves, William Jordan, Edward Moore, Allen Sanborn, Donald Johnston, Vincent Gallagher, Clyde King, Sherman Clark

2. Great Britain, 6:05.0, Ewart Horsfall, Guy O. Nickalls, Richard Lucas, Walter James, John Campbell, Sebastian Earl, Ralph Shove, Sidney Swann, Robin Johnstone

3. Norway, 6:36.0, Theodor Nag, Conrad Olsen, Adolf Nilsen, Haakon Ellingsen, Thore Michelsen, Arne Mortensen, Karl Nag, Tollef Tollefsen, Thoralf Hagen

1912 1. Great Britain, 6:15.0, (Leander Club), Edgar Burgess, Sidney Swann, Leslie Wormald, Ewart Horsfall, James Gillan, Arthur Garton, Alister Kirby, Philip Fleming, Henry Wells

2. Great Britain, (New College), William Fison, William Parker, Thomas Gillespie, Beaufort Burdekin, Frederick Pitman, Arthur Wiggins, Charles Littlejohn, Robert Bourne, John Walker

3. Germany, (Berliner R.V. 1876), Otto Liebing, Max Broeske, Max Vetter, Willi Bartholomae, Fritz Bartholomae, Werner Dehn, Rudolf Reichelt, Hans Matthiae, Kurt Runge

1908 1. Great Britain, 7:52.0, (Leander Club), Albert Gladstone, Frederick Kelly, Banner Johnstone, Guy Nickalls, Charles Burnell, Ronald Sanderson, Raymond Etherington-Smith, Henry Bucknall, Gilchrist MacLagan

2. Belgium, (Royal C.N., Gand), Oscar Taelman, Marcel Morimont, Remy Orban, Georges Mijs, Francois Vergucht, Polydore Veirman, Oscar De Somville, Rodolphe Poma, Alfred Valandeghem

3. Canada, (Argonaut R.C.), Irvine Robertson, George F. Wright, Julius A. Thomson, Walter A. Lewis, Gordon B. Balfour, Becher R. Gale, Charles Riddy, Geoffrey Taylor, Douglas E. Kertland

3. Great Britain, (Cambridge University B.C.), Frederick Jerwood, Eric Powell, Guy Carver, Edward Williams, Henry Goldsmith, Harold Kitching, John Burn, Douglas Stuart, Richard Boyle

1906 **Not held**

1904 1. USA, 7:50.0, (Vesper B.C.), Louis Abell, Joseph F. Dempsey, M.D. Gleason, Frank Schell, James Flanigan, Charles E. Armstrong, Harry H. Lott, Frederick Cresser, John Exley

2. Canada (Argonaut R.C., Toronto), Joseph Wright, Donald MacKenzie, William Wadsworth, George Strange, Phil Boyd, C.R. "Pat" Reiffenstein, Colonel W. Rice, R. . . . Bailey, Thomas Loudon

1900 1. USA, 6:09.8, (Vesper B.C., Philadelphia), Louis Abell, Harry DeBaecke, William Carr, John Exley, John Geiger, Edward Hedley, James Juvenal, Roscoe Lockwood, Edward Marsh

2. Belgium, 6:13.8, (Royal Club Nautique de Gand), Marcel van Crombrugghe, Maurice Hemelsoet, Oscar De Cock, Maurice Verdonck, Prospere Bruggeman, Oscar De Somville, Frank Odberg, Jules De Bisschop, Alfred Vanlandeghem

3. Netherlands, 6:23.0, (Minerva Amsterdam), Walter Mejer Timmerman-Thijssen, Ruurd G. Leegstra, Johannes W. van Dijk, Henricus Tromp, Hendrik K. Offerhaus, Roelof Klein, Francois A. Brandt, Walter Middelberg, Dr. Hermanus Brockmann

1896 **Not held**

WOMEN'S ROWING EVENTS

▼

HIGHLIGHTS

Rowing events for women were finally included in the Olympic program in 1976. In its short history, women's Olympic rowing has been dominated by Eastern Europeans, including East Germans, Bulgarians, Romanians, and Soviets. The US women's eights captured a bronze in 1976 ahead of the Canadian eight and behind East Germany and the USSR. And US single sculler Joan Lind brought a silver medal home from the Montréal Games.

In 1984 the Rumanian women stroked to five gold medals and one silver in their six races. That year the US eights team took the gold medal, US single-sculler Charlotte Geer brought home a silver in her event, and the US quadruple sculls crew also rowed to a silver. The Netherlands and Canada medalled in double sculls in 1984, and Canada picked up silvers in the coxless pairs and coxed four, while the Netherlands captured a bronze in the eights.

US single-sculler Anne Marden took the silver medal behind Jutta Behrendt of East Germany in 1988. East Germany pulled away with most of the women's rowing gold in Seoul, except the coxless pair, which went to a Romanian crew.

Medalists

Rowing — Women's Single Sculls

1988
1. Jutta Behrendt, East Germany, 7:47.19
2. Anne Marden, USA, 7:50.28
3. Magdalena Gueorguieva, Bulgaria, 7:53.65

1984
1. Valeria Racila, Romania, 3:40.68
2. Charlote Geer, USA, 3:43.89
3. Ann Haesebrouck, Belgium, 3:45.72

1980
1. Sanda Toma, Romania, 3:40.69
2. Antonina Makhina, Soviet Union, 3:41.65
3. Martina Schroeter, East Germany 3:43.54

1976
1. Christine Scheiblich, East Germany, 4:05.56
2. Joan Lind, USA, 4:06.21
3. Elena Antonova, Soviet Union, 4:10.24

3. Bulgaria, 7:06.03, Violeta Ninova, Stefka Madina

1984
1. Romania, 3:26.75, Manoara Popescu, Elisabeta Oleniuc
2. Netherlands, 3:29.13, Greet Hellemans, Nicolette Hellemans
3. Canada, 3:29.82, Daniele Laumann, Silken Laumann

1980
1. Soviet Union, 3:16.27, Yelena Khloptseva, Larissa Popova
2. East Germany, 3:17.63, Cornelia Linse, Heidi Westphal
3. Romania, 3:18.91, Olga Homeghi, Valeria Rosca

1976
1. Bulgaria, 3:44.38, Svetla Ozetova, Zdravko Yordanova-Barboulova
2. East Germany, 3:47.86, Sabine Jahn, Petra Boesler
3. Soviet Union, 3:49.93, Leonora Kaminskaite, Genovaite Ramoshkene

Rowing — Women's Double Sculls

1988
1. East Germany, 7:00.48, Birgit Peter, Martina Schroeter
2. Romania, 7:04.36, Elisabeta Lipa, Veronica Cogeanu

Rowing — Women's Coxless Pair

1988
1. Romania, 7:28.13, Rodica Arba, Olga Homeghi
2. Bulgaria, 7:31.95, Radka Stoyanova, Lalka Berberova

380

3. New Zealand, 7:35.68, Nicola Payne, Lynley Hannen

1984 1. Romania, 3:32.60, Rodica Arba, Elena Horvat
2. Canada, 3:36.06, Betty Craig, Tricia Smith
3. West Germany, 3:40.50, Ellen Becker, Iris Volkner

1980 1. East Germany, 3:30.49, Ute Steindorf, Cornelia Klier
2. Poland, 3:30.95, Malgorzata Dluzewska, Czeslawa Koscianska
3. Bulgaria, 3:32.39, Siika Barboulova, Stoianka Kurbatova

1976 1. Bulgaria, 4:01.22, Siika Kelbecheva-Barboulova, Stoyanka Grouicheva
2. East Germany, 4:01.64, Angelica Noack, Sabine Daehne
3. West Germany, 4:02.35, Edith Eckbauer, Thea Einoeder

Rowing — Women's Quadruple Sculls

1988 1. East Germany, 6:21.06, Kerstin Foerster, Kristina Mundt, Beate Schramm, Jana Sorgers
2. Soviet Union, 6:23.47, Irina Kalimbet, Svetlana Mazyi, Inna Frolova, Antonina Doumtcheva
3. Romania, 6:23.81, Anisoara Balan, Anisoara Minea, Veronica Cogeanu, Elisabeta Lipa

1984 1. Romania, 3:14.11, Maricica Taran, Anisoara Sorohan, Ioana Badea, Sofia Corban, Ecaterina Oancia
2. USA, 3:15.57, Anne Marden, Lisa Rohde, Joan Lind, Virginia Gilder, Kelly Rickon
3. Denmark, 3:16.02, Hanne Mandsf Eriksen, Birgitte Hanel, Charlotte Koefoed, Bodil Steen Rasmussen, Jette Hejli Soerensen

1980 1. East Germany, 3:15.32, Sybille Reinhardt, Jutta Ploch, Jutta Lau, Roswietha Zobelt, Liane Buhr-Weigelt
2. Soviet Union, 3:15.73, Antonina Pustovit, Yelena Matievskaya, Olga Vasilchenko, Nadezhda Lyubimova, Nina Cheremisina
3. Bulgaria, 3:16.10, Mariana Serbezova, Roumeliana Boneva, Dolores Nakova, Ani Bakova, Stanka Georgieva

1976 1. East Germany, 3:29.99, Anke Borchmann, Jutta Lau, Viola Kowalschek-Poley, Roswietha Zobelt, Liane Buhr-Weigelt
2. Soviet Union, 3:32.49, Anna Kondrachina, Mira Bryunina, Larissa Aleksandrova, Galina Ermolaeva, Nadezhda Chernyscheva
3. Romania, 3:32.76, Ioana Tudoran, Maria Micsa, Felicia Afrasiloaia, Elisabeta Lazar, Elena Giurca

Rowing — Women's Coxed Four

1988 1. East Germany, 6:56.00, Martina Walther, Gerlinde Doberschuetz, Carola Hornig, Birte Siech, Sylvia Rose

2. People's Republic of China, 6:58.78, Zhang Xianghua, Hu Yadong, Yang Xiao, Zhou Shouying, Li Ronghua
3. Romania, 7:01.13, Marioara Trasca, Veronica Necula, Herta Anitas, Doina Iilian Balan, Escatering Oancia

1984 1. Romania, 3:19.30, Florica Lavric, Maria Fricioiu, Chira Apostol, Olga Bularda, Viorica Ioja
2. Canada, 3:21.55, Marilyn Brain, Angie Schneider, Barbara Armbrust, Jane Tregunno, Lesley Thompson
3. Australia, 3:23.29, Robyn Grey-Gardner, Karen Brancourt, Susan Chapman, Margot Foster, Susan Lee

1980 1. East Germany, 3:19.27, Ramona Kapheim, Silvia Frohlich, Angelika Noack, Romy Saalfeld, Kirsten Wenzel
2. Bulgaria, 3:20.75, Ginka Gurova, Mariika Modeva, Rita Todorova, Iskra Velinova, Nadezhda Filipova
3. Soviet Union, 3:20.92, Maria Fadeyeva, Galina Sovetnikova, Marina Studneva, Svetlana Semyonova, Nina Cheremisina

1976 1. East Germany, 3:45.08, Karin Metze, Bianka Borrman-Schwede, Gavrielle Koehn-Lohs, Andrea Kurth-Sredzki, Sabine Schubert-Hess
2. Bulgaria, 3:48.24, Guinka Guiourova, Liliana Vasseva, Reni Yordahova, Mariika Modeva, Kapka Georguieva-Panayotova
3. Soviet Union, 3:49.38, Nadezhda Sevostyanova, Ljudmila Korkhina, Galina Mishenina, Anna Pasokha, Lydia Krylova

1896-1972 Not held

Rowing — Women's Eight Oars

1988 1. East Germany, 6:15.17, Annegret Strauch, Judith Zeidler, Kathrin Haacker, Ute Wild, Anja Kluge, Beatrix Schroer, Ramona Balthasar, Uta Stange, Daniela Neunast
2. Romania, 6:17.44, Doina Lilian Balan, Marioara Trasca, Veronica Necula, Herta Anitas, Adriana Bazon, Mihaela Armasescu, Rodica Arba, Olga Homeghi, Ecaterina Oancia
3. People's Republic of China, 6:21.83, Xiuhua Zhou, Yali Zhang, Yanwen He, Yaqin Han, Xianghua Zhang, Shouhging Zhou, Xiao Yang, Yadong Hu

1984 1. USA, 2:59.80, Shyril O'Steen, Harriet Metcalf, Caroll Bower, Carie Graves, Jeanne Flanagan, Kristine Norellus, Kristen Thorsness, Kathryn Keeler, Betsy Beard
2. Romania, 3:00.87, Doina Balan, Marioara Trasca, Aurora Plesca, Aneta Mihaly, Adriana Chelariu, Mihaela Armasescu, Camelia Diaconescu, Lucia Sauca, Viorica Ioja

3. Netherlands, 3:02.92, Nicolette Hellemans, Lynda Cornet, Harriet Van Ettekoven, Greet Hellemans, Marieke Van Drogenbroek, Anne Marie Quist, Catharina Neelissen, Willemien Vaandrager, Martha Laurijsen

1980 **1.** East Germany, 3:03.32, Martina Boesler, Kersten Neisser, Christiane Kopke, Birgit Schutz, Gabriele Kuhn, Ilona Richter, Marita Sandig, Karin Metze, Marina Wilke

2. Soviet Union, 3:04.29, Olga Pivovarova, Nina Umanets, Nadezhda Prishchepa, Valentina Zhulina, Tatyana Stetsenko, Yelena Tereshina, Nina Preobrazhenskaya, Mariya Pazyun, Nina Frolova

3. Romania, 3:05.63, Angelica Aposteanu, Marlena Zagoni, Rodica Frintu, Florica Bucur, Rodica Puscatu, Ana Illiuta, Maria Constantinescu, Elena Bondar, Elena Dobritoiu

1976 **1.** East Germany, 3:33.32, Viola Landroight-Goretzki, Christiane Koepe-Knetsch, Ilona Doerfel-Richter, Brigitte Ahrenholz, Monika Leschhorn-Kallies, Henrietta Ebert, Helma Lehmann, Irina Weisse-Mueller, Marina Jaehrling-Wilke

2. Soviet Union, 3:36.17, Lyubov Talalayeva, Nadezhda Roshchina, Klavdiya Kozenkova, Elena Zubko, Olga Kolkova, Nelli Tarakanova, Nadezhda Rozgon, Olga Guzenko, Olga Pugovskaya

3. USA, 3:38.68, Jacqueline Zoch, Anita DeFrantz, Carie Graves, Marion Greig, Anne Warner, Peggy McCarthy, Carol Brown, Gail Ricketson, Lynn Silliman

382

SHOOTING

WARM-UP

Shooting competitions began in the fourteenth century. Not so coincidentally, the firearm was invented during this period as well. The first documented shooting contest was held in 1477 in Eichstadt, Germany, using blunderbusses. After pistols were developed, handguns became standard equipment in the military, and competitions eventually involved both rifles and handguns.

Shooting is a traditional Olympic event. In the 1896 Games in Athens, five shooting events were included among the nine sports on the program. Also included in the 1900 Games at Paris, these first Olympic shooting contests served as a prelude to the emergence and organization of shooting as an international sport.

fact: Shooting is also part of the Biathlon, a Winter Games event, and the Modern Pentathlon, another Summer Games event.

In 1907, eight countries established the Union Internationale de Tir (UIT), which became the governing body of the sport, at the Swiss Federal Shooting Festival in Zurich. The founding nations were Argentina, Austria, Belgium, France, Greece, Italy, the Netherlands, and Switzerland. Annual world championships were developed under the guidance of this organization, with programs devoted exclusively to rifle shooting at 300 meters and pistol matches at 50 meters.

By 1913, eleven nations took part in a World Championship event at Camp Perry, near Port Clinton, Ohio. Shooting contests involving many more contestants (known as World Wars I and II) interrupted the World Championships and temporarily disrupted the UIT, which remains the ruling body of international shooting competitions.

Although shooting is a traditional Olympic event, the sport has changed a great deal over the years. International, or Olympic-style, shooting combines aspects of its military origins with a more leisurely and European aristocratic tradition. Over the years, preparation and training has moved away from

383

shooting's original military orientation to an emphasis today placed entirely on shooting as a sport.

From the five original events included in the 1896 Olympic Games to the 13 events scheduled for the 1992 Games in Barcelona, the number of events as well as the number of competitors has changed constantly. For example, while nine shooting events were held at the 1972 Games at Munich, a reduction to seven was made at the 1976 Montréal and 1980 Moscow Games. In Los Angeles in 1984, the number of events shot up to 11, including the air rifle for men.

An historic first was created at LA, when three women-only events were added: standard rifle, air rifle, and pistol match. In 1976 at Montréal, women were allowed to compete in the men's events, and Margaret Murdock of the United States won a silver medal in the three-position competition. Montréal was also notable for the addition of skeet shooting to the program, an event that traces its origins to the United States.

Adding to the continual change and development of the sport are technical improvements to guns, ammunition, and equipment. Modern forms of training and the steady increase in the number of participating nations ensure that the sport continues to evolve. In the 1992 Olympics, shooting will attract the third-largest number of competitors to the Summer Games.

▼

SPECTATORS' GUIDE

More shooting events will be held during the 1992 Olympic Games than ever before. Rapid-fire pistol, trap, skeet, and running target competitions offer viewers the most exciting experience. Time and distance are the key factors in shooting.

Medal winners in each event are determined in a final-round shoot-off. The top eight finishers in rifle and pistol events, and the top six in running target, fire a 10-shot final round under strict time limits. In the shotgun events, the top six compete in a 25-target final round.

In all finals, each competitor's score is announced to spectators, and aggregate place-standings are tabulated after every shot. In smallbore rifle, air rifle, and air pistol events, targets are scored in tenths of a point, with 10.9 being a perfect shot.

If aggregate scores are tied, the shooter with the highest final score is awarded the higher place. If aggregate scores are tied and final scores are also equal, then a sudden-death shoot-off is fired.

Air Pistol: Separate men's and women's events are held with air or gas-powered .17 caliber pistols from 10 meters. One shot is fired per target, a bullseye with a one-half inch ten-ring. The course of fire is 60 shots in two hours and 15 minutes for men; 40 shots in one and one-half hours for women. A perfect score is 600 for men (585 is considered a world-class score); 400 for women (385 is considered world-class).

Free Pistol: This men's event is shot with a .22 caliber pistol. Regulations require only that it be a .22 caliber pistol with metallic sights. This is the only Olympic-style pistol event fired at 50 meters, and shooters fire five shots per target, a bullseye with a two-inch 10-ring. The course of fire is 60 shots in two hours and 30 minutes. A perfect score is 600, with 565 as world class.

Rapid-fire Pistol: Using a .22 caliber pistol from 25 meters, men fire one shot at each of five adjacent targets. The targets, a bullseye with a four-inch center, begin on edge and then turn to face the competitor for either eight, six, or four seconds. As an added difficulty, competitors must hold their pistols downward at a 45-degree angle until the targets turn to face them. The course of fire is 60 shots, fired in two courses of 30 shots; in each course, competitors twice fire five shots in eight seconds, six seconds, then four seconds. A perfect score is 600, with 592 as world class.

Sport Pistol: Women fire .22 caliber standard pistols from 25 meters. The course of fire is 60 shots, divided into a 30-shot precision phase and a 30-shot duel. The precision, or slow-fire stage, is fired in six series of five shots, and competitors are allowed six minutes per series. In the 30-shot duel, or rapid-fire stage, the target, a bullseye with a four-inch center for duel (and a two-inch center for precision), begins on edge, turns to face the shooter for three seconds, then turns away for seven seconds. A perfect score is 600, with 588 as world class.

fact: Small-bore competition flourished during the Depression between the World Wars, when small-bore ammunition was the easiest to afford.

Men's Smallbore Free Rifle Prone: This event is shot at 50 meters with .22 caliber rifles weighing up to 17.6 pounds. Athletes fire one shot per target, a bullseye with a 10.4 millimeter center (roughly the size of a dime), from the prone (lying down) position. As with all rifle events described, metallic sights are used. The course of fire is 60 shots in one hour and 45 minutes. A perfect score is 600, with 597 as world class.

Three-Position: Separate events are fired for men and women. Men use .22 caliber free rifles not weighing more than 17.6 pounds. Women fire .22 caliber standard rifles not exceeding 12.12 pounds. The target, a bullseye with a 10.4 millimeter center, is fired upon from the prone, standing, and kneeling positions. Athletes fire one shot per target from 50 meters. The course of fire is 120 shots for men—40 shots per position with the following time limits: one and one-quarter hour for prone, one hour and 45 minutes for standing, and one and one-half hours for kneeling. 60 shots for women—20 per position. Women are allowed a total of two and one-half hours for all three positions. A perfect score is 1200 for men, with 1165 as world class; 600 for women, with 580 as world class.

Air Rifle: Separate events are fired for men and women, with all competitors firing air- or gas-powered .17 caliber rifles weighing up to 12.12 pounds. Competitors fire one shot per target, a bullseye with a one-half millimeter center (roughly the size of the head of a pin), from a standing position at a distance of 10 meters. The course of fire is 60 shots in two hours for men; 40 shots in one hour and 30 minutes for women. A perfect score is 600 for men, with 588 as world class; 400 for women, with 393 as world class.

Running Target: Men shoot .17 caliber air rifles with telescope sights (not exceeding four-power) at paper targets moving across a track ten meters away. The target has two bullseyes spaced roughly six inches apart; an aiming dot placed between them aids the shooter in tracking. The course of fire is 60 shots divided into 30 slow runs (5 seconds to track, aim, and fire) and 30 fast runs (2.5 seconds to track, aim, and fire). A perfect score is 600, with 570 as world class.

Trap: Men and women compete together with 12-gauge shotguns. Breakable four-inch clay targets are thrown from an underground bunker a minimum distance of 70 meters and at speeds of up to 110 miles per hour. Competitors mount their shotguns on their shoulders before calling for the target and are allowed two shots per target. The course of fire is 200 targets in eight rounds of 25. Targets may be shot in two days of 100 targets, or three days of 75, 75, and 50 targets. A perfect score is 200, with 198 as world class.

Skeet: Men and women compete together with 12-gauge shotguns. Single or double clay targets are thrown at least 65 meters from the high or low house on either side of the semicircular field. Competitors fire one shot per target from each of eight stations. Unlike international trap, the competitor must hold the shotgun at hip level until the target appears, which can be anywhere from 0–3 seconds after called. The course of fire is same as trap. A perfect score is same as trap.

For all events, medal winners in each event are determined in a final round shoot-off. The top eight finishers in rifle and pistol events, and the top six in running target, fire a 10-shot final round under strict time limits. In the shotgun events, the top six compete in a 25-target final round.

In all finals, each competitor's score is announced to spectators, and aggregate place standings are tabulated after every shot. In smallbore rifle, air rifle, and air pistol events, targets are scored in tenths of a point, with 10.9 being a perfect shot.

If aggregate scores are tied, the shooter with the highest final score is awarded the higher place. If aggregate scores are tied and final scores are also equal, then a sudden-death shoot-off is fired.

AIRGUN is a gun that discharges lead pellets through compressed air or carbon dioxide.

BORE is the interior diameter of a gun barrel.

BULL is the central blackened portion of a target that appears as a dot to the shooter who is taking aim. The center ring is a ten or "bullseye."

BUNKER in trapshooting is the underground "dugout" in front of the firing line that houses the clay target throwing machine.

CALIBER is the interior diameter of a rifle or pistol barrel.

CARTRIDGE is the complete unit of ammunition, including the projectile, case, powder, and primer.

CHALLENGE is a shooter's petition that a target be rescored.

CHAMBER is the rear portion of the gun barrel into which a cartridge is inserted for firing.

CROSSFIRE is a shot accidentally fired on a target assigned to another competitor.

FIRING LINE is the line from which competitors position themselves to shoot their targets.

FREE PISTOL is a .22 caliber pistol relatively "free" of restrictions.

FREE RIFLE is a smallbore or centerfire rifle used in international competition that is relatively "free" of restrictions.

METALLIC SIGHT includes the devices on the front and rear ends of a gun barrel used to assist aim.

OFFHAND is another term for the standing shooting position.

PITS, in .22 caliber firing ranges, are the man-made berms or walls rising behind the targets to absorb bullets.

SIGHTERS are practice shots fired at the beginning of a match to check sight adjustments; they do not count in the match score.

STRING is a series of shots, normally five or ten.

STOCK is the wooden, metal, plastic, or fiberglass portion of a rifle or shotgun, to which the barrel, action, trigger assembly, etc., are seated.

TEN-RING is the innermost ring of the black section of the target.

Shooting

HOPEFULS

The Soviet Union and other Eastern European nations, with their history of excellent Olympic marksmanship, should claim most of the shooting medals again in Barcelona. In 1991 at the US International Shooting Championships, the Soviet Union took 44 medals, including two golds that Valentina Cherkasova won as she set two world records in women's air rifle events. Korea and the USA (which is considered to have the best team in the Western hemisphere) won four medals each, and Australia brought home three. David Edmondson, who gave the USA three of its four medals (his were all golds), has his sights set on an Olympic medal in the running target events. World champion Glen Dubis, whose specialty is rifle shooting, and US champion Bob Foth, who shoots well in smallbore free rifle events, also aim to help the men's team.

Promising women shooters include Connie Petracek, who set a national record and won a gold medal at the 1991 US Internationals, and Deena Wigger—daughter of four-time Olympian Lones Wigger—who won two bronze medals at the championships.

Schedule

The tentative shooting schedule is as follows:

Sunday, July 26
Final, air rifle, women
Finals, free pistol, men
Clay target, skeet

Monday, July 27
Sport pistol, precision, women
Finals, sport pistol, rapid fire, women
Finals, air rifle, men
Clay target, skeet

Tuesday, July 28
Finals, air pistol, men
Semifinals & finals clay target, skeet

Wednesday, July 29
Finals, smallbore free rifle, men (English)
Rapid fire pistol, men

Thursday, July 30
Semifinals & finals, rapid fire, pistol, men
Finals, smallbore free rifle 3 positions, women

Friday, July 31
Finals, smallbore free rifle, 3 position, men
Clay target, men
Running game target, men

Saturday, August 1
Finals, air pistol, women
Finals, running game target, men
Clay target, trap

Sunday, August 2
Semifinals & finals, clay target, trap

388

HIGHLIGHTS

Shooting events were sure to be included among the nine original sports in the Olympics, since Baron de Coubertin, the founder of the Modern Games, had been a pistol-shooter in his youth. The first Olympic gold medalist was Pantelis Karasevdas, from Greece, in the free rifle event. Greece took two other golds in 1896, and America won the two remaining events.

Perhaps the most memorable—if somewhat distasteful—victory in 1900 was that of Léon de Lunden, from Belgium, who became an Olympic victor for slaying a record 21 pigeons in the one-and-only live pigeon shooting event. France—who entered 173 participants—and Switzerland dominated the other events that year.

Shooting was omitted from the program in 1904, but returned for the London Games in 1908, when seventy competitors from the host country participated. The Russians, who had alerted officials that they would be competing, arrived in time to help with the clean-up. Following the Julian calendar, rather than the Gregorian calendar—which the Games followed—they arrived twelve days late. In the Russians' absence, Oscar Swahn won his first Olympic gold medal, in running dear shooting, a discontinued event. The sixty-year-old Swede hadn't experienced his last Olympic victory. Swahn medalled in the same event in 1920 and again in 1924, the final time this event was held.

In 1908, the US dominated the military revolver teams event, which was later discontinued. The 1912 and 1920 Games were an exercise in déjà vu: American Alfred Lane and marine Sergeant. Morris Fisher won more than one gold ... at both Games. Also in 1912, the ten-time Russian pistol champion, Nikolai Kolomenkin, placed eighth in the free pistol event; not as impressive as his gold medal as a figure skater in the 1908 Games. The 1920 free pistol event was marked by good sportsmanship: Brazilian Alfranio da Costa won silver with a pistol lent to him by the American team. Alfred Lane, who had given da Costa his ammunition, came in third.

fact: The rapid fire pistol target resembles a small human figure.

Perhaps the most noteworthy shooting event of the 1924 Games was the rapid fire shooting event. When 8 of the 55 competitors achieved perfect scores, another round was called; this, too, produced eight perfect scores. Yet another round was called. This went on until the sixth round, when two shooters still maintained perfect scores. In the final round, Henry Bailey, a US Marine Corps sergeant, lost part of his eight seconds removing a cartridge from his .22, which had malfunctioned. Nevertheless, his five remaining shots were on target—enough to earn him the 1924 gold medal.

No shooting events appeared in the 1928 Games, but the sport returned—although with only two events—in 1932. Yet another good sportsman brightened the 1932 LA Games: Hungarian Antonius Lemberkovits hit a bullseye in the small-bore rifle, prone event, but was credited with a complete miss because he alerted judges that he had aimed at the wrong target. In the same event in the 1936 Games, Norwegian Willy Rögeberg captured the gold with a perfect-300 score, the first such score to be recorded in international competition.

In 1948, Hungarian Károly Tákacs—the European pistol champion of the 1930s—won the rapid fire pistol event, and won it again in 1952, becoming one of only five competitors to have defended an Olympic shooting title successfully. What is most unusual about Tákacs, though, is that he won the event left-handed; originally a right-handed shooter, he lost the use of his right arm when a grenade exploded in his hand in 1938, during army training.

In 1952, Canadian George Généreux won the gold medal in the trap shooting event by one point; Swede Knut Holmquist, who missed the penultimate shot of his last round, earned the silver medal, while his compatriot, Hans Liljedahl, won the bronze. Winning the event at the age of seventeen, Généreux is the youngest gold medalist in the sport of shooting. Also at the Helsinki Games, Huelet Benner became the first American in 32 years to win a pistol event.

fact: Consistency is the most important element in winning shooting competitions.

At the 1956 Games, Gerald Ouellette won the small-bore, prone event and set a world record—they thought—with a perfect-600 score. When the course was discovered to measure 48 1/2m instead of the standard 50m, Ouellette's record was disallowed.

In 1960, American William McMillan won the rapid fire pistol event, and went on to a record of competing in six games. Swede Torsten Ullman, who had won the free pistol event in Berlin, placed in the top ten of the event in every Games up to and including the Rome Games, where he finished fourth at the age of 52. Finland's Pentti Linnosvuo won the gold medal in the rapid fire pistol event; having won the free pistol event in 1956, he became the second shooter in the history of the Games to win the gold in both events.

Women competed in shooting for the first time in 1968, albeit without separate categories. Poland, Peru, and Mexico each entered one woman in the men's events; the first to compete, Nuria Ortiz of Mexico finished thirteenth in the skeet event. The 1972 small bore, prone event winner, Ho Jun Li, from North Korea, made history not so much for his medal as for his professed secret to success: he claimed to pretend to aim at a capitalist.

1976 was the year in which the sport of shooting inducted a member into the Hall of Shame: Paul Cerutti of Monaco—who finished 43rd out of 44 competitors—was disqualified for drug use. At 65 years old, Cerutti is the oldest

Games competitor, as far as records indicate, to have been disqualified for drug use. Also that year, American Margaret Murdock became the first woman to medal in shooting.

The USSR and East Germany swept the Moscow Games: the Soviets took three golds, a silver and a bronze, while the East Germans took five silvers and a bronze. In the small bore rifle, prone event, Hungarian Károly Varga captured the gold despite having broken his shooting hand just prior to the Games.

In 1984, the US cultivated a bumper crop in terms of medals: two gold, one silver, and one bronze medal went to the US men's team, while a gold and a bronze went to the US women—who, at long last, competed in their own classes. China boasted an even better year: Xu Heifing captured the gold medal for pistol shooting, and five other medals went to the Chinese team, including two more golds.

1988 produced the first Olympic shooter to win consecutive medals in the men's small-bore rifle, three position event. Malcolm Cooper, from Great Britain, outshot his countryman Alister Allan by 3.7 points, in his second victory over Allan, who had placed third in 1984. The US men's team took home only one medal from Seoul—Edward Etzel's smallbore free rifle, prone—and the US women failed to medal at all.

![Medalists]

Shooting — Men's Air Pistol

1988   1. Taniou Kiriakov, Bulgaria, 687.9
2. Erich Buljung, USA, 687.9 (EWR)
3. Haifeng Xu, People's Republic of China, 684.5

Shooting — Men's Free Pistol

1988   1. Sorin Babii, Romania, 660
2. Ragnar Skanaker, Sweden, 657
3. Igor Bassinski, Soviet Union, 657
1984   1. Haifeng Xu, China, 566
2. Ragnar Skanaker, Sweden, 565
3. Yifu Wang, China, 564
1980   1. Aleksandr Melentiev, Soviet Union, 581 (WR)
2. Harald Vollmar, East Germany, 568
3. Lubcho Diakov, Bulgaria, 565
1976   1. Uwe Potteck, East Germany, 573 (WR, OR)
2. Harald Vollmar, East Germany, 567
3. Rudolf Dollinger, Austria, 562
1972   1. Ragnar Skanaker, Sweden, 567 (OR)
2. Dan Iuga, Romania, 562
3. Rudolf Dollinger, Austria, 560
1968   1. Grigori Kossykh, Soviet Union, 562/30 (OR)
2. Heinz Mertel, West Germany, 562/26 (OR)
3. Harald Vollmar, East Germany, 560

1964   1. Vaino Markkanen, Finland, 560 (EOR)
2. Franklin Green, USA, 557
3. Yoshihisa Yoshikawa, Japan, 554/26
1960   1. Aleksei Gustchin, Soviet Union, 560 (OR)
2. Makhmud Umarov, Soviet Union, 552/26
3. Yoshihisa Yoshikawa, Japan, 552/20
1956   1. Pentti Linnosvuo, Finland, 556/26 (OR)
2. Makhmud Umarov, Soviet Union, 556/24 (OR)
3. Offutt Pinion, USA, 551
1952   1. Huelet Benner, USA, 553 (OR)
2. Angel Leon De Gozalo, Spain, 550
3. Ambrus Balogh, Hungary, 549
1948   1. Edwin Vasquez Cam, Peru, 545
2. Rudolf Schnyder, Switzerland, 539/60/21
3. Torsten Ullman, Sweden, 539/60/16
1936   1. Torsten Ullman, Sweden, 559 (WR)
2. Erich Krempel, Germany, 544
3. Charles Des Jammonieres, France, 540
1924-1932   **Not held**
1920   1. Karl Frederick, USA, 496
2. Afranio Da Costa, Brazil, 489
3. Alfred Lane, USA, 481
1912   1. Alfred Lane, USA, 499
2. Peter Dolfen, USA, 474
3. Charles E. Stewart, Great Britain, 470
1908   **Not held**
1906   1. Georgios Orphanidis, Greece, 221

2. Jean Fouconnier, France, 219
3. Aristides Rangavis, Greece, 218
1904 **Not held**
1900 1. Conrad Roderer, Switzerland, 503
2. Achille Paroche, France, 466
3. Konrad Staheli, Switzerland, 453
1896 1. Sumner Paine, USA, 442
2. Holger Nielsen, Denmark, 285
3. Nikoalos Morakis, Greece

Shooting — Men's Rapid-Fire Pistol

1988 1. Afanasi Kouzming, Soviet Union, 698 (WR)
2. Ralf Schumann, East Germany, 696
3. Zoltan Kovacs, Hungary, 693
1984 1. Takeo Kamachi, Japan, 595
2. Corneliu Ion, Romania, 593
3. Rauno Bies, Finland, 591/146
1980 1. Corneliu Ion, Romania, 596/148/147/148
2. Jurgen Wiefel, East Germany, 596/148/147/147
3. Gerhard Petritsch, Austria, 596/146
1976 1. Norbert Klaar, East Germany, 597 (OR)
2. Jurgen Wiefel, East Germany, 596
3. Roberto Ferraris, Italy, 595
1972 1. Jozef Zapedzki, Poland, 595 (OR)
2. Ladislav Falta, Czechoslovakia, 594
3. Viktor Torshin, Soviet Union, 593
1968 1. Jozef Zapedzki, Poland, 593 (OR)
2. Marcel Rosca, Romania, 591/147
3. Renart Suleimanov, Soviet Union, 591/146
1964 1. Pentti Linnosvuo, Finland, 592 (OR)
2. Ion Tripsa, Romania, 591
3. Lubomir Nacovsky, Czechoslovakia, 590
1960 1. William McMillan, USA, 587/147 (EOR)
2. Pentti Linnosvuo, Finland, 587/139
3. Aleksandr Zabelin, Soviet Union, 587/135
1956 1. Stefan Petrescu, Romania, 587 (OR)
2. Yergeny Cherkassov, Soviet Union, 585
3. Gheorghe Lichiardopol, Romania, 581
1952 1. Karoly Takacs, Hungary, 579
2. Szilard Kun, Hungary, 578
3. Gheorghe Lichiardopol, Romania, 578
1948 1. Karoly Takacs, Hungary, 580 (WR)
2. Carlos E. Diaz Saenz Valiente, Argentina, 571
3. Sven Lundqvist, Sweden, 569
1936 1. Cornelius Van Oyen, Germany, 36
2. Heinz Hax, Germany, 35
3. Torsten Ullman, Sweden, 34
1932 1. Renzo Morigi, Italy, 36
2. Heinz Hax, Germany, 36
3. Domenico Matteucci, Italy, 36
1928 **Not held**
1924 1. H. M. Bailey, USA, 18
2. Vilhelm Carlberg, Sweden, 18
3. Lennart Hannelius, Finland, 18
1920 1. Guilherme Paraense, Brazil, 274
2. Raymond Bracken, USA, 272
3. Fritz Zulauf, Switzerland, 269
1912 1. Alfred Lane, USA, 287
2. Paul Palen, Sweden, 286

3. Johan Hubner Von Holst, Sweden, 283
1908 1. Paul Van Asbroeck, Belgium, 490
2. Reginald Storms, Belgium, 487
3. James E. Gorman, USA, 485
1906 1. Maurice Lecoq, France, 250
2. Leon Moreaux, France, 249
3. Aristides Rangavis, Greece, 245
1904 **Not held**
1900 1. Maurice Larrouy, France, 58
2. Leon Moreaux, France, 57
3. Eugene Balme, France, 57
1896 1. Jean Phrangoudis, Greece, 344
2. Georgios Orphanidis, Greece, 249
3. Holger Nielsen, Denmark

Shooting — Men's Running Game Target

1988 1. Tor Heiestad, Norway, 689 (OR)
2. Shiping Huang, People's Republic of China, 687
3. Guennadi Avramenko, Soviet Union, 686
1984 1. Yuwei Li, China, 587
2. Helmut Bellingrodt, Colombia, 584
3. Shiping Huang, China, 581
1980 1. Igor Sokolov, Soviet Union, 589 (WR)
2. Thomas Pfeffer, East Germany, 589
3. Aleksandr Gazov, Soviet Union, 587
1976 1. Aleksandr Gazov, Soviet Union, 579 (WR)
2. Alexandr Kedyrov, Soviet Union, 576
3. Jerzy Greszkiewicz, Poland, 571
1972 1. Yakov Zhelezniak, Soviet Union, 569 (WR)
2. Helmut Bellingrodt, Colombia, 565
3. John Kynoch, Great Britain, 562
1904-
1968 **Not held**
1900 1. Louis Debray, France, 20
2. P. Nivet, France, 20
3. Comte De Lambert, France, 19
1896 **Not held**

Shooting — Men's Air Rifle

1988 1. Goran Maksimovic, Yugoslavia, 695.6 (OR)
2. Nicolas Berthelof, France, 694.2
3. Johann Reiderer, West Germany, 694.0
1984 1. Philippe Heberle, France, 589
2. Andreas D. I. Kronthaler, Austria, 587
3. Barry Dagger, Great Britain, 587
1896-
1980 **Not held**

Shooting — Men's Smallbore Free Rifle, Prone

1988 1. Miroslav Varga, Czechoslovakia, 703.9 (EWR)
2. Young-chul Cha, South Korea, 702.8
3. Attila Zahonyi, Hungary, 701.9
1984 1. Edward Etzel, USA, 599
2. Michel Bury, France, 596
3. Michael Sullivan, Great Britain, 596
1980 1. Karoly Varga, Hungary, 599 (EWR)

2. Hellfried Heilfort, East Germany, 599 (EWR)
3. Petur Zaprianov, Bulgaria, 598
1976 1. Karlheinz Smieszek, West Germany, 599 (WR,OR)
2. Ulrich Lind, West Germany, 597
3. Gennady Lushnikov, Soviet Union, 595
1972 1. Ho-Jun Li Democratic People's Republic of Korea, 599 (WR)
2. Victor Auer, USA, 598
3. Nicolae Rotaru, Romania, 598
1968 1. Jan Kurka, Czechoslovakia, 598 (EWR)
2. Laszlo Hammerl, Hungary, 598 (EWR)
3. Ian Ballinger, New Zealand, 597
1964 1. Laszlo Hammerl, Hungary, 597 (WR)
2. Lones Wigger, USA, 597 (WR)
3. Tommy Pool, USA, 596
1960 1. Peter Kohnke, West Germany, 590
2. James Hill, USA, 589
3. Enrico Forcella Pelliccioni, Venezuela, 587
1956 1. Gerald R. Ouellette, Canada, 600
2. Vassili Borissov, Soviet Union, 599
3. Gilmour S. Boa, Canada, 598
1952 1. Iosif Sirbu, Romania, 400/33 (EWR)
2. Boris Andreyev, Soviet Union, 400/28 (EWR)
3. Arthur Jackson, USA, 399
1948 1. Arthur Cook, USA, 599/43 (WR)
2. Walter Tomsen, USA, 599/42 (WR)
3. Jonas Jonsson, Sweden, 597
1936 1. Willy Rogeberg, Norway, 300 (WR)
2. Ralf Berzsenyi, Hungary, 296
3. Wladyslaw Karas, Poland, 296
1932 1. Bertil Ronnmark, Sweden, 294
2. Gustavo Huet, Mexico, 294
3. Zoltan Hradetzky-Soos, Hungary, 293
1928 Not held
1924 1. Pierre Coquelin De Lisle, France, 398 (prone)
2. Marcus Dinwiddie, USA, 396 (prone)
3. Josias Hartmann, Switzerland, 394 (prone)
1920 1. Lawrence A. Nuesslein, USA, 391 (standing)
2. Arthur Rothrock, USA, 386 (standing)
3. Dennis Fenton, USA, 385 (standing)
1912 1. Frederick Hird, USA, 194 (any position)
2. William Milne, Great Britain, 193 (any position)
3. Harry Burt, Great Britain, 192 (any position)
1908 1. A. A. Carnell, Great Britain, 387 (any position)
2. Harry R. Humby, Great Britain, 386 (any position)
3. G. Barnes, Great Britain, 385 (any position)
1896-
1906 Not held

Shooting — Men's Smallbore Rifle, Three-Position

1988 1. Malcolm Cooper, Great Britain, 1279.3
2. Alister Allan, Great Britain, 1275.6
3. Kirill Ivanov, Soviet Union, 1275.0
1984 1. Malcolm Cooper, Great Britain, 1173

2. Daniel Nipkow, Switzerland, 1163
3. Alister Allan, Great Britain, 1162
1980 1. Viktor Vlasov, Soviet Union, 1173 (WR)
2. Bernd Hartstein, East Germany, 1166
3. Sven Johansson, Sweden, 1165
1976 1. Lanny Bassham, USA, 1162
2. Margaret Murdock, USA, 1162
3. Rainer Seibold, West Germany, 1160
1972 1. John Writer, USA, 1166 (WR)
2. Lanny Bassham, USA, 1157
3. Werner Lippoldt, East Germany, 1153
1968 1. Bernd Klingner, West Germany, 1157
2. John Writer, USA, 1156
3. Vitali Parkhimovich, Soviet Union, 1154
1964 1. Lones Wigger, USA, 1164 (WR)
2. Velitschko Christov, Bulgaria, 1152
3. Laszlo Hammerl, Hungary, 1151
1960 1. Viktor Shamburkin, Soviet Union, 1149 (EWR)
2. Marat Niyasov, Soviet Union, 1145
3. Klaus Zahringer, West Germany, 1139
1956 1. Anatoli Bogdanov, Soviet Union, 1172 (OR)
2. Otakar Horinek, Czechoslovakia, 1172 (OR)
3. John Sundberg, Sweden, 1167
1952 1. Erling Kongshaug, Norway, 1164/53
2. Vilho Ylonen, Finland, 1164/49
3. Boris Andreyev, Soviet Union, 1163
1896-
1948 Not held

Shooting — Olympic Skeet (Open)

1988 1. Axel Wegner, East Germany, 222 (EOR)
2. Alfonso De Iruarrizaga, Chile, 221 (EOR)
3. Jorge Guardiola, Spain, 220
1984 1. Matthew Dryke, USA, 198
2. Ole Riber Rasmussen, Denmark, 196/25
3. Luca Scribani Italy, 196/23
1980 1. Hans Kjeld Rasmussen, Denmark, 196/25/25
2. Lars-Goran Carlsson, Sweden, 196/25/24
3. Roberto Castrillo, Cuba, 196/25/23
1976 1. Josef Panacek, Czechoslovakia, 198 (EOR)
2. Eric Swinkels, Netherlands, 198 (EOR)
3. Wieslaw Gwalikowski, Poland, 196
1972 1. Konrad Wirnhier, West Germany, 195/25
2. Yevgeny Petrov, Soviet Union, 195/24
3. Michael Buchheim, East Germany, 195/23
1968 1. Yevgeny Petrov, Soviet Union, 198/25 (EWR)
2. Romano Garagnani, Italy, 198/25 (EWR)
3. Konrad Wirnhier, West Germany, 198/24/23 (EWR)
1896-
1964 Not held

393

Shooting — Women's Air Pistol

1988 1. Jasna Sekaric, Yugoslavia, 489.5 (WR)
2. Nino Saloukvadze, Soviet Union, 487.5
3. Marina Dobrantcheva, Soviet Union, 485.2

Shooting — Women's Sport Pistol

1988 1. Nino Salukvadze, Soviet Union, 690.0 (OR)
2. Tomoko Hasegawa, Japan, 686.0
3. Jasna Sekaric, Yugoslavia, 686.0 (OR)
1984 1. Linda Thom, Canada, 585/198
2. Ruby Fox, USA, 585/197
3. Patricia Dench, Australia, 583/196
**1896-
1980** Not held

Shooting — Olympic Trap (Open)

1988 1. Dmitri Monakov, Soviet Union, 222
2. Miloslav Bednarik, Czechoslovakia, 222
3. Frans Peeters, Belgium, 219
1984 1. Luciano Giovannetti, Italy, 192/24
2. Francisco Boza, Peru, 192/23
3. Daniel Carlisle, USA, 192/22
1980 1. Luciano Giovannetti, Italy, 198
2. Rustam Yambulatov, Soviet Union, 196/24/25
3. Jorg Damme, East Germany, 196/24/24
1976 1. Donald Haldeman, USA, 190
2. Armando Silva Marquese, Portugal, 189
3. Ubaldesco Baldi, Italy, 189
1972 1. Angelo Scalzone, Italy, 199 (WR)
2. Michel Carrega, France, 198
3. Silvano Basagni, Italy, 195
1968 1. John R. Braithwaite, Great Britain, 198 (EWR)
2. Thomas Garrigus, USA, 196/25/25
3. Kurt Czekalla, East Germany, 196/25/23
1964 1. Ennio Mattarelli, Italy, 198 (OR)
2. Pavel Senichev, Soviet Union, 194/25
3. William Morris, USA, 194/24
1960 1. Ion Dumitrescu, Romania, 192
2. Galliano Rossini, Italy, 191
3. Sergei Kalinin, Soviet Union, 190
1956 1. Galliano Rossini, Italy, 195 (OR)
2. Adam Smelczynski, Poland, 190
3. Alessandro Ciceri, Italy, 188
1952 1. George P. Genereux, Canada, 192
2. Knut Holmqvist, Sweden, 191

3. Hans Liljedahl, Sweden, 190
**1928-
1948** Not held
1924 1. Gyula Halasy, Hungary, 98/8 (OR)
2. Konrad Huber, Finland, 98/7 (OR)
3. Frank Hughes, USA, 97
1920 1. Mark Arie, USA, 95
2. Frank Troeh, USA, 93
3. Frank Wright, USA, 87
1912 1. James Graham, USA, 96
2. Alfred Goeldel, Germany, 94
3. Harry Blau, Russia, 91
1908 1. Walter H. Ewing, Canada, 72
2. George Beattie, Canada, 60
3. Alexander Maunder, Great Britain, 57
3. Anastasios Metaxas, Greece, 57
1906 1. Gerald Merlin, Great Britain, 24 (single shot)
1. Sidney Merlin, Great Britain, 15 (double shot)
2. Anastasios Metaxas, Greece, 13 (double shot)
2. Ioannis Peridis, Greece, 23 (single shot)
3. Gerald Merlin, Great Britain, 12 (double shot)
3. Sidney Merlin, Great Britain, 21 (single shot)
1904 Not held
1900 1. Roger De Barbarin, France, 17
2. Rene Guyot, France, 17
3. Justinien De Clary, France, 17
1896 Not held

Shooting — Women's Air Rifle

1988 1. Irina Chilova, Soviet Union, 498.5 (OR)
2. Silvia Sperber, West Germany, 497.5
3. Anna Maloukhina, Soviet Union, 495.8
1984 1. Pat Spurgin, USA, 393
2. Edith Gufler, Italy, 391
3. Xiao Xuan Wu, China, 389
**1896-
1980** Not held

Shooting — Women's Smallbore Rifle, Three-Position

1988 1. Silvia Sperber, West Germany, 685.6 (OR)
2. Vessela Letcheva, Bulgaria, 683.2
3. Valentina Tcherka Ssova, Soviet Union, 681.4
1984 1. Xiao Xuan Wu, China, 581
2. Ulrike Holmer, West Germany, 578
3. Wanda Jewel, USA, 578
**1896-
1980** Not held

▼

SOCCER

WARM-UP

Today, it is the world's most popular sport, thanks to successful 18th- and 19th-century British Empire expansion. Yet soccer, or *futbol* (football) as it is known in all parts of the world outside the US and Canada, has been around in one form or another for thousands of years. And so, likewise, has the violence associated with the sport.

In 80 BC China, a popular game of the day involved one goal, formed with two bamboo poles thirty or more feet high, with an opening one-foot in diameter. Players took turns trying to kick a ball through the opening, scoring points for each success.

In ancient Greece and Rome, several types of balls were used in games. One, the *follis*, was a large ball filled with hair and otherwise similar to a modern soccer ball. In the Roman game of *follis*, the object was to toss the ball in the air and keep it up by using the hands. A smaller ball, the *harpastum*, was used in another game played with the hands. Participants tossed the ball to one another while others tried to intercept it or tackle the player who caught it. But neither the *follis* or *harpastum* was ever kicked on purpose.

In ancient Florence, a game called *calcio* was very big. *Calcio* involved 27 players on a side and one ball. The object was to pass, kick, or carry the ball across the goal. The game was more like the English version of mob football, in which the real goal was to kick your neighbor.

Legend has it that Roman legionnaires would celebrate a victory by kicking around the severed heads of their foes. Apparently villagers in Britain witnessed this great fun and decided they had the basis of a game. Using an inflated bladder for a ball and village streets for a field, *futbol* was born. Or another legend: around 1050, workmen digging in an old battlefield came across the skull of a Dane. How they knew it was the skull of a Dane, we do not know. The workmen, angered at Danes in general for occupying England during the period, began kicking the skull around the battlefield and at some point, directed it at targets for points. Interestingly enough, "heading" is a big part of the game now, although you don't necessarily have to lose one to be effective.

Football's first mention in English literature appeared in a history of London written in 1174. During the 12th and 13th centuries, a game loosely resembling modern soccer, but involving more physical violence among participants, was played throughout England. The object was to advance the ball to the opponent's goal, playing on an ad hoc field that often wove through the middle of a town. At any given moment, a football game might rush through town, damaging storefronts and homes. Players used arms, legs, heads, and brute force to move the ball forward. With its potential for mayhem, the game attracted the thug element (which apparently in Old England was rather profuse), so authorities sought to shut it down. In 1314, King Edward II of England outlawed football, on the basis that it was a waste of people's time. Similar actions were later taken by Richard II and Henry VIII (who, incidentally, chose better ways of wasting his time).

But regardless of what the authorities did, the game continued to flourish. Eventually, it was confined to a preestablished field, which appeased the town dwellers who did not embrace spontaneous soccer action exploding in front of their homes or businesses. Standardized rules were adopted, so that by the end of the 15th century the game was described as one in which the ball was propelled by striking it with the feet. In 1580, the game appeared on British college campuses as an intramural sport, and 40 years later as an intercollegiate event.

In the 1800s, football was introduced in Britain's public schools, where it became further refined. But the question of hand use during the game was still open. At the schools, such as Westminster, where the playgrounds were smaller, the kicking version of soccer dominated. At Rugby School, however, the wide open spaces of the campus invited carrying the ball. It was left to William Webb Elias to turn fantasy into reality, as he elected during a football game to run with the ball, creating another game in the process, rugby.

The modern game started with the foundation of the Football Association (of England) in 1863. By 1883, England, Ireland, Scotland, and Wales had founded the International Board, which has become the game's sole rule-making council. In 1904, the Fédération Internationale de Football Associations (FIFA) was founded, becoming soccer's worldwide administrative body.

fact: The term soccer stems from 1890s British University slang; derived from association football, it takes the *soc* and adds an *-er* suffix.

Soccer was the first team sport added to the Olympics. Great Britain dominated the early tournaments, winning three of the first four. Although the sport made its medal debut in 1900, it was not until 1908 that the tournament attracted reasonable international representation.

After World War I, as the sport grew internationally, British dominance ended, while the South American style came into vogue, with Uruguay taking the 1924 and 1928 Olympics (the only tournaments at which a non-European team has won). At the same time, controversy increased over what constituted a professional or amateur player, a debate that has dogged the Olympic tournament for years. In 1932, soccer was pulled from the program at Los Angeles as the issue of pseudo-amateurs in the Games reached the boiling point. Olympic soccer is now dominated by Eastern European teams that do not have to compete with professional leagues for players.

In 1930, the first World Cup was held, coming two years after the Olympics, and the two events have followed this staggered four-year sequence ever since. Held in Uruguay, 13 countries participated, including the US and four teams from Europe: France, Belgium, Romania, and Yugoslavia. The US slipped into the semifinals (its highest placement to date in the World Cup) before losing 6–1 to the Argentines, the bronze medal winners in the 1928 Olympics. The host Uruguayans became the first World Cup world champions.

Although America has never won an Olympic medal in soccer or taken the World Cup, the popularity of the game continues to increase in the United States. According to a 1989 survey released by the Soccer Industry Council of America, more than 15 million Americans over the age of six played soccer at least once during 1989. The sport is administered by the US Soccer Foundation, founded in 1913. In 1994, the US will host the World Cup, an event that many in the soccer community believe will greatly increase the popularity of the sport in America. The US will be making its fourth appearance in World Cup play.

SPECTATORS' GUIDE

Let's talk kicking, shall we? Kicking the ball, we are pleased to discover, is an important part of soccer. The basic soccer kick is made with the foot turned sideways, using the instep rather than the toe. The technique assures greater accuracy because more of the foot is in contact with the ball. This comes as no surprise to the National Football League, in which many teams employ a soccer-style kicker for that very reason. The best kickers can make the ball travel more than 70 miles per hour. Lateral passing, or flick passing, can be accomplished by kicking the ball with the outside of the foot.

Games are divided into 45-minute halves. The game begins with a coin toss; the winner elects either to pick which goal to defend or to take the kickoff. The kickoff has little meaning in soccer, so the winner of the coin toss usually elects to choose which goal to defend.

While goals are few and far between (perhaps the chief reason for the still dispassionate American view of the game), scoring opportunities are frequent. Tempo is one of the keys to watch—which team is completing more passes, who is getting off the most shots on goal, which side is controlling the ball at midfield with the most consistency.

Ball control is a fundamental part of soccer. In addition to the feet, soccer players use their heads and chests for passing and controlling the ball. A popular strategy during corner kicks is for one or more players to hang in front of the net hoping to get a piece of the ball with his head and jam it past the goalie.

As a player moves up the field with the ball, he often resorts to dribbling. Dribbling is accomplished via a series of short kicks as the player alternately hits the ball with first one instep and then the other. Attackers take much of their running diagonally across the field, rather than straight down, since this creates more problems for the defense.

The field on which all that dribbling occurs is somewhat larger than an American football field, about 120 yards long and 75 yards wide. The goals are eight feet high and 24 feet wide, with a six by 20 foot penalty area in front. The ball is 8.5 inches in diameter and weighs between 14 and 16 ounces.

fact: Soccer was played in the evening floodlights as far back as 1878.

Each team fields 11 players. Of these 11, only the goalie is allowed to use his hands during play, and only when he occupies his penalty area. When in possession of the ball, the goalie is allowed four steps before he must get rid of it.

Soccer allows one exception to the no-hands rule, and that is on **throw-ins**, when the ball is put in play from out-of-bounds (note that a ball on a line is considered in play). If the ball crosses either sideline, a player on the team that did not knock it out must throw the ball back into play, holding the ball with both hands and throwing it over his head while both feet are planted.

The clock can only be stopped at the referee's discretion, usually for serious injuries. The single referee is joined by two linesmen, who together police the game, watching for the ball bounding over the sidelines, players streaking offside, and the presence of one of the nine deadly fouls.

The nine serious fouls in soccer include dangerous charging, charging from behind, holding, striking, pushing, tripping, kicking or jumping at an opponent, and handling the ball (for a foul to be called, the handling must be judged by the referee or linesman to be intentional). These offenses will result in a direct free kick against the guilty team, or a penalty kick if the foul occurred in the penalty area. During a penalty kick, the ball is placed 12 yards from the goal, and the player taking the kick has only the goalkeeper to beat. The goalie must stand on his goal line and is not allowed to move his feet until the ball is kicked.

Under international rules, penalty-kick shootouts are not held to break ties. A team is permitted two substitutes during a match, and once a player is removed, he cannot return.

At the Olympics, 16 teams compete for the gold in a single elimination tournament. The defending champion and the host country receive automatic berths, while the other 14 teams are survivors of a worldwide qualifying tournament. Currently, no women's Olympic tournament is played.

BANANA SHOT: A hard shot at goal in which the ball is kicked off center, giving it a spin the makes it curve in flight; usually used on free kicks near the goal.

BEND: To kick the ball off center, so that it curves in flight.

BOOT: To kick the ball awkwardly.

BOX: The penalty area (the 18-yard box); also, less frequently, the goal area (the six-yard box).

CANNONBALL SHOT: Any very fast and powerful shot on goal.

CENTER CIRCLE: A circle of ten yard's radius marked out around the center spot of the field; at the moment of kickoff, players on the team not taking the kick must be outside the circle. Kickoffs also start the second half and follow scores, with the team that gave up the goal taking the kick.

CHALLENGE: To approach a player who has possession of the ball in order to force the player to commit to either a pass or a run.

CHARGE: Physical contact of the shoulder-to-shoulder variety with an opponent in an attempt to force him off the ball; can result in a foul call if contact is excessive.

CLOGGER: A player who tackles in a physical way.

CORNER KICK: What the attacking side is awarded when a defending player kicks the ball over his own goal line (other than into the goal). The ball is placed in the corner area and kicked, usually in the air, so that it will reach the opposing goal mouth, where the attackers gather, hoping to head or kick it into the goal.

FREE KICK: Two kinds of free kicks are awarded—**indirect** (from which a goal cannot be scored unless the ball has been played or touched by a player other than the kicker before passing through the goal) and **direct** (from which a goal can be scored directly from the kicker's foot). Opposing players must stand at least 10 yards away from the ball while the kick is being taken.

GOAL AREA: A rectangular area, marked by a line, in front of each goal, measuring twenty yards wide and six yards deep; inside this area the goalie cannot be charged.

GOAL KICK: When the attacking team plays the ball over the opponent's goal line, play is restarted by the defending team receiving a chance to kick it out of there; the ball is then placed at the edge of the goal area and kicked by the goalie or a defender.

Soccer

MARK: In man-to-man coverage, the defender is said to mark the attacker; the closer he plays to him, the tighter the marking.

OFFSIDE: The offside rule requires than an attacker must have at least two opponents (one of whom can be the goalie) between himself and the opposing goal line when the ball is passed to him and he is on the defender's half of the field. If the attacker is running toward the opposing goal and the ball is front of him, he cannot be called for offside.

OVERHEAD KICK: Also called a somersault or bicycle kick; useful when a player finds himself facing the wrong way with no time to turn around. The player flips into the air, throwing his feet up and his torso down. When contact is made with the ball, the body is parallel to the ground and some three or four feet above it.

PENALTY AREA: An area at each end of the field bounded by two lines drawn at right angles to the goal line, 18 yards from each goalpost, that extend into the field of play for a distance of 18 yards and are met by a line running parallel with the goal line.

STOPPER: Denotes a defender who is tightly marking a striker.

STRIKER: Any of the central attacking players in the 4–2–4, 4–3–3, and 4–4–2 formations.

TOUCHLINE: Also called sideline; the line at each side of the field. A ball going over the touchline is said to have gone into touch.

▼

HOPEFULS

The traditional European domination of soccer, along with Brazil's prowess in the sport, will be evident at the 1992 Olympics. While the USA doesn't really count on a medal (though they are nearly certain of a place on the competition roster), the team's remarkable improvement in 1991 has fueled its hope for a respectable final placement.

Team USA, which sustained a six-game winning streak in 1991, scored its greatest victory to date during the August, 1991, Pan American Games when it defeated Mexico for the gold medal. Even reaching the final rounds was a first: the US had never played for a gold medal at this level before. Its only prior Pan Am medal was a bronze in 1959. Much of Team USA's success in Barcelona may depend on forward Dante Washington, who leads the US Under-23 team in Olympic qualifying, and midfielder Chris Henderson, a likely starter for the US Olympic team.

The tentative soccer schedule is as follows:

Friday, July 24
Preliminary rounds

Saturday, July 25
Preliminary rounds

Sunday, July 26
Preliminary rounds

Monday, July 27
Preliminary rounds

Tuesday, July 28
Preliminary rounds

Wednesday, July 29
Preliminary rounds

Thursday, July 30
Preliminary rounds

Saturday, August 1
Quarterfinal matches

Sunday, August 2
Quarterfinal matches

Wednesday, August 5
Semifinal matches

Friday, August 7
Final match (3rd & 4th places)

Saturday, August 8
Final match (1st & 2nd places)

Soccer

▼

HIGHLIGHTS

Although at the time not officially recognized as an Olympic sport, two soccer matches were played in 1896 at Athens: a Greek team from Smyrna was defeated in the final by a Danish team by a score of 15–0. Soccer was considered a demonstration sport at Paris in 1900, when London defeated the host city's team with a score of 4–0. The host city's team in the St. Louis Games, too, was defeated, this time by the Galt Football Club of Canada. The third place team, also from the US, scored one goal ... for the opposing team.

Finally, in 1908, the host city's team claimed a victory: Britain outscored Denmark, who in turn soundly beat the two French teams. Ten of Denmark's 17 goals in their match against the French B team—which scored once—were netted by Sophus Nielsen. Britain successfully defended the title in Stockholm in 1912; their opponents, a Danish team, were forced to play with only ten men when the eleventh was sidelined by injury.

1920 produced the first of what would be a series of incidents in the field: the Belgian team was awarded the victory when a Czech player—who had kicked a Belgian player rather than the ball—was ejected from the game. His teammates followed, and the gold went to Belgium.

Uruguay, the only non-European team to win the final up until then, took the gold medal home in both 1924 and in 1928; oddly, they never participated in Olympic soccer again. In the 1924 match, Uruguay played against Switzerland, with a French referee. Initially, the game was assigned a Dutch referee; Uruguay

401

promptly protested, having beaten the Dutch team, amid some controversy, in the semifinals. Some 60,000 people jammed the stadium to watch the final match, and the 5000 would-be spectators outside the stadium sustained a number of injuries.

Uruguay's 1928 victory over Argentina was less turbulent, although the final had to be replayed because of a tied score in the first match. Conspicuous by its absence, Great Britain entered neither the 1924 nor the 1928 Games because of its grudges with the Football Association and with the FIFA.

Soccer was omitted from the 1932 Games, and reintroduced itself at the Berlin Games with little aplomb. Two Americans were injured in the first match between the US and Italy, who played with a full compliment of players, despite the fact that the referee had ordered one of the Italians to leave the game.

fact: The BBC began broadcasting live soccer commentary in 1927.

What came later in the tournament was mayhem: in the second overtime in the quarterfinal match between Peru and Austria, Peruvian fans stormed the field and attacked an Austrian player; the Peruvian team seized the opportunity to score two goals, and, not surprisingly, the results were protested. Officials ordered a rematch between Peru and Austria—to be played under lock and key, with no crowds to interfere—and the Peruvian team refused to play. In fact, all of Peru's athletes withdrew from the Games, and the Colombians followed. Meanwhile, in Lima, demonstrators were hurling insults and stones at the German consulate. With the Peruvians absent, the final was contested between the Austrians and the Italians, who, in overtime, won the gold.

The 1948 final match turned out to be a firemen's ball: the Swedish team—which included three brothers and three firemen—won the match over Yugoslavia. By 1952, soccer had become such a popular Olympic sport that pre-Games tournaments were held to decide which 16 teams would compete. In Helsinki, Hungary won the first of three victories, defeating Yugoslavia in 1952, Czechoslovakia in 1964, and Bulgaria in 1968. The Soviets won in Melbourne against the Yugoslavian team, 1-0, thanks to a disallowed Yugoslavian goal.

Yugoslavia—who until 1960 had always been the bridesmaid and never the bride, and whose team made the quarterfinal by virtue of a coin toss—enjoyed its day in the sun at the Rome Games. Yugoslavia defeated Denmark in the final match—even though their team captain had been expelled from the game for having insulted a referee.

The 1964 match has become infamous not because of the ultimate resolution of the tournament—in which Hungary defeated Czechoslovakia—but for the tragic outcome of one of the qualifying matches. The match between Peru and Argentina—held in Lima—was suspended when unruly crowds protested the referee's decision to disallow the Peruvian team's tying goal because of rough play. The rioting that followed was so violent that the Peruvian government declared a state of siege; 328 people were left dead, and another 500 were injured.

Crowds in the final match in Mexico City were tame compared to the Lima debacle, but were unruly nonetheless, throwing cushions at the field to express their lack of sympathy with the referees. When a Bulgarian player was expelled for rough play, a domino effect seemed to take place, and two other Bulgarian expulsions followed, leaving a skeleton team of only 8 players. Eight was not enough, and the Hungarians won the final with a score of 4–1.

Although the US was one of the first teams eliminated from the Munich Games, they had at least qualified. 1972 provided a rainy day for Hungary—who had lost only one Olympic match since 1960—when rainstorms and windy weather turned the tables on them in the second half of the final. The Polish team, with the wind at their back during the final half, scored two goals against Hungary, winning the gold.

Attempting to defend their title in Montréal, the Polish team was defeated by the East Germans, when the latter scored their third and final goal with six minutes to go. The Moscow Games were not entirely up to snuff—seven of the sixteen qualifying teams declined to participate—and only one goal was scored in the final match, allowing the Czechs a victory over the East Germans; for third place, the Soviets defeated the Yugoslavs.

In the boycott year of 1984, for the first time since the Swedish team had won in 1948, a non-Communist country won the gold: in a final match against Brazil, the French team took the first-place medal. The Yugoslavian team won the bronze.

By the 1988 Olympics, the US had won only two of thirteen matches, and had been outscored by as much as 53–8. In Seoul, however, they made it up to the quarterfinal: having tied with the South Korean team, they proceeded to take on the Soviets, who ultimately beat them 4–2. In the finals, the Soviets outscored the Brazilian team. The bronze-medaling team in 1988 was from Germany—this time from the West.

Medalists

Soccer (Football)

1988 1. Soviet Union, A. Borodiouk, I. Dovrosvolski, Serguei Fokine, S. Gorloukovitch, Arvidas Ianonis, E. Iarovenko, G. Ketachvili, Dmitri Kharine, E. Kouznetsov, V. Lioutyi, Victor Lossev, Mikhailitchenko, A. Narbekovas, Igor Ponomarev, A. Proundnikov, Iouri Savitchev, Igor Skliarov, V. Tatartchouk, A. Cherednik, V. Tichtchenko

2. Brazil, Aloisio Alves, Jose Araujo, Jorge Campos, Valdo Candido, Andre Cruz, Romario Farias, Jose Ferreira, Ademir Kaefer, I. Nascimento, Sergio Luiz, Jose Oliveira, R. Raimundo, Edmar Santos, Joao Santos, Geovani Silva, Jorge Silva, Hamilton Souza, Milton Souza, C. Taffarel, Luiz Winck

3. West Germany, Rudi Bommer, Holger Fach, Wolfgang Funkel, Armin Goertz, R. Grahammer, Thomas Haessler, Thomas Hoerster, Olaf Janssen, Uwe Kamps, G. Kleppinger, J. Klinsmann, Frank Mill, Oliver Reck, K. Riedle, Gunnar Sauer, C. Schreier, Michael Schulz, Ralf Sievers, Fritz Walter, Wolfram Wuttke

1984 1. France, Albert Rust, William Ayache, Michel Bibard, Dominique Bijotat, Francois Brisson, Patrick Cubaynes, Patrice Garande, Phillipe Jeannol, Guy Lacombe, Jean-Claude Lemoult, Jean-Phillipe Rohr, Didier Senac, Jean-Christoph Thouvenel, Jose Toure, Daniel Xuereb, Jean-Louis Zanon, Michel Bensoussan

2. Brazil, Gilmar Rinaldi, Ronaldo Silva, Jorge Luiz Brum, Mauro Galvao, Ademir Rock Kaeser, Andre Luiz Ferreira, Paulo Santos, Carlos Verri, Joao Leiehardt Neto, Augilmar Oliveira, Silvio Paiva, Luiz Dias, Luiz Carlos Winck, Davi Cortez Silva, Antonio Jose Gil, Francisco Vidal, Milton Cruz

3. Yugoslavia, Ivan Pudar, Vlado Capljic, Mirsad Baljic, S. Katanec, Marko Elsner, Ljubomir Radanovic, Admir Smajic, Nenad Gracan, Milko Djurovski, Mehmed Basdarevic, Borislav Cvetkovic, Tomislav Ivkovic, Jovica Nikolic, Stjepan Devec, Branko Miljus, Dragan Stojkovic, Mitar Mrkela

1980 1. Czechoslovakia, Stanislav Seman, Ludek Macela, Josef Mazura, Libor Radimec, Zdenek Rygel, Petr Nemec, Ladislav Vizek, Jan Berger, Jindrich Svoboda, Lubos Pokluda, Werner Licka, Rostislav Vaclavicek, Jaroslav Netolicka, Oldrich Rott, Frantisek Stambacher, Frantisek Kunzo

2. East Germany, Bodo Rudwaleit, Artur Ullrich, Lothar Hause, Frank Uhlig, Frank Baum, Rudiger Schnuphase, Frank Terletzki, Wolfgang Steinbach, Jurgen Bahringer, Werner Peter, Dieter Kuhn, Norbert Trieloff, Matthias Liebers, Bernd Jakubowski, Wolf-Ridiger Netz, Matthias Muller

3. Soviet Union, Rinat Dasaev, Tengiz Sulakvelidze, Aleksandr Chivadze, Vigaz Khidiyatullin, Oleg Romantsev, Sergei Shavlo, Sergei Andreev, Vladimir Bessonov, Yuri Gavrilov, Fyodor Cherenkov, Valeri Gazzaev, Vladimir Pilguj, Sergei Baltacha, Sergei Nikulin, Khoren Oganesyan, Aleksandr Prokopenko

1976 1. East Germany, Jurgen Croy, Gerd Weber, Hans-Jurgen Dorner, Konrad Weise, Lothar Kurbjuweit, Reinhard Lauck, Gert Heidler, Reinhard Hafner, Hans-Jurgen Riediger, Bernd Bransch, Martin Hoffman, Gerd Kische, Wolfram Lowe, Hartmut Schade, Dieter Riedel, Hans-Ullrich Grapenthin, Wilfried Grobner

2. Poland, Jan Tomaszewski, Antoni Szymanowski, Jerzy Gorgon, Wojciech Rudy, Wladyslaw Zmuda, Zygmunt Maszczyk, Grzegroz Lato, Henryk Kasperczak, Kazimierz Deyna, Andrzej Szarmach, Kazimierz Kmiecik, Piotr Mowlik, Henryk Wawrowski, Henryk Wieczorek, Leslaw Cmikiewicz, Jan Beniger, Roman Ogaza

3. Soviet Union, Vladimir Astapovskiy, Anatoli Konkov, Viktor Matvienko, Mikhail Fomenko, Stefan Reshko, Vladimir Troshkin, David Kipiani, Vladimir Onishenko, Viktor Kolotov, Vladimir Veremeev, Oleg Blochin, Leonid Buriak, Vladimir Feodorov, Aleksandr Minayev, Viktor Zyiaginchev, Leonid Nazarenko, Aleksandr Prokhorov

1972 1. Poland, Hubert Kostka, Zbigniew Gut, Jerzy Gorgon, Zygmunt Maszczyk, Jerzy Kraska, Kazimierz Dejna, Ryszard Szymczak, Zygfryd Szoltysik, Wlodzimierz Lubanski, Robert Gadocha, Antoni Szymanowski, Marian Ostafinski, Kazimierz Kmiecik, Joachim Marx, Grzegorz Lato, Zygmunt Anczok, Leslaw Cmikiewicz

2. Hungary, Istvan Geczi, Peter Vepi, Miklos Pancsics, Laszlo Balint, Peter Juhasz, Ede Dunai, Lajos Ku, Lajos Szucs, Mihaly Kozma, Antal Dunai, Bela Varadi, Kalman Toth, Lajos Kocsis, Jozsef Kovacs, Laszlo Branikovits, Csaba Vidats, Adam Rothermel

3. East Germany, Jurgen Croy, Frank Ganzera, Lothar Kurbjuweit, Konrad Weise, Manfred Zapf, Bernd Bransch, Jurgen Pommerenke, Wolfgang Seguin, Eberhard Vogel, Hans-Jurgen Kreische, Jurgen Sparwasser, Peter Ducke, Joachim Streich, Ralf Schulenberg, Reinhard Hafner, Harald Irmscher, Siegemar Watzlich

3. Soviet Union, Oleg Blochin, Murtaz Hurcilava, Yuri Istomin, Vladimir Kaplichnyi, Viktor Kolotov, Yevgeny Lovchev, Sergei Olshanskiy, Yevgeny Rudakov, Vyacheslav Semenov, Gennady Yevrushikhin, Oganes Zanazanian, Andrei Yakubik, Arkadiy Andriasian

1968 1. Hungary, Karoly Fater, Dezso Novak, Lajos Dunai, Miklos Pancsics, Ivan Menczel, Lajos Szucs, Laszlo Fazekas, Antal Dunai, Laszlo Nagy, Erno Nosko, Istvan Juhasz, Lajos Kocsis, Istvan Basti, Laszlo Keglovich, Istvan Sarkozi

2. Bulgaria, Stojan Jordanow, Atanas Gerow, Georgi Christakijew, Milko Gaidarski, Kiril Iwkow, Iwailo Georgijew, Tswetan Dimitrow, Jewgeni Jantschowski, Petar Schekow, Atanas Christow, Asparuch Donew, Kiril Christow, Todor Nikolow, Michail Gionin, Jantscho Dimitrow, Georgi Iwanow, Iwan Safirow, Georgi Wassiljew

3. Japan, Kenzo Yokoyama, Hiroshi Katayama, Yoshitada Yamaguchi, Mitsuo Kamata, Takaji Mori, Aritatsu Ogi, Teruki Miyamoto, Masashi Watanabe, Kunishige Kamamoto, Ikuo Matsumoto, Ryuichi Sugiyama, Masakatsu Miyamoto, Yasuyuki Kuwahara, Shigeo Yaegashi

1964 1. Hungary, Antal Szentmihalyi, Dezso Novak, Kalman Ihasz, Gusztav Szepesi, Arpad Orban, Ferenc Nogradi, Janos Farkas, Tibor Csernai, Ferenc Bene, Imre Komora, Sandor Katona, Jozsef Gelei, Karoly Palotai, Zoltan Varga

2. Czechoslovakia, Frantisek Schmucker, Anton Urban, Karel Z. Picman, Josef Vojta, Vladimir Weiss, Jan Geleta, Jan Brumovsky, Ivan Mraz, Karel Lichtnegl, Vojtech Masny, Frantisek Vlosek, Anton Svajlen, Karel Knesl, Stefan Matlak, Karel Nepomucky, Frantisek Knebort, Ludevit Cvetler

3. East Germany, Hans Jurgen Heinsch, Peter Rock, Manfred Geisler, Herbert Pankau, Manfred Walter, Gerhard Korner, Otto Frassdorf, Henning Frenzel, Jurgen Noldner, Eberhard Vogel, Horst Weigang, Klaus Urbanczyk, Bernd Bauchspress, Klaus-Dieter Sechaus, Werner Unger, Wolfgang Barthels, Klaus Lisiewicz, Dieter Engelhardt, Hermann Stocker

1960 1. Yugoslavia, Blagoje Vidinic, Novak Roganovic, Fahrudin Jusufi, Zeljko Perusic, Vladimir Durkovic, Ante Zanetic, Andrija Ankovic, Zeljko Matus, Milan Galic, Tomislav Knez, Borivoje Kostic, Milutin Soskic, Velimir Sombolac, Aleksandar Kozlina, Silvester Takac, Dusan Maravic

2. Denmark, Henry From, Poul Andersen, Poul Jensen, Bent Hansen, Hans C. Nielsen, Flemming Nielsen, Poul Pedersen, Tommy Troelsen, Harald Nielsen, Henning Enoksen, Jorn Sorensen, John Danielsen

3. Hungary, Gabor Torok, Zoltan Dudas, Jeno Dalnoki, Erno Solymosi, Pal Varhidi, Ferenc Kovacs, Imre Satori, Janos Gorocs, Florian Albert, Pal Orosz, Janos Dunai, Lajos Farago, Dezso Novak, Oszkar Vilezsal, Gyula Rakosi, Laszlo Pal, Tibor Pal

1956 1. Soviet Union, Lev Yashin, Anatoli Bashashkin, Mikhail Ogognikov, Boris Kuznyetsov, Igor Netto, Anatoli Maslyonkin, Boris Tatushin, Anatoli Issayev, Nikita Simonyan, Sergei Salnikov, Anatoli Ilyun, Nikolai Tichenko, Aleksei Paramonov, Eduard Streltsov, Valentin Ivanov, Vladimir Ryjkin, Yosif Betsa, Boris Rasinsky

2. Yugoslavia, Petar Radenkovic, Mladen Koscak, Nikola Radovic, Ivan Santek, Ljubisa Spajic, Dobroslav Krstic, Dragoslav Sekularac, Zlatko Papec, Sava Antic, Todor Veselinovic, Muhamed Mujic, Blagoje Vidinic, Ibrahim Biogradlic, Luka Liposinovic

3. Bulgaria, Josif Josifow, Kiril Rakarow, Nikola Kowatschew, Stefan Stefanow, Mnaol Manolow, Gawril Stojanow, Dimiter Milanow, Georgi Dimitrow, Panajot Panajotow, Iwan Kolew, Todor Dijew, Georgi Naydenow, Miltscho Goranow, Krum Janew

1952 1. Hungary, Gyula Grosics, Jeno Buzanszky, Mihaly Lantos, Jozsef Bozsik, Gyula Lorant, Jozsef Zakarias, Nandor Hidegkuti, Sandor Kocsis, Peter Palotas, Ferenc Puskas, Zoltan Czibor, Jeno Dalnoki, Imre Kovacs I, Laszlo Budai II , Lajos Csordas

2. Yugoslavia, Vladimir Beara, Branislav Stankovic, Tomislav Crnkovic, Zlatko Cajkovski, Ivan Horvat, Vujadin Boskov, Tihomir Ognjanov, Rajko Mitic, Bernard Vukas, Stjepan Bobek, Branko Zebec

3. Sweden, Karl Svensson, Lennart Samuelsson, Erik Nilsson, Olof Ahlund, Bengt Gustavsson, Gosta Lindh, Sylve Bengtsson, Gosta Lofgren, Ingvar Rydell, Yngve Brodd, Gosta Sandberg, Holger Hansson

1948 1. Sweden, Torsten Lindberg, Knut Nordahl, Erik Nilsson, Birger Rosengren, Bertil Nordahl, Sune Andersson, Kjell Rosen, Gunnar Gren, Gunnar Nordahl, Henry Carlsson, Nils Liedholm, Borje Leander

2. Yugoslavia, Ljubomir Lovric, Miroslav Brozovic, Branislav Stankovic, Zlatko Cajkovski, Miodrag Jovanovic, Aleksandar Atanackovic, Zvonko Cimermancic, Rajko Mitic, Stjepan Bobek, Zeljko Cajkovski, Bernard Vukas, Franjo Sostaric, Prvoslav Mihajlovic, Franjo Wolfl, Kosta Tomasevic

3. Denmark, Ejgil Nielsen, Viggo Jensen, Knud B. Overgaard, Axel Pilmark, Dion Ornvold, Ivan Jensen, Johannes Ploger, Knud Lundberg, Carl A. Praest, John Hansen, Jorgen Sorensen, Holger Seebach, Karl A. Hansen

1936 1. Italy, Bruno Venturini, Alfredo Foni, Pietro Rava, Giuseppe Baldo, Achille Piccini, Ugo Locatelli, Annibale Frossi, Libero Marchini, Sergio Bertoni, Carlo Biagi, Francesco Gabriotti, Luigi Scarabello, Giulio Cappelli, Alfonso Negro

2. Austria, Eduard Kainberger, Ernst Kunz, Martin Kargl, Anton Krenn, Karl Wahlmuller, Max Hofmeister, Walter Werginz, Adolf Laudon, Klement Steinmetz, Karl Kainberger, Franz Fuchsberger, Franz Mandl, Josef Kitzmuller

3. Norway, Henry Johansen, Nils Eriksen, Oivind Holmsen, Frithjof Ulleberg, Jorgen Juve, Rolf Holmberg, Magdalon Monsen, Reidar Kvammen, Alf Martinsen, Odd Frantzen, Arne Brustad, Fredrik Horn, Sverre Hansen, Magnar Isaksen

1932 **Not held**

405

Summer

1928 1. Uruguay, Andres Mazali, Jose
Nasazzi, Pedro Arispe, Jose L.
Andrade, Lorenzo Fernandez, Juan
Piriz, Alvaro Gestido, Santos
Urdinaran, Hector Castro, Pedro
Petrone, Pedro Cea, Antonio
Campolo, Adhemar Canavesi, Juan
Arremon, Rene Borjas, Hector
Scarone, Robert Figueroa
2. Argentina, Angel Bosio, Fernando
Paternoster, Ludovico Bidoglio, Juan
Evaristo, Luis F. Monti, Segundo
Medici, Raimundo Orsi, Enrique
Gainzarain, Manuel Ferreyra, Domingo
Tarasconi, Adolfo Carricaberry,
Feliciano A. Perducca, Octavio Diaz,
Robert Cherro, Rodolfo Orlandini, Saul
Calandra
3. Italy, Giampiero Combi, Delfo Bellini,
Umberto Caligaris, Alfredo Pitto, Fulvio
Bernardini, Pietro Genovesi, Adolfo
Baloncieri, Elvio Banchero, Angelo
Schiavio, Mario Magnozzi, Virgilio F.
Levratto, Giovanni Depra, Virginio
Rosetta, Silvio Pietroboni, Antonio
Janni, Enrico Rivolta, Gino Rossetti
1924 1. Uruguay, Andres Mazali, Jose
Nasazzi, Pedro Arispe, Jose L.
Andrade, Jose Vidal, Alfredo Ghierra,
Santos Urdinaran, Hector Scarone,
Pedro Petrone, Pedro Cea, Angel
Romano, Umberto Tomasina, Jose
Naya, Alfredo Zibechi, Antoni o
Urdinaran
2. Switzerland, Hans Pulver, Adolphe
Reymond, Rudolf Ramseyer, August
Oberhauser, Paul Schmiedlin, Aron
Pollitz, Karl Ehrenbolger, Robert
Pache, Walter Dietrich, Max
Abegglen, Paul Fassler, Felix Bedouret,
Adolphe Mengotti, Paul Sturzenegger,
Edmond Kramer
3. Sweden, Sigfrid Lindberg, Axel
Alfredsson, Fritjof Hillen, Gunnar
Holmberg, Sven Friberg, Harry
Sundberg, Evert Lundqvist, Sven
Rydell, Per Kaufeldt, Tore Keller,
Rudolf Kock, Gustaf Carlson, Charles
Brommesson, Thorsten Svensson, Albin
Dahl, Konrad Hirsch, Sven Lindqvist,
Sten Mellgren
1920 1. Belgium, Jan De Bie, Armand
Swartenbroeks, Oscar Verbeeck,
Joseph Musch, Emile Hanse, Andre
Fierens, Louis van Hege, Henri Larnoe,
Mathieu Bragard, Robert Coppee,
Desire Bastin, Felix Balyu, Fernand
Nisot, Georges Hebdin
2. Spain, Ricardo Zamora, Pedro
Vallana, Mariano Arrate, Jose
Samitier, Jose M. Belausteguigoitia,
Agustin Sancho, Ramon Eguiazabal,
Felix Sesumaga, Patricio Arabolaza,
Rafael Moreno, Domingo Acedo, Juan
Artola, Francisco Pagazaurtundua,
Louis Otero, Joaquin Vasquez, Ramon
Moncho Gil, Sabino Bilbao, Silverio
Izaguirre

3. Netherlands, Robert McNeill, Henri L.
B. Denis, Bernard W. J. Verweij,
Leonard F. G. Bosschart, Frederik C.
Kuipers, Hermanus H. Steeman, Oscar
E. van Rappard, Jan L. van Dort,
Bernardus Groosjohan, Herman C. F.
van Heijden, Jacob E. Bulder,
Johannes D. de Natris, Evert J.
Bulder, Adrianus G. Bieshaar
1912 1. Great Britain, Ronald Brebner, Thomas
Burn, Arthur Knight, Douglas
McWhirter, Henry C. Littlewort, Joseph
Dines, Arthur Berry, Vivian Woodward,
Harold Walden, Gordon Hoare, Ivan
Sharpe, Edward Hanney, Gordon
Wright, Harold Stamper
2. Denmark, Sophus Hansen, Nils
Middelboe, Harald Hansen, Charles
Buchwald, Emil Jorgensen, Paul Berth,
Oscar Nielsen-Norlund, Axel Thufason,
Anton Olsen, Sophus Nielsen, Vilhelm
Wolffhagen, Hjalmar Christoffersen,
Aksel Petersen, Ivar Lykke Seidelin,
Poul Nielsen
3. Netherlands, Marius J. Gobel, David
Wijnveldt, Piet Bouman, Gerardus
Fortgens, Constant W. Feith, Nicolaas
de Wolf, Dirk N. Lotsy, Johannes W.
Boutmy, Jan G. van Breda Kolff, Huug
de Groot, Caesar H. ten Cate, Jan
van der Sluis, Jan Vos, Nico Bouvy,
Johannes M. de Korver
1908 1. Great Britain, Horace B. Bailey,
William Corbett, Herbert Smith,
Kenneth Hunt, Frederick W. Chapman,
Robert Hawkes, Arthur Berry, Vivian
Woodward, Hubert Stapley, Claude
Purnell, Harold Hardman
2. Denmark, Ludvig Drescher, Charles
Buchwald, Harald Hansen, Harald
Bohr, Kristian Middelboe, Nils
Middelboe, Oscar Nielsen-Norland,
August Lindgreen, Sophus Nielsen,
Vilhelm Wolffhagen, Bjorn Rasmussen,
Marius Andersen, Johannes Gandil
3. Netherlands, Reinier B. Beeuwkes,
Karel Heijting, Lou Otten, Johan W. E.
Sol, Johannes M. de Korver, Emil G.
Mundt, Jan H. Welcker, Edu
Snethlage, Gerard S. Reeman, Jan
Thomee, Georges F. de Bruyn Kops,
Johan A. F. Kok
1906 1. Denmark, Viggo Andersen, Peter
Petersen, Charles Buchwald, Parmo
Ferslew, Stefan Rasmussen, Aage
Andersen, Oscar Nielsen-Norland,
Carl F. Petersen, Holger Fredriksen,
August Lundgreen, Henry Rambusch,
Hjalmar Heerup
2. International (Smyrna), Edwin
Charnaud, Zareck Couyoumdzian,
Edouard Giraud, Jacques Giraud,
Henri Joly, Percy de la Fontaine,
Donald Whittal, Albert Whittal,
Godfrey Whittal, Herbert Whittal,
Edward Whittal

406

3. Greece (Thessaloniki), Georgios Vaporis, Nicolaos Pindos, A. Tegos, Nicolaos Pentzikis, Ioannis Kyrou, Georgios Sotiriadis, V. Zarkadis, Dimitrios Michitsopoulos, A. Karangonidis, Ioannis Abbot, Ioannis Saridakis

1904 1. Canada, (Galt F. C. Ontario), Ernest Linton, George Ducker, John Gourley, John Fraser, Albert Johnson, Robert Lane, Tom Taylor, Frederick Steep, Alexander Hall, Gordon McDonald, William Twaits

2. USA, (Christian Brothers College), Louis Menges, Oscar B. Brockmyer, Thomas T. January, John H. January, Charles January, Peter J. Ratican, Warren G. Brittingham, Alexander Cudmore, Charles A. Bartliff, Joseph P. Lydon, Raymond Lawler

3. USA, (St. Rose. St. Louis), Frank Frost, George Crook, Henry W. Jameson, Joseph Brady, Dierkes, Martin T. Dooling, Cormic F. Cosgrove, O'Connell, Claude Jameson, Harry Tate, Thomas Cooke, Johnson

1900 1. Great Britain, J. H. Jones, Grosling, Claude Percy Buckenham, W. Quash, T. E. Burridge, A. Chalk, Haslam, J. Zealley, J. Nicholas, Spackman, R. P. Turner

2. France, Huteau, Bach, Pierre Allemane, Gaillard, Bloch, Macaire, Fraysse, Garnier, Lambert, Grandjean, Fernand Canelle, Dupare, Peltier

3. Belgium, Marcel Leboutte, R. Kelecom, Ernest Moreau, Alphonse Renier, Georges Pelgrims, E. Neefs, Erich Thornton, Albert Delbecque, H. Spannoghe, van Heuckelum, Londot

1896 **Not held**

SWIMMING

WARM-UP

Although the English generally are credited with introducing swimming as a sport in the late 1830s, races were held in Japan nearly two thousand years earlier. And in 1603 the Japanese formed the first national swimming organization.

But long before the first races were held, people went swimming. Plato remarked that anyone who couldn't swim lacked education. Julius Caesar, Alexander the Great, and Charlemagne were known for their swimming prowess, as well as their ability to conquer large parts of the world. The Old Testament describes people swimming in the Nile, and Greek mythology relates the tale of Leander swimming the Hellespont to enjoy the company of his lover. Lord Byron later crossed the same Hellespont in 1810 and the Tagus in 1818, both significant feats of swimming endurance.

Since the first human encounter a body of water blocking his or her way, people have been swimming (or perhaps first, drowning). Swimming for speed probably began when a waterborne human first encountered a large aquatic creature with dinner on its mind. But swimming didn't become a competitive sport resembling its modern form until the 19th century. In one of the first races on record, two Native Americans were brought to London in 1844 to compete for a silver medal offered by the National Swimming Society in England. The transatlantic competitors introduced the overhand (crawl) stroke to Britain, although the stuffy English clung to the slower breaststroke for another 40 years, insisting that endurance, not speed, was the issue.

fact: A competitive pool must contain a minimum of eight lanes, each lane seven to nine feet wide.

In 1878, an Englishman by the name of Frederick Cavill moved to Australia. There he built that country's first swimming pool. But for pool building he's not remembered. On a trip through the South Seas, Cavill observed some natives swimming, and particularly noted the leg action that provided them with an extra kick. Returning to Australia, he demonstrated the leg kick to other swimmers, who appreciated the additional power that the kick provided. At the turn of the century, the leg kick was introduced to the US and England by two of Cavill's sons, and the resulting stroke became known as the Australian crawl, revolutionizing swimming competitions.

A little more than 20 years after Captain Matthew Webb's pioneering swim across the English Channel (using the breaststroke), swimming was included on the initial Olympic Games program in 1896. Six countries sent 18 swimmers to compete for swimming titles in the 100, 500, and 1200 meter races, plus a special 100-meter race for sailors only. The events were restricted to men; women entered the Olympic swimming fray in 1912, taking part in three events: the 100-meter freestyle, the 4 x 100-meter relay, and high diving.

Following the 1896 debut, the next two Olympics were rather disorganized affairs, featuring programs essentially crafted by the host cities. At the 1900 Games, swimming events were held in the Seine, while an underwater race was held at the 1904 Games in St. Louis. The pool in St. Louis was in the middle of an artificial lake, making good seats scarce for spectators.

The 1908 Games in London were much better organized, providing the swimmers with a specially built pool 100 meters long and 17 meters wide. At this Olympiad, the Fédération Internationale de Natation Amateur (FINA), the governing body for competitive swimming, diving, water polo, and synchronized swimming, was formed. Under FINA's leadership, the sport became better organized and more popular, and now reigns as one of the dominant Olympic attractions.

▼

SPECTATORS' GUIDE

In the Olympics, swimmers compete in 13 individual events as well as three relays for men and two relays for women. The events are held in a 50-meter pool, also called the long course.

Many races are lost in poor starts and turns. In the start, the swimmer is called to starting position by the starter, who visually checks that all swimmers are down and still. Then, once the starter is satisfied, the race is started by either a gun or an electronic tone. If the starter believes that one of the swimmers has jumped early, the race will be recalled and the offending swimmer disqualified.

fact: The front edge of the starting blocks are 30 inches above the surface of the water.

Quick turns are essential. In all events the swimmer must touch the wall, but in the freestyle and the backstroke, the swimmer may somersault as he or she reaches the wall, touching only with the feet. In the other two competitive strokes, the swimmer must touch the wall with one or both hands before executing the turn.

The sprint races (50m and 100m) are all-out scrambles from start to finish. The slightest mistake can cost precious hundredths of seconds and, ultimately, the race.

The 200m events are a controlled sprint, as the swimmers pace themselves during the first part of the race.

The 400m, 800m, and 1500m freestyles require the swimmers to remain constantly aware of where they are and how tired they are becoming. Swimming the first portion of the race at too fast a pace can sap a swimmer's strength and cause a poor finish. Swimming the first portion of the race too slowly can separate the swimmer from the leading pack and make catching up impossible.

Two methods are used by swimmers for the distance races. They may elect to swim the race evenly (like Janet Evans), holding the same pace throughout the race. Or they may "negative split" the race, covering the second half faster than the first, the most popular method in the early 1980s.

In the **freestyle**, competitors may use any strokes they wish, and their wish is usually the Australian crawl, characterized by the alternate overhand motion of the arms. Individual freestyle events for men and women include 50m, 100m, 200m, and 400m. Women also swim an 800m individual race, while the men engage in a 1500m event. Additionally, both women and men swim 400m and 800m freestyle relays, in which no individual may swim more than one leg of the race.

fact: Water temperature in competitive pools must be between 78 and 80 degrees Fahrenheit (25.5 to 26.6 degrees Celcius).

The **butterfly** features the simultaneous overhead stroke of the arms combined with the dolphin kick, and both the arms and legs move up and down together. No flutter kicking is allowed. The butterfly, perhaps the most beautiful and physically demanding stroke, was developed in the early 1950s as a loophole in the breaststroke rules and in 1956 became an Olympic event at the Melbourne Games. Butterfly races include a men's and women's 100m and 200m.

Popularized by Harry Hebner of the United States in the 1912 Olympics, the **backstroke** requires the swimmer to remain on his or her back at all times. The backstroke is the only race in which the competitors are in the water at the start, taking a handgrip on the edge of the pool while resting on their back. The stroke is an alternating motion of the arm, resembling an upside-down crawl. Starting in 1991, a swimmer no longer must touch the wall with his or her hand before executing the turn maneuver, a change that may cause many Olympic backstroke records to fall. Backstroke events include the men's and women's 100m and 200m races.

One of the most difficult strokes to master is the **breaststroke**, which requires simultaneous movements of the arms on the same horizontal plane. The hands are pushed forward from the breast or under the surface of the water and brought backward in the propulsive stage of the stroke simultaneously.

The kick is a simultaneous thrust of the legs called a "frog" or breaststroke kick. No flutter or dolphin kicking is allowed. At each turn a swimmer must touch with both hands at the same time. The breaststroke races include a men's and women's 100m and 200m.

The **individual** medley features all four competitive strokes. The swimmer begins with the butterfly, changes to the backstroke for another quarter, then breastroke, and finally finishes with the freestyle. The new "no-touch" backstroke turn may not be used in the backstroke to breaststroke exchange in an individual medley race. Both men and women swim 200m and 400m individual medleys.

And then we have the **medley relay**: all four strokes are swum by four different swimmers, covering 100m each. No swimmer may swim more than one leg of the relay, which is swum in backstroke, breaststroke, butterfly, then freestyle order. The men and women each compete in their own 400m race. An important part of any relay race is the exchange between the swimmer in the water and the next swimmer on the relay team. In a perfect exchange, the finishing swimmer's hand will alight on the touch pad at the same time as the starting swimmer's feet are still just touching the starting block, with the body extended over the water in the last instant before takeoff.

The first leg of a relay can be counted for a record, because while swimming an individual event or the lead-off leg of a relay, a swimmer cannot move on the blocks. To do so is called **rolling**, and constitutes a false start. On the subsequent legs of a relay, a swimmer can roll, as long as the person does not leave the block before the swimmer in the water touches the wall. As a result, relay splits tend to be faster than corresponding individual times and are not eligible for record consideration.

Swim Speak

BANANA HEAT: Slang term for the consolation final of an event.

GRAVITY WAVE: Wave action caused by the swimmers' bodies moving through the water. Gravity waves move down and forward from the swimmer, bounce off the bottom of the pool, and return to the surface in the form of turbulence.

LANE: The area of the pool in which each swimmer competes during a race.

LANELINES: The dividers used to delineate the individual lanes. These are made of individual finned disks strung on a cable, rotating on the cable when hit by a wave. The rotating disks dissipate surface tension waves in a competitive pool.

NEGATIVE SPLIT: A race strategy in the distance freestyle events, in which a swimmer covers the second half of the race faster than the first half.

RELAY EXCHANGE: The exchange between the swimmer in the water and the next swimmer on the relay team. In a perfect exchange, the finishing swimmer's hand will alight on the touch pad at the same time as the starting swimmer's feet are still just touching the starting block, with the body extended over the water in the last instant before takeoff.

ROLL: To move on the blocks prior to the starting signal. A roll is usually caught by the starter, but swimmers will often try to guess the starter's cadence and get a good start. Similar to illegal procedure in football.

SHAVE: With a haircut, formerly two bits. Prior to a major competition, a swimmer will shave his or her entire body, lessening the resistance between skin and water.

SPLIT: A swimmer's intermediate time in a race; splits are registered every 50 meters and are used to determine if a swimmer is on a record pace.

TOUCHPAD: The area at the end of each lane in the pool where a swimmer's time is registered and sent electronically to the timing system.

▼

HOPEFULS

Men's Events

With an exceptionally deep pool of new and veteran talent from which to draw, Team USA should once again lead the men's swimming events in Barcelona. Olympic medalist Matt Biondi, whose seven medals in the 1988 Games included five golds (a feat second only to Mark Spitz's record seven golds in 1972), isn't certain whether he'll represent the USA again in competitive swimming or in water polo, or at all. He has continued swimming competitively through 1991, though—an indication that he may swim again for the US team—and his three gold medals at the 1991 World Aquatic Championships indicate that his form is still up to par.

Other Olympic veterans—all world-record holders in their best events—include 1988 silver medalist Tom Jager, who is recognized as the best 50m freestyle swimmer in the world, Mike Barrowman, who repeatedly breaks his own records in the 200m breaststroke, and 100m backstroke record holder David Berkoff. Possible newcomers to the Olympic swimming team include 1991 NCAA champion Melvin Stewart, who set a world record in the 200m butterfly at the 1991 World Aquatic Championships, backstroke swimmer Jeff Rouse, and breaststroke swimmer Eric Wunderlich.

In addition, 1972's Olympic star Mark Spitz began retraining in 1991 with the hope of rejoining the Olympic team. Since he was consistently outpaced by swimmers like Biondi and Jager in 1991 meets, though, an Olympic comeback seems unlikely. Still, the US can always hope for a showing from its sentimental favorite.

The US men led the three relay events in Seoul with three golds, but East and West Germany followed with three relay medals between them. A unified Germany will remain strong with two Olympic gold medalists. Michael Gross, who has dominated the 200m butterfly since 1982, won that event for West Germany at the Seoul Games but finished second behind the USA's Stewart at the 1991 World competition. Gross had retired from competition after the 1988 Olympics but later returned to swim for a unified Germany. And Olympic 400m freestyle gold medalist Uwe Dassler, formerly of East Germany, remains the champion of that event with his 1991 World Cup win. Another German, Joerg Hoffman, proved his prowess in the 1500m freestyle at the 1991 World games when he beat the world record in that event by more than four seconds.

Olympic gold medalist Vladimir Salnikof, who won a World Aquatic silver medal in the 1500m freestyle, and European champion Vladislav Kulikov, who won a World Aquatic bronze in the 100m butterfly, will contribute to the typically strong Soviet team.

Hungary will be well represented by two-time Olympic gold medalist Tamás Darnyi, who set a world record in the 200m medley at the World Aquatic competition, and Norbert Rozsa, who broke his own world record in the 100m breaststroke at the 1991 European Championships.

Canada will rely on 1991 World Cup backstroke champ Mark Tewksbury, who led the 1988 Olympic team to its second-place finish in the medley relay. And Spain will be rooting for Spanish-American Martin Zubero (he represents Spain in international competition), who shattered the oldest record in men's swimming when he swam the 200m backstroke in 1 minute, 57.30 seconds at the 1991 Phillips 66 National Swimming Championships. The record had stood since 1985.

Matt Biondi

As a child, Matt Biondi admired Olympic champions, never dreaming that one day he would become one himself. Yet the six-foot-seven, 210-pound University of California graduate rose to stardom during the 1988 Summer Games, walking off with five gold, one silver, and one bronze medal—a haul eclipsed only by the 1972 performance of Mark Spitz.

Most Olympic swimmers begin preparing for the games as mere youngsters, practicing endlessly at childhood swim meets. Biondi—who was born in Moraga, California, on October 8, 1965—began swimming competitively at the comparatively late age of fifteen. Three years later, in 1984, he made the Olympic team. A graduate of Campolinda High in Moraga, Biondi played basketball and water polo in addition to swimming races. He was almost a well-kept secret when he earned a spot on the team that went to Los Angeles.

It was in Los Angeles in 1984 that Biondi earned his first gold medal, as part of the 400m freestyle relay team. He entered the University of California and continued his cross-training as a race swimmer and water polo player, helping his school to win several NCAA water polo championships even as he was breaking records in 100- and 200-yard freestyle races.

Biondi was considered one of the most promising stars of the 1988 Olympic team, and he lived up to his advance billing. He earned golds in the 4 x 200m freestyle relay, the 100m freestyle, the 4 x 100m freestyle relay, the 50m freestyle, and the 400m medley relay. In the process he also set or helped to set four world records. His silver medal came in the 100m fly, and he earned a bronze in the 200m freestyle. Afterwards, he told the *Charlotte Observer:* "One time, I wanted to show the world at a meet like this what Matt Biondi is about."

Although he once professed no interest in the 1992 Games, Biondi is still in training and will almost certainly be a figure in Barcelona. The multiple medal winner and record-breaker believes that his most valuable lessons as a swimmer came from dolphins he swam among in the Bahamas. "Watching them made me aware of how water moves across my body," he says. "The best swimmers are the ones who know how to swim through the water, to feel the water. Watching the dolphins heightened my awareness." —*M.K.*

Tom Jager

It is the equivalent of the sprinter's 50-yard dash—the 50m freestyle swim, a mad, one-lap race that demands both physical prowess and psychological toughness. The best swimmer in this event overall—and the first to finish the race in less than 20 seconds—is Tom Jager. The 26-year-old Jager waits impatiently for the 1992 Olympic Games in Barcelona, where he hopes finally to beat his chief rival, Matt Biondi, for a gold medal.

Jager was born October 4, 1964, in East St. Louis, Illinois. He grew up in Collinsville, Illinois, and had to travel 45 minutes each way—and cross a state line—to find the nearest swim club in Ballwin, Missouri. Nevertheless, he developed into a dominant swimmer at a young age and won an athletic scholarship to the University of California, Los Angeles, where he earned a degree in psychology in 1987.

While at UCLA, Jager won five NCAA titles, in the 50- and 100-yard freestyle and in the 100-yard backstroke. He often went head-to-head with

Biondi, and the two young swimmers took turns breaking each others' records. Jager made the 1984 Olympic team as an alternate, where he told *Sports Illustrated* he was treated as "expendable" even though he swam 100m freestyle legs in preliminary rounds for two gold-medal-winning relay teams. It was a full year after the 1984 Games in Los Angeles that Jager was finally awarded a gold medal for his contribution. Jager stills recalls this slight when he wants to get pumped up for a big race.

The 1988 Olympics were the first since 1904 to feature a 50m freestyle race. The 6-foot, 3-inch, 180-pound Jager was the favorite to win the sprint, but he lost both the race and a record to Biondi. Biondi also beat Jager at the 1990 Goodwill Games, but on a day-to-day basis, Jager is certainly the better swimmer at that length.

In fact, Jager and Biondi have become business partners in a manner of speaking, staging races for prize money as tune-ups for the 1992 games. Both swimmers agree that these races—usually sponsored by a major product manufacturer—help to promote swimming as an exciting competitive sport with cash incentives. After an Iowa City race in 1990, in which he finished the 50 at a staggering 19.12 seconds, Jager told *Sports Illustrated* that he is encouraged by the number of children he sees at such sponsored events. He hopes some of them choose swimming as a sport in which to excel. "Instead of just looking at the bottom of the pool and thinking about swimming back and forth," he said, "now kids can think, 'I can't wait—someday I'll be swimming for the car.'" —*M.K.*

Women's Events

The East German women dominated the 1988 Olympics with eight individual gold medals and both team relay titles. A united German team, in apparent disarray without many of the former East Germans, may not be as good but will still demonstrate a great deal of talent. Olympic medalist Daniela Hunger, who won the 200m medley at Seoul, is still competing but finished eighth in the 50m freestyle at the 1991 World Aquatic Championships. European 50m freestyle champion Simone Osygus took the 1991 World Cup titles in the 50m and 200m freestyle events, and Christiana Siebert and Marion Zoller took World Cup silvers in the 100m butterfly and 50m backstroke, respectively.

China's team has dramatically improved (amidst rumors of drug enhance-ment—a charge previously directed toward the East Germans), as evidenced by the 1990 performance of two women who broke the 59-second barrier in the 100m butterfly, a record that had gone unbroken for nine years. Olympic 100m freestyle silver medalist Zhuang Yong improved her performance with gold medals in the 100m freestyle at the 1991 World University Games, and in the 50m freestyle at the 1991 World Aquatic games. Especially promising is Lin Li, who took three titles (two medleys and the 200m backstroke) at the 1991 World University Games. World Cup 100m butterfly champion Te Hong and 50m freestyle world record holder Yang Wenyi contribute to China's improving team.

Matt Biondi swam to seven medals in the 1988 Games, including five golds, and was still in training in 1991, a possible contender for the US swimming team in Barcelona.

Distance swimmer Janet Evans brought three gold medals home to the US from the Games at Seoul, and is almost certain to medal again in 1992.

The US women's team, who in 1988 relied on distance swimmer Janet Evans to bring home the country's three Olympic gold medals, has developed an exceptionally well-rounded team. Evans, who remains undefeated in distance freestyle races since 1987, secured two freestyle golds and a freestyle silver in the 1991 World Aquatic competition.

One new US hopeful is Summer Sanders, Evans' former Stanford University teammate and her main competitor in the medley. Sanders won three titles, upsetting Evans in the 400m medley, at the 1990 Goodwill Games, and she won a 200m butterfly gold, 200m medley silver, and 400m medley bronze at the 1991 World Aquatic competition.

NCAA freestyle champion Nicole Haislett is one of the best young sprinters in the USA, with a Goodwill Games title in the 100m freestyle, 1990 US Open titles in the 50m and 100m freestyle races, and a 100m freestyle title and two relay gold medals from the 1991 World Aquatic Championships. Mary Ellen Blanchard—the granddaughter of 1945 Heisman Trophy winner Doc Blanchard—has set records in breaststroke events, and Janie Wagstaff reached gold medals in the 100m and 200m backstroke at the 1990 US Open. Additionally, Angel Myers, who was suspended from the 1988 Olympic team after testing positive for steroids (a charge she denies), returned to competition in 1991.

Olympic hopefuls who might infiltrate the German-Chinese-American domination of women's swimming include Hungary's Olympic gold medalist Kristina Egerszegi, who beat a world backstroke record by nearly two seconds during the 1991 European Championships, and France's Olympic bronze medalist Catherine Plewinski, who placed second in the 50m freestyle at both the 1991 European Championships and the World Aquatic Championships.

Janet Evans

Facing stiff competition, Janet Evans will try to retain her title of America's top woman swimmer as she moves into the 1992 Olympics. Evans took the 1988 Summer Olympics by storm at the tender age of seventeen by winning three gold medals, setting one world record, one American record, and one Olympic record. She has not lost an important distance freestyle race since, although several promising contenders are literally at her heels.

Charlotte Observer staff writer Joe Posnanski notes that in 1988, Evans "was an original America's sweetheart, an Olympic gold-medal winner with a poster-perfect smile and the best freestyle stroke in women's swimming." Critics compared the teenager to Mark Spitz, of course, but she also drew comparisons to Michael Jordan, Joe Montana, and Roger Clemens. Evans finds this unfair and claims that audiences now expect her to dazzle each time she jumps into a swimming pool. The years since 1988 have proved a great challenge to the young star.

Evans, who was born August 28, 1971, was still in high school when she entered the 1988 Olympics. She was no stranger to the world of high-stakes swimming races, however. As early as 1985 she had placed sixth in a nationally ranked 400m individual medley and sixth in a 1500m freestyle. At the 1986 Goodwill Games she finished third in both the 800m and 1500m freestyles, and by the following year she was winning regularly at the US Open and the Olympic Trials. She set her first world records in 1987 as well, in both the 1500m and 800m freestyles.

Still, at seventeen, five feet tall, and barely 100 pounds, she was the youngest and the smallest member of the 1988 American Olympic women's swimming team. She earned gold medals in the 400m individual medley, the 400m freestyle, and the 800m freestyle. Her world record-setting time in the 400m freestyle still stands, while her time in the 400 IM was recently bettered by future Olympian Summer Sanders. Posnanski observes that, during the 1988 games, Evans "blew away the other swimmers and mesmerized fans."

A certified heroine overnight, Evans was offered a number of attractive product endorsement contracts and other publicity-grabbing opportunities. Instead, she decided to attend Stanford University, a college known for producing Olympic-caliber swimmers. Evans spent three years at Stanford, but her performance there did not always suit her. She occasionally broke her own records, but she also occasionally began to lose races when pitted against other powerhouse swimmers like Sanders. In April, 1991, Evans dropped out of Stanford. "I definitely knew I had to leave the swim program—the training just didn't feel correct," she told the *Charlotte Observer*.

Evans joined Texas Aquatics, the team coached by Mark Schubert, the US Olympic team coach. Since turning to Texas Aquatics, she seems more confident and brighter in outlook. "I don't want to try to recapture what I did in 1988," she says. "I don't think all this stuff is that hard. I go to big meets and, well, I have confidence. I've done it all before. I don't think that's arrogant. I'm older now, and I've just been through it all."

Under the tutelage of Schubert, and just turning twenty, Evans is almost certain to win a berth on the 1992 Olympic team, should she remain free of injury. The winner of the 1989 Sullivan Award as the nation's top amateur athlete is often asked how she can possibly become better than she was in 1988. Her answer is simple and to the point: "I think I can.... I think everything works out for the best in the end. Besides ... seventeen is too young to quit."
—M.K.

Schedule

The tentative swimming schedule is as follows:

Sunday, July 26
Heats, 100m freestyle, women
Heats, 100m breaststroke, women
Heats, 400m individual medley, women

Heats, 200m freestyle, men
Finals, 100m freestyle, women
Finals, 100m breaststroke, women
Finals, 400m individual medley, women

Finals, 200m freestyle, men

Monday, July 27
Heats, 100m butterfly, men
Heats, 200m freestyle, women
Heats, 400m individual medley, men
Heats, 200m breaststroke, women
Heats, 4x200m freestyle relay, men
Finals, 100m butterfly, men
Finals, 100m freestyle, women
Finals, 200m freestyle, women
Finals, 400m individual medley, men
Finals, 200m breaststroke, women
Finals, 4x200m freestyle relay, men

Tuesday, July 28
Heats, 400m freestyle, women
Heats, 100m freestyle, men
Heats, 100m backstroke, women
Heats, 200m backstroke, men
Heats, 4x100m freestyle relay, women
Finals, 400m freestyle, women
Finals, 100m freestyle, men
Finals, 100m backstroke, women
Finals, 200m backstroke, men
Finals, 4x100m freestyle relay, women

Wednesday, July 29
Heats, 400m freestyle, men
Heats, 100m butterfly, women
Heats, 200m breastroke, men
Heats, 100m breastroke, women
Heats, 4x100m medley, relay, men
Heats, 800m freestyle, women

Finals, 400m freestyle, men
Finals, 100m butterfly, women
Finals, 200m breaststroke, men
Finals, 100m breaststroke, women
Finals, 4x100m freestyle relay, men

Thursday, July 30
Heats, 200m individual medley, women
Heats, 200m butterfly, men
Heats, 100m backstroke, men
Heats, 4x100m medley relay, women
Heats, 50m freestyle, men
Heats, 1500m freestyle, men
Final, 200m individual medley, women
Final, 200m butterfly, men
Final, 50m freestyle, men
Final, 800m freestyle, women
Final, 100m backstroke, men
Final, 4x100 medley relay, women

Friday, July 31
Heats, 200m individual medley, men
Heats, 200m butterfly, women
Heats, 200m backstroke, women
Heats, 4x100m medley relay, men
Heats, 50m freestyle, women
Final, 200m individual medley, men
Final, 200m butterfly, women
Final, 50m freestyle, women
Final, 1500m freestyle, men
Final, 200m backstroke, women
Final, 4x100 medley relay, men

Swimming

MEN'S SWIMMING EVENTS

▼

HIGHLIGHTS

In 1896, when only four swimming events were included in the Games, Alfréd Hajós became the first swimmer to win an Olympic title, winning first the 100m freestyle and then the 1200m as well. Twenty-eight years later, in Paris, Hajós won a silver Olympic medal, this time for a more sedentary adventure, stadium architecture.

Britain's John Jarvis was a double winner in 1900, when he took the 1000m and 4000m events, while the Australian Frederick Lane captured the 200 meters. Four years later, in St. Louis, the home team scored its first victory, as Charlie Daniels swam his way to five medals. Zoltán von Halmay, a Hungarian, beat out Daniels, the medium-distance title holder, in the sprint.

fact: Charlie Daniels is credited with evolving the American crawl from the Australian two-beat crawl.

In 1908, Daniels returned—to swim in water that was neither heated nor filtered—this time to win the 100m sprint, while von Halmay placed second. Daniels had become the leading proponent of the new crawl stroke. The 1912 Games introduced Duke Kahanamoku and his brother Samuel, descendants of a Hawaiian chief, as prominent US swimmers. Duke, the older of the two, swam to a 100m first place, which he managed to defend in Antwerp in 1920, where the Americans won five gold medals.

1924 marked the Olympic debut of a tall, slim, and shy Johnny Weissmuller, who won three of the six gold medals awarded to the US in Paris: he captured the 100m and 400m freestyles, and swam a leg of the winning 800m relay team. The now-veteran Kahanamoku brothers came in second and third in the 100m freestyle, giving the US a clean sweep of the event. Although soon-to-be-Tarzan-the-ape-man Weissmuller did manage to win another two gold medals at Amsterdam in 1928—again for the 100m freestyle and the 800m relay team— Japan was moving ahead as a dominant power, and Yoshiyuki Tsuruta won the 200m breaststroke. Weissmuller also played on two US Olympic Water Polo teams.

fact: Johnny Weissmuller never lost a race in 10 years of amateur swimming at distances from 50 yards to 1/2 mile.

By 1932, the American supremacy was thoroughly undermined, when the Japanese men won five of the six races, along with various other lesser wins. Winning four individual medals, the young Japanese team also lowered the freestyle relay record by 38 seconds. Buster Crabbe, another Tarzan-to-be, won the only US medal by defeating world record holder Jean Taris of France in the 400m freestyle.

It wasn't much better for the Yanks in 1936, although they doubled their gold haul with Jack Medica winning the 400m freestyle and Adolph Kiefer the backstroke. Japan, in the meantime, won yet another four races, including the relay. After the war, the Americans enjoyed another moment in the sun (with the Japanese absent from the Games), when they captured six golds at London in 1948, including a sweep of the three freestyle races. That same year, almost all the Olympic records—and some world records—were broken.

Freestyle again proved to be the primary vein of gold for the US in 1952 when Clarke Scholes won the 100m; Ford Konno won the 1500, lowering the Olympic record by 42 seconds, later swimming on the successful relay team. Australia, which had won a total of only three medals since the very beginning of the Games, captured a gold when John Davies outswam American Bowen Stassforth in the 200m breaststroke.

The 1956 Games, held in Melbourne, were ruled by the newly established Australians. With Murray Rose sweeping both the 400m and 1500m freestyles, the Aussies captured five gold medals; for the first time since 1900 America was shut out in the freestyle, as Australia also captured the relay and Jon Henricks took the 100 meters. In fact, all that prevented the US from being totally wiped out was the introduction that year of the butterfly to the Olympic program. Bill Yorzyk began the American domination of that stroke by winning at 200 meters.

Good fortune—not to mention skill—followed the Australians to Rome in 1960. John Devitt was declared winner of the 100m freestyle even though the electronic timer caught American Lance Larson in a faster time, allowing Australia to sweep the individual freestyle races once again, as Rose made a successful defense of the 400m and John Konrads won the 1500m. But the US salvaged both relays, including the 400m medley, conducted for the first time. The latter event has been the exclusive property of the US in the Olympics, with the obvious exception of 1980, when an Australian won the event; Americans have also been unbeaten in the 800m freestyle relay since 1960, and in the 400m freestyle relay since it was introduced in 1960.

In 1964, when the men's program had grown to 10 events, America indisputably reclaimed its position as the No. 1 power. Don Schollander became the first Olympian to win four gold medals in a single Olympics, and his teammates added three more victories. When a minor controversy developed over the third place in the 100m freestyle, the unofficial electronic timers provided by the Japanese were consulted; although Germany's Hans-Joachim Klein and America's Gary Ilman had stopped the clock together at the same hundredth of a second, Klein had finished one one-thousandth of a second sooner, thus earning the bronze medal.

fact: Only track and field numbers more US Olympic medals to its credit then men's or women's swimming.

The Americans went to Mexico City as heavy favorites, in 1968, and indeed they won 10 of 15 swimming events. Mike Burton and Charley Hickcox each won two individual events, Burton taking the 400m and 1500m freestyles and Hickcox the 200m and 400m individual medleys. That year, however, the 100m freestyle victory went to Australian Michael Wenden, who landed the most decisive 100m victory in 40 years. In third place in that same race, Mark Spitz quietly earned one of the first of his Olympic medals.

Limited to two gold medals for his work on the 1968 relay teams, Spitz stormed the 1972 Games in Munich, capturing four individual races (the freestyle sprints and both butterfly events) and swimming on three successful relay teams. As if that weren't enough, all seven events broke world record times. While Mike Burton successfully defended his 1500m title, America's final gold went to John Hencken in the 200m breaststroke; one of America's principal antagonists, Swede Gunnar Larsson, won both medleys this time around. And sixteen-year-old Rick DeMont, swimming for the US, finished first in the 400m freestyle, but was disqualified because the prescription medicine he was taking for asthma was ruled to be illegal.

In Montréal in 1976, the US conducted a near-shutout, taking 12 of the 13 gold medals and 10 of the 11 silvers. The only man to foil both sweeps was British breaststroker David Wilkie (who happened to have attended school in the US). Of the 27 men on the US team, 19 earned individual medals, and the Americans set 18 world records, seven times setting a mark in the heats and then lowering it again in the finals. Unlike 1972, when Mark Spitz hogged the limelight, the 1976 performance was more a team effort; the big winner of the Games, however, was John Naber, who won four golds (in the 100m and 200m backstroke, and two medleys), and a silver (in the 200m freestyle).

In the absence of the US at Moscow, it was the host country who dominated the men's swimming program, capturing seven gold, seven silver, and three bronze. Prior to 1980, the Soviet men had never won a swimming gold. Vladimir Salnikov led the way with three gold and compatriot Sergei Kopliakov took two gold and a silver. With a time of 14 minutes, 58.27 seconds for the 1500m freestyle, Salnikov became the first person to break the 15-minute barrier. Whereas American men accounted for 11 world records in 1976 at Montréal, Salnikov's 1500m mark was the only world standard to fall in what was considered to be a "fast pool" at Moscow.

American swimmer Rowdy Gaines, hurt by the 1980 boycott, won three golds at age of 25 in 1984. His 1980 teammate, Steve Lunquist, also came back in 1984, for a pair of golds in the 100m breastroke and the 400m medley relay. That year the Canadians, who hadn't won a gold in swimming since 1912, picked up seven medals on the men's team, including golds for Alex Baumann and Victor Davis, as well as two silvers and two bronzes. Australian swimmers earned 13 medals that year, the most since 1960, when the team from Down Under also won 13. These included men's medals in the 100m freestyle (silver), the 100m breaststroke (bronze), the 200m breaststroke (silver), the 100m butterfly (bronze), and the 200m butterfly (gold), to name but a few.

422

Another swimming phenomenon of 1984, West Germany's Michael Gross, entered the Games as the only male swimmer since Mark Spitz to hold world records in two strokes at the same time. His countryman, Thomas Fahrner, failed to qualify for the 400m freestyle and was so angry with himself that in the consolation race he broke the just-set Olympic record in the event; record, but no medal.

In 1988, US butterflyer/freestyler Matt Biondi burst on the scene to set or help to set four world records, piling up a total of five gold medals, one silver, and one bronze, the best performance in swimming since Mark Spitz's haul in 1972. He added these to the gold medal he'd won as a member of the 4 x 100 freestyle relay in 1984. Meanwhile, the American men relayers shattered world records.

Other swimming greats competing in 1988 included West German Michael Gross, who won the 200m butterfly, Artur Wojdat of Poland, who took third in the 400m freestyle, Anders Holmertz of Sweden, who took second in the 200m freestyle, and Australian Duncan Armstrong, who won the 200m freestyle, and placed second in the 400m. Tamás Darnyi of Hungary swept the 200m and 400m individual medleys, smashing his own world records in those events; he also competed in the 200m backstroke, his strongest discipline.

US backstroker David Berkoff adapted an underwater maneuver for the start of his race after seeing US swimmer Jesse Vassallo experiment with the innovation in 1984; he stayed underwater for 35 meters after the start of the race, then surfaced half a body length ahead of the rest of the pool. Berkoff's silver in the 100m backstroke heralded a new direction for backstrokers worldwide.

From Poolside to Film Stardom

Three US swimmers during the 1920s and 1930s won Olympic medals, then launched film careers.

Duke Paoa Kahanamoku was named for the Duke of Edinburgh, who happened to be in Honolulu when the future swimmer was born August 24, 1890. He won the 100m freestyle in 1912 and 1920, surviving a re-swim after an apparent lane violation by another competitor (this was before lane markers were used). At the 100m freestyle in Paris in 1924, he and brother Samuel flanked Johnny Weismuller, who feared they would team up against him. Instead, Duke told Johnny the most important goal was getting the "American flag up there three times." Weismuller won; the brothers placed second and third. Kahanamoku, who often played Hawaiian kings in the movies, also helped popularize surfing. The Duke died in Honolulu on January 22, 1968.

As an infant, Johnny Weismuller, born on June 2, 1904, was thought to have heart trouble, a condition that seems not to have held him back. Just before the 1924 Paris Olympics, Weismuller became the first man ever to swim 100 meters in under one minute, at 57.4 seconds. Just 20, Weismuller won four medals in Paris, and two more four years later in Amsterdam. His style was then unique: riding high in the water and alternating sides when lifting his head to breathe—

the better to see his opponents. He held 52 US titles and 28 world records. Later, Weismuller became one of Hollywood's Tarzans (and probably the most popular one), debuting in *Tarzan, the Ape Man,* in 1932 and starring in 18 other Tarzan flicks. He died in Acapulco on January 20, 1984.

Clarence "Buster" Crabbe credits his discovery by Hollywood moguls to the one-tenth of a second victory he won over France's Jean Taris in the 400m freestyle at the 1932 Los Angeles Olympics. Crabbe also won a bronze in the 1500m freestyle in 1928. Like Weismuller, Crabbe starred as Tarzan, then went on to play Flash Gordon and Buck Rogers. He died April 23, 1983, in Scottsdale, Arizona. —*H.D.*

Mark Spitz

In his heyday he was unchallenged as the best swimmer in the world: Mark Spitz, winner of seven gold medals and holder of seven world records at the 1972 Olympics in Munich. Not only was Spitz, then in his early twenties, considered the greatest Olympic swimmer ever, he was an ideal celebrity, an all-American hero "who happened to look like a cross between Omar Sharif and the Marlboro Man," to quote the *Chicago Tribune.* Posters of the handsome Spitz with his medals splayed across his chest became the best-selling Olympic souvenir item ever.

Now in his forties—and contemplating a comeback—Spitz looks back at those years as if they passed in a dream. "As a kid, I ended up in the sport of swimming through osmosis," he told the *Washington Post.* "I went out, sort of swam, was on a team, I got better, I got good, I got great, then I held world records. I never had a chance to sit back and reflect: What would I be doing if I wasn't doing this?"

Spitz never reflected on his talent because it came almost naturally. He was born February 10, 1950, in Modesto, California, and began swimming competitively at the age of eight. He spent the next ten years roaming Northern California in search of top-flight swim clubs where he could hone his abilities. He continued his swimming in college at the University of Indiana and quickly gained a national reputation, although he quietly assured fans that he wanted to study to be a dentist.

Ron Ballatore, current swimming coach at the University of California, Los Angeles, remembered that as a young Olympic hopeful, Spitz showed tremendous potential. He could deceive his trainers by swimming far faster in meets than in practice, he tested better than any other United States swimmer on stroke efficiency, and both his hands and legs worked flawlessly to propel him forward in a variety of strokes. Ballatore said: "It is hard to explain. He's like an artist in the water. Many people can copy his stroke, but it doesn't mean it is going to work for them."

Spitz suffered a disappointing—if you can call it that—outing in the 1968 Olympics in Mexico City. During that meet, he earned only two gold medals, both for relays. His day to shine came in 1972, in Munich, where he entered seven

424

events and won all seven of them in record-setting times. His victories came in the 100m freestyle, the 200m freestyle, the 100m butterfly, the 200m butterfly, the 400m freestyle relay, the 800m freestyle relay, and the 400m medley relay. His success was arguably one of America's finest moments in Olympic history.

At the height of his fame, Spitz stopped swimming and opened a real estate development business with the money he earned on product endorsements. He drifted slowly back into obscurity as, one by one, his records fell at subsequent Olympic Games. Then, in 1990, the forty-year-old Spitz announced that he would train for a spot on the 1992 Olympic team. Battling a back injury and all the years of inactivity, he strove to regain his old form, at least in short-distance butterfly sprints. "There aren't that many skeptics," he told the *Atlanta Constitution* of his proposed comeback. "Deep down inside they all kind of wish and hope I can do it. They're kind of reliving my past and their own past. It's sort of like all the couch potatoes united."

Some skeptics did remain, however. One suggested that Spitz's chances of regaining his 1972 glory "are about the same as Richard Nixon's." Nevertheless, Spitz's 1972 time for the 100m butterfly—54.27 seconds—is not far from the current record of 53 seconds. What remains to be seen is whether he can recapture the youthful vigor that took him to unprecedented heights in swimming. Preliminary races have been disappointing, but Spitz retains a spark of hope that he may see another Olympic meet. The athlete told the *Chicago Tribune* that he has received widespread support from greying baby boomers, who see him as the representative of a generation that resists falling into ruts.

"I am probably in the best shape cardiovascular-wise and physically than anybody my age—and I don't care what the heck sport you're talking about," Spitz says. "If I don't make the [1991] Olympic Trials, nobody my age ever will be able to. That's about as bold a statement as I'll say." —*M.K.*

Medalists

Swimming — Men's 50-Meter Freestyle

1988
1. Matthew Biondi, USA, 22.14 (WR)
2. Thomas Jager, USA, 22.36
3. Gennadi Prigoda, Soviet Union, 22.71
1906-1984 Not held
1904 1. Zoltan von Halmay, Hungary, 28.0
2. J. Scott Leary, USA, 28.6
3. Charles Daniels, USA
1896-1900 Not held

Swimming — Men's 100-Meter Freestyle

1988 1. Matthew Biondi, USA, 48.63 (OR)

2. Christopher Jacobs, USA, 49.08
3. Stephan Caron, France, 49.62
1984 1. Ambrose Gaines, USA, 49.80 (OR)
2. Mark Stockwell, Australia, 50.24
3. Per Johansson, Sweden, 50.31
1980 1. Jorg Woithe, East Germany, 50.40
2. Per Holmertz, Sweden, 50.91
3. Per Johansson, Sweden, 51.29
1976 1. Jim Montgomery, USA, 49.99 (WR, OR)
2. Jack Babashoff, USA, 50.81
3. Peter Nocke, West Germany, 51.31
1972 1. Mark Spitz, USA, 51.22 (WR)
2. Jerry Heidenreich, USA, 51.65
3. Vladimir Bure, Soviet Union, 51.77
1968 1. Michael Wenden, Australia, 52.2 (WR)
2. Ken Walsh, USA, 52.8
3. Mark Spitz, USA, 53.0
1964 1. Don Schollander, USA, 53.4 (OR)

425

2. Robert McGregor, Great Britain, 53.5
3. Hans-Joachim Klein, West Germany, 54.0

1960 1. John Devitt, Australia, 55.2 (OR)
2. Lance Larson, USA, 55.2 (OR)
3. Manuel Dos Santos, Brazil, 55.4

1956 1. Jon Henricks, Australia, 55.4 (OR)
2. John Devitt, Australia, 55.8
3. Gary Chapman, Australia, 56.7

1952 1. Clarke Scholes, USA, 57.4
2. Hiroshi Suzuki, Japan, 57.4
3. Goran Larsson, Sweden, 58.2

1948 1. Walter Ris, USA, 57.3 (OR)
2. Alan Ford, USA, 57.8
3. Geza Kadas, Hungary, 58.1

1936 1. Ferenc Csik, Hungary, 57.6
2. Masanori Yusa, Japan, 57.9
3. Shigeo Arai, Japan, 58.0

1932 1. Yasuji Miyazaki, Japan, 58.2
2. Tatsugo Kawaishi, Japan, 58.6
3. Albert Schwartz, USA, 58.8

1928 1. John Weissmuller, USA, 58.6 (OR)
2. Istvan Barany, Hungary, 59.8
3. Katsuo Takaishi, Japan, 1:00.0

1924 1. John Weissmuller, USA, 59.0 (OR)
2. Duke Paoa Kahanamoku, USA, 1:01.4
3. Samuel Kahanamoku, USA, 1:01.8

1920 1. Duke Paoa Kahanamoku, USA, 1:01.4 (WR)
2. Pua Kela Kealoha, USA, 1:02.2
3. William Harris, USA, 1:03.2

1912 1. Duke Paoa Kahanamoku, USA, 1:03.4
2. Cecil Healy, Australia, 1:04.6
3. Kenneth Huszagh, USA, 1:05.6

1908 1. Charles Daniels, USA, 1:05.6 (WR)
2. Zoltan von Halmay, Hungary, 1:06.2
3. Harald Julin, Sweden, 1:08.0

1906 1. Charles Daniels, USA, 1:13.4 (WR)
2. Zoltan von Halmay, Hungary, 1:14.2
3. Cecil Healy, Australia

1904 1. Zoltan von Halmay, Hungary, 1:02.8
2. Charles Daniels, USA
3. J. Scott Leary, USA

1900 **Not held**

1896 1. Alfred Hajos, Hungary, 1:22.2 (OR)
2. Efstathios Choraphas, Greece, 1:23.0
3. Otto Herschmann, Austria

Swimming — Men's 200-Meter Freestyle

1988 1. Duncan Armstrong, Australia 1:47.25 (WR)
2. Anders Holmertz, Sweden, 1:47.89
3. Matthew Biondi, USA, 1:47.99

1984 1. Michael Gross West Germany, 1:47.44
2. Michael Heath, USA, 1:49.10
3. Thomas Fahrner, West Germany, 1:49.69

1980 1. Sergei Kopliakov, Soviet Union, 1:49.81 (OR)
2. Andrei Krylov, Soviet Union, 1:50.76
3. Graeme Brewer, Australia, 1:51.60

1976 1. Bruce Furniss, USA, 1:50.29 (WR, OR)
2. John Naber, USA, 1:50.50
3. Jim Montgomery, USA, 1:50.58

1972 1. Mark Spitz, USA, 1:52.78 (WR)
2. Steven Genter, USA, 1:53.73
3. Werner Lampe, W. Germany, 1:53.99

1968 1. Michael Wenden, Australia, 1:55.2 (OR)
2. Don Schollander, USA, 1:55.8
3. John Nelson, USA, 1:58.1

1906-1964 **Not held**

1904 1. Charles Daniels, USA, 2:44.2
2. Francis Gailey, USA, 2:46.0
3. Emil Rausch, Germany, 2:56.0

1900 1. Frederick C. V. Lane, Australia, 2:25.2 (OR)
2. Zoltan von Halmay, Hungary, 2:31.4
3. Karl Ruberl, Austria, 2:32.0

1896 **Not held**

Swimming — Men's 400-Meter Freestyle

1988 1. Uwe Dassler, East Germany, 3:46.95 (WR)
2. Duncan Armstrong, Australia, 3:47.15
3. Artur Wojdat, Poland, 3:47.34

1984 1. George Dicarlo, USA, 3:51.23 (OR)
2. John Mykkanen, USA, 3:51.49
3. Justin Lemberg, USA, 3:51.79

1980 1. Vladimir Salnikov, Soviet Union, 3:51.31 (OR)
2. Andrei Krylov, Soviet Union, 3:53.24
3. Ivar Stukolkin, Soviet Union, 3:53.95

1976 1. Brian Goodell, USA, 3:51.93 (WR, OR)
2. Tim Shaw, USA, 3:52.54
3. Vladimir Raskatov, Soviet Union, 3:55.76

1972 1. Bradford Cooper, Australia, 4:00.27 (OR)
2. Steven Genter, USA, 4:01.94
3. Tom McBreen, USA, 4:02.64

1968 1. Michael Burton, USA, 4:09.0 (OR)
2. Ralph Hutton, Canada, 4:11.7
3. Alain Mosconi, France, 4:13.3

1964 1. Don Schollander, USA, 4:12.2 (WR)
2. Frank Wiegand, East Germany, 4:14.9
3. Allan Wood, Australia, 4:15.1

1960 1. Murray Rose, Australia, 4:18.3 (OR)
2. Tsuyoshi Yamanaka, Japan, 4:21.4
3. John Konrads, Australia, 4:21.8

1956 1. Murray Rose, Australia, 4:27.3 (OR)
2. Tsuyoshi Yamanaka, Japan, 4:30.4
3. George Breen, USA, 4:32.5

1952 1. Jean Boiteux, France, 4:30.7 (OR)
2. Ford Konno, USA, 4:31.3
3. Per-Olof Ostrand, Sweden, 4:35.2

1948 1. William Smith, USA, 4:41.0 (OR)
2. James McLane, USA, 4:43.4
3. John Marshall, Australia, 4:47.4

1936 1. Jack Medica, USA, 4:44.5 (OR)
2. Shumpei Uto, Japan, 4:45.6
3. Shozo Makino, Japan, 4:48.1

1932 1. Clarence Crabbe, USA, 4:48.4 (OR)
2. Jean Taris, France, 4:48.5
3. Tsutomu Oyokota, Japan, 4:52.3

1928 1. Alberto Zorilla, Argentina, 5:01.6 (OR)
2. Andrew Charlton, Australia, 5:03.6
3. Arne Borg, Sweden, 5:04.6

1924 1. John Weissmuller, USA, 5:04.2 (OR)
2. Arne Borg, Sweden, 5:06.6
3. Andrew Charlton, Australia, 5:06.6

1920 1. Norman Ross, USA, 5:26.8
2. Ludy Langer, USA, 5:29.0
3. George Vernot, Canada, 5:29.6

426

1912   1. George Hodgson, Canada, 5:24.4
     2. John Hatfield, Great Britain, 5:25.8
     3. Harold Hardwick, Australia, 5:31.2
1908   1. Henry Taylor, Great Britain, 5:36.8
     2. Frank Beaurepaire, Australia, 5:44.2
     3. Otto Scheff, Austria, 5:46.0
1906   1. Otto Scheff, Austria, 6:23.8
     2. Henry Taylor, Great Britain, 6:24.4
     3. John Jarvis, Great Britain, 6:27.2
1904   1. Charles Daniels, USA, 6:16.2
     2. Francis Gailey, USA, 6:22.0
     3. Otto Wahle, Austria, 6:39.0
1900   **Not held**
1896   1. Paul Neumann, Australia, 8:12.6
     2. Antonios Pepanos, Greece, 30 m behind
     3. Efstathios Choraphas, Greece

Swimming — Men's 1,500-Meter Freestyle

1988   1. Vladimir Salnikov, Soviet Union, 15:00.40
     2. Stefan Pfeiffer, West Germany, 15:02.69
     3. Uwe Dassler, East Germany, 15:06.15
1984   1. Michael O'Brien, USA, 15:05.20
     2. George DiCarlo, USA, 15:10.59
     3. Stefan Pfeiffer, West Germany, 15:12.11
1980   1. Vladimir Salnikov, Soviet Union, 14:58.27 (WR)
     2. Aleksandr Chaev, Soviet Union, 15:14.30
     3. Maxwell Metzker, Australia, 15:14.49
1976   1. Brian Goodell, USA, 15:02.40 (WR, OR)
     2. Bobby Hackett, USA, 15:03.91
     3. Stephen Holland, Australia, 15:04.66
1972   1. Michael Burton, USA, 15:52.58 (WR)
     2. Graham Windeatt, Australia, 15:58.48
     3. Douglas Northway, USA, 16:09.25
1968   1. Michael Burton, USA, 16:38.9 (OR)
     2. John Kinsella, USA, 16:57.3
     3. Gregory Brough, Australia, 17:04.7
1964   1. Robert Windle, Australia, 17:01.7 (OR)
     2. John Nelson, USA, 17:03.0
     3. Allan Wood, Australia, 17:07.7
1960   1. John Konrads, Australia, 17:19.6 (OR)
     2. Murray Rose, Australia, 17:21.7
     3. George Breen, USA, 17:30.6
1956   1. Murray Rose, Australia, 17:58.9
     2. Tsuyoshi Yamanaka, Japan, 18:00.3
     3. George Breen, USA, 18:08.2
1952   1. Ford Konno, USA, 18:30.3 (OR)
     2. Shiro Hashizume, Japan, 18:41.4
     3. Tetsuo Okamoto, Brazil, 18:51.3
1948   1. James McLane, USA, 19:18.5
     2. John Marshall, Australia, 19:31.3
     3. Gyorgy Mitro, Hungary, 19:43.2
1936   1. Noboru Terada, Japan, 19:13.7
     2. Jack Medica, USA, 19:34.0
     3. Shumpei Uto, Japan, 19:34.5
1932   1. Kusuo Kitamura, Japan, 19:12.4 (OR)
     2. Shozo Makino, Japan, 19:14.1
     3. James Cristy, USA, 19:39.5
1928   1. Arne Borg, Sweden, 19:51.8 (OR)
     2. Andrew Charlton, Australia, 20:02.6
     3. Clarence Crabbe, USA, 20:28.8

1924   1. Andrew Charlton, Australia, 20:06.6 (WR)
     2. Arne Borg, Sweden, 20:41.4
     3. Frank Beaurepaire, Australia, 21:48.4
1920   1. Norman Ross, USA, 22:23.2
     2. George Vernot, Canada, 22:36.4
     3. Frank Beaurepaire, Australia, 23:04.0
1912   1. George Hodgson, Canada, 22:00.0 (WR)
     2. John Hatfield, Great Britain, 22:39.0
     3. Harold Hardwick, Australia, 23:15.4
1908   1. Henry Taylor, Great Britain, 22:48.4 (WR)
     2. Thomas Battersby, Great Britain, 22:51.2
     3. Frank Beaurepaire, Australia, 22:56.2
1906   1. Henry Taylor, Great Britain, 28:28.0
     2. John Jarvis, Great Britain, 30:07.6
     3. Otto Scheff, Austria, 30:53.4
1904   1. Emil Rausch, Germany, 27:18.2
     2. Geza Kiss, Hungary, 28:28.2
     3. Francis Gailey, USA, 28:54.0
1900   1. John Jarvis, Great Britain, 13:40.2
     2. Otto Wahle, Austria, 14:53.6
     3. Zoltan von Halmay, Hungary, 15:16.4
1896   1. Alfred Hajos, Hungary, 18.22.2 (OR)
     2. Jean Andreou, Greece, 21:03.4
     3. Efstathios Choraphas, Greece

Swimming — Men's 100-Meter Backstroke

1988   1. Daichi Suzuki, Japan, 55.05
     2. David Berkoff, USA, 55.18
     3. Igor Polianski, Soviet Union, 55.20
1984   1. Richard Carey, USA, 55.79
     2. David Wilson, USA, 56.35
     3. Mike West, Canada, 56.49
1980   1. Bengt Baron, Sweden, 56.53
     2. Viktor Kuznetsov, Soviet Union, 56.99
     3. Vladimir Dolgov, Soviet Union, 57.63
1976   1. John Naber, USA, 55.49 (WR, OR)
     2. Peter Rocca, USA, 56.34
     3. Roland Matthes, East Germany, 57.22
1972   1. Roland Matthes, East Germany, 56.58 (OR)
     2. Mike Stamm, USA, 57.70
     3. John Murphy, USA, 58.35
1968   1. Roland Matthes, East Germany, 58.7 (OR)
     2. Charles Hickcox, USA, 1:00.2
     3. Ron Mills, USA, 1:00.5
1964   **Not held**
1960   1. David Theile, Australia, 1:01.9 (OR)
     2. Frank McKinney, USA, 1:02.1
     3. Robert Bennett, USA, 1:02.3
1956   1. David Theile, Australia, 1:02.2 (OR)
     2. John Monckton, Australia, 1:03.2
     3. Frank McKinney, USA, 1:04.5
1952   1. Yoshinobu Oyakawa, USA, 1:05.4 (OR)
     2. Gilbert Bozon, France, 1:06.2
     3. Jack Taylor, USA, 1:06.4
1948   1. Allen Stack, USA, 1:06.4
     2. Robert Cowell, USA, 1:06.5
     3. Georges Vallerey, France, 1:07.8
1936   1. Adolf Kiefer, USA, 1:05.9 (OR)
     2. Albert Van de Weghe, USA, 1:07.7
     3. Masaji Kiyokawa, Japan, 1:08.4
1932   1. Masaji Kiyokawa, Japan, 1:08.6

2. Toshio Irie, Japan, 1:09.8
3. Kentaro Kawatsu, Japan, 1:10.0
1928 1. George Kojac, USA, 1:08.2 (WR)
2. Walter Laufer, USA, 1:10.0
3. Paul Wyatt, USA, 1:12.0
1924 1. Warren Paoa Kealoha, USA, 1:13.2
(OR)
2. Paul Wyatt, USA, 1:15.4
3. Karoly Bartha, Hungary, 1:17.8
1920 1. Warren Paoa Kealoha, USA, 1:15.2
2. Ray Kegeris, USA, 1:16.2
3. Gerard Blitz, Belgium, 1:19.0
1912 1. Harry Hebner, USA, 1:21.2
2. Otto Fahr, Germany, 1:22.4
3. Paul Kellner, Germany
1908 1. Arno Bieberstein, Germany, 1:24.6
(WR)
2. Ludvig Dam, Denmark, 1:26.6
3. Herbert Haresnape, Great Britain,
1:27.0
1906 Not held
1904 1. Walter Brack, Germany, 1:16.8
2. Georg Hoffmann, Germany
3. Georg Zacharias, Germany
1896-
1900 Not held

Swimming — Men's 200-Meter Backstroke

1988 1. Igor Polianski, Soviet Union, 1:59.37
2. Frank Baltrusch, East Germany,
1:59.60
3. Paul Kingsman, New Zealand, 2:00.48
1984 1. Richard Carey, USA, 2:00.23
2. Frederic Delcourt France, 2:01.75
3. Cameron Henning, Canada, 2:02.37
1980 1. Sandor Wladar, Hungary, 2:01.93
2. Zoltan Verraszto, Hungary, 2:02.40
3. Mark Kerry, Australia, 2:03.14
1976 1. John Naber, USA, 1:59.19 (WR, OR)
2. Peter Rocca, USA, 2:00.55
3. Dan Harrigan, USA, 2:01.35
1972 1. Roland Matthes, East Germany,
2:02.82 (EWR)
2. Mike Stamm, USA, 2:04.09
3. Mitchell Ivey, USA, 2:04.33
1968 1. Roland Matthes, East Germany, 2:09.6
(OR)
2. Mitchell Ivey, USA, 2:10.6
3. Jack Horsley, USA, 2:10.9
1964 1. Jed Graef, USA, 2:10.3 (WR)
2. Gary Dilley, USA, 2:10.5
3. Robert Bennett, USA, 2:13.1
1904-
1960 Not held
1900 1. Ernst Hoppenberg, Germany, 2:47.0
2. Karl Ruberl, Austria, 2:56.0
3. Johannes Drost, Netherlands, 3:01.0
1896 Not held

Swimming — Men's 100-Meter Breaststroke

1988 1. Adrian Moorhouse, Great Britain,
1:02.04
2. Karoly Guttler, Hungary, 1:02.05
3. Dmitri Volkov, Soviet Union, 1:02.20
1984 1. Steve Lundquist, USA, 1:01.65

2. Victor Davis, Canada, 1:01.99
3. Peter Evans, Australia, 1:02.97
1980 1. Dunkan Goodhew, Great Britain,
1:03.34
2. Arsen Miskarov, Soviet Union, 1:03.82
3. Peter Evans, Australia, 1:03.96
1976 1. John Hencken, USA, 1:03.11 (WR, OR)
2. David Wilkie, Great Britain, 1:03.43
3. Arvidas Iuozaytis, Soviet Union,
1:04.23
1972 1. Nobutaka Taguchi, Japan, 1:04.94
(WR)
2. Tom Bruce, USA, 1:05.43
3. John Hencken, USA, 1:05.61
1968 1. Donald McKenzie, USA, 1:07.7 (OR)
2. Vladimir Kossinsky, Soviet Union,
1:08.0
3. Nikolai Pankin, Soviet Union, 1:08.0
1896-
1964 Not held

Swimming — Men's 200-Meter Breaststroke

1988 1. Jozsef Szabo, Hungary, 2:13.52
2. Nick Gillingham, Great Britain,
2:14.12
3. Sergio Lopez, Spain, 2:15.21
1984 1. Victor Davis, Canada, 2:13.34 (WR)
2. Glenn Beringen, Australia, 2:15.79
3. Etienne Dagon, Switzerland, 2:17.41
1980 1. Robertas Zulpa, Soviet Union, 2:15.85
2. Alban Vermes, Hungary, 2:16.93
3. Arsen Miskarov, Soviet Union, 2:17.28
1976 1. David Wilkie, Great Britain, 2:15.11
(WR, OR)
2. John Hencken, USA, 2:17.26
3. Rick Colella, USA, 2:19.20
1972 1. John Hencken, USA, 2:21.55 (WR)
2. David Wilkie, Great Britain, 2:23.67
3. Nobutaka Taguchi, Japan, 2:23.88
1968 1. Felipe Munoz, Mexico, 2:28.7
2. Vladimir Kossinsky, Soviet Union,
2:29.2
3. Brian Job, USA, 2:29.9
1964 1. Ian O'Brien, Australia, 2:27.8 (WR)
2. Georgy Prokopenko, Soviet Union,
2:28.2
3. Chester Jastremski, USA, 2:29.6
1960 1. William Mulliken, USA, 2:37.4
2. Yoshihiko Osaki, Japan, 2:38.0
3. Wieger Mensonides, Netherlands,
2:39.7
1956 1. Masaru Furukawa, Japan, 2:34.7 (OR)
2. Masahiro Yoshimura, Japan, 2:36.7
3. Charis Yunichev, Soviet Union, 2:36.8
1952 1. John Davies, Australia, 2:34.4 (OR)
2. Bowen Stassforth, USA, 2:34.7
3. Herbert Klein, West Germany, 2:35.9
1948 1. Joseph Verdeur, USA, 2:39.3 (OR)
2. Keith Carter, USA, 2:40.2
3. Robert Sohl, USA, 2:43.9
1936 1. Tetsuo Hamuro, Japan, 2:41.5 (OR)
2. Erwin Sietas, Germany, 2:42.9
3. Reizo Koike, Japan, 2:44.2
1932 1. Yoshiyuki Tsuruta, Japan, 2:45.4
2. Reizo Koike, Japan, 2:46.6
3. Teofilo Yldefonzo, Philippines, 2:47.1
1928 1. Yoshiyuki Tsuruta, Japan, 2:48.8 (OR)
2. Erich Rademacher, Germany, 2:50.6

428

3. Teofilo Yldefonzo, Philippines, 2:56.4
1924   1. Robert Skelton, USA, 2:56.6
      2. Joseph De Combe, Belgium, 2:59.2
      3. William Kirschbaum, USA, 3:01.0
1920   1. Hakan Malmroth, Sweden, 3:04.4
      2. Thor Henning, Sweden, 3:09.2
      3. Arvo Aaltonen, Finland, 3:12.2
1912   1. Walther Bathe, Germany, 3:01.8 (OR)
      2. Willy Lutzow, Germany, 3:05.0
      3. Kurt Malisch, Germany, 3:08.0
1908   1. Frederick Holman, Great Britain, 3:09.2 (WR)
      2. William Robinson, Great Britain, 3:12.8
      3. Pontus Hanson, Sweden, 3:14.6
1896-
1906   Not held

Swimming — Men's 100-Meter Butterfly

1988   1. Anthony Nesty, Suriname, 53.00 (OR)
      2. Matthew Biondi, USA, 53.01
      3. Andy Jameson, Great Britain, 53.30
1984   1. Michael Gross, West Germany, 53.08 (WR)
      2. Pedro Pablo Morales, USA, 53.23
      3. Glenn Buchanan, Australia, 53.85
1980   1. Par Arvidsson, Sweden, 54.92
      2. Roger Pyttel, East Germany, 54.94
      3. David Lopez, Spain, 55.13
1976   1. Matt Vogel, USA, 54.35
      2. Joe Bottom, USA, 54.50
      3. Gary Hall, USA, 54.65
1972   1. Mark Spitz, USA, 54.27 (WR)
      2. Bruce Robertson, Canada, 55.56
      3. Jerry Heidenreich, USA, 55.74
1968   1. Douglas Russell, USA, 55.9 (OR)
      2. Mark Spitz, USA, 56.4
      3. Ross Wales, USA, 57.2
1896-
1964   Not held

Swimming — Men's 200-Meter Butterfly

1988   1. Michael Gross, West Germany, 1:56.94 (OR)
      2. Benny Nielsen, Denmark, 1:58.24
      3. Anthony Mosse, New Zealand, 1:58.28
1984   1. Jon Sieben, Australia, 1:57.04 (WR)
      2. Michael Gross, West Germany, 1:57.40
      3. Rafael Vidal Castro, Venezuela, 1:57.51
1980   1. Sergei Fesenko, Soviet Union, 1:59.76
      2. Philip Hubble, Great Britain, 2:01.20
      3. Roger Pyttel, East Germany, 2:01.39
1976   1. Mike Bruner, USA, 1:59.23 (WR,OR)
      2. Steven Gregg, USA, 1:59.54
      3. Bill Forrester, USA, 1:59.96
1972   1. Mark Spitz, USA, 2:00.70 (WR)
      2. Gary Hall, USA, 2:02.86
      3. Robin Backhaus, USA, 2:03.23
1968   1. Carl Robie, USA, 2:08.7
      2. Martin Woodroffe, Great Britain, 2:09.0
      3. John Ferris, USA, 2:09.3

1964   1. Kevin Berry, Australia, 2:06.6 (WR)
      2. Carl Robie, USA, 2:07.5
      3. Fred Schmidt, USA, 2:09.3
1960   1. Michael Troy, USA, 2:12.8 (WR)
      2. Neville Hayes, Australia, 2:14.6
      3. J. David Gillanders, USA, 2:15.3
1956   1. William Yorzyk, USA, 2:19.3 (OR)
      2. Takashi Ishimoto, Japan, 2:23.8
      3. Gyorgy Tumpek, Hungary, 2:23.9
1896-
1952   Not held

Swimming — Men's 200-Meter Individual Medley

1988   1. Tamas Darnyi, Hungary, 2:00.17 (WR)
      2. Patrick Kuehl, East Germany, 2:01.61
      3. Vadim Iarochtchouk, Soviet Union, 2:02.40
1984   1. Alex Baumann, Canada, 2:01.42 (WR)
      2. Pedro Pablo Morales, USA, 2:03.05
      3. Neil Cochran, Great Britain, 2:04.38
1976-
1980   Not held
1972   1. Gunnar Larsson, Sweden, 2:07.17 (WR)
      2. Tim McKee, USA, 2:08.37
      3. Steven Furniss, USA, 2:08.45
1968   1. Charles Hickcox, USA, 2:12.0 (OR)
      2. Gregory Buckingham, USA, 2:13.0
      3. John Ferris, USA, 2:13.3
1896-
1964   Not held

Swimming — Men's 400-Meter Individual Medley

1988   1. Tamas Darnyi, Hungary, 4:14.75 (WR)
      2. David Wharton, USA, 4:17.36
      3. Stefano Battistelli, Italy, 4:18.01
1984   1. Alex Baumann, Canada, 4:17.41 (WR)
      2. Ricardo Prado, Brazil, 4:18.45
      3. Robert Woodhouse, Australia, 4:20.50
1980   1. Aleksandr Sidorenko, Soviet Union, 4:22.89 (OR)
      2. Sergei Fesenko, Soviet Union, 4:23.43
      3. Zoltan Verraszto, Hungary, 4:24.24
1976   1. Rod Strachan, USA, 4:23.68 (WR, OR)
      2. Tim McKee, USA, 4:24.62
      3. Andrei Smirnov, Soviet Union, 4:26.90
1972   1. Gunnar Larsson, Sweden, 4:31.98 (OR)
      2. Tim McKee, USA, 4:31.98 (OR)
      3. Andras Hargitay, Hungary, 4:32.70
1968   1. Charles Hickcox, USA, 4:48.4
      2. Gary Hall, USA, 4:48.7
      3. Michael Holthaus, West Germany, 4:51.4
1964   1. Richard Roth, USA, 4:45.4 (WR)
      2. Roy Saari, USA, 4:47.1
      3. Gerhard Hetz, West Germany, 4:51.0
1896-
1960   Not held

Swimming — Men's 4x100-Meter Freestyle Relay

1988   1. USA, 3:16.53, (WR), Christopher Jacobs Troy Dalbey, Thomas Jager, Matthew Biondi

429

2. Soviet Union, 3:18.33, Gennadi Prigoda, Iouri Bachkatov, Nikolai Evseev, Vladimir Tkashenko
3. East Germany, 3:19.82, Dirk Richter, Thomas Flemming, Lars Hinneburg, Steffen Zesner
1984 1. USA, 3:19.03 (WR), Christopher Cavanaugh, Michael Heath, Matthew Biondi, Ambrose Gaines
2. Australia, 3:19.68, Gregory Fasala, Neil Brooks, Michael Delany, Mark Stockwell
3. Sweden, 3:22.69, Thomas Leidstrom, Bengt Baron, Mikael Orn, Per Johansson
1976-
1980 **Not held**
1972 1. USA, 3:26.42 (WR), David Edgar, John Murphy, Jerry Heidenreich, Mark Spitz
2. Soviet Union, 3:29.72, Vladimir Bure, Viktor Mazanov, Viktor Aboimov, Igor Grivennikov
3. East Germany, 3:32.42, Roland Matthes, Wilfried Hartung, Peter Bruch, Lutz Unger
1968 1. USA, 3:31.7, Zachary Zorn, Stephen Rerych, Mark Spitz, Kenneth Walsh (WR)
2. Soviet Union, 3:34.2, Semyon Belits-Geiman, Viktor Mazanov, Georgy Kulikov, Leonid Ilyichev
3. Austria, 3:34.7, Gregory Rogers, Robert Windle, Robert Cusack, Michael Wenden
1964 1. USA, 3:33.2 (WR), Stephen Clark, Michael Austin, Gary Ilman, Don Schollander
2. East Germany, 3:37.2, Horst Loffler, Frank Wiegand, Uwe Jacobsen, Hans-Joachim Klein
3. Austria, 3:39.1, David Dickson, Peter Doak, John Ryan, Robert Windle
1896-
1960 **Not held**

Swimming — Men's 4x100-Meter Medley Relay

1988 1. USA, 3:36.93, (WR), David Berkoff, Richard Schroeder, Matthew Biondi, Christopher Jacobs
2. Canada, 3:39.28, Mark Tewksbury, Victor Davis, Thomas Ponting, Donald Alexander Goss
3. Soviet Union, 3:39.96, Igor Polianski, Dmitri Volkov, Vadim Iarochtchouk, Gennadi Prigoda
1984 1. USA, 3:39.30 (WR,OR), Richard Carey, Steve Lundquist, Pedro Pablo Morales, Ambrose Gaines
2. Canada, 3:43.23, Mike West, Victor Davis, Thomas Ponting, Sandy Goss
3. Australia, 3:43.25, Mark Kerry, Peter Evans, Glenn Buchanan, Mark Stockwell
1980 1. Australia, 3:45.70, Mark Kerry, Peter Evans, Mark Tonelli, Neil Brooks
2. Soviet Union, 3:45.92, Viktor Kuznetsov, Arsen Miskarov, Yevgeny Seredin, Sergei Kopliakov

3. Great Britain, 3:47.71, Gary Abraham, Dunkan Goodhew, David Lowe, Martin Smith
1976 1. USA, 3:42.22 (WR, OR), John Naber, John Hencken, Matt Vogel, Jim Montgomery
2. Canada, 3:45.94, Stephen Pickell, Graham Smith, Clay Evans, Gary MacDonald
3. West Germany, 3:47.29, Klaus Steinbach, Walter Kusch, Michael Kraus, Peter Nocke
1972 1. USA, 3:48.16 (WR), Mike Stamm, Tom Bruce, Mark Spitz, Jerry Heidenreich
2. East Germany, 3:52.12, Roland Matthes, Klaus Katzur, Hartmut Flockner, Lutz Unger
3. Canada, 3:52.26, Eric Fish, William Mahony, Bruce Robertson, Robert Kasting
1968 1. USA, 3:54.9 (WR), Charles Hickcox, Donald McKenzie, Douglas Russell, Kenneth Walsh
2. East Germany, 3:57.5, Roland Matthes, Egon Henninger, Horst-Gunter Gregor, Frank Wiegand
3. Soviet Union, 4:00.7, Yuri Gromak, Vladimir Kossinsky, Vladimir Nemshilov, Leonid Ilyichev
1964 1. USA, 3:58.4 (WR), H. Thompson Mann, William Craig, Fred Schmidt, Stephen Clark
2. West Germany, 4:01.6, Ernst-Joachim Kuppers, Egon Henninger, Horst-Gunter Gregor, Hans-Joachim Klein
3. Australia, 4:02.3, Peter Reynolds, Ian O'Brien, Kevin Berry, David Dickson
1960 1. USA, 4:05.4 (WR), Frank McKinney, Paul Hait, Lance Larson, F. Jeffrey Farrell
2. Australia, 4:12.0, David Theile, Terry Gathercole, Neville Hayes, Geoffrey Shipton
3. Japan, 4:12.2, Kazuo Tomita, Koichi Hirakida, Yoshihiko Osaki, Keigo Shimizu
1896-
1956 **Not held**

Swimming — Men's 4x200-Meter Freestyle Relay

1988 1. USA, 7:12.51 (WR), Troy Dalbey, Matt Cetlinski, Doug Gjertser, Matthew Biondi
2. East Germany, 7:13.68, Uwe Dassler, Sven Lodziewski, Thomas Flemming, Steffen Zesner
3. West Germany, 7:14.35, Erik Hochstein, Thomas Fahrner, Rainer Henkel, Michael Gross
1984 1. USA, 7:15.69 (WR), Michael Heath, David Larson, Jeffrey Float, Lawrence Bruce Hayes
2. West Germany, 7:15.73, Thomas Fahrner, Dirk Korthals, Alexander Schowtka, Michael Gross
3. Great Britain, 7:24.78, Neil Cochran, Paul Easter, Paul Howe, Andrew Astbury

430

1980 1. Soviet Union, 7:23.50, Sergei Kopliakov, Vladimir Salnikov, Ivar Stukolkin, Andrei Krylov
2. East Germany, 7:28.60, Frank Pfutze, Jorg Woithe, Detlev Grabs, Rainer Strohbach
3. Brazil, 7:29.30, Jorge Luiz Fernandes, Marcus Laborne Mattioli, Ciro Marques Delgado, Djan Garrido Madruga

1976 1. USA, 7:23.22 (WR, OR), Bruce Furniss, Mike Bruner, John Naber, Jim Montgomery
2. Soviet Union, 7:27.97, Vladimir Raskatov, Andrei Bogdanov, Sergei Kopliakov, Andrei Krylov
3. Great Britain, 7:32.11, Alan MacClatchey, David Dunne, Gordon Downie, Brian Brinkley

1972 1. USA, 7:35.78 (WR), John Kinsella, Frederick Tyler, Steven Genter, Mark Spitz
2. West Germany, 7:41.69, Klaus Steinbach, Werner Lampe, Hans-Gunter Vosseler, Hans Fassnacht
3. Soviet Union, 7:45.76, Igor Grivennikov, Viktor Masanov, Georgy Kulikov, Vladimir Bure

1968 1. USA, 7:52.33, John Nelson, Stephen Rerych, Mark Spitz, Donald Schollander
2. Australia, 7:53.77, Gregory Rogers, Graham White, Robert Windle, Michael Wenden
3. Soviet Union, 8:01.66, Vladimir Bure, Semyon Belits- Geiman, Georgy Kulikov, Leonid Ilyichev

1964 1. USA, 7:52.1 (WR), Stephen Clark, Roy Saari, Gary Ilman, Don Schollander
2. West Germany, 7:59.3, Horst-Gunter Gregor, Gerhard Hetz, Frank Wiegand, Hans-Joachim Klein
3. Japan, 8:03.8, Makoto Fukui, Kunihiro Iwasaki, Toshio Shoji, Yukiaki Okabe

1960 1. USA, 8:10.2 (WR), George Harrison, Richard Blick, Michael Troy, F. Jeffrey Farrell
2. Japan, 8:13.2, Makoto Fukui, Hiroshi Ishii, Tsuyoshi Yamanaka, Tatsuo Fujimoto
3. Australia, 8:13.8, David Dickson, John Devitt, Murray Rose, John Konrads

1956 1. Australia, 8:23.6 (WR), Kevin O'Halloran, John Devitt, Murray Rose, Jon Henricks
2. USA, 8:31.5, Richard Hanley, George Breen, William Woolsey, Ford Konno
3. Soviet Union, 8:34.7, Vitali Sorokin, Vladimir Strushanov, Gennady Nikolayev, Boris Nikitin

1952 1. USA, 8:31.1 (OR), Wayne Moore, William Woolsey, Ford Konno, James McLane
2. Japan, 8:33.5, Hiroshi Suzuki, Yoshihiro Hamaguchi, Toru Goto, Teijiro Tanikawa
3. France, 8:45.9, Joseph Bernardo, Aldo Eminente, Alexandre Jany, Jean Boiteux

1948 1. USA, 8:46.0 (WR), Walter Ris, James McLane, Wallace Wolf, William Smith

2. Hungary, 8:48.4, Elemer Szathmary, Gyorgy Mitro, Imre Kadas Geza Kadas
3. France, 9:08.0, Joseph Bernardo, Henri Padou, Jr., Rene Cornu, Alexandre Jany

1936 1. Japan, 8:51.5 (WR), Masanori Yusa, Shigeo Sugiura, Masaharu Taguchi, Shigeo Arai
2. USA, 9:03.0, Ralph Flanagan, John Macionis, Paul Wolf, Jack Medica
3. Hungary, 9:12.3, Arpad Lengyel, Oszkar Abay-Nemes, Odon Grof, Ference Csik

1932 1. Japan, 8:58.4 (WR), Yasuji Miyazaki, Masanori Yusa, Takashi Yokoyama, Hisakichi Toyoda
2. USA, 9:10.5, Frank Booth, George Fissler, Marola Kalili, Manuella Kalili
3. Hungary, 9:31.4, Andras Wannie, Laszlo Szabados, Andras Szekely, Istvan Barany

1928 1. USA, 9:36.2, Austin Clapp, Walter Laufer, George Kojac, John Weissmuller (WR)
2. Japan, 9:41.4, Hiroshi Yoneyama, Nobuo Arai, Tokuhei Sada, Katsuo Takaishi
3. Canada, 9:47.8, F. Munro Bourne, James Thompson, Garnet Ault, Walter Spence

1924 1. USA, 9:53.4 (WR), Wallace O'Connor, Harry Glancy, Ralph Breyer, John Weissmuller
2. Australia, 10:02.2, Maurice Christie, Ernest Henry, Frank Beaurepaire, Andrew Charlton
3. Sweden, 10:06.8, Georg Werner, Orvar Trolle, Ake Borg, Arne Borg

1920 1. USA, 10:04.4 (WR), Perry McGillivray, Pua Kela Kealoha, Norman Ross, Duke Paoa Kahanamoku
2. Australia, 10:25.4, Henry Hay, William Herald, Ivan Stedman, Frank Beaurepaire
3. Great Britain, 10:37.2, Leslie Savage, E. Percy Peter, Henry Taylor, Harold E. Annison

1912 1. Australia, 10:11.6 (WR), Cecil Healy, Malcolm Champion, Leslie Boardman, Harold Hardwick
2. USA, 10:20.2, Kenneth Huszagh, Harry Hebner, Perry McGillivray, Duke Paoa Kahanamoku
3. Great Britain, 10:28.2, William Foster, Thomas Battersby, John Hatfield, Henry Taylor

1908 1. Great Britain, 10:55.6 (WR), John Derbyshire, Paul Radmilovic, William Foster, Henry Taylor
2. Hungary, 10:59.0, Jozsef Munk, Imre Zachar, Bela von Las Torres, Zoltan von Halmay
3. USA, 11:02.8, Harry Hebner, Leo Goodwin, Charles Daniels, Leslie G. Rich

1906 1. Hungary, 16:52.4, Jozsef Onody, Henrik Hajos, Geza Kiss, Zoltan von Halmay
2. Germany, 17:16.2, Ernst Bahnmeyer, Oscar Schiele, Emil Rausch, Max Pape

431

3. Great Britain, William Henry, John
Derbyshire, Henry Taylor, John Jarvis

**1896-
1904 Not held**

WOMEN'S SWIMMING EVENTS

▼

HIGHLIGHTS

Women were first allowed to swim in the Olympics in 1912, and Australia's Fanny Durack—wearing a long woollen swimsuit with a skirt—won the 100m freestyle to become the first female champion in the Games; impressively, her time was the same as the men's winner's. The US was a consistent power almost from the start: in 1920, Ethelda Bleibtrey achieved a personal sweep by winning both individual races and joining the successful relay team. During the period from 1920 to 1936, the Americans collected a total of 31 of a possible 59 medals. American women took all the swimming titles in 1924, except for the breaststroke, which British Lucy Morton captured.

Four years later, in Amsterdam, a German woman won the 200m breaststroke, while Dutch swimmer Marie Braun, whose mother trained her and other swimmers, won the 100m backstroke. The US placed well, taking the 100m and 400m freestyle and the 400m freestyle relay. Faring a little better than the men in 1932, the American women were led by Helene Madison, and managed to win the 100m and 400m freestyle, the backstroke event, and the 400m freestyle relay.

fact: US backstroker Eleanor Holm, a gold medalist in 1932, was disqualified from the Berlin Games "for sipping champagne with officials."

In Berlin in 1936, the Dutch team proved to be America's nemesis, with a star performer in Rie Mastenbroek, who won the 100m and 400m freestyle. The second-place finisher, Ragnhild Hveger, was only fifteen and a half, and later went on to set all freestyle records except the 100m; in fact, between 1936 and 1942, Hveger demolished forty-two world records.

In London, in 1948, Denmark's Greta Andersen won the 100m freestyle, and later turned professional, swimming the English Channel six times; at the age of 36, she set the England-to-France record in 13 hours, 14 minutes. The US came from behind in the 400m freestyle relay, thanks to Ann Curtis, whose unofficial time bettered the 12-year-old world record time for the 100 meters.

432

Mark Spitz, who won a record seven gold medals swimming at the
Munich Games in 1972, revived his Olympic hopes at the age of 41,
aiming for a butterflyer's berth on the Barcelona–bound US team.

US swimmer Tracy Caulkins is the only swimmer ever, man or woman, to own American records in every stroke. She was ready to impress Olympic fans in 1980, but was stymied by the US boycott of the Moscow Games. Caulkins captured three Olympic golds in 1984.

The American women were hardly able to place in 1952, when Hungarian women took most of the titles, except the 100m backstroke, which South African Joan Harrison won.

In Melbourne in 1956, Australian Dawn Fraser was nineteen years old; she dominated the freestyle sprints until her retirement in 1964, after becoming the first woman to freestyle a sub-minute 100 meters. While Fraser won the 100m freestyle, she placed second in the 400m to fellow countrywoman Lorraine Crapp, who had just before the Games become the first woman to swim the 400 meters in less than 5 minutes. The first butterfly event was swept by the US, whose first-place finisher, Shelly Mann, had taken up swimming as therapy for childhood polio.

An American resurgence began in 1960, when Chris von Saltza led a group of so-called "water babies" who averaged 16 years old. Von Saltza finished second to Dawn Fraser in the 100m freestyle, then upset the Australian in the 400m, and then swam on two winning relay teams. Fraser captured the 100m for the third consecutive time at Tokyo in 1964, but Ginny Duenkel led an American 1–2–3 sweep in the 400m freestyle and Donna deVarona did likewise in the individual medley. Cathy Ferguson won the backstroke and the US captured both relays.

fact: In 1965 US swimmer Donna deVarona was the first women to break into network television in the sports broadcasting field.

In 1968, the American women captured 11 of the 14 events, and 16-year-old Debbie Meyer, who won three golds that year in the 200m, 400m, and 800m freestyles, was named the USA amateur athlete for 1968. Claudia Kolb, Kaye Hall, and Sue Pedersen each came away with two gold medals. Kolb won the new 200m medley as well as the 400m, Hall won the 100m backstroke and swam on the medley relay, and Pedersen took a leg on both relay teams. The 1968 Games were also marked by Jan Henn's victory in the 100m freestyle, the first American to win that event since Helene Madison in 1932. The events not taken that year by the Americans were awarded to Yugoslavia, in the 100m breaststroke, Australia, in the 100m butterfly, and the Netherlands, in the 200m butterfly; a pair of second-place finishes in the two backstrokes marked the first silver medals ever won by a Canadian woman swimmer.

Between them, the US and Australia won 13 of the 14 women's events at Munich in 1972. The individual star was Australia's Shane Gould, who competed in a record 12 races, including heats and finals. For her effort, she took home three gold (the 200m and 400m freestyle and the 200m individual medley), a silver and a bronze. Keena Rothhanner, a 15-year-old Californian, thwarted Gould in the 800m freestyle with a world-record time of 8:53.7, and Sandra Neilson and

Shirley Babashoff both beat out the dynamic Aussie in the 100m freestyle. Melissa Belote, another 15-year-old, won both backstroke races for the US. As successful as the US men swimmers were at Montréal in 1976, their female counterparts were struggling to remain competitive; while the men lost only one race, the women won only one. East Germany took the 1976 events by a landslide (as it were), winning 11 of 13 events, establishing what would become a long term of East German domination. The only US success came in the final race, the 400m freestyle relay. Meanwhile, the American camp put forth insinuations that the muscular East Germans looked more like men and that their training methods were too autocratic. Kornelia Ender was the outstanding performer with four gold medals, barely missing a fifth in the relay; with a total of five medals, she and Shirley Babashoff share the distinction of being the only women to medal five times in swimming in a single Games. She also provided the media with a sentimental story because of a reunion with her grandmother, who had defected to the US in 1959. Two of Ender's victories came within the space of 26 minutes, as she first tied the world record in the 100m butterfly, then came back to set a world record in the 200m freestyle.

It was the same old story in 1980, although this time the Americans weren't around to have their faces pushed into the water. For the second Olympics in a row, the East Germans captured 11 of 13 events, and at Moscow they swept all of the medals in six of the 11 individual races. Freestyler Barbara Krause, who had missed the 1976 Games because of illness, backstroke specialist Rica Reinisch, only 15 years old at the time, and Caren Metschuck each won three gold medals. The East German women set six world records, with Reinisch helping to account for half of them, two in the backstroke events and one in the 400m medley relay.

In 1984 US swimmer Nancy Hogshead was the big winner in women's swimming, earning four medals. Her temmate, Tracy Caulkins, had been hurt by the 1980 US boycott of the Games, but held on to claim three gold medals at the 1984 Games. Another swimmer affected by the 1980 boycott, butterflyer Mary T. Meagher, won three gold medals in 1984 and captured the 200m butterfly bronze in 1988. But 1984 was the first since 1952 that the Olympics failed to produce at least one women's swimming world record. And for the first time ever, two gold medals were awarded in a single Olympic swimming race, in the women's 100-meter freestyle, the first-place time shared by Americans Hogshead and Carrie Steinseifer, Olympic bunkmates. Also that year, Canada's first swimming medals since 1912 included three medals for the women's team: a gold and a silver captured by Anne Ottenbrite and a relay bronze. While their male counterparts earned the most medals since the 1960 Games, the Australian women contributed their share, winning the silver in the 200m butterfly and the 400m individual medley, along with the bronze in the 200m individual medley.

fact: US swimmer Tracy Caulkins is the only swimmer ever, man or woman, to own American records in every stroke. *USA Today* named her "Swimmer of the Decade."

In 1988 East German Kristin Otto accumulated swimming medals as has no woman in Olympic history, taking the 100m freestyle, the 100m backstroke, the 100m butterfly, and the 50m freestyle, then leading her relay teams to gold medals in the 4 x 100 freestyle and the 4 x 100 medley.

The East German women might have swept the Seoul Games if it hadn't been for US triple-gold medalist Janet Evans. She triumphed in the 400m individual medley, the 400m freestyle, and the 800m freestyle, becoming the fifth woman to win three or more individual swimming gold medals at one Olympics. In fact, she was the only American woman to win any individual gold. Evans's mark in the 400m freestyle beat the record Mark Spitz set in that event in 1968, and her 800m freestyle time would have won any men's race until 1973.

Also swimming strong in 1988 were Tania Dangalakova of Bulgaria in the 100m breaststroke and Krisztina Egerszegi of Hungary in the 200m backstroke, both of whom took home the gold.

Shane Gould

When Shane Gould got home from the 1972 Munich Summer Olympics, she said, "I'm tired. I'm looking forward to school. I wish to be an ordinary teenager." Not an easy order when, at 15, you've won five Olympic medals, including three golds that set world-record times. The young Australian phenomenon had American women swimmers so spooked at Munich, they wore t-shirts that read: "All that glitters is not Gould." It didn't help much.

Gould, born September 4, 1956 in Brisbane, Queensland, could swim underwater with her eyes closed at the age of three. At six she began professional lessons and at thirteen started the serious training that would bring her to international acclaim and the amazingly low heart rate of 40 beats per minute. By 1971, she held every women's freestyle record up to 1500 meters.

Her 1972 Olympic victories came in the 200m and 400m freestyles, and the 200m individual medley. She took a silver medal in the 800m and a bronze in the 100m freestyle races, which were her first freestyle losses in two years. Gould's parents were nearly as big a presence as their daughter at the Games. Her mother, Shirley Gould, had already written a book, *Swimming the Shane Gould Way.*

Tired of the regimen, Gould announced her retirement the following year. Three years after the Olympics, Gould, then 18, married 25-year-old Bible student Neil Innes. After the outdoor wedding, Gould said, "Instead of saying the formal vows, we made up our own. It seemed to be in line with what we believe. We like the open air and surfing." —*H.D.*

435

Tracy Caulkins

Few people "retire" at the age of twenty-one, but that is exactly what Tracy Caulkins has done. The University of Florida swimming great who won three gold medals at the 1984 Summer Olympics is an athlete who is content these days to watch her own records fall as a new generation prepares for future Games.

Caulkins was born on January 11, 1963, in Winona, Minnesota. She grew up in Nashville, Tennessee, and attended Harpeth Hall Academy, a private school. She began swimming competitively as a youngster. In 1981 she enrolled at the University of Florida, where, over a period of four years, she turned in a stunning record as an amateur athlete. Her achievements include 48 national long and short course titles—the most won by any swimmer in US history—62 American records, 15 individual American records, and participation in 11 American record-setting relay teams. From 1980 until 1984 she was widely considered the best and fastest woman swimmer in America.

Caulkins actually earned a position on the Olympic team in 1980, even before she entered college. That year the United States government decided to boycott the games. All of the Olympic athletes were disappointed, but none more so than Caulkins. She has said that she trained even harder during her college years so that she could prove herself beyond any doubt at the 1984 Games in Los Angeles.

While at Florida, Caulkins won the Broderick Cup as outstanding collegiate woman athlete of the year in both 1983 and 1984. Although she was a consistent winner throughout her college years—and a winner in the 200m and 400m individual medleys at the 1982 Pan American Games—her best year as an NCAA swimmer came in 1984. That year she set NCAA records in all four of her individual events (the 200m IM, 400m IM, 100m breaststroke, and 200m fly). She also helped the Florida team to win the 800m freestyle relay and the 400m freestyle relay, both in NCAA record-setting times.

In preparation for the 1984 Olympic trials, Caulkins swam five hours a day, six days per week. The intense practice and long record of first place finishes paid off handsomely during the Games, where she won the 400m IM, setting an American record, and the 200m IM, establishing an Olympic record. Her third gold medal came as part of a victorious 400m relay team. After the Games ended, the United States Olympic Team recognized Caulkins as "female athlete of the year," a fitting tribute.

For some time several of Caulkins's records remained unbroken, especially the 200-yard individual medley. That record was only recently bested by Summer Sanders, a 1992 Olympic hopeful. Caulkins expresses no regrets as her successors in competitive swimming gradually beat her in the numbers game. "There's a lot of depth with these girls leading the way to '92," she told the Associated Press. "I thought, 'Why are [my] records not falling?' It shows a lot of progress when they do. The women here are not satisfied with just winning."

Caulkins was inducted into the International Swimming Hall of Fame in 1990. The University of Florida has also honored her accomplishments by naming a double swimming scholarship after her and by awarding a Tracy Caulkins Award to Florida's best female swimmer each year. —*M.K.*

Medalists

Swimming

Swimming — Women's 50-Meter Freestyle

1988
1. Kristin Otto, East Germany, 25.49 (OR)
2. Yang Wenyi, People's Republic of China, 25.64
3. Katrin Meissner, East Germany, 25.71
3. Jill Sterkel, USA, 25.71

Swimming — Women's 100-Meter Freestyle

1988
1. Kristin Otto, East Germany, 54.93
2. Yong Zhuang, People's Republic of China, 55.47
3. Catherine Plewinski, France, 55.49
1984
1. Nancy Hogshead, USA, 55.92
1. Carrie Steinseifer, USA, 55.92
3. Annemarie Verstappen, Netherlands, 56.08
1980
1. Barbara Krause, East Germany, 54.79 (WR)
2. Caren Metschuck, East Germany, 55.16
3. Ines Diers, East Germany, 55.65
1976
1. Kornelia Ender, East Germany, 55.65 (WR, OR)
2. Petra Priemer, East Germany, 56.49
3. Enith Brigitha, Netherlands, 56.65
1972
1. Sandra Neilson, USA, 58.59 (OR)
2. Shirley Babashoff, USA, 59.02
3. Shane Gould, Australia, 59.06
1968
1. Jan Henne, USA, 1:00.0
2. Susan Pedersen, USA, 1:00.3
3. Linda Gustavson, USA, 1:00.3
1964
1. Dawn Fraser, Australia, 59.5 (OR)
2. Sharon Stouder, USA, 59.9
3. Kathleen Ellis, USA, 1:00.8
1960
1. Dawn Fraser, Australia, 1:01.2 (OR)
2. Christine Von Saltza, USA, 1:02.8
3. Natalie Steward, Great Britain, 1:03.1
1956
1. Dawn Fraser, Australia, 1:02.0 (WR)
2. Lorraine Crapp, Australia, 1:02.3
3. Faith Leech, Australia, 1:05.1
1952
1. Katalin Szoke, Hungary, 1:06.8
2. Johanna Termeulen, Netherlands, 1:07.0
3. Judit Temes, Hungary, 1:07.1
1948
1. Greta Andersen, Denmark, 1:06.3
2. Ann Curtis, USA, 1:06.5
3. Marie-Louise Vaessen, Netherlands, 1:07.6
1936
1. Hendrika Mastenbroek, Netherlands, 1:05.9 (OR)
2. Jeanette Campbell, Argentina, 1:06.4
3. Gisela Arendt, Germany, 1:06.6
1932
1. Helene Madison, USA, 1:06.8 (OR)

2. Willemijntje den Ouden, Netherlands, 1:07.8
3. Eleanor Saville-Garatti, USA, 1:08.2
1928
1. Albina Osipowich, USA, 1:11.0 (OR)
2. Eleanor Garatti, USA, 1:11.4
3. M. Joyce Cooper, Great Britain, 1:13.6
1924
1. Ethel Lackie, USA, 1:12.4
2. Mariechen Wehselau, USA, 1:12.8
3. Gertrude Ederle, USA, 1:14.2
1920
1. Ethelda Bleibtrey, USA, 1:13.6 (WR)
2. Irene Guest, USA, 1:17.0
3. Frances Schroth, USA, 1:17.2
1912
1. Fanny Durack, Australia, 1:22.2
2. Wilhelmina Wylie, Australia, 1:25.4
3. Jennie Fletcher, Great Britain, 1:27.0
1896-1908 Not held

Swimming — Women's 200-Meter Freestyle

1988
1. Heike Friedrich, East Germany, 1:57.65 (OR)
2. Silvia Poll, Costa Ria, 1:58.67
3. Manuela Stellmach, East Germany, 1:59.01
1984
1. Mary Wayte, USA, 1:59.23
2. Cynthia Woodhead, USA, 1:59.50
3. Annemarie Verstappen, Netherlands, 1:59.69
1980
1. Barbara Krause, East Germany, 1:58.33 (OR)
2. Ines Diers, East Germany, 1:59.64
3. Carmela Schmidt, East Germany, 2:01.44
1976
1. Kornelia Ender, East Germany, 1:59.26 (WR, OR)
2. Shirley Babashoff, USA, 2:01.22
3. Enith Brigitha, Netherlands, 2:01.40
1972
1. Shane Gould, Australia, 2:03.56 (WR)
2. Shirley Babashoff, USA, 2:04.33
3. Keena Rothhammer, USA, 2:04.92
1968
1. Debbie Meyer, USA, 2:10.5 (OR)
2. Jan Henne, USA, 2:11.0
3. Jane Barkman, USA, 2:11.2
1896-1964 Not held

Swimming — Women's 400-Meter Freestyle

1988
1. Janet Evans, USA, 4:03.85 (WR)
2. Heike Friedrich, East Germany, 4:05.94
3. Anke Moehring, East Germany, 4:06.62
1984
1. Tiffany Cohen, USA, 4:07.10 (OR)

437

2. Sarah Hardcastle, Great Britain, 4:10.27
3. June Croft, Great Britain, 4:11.49

1980 1. Ines Diers, East Germany, 4:08.76 (OR)
2. Petra Schneider, East Germany, 4:09.16
3. Carmela Schmidt, East Germany, 4:10.86

1976 1. Petra Thuemer, East Germany, 4:09.89 (WR,OR)
2. Shirley Babashoff, USA, 4:10.46
3. Shannon Smith, Canada, 4:14.60

1972 1. Shane Gould, Australia, 4:19.04 (WR)
2. Novella Calhgaris, Italy, 4:22.44
3. Gudrun Wegner, East Germany, 4:23.11

1968 1. Debbie Meyer, USA, 4:31.8 (OR)
2. Linda Gustavson, USA, 4:35.5
3. Karen Moras, Australia, 4:37.0

1964 1. Virginia Duenkel, USA, 4:43.3 (OR)
2. Marilyn Ramenofsky, USA, 4:44.6
3. Terri Lee Stickles, USA, 4:47.2

1960 1. Christine Von Saltza, USA, 4:50.6 (OR)
2. Jane Cederqvist, Sweden, 4:53.9
3. Catharina Lagerberg, Netherlands, 4:56.9

1956 1. Lorraine Crapp, Australia, 4:54.6 (OR)
2. Dawn Fraser, Australia, 5:02.5
3. Sylvia Ruuska, USA, 5:07.1

1952 1. Valeria Gyenge, Hungary, 5:12.1 (OR)
2. Eva Novak, Hungary, 5:13.7
3. Evelyn Kawamoto, USA, 5:14.6

1948 1. Ann Curtis, USA, 5:17.8 (OR)
2. Karen-Margrete Harup, Denmark, 5:21.2
3. Catherine Gibson, Great Britain, 5:22.5

1936 1. Hendrika Mastenbroek, Netherlands, 5:26.4 (OR)
2. Ragnhild Hveger, Denmark, 5:27.5
3. Lenore Wingard-Kight, USA, 5:29.0

1932 1. Helene Madison, USA, 5:28.5 (WR)
2. Lenore Kight, USA, 5:28.6
3. Jennie Makaal, South Africa, 5:47.3

1928 1. Martha Norelius, USA, 5:42.8 (WR)
2. Maria Johanna Braun, Netherlands, 5:57.8
3. Josephine McKim, USA, 6:00.2

1924 1. Martha Norelius, USA, 6:02.2 (OR)
2. Helen Wainwright, USA, 6:03.8
3. Gertrude Ederle, USA, 6:04.8

1920 1. Ethelda Bleibtrey, USA, 4:34.0 (WR)
2. Margaret Woodbridge, USA, 4:42.8
3. Frances Schroth, USA, 4:52.0

1896-
1912 **Not held**

Swimming — Women's 800-Meter Freestyle

1988 1. Janet Evans, USA, 8:20.20 (OR)
2. Astrid Strauss, East Germany, 8:22.09
3. Julie McDonald, Australia, 8:22.93

1984 1. Tiffany Cohen, USA, 8:24.95 (OR)
2. Michele Richardson, USA, 8:30.73
3. Sarah Hardcastle, Great Britain, 8:32.60

1980 1. Michelle Ford, Australia, 8:28.90 (OR)
2. Ines Diers, East Germany, 8:32.55

3. Heike Dahne, East Germany, 8:33.48

1976 1. Petra Thuemer, East Germany, 8:37.14 (WR, OR)
2. Shirley Babashoff, USA, 8:37.59
3. Wendy Weinberg, USA, 8:42.60

1972 1. Keena Rothhammer, USA, 8:53.68 (WR)
2. Shane Gould, Australia, 8:56.39
3. Novella Calligaris, Italy, 8:57.46

1968 1. Debbie Meyer, USA, 9:24.0 (OR)
2. Pamela Kruse, USA, 9:35.7
3. Maria Teresa Ramirez, Mexico, 9:38.5

1896-
1964 **Not held**

Swimming — Women's 100-Meter Backstroke

1988 1. Kristin Otto, East Germany, 1:00.89
2. Krisztina Egerszegi, Hungary, 1:01.56
3. Cornelia Sirch, East Germany, 1:01.57

1984 1. Theresa Andrews, USA, 1:02.55
2. Betsy Mitchell, USA, 1:02.63
3. Jolanda de Rover, Netherlands, 1:02.91

1980 1. Rica Reinisch, East Germany, 1:00.86 (WR)
2. Ina Kleber, East Germany, 1:02.07
3. Petra Riedel, East Germany, 1:02.64

1976 1. Ulrike Richter, East Germany, 1:01.83 (OR)
2. Brigit Treiber, East Germany, 1:03.41
3. Nancy Garapick, Canada, 1:03.71

1972 1. Melissa Belote, USA, 1:05.78 (OR)
2. Andrea Gyarmati, Hungary, 1:06.26
3. Susie Atwood, USA, 1:06.34

1968 1. Kaye Hall, USA, 1:06.2 (WR)
2. Elaine Tanner, Canada, 1:06.7
3. Jane Swagerty, USA, 1:08.1

1964 1. Cathy Ferguson, USA, 1:07.7 (WR)
2. Christine Caron, France, 1:07.9
3. Virginia Duenkel, USA, 1:08.0

1960 1. Lynn Burke, USA, 1:09.3 (OR)
2. Natalie Steward, Great Britain, 1:10.8
3. Satoko Tanaka, Japan, 1:11.4

1956 1. Judith Grinham, Great Britain, 1:12.9 (OR)
2. Carin Cone, USA, 1:12.9
3. Margaret Edwards, Great Britain, 1:13.1

1952 1. Joan Harrison, South Africa, 1:14.3
2. Geertje Wielema, Netherlands, 1:14.5
3. Jean Stewart, New Zealand, 1:15.8

1948 1. Karen Margrete Harup, Denmark, 1:14.4 (OR)
2. Suzanne Zimmerman, USA, 1:16.0
3. Judy Davies, Australia, 1:16.7

1936 1. Dina W. Senff, Netherlands, 1:18.9
2. Hendrika Mastenbroek, Netherlands, 1:19.2
3. Alice Bridges, USA, 1:19.4

1932 1. Eleanor Holm, USA, 1:19.4
2. Philomena Mealing, Australia, 1:21.3
3. E. Valerie Davies, Great Britain, 1:22.5

1928 1. Maria Johanna Braun, Netherlands, 1:22.0
2. Ellen E. King, Great Britain, 1:22.2
3. M. Joyce Cooper, Great Britain, 1:22.8

438

1924 1. Sybil Bauer, USA, 1:23.2 (OR)
      2. Phyllis Harding, Great Britain, 1:27.4
      3. Aileen Riggin, USA, 1:28.2
1896-
1920 Not held

Swimming — Women's 200-Meter Backstroke

1988 1. Krisztina Egerszegi, Hungary, 2:09.29
         (OR)
      2. Kathrin Zimmermann, East Germany,
         2:10.61
      3. Cornelia Sirch, East Germany, 2:11.45
1984 1. Jolanda De Rover, Netherlands,
         2:12.38
      2. Amy White, USA, 2:13.04
      3. Aneta Patrascoiu, Romania, 2:13.29
1980 1. Rica Reinisch, East Germany, 2:11.77
         (WR)
      2. Cornelia Polit, East Germany, 2:13.75
      3. Brigit Treiber, East Germany, 2:14.14
1976 1. Ulrike Richter, East Germany, 2:13.43.
         (OR)
      2. Brigit Treiber, East Germany, 2:14.97
      3. Nancy Garapick, Canada, 2:15.60
1972 1. Melissa Belote, USA, 2:19.19 (WR)
      2. Susie Atwood, USA, 2:20.38
      3. Donna Marie Gurr, Canada, 2:23.22
1968 1. Pokey Watson, USA, 2:24.8 (OR)
      2. Elaine Tanner, Canada, 2:27.4
      3. Kaye Hall, USA, 2:28.9
1896-
1964 Not held

Swimming — Women's 100-Meter Breaststroke

1988 1. Tania Dangalakova, Bulgaria, 1:07.95
         (OR)
      2. Antoaneta Frenkeva, Bulgaria, 1:08.74
      3. Silke Hoerner, East Germany, 1:08.83
1984 1. Petra Van Staveren, Netherlands,
         1:09.88 (OR)
      2. Anne Ottenbrite, Canada, 1:10.69
      3. Catherine Poirot, France, 1:10.70
1980 1. Ute Geweniger, East Germany,
         1:10.22
      2. Elvira Vasilkova, Soviet Union, 1:10.41
      3. Susanne Schultz Nielsson, Denmark,
         1:11.16
1976 1. Hannelore Anke, East Germany,
         1:11.16
      2. Liubov Rusanova, Soviet Union,
         1:13.04
      3. Marina Koshevaia, Soviet Union,
         1:13.30
1972 1. Catherine Carr, USA, 1:13.58 (WR)
      2. Galina Stepanova-Prozumenshikova,
         Soviet Union, 1:14.99
      3. Beverly Whitfield, Australia, 1:15.73
1968 1. Djurdjica Bjedov, Yugoslavia, 1:15.8
         (OR)
      2. Galina Prozumenshikova, Soviet Union,
         1:15.9
      3. Sharon Wichman, USA, 1:16.1
1896-
1964 Not held

Swimming — Women's 200-Meter Breaststroke

1988 1. Silke Hoerner, East Germany, 2:26.71
         (WR)
      2. Xiaomin Huang, People's Republic of
         China, 2:27.49
      3. Antoaneta Frenkeva, Bulgaria, 2:28.34
1984 1. Anne Ottenbrite, Canada, 2:30.38
      2. Susan Rapp, USA, 2:31.15
      3. Ingrid Lempereur, Belgium, 2:31.40
1980 1. Lina Kochushite, Soviet Union, 2:29.54
         (OR)
      2. Svetlana Varganova, Soviet Union,
         2:29.61
      3. Yulia Bogdanova, Soviet Union,
         2:32.39
1976 1. Marina Koshevaia, Soviet Union,
         2:33.35 (WR, OR)
      2. Marina Iurchenia, Soviet Union,
         2:36.08
      3. Liubov Rusanova, Soviet Union,
         2:36.22
1972 1. Beverly Whitfield, Australia, 2:41.71
         (OR)
      2. Dana Schoenfield, USA, 2:42.05
      3. Galina Stepanowa-Prozumenshikova,
         Soviet Union, 2:42.36
1968 1. Sharon Wichman, USA, 2:44.4 (OR)
      2. Djurdjica Bjedov, Yugoslavia, 2:46.4
      3. Galina Prozumenshikova, Soviet Union,
         2:47.0
1964 1. Galina Prozumenshikova, Soviet Union,
         2:46.4 (OR)
      2. Claudia Kolb, USA, 2:47.6
      3. Svetlana Babanina, Soviet Union,
         2:48.6
1960 1. Anita Lonsbrough, Great Britain,
         2:49.5 (WR)
      2. Wiltrud Urselmann, West Germany,
         2:50.0
      3. Barbara Gobel, East Germany, 2:53.6
1956 1. Ursula Happe, West Germany, 2:53.1
         (OR)
      2. Eva Szekely, Hungary, 2:54.8
      3. Eva-Maria Ten Elsen, East Germany,
         2:55.1
1952 1. Eva Szekely, Hungary, 2:51.7 (OR)
      2. Eva Novak, Hungary, 2:54.4
      3. Helen Gordon, Great Britain, 2:57.6
1948 1. Petronella van Vliet, Netherlands,
         2:57.2
      2. Beatrice Lyons, Australia, 2:57.7
      3. Eva Novak, Hungary, 3:00.2
1936 1. Hideko Maehata, Japan, 3:03.6
      2. Martha Geneger, Germany, 3:04.2
      3. Inge Sorensen, Denmark, 3:07.8
1932 1. Claire Dennis, Australia, 3:06.3 (OR)
      2. Hideko Maehata, Japan, 3:06.4
      3. Else Jacobsen, Denmark, 3:07.1
1928 1. Hilde Schrader, Germany, 3:12.6
      2. Mietje Baron, Netherlands, 3:15.2
      3. Lotte Muhe, Germany, 3:17.6
1924 1. Lucy Morton, Great Britain, 3:33.2
         (OR)
      2. Agnes Geraghty, USA, 3:34.0
      3. Gladys Carson, Great Britain, 3:35.4
1896-
1920 Not held

439

Swimming — Women's 100-Meter Butterfly

1988 1. Kristin Otto, East Germany, 59.00 (OR)
2. Birte Weigang, East Germany, 59.45
3. Hong Qian, People's Republic of China, 59.52
1984 1. Mary T. Meagher, USA, 59.26
2. Jenna Johnson, USA, 1:00.19
3. Karin Seick, West Germany, 1:01.36
1980 1. Caren Metschuck, East Germany, 1:00.42
2. Andrea Pollack, East Germany, 1:00.90
3. Christiane Knacke, East Germany, 1:01.44
1976 1. Kornelia Ender, East Germany, 1:00.13 (EWR)
2. Andrea Pollack, East Germany, 1:00.98
3. Wendy Boglioli, USA, 1:01.17
1972 1. Mayumi Aoki, Japan, 1:03.34 (WR)
2. Roswitha Beier, East Germany, 1:03.61
3. Andrea Gyarmati, Hungary, 1:03.73
1968 1. Lynette McClements, Australia, 1:05.5
2. Ellie Daniel, USA, 1:05.8
3. Susan Shields, USA, 1:06.2
1964 1. Sharon Stouder, USA, 1:04.7 (WR)
2. Ada Kok, Netherlands, 1:05.6
3. Kathleen Ellis, USA, 1:06.0
1960 1. Carolyn Schuler, USA, 1:09.5 (OR)
2. Marianne Heemskerk, Netherlands, 1:10.4
3. Janice Andrew, Australia, 1:12.2
1956 1. Shelley Mann, USA, 1:11.0 (OR)
2. Nancy Ramey, USA, 1:11.9
3. Mary Sears, USA, 1:14.4
1896-1952 Not held

Swimming — Women's 200-Meter Butterfly

1988 1. Kathleen Nord, East Germany, 2:09.51
2. Birte Weigang, East Germany, 2:09.91
3. Mary T. Meagher, USA, 2:10.80
1984 1. Mary T. Meagher, USA, (OR) 2:06.90
2. Karen Phillips, Australia, 2:10.56
3. Ina Beyermann, West Germany, 2:11.91
1980 1. Ines Geissler, East Germany, 2:10.44 (OR)
2. Sybille Schonrock, East Germany, 2:10.45
3. Michelle Ford, Australia, 2:11.66
1976 1. Andrea Pollack, East Germany, 2:11.41 (OR)
2. Ulrike Tauber, East Germany, 2:12.50
3. Rosemarie Gabriel, East Germany, 2:12.86
1972 1. Karen Moe, USA, 2:15.57 (WR)
2. Lynn Colella, USA, 2:16.34
3. Ellie Daniel, USA, 2:16.74
1968 1. Ada Kok, Netherlands, 2:24.7 (OR)
2. Helga Lindner, East Germany, 2:24.8
3. Ellie Daniel, USA, 2:25.9

1896-1964 Not held

Swimming — Women's 200-Meter Individual Medley

1988 1. Daniela Hunger, East Germany, 2:12.59 (OR)
2. Elena Dendeberova, Soviet Union, 2:13.31
3. Noemi Ildiko Lung, Romania, 2:14.85
1984 1. Tracy Caulkins, USA, 2:12.64 (OR)
2. Nancy Hogshead, USA, 2:15.17
3. Michele Pearson, Australia, 2:15.92
1976-1980 Not held
1972 1. Shane Gould, Australia, 2:23.07 (WR)
2. Kornelia Ender, East Germany, 2:23.59
3. Lynn Vidali, USA, 2:24.06
1968 1. Claudia Kolb, USA, 2:24.7 (OR)
2. Susan Pedersen, USA, 2:28.8
3. Jan Henne, USA, 2:31.4
1896-1964 Not held

Swimming — Women's 400-Meter Individual Medley

1988 1. Janet Evans, USA, 4:37.76
2. Noemi Ildiko Lung, Romania, 4:39.46
3. Daniela Hunger, East Germany, 4:39.76
1984 1. Tracy Caulkins, USA, 3:39.24
2. Suzanne Landells, Australia, 4:48.30
3. Petra Zindler, West Germany, 4:48.57
1980 1. Petra Schneider, East Germany, 4:36.29 (WR)
2. Sharron Davies, Great Britain, 4:46.83
3. Agnieszka Czopek, Poland, 4:48.17
1976 1. Ulrike Tauber, East Germany, 4:42.77 (WR, OR)
2. Cheryl Gibson, Canada, 4:48.10
3. Becky Smith, Canada, 4:50.48
1972 1. Gail Neall, Australia, 5:02.97 (WR)
2. Leslie Cliff, Canada, 5:03.57
3. Novella Calligaris, Italy, 5:03.99
1968 1. Claudia Kolb, USA, 5:08.5 (OR)
2. Lynn Vidali, USA, 5:22.2
3. Sabine Steinbach, East Germany, 5:25.3
1964 1. Donna De Varona, USA, 5:18.7 (OR)
2. Sharon Finneran, USA, 5:24.1
3. Martha Randall, USA, 5:24.2
1896-1960 Not held

Swimming — Women's 4x100-Meter Freestyle Relay

1988 1. East Germany, 3:40.63 (OR), Kristin Otto, Katrin Meissner, Daniela Hunger, Manuela Stellmach
2. Netherlands, 3:43.39, Marianne Muis, Mildred Muis, Connie Van Bentum, Karin Brienesse
3. USA, 3:44.25, Mary Wayte, Mitzi Kremer, Laura Walker, Dara Torres

440

1984
1. USA, 3:43.43, Jenna Johnson, Carrie Steinseifer, Dara Torres, Nancy Hogshead
2. Netherlands, 3:44.40, Annemarie Verstappen, Elles Vosles, Desi Reijers, Connie Van Bentum
3. West Germany, 3:45.56, Iris Zscherpe, Suzanne Schuster, Christiane Pielke, Karin Seick

1980
1. East Germany, 3:42.71 (WR), Barbara Kruase, Caren Metschuck, Ines Diers, Sarina Hulsenbeck
2. Sweden, 3:48.93, Carina Ljungdahl, Tina Gustafsson, Agneta Maartensson, Agneta Eriksson
3. Netherlands, 3:49.51, Connie Van Bentum, Wilma van Velsen, Reggie de Jong, Annelies Maas

1976
1. USA, 3:44.82, (WR), Kim Peyton, Wendy Boglioli, Jill Sterkel, Shirley Babashoff
2. East Germany, 3:34.50, Kornelia Ender, Petra Priemer, Andrea Pollack, Claudia Hempel
3. Canada, 3:48.81, Gail Amundrud, Barbara Clark, Becky Smith, Anne Jardin

1972
1. USA, 3:55.19 (WR), Sandra Neilson, Jennifer Kemp, Jane Barkman, Shirley Babashoff
2. East Germany, 3:55.55, Gabriele Wetzko, Andrea Eife, Elke Sehmisch, Kornelia Ender
3. West Germany, 3:57.93, Jutta Weber, Heidemarie Reineck, Gudrun Beckmann, Angela Steinbach

1968
1. USA, 4:02.5 (OR), Jane Barkman, Linda Gustavson, Susan Pedersen, Jan Henne
2. East Germany, 4:05.7, Martina Grunert, Uta Schmuck, Roswitha Krause, Gabriele Wetzko
3. Canada, 4:07.2, Angela Coughlan, Marilyn Corson, Elaine Tanner, Marion Lay

1964
1. USA, 4:03.8 (WR), Sharon Stouder, Donna De Varona, Lillian "Pokey" Watson, Kathleen Ellis
2. Australia, 4:06.9, Robyn Thorn, Janice Murphy, Lynette Bell, Dawn Fraser
3. Netherlands, 4:12.0, Pauline van der Wildt, Catharina Beumer, Winnie van Weerdenburg, Erica Terpstra

1960
1. USA, 4:08.9 (WR), Joan Spillane, Shirley Stobs, Carolyn Wood, Susan Christine Von Saltza
2. Australia, 4:11.3, Dawn Fraser, Ilsa Konrads, Lorraine Crapp, Alva Colqhoun
3. West Germany and East Germany 4:19.7, Christel Steffin, Heidi Pechstein, Gisela Weiss, Ursula Brunner

1956
1. Australia, 4:17.1 (WR), Dawn Fraser, Faith Leech, Sandra Morgan, Lorraine Crapp
2. USA, 4:19.2, Sylvia Ruuska, Shelley Mann, Nancy Simons, Joan Rosazza
3. South Africa, 4:25.7, Jeanette Myburgh, Susan Roberts, Natalie Myburgh, Moira Abernathy

1952
1. Hungary, 4:24.4 (WR), Ilona Novak, Judit Temes, Eva Novak, Katalin Szoke
2. Netherlands, 4:29.0, Marie-Louise Linssen-Vaessen, Koosje van Voorn, Johanna Termeulen, Irma Heijting-Schuhmacher
3. USA, 4:30.1, Jacqueline La Vine, Marilee Stepan, Joan Alderson, Evelyn Kawamoto

1948
1. USA, 4:29.2 (OR), Marie Corridon, Thelma Kalama, Brenda Helser, Ann Curtis
2. Denmark, 4:29.6, Eva Riise, Karen-Margrete Harup, Greta Andersen, Fritze Carstensen
3. Netherlands, 4:31.6, Irma Schuhmacher, Margot Marsman, Marie-Louise Vaessen, Johanna Termeulen

1936
1. Netherlands, 4:36.0 (OR), Johanna Selbach, Catherina Wagner, Willemijntje den Ouden, Hendrika Mastenbroek
2. Germany, 4:36.8, Ruth Halbsguth, Leni Lohmar, Ingeborg Schmitz, Gisela Arendt
3. USA, 4:40.2, Katherine Rawls, Bernice Lapp, Mavis Freeman, Olive McKean

1932
1. USA, 4:38.0 (WR), Josephine McKim, Helen Johns, Eleanor Saville-Garatti, Helene Madison
2. Netherlands, 4:47.5, Maria Vierdag, Maria Oversloot, Cornelia Ladde, Willemijntje den Ouden
3. Great Britain, 4:52.4, E. Valerie Davies, Helen Varcoe, M. Joyce Cooper, Edna Hughes

1928
1. USA, 4:47.6 (WR), Adelaide Lambert, Eleanor Garatti, Albina Osipowich, Martha Norelius
2. Great Britain, 5:02.8, M. Joyce Cooper, Sarah Stewart, I. Vera Tanner, Ellen E. King
3. South Africa, 5:13.4, Kathleen Russell, Rhoda Rennie, Marie Bedford, Frederica J. van der Goes

1924
1. USA, 4:58.8 (WR), Gertrude Ederle, Euphrasia Donnelly, Ethel Lackie, Mariechen Wehselau
2. Great Britain, 5:17.0, Florence Barker, Grace McKenzie, I. Vera Tanner, Constance Jeans
3. Sweden, 5:35.6, Aina Berg, Vivian Pettersson, Gulli Everlund, Hjordis Topel

1920
1. USA, 5:11.6 (WR), Margaret Woodbridge, Frances Schroth, Irene Guest, Ethelda Bleibtrey
2. Great Britain, 5:40.6, Hilda James, Constance Jeans, Charlotte Radcliffe, Grace McKenzie
3. Sweden, 5:43.6, Aina Berg, Emy Machnow, Carin Nilsson, Jane Gylling

1912
1. Great Britain, 552.8 (WR), Bella Moore, Jennie Fletcher, Annie Speirs, Irene Steer
2. West Germany, 6:04.6, Vally Dressel, Louise Otto, Hermine Stindt, Grete Rosenberg
3. Austria, 6:17.0, Margarete Adler, Klara Milch, Josephine Sticker, Berta Zahourek

441

Swimming — Women's 4x100- Meter Medley Relay

1988 1. East Germany, 4:03.74 (OR), Kristin Otto, Silke Hoerner, Birte Weigang, Katrin Meissner
2. USA, 4:07.90, Beth Barr, Tracey McFarlane, Janel Jorgensen, Mary Wayte
3. Canada, 4:10.49, Lori Melien, Allison Higson, Jane Kerr, Andrea Nugent

1984 1. USA, 4:08.34, Theresa Andrews, Tracy Caulkins, Mary T. Meagher, Nancy Hogshead
2. West Germany, 4:11.97, Svenja Schlicht, Ute Hasse, Ina Beyermann, Karin Seick
3. Canada, 4:12.98, Reema Abdo, Anne Ottenbrite, Michele McPherson, Pamela Rai

1980 1. East Germany, 4:06.67 (WR), Rica Reinisch, Ute Geweniger, Andrea Pollack, Caren Metschuck
2. Great Britain, 4:12.24, Helen Jameson, Margaret Kelly, Ann Osgerby, June Croft
3. Soviet Union, 4:13.61, Yelena Kruglova, Elvira Vasilkova, Alla Grishchenkova, Natalia Strunnikova

1976 1. East Germany, 4:07.95 (WR, OR), Ulrike Richter, Hannelore Anke, Andrea Pollack, Kornelia Ender
2. USA, 4:14.55 Linda Jezek, Lauri Siering, Camille Wright, Shirley Babashoff

3. Canada, 4:15.22, Wendy Hugg, Robin Corsiglia, Susan Sloan, Anne Jardin

1972 1. USA, 4:20.75 (WR), Melissa Belote, Catherine Carr, Deena Deardurff, Sandra Neilson
2. East Germany, 4:24.91, Christine Herbst, Renate Vogel, Roswitha Beier, Kornelia Ender
3. West Germany, 4:26.46, Silke Pielen, Verena Eberle, Gudrun Beckmann, Heidemarie Reineck

1968 1. USA, 4:28.3 (OR), Kaye Hall, Catie Ball, Ellie Daniel, Susan Pedersen
2. Australia, 4:30.0, Lynette Watson, Lynette McClements, Judy Playfair, Janet Steinbeck
3. West Germany, 4:36.4, Angelika Kraus, Uta Frommater, Heike Hustede, Heidemarie Reineck

1964 1. USA, 4:33.9 (WR), Cathy Ferguson, Cynthia Goyette, Sharon Stouder, Kathleen Ellis
2. Netherlands, 4:37.0, Cornelia Winkel, Klena Bimolt, Ada Kok, Erica Terpstra
3. Soviet Union, 4:39.2, Tatyana Savelyeva, Svetlana Babanina, Tatyana Devyatova, Natalia Ustinova

1960 1. USA, 4:41.1 (WR), Lynn Burke, Patty Kempner, Carolyn Schuler, Susan Christine Von Saltza
2. Australia, 4:45.9, Marilyn Wilson, Rosemary Lassig, Janice Andrew, Dawn Fraser
3. East Germany and West Germany, 4:47.6, Ingrid Schmidt, Ursula Kuper, Barbel Fuhrmann, Ursel Brunner

1896-1956 Not held

1896-1908 Not held

442

SYNCHRONIZED SWIMMING

WARM-UP

D escribed as a cross between Esther Williams movies and advanced figure skating, synchronized swimming is a sport requiring overall body strength and agility, grace and beauty, split-second timing, musical interpretation, and a bit of the dramatic. You also have to know how to hold your breath underwater.

Added to the Olympics menu in 1984, synchro competitions were first held in England at the turn of the century. In the US, Katherine Curtis, a swimmer at the University of Wisconsin in the early 1920s, is credited with developing the modern version of the sport, then called water ballet. The term *synchronized swimming* was first used by a radio announcer at the 1934 World's Fair in Chicago. And following the popularity of Billy Rose's Aquacade at the New York World's Fair in 1939, Hollywood created the first synchronized-swimming movie star, Esther Williams.

In 1945, the Amateur Athletic Union recognized synchronized swimming as a sport, and a year later, the first National Synchronized Swimming Championships were held. In the 1950s, the Pan-American Games offered synchro events, and soon world championships were held. The 1952 Olympic Games offered synchro as a demonstration sport, the same year that it was recognized by the Fédération Internationale de Natation Amateur (FINA), the governing body for swimming competitions.

Today, three events are internationally recognized in synchronized swimming: solo, duet (two swimmers), and team (eight swimmers). For the 1992 Olympics, solo and duet competitions will be held. In 1996, however, the team competition will replace the solo and duet features. "The team event is the premier event in synchronized swimming," asserts Betty Watanabe, executive director of the program commission of the International Olympic Committee. "Synchronizing eight individuals together is what synchronized swimming is all about."

▼

SPECTATORS' GUIDE

Contestants have to hold their breath for long periods, with up to 60% of the 3.5-minute routine performed underwater. Tracie Ruiz-Conforto, silver medalist in the 1988 solo competition (and gold in the solo and duet in 1984), explains that to score well, "You have to have charisma, enthusiasm, and flair. You have to be dynamic. The judges look at 50 performances, and you want to do something so they don't get bored."

Synchronized swimming consists of routine and figure competitions, each accounting for 50% of the final score. The rules are similar to the sports' counterparts, figure skating and gymnastics, and comprehending the scoring system is on the same level of difficulty. During a routine, the swimmer cannot touch the side or bottom of the pool.

For the **routine competition**, swimmers are free to choose music and choreography. Routines are enhanced by the use of original and expressive movements, patterns, rhythms, and audience contact. A panel of seven judges awards points from 0 to 10 in one-tenth point increments in two categories, technical merit and artistic impression. *Technical merit* includes execution, the ability of the swimmers to match each other's moves (synchronization), and degree of difficulty, which covers such items as time underwater, amount of body weight extended above the water surface, and complexity of the routine. *Artistic impression* covers creativity of the choreography, the use of movement to interpret the music, and the poise and confidence with which the routine is presented.

The highest and lowest of the scores awarded by the judges in the two categories are canceled and the remaining scores averaged. The technical merit total is multiplied by six and the artistic impression score by four. The total of these two equals the routine score.

In the **figure competition**, each athlete is required to perform four of a possible 28 figures individually, without music, before a panel of judges. With such exotic names as alba, aurora, gaviata, nova, catalina, flamingo, swordfish, and heron, the figures are designed to determine the swimmer's ability to control movement and demonstrate balance, flexibility, and timing. Judges award points from 0 to 10 in one-tenth point increments (e.g., 7.3 or 8.1), based on the accuracy of the performance, as well as the timing, height, stability, and control demonstrated.

To determine the overall figure score for each competitor, the judges' awards are multiplied by the varying degrees of difficulty and the four are then combined for a total figure score. The scores are added to the routine totals to determine a final composite score. For duet and team events, the figure scores of the competitors actually performing the routine are averaged before adding the routine score. The scoring system is identical for both the preliminaries and the finals.

Basic Synchro Positions

BALLET LEG: Body and one leg horizontal, with the foot and face at the surface. The hips as close to the surface as possible. One leg perpendicular to the surface.

BENT KNEE/VERTICAL: In front layout, back layout, vertical, or arched position. One leg is bent with the toe of that leg at the inside of the other leg, at or above the knee. In the bent knee used to raise or lower a ballet leg, only the knee shall be bent until the thigh of this leg is perpendicular to the surface, the toe remaining at the inside of the other leg.

CRANE: Head downward, with the head, body, and one leg vertical and the other leg horizontal and parallel to the surface.

FLAMINGO: One leg vertical, perpendicular to the surface; the other leg is drawn toward the chest, with its mid-calf opposite the vertical leg, and its foot at the surface. The face is at the surface, and horizontal, with the hips as close to the surface as possible.

FRONT PIKE: The trunk and head are vertical, head downward. The heels, thighs, and buttocks are at the surface, with the legs perpendicular to the body.

SPLIT: Legs evenly split forward and backward with both feet and hips as near the surface as possible. Back arches, with shoulders, head, and hip as close to a vertical line as possible.

TUCK: Body as compact as possible, with the back rounded, heels close to buttocks, face close to the knees, with the knees together.

VERTICAL: Body vertical, head downward. Head, hips, and ankle(s) in line.

▼

HOPEFULS

Since the synchronized swimming event was added to Olympic competition in 1984, the USA and Canada have won all eight gold and silver medals (two each in the individual and duet competitions), and Japan has taken all four bronze medals.

Twins Karen and Sarah Josephson, who won the 1988 silver for the **USA** in the duet event, have placed first in every national event they've entered together since 1985, and have placed either first or second in every international event. At Barcelona, they'll be swimming for a gold. Kristen Babb-Sprague is the USA's most promising soloist, with a 1991 silver medal from the World Aquatic Championships and gold or silver medals in every event she's entered since 1987.

World Champion Sylvie Frechette of **Canada** plans to make her Olympic debut at Barcelona, along with duo swimmers Kathy Glen and Lisa Alexander, who won the World Aquatic bronze in 1991.

Japan's 1988 Olympian Mikako Kotani, who won the solo and shared the duet medal at Seoul, will attempt to repeat her World Aquatic silver medal duet with Aki Takayama at the 1992 Olympic Games.

Schedule

The tentative synchronized swimming schedule is as follows:

Sunday, August 2
Solo preliminaries

Monday, August 3
Duet preliminaries

Wednesday, August 5
Routines

Thursday, August 6
Solo finals

Friday, August 7
Duet final

HIGHLIGHTS

First included as an official event in the LA Games, synchronized swimming did not receive entirely unanimous support from IOC officials. Nonetheless, it was so successful in 1984 that it continues to be part of the Olympic program.

The American team performed exceptionally well in 1984, when both the individual and duet gold medals stayed in the States: Tracie Ruiz won the individual event with a score of 198.467, followed by Canada's Carolyn Waldo, with 195.300 points, and Miwako Motoyoshi, from Japan, with 187.050 points. In the duet event, The US team—which included Ruiz—took another gold medal, with a score of 195.584, followed by the Canadian team, with 194.234 and the Japanese team, with 187.992.

446

In 1988, Canada and the US traded places, this time with the Maple Leaf team taking both golds. Carolyn Waldo, of Canada, scored an unprecedented 200.150 in the individual event, followed by the now-married American, Tracie Ruiz-Conforto, with 197.633, a little below her previous year's score. Japan, the perennial bronze medalist, came in third with Mikako Kotani's score of 191.850. In the duet event, the Canadian team outscored the US, while yet another bronze went to the Japanese team.

Medalists

Synchronized Swimming — Solo

1988	1. Carolyn Waldo, Canada, 200.150
	2. Tracie Ruiz-Conforto, USA, 197.633
	3. Mikako Kotani, Japan, 191.850
1984	1. Tracie Ruiz, USA, 198.467
	2. Carolyn Waldo, Canada, 195.300
	3. Miwako Motoyoshi, Japan, 187.050
1896-	
1980	**Not held**

Synchronized Swimming — Duet

1988	1. Canada, 197.717, Michelle Cameron, Carolyn Waldo
	2. USA, 197.284, Sarah Josephson, Karen Josephson
	3. Japan, 190.159 Miyako Tanaka, Mikako Kotani
1984	1. USA, 195.584, Candy Costie, Tracie Ruiz
	2. Canada, 194.234, Sharon Hambrook, Kelly Kryczka
	3. Japan, 187.992, Saeko Kimura, Miwako Motoyoshi

447

TABLE TENNIS

WARM-UP

The most popular racket sport in the world (and the world's second largest participation sport) made its debut as a full medal sport in the 1988 Summer Olympic Games in Seoul. More than 10 million players annually participate in sanctioned tournaments worldwide.

Table tennis began around the turn of the century as a genteel parlor game, a far cry from today's blitzkrieg smash-o-rama. Although there is little evidence to suggest it, table tennis likely started on college campuses and in military recreational halls.

In the 1890s, Parker Brothers, a sports equipment manufacturer in Salem, Massachusetts, marketed a game called "Indoor Tennis." While mildly received in the US, the game was exported to England, where is became popular. The game was played with small rackets and a firm light ball covered with a knitted web. The small net could be stretched across a dining room table, or between chairs if played on the floor.

An Englishman by the name of James Gibb added a celluloid ball (that he had bought in America) to the game. A game called "Gossima" was manufactured in England, and soon came to be known by the onomatopoeic tag of *Ping Pong*. Ping for when the racket hit the ball; pong for the ball striking the table. The name was patented in England and the US by Parker Brothers.

fact: Early paddles were made of such materials as cork, vellum, cardboard, and wood, and covered with cloth, leather, or sandpaper.

In 1903, another Englishman, E.C. Goode, improvised a new racket by sticking a piece of pimpled rubber to the standard type of wooden paddle. The game caught on extremely well in Britain, particularly among the upper class. Soon, however, the craze subsided and Ping Pong became something of a forgotten recreation.

In the 1920s, groups in several European countries revived the game, reintroducing it as table tennis due to Parker's proprietary interest in the trademark Ping Pong. In 1923, the English Table Tennis Association formed, and in 1926 the International Table Tennis Federation (ITTF) was founded in Berlin, with Austria, Czechoslovakia, Denmark, England, Germany, Hungary, India, Sweden, and Wales as members. By the 1930s, table tennis had evolved into a highly competitive international sport, and had captured a large US audience. As a result, the United States Table Tennis Association (USTTA) was formed in 1933.

By 1936, the United States was the first country to win both the Swaythling and Corbillon Cups, awarded to the world's best men's and women's teams, respectively. The USTTA remains the national governing body for the sport in the United States and is affiliated with the International Table Tennis Federation (ITTF).

The game is thought to have been introduced to Japan in the early part of this century by an English cleric. The Japanese Ping Pong Association, founded in the 1920s, joined the ITTF in 1929. From the 1920s to the 1950s, international play was dominated by Hungary in particular, as well as by Austria, Czechoslovakia, England, and Germany. In 1954, however, the oriental era of ping pong began. Between 1952 and 1971, for instance, the Japanese won the Swaythling Cup seven times, the Corbillon Cup eight times, the men's singles six times, the men's doubles three times, and the mixed doubles seven times. During the 1960s, the Chinese began to challenge Japanese supremacy on the green table, and today more than four million Chinese play the game. The Koreans have also become formidable in international play.

Table tennis has been a part of the Pan American Games since 1979, when it was a demonstration sport. The US team dominated the 1983 Pan Am Games, winning five gold medals and one bronze in seven events. A very young 1987 US Pan American team won three gold and three silver medals, once again dominating the competition.

▼

SPECTATORS' GUIDE

Table tennis has undergone constant change throughout its history. Today's players are indeed playing a different game than was played in the 1930s. Past world championship games sometimes lasted for several hours. Today, the average match at the top levels of competition lasts about 30 minutes, as players smash the ball past each other at speeds exceeding 100 miles per hour.

Four events are on the 1992 table tennis Olympic program—men's and women's singles and doubles.

The table is nine feet in length, five feet in width, and two and one-half feet high. The net is six inches high. The ball is made of celluloid and approximately 1.5 inches in diameter and weighs roughly 2.5 grams.

Each player whacks at the ball with a small racket. A racket may be of any size, shape, or weight. Its surface must be dark colored and matte, and the blade made of wood. The blade may be covered with plain ordinary pimpled rubber of a total thickness of 2mm, or with "sandwich" consisting of a layer of cellular rubber surfaced by pimpled rubber with pimples either inward or outward with a total thickness of not more than 4mm.

The rules of the game are fairly straightforward. Generally, the first player to score 21 points (one point at a time) wins. In the event of a deuce at 20, the players alternate serves until one scores two consecutive points. A match is two games out of three or three games out of five. The player winning the toss has choice of service or end of table. The first player serves five times, then receives five times, and so on. On the serve, the ball must be thrown straight up at least six inches from a flat, open palm and cannot be hit until it begins to descend.

The period when the ball is in play is called a "rally." Volleying, or striking the ball in play before it has touched the playing surface on the player's side of the table, is not allowed. The ball is deemed out of play once it has touched any object other than the net, its supports, the playing surface, the racquet, or the racquet hand below the wrist.

fact: Table tennis was banned in the Soviet Union from around 1930 to 1950, allegedly because it was harmful to the eyes.

Players display a variety of styles in the hotly competitive game. The **defender** pushes, chops, and blocks to let his opponent make a mistake. Relying on his ability to return every ball, the defender literally wears down his opponent. The **pick hitter** is basically a defender but occasionally hits the ball past his opponent when there is an opening. The **all-out attacker** hits every ball and tries to kill as many as he can, hoping to win by overpowering his opponent. The benevolent-sounding **looper** is the offensive counterpart to the pick hitter. He uses the loop until the ball pops up enough to kill.

And tactics? **Short serves** to the forehand are very difficult to return. Against a top player, a very short, very low serve is the safest way to get the ball into play. **Three- and five-ball attack** strategies attempt to end the point by the third or fifth ball over the net. In a three-ball attack the server attempts to kill the serve return. A typical five-ball attack begins with a serve, then a return, then a loop, return, then kill.

Psychological ploys are often used in table tennis. Watch for players toweling themselves off, tying their shoes, or in some other way attempting to change the pace of the game.

THE PUSH is used to return a ball that has underspin on it or when balls are too low or too far over the table. It is seldom used by experts.

THE BLOCK is used to return a hard shot or when a player is out of position.

THE KILL is the fastest shot in table tennis and almost impossible to return. Kill shots average 80 miles per hour and may reach 105 mph.

THE HIT or counterdrive is a slower version of the kill shot.

THE LOOP is relatively new. With a long sweeping upward motion, the looper just grazes the ball and puts a tremendous amount of topspin on it. A good loop goes straight up if it strikes a vertical paddle. The main use of the loop is as a set-up shot for the kill shot.

THE CHOP is used to force a player to hit the ball into the net. The downward stroke puts underspin on the ball and makes it difficult to return.

THE SHAKEHANDS is the most popular grip. The player basically "shakes hands" with the racket.

THE PENHOLD gives a good forehand but a weaker backhand. The racket is held as if holding a pen, with the racket tip pointing downward.

THE SEEMILLER is an unorthodox grip used successfully by five-time US National Champion Danny Seemiller. It is a version of the shakehands grip, with the racket rotated so that the forehand side of the racket can be used on the backhand side. The grip enables the player to switch surfaces for any given shot.

▼

HOPEFULS

At table tennis's competitive debut at the 1988 Olympic Games, the Korean and Chinese teams took all but three of the nine medals awarded, and they'll almost certainly perform as well in 1992. Sweden and Yugoslavia also yield impressive teams. The US—not generally considered a high-ranking competitor in table tennis—hopes to improve its status with Olympic veterans and Pan American gold medalists Insook Bhushan, Diana Gee, and Sean O'Neill, as well as top-ranked US player Jim Butler.

The tentative table tennis schedule is as follows:

Tuesday, July 28
16 games, doubles, 1st round, women
16 games, doubles, 1st round, men

Wednesday, July 29
32 games, singles, 1st round, women
16 games, doubles, 1st round, women
16 games, doubles, 1st round, men

Thursday, July 30
32 games, singles, 1st round, women
16 games, singles, 1st round, men
8 games, doubles, 1st round, men
16 games, singles, 1st round, women
16 games, doubles, 1st round, women

Friday, July 31
32 games, singles, 1st round, men
16 games, singles, 1st round, women
4 games, doubles, quarterfinal, women
8 games, doubles, 1st round, men

16 games, singles, 1st round, women

Saturday, August 1
32 games, singles, 1st round, men
8 games, singles, 2nd round, women
4 games, doubles, quarterfinal, men
2 games, doubles, semifinals, women

Sunday, August 2
8 games, singles, 2nd round, men

Monday, August 3
Finals, doubles, women
4 games, singles, semifinals, women
2 games, doubles, semifinals, men

Tuesday, August 4
Finals, doubles, men
4 games, singles, quarterfinal, men
2 games, singles, semifinals, women

Wednesday, August 5
Finals, singles, women
2 games, singles, semifinals, men

Thursday, August 6
Finals, singles, men

Table Tennis

▼

HIGHLIGHTS

Although first recognized by the IOC as an Olympic sport in 1977, table tennis was not included in the Games—even as a demonstration sport—until 1988. The host country was victorious in a number of events: South Korea won the gold in the women's doubles, both gold and silver in the men's singles, and the bronze in men's doubles. China captured the most medals at Seoul, sweeping the medals in women's singles, taking a silver in women's doubles, and grabbing a gold in the men's doubles, but they failed to medal in the men's singles, where the bronze was taken by a Swedish player. The remaining medals—a silver in the men's doubles and a bronze in the women's doubles—went to Yugoslavia.

The field of competitors was limited to 64 men and 48 women, which included three American players: Insook Bhushan, Sean O'Neill, and Diana Gee. With only one man among them, the US team did not compete in men's doubles. In women's singles, Bhushan completed the competition with a 2–3 record and came in fourth in her grouping, while Diana Gee finished fifth. Seeded third in her six-player group, Bhushan beat an Australian, a Tunisian, and a Dominican woman. In the women's doubles, Bhushan and Gee finished with a record of 1–5 to take sixth place. Sean O'Neill, with a 2–5 win/loss record, finished sixth in his grouping in men's singles.

Medalists

Table Tennis — Men's Singles

1988   1. Nam-Kyu Yoo, South Korea
2. Ki-Taik Kim, South Korea
3. Erik Lindh, Sweden

Table Tennis — Men's Doubles

1988   1. People's Republic of China, Longcan Chen, Qingguang Wei
2. Yugoslavia, Ilija Lupulesku, Zoran Primorac
3. South Korea, Jae-Hyung Ahn, Nam-Kyu Yoo

Table Tennis — Women's Singles

1988   1. Jing Chen, People's Republic of China
2. Huifen Li, People's Republic of China
3. Zhimin Jiao, People's Republic of China

Table Tennis — Women's Doubles

1988   1. South Korea, Jung-Hwa Hyun, Young-Ja Yang
2. People's Republic of China, Jing Chen, Zhimin Jiao
3. Yugoslavia, Jasna Fazlic, Gordana Perkucin

▼

TEAM HANDBALL

WARM-UP

To US Olympic fans, team handball is not one of the glamour sports of the Games, although more than three million players worldwide are registered with the international handball association. Adding to the apparent nonchalance is the confusion about what team handball is; it is not at all like the "handball" sport played in a small room by four people.

In Europe the game is called "handball," while in the US it goes by the moniker of "team handball," due to the existence of that other, four-wall, game. Team handball combines elements of other, better-known games: it's been called ice hockey without sticks and ice, water polo without water, and indoor soccer without kicking. Although it's never been called baseball without bats or tennis without rackets, team handball does incorporate many elements of basketball, although not the basket.

fact: Though team handball as we know it is a modern invention, a fourth-century mosaic in Sicily's Piazza Armerina depicts bikini-clad women playing what looks like a form of handball.

Team handball was invented about the same time as basketball in the 1890s by a group of Danish track and field athletes looking for an effective indoor exercise during the cold Scandinavian winter. They placed two soccer balls at each end of a gymnasium floor and began playing a soccer-type game using the hands instead of the feet. In 1906, Danish teacher Holger Nielsen formalized the first rules and organized competitions.

Germans tried the same sort of game outdoors that summer, as did members of several other European countries. The Scandinavian version called for an indoor court and six players a side, plus a goalkeeper; elsewhere, teams used 10 or 11 players per side in the great outdoors.

In 1924, the many variations of the game were standardized by the International Handball Federation (IHF). In 1928, representatives of 11 handball nations met at the Olympic Games, formed the International Amateur Handball

455

Federation and printed the first official international rules. In 1936 at Berlin, team handball, with 11 to a team playing on a soccer field, officially became an Olympic sport, with Germany, Austria, Switzerland, Hungary, Romania, and the United States competing.

Meanwhile, the Scandinavians continued to refine indoor, seven-a-side handball. The first world championship for handball (both seven and 11 a side) was held in 1938.

At the 1948 Games, however, handball was taken off the program. The 11-a-side game was waning in popularity, while seven-a-side was still becoming established as an international sport. Basketball tactics and jargon were integrated into the sport during this period, reflected in such handball/basketball terms as dribble, pivot, post, and man-to-man.

The formation of the US Team Handball Federation (USTHF) in 1959 marked the beginning of team handball in the United States. Men's team handball was reintroduced to the Olympic program in 1972, and the women's event followed four years later.

▼

SPECTATORS' GUIDE

Team handball combines the skills of running, jumping, catching, and throwing into a fast-moving game. The basic objective of the game is to score a goal by using passing and good teamwork. A successful scoring attempt results in a point, and the final scores in the game run in the high teens or low twenties. 12 teams compete in the men's tournament and eight in the women's.

The court is slightly larger than a basketball court, measuring 40 meters in length (131 feet) and 20 meters from sideline to sideline (65.5 feet). The goal is some seven feet high and 10 feet wide. The most significant line on the court is the six-meter line, or **goal area line**. The area enclosed by the line is called the goal area, or **circle**. Only the goalie is allowed to stand inside the goal area. However, an offensive or defensive player may be in the air over the circle as long as they take off from outside of the goal area line. Once they land in the circle, players cannot interfere with play in any way and must exit as quickly as possible. If a goal is scored while the goal scorer or a teammate is in the circle, the goal does not count. If the defense gains an advantage by being in the circle, a penalty throw is awarded to the offense.

The ball is some 60 centimeters (23 inches) in circumference and weighs 16 ounces.

The game is played in 30-minute halves, with no timeouts except for injuries or other major interruptions, as determined by the referees. Each team fields seven players (six court players and one goalie). All players may roam over the entire court. The essential line-up includes a player at left backcourt, center, and right backcourt. Forward positions include a left wing, a circle runner, and a right wing.

The backcourt players are usually tall and good leapers who shoot from the backcourt over the defense. The center is a play maker who directs the offense. The wings are smaller, quicker players who shoot from difficult angles. And the circle runners are large, aggressive tight-end types who screen and pick to disorganize the defense, awaiting the opportunity of blasting a shot from the six-meter line.

The offense usually runs set plays, but free-lance play is encouraged, particularly in quick or fast-break situations. The pace of the game runs the gamut from "slow down and set up" to "run and gun."

A coin flip determines the first possession of the ball, and the game begins with a throw-off, or pass, at center court. The same procedure is followed after each goal. Before passing or shooting, a player is permitted to run three steps with the ball or hold it for three seconds. They also may dribble as much as they like, although the game is not as dribble-oriented as basketball. Double dribbling results in a free throw for the opposing team. A player cannot kick the ball.

A player is allowed to use the body to obstruct an opponent either with or without the ball. However, using the arms or legs to obstruct, push, hold, trip, or hit is not allowed. A free throw is awarded if an offensive player charges into a defensive player.

fact: As in hockey, excessive roughness can result in a two-minute penalty.

A **throw-in** is awarded to an opponent when one team loses the ball out of bounds. The defense must be three meters away when the ball is thrown in.

Free throws are awarded for minor infringements of the rules, similar to the basketball version. The free throw is taken immediately, without the referee handling the ball, from the place where the violation occurred. The defense must remain three meters away. The thrower must keep one foot continuously in contact with the court, and must make a throw or pass within three seconds. A goal may be scored directly from a free throw. If a minor foul occurs between the goal line and the free throw line (nine meters from the goal line), the free throw is taken from the free throw line just opposite from where the foul took place.

For more serious fouls, such as those that occur while a player is shooting, a **penalty throw** is awarded. When the penalty throw is taken, one foot must remain in contact with the floor behind the seven-meter penalty line until the ball is released.

HOPEFULS

The Soviet men and the Korean women are expected to defend their 1988 titles with their teams' usual agility and unity. Both countries field strong teams in both the men's and women's events; in 1988, the Soviets also took the bronze in the women's event, and the South Koreans also won the silver in the men's event. The US men finished last and the US women next-to-last in the Olympics at Seoul, and although a rigorous pre-Olympic competition schedule has improved their performance, they were still uncertain in 1991 whether they would make the competition roster for Barcelona.

Schedule

The tentative team handball schedule is as follows:

Monday, July 27
6 games, preliminaries, men

Wednesday, July 29
6 games, preliminaries, men

Thursday, July 30
4 games, preliminaries, women

Friday, July 31
6 games, preliminaries, men

Saturday, August 1
4 games, preliminaries, women

Sunday, August 2
6 games, preliminaries, men

Monday, August 3
4 games, preliminaries, women

Tuesday, August 4
6 games, preliminaries, men

Thursday, August 6
2 games, semifinals, women
2 games, semifinals, men

Friday, August 7
2 games, semifinals, women
(5th–8th places)
2 games, semifinals, men
(9th–12th places)
2 games, finals, men (5th–8th places)

Saturday, August 8
1 game, final, women (3rd & 4th places)
1 game, final, women
1 game, final, men (3rd & 4th places)
1 game, final, men

HIGHLIGHTS

Team handball first appeared and then reappeared in Games held in Germany. In the 1936 Olympics, the host country—which had opted to include the sport in the Berlin Games—easily defeated the opposition: the US was beaten 29–1, and only Austria managed to close the score a little with a losing score of 8–6. Absent from the Games until Munich, the seven-man event was no longer dominated by Germany—with Yugoslavia, Czechoslovakia, and Romania taking the gold, silver, and bronze, East Germany came in fourth while West Germany finished sixth.

Romania, whose team held the world championship title in 1972 and 1976, improved their 1972 bronze with a 1976 silver, still shy of the gold. The Soviets, who had placed fifth in 1972, captured the 1976 gold; they dominated the final from halftime on, winning with a score of 19–15. In the first women's handball match, the Soviets dominated as well, defeating East Germany; Hungary came in third, while the Romanian women's team came in fourth.

At the Moscow Games the women's gold medal was taken by the host country, while East Germany took the men's gold. The last point of the game was scored by East German Hans-Georg Beyer, who came from an Olympic family: also during the Moscow Games, his brother, Udo, medaled in the shot put, and his sister, Gisela, took fourth place in the discus. On the bronze-medaling East German women's team, Roswitha Krause competed in her second Games, having captured a silver medal in the freestyle swimming relay in Mexico City.

Yugoslavia dominated the 1984 Games, taking both the men's and women's gold. The West German men's team came in second, while the Romanians placed third. In the women's events, the Republic of Korea captured the silver medal, while the People's Republic of China took the bronze.

In 1988, the host country again kept a gold medal: South Korea won the gold in the women's event. In the same event, a new player entered the Hall of Olympic medalists in handball: the Norwegian women's team took second place ahead of the Soviets. The men's event featured a familiar cast of medalists: while the host country won the silver, the Soviets took the gold and the Yugoslavian team earned the bronze.

The US men's team suffered a number of disappointments through its six matches. In the initial match against Iceland, the US team lost 15–22; the following match, the US went up against the previous year's gold medalist, Yugoslavia. Most interestingly, the US coach was not only Yugoslavian-born, but had coached the winning 1984 team. The US started off well but slipped in the second half, losing with a score of 23–31. No one was surprised by the Soviets' 14–26 victory in the next match, but the round with Sweden—which the US had hoped to win—produced a stunning loss, with a score of 12–26. Having lost their fifth match against Algeria, the US incurred its most devastating loss, in a 21–24 match against Japan, whose team they had considered to be eminently beatable.

Team Handball — Men's Team

1988 1. Soviet Union, V. Atavin, K. Charovarov, Youri Chevtson, L. Dorochenko, Vareli Gopin, A. Karchakevish, Andrei Lavrov, Youri Nesterov, V. Novitski, A. Rymanov, G. Sviridenko, Igor Tcooumak, A. Tioumentsev, A. Toutchkine, M. Vassiliev

2. South Korea, Suk-Jae Choi, Jae-Won Kang, Jae-Hwan Kim, Man- Ho Kim, Suk-Chang Koh, Kyung-Mo Lee, Sang-Hyo Lee, Jin-Suk Lim, Youg- Li Oh, Do-Hun Park, Young-Dae Park, Hyun-Suk Roh, Jae-Hong Shim, Young-Suk Sin, Tae-Il Yoon

3. Yugoslavia, Mirko Basic, Jozef Holpert, Boris Jarak, S. Kuzmanovski, Muhamed Memic, A. Nacinovic, Goran Perkovac, Zlatko Portner, Iztok Puc, Rolando Pusnik, Momir Rnic, Z. Saracevic, Irfan Smajlagic, Ermin Velic, Veselin Vujovic

1984 1. Yugoslavia, Zlatan Arnautovic, Momir Rnic, Veselin Vukovic, Milan Kalina, Jovan Elezovic, Zdravko Zovko, Branko Strbac, Pavo Jurina, Veselin Vujovic, Slobodan Kuzmanovski, Mirko Basic, Dragan Mladenovic, Zdravko Radjenovic, Mile Isakovic, Rolando Pusnik

2. West Germany, Andreas Thiel, Arnulf Meffle, Rudiger Neitzel, Martin Schwalb, Dirk Rauin, Michael Paul, Michael Roth, Thomas Happe, Erhard Wunderlich, Thomas Springel, Klaus Woller, Jochen Fraatz, Uwe Schwenker, Siegfried Roch, Ulrich Roth

3. Romania, Nicolae Munteanu, Marian Dumitru, Iosif Boros, Maricel Voinea, Vasile Stinga, George Dogarescu, Gheorghe Covaciu, Comel Durau, Dumitru Berbece, Alexandru Folker, Neculai Vasilca, Alexandru Buligan, Vasile Oprea, Mircea Bedivan, Adrain Simion

1980 1. East Germany, Siegfried Voigt, Gunter Dreibrodt, Peter Rost, Klaus Gruner, Hans-Georg Beyer, Dietmar Schmidt, Hartmut Kruger, Lothar Doering, Ernst Gerlach, Frank-Michael Wahl, Ingolf Wiegert, Wieland Schmidt, Rainer Hoft, Hans-Georg Jaunich

2. Soviet Union, Mikhail Ishchenko, Viktor Makhorin, Sergei Kushniryuk, Aleksandr Karshakevich, Vladimir Kravzov, Vladimir Belov, Anatoli Fedyukin, Aleksandr Anpilogov, Yevgeny Chernyshov, Aleksei Zhuk, Nikolai Tomin, Yuri Kidyaev, Vladimir Repiev, Valdemar Novitsky

3. Romania, Nicolae Munteanu, Marian Dumitru, Iosif Boros, Maricel Vionea, Vasile Stinga, Radu Voina, Cezar Draganita, Cornel Durau, Stefan Birtalan, Alexandru Folker, Neculai Vasilca, Lucian Vasilache, Adrian Cosma, Claudiu Eugen Ionescu

1976 1. Soviet Union, 19, 18:20, Mikhail Ishchenko, Anatoli Fedyukin, Vladimir Maximov, Segei Kushniryuk, Vassili Ilyin, Vladimir Kravzov, Yuri Klimov, Yuri Lagutin, Aleksandr Anpilogov, Yevgeny Chernyshov, Valeri Gassiy, Anatoli Tomin, Yuri Kidyaev, Aleksandr Rezanov

2. Romania, 15, 18:20, Cornel Penu, Gavril Kicsid, Cristian Gatu, Cezar Draganita, Radu Voina, Stefan Birtalan, Adrian Cosma, Constantin Tudosie, Nicolae Munteanu, Werner Stockl, Mircea Grabovschi, Ghita Licu

3. Poland, 21, 23.22, Andrzej Szymczak, Piotr Ciesla, Zdzislaw Antczak, Zygfryd Kuchta, Jerzy Klempel, Janusz Brzozowski, Ryszard Przbysz, Jerzy Melcer, Andrzej Sokolowski, Jan Gmyrek, Henryk Rozmiarek, Alfred Kaluzinski, Wlodzimierz Zielinski, Mieczyslaw Wojczak

1972 1. Yugoslavia, Zoran Zivkovic, Abaz Arslanagic, Miroslav Pribanic, Petar Fajfric, Milorad Karalic, Djoko Lavrnic, Slobodan Miskovic, Hrvoje Horvat, Branislav Pokrajac, Zdravko Miljak, Milan Lazarevic, Nebojsa Popvic, Zdenko Zorko, Albin Vidovic

2. Czechoslovakia, Frantisek Kralik, Petr Pospisil, Ivan Satrapa, Vladimir Jary, Jiri Kavan, Andrej Lukosik, Vladimir Haber, Jindrich Krepindl, Ladislav Benes, Vincent Lafko, Jaroslav Konecny, Pavel Mikes, Frantisek Bruna, Zdenek Skara, Jaroslav Skarvan, Arnost Klimcik

3. Romania, Cornel Penu, Alexandru Dinca, Gavril Kicsid, Ghita Licu, Christian Gatu, Roladn Gunesch, Radu Voina, Simion Schobel, Gheorghe Gruia, Werner Stockl, Dan Marin, Adrian Cosma, Valentin Samungi, Constantin Tudose, Stefan Birtolan

1956-
1968 Not held
1952 Demonstration game only. (Sweden 19, Denmark 11)
1948 Not held
1936 1. Germany, Heinz Korvers, Arthur Knautz, Willy Bandholz, Hans Keiter, Wilhelm Brinkmann, Gerog Dascher, Erich Herrmann, Hans Theilig, Helmut Berthold, Alfred Klinger, Fritz Fromm, Karl Kreutzberg, Heinrich Keimig, Wilhelm Muller, Kurt Dossin, Rudolf Stahl, Hermann Hansen, Fritz Sengler, Edgar Reinhardt, Gunther Ortmann, Wilhelm Baumann, Helmut Braselmann

2. Austria, Alois Schnabel, Franz Bartl, Johann Tauscher, Otto Licha, Emil Juracka, Leopold Wohlrab, Jaroslav Volak, Alfred Schmalzer, Ludwig Schubert, Ferdinand Kiefler, Anton Perwein, Fritz Maurer, Franz Brunner, Fritz Wurmbock, Siegfried Purner, Hans Zehetner, Hans Houska, Franz Bistricky, Franz Berghammer, Walter Reisp, Josef Krejci, Siegfried Powolny
3. Switzerland, Willi Gysi, Robert Studer, Erich Schmitt, Rolf Faes, Erland Herkenrath, Burkhard Gantenbein, Werner Meyer, Max Streib, Georg Mischon, Ernst Hufschmid, Eugen Seiterle, Edy Schmid, Max Blosch, Werner Scheurmann, Willy Schafer, Willy Hufschmid, Rudolf Wirz

1896-1932   **Not held**

Team Handball — Women's Team

1988   1. South Korea, Hyun-Sook Han, Mi-Sook Ki, Choon-Rye Kim, Hyun- Mee Kim, Kyung-Soon Kim, Myung-Soon Kim, Young-Sook Kim, Ki-Soon Lee, Mi-Young Lee, Mi-Kyung Lim, Hyun-Sook Park, Mi-Na Son, Ji-Hyun Song, Min-Hee Suk, Kyung-Hwa Sung
2. Norway, K. Andersen, Berit Digre, Marte Eliasson, Susann Goksor, Trine Haltvik, Hanne Hegh, Hanne Hogness, Vibeke Johnsen, Kristin Midthun, Karin Pettersen, Karin Singstao, A. Skottvoll, Ingrid Steen, Heidi Sundal, C. Svendsen
3. Soviet Union, Imova N. Aniss, Marina Bazanova, T. Djandagava, Elina Gouszeva, Larissa Karlova, N. Lapitskaia, S. Mankova, N. Mitruiuk, N. Morskova, E. Nemachkalo, N. Rousnatchenko, Olga Semenova, Z. Tourtchina, E. Tovstogan, Tatiana Gorb

1984   1. Yugoslavia, Jasna Ptujec, Mirjana Ognjenovic, Ljubinka Jankovic, Svetlana Anastasovski, Svetlana Dasic-Kitic, Alenka Cuderman, Svetlana Mugosa, Mirjana Djunca, Biserka Visnjic, Slavica Djukic, Jasna Kolar-Merdan, Ljiljana Mugosa

2. Republic of Korea, Kyung-Soon Kim, Soon-Ei Lee, Hyoi-Soon Jeong, Mi-Sook Kim, Hwa-Soo Han, Ok-Hwa Kim, Choon-Yei Kim, Soon-Bok Jeung, Byung-Soon Yoon, Young-Ya Lee, Kyung-Hwa Sung, Soo-Kyung Youn
3. People's Republic of China, Xingjiang Wu, Jianping He, Juefeng Zhu, Weihong Zhang, Xiumin Gao, Linwei Wang, Liping Liu, Xiulan Sun, Yumei Liu, Lan Li, Mingxing Wang, Zhen Chen

1980   1. Soviet Union, Natalia Timoshkina, Larissa Karlova, Irina Palchikova, Zinaida Turchina, Tatiana Kochergina Makerez, Ljudmila Poradnik Bobrus, Larissa Savkina, Aldona Nenenene-Chesaitite, Yulia Safina, Olga Zubareva, Valentina Lutaeva, Lyubov Odinokova-Berechnaya, Sigita Strechen
2. Yugoslavia, Ana Titlic, Slavica Jeremic, Zorica Vojinovic, Radmila Drljaca, Katica Iles, Mirjana Ognjenovic, Svetlana Anastasovski, Rada Savic, Svetlana Kitic, Mirjana Djurica, Biserka Visnjic, Vesna Radovic, Jasna Merdan, Vesna Milosevic
3. East Germany, Hannelore Zober, Katrin Kruger, Evelyn Matz, Roswitha Krause, Christina Rost, Petra Uhlig, Claudia Wunderlich, Sabine Rother, Kornelia Kunisch, Marion Tietz, Kristina Richter, Waltraud Kertzschmar, Birgit Heinecke, Renate Rudolph

1976   1. Soviet Union, Natalia Sherstyuk, Rafiga Shabanova, Lyubov Berezhnaya, Zinaida Turchina, Tatiana Makarez, Maria Litoshenko, Ljudmila Bobrus, Tatiana Gluschenko, Ljudmila Shubina, Galina Zakharova, Aldona Chesaitite, Nina Lobova, Ljudmila Pantchuk, Larissa Karlova
2. East Germany, Hannelore Zober, Gabriele Badorek, Evelyn Matz, Roswitha Krause, Christina Rost, Petra Uhlig, Christina Voss, Liane Michaellis, Silvia Siefert, Marion Tietz, Kristina Richter, Eva Paskuy, Waltraud, Kretzchmar, Hannelore Burosch
3. Hungary, Agota Bujdoso, Marta Magyeri, Borbala Toth-Harsanyi, Katalin Laki, Amalia Sterbinszky, Ilona Nagy, Klara Csik, Rozalia Lelkes, Maria Vadasz, Erzsebet Nemeth, Eva Angyal, Maria Berzsenyi, Marianna Nagy, Zsuzsanna Kezi

TENNIS

WARM-UP

Back as an Olympic sport after a 64-year siesta, tennis is a grand old game with roots that go back to the Stone Age, when human beings first discovered the thrill of hitting rocks with a club over dirt and stone barricades. Even further along in the history of human development, a person on the other side returned the rock. Soon, the volley was invented.

It was the French who gave shape to the semi-modern game of tennis. The word tennis may be derived from the French *tenez*, meaning "take it" or "play." Tennis is derivative of a game similar to handball, which was played in ancient Greece, Rome, Egypt, Persia, and Arabia. During the 10th century or so, legend has it, a wandering minstrel introduced the game to the French Court. Evidence also suggests that it was a recreation in monastic cloisters as early as the 11th century. The game was amenable to either outdoor or indoor play. Indoors, a rope cord stretched across the room served as the net, while outdoors, a mound of dirt served to divide the court.

Players used their open hands to swat a cloth bag stuffed with hair back and forth. The game became known as *jeu de paume*, or "sport of the hands" (or palm). Outside France, it was known as *real* (royal) tennis.

Although Louis IV (who ruled what was considered France during the 10th century) banned tennis as undignified (much as the English kings attempted to do so with soccer), the sport continued to attract interest. Throughout the Middle Ages, ecclesiastical bans were imposed by bishops and so forth, in the hope of inhibiting tennis-crazed monks. "Born to serve" had taken on an entirely new meaning.

By the 14th century, tennis had swum the channel to the British Isles, where first it may have washed up in Scotland and was known as *caitchspeel*. Within a hundred years it was established as a royal game, although it was not to Richard II's tastes. Richard the Deuce, who thought that soccer was a great waste of time, felt likewise about tennis, believing that his soldiers were misplacing their priorities. England, he reckoned, could be invaded while his army was playing tennis. And a soldier did not improve upon his bow and arrow technique while swatting a small ball around a court. Henry VII and Henry VIII, however, both enthusiastically embraced the game. Of the courts that Henry VIII built, the one at Hampton is the oldest of the 17 ancient tennis courts surviving in England.

An all-wood racket, similar to a table tennis racket, was added to the game as it became fashionable throughout Europe in the later Middle Ages. By 1500, a racket with a wooden handle and a head strung with sheep gut had been developed. In 16th-century France, tennis became the national game. Nearly every town featured a tennis court (or several), and Paris boasted more than 1000.

But by 1600, interest in the game had dissipated, for reasons unknown. For the next two hundred years, tennis was a seldom-played game. Then in the 19th century, the sport was rediscovered in England.

In 1858, Major T.H. Gem and J.B. Perera marked out a tennis court at Edgbaston, Birmingham, England. There they began to adapt real tennis to an open-air court on grass. The modern game took another giant leap forward in 1873, when Major Walter Wingfield introduced a game called *sphairistike* (the Greek root for "ball.") in England. Only the server could score and a game was 15 points, played on an hourglass-shaped court divided by a net seven feet high. Wingfield had the foresight to patent his equipment, which essentially consisted of tape that he used to mark out the court.

The All-England Croquet Club took an interest in the sport, and club officials, always short of funds, decided to hold a championship to raise money for the club. Three members drew up the rules, and the first Wimbledon lawn tennis championships were held in 1877 on the original ground at Worple Road.

In 1874, the game was introduced in the United States by Mary Outerbridge, who was initiated in the game while vacationing in Bermuda. Upon her return she brought with her two rackets, a ball, and a net, and began the long search for a singles partner. Through her efforts, the first court was established on the lawn of the Staten Island Cricket and Baseball Club.

The game caught on quickly in the States, leading to the formation of the US Lawn Tennis Association in 1881. One of the oldest international competitions, the Davis Cup, traces its roots to the United States. In 1900, Dwight Filley Davis, then a 21-year-old just graduated from Harvard College and a leading American player, started the International Lawn Tennis Challenge Trophy. He envisioned a yearly team tournament for men that would advance friendship and goodwill internationally among sportsmen who visited one another's countries for matches. The endeavor succeeded, and the sterling silver bowl became known as the Davis Cup. In the spirit of the Davis Cup, the Federation Cup was launched in 1963 by the International Lawn Tennis Federation as a worldwide team competition for women.

fact: Chris Evert was unbeaten in 26 singles matches in Wightman Competition, and compiled an 8-4 doubles record in 13 years.

In 1923, the Wightman Cup was established, providing an arena for teams of British and American women to compete against one another. Coincidentally, the first captain of the American team was Hazel Wightman (Hazel Hotchkiss), one of the better players in the world then (and an Olympic champion in 1924), who led the US squad to victory. Currently the United States leads in the series, 51 matches to 10.

During the first modern Olympics in 1896, men's singles and doubles events were on the program. In 1900, a mixed event and women's singles were added, and in 1904, subtracted. Tennis disappeared from the Olympic menu after the 1924 Paris Games until its revival as a demonstration sport at Mexico in 1968. The game was dropped after the Paris Olympics due to the ongoing problem (in many sports besides tennis) of deciding where the dividing line was between amateur and professional. Before reaching full-medal status at Seoul, tennis was again a demonstration event in LA in 1984.

Today, in addition to Wimbledon, the major international individual championships include the US Open Championships, with the first tournament held in 1881; the French Open Championships, dating from 1891; and the Australian Open Championships, which were first held in 1905.

To win all of these championships in a single season is known as a Grand Slam. The first to achieve one was California's Don Budge in 1938.

Other Grand Slammers include Maureen Connolly of San Diego in 1953, Australians Rod Laver in 1962 and 1969 and Margaret Smith Court in 1970, and Germany's Steffi Graf in 1988.

▼

SPECTATORS' GUIDE

Four Olympic events are held: men's and women's singles and doubles. Both men's and women's events allow a maximum of 96 competitors, and the matches in Barcelona will take place on clay courts. Play consists of a series of elimination rounds. The losers in the two semifinal matches for each event are both awarded bronze medals; no consolation match is held.

The equipment consists of a racket, ball, court, and net. The court measures 36 feet wide (10.97m) by 78 feet long (23.77m). For singles play, the sideline boundaries are pinched in at the 27 foot mark (8.23m). The height of the net is three feet at center court. Rackets, made of metal or wood, weigh between 12 and 15 ounces and are approximately 27 inches long. Tennis balls, the favorite chewing toy of puppies everywhere, are made from rubber molded into two cups that are cemented together and covered with wool felt. The ball is inflated with compressed air or gas, is approximately 2.5 inches in diameter, and weighs two ounces. When dropped from 100 feet, it should bounce 55 feet. By comparison, a watermelon dropped by David Letterman from 100 feet will only bounce some five feet.

The rules of tennis are relatively simple. The server starts play by sending the ball over the net into the service court. A player will serve for an entire game, upon which the service goes to his or her opponent, so that the server becomes the receiver and the receiver the server.

fact: Players may use underhand or overhand serves at their discretion. The server may stand anywhere in back of the baseline between the imaginary extensions of the center mark and the singles sideline.

For the service to be good, the ball must cross the net without bouncing and pitch into the service court diagonally opposite. If the service or server infringes any rule, a fault is called and the server is permitted a second serve. If the second serve is a fault, the server loses a point.

A player wins a point when the opponent fails to return the ball over the net before it touches the ground twice on the opponent's side of the net. Points are also won when the opponent returns the ball so that it first hits the ground outside of the boundaries of the court or a permanent fixture outside the court (umpire stand, etc.) or goes into the net. The ball cannot be hit twice with a racket on any return. A return is good if it bounces within the opponent's court after crossing the net. A ball hit on any portion of the sidelines or baselines is considered in bounds. The ball may touch the net or cross outside the post as long as it lands in the correct court.

In doubles, the order of service is decided this way: the pair who have to serve in the first game of each set shall decide which partner shall do so, and the opposing pair shall decide similarly for the second game. The partner of the player who served in the first game shall serve in the third; and the partner of the player who served in the second game shall serve in the fourth, and so on for all subsequent games of the set.

A match is scored in games and sets. The first point is 15, the second 30, the third 40, and the fourth wins the game unless there is a deuce, which is called at the score of 40-all. After deuce, the next point won is scored as an advantage to the player who won it, and if he or she wins the following point, he or she wins the game. Should the opponent redress the balance, the score returns to deuce and the game continues.

A player must win a set by two games, and the first player to win six games wins the set. If each player has won five games, two scenarios are possible: one player can win the next two games and win the set, or they can tie at six-all and play a tiebreaker. In a tiebreaker, the first player to reach seven points (again being ahead by two) wins the tiebreaker and the set.

Players change ends after every odd numbered game in each set.

Tennis Talk

ACE: A ball that is served so excellently that the opponent fails to touch it with the racket.

ALL: Score all tied up.

BACK COURT: The area between the service line and the baseline.

BACKHAND: The stroke use to return balls hit to the left of a right-handed player, and to the right of a left-handed player.

BASELINE: The end boundary line of a tennis court, located 39 feet from the net.

DEUCE: A score of 40–40.

DINK: A ball hit so that it floats back really soft.

DROP SHOT: A softly hit shot that barely crosses the net.

EARNED POINT: A point won by skillful playing rather than by a player's mistake.

ERROR: A point that ends by an obvious mistake rather than by skillful playing.

FAULT: A serve error.

FORECOURT: The area between the net and the service line.

GROUND STROKES: Strokes made after the ball has bounced, either forehand or backhand.

HOLD SERVE: To serve and win the game.

KILL: To smash the ball down very hard, usually resulting in a point.

LET: A serve that hits the top of the net or an interruption that forces a replay of the point.

LOB: A ball hit high enough in the air to pass over the head of the player at the net.

LOVE: Zero or no score.

MATCH POINT: The point that, if won, wins the match for a player.

POACH: A strategy whereby the net player in doubles moves over to his serving partner's side of the court to make a volley.

SERVICE LINE: The line that outlines the base of the service court; parallel to the baseline and 21 feet from the net.

SET: That part of a match that is completed when one player or side wins at least six games and is ahead by at least two games, or has won the tie break.

SET POINT: The point that, if won, wins the set.

SMASH: A hard, overhead shot.

STRAIGHT SETS: Winning a match without the loss of a set.

VOLLEY: To hit the ball before it bounces.

HOPEFULS

Men's Tennis

A series of upsets and reversals leading to the 1992 Olympic tennis tournaments—evidence not of a lack of talent but an abundance of it—will make the men's games interesting to follow. Olympic bronze medalist Stefan Edberg of Sweden will hope to follow his stunning 1991 US Open win with an Olympic championship. Edberg, who has won two Wimbledon titles and two Australian Opens, had bombed out of the first round in the previous US Open. The very next year, though, in a lopsided final against USA's Jim Courier, Edberg won the tournament and became the first-ranked tennis player in the world.

Courier, the third-ranked player after his loss to Edberg, had won the 1991 French Open and, despite his loss to Edberg at the August-September US Open, remains a strong, confident player. The USA, which can include four men on its Olympic team, does not boast a lone superstar tennis player but a varied group of talented men. Andre Agassi and Pete Sampras remained among the top 10 players throughout 1991, though Agassi was eliminated early from the 1991 US Open and Sampras failed to defend his 1990 US Open title. Former French Open champion Michael Chang, Olympic bronze medalist Brad Gilbert, Patrick McEnroe, and David Wheaton contribute to the US pool of young talent, and veterans John McEnroe and Jimmy Connors, while still pleasing and infuriating fans and officials, can't quite match the consistency of the younger players.

fact: The longest singles match, 126 games, ever played was between Roger Taylor of England and Wieslaw Gasiorek of Poland in 1966 during the King's Cup Competition. Taylor won. Taylor also played one of the longer sets in history in that same competition, winning in 64 games.

Germany will undoubtedly come out strong with powerful players Boris Becker, 1991 Australian Open champion and Wimbledon finalist, and Wimbledon champ Michael Stich.

At home in Spain, Sergi Bruguera and the Sanchez brothers, Javier and Olympic silver medalist Emilio (along with sister Arantxa on the women's team), will be the favorites.

Yugoslavia's best, Goran Ivanisevic and Goran Prpic—both Croatian—weren't sure partway into 1991 whether they'd continue to represent Yugoslavia because of political developments at home.

Women's Tennis

The wealth of talent in women's tennis will yield some great matches in Barcelona. Defending Olympic champion Steffi Graf of Germany is again favored to win. Her formidable forehand and impressive championship record—including a Grand Slam sweep in 1988 and three Wimbledon titles—have kept her at number two in the rankings during most of 1991.

Yugoslavia's Monica Seles, a four-time Grand Slam event winner, will be Graf's toughest opponent—if she qualifies for Olympic competition. Her eligibility has been in doubt since she withdrew from the 32-nation Federation Cup in July of 1991, pleading injury. (Two other top women's players, USA's Martina Navratilova and Argentina's Olympic silver medalist Gabriela Sabatini, also missed the Fed Cup and cannot compete at the Barcelona Games.)

US fans will undoubtedly watch for their latest favorite, Jennifer Capriati, who at 15 reached the semifinals at the 1991 Wimbledon Tournament, then won two consecutive titles (the Mazda Classic and the Canadian Open), reached the semifinals of the 1991 US Open, and has beaten all the top 10 women's players but Graf. Since the USA can only send three women tennis players to Barcelona, they'll have to choose between Capriati, Olympic bronze medalist Zina Garrison, Gigi Fernandez, and Mary Joe Fernandez, whose steady but non-aggressive game has led her to the finals or semifinals of every Grand Slam event.

Spain will look strong with hometown favorites Conchita Martinez and Arantxa Sanchez Vicario, whose high-powered performance brought her to at least the semifinals of all but two of the thirteen events she entered in 1991 (at Wimbledon and the US Open, she reached the quarterfinals).

Bulgaria's Olympic bronze medalist Manuela Maleeva-Fragniere now competes for Switzerland, but there remain two other promising Maleevas to represent Bulgaria: Katerina and Magdalena. Jana Novotna, who shared the Olympic doubles silver with Helena Sukova, and Radka Zrubakova could make an impressive showing for Czechoslovakia. And Indonesia may yield a surprise star, Yayuk Basuki, whose ranking among the pros skyrocketed in 1991 from 273 to 39.

Steffi Graf

Achievement comes early in some sports, a bit later in others. Distance runners often don't reach their peak until their late twenties or early thirties. Athletes well into their forties have competed in events such as the discus. On the other hand, tennis players start young. Case in point: Steffi Graf, born in Bruhl, Germany, in 1969. Only the fifth player in history to win tennis's coveted Grand Slam (with victories in the Australian, French, and US Opens and at Wimbledon in the same year), Graf started swinging a racket at the tender age of three, while her contemporaries continued to lounge in the sandbox of their choice.

Her father, Peter Graf, a nationally ranked West German semiprofessional tennis player, thought his toddler daughter only wanted to emulate him. But her insistence eventually won him over. He cut off one of his tennis rackets and showed her how to hit the ball. After that, Steffi's mother, Heidi, reports, "we broke a lot of lamps."

But Steffi progressed quickly under her father's tutelage. She won her first tournament at six, dominated her age group for several years, and at 13 won the German junior championship in the 18-and-under division. She quit school in 1982 and joined the professional tour, becoming the second-youngest player to receive an international ranking. At the 1984 Olympics in Los Angeles, where tennis was still a demonstration sport, Graf won the women's gold medal, even though at the age of 15 she was the youngest competitor in the event.

In 1987 Graf defeated Martina Navratilova and captured her first professional tournament—the French Open—becoming the youngest player ever to do so. By mid-1987, she had achieved the number-one ranking. Thus was the table set for Graf in 1988, a year that many experts have called the finest ever for any tennis player.

In January Graf captured the Australian Open, defeating Chris Evert in the finals, then in March Graf volleyed to victory in the French Open. Prior to Wimbledon, she practiced with a male left-hander in preparation for an expected finals match against the formidable Navratilova, who was competing for a record ninth Wimbledon title. As expected, the two faced off at center court in the final round. After a somewhat shaky start, Graf settled her game, taking the match by winning 12 of the last 13 games. She concluded the Grand Slam in September with a hard-fought victory over Gabriela Sabatini at the US Open.

Only a few days later, Graf was in Seoul, South Korea, where tennis was to be played as a full medal Olympic sport for the first time in 64 years. Again she started slowly, struggling in her early-round matches. Perhaps Graf suffered from an emotional and physical letdown following the Grand Slam quest. But she recovered for the semifinals, in which she played an inspired match against American Zina Garrison, and went into the gold-medal round pitted, once again, against Sabatini. This time, Graf quickly found her rhythm and Sabatini discovered the blues, losing 6–3, 6–3. A year shy of 20, Graf had grabbed the gold.

Steffi Graf continues to be a dominant force in her sport. And she enjoys all-around ability that should allow her to remain a strong contender for many years to come. Her topspin forehand may be the best in the history of women's tennis, and her powerful serve and lightning speed give her tremendous edges against opponents. As Navratilova has said, "I think she can do pretty much anything." —*P.G.*

Schedule

The tentative tennis schedule is as follows:

Tuesday, July 28
32 matches, men & women
1st round, singles

Wednesday, July 29
32 matches, men & women
1st round, singles

Thursday, July 30
32 matches, men & women
2nd round, singles, 1st round doubles

Friday, July 31
32 matches, men & women
2nd round singles, 1st round doubles

Saturday, August 1
20 matches, men & women
3rd round singles, 2nd round doubles

Sunday, August 2
12 matches, men & women
3rd round singles, 2nd round doubles

Monday, August 3
4 matches, quarterfinals
women singles & men doubles
4 matches, quarterfinals
men & women singles

Tuesday, August 4
4 matches, quarterfinals
men singles & doubles, women doubles
4 matches, quarterfinal
men singles, women doubles

Wednesday, August 5
4 matches, semifinals
men doubles, women singles

Thursday, August 6
4 matches, semifinals
men singles, women doubles

Friday, August 7
2 matches, finals
men doubles, women singles

Saturday, August 8
2 matches, finals
women doubles & men singles

HIGHLIGHTS

Last included in the 1924 Olympics, tennis had been played in every Games since Athens. Irish-born John Pius Boland won the first gold medal, for Great Britain, in singles. What is perhaps most interesting about his performance is that he had traveled from Oxford to attend the Games ... as a spectator. Winning the men's doubles as well—with a German partner, Fritz Traun—Boland protested when the English flag was raised for his victory, and an Irish flag was raised in its stead.

When, in 1900, the women's singles event was added, Charlotte Cooper, from Great Britain, became the first woman to medal in tennis—or any sport, for that matter. 1912 was hardly a banner year, since the events were held—albeit on indoor courts—at the same time as the Wimbledon Games.

Impressive performances were the order of the 1920 Games, however: Suzanne Lenglen from France—one of the all-time greatest women tennis players ever—captured the gold medal by losing only four games of the ten sets it took to win the singles title. That same year, the women's doubles event was added, and Great Britain took both the gold and silver. The US made a dazzling show at the 1924 Games, winning the gold for both the men's singles and doubles, the gold and silver in mixed doubles, and the gold in both women's events, before the sport went on hiatus from the Games.

When tennis returned to the official program in 1988, the US fared well—though perhaps not quite so well as it had in 1924. The US captured two golds—in the men's and women's doubles, a silver and bronze in the men's singles, and a bronze in the women's singles. Ken Flack and Robert Seguso made up the men's doubles, while Pam Shriver and Zina Garrison paired for the women's event. West German Steffi Graf beat out Argentinean Gabriela Sabatini in the women's singles, in which Garrison took third. The other medals were divided among a smattering of countries, including Czechoslovakia, Spain, Sweden, Bulgaria, and Australia.

Medalists

Tennis — Men's Singles

1988
1. Miloslav Mecir, Czechoslovakia
2. Tim Mayotte, USA
3. Stefan Edberg, Sweden
3. Brad Gilbert, USA

1928-1984 Not held

1924
1. Vincent Richards, USA
2. Henri Cochet, France
3. Umberto De Morpurgo, Italy

1920
1. Louis Raymond, South Africa
2. Ichiya Kumagae, Japan
3. Charles Winslow, Great Britain

1912
1. Charles Winslow, South Africa, outdoor
1. Andre Govert, France, indoor
2. Harold Kitson, South Africa, outdoor
2. Charles Dixon, Great Britain, indoor
3. Oscar Kreuzer, Germany, outdoor
3. Anthony Wilding, New Zealand, indoor

1908
1. Josiah Ritchie, Great Britain, outdoor
1. Wentworth Gore, Great Britain, indoor

2. Otto Froitzheim, Germany, outdoor
2. George Caridia, Great Britain, indoor
3. Wilberforce Eves, Great Britain, outdoor
3. Josiah Ritchie, Great Britain, indoor

1906 1. Max Decugis, France
2. Maurice Germot, France
3. Zdenek Zemia, Bohemia (Czech)

1904 1. Beals Wright, USA
2. Robert LeRoy, USA

1900 1. Hugh Doherty, Great Britain
2. Harold Mahony, Great Britain
3. Reginald Doherty, Great Britain
3. A.B. Norris, Great Britain

1896 1. John Boland, Great Britain
2. Demis Kasdaglis, Great Britain

Tennis — Men's Doubles

1988 1. USA, Ken Flach, Robert Seguso
2. Spain, Emilio Sanchez, Sergio Casal
3. Sweden, Stefan Edberg, Anders Jarryd
3. Czechoslovakia, Miloslav Mecir, Milan Srejber

1928-
1984 Not held
1924 1. USA
2. France
3. France

1920 1. Great Britain
2. Japan
3. France

1912 1. South Africa, outdoor
1. France, indoor
2. Austria, outdoor
2. Sweden, indoor
3. France, outdoor
3. Great Britain, indoor

1908 1. Great Britain, outdoor
1. Great Britain, indoor
2. Great Britain, outdoor
2. Great Britain, indoor
3. Great Britain, outdoor
3. Sweden, indoor

1906 1. France
2. Greece
3. Bohemia (Czech)

1904 1. USA
2. USA

1900 1. Great Britain
2. USA/France
3. France
3. Great Britain

1896 1. Great Britain/Germany
2. Greece

Tennis — Women's Singles

1988 1. Steffi Graf, West Germany

2. Gabriela Sabatini, Argentina
3. Zina Garrison, USA
3. Manuela Maleeva, Bulgaria

1928-
2984 Not held
1924 1. Helen Wills, USA
2. Julie Vlasto, France
3. Kitty McKane, Great Britain

1920 1. Suzanne Lenglen, France
2. Dorothy Holman, Great Britain
3. Kitty McKane, Great Britain

1912 1. Maarguerite Broquedis, France, outdoor
1. Ethel Hannam, Great Britain, indoor
2. Dora Koring, Germany, outdoor
2. Thora Castenschiold, Denmark, indoor
3. Molla Bjurstedt, Norway, outdoor
3. Mabel Parton, Great Britain, indoor

1908 1. Dorothea Chambers, Great Britain, outdoor
1. Gwen Eastlake-Smith, Great Britain, indoor
2. Dorothy Boothby, Great Britain, outdoor
2. Angela Greene, Great Britain, indoor
3. Martha Adlerstrahle, Sweden, outdoor
3. Molla Bjurstedt, Norway, indoor

1906 1. Esmee Simiriotou, Greece
2. Sophia Marinou, Greece
3. Euphrosine Paspati, Greece

1904 Not held
1900 1. Charlotte Cooper, Great Britain
2. Helene Prevost, France
3. Marion Jones, USA
3. Hedwiga Rosenbaumova, Bohemia (Czech)

Tennis — Women's Doubles

1988 1. USA, Zina Garrison, Pam Shriver
2. Czechoslovakia, Jana Novotna, Helena Sukova
3. West Germany, Steffi Graf, Claudia Kohde-Kilsch
3. Australia, Elizabeth Smylie, Wendy Turnbull

1928-
1984 Not held
1924 1. USA
2. Great Britain
3. Great Britain

1920 1. Great Britain
2. Great Britain
3. France

1896-
1912 Not held

473

Continually breaking his own records, Soviet Sergei Bubka has been the world's best pole vaulter since 1984. In 1991 he cleared the 20-foot barrier, and the sky may be the limit when he defends his Olympic title in 1992.

TRACK AND FIELD (ATHLETICS)— JUMPING

WARM-UP

As soon as humans began jumping, running, and throwing things, they began jumping, running, and throwing things higher, faster, and farther than (and occasionally at) each other. Well, actually, they probably first developed those skills to obtain or avoid becoming food, but individual competition surfaced early on and remains the heart of the modern Olympic Games.

fact: Track and field accounts for more US Olympic medals than any other sport.

The long jump became one of five sports that made up the pentathlon in 708 BC during the ancient Greek Olympics in Peloponnesus. Greek long jumpers used jumping weights, called halters. Artwork representing the Games shows the weights being swung backwards by athletes, apparently to gain a better landing position. (English long jumpers in the 19th century jumped carrying dumbbells, which they released when airborne to change mass, oddly enough.)

Evidence suggests that one Greek Olympian named Chionis jumped to a distance of 23 feet, 1.5 inches in 656 BC.

Not bad for his day. Contemporary long jumpers are floating to just over 29 feet these days.

The Greeks, including Chionis, also recorded some jumps in the 50-foot (15–16 meters) range, which leads sports historians to believe these were a series of jumps, perhaps an ancient version of the triple jump or standing broad jumps. It is not clear if the Greeks practiced a running jump or a standing one. Some ancient vases with scenes depicting the games show both standing jumps and running jumpers carrying halters.

Jumping events are believed to stem from Celtic roots as well. Vaulting, which apparently sprang from the use of small sticks or poles to jump streams, was part of the ancient Irish Tailteann Games that took place in 1829 BC.

Jumping continued in competitions in Ireland and in the Highland Games of Scotland. When English track and field organizers set minimum standards for

475

performances in 1834, athletes had to long jump at least 20 feet and high jump at least five feet, seven inches to qualify.

At the first modern Olympic Games in 1896, pole vault, long jump, high jump, and triple jump were among the six field events. The long jump was one of two field events added for women in the 1928 Olympics. Before that, standing jumping events (for men) were included in addition to the running versions. The standing high jump and long jump were held 1900–12, and the standing triple jump took place in the 1900 and 1904 games. American Ray Ewer dominated the three events. He won 10 gold medals in four different Olympics, overcoming polio as a child to become a superb athlete.

Innovation led to improved performances in the jumping events, especially the pole vault and high jump. In vaulting it was changes to the pole, and in high jump, new styles of jumping.

The first vaulting poles were probably large sticks or tree limbs. Vaulters in the 19th century used wooden poles, and bamboo was even better until World War II interrupted (among other things) bamboo supplies from Japan. Metal poles were used for about a decade, though aluminum is less flexible than bamboo.

Fiberglass poles were introduced in the mid-1950s, and soon vaulters were soaring higher than ever. The fiberglass pole permitted handholds of 15 feet (4.57m) and this made vaults of 18 feet (5.48m) possible.

fact: Ellery Clark, a double-gold medalist in the high and long jump at the first (1896) Olympics, is still the only person to have won those two events at the same Summer Games.

Early high jumpers favored the scissors style, with the legs moving and the torso remaining vertical to the bar. In 1912, American George Horine broke a record with his western roll, in which the jumper passes over the bar lying on his side with knees together. That was refined further to the belly roll, with the jumper going over the bar face down. Another roll change was the straddle. In this style, the jumper's arm and leading leg crossed over the bar and started down as the other arm and leg were still rising. Two straddler style jumpers were Charles Dumas, an American who in 1956 was first to clear seven feet, and Valeri Brumel, a Soviet who dominated high jumping in the 1960s.

American jumper Dick Fosbury won an Olympic gold in 1968 and won over most fellow jumpers with his Fosbury flop. Fosbury used a circular run to approach the bar, then leapt head first and cleared the height with his back facing the bar and his legs trailing. Javier Sotomayor of Cuba cleared eight feet with a flop in 1989.

Foam landing pads replaced those made of sand and allowed jumpers and vaulters to land on their back without injury. Unfortunately, new high-cost landing areas could force smaller, poorer nations from keeping up in international competition.

▼

SPECTATORS' GUIDE

High Jump: In the high jump, the athlete tries to propel his body over a bar that rests across two uprights. The approach can be from any angle along a semi-circular runway. If the jumper hits the bar and causes it to fall, that jump is scored a miss. A contestant can pass, or decline to jump, at any height. Three successive misses, even at different heights, eliminates the jumper.

In case of ties, the high jumper with the fewest misses at the last height cleared wins. If there is still a tie, the competitor with the fewest total misses wins. If there is still a tie, the athlete who has taken the fewest attempts, successful or not, wins. If there is still a tie, excepting a tie for first place, each athlete is given an extra jump. If the deadlock is still not resolved, then the bar is raised or lowered and the contestants jump until the tie is broken.

Another rule is that jumpers must take off from one foot. There have been some challenges to this rule. In 1954, American gymnastics tumbler Dick Browning is reported to have somersaulted over a bar set at seven feet six inches (2.28m). In 1962, another jumper did a back handspring with a back flip over a bar set at seven feet four inches (2.23m). He landed on his feet.

There are also limits on the thickness of a jumper's shoe and sole ever since, in the 1950s, contestants began breaking records with the aid of built-up shoes, using a vaulting effect.

Olympic officials have had to struggle to keep up with the varying styles of high jumpers. In 1932, they objected to the diving style—head and shoulders first—of American Mildred "Babe" Didrikson. She finished first but was awarded the silver because of this unorthodoxy. She did win golds in the javelin and 80m hurdles that year.

Much of the emphasis in style changes has been on finding a lower center of gravity, thus more control over movement. With the upright scissors style of the earlier part of the century, a jumper's center of gravity passed over the bar and offered little control. The western roll of 1912 and related belly roll improved control better still.

Dick Fosbury's famous flop allowed the jumper's center of gravity to actually pass under the bar. More than 20 years later, the Fosbury Flop is still popular.

Track and Field (Athletics)—Jumping

fact: At the 1936 Berlin Olympics, gold medal winners were presented with one-year-old potted oak seedlings, adorned with the motto, "Grow to the honor of victory! Summon to further achievement!" A few of the oaks are still alive, including one of the three brought back by Jesse Owens.

Psyching out one's opponent is not uncommon in field events, mostly because the wait between jumps or throws can toy with the fragile and frayed nerves of athletes. A winner is one who can avoid being rattled by the pressure from any source. Likewise, the power of positive thinking is important. As world high jump recordholder Dwight Stones has said, "The body doesn't know it has limits. It's your brain that screws everything up."

Pole Vault: In the pole vault, an athlete uses a long flexible pole to push himself, as if catapulted, over a bar three times his size. The vaulter sprints along a short runway track and jams the pole into a box beneath the bar. He raises the pole and his forward running speed shifts into upward motion. He hangs upside down as he rises off the ground at the end of a bending pole. He turns and pushes off the pole with his arms and, if the vault is successful, passes over the bar legs first and face down before landing in a pit of foam.

Sounds gravity-defying, doesn't it?

Contestants are allowed three tries at each height, which is gradually increased. Three misses at any height disqualifies a pole vaulter. A miss is charged if an athlete knocks over the bar, passes to the side or underneath it, touches the ground beyond with the pole, switches his hands on the pole, or moves his upper hand on the pole after leaving the ground. A vaulter who takes more than two minutes after getting clearance to begin an attempt is also charged with a miss.

Vaulters are usually fast runners with powerful upper bodies and good all-around gymnastics ability.

During WWII, when bamboo poles were not available, pole vaulters used steel or aluminum poles, which lacked the flexibility of bamboo but were more consistent. Poles made of fiberglass were introduced as early as 1956, though it was several years before vaulters learned properly how to use them. When they did, vaults mounted higher and higher.

Fiberglass offers both consistency and flexibility. Fiberglass poles bend several feet, then snap back when the athlete's feet are pointed up and approaching the pole. The flexibility of a pole determines the height at which it can be gripped. The stiffer the pole, and the lighter the vaulter, the greater the whip and potential for height. Still, it takes strength to bend the pole sufficiently.

Sergei Bubka, a Soviet pole vaulter who won the Olympic gold medal in 1988, has said that the speed of the take-off and strength in the jump are all-important.

Long jump: Formerly called a broad jump, a valid one must be made from behind the far edge of a take-off board, which is about eight inches (20cm) wide, and level to the ground. The jump is measured from the nearest impression in the sand made by the jumper's body to the nearest edge of the board. Jumpers approach the board along a runway. The board contains a strip of plasticine four inches (10cm) wide on the runway side of the board so judges can detect fouls. The plasticine is raised about one-third inch (7mm) above the board and will show any contact by the jumper's shoe.

The competition begins with a qualifying round, the results from which are not carried over to the final. In the final, each contestant is allowed three jumps, then the best eight jumpers are allowed three more jumps. If a jump is aided by wind of more than two meters per second (4.473 miles per hour), the jump counts but is not recognized as a record.

Americans have dominated the Olympic men's long jump. They have won it 17 of 20 times, losing once because of a boycott. Bob Beamon's 29 feet, 2.5 inches jump in the 1968 Olympics is considered one of the greatest track and field performances ever. That world record leap, which took place in the "rare air" Olympics in Mexico City, was tops for 23 years.

In the early part of the 20th century, long jumpers were speedsters with great spring. Jumpers now have added strength training to their repertoire to increase distance.

Triple Jump: This is similar to the long jump except for the mechanics of the actual jump. It's also known as the hop, step and jump because the athlete makes a running start, hops, lands on the same foot from which he took off, takes one step onto the other foot, then jumps. The leap is ruled a foul if a trailing foot touches the ground.

Jumpers sprint down a runway and must jump before reaching a takeoff line, same as in the long jump. The final maneuver of the triple jump leaves the athlete in the sand pit, from which the distance is measured.

Japanese jumpers dominated this men-only event through the 1930s, while a Brazilian named Adhemar Ferreira da Silva won gold medals in the event in 1952 and 1956. Eastern Europeans then ruled the event through the 1960s, led by the Soviet jumper Viktor Saneyev.

HOPEFULS

Men's Events

US long jumper Mike Powell, whose talent had long been eclipsed by that of Carl Lewis, finally grabbed some glory of his own at the 1991 World Track and Field Championships in Tokyo when he broke the sport's oldest record, set by Bob Beamon in the 1968 Olympics. By jumping 29 feet, 4.5 inches—two full inches farther than Beamon—Powell also broke Lewis's record-setting 10-year, 65-meet winning streak in the event.

Oddly enough, Lewis gave the best four jumps of his life at that World meet, losing nonetheless to Powell. A repeat of Seoul's 1988 long jump results is quite possible at Barcelona, with Lewis, Powell, and Larry Myricks sweeping the medals for the USA.

In the pole vault, the world will be watching the Soviet Union's undisputed czar of vaulting, Sergi Bubka. Undefeated since 1984, Bubka became the first to accomplish a 20-foot jump and continually breaks his own world records.

The Olympic triple jump title could go to either of two Americans: Kenny Harrison, who won the event at the Tokyo World games, or Michael Conley, who finished third at the Worlds but in 1984 brought home the Olympic silver in the event. Stiff competition, though, may come from the Soviet Union's Leonid Voloshin.

In the high jump, Americans Charles Austin (the current world champion) and Hollis Conway (the silver medalist at Seoul) and Cuban Javier Sotomayor are the athletes to watch.

Sergei Bubka

A name to remember for the Barcelona Games: Bubka. Sergei Bubka has been the world's best pole vaulter since 1984, when he set the first of his nearly thirty world records. Track insiders call Bubka the "Czar of Vaulting" because the records he is breaking—the most by any individual in a single track and field event in history—are all his own. No one else can come near him. No one has in years.

Bubka was the first man to clear the magical 20-foot barrier in the pole vault. He has done so both indoors and outdoors in 1991, a year that also saw him break his records three times in an eight-day span. As *Boston Globe* correspondent Joe Concannon sees it, Bubka "simply seems to overpower his event. He doesn't tip the bar, he clears it with room to spare. ... He heads for the skies in earnest."

Bubka is probably one of the last of the Olympic stars to emerge from the communist-dominated Soviet system. He was born in Voroshilograd in the Ukraine on November 4, 1963, and was identified early as an athlete with

480

potential. He took to pole vaulting when he was 15, working with Vitaly Petrov, a coach from his hometown.

At the advent of the 1984 Olympics, Bubka was already the world record holder, having set a new height of 19 feet, 4.5 inches just two weeks before festivities began in Los Angeles. A Soviet boycott of the 1984 Games kept Bubka from competing, and the gold medal winner, France's Pierre Quinon, won with a jump six inches short of his Soviet counterpart's. No boycott barred Bubka from competing in the 1988 Olympics. He handily won the gold in Seoul, and, since 1984, has not been beaten anywhere.

Needless to say, Bubka is one of the Soviet Union's most famous and celebrated modern athletes. He has been allowed to take an American sponsor— Nike—and win prize money each time he competes, retaining all but ten percent of his hefty earnings. He is also allowed to continue his training in the Ukraine rather than move to Moscow. Still, for years he has given few interviews to the West and has returned promptly to his homeland whenever the competitions ended. That has changed now.

Numerous Soviet states are clamoring for independence, including the Ukraine. "There are some big changes in Russia," Bubka told the *Boston Globe* just prior to the 1991 World Championships. "Which flag I compete under, I don't know. So many things are happening in the Soviet Union, and I believe things will not be settled down quickly." Bubka has even stated openly that he may move to a Western nation—possibly France—while his troubled country sorts out its politics.

Should he stay healthy, Bubka is a certain medalist at the 1992 games. He jumped seven inches higher than his nearest competitor in 1991. The phenomenal Ukrainian is not indestructible, however. In 1990 he suffered back trouble, and during the World Championships in 1991 he was forced to take injections of painkiller in his left foot in order to compete. Even with the injuries he still won the gold medal—but injuries and age may take their toll before Barcelona.

Still, Bubka will enter the record books as the first pole vaulter to clear 20 feet, the first track star to set more than 28 records in his event, and, perhaps, the last sports hero of the old Soviet regime. He works with a new coach now, Alexander Salamachim, and plans to keep right on breaking records. Asked how high he might vault some day, Bubka winced and told the *Philadelphia Inquirer*, "Maybe 6.20, 6.25 meters [20 feet, 6 inches]."

Some say he has reached those heights already, in practice.

Washington Post correspondent Frank Costello writes: "On a bad day [Bubka] still outclasses the rest of the vaulters in the world. He is perhaps the greatest athlete in all of track and field." —*M.K.*

Women's Events

A strong competitor in jumping, running, and field events, USA's Jackie Joyner-Kersee is a multi-talented athlete. Her winning long jump in the 1988 Seoul

Games set an Olympic record, and her gold medal at the 1991 World Championships in Tokyo proves her readiness for the 1992 Olympic Games at Barcelona. Finishing just behind Joyner-Kersee at both the 1988 Games and the Tokyo World competition, though, was Germany's Heike Drechsler, who will be hungry for a win when the two next meet.

The high jump could see a showdown between 1988 Olympic silver medalist Stefka Kostavinova of Bulgaria and Germany's Heike Henkel, whose championship jump at the Tokyo World games was more than two inches higher than that of her runner-up, Soviet Yelena Yelesina.

Schedule

The tentative track and field (athletics) schedule for jumping events is as follows:

Friday, July 31
High jump, qualifying, men

Saturday, August 1
Triple jump, qualifying, men

Sunday, August 2
High jump, final, men

Monday, August 3
Triple jump, final, men

Wednesday, August 5
Pole vault. qualifying, men

Long jump, qualifying, men

Thursday, August 6
High jump, qualifying, women
Long jump, qualifying, women
Long jump, finals, men

Friday, August 7
Pole vault, finals, men
Long jump, finals, women

Saturday, August 8
High jump, finals, women

MEN'S JUMPING EVENTS

▼

HIGHLIGHTS

Long jump: The Athens games provided an American shutout in the long jump, then known as the broad jump: Ellery Clark won the gold, while teammates Robert Garrett and James Connolly took the silver and bronze. The star of the 1900 long jump, Alvin Kraenzlein, is distinguished as the athlete who received the most individual titles (four) at a single Games. 1900's second-place finisher, Meyer Prinstein, also an American, went on to win the long jump at the St. Louis Games and again in 1906.

The London and Stockholm Games set new Olympic records, with Americans Francis "Frank" Irons winning the gold at London, and Albert

Gutterson at Stockholm. The Antwerp Games marked the first non-American gold medalist, when William Petersen of Sweden leapt 23ft, 5.5 in, to beat out American Carl Johnson.

The Paris Games marked yet another Olympic first when American William De Hart Hubbard became the first black to win an individual Olympic gold medal. In second place, American Edward Gourdin jumped only 23ft, 10.25in—short of the world record-setting mark he had posted prior to the Games, when he broke the twenty-year record of Peter O'Connor. Also at the Paris Games, Bob LeGendre, who had failed to make the US long jump team, wasted a world record-breaking long jump of 25:5.75—which would have won the open competition—on the pentathlon competition, where he finished third.

Although American Edward Hamm won the 1928 competition and set a new Olympic record in the long jump, it was Haiti's second-place finisher, Silvio Cator, who went on to be the first long jumper to surpass the 26-foot benchmark. A number of Americans distinguished themselves in track and field at the Games in 1932, including Edward Gordon, whose long jump won the gold.

Everyone knew the name of Jesse Owens by the time of the 1936 Berlin Games, since he had set a new world record the previous year. What they didn't know was that it would take twenty-five years for that record to be surpassed—pretty remarkable considering the short life of many of the other world records. Although Owens' Olympic jump fell short of his world record distance, he easily set a new Olympic record and won the gold medal.

Continuing the American domination of long jumping, the US won the gold in four more Games: Willie Steele won in 1948, Jerome Biffle in 1952, Gregory Bell in 1956, and Ralph Boston in 1960. It was Boston who finally broke Jesse Owens' seemingly immortal record jump, just two weeks before the Rome Games began. Boston set a new Olympic record at 26ft, 7.75in, while fellow American Irvin "Bo" Roberson followed close on his heels with a 26ft, 7.25in jump; Soviet bronze medalist Igor Ter-Ovanesyan also surpassed the 26-foot mark by 4.5 inches. The Rome meet marked the first time that four men had outjumped the 26-foot mark.

In Tokyo in 1964, Great Britain's Lynn Davies stole the title from the previous Games' gold and silver medalists, much to everyone's surprise, making him the first Welshman to capture a gold medal at the Games.

The 1968 meet featured a star-studded lineup: Ralph Boston, Lynn Davies, and Igor Ter-Orvanesyan, all of whom had medaled in 1964, were there, and they were all in top form. And then there was Bob Beamon—on suspension from the University of Texas at El Paso for refusing to compete against Brigham Young University because of their racial policies—who was informally receiving advice from Boston. Known for fouling often, Beamon managed a perfect takeoff on his first jump, thanks to advice from Boston. Clearly Beamon's jump was a good one, even to the naked eye. Not relying on the high-tech measuring apparatus at their disposal, officials used a measuring tape to confirm that Beamon had, indeed, jumped 21.75 inches beyond the world record, and when the magnitude of what he had done finally sunk in, Beamon suffered what is called a "cataplectic seizure"—that is, he fell to his knees in shock.

Beamon's jump is still considered to be one of the greatest of all track and field accomplishments, having stood for 23 years.

In Munich, American Randy Williams's 27ft, 0.5 inches might have seemed anti-climatic in the long jump pit; nonetheless, Williams won a gold medal, followed by German Hans Baumgartner in second place and American Arnie Robinson in third. Robinson returned four years later to win the gold, marking the tenth time in a dozen Games that an African-American had won the event, and he did so in the first round, marking the third consecutive Olympics in which the long jump had been won in the first round.

1980 was yet another benchmark year. No one—including Bob Beamon—had ever long jumped 28 feet in an Olympic meet: Beamon had sailed right past the 28 foot mark. Lutz Dombrowski, East Germany's gold medalist at the Moscow Games, was the first man to achieve an Olympic jump in the 28-foot range, jumping 28ft, 0.25in. His countryman, Frank Paschek, placed second with a 26ft, 11.25in leap, followed by the Soviet Valery Podluzhniy.

Carl Lewis took the gold in Los Angeles in 1984 and successfully defended his title in Seoul four years later, when the Americans again swept the medals: Mike Powell earned a silver medal while Larry Myricks picked up a bronze.

Triple jump: Irish-American James Connolly became the first thoroughly modern Olympic champion when he won the triple jump—then known as the hop, step and jump—on April 6, 1896. The last to jump, Connolly threw his cap down a yard beyond the leading jumper's mark and, lucky for him, proceeded to best Frenchman Alexandre Tuffere's mark of 42ft, 8in with a jump of 44ft, 11.75in.

Meyer Prinstein increased his medal haul by winning the 1900 and 1904 triple jump events (while James Connolly placed second in Paris); by the end of his Olympic career, Prinstein had earned a silver and two gold medals in the long jump, in addition to his two triple jump golds.

Despite American domination in other jumping events, the US would not receive another gold medal in the triple jump until 1984. The 1908 London Games triple jump winner was an Irishman, Timothy Ahearne, who set a new Olympic record of 48ft, 11.25in. The Swedes shut out the competition, taking all the medals in the event in 1912, but took only a silver and bronze away from the Antwerp Games, where a Finn captured the gold medal. Australian Anthony Winter established a world record in Paris with a 50ft, 11.25 jump, and Japanese Mikio Oda became the first Asian to win a gold medal when he won the triple jump at the Amsterdam Games.

Another Japanese jumper captured the gold in Los Angeles, setting a world record with his 51ft, 7in jump; Chuhei Nambu had the added distinction of being the world record holder in the long jump as well.

Once again, in Berlin, Japanese jumpers captured the gold and silver medals, and Naoto Tajima's world record of 52ft, 6in withstood the 1948 Olympic

484

meet, in spite of Japan's absence. However, Japan would never regain its prominence in the Olympic triple jump event.

Brazil's Adhemar Ferreira da Silva went into the Helsinki Games as the world record holder, and left with a gold medal and a new world record—during his six jumps, he had broken his world record four times. The bronze medalist, Arnoldo Devonish, was the first Venezualan athlete to earn an Olympic medal.

Da Silva earned a second gold medal in the triple jump at Melbourne, resetting the Olympic record, and when Icelander Vilhjálmur Einarsson won the silver medal at Melbourne, he became the first medalist from his country. The Rome meet proved to be no contest when Poland's Józef Schmidt—who had been the first man to break the 55-foot barrier—leapt 55ft, 2in. Schmidt recaptured the gold in Tokyo in 1964, setting a new Olympic record at 55ft, 3.5in, despite having undergone knee surgery less than two months before the Games.

Schmidt's world record stood at the start of the Mexico City Games, but it was to fall more than once during the course of the 1968 triple jump event. Soviet Viktor Saneyev vaulted to a new world record of 57ft, 0.75in, while Brazilian Nelson Prudencio and Italian Giuseppe Gentile took second and third place. Saneyev reigned as the king of the triple jump in Munich and Montréal, making him one of a select few track and field athletes to have earned three or more individual gold medals in a single event.

In second place at the Moscow Games, Saneyev just missed winning his fourth consecutive gold medal. Another Soviet, Jaak Uudmäe, made the gold-medaling jump, while Brazilian Joao Carlos de Oliveira—whose world record remained unchallenged—won the bronze.

For the first time since 1904, the US won the triple jump gold medal in 1984, thanks to Al Joyner, whose name was splashed throughout Olympic records, with or without a hyphen. Joyner's teammate, Mike Conley, added to the US medals, taking the silver as well. 1984 didn't prove to initiate a winning streak for the US, though, and the American team was shut out from medaling at the Seoul Games: Bulgarian Hristo Markov won the event, followed by Soviets Igor Lapchine and Alexandre Kovalenko.

High jump: A noteworthy medal haul was taken by America's Robert Garrett in 1896, when he added silvers in the high and long jumps to his golds in the shot and discus. Tied for second place was his teammate James Connolly, the winner of the triple jump; Ellery Clark, also from the States, won the event with a 5ft, 11.25in jump.

The Americans continued to dominate the long jump for the next several Games: Irving Baxter set a new Olympic record in 1900 at 6ft, 2.75in; Samuel Jones set no record but won the gold medal in 1904; Harry Porter lifted the Olympic record to 6ft, 3in in 1908, and Alma Richards raised the record yet another inch in 1912—the year when Jim Thorpe tied for fourth place.

The 1920 gold went to Richmond Landon, and 1924's went to decathlon silver medalist Harold Osborn. In Paris in 1924, the US matched the Finns' distance-running ability with its field-event strength. American Harold Osborn—

who won the 1924 decathlon—won the high jump competition using the back lay-out version of the Western roll at the Paris Games, and consequently sparked a controversy that resulted in a rule change.

American Robert King posted the best jump of 1928; interestingly, the next four jumpers behind King all leapt 6ft, 3.25in, and places had to be decided by a jump-off.

Not until LA, ironically, in 1932, did a non-American win the high jump—but not by much. Canadian Duncan McNaughton won the gold, thanks to a jump-off, although the top four jumpers all leapt exactly 6ft, 5.5in. Under current tie-breaking rules, McNaughton would have received only a bronze medal, and the second-place finisher, American Robert Van Osdel, would have won the gold.

When the US swept the high jump medals in 1936, Nazi leader Adolf Hitler—who was already in trouble with the IOC for summoning the German shot-put winner for a special tribute, against Olympic protocol—had already left the stadium. Cornelius Johnson, in first place, set an Olympic record, which lasted until another American, Walter Davis, broke it in 1952.

An Australian, John Winter, won the 1948 high jump, and the silver and bronze medals—both awarded to athletes who had jumped 6ft, 4.75in—were decided by calculating the number of misses, rather than by a jump-off. In Helsinki, American Walter Davis jumped a half-inch higher than his height to win the gold medal and set a new Olympic record at 6ft, 8.5in. It wasn't much of a surprise when this record was broken by American Charlie Dumas, who won the gold and set a new Olympic record in Melbourne, since he had managed to clear the seemingly unbeatable 7-foot mark in the US Olympic trials. (Les Steers's world record jump of 6ft, 11in stood from 1941 until 1953, when Walt Davis still fell a half inch short of the seven-foot mark.)

By 1960, the mystical barrier had utterly lost its spell, and the field included a number of athletes who had cleared 7 feet. All three medalists surpassed the seven-foot mark, with Soviets Robert Shavlakadze and Valery Brumel placing first and second, and American John Thomas third. Charles Dumas, with a 6ft, 8in jump, managed only to place sixth.

John Thomas improved his position in Tokyo, earning the silver medal and sharing the Olympic record with Soviet Valery Brumel. While both had jumped 7ft, 1.75in, Brumel was awarded the gold since he had fewer misses. The 1960 gold medalist, Shavlakadze, managed only to place fifth, and American John Rambo earned a bronze.

Mexico City's rarified air sparked a number of rare achievements: the "Fosbury flop" became the talk of the town of the 1968 Games when American Dick Fosbury won the gold medal with an Olympic record-breaking jump of 7ft, 4.25in. Soviet Yuri Tarmak won the gold in Munich, but still fell one inch short of Fosbury's mark. At Montréal in 1976, Dwight Stones, who had placed third in the Munich Games, managed only to place third again, although the world record he had set prior to the 1976 Games remained untouched. Poland's Jacek Wszola set a new Olympic record that year with his gold-winning 7ft, 4.5in jump.

Wszola was considered to be a prime candidate for the gold in Moscow, but a relatively unknown East German by the name of Gerd Wessig—who had made the East German team two weeks before the Games—upset the competition. Wessig easily won the gold medal with a 7ft, 8.75in jump—a full 1.75in above Wszola's second-place jump—and he became the first man to establish a high jump world record at the Games.

Dietmar Moegenburg won the 1984 event for West Germany, followed by Patrik Sjoberg of Sweden, and, in an unusual showing, Zhu Jianhua of China took the bronze. Sjoberg managed only to tie for third in Seoul, with Soviet Roudolf Povarnitsyne, while Hollis Conway of the US captured the silver medal. Soviet Guennadi Avdeenko set an Olympic record as he vaulted to the gold in Seoul.

Pole vault: The first pole vault competition was won by American William Welles Hoyt, and it was another seventy-six years before a non-American would win the event in the Olympics. Irving Baxter won the pole vault in Paris in 1900 amid much controversy: a number of the competitors objected to the fact that the event was being held on a Sunday, and they refused to participate. And two of the US team's best vaulters had been misinformed that the event would be rescheduled and consequently missed the competition. When a consolation competition was staged, Baxter's teammate, D.S. Horton, bettered his jump by 5.75 inches.

Charles Dvorak, the other American who had been misinformed of a rescheduled event by the Olympic officials, went on to win the 1904 event in Saint Louis. The Americans swept the event that year, taking first through sixth place. In the following Games, Edward Cooke and Alfred Gilbert managed to establish an Olympic record despite having to compete amid the havoc that the marathon finish had created; both shared first place with a 12ft, 2in jump. Gilbert went on to post-Olympic fame to create the ubiquitous Erector set.

Harry Babcock set an Olympic record in Stockholm, while his teammates Frank Nelson and Marcus Wright helped America sweep the medals again. Then, in Antwerp, Frank Foss set a new world record with a 13ft, 5in jump—giving him the largest margin of victory in Olympic history. Denmark's Henry Petersen managed only 12ft, 1.5in for second place.

fact: When the vaulter is only halfway between take-off and the bar, and the pole is bent and ready to snap back, the vaulter's body must be curled completely upside down in perfect alignment with the pole, or the force from the pole's upward swing will be lost.

The US made a clean sweep of the Paris and Amsterdam Games, and was expected to do so again in LA when a surprise contender from Japan, Shuhei

Nishida, jumped just a half inch less than the American gold medalist, William Miller. The following Games, in Berlin, Nishida was again awarded silver, and another Japanese vaulter, Sueo Oe, was given the bronze, despite the fact that both had vaulted 13ft, 11.25in. Back in Japan, the two winners had their medals re-worked so that each was half silver and half bronze.

The US hegemony remained unchallenged for the next few years, with O. Guinn Smith winning the event at London, and Robert Richards at Helsinki and again at Melbourne, which made him the only man to win two gold medals—three medals, in toto—for pole vaulting. In recognition of his accomplishments, Richards was pictured on the front of Wheaties cereal boxes.

Almost nine hours of grueling vaulting decided the Tokyo competition, which made a gold medalist out of the world record holder, Texan Frederick Hansen. Though Hansen established a new Olympic record, his world record—which marked the seventeenth time the world record had been broken since the Rome Games—remained intact. The Tokyo Games marked the first time flexible fiberglass poles were used. The US went home from Mexico City with another gold medal, but clearly the Americans were not unchallenged: American Robert Seagren, West German Claus Schiprowski, and East German Wolfgang Nordwig all shared the Olympic record at 17ft, 8.5in, and medals were determined based on the number of misses.

Wolfgang Nordwig, who had won the bronze in 1968, returned to the Munich Games to win the first pole vaulting gold medal ever awarded to a non-American, while Robert Seagren and Jan Johnson kept the US in the medals by winning the silver and bronze. The US managed only a bronze medal in Montréal, when David Roberts jumped 18ft, 0.5in—just as had the Polish gold medalist and the Finnish silver medalist; once again, places were determined by the number of misses. As fate would have it, had Roberts not missed his first attempt at 17ft, 6.75in, he would have won the gold medal.

When the 1980 Games began, a new two-week-old world record of 18ft, 11in existed; set by Philippe Houvion of France, the record was short lived. Poland's Wladyslaw Kozakiewicz jumped an extra half inch to set another world record—the second pole vaulting world record to be established during an Olympics—allowing erstwhile world record holder Houvion to place only fourth, with a jump of 18ft, 6.5in, by virtue of number of misses.

The 1984 Games introduced a new gold medalist when Pierre Quinon of France out-vaulted the competition; Americans Mike Tully and Earl Bell placed second and third. The Seoul Games proved to be a total sweep for the Soviets: Grigori Egorov captured the bronze, Radion Gataoulline the silver, and Sergei Bubka—who grips the fiberglass pole closer to the end than any other pole vaulter—set an Olympic record to win the Seoul gold medal.

488

Track and Field — Men's High Jump

1988 1. Guennadi Avdeenko, Soviet Union, 2.38 (OR)
2. Hollis Conway, USA, 2.36
3. Roudolf Povarnitsyne, Soviet Union, 2.36
3. Patrik Sjoberg, Sweden, 2.36
1984 1. Dietmar Moegenburg, FRG, 2.35
2. Patrik Sjoberg, Sweden, 2.33
3. Zhu Jianhua, China, 2.31
1980 1. Gerd Wessig, East Germany, 2.36 (WR)
2. Jacek Wszola, Poland, 2.31
3. Jorg Freimuth, East Germany, 2.31
1976 1. Jacek Wzsola, Poland, 2.25 (OR)
2. Greg Joy, Canada, 2.23
3. Dwight Stones, USA, 2.21
1972 1. Yuri Tarmak, Soviet Union, 2.23
2. Stefan Junge, G.D.R., 2.21
3. Dwight Stones, USA, 2.21
1968 1. Dick Fosbury, USA, 2.24 (OR)
2. Ed Caruthers, USA, 2.22
3. Valentin Gavrilov, Soviet Union, 2.20
1964 1. Valeri Brumel, Soviet Union, 2.18 (OR)
2. John Thomas, USA 2.18 (OR)
3. John Rambo, USA, 2.16
1960 1. Robert Shavlakadze, Soviet Union, 2.16 (OR)
2. Valeri Brumel, Soviet Union, 2.16
3. John Thomas, USA, 2.14
1956 1. Charles Dumas, USA, 2.12 (OR)
2. Charles Porter, Australia, 2.10
3. Igor Kashkarov, Soviet Union, 2.08
1952 1. Walter Davis, USA, 2.04 (OR)
2. Kenneth Wiesner, USA, 2.01
3. Jose Telles da Conceicao, Brazil, 1.98
1948 1. John Winter, Australia, 1.98
2. Bjorn Paulson, Norway, 1.95
3. George Stanich, USA, 1.95
1936 1. Cornelius Johnson, USA, 2.03 (OR)
2. David Albritton, USA, 2.00
3. Delos Thurber, USA, 2.00
1932 1. Duncan McNaughton, Canada, 1.97
2. Robert Van Osdel, USA, 1.97
3. Simeon Toribio Philippines, 1.97
1928 1. Robert King, USA, 1.94
2. Benjamin Hedges, USA, 1.91
3. Claude Menard, France, 1.91
1924 1. Harold Osborn, USA, 1.98 (OR)
2. Leroy Brown, USA, 1.95
3. Pierre Lewden, France, 1.92
1920 1. Richmond Landon, USA, 1.935 (OR)
2. Harold Muller, USA, 1.90
3. Bo Ekelund, Sweden, 1.90
1912 1. Alma Richards, USA, 1.93 (OR)
2. Hans Liesche, Germany, 1.91
3. George Horine, USA, 1.89
1908 1. Harry Porter, USA, 1.905 (OR)
2. Geo Andre, France, 1.88
2. Con Leahy, Great Britain/Ireland, 1.88
2. Istvan Somodi, Hungary, 1.88
1906 1. Con Leahy, Great Britain/Ireland, 1.775
2. Lajos Gonczy, Hungary, 1.75

3. Themistoklis Diakidis, Greece, 1.725
3. Herbert Kerrigan, USA, 1.725
1904 1. Samuel Jones, USA, 1.803
2. Garrett Serviss, USA, 1.778
3. Paul Weinstein, Germany, 1.778
1900 1. Irving Baxter, USA, 1.90 (OR)
2. Patrick Leahy, Great Britain/Ireland, 1.78
3. Lajos Gonczy, Hungary, 1.75
1896 1. Ellery Clark, USA, 1.81
2. James Connolly, USA, 1.65
3. Robert Garrett, USA, 1.65

Track and Field — Men's Pole Vault

1988 1. Sergei Bubka, Soviet Union, 5.90 (OR)
2. Radion Gataoulline, Soviet Union, 5.85
3. Grigori Egorov, Soviet Union, 5.80
1984 1. Pierre Quinon, France, 5.75
2. Mike Tully, USA, 5.65
3. Earl Bell, USA, 5.60
1980 1. Wladyslaw Kozakiewicz, Poland, 5.78 (WR)
2. Tadeusz Slusarski, Poland, 5.65
3. Konstantin Volkov, Soviet Union, 5.65
1976 1. Tadeusz Slusarski, Poland, 5.50 (EOR)
2. Antti Kalliomaki, Finland, 5.50 (EOR)
3. Dave Roberts, USA, 5.50 (EOR)
1972 1. Wolfgang Nordwig, East Germany, 5.50 (OR)
2. Bob Seagren, USA, 5.40
3. Jan Johnson, USA, 5.35
1968 1. Bob Seagren, USA, 5.40 (OR)
2. Claus Schiprowski, West Germany, 5.40 (OR)
3. Wolfgang Nordwig, East Germany, 5.40 (OR)
1964 1. Fred Hansen, USA, 5.10 (OR)
2. Wolfgang Reinhardt, West Germany, 5.05
3. Klaus Lehnertz, West Germany, 5.00
1960 1. Donald Bragg, USA, 4.70 (OR)
2. Ronald Morris, USA, 4.60
3. Eeles Landstrom, Finland, 4.55
1956 1. Robert Richards, USA, 4.56 (OR)
2. Robert Gutowski, USA, 4.53
3. Georgios Roubanis, Greece, 4.50
1952 1. Robert Richards, USA, 4.55 (OR)
2. Donald Laz, USA, 4.50
3. Ragnar Lundberg, Sweden, 4.40
1948 1. Guinn Smith, USA, 4.30
2. Erkki Kataja, Finland, 4.20
3. Robert Richards, USA, 4.20
1936 1. Earle Meadows, USA, 4.35 (OR)
2. Shuhei Nishida, Japan, 4.25
3. Sueo Oe, Japan, 4.25
1932 1. William Miller, USA, 4.315 (OR)
2. Shuhei Nishida, Japan, 4.30
3. George Jefferson, USA, 4.20
1928 1. Sabin Carr, USA, 4.20 (OR)
2. William Droegemuller, USA, 4.10
3. Charles McGinnis, USA, 3.95
1924 1. Lee Barnes, USA, 3.95
2. Glenn Graham, USA, 3.95
3. James Brooker, USA, 3.90

489

1920   1. Frank Foss, USA, 4.09 (WR)
        2. Henry Petersen, Denmark, 3.70
        3. Edwin Myers, USA, 3.60
1912   1. Harry Babcock, USA, 3.95 (OR)
        2. Frank Nelson, USA, 3.85
        2. Marcus Wright, USA, 3.85
        3. William Happenny, Canada, 3.80
        3. Frank Murphy, USA, 3.80
        3. Bertil Uggla, Sweden, 3.80
1908   1. Edward Cooke, USA, 3.71 (OR)
        1. Alfred Gilbert, USA, 3.71 (OR)
        3. Edward B. Archibald, Canada, 3.58
        3. Charles Jacobs, USA, 3.58
        3. Bruno Soderstrom, Sweden, 3.58
1906   1. Fernand Gonder, France, 3.50
        2. Bruno Soderstrom, Sweden, 3.40
        3. Ernest Glover, USA, 3.35
1904   1. Charles Dvorak, USA, 3.505
        2. LeRoy Samse, USA, 3.43
        3. Louis Wilkins., USA, 3.43
1900   1. Irving Baxter, USA, 3.30
        2. Michael Colket, USA, 3.25
        3. Carl-Albert Andersen, Norway, 3.20
1896   1. William Hoyt, USA, 3.30
        2. Albert Tyler, USA, 3.25
        3. Evangelos Damaskos, Greece, 2.85

Track and Field — Men's Long Jump

1988   1. Carl Lewis, USA, 8.72
        2. Mike Powell, USA, 8.49
        3. Larry Myricks, USA, 8.27
1984   1. Carl Lewis, USA, 8.54
        2. Gary Honey, Australia, 8.24
        3. Giovanni Evangelisti, Italy, 8.24
1980   1. Lutz Dombrowski, East Germany, 8.54
        2. Frank Paschek, East Germany, 8.21
        3. Valeri Podluzhnyi, Soviet Union, 8.18
1976   1. Arnie Robinson, USA, 8.35
        2. Randy Williams, USA, 8.11
        3. Frank Wartenberg, East Germany, 8.02
1972   1. Randy Williams, USA, 8.24
        2. Hans Baumgartner, West Germany, 8.18
        3. Arnie Robinson, USA, 8.03
1968   1. Bob Beamon, USA, 8.90 (WR)
        2. Klaus Beer, East Germany, 8.19
        3. Ralph Boston, USA, 8.16
1964   1. Lynn Davies, Great Britain, 8.07
        2. Ralph Boston, USA, 8.03
        3. Igor Ter-Ovanesyan, Soviet Union, 7.99
1960   1. Ralph Boston, USA, 8.12 (OR)
        2. Irvin Roberson, USA, 8.11
        3. Igor Ter-Ovanesyan, Soviet Union, 8.04
1956   1. Greg Bell, USA, 7.83
        2. John Bennett, USA, 7.68
        3. Jorma Valkama, Finland, 7.48
1952   1. Jerome Biffle, USA, 7.57
        2. Meredith Gourdine, USA, 7.53
        3. Odon Foldessy, Hungary, 7.30
1948   1. Willie Steele, USA, 7.825
        2. Thomas Bruce, Australia, 7.555
        3. Herbert Douglas, USA, 7.545
1936   1. Jesse Owens, USA, 8.06 (OR)
        2. Luz Long, Germany, 7.87
        3. Naoto Tajima, Japan, 7.74

1932   1. Edward Gordon, USA, 7.64
        2. C. Lambert Redd, USA, 7.60
        3. Chuhei Nambu, Japan, 7.45
1928   1. Edward Hamm, USA, 7.73 (OR)
        2. Silvio Cator, Haiti, 7.58
        3. Alfred Bates, USA, 7.40
1924   1. William DeHart Hubbard, USA, 7.445
        2. Edward Gourdin, USA, 7.275
        3. Sverre Hansen, Norway, 7.26
1920   1. William Petersson, Sweden, 7.15
        2. Carl Johnson, USA, 7.095
        3. Eric Abrahamsson, Sweden, 7.08
1912   1. Albert Gutterson, USA, 7.60 (OR)
        2. Calvin Bricker, Canada, 7.21
        3. Georg Aberg, Sweden, 7.18
1908   1. Francis Irons, USA, 7.48 (OR)
        2. Daniel Kelly, USA, 7.09
        3. Calvin Bricker, Canada, 7.085
1906   1. Meyer Prinstein, USA, 7.20
        2. Peter O'Connor, Great Britain/Ireland, 7.025
        3. Hugo Friend, USA, 6.96
1904   1. Meyer Prinstein, USA, 7.34 (OR)
        2. Daniel Frank, USA, 6.89
        3. Robert Stangland, USA, 6.88
1900   1. Alvin Kraenzlein, USA, 7.185 (OR)
        2. Meyer Prinstein, USA, 7.175
        3. Patrick Leahy, Great Britain/Ireland, 6.95
1896   1. Ellery Clark, USA, 6.35
        2. Robert Garrett, USA, 6.18
        3. James Connolly, USA, 6.11

Track and Field — Men's Triple Jump

1988   1. Hristo Markov, Bulgaria, 17.61
        2. Igor Lapchine, Soviet Union, 17.52
        3. Alexandre Kovalenko, Soviet Union, 17.42
1984   1. Al Joyner, USA, 17.26
        2. Mike Conley, USA, 17.18
        3. Keith Connor, Great Britain, 16.87
1980   1. Jaak Uudmae, Soviet Union, 17.35
        2. Viktor Saneyev, Soviet Union, 17.24
        3. Joao Carlos de Oliveira, Brazil, 17.22
1976   1. Viktor Saneyev, Soviet Union, 17.29
        2. James Butts, USA, 17.18
        3. Joao Carlos de Oliveira, Brazil, 16.90
1972   1. Viktor Saneyev, Soviet Union, 17.35
        2. Jorg Drehmel, East Germany, 17.31
        3. Nelson Prudencio, Brazil, 17.05
1968   1. Viktor Saneyev, Soviet Union, 17.39 (WR)
        2. Nelson Prudencio, Brazil, 17.27
        3. Giuseppe Gentile, Italy, 17.22
1964   1. Jozef Schmidt, Poland, 16.85 (OR)
        2. Oleg Fyedoseyev, Soviet Union, 16.58
        3. Viktor Kravchenko, Soviet Union, 16.57
1960   1. Jozef Schmidt, Poland, 16.81
        2. Vladimir Goryayev, Soviet Union, 16.63
        3. Vitold Kreyer, Soviet Union, 16.43
1956   1. Adhemar Ferreira da Silva, Brazil, 16.35 (OR)
        2. Vilhjalmur Einarsson, Iceland, 16.26
        3. Vitold Kreyer, Soviet Union, 16.02
1952   1. Adhemar Ferreira da Silva, Brazil, 16.22 (WR)

490

2. Leonid Sherbakov, Soviet Union, 15.98
3. Arnoldo Devonish, Venezuela, 15.52
1948 1. Arne Ahman, Sweden, 15.40
2. George Avery, Australia, 15.365
3. Ruhi Sarialp, Turkey, 15.025
1936 1. Naoto Tajima, Japan, 16.00 (WR)
2. Masao Harada, Japan, 15.66
3. John Metcalfe, Australia, 15.50
1932 1. Chuhei Nambu, Japan, 15.72 (WR)
2. Erik Svensson, Sweden, 15.32
3. Kenkichi Oshima, Japan, 15.12
1928 1. Mikio Oda, Japan, 15.21
2. Levi Casey, USA, 15.17
3. Vilho Tuulos, Finland, 15.11
1924 1. Anthony Winter, Australia, 15,525 (WR)
2. Luis Bruneto, Argentina, 15.425
3. Vilho Tuulos, Finland, 15.37
1920 1. Vilho Tuulos, Finland, 14.505
2. Folke Jansson, Sweden, 14.48
3. Eric Almlof, Sweden, 14.27
1912 1. Gustaf Lindblom, Sweden, 14.76

2. Georg Aberg, Sweden, 14.51
3. Eric Almlof, Sweden, 14.17
1908 1. Timothy Ahearne, Great Britain/Ireland, 14.92 (OR)
2. J. Garfield MacDonald, Canada, 14.76
3. Edvard Larsen, Norway, 14.395
1906 1. Peter O'Connor, Great Britain/Ireland, 14.075
2. Con Leahy, Great Britain/Ireland, 13.98
3. Thomas Cronan, USA, 13.70
1904 1. Meyer Prinstein, USA, 14.35
2. Frederick Englehardt, USA, 13.90
3. Robert Stangland, USA, 13.365
1900 1. Meyer Prinstein, USA, 14.47 (OR)
2. James Connolly, USA, 13.97
3. Lewis P. Sheldon, USA, 13.64
1896 1. James Connolly, USA, 13.71
2. Alexandre Tuffere, France, 12.70
3. Ioannis Persakis, Greece, 12.52

WOMEN'S JUMPING EVENTS

▼

HIGHLIGHTS

High jump: Not until Amsterdam in 1928 were women permitted to compete in jumping events at the Games; the high jump was added to the women's program in 1928, but the long jump would not be added for another two decades. The first women's high jump gold was awarded to Canadian Ethel Catherwood, aka "The Saskatoon Lily," who was an eighteen-year-old beauty known for facing the bar smiling before she launched a successful jump. Asked whether she would pursue a career in Tinseltown, she responded, "I'd rather gulp poison than try my hand at motion pictures."

American Mildred "Babe" Didriksen—later known for her golfing prowess as Babe Zaharias—captured a unique assortment of medals in 1932 when she won the silver for the high jump, in addition to golds in the 80m hurdles and javelin. Both she and fellow American Jean Shiley jumped 5ft, 5.25in—after already having tied in the LA Olympic trials—at which point the judges ruled her technique illegal. The rule that penalized her "diving" technique in the high jump—which relegated her to second place—was rescinded in 1937. While Babe had to settle for the silver medal, she was recognized in the world record.

While Ibolya Csák of Hungary was awarded the 1936 gold medal, Great Britain's Dorothy Odam—who had matched her jump—was forced to settle for second place after a jump-off. Had current tie-breaking rules been applied, the 16-year-old Odam would have taken the gold. Germany's Dora Ratjen placed fourth

491

in the 1936 high jump but was barred from further competition in 1938, when she was discovered to be the wrong gender.

The odds were against Dorothy Odam—now Dorothy Tyler—again in the 1948 London Games when she lost a tie with Alice Coachman, even though she had fewer misses. Coachman, the first black woman to win an Olympic gold, shared an Olympic record with Tyler. That same year, French concert pianist Micheline Ostermeyer added a bronze in the high jump to her golds in the discus and shot in 1948.

After placing fifth in Melbourne, Rumanian Iolanda Balas leapt over the competition in Rome in 1960 by jumping an Olympic record-setting 6ft, 0.75in. The first woman to jump over 6 feet, Balas set 14 world records in the following ten and a half years. The year after the Rome Games, Balas bounded 6ft, 3.25in, a benchmark that wouldn't be approached for another decade.

When Ulrike Meyfarth of West Germany won the high jump in 1972, she became the youngest Olympic individual event champion. Jumping 2.75 inches higher than she ever had, Meyfarth equaled the world record at Munich.

In Montréal, Meyfarth, along with three other women who had 6ft, 3in jumps in their repertoire, were eliminated from the qualifying rounds. Three hours into the competition, eighteen women had jumped six feet—a feat that hadn't been achieved before 1960. Rosemarie Ackermann, from East Germany, won the gold, becoming the first woman to jump two meters over her own height.

Jumping just shy of an inch less than she had in Montréal, Ackermann managed only to place fourth in Moscow, where Italian Sara Simeoni earned a gold with an Olympic record-breaking jump of 6ft, 5.5in. Shortly before the Games, Soviet Marina Sysoyeva had reset the women's world record for jumping over one's height, setting the mark at 10.25 inches.

For the first time since 1956, the US was in the money when Joni Huntley captured a bronze medal in 1984; Sara Simeoni of Italy took the silver, while West Germany's Ulrike Mayfarth set an Olympic record for first place. Finally, in Seoul, American women took home another gold medal when Louise Ritter re-set the Olympic record. Also that year, Bulgarian Stefka Kostavinova captured the silver, while Soviet Tamara Bykova won the bronze.

Long jump: When women were finally permitted to compete in the Olympics in the long jump in 1948, the number of events in which they were allowed to compete at a single Games was still limited. So Fanny Blankers-Koen, the German world-record holder in the long jump, competed in other events at the London Games. 1948's winner, Hungarian Olga Gyarmati, jumped 18ft, 8.25in—almost two feet shy of Blankers-Koen's world record.

New Zealand's Yvette Williams set a new Olympic record—still considerably shy of the Blankers-Koen's world record—at 20ft, 5.75in. The second place finisher, Soviet Aleksandra Chudina, also took the silver in the javelin, and the bronze in the high jump.

Willye White was the first American woman to medal in the long jump, winning the silver medal at the 1956 Melbourne Games with a jump of 19ft,

11.75in. Jumping more than a foot farther than White, Poland's Elzbieta Krzesinska set a new world record at 20ft, 10in. Her record was bested in Rome, where she managed only a 20ft, 7in jump for second place; Soviet Vyera Krepkina set a new Olympic record at 20ft, 10.75in, earning the gold but falling shy of the new women's world record of 21ft. Still not bad for someone better known as a sprinter: Krepkina was the co-holder of the women's world record for the 100m.

Until 1964, no British woman had ever won an Olympic gold medal in track and field. Great Britain's Mary Rand, however, left Tokyo with the long jump gold medal—not to mention a pentathlon silver and a 4 x 100m relay bronze. Jumping into a 1.69m-per-second wind, Rand managed to break the world record with a 22ft, 2.25in flight.

That was far, but not far enough to stand through the next Olympiad, in which Romanian Viorica Viscopoleanu added another 2.25in to the world record, easily winning the gold medal with her 22ft, 4.5 in jump—nine inches better than she had ever jumped. Behind her, Sheila Sherwood won another medal for Great Britain, taking a silver for her 21ft, 11in jump.

The Munich crowds jumped for joy when Heidemarie Rosendahl leapt for the host country's first gold medal of 1972; Rosendahl tripled her medal haul later in Munich with a pentathlon silver and a 4 x 100m relay gold. In second place that year, Diana Yorgova won Bulgaria's first track and field medal.

The US earned its second women's long jump medal in 1976 when Kathy McMillan earned the silver with a 21ft, 10.25in leap; East Germany's Angela Voigt won the gold that year. The 1980 Olympic long jump competition provided quite an upset when the third-string Soviet jumper, Tatiana Kolpakova, bested her compatriots—not to mention herself—by setting a new Olympic record of 23ft, 2in—nine inches further than she had ever jumped.

1984 proved to be a good year for the Romanian women, who stole both first and second place, while Great Britain's Susan Hearnshaw captured the bronze. And finally, in Seoul, the Joyner name appeared again on Olympic records, this time when Jackie Joyner-Kersee—Florence Griffith Joyner's sister-in-law and Al Joyner's sister—set a new Olympic benchmark to win the gold, while East Germans Heike Drechsler and Galina Tchistiakova trailed in second and third place.

Track and Field (Athletics)—Jumping

Track and Field — Women's High Jump

1988 1. Louise Ritter, USA, 2.03 (OR)
2. Stefka Kostavinova, Bulgaria, 2.01
3. Tamara Bykova, Soviet Union, 1.99
1984 1. Ulrike Mayfarth, West Germany, 2.02 (OR)
2. Sara Simeoni, Italy, 2.00

3. Joni Huntley, USA, 1.97
1980 1. Sara Simeoni, Italy, 1.97 (OR)
2. Urszula Kielan, Poland, 1.94
3. Jutta Kirst, East Germany, 1.94
1976 1. Rosemarie Ackermann, East Germany, 1.93 (OR)
2. Sara Simeoni, Italy, 1.91
3. Yordanka Blagoyeva, Bulgaria, 1.91

493

1972	1. Ulrike Meyfarth, West Germany, 1.92 (EWR)
	2. Yordanka Blagoyeva, Bulgaria, 1.88
	3. Ilona Gusenbauer, Austria, 1.88
1968	1. Miloslava Rezkova, Czechoslovakia, 1.82
	2. Antonina Okorokova, Soviet Union, 1.80
	3. Valentina Kozyr, Soviet Union, 1.80
1964	1. Iolanda Balas, Romania, 1.90 (OR)
	2. Michele Brown-Mason, Australia, 1.80
	3. Taisiya Chenchik, Soviet Union, 1.78
1960	1. Iolanda Balas, Romania, 1.85
	2. Jaroslawa Jozwiakowska, Poland, 1.71
	2. Dorothy Shirley, Great Britain, 1.71
1956	1. Mildred McDaniel, USA, 1.76 (WR)
	2. Thelma Hopkins, Great Britain, 1.67
	2. Maria Pissaryeva, Soviet Union, 1.67
1952	1. Esther Brand, South Africa, 1.67
	2. Sheila Lerwill, Great Britain, 1.65
	3. Aleksandra Chudina, Soviet Union, 1.63
1948	1. Alice Coachman, USA, 1.68 (OR)
	2. Dorothy Tyler-Odam, Great Britain, 1.68 (OR)
	3. Micheline Ostermeyer, France, 1.61
1936	1. Ibolya Csak, Hungary, 1.60
	2. Dorothy Odam, Great Britain, 1.60
	3. Elfriede Kaun, Germany, 1.60
1932	1. Jean Shiley, USA, 1.657 (WR)
	2. Mildred "Babe" Didrikson, USA, 1.657 (WR)
	3. Eva Dawes, Canada, 1.60
1928	1. Ethel Catherwood, Canada, 1.59
	2. Carolina Gisolf, Netherlands, 1.56
	3. Mildred Wiley, USA, 1.56
1896–1924	Not held

Track and Field — Women's Long Jump

1988	1. Jackie Joyner-Kersee, USA, 7.40 (OR)
	2. Heike Drechsler, East Germany, 7.22
	3. Galina Tchistiakova, Soviet Union, 7.11
1984	1. Anisoara Cusmir-Stanciu, Romania, 6.96
	2. Vali Ionescu, Romania, 6.81
	3. Susan Hearnshaw, Great Britain, 6.80
1980	1. Tatiana Kolpakova, Soviet Union, 7.06 (OR)
	2. Brigitte Wujak, East Germany, 7.04
	3. Tatiana Skachko, Soviet Union, 7.01
1976	1. Angela Voigt, East Germany, 6.72
	2. Kathy McMillan, USA, 6.66
	3. Lydia Alfeyeva, Soviet Union, 6.60
1972	1. Heidemarie Rosendahl, West Germany, 6.78
	2. Diana Jorgova, Bulgaria, 6.77
	3. Eva Suranova, Czechoslovakia, 6.67
1968	1. Viorica Viscopoleanu, Romania, 6.82 (WR)
	2. Sheila Sherwood, Great Britain, 6.68
	3. Tatyana Talisheva, Soviet Union, 6.66
1964	1. Mary Rand, Great Britain, 6.76 (WR)
	2. Irena Kirszenstein, Poland, 6.60
	3. Tatyana Schelkanova, Soviet Union, 6.42
1960	1. Vyera Krepkina, Soviet Union, 6.37 (OR)
	2. Elzbieta Krzesinska, Poland, 6.27
	3. Hildrun Claus, East Germany, 6.21
1956	1. Elzbieta Krzesinska, Poland, 6.35 (EWR)
	2. Willye White, USA, 6.09
	3. Nadezhda Dvalischvili, Soviet Union, 6.07
1952	1. Yvette Williams, New Zealand, 6.24 (OR)
	2. Aleksandra Chudina, Soviet Union, 6.14
	3. Shirley Cawley, Great Britain, 5.92
1948	1. Olga Gyarmati, Hungary, 5.695
	2. Noemi Simonetto De Portela, Argentina, 5.60
	3. Ann-Britt Leyman, Sweden, 5.575
1896–1936	Not held

TRACK AND FIELD (ATHLETICS)— RUNNING

WARM-UP

The games of ancient Greece, held at Olympia in Peloponnesus every four years, began with running races, drawing contestants and spectators from surrounding city-states. For variety, the Greeks occasionally required the runners to dress in infantry armor and compete over a two-stadium course, though this was later modified so runners carried only a soldier's shield.

The first recorded Olympic champion was named Coroebus, a sprinter who competed in 776 BC and won the stadion, a race run over a course of 630 feet (about 193 meters).

A few centuries later, in 394 AD, the Olympic Games were banned as unchristian, and little record survives of formal running contests for the next 800 years. Undoubtedly, though, a few heathens managed to sneak in some clandestine contests, and soldiers probably continued to compete in races to test speed and endurance.

fact: In 1932, Volmari Iso-Hollo of Finland won the 3000m steeplechase with a time of 10:33.4, even though it was later discovered he ran an extra lap because of a lap counter's error. Four years later he won another gold medal in the same event with a time of 9:03.8.

Track and field as a sport was revived in England in the 12th century, and much later—in 1871—the first modern athletic club was formed in Suffolk, England. The first college track meet had already taken place in 1864, pitting Oxford versus Cambridge.

Some English athletic enthusiasts set minimum standards for athletes in 1834, which included a five-minute mile and a 10-minute, two-mile run.

The first Greek tracks were banked and earthen, probably with holes in the ground for blocks. In longer races, runners turned around a pillar at the halfway mark before heading for the finish line.

The first English running tracks were turnpike roads or horse racing tracks. These running tracks eventually became circular and were made of cinder. England boasted more running tracks than all of Europe combined by 1896, and it was an Englishman who designed the track at Athens used in the first modern Olympics held that year.

The 1896 Olympic Games included 100m, 400m, 800m, and 1500m runs, the 110m hurdle event, and a marathon. Though not part of the ancient Games, the marathon commemorates the 25-mile run by Greek soldier and Olympic star Pheidippides. He'd run from Marathon to Athens with news of the Athenian victory over the Persians. "Rejoice, we conquer," he announced. Then, according to legend, he fell over dead.

The conquering Athenians rejoiced following the 1896 Olympic marathon as well—along with the winner himself, Spyridon Louis, whose post-race fate was much less dire than that of Pheidippides. As Louis entered the stadium on the final lap, Greek princes Constantine and George ran from their seats to the track to accompany him.

It was not until 1924 that Olympic Games organizers allowed women to compete in track and field events. (Until then, swimming and tennis were the only women's events.) Five events were added that year: 100m and 800m runs, high jump, discus, and 4 x 100m relay.

Controversy, emerged though, over the 800m race. The distance was considered dangerously long for women. A 17-year-old German, Lina Radke, won in just over two minutes, but several racers collapsed during the race and Olympic officials banned the race from future games. Amazingly, the ban lasted 36 years.

fact: In 1932, Stella Walasiewicz won the women's 100m gold, but a 1980 autopsy found her to have male characteristics. Her world record time of 11.9 stood until 1952.

The women's 800m did not return until Rome in 1960, and its absence may have slowed the development of women distance runners. More recently, a women's 10,000m was added in 1988, and the marathon in 1984.

The winning time in the 100 meters in 1896 was 12 seconds. World record time is now about 9.9 seconds. Runners are stronger, faster, and better conditioned, and their track equipment is better. Starting blocks have replaced holes dug in the ground for sprinters. Racing spikes are lighter, and times are recorded electronically. The synthetic track surface, first featured in the 1968 Olympics, is more consistent than cinder and helps yield better running times.

Called Tartan, the surface was originally developed for racehorse training during inclimate weather.

▼

SPECTATORS' GUIDE

Races begin at the sound of a starter's pistol. When runners are ready, the starter calls, "On your marks." In races of 400m or less, the starter calls, "Set." Then the pistol fires. A runner who jumps the gun causes a false start, and two false starts disqualify a runner.

Runners in races over one lap are notified of the last lap by a bell. A runner finishes when any part of the body other than the head or limbs crosses the vertical plane of the finish line.

Weather affects both the runner and the race. In sprints, warm weather is preferable to cold because it keeps muscles looser. Hot weather can add to the difficulties of a marathon runner. A sprint race is considered wind-aided if the breeze blows at the competitors' backs at more than two meters per second.

Sprints: A sprint is a race run at full speed over a short distance, such as the 100m and 200m dashes. A quick start is as important as speed in running a successful race. Before the race begins, runners set their feet against metal starting blocks in a kneeling position. They raise their knees at the "Set" command. When the gun sounds, they push off hard and lengthen their strides as they reach full speed. Runners generally lean into the finish line to try to gain an advantage on competitors.

The 200 meters features a staggered start. Runners start several meters apart in adjoining lanes to compensate for running around a curve. Most sprinters prefer the middle lanes, which keep them away from the tighter turn of inside lanes while allowing them to see opponents. The larger the runner physically, the more likely she is to prefer a lane toward the outside, where turns aren't as sharp to negotiate.

Middle distance events: For these 400m, 800m, and 1500m races, runners must have speed and endurance. The 400m features a staggered start, and runners go one lap around the track, remaining in their assigned lanes for the entire race. Runners must set their own pace rather than marking their speed against a competitor's.

The 800m and 1500m involve kick, or speed, versus steady-pace tactics. Jim Ryun preferred to finish strong. But Filbert Bayi began to change the style of middle distance running by setting a very fast pace early, then holding on with amazing strength. The increased strength of Bayi and others, like Alberto Juantorena of Cuba, have begun to make 800m similar to the 400m—more like a sprint than a middle distance run. These improved runners don't wait around for a strong finishing kick; they start early.

In the 800m, runners circle the track twice and must stay in their lanes for the first half-lap. Thereafter, runners converge in a pack. Position becomes important because every inch or centimeter from the inside curve adds distance to the race. In 1968, American Lee Evans set a record in this event, 43.86, which lasted 10 years.

In 1960, New Zealander David Snell's training regimen began to be widely copied after he won the 800m despite relative inexperience. Under coach Arthur Lydiard, Snell ran 100 miles a week. This was considered revolutionary. Until then, middle distance training consisted of a series of much shorter runs. The new methods helped improve both middle distance and distance performances.

The 1500m is 110 meters or 120 yards shorter than a mile. Roger Bannister's sub-four-minute mile preceded several other runners' equally barrier-breaking performances in the 1500m race.

Distance events: Women compete in a 3000m run, men compete in a 5000m run, and both compete in the 10,000m event. The 10,000m, which is equal to 6.2 miles, has been a men's event since at least the 1920s but only became a women's Olympic event in 1988.

In longer distances like the 10,000m, unnecessary motion is avoided. Knee action is slight, arm movements are reduced to a comfortable minimum, and strides are much shorter than those used by sprinters or middle distance runners. When in full stride, the distance runner lands on the ball of his or her foot, lowers the heel briefly, then drives forward off the toes.

Dominant runners are able to shatter their opponents with sudden bursts of speed at various stages of the race. They can run an extremely fast lap, then cruise for a while, then run another fast lap, while still holding back strength for a finishing kick.

Marathon: This is the longest Olympic running race, 26 miles, 385 yards. It is one of the most grueling as well. The race starts and finishes inside the stadium. In between, it is a road race and runners must contend with hills and concrete rather than a consistent, flat oval track.

Though the first women's Olympic marathon didn't take place until 1984, the first men's marathon was in 1896, from the Greek city of Marathon to Athens. Twelve years later, at the Games in London, the race's distance was extended slightly so British royalty could watch the start in front of Windsor Castle.

The marathon requires competitors to run hard when necessary while conserving strength for any possible difficulties ahead. As in all distance races, pace is important. Runners must also be able to ascend hills with efficient strides, and descend them evenly.

Weather can be a factor. Some runners can handle warm temperatures, or cool ones, better than others. But a temperature above 70 degrees Farenheit is considered difficult on any runner.

Steeplechase: This challenging event covers 3000 meters. Runners must contend with a course full of obstacles, among them 28 hurdles and seven water jumps. The hurdles are three feet (91.4cm) high and solid—they can't be knocked over. The top surface of the hurdles is five inches wide so runners can step on them, though most do not. The water jumps are preceded by a hurdle. Beyond the hurdle is a pool of water 12 feet (3.7m) square and, at the deepest point closest to the hurdle, 27 inches (70cm) deep. The bottom of the pool slopes up, and runners often use the water's surface to soften their landings.

Steeplechasers are distance runners and, because of the uniqueness of the event, specialists. They generally don't compete in other events, though there have been exceptions. The Finn Ville Ritola and the Kenyan Kip Keino, both runners but novice steeplechasers, won the event in 1924 and 1972, respectively.

Hurdles: These are basically sprint races made tougher with a series of barriers. Women run the 100m and 400m hurdles, the latter only since 1984. The hurdles stand two feet, nine inches in the shorter race and two feet, six inches in the longer. For men, the barriers stand three feet in the 400m, and three feet, six inches in the 110m.

Hurdlers start their race like sprinters, getting up to speed as quickly as possible. In approaching a hurdle they jump and lean forward, trying to clear the barrier without breaking their running stride. The first leg over the hurdle hits the ground sharply while the second clears the hurdle at almost a rightangle to the body. Runners are not penalized for pushing over hurdles, though contact with the uprights often slows them. There are 10 hurdles in each race. High hurdlers take three steps between, and runners in the 400m take 13 to 15, the longer the stride the better. It takes dexterity and great timing to be a hurdler, and not all sprinters are successful hurdlers.

The hurdles themselves are made of wood and metal, and they can be knocked over with a force of eight pounds (four kilograms).

Track and Field (Athletics)—Running

Relays: Track teams are often made up of sprinters and middle distance runners who can also run relays or the hurdles. So countries with medal-winning sprinters will often field a strong relay team as well. The events for both men and women are the 4 x 100 meters and the 4 x 400 meters.

Four runners make up a relay team, and each runs a leg, a quarter of the race's distance. When each runner finishes a leg, he or she passes a hollow tube called the baton to the next runner. A key to winning a relay race is an efficient and effective baton passage. The two runners must exchange the baton within a passing zone, and the team is disqualified if the exchange takes place outside the zone, or for failing to carry the baton across the finish line.

Ideally, the baton passer and baton receiver should be in full stride when the hand-off takes place. The receiver needs to reach full speed quickly. Typically, the receiver will be facing forward with his or her hand outstretched behind. Though speed is important, a team skilled in passing the baton can often beat a faster team that exchanges poorly.

Walking: This is one of the most unheralded of Olympic track events. It makes for an unusual spectacle as well, with men swaying down the street, seemingly half-walking and half-running, shoulders pumping and hips rolling.

There is a reason for this display, of course. It is to prove the competitors are walking and not running, the latter being faster but illegal. The rules require the walker's front foot to touch the ground before his rear foot leaves the ground. Also, while the foot is on the ground, the leg must be bent for a moment. If it is not, the walker is warned the first time, then disqualified by a judge. The offense is called "lifting."

This, then, leads to the odd form. Walking is much less popular than marathon running, but it undoubtedly takes the same endurance and stamina.

The 1908 Olympics featured a 10,000m and a 10-mile walk, and currently two walking events are staged, both for men: the 20,000m and the 50,000m walk. The 50,000m walk was dropped from the 1976 Olympics, then added again after competitors complained.

Official world records in walking races can be set only on a track. Olympic races take place on the road, so they are not eligible for world record consideration.

Walking rules are difficult to judge, and walkers are believed to have generally increased the amount of unbroken contact with the ground. Times have increased significantly over the years—20 percent during the last 40 years in the 50,000m walk, compared to about 5.5 percent in the marathon run.

HOPEFULS

Men's Events

If Sprinter Ben Johnson makes Canada's 1992 Olympic team, track fans will look forward to another showdown between Johnson and sprint champion Carl Lewis of the US. Their rivalry began in 1980 and ended—at least temporarily—at the 1988 Olympic Games, when a drug test disclosed that steroids had helped Johnson execute his record-setting gold-medal 100m dash. Johnson was banned from competition for two years, and second-place finisher Lewis was awarded the gold. Perhaps beating both of them, though, will be Americans Leroy Burrell, 1990's top 100m sprinter, and Michael Johnson, the current 200m champion.

Michael Johnson is also talented in the middle distance runs, along with fellow Americans Antonio Pettigrew, the 400m world champion, Danny Everett, an Olympic and World bronze medalist in the 400m, and Mark Everett, a World bronze medalist in the 800m. Even more promising in the longer runs, though, are world champions Billy Konchellah of Kenya in the 800m, and Noureddine Morceli of Algeria in the 1500m.

Kenya dominates the distance runs with world champs Yobes Ondieki in the 5000m and Moses Tanui in the 10,000m. In the marathon, watch for Japan's Hiromi Taniguchi, who completed the Tokyo World marathon nearly half a minute ahead of silver medalist Ahmed Salah of Djibouti and bronze medalist Steve Spence of the USA.

After reaching the silver medal in the 1984 Olympics but missing the 1988 Games due to injury, USA's three-time world hurdling champion Greg Foster wants to run for a 110m gold in 1992. His main US competitor, Roger Kingdom, won the Olympic gold in both 1984 and 1988 but may try the decathlon in 1992. In the 400m hurdle, Zambia's world champion Samuel Matete, Jamaica's Winthrop Graham, and Great Britain's Kriss Akabussi look promising.

Ben Johnson

From 1985 until 1988, Ben Johnson dominated in the 100m sprint. He was proclaimed the fastest man on earth and was hailed as Canada's finest athlete. His confession to steroid use soon after he was caught abusing at the 1988 Games came as a blow to track fans worldwide.

Yet no athlete cherishes higher hopes of making the 1992 Olympic Games than Ben Johnson. The Canadian sprinter feels he has to rescue his reputation, tarnished by the discovery that steroid use had contributed to his record-setting gold medal victory in Seoul.

Maclean's contributor Bob Levin writes: "[Johnson] was a rocket, a role model, a national hero. . . . To Canadians, he was never Johnson, just Ben. . . . But when the steroid scandal burst upon the world, . . . Canadians, who had risen

501

as one to applaud Johnson's triumph, doubled over in sickened disbelief, taking Johnson's humiliation as their own. Children wept openly. Many people clutched at faint hopes of some innocent explanation. Others branded Ben a betrayer, a cheat." Small wonder that Johnson has spent the ensuing years crusading against drug use and predicting that he will return and win sprints without the help of drugs.

A native of Falmouth, Jamaica, Johnson was born December 30, 1961. The fifth of six children, he spent his early years running and swimming in the ocean. Inflicted with a speech impediment, he was an average student in Jamaican schools. His interests lay elsewhere, with the local track clubs to which his older brothers belonged.

In 1972 Johnson's mother moved her family to a two-bedroom flat in suburban Toronto, hoping her younger children could get a better education in Canada. The move was difficult for Johnson, who not only stuttered but could hardly speak English. Nevertheless, he managed to graduate from Yorkdale High. In 1977 he joined the Scarborough (now Mazda) Optimist Track Club, where he was coached by Charles Francis, a former Olympic sprinter. Under Francis's eye, Johnson gained forty-three pounds and six inches of height in only six months— and he became a formidable runner as well.

Johnson encountered American Carl Lewis for the first time during the 1980 Pan-American Junior Championships. Lewis beat Johnson on that occasion, and a bitter rivalry ensued between the two runners. Johnson determined to become better than Lewis, and the Canadian was bitterly disappointed when Lewis won four gold medals in the 1984 Olympics. Johnson had to settle for two bronze medals at Los Angeles, but he vowed to improve—and he did.

A year later, Johnson won the 100m dash at the World Championships. At the 1986 Goodwill Games in Moscow he won again, setting a record with a 9.95-second time. The following year he was an undisputed champion with four indoor world records and a stunning 9.83-second finish in the outdoor World Championships in Rome. He came to the 1988 Olympics in Seoul heavily favored to win the 100m race.

And win he did, amazing everyone with a time of 9.79 seconds. The joy of victory was extremely short-lived, however. In a post-race test, traces of the drug stanozolol appeared in his urine. In the worst scandal in Olympic history, Johnson was stripped of his medal (it went to Lewis, who finished second) and was suspended from competition for two years by the International Amateur Athletic Federation.

Johnson denied any steroid use until coach Francis testified about it in court. Then the athlete admitted that he had been taking drugs since 1981. The scandal brought financial ruin and personal humiliation, but Johnson vowed to make a clean comeback. "Whatever I lost doesn't mean a thing," he told the *Philadelphia Inquirer.* "My health is the most important thing. If I had kept taking [steroids], I could have had side effects with my liver."

Visibly smaller and thinner than he was in 1988, Johnson has been racing regularly since his re-instatement in 1990. He desperately wants to make the Canadian team in 1992, feeling he has a great deal to prove to his adopted country and to himself. "People won't forget," he told the *Chicago Tribune*, "but they're going to say, 'Great. After his downfall, the guy took care of his problems and won again.' That will be the biggest thrill of my life." *—M.K.*

Women's Events

The women's marathon should yield an exciting outcome in 1992. Two veteran Olympians plan to run this event for the first time, two Olympic medalists hope to defend their titles, and the current world champion would like to prove herself in Olympic competition as well.

American Francie Larrieu Smith, now almost forty years old, was once the best middle-distance runner in the country and in 1990 became America's best marathon runner. Though she still runs 10,000m distance races as well, Larrieu Smith believes her finest Olympic performance would be in the marathon.

After dominating sprints in 1988 with Olympic golds in the 100m dash, 200m run, and 400m relay, Florence Griffith Joyner began training for the marathon. She and Larrieu Smith would have to outrun Portugal's defending champion Rosa Mota, though, as well as Germany's bronze medalist Katrin Dörre and Poland's Wanda Panfil, who won the event at the Tokyo World competition.

Joyner's absence from the sprints could allow fellow American Evelyn Ashford to reclaim her Olympic title in the 100m dash, which she lost to Joyner in 1988. Germany's Heike Drechsler, who also competes against Joyner's sister-in-law Jackie in the long jump, could advance her 1988 third-place standing. And another German, Katrin Krabbe, became champion of both the 100m and 200m sprints at the Tokyo World games in 1991 and hopes to match that achievement at Barcelona.

USA's Mary Decker Slaney, one of the world's best—and unluckiest—middle distance runners since the 1970s, still hasn't won in the Olympics. After several operations for Achilles tendon and other leg injuries, Decker Slaney continues to hope for an Olympic medal. To earn one in 1992, though, she'll have to compete against world champions Marie-Josée Perec of France, Soviet Lilia Nurutdinova, and Algerian Hassiba Boulmerka.

Kenyan women are showing promise in the distance events, with 1988 Olympian Susan Sirma finishing third in the 3000m at the 1991 World Competitions and Delillah Asiago winning 10-kilometer road races—including the Bolder Boulder and Advil Women's Mini-Marathon in New York City—the same year. World champions Tatyana Dorovskikh of the Soviet Union and Liz McColgan of Great Britain, though, will be tough to beat.

Soviet 400m hurdler Tatyana Ledovskaya, an Olympic silver medalist in 1988, became the world champion in 1991 and hopes to reach the Olympic championship next. And another Soviet, Lyudmila Narozhilenko, won the 100m world championship at Tokyo and will try for the Olympic title in 1992.

503

Francie Larrieu Smith

Once considered the greatest middle-distance runner in American history, Francie Larrieu Smith may make a mark yet again at the Olympic Games in 1992.

Larrieu Smith, who is very near the age of 40, relatively ancient by Olympics standards, has made three previous Olympic teams, won 22 national championships in track, cross country, and road racing, and set 17 outdoor American track records. Most remarkably, she set her first record in 1969 at the age of 16 and turned in her most recent record—at 10,000 meters—in April of 1991. If she makes the 1992 American Olympic team, she will tie Al Oerter's record for participation in Olympic Games.

Youth is a very valuable commodity in athletics. Larrieu Smith knows that many observers had written her off in the 1980s after the appearance of Mary Decker Slaney and a number of other younger runners. Larrieu Smith has almost literally found a second wind with a new coach, Robert Vaughan, and a new event—the marathon.

Still a powerhouse at 10,000 meters, the athlete has recently begun running select marathons as well. In 1990 she became the top-ranked American woman for the marathon, after a second-place finish in London behind Rosa Mota, the defending Olympic women's champion. "I really, truly believe that if I have any chance in the Olympics, it's probably in the marathon," says Larrieu Smith.

Larrieu Smith can hardly remember a time when she was not obsessed with running. Born November 23, 1952, in the San Francisco Bay area, she was part of a large, extremely athletic family. When she was 12, her brother Ron ran the 10,000m race in the Tokyo Olympics. Watching him only deepened her determination to do the same thing.

As a teenager, she trained single-mindedly with the Santa Clara Club and later with the San Jose Cindergals, while finishing school at Fremont High in Sunnyvale, California. At the tender age of 16 she found herself in Europe, running in a four-woman 1500m race against three veterans, including the world record holder. She finished third, tying the American record. "I was learning to believe in myself and my capabilities," she recalls.

Larrieu Smith made her first Olympic team in 1972 and was the youngest member of the track and field squad. She failed to make the finals in her event, the 1500m, because she was "awestruck," according to a *Dallas Morning News* profile. She made the Olympic team again in 1976, but caught the flu and once again missed the finals. In 1980 she was one of the Olympians who had to sit the Games out because of a government-mandated boycott.

The Olympics were only a small part of Larrieu Smith's agenda during the 1970s. She attended the University of California, Los Angeles, and spent summers competing in middle distance races in Europe. Throughout the decade she was the top-ranked American in either the 1500m or the 3000m races no less than ten times. At various points, she held more than 30 American records.

New competition arrived in the 1980s in the form of Decker Slaney and other runners. "I was going to the starting line, and people were beating me," the athlete told *Runner's World.* "And I didn't even know their names." Larrieu Smith considered retiring, but she found her life without running to be unfocused. She married her second husband, exercise physiologist Jimmy Smith, took Vaughan as a coach, and began to consider a new career at longer distances.

She failed to make the 1984 Olympic team, but she did attend her third Olympics in 1988, finishing fifth in the 10,000m run. Remarkably, she has since become even better at 10,000 meters, setting a new American record of 31:28.9 at the 1991 Texas Relays.

As 1992 looms, Larrieu Smith says she does not consider her age an impediment. "I think I'm structurally sound," the five-foot-four inch, 104-pound athlete told *Runner's World.* "Although I look in the mirror, and I see that I'm aging, I do not in any way think of myself any differently than when I was 24 years old and chasing around Europe."

Larrieu Smith also said that winning an Olympic medal once was her highest aspiration. "It used to be all of why I ran," she admitted. "But along the road, I just fell in love with running." —*M.K.*

The Sisters-in-Law

Some families have all the luck. As if Olympic gold medals weren't hard enough to come by, sisters-in-law Florence Griffith Joyner and Jackie Joyner Kersee have five between them, among a long list of other awards, honors, and records.

Florence was born December 21, 1959, in Los Angeles, California, the daughter of Robert and Florence Griffith. In 1987 she married Jackie's brother, Al Joyner, a winner himself of the gold medal in the triple jump at the 1984 Olympics. They have one daughter, Mary Ruth.

Florence Griffith Joyner's love of running began early: she started competing in track meets at the age of seven. In high school, she set records in sprints and in the long jump and then won two NCAA titles while attending California State University, Northridge, and UCLA. Along the way, she developed a flair for unusual fashions, often wearing clothing she designed herself. At the 1984 Los Angeles Olympics, she sported six-inch-long fingernails painted red, white, and blue. She also won a silver medal in the 200m race.

But Griffith Joyner was unhappy with the second-place finish and, demoralized, went into semi-retirement, working as a customer-service representative at a bank and doing hair styling at night. Her competitive nature resurfaced, however, and she resumed training in time for the 1988 Olympics in Seoul. As she said of that period: "I had to take inventory. It was time to run better or move on."

She ran better. At Seoul "Flo-Jo," as she came to be called, took gold medals in the 100m dash and the 200m race and shared the gold medal in the 400m relay and the silver medal in the 1600m relay. She capped off 1988 by winning the Sullivan Award as the outstanding amateur athlete in the United

Track and Field (Athletics)—Running

States. Griffith Joyner is currently in training for a new event, the women's marathon, for the 1992 Olympics.

Sister-in-law Jackie Joyner-Kersee (who, in 1986, married coach Bob Kersee, now head of the track and field program at UCLA) has been called the world's greatest female athlete. She was born March 3, 1962, in East St. Louis, Illinois, daughter of Al and Mary Joyner. She, too, was a standout athlete at an early age, competing in the local track club in running and the long jump. She graduated in the top 10 percent of her high school class and entered UCLA on an athletic scholarship in 1980.

She starred on the UCLA women's basketball team, appearing as a starter for four seasons, but was steered toward concentrating on track events by Bob Kersee. In 1985, she set a collegiate record in the long jump: 22 feet, 11.25 inches. She also competed in the 400m hurdles and the triple jump, developing into perhaps the finest heptathlete in history. (The heptathlon is a seven-event contest that includes running, jumping, and throwing events.)

At the 1984 Olympics, Joyner-Kersee captured the silver medal in the heptathlon, setting a US record of 6520 points. In 1986, she scored an astounding 7148 points in the heptathlon at the Goodwill Games in Moscow, becoming the first American sportswoman ever to set a multi-event world record. For her performance she was awarded the 1986 Sullivan Award.

By the time of the 1988 Seoul Olympics, Joyner-Kersee was clearly the dominant force in her events, winning gold medals in the heptathlon and in the long jump. In 1989 Joyner-Kersee was awarded an honorary doctorate from the University of Missouri and is now, as usual, in training for the Olympics. —*P.G.*

Schedule

The tentative track and field (athletics) schedule for running events is as follows:

Friday, July 31
100m, 1st round, men
100m, 1st round, women
800m, 1st round, women
100m, 2nd round, men
100m, 2nd round, women
Marathon, women (start & finish)
800m, 1st round, men
3000m, 1st round, women
10000m, 1st round, men

Saturday, August 1
400m, 1st round, men
400m hurdles, 1st round, women
100m, semifinals, final, women
100m, semifinals, final, men

800m, 2nd round, men
800m, semifinals, women
20K walk, final, men (start & finish)
20K walk, final, women (start & finish)
10000m, 1st round, women

Sunday, August 2
110m hurdles, 1st round, men
400m, 1st round, women
110m hurdles, 2nd round, men
400m, 2nd round, men
400m hurdles, semifinals, women
800m, semifinals, men
800m, finals, women

3000m, finals, women

Monday, August 3
200m, 1st round, men
200m, 1st round, women
1500m, 1st round, men
400m hurdles, 1st round, men
110m hurdles, semifinals and
   finals, men
200m, 2nd round, women
200m 2nd round, men
400m, 2nd round, women
400m semifinal, men
10K walk, women (start and
   finish)
3000m steeplechase, 1st round,
   men
400m hurdles, finals, women
10000m finals, men

Wednesday, August 5
1500m 1st round, women
100m hurdles, 1st round, women
100m hurdles, 2nd round, women
200m semifinals and finals,
   women
200m, semifinals and finals, men
400m hurdles, semifinals, men
400m, semifinals, women
400m, finals, men
3000m steeplechase, semifinals,
   men
800m, finals, men

5000m, 1st round, men

Thursday, August 6
100m hurdles, semifinals & finals,
   women
400m, finals, women
400m hurdles, finals, men
1500m, semifinals, women
1500m, semifinals, men
5000m, semifinals, men

Friday, August 7
50k walk, men (start and finish)
4x100m, 1st round, men
4x100m, 1st round, women
4x400m, 1st round, men
4x400m, semifinals, men
4x400m, 1st round, women
4x400m, semifinals, men
3000m steeplechase, finals, men
10000m, finals, women

Saturday, August 8
4x100m, finals, women
4x100m, finals, men
1500m, finals, women
1500m, finals, men
5000m, finals, men
4x400m, finals, women
4x400m, finals, men

Sunday, August 9
Marathon, men (start & finish)

MEN'S RUNNING EVENTS

▼

HIGHLIGHTS

Sprints, 400 Meters, and Relays

Thomas Burke of the US won the first 100m race of the Modern Olympics; four years later the US came in 1–2 in the 100m, with Frank Jarvis and John Walter Tewksbury ahead of Australian Stanley Rowley; Rowley also won bronze medals in the 60m and 200m.

Tewksbury (who also medalled in the 60m sprint and two hurdle events) grabbed the 200m gold ahead of India's Norman Pritchard. US sprinter Archie

Hahn won three gold medals in 1904, including the 100m and 200m, in which he led US sweeps. Hahn later wrote the book *How to Sprint.*

Born in Ireland, Robert Kerr represented Canada in the 200m at the 1908 Games, where he ran away with the 100m bronze and the 200m gold ahead of two US sprinters. The 400m in 1908 was total chaos, resulting in protests, disqualifications, and a lone medalist. The US swept the 100m again in 1912, then took the event 1–2 in 1920; the US also took the 200m 1–2, with Charley Paddock accepting the silver behind Allen Woodring.

1924 was the Olympics of Harold Abrahams, England's storied winner in the 100m, recalled in the vivid, if not entirely accurate, film *Chariots of Fire.* Abrahams faced stiff competition in US runners Charley Paddock (the world-record holder and defending Olympic champion), Jackson Scholz, and Loren Murchison. The field was even at first, but when Abrahams pulled away for the gold, New Zealand's Arthur Porritt—who went on to serve as that country's Governor-General—took the bronze behind Scholz.

Also featured as a character in *Chariots of Fire* was the winner of the 400m in 1924, Eric Liddell, a rugby champion from Scotland who changed the way the race was run by setting out at a blistering pace for the race's first half. Liddell also won the 200m bronze in 1924; Charley Paddock was back for the 200m silver behind Jackson Scholz, and Abrahams came in sixth.

At the Amsterdam Games in 1928 Canadian Percy Williams became a national hero with his gold medals in the 100m and 200m. That year, sprinter Ray Barbuti's victory in the 400m was the only individual gold won by the US; James Ball of Canada took the 400m silver. But American sprinter Frank Wykoff won the first of his three relay gold medals in 1928; in 1936 he became the first sprinter to win gold medals in three Games.

US sprinter Eddie Tolan won double gold in 1932, setting records in the 100m and 200m. A master of the late-race spurt, US runner Ralph Metcalfe silver medalled in the 100m behind Tolan, but the finish was so close, the call could really have gone either way. The US swept the 200m, with Tolan taking the gold and Metcalfe the bronze behind George Simpson; Metcalfe may have started three of four feet too far back in his lane. Teammate Bill Carr also claimed a gold and a record in the 400m, then added another gold in the 4 x 100 relay. Carr's chief rival, Benjamin Eastman, settled for the 400m silver, and Canadian Alexander Wilson took home the bronze.

Metcalfe again took the silver in the 100m in 1936, behind an American legend. The Berlin Games of 1936, Hitler notwithstanding, belonged to US athlete Jesse Owens, who cleaned up in the 100m, the 200m, and the 4 x 100m relay, as well as the broad jump (now called the long jump). Owens's Olympic marks proved their greatness by their staying power: his 100m record lasted until 1952, his 200m record until 1956, his long jump record until 1960. Silver medalist behind Owens in the 200m was Matthew "Mack" Robinson, older brother of baseball great Jackie Robinson. British sprinter Arthur Godfrey Brown also made a good showing at the Berlin Games in the 400m and the 4 x 400m relay.

At the London Games in 1948, US hurdler Harrison Dillard entered the 100m when he failed to qualify for his main event. Dillard found inspiration in Jesse Owens, who had presented Dillard with the pair of running shoes that he wore at the Berlin Games. Dillard duly ran off with the 1948 100m gold ahead of all of the favorites, including Melvin Patton; his teammate, H. Norwood "Barney" Ewell, initially thought he had the gold, but happily settled for silver in a sportsmanlike demonstration that impressed onlookers. The third-place runner, Lloyd LaBeach, became Panama's first Olympic medalist. Patton and Ewell won 1–2 in the 200m, with LaBeach gaining another bronze for Panama. Jamaican Arthur Wint took the 400m title in 1948, ahead of his countryman, Herbert McKenley, who was favored.

McKenley repeated his silver medal in the 400m, 18 inches behind another Jamaican, and also captured a surprise silver in the 100m in 1952, when two of the favorites were unable to compete. McKenley almost ran away with the 100m gold, but a photo-finish awarded the title to American unknown Lindy Remigino. The favorite, Emmanuel McDonald Bailey of Great Britain, took the 100m bronze. The 200m at Helsinki was swept by the US, with Andrew Stanfield, W. Thane Baker, and Jamer Gathers coming in 1–2–3; Stanfield and Baker were on board for another US sweep of the 200m in 1956. That year the US took the 100m 1–2, with the bronze going to Australian champion Hector Hogan; gold medalist in the 100m and 200m in Melbourne was Bobby Morrow. The US picked up another gold in the 400m, earned by Charles Jenkins.

The US relay team was disappointed in Rome when sprinter Ray Norton messed up a baton pass; he also finished last in the sprint events he was expected to win. The 1960 100m title went to Armin Hary, the first German male to win an Olympic track gold; he was known for a "blitz start" that carried him to victory. The 200m title was captured for the ecstatic home crowd by Italian Livio Berruti. Otis Davis of the US claimed the 400m gold.

US sprinters Bob Hayes and Henry Carr made their mark at the 1964 Tokyo Games, when electronic timing was used for the first time. Hayes took the gold in the 100m, ahead of Cuba's first-time track medalist Enrique Figuerola Camue, who beat out Hayes's teammate Harry Jerome. Carr struck gold in the 200m ahead of teammate Otis Drayton and bronze medalist Edwin Roberts from Trinidad and Tobago. Injured in 1960, US runner Michael Larrabee kicked to a gold finish in the 400m.

Sprinters may have been helped by the high altitude at the Mexico City Games, setting world records in many events. Jimmy Hines took the 100m (ahead of Jamaica's Lennox Miller and US runner Charles Greene), Tommie Smith the 200m, and Lee Evans (leading a US sweep) the 400m, all in record time, all for the US. The 100m race in 1968 was the first all-black final in Olympic history.

It was also in 1968 that Smith and American bronze-medalist sprinter John Carlos, both members of the Olympic Project for Human Rights, stirred controversy when they stood barefoot on the medal podium, black-gloved fists silently raised in the black power salute. They were ousted from the Olympic Village and removed from the US team. Pre-war track star Jesse Owens initially backed the USOC in this controversy, but in 1972 reversed his support. Sports journalist Brent Musburger, then a columnist in Chicago, reportedly called Smith and Carlos "black-skinned storm troopers." Some reconciliation must have occurred over time: in 1984 John Carlos worked for the Los Angeles Olympic Organizing Committee preparing for the Summer Games.

At the Munich Games of 1972, two favored American sprinters failed to show up for their 100m trials when their coach apparently relied on the wrong time schedule. US runners Vince Matthews and Wayne Collett, after finishing 1–2 in the 400m, displayed their own variation of the civil rights demonstration by chatting and moving about on the victory stand during their medal ceremony, instead of standing at attention. The IOC instantly banned them "for life," and the US was left without enough runners to compete in the 4 x 400 relay.

Jamaica's Lennox Miller was back for the 100m bronze in 1972. That year the Soviet Union fielded its first sprinting hero, Valery Borzov, who streaked off with the gold in the 100m and the 200m events, and later married solid-gold Soviet gymnast Lyudmila Turischeva. Bronze medalist in the 200m at Munich, Pietro Mennea exposed the crowd to his jockstrap while donning his running shorts; he competed in the 200m without medalling in 1976, then came back for the gold in that event in 1980.

The Soviet Borzov was back for the 100m bronze in 1976, behind Trinidad's Hasely Crawford and Jamaican silver medalist Donald Quarrie. Quarrie took the gold in the 200m ahead of two US runners. Two US runners also finished the 400m behind Cuban runner Alberto Juantorena, who also took a gold in the 800m.

fact: Alberto Juantorena's stride measured nine feet.

Scottish sprinter Allan Wells ignored the boycott of the Moscow Games to take the 100m for Great Britain ahead of Cuba's Silvio Leonard; Wells had only begun using starting blocks that year. In the 200m Wells took the silver ahead of Jamaica's defending champ, Donald Quarrie. The 400m title was won by a Soviet unknown, Viktor Markin. In the 1980 4 x 100 relay French twins Patrick and Pascal Barré sprinted their team to a bronze medal.

In 1984 US sprinter Carl Lewis took the 100m gold ahead of teammate Sam Graddy; the bronze medalist that year was Canada's Ben Johnson. Lewis also broke Tommie Smith's 1968 Olympic record in the 200m, and that year for the fifth time the US swept the event, winning all three Olympic medals. Italy's Pietro Mennea ran the 200m for his fourth straight Olympics in 1984; defending the title he won in 1980, he placed seventh. In the 400m, the US captured the gold and bronze, leaving the silver to Gabriel Tiacoh of the Côte d'Ivoire.

fact: The only track and field world record established at the 1984 Games came in the 4 x 100 relay.

Up to 1988, no man had ever successfully defended an Olympic 100m title, and at first Carl Lewis watched as Canada's Ben Johnson crossed the finish-line ahead of him. But Lewis was ultimately to retain the 100m gold, when Johnson was disqualified for illegal drug use. Lewis finished ahead of Britain's Linford Christie; 1988 bronze medalist Calvin Smith turned in a time equal to Lewis's 1984 gold time. Lewis lost his 200m Olympic title, taking the silver medal in the 200m in Seoul behind teammate Joe DeLoach; Brazil's Robson de Silva captured the bronze. Steven Lewis led a US sweep of the 400m at Seoul.

Middle Distance, Long Distance, and Cross Country

Australian Eddie Flack won the first 800m race of the modern Games, and put together a winning sprint at the end of the 1500m to capture that event as well. British runner Alfred Tysoe captured the 800m title in 1900. Four years later the US swept the event, led by James Lightbody in a come-from-behind victory. Lightbody also led a US sweep of the 1500m.

US runner Mel Sheppard, who not long before the 1908 Games had been rejected by the New York City police as being physically unfit, won the 1500m in Olympic record time, and took the 800m in world record time. In 1912, 18-year-old American Ted Meredith won the 800m gold, just edging Sheppard, who came in for the silver; Ira Davenport completed the US 800m sweep. British runner Arnold Jackson passed the field in the 1500m in a final burst that prevented an American sweep of the event in 1912. Another British runner, Albert Hill, mined double gold in 1920 with the 800m and 1500m titles.

The first "flying Finn," Hannes Kolehmainen, flew in to the 1912 Games, where he took golds in the 5000m and the 10,000m, as well as the 8,000m cross-country. He was back in 1920 to win the marathon. But his memory is overshadowed by that of Finland's emerging legend, Paavo Nurmi, a bony man with receding hairline, high cheekbones, a sour expression or, at best, no expression at all. At the 1920 Games he was the prototype Flying Finn, winning the 10,000-meter cross-country race and the 10,000-meter track race.

In the decade between 1921 and 1931 Nurmi broke the world outdoor record 16 times at races from 1500 meters up to 20,000 meters. He won nine gold medals and three silvers in the Olympics from 1920 through 1928; he was tossed out of the 1932 Games after the Germans protested that he had taken excessive expenses the year before.

In 1924 Nurmi was at his peak, winning the 1500m, the 5000m, the 10,000m cross-country and the 3000m team races. That year Finland won every race of 1500 meters or longer, and Nurmi's teammate, Ville Ritola, ran 39,000 meters in heats and finals during one week on his way to victories in the 10,000m flat race and 3000m steeplechase, plus second-place finishes in the 5000m, the

Track and Field (Athletics)—Running

10,000 cross-country, and the 3000m team race. The 1924 800m race was won by British runner Douglas Lowe, who successfully defended his title in 1928. Nurmi won his last Olympic gold in 1928, in the 10,000.

Italy's Luigi Beccali stood out in the 1500m race in 1932, besting such notables as Glenn Cunningham of the US and Jack Lovelock of New Zealand. Canadians Alexander Wilson and Philip Edwards (who was bronze medalist in the 1500m) took the silver and bronze in the 800m in 1932 behind Britain's Thomas Hampson; Edwards defended his 800m bronze successfully in Berlin, while Beccali had to settle for bronze in the 1500m in 1936. That year's 1500m winner was New Zealand's John Lovelock.

Swedish runners finished 1–2 in the 1500m in London, while US runner Malvin Whitfield pulled ahead of Jamaica's Arthur Wint for the 800m title in 1948. The pair finished 1–2 in the half-mile in Helsinki as well, with Whitfield matching his 1948 time, and Wint bettering his.

Versatile Czech runner Emil Zátopek made his first appearance at the 1948 Games in London; he claimed the gold in the 10,000m and a silver in the 5000m. Zátopek's wife, Dana, won the women's javelin that year, making the first husband-wife double gold in track and field. Zátopek was the biggest story of the 1952 Games, claiming the gold in the 5000m, the 10,000m, and the marathon, a monumental triple.

British runner Roger Bannister competed in the 1500m at Helsinki but did not medal; the first-place finisher in that race, Josy Barthel of Luxembourg, claimed his country's first Olympic medal. Bannister was spurred by his defeat to train harder, and two years later broke the four-minute mile. The first Olympic encounter of sub-four-minute milers was staged in the 1500m at the Melbourne Games, with Ireland's Ron Delany claiming the gold.

Soviet runners exploded on the scene in 1956, and in the 5000m and 10,000m races the gold medals went to Vladimir Kuts, the first Soviet male to win a track and field gold medal. That year US runner Tom Courtney twice lost his lead in the stretch of the 800m, and regained it twice to win; he was so exhausted by the effort that he was unable to claim his medal four hours later.

The 1960 Games saw the surprise victory of New Zealand's Peter Snell in the 800m, thanks in part to a rigorous training program, then experimental, that included up to 100 miles of running per week. Silver medalling behind Snell was world record–holder Roger Moens of Belgium. In the 1500m it was Australian favorite Herb Elliott ahead of France's Michel Jazy. Snell took the 800m and the 1500m in 1964, the first runner to achieve a double gold since 1920; behind him in the 800m was Canadian William Crothers, and bronze medalist Wilson Kiprugut (claiming Kenya's first medal), while silver medalling in the 1500m was Czech Josef Odlozil.

In the 10,000m race at the Tokyo Games, favorite Ron Clark of Australia was shocked when Billy Mills of the US triumphed, coming seemingly out of nowhere. "Hell, I never heard of Mills," Clarke remarked. Tunisia's Mohamed

Gammoudi slipped ahead of Clarke for the silver that year. Another American upset came in the 5000m, where Bob Schul ran off with the gold.

Runners in the longer-distance events were handicapped by the high altitude at the Mexico City Games, where they went into oxygen deficit in the thin air. Kenya's Wilson Kiprugut was edged out of the 800m gold by Australian Ralph Doubell. US runner Jim Ryun, the dominant miler for three years prior to the Games, was done in by both thin air and shrewd teamwork on the part of Kenyans Ben Jipcho and Kip Keino during the 1500m. Jipcho, unheralded at the time, set a searing pace, with the intent of sapping Ryun's strength early, thus allowing Keino to relax during the early stages of the race, then cruise past the weary Ryun at the end. Ryun won a medal—a silver—and was hounded by the press and public, who craved more precious metal. Ryun, back for more in 1972, seemed cursed by the Olympic gods; he tripped and fell in the 1500m final at Munich, and Keino successfully defended his title.

Ryun's teammate, Rick Wohlhuter, was favored to win the 800m in 1972 but fell in his trial heat; relative unknown Dave Wottle, wearing his trademark white golf cap, showed a devastating kick to salvage the 800m gold for the US team that year, besting the favorite, Soviet Yevgeny Arzhanov. Finland's Lasse Viren ran off with double gold in the 5000m and 10,000m, in Munich, despite taking a fall early in the 10,000m final.

The Montréal Games were boycotted by African nations protesting the participation of New Zealand, who had played rugby against South Africa (during the height of apartheid). The great match-up between milers John Walker of New Zealand and Filbert Bayi of Tanzania was not to be; Walker took the 1500m gold at a dreadfully plodding pace. Lasse Viren provided excitement, mining double gold again in the 5000m and 10,000m; he even competed in the marathon, but did not medal. Cuba's massive Alberto Juantorena barreled to a unique double win in the 400m, as favorite, and the 800m, as upset.

With the absence of US athletes from the 1980 Games, the only closely watched track events were the 800m and 1500m races, where British greats Sebastian Coe and Steve Ovett at last met head on, partly because they were among a handful of British athletes who went against their government's request that they, too, boycott Moscow.

At the time, the two shared the world 1500m record and Ovett had recently broken Coe's world mile record. And an additional element was the way the two avoided each other in competition—not to mention on the sidelines. They didn't speak to each other, they were strikingly different personalities, Coe the good guy, Ovett the villain. Coe was the speed man, Ovett the strength man, so that Coe was favored in the 800m, Ovett in the 1500m. But the 800m was run first, and Ovett won. Then they ran the 1500m, and Coe won. Those two races were the emotional high point of the Moscow Games.

In 1984 Coe became the first man ever to win two Olympic 1500m races, capturing the title ahead of countryman Steve Cram. Coe also silver medaled in

Track and Field (Athletics)—Running

the 800m behind Brazil's Joaquim Cruz. Moroccan Said Aouita captured the 5000m in 1984, while Italy's Alberto Cova triumphed in the 10,000m.

Defending his 800m title, Brazil's Joaquim Cruz settled for silver behind Kenya's Paul Ereng in Seoul. Kenya's Peter Rono captured the 1500m ahead of Britain's Peter Elliott. Kenya took yet another gold in the 5000m when John Ngugi posted the winning time ahead of two Germans, but had to settle for a Kenyan bronze in the 10,000m, where Morocco's Brahim Boutaib excelled.

Marathon and Walking

At the first Games in 1896, the Greeks cheered local hero Spiridon Loues, who won his country's only track and field gold medal that year in a most fitting event, the marathon. In 1904 the apparent winner of the marathon, Fred Lorz, mentioned that he had experienced part of the race from an automobile, and the gold was awarded to US runner Tommy Hicks.

The marathon distance was standardized during the London Olympics of 1908. The English royal family wanted to watch the start of the race, and the distance from the private lawns of Windsor Castle to the Olympic stadium finish line was 26 miles, 385 yards. The marathon's distance was thus fixed.

That year the marathon was again dramatic, as 22-year-old Dorando Pietri, a candy maker from Italy, took the lead from South Africa's Charles Hefferon with some two miles remaining. Half of the field of 56 had dropped out. Boston's Johnny Hayes was in the process of catching Hefferon. Pietri triumphantly entered the stadium and then—yikes!—turned the wrong way. Suddenly the heat and the race's toll grabbed Pietri all at once. An invisible bear had jumped out of an invisible forest and landed on his back, as distance runners used to say. Pietri staggered, fell, got up, turned around, and staggered again. He fell again, only yards from the finish line. The spectators leaned forward as the action mounted, and trackside officials moved in, propping up the tiny runner as he wobbled across the finish line. Hayes, meanwhile, was striding toward the finish himself. After a lengthy discussion, officials decided Pietri had been unfairly aided across the line, giving the victory to Hayes.

The 1920 marathon title went to Hannes Kolehmainen, a triple-gold medalist in 1912. Fifty years later Czech runner Emile Zátopek also claimed a triple gold with a victory in the marathon, an event he'd never run before, as well as the 5000m and the 10,000m. For his marathon feat Zátopek became known as the Iron Czech.

Korea's great marathoner Sohn Kee Chung was forced to accept a gold medal for Japan at the Games of 1936, when Korea was under Japanese colonial rule; at age 76 he carried the Olympic flame into the stadium at the opening of the Seoul Games in 1988.

Ethiopia's Abebe Bikila ran barefoot down the Appian Way at the Rome Games of 1960, attaining the Arch of Constantine ahead of the field for a marathon gold. Bikila was back, with shoes on, to repeat for the gold in Tokyo.

Of the Americans' performances in 1972 at the Munich Games, none had the overall impact of that turned in by Frank Shorter, a Yale man who had dabbled in medical school and law school while training 20 miles a day. Shorter's marathon victory pulled an entire nation with it; television beamed almost every step back to the US, where thousands apparently decided to see how far *they* could run. And within five years, distance running became the most fashionable of American leisure-time sports. Shorter was back for the marathon silver in 1976 at the Montréal Games, and several months later began producing his own line of running gear.

In Moscow Frank Shorter's 1976 silver-medal time would have been good as gold in the marathon, an unimpressive event at the boycotted games. Portugal's Carlos Lopes was 37 when he won the gold in the marathon in 1984. He had narrowly missed a gold in the 10,000 meters in 1976 when Finland's Lasse Viren outsprinted him in the last lap. Ireland's John Treacy took the silver in 1984. The 1988 marathon title went to Gelindo Bordin of Italy, ahead of runners from Kenya and Djbouti.

The oldest track gold medalist was Tebbs Lloyd Johnson of Great Britain, who was 48 when he walked off with the 1952 gold in the 3500m walk, the only time that event was held.

Hurdles and Steeplechase

US hurdler Alvin Kraenzlein won two golds at the 1900 Games, in high and low hurdles, to add to two other golds he won in the 60m dash and the long jump. In 1904 US hurdler Harry Hillman won three golds in three hurdle events.

Lord Burghley, the sixth marquess of Exeter, won the gold medal in the 1928 Olympics in Amsterdam; he later served as a member of the IOC, turning up as a character in the film *Chariots of Fire.*

US hurdler George Saling leaped for gold in the 110m event in 1932, while teammate Glenn Hardin lost the gold by two feet in the 400m hurdles to Ireland's Robert Tisdall, who knocked over the last hurdle (and thus under the old rules could not set a record); Hardin's second-place performance was good for an Olympic record but only a silver medal.

Top-ranked US hurdler Harrison Dillard fell in his qualifying race and failed to make the US team in 1948; he competed in the 100m sprint that year instead, claiming the gold. Dillard was able to come back for his event, the 110m hurdles, in 1952 and claim that gold, too.

The hurdler to beat in 1968 was Great Britain's David Hemery, who looked like he'd invented hurdles winning the 400m event. In 1972 Uganda's John Akii-Bua set a world record in the 400m hurdles.

US hurdler Edwin Moses cruised to his first gold in the 400m hurdles at Montréal in 1976, sat out the 1980 Games, then repeated for gold in 1984.

Amadou Dia Ba of Senegal claimed the 400m silver medal in 1988, behind Andre Phillips of the US and ahead of then legendary Moses. Moses's record, set

515

in 1976, was broken by Phillips in 1988. In fact, Moses ran faster for the bronze in 1988 than he had for either of his gold medals.

In the high hurdles, Lee Calhoun of the US was the first man to win two golds in that event, in 1956 and 1960. US hurdler Roger Kingdom repeated that feat, taking the event in Los Angeles by 0.03 seconds over his teammate Greg Foster, then in 1988 setting an Olympic record, winning by an amazing three meters over the UK's Colin Jackson and US hurdler Tonie Campbell.

Steeplechase distance wasn't standardized in the early Games. At one time there was a 5000m team steeplechase, and then a 3000m team steeplechase. In 1904 US runner James Lightbody won three golds in three steeplechase events. In 1952 Russian steeplechaser Vladimir Kazantsen was leading until the last water jump of the race, when US FBI agent Horace Ashenfelter caught him and went on to win in world-record time.

Paavo Nurmi

The "Flying Finn" may be the most famous, most innovative, most stubborn runner of all time. He won nine Olympic gold medals, set 29 world records and competed in three separate Olympics: 1920, 1924, and 1928.

Nurmi legends make for some of the best Olympic lore. In Paris in 1924, "The Phantom Finn" (as he was also known) had only half an hour to rest between the finals of the 1500m and 5000m races. He won them both.

Finnish athletic officials, facing an embarrassment of riches in the 1924 Games, barred Nurmi from defending his 10,000m title of 1920 to give countryman Ville Ritola a crack at the gold. Ritola won. But, according to legend, Nurmi, carrying a stopwatch, ran a one-man exhibition on a nearby track, beating Ritola's time by 40 seconds.

Nurmi, born June 13, 1897, in Turku, Finland, habitually ran with a stopwatch, both while training and competing. He was one of the first to practice pacing in a scientific manner. Nurmi began a self-imposed running regimen at age 12, loping through Finnish forests for endurance. He entered the Finnish military in 1919 and was known to run entire 20-kilometer marches with full pack and rifle plus an 11-pound sack of sand.

Nurmi's last public appearance on a track came in 1952 at the age of 55, when he carried the Olympic torch into the arena for the Helsinki Games. The appearance came 20 years after he was banned from competing in the 1932 Games by the International Amateur Athletic Foundation because of supposed professionalism. Having become financially secure through real estate investing, he died in Helsinki on October 2, 1973. The great Finn is commemorated with a bronze statue that stands outside the Helsinki Olympic stadium. —*H.D.*

Chariots of Fire: Abrahams and Liddell, Coe and Ovett

Chariots of Fire is a inspirational movie, with Vangelis's mythic soundtrack providing some of the best running-on-the-beach music ever. Even if you don't

Finnish distance runner Paavo Nurmi, who earned Olympic medals from 1920 to 1928, lit the Olympic flame to open the Helsinki Games in 1952.

After training intensely for four years, British sprinter Harold Abrahams captured the 100m gold medal at the 1924 Games; his story inspired the film *Chariots of Fire*.

usually trot on the beach, you'll want to after listening to this. But as literal track history, portraying the life and times of Olympians Harold Abrahams and Eric Liddell, the movie puts forth the usual cinematic discrepancies. Some events are compressed, others fabricated. What the movie does stay truthful to, however, is the complex and separate visions that drove Abrahams and Liddell at the 1924 Paris Games.

Abrahams, who was Jewish, surely did feel the sting of anti-Semitism. But he was also competing against the memory of his older brothers' achievements, including one who competed in Stockholm in 1912. Abrahams ran at the Antwerp Games in 1920 but lost in the quarterfinals of the 100m. During the next four years he worked relentlessly at his sprinting style; he carried a piece of string to measure where his first step should fall after the start. At the 100m in Paris, the training helped him defeat the favored American runners.

Liddell had been born in China to missionary parents of Scottish origin. He was as natural at athletics—training was only a sometime thing for the former rugby star—as he was at preaching. At Paris, he declined the opportunity to run three races, including two relays, because they fell on Sundays and conflicted with his religious beliefs. That allowed him to focus on the 400m race, which he won by the wide margin of five meters. He also won a bronze in the 200m sprint. But he was loudly criticized by countrymen for denying Scotland a rare shot at more Olympic medals.

Abrahams was forced into retirement not long after the 1924 Games when he injured his thigh during a long jump. He became a lawyer, worked in radio, and served as president of the British Amateur Athletic Association. Abrahams died in 1978.

A year after winning his medals, Liddell went back to China to help his father's missionary work. He was imprisoned during World War II and died of a brain tumor in a Japanese internment camp on February 21, 1945. A six-foot column of Scottish granite was erected near the site of his death in 1991.

Let's take another listen to that *Chariots of Fire* soundtrack. Fifty-six years after Paris, two more British subjects were linked again by the urge to run in the Olympics. The 800m race in Moscow was to be a classic match-up between Steve Ovett and Sebastian Coe. Ovett had won their last head-to-head encounter in 1978, but the two runners had avoided each other ever since. Coe was one of the great runners of the period. The media hyped the battle between the two track stars, and anticipation was high that a classic duel was in the making.

But the 800m race was anticlimactic. The pace was plodding, though Ovett eventually broke away from the pack to win. Coe put himself in poor positions in outside lanes before ending with a sprint for the silver medal. In a book he later wrote about the Olympic games, Coe revealed, "I still can't watch the 800 meters final on video, even after all this time, without kicking myself. I clearly lost concentration."

But in the 1500m race, Coe found a measure of revenge. Ovett should have been the favorite, having won 42 straight races in that distance range. But Coe was determined not to repeat the mistakes he made in the 800m. This time, Coe stayed near the front, finally passing East German Jürgen Straub 200 meters before the finish. Ovett placed third.

Coe defended his title in the 1500m four years later in Los Angeles, defeating another Brit, Steve Cram. Ovett enjoyed less luck repeating. Battling bronchitis, he was the last to qualify for the 800m final, and then placed eighth out of eight runners. He collapsed after the race and spent two days in hospital. —H.D.

Edwin Moses

Edwin Moses was a twenty-year-old physics major at Morehouse College who had pretty much taught himself to run hurdles when he attended the 1976 Summer Olympics in Montréal. In those Games, Moses set a world record of 47.64 seconds in his event, winning a gold medal and beginning a career as an Olympic athlete that has lasted to this day. While other athletes—amateur and professional—came and went, Moses endured as *the* star of the 400m hurdles, at one point winning a staggering 107 consecutive races.

Ironically, Moses was attending Morehouse on an academic rather than an athletic scholarship, and the college did not even have a track. Running hurdles was a hobby for him, a way to keep fit while he earned his physics degree. After Montréal, which was his first international meet, he began to devote himself wholeheartedly to the sport. For ten years he was nearly untouchable.

Moses developed a 13-step rhythm between each hurdle that he was able to maintain throughout the course. While his competitors would tire in the stretch and begin to take 15 or 16 steps, Moses remained in what seemed like an effortless flow from jump to jump. He was highly favored to win the 400m hurdles in the 1980 Olympics in Moscow, but the government-mandated boycott kept him sidelined from the event. Other international competitions remained open to him, however, and he attended almost all of them, winning with a consistency that confounded his opponents. His 1983 world record of 47.02 seconds was considered unbeatable.

Moses arrived at the 1984 Olympics a heavy favorite. In Los Angeles he hurdled to a second gold medal, despite a poor start and—by his standards—a mediocre pace. At that time he was in the midst of a winning streak that stretched to 107 before the 1984 silver medalist Danny Harris did the undoable, beating Moses at a race in Madrid. After that loss Moses came back with 10 more consecutive victories, for a total of 117 wins in 119 starts from 1977 until 1987.

The statistics are tarnished somewhat by the fact that, as he aged, Moses picked and chose his races carefully. Some observers contended that he was avoiding the other top-level hurdlers—such as Harris—but Moses answered that he was pacing himself, saving his strength for the most important matches. However, as the 1988 Games approached, and Moses found himself over 30, the athlete "began to think of himself less as a competitor than as conservator of the

Scots runner Eric Liddell was also featured as a character in *Chariots of Fire*. His performance at the 1924 Games brought him a gold medal in the 400m and a bronze in the 200m.

In another great match–up of UK runners, at the 1980 Games Sebastian Coe, center, captured the gold in the 1500m ahead of arch–rival Steve Ovett, #279. In the 800m that year it was Ovett for the gold and Coe for the silver.

US hurdler Edwin Moses won his first gold medal in the 400m at the 1976 Olympics, then had to sit out the Moscow Games, and recaptured the gold in 1984. He outdid his previous winning times in Seoul, but the performance was only good for a bronze in 1988.

[winning] streak," to quote *Sports Illustrated* correspondent Pat Butcher. At any rate, Moses settled for the bronze in Seoul, behind teammate Andre Phillips and suprise silver medalist El Hedj Dia Ba of Senegal.

But another sport beckoned Edwin Moses—bobsledding. He told *Sports Illustrated* that he "got the fever" to try bobsledding after attending the 1988 Winter Games in Calgary. Since then, Moses and partner Brian Shimer have become the most respected two-man team composed of athletes from other sports. Shimer and Moses were the only Americans to win a medal at the 1991 World Cup bobsled competition. They earned their prize, a bronze, in Winterberg, Germany, but failed to make the US Olympic team for 1992.

Moses told *Sports Illustrated* that he plans to make a comeback as a hurdler for the 1992 Summer Games. He also wants to continue his work on the bobsled, where his degree in physics provides practical solutions to problems of acceleration and momentum. He has also been active on the sidelines as an advocate of the trust system for paying amateur athletes. One day, he says, he wants to be a member of the US Olympic Committee. "I don't want to sit on the sidelines," the two-time gold medal winner proclaims. "It's not my nature. I need to be involved." —*M.K.*

Medalists

Track and Field — Men's 100 Meters

1988
1. Carl Lewis, USA, 9.92 (OR). (Ben Johnson, Canada, ran 9.79 but was disqualified.)
2. Linford Christie, Great Britain, 9.97
3. Calvin Smith, USA, 9.99

1984
1. Carl Lewis, USA, 9.99
2. Sam Graddy, USA, 10.19
3. Ben Johnson, Canada, 10.22

1980
1. Allan Wells, Great Britain, 10.25
2. Silvio Leonard, Cuba, 10.25
3. Peter Petrov, Bulgaria, 10.39

1976
1. Hasely Crawford, Trinidad and Tobago, 10.06
2. Donald Quarrie, Jamaica, 10.08
3. Valeri Borzov, Soviet Union, 10.14

1972
1. Valery Borsov, Soviet Union, 10.14
2. Robert Taylor, USA, 10.24
3. Lennox Miller, Jamaica, 10.33

1968
1. Jim Hines, USA, 9.95 (WR)
2. Lennox Miller, Jamaica, 10.0
3. Charles Greene, USA, 10.0

1964
1. Robert Hayes, USA, 10.0 (EWR)
2. Enrique Figuerola, Cuba, 10.2
3. Harry Jerome, Canada, 10.2

1960
1. Armin Hary, West Germany, 10.2 (OR)
2. David Sime, USA, 10.2
3. Peter Radford, Great Britain, 10.3

1956
1. Robert Morrow, USA, 10.5
2. Thane Baker, USA, 10.5

3. Hector Hogan, Australia, 10.6

1952
1. Lindy Remigino, USA, 10.4
2. Herbert McKenley, Jamaica, 10.4
3. Emmanuel McDonald Bailey, Great Britain, 10.4

1948
1. Harrison Dillard, USA, 10.3 (EOR)
2. Norwood Ewell, USA, 10.4
3. Lloyd LaBeach, Panama, 10.4

1936
1. Jesse Owens, USA, 10.3
2. Ralph Metcalfe, USA, 10.4
3. Martinus Osendarp, Netherlands, 10.5

1932
1. Eddie Tolan, USA, 10.3 (OR)
2. Ralph Metcalfe, USA, 10.3
3. Arthur Jonath, Germany, 10.4

1928
1. Percy Williams, Canada, 10.8
2. Jack London, Great Britain, 10.9
3. Georg Lammers, Germany, 10.9

1924
1. Harold Abrahams, Great Britian, 10.6 (OR)
2. Jackson Scholz, USA, 10.7
3. Arthur Porritt, New Zealand, 10.8

1920
1. Charles Paddock, USA, 10.8
2. Morris Kirksey, USA, 10.8
3. Harry Edward, Great Britain, 11.0

1912
1. Ralph Craig, USA, 10.8
2. Alvah Mayer, USA, 10.9
3. Donald Lippincott, USA, 10.9

1908
1. Reginald Walker, South Africa, 10.8 (OR)
2. James Rector, USA, 10.9
3. Robert Kerr, Canada, 11.0

1906
1. Archie Hahn, USA, 11.2
2. Fay Moulton, USA, 11.3
3. Nigel Barker, Australia, 11.3

519

1904 1. Archie Hahn, USA, 11.0
      2. Nathaniel Cartmell, USA, 11.2
      3. William Hogenson, USA, 11.2
1900 1. Francis Jarvis, USA, 11.0
      2. John Walter Tewksbury, USA 11.1
      3. Stanley Rowley, Australia, 11.2
1896 1. Thomas Burke, USA, 12.0
      2. Fritz Hofmann, Germany, 12.2
      3. Alajos Szokolyi, Hungary, 12.6

Track and Field — Men's 200 Meters

1988 1. Joe DeLoach, USA, 19.75 (OR)
      2. Carl Lewis, USA, 19.79
      3. Robson de Silva, Brazil, 20.04
1984 1. Carl Lewis, USA, 19.80 (OR)
      2. Kirk Baptiste, USA, 19.96
      3. Thomas Jefferson, USA, 20.26
1980 1. Pietro Mennea, Italy, 20.19
      2. Allan Wells, Great Britain, 20.21
      3. Donald Quarrie, Jamaica, 20.29
1976 1. Donald Quarrie, Jamaica, 20.23
      2. Millard Hampton, USA, 20.29
      3. Dwayne Evans, USA, 20.43
1972 1. Valery Borsov, Soviet Union, 20.00
      2. Larry Black, USA, 20.19
      3. Pietro Mennea, Italy, 20.30
1968 1. Tommie Smith, USA, 19.83 (WR)
      2. Peter Norman, Australia, 20.0
      3. John Carlos, USA, 20.0
1964 1. Henry Carr, USA, 20.3 (OR)
      2. Otis Drayton, USA, 20.5
      3. Edwin Roberts, Trinidad and Tobago, 20.6
1960 1. Livio Berruti, Italy, 20.5 (EWR)
      2. Lester Carney, USA, 20.6
      3. Abdoulaye Seye, France, 20.7
1956 1. Robert Morrow, USA, 20.6 (OR)
      2. Andrew Stanfield, USA, 20.7
      3. Thane Baker, USA, 20.9
1952 1. Andrew Stanfield, USA, 20.7
      2. Thane Baker, USA, 20.8
      3. James Gathers, USA, 20.8
1948 1. Mel Patton, USA, 21.1
      2. Norwood Ewell, USA, 21.1
      3. Lloyd LaBeach, Panama, 21.2
1936 1. Jesse Owens, USA, 20.7 (OR)
      2. Matthew Robinson, USA, 21.1
      3. Martinus Osendarp, Netherlands, 21.3
1932 1. Eddie Tolan, USA, 21.2 (OR)
      2. George Simpson, USA, 21.4
      3. Ralph Metcalfe, USA, 21.5
1928 1. Percy Williams, Canada, 21.8
      2. Walter Rangeley, Great Britain, 21.9
      3. Helmut Kornig, Germany, 21.9
1924 1. Jackson Scholz, USA, 21.6
      2. Charles Paddock, USA, 21.7
      3. Eric Liddell, Great Britain, 21.9
1920 1. Allen Woodring, USA, 22.0
      2. Charles Paddock, USA, 22.1
      3. Harry Edward, Great Britain, 22.2
1912 1. Ralph Craig, USA, 21.7
      2. Donald Lippincott, USA, 21.8
      3. William Applegarth, Great Britain, 22.0
1908 1. Robert Kerr, Canada, 22.6
      2. Robert Cloughen, USA, 22.6
      3. Nathaniel Cartmell, USA, 22.7
1906 Not held

1904 1. Archie Hahn, USA, 21.6 (OR)
      2. Nathaniel Cartmell, USA, 21.9
      3. William Hogenson, USA
1900 1. John Walter Tewksbury, USA, 22.2
      2. Norman Pritchard, India, 22.8
      3. Stanley Rowley, Australia, 22.9
1896 Not held

Track and Field — Men's 400 Meters

1988 1. Steven Lewis, USA, 43.87
      2. Butch Reynolds, USA, 43.93
      3. Danny Everett, USA, 44.09
1984 1. Alonzo Babers, USA, 44.27
      2. Gabriel Tiacoh, Cote d'Ivorie, 44.54
      3. Antonio McKay, USA, 44.71
1980 1. Viktor Markin, Soviet Union, 44.60
      2. Richard Mitchell, Australia, 44.84
      3. Frank Schaffer, East Germany, 44.87
1976 1. Alberto Juantorena, Cuba, 44.26
      2. Frederick Newhouse, USA, 44.40
      3. Herman Frazier, USA, 44.95
1972 1. Vincent Matthews, USA, 44.66
      2. Wayne Collett, USA, 44.80
      3. Julius Sang, Kenya, 44.92
1968 1. Lee Evans, USA, 43.86 (WR)
      2. Larry James, USA, 43.9
      3. Ronald Freeman, USA, 44.4
1964 1. Michael Larrabee, USA, 45.1
      2. Wendell Mottley, Trinidad and Tobago, 45.2
      3. Andrzej Badenski, Poland, 45.6
1960 1. Otis Davis, USA, 44.9 (WR)
      2. Carl Kaufmann, West Germany, 44.9 (WR)
      3. Malcolm Spence, South Africa, 45.5
1956 1. Charles Jenkins, USA, 46.7
      2. Karl-Friedrich Haas, West Germany, 46.8
      3. Voitto Hellsten, Finland, 47.0
      3. Ardalion Ignatyev, Soviet Union, 47.0
1952 1. George Rhoden, Jamaica, 45.9 (OR)
      2. Herbert McKenley, Jamaica, 45.9
      3. Ollie Matson, USA, 46.8
1948 1. Arthur Wint, Jamaica, 46.2
      2. Herbert McKenley, Jamaica, 46.4
      3. Malvin Whitfield, USA, 46.9
1936 1. Archie Williams, USA, 46.5
      2. A. Godfrey Brown, Great Britain, 46.7
      3. James LuValle, USA, 46.8
1932 1. William Carr, USA, 46.2 (WR)
      2. Benjamin Eastman, USA 46.4
      3. Alexander Wilson, Canada, 47.4
1928 1. Raymond Barbuti, USA, 47.8
      2. James Ball, Canada, 48.0
      3. Joachim Buchner, Germany, 48.2
1924 1. Eric Liddell, Great Britain, 47.6 (OR)
      2. Horatio Fitch, USA, 48.4
      3. Guy Butler, Great Britain, 48.6
1920 1. Bevil Rudd, South Africa, 50.0
      2. Guy Butler, Great Britain, 49.9
      3. Nils Engdahl, Sweden, 50.0
1912 1. Charles Reidpath, USA, 48.2 (OR)
      2. Hanns Braun, Germany, 48.3
      3. Edward Lindberg, USA, 48.4
1908 1. Wyndham Halswelle, Great Britain, 50.0
1906 1. Paul Pilgrim, USA, 53.2

2. Wyndham Halswelle, Great Britain,
53.8
3. Nigel Barker, Australia, 54.1
1904 1. Harry Hillman, USA, 49.2 (OR)
2. Frank Waller, USA, 49.9
3. Herman Groman, USA, 50.0
1900 1. Maxwell Long, USA,, 49.4 (OR)
2. William Holland, USA, 49.6
3. Ernst Schulz, Denmark, 15m behind
1896 1. Thomas Burke, USA, 54.2
2. Herbert Jamison, USA, 14m behind
3. Charles Gmelin, Great Britain

Track and Field — Men's 800 Meters

1988 1. Paul Ereng, Kenya, 1:43.45
2. Joaquim Cruz, Brazil, 1:43.90
3. Said Aouita, Morocco, 1:44.06
1984 1. Joaquim Cruz, Brazil, 1:43.00 (OR)
2. Sebastian Coe, Great Britain, 1:43.64
3. Earl Jones USA, 1:43.83
1980 1. Steven Ovett, Great Britain, 1:45.4
2. Sebastian Coe, Great Britain, 1:45.9
3. Nikolai Kirov, Soviet Union, 1:46.0
1976 1. Alberto Juantorena, Cuba, 1:43.50
(WR, OR)
2. Ivo Van Damme, Belgium, 1:43.86
3. Richard Wohlhuter, USA, 1:44.12
1972 1. David Wottle, USA, 1:45.9
2. Yevgeny Arzhanov, Soviet Union,
1:45.9
3. Mike Boit, Kenya, 1:46.0
1968 1. Ralph Doubell, Australia, 1:44.3 (EWR)
2. Wilson Kiprugut, Kenya, 1:44.5
3. Thomas Farrell, USA, 1:45.4
1964 1. Peter Snell, New Zealand, 1:45.1 (OR)
2. William Crothers, Canada, 1:45.6
3. Wilson Kiprugut, Kenya, 1:45.9
1960 1. Peter Snell, New Zealand, 1:46.3 (OR)
2. Roger Moens, Belgium, 1:46.5
3. George Kerr, Antilles, 1:47.1
1956 1. Tom Courtney, USA 1:47.7 (OR)
2. Derek Johnson, Great Britain, 1:47.8
3. Audun Boysen, Norway, 1:48.1
1952 1. Malvin Whitfield, USA, 1:49.2 (EOR)
2. Arthur Wint, Jamaica, 1:49.4
3. Heinz Ulzheimer, Germany 1:49.7
1948 1. Malvin Whitfield, USA, 1:49.2 (OR)
2. Arthur Wint, Jamaica, 1:49.5
3. Marcel Hansenne, France, 1:49.8
1936 1. John Woodruff, USA, 1:52.9
2. Mario Lanzi, Italy, 1:53.3
3. Philip Edwards, Canada, 1:53.6
1932 1. Thomas Hampson, Great Britain,
1:49.7 (WR)
2. Alexander Wilson, Canada, 1:49.9
3. Philip Edwards, Canada, 1:51.5
1928 1. Douglas Lowe, Great Britain, 1:51.8
(OR)
2. Erik Bylehn, Sweden, 1:52.8
3. Hermann Engelhard, Germany, 1:53.2
1924 1. Douglas Lowe, Great Britain, 1:52.4
2. Paul Martin, Switzerland, 1:52.6
3. Schuyler Enck, USA, 1:53.0
1920 1. Albert Hill, Great Britain, 1:53.4
2. Earl Eby, USA, 1:53.6
3. Bevil Rudd, South Africa, 1:54.0
1912 1. James Meredith, USA, 1:51.9 (WR)
2. Melvin Sheppard, USA, 1:52.0

3. Ira Davenport, USA, 1:52.0
1908 1. Melvin Sheppard, USA, 1:52.8 (WR)
2. Emilio Lunghi, Italy, 1:54.2
3. Hanns Braun, Germany, 1:55.2
1906 1. Paul Pilgrim, USA, 2:01.5
2. James Lightbody, USA, 2:01.6
3. Wyndham Halswelle, Great Britain,
2:03.0
1904 1. James Lightbody, USA, 1:56.0 (OR)
2. Howard Valentine, USA, 1:56.3
3. Emil Breitkreutz, USA, 1:56.4
1900 1. Alfred Tysoe, Great Britain, 2:01.2
2. John Cregan, USA, 2:03.0
3. David Hall, USA
1896 1. Edwin Flack, Australia, 2:11.0
2. Nandor Dani, Hungary, 2:11.8
3. Dimitrios Golemis, Greece, 90m
behind

Track and Field — Men's 1,500 Meters

1988 1. Peter Rono, Kenya, 3:35.96
2. Peter Elliott, Great Britain, 3:36.15
3. Jens-Peter Herold, East Germany,
3:36.21
1984 1. Sebastian Coe, Great Britain, 3:32.53
(OR)
2. Steve Cram, Great Britain, 3:33.40
3. Jose Abascal, Spain, 3:34.30
1980 1. Sebastian Coe, Great Britain, 3:38.4
2. Jurgen Straub, Great Britain, 3:38.8
3. Steven Ovett, Great Britain, 3:39.0
1976 1. John Walker, New Zealand, 3:39.17
2. Ivo Van Damme, Belgium, 3:39.27
3. Paul-Heinz Wellmann, West Germany,
3:39.33
1972 1. Kipchoge Keino, Kenya, 3:36.8
1. Pekkha Vasala, Finland, 3:36.3
3. Rod Dixon, New Zealand, 3:37.5
1968 1. Kipchoge Keino, Kenya, 3:34.9 (OR)
2. Jim Ryun, USA, 3:37.8
3. Bodo Tummler, West Germany, 3:39.0
1964 1. Peter Snell, New Zealand, 3:38.1
2. Josef Odlozil, Czechoslovakia, 3:39.6
3. John Davies, New Zealand, 3:39.6
1960 1. Herbert Elliott, Australia, 3:35.6 (WR)
2. Michel Jazy, France, 3:38.4
3. Istvan Rozsavolgyi, Hungary, 3:39.2
1956 1. Ron Delany, Ireland, 3:41.2 (OR)
2. Klaus Richtzenhain, East Germany,
3:42.0
3. John Landy, Australia, 3:42.0
1952 1. Josef Barthel, Luxembourg, 3:45.1
(OR)
2. Robert McMillen, USA, 3:45.2
3. Werner Lueg, Germany, 3:45.4
1948 1. Henry Eriksson, Sweden, 3:49.8
2. Lennart Strand, Sweden, 3:50.4
3. Willem Slijkhuis, Netherlands, 3:50.4
1936 1. John Lovelock, New Zealand, 3:47.8
(WR)
2. Glenn Cunningham, USA, 3:48.4
3. Luigi Beccali, Italy, 3:49.2
1932 1. Luigi Beccali, Italy, 3:51.2 (OR)
2. John Cornes, Great Britain, 3:52.6
3. Philip Edwards, Canada, 3:52.8
1928 1. Harri Larva,, Finland, 3:53.2 (OR)
2. Jules Ladoumegue, France, 3:53.8
3. Eino Purje-Borg, Finland, 3:56.4

521

1924	1. Paavo Nurmi, Finland, 3:53.6 (OR)
	2. Willy Scharer, Switzerland, 3:55.0
	3. Henry Stallard, Great Britain, 3:55.6
1920	1. Albert Hill, Great Britain, 4:01.8
	2. Philip Baker, Great Britain, 4:02.4
	3. Lawrence Shields, USA, 4:03.1
1912	1. Arnold Jackson, Great Britain, 3:56.8 (OR)
	2. Abel Kiviat, USA, 3:56.9
	3. Norman Taber, USA, 3:56.9
1908	1. Melvin Sheppard, USA, 4:03.4 (OR)
	2. Harold Wilson, Great Britain, 4:03.6
	3. Norman Hallows, Great Britain, 4:04.0
1906	1. James Lightbody, USA, 4:12.0
	2. John McGough, Great Britain/Ireland, 4:12.6
	3. Kristian Hellstrom, Sweden, 4:13.4
1904	1. James Lightbody, USA, 4:05.4 (WR)
	2. W. Frank Verner, USA, 4:06.8
	3. Lacey Hearn, USA
1900	1. Charles Bennett, Great Britain, 4:06.2 (WR)
	2. Henri Deloge, France, 4:06.6
	3. John Bray, USA, 4:07.2
1896	1. Edwin Flack, Australia, 4:33.2
	2. Arthur Blake, USA, 4:34.0
	3. Albin Lermusiaux, France, 4:36.0

Track and Field — Men's 5,000 Meters

1988	1. John Ngugi, Kenya, 13:11.70
	2. Dieter Baumann, West Germany, 13:15.52
	3. Hansjoerg Kunze, East Germany, 13:15.73
1984	1. Said Aouita, Morocco, 13:05.59 (OR)
	2. Markus Ryffel, Switzerland, 13:07.54
	3. Antonio Leitao, Portugal, 13:09.20
1980	1. Miruts Yifter, Ethiopia, 13:21.0
	2. Suleiman Nyambui, Tanzania, 13:21.6
	3. Kaarlo Maaninka, Finland, 13:22.0
1976	1. Lasse Viren, Finland, 13:24.76
	2. Dick Quax, New Zealand, 13:25.16
	3. Klaus-Dieter Hildenbrand, West Germany, 13:25.38
1972	1. Lasse Viren, Finland, 13:26.4 (OR)
	2. Mohamed Gammoudi, Tunisia, 13:27.4
	3. Ian Stewart, Great Britain, 13:27.6
1968	1. Mohamed Gammoudi, Tunisia, 14:05.0
	2. Kipchoge Keino, Kenya, 14:05.2
	3. Naftali Temu, Kenya, 14:06.4
1964	1. Robert Schul, USA, 13:48.8
	2. Harald Norpoth, West Germany, 13:49.6
	3. William Dellinger, USA, 13:49.8
1960	1. Murray Halberg, New Zealand, 13:43.4
	2. Hans Grodotzki, East Germany, 13:44.6
	3. Kazimierz Zimmy, Poland, 13:44.8
1956	1. Vladimir Kuts, Soviet Union, 13.39.6 (OR)
	2. Gordon Pirie, Great Britain, 13:50.6
	3. Derek Ibbotson, Great Britain, 13.54.4
1952	1. Emil Zatopek, Czechoslovakia, 14:06.6 (OR)
	2. Alain Mimoun O'Kacha, France, 14:07.4

	3. Herbert Schade, West Germany, 14:08.6
1948	1. Gaston Reiff, Belgium, 14:17.6 (OR)
	2. Emil Zatopek, Czechoslovakia, 14:17.8
	3. Willem Slijkhuis, Netherlands, 14:26.8
1936	1. Gunnar Hockert, Finland, 14:22.2 (OR)
	2. Lauri Lehtinen, Finland, 14:25.8
	3. Henry Jonsson, Sweden, 14:29.0
1932	1. Lauri Lehtinen, Finland, 14:30.0 (OR)
	2. Ralph Hill, USA, 14:30.0
	3. Lauri Virtanen, Finland, 14:44.0
1928	1. Ville Ritola, Finland, 14:38.0
	2. Paavo Nurmi, Finland, 14:40.0
	3. Edvin Wide, Sweden, 14:41.2
1924	1. Paavo Nurmi, Finland, 14:31.2
	2. Ville Ritola, Finland, 14:31.4
	3. Edvin Wide, Sweden, 15:01.8
1920	1. Joseph Guillemot, France, 14.55.6
	2. Paavo Nurmi, Finland, 15:00.0
	3. Eric Backman, Sweden, 15:13.0
1912	1. Johannes Kolehmainen, Finland, 14:36.6 (WR)
	2. Jean Bouin, France, 14:36.7
	3. George Hutson, Great Britain, 15:07.6
1896– 1908	**Not held**

Track and Field — Men's 10,000 Meters

1988	1. Brahim Boutaib, Morocco, 27:21.46 (OR)
	2. Salvatore Antibo, Italy, 27:23.55
	3. Kipkemboi Kimeli, Kenya, 27:25.16
1984	1. Alberto Cova, Italy, 27:47.54
	2. Michael McLeod, Great Britain, 28:06.22
	3. Michael Musyoki, Kenya, 28:06.46
1980	1. Miruts Yifter, Ethiopia, 27:42.7
	2. Kaarlo Maaninka, Finland, 27:44.3
	3. Mohammed Kedir, Ethiopia, 27:44.7
1976	1. Lasse Viren, Finland, 27:40.38
	2. Carlos Lopez, Portugal, 27:45.17
	3. Brendan Foster, Great Britain, 27:54.92
1972	1. Lasse Viren, Finland, 27:38.4 (WR)
	2. Emiel Puttemans, Belgium, 27:39.6
	3. Miruts Yifter, Ethiopia, 27:41.0
1968	1. Naftali Temu, Kenya, 29:27.4
	2. Mamo Wolde, Ethiopia, 29:28.0
	3. Mohamed Gammoudi, Tunisia, 29:34.2
1964	1. William Mills, USA, 28:24.4 (OR)
	2. Mohamed Gammoudi, Tunisia, 28:24.8
	3. Ronald Clarke, Australia, 28:25.8
1960	1. Pyotr Bolotnikov, Soviet Union, 28:32.2 (OR)
	2. Hans Grodotzki, East Germany, 28:37.0
	3. David Power, Australia, 28:38.2
1956	1. Vladimir Kuts, Soviet Union, 28:45.6 (OR)
	2. Jozsef Kovacs, Hungary, 28:52.4
	3. Allan Lawrence, Australia, 28:53.6
1952	1. Emil Zatopek, Czechoslovakia, 29:17.0 (OR)
	2. Alain Mimoun O'Kacha, France, 29:32.8
	3. Aleksandr Anufriev, Soviet Union, 29:48.2

522

1948	1. Emil Zatopek, Czechoslovakia, 29:59.6 (OR)
	2. Alain Mimoun O'Kacha, France, 30:47.4
	3. Bertil Albertsson, Sweden, 30:53.6
1936	1. Ilmari Salminen, Finland, 30:15.4
	2. Arvo Askola, Finland, 30:15.6
	3. Volmari Iso-Hollo, Finland, 30:20.2
1932	1. Janusz Kusocinski, Poland, 30:11.4 (OR)
	2. Volmari Iso-Hollo, Finland, 30:12.6
	3. Lauri Virtanen, Finland, 30:35.0
1928	1. Paavo Nurmi, Finland, 30.18.8 (OR)
	2. Ville Ritola, Finland, 30:19.4
	3. Edvin Wide, Sweden, 31:00.8
1924	1. Ville Ritola, Finland, 30:23.2 (WR)
	2. Edvin Wide, Sweden, 30:55.2
	3. Eero Berg, Finland, 31:43.0
1920	1. Paavo Nurmi, Finland, 31:45.8
	2. Joseph Guillemot, France, 31:47.2
	3. James Wilson, Great Britain, 31:50.8
1912	1. Johannes Kolehmainen, Finland, 31:20.8
	2. Louis Tewanima, USA, 32:06.6
	3. Albin Stenroos, Finland, 32:21.8
1896-1908	Not held

Track and Field — Men's Marathon

1988	1. Gelindo Bordin, Italy, 2:10:32
	2. Douglas Wakiihuri, Kenya, 2:10:47
	3. Houssein Ahmed Saleh, Djibouti, 2:10:59
1984	1. Carlos Lopez, Portugal, 2:09:21 (OR)
	2. John Treacy, Ireland, 2:09:56
	3. Charles Spedding, Great Britain, 2:09:58
1980	1. Waldemar Cierpinski, East Germany, 2:11:03.0
	2. Gerard Nijboer, Netherlands, 2:11:20.0
	3. Setymkul Dzhumanazarov, Soviet Union, 2:11:35.0
1976	1. Waldemar Cierpinski, East Germany, 2:09:55.0 (OR)
	2. Frank Shorter, USA, 2:10:45.8
	3. Karel Lismont, Belgium, 2:11:12.6
1972	1. Frank Shorter, USA, 2:12:19.8
	2. Karel Lismont, Belgium, 2:14:31.8
	3. Mamo Wolde, Ethiopia, 2:15:08.4
1968	1. Mamo Wolde, Ethiopia, 2:20:26.4
	2. Kenji Kimihara, Japan, 2:23:31.0
	3. Michael Ryan, New Zealand, 2:23:45.0
1964	1. Abebe Bikila, Ethiopia, 2:12:11.2 (WB)
	2. Basil Heatley, Great Britain, 2:16:19.2
	3. Kokichi Tsuburaya, Japan, 2:16:22.8
1960	1. Abebe Bikila, Ethiopia, 2:15:16.2 (WB)
	2. Rhadi Ben Abdesselam, Morocco, 2:15:41.6
	3. Barry Magee, New Zealand, 2:17:18.2
1956	1. Alain Mimoun O'Kacha, France, 2:25:00.0
	2. Franjo Mihalic, Yugoslavia, 2:26:32.0
	3. Veikko Karvonen, Finland, 2:27:47.0
1952	1. Emil Zatopek, Czechoslovakia, 2:23:03.2 (OR)

	2. Reinaldo Gorno, Argentina, 2:25:35.0
	3. Gustaf Jansson, Sweden, 2:26:07.0
1948	1. Delfo Cabrera, Argentina, 2:34:51.6
	2. Thomas Richards, Great Britain, 2:35:07.6
	3. Etienne Gailly, Belgium, 2:35:33.6
1936	1. Kitei Son, Japan/Republic of Korea, 2:29:19.2 (OR)
	2. Ernest Harper, Great Britain, 2:31:23:2
	3. Shoryu Nan, Japan/Republic of Korea, 2:31:42.0
1932	1. Juan Zabala, Argentina, 2:31:36.0 (OR)
	2. Samuel Ferris, Great Britain, 2:31:55:0
	3. Armas Toivonen, Finland, 2:32:12.0
1928	1. Boughera El Ouafi, France, 2:32:57.0
	2. Miguel Plaza, Chile, 2:33:23.0
	3. Martti Marttelin, Finland, 2:35:02.0
1924	1. Albin Stenroos, Finland, 2:41:22.6
	2. Romeo Bertini, Italy, 2:47:19.6
	3. Clarence DeMar, USA, 2:48:14.0
1920	1. Johannes Kolehmainen, Finland, 2:32:35.8 (WB)
	2. Juri Lossman, Estonia, 2:32:48.6
	3. Valerio Arri, Italy, 2:36:32.8
1912	1. Kenneth McArthur, South Africa, 2:36:54.8
	2. Christian Gitsham, South Africa, 2:37:52.0
	3. Gaston Strobino, USA, 2:38:42.4
1908	1. John Hayes, USA, 2:55:18.4 (OR)
	2. Charles Hefferon, South Africa, 2:56:06.0
	3. Joseph Forshaw, USA, 2:57:10.4
1906	1. W. John Sherring, Canada, 2:51:23.6
	2. John Svanberg, Sweden, 2:58:20.8
	3. William Frank, USA, 3:00:46.8
1904	1. Thomas Hicks, USA, 3:28:53
	2. Albert Coery, USA, 3:34:52
	3. Arthur Newton, USA, 3:47:33
1900	1. Michel Theato, France, 2:59:45
	2. Emilie Champion, France, 3:04:17
	3. Ernst Fast, Sweden, 3:37:14
1896	1. Spyridon Louis, Greece, 2:58:50
	2. Charilaos Vasilakos, Greece, 3:06:03
	3. Gyula Kellner, Hungary, 3:06:35

Track and Field — Men's 110-Meter Hurdles

1988	1. Roger Kingdom, USA, 12.98 (OR)
	2. Colin Jackson, Great Britain, 13.28
	3. Tonie Campbell, USA, 13.38
1984	1. Roger Kingdom, USA, 13.20 (OR)
	2. Greg Foster, USA, 13.23
	3. Arto Bryggare, Finland, 13.40
1980	1. Thomas Munkelt, East Germany, 13.39
	2. Alejandro Casanas, Cuba, 13.40
	3. Aleksandr Puchkov, Soviet Union, 13.44
1976	1. Guy Drut, France, 13.30
	2. Alejandro Casanas, Cuba, 13.33
	3. Willie Davenport, USA, 13.38
1972	1. Rod Milburn, USA, 13.24 (EWR)
	2. Guy Drut, France, 13.34
	3. Thomas Hill, USA, 13.48
1968	1. Willie Davenport, USA, 13.3 (OR)
	2. Erv Hall, USA, 13.4
	2. Ervin Hall, USA, 13.4

523

Summer

3. Eddy Ottoz, Italy, 13.4
1964 1. Hayes Jones, USA, 13.6
2. H. Blaine Lindgren, USA, 13.7
3. Anatoli Mikhailov, Soviet Union, 13.7
1960 1. Lee Calhoun, USA, 13.8
2. Willie May, USA, 13.8
3. Hayes Jones, USA, 14.0
1956 1. Lee Calhoun, USA, 13.5 (OR)
2. Jack Davis, USA, 13.5
3. Joel Shankle, USA, 14.1
1952 1. Harrison Dillard, USA, 13.7 (OR)
2. Jack Davis, USA, 13.7
3. Arthur Barnard, USA, 14.1
1948 1. William Porter, USA, 13.9 (OR)
2. Clyde Scott, USA, 14.1
3. Craig Dixon, USA, 14.1
1936 1. Forrest Towns, USA, 14.2
2. Donald Finlay, Great Britain, 14.4
3. Frederick Pollard, USA, 14.4
1932 1. George Saling, USA, 14.6
2. Percy Beard, USA, 14.7
3. Donald Finlay, Great Britain, 14.8
1928 1. Sydney Atkinson, South Africa, 14.8
2. Stephen Anderson. USA, 14.8
3. John Collier, USA, 14.9
1924 1. Daniel Kinsey, USA, 15.0
2. Sydney Atkinson, South Africa, 15.0
3. Sten Pettersson, Sweden, 15.4
1920 1. Earl Thomson, Canada, 14.8 (WR)
2. Harold Barron, USA, 15.1
3. Frederick Murray, USA, 15.2
1912 1. Frederick Kelly, USA, 15.1
2. James Wendell, USA, 15.2
3. Martin Hawkins, USA, 15.3
1908 1. Forest Smithson. USA, 15.0 (WR)
2. John Garrels, USA, 15.7
3. Arthur Shaw, USA
1906 1. Robert Leavitt, USA, 16.2
2. A. H. Healey, Great Britain, 16.2
3. Vincent Duncker, South Africa, 16.3
1904 1. Frederick Schule, USA, 16.0
2. Thaddeus Shideler, USA, 16.3
3. Lesley Ashburner, USA, 16.4
1900 1. Alvin Kraenzlein, USA, 15.4 (OR)
2. John McLean, USA, 15.5
3. Fred Moloney, USA
1896 1. Thomas Curtis, USA, 17.6
2. Grantley Goulding, Great Britain, 17.7

Track and Field — Men's 400-Meter Hurdles

1988 1. Andre Phillips, USA, 47.19 (OR)
2. El Hedj Dia Ba, Senegal, 47.23
3. Edwin Moses, USA, 47.56
1984 1. Edwin Moses, USA, 47.75
2. Danny Harris USA, 48.13
3. Harald Schmid, FRG, 48.19
1980 1. Volker Beck, East Germany, 48.70
2. Vasili Arkhipenko, Soviet Union, 48.86
3. Gary Oakes, Great Britain, 49.11
1976 1. Edwin Moses, USA, 47.64 (WR, OR)
2. Michael Shine, USA, 48.69
3. Yevgeny Gavrilenko, Soviet Union, 49.45
1972 1. John Akii-Bua, Uganda, 47.82 (WR)
2. Ralph Mann, USA, 48.51
3. David Hemery, Great Britain, 48.52
1968 1. David Hemery, Great Britain, 48.1 (WR)

2. Gerhard Hennige, West Germany, 49.0
3. John Sherwood, Great Britain, 49.0
1964 1. Warren Cawley, USA, 49.6
2. John Cooper, Great Britain, 50.1
3. Salvatore Morale, Italy, 50.1
1960 1. Glenn Davis, USA, 49.3 (OR)
2. Clifton Cushman, USA, 49.6
3. Richard Howard, USA, 49.7
1956 1. Glenn Davis, USA, 50.1 (OR)
2. Eddie Southern, USA, 50.8
3. Josh Culbreath, USA, 51.6
1952 1. Charles Moore, USA, 50.8 (OR)
2. Juri Lituyev, Soviet Union, 51.3
3. John Holland, New Zealand, 52.2
1948 1. Roy Cochran, USA, 51.1 (OR)
2. Duncan White, Ceylon, 51.8
3. Rune Larsson, Sweden, 52.2
1936 1. Glenn Hardin, USA, 52.4
2. John Loaring, Canada, 52.7
3. Miguel White, Philippines, 52.8
1932 1. Robert Tisdall, Ireland, 51.7
2. Glenn Hardin, USA, 51.9 (WR)
3. F. Morgan Taylor, USA, 52.0
1928 1. David Burghley, Great Britain, 53.4 (OR)
2. Frank Cuhel, USA, 53.6
3. F. Morgan Taylor, USA, 53.6
1924 1. F. Morgan Taylor, USA, 52.6
2. Erik Vilen, Finland, 53.8 (OR)
3. Ivan Riley, USA, 54.2
1920 1. Frank Loomis, USA, 54.0 (WR)
2. John Norton, USA, 54.3
3. August Desch, USA, 54.5
1912 **Not held**
1908 1. Charles Bacon, USA, 55.0 (WR)
2. Harry Hillman, USA, 55.3
3. Leonard Tremeer, Great Britain, 57.0
1906 **Not held**
1904 1. Harry Hillman, USA, 53.0
2. Frank Waller, USA, 53.2
3. George Poage, USA
1900 1. John Walter Tewksbury, USA, 57.6
2. Henri Tauzin, France, 58.3
3. George Orton, Canada
1896 **Not held**

Track and Field — 3,000-Meter Steeplechase

1988 1. Julius Kariuki, Kenya, 8:05.51 (OR)
2. Peter Koech, Kenya, 8:06.79
3. Mark Rowland, Great Britain, 8:07.96
1984 1. Julius Korir, Kenya, 8:11.80
2. Joseph Mahmoud, France, 8:13.31
3. Brian Diemer, USA, 8:14.06
1980 1. Bronislav Malinovski, Poland, 8:09.7
2. Filbert Bayi, Tanganyika, 8:12.5
3. Eshetu Tura, Ethiopia, 8:13.6
1976 1. Anders Garderud, Sweden, 8:08.2 (WR, OR)
2. Bronislav Malinovski, Poland, 8:09.2
3. Frank Baumgartl, East Germany, 8:10.4
1972 1. Kipchoge Keino, Kenya, 8:23.6 (OR)
2. Benjamin Jipcho, Kenya, 8:24.6
3. Tapio Kantanen, Finland, 8:24.8
1968 1. Amos Biwott, Kenya, 8:51.0
2. Benjamin Kogo, Kenya, 8:51.6
3. George Young, USA, 8:51.8

524

1964   1. Gaston Roelants, Belgium, 8:30.8 (OR)
         2. Maurice Herriott, Great Britain, 8:32.4
         3. Ivan Belyayev, Soviet Union, 8:33.8
1960   1. Zdzislaw Krzyszkowiak, Poland, 8:34.2
          (OR)
         2. Nikolai Sokolov, Soviet Union, 8:36.4
         3. Semyon Rzhischin, Soviet Union,
          8:42.2
1956   1. Christopher Brasher, Great Britain,
          8:41.2 (OR)
         2. Sandor Rozsnyoi, Hungary, 8:43.6
         3. Ernst Larsen, Norway, 8:44.0
1952   1. Horace Ashenfelter, USA, 8:45.4 (WR)
         2. Vladimir Kazantsev, Soviet Union,
          8:51.6
         3. John Disley, Great Britain, 8:51.8
1948   1. Thore Sjostrand, Sweden, 9:04.6
         2. Erik Elmsater, Sweden, 9:08.2
         3. Gote Hagstrom, Sweden, 9:11.3
1936   1. Volmari Iso-Hollo, Finland, 9:03.8
          (WR)
         2. Kaarlo Tuominen, Finland, 9:06.8
         3. Alfred Dompert, Germany, 9:07.2
1932   1. Volmari Iso-Hollo, Finland, 10:33.4
         2. Thomas Evenson, Great Britian,
          10:46.0
         3. Joseph McCluskey, USA, 10:46.2
1928   1. Toivo Loukola, Finland, 9:21.8 (WR)
         2. Paavo Nurmi, Finland, 9:31.2
         3. Ove Andersen, Finland, 9:35.6
1924   1. Ville Ritola, Finland, 9:33.6 (EWR)
         2. Elias Katz, Finland, 9:44.0
         3. Paul Bontemps, France, 9:45.2
1920   1. Percy Hodge, Great Britain, 10:00.4
          (OR)
         2. Patrick Flynn, USA, 100m behind
         3. Ernesto Ambrosini, Italy, 130m behind
1912   **Not held**
1908   1. Arthur Russell, Great Britain, 10:47.8
         2. Archie Robertson, Great Britain,
          10:48.4
         3. John Eisele, USA, 20m behind
1906   **Not held**
1904   1. James Lightbody, USA, 7:39.6
         2. John Daly, Great Britain/Ireland,
          7:40.6
         3. Arthur Newton, USA, 25m behind
1900   1. George Orton, Canada, 7:34.4
         2. Sidney Robinson, Great Britain, 7:38.0
         3. Jacques Chastanie, France
1896   **Not held**

Track and Field — Men's 4x100-Meter Relay

1988   1. Soviet Union, 38.19, Victor Bryzgine,
          Vladimir Krylov, Vladimir Mouraviev,
          Vitali Savine
         2. Great Britain, 38.40, Elliot Bunney,
          John Regis, Michael McFarlane, Linford
          Christie
         3. France, 38.47, Bruno Marie-Rose,
          Daniel Sangouma, Gilles Queneherve,
          Max Moriniere
1984   1. USA, 37.83, (WR,OR) Sam Graddy,
          Ron Brown, Calvin Smith, Carl Lewis
         2. Jamaica, 38.62, Albert Lawrence,
          Gregory Meghoo, Donald Quarrie,
          Ray Stewart

         3. Canada, 38.70, Ben Johnson, Tony
          Sharpe, Desai Williams, Sterling Hinds
1980   1. Soviet Union, 38.26, Vladimir
          Muraviov, Nikolai Sidorov, Aleksandr
          Aksinin, Andrei Prokofiev
         2. Poland, 38.33, Krzysztof Zwolinski,
          Zenon Licznerski, Leszek Dunecki,
          Marian Woronin
         3. France, 38.53, Antoine Richard, Pascal
          Barre, Patrick Barre, Herman Panzo
1976   1. USA, 38.33, Harvey Glance, John
          Jones, Millard Hampton, Steven
          Riddick
         2. East Germany, 38.66, Manfred Kokot,
          Joerg Pfeifer, Klaus-Dieter Kurrat,
          Alexander Thieme
         3. Soviet Union, 38.78, Aleksandr
          Aksinin, Nikolai Kolesnikov, Yuri Silvos,
          Valeri Borzov
1972   1. USA, 38.19, (WR) Larry Black, Robert
          Taylor, Gerald Tinker, Eddie Hart
         2. Soviet Union, 38.50, Aleksandr
          Kornelyuk, Vladimir Lovetski, Yuri
          Silovs, Valeri Borzov
         3. West Germany, 38.79, Jobst Hirscht,
          Karlheinz Klotz, Gerhard Wucherer,
          Klas Ehl
1968   1. USA, 38.2, (WR) Charles Greene,
          Melvin Pender, Ronnie Ray Smith, Jim
          Hines
         2. Cuba, 38.3, Hermes Ramirez, Juan
          Morales, Pablo Montes, Enrique
          Figuerola
         3. France, 38.4, Gerard Fenouil, Jocelyn
          Delecour, Claude Piquemal, Roger
          Bambuck
1964   1. USA, 39.0, (WR) O. Paul Drayton,
          Gerald Ashworth, Richard Stebbins,
          Robert Hayes
         2. Poland, 39.3, Andrzej Zielinski,
          Wieslaw Maniak, Marian Foik, Marian
          Dudziak
         3. France, 39.3, Paul Genevay, Bernard
          Laidebeur, Claude Piquemal, Jocelyn
          Delecour
1960   1. East Germany, 39.5, (EWR) Bernd
          Cullmann, Armin Hary, Walter
          Mahlendorf, Martin Lauer
         2. Soviet Union, 40.1, Gusman Kosanov,
          Leonid Bartenyev, Yuri Konovalov,
          Edvin Ozolin
         3. Great Britain, 40.2, Peter Radford,
          David Jones, David Segal, Neville
          Whitehead
1956   1. USA, 39.5, (WR) Ira Murchison,
          Leamon King, Thane Baker, Robert
          Morrow
         2. Soviet Union, 39.8, Boris Tokaryev,
          Vladimir Sukharyev, Leonid Bartenyev,
          Yuri Konovalov
         3. East Germany, 40.3, Lothar Knorzer,
          Leonhard Pohl, Heinz Futterer,
          Manfred Germar
1952   1. USA, 40.1, Dean Smith, Harrison
          Dillard, Lindy Remigino, Andrew
          Stanfield
         2. Soviet Union, 40.3, Boris Tokaryev,
          Levan Kalyayev, Levan Sanadze,
          Vladimir Sukharyev
         3. Hungary, 40.5, Laszlo Zarandi, Geza
          Varasdi, Gyorgy Csanyi, Bela
          Goldovanyi

1948 1. USA, 40.6, Norwood Ewell, Lorenzo Wright, Harrison Dillard, Mel Patton
2. Great Britain, 41.3, John Archer, John Gregory, Alistair McCorquodale, Ken Jones
3. Italy, 41.5, Michele Tito, Enrico Perucconi, Antonio Siddi, Carlo Monti

1936 1. USA, 39.8, (WR) Jesse Owens,, Ralph Metcalfe, Foy Draper, Frank Wykoff
2. Italy, 41.1, Orazio Mariani, Gianni Caldana, Elio Ragni, Tullio Gonnelli
3. Germany, 41.2, Wilhelm Leichum, Erich Borchmeyer, Erwin Gillmeister, Gerd Hornberger

1932 1. USA, 40.0, (WR) Robert Kiesel, Emmett Toppino, Hector Dyer, Frank Wykoff
2. Germany, 40.9, Helmut Kornig, Friedrich Hendrix, Erich Borchmeyer, Arthur Jonath
3. Italy, 41.2, Giuseppe Castelli, Ruggero Maregatti, Gabriele Salviati, Edgardo Toetti

1928 1. USA, 41.0, (EWR) Frank Wykoff, James Quinn, Charles Borah, Henry Russell
2. Germany, 41.2, Georg Lammers, Richard Corts, Hubert Houben, Helmut Kornig
3. Great Britain, 41.8, Cyril Gill, Ellis Smouha, Walter Rangeley, Jack London

1924 1. USA, 41.0, (WR) Francis Hussey, Louis Clarke, Loren Murchison, Alfred Leconey
2. Great Britain, 41.2, Harold Abrahams, Walter Rangeley, Lancelot Royle, William Nichol
3. Netherlands, 41.8, Jacob Boot, Henricus Broos, Jan de Vries, Marinus van den Berge

1920 1. USA, 42.2, (WR) Charles Paddock, Jackson Scholz, Loren Murchison, Morris Kirksey
2. France, 42.6, Rene Tirard, Rene Lorain, Rene Mourlon, Emile Ali Khan
3. Sweden, 42.9, Agne Holmstrom, William Petersson, Sven Malm, Nils Sandstrom

1912 1. Great Britain, 42.4, (OR) David Jacobs, Henry Macintosh, Victor d'Arcy, William Applegarth
2. Sweden, 42.6, Ivan Moller, Charles Luther, Ture Persson, Knut Lindberg

**1896-
1908** **Not held**

Track and Field — Men's 4x400-Meter Relay

1988 1. USA, 2:56.16, (EWR) Danny Everett, Steve Lewis, Kevin Robinzine, Butch Reynolds
2. Jamaica, 3:00.30, Howard Davis, Devon Morris, Winthrop Graham, Bertland Cameron
3. West Germany, 3:00.56, Norbert Dobeleit, Edgar Itt, Jorg Vaihinger, Raif Lubke

1984 1. USA, 2:57.91, Sunder Nix, Ray Armstead, Alonzo Babers, Antonio McKay

2. Great Britain, 2:59.13, Kriss Akabusi, Garry Cook, Todd Bennett, Philip Brown
3. Nigeria, 2:59.32, Sunday Uti, Moses Ugbusien, Rotimi Peters, Innocent Egbunike

1980 1. Soviet Union, 3:01.1, Remigius Valiulis, Mikhail Linge, Nikolai Chernetski, Viktor Markin
2. East Germany. 3:01.3, Klaus Thiele, Andreas Knebel, Frank Schaffer, Volker Beck
3. Italy, 3:04.3, Stefano Malinverni, Mauro Zuliani, Roberto Tozzi, Pietro Mennea

1976 1. USA, 2:59.52, Herman Frazier, Benjamin Brown, Frederick Newhouse, Maxie Parks
2. Poland, 3:01.43, Ryszard Podlas, Jan Werner, Zbigniew Jaremski, Jerzy Pietrzyk
3. West Germany, 3:01.98, Franz-Peter Hofmeister, Lothar Krieg, Harald Schmid, Bernd Herrmann

1972 1. Kenya, 2:59.8, Charles Asati, H. Munyoro Nyamau, Robert Ouko, Julius Sang
2. Great Britain, 3:00.5, Martin Reynolds, Alan Pascoe, David Hemery, David Jenkins
3. France, 3:00.7, Gilles Bertould, Daniel Velasquez, Francis Kerbiriou, Jacques Carette

1968 1. USA, 2:56.16 (WR), Vincent Matthews, Ronald Freeman, Larry James, Lee Evans
2. Kenya, 2:59.6, Daniel Rudisha, Matesi Munyoro, Naftali Bon, Charles Asati
3. West Germany, 3:00.5, Helmar Muller, Manfred Kinder, Gerhard Hennige, Martin Jellinghaus

1964 1. USA, 3:00.7, (WR) Ollan Cassell, Michael Larrabee, Ulis Williams, Henry Carr
2. Great Britain, 3:01.6, Timothy Graham, Adrian Metcalfe, John Cooper, Robbie Brightwell
3. Trinidad and Tobago, 3:01.7, Edwin Skinner, Kent Bernard, Edwin Roberts, Wendell Mottley

1960 1. USA, 3:02.2, (WR) Jack Yerman, Earl Young, Glenn Davis, Otis Davis
2. West Germany, 3:02.7, Hans-Joachim Reske, Manfred Kinder, Johannes Kaiser, Carl Kaufmann
3. British West Indies, 3:04.0, Malcolm Spence, James Wedderburn, Keith Gardner, George Kerr

1956 1. USA, 3:04.8, Louis Jones, Jesse Mashburn, Charles Jenkins, Tom Courtney
2. Australia, 3:06.2, Leon Gregory, David Lean, Graham Gipson, Kevin Gosper
3. Great Britain, 3:07.2, John Salisbury, Michael Wheeler, F. Peter Higgins, Derek Johnson

1952 1. Jamaica, 3:03.9, (WR) Arthur Wint, Leslie Laing, Herbert McKenley, George Rhoden
2. USA, 3:04.0, Ollie Matson, Gerald Cole, Charles Moore, Malvin Whitfield

3. West Germany, 3:06.6, Hans Geister, Gunter Steines, Heinz Ulzheimer, Karl-Friedrich Haas

1948 1. USA, 3:10.4, Arthur Harnden, Clifford Bourland, Roy Cochran, Malvin Whitfield
2. France, 3:14.8, Jean Kerebel, Francis Schewetta, Robert Chef d'hotel, Jacques Lunis
3. Sweden, 3:16.0, Kurt Lundqvist, Lars Wolfbrandt, Folke Alnevik, Rune Larsson

1936 1. Great Britain, 3:09.0, Frederick Wolff, Godfrey Rampling, William Roberts, A. Godfrey Brown
2. USA, 3:11.0, Harold Cagle, Robert Young, Edward O'Brien Alfred Fitch
3. Germany, 3:11.8, Helmut Hamann, Friedrich von Stulpnagel, Harry Voigt, Rudolf Harbig

1932 1. USA, 3:08.2, (WR) Ivan Fuqua, Edgar Ablowich, Carl Warner, William Carr
2. Great Britain, 3:11.2, Crew Stoneley, Thomas Hampson, David Burghley, Godfrey Rampling
3. Canada, 3:12.8, Raymond Lewis, James Ball, Philip Edwards, Alexander Wilson

1928 1. USA, 3:14.2, (WR) George Baird, Emerson Spencer, Fred Alderman, Raymond Barbuti
2. Germany, 3:14.8, (WR) Otto Neumann, Richard Krebs, Harry Storz, Hermann Engelhard
3. Canada, 3:15.4, Alexander Wilson, Philip Edwards, Stanley Glover, James Ball

1924 1. USA, 3:16.0, (WR) Con Cochrane, Alan Helffrich, Olivier McDonald, William Stevenson
2. Sweden, 3:17.0, Artur Svensson, Erik Bylehn, Gustaf Wejnarth, Nils Engdahl
3. Great Britain, 3:17.4, Edward Toms, George Renwick, Richard Ripley, Guy Butler

1920 1. Great Britain, 3:22.2, Cecil Griffiths, Robert Lindsay, John Ainsworth-Davis, Guy Butler
2. South Africa, 3:24.2, Harry Davel, Clarence Oldfield, Jack Oosterlaak, Bevil Rudd
3. France, 3:24.8, Geo Andre, Gaston Fery, Maurice Delvart, Jean Devaux

1912 1. USA, 3:16.6 (WR) Melvin Sheppard, Edward Lindberg, James Meredith, Charles Reidpath
2. France, 3:20.7, Charles Lelong, Robert Schurrer, Pierre Failliot, Charles Poulenard
3. Great Britain, 3:23.2, George Nicol, Ernest Henley, James Soutter, Cyril Seedhouse

1908 1. USA, 3:29.4, William Hamilton, Nathaniel Cartmell, John Taylor, Melvin Sheppard
2. Germany, 3:32.4 Arthur Hoffman, Hans Eicke, Otto Trieloff, Hanns Braun
3. Hungary, 3:32.5 Pal Simon, Frigyes Mezey-Wiesner, Jozsef Nagy, Odon Bodor

1896-
1906 **Not held**

Track and Field — Men's 20 km Walk

1988 1. Jozef Pribilinec, Czechoslovakia, 1:19:57 (OR)
2. Ronald Weigel, East Germany, 1:20:00
3. Maurizio Damilano, Italy, 1:20:14

1984
1. Ernesto Canto, Mexico, 1:23:13 (OR)
2. Raul Gonzalez, Mexico, 1:23:20
3. Maurizio Damilano, Italy, 1:23:26

1980 1. Maurizio Damilano, Italy, 1:23:35.5 (OR)
2. Pyotr Pochinchuk, Soviet Union, 1:24:45.4
3. Roland Wieser, East Germany, 1:25:58.2

1976 1. Daniel Bautista, Mexico, 1:24:40.6 (OR)
2. Hans Reimann, East Germany, 1:25:13.8
3. Peter Frenkel, East Germany, 1:25:29.4

1972 1. Peter Frenkel, East Germany, 1:26;42.4 (OR)
2. Vladimir Golubnichi, Soviet Union, 1:26:55.2
3. Hans Reimann, East Germany, 1:27:16.6

1968 1. Vladimir Golubnichi, Soviet Union, 1:33:58.4
2. Jose Pedraza, Mexico, 1:34:00.0
3. Nikolai Smaga, Soviet Union, 1:34:03.4

1964 1. Kenneth Matthews, Great Britain, 1:29:34.0
2. Dieter Lindner, East Germany, 1:31:13.2
3. Vladimir Golubnichi, Soviet Union, 1:31:59.4

1960 1. Vladimir Golubnichi, Soviet Union, 1:34:07.2
2. Noel Freeman, Australia, 1:34:16.4
3. Stanley Vickers, Great Britain, 1:34:56.4

1956 1. Leonid Spirin, Soviet Union, 1:31:27.4
2. Antanas Mikenas, Soviet Union, 1:32:03.0
3. Bruno Junk, Soviet Union, 1:32:12.0

1896-
1952 **Not held**

Track and Field — Men's 50 km Walk

1988 1. Viacheslav Ivanenko, Soviet Union, 3:38:29 (OR)
2. Ronald Weigel, East Germany, 3:28:56
3. Hartwig Gauder, East Germany, 3:39:45

1984 1. Raul Gonzalez, Mexico, 3:47:26
2. Bo Gustafsson, Sweden, 3:53:19
3. Alessandro Belluci, Italy, 3:53:45

1980 1. Hartwig Gauder, East Germany, 3:49:24.0 (OR)
2. Jorge Llopart, Spain, 3:51:25.0

527

3. Yevgeny Ivchenko, Soviet Union,
3:56:32.0
1976 **Not held**
1972 1. Bernd Kannenberg, West Germany,
3:56:11.6 (OR)
1. Veniamin Soldatenko, Soviet Union,
3:58:24.0
3. Larry Young, USA, 4:00:46.0
1968 1. Christoph Hohne, East Germany,
4:20:13.6
2. Antal Kiss, Hungary, 4:30:17.0
3. Larry Young, USA, 4:31:55.4
1964 1. Abdon Pamich, Italy, 4:11:12.4 (OR)
2. Paul Nihill, Great Britain, 4:11:31.2
3. Ingvar Pettersson, Sweden, 4:14:17.4
1960 1. Donald Thompson, Great Britain,
4:25:30.0 (OR)
2. John Ljunggren, Sweden, 4:25:47.0
3. Abdon Pamich, Italy, 4:27:55.4
1956 1. Norman Read, New Zealand,
4:30:42.8

2. Yevgeny Maskinskov, Soviet Union,
4:32:57.0
3. John Ljunggren, Sweden, 4:35:02.0
1952 1. Giuseppe Dordoni, Italy, 4:28:07.8
(OR)
2. Josef Dolezal, Czechoslovakia,
4:30:17.8
3. Antal Roka, Hungary, 4:31:27.2
1948 1. John Ljunggren, Sweden, 4:41:52
2. Godel Gaston, Switzerland, 4:48:17
3. Tebbs Lloyd-Johnson, Great Britain,
4:48:31
1936 1. H. Harold Whitlock, Great Britain,
4:30:41.4 (OR)
2. Arthur Schwab, Switzerland, 4:32:09.2
3. Adalberts Bubenko, Latvia, 4:32:42.2
1932 1. Thomas Green, Great Britain, 4:50:10
2. Janis Dalinsch, Latvia, 4:57:20
3. Ugo Frigerio, Italy, 4:59:06
1896-
1928 **Not held**

WOMEN'S RUNNING EVENTS

▼

HIGHLIGHTS

Sprints, 400 Meters, and Relays

In 1928 the 100m, the initial Olympic women's track and field event, was won by Elizabeth Robinson of the US. A few years after the Amsterdam Games, Robinson was severely injured in a plane crash, and her prospects of returning to competition were bleak. Astonishingly, she managed a comeback and went on to capture another gold medal in Berlin as a member of the American 4 x 100 relay team.

A poignant Olympic story relates that the German women's relay team of 1936 couldn't lose; that is, until Marie Dollinger and a teammate dropped the baton. The world was watching, and so was Hitler. The American team—anchored by 1928's 100m winner Betty Robinson and 1936's 100m winner Helen Stephens—seized the golden opportunity, winning by eight yards. Dollinger's daughter, Brunhilde Hendrix, ran the relay final in 1960 for Germany, and happily brought home a silver medal.

Polish-born Stella Walasiewicz (later Walsh, as an American citizen), won the 100m gold in 1932 and the 100m silver in 1936, and minced no words when she referred to the young American upstart, Helen Stephens, who beat her in the 1936 Games, calling her a "greenie from the sticks." Walsh's story came to a tragic end—and her record was amended—when she was caught in the middle of a holdup; the post-shooting autopsy revealed that Stella Walsh was a man.

Fanny Blankers-Koen was the belle of the ball in 1948; having been on the 1936 Dutch team, Blankers had married, had two children, and established six world records in the 12-year interim. Some thought she was too old to compete well in London, but her four-medal haul—that's almost half of that year's women's track and field medals—soon silenced them. Blankers-Koen won the 100m, the 80m hurdles, the 200m, and the 4 x 100m relay. Too bad she wasn't allowed to compete in her strongest event, the long jump: her best jump beat the gold medal distance by twenty inches. Blankers-Koen also held the world record in the high jump.

Fifteen-year-old US sprinter Barbara Jones ran a leg in 1952's 4 x 100 relay team, becoming the youngest track gold medal winner. Also that year, Australian Marjorie Jackson tied the 17-year-old record for the 200m that had been set by Stella Walsh. Jackson tied his-or-her record in the first round, and broke it in the first semifinal; in the final, having no more record to challenge, she left her competition in the dust four yards back.

Australia's Betty Cuthbert struck gold in 1956 at the tender age of 18, winning the 100m and 200m, and helping her team to the relay gold. 1956 was the first time in the history of the Games that the first and second place finisher of the 100m were in the same person and the same order as for the 200 meters, as Christa Stubnick of East Germany took the silver in both races. At the wizened age of 22, Cuthbert triumphed again in the 400m in 1960.

Wilma Rudolph was 1960's champion, winning a total of three gold medals, at that time the most ever by a US woman. Touted as the world's fastest woman, Rudolph was clocked in the final at 11.0 flat. Although she had beaten the world record time, her time was disallowed because the favoring wind was .752 meters per second above the acceptable limit.

Rudolph was followed by sprint champion Wyomia Tyus, who captured the 100m in Tokyo. Tyus was the first athlete, man or woman, to win back-to-back titles in the 100m in the Olympics when she defended her gold in 1968.

Poland's Irena Szewinska-Kirszenstein captured a silver medal in the 200m in 1964, came back for the gold in 1968—setting a world record in the 200 with a time of 22.5— then completed the set with a bronze in 1972. She also shared in the team gold of the Polish 4 x 100m relay team in 1964, won the silver medal in 1964's long jump, and dashed to a bronze in the 100m in 1968. In 1976, she capped her very successful Olympic career with a gold in the 400m. Szewinska-Kirszenstein was the first woman to win medals at three successive Games, and also in five different events.

East Germany's Bärbel Eckert, later competing as Bärbel Wöckel, captured four gold medals from 1976 to 1980, in the 200m and the 4 x 100m relay. Competing in 1976 at the age of 21 as a third-string sprinter, she surprised everyone when—after equaling her personal best in the quarterfinals—she won the final with an Olympic record for the 200 meters. In 1980, even though Wöckel had not won a single heat, she made it to the 200m finals, and sprinted to the front in the final turn to take another gold.

Wilma Rudolph's 1960 performance was matched in 1984 by Valerie Brisco-Hooks. Brisco-Hooks became the only 200m and 400m double winner of either gender in all Olympic history. Evelyn Ashford set an Olympic record in the 100m in 1984; Florence Griffith Joyner broke that record in 1988 in the preliminaries, and ran even faster in the finals, but Griffith Joyner's time didn't count for the record because the tail wind was above the allowable maximum. Griffith Joyner nonetheless won the gold, while Ashford took home the silver in 1988.

In 1988, the USA's 4 x 100m relay team of Alice Brown, Sheila Echols, Griffith Joyner, and Ashford claimed the gold, followed by the East German and Soviet teams. In the 4 x 400m race, the Soviet Union ran for the gold and the USA (Brisco-Hooks, Griffith Joyner, Denean Howard-Hill, and Diane Dixon) settled for silver, trailing the Soviets by less than half a second.

Middle Distance, Long Distance, and Cross Country

The women's 800m was run at the first Games to admit women for track events, in 1928. The sight of ill-trained women staggering toward the finish of the 800m caused the event to be banished from the Olympic program until 1960. Even in 1960, Australian Dixie Willis, who had led the race until the final 150 meters, staggered off the track, allowing Soviet Lyudmila Shevtsova to sprint to the gold and an Olympic record. British runner Ann Packer took the gold in that event in 1964, even though the 800 was not her event; she had already captured the 400m silver that year.

The 1968 800m was best remembered for the unfortunate story of the Yugoslavian record holder, Vera Nikolić. Apparently on the verge of suicide because of the pressure of being Yugoslavia's only hope for a track and field medal, Nikolić was rumored to have been prevented from jumping off a bridge by her coach. American Madeline Manning won the event that year.

Thirteen women beat the pre-Olympic world record in the 1972 semifinals for the 1500m. Twenty-nine-year-old Soviet Lyudmila Bragina maintained a 12-meter lead over the pack during the entire final lap, winning the gold and setting a world record.

At the Montréal Games, Bragina managed only fifth place in the 1500m. Fellow Soviet Tatayana Kazankina, who had broken Bragina's world record the previous month, ran a tactical race to capture the gold, but set no record.

In 1984 Romanian Maricica Puica won the gold in the 3000m race and a bronze in the 1500m. The International Olympic Committee finally allowed the women's 10,000m race for the 1988 Games, and Olga Bondarenko of the Soviet Union promptly ran for the gold, setting an Olympic record in the process.

Marathon and Walking

The USA's Joan Benoit won the first Olympic women's marathon in 1984. That year, Switzerland's Gabriela Andersen Schiess staggered to the finish line, unaided and obviously in trouble, sparking debate about whether someone should have gone out and saved her from those last agonizing steps, when she seemed not only near collapse, but possibly near death. She reeled over the line in 37th place. In 1988 Portugal's Rosa Mota, bronze medalist in 1984, won the gold but did not break Benoit's Olympic record.

Hurdles

In 1932, at the second Olympics open to women, US hurdler Babe Didrikson won a gold in the hurdles to add to her gold in the javelin and a silver in the high jump (changed from gold when her style was ruled illegal).

Didrikson's multiple-medaling performance seemed to foreshadow things to come. Holland's Fanny Blankers-Koen earned a hurdling gold in 1948 to complement her other Olympic spoils. With four firsts, she became distinguished as the woman with the most gold medals earned at a single Games.

Australian Shirley Strickland took the bronze in the hurdles in 1948, then competing as Shirley de la Hunty captured the hurdles gold in 1952 and 1956, to add to a 1956 relay gold, a 1948 relay silver, and two bronzes in the 100m (1948 and 1952). Photo studies show that Strickland also came in third in the 200m event of 1948, but the result has not yet been officially changed.

In 1960 Soviet hurdler Irina Press captured the 80m gold, while her sister, Tamara, won the shot put title, giving the two the impressive distinction of being the Olympics' most successful sisters... or maybe brothers.

At Munich in 1972, Israeli Esther Shakhamorov cherished hopes of becoming her country's first Olympic finalist by competing in the 100m hurdles. When she withdrew following the shocking terrorist attack on Israeli athletes, East Germany's Annelie Ehrhardt had no real competition, and proceeded to set a world record in the hurdles.

Having married in the interim, Shakhamorov competed in Montréal as Esther Rot, and managed to become Israel's first Olympic finalist by placing fifth in the 100m hurdles competition. An imbroglio during the second heat had Soviet Lyubov Kononova bumping into Romanian Valeria Stefanescu in the lane next to her. It was Johanna Schaller, from East Germany, however, who won the race in 12.77.

USA's Benita Fitzgerald-Brown won the 100m hurdles in 1984, while Bulgaria's Jordanka Donkova took the gold in 1988. Casablanca native Nawal El Moutawakel leaped to gold in 1984's 400m hurdles, setting an Olympic record and giving Morocco its first gold medal of the modern Olympics; this was thought to be the only medal ever won by an Arab woman. USA's Judi Brown trailed for silver. In the 1988 400m hurdles, Debra Flintoff-King of Australia set an Olympic record and claimed the gold, although she was a scant one one-hundredth of a second ahead of Tatiana Ledovskaia of the Soviet Union.

The Fall Seen Round the World: The Decker-Budd Duel

On some occasions, due to circumstance and fate, the most deserving amateur athletes fail to win an Olympic medal. Such has been the case with Mary Decker

Slaney, one of the greatest middle distance runners of all time, and a competitor with a fierce desire to succeed.

In 1984 she was Mary Decker, World Champion at the 3000m distance, and a highly regarded hopeful for the gold medal. Her race that year ended in heartbreak and frustration, when a relative newcomer from South Africa, barefoot Zola Budd, tripped her on the track.

Ray Didinger, covering the Olympics in Los Angeles for the *Philadelphia Daily News*, put it this way: "It was a matchup made for Hollywood's Summer Games: Decker, the world champion, ... chasing the one honor she never had won; vs. Budd, the 17-year-old waif who learned to run amid the ostriches in her native land.... This was supposed to be Mary Decker's night of triumph, the night when she wore the Olympic gold medal home and put her career in order. Instead, she added yet another chapter to a life story written in tears. If you saw it, you aren't likely to forget."

Mary Decker, born on August 4, 1958, and a native of Bunnvale, New Jersey, began running when she was 11, just after her family moved to California. She trained and raced relentlessly, once competing in a marathon, a 440, an 880, a mile race, and a two-mile race all in one day. In 1974, the 15-year-old Decker caused an international sensation during a 4 x 800m relay in the Soviet Union. Shoved off the track by a Soviet runner, she responded by throwing her baton at the offender not once but twice. Both teams were disqualified, and Decker was admonished for her unsportsmanlike behavior. Many Americans were quick to forgive her, under the circumstances.

Soon after that incident, Decker's intense devotion to running nearly crippled her. Her muscles grew faster than her bones, causing severe pain and cramping. The condition—called compartment syndrome—caused her to miss the 1976 Olympics and almost ruined her career. Fortunately for her, she was finally able to undergo corrective surgery, and she returned to her sport.

In 1980 she set her first outdoor world record, running the mile in 4:21.7. She easily qualified for the Olympic team but had to sit the Games out yet again because the United States boycotted. After a grueling European tour some months later, she underwent yet more surgery to repair a partial tear of her Achilles' tendon.

When that injury healed, Decker quickly regained her place among the best middle distance champions in the world. At one point in 1983, she held every United States record from 800 to 10,000 meters, and she had bettered her own world record in the mile by three seconds. At the 1983 World Championships in Helsinki, she won both the 3000 and the 1500 meter races. Immediately, "Little Mary," who had undergone leg surgery half a dozen times, became the favorite to win the gold medal in the 3000m race in Los Angeles.

One of Decker's numerous fans was a rural South African runner named Zola Budd. Born in 1966 in Bloemfontein, Orange Free State, Budd trained racing barefoot on the quiet farm where she grew up. She showed such talent that her parents sought professional coaching for her, and by 1983 she was ranked number one in the world at 5000 meters. Budd's frustrations were not health problems but political ones—South Africa was banned from participation in the Olympic Games because of its legislated racism. Budd took small solace in the picture of Mary Decker she kept pinned to the wall next to her bed.

Shortly before the 1984 Olympic Games, Budd's family found a loophole. Since her paternal grandfather had been a citizen of Britain, Budd and her family were allowed to emigrate. Her citizenship was granted in two weeks, and all of her moving expenses were paid by the *Daily Mail* newspaper in London. Suddenly the quiet teenager found herself the object of scorn for her homeland's racial policies. She was also hardly welcome amongst British women runners, who resented her sudden intrusion. Not long after arriving in Los Angeles to compete in the games as a member of Team Great Britain, Budd learned that her South African citizenship had been revoked.

Thus both women took the track in Los Angeles with a wealth of pressures. Decker had dominated her sport but had never won an Olympic award. Budd was unaccustomed to running with others of her ability—a defect that brought tragic consequences.

The 3000m final in Los Angeles had just passed its mid-point when the collision occurred. Budd was in the lead, followed closely by Decker and Romanian Maricica Puica. At about the 1700-meter mark, Budd may have tried to move inside without sufficient room; Decker hit one of Budd's legs, throwing Budd slightly off balance. Five strides later the two runners bumped again, with more serious consequences. This time Budd landed awkwardly, and Decker—running full tilt—tripped over Budd's right leg, lost her balance, and sprawled into the infield. The hard fall caused Decker to pull a hip muscle. She could not rise on her own from the ground.

Decker was inconsolable after the race and would accept no apologies from Budd. The American openly blamed Budd for the accident. Initially Budd was disqualified—she finished seventh—but after further review by videotape, a jury voted to reinstate her.

Decker did not run again in 1984, but the following year she defeated both Budd and Puica in a mile race in Zurich, setting yet another world record. The incident at the Olympics continued to haunt Decker, however—her coaches constantly faulted her for setting fast paces off the block in order to get ahead of the pack. The strategy began to backfire, and never more so than in the 1988 Olympics, where she finished a badly beaten 10th in the 3000m finals.

Now, despite yet another four operations on her Achilles tendon, Mary Decker Slaney, who will turn 34 during the Barcelona Games, hopes to run in the 1992 Olympics. She told the *Philadelphia Inquirer* that the wrenching disappointments were all part of her past, and now she only wants to compete and win again. "What keeps me coming back is that I truly love the sport," she said. "I really believe in my heart that I haven't run as fast as I can. I can't ever see myself not running. I love working out."

Zola Budd, who was recently married, has retired from competition and returned to Bloemfontein. —*M.K.*

Joan Benoit Samuelson

In April, 1979, on the way to compete in her first Boston Marathon, Joan Benoit found herself caught in a traffic jam. She jumped out of her friend's car, ran two miles to the starting line, and 26 miles later won the race with a record-setting time of 2:35:15.

This same determination drove her to enter a marathon in September, 1982, just months after surgery on both Achilles tendons. She won that race in 2:26:11, breaking the record for American women by two minutes. And she ran to victory in the 1984 US Olympic trials with a time of 2:31:04, just 17 days after undergoing arthroscopic surgery on her knee.

The diminutive Joan Benoit Samuelson—she stands 5 feet, 3 inches, and weighs 105 pounds—has set new standards of both speed and courage for long-distance runners with her victories in the 1979 and 1983 Boston Marathons. And she secured her place in history by winning the gold medal in the first women's Olympic marathon at the Los Angeles Games in 1984, in an incredible 2:24:52.

The Olympic marathon started off slowly—too slowly, thought Benoit. She took the lead at the three-mile mark and wondered why she was so outpacing her competitors. Toward the end, she maintained a more comfortable pace, conserving energy in case she needed to repel a last-minute challenge. That never happened: Benoit entered the Los Angeles Coliseum to the thunderous ovation of 77,000 spectators.

Asked later to recall her thoughts during the final yards of the marathon, she said: "I couldn't believe no one had challenged me. . . . I couldn't imagine that it was almost over." Her time was the third-fastest ever run by a woman in a marathon.

The daughter of Andre (who runs an apparel store in Portland, Maine) and Nancy Benoit, Joan Benoit Samuelson was born on May 16, 1957. She became a dedicated athlete, concentrating primarily on skiing until she broke her leg in a slalom race. As part of her rehabilitation program, she began running, eventually turning in a 5:15 mile in her senior year of high school. At Bowdoin College, where she earned a bachelor's degree in 1979, and North Carolina State University, she was highly ranked as a distance runner, which ultimately led to her outstanding performance in numerous marathons and culminated in her Olympic victory.

On September 29, 1984, Joan Benoit married Scott Samuelson. They have two children, Abigail and Anders. She ran the 1987 Boston Marathon while three months pregnant with her first child and competed in that event in 1991 one month after she had stopped nursing her second. Since giving birth to Abigail in 1987 she has been plagued with chronic lower back pain. But as she says, "I'm learning to work with it. I make the best of what I have."

Although she has had to contend with a long list of injuries, Samuelson must still be considered a serious distance-running threat. Her performance in the 1991 Boston Marathon, with a time of 2:26:54, qualified her for the 1992 Olympic trials. "I knew I'd be back as soon as I got over those [medical] problems," she said after her fourth-place finish. "All I had to do was to get my head in the thick of things." —*P.G.*

Medalists

Track and Field — Women's 100 Meters

1988
1. Florence Griffith Joyner, USA, 10.54 (OR)
2. Evelyn Ashford, USA, 10.83
3. Heike Drechsler, East Germany, 10.85

1984
1. Evelyn Ashford, USA, (OR) 10.97
2. Alice Brown, USA, 11.13
3. Merlene Ottey-Page, Jamaica, 11.16

1980
1. Lyudmila Kondratyeva, Soviet Union, 11.06
2. Marlies Gohr, East Germany, 11.07
3. Ingrid Auerswald, East Germany, 11.14

1976
1. Annegret Richter, West Germany, 11.08
2. Renate Stecher, East Germany, 11.13
3. Inge Helten, West Germany, 11.17

1972
1. Renate Stecher, East Germany, 11.07
2. Raelene Boyle, Australia, 11.23
3. Silvia Chibas, Cuba, 11.24

1968
1. Wyomia Tyus, USA, 11.0 (WR)
2. Barbara Ferrell, USA, 11.1
3. Irena Szewinska-Kirszenstein, Poland, 11.1

1964
1. Wyomia Tyus, USA, 11.4
2. Edith McGuire, USA, 11.6
3. Ewa Klobukowska, Poland, 11.6

1960
1. Wilma Rudolph, USA, 11.0
2. Dorothy Hyman, Great Britain, 11.3
3. Giuseppina Leone, Italy, 11.3

1956
1. Betty Cuthbert, Australia, 11.5
2. Christa Stubnick, East Germany, 11.7
3. Marlene Matthews, Australia, 11.7

1952
1. Marjorie Jackson, Australia, 11.5 (EWR)
2. Daphne Hasenjager-Robb, South Africa, 11.8
3. Shirley De La Hunty-Strickland, Australia, 11.9

1948
1. Francina Blankers-Koen, Netherlands, 11.9
2. Dorothy Manley, Great Britain, 12.2
3. Shirley Strickland, Australia, 12.2

1936
1. Helen Stephens, USA, 11.5
2. Stanislawa Walasiewicz, Poland, 11.7
3. Kathe Krauss, Germany, 11.9

1932
1. Stanislawa Walasiewicz, Poland, 11.9 (EWR)
2. Hilda Strike, Canada, 11.9
3. Wilhelmina Von Bremen, USA, 12.0

1928
1. Elizabeth Robinson, USA, 12.2 (EWR)
2. Fanny Rosenfeld, Canada, 12.3
3. Ethel Smith, Canada, 12.3

1896-1924
Not held

Track and Field — Women's 200 Meters

1988
1. Florence Griffith Joyner, USA, 21.34 (WR)
2. Grace Jackson, Jamaica, 21.72
3. Heike Drechsler, East Germany, 21.95

1984
1. Valerie Brisco-Hooks, USA, 21.81 (OR)
2. Florence Griffith, USA, 22.04
3. Merlene Ottey-Page, Jamaica, 22.09

1980
1. Barbel Eckert Wockel, East Germany, 22.03 (OR)
2. Natalya Bochina, Soviet Union, 22.19
3. Merlene Ottey, Jamaica, 22.20

1976
1. Barbel Eckert, East Germany, 22.37 (OR)
2. Annegret Richter, West Germany, 22.39
3. Renate Stecher, East Germany, 22.47

1972
1. Renate Stecher, East Germany, 22.40 (EWR)
2. Raelene Boyle, Australia, 22.45
3. Irena Szewinska-Kirszenstein, Poland, 22.74

1968
1. Irena Szewinska-Kirszenstein, Poland, 22.5 (WR)
2. Raelene Boyle, Australia, 22.7
3. Jennifer Lamy, Australia, 22.8

1964
1. Edith McGuire, USA, 23.0 (OR)
2. Irena Kirszenstein, Poland, 23.1
3. Marilyn Black, Australia, 23.1

1960
1. Wilma Rudolph, USA, 24.0
2. Jutta Heine, West Germany, 24.4
3. Dorothy Hyman, Great Britain, 24.7

1956
1. Betty Cuthbert, Australia, 23.4 (EOR)
2. Christa Stubnick, East Germany, 23.7
3. Marlene Matthews, Australia, 23.8

1952
1. Marjorie Jackson, Australia, 23.7
2. Bertha Brouwer, Netherlands, 24.2
3. Nadezhda Khnykina, Soviet Union, 24.2

1948
1. Francina Blankers-Koen, Netherlands, 24.4
2. Audrey Williamson, Great Britain, 25.1
3. Audrey Patterson, USA, 25.2

535

Summer

1896-
1936   Not held

Track and Field — Women's 400 Meters

1988   1. Olga Bryzguina, Soviet Union, 48.65 (OR)
        2. Petra Mueller, East Germany, 49.45
        3. Olga Nazarova, Soviet Union, 49.90
1984   1. Valerie Brisco-Hooks, USA, 48.83 (OR)
        2. Chandra Cheeseborough, USA, 49.05
        3. Kathryn Cook, Great Britain, 49.42
1980   1. Marita Koch, East Germany, 48.88 (OR)
        2. Jarmila Kratochvilova, Czechoslovakia, 49.46
        3. Christina Lathan, East Germany, 49.66
1976   1. Irena Szewinska-Kirszenstein, Poland, 49.29 (WR, OR)
        2. Christina Brehmer, East Germany, 50.51
        3. Ellen Streidt, East Germany, 50.55
1972   1. Monika Zehrt, East Germany, 51.08 (OR)
        2. Rita Wilden, West Germany, 51.21
        3. Kathy Hammond, USA, 51.64
1968   1. Colette Besson, France, 52.0 (EOR)
        2. Lillian Board, Great Britain, 52.1
        3. Natalja Pechenkina, Soviet Union, 52.2
1964   1. Betty Cuthbert, Australia, 52.0 (OR)
        2. Ann Packer, Great Britain, 52.2
        3. Judith Amoore, Australia, 53.4
1896-
1960   Not held

Track and Field — Women's 800 Meters

1988   1. Sigrun Wodars, East Germany, 1:56.10
        2. Christine Wachtel, East Germany, 1:56.64
        3. Kim Gallagher, USA, 1:56.91
1984   1. Doina Melinte, Romania, 1:57.60
        2. Kim Gallagher, USA, 1:58.63
        3. Fita Lovin, Romania, 1:58.83
1980   1. Nadezhda Olizarenko, Soviet Union, 1:53.42 (WR)
        2. Olga Mineyeva, Soviet Union, 1:54.9
        3. Tatyana Providokhina, Soviet Union, 1:55.5
1976   1. Tatyana Kazankina, Soviet Union, 1:54.94 (WR, OR)
        2. Nikolina Shtereva, Bulgaria, 1:55.42
        3. Elfi Zinn, East Germany, 1:55.60
1972   1. Hildegard Falck, West Germany, 1:58.55 (OR)
        2. Niole Sabaite, Soviet Union, 1:58.65
        3. Gunhild Hoffmeister, East Germany, 1:59.19
1968   1. Madeline Manning, USA, 2:00.9 (OR)
        2. Ileana Silai, Romania, 2:02.5
        3. Maria Gommers, Netherlands, 2:02.6
1964   1. Ann Packer, Great Britain, 2:01.1 (OR)
        2. Maryvonne Dupureur, France, 2:01.9
        3. Ann Chamberlain, New Zealand, 2:02.8

1960   1. Lyudmila Shevtsova, Soviet Union, 2:04.3 (EWR)
        2. Brenda Jones, Australia, 2:04.4
        3. Ursula Donath, East Germany, 2:05.6
1932-
1956   Not held
1928   1. Lina Radke, Germany, 2:16.8 (WR)
        2. Kinue Hitomi, Japan, 2:17.6
        3. Inga Gentzel, Sweden, 2:17.8
1896-
1924   Not held

Track and Field — Women's 1,500 Meters

1988   1. Paula Ivan, Romania, 3:53.96 (OR)
        2. Lailoute Baikauskaite, Soviet Union, 4:00.24
        3. Tatiana Samolenko, Soviet Union, 4:00.30
1984   1. Gabriella Dorio, Italy, 4:03.25
        2. Doina Melinte, Romania, 4:03.76
        3. Maricica Puica, Romania, 4:04.15
1980   1. Tatyana Kazankina, Soviet Union, 3:56.6 (OR)
        2. Christiane Wartenberg, East Germany, 3:57.8
        3. Nadezhda Olizarenko, Soviet Union, 3:59.6
1976   1. Tatyana Kazankina, Soviet Union, 4:05.48
        2. Gunhild Hoffmeister, East Germany, 4:06.02
        3. Ulrike Klapezynski, East Germany, 4:06.09
1972   1. Ljudmila Bragina, Soviet Union, 4:01.4 (WR)
        2. Gunhild Hoffmeister, East Germany, 4:02.8
        3. Paola Cacchi-Pigni, Italy, 4:02.9
1896-
1968   Not held

Track and Field — Women's 3,000 Meters

1988   1. Tatiana Samolenko, Soviet Union, 8:26.53 (OR)
        2. Paula Ivan, Romania, 8:27.15
        3. Yvonne Murray, Great Britain, 8:29.02
1984   1. Maricica Puica, Romania, 8:35.96 (OR)
        2. Wendy Sly, Great Britain, 8:39.47
        3. Lynn Williams, Canada, 8:42.14
1896-
1980   Not held

Track and Field — Women's 10,000 Meters

1988   1. Olga Bondarenko, Soviet Union, 31:05.21 (OR)
        2. Elizabeth McColgan, Great Britain, 31:08.44
        3. Elena Joupieva, Soviet Union, 31:19.82
1896-
1984   Not held

536

Track and Field — Women's Marathon

1988 1. Rosa Mota, Portugal, 2:25.40
2. Lisa Martin, Australia, 2:25.53
3. Kathrin Doerre, East Germany, 2:26.21
1984 1. Joan Benoit, USA, 2:24.52
2. Grete Waitz, Norway, 2:26.18
3. Rosa Mota, Portugal, 2:26.57
1896-
1980 Not held

Track and Field — Women's 100-Meter Hurdles

1988 1. Jordanka Donkova, Bulgaria, 12.38 (OR)
2. Gloria Siebert, East Germany, 12.61
3. Claudia Zackiewicz, West Germany, 12.75
1984 1. Benita Fitzgerald-Brown, USA, 12.84
2. Shirley Strong, Great Britain, 12.88
3. Michele Chardonnet, France, 13.06
3. Kim Turner, USA, 13.06
1980 1. Vera Komisova, Soviet Union, 12.56 (OR)
2. Johanna Klier, East Germany, 12.63
3. Lucyna Langer, Poland, 12.65
1976 1. Johanna Schaller, East Germany, 12.77
2. Tatiana Anisimova, Soviet Union, 12.78
3. Natalia Lebedeva, Soviet Union, 12.80
1972 1. Annelie Ehrhardt, East Germany, 12.59 (OR)
2. Valeria Bufanu, Romania, 12.84
3. Karin Balzer, East Germany, 12.90
1968 1. Maureen Caird, Australia, 10.3 (OR)
2. Pamela Kilborn, Australia, 10.4
3. Chi Cheng, Taiwan, 10.4
1964 1. Karin Balzer, East Germany, 10.5
2. Teresa Ciepla, Poland, 10.5
3. Pamela Kilborn, Australia, 10.5
1960 1. Irina Press, Soviet Union, 10.8
2. Carol Quinton, Great Britain, 10.9
3. Gisela Birkemeyer-Kohler, East Germany, 11.0
1956 1. Shirley De La Hunty-Strickland, Australia, 10.7 (OR)
2. Gisela Kohler, East Germany, 10.9
3. Norma Thrower, Australia, 11.0
1952 1. Shirley De La Hunty-Strickland, Australia, 10.9 (WR)
2. Maria Golubnichaya, Soviet Union, 11.1
3. Maria Sander, West Germany, 11.1
1948 1. Francina Blankers-Koen, Netherlands, 11.2 (OR)
2. Maureen Gardner, Great Britain, 11.2
3. Shirley Strickland, Australia, 11.4
1936 1. Trebisonda Valla, Italy, 11.7
2. Anni Steuer, Germany, 11.7
3. Elizabeth Taylor, Canada, 11.7
1932 1. Mildred "Babe" Didrikson, USA, 11.7 (WR)
2. Evelyne Hall, USA, 11.7
3. Marjorie Clark, South Africa, 11.8

1896-
1928 Not held

Track and Field — Women's 400-Meter Hurdles

1988 1. Debra Flintoff-King, Australia, 53.17 (OR)
2. Tatiana Ledovskaia, Soviet Union, 53.18
3. Ellen Fiedler, East Germany, 53.63
1984 1. Nawal El Moutawakel, Morocco, 54.61 (OR)
2. Judi Brown, USA, 55.20
3. Christina Cojocaru, Romania, 55:41
1896-
1980 Not held

Track and Field — Women's 4x100-Meter Relay

1988 1. USA, 41.98, Alice Brown, Sheila Echols, Florence Griffith Joyner, Evelyn Ashford
2. East Germany, 42.09, Silke Moeller, Kerstin Behrendt, Ingrid Lange, Marlies Goehr
3. Soviet Union, 42.75, Lyudmila Kondrayeva, Galina Maltchougina, Marina Jirova, Natalia Pomochtchnikova
1984 1. USA, 41.65, Alice Brown, Jeannette Bolden, Chandra Cheeseborough, Evelyn Ashford
2. Canada, 42.77, Angella Bailey, Marita Payne, Angella Taylor, France Gareau
3. Great Britain, 43.11, Simone Jacobs, Kathryn Cook, Beverley Callender, Heather Oakes
1980 1. East Germany, 41.60, (WR) Romy Muller, Barbel Wockel Eckert, Ingrid Auerswald, Marlies Gohr
2. Soviet Union, 42.10, Vera Komisova, Lyudmila Maslakova-Zharkova, Vera Anisimova, Natalya Bochina
3. Great Britain, 42.43, Heather Hunte, Kathryn Smallwood, Beverley Goddard, Sonia Lannaman
1976 1. East Germany, 42.55 (OR), Marlies Oelsner, Barbel Eckert Wockel Renate Stecher Meissner, Carla Bodendorf
2. West Germany, 42.59, Elvira Possekel, Inge Helten, Annegret Richter, Annegret Kroninger
3. Soviet Union, 43.09, Tatyana Prorochenko, Lyudmila Maslakova-Zharkova, Nadezhda Besfamilnaya, Vera Anisimova
1972 1. West Germany, 42.81, (EWR) Christiane Krause, Ingrid Mickler, Annegret Richter, Heidemarie Rosendahl
2. East Germany, 42.95, Evelyn Kaufer, Christina Heinich, Barbel Struppert, Renate Stecher
3. Cuba, 43.36, Marlene Elejarde, Carmen Valdes, Fulgencia Romay, Silvia Chibas

1968 1. USA, 42.8, (WR) Barbara Ferrell,
Margaret Bailes, Mildrette Netter,
Wyomia Tyus
2. Cuba, 43.3, Marlene Elejarde,
Fulgencia Romay, Violetta Quesada,
Miguelina Cobian
3. Soviet Union, 43.4, Lyudmila
Zharkova, Galina Bukharina, Vyera
Popkova, Lyudmila Samotysova
1964 3. Great Britain, 44.0, Janet Simpson,
Mary Rand, Daphne Arden, Dorothy
Hyman
1. Poland, 43.6 Teresa Ciepla-
Wieczorek, Irena Kirszenstein, Halina
Gorecka-Richter, Ewa Klobukowska
2. USA, 43.9, Willye White, Wyomia
Tyus, Marilyn White, Edith McGuire
1960 1. USA, 44.5, Martha Hudson, Lucinda
Williams, Barbara Jones, Wilma
Rudolph
2. West Germany, 44.8, Martha
Langbein, Anni Biechl, Brunhilde
Hendrix, Jutta Heine
3. Poland, 45.0, Teresa Wieczorek,
Barbara Janiszewska, Celina
Jesionowska, Halina Richter
1956 1. Australia, 44.5, (WR) Shirley De La
Hunty-Strickland, Norma Croker, F leur
Mellor, Betty Cuthbert
2. Great Britain, 44.7, Anne Pashley,
Jean Scrivens, June Paul-Foulds,
Heather Armitage
3. USA, 44.9, Mae Faggs, Margaret
Matthews, Wilma Rudolph, Isabelle
Daniels
1952 1. USA, 45.9, (WR) Mae Faggs, Barbara
Jones, Janet Moreau, Catherine Hardy
2. West Germany, 45.9, (WR) Ursula
Knab, Maria Sanders, Helga Klein,
Marga Petersen
3. Great Britain, 46.2, Sylvia Cheeseman,
June Foulds, Jean Desforges, Heather
Armitage
1948 1. Netherlands, 47.5, Xenia Stad-de
Jong, Jeanette Witziers-Timmer, Gerda
Van Der Kade-Koudijs, Francina
Blankers-Koen
2. Australia, 47.6, Shirley Strickland, June
Maston, Betty McKinnon, Joyce King
3. Canada, 47.8, Viola Myers, Nancy
Mackay, Diane Foster, Patricia Jones
1936 1. USA, 46.9, Harriet Bland, Annette
Rogers, Elizabeth Robinson, Helen
Stephens
2. Great Britain, 47.6, Eileen Hiscock,
Violet Olney, Audrey Brown, Barbara
Burke
3. Canada, 47.8, Dorothy Brookshaw,
Mildred Dolson, Hilda Cameron,
Aileen Meagher
1932 1. USA, 46.9, (WR) Mary Carew, Evelyn
Furtsch, Annette Rogers, Wilhelmina
Von Bremen
2. Canada, 47.0, Mildred Frizzel, Lilian
Palmer, Mary Frizzel, Hilda Strike

3. Great Britain, 47.6, Eileen Hiscock,
Gwendoline Porter, Violet Webb,
Nellie Halstead
1928 1. Canada, 48.4 (WR), Fanny Rosenfeld,
Ethel Smith, Florence Bell, Myrtle Cook
2. USA, 48.8, Mary Washburn, Jessie
Cross, Lorata McNeil, Elizabeth
Robinson
3. Germany, 49.0, Rosa Kellner, Leni
Schmidt, Anni Holdmann, Leni Junker
1896-
1924 **Not held**

Track and Field — Women's 4x400-Meter Relay

1988 1. Soviet Union, 3:15.18 (WR), Tatiana
Ledovskaia, Olga Nazarova, Maria
Piniguina, Olga Bryzguina
2. USA, 3:15.51, Denean Howard-Hill,
Diane Dixon, Valerie Brisco-Hooks,
Florence Griffith Joyner
3. East Germany, 3:18.29, Dagmar
Neubauer, Kirsten Emmelmann, Sabine
Busch, Petra Mueller
1984 1. USA, 3:18.39 (OR), Lillie Leatherwood,
Sherri Howard, Valerie Brisco-Hooks,
Chandra Cheeseborough
2. Canada, 3:21.21, Charmaine Crooks,
Jillian Richardson, Molly Killingbeck,
Marita Payne
3. West Germany, 3:22.98, Heike
Schulte- Mattler, Ute Thimm, Heide
Gaugel, Gaby Bussmann
1980 1. Soviet Union, 3:20.2, Tatyana
Prorochenko, Tatyana Goishchik, Nina
Zyuskova, Irina Nazarova
2. East Germany, 3:20.4, Gabriele Lowe,
Barbara Krug, Christina Lathan, Marita
Koch
3. Great Britain, 3:27.5, Linsey
MacDonald, Michelle Probert, Joslyn
Hoyte-Smith, Janine Macgregor
1976 1. East Germany, 3:East Germany,
3:19.23 (WR,OR), Doris Brachmann
Maletzki, Brigitte Koehn Rohde,
Christina Lathan Bremer, Ellen Streidt
2. USA, 3:22.81, Debra Sapenter, Sheila
Ingram, Pamela Jiles, Rosalyn Bryant
3. Soviet Union, 3:24.24, Inta
Klimovocha, Ljudmila Aksenina, Natalia
Sokolova, Nadezhda Ilyina
1972 1. East Germany, 3:23.0 (WR), Dagmar
Kasling, Rita Kuhne, Helga Seidler,
Monika Zehrt
2. USA, 3:25.2, Mabel Fergerson,
Madeline Jackson-Manning, Cheryl
Toussaint, Kathy Hammond
3. West Germany, 3:26.5, Anette Ruckes,
Inge Bodding, Hildegard Falck, Rita
Wilden
1896-
1968 **Not held**

538

TRACK AND FIELD (ATHLETICS)— THROWING AND MIXED EVENTS

WARM-UP

Go back a few thousand years and you'll find throwing events taking place on the battlefield, not in the sports stadium.

Humans depended on the spear-like javelin for hunting and warring. The round-and-round motion of the hammer throw worked nicely in launching, say, a primitive firebomb. The form of the discus thrower is not unlike that of a grenade tosser.

It's better that we keep these athletes competing in the stadium.

The Tailteann Games of ancient Ireland included something called "roth cleas," or wheel feat, which was the hurling of a weight attached to a length of rope, something like the modern-day hammer throw.

The javelin and discus throws are among the oldest competitions organized by the Greeks. Both were part of the pentathlon that was added to the ancient Olympia Games in 708 BC. The famous Greek statue Discobus portrays a discus thrower, though the discus he carries is much larger than today's.

It is believed that the Greeks used a plate of bronze for their discus, and it was thrown using a running turn. Likewise, the ancient Greek version of the javelin throw is quite similar to modern technique. The Greeks attached a loop to the shaft of the spear, apparently to give greater pulling power and accuracy. Unlike modern-day Olympians, though, they threw the javelin for accuracy, not distance.

Napoleon ordered the study of javelin as a possible weapon of war in the 19th century, and a few centuries earlier, British King Henry the VIII had his portrait painted throwing a wooden hammer.

Hammer throwing was popular for centuries in Britain. Like the shot put, it remains part of the modern Scottish Highland Games. Its popularity carried over to America, where the hammer evolved from a clumsy, wood-shafted implement to a clumsy, metallic implement. Americans also experimented in building a hammer from shafts of knotted grape vines.

The first few modern Olympic Games featured several throwing events long since discontinued. There was stone throwing, in which athletes used a javelin toss–like technique to propel a 14-pound rock, and there were two-handed

539

versions of the shot, discus, and javelin throws. Contestants threw with their left and right hands, and were scored based on an aggregate total of the two.

Discus was the only throwing event included when women began competing in track and field sports during the 1928 Olympics. The first female track and field gold medalist was Halina Konopacka of Poland, the discus winner.

In the 1988 Olympic Games, Eastern European athletes won every men's throwing even except the javelin, which was won by a Finn.

Some observers believe that anabolic steroids, now illegal in Olympic competition, were widely used by athletes in "heavy" sports like the throwing events and weightlifting as far back as the mid-1960s to stimulate muscle growth and increase work capacity. If true, the drugs no doubt helped to increase record performances.

fact: While the ancient Greeks tended to immortalize their pentathlon athletes, decathlon champs in America tend to end up in bad movies. Jim Thorpe was an extra in several Westerns. Bob Mathias acted with bombshell Jayne Mansfield in *It Happened in Athens*. Rafer Johnson and C.K. Yang also did some acting, and Bruce Jenner, who won in 1976, starred in a very forgettable film called *Can't Stop the Music*.

Throwing events were combined with running and jumping events early on. The Greeks held the first known pentathlon in 708 BC, which included javelin and discus throws, wrestling, long jump, and foot racing. Ireland staged all-around athletic competitions in the mid-19th century, and the Americans began the same in 1884. A decathlon (not as we know it today) was added to the 1904 Olympics in St. Louis as a men's event. It disappeared until 1912, when the events were reestablished. The women's pentathlon was added in 1964, and in 1980 two more events were added and it became the heptathlon. The Scandinavians organized a decathlon that included the same 10 events as in modern Olympic competition.

Bill Toomey, an American, won the decathlon in 1968 after stressing training for every event. His lead was followed by most decathletes who followed. Daley Thompson, a Briton, set four world records and won the decathlons of 1980 and 1984. German and Soviet women dominated the pentathlon until 1980. Worldwide, decathlon and heptathlon winners are considered the best of the best.

SPECTATORS' GUIDE

Discus: Today's discus is made from wood and metal and shaped like a flying saucer. It has a metal rim and metal center for added weight. The men's discus is about 22 centimeters (0.66 inches) and weighs two kilograms (4 pounds, 6.5 ounces). The women's discus weighs one kilogram and measures 18 centimeters (7.13 inches).

The athlete holds the discus flat against the palm and forearm while standing in the 2.5m (eight foot, 2.25-inch) throwing circle. The throw begins with one and a half spins that leads to a sidearm release.

The discus spins through the air at an upward angle, the spin helping to propel it farther. Throws with a strong wind will carry the discus farther, but there is no rule against wind-aided throws. This makes it difficult to compare the distances of throws.

fact: The discus throw is the only track and field event in which a world record has never been set in the Olympics.

Once the athlete enters the throwing circle, he or she must not leave until the discus has landed. Throws are measured from the landing point to the inside edge of the circle.

Too much spin on the thrower's part causes an uneven launch. Early discus throwers were strong but slow athletes who depended on pure power for throw length. Smaller but quicker athletes began to get better results by concentrating on form and spin. The winning distance for the discus has more than doubled since the modern Games began in 1896, when the winning throw was 95 feet, 7.5 inches.

Al Oerter is probably the greatest discus thrower of modern times. He favored a controlled spin in his throws, and he won four Olympic gold medals, beginning in 1956 at age 20.

Shot put: The shot is a ball of solid metal that weighs 16 pounds for men, and eight pounds, 13 ounces for women. The goal of this event is to "put" the shot as far as possible.

Because shots lose weight in use—tiny particles get chipped off when they land—the balls are weighed before each use. Additional tungsten chips can be added through a plugged hole to bring the shot back up to legal weight.

The shot must be pushed, or put, not thrown. The shot must not drop during the put below the athlete's shoulder. The putting technique begins with the contestant holding the shot in his or her hand, which rests against the shoulder. This is followed by a series of hops inside the putting circle, which is

Track and Field (Athletcis)—Throwing and Mixed Events

541

seven feet (2.1m) in diameter. The athlete then springs powerfully from a near-crouch, unleashes his or her arm, and lets loose the shot with a powerful push.

fact: An American shot putter named Herman Brix finished second in at the Amsterdam Olympics of 1928, then became the first of several Olympic athletes to portray Tarzan in the movies.

The athlete must remain within the circle during the throw. The ring is bounded by a board four inches (10cm) high at the top of the circle. The purpose is to allow the competitor's foot to hit the board without pushing beyond the circle to be disqualified.

Measurement is from the point of impact to the inside circumference of the putting circle.

Like discus throwers, shot putters were originally physically powerful athletes who lacked technique. That changed as speed became important and as weight training improved performances. Additionally, shot putters were among the first athletes to abuse steroids, and many performances improved accordingly.

Up until the early 20th century, most shot putters used the side-on hop favored by Scottish athletes since the beginning of the 19th century. A new putting technique was developed by American Parry O'Brien, who started with his back to the putting field to give more momentum before releasing the shot. He won gold medals in 1952 and 1956. And some putters use a relatively new technique of making one complete spin in the ring before putting.

Hammer throw (men only): The hammer is a 16-pound metal ball attached to nearly four feet (121.5 cm) of a spring steel wire that leads to grips. The name apparently derives from the Scottish and English sport of sledgehammer throwing.

The throwing circle is seven feet (2.1m) in diameter. Inside the circle, with his feet stationary, the thrower grasps the handle in both hands and begins to swing the hammer. He swings the hammer in an arc so it passes below his knees and above his head several times. Before releasing the hammer he swings his body around to build up even more force, up to 500 pounds (227kg). Measurement of the throw is from the dent in the ground where the hammer landed to the inside circumference of the circle. A cage protects spectators from wild throws. Throws that land outside a marked field are not allowed.

Irish Americans won the hammer toss at the Olympics from 1896–1924. John Flanagan, a New York City policeman and Irish emigrant, won three golds, and Matt McGrath, also a policeman, won a gold and a silver.

Europeans dominated the sport then until the mid-1950s. Soviet hammer throwers swept the event in the 1976, 1980, and 1988 Olympics.

Javelin: A men's javelin must weigh at least 800 grams (one pound, 12.25 ounces) and measure 2.6–2.7 meters (eight feet, 6.25 inches and eight feet, 10.25 inches). A women's javelin weighs at least 600 grams (26.16 ounces) and measures 2.2–2.3 meters (seven feet, 2.66 inches and seven feet, 6.5 inches). The shaft can be either wood or metal, though the tip is always steel. For a throw to be counted, the metal tip must break the turf, and the distance is measured form the first touch-down point to a scratch line at the end of the thrower's runway.

fact: Spinning before throwing the javelin is illegal because it endangers spectators.

Unlike competitors in other throwing events, javelin throwers wear spikes. They begin with a sprint down the runway, carrying the spear-like instrument by a grip in the shaft's center. As they near the line, throwers turn to one side, pull back the javelin and throw. Crossing the scratch line disqualifies the throw.

In the Middle Ages, the javelin was thrown for accuracy. Throwing for distance was developed in Hungary and Germany in the mid-1800s. Most modern developments in the sport came in Sweden and Finland. Throwers from these two countries won all the Olympic competitions in javelin until 1936.

Franklin Held, an American, helped develop a more aerodynamic javelin. It floated farther but sometimes landed flat rather than at the point. He used this javelin to extend the world record to 263 feet. An East German athlete threw the javelin 16 feet, eight inches beyond the world record at the time, and in 1986 an amateur sports federation placed limits on the javelin that emphasize aerodynamics over distance.

Mixed or combined events: Both the decathlon and the heptathlon are two-day competitions that stress stamina and versatility.

The decathlon is the men's event and consists of the 100m dash, long jump, shot put, high jump, and 400m run in the first day. Day two continues with the 110m hurdles, discus throw, pole vault, javelin throw, and 1500m run.

The heptathlon for women includes the following on day one: 200m run, 100m hurdles, high jump, and shot put. Day two sports are the long jump, javelin throw, and 800m run.

Points are scored according to a set of tables approved by the International Amateur Athletic Federation. Athletes do not have to win every event, but rather finish well in the largest number of sports.

Track and Field (Athletcis)—Throwing and Mixed Events

HOPEFULS

Men's Events

World shot put champion Werner Günthör hopes to replace his 1988 Olympic bronze with a gold in 1992, and vying for the discus title could be Tokyo World medalists Lars Riedel of Germany, Erik De Bruin of the Netherlands, and Attila Horvath of Hungary. Soviet Yuriy Sedykh, who has already won two Olympic golds and a silver in the hammer throw, is still in top form and may grab a fourth Olympic medal in 1992. Finland's Seppo Raty, a third-place javelin thrower at Seoul, advanced to second place at the Tokyo World games and may continue his climb at Barcelona.

Germany's Olympic gold-medal decathlete Christian Schenk, despite finishing third at the 1991 World Championships, looks able to defend his Olympic title in 1992. But USA's world champion Dan O'Brien, Canada's runner-up Mike Smith, and—if he decides to try this event—US hurdler Roger Kingdom could put up a good fight.

Women's Events

Though a leg injury left heptathlete Jackie Joyner-Kersee unable to defend her world championship at the 1991 Tokyo World games, she hopes to defend her Olympic gold in 1992. Sabine Braun, Germany's Olympic silver medalist, won the heptathlon at Tokyo and will be Joyner-Kersee's toughest competition in Barcelona.

Schedule

The tentative track and field (athletics) schedule for throwing and combined events is as follows:

Friday, July 31
Shot put, qualifying rounds, men
Javelin throw, qualifying, women
Shot put, final, men

Saturday, August 1
Heptathlon, 100m hurdles, high jump
Hammer throw, qualifying, men
Heptathlon, shot put, 200m
Javelin throw, final, women

Sunday, August 2
Heptathlon, long jump

Discus throw, qualifying, women
Hammer throw, final, men
Heptathlon, javelin, 800m

Monday, August 3
Discus throw, qualifying, men
Discus throw, final, women

Wednesday, August 5
Decathlon, 100m, long jump, shot put
Shot put, qualifying, women
Decathlon, high jump, 400m
Discus throw, finals, men

544

Thursday, August 6
Decathlon 110m hurdles
Discus throw, pole vault
Decathlon, javelin, 1500m

Friday, August 7
Javelin, qualifying, men
Shot put, finals, women

Saturday, August 8
Javelin, finals, men

MEN'S THROWING AND MIXED EVENTS

▼

HIGHLIGHTS

Shot Put

Everyone knows Johnny Weissmuller as Tarzan, and a lot of people know Buster Crabbe as the apeman, but not only swimmers make good Tarzans. In Amsterdam in 1928, American shot-putter Herman Brix finished second in his event, but went on to be the first of many Olympic athletes to play Tarzan on the silver screen. You won't find the name Brix in the credits, though: look for his tinseltown name, Bruce Bennet.

It was a shot-putter that got Hitler in trouble with the IOC in Berlin in 1936 ... sort of. When a tall, blond German shot-putter won the event on the first day of the Games, Hitler summoned the athlete to congratulate him, or tell him he thought it was mighty Aryan of him to win the first medal, or something like that; the IOC frowned on such behavior, advising Hitler that it wasn't protocol for him to greet winners, but if he did he would have to greet them all. The message didn't seem to hit home, though: Hitler failed to congratulate African-American athletes, including Jesse Owens.

US shot putter Randy Matson claimed the gold in 1968. Twenty years later Randy Barnes of the US produced a magnificent come-through throw of 73' 5 1/2" to momentarily take the lead, but East German Ulf Timmermann summoned a historic throw of 73' 8 3/4" to regain the lead and the gold.

Hammer Throw

American policeman John J. Flanagan was the first Olympic hammer throw champion; competing in the 1900 Games in Paris, he won his second gold medal, even though the event was marred by the insouciant treatment the track and field events had been given by the Parisian organizers; many of the athletes' throws wound up in the trees that year, due to poor planning of the field. Flanagan won his third consecutive hammer throw in London in 1908. The following year, at the age of 41, he threw the hammer 184 feet 4 inches to become the oldest world record breaker in track and field history.

545

Track and Field (Athletcis)—Throwing and Mixed Events

When Harold Connolly hammered the competition at Melbourne in 1956, he became the first American to win the hammer throw since 1924 (when Frederick Tootell had won). What's even more interesting, though, is that he married the women's discus champion, Olga Fikotova of Czechoslovakia, who was allowed to emigrate for the marriage. Connolly went on to participate in four Games, but divorced his Czech wife in 1975, later marrying another Olympian, Pat Daniels.

Soviet hammer thrower Uri Sedykh is the only man to win the event twice; his characteristic performance produced his best throw on his first try. Sedykh was going for his third gold in 1988, but had to accept the silver behind teammate Sergei Litvinov; Uri Tamm completed a Soviet sweep of the event.

Discus

American Robert Garrett became the first discus champion of the modern Games when he won the event in Athens in 1896. He was also the first shot put champion. In his spare time, he silvered in the high and long jumps. That guy really knew how to throw his weight around.

In Melbourne, in 1956, American Al Oerter won the gold medal for throwing the discus a record distance; earning another three gold medals in the event, Oerter has the unique distinction of winning four successive gold medals in the discus. And, by the way, he won the 1964 event despite a ruptured muscle.

Based on world rankings just prior to the Moscow Games, the US boasted the best four discus throwers, in addition to a variety of other frustrated track and field hopefuls. Soviet Viktor Rashchupkin was the victor that year. 1984's gold medalist, West German Rolf Danneberg, came back for a bronze in Seoul.

Decathlon

The decathlon gets little attention between Olympic years, when suddenly it becomes the test to see who's the world's best all-around athlete. In Stockholm in 1912, no doubt existed about who the world's best all-around athlete was. By the time the Stockholm Games were over, King Gustav V of Sweden had told American decathlete Jim Thorpe: "You, sir, are the greatest athlete in the world." Thorpe won the 10-event decathlon, finishing an astounding 700 points ahead of the runner-up. And that's not all: he won the five-event pentathlon as well—winning four of the five events. Thorpe's timing wasn't bad, either: many heads wearing crowns were in the audience, including those from Russia, Germany, Austria-Hungary, Greece and Italy, not to mention Thorpe's buddy, Gustav.

There was this one hitch, though: Olympic officials declared Thorpe a professional and stripped him of all his medals. Seventy years later, when the IOC decided that playing a little summer baseball for a few dollars didn't make you a professional ringer, Thorpe's medals were restored in a posthumous presentation to the Thorpe family.

Bob Mathias of Tulare, California, was a babe of seventeen when he competed in London in 1948 in the decathlon. He finished the first day of the decathlon in third place, behind Enrique Kistenmacher of Argentina and Ignace Heinrich of France. Not bad for someone who had learned two of the events—the pole vault and javelin—only months before the competition. But Mathias hadn't competed in his best events yet; his 110m hurdles time and his discus distance pulled him into the lead, and by the time he finished the javelin, pole vault, and 1500 meters, he'd won himself a gold necklace. As if there weren't enough drama in the ten-event sport, Mathias finished in rain and darkness, and officials had to use flashlights to mark his javelin throws. Mathias—who later became a US congressman—was and is the youngest Olympic gold medalist. He repeated his decathlon gold performance in 1952.

Decathlon drama heated up in Rome in 1960, when two UCLA teammates, American Rafer Johnson and China's C.K. Yang, tried to best each other ten times over. Yang bested Johnson in six running and jumping events, but Johnson, silver medalist in 1956, had finished so far ahead of the smallish Yang in the weight events that Johnson needed only to stay within 10 seconds of Yang in the final event, the 1500 meters, to win. Johnson finished a second and a half behind Yang to earn the gold. And that wouldn't be the last time Johnson would run in the Olympics: he served as the final torchbearer in 1984, lighting the Olympic flame to start the Los Angeles Games.

British decathlete Daley Thompson began competing in 1977 and won every decathlon he entered through 1984; Thompson describes the decathlon as "nine Mickey Mouse events and a 1500m." Earning Olympic gold medals in 1980 and 1984, Thompson tried again in 1988; however, when his pole-vault broke in half during the competition, he re-injured an adductor muscle. All hopes of a medal in Seoul were dashed.

Several decathletes have gone on to acting performances, or politics—not to mention cereal celebrity in the guise of Wheaties box fame. Such cereal athletes include Jim Thorpe, Bob Mathias, Rafer Johnson, C.K. Yang, Dennis Weaver, and Bruce Jenner.

Al Oerter

Al Oerter's feat will almost certainly never be surpassed in the annals of Olympic history. Oerter—a discus thrower—is the only athlete who has ever won four gold medals in four consecutive Olympiads. *Philadelphia Inquirer* correspondent Frank Dolson notes that Oerter's accomplishment represents "what many consider—with good reason—the greatest athletic achievement of our time. Not the most highly publicized. And certainly not the most highly rewarded in monetary terms. But to an athlete who epitomizes the amateur spirit, surely the most satisfying."

Born in 1936, Alfred Oerter competed in his first Olympics in Melbourne in 1956. At the time he was a sophomore at the University of Kansas, although he had grown up in West Babylon, New York. During those Games, the favorite for the gold was world record-holder Fortune Gordien. When Oerter's turn came to throw, his three turns outstripped all of his competitors by five feet. It was the beginning of a long period of dominance for the determined Oerter.

He won the gold again in Rome in 1960, again in Tokyo in 1964, and again in Mexico City in 1968. Injuries from automobile accidents and muscle pulls never seemed to daunt him, even though his glory years came before the advent of sophisticated sports medicine. Amazingly, his best official discus throw came not during these years but in 1980, when he posted a 227-foot, 11-inch hurl.

In 1968 Oerter retired from the Games. He was married and raising children and held a full-time job in a computer business. The lure of competition proved irresistible, however, and in 1980—at the age of 44—he qualified once again for the Olympic team. He was one of the many athletes who had to miss the Games because of a government-mandated boycott, but he announced that he would try again in 1984. Once again he qualified for the trials, but a torn Achilles' tendon ruined his chances.

The best he could do in 1984 was to carry the flag into the Los Angeles Arena as part of the opening ceremonies. He also presented the discus throwers with their medals. "Being around good, intense competition really started fueling this interest in 1988," he told the *Philadelphia Daily News* soon after the Games.

At the age of fifty, and a grandfather, Oerter was still training regularly with the hopes of gaining yet another Olympic berth. The fact that he was unable to do so does not detract from his extraordinary Olympic achievement. As Dolson puts it, "The Games have changed in many ways since Oerter won his first gold medal.... They're bigger and more political and more commercial..... The sports-for-sports-sake attitude of yesterday has turned, in too many cases, into the take-the-money-and-run attitude of today. But just when you begin to doubt whether there's really a place for the Olympic Games and the Olympic ideals in today's world, you run into an Al Oerter and you realize that the spirit that feeds the Olympic flame hasn't burned out yet." —*M.K.*

Medalists

Track and Field — Men's Shot Put

1988
1. Ulf Timmerman, East Germany, 22.47 (OR)
2. Randy Barnes, USA, 22.39
3. Werner Guenthoer, Switzerland, 21.99

1984
1. Alessandro Andrei, Italy, 21.26
2. Michael Carter, USA, 21.09
3. David Laut, USA, 20.97

1980
1. Vladimir Kiselyov, Soviet Union, 21.35 (OR)
2. Aleksandr Baryshnikov, Soviet Union, 21.08

1976
1. Udo Beyer, East Germany, 21.05
2. Yevgeny Mironov, Soviet Union, 21.03
3. Alexsandr Baryshnikov, Soviet Union, 21.00

3. Udo Beyer, East Germany, 21.06

1972
1. Wladyslaw Komar, Poland, 21.18 (OR)
2. George Woods, USA, 21.17
3. Hartmut Briesenick, East Germany, 21.14

1968
1. Randy Matson, USA, 20.54
2. George Woods, USA, 20.12
3. Eduard Gushchin, Soviet Union, 20.09

1964
1. Dallas Long, USA, 20.33 (OR)
2. Randy Matson, USA, 20.20

3. Vilmos Varju, Hungary, 19.39
1960 1. William Nieder, USA, 19.68 (OR)
2. Parry O'Brien, USA, 19.11
3. Dallas Long, USA, 19.01
1956 1. Parry O'Brien, USA, 18.57 (OR)
2. William Nieder, USA, 18.18
3. Jiri Skobla, Czechoslovakia, 17.65
1952 1. Parry O'Brien, USA, 17.41 (OR)
2. Darrow Hooper, USA, 17.39
3. James Fuchs, USA, 17.06
1948 1. Wilbur Thompson, USA, 17.12 (OR)
2. F. James Delaney, USA, 16.68
3. James Fuchs, USA, 16.42
1936 1. Hans Woellke, Germany, 16.20 (OR)
2. Sulo Barlund, Finland, 16.12
3. Gerhard Stock, Germany, 15.66
1932 1. Leo Sexton, USA, 16.005 (OR)
2. Harlow Rothert, USA, 15.75
3. Frantisek Douda, Czechoslovakia,
15.61
1928 1. John Kuck, USA, 15.87 (WR)
2. Herman Brix, USA, 15.75
3. Emil Hirschfeld, Germany, 15.72
1924 1. Clarence Houser, USA, 14.995
2. Glenn Hartranft, USA, 14.895
3. Ralph Hills, USA, 14.64
1920 1. Ville Porhola, Finland, 14.81
2. Elmer Niklander, Finland, 14.155
3. Harry Liversedge, USA, 14.15
1912 1. Patrick McDonald, USA, 15.34 (OR)
2. Ralph Rose, USA, 15.25
3. Lawrence Whitney, USA, 13.93
1908 1. Ralph Rose, USA, 14.21
2. Dennis Horgan, Great Britain, 13.62
3. John Garreis, USA, 13.18
1906 1. Martin Sheridan, USA, 12.325
2. Mihaly David, Hungary, 11.83
3. Eric Lemming, Sweden, 11.26
1904 1. Ralph Rose, USA, 14.81 (WR)
2. William Coe, USA, 14.40
3. Leon Feuerbach, USA, 13.37
1900 1. Richard Sheldon, USA 14.10 (OR)
2. Josiah McCracken, USA, 12.85
3. Robert Garrett,. USA, 12.37
1896 1. Robert Garrett, USA, 11.22
2. Miltiades Gouskos, Greece, 11.20
3. Georgios Papasideris, Greece, 10.36

Track and Field — Men's Discus Throw

1988 1. Jurgen Schult, East Germany, 68.82 (OR)
2. Romas Oubartas, Soviet Union, 67.48
3. Rolf Danneberg, West Germany, 67.38
1984 1. Rolf Danneberg, West Germany, 66.60
2. Mac Wilkins, USA, 66.30
3. John (Boog) Powell, USA, 65.46
1980 1. Viktor Rashchupkin, Soviet Union, 66.64
2. Imrich Bugar, Czechoslovakia, 66.38
3. Luis Delis, Cuba, 66.32
1976 1. Mac Wilkins, USA, 67.50
2. Wolfgang Schmidt, East Germany, 66.22
3. John (Boog) Powell, USA, 65.70
1972 1. Ludvik Danek, Czechoslovakia, 64.40
2. Jay Silvester, USA, 63.50

3. Rickard Bruch, Sweden, 63.40
1968 1. Al Oerter, USA, 64.78 (OR)
2. Lothar Milde, East Germany, 63.08
3. Ludvik Danek, Czechoslovakia, 62.92
1964 1. Al Oerter, USA, 61.00 (OR)
2. Ludvik Danek, Czechoslovakia, 60.52
3. David Weill, USA, 59.49
1960 1. Al Oerter, USA, 59.18 (OR)
2. Richard Babka, USA, 58.02
3. Richard Cochran, USA, 57.16
1956 1. Al Oerter, USA, 56.36 (OR)
2. Fortune Gordien, USA, 54.81
3. Desmond Koch, USA, 54.40
1952 1. Sim Iness, USA, 55.03 (OR)
2. Adolfo Consolini, Italy, 53.78
3. James Dillion, USA, 53.28
1948 1. Adolfo Consolini, Italy, 52.78 (OR)
2. Giuseppe Tosi, Italy, 51.78
3. Fortune Gordien, USA, 50.77
1936 1. Kenneth Carpenter, USA, 50.48 (OR)
2. Gordon Dunn, USA, 49.36
3. Giorgio Oberweger, Italy, 49.23
1932 1. John Anderson, USA, 49.49 (OR)
2. Henry Laborde, USA, 48.47
3. Paul Winter, France, 47.85
1928 1. Clarence Houser, USA, 47.32 (OR)
2. Antero Kivi, Finland, 47.23
3. James Corson, USA, 47.10
1924 1. Clarence Houser, USA, 46.15 (OR)
2. Vilho Niittymaa, Finland, 44.95
3. Thomas Lieb, USA, 44.83
1920 1. Elmer Niklander, Finland, 44.685
2. Armas Taipale, Finland, 44.19
3. Augustus Pope, USA, 42.13
1912 1. Armas Taipale, Finland, 45.21 (OR)
2. Richard Byrd, USA, 42.32
3. James Duncan, USA, 42.28
1908 1. Martin Sheridan, USA, 40.89 (OR)
2. Merritt Griffin, USA, 40.70
3. Marquis Horr, USA, 39.445
1906 1. Martin Sheridan, USA, 41.46
2. Nicolaos Georgantas, Greece, 38.06
3. Werner Jarvinen, Finland, 36.82
1904 1. Martin Sheridan, USA, 39.28 (OR)
2. Ralph Rose, USA, 39.28
3. Nicolaos Georgantas, Greece, 37.68
1900 1. Rudolf Bauer, Hungary, 36.04 (OR)
2. Frantisek Janda-Suk, Bohemia, 35.25
3. Richard Sheldon, USA, 34.60
1896 1. Robert Garrett, USA, 29.15
2. Panagiotis Paraskevopoulos, Greece, 28.955
3. Sotirios Versis, Greece, 28.78

Track and Field — Men's Hammer Throw

1988 1. Serguei Litvinov, Soviet Union, 84.80 (OR)
2. Yuriy Sedykh, Soviet Union, 83.76
3. Iouri Tamm, Soviet Union, 81.16
1984 1. Juha Tiainen, Finland, 78.0
2. Karl-Hans Riehm, West Germany, 77.9
3. Klaus Ploghaus, West Germany, 76.68
1980 1. Yuriy Sedykh, Soviet Union, 81.80 (WR)
2. Sergei Litvinov, Soviet Union, 80.64
3. Iouri Tamm, Soviet Union, 78.96
1976 1. Yuriy Sedykh, Soviet Union, 77.52 (OR)

549

2. Aleksei Spiridonov, Soviet Union, 76.08
3. Anatoli Bondarchuk, Soviet Union, 75.48

1972 1. Anatoli Bondarchuk, Soviet Union, 75.50 (OR)
2. Jochen Sachse, East Germany, 74.96
3. Vasily Khmelevski, Soviet Union, 74.04

1968 1. Gyula Zsivotzky, Hungary, 73.36 (OR)
2. Romuald Klim, Soviet Union, 73.28
3. Lazar Lovasz, Hungary, 69.78

1964 1. Romuald Klim, Soviet Union, 69.74 (OR)
2. Gyula Zsivotzky, Hungary, 69.09
3. Uwe Beyer, West Germany, 68.09

1960 1. Vasily Rudenkov, Soviet Union, 67.10 (OR)
2. Gyula Zsivotzky, Hungary, 65.79
3. Tadeusz Rut, Poland, 65.64

1956 1. Harold Connolly, USA, 63.19 (OR)
2. Mikhail Krivonosov, USA, 63.03
3. Anatoly Samotsvetov, Soviet Union, 62.56

1952 1. Jozsef Csermak, Hungary, 60.34 (WR)
2. Karl Storch, West Germany, 58.86
3. Imre Nemeth, Hungary, 57.74

1948 1. Imre Nemeth, Hungary, 56.07
2. Ivan Gubijan, Yugoslavia, 54.27
3. Robert Bennett, USA, 53.73

1936 1. Karl Hein, Germany, 56.49 (OR)
2. Erwin Blask, Germany, 55.04
3. Fred Warngard, Sweden, 54.83

1932 1. Patrick O'Callaghan, Ireland, 53.92
2. Ville Porhola, Finland, 52.27
3. Peter Zaremba, USA, 50.33

1928 1. Patrick O'Callaghan, Ireland, 51.39
2. Ossian Skiold, Sweden, 51.29
3. Edmund Black, USA, 49.03

1924 1. Frederick Tootell, USA, 53.295
2. Matthew McGrath, USA, 50.84
3. Malcolm Nokes, Great Britain, 48.875

1920 1. Patrick Ryan, USA, 52.875
2. Carl Johan Lind, Sweden, 48.43
3. Basil Bennet, USA, 48.25

1912 1. Matthew McGrath, USA, 54.74 (OR)
2. Duncan Gillis, Canada, 48.39
3. Clarence Childs, USA, 48.17

1908 1. John Flanagan, USA, 51.92 (OR)
2. Matthew McGrath, USA, 51.18
3. Cornelius Walsh, USA, 48.51

1906 **Not held**
1904 1. John Flanagan, USA, 51.23 (OR)
2. John DeWitt, USA, 50.265
3. Ralph Rose, USA, 45.73

1900 1. John Flanagan, USA, 49.73
2. Truxton Hare, USA, 49.13
3. Josiah McCracken, USA, 42.46

1896 **Not held**

Track and Field — Men's Javelin Throw

1988 1. Tapio Korjus, Finland, 84.28
2. Jan Zelezny, Czechoslovakia, 84.12
3. Seppo Raty, Finland, 83.26

1984 1. Arto Harkonen, Finland, 86.76
2. David Ottley, Great Britain, 85.74
3. Kenth Eldebrink, Sweden, 83.72

1980 1. Dainis Kula, Soviet Union, 91.20

2. Aleksandr Makarov, Soviet Union, 89.64
3. Wolfgang Hanisch, East Germany, 86.72

1976 1. Miklos Nemeth, Hungary, 94.58 (WR, OR)
2. Hannu Siitonen, Finland, 87.92
3. Gheorghe Megelea, Romania, 87.16

1972 1. Klaus Wolfermann, West Germany, 90.48 (OR)
2. Janis Lusis, Soviet Union, 90.46
3. William Schmidt, USA, 84.42

1968 1. Janis Lusis, Soviet Union, 90.10 (OR)
2. Jorma Kinnunen, Finland, 88.58
3. Gergely Kulcsar, Hungary, 87.06

1964 1. Pauli Nevala, Finland, 82.66
2. Gergely Kulcsar, Hungary, 82.32
3. Janis Lusis, Soviet Union, 80.57

1960 1. Viktor Tsibulenko, Soviet Union, 84.64
2. Walter Kruger, East Germany, 79.36
3. Gergely Kulcsar, Hungary, 78.57

1956 1. Egil Danielsen, Norway, 85.71 (WR)
2. Janusz Sidlo, Poland, 79.98
3. Viktor Tsibulenko, Soviet Union, 79.50

1952 1. Cyrus Young, USA, 73.78 (OR)
2. William Miller, USA, 72.46
3. Toivo Hyytiainen, Finland, 71.89

1948 1. Tapio Rautavaara, Finland, 69.77
2. Steve Seymour, USA, 67.56
3. Jozsef Varszegi, Hungary, 67.03

1936 1. Gerhard Stock, Great Britain, 71.84
2. Yrjo Nikkanen, Finland, 70.77
3. Kalervo Toivonen, Finland, 70.72

1932 1. Matti Jarvinen, Finland, 72.71 (OR)
2. Matti Sippala, Finland, 69.80
3. Eino Penttila, Finland, 68.70

1928 1. Erik Lundkvist, Sweden, 66.60 (OR)
2. Bela Szepes, Hungary, 65.26
3. Olav Sunde, Norway, 63.97

1924 1. Jonni Myyra, Finland, 62.96
2. Gunnar Lindstrom, Sweden, 60.92
3. Eugene Oberst, USA, 58.35

1920 1. Jonni Myyra, Finland, 65.78 (OR)
2. Urho Peltonen, Finland, 63.50
3. Pekka Johansson-Jaale, Finland, 63.095

1912 1. Eric Lemming, Sweden, 60.64 (WR)
2. Julius Saaristo, Finland, 58.66
3. Mor Koczan, Hungary, 55.50

1908 1. Eric Lemming, Sweden, 54.825 (WR)
2. Arne Halse, Norway, 50.57
3. Otto Nilsson, Sweden, 47.105

1906 1. Eric Lemming, Sweden, 53.90 (WR)
2. Knut Lindberg, Sweden 45.17
3. Bruno Soderstrom, Sweden, 44.92

1896 **Not held**

Track and Field — Men's Decathlon

1988 1. Christian Schenk, East Germany, 8,488
2. Torsten Voss, East Germany, 8,399
3. Dave Steen, Canada, 8,328

1984 1. Daley Thompson, Great Britain, 8,798 (EWR)
2. Jurgen Hingsen, West Germany, 8,673
3. Siegfried Wentz, West Germany, 8,412

1980 1. Daley Thompson, Great Britain, 8,495
2. Yuri Kutsenko, Soviet Union, 8,331

US decathlete Jim Thorpe was called "the greatest athlete in the world" when he captured the 1912 decathlon gold. His medal was later stripped from him, then restored posthumously.

Mildred "Babe" Didriksen is the only woman to medal in running, throwing, and jumping events, mining gold at the 1932 Games in the 80m hurdles and the javelin and settling for silver (penalized for her unorthodox style) in the high jump.

	3. Sergei Zhelanov, Soviet Union, 8,135	
1976	**1.** Bruce Jenner, USA, 8,618 (WR)	
	2. Guido Kretschmer, West Germany, 8,411	
	3. Nikolai Avilov, Soviet Union, 8,369	
1972	**1.** Nikolai Avilov, Soviet Union, 8,454 (WR)	
	2. Leonid Litvinenko, Soviet Union, 8,035	
	3. Ryszard Katus, Poland, 7,984	
1968	**1.** Bill Toomey, USA, 8,193 (OR)	
	2. Hans-Joachim Walde, West Germany, 8,111	
	3. Kurt Bendlin, West Germany, 8,064	
1964	**1.** Willi Holdorf, West Germany, 7,887	
	2. Rein Aun, Soviet Union, 7,842	
	3. Hans-Joachim Walde, West Germany, 7,809	
1960	**1.** Rafer Johnson, USA, 8,001 (OR)	
	2. Chuan-Kwang Yang, Taiwan, 7,930	
	3. Vassily Kuznyetsov, Soviet Union, 7,624	
1956	**1.** Milton Campbell, USA, 7,708 (OR)	
	2. Rafer Johnson, USA, 7,568	
	3. Vassily Kuznyetsov, Soviet Union, 7,461	
1952	**1.** Robert B. Mathias, USA, 7,731 (WR)	
	2. Milton Campbell, USA, 7,132	
	3. Floyd Simmons, USA, 7,069	
1948	**1.** Robert B. Mathias, USA, 6,826	
	2. Ignace Heinrich, France, 6,740	
	3. Floyd Simmons, USA, 6,711	

1936 1. Glenn Morris, USA, 7,421 (WR)
2. Robert Clark, USA, 7,226
3. Jack Parker, USA, 6,918
1932 1. James Bausch, USA, 6,896 (WR)
2. Akilles Jarvinen, Finland, 7,038
3. Wolrad Eberle, Germany, 6,830
1928 1. Paavo Yrjola, Finland, 6,774 (WR)
2. Akilles Jarvinen, Finland, 6,815
3. J. Kenneth Doherty, USA, 6,593
1924 1. Harold Osborn, USA, 6,668 (WR)
2. Emerson Norton, USA, 6,340
3. Alexander Klumberg, Estonia, 6,260
1920 1. Helge Lovland, Norway, 5,970
2. Brutus Hamilton, USA, 5,940
3. Bertil Ohlson, Sweden, 5,825
1912 1. James Thorpe, USA, 6,765 (WR)
(previously disqualified, Jim Thorpe's medals were restored in 1982)
2. Hugo Wieslander, Sweden, 6,161
3. Charles Lomberg, Sweden, 5,943
4. Gosta Holmer, Sweden, 5,956
1906–1908 **Not held**
1904 1. Thomas Kiely, Great Britain/Ireland, 6,036
2. Adam Gunn, USA, 5,907
3. Truxton Hare, USA, 5,813
1896–1900 **Not held**

WOMEN'S THROWING AND MIXED EVENTS

▼

HIGHLIGHTS

Javelin

A woman of many talents, America's Babe Didriksen added a javelin gold to her 80m hurdle gold and her high jump silver in 1932. Although her medal haul eclipsed other performances that year (no other woman holds triple medals in running, jumping, and throwing events), a number of notable American field performances occurred among both men and women, including James Bausch in the decathlon, John Anderson in the discus, Lillian Copeland in the women's discus, and Leo Sexton in the shot put.

In Helsinki in 1952, while runner Emil Zátopek, a Czech army officer, won the gold in the 10,000m and the silver in the 5000m, Dana Zátopek, Emil's wife, won the women's javelin. Dana and Emil thus marched into history as the first husband-wife Olympic double in track and field. And if that didn't earn them a place in the Twilight Zone: they were born on the same day.

Shot Put

The women's shot put boasts an Olympic first: when, in Rome in 1960, Soviet sisters Irina Press and Tamara Press won golds in their events, they became the first sisters to win the Olympic gold. While Irina won the 80m hurdles, sister Tamara pressed for gold in the shot put. Between the two of them, the two Leningrad lasses set 26 world records and won five Olympic golds, and one silver. The thing is—there seems to be some dispute about their hormonal makeup; anyway, their record as Olympic siblings would probably still stand.

The first Bulgarian track and field gold medal was awarded to Ivanka Hristova, who, at the age of 34, set an Olympic record. And the competition that year were no slouches: there was one world record holder and three former record holders. In second place, Soviet Nadezhda Chizhova completed her necklace set, adding the silver to the gold and bronze she already owned.

Discus

When women's track and field events were finally added to the Olympic program in 1928—much to Coubertin's chagrin—Poland's Halina Konopacka earned the double honor of winning the discus event, and becoming the first woman to win an Olympic gold medal in track and field.

Frenchwoman Micheline Ostermeyer earned an unusual assortment of necklaces when she won the shot put and the discus, and took a bronze medal in the high jump in 1948. Not bad for a concert pianist.

The discus knows no limits, it seems: the oldest female Olympic champion threw the discus in Mexico City in 1968: Rumanian Lia Manoliu was 36 when she treated herself to a gold necklace. A glutton for the Games, she is a co-holder of the record for female attendance, having attended six Games (1952–1968).

And the women's discus event has contributed its share of infamy to the Olympic Hall of Shame: in 1976, Poland's discus champ Danuta Rosani was the first Olympic athlete to be DQ'd because she didn't just say no. Anabolic steroids have probably been present in athletics since the mid-1960s, and heavy throwers have historically been big fans of improperly pumping up; without the ready-made hormones, the record books might have told a different story.

Heptathlon

The women's heptathlon's previous incarnation, the pentathlon, boasts a record for the shortest time that an athlete has held an Olympic record. In 1980, Soviet pentathlete Olga Rukavishnikova enjoyed four-tenths of a second of fame. Wonder what Andy Warhol would say about that.

US athlete Jackie Joyner-Kersee missed winning the heptathlon—which in 1984 replaced the pentathlon—in Los Angeles by a mere five points. That year, Glynnis Nunn of Australia won the inaugural event, and West Germany's Sabine Everts took home the bronze. In 1988, however, Joyner-Kersee proved her mettle when she posted a world-record heptathlon score of 7291 points. In second place, East German Sabine John trailed with only 6897 points, while her compatriot Anke Behmer followed with 6858 for the bronze.

Babe Didriksen

Mildred "Babe" Didriksen even typed fast: 85 words per minute for a Dallas insurance company before she became an American icon. Her only complaint about the 1932 Los Angeles Games was that she was permitted to enter just three events, even though she had qualified at US trials for five. After she arrived, the thin 18-year-old blonde from Port Arthur, Texas, told reporters, "I came out here to beat everybody in sight, and that is exactly what I'm going to do." Confidence was never a problem for Babe, and she was nearly as good as her word.

Didriksen defeated two German favorites in the javelin throw, set a world record in the 80m hurdles and tied for first with countrywoman Jean Shiley in the high jump. But—to break the tie—judges ruled that Didriksen's technique had been illegal. She was awarded the silver, even though her jump matched Shiley's world record.

Didriksen quickly turned professional everything, touring America playing harmonica, telling jokes, posing in auto ad campaigns, pitching for the House of David baseball team, and throwing an inning in an exhibition game for the St. Louis Cardinals against the Philadelphia Athletics. She became the most successful female golfer ever, winning 14 consecutive tournaments at one point. Romance entered her life in the person of wrestler George Zaharias, whom she later married.

In 1950, the Associated Press named her the greatest female athlete of the first half-century. But in 1953, Didriksen was diagnosed with cancer. Doctors performed an emergency colostomy. Displaying the colossal drive that made her a champion, Didriksen returned to the golf circuit three months later. The next year she again accomplished the improbable, winning the US Open by 12 strokes. But soon the cancer returned, this time inoperable. On September 17, 1956, the amazing athletic career and life of Babe Didriksen ended at the age of 42. —H.D.

Medalists

Track and Field — Women's Shot Put

1988
1. Natalia Lisovskaya, Soviet Union, 22.24
2. Kathrin Neimke, East Germany, 21.07
3. Meisu Li, People's Republic of China, 21.06

1984
1. Claudia Losch, West Germany, 20.48
2. Mihaela Loghin, Romania, 20.47
3. Gael Martin, Australia, 19.19

1980
1. Ilona Slupianek, East Germany, 22.41
2. Svetlana Krachevskaya, Soviet Union, 21.42
3. Margitta Pufe, East Germany, 21.20

1976
1. Ivanka Hristova, Bulgaria, 21.16 (OR)
2. Nadezhda Chizhova, Soviet Union, 20.96
3. Helena Fibingerova, Czechoslovakia, 20.67

1972
1. Nadezhda Chizhova, Soviet Union, 21.03 (WR)

553

2. Margitta Gummel-Helmbolt, East Germany, 20.22
3. Ivanka Hristova, Bulgaria, 19.35

1968 1. Margitta Gummel-Helmbolt, East Germany, 19.61 (WR)
2. Marita Lange, East Germany, 18.78
3. Nadezhda Chizhova, Soviet Union, 18.19

1964 1. Tamara Press, Soviet Union, 18.14 (OR)
2. Renate Garisch-Culmberger, East Germany, 17.61
3. Galina Zybina, Soviet Union, 17.45

1960 1. Tamara Press, Soviet Union, 17.32 (OR)
2. Johanna Luttge, East Germany, 16.61
3. Earlene Brown, USA, 16.42

1956 1. Tamara Tyshkevich, Soviet Union, 16.59 (OR)
2. Galina Zybina, Soviet Union, 16.53
3. Marianne Werner, West Germany, 15.61

1952 1. Galina Zybina, Soviet Union, 15.28 (WR)
2. Marianne Werner, West Germany, 14.57
3. Klaudia Tochenova, Soviet Union, 14.50

1948 1. Micheline Ostermeyer, France, 13.75
2. Amelia Piccinini, Italy, 13.09
3. Ine Schaffer, Austria, 13.08

1896-
1936 Not held

Track and Field — Women's Discus

1988 1. Martina Hellmann, East Germany, 72.30 (OR)
2. Diana Gansky, East Germany, 71.88
3. Tzvetanka Hristova, Bulgaria, 69.74

1984 1. Ria Stalman, Netherlands, 65.36
2. Leslie Deniz, USA, 64.86
3. Florenta Craciunescu, Romania, 63.64

1980 1. Evelin Jahl-Schlaak, East Germany, 69.96 (OR)
2. Maria Petkova, Bulgaria, 67.90
3. Tatiana Lesovaya, Soviet Union, 67.40

1976 1. Evelin Schlaak, East Germany, 69.00 (OR)
2. Maria Vergova, Bulgaria, 67.30
3. Gabriele Hinzmann, East Germany, 66.84

1972 1. Faina Melnik, Soviet Union, 66.62 (OR)
2. Argentina Menis, Romania, 65.06
3. Wassilka Stoeva, Bulgaria, 64.34

1968 1. Lia Manoliu, Romania, 58.28
2. Liesel Westermann, West Germany, 57.76
3. Jolan Kleiber, Hungary, 54.90

1964 1. Tamara Press, Soviet Union, 57.27 (OR)
2. Ingrid Lotz, East Germany, 57.21
3. Lia Manoliu, Romania, 56.97

1960 1. Nina Ponomaryeva-Romaschkova, Soviet Union, 55.10 (OR)
2. Tamara Press, Soviet Union, 52.59
3. Lia Manoliu, Romania, 52.36

1956 1. Olga Fikotova, Czechoslovakia, 53.69 (OR)
2. Irina Beglyakova, Soviet Union, 52.54
3. Nina Ponomaryeva-Romaschkova, Soviet Union, 52.02

1952 1. Nina Romaschkova, Soviet Union, 51.42 (OR)
2. Yelisaveta Bagryantseva, Soviet Union, 47.08
3. Nina Dumbadze, Soviet Union, 46.29

1948 1. Micheline Ostermeyer, France, 41.92
2. Edera Gentile-Cordiale, Italy, 41.17
3. Jacqueline Mazeas, France, 40.47

1936 1. Gisela Mauermeyer, Germany, 47.63 (OR)
2. Jadwiga Wajsowna, Poland, 46.22
3. Paula Mollenhauer, Germany, 39.80

1932 1. Lillian Copeland, USA, 40.58 (OR)
2. Ruth Osburn, USA, 40.12
3. Jadwiga Wajsowna, Poland, 38.74

1928 1. Halina Konopacka, Poland, 39.62 (WR)
2. Lillian Copeland, USA, 37.08
3. Ruth Svedberg, Sweden, 35.92

1896-
1924 Not held

Track and Field — Women's Javelin

1988 1. Petra Felke, East Germany, 74.68 (OR)
2. Fatima Whitbread, Great Britain, 70.32
3. Beate Koch, East Germany, 67.30

1984 1. Tessa Sanderson, Great Britain, 69.56 (OR)
2. Tiina Lillak, Finland, 69.00
3. Fatima Whitbread, Great Britain, 67.14

1980 1. Maria Colon, Cuba, 68.40 (OR)
2. Saida Gunba, Soviet Union, 67.76
3. Ute Hommola, East Germany, 66,56

1976 1. Ruth Fuchs, East Germany, 65.94 (OR)
2. Marion Becker, West Germany, 64.70
3. Kathy Schmidt, USA, 63.96

1972 1. Ruth Fuchs, East Germany, 63.88 (OR)
2. Jaqueline Todten, East Germany, 62.54
3. Kathy Schmidt, USA, 59.94

1968 1. Angela Nemeth, Hungary, 60.36
2. Mihaela Penes, Romania, 59.92
3. Eva Janko, Austria, 58.04

1964 1. Mihaela Penes, Romania, 60.54
2. Marta Rudas, Hungary, 58.27
3. Yelena Gorchakova, Soviet Union, 57.06

1960 1. Elvira Ozolina, Soviet Union, 55.98 (OR)
2. Dana Zatopkova, Czechoslovakia, 53.78
3. Birute Kalediene, Soviet Union, 53.45

1956 1. Inese Jaunzeme, Soviet Union, 53.86 (OR)
2. Marlene Ahrens, Chile, 50.38
3. Nadezhda Konyayeva, Soviet Union, 50.28

1952 1. Dana Zatopkova, Czechoslovakia, 50.47 (OR)

2. Aleksandra Chudina, Soviet Union, 50.01
3. Yelena Gorchakova, Soviet Union, 49.76

1948 1. Herma Bauma, Austria, 45.57 (OR)
2. Kaisa Parviainen, Finland, 43.79
3. Lily Carlstedt, Denmark, 42.08

1936 1. Tilly Fleischer, Germany, 45.18 (OR)
2. Luise Kruger, Germany, 43.29
3. Maria Kwasniewska, Poland, 41.80

1932 1. Mildred "Babe" Didrikson, USA, 43.68 (OR)
2. Ellen Braumuller, Germany, 43.49
3. Tilly Fleischer, Germany, 43.00

1896-
1928 Not held

Track and Field — Women's Pentathlon

1980 1. Nadezhda Tkachenko, Soviet Union, 5083 (WR)
2. Olga Rukavishnikova, Soviet Union, 4937
3. Olga Kuragina, Soviet Union, 4875

1976 1. Siegrun Siegl, East Germany, 4745

2. Christine Laser, East Germany, 4745
3. Burglinde Pollak, East Germany, 4740

1972 1. Mary Peters, Great Britain, 4801 (WR)
2. Heidemarie Rosendahl, West Germany, 4791
3. Burglinde Pollak, East Germany, 4768

1968 1. Ingrid Becker, West Germany, 5098
2. Liese Prokop, Austria, 4966
3. Annamaria Toth, Hungary, 4959

1964 1. Irina Press, Soviet Union, 5246 (WR)
2. Mary Rand, Great Britain, 5035
3. Galina Bystrova, Soviet Union, 4956

1896-
1960 Not held

Track and Field — Women's Heptathlon

1988 1. Jackie Joyner-Kersee, USA, 7,291 (WR)
2. Sabine John, East Germany, 6,897
3. Anke Behmer, East Germany, 6,858

1984 1. Glynis Nunn, Australia, 6,390 (OR)
2. Jackie Joyner, USA, 6,385
3. Sabine Everts, West Germany, 6,363

Master of a deadly spike, captain Karch Kiraly led the US men's team to volleyball gold medals in 1984 and 1988.

VOLLEYBALL

WARM-UP

"Awesome serve, dude!"

Whether played on the beach, the gym, or the Olympic stage, volleyball carries a made-in-the-USA tag. Volleyball was invented in 1895 by William G. Morgan, the athletic director of the YMCA training school in Holyoke, Massachusetts. The game, known then as minonette, spread quickly to other YMCAs in the region, where it competed with that other new-fangled sport, basketball. In fact, Morgan invented the game as an alternative for middle-aged fitness fans who found basketball too strenuous.

Via the international YMCA network, the game spread slowly throughout the world, with the exception of the Orient, where volleyball enjoyed its most enthusiastic reception. By 1896 the game was played five a side in the US, while in Japan each team fielded nine members, creating havoc in the backcourt. By 1918 the current six-a-side game was established, as was the counter-clockwise rotation on service.

In 1923, the first All-USA Championship was held, and national organizations for the game were founded in Russia and Japan during the next five years.

Exported overseas by American servicemen, volleyball became popular throughout the world by the end of World War II. The game required little organization and minimal equipment, and followed simple rules. It could be played outdoors and indoors, with as few as two people to a side. Responding to the increasing awareness of the sport worldwide, the Fédération Internationale de Volleyball (FIVB) was organized in 1948. A year later, the initial World Championships were held in Prague, Czechoslovakia. Buoyed by the general public's acceptance of the game, the FIVB began lobbying to add volleyball to the Olympic Games, a dream that came true in Tokyo 15 years later.

In the 1960s, the Japanese, the sport's most enthusiastic promoters, ruled supreme over the volleyball world. At that first Olympic volleyball tournament in Tokyo in 1964, the Japanese proved to be the dominant volleyball force in the world, with the women's team winning the gold and the men the bronze. In 1968 the men's team took the silver medal at Mexico City before capturing the gold once again at Munich in 1972. Following that triumph, the Japanese men's team was overtaken by more zealous international competition and have not won a medal since. Japanese women, meanwhile, remained a potent international volleyball force, winning the silver in 1968 and 1972, gold in 1976, and bronze in 1984.

The sport officially began its ascension in the US with the 1984 Olympic Games, where the men captured the gold and the women the silver, the first medals that the Americans had earned in the competition. The US men went on to win the 1988 gold, as well as the 1985 World Cup, 1986 World Championship, and the 1983 and 1987 Pan American Games titles. The women's team captured the bronze medals at the 1982 and 1990 World Championships, as well as the 1987 Pan American Games.

Competition on the international level now includes the FIVB-supported World League, which began in 1990. The World League involves 10 teams and $2 million in prize money, with the season extending from mid-May to mid-July.

▼

SPECTATORS' GUIDE

Going for the gold in Barcelona will be 12 men's and eight women's teams. The USA's men's team has qualified for the 1992 Games thanks to the gold medal performance at the last Olympics, while at press time, the US women were still attempting to qualify. Played at its highest level in the international arena, the game bears little resemblance to the popular backyard and beach styles, but is instead a demonstration of speed and power, along with exacting team coordination.

Volleyball is played by two teams of six players each, on a court measuring 18 meters (59 feet) long and nine meters (29 feet six inches) wide. The court is divided by a center line into two equal courts; above the line is the net. The net is one meter (39 inches) in width and 9.5 meters (32 feet) in length. In men's competition, the top of the net is 2.43 meters (seven feet, 11.5 inches) above the floor, while in women's matches the height is 2.24 meters (seven feet, 4.25 inches).

The ball, slightly smaller than a basketball, is 25 to 27 inches in circumference and weighs nine to 10 ounces.

Matches are best three-of-five games (or sets, as they are sometimes called). The winner of a game is the first to score 15 points, with a minimum of a two-point advantage. If the score is tied at 14, then the first team to go ahead by two points (i.e., 16–14, 18–16, etc.) is the winner. Only the team that serves can score a point. When the nonserving team wins a rally, it merely gains possession of the serve. A team rotates counter-clockwise after gaining the serve. Teams change sides between games, except before the fifth game, in which a coin toss decides.

Each point begins with three players at the net and three in the backcourt, although after the serve, a player may move anywhere on his or her side of the net.

The object of the game is to cause the ball to strike the floor on the opponent's side of the court. The fastest way of accomplishing this is to spike the ball, as one of the front court players reaches high into the air and drives the ball down at speeds reaching more than 100 miles per hour. Strategy is an important ingredient for a winning volleyball team. Players fake spikes and passes, attempting to pull the opponent into the wrong defensive arrangement. The spike is a primary weapon, but its threat often is as unsettling as its actual use.

On any given play, each team is allowed a maximum of three hits. Each time a player touches the ball or is touched by the ball, it counts as a hit. The ball may come in contact with any part of the body above and including the waist. The ball must be clearly hit and cannot come to rest (lifted, pushed, carried, or thrown). Generally the sequence of the hits is return of serve, set, and spike.

fact: Hirofumi Diamatsu, infamous coach of Japan's 1964 gold-medal women's team, introduced the rolling receive, in which a player dives, hits the ball, rolls over, and jumps back up. He also hit, kicked, and insulted his players, and made them practice at least six hours a day, seven days a week.

The exception to the three-hit rule is the block. When a defending player goes up at the net and physically blocks a shot, the block does not count as a contact. And though a player normally is not allowed to touch the ball two times consecutively, a blocker may make first contact with the ball after the attempted block.

Setting is a pass used to "set up" a point-winning shot. The player making the second hit in a three-hit sequence lofts the ball softly into the air with little spin toward a teammate by the net, who spikes the ball at its apex toward the opposing team. The softness and trajectory of a good set permit the player receiving the pass to much more accurately place the ball between defenders on the opposing side and negate the return.

A team is permitted six player-substitutions during a game. The substitutions may be made before any point for any position on the floor. A substitute can only be substituted into a game once. A starting player may leave the game once and re-enter only in his or her starting position.

How to Lose the Serve or Give up a Point

A team gives up a point or loses the serve under the following conditions:

▼ A player initiates contact with the ball before it crosses the plane of the net.

▼ A player crosses the vertical plane of the net and touches the court or an opponent.

▼ The ball touches the ground on that team's side of the court, within the boundaries.

▼ A player hits the ball so that it lands out of bounds. If the ball is on the line, the ball is in play.

▼ A player serving hits the ball out of bounds or into the net.

▼ A team makes more than three contacts with the ball in succession.

▼ A player touches the ball twice consecutively, except in the case of a blocker.

▼ A player touches the net.

▼ A player steps over the center line during play.

▼ A backline player in the attack area returns the ball from above net height. The players in the backcourt cannot spike the ball unless they are at least 10 feet behind the net.

▼

HOPEFULS

The US men hope to defend their second Olympic gold at Barcelona, while the ever-strong Soviet and Chinese women will probably vie for the women's title. The American men may face a tough battle without former Olympians Karch Kiraly, Steve Timmons, and others who have left for Italy or the beaches of California to play professionally. Their weakness showed in 1989, when they placed fourth in the World Cup tournaments, and in 1990, when they again placed fourth in the Goodwill Games and thirteenth at the World Championships.

With promising additions, though, including 1991 NCAA champion player Brent Hillard and two-time NCAA player of the year Bryan Ivie, and some former Olympians who will rejoin the team, the USA will fight hard for its third straight gold. The American women—if they earn a place on the roster through pre-Olympic competitions—will field an impressive team, with three players from the NCAA title team (UCLA), Jenny Evans, Natalie Williams, and Elaine Youngs, and several former Olympians, including Deitre Collins, Kim Oden, and Paula Weishoff.

The tentative volleyball schedule is as follows:

Sunday, July 26
6 matches, preliminaries, men

Tuesday, July 28
6 matches, preliminaries, men

Wednesday, July 29
4 matches, preliminaries, women

Thursday, July 30
6 matches, preliminaries, men

Friday, July 31
4 matches, preliminaries, women

Saturday, August 1
6 matches, preliminaries, men

Sunday, August 2
4 matches, preliminaries, women

Monday, August 3
6 matches, preliminaries, men

Tuesday, August 4
1 match, final, women (7th & 8th places)
2 matches, quarterfinals, women

Wednesday, August 5
4 matches, quarterfinal, men
2 matches, finals, men (9th-12th places)

Thursday, August 6
1 match, final, women (5th & 6th places)
2 matches, classifications, men
2 matches, semifinals, women

Friday, August 7
1 match, final, women (3rd & 4th places)
Semifinals, men
2 matches, finals, men (5th-8th places)
1 match, semifinals, men
1 match, final, women

Sunday, August 9
1 match, final, men (3rd & 4th places)
1 match, final, men (1st & 2nd places)

Volleyball

▼

HIGHLIGHTS

Between the introduction of volleyball into the Games in 1964 and the LA Games, the Soviet Japanese–shared hegemony of the sport was hardly challenged: the Soviets took a total of ten medals, and the Japanese took eight, while the next-closest competitor, Poland, counted only three medals to its name. In fact, the Soviet domination was so thoroughgoing that the men lost only four of 39 matches, and their women's team lost only two of 28 matches during that time span.

During the Soviet absence from the LA Games, a new reign was in the making. The US, which until 1984 had not even been able to qualify a team—despite the sport's American origins—won its first medals ever: a silver in the women's event, and a gold in the men's. The name of Karch Kiraly, the US team's standout setter-hitter, has become synonymous with the LA Games.

The US team, which had been led in 1984 by head coach Doug Beal, enjoyed an auspicious between-Games period: the men's 1985 World Cup, the

1986 World Championship, the 1987 Pan Am gold. In 1988, under head coach Marv Dunphy, the US team was primed for another victory.

The Japanese team, however, had set its sights on the gold, and was ahead of the US early in the first game, by a score of 11–7. Coming from behind, the US managed victory by a two-point margin, defeating the Japanese in the next two matches by a decisive score of 15–2. The US team, with Karch Kiraly—by then proclaimed the world's greatest player—earned its second gold medal, even with the Soviets present. The US women's team, however, didn't fare so well: medals were taken by the Soviet Union, Peru, and the People's Republic of China.

Volleyball King Kiraly

Every so often, an athlete comes to dominate a sport so completely as to leave other competitors merely shaking their heads in amazement. Such an athlete is Karch Kiraly. His standing as perhaps the best volleyball player in history is backed by the sport's international governing body, which felt compelled to invent a special one-time award citing Kiraly for both his ability and his unparalleled contributions to the game.

So Kiraly is a volleyball superstar. The funny thing is, volleyball in the US is looked upon as beach and backyard barbecue recreation, right up there with badminton and croquet. Kiraly will never vie with Michael Jordan or Bo Jackson for the next big athletic shoe commercial. And even though the brand of volleyball played by Kiraly has as much in common with the recreational version as a Grand Prix race has with a drive in the family sedan, the sport was never taken very seriously by the American public. Battling uphill all the way, Kiraly has fought to change that view. And he's winning.

Born in 1961, Kiraly is the son of a Hungarian refugee physician, Laszlo, and Toni Kiraly. Raised in Santa Barbara, California, where volleyball is taken more seriously than in other parts of the country, Kiraly began playing volleyball with his father in two-man team tournaments. He made a name for himself throughout his school years—both as a volleyballer and as an academic standout. He attended UCLA, where he carried a 3.55 grade point average on the way to a degree in biochemistry. His talents were also obvious on the volleyball court, where he starred on the school team. That particular UCLA volleyball team enjoyed some success, taking 124 of 129 matches and capturing three national championships.

Kiraly was one of several talented volleyball players recruited from UCLA and USC in 1980 and 1981 by the US Olympic men's team. In a sport dominated by Japan, China, and the Soviet Union, the United States had long taken a backseat, never winning an Olympic medal or finishing higher than sixth in the world championships. US coach Doug Beal desperately wanted to change that.

Beal developed a revolutionary strategy based on Kiraly's extraordinary ability, particularly his outstanding passing skills. At the 1984 Olympics in Los Angeles, the upstart US team, with Kiraly serving as captain, upset the favored contenders for the gold medal. They then went on to win the World Cup in 1985, the World Championships in 1986, and the Pan Am Games in 1987. Then, this time with the Soviet Union present, the Kiraly-led US team successfully defended their title at the 1988 Olympics in Seoul, where Kiraly was named Most Valuable Player.

Throughout his tenure with Team USA, Kiraly repeatedly turned down offers to join professional volleyball teams in the United States and Europe. Amateur no longer, in 1990 Kiraly participated in the Italian Indoor League and is now performing on the pro beach tour. He's won the prestigious Manhattan Beach Open, the granddaddy of all professional beach tournaments, three times in the past four years and four times overall. The beach tour is played extensively in Southern California, where Kiraly and wife Janna live and hope to raise a family.

And, as he says, "It's nice at the beach. You don't have to wear a shirt." — P.G.

Volleyball

Medalists

Volleyball — Men's Team

1988 1. USA, Craig Buck, Robert Ctvrtlik, Scott Fortune, Charles "Karch" Kiraly, Ricci Luyties, Robert Doug Partie, Jon Root, Eric Sato, David Saunders, Jeff Stork, Troy Tanner, Steve Timmons
2. Soviet Union, I. Antonov, V. Chkourikhine, A. Kouzentsov, E. Krasilnikov, Valeri Lossev, I. Pantchenko, Igor Rounov, Iouri Sapega, A. Sorokolet, I. Tcherednik, Raimond Vilde, V. Zaitsev
3. Argentina, D. Castellani, Daniel M. Colla, H. Conte, J. Cuminetti, E. De Palma, Alejandro Diz, W. Kantor, E. Martinez, R. Quiroga, J. Uriarte, Carlos J. Weber, C. Zulianello

1984 1. USA, Dusty Dvorak, Dave Saunders, Steve Salmons, Paul Sunderland, Rich Duwelius, Steve Timmons, Craig Buck, Marc Waldie, Chris Marlowe, Aldis Berzins, Pat Powers, Karch Kiraly
2. Brazil, Bernardo Rezende, Mario Xando Oliveria Neto, Antonio Ribeiro, Jose Junior Montanaro, Ruy Campos Nascimento, Renan Dal Zotto, William Silva, Amauri Ribeiro, Marcus Freire, Domingos Lamapariello Neto, Bernard Rajzman, Fernando D'Avila
3. Italy, Marco Negri, Pier Paolo Lucchetta, Gian Carlo Dametto, Franco Bertoli, Francesco Dall'Olio, Piero Rebaudengo, Giovanni Errichiello, Guido De Luigi, Fabio Vullo, Giovanni Lanfranco, Paolo Vecchi, Andrea Lucchetta

1980 1. Soviet Union, Yuri Panchenko Vyacheslav Zaitsev, Aleksandr Savin, Vladimir Dorokhov, Aleksandr Yermilov, Pavel Selivanov, Oleg Moliboga, Vladimir Kondra, Vladimir Chernyshev, Fyodor Lashchenov, Valeri Krivov, Vilyar Loor
2. Bulgaria, Stoyan Counchev, Hristo Stoyanov, Dimitar Zlatanov, Dimitar Dimitrov, Petko Petkov, Mitko Todorov, Kaspar Simeonov, Emil Vulchev, Hristo Illiev, Yordan Angelov, Tsano Tsanov, Stefan Dimitrov
3. Romania, Corneliu Oros, Laurentiu Dumanoiu, Dan Girleanu, Nicu Stoian, Sorin Macavei, Constantin Sterea, Neculae Vasile Pop, Gunter Enescu, Valter-Korneliu Chifu, Marius Chata-Chitiga

1976 1. Poland, Wlodzimierz Stefanski, Bronislaw Bebel, Lech Lasko, Edward Skorek, Tomasz Wojtowicz, Wieslaw Gawlowski, Mieczyslaw Rybaczewski, Zbigniew Lubiejewski, Ryszard Bosek, Wlodzimierz Sadalski, Zbigniew Zarzycki, Marek Karbarz
2. Soviet Union, Anatoli Polishuk, Vyacheslav Zaitsev, Efim Chulak, Vladimir Dorohov, Aleksandr Ermilov, Pavel Selivanov, Oleg Moliboga, Vladimir Kondra, Yuri Starunski, Vladimir Chernyshev, Vladimir Ulanov, Aleksandr Savin, Yuri Chesnokov, Vladimir Patkin
3. Cuba, Leonel Marshall, Victoriano Sarmientos, Ernesto Maritnez, Victor Garcia, Carlosy Salas, Raul Virches, Jesus Savigne, Lorenzo Martinez, Diego Lapera, Antonio Rodriguez, Alfredo Figueredo, Jorge Perez

563

1972
1. Japan, Katsutoshi Nekoda, Kenji Kimura Yoshihide Fukao, Jungo Morita, Tadayoshi Yokota, Seiji Oko, Kenji Shimaoka, Yuzo Nakamura, Masayuki Minami, Tetsuo Sato, Yasuhiro Noguchi, Tetsuo Nishimoto
2. East Germany, Arnold Schulz, Wolfgang Webner, Siegfried Schneider, Wolfgang Weise, Rudi Schumann, Eckehard Pietzsch, Wolfgang Lowe, Wolfgang Maibohm, Rainer Tscharke, Jurgen Maune, Horst Peter, Horst Hagen
3. Soviet Union, Victor Borsch, Vyacheslav Domani, Vladimir Patkin, Leonid Zaiko, Yuri Starunski, Aleksandr Saprykine, VLadimir Kondra, Efim Chulak, Vladimir Poutiatov, Valeri Kravchenko, Yevgeny Lapinsky, Yuri Poyarkov

1968
1. Soviet Union, Eduard Sibiryakov, Valeri Kravchenko, Vladimir Belyayev, Yevgeny Lapinsky, Oleg Antropov, Vasiliyus Matuschevas, Viktor Mikhalchuk, Vladimir Ivanov, Yvan Bugayenkov, Georgi Mondzolevsky
2. Japan, Masayuki Minami, Katsutoshi Nekoda, Mamoru Shiragami, Isao Koizumi, Kenji Kimura, Yasuaki Mitsumori, Jungo Morita, Tadayoshi Yokota, Seiji Oko, Tetsuo Sato, Kenji Shimaoka
3. Czechoslovakia, Antonin Prochazka, Jiri Svoboda, Lubomir Zajicek, Joserf Musil, Josef Smolka, Vladimir Petlak, Petr Kop, Frantisek Sokol, Bohumil Golian, Zdenek Groessl, Pavel Schenk, Drabomir Koudelka

1964
1. Soviet Union, Yvan Buagyenkov, Nikolai Burobin, Yuri Chesnokov, Vascha Kacharava, Valeri Kalatschikhin, Vitali Kovalenko, Stanislav Lyugaylo, Gerogy Mondzolevsky, Yuri Poyarkov, Eduard Sibiryakov, Yuri Vengerovsky, Dmitri Voskoboynikov
2. Czechoslovakia, Milan Cuda, Bohumil Golian, Zdenek Humhal, Petr Kop, Josef Labuda, Josef Musil, Karel Paulus, Boris Perusic, Pavel Schenk, Vaclav Smidl, Josef Sorm, Ladislav Toman
3. Japan, Yutaka Demachi, Tsutomu Koyama, Sadatoshi Sugahara, Naohiro Ikeda, Yasutaka Sato, Toshiaki Kosedo, Tokihiko Higuchi, Masayuki Minami, Takeshi Tokutomi, Teruhisa Moriyama, Yuzo Nakamura, Katsutoshi Nekoda

1896-1960 Not held

Volleyball — Women's Team

1988
1. Soviet Union, Olga Chkournova, S. Korytova, Marina Koumych, T. Krainova, O. Krivocheeva, M. Nikoulina, V. Oguienko, E. Ovtchinnikova, I. Parkhomtchouk, T. Sidorenko, Irina Smirnova, Elena Volkova
2. Peru, Luisa Cervera, A. De La Guerra, Demisse Fajardo, Miriam Gallardo, Rosa Garcia, Isabel Heredia, Katherine Horny, Natalia Malaga, Gabriela Perez Del Solar, Cecilia Tilt, Gina Torrealva, Cenaida Uribe
3. People's Republic of China, Yongmei Cui, Yuzhu Hou, Ying Jiang, Guojun Li, Yueming Li, Huijuan Su, Yajun Wang, Dan Wu, Xiaojun Yang, Xilan Yang, Hong Zhao, Meizhu Zheng

1984
1. People's Republic of China, Ping Lang, Yan Liang, Ling Zhu, Yuzhu Hou, Xiaolan Zhou, Xilan Yang, Huijuan Su, Ying Jiang, Yanjun Li, Xiaojun Yang, Meizhu Zheng, Rongfang Zhang
2. USA, Paula Weishoff, Susan Woodstra, Riat Crockett, Laurie Flachmeier, Carolyn Becker, Flora Hyman, Rose Magers, Julie Vollertsen, Debbie Green, Kimberly Ruddins, Jeanne Beauprey, Linda Chisholm
3. Japan, Yumi Egami, Kimie Morita, Yuko Mitsuya, Miyoko Hirose, Kyoko Ishida, Yoko Kagabu, Norie Hiro, Kayoko Sugiyama, Sachiko Otani, Keiko Miyajima, Emiko Odaka, Kumi Nakada

1980
1. Soviet Union, Nadazhda Radzevich, Natalia Razumova, Olga Solovova, Yelena Akhaminova, Larissa Pavlova, Lyubov Kozyreva, Svetlana Nikishina, Ljudmila Chernysheva, Svetlana Badulina, Lydia Loginova
2. East Germany, Ute Kkostrzewa, Andrea Heim, Annette Schultz, Christine Mummhardt, Hieke Lehmann, Barbara Czekalla, Karla Roffeis, Martina Schmidt, Anke Westendorf, Karin Puschel, Brigitte Fetzer, Katharina Bullin
3. Bulgaria, Tania Dimitrova, Valentina Ilieva, Galina Stancheva, Silva Petrunova, Anka Hristolova, Verka Borisova, Margarita Gherasimova, Roumiana Kaicheva, Maya Georgieva, Tania Gogova, Tzvetana Bozhurina, Rossitza Dimitrova

1976
1. Japan, Takako Iida, Mariko Okamato, Echiko Maedo, Noriko Matsuda, Takako Shirai, Kiyomi Kato, Yuko Arakida, Katsuko Kanesaka, Mariko Yoshida, Shoko Takayanagi, Hiromi Yano, Juri Yokoyama
2. Soviet Union, Anna Rostova, Lyudmila Shetinina, Lilia Osadchaya, Natalya Kushnir, Olga Kozakova, Nina Smoleeva, Lyubov Rudovskaya, Larisa Bergen, Inna Ryskal, Lyudmila Chernysheva, Zoya Iusova, Nina Muradian
3. Republic of Korea, Soon-Bok Lee, Jung-Hye Yu, Kyung-Ja Byon, Soo-Nok Lee, Myung-Sun Baik, Hee-Sook Chang, Kum-Ja Ma, Young-Nae Yun, Kyung-Hwa Yu, Mi-Kum Park, Soo-Nok Jung, Jea-Jung Jo

1972 1. Soviet Union, Inna Ryskal, Vera Douiounova, Tatiana Tretiakova, Nina Smoleeva, Roza Salikhova, Ljudmila Buldakova, Tatiana Gonobobleva, Lyubov Turina, Galina Leontieva, Tatiana Sarycheva
2. Japan, Sumie Oinuma, Noriko Yamashita, Seiko Shimakage, Makiko Furukawa, Takako Iida, Katsumi Matsumura, Michiko Shiokawa, Takako Shirai, Mariko Okamoto, Keiko Hama, Yaeko Yamazaki, Toyoko Iwahara
3. Democratic People's Republic of Korea, Chun-Ok Ri, Myong-Suk Kim, Zung-Bok Kim, Ok-Sun Kang, Yeun-Ja Kim, He-Suk Hwang, Ok-Rim Jang, Myong-Suk Paek, Chun-ja Ryom, Su-Dae Kim, Ok-Jin Jong

1968 1. Soviet Union, Ljudmila Buldakova, Ljudmila Mikhailovskaya, Vera Lantratova, Vera Galushka, Tatiana Sarycheva, Tatiana Ponyayeva, Nina Smoleeva, Inna Ryskal, Galina Leontieva, Roza Salikhova, Valentina Vinogradova
2. Japan, Setsuko Yoshida, Suzue Takayama, Toyoko Iwahara, Yukiyo Kojima, Sachiko Fukunaka, Kunie Shishikura, Setsuko Inoue, Sumie Oinuma, Keiko Hama

3. Poland, Krystyna Czajkowska, Jozefa Ledwigowa, Elzbieta Porzec, Wanda Wiecha, Zofia Szczesniewska, Krystyna Jakubowska, Lidia Chmielnicka, Barbara Niemczyk, Halina Aszkielowicz, Krystyna Krupowa, Jadwiga Ksiazek, Krystyna Ostromecka

1964 1. Japan, Masae Kasai, Emiko Miyamoto, Kinuko Tanida, Yuriko Handa, Yoshiko Matsumura, Sata Isobe, Katsumi Matsumura, Yoko Shinozaki, Setsuko Sasaki, Yuko Fujimoto, Masako Kondo, Ayano Shibuki
2. Soviet Union, Nelly Abramova, Astra Biltauer, Ljudmila Buldakova, Lyudmila Gureyeva, Valentina Kamenek, Marita Katusheva, Ninel Lukanina, Valentina Mishak, Tatiana Roschina, Inna Ryzkal, Antonina Ryschova, Tamara Tikhonina
3. Poland, Krystyna Czajkowska, Maria Golimowska, Krystyna Jakubowska, Danuta Kordaczuk, Krystyna Krupowa, Jozefa Ledwigowa, Jadwiga Marko, Jadwiga Rutkowska, Maria Sliwkowa, Zofia Szczesniewska

1896–1960 Not held

Terry Schroeder captained the US water polo team to silver medals in 1984 and 1988, posed nude for the male statue that graces Los Angeles's Olympic Gateway Park, and figures to contend for the gold in 1992.

WATER POLO

WARM-UP

Known as "football in the water," or "aquatic soccer" or "hockey without sticks or skates or ice" (wait! that's team handball!), water polo has a history similar to soccer's, in that the early games of both sports were invitations for mayhem and violence. Invented in England during the 1870s by resort owners as a means of attracting guests, water polo first found favor with goons hellbent on discovering the quiet, novel joy of pulverizing an opponent in the water, as opposed to the usual roughhousing on land. Participants straddled wooden barrels and slapped at a ball with kayak paddles. The game grew so physical and dangerous that it was once barred from US collegiate competition.

Soon enough, paddles and barrels were dropped as equipment, leaving the ball, the water, and the object of desire: the goal. Although many of the early players were unable to swim, this did not greatly impede their game. Water polo was played in waters fit for advanced wading; the chief talent of a good player was knowing how to protect himself below the water line. Inasmuch as the water presented a natural screen, much of the unauthorized activity and near drownings could be negotiated out of sight of the referee.

Although on the Olympic program by 1900, the sport was slow in developing in Europe and the United States. The first US national champion was recognized in 1906 when the sport was known as softball polo, a version that put a premium on rough, unethical conduct. It was eventually discarded in favor of hardball polo, the basis for the current game.

Two key developments occurred in the 1920s that introduced the need for more skill, thereby helping water polo mature into a legitimate sport. The first was the use of larger and deeper pools, creating a need for players to acquire swimming ability, and the other was the development in Hungary of a method of passing the ball from player to player without allowing it to touch the water.

In the US, the game is still a California phenomenon, with much of the Olympic squad usually hailing from that state. The University of California, for instance, has won eight NCAA titles in the last two decades, maintaining the top collegiate water polo program in the country. And the US has become a power at the Olympic level, winning the silver medal in 1984 and 1988.

SPECTATORS' GUIDE

Water polo is similar to soccer, in that the basic object is to put the ball into the other team's net. Good passing technique is a necessity. The ball is advanced by passing or dribbling, and shots on goal are generally taken with brutal speed. A player is not allowed to touch the ball with both hands simultaneously. Goals can be scored off any part of the body, except a clenched fist. Also prohibited are striking the ball with a clenched fist and holding the ball underwater when tackled.

The water in the pool must be at least 5 feet, 11 inches in depth, and the distance between goal lines is just under 100 feet. The width of the playing area is 65 feet, seven inches. A team consists of the goalkeeper and six others, playing a game with four periods of seven minutes each, allowing a two-minute interval between periods for changing ends.

Minor offenses, such as splashing water in the face of an opponent (take that, you dirty animal), pushing, punching the ball, playing the ball with both hands, or wasting time, result in a free throw being awarded to the opposing team. A major foul results in a free throw and the exclusion of the guilty player from the pool for 45 seconds or until a goal is scored (much like the ice hockey power play). Major fouls include kicking or striking an opponent, holding, sinking, and unwarranted brutality.

A team earns two points for a victory and one for a tie. In the event of a deadlock in the standings, the first tie-breaker is goal difference. The event consists of preliminary rounds, semifinals, and the final.

HOPEFULS

It looks like the Yugoslavian water polo team may continue its winning streak at Barcelona, having pretty much drowned most of its competition throughout the 1980s. In both the 1984 and 1988 Olympic matches the Yugoslavians managed to meet and surpass the Americans' initial lead, and in the 1991 World Aquatic Championships they beat Spain for the title. With young stars Erich Fischer and David Imbernino, though, along with two-time Olympic goalie Craig Wilson and three-time Olympic veteran Terry Schroeder, the US team recaptured some of its honor in 1991.

Schroeder, captain of the last Olympic team, had retired after the team's second heartbreaking defeat to Yugoslavia, only to come out of retirement two years later. In 1991 he captained the US team to a long-awaited win over Yugoslavia, securing the gold at the FINA World Cup competition in Barcelona. Schroeder hopes to duplicate the performance at his fourth Olympic Games.

Terry Schroeder

Terry Schroeder didn't get out of the pool after the heart-crushing overtime defeat to the Yugoslavian team in the gold-medal water polo final at the 1988 Games in Seoul. He just swam—slowly, back and forth. Back. And forth.

"I guess maybe I was wishing the game wasn't over," he said after he finally emerged. "I was wishing my career wasn't over. But they are, and life goes on. I have to get on with my life."

Schroeder, then 30, of Agoura Hills, California, retired. He returned to his alma mater, Pepperdine University, to coach the water polo team. He returned to a career as a chiropractor.

He certainly had accomplished enough in his sport. He had competed internationally since 1978. He had been named to the 1980, 1984, and 1988 Olympic teams, captaining the latter two. He had been named player of the world in 1981 and 1985 by *Swimming* magazine. He had carried the US flag at the closing ceremonies of the 1988 Olympics. He was generally considered one of the greatest two-meter players in the history of the sport.

He also had been immortalized in art: Schroeder was the nude model for the statue of the male torso at the Olympic Gateway Park in front of the LA Coliseum.

Yes, back then, dripping water and disappointment, Schroeder, who graduated magna cum laude with a BS in sports medicine in 1981, was ready to concentrate on his career as a chiropractor—along with his wife, Lori, also a chiropractor, and 57 other chiropractors in the Schroeder family.

Well, sort of.

"When you leave the game," Schroeder has said, "you want to make sure you gave 100 percent and that you have no excuses."

He had none. No excuses. Problem was, he didn't have a gold medal, either.

It came as a surprise to few—if any—then, when Schroeder came out of retirement two years later, shortly after working as water polo analyst for Turner Broadcasting at the Goodwill Games in Seattle in the summer of 1990. Being at the pool wasn't exactly like being in it.

Need a better reason to unretire? How about this: Seems as though losing the gold medal twice to the Yugoslavs—the US lost to them in 1984, too—is the sort of pain in the neck even a chiropractor can't excise.

"My Olympic experiences have been fantastic," Schroeder told David Leon Moore of *USA Today* in January, 1991. "But there's still that inner drive that makes me want to reach out for that gold medal."

Schroeder, 6' 3" and 215 pounds, and his teammates led the Yugoslavs, 5-2, in 1988 and by the same score in 1984 as well, before losing.

Schroeder quickly shook off the effects of his retirement, discovering that he could still cut it in one of sports' most physically demanding games.

He was named captain of the 1991 US team, which won a gold medal at the FINA World Cup competition in Barcelona, the site of the 1992 Games, and a silver medal at the Pan Am Games in Cuba.

"I think I'm still playing well, and I still love playing," Schroeder said. "I still think I can help the team."

Schroeder said he wouldn't have returned without his wife's support.

Said Lori: "It didn't really surprise me. I think all along he wanted to play." No kidding. —*E.K.*

Schedule

The tentative water polo schedule is as follows:

Saturday, August 1
6 preliminary rounds

Sunday, August 2
6 preliminary rounds

Monday, August 3
3 preliminary rounds

Wednesday, August 5
6 preliminary rounds

Thursday, August 6
6 preliminary rounds

Saturday, August 8
6 semifinals rounds

Sunday, August 9
3 semifinal rounds
1 semifinal round, 2 final rounds, final

▼

HIGHLIGHTS

Water polo medals have traditionally been dominated by the Hungarians—who have mined a total of 12 medals, seven of them gold—while the next-in-line medalist, the US, has a total of seven, with one gold. The Hungarian Olympic presence has been marked by a variety of standout performances and interesting sidelights. A number of the Hungarian victories were awarded simply by virtue of a higher goal differential: in Berlin in 1936, Hungary and Germany were tied 2–2; in Helsinki in 1952, Yugoslavia and Hungary were tied 2–2; and again in Tokyo in 1964, the two were tied . . . and each time Hungary made away with the gold because of the goal differential.

Some of Hungary's more notable players include Dezsö Gyarmati, who medaled in five different Games (and whose wife, Eva, won a gold and silver in swimming events in 1952 and 1956), and Oliver Halassy, who played on three

570

Olympic water polo teams (including two gold-medaling teams)—despite the fact that one of his legs had been amputated below the knee due to a childhood accident.

Hungarian sportsmanship hasn't always been impeccable. In the 1972 Munich Games, in a match between Hungary and Italy, eight Hungarian players were suspended in a mere 38 seconds. That must be some kind of record. A much more serious imbroglio developed in the pool in 1956 when the Hungarian team competed against the Soviets. The match began with not a little acrimony: 200,000 Soviet troops had invaded Hungary just over one month prior to the match-not-made-in-heaven. Hailed as an underwater boxing match, the subaquatic war was called with Hungary in the lead 4–0; the Hungarian team was proclaimed victorious, and police were summoned to prevent rioting among the 5500 Soviet-unsympathetic spectators.

The Hungarian presence has not been felt in recent Games: Yugoslavia captured the gold in the 1984 and 1988 Games, while the US took silver both times. America's first medals came in 1904, when the US team literally swept the pool, taking gold, silver, and bronze. The victory is somewhat tarnished, however, by the fact that because the Americans insisted on playing the American way—using a soft, underinflated ball—at the St. Louis Games, no other countries participated. Paris in 1924 produced America's most famous water polo player (albeit best known for his swimming prowess): as a member of the US water polo team, the soon-to-be-known-as-Tarzan Johnny Weissmuller collected a bronze medal to add to his three swimming golds.

Medalists

Water Polo

1988
1. Yugoslavia, Dragan Andric, M. Bezmalinovic, Perica Bukic, Veselin Djuho, Igor Gocanin, Deni Lusic, Igor Milanovic, T. Paskvalin, R. Posinkovic, G. Radjenovic, Dubravko Simenc, A. Sostar, Mirko Vicevic
2. USA, James Bergeson, Greg Boyer, Jeff Campbell, Jody Campbell, Peter Campbell, Chris DuPlanty, Mike Evans, Doug Kimball, Craig Klass, Alan Mouchawar, Kevin Robertson, Terry Schroeder, Craig Wilson
3. Soviet Union, D. Apanasenko, V. Berendiouga, E. Charonov, M. Giorgadze, Evgeni Grichine, Mikhail Ivanov, Serguei Kotenko, S. Markotch, G. Mchvenieradze, N. Mendygaliev, Sergei Naoumov, Nikolai Smirnov

1984
1. Yugoslavia, Milorad Krivokapic, Deni Lusic, Zoran Petrovic, Bozo Vuletic, Veselin Djuho, Zoran Roje, Milivoj Bebic, Perica Bukic, Goran Sukno, Tomislav Paskvalin, Igor Milanovic, Dragan Andric, Andrija Popovic
2. USA, Craig Wilson, Kevin Robertson, Gary Figueroa, Peter Campbell, Douglas Burke, Joseph Vargas, Jon Svendsen, John Siman, Andrew McDonald, Terry Schroeder, Jody Campbell, Timothy Shaw, Christopher Dorst
3. West Germany, Peter Rohle, Thomas Loebb, Frank Otto, Rainer Hoppe, Armando Fernandez, Thomas Huber, Jurgen Schroeder, Rainer Osselmann, Hagen Stamm, Roland Freund, Dirk Theismann, Santiago Chalmovsky, Werner Obschernikat

1980
1. Soviet Union, Yevgeny Sharonov, Sergei Kotenko, Vladimir Akimov, Yevgeny Grishin, Mait Riysman, Aleksandr Kabanov, Aleksei Barkalov, Erkin Shagaev, Georgi Mshvenieradze, Mikhail Ivanov, Vyacheslav Sobchenko

571

1976

2. Yugoslavia, Luka Vezilic, Zoran Gopcevic, Damir Polic, Ratko Rudic, Zoran Mustur, Zoran Roje Milivoj Bebic, Slobodan Trifunovic, Bosko Lozica, Predrag Manojlovic, Milorad Krivokapic

3. Hungary, Endre Molnar, Istvan Szivos, Attila Sudar, Gyorgy Gerendas, Gyorgy Horkai, Gabor Csapo, Istvan Kiss, Istvan Udvardi, Laszlo Kuncz, Tamas Farago, Karoly Hauszler

1976 1. Hungary, Endre Molnar, Istvan Szivos, Tamas Farago, Laszlo Sarosi, Gyorgy Horkai, Gabor Csapo, Attila Sudar, Gyorgy Kenex, Gyorgy Gerendas, Ferenc Konrad, Tibor Cservenyak

2. Italy, Alberto Alberani, Rolando Simeoni, Silvio Baracchini, Sante Marsili, Marcello Del Duca, Gianni De Magistris, Alessandro Ghibellini, Luigi Castagnola, Riccardo De Magistris, Vincenzo D'Angelo, Umberto Panerai

3. Netherlands, Evert Kroon, Nico Landweerd, Jan Evert Veer, Hans van Zeeland, Ton Buunk, Piet de Zwarte, Hans Smits, Rik Toonen, Gyze Stroboer, Andy Hoepelman, Alex Boegschoten

1972 1. Soviet Union, Vadim Gulyaev, Anatoly Akimov, Aleksandr Dreval, Aleksandr Dolgushin, Vladimir Shmudski, Aleksandr Kabanov, Aleksei Barkalov, Aleksandr Shidlovsky, Nikolai Melnikov, Leonid Osipov, Vyacheslav Sobchenko

2. Hungary, Endre Molnar, Tibor Cservenyak, Dr. Andras Bodnar, Istvan Gorgenyi, Zoltan Kasas, Tamas Farago, Laszlo Sarosi, Istvan Szivos, Istvan Magas, Denes Pocsik, Dr. Ferenc Konrad

3. USA, James Slatton, Stanley Cole, Russell Webb, Barry Weitzenberg, Gary Sheerer, Bruce Bradley, Peter Asch, James Ferguson, Steven Barnett, John Parker, Eric Lindroth

1968 1. Yugoslavia, Karlo Stipanic, Ivo Trumbic, Ozren Bonacic, Uros Marovic, Ronald Lopatny, Zoran Jankovic, Miroslav Poljak, Dejan Dabovic, Djordje Perisic, Mirko Sandic, Zdravko Hebel

2. Soviet Union, Vadim Gulyaev, Givi Chikvanaya, Boris Grishin, Aleksandr Dolgushin, Aleksei Barkalov, Yuri Grigorovsky, Vladimir Semyonov, Aleksandr Shidlovsky, Vyacheslav Skok, Leonid Osipov, Oleg Bovin

3. Hungary, Endre Molnar, Mihaly Mayer, Istvan Szivos, Janos Konrad II, Laszlo Sarosi, Laszlo Felkai, Ferene Konrad III, Denes Pocsik, Andras Bodnar, Zoltan Domotor, Janos Steinmetz

1964 1. Hungary, Miklos Ambrus, Laszlo Felkai, Janos Konrad, Zoltan Domotor, Tivadar Kanizsa, Peter Rusoran II, Gyorgy Karpati, Otto Boros, Mihaly Mayer, Denes Pocsik, Andras Bodnar, Dezso Gyarmati

2. Yugoslavia, Milan Muskatirovic, Ivo Trumbic, Vinko Rosic, Zlatko Simenc, Bozidar Stanisic, Ante Nardeli, Zoran Jankovic, Mirko Sandic, Ozren Bonacic, Frane Nonkovic, Karlo Stipanic

3. Soviet Union, Igor Grabovsky, Vladimir Kuznyetsov, Boris Grishin, Boris Popov, Nikolai Kalashnikov, Zenon Bortkevich, Nikolai Kuznyetsov, Viktor Ageyev, Leonid Osipov, Vladimir Semyonov, Eduard Yegorov

1960 1. Italy, Dante Rossi, Giuseppe D'Altrui, Eraldo Pizzo, Gianni Lonzi, Franco Lavoratori, Rosario Parmegiani, Danio Bardi, Brunello Spinelli, Salvatore Gionta, Amadeo Ambron, Giancarlo Guerrini, Luigi Mannelli

2. Soviet Union, Leri Gogoladze, Givi Chikvanaya, Vyacheslav Kurennoi, Anatoly Kartashov, Yuri Grigorovsky, Pyotr Mshvenieradze , Vladimir Semyonov, Boris Goikhman, Yevgeny Salzyn, Viktor Ageyev, Vladimir Novikov

3. Hungary, Otto Boros, Istvan Hevesi, Mihaly Mayer, Dezso Gyarmati, Tivadar Kanizsa, Zoltan Domotor, Laszlo Felkai, Laszlo Jeney, Andras Katona, Kalman Markovits, Peter Rusoran II, Gyorgy Karpati, Janos Konrad, Andras Bodnar

1956 1. Hungary, Otto Boros, Istvan Hevesi, Dezso Gyarmati, Kalman Markovits, Antal Bolvari, Mihaly Mayer, Gyorgy Karpati, Laszlo Jeney, Istvan Szivos, Tivadar Kanizsa, Ervin Zador

2. Yugoslavia, Zdravko Kovacic, Ivo Cipci, Hrvoje Kacic, Marjan Zurej, Zdravko Jezic, Lovro Radonjic, Tomislav Franjkovic, Vladimir Ivkovic

3. Soviet Union, Boris Goikhman, Viktor Ageyev, Yuri Schlyapin, Vyacheslav Kurennoi, Pyotr Breus, Pyotr Mshvenieradze, Nodar Gyakharia, Mikhail Ryschak, Valentin Prokopov, Boris Markarov

1952 1. Hungary, Laszlo Jeney, Gyorgy Vizvari, Dezso Gyarmati, Kalman Markovits, Antal Bolvari, Istvan Szivos, Gyorgy Karpati, Robert Antal, Dezso Fabian, Karoly Szittya, Dezso Lemhenyi, Istvan Hasznos, Miklos Martin

2. Yugoslavia, Zdravko Kovacic, Veljko Bakasun, Ivo Stakula, Ivo Kurtini, Bosko Vuksanovic, Zdravko Jezic, Lovro Radonjic, Marko Brainovic, Vlado Ivkovic

3. Italy, Raffaello Gambino, Vincenzo Polito, Cesare Rubini, Carlo Peretti, Ermenegildo Arena, Maurizio Mannelli, Renato De Sanzuane, Renato Traiola, Geminio Ognio, Salvatore Gionta, Lucio Ceccarini

1948 1. Italy, Pasquale Buonocore, Emilio Bulgarelli, Cesare Rubini, Geminio Ognio, Ermenegildo Arena, Aldo Ghira, Gianfranco Pandolfini, Mario Maioni, Tullio Pandolfini

2. Hungary, Endre Gyorfi, Miklos Holop, Dezso Gyarmati, Karoly Szittya, Oszkar Csuvik, Istvan Szivos, Dezso Lemhenyi, Laszlo Jeney, Dezso Fabian, Jeno Brandi
3. Netherlands, Johannes J. Rohner, Cornelis Korevaar, Cor Braasem, Hans Stam, Albert F. Ruimschotel, Rudolph van Feggelen, Fritz Smol, Pieter J. Salomons, Hendrikus Keetelaar

1936 1. Hungary, Gyorgy Brody, Kalman Hazai, Marton Homannai, Oliver Halassy, Jeno Brandi, Janos Nemeth, Mihaly Bozsi, Gyorgy Kutasi, Miklos Sarkany, Sandor Tarics, Istvan Molnar
2. Germany, Paul Klingenburg, Bernhard Baier, Gustav Schurger, Fritz Gunst, Josef Hauser, Hans Schneider, Hans Schulze, Fritz Stolze, Heinrich Krug, Alfred Kienzle, Helmuth Schwenn
3. Belgium, Henri Disy, Joseph De Combe, Henri Stoelen, Fernand Issele, Albert Casteleyns, Gerard Blitz, Pierre Coppieters, Henri De Pauw, Edmond Michiels

1932 1. Hungary, Gyorgy Brody, Sandor Ivady, Marton Homonnai, Oliver Halassy, Jozsef Vertesy, Janos Nemeth, Ferenc Keseru I, Alajos Keseru II, Istvan Barta, Miklos Sarkany
2. Germany, Erich Rademacher, Fritz Gunst, Otto Cordes, Emil Benecke, Joachim Rademacher, Heiko Schwartz, Hans Schulze, Hans Eckstein
3. USA, Herbert Wildman, Calvert Strong, Charles Finn, Harold McAlister, Philip Daubenspeck, Austin Clapp, Wallace O'Connor

1928 1. Germany, Erich Rademacher, Otto Cordes, Emil Benecke, Fritz Gunst, Joachim Rademacher, Karl Bahre, Max Amann, Johann Blank
2. Hungary, Istvan Barta, Sandor Ivady, Alajos Keseru II, Marton Homonnai, Ferenc Keseru I, Jozsef Vertesy, Oliver Halassy
3. France, Paul Dujardin, Jules Keignaert, Henri Padou, Emile Bulteel, Achille Tribouillet, Henri Cuvelier, Albert Vandeplancke, Ernest Rogez, Albert Thevenon

1924 1. France, Paul Dujardin, Noel Delberghe, Georges Rigal, Henri Padou, Robert Desmettre, Albert Mayaud, Albert Delborgies
2. Belgium, Albert Durant, Joseph De Combe, Maurice Blitz, Joseph Pletincx, Pierre Dewin, Gerard Blitz, Joseph Cludts, Georges Fleurix, Paul Gailly, Jules Thiry, Pierre Vermetten
3. USA, Frederick Lauer, Oliver Horn, Clarence Mitchell, George Schroth, Herbert Vollmer, John Weissmuller, Arthur Austin, John Norton, Wallace O'Connor

1920 1. Great Britain, Charles Smith, Noel Purcell, Christopher Jones, Charles Bugbee, William Dean, Paul Radmilovic, William Peacock

2. Belgium, Albert Durant, Paul Gailly, Pierre Nijs, Joseph Pletincx, Maurice Blitz, Rene Bauwens, Gerard Blitz, Pierre Dewin
3. Sweden, Theodor Naumann, Pontus Hanson, Max Gumpel, Vilhelm Anderson, Nils Backlund, Robert Andersson, Erik Andersson, Harald Julin, Erik Bergqvist

1912 1. Great Britain, Charles Smith, George Cornet, Charles Bugbee, Arthur Hill, George Wilkinson, Paul Radmilovic, Isaac Bentham
2. Sweden, Torsten Kumfeldt, Harald Julin, Max Gumpel, Pontus Hanson, Vilhelm Anderson, Robert Andersson, Erik Bergqvist
3. Belgium, Albert Durant, Herman Donners, Victor Boin, Joseph Pletincx, Oscar Gregoire, Herman Meyboom, Felicien Courbet, Jean Hoffmann, Pierre Nijs

1908 1. Great Britain, Charles Smith, George Nevinson, George Cornet, Thomas Thould, George Wilkinson, Paul Radmilovic, Charles Forsyth
2. Belgium, Albert Michant, Herman Meyboom, Victor Boin, Joseph Pletincx, Fernand Feyaerts, Oscar Gregoire, Herman Donners
3. Sweden, Torsten Kumfeldt, Axel Runstrom, Harald Julin, Pontus Hanson, Gunnar Wennerstrom, Robert Andersson, Erik Bergvall

1906 **Not held**
1904 1. USA (New York Athletic Club), David Bratton, George Van Cleef, Leo "Budd" Goodwin, Louis Handley, David Hesser, Joseph Ruddy, James Steen
2. USA (Chicago Athletic Club), R. E. Breach, James Steever, Swatek, Charles Healy, Frank Kehoe, David Hammond, William Tuttle
2. USA (Missouri Athletic Club), John Meyers, Manfred Toeppen, Gwynne Evans, Amadee Reyburn, Fred Schreiner, A. M. Goessling, W. R. Orthwein

1900 1. Great Britain, (Osborne Swimming Club, Manchester), Arthur Robertson, Thomas Coe, Eric Robinson, Peter Kemp, George Wilkinson, John H. Derbyshire, William Lister
2. Belgium, (Club de Natation de Bruxelles), Albert Michant, Fernand Fayaerts, Henri Cohen, Victor De Behr, Oscar Gregoire, Victor Sonnemans, Jean De Backer
3. France (II), (Pupilles de Neptune de Lille), Coulon, Fardelle, Favier, Leriche, Louis Martin, Charles Treffel, Desire Merchez
3. France (I), (Libellule de Paris), Henri Peslier, Thomas Burgess, Decuyper, Pesloy, Paul Vasseur, Devenot, Louis Lauffray

1896 **Not held**

573

WEIGHTLIFTING

WARM-UP

Strong men lifting unbelievable weights are the stuff of myth and legend. Atlas, Hercules, and Samson were legendary men of remarkable strength. Together, strength and virtue have created unforgettable ideals.

Legends also indicate that competitions between strong men go back for thousands of years. Weightlifting was part of the regimen of the classical Greek athlete, who used stone or lead weights that were held in one hand and later came to be known as dumbbells.

Weightlifting as a competitive sport may have begun in the eighteenth century in countries such as Germany, France, Switzerland, and Austria, as well as the Scandinavian countries. Widely regarded as showmen, weightlifters often performed in sideshows and music halls.

Athletic clubs for strong men first appeared in the 1860s. Early competitors did not enjoy the advantage of adjustable weights, so rankings were determined by lifting a certain weight several times. The first form of two-handed weight was a metal bar with balls at each end made of solid iron or filled with sand, pebbles, lead shot, or pieces of metal.

Weightlifting became a respected sport with its inclusion in the Olympic program of 1896. The first official World Championships involving one- and two-hand events were held in Vienna in 1898.

The International Weightlifting Federation (IWF) was founded in Paris in 1920 with 14 members. Prior to 1920, weightlifting was governed by the International Gymnastics Federation (FIG).

Weightlifting took its modern-day form of competition in 1928, when the excercises done with one hand were abolished and the disc barbells appeared. The 1928 Olympics at Amsterdam included the press, the snatch, and the jerk, all done with two hands.

With the exception of the 1900, 1908, and 1912 Olympic Games, weightlifting has always been a part of the Olympic program. Before the current rule of determining the winner of a tie by placing the lighter competitor first, two gold medals were awarded for ties. This happened in 1928 and 1936 in the lightweight event.

The press was eliminated from Olympic competition for the 1972 Games in Munich. The event had proved difficult to adjudicate, and controversies arose over deviations between the valid lay-back style and the "Military Press."

Results in weightlifting are increasingly dramatic, and year after year new records are established. The United States dominated the weightlifting events from 1948 through 1956. The Soviet Union dominated the 1960 Games at Rome and have continued their dominance ever since.

▼

SPECTATORS' GUIDE

Two lift events are contested in the Olympics, the snatch and the clean-and-jerk. A lifter's total represents the combined weight of his best snatch and clean-and-jerk. Only the heaviest successful snatch and clean-and-jerk are used when tabulating the final score. Medals are awarded for totals only in ten different body-weight classifications, as follows: 52kg (115lb), 56kg (123lb), 60kg (132lb), 67.5kg (149lb), 75kg (165lb), 82.5kg (182lb), 90kg (198lb), 100kg (220lb), 110kg (243lb), and over 110kg.

The snatch is the more technical and more explosive of the two lifts. It is performed in one continuous movement: the bar is brought from the platform to a position overhead using one fluid motion. The lifter pulls the bar to about chest height and then, in the moment before the bar starts to descend, pulls his body into a squat position under the bar, securing it overhead with arms held straight. The lifter must stand and wait for the referee's signal, called a "down" signal, to lower the bar.

More weight is lifted in the clean-and-jerk than in the snatch. Two separate efforts are involved. First, in the "clean," the lifter must pull the weight from the platform to his shoulders in one motion. The bar is pulled to about waist level, keeping it close to the body and even close enough to brush the thighs. Then, before the bar starts to descend, the lifter pulls his body beneath the bar, secures the bar on his shoulders or chest, and then stands erect. The "jerk" then follows in which the lifter thrusts the bar from his shoulders to a position overhead, again in one motion, and splits his legs front and back. The lifter then brings his feet together and awaits the signal from the referee to lower the bar.

In both events, the down signal is given once the lifter is motionless.

Each lifter is allowed three chances to successfully perform each lift. If a lifter misses all three opportunities in the snatch, he is allowed to continue in the clean-and-jerk but is ineligible for final placing.

The starting weight is up to each individual lifter. Since each contestant is limited to three lifts in the snatch and three in the clean-and-jerk, he must choose carefully. In some cases, lifters will pass on the lower weights, but this strategy can backfire if the lifter is not able to make a lift at his first weight.

The lifting order for the competition is determined by the weight each individual lifter chooses to start with. In the case of identical weight requests, the order is determined by lot number.

The weight lifted for each attempt must increase by a minimum of 2.5 kg. In the case of attempting to break a record, a fourth attempt may be granted, and the weight increase may be as little as .5 kg.

Each lifter is accorded a 90 second time limit in which to mount the platform and begin the lift. If the lifter is making consecutive attempts, then three minutes are allowed between lifts.

If upon completion of a weight class, two lifters have identical totals, the lifter with the lower bodyweight is awarded the higher place.

Three referees judge each lift, a head referee and two side referees. Referees watch carefully for incorrect movements and rules violations. When officials disagree, the majority rules.

A judgement of "no lift" may occur when the bar touches the legs; during any unfinished attempt in which the bar has arrived at the height of the knees; when any part of the body except the feet touches the platform; if the bar stops in its upward path before arriving at the shoulders in the snatch or arm's length in the clean-and-jerk; when the bar is placed on the chest before the turning over of the elbows.

Common errors causing bad lifts include the press out, which occurs when the lifter bends his arms while holding the bar overhead and then presses out to make them straight; touching the platform with any part of the body except the feet; failure to control the bar; and touching the arm or elbow on the knee or leg in the clean part of the clean-and-jerk.

▼

HOPEFULS

Despite possible cuts in athletic funding and training due to recent political struggles, the Soviet Union and other Eastern European nations are expected to maintain their grip on the Olympic weightlifting medals in 1992. US lifters have fared poorly in the sport since the Soviets began dominating in the 1960s, but in recent years they've shown improvement. In 1990 four-time World Team member Richard Schutz finished ninth at the World Championships—the USA's best placement since 1976—and in 1991 Chris LeRoux became the first American to win a medal in the Junior World Championships. Roberto "Tony" Urrutia, a three-time world champion who finished eighth for the US at Seoul, should be the USA's strongest hope. Newcomers to watch include super heavyweight Mark Henry, who had been lifting for less than a year before winning the 1991 US Olympic Festival bronze medal, and Outstanding National Champion Bryan Jacob, who set two US records at the 1991 festival.

Schedule

The tentative weightlifting schedule is as follows:

Sunday, July 26
Flyweight (up to 52kg.)

Monday, July 27
Bantamweight (up to 56 kg.)

Tuesday, July 28
Featherweight (up to 60kg.)

Wednesday, July 29
Lightweight (up to 67.5 kg.)

Thursday, July 30
Middleweight (up to 75kg.)

Friday, July 31
Light heavyweight (up to 82.5 kg.)

Saturday, August 1
Middle heavyweight (up to 90kg.)

Sunday, August 2
First heavyweight (up to 100kg.)

Monday, August 3
Second heavyweight (up to 110kg.)

Tuesday, August 4
Super heavyweight (over 110kg.)

▼

HIGHLIGHTS

In weightlifting's first appearance at the Athens Games, Viggo Jensen of Denmark and Launceston Eliot of Great Britain both lifted the same weight in the two-arm competition. Viggo, however, was awarded the gold medal—thus becoming the first Olympic weightlifting champion—by virtue of the fact that Eliot had shuffled one of his feet during the lift. This would hardly be the last time such a fortuitous detail would be the criterion for victory.

During the Golden Age of American domination, the US earned four gold medals in each of the 1948, 1952, and 1956 Games, in addition to various silver and bronze medals. But America's Golden era quickly grew lackluster at the 1960 Rome Games, where the Soviets captured five of the six gold medals, initiating a trend of Eastern European domination.

Weightlifting, it seems, is as much weight watching as anything: the difference between 300-odd pound athletes as measured in ounces can mean the difference between victory and defeat, or even between being allowed to compete or not. In the Melbourne Games in 1956, American Charles Vinci—who stood

4'10—weighed 1 1/2 pounds more than his category allowed. He was able to compete after an hour of perspiration-inducing running—and a last-minute haircut. In the 1968 Games in Mexico City, Iran's Seresht Mohammed Nassiri and Hungarian Imre Földi both lifted a total of exactly 367.5 kg; Nassiri, however, snatched the gold because he weighed ten ounces less than Földi. Ironically, this had happened in Berlin in 1936, and, when the decision was protested, both athletes received gold medals.

Perhaps one of the most interesting weightwatching stories is that of American Tamio "Tommy" Kono—the archetypal wimpy-kid-turned-muscle-man—who, depending on the needs of the US weightlifting squad, bulked up and down to compete in lighter or heavier categories. If the US needed a heavyweight, he ate seven meals a day, if they needed a lightweight, he dieted on three. Kono won two Olympic golds in 1952 and 1956, and a silver in 1960, all in different weight categories.

Recent Games have continued to be dominated by non-Western muscle-men. The US managed to lift two medals at the LA Games: a bronze for Guy Carlton in the 110 kg category, and a silver for Mario Martinez in the over 110 kg category. Romania and China took most of the medals in 1984, with Romania garnering eight and China six.

Drugs have for a long time been a problem among those who are improperly pumped up. 1988 produced another doping debacle, this time involving the heavily favored Bulgarian team: after Mitko Grabley and Angel Guenchev were stripped of their gold medals for failing a test revealing probable steroid use, the entire Bulgarian team pulled out of the Seoul Games.

Turkish weightlifter Naim Sulemanoglu, the "Pocket Hercules," became a favorite of the 1988 Games for a host of reasons. Ethnically Turkish, in 1986 he defected from Bulgaria, where his parents and two brothers were still trapped when he captured the gold in Seoul. His performance in the 132 1/4-pound division would have won him a silver medal in the heavyweight division in the 1960 Games, and in 1956 it would have earned him a victory over Olympic heavyweight champ Paul Anderson, who weighed more than 300 pounds. Sulemanoglu was the first man to lift 2 1/2 times his weight in the snatch lift; with a herculean 342.5 kg lift, he made clean away with the gold in his weight class: the Bulgarian silver medalist, Stefan Topourov, lifted only 312.5 kg.

Medalists

Weightlifting — 52 kg

1988
1. Sevdalin Marinov, Bulgaria, 270.0 kg (WR)
2. Byung-Kwan Chun, South Korea, 260.0 kg
3. Zhuoqiang He, People's Republic of China, 257.5 kg

1984
1. Guoqiang Zeng, People's Republic of China, 235.0 kg
2. Peishun Zhou, People's Republic of China, 235.0 kg
3. Kazushito Manabe, Japan, 232.5 kg

1980
1. Kanybek Osmonaliev, Soviet Union, 245.0 kg (OR)

2. Bong Chol Ho, Democratic People's Republic of Korea, 245.0 kg
3. Gyong Si Han, Democratic People's Republic of Korea, 245.0 kg

1976 1. Alexander Voronin, Soviet Union, 242.5 kg (EWR)
2. Gyorgy Koszegi, Hungary, 237.5 kg
3. Mohammad Nassiri, Iran, 235.0 kg

1972 1. Zygmunt Smalcerz, Poland, 337.5 kg
2. Lajos Szucs, Hungary, 330.0 Kg
3. Sandor Holczreiter, Hungary, 327.5 Kg

1896-1968 Not held

Weightlifting — 56 kg

1988 1. Oxen Mirzoian, Soviet Union, 292.5 kg (OR); Mitko Grablev of Bulgaria won but was disqualified.
2. Yingqiang He, People's Republic of China, 287.5 kg
3. Shoubin Liu, People's Republic of China, 267.5 kg

1984 1. Shude Wu, People's Republic of China, 267.5 kg
2. Runming Lai, People's Republic of China, 265.0 kg
3. Masahiro Kotaka, Japan, 252.5 kg

1980 1. Daniel Nunez, Cuba, 275.0 kg (WR)
2. Yurik Sarkisian, Soviet Union, 270.0 kg
3. Tadeusz Dembonczyk, Poland, 265.0 kg

1976 1. Norair Nourikian, Bulgaria, 262.5 kg (WR)
2. Grzegorz Cziura, Poland, 252.5 kg
3. Kenkichi Ando, Japan, 250.0 kg

1972 1. Imre Foldi, Hungary, 377.5 kg (WR)
2. Mohammad Nassiri, Iran, 370.0 kg
3. Gennady Chetin, Soviet Union, 367.5 kg

1968 1. Mohammad Nassiri, Iran, 367.5 kg (EWR)
2. Imre Foldi, Hungary, 367.5 kg (EWR)
3. Henryk Trebicki, Poland, 357.5 kg

1964 1. Aleksei Vakhonin, Soviet Union, 357.5 kg (WR)
2. Imre Foldi, Hungary, 355.0 kg
3. Shiro Ichinoseki, Japan, 347.5 kg

1960 1. Charles Vinci, USA, 345.0 kg (EWR)
2. Yoshinobu Miyake, Japan, 337.5 kg
3. Esmail Elm Khan, Iran, 330.0 kg

1956 1. Charles Vinci, USA, 342.5 kg (WR)
2. Vladimir Stogov, Soviet Union, 337.5 kg
3. Mahmoud Namdjou, Iran, 332.5 kg

1952 1. Ivan Udodov, Soviet Union, 315.0 kg (OR)
2. Mahmoud Namdjou, Iran, 307.5 kg
3. Ali Mirzai, Iran, 300.0 kg

1948 1. Joseph De Pietro, USA, 307.5 kg (WR)
2. Julian Creus, Great Britain, 297.5 kg
3. Richard Tom, USA, 295.0 Kg

1896-1936 Not held

Weightlifting — 60 kg

1988 1. Naim Suleymanoglu, Turkey, 342.5 kg (WR)

2. Stefan Topourov, Bulgaria, 312.5 kg
3. Huenming Ye, People's Republic of China, 287.5 kg

1984 1. Weiqiang Chen, People's Republic of China, 282.5 kg
2. Gelu Radu, Romania, 280.0 kg
3. Wen-Yee Tsai, Taiwan, 272.5 kg

1980 1. Viktor Mazin, Soviet Union, 290.0 kg (OR)
2. Stefan Dimitrov, Bulgaria, 287.5 kg
3. Marek Seweryn, Poland, 282.5 kg

1976 1. Nikolai Kolesnikov, Soviet Union, 285.0 kg (EWR)
2. Georgi Todorov, Bulgaria, 280.0 kg
3. Kazumasu Hirai, Japan, 275.0 kg

1972 1. Norair Nurikjan, Bulgaria, 402.5 kg (EWR)
2. Dito Shanidze, Soviet Union, 400.0 kg
3. Janos Benedek, Hungary, 390.0 kg

1968 1. Yoshinobu Miyake, Japan, 392.5 kg
2. Dito Shanidze, Soviet Union, 387.5 kg
3. Yoshiyuki Mijake, Japan, 385.0 kg

1964 1. Yoshinobu Miyake, Japan, 397.5 kg (WR)
2. Isaac Berger, USA, 382.5 kg
3. Mieczyslaw Nowak, Poland, 377.5 kg

1960 1. Yevgeny Minayev, Soviet Union, 372.5 kg (EWR)
2. Isaac Berger, USA, 362.5 kg
3. Sebastiano Mannironi, Italy, 352.5 kg

1956 1. Isaac Berger, USA, 352.5 kg (WR)
2. Yevgeny Minayev, Soviet Union, 342.5 kg
3. Marian Zielinski, Poland, 335.0 kg

1952 1. Rafael Chimishkyan, Soviet Union, 337.5 kg (WR)
2. Nikolai Saksonov, Soviet Union, 332.5 kg
3. Rodney Wilkes, Trinidad and Tobago, 322.5 kg

1948 1. Mahmoud Fayad, Egypt, 332.5 kg (WR)
2. Rodney Wilkes, Trindad and Tobago, 317.5 kg
3. Jaffar Salmasi, Iran, 312.5 kg

1936 1. Anthony Terlazzo, USA, 312.5 kg (WR)
2. Saleh M. Soliman, Egypt, 305.0 kg
3. Ibrahim H. Shams, Egypt, 300.0 kg

1932 1. Raymond Suvigny, France, 287.5 kg (EOR)
2. Hans Wolpert, Germany, 282.5 kg
3. Anthony Terlazzo, USA, 280.0 kg

1928 1. Franz Andrysek, Austria, 287.5 kg
2. Pierino Gabetti, Italy, 282.5 kg
3. Hans Wolpert, Germany, 282.5 kg

1924 1. Pierino Gabetti, Italy, 402.5 kg
2. Andreas Stadler, Austria, 385.0 kg
3. Artur Reinmann, Switzerland, 382.5 kg

1920 1. Frans De Haes, Belgium, 220.0 kg
2. Alfred Schmidt, Estonia, 212.5 kg
3. Eugene Ryther, Switzerland, 210.0 kg

1896-1912 Not held

Weightlifting — 67.5 kg

1988 1. Angel Guenchev, Bulgaria (disqualified)
1. Joachim Kunz, East Germany, 340.0 kg

2. Israel Militossian, Soviet Union, 337.5 kg
3. Jinhe Li, People's Republic of China, 325.0 kg
1984 1. Yao Jingyuan, People's Republic of China, 320.0 kg
2. Andrei Socaci, Romania, 312.5 kg
3. Jouni Gronman, Finland, 312.5 kg
1980 1. Yanko Rusev, Bulgaria, 342.5 kg (WR)
2. Joachim Kunz, East Germany, 335.0 kg
3. Mincho Pashev, Bulgaria, 325.0 kg
1976 1. Zbigniew Kaczmarek, Poland, 307.5 kg
2. Piotr Korol, Soviet Union, 305.0 kg
3. Daniel Senet, France, 300.0 kg
1972 1. Muckarbi Kirzhinov, Soviet Union, 460.0 kg (WR)
2. Mladen Kutschew, Bulgaria, 450.0 kg
3. Zbigniew Kaczmarek, Poland, 437.5 kg
1968 1. Waldemar Baszanowski, Poland, 437.5 kg (OR)
2. Parviz Jalayer, Iran, 422.5 kg
3. Marian Zielinski, Poland, 420.0 kg
1964 1. Waldemar Baszanowski, Poland, 432.5 kg (WR)
2. Vladimir Kaplunov, Soviet Union, 432.5 kg (WR)
3. Marian Zielinski, Poland, 420.0 kg
1960 1. Viktor Buschuyev, Soviet Union, 397.5 kg (WR)
2. Howe-Liang Tan, Singapore, 380.0 kg
3. Abdul Wahid Aziz, Iraq, 380.0 kg
1956 1. Igor Rybak, Soviet Union, 380.0 kg (OR)
2. Rafael Khabutdinov, Soviet Union, 372.5 kg
3. Chang-hee Kim, Republic of Korea, 370.0 kg
1952 1. Tamio "Tommy" Kono, USA, 362.5 kg (OR)
2. Yevgeny Lopatin, Soviet Union, 350.0 kg
3. Verne Barberis, Australia, 350.0 kg
1948 1. Ibrahim H. Shams, Egypt, 360.0 kg (OR)
2. Appia Hamouda, Egypt, 360.0 kg (OR)
3. James Halliday, Great Britain, 340.0 kg
1936 1. Robert Fein, Austria, 342.5 (WR)
1. Anwar M. Mesbah, Egypt, 342.5 kg (WR)
3. Karl Jansen, Germany, 327.5 kg
1932 1. Rene Duverger, France, 325.0 kg (EWR)
2. Hans Haas, Austria, 307.5 kg
3. Gastone Pierini, Italy, 302.5 kg
1928 1. Hans Haas, Austria, 322.5 kg
1. Kurt Helbig, Germany, 322.5 kg
3. Fernand Arnout, France, 302.5 kg
1924 1. Edmond Decottignies, France, 440.0 kg
2. Anton Zwerina, Austria, 427.5
3. Bohumil Durdis, Czechoslovakia, 425.0 kg
1920 1. Alfred Neuland, Estonia, 257.5
2. Louis Williquet, Belgium, 240.0 kg
3. Florimond Rooms, Belgium, 230.0 kg
1896-
1912 **Not held**

Weightlifting — 75 kg

1988 1. Borislav Guidikov, Bulgaria, 375.0 kg
2. Ingo Steinhoefel, East Germany, 360.0 kg
3. Alexander Varbanov, Bulgaria, 357.5 kg
1984 1. Karl-Heinz Radschinsky, West Germany, 340.0 kg
2. Jacques Demers, Canada, 335.0 kg
3. Dragomir Cioroslan, Romania, 332.5 kg
1980 1. Assen Zlatev, Bulgaria, 360.0 kg (WR)
2. Aleksandr Pervy, Soviet Union, 357.5 kg
3. Nedelcho Kolev, Bulgaria, 345.0 kg
1976 1. Yordan Mitkov, Bulgaria, 335.0 kg (OR)
2. Vartan Militosyan, Soviet Union, 330.0 kg
3. Peter Wenzel, East Germany, 327.5 kg
1972 1. Yordan Bikow, Bulgaria, 485.0 kg (WR)
2. Mohamed Trabulsi, Lebanon, 472.5 kg
3. Anselmo Silvino, Italy, 470.0 kg
1968 1. Viktor Kurentsov, Soviet Union, 475.0 kg (OR)
2. Masashi Ouchi, Japan, 455.0 kg
3. Karoly Bakos, Hungary, 440.0 kg
1964 1. Hans Zdrazila, Czechoslovakia, 445.0 kg (EWR)
2. Viktor Kurentsov, Soviet Union, 440.0 kg
3. Masashi Ouchi, Japan, 437.5 kg
1960 1. Aleksandr Kurynov, Soviet Union, 437.5 kg (WR)
2. Thomas Kono, USA, 427.5 kg
3. Gyozo Veres, Hungary, 405.0 kg
1956 1. Fyodor Bogdanovsky, Soviet Union, 420.0 kg (WR)
2. Peter George, USA, 412.5 kg
3. Ermanno Pignatti, Italy, 382.5 kg
1952 1. Peter George, USA, 400.0 kg (OR)
2. Gerard Gratton, Canada, 390.0 kg
3. Sung-jip Kim, Republic of Korea, 382.5 kg
1948 1. Frank Spellman, USA, 390.0 kg (OR)
2. Peter George, USA, 382.5 kg
3. Sung-jip Kim, Republic of Korea, 380.0 kg
1936 1. Khadr Sayed El Touni, Egypt, 387.5 kg (WR)
2. Rudolf Ismayr, Germany, 352.5 kg
3. Adolf Wagner, Germany, 352.5 kg
1932 1. Rudolf Ismayr, Germany, 345.0 kg
2. Carlo Galimberti, Italy, 340.0 kg
3. Karl Hipfinger, Austria, 337.5 kg
1928 1. Roger Francois, France, 335.0 kg (WR)
2. Carlo Galimberti, Italy, 332.5 kg
3. August Scheffer, Netherlands, 327.5 kg
1924 1. Carlo Galimberti, Italy, 492.5 kg
2. Jaan Kikkas, Estonia, 450.0 kg
2. Alfred Neuland, Estonia, 455.0 kg
1920 1. Henri Gance, France, 245.0 kg
2. Pietro Bianchi, Italy, 237.5 kg
3. Albert Pettersson, Sweden, 237.5 kg
1896-
1912 **Not held**

Weightlifting — 82.5 kg

1988 1. Israil Arsamakov, Soviet Union, 377.5 kg
2. Istvan Messzi, Hungary, 370.0 kg
3. Hyung-Kun Lee, South Korea, 367.5 kg
1984 1. Petre Becheru, Romania, 355.0 kg
2. Robert Kabbas, Australia, 342.5 kg
3. Ryoji Isaoka, Japan, 340.0 kg
1980 1. Yurik Vardanjan, Soviet Union, 400.0 kg
2. Blagoi Blagoev, Bulgaria, 372.5 kg
3. Dusan Poliacik, Czechoslovakia, 367.5 kg
1976 1. Valeri Shary, Soviet Union, 365.0 kg (OR)
2. Blagoi Blagoev, Bulgaria, 362.5 kg
3. Trendafil Stoichev, Bulgaria, 360.0 kg
1972 1. Leif Jenssen, Norway, 507.5 kg (OR)
2. Norbert Ozimek, Poland, 497.5 kg
3. Gyorgy Horvath, Hungary, 495.0 kg
1968 1. Boris Selitsky, Soviet Union, 485.0 kg (EWR)
2. Vladimir Belyayev, Soviet Union, 485.0 kg (EWR)
3. Norbert Ozimek, Poland, 472.5 kg
1964 1. Rudolf Plukfelder, Soviet Union, 475.0 kg (OR)
2. Geza Toth, Hungary, 467.5 kg
3. Gyozo Veres, Hungary, 467.5 kg
1960 1. Ireneusz Palinski, Poland, 442.5 kg
2. James George, USA, 430.0 kg
3. Jan Bochenek, Poland, 420.0 kg
1956 1. Tamio "Tommy" Kono, USA, 447.5 kg (WR)
2. Vassili Stepanov, Soviet Union, 427.5 kg
3. James George, USA, 417.5 kg
1952 1. Trofim Lomakin, Soviet Union, 417.5 kg (EOR)
2. Stanley Stanczyk, USA, 415.0 kg
3. Arkadi Vorobyov, Soviet Union, 407.5 kg
1948 1. Stanley Stanczyk, USA, 417.5 kg (OR)
2. Harold Sakata, USA, 380.0 kg
3. Gosta Magnusson, Sweden, 375.0 kg
1936 1. Louis Hostin, France, 372.5 kg (OR)
2. Eugen Deutsch, Germany, 365.0 kg
3. Ibrahim Wasif, Egypt, 360.0 kg
1932 1. Louis Hostin, France, 365.0 kg (EWR)
2. Svend Olsen, Denmark, 360.0 kg
3. Henry Duey, USA, 330.0 kg
1928 1. El Sayed Nosseir, Egypt, 355.0 kg (WR)
2. Louis Hostin, France, 352.5 kg
3. Johannes Verheijen, Netherlands, 337.5 kg
1924 1. Charles Rigoulot, France, 502.5 kg
2. Fritz Hunenberger, Switzerland, 490.0 kg
3. Leopold Friedrich, Austria, 490.0 kg
1920 1. Ernest Cadine, France, 290.0 kg
2. Fritz Hunenberger, Switzerland, 275.0 kg
3. Erik Pettersson, Sweden, 272.5 kg
1896-1912 Not held

Weightlifting — 90 kg

1988 1. Anatoli Khrapatyi, Soviet Union, 412.5 kg
2. Nail Moukhamediarov, Soviet Union, 400.0 kg
3. Slawomir Zawada, Poland, 400.0 kg
1984 1. Nicu Vlad, Romania, 392.5 kg (OR)
2. Dumitru Petre, Romania, 360.0 kg
3. David Mercer, Great Britain, 352.5 kg
1980 1. Peter Baczaka, Hungary, 377.5 kg
2. Roumen Aleksandrov, Bulgaria, 375.0 kg
3. Frank Mantek, East Germany, 370.0 kg
1976 1. David Rigert, Soviet Union, 382.5 kg (OR)
2. Lee James, USA, 362.5 kg
3. Atanas Shopov, Bulgaria, 360.0 kg
1972 1. Andon Nikolov, Bulgaria, 525.0 kg (OR)
2. Atanas Schopov, Bulgaria, 517.5 kg
3. Hans Bettembourg, Sweden, 512.5 kg
1968 1. Kaarlo Kangasniemi, Finland, 517.5 kg (OR)
2. Jan Talts, Soviet Union, 507.5 kg
3. Marek Golab, Poland, 495.0 kg
1964 1. Vladimir Golovanov, Soviet Union, 487.5 kg (WR)
2. Louis Martin, Great Britain, 475.0 kg
3. Ireneusz Palinski, Poland, 467.5 kg
1960 1. Arkadi Vorobyov, Soviet Union, 472.5 kg (WR)
2. Trofim Lomakin, Soviet Union, 457.5 kg
3. Louis Martin, Great Britain, 445.0 kg
1956 1. Arkadi Vorobyov, Soviet Union, 462.5 kg (WR)
2. David Sheppard, USA, 442.5 kg
3. Jean Debuf, France, 425.0 kg
1952 1. Norbert Schemansky, USA, 445.0 kg (WR)
2. Grigori Novak, Soviet Union, 410.0 kg
3. Lennox Kilgour, Trinidad and Tobago, 402.5 kg
1896-1948 Not held

Weightlifting — 100 kg

1988 1. Pavel Kouznetsov, Soviet Union, 425.0 kg (OR) (Andov Szanyi was disqualified)
2. Nicu Vlad, Romania, 402.5 kg
3. Peter Immesberger, West Germany, 395.0 kg
1984 1. Rolf Milser, West Germany, 385.0 kg
2. Vasile Gropa, Romania, 382.5 kg
3. Pekka Niemi, Finland, 367.5 kg
1980 1. Ota Zaremba, Czechoslovakia, 395.0 kg (OR)
2. Igor Nikitin, Soviet Union, 392.5 kg
3. Alberto Blanco Fernandez, Cuba, 385.0 kg

Weightlifting — 110 kg

1988 1. Yuri Zakharevitch, Soviet Union, 455.0 kg (WR)
2. Jozsef Jacso, Hungary, 427.5 kg

3. Ronny Weller, East Germany, 425.0 kg
1984 1. Norberto Oberburger, Italy, 390.0 kg
2. Stefan Tasnadi, Romania, 380.0 kg
3. Guy Carlton, USA, 377.5 kg
1980 1. Leonid Taranenko, Soviet Union, 422.5 kg (WR)
2. Valentin Hristov, Bulgaria, 405.0 kg.
3. Gyorgy Szalai, Hungary, 390.0 kg
1976 1. Valentin Khristov, Bulgaria, 400.0 kg
2. Yuri Zaitsev, Soviet Union, 385.0 kg
3. Krastic Sermedjiev, Bulgaria, 385.0 kg
1972 1. Jan Talts, Soviet Union, 580.0 kg (OR)
2. Aleksandr Kraichev, Bulgaria, 562.5 kg
3. Stefan Grutzner, East Germany, 555.0 kg
1968 1. Leonid Schabotinski, Soviet Union, 572.5 kg (EOR)
2. Serge Reding, Belgium, 555.0 kg
3. Joe Dube, USA, 555.0 kg
1964 1. Leonid Zhabotinsky, Soviet Union, 572.5 kg (OR)
2. Yuri Vlassov, Soviet Union, 570.0 kg
3. Norbert Schemansky, USA, 537.5 kg
1960 1. Yuri Vlassov, Soviet Union, 537.5 kg (WR)
2. James Bradford, USA, 512.5 kg
3. Norbert Schemansky, USA, 500.0 kg
1956 1. Paul Anderson, USA, 500.0 kg (OR)
2. Humberto Selvetti, Argentina, 500.0 kg (OR)
3. Alberto Pigaiani, Italy, 452.5 kg
1952 1. John Davis, USA, 460.0 kg (OR)
2. James Bradford, USA, 437.5 kg
3. Humberto Selvetti, Argentina, 432.5 kg
1948 1. John Davis, USA, 452.5 kg (OR)
2. Norbert Schemansky, USA, 425.0 kg
3. Abraham Charite, Netherlands, 412.5 kg
1936 1. Josef Manger, Germany, 410.0 kg (WR)
2. Vaclav Psenicka, Czechoslovakia, 402.5 kg
3. Arnold Luhaar, Estonia, 400.0 kg
1932 1. Jaroslav Skobla, Czechoslovakia, 380.0 kg (OR)
2. Vaclav Psenicka, Czechoslovakia, 377.5 kg
3. Josef Strassberger, Germany, 377.5 kg
1928 1. Josef Strassberger, Germany, 372.5 kg (WR)
2. Arnold Luhaar, Estonia, 360.0 kg
3. Jaroslav Skobla, Czechoslovakia, 357.5 kg
1924 1. Giuseppe Tonani, Italy, 517.5 kg
2. Franz Aigner, Austria, 515.0 kg
3. Harald Tammer, Estonia, 497.5 kg
1920 1. Filippo Bottino, Italy, 270.0 kg
2. Joseph Alzin, Luxembourg, 255.0 kg
3. Louis Bernot, France, 250.0 kg
1908-
1912 **Not held**
1906 1. Josef Steinbach, Austria - one-hand lift, 76.55 kg
1. Dimitrios Tofalos, Great Britain - two-hand lift, 142.5 kg

2. Tullio Camilotti, Italy - one-hand lift, 73.75 kg
2. Josef Steinbach, Austria - two-hand lift, 136.5 kg
3. Alexandre Maspoli, France - two-hand lift, 129.5 kg
3. Heinrich Rondi, Germany - two-hand lift, 129.5 kg
3. Heinrich Schneidereit, Germany - two-hand lift, 129.5 kg
3. Heinrich Schneidereit, Germany - one-hand lift, 70.75 kg
1904 1. Perikles Kakousis, Greece - two-hand lift, 111.70 kg
1. Oscar Paul Osthoff, USA - one-hand lift, 48 P.
2. Oscar Paul Osthoff, USA - two-hand lift, 84.37 kg
2. Frederick Winters, USA - one-hand lift, 45 P.
3. Frank Kungler, USA - two-hand lift, 79.61 kg
3. Frank Kungler, USA - one-hand lift, 10 P.
1900 **Not held**
1896 1. Launceston Elliott, Great Britain - one-hand lift, 71.0 kg
1. Viggo Jensen, Denmark - two-hand lift, 111.5 kg
2. Launceston Elliott, Great Britain - two-hand lift, 111.5 kg
2. Viggo Jensen, Denmark - one-hand lift, 57.2 kg
3. Alexandros Nikolopoulos, Greece - one-hand lift, 57.2 kg
3. Sotirios Versis, Greece - two-hand lift, 100.0 kg

Weightlifting — Over 110 kg

1988 1. Alexandre Kourlovitch, Soviet Union, 462.5 kg
2. Manfred Nerlinger, West Germany, 430.0 kg
3. Martin Zawieja, West Germany, 407.5 kg
1984 1. Dean "Dinko" Lukin, Australia, 412.5 kg
2. Mario Martinez, USA, 410.0 kg
3. Manfred Nerlinger, West Germany, 397.5 kg
1980 1. Sultan Rakhmanov, Soviet Union, 440.0 kg
2. Jurgen Heuser, East Germany, 410.0 kg
3. Tadeusz Rutkowski, Poland, 407.5 kg
1976 1. Vassili Alekseyev, Soviet Union, 440.0 kg
2. Gerd Bonk, East Germany, 405.0 kg
3. Helmut Losch, East Germany, 387.5 kg
1972 1. Vassili Alekseyev, Soviet Union, 230.0 kg (OR)
2. Rudolf Mang, West Germany, 610.0 kg
3. Gerd Bonk, East Germany, 572.5 kg
1896-
1968 **Not held**

583

US freestyle wrestler John Smith, top, pinned down a gold medal in Seoul and goes to Barcelona a certified "Master of Technique," as voted by the international wrestling federation.

WRESTLING

WARM-UP

Statues, stone slabs, and wall paintings from ancient civilizations indicate that wrestling is as old as civilization itself. Bearing no relationship to the modern performance art of professional wrestling, it was once an honored pastime and practiced by royalty in ancient Japan, China, India, Babylon, Egypt, and elsewhere.

Wrestling as a competitive sport first appeared in ancient Greece. Records indicate that events between men were introduced in the 18th Olympic Games (708 BC)

Wrestling was a part of the first modern-day Olympic Games held in 1896. Only one category, heavyweight, was contested that year, and the sport was left out of the 1900 Games. However, wrestling grew in importance in the years prior to World War I.

Although wrestling is an ancient sport, it has known countless variations as different countries practice their own versions: sumo in Japan, sambo in Russia, kushti in Iran, yagli in Turkey, and schwingen in Switzerland.

The two forms of wrestling practiced in the Olympics are freestyle and Greco-Roman. Freestyle events in seven weight categories were contested in the 1904 Games. Greco-Roman was introduced at the 1908 London Games with competitions in four weight categories. The primary distinction between freestyle and Greco-Roman is that Greco-Roman wrestlers may not grasp the legs of their opponents nor use their legs in any aggressive action.

By 1912, when the Games were held in Stockholm, freestyle competition was dropped in favor of Greco-Roman, indicating that style's popularity in the Scandinavian countries. It was during the 1912 Games that the longest final ever staged in a combat sport occurred. The light-heavyweight match was called after nine hours of wrestling.

The International Amateur Wrestling Federation (FILA) was founded in 1912, and in the years following World War I wrestling became increasingly regulated. International rules were established, and World and European Championships were eventually held on an annual basis.

Wrestling expanded after World War II, with 266 competitors from 27 nations entering the 1948 Olympic Games at London. The USSR wrestlers made their debut in 1952 and took most of the medals. Turkey and Japan made strong showings in subsequent Games, and in 1972, two weight categories were added to bring the total to ten. These new categories were a new weight group under 48kg (105lb) and a super-heavyweight category over 100kg (220lb).

SPECTATORS' GUIDE

Recent rules changes have made wrestling a more interesting spectator sport. Starting in 1989, a match became a one-period, five-minute contest. Matches had previously consisted of two rounds of three minutes each, and prior to that were three rounds of three minutes each. By limiting the matches to shorter time periods, officials hoped to introduce more action and lessen the emphasis on endurance.

Wrestlers are arranged in ten weight categories, from under 48kg (105lb) to over 100kg (220lb). Two styles of wrestling are contested in the Olympics, Greco-Roman and freestyle. Both have similar rules and scoring, but in Greco-Roman the wrestlers may not use or touch the legs. Each style has developed its own moves and strategies.

Wrestlers compete on a circular mat, including a nine-meter circular competition area and a two-meter passivity zone at the edge. Each bout starts with the wrestlers standing on their feet. They attempt to take their opponent down to score points. Wrestling also occurs with both wrestlers down on the mat; this is known as par terre.

The main objective in wrestling is to pin your opponent. This is achieved by holding his shoulder blades to the mat for one-half of one second. Automatically ending the match, the pin is similar to a knockout in boxing. A pin is also known as a fall.

Most matches are won on points, which are awarded for performing techniques or moves within the rules. If a wrestler earns 15 or more points than his opponent at any time, the bout is stopped. This is known as a technical fall and is similar to the TKO in boxing.

Another way to end a bout is through passive disqualification. When a wrestler is not aggressive or does not work to score points, the officials penalize him with a caution. Three cautions against any wrestler results in an automatic loss of the match.

Points are scored in three basic ways. The first is through a takedown, when a wrestler takes his opponent to the mat. This is worth one point but can be worth more if the opponent is brought down on his back. A high amplitude takedown, where an opponent goes through the air to land on his back, is worth five points.

A second way to score points is to turn the opponent's shoulders to the mat. This is called exposure. Points are scored once the back area breaks a 90-degree angle.

A third scoring maneuver is called a reversal. A point is awarded when the man underneath completely reverses his position and comes to the top position.

The most popular takedown techniques in freestyle are the single-leg and double-leg takedowns. Popular throws include bodylocks and headlocks. The gut wrench is the most popular turning maneuver and involves rolling over the opponent's back after locking around his waist.

In Greco-Roman, popular takedowns include arm throws, arm drags, slidebys, and snapdowns. Body lifts and saltos are among the spectacular throws seen in Greco-Roman wrestling.

▼

HOPEFULS

Look for the ever-powerful Soviet and US teams to grapple for the medals in Barcelona. Though the Soviet Union is expected to offer a team as powerful and hungry as ever, the USA will be ready to meet their challenge, having scored their biggest team victory in 30 years over the Soviets at the 1990 Goodwill Games.

The USA's best hope, arguably the best freestyle wrestler of all time in his weight class, is 136.5-pound John Smith. The winner of a 1988 Olympic gold, three world championships, two Goodwill Games titles, and the 1991 Sullivan Award as the top US amateur athlete, Smith is ready and able to defend his Olympic championship.

Adding depth to the US freestyle team are Brian Baumgartner, a 286-pound Olympic gold and silver medalist; Kenny Monday, 163-pound Olympic gold medalist and 1989 world champion; and Chris Campbell, a 1981 world champ and three-time world cup winner who is coming out of athletic retirement with the hope of competing in his first Olympic Games. Dennis Koslowski, who won the 1988 Olympic bronze medal, will again compete for a Greco-Roman title.

John Smith

It takes a lot of world titles, more than a few prestigious awards, and a complete and sustained dominance over the competition for many years before a wrestler can assume the status of a national sports hero, and John Smith of Del City, Oklahoma, has earned the honor.

Arguably the greatest wrestler in American history, Smith became the first American in this tough, but underappreciated sport, to win four world titles when he ripped through his opponents in the 136.5-pound weight class at the 1990 World Championships by a combined total score of 58-4. Smith's performance that year in Tokyo was so impressive that FILA, the international wrestling federation, voted him the prestigious title of "Master of Technique."

In 1991 Smith earned further distinction when he outpolled the great Notre Dame football player Raghib "Rocket" Ismail and several others to win the 61st Sullivan Award as America's top amateur athlete.

And while the Sullivan Award certainly helped bring Smith's stellar career to national prominence, coach Bobby Douglas put it into perspective for the average sports fan. Smith, said Douglas, who will coach the US Olympic freestyle wrestlers at Barcelona in 1992, "is the Mike Tyson of wrestling."

But for Smith, a soft-spoken 26-year-old from a large, sports-oriented family, success is no reason to stop working. "Being the best at something, God, that's a great feeling," he admits. "You don't think about it too long, though. It's easy to let your priorities slip."

For the second-oldest son of Lee Roy Smith, a retired Oklahoma Transportation Department worker, and his wife Madalene, a down-to-earth, iron-willed mother, such humility came naturally. It also didn't hurt for young John to have an older brother to worship while growing up. The younger Lee Roy Smith was himself a multi-national title holder and has pushed John's career along as his brother's coach, mentor, and—sometimes—tormentor. "John learned to be fast wrestling Lee Roy," the boys' father said. "If he beat him, Lee Roy would hit him. John learned to take him down and take off running."

"I learned a lot from [Lee Roy] about how to prepare for competition," John has said. "I saw the fire in his eyes, the determination .... I started to wrestle because I wanted to be like him."

Smith wrestled well enough in high school to gain a scholarship to Oklahoma State, but it was not until he suffered his first major collegiate defeat that his career really began to blossom. As a sophomore wrestling in the 1985 NCAA championship finals, Smith was beaten 5–2 by Wisconsin's Jim Jordan, a quick, slick wrestler whose style Smith decided he would adopt for himself. Not as strong or muscular as most wrestlers, Smith began to play to his own strengths: speed, intelligence, and an attacking, unorthodox style that kept his opponents off-balance. The hard hours of practice eventually led to Smith's signature move, a lightning-fast single leg takedown that has proven virtually unstoppable.

Since he first began competing in international meets in 1986, Smith has compiled a 150–3 record. He has added world titles in the 1986 and 1990 Goodwill Games, and at the 1988 Olympics in Seoul he defeated the stocky Stephan Sarkissian of the Soviet Union 4–0 to win the gold.

Not quite ready to rest on his laurels, Smith has his sights set firmly on a repeat performance at Barcelona and a chance to lay undisputed claim to the lofty prestige as the world's best wrestler in any weight class. "I would like to win five or six straight world titles," Smith has said. "I would like to put that record out of reach." —*D.C.*

Schedule

The tentative wrestling (Greco-Roman style) schedule is as follows:

Sunday, July 26
Preliminaries, 52, 68, 100kg.

Monday, July 27
Preliminaries, 48, 52, 68, 74,
100, over 100 kg.

Tuesday, July 28
Preliminaries, 48, 57, 62, 68,
74, 82, 90, 100 over 100kg.

Finals 52, 68, 100kg.

Wednesday, July 29
Preliminaries, 48, 57, 62, 74, 82,
90, over 100kg.
Finals, 48, 74, over 100kg.

Thursday, July 30
Preliminaries, 57, 62, 82, 90kg.
Finals, 57, 62, 82, 90kg.

The tentative wrestling (freestyle) schedule is as follows:

Monday, August 3
Preliminaries, 52, 68, 100kg.

Tuesday, August 4
Preliminaries, 48, 52, 68,
74, 100, over 100kg.

Wednesday, August 5
Preliminaries, 48, 52, 57, 62, 68,
74, 82, 90, over 100kg.
Finals, 52, 68, 100kg.

Thursday, August 6
Preliminaries, 48, 57, 62,
74, 82, 90, over 100kg.
Finals, 48, 74, over 100kg.

Friday, August 7
Preliminaries, 57, 62, 82, 90kg.
Finals, (7th-12th places) 57, 62,
82, 90kg.
Finals, 57, 62, 82, 90kg.

▼

HIGHLIGHTS

Carl Schuhmann, who stood a mere 64 inches tall, became the first wrestling victor of the modern Games in 1896; competing in an event with no bodyweight limit, the German defeated Great Britain's weightlifting champion Launceston Eliot in the preliminaries. The wrestling title was not Schuhmann's only Olympic victory: he was a gymnastics triple gold medalist as well.

The host Americans dominated the sport upon its return to the Games in St. Louis, taking literally every title in each of the seven freestyle weight categories that year. At the 1908 Games, the Americans had to share the medals, primarily with Great Britain, which took three of the five golds, and various other titles. The US held on to two golds this time around, one of which was won by 63.5 inch Yale student George Dole in the featherweight division; he was the only non-British wrestler in that division.

fact: In the Middle Ages a typical prize for a victorious wrestler in England was a ram.

When Greco-Roman events replaced freestyle events in the 1912 Games, the gold medals were shared between the Finns, who took three, and the Swedes, who claimed two. The longest match in Olympic history took place that year. In the Greco-Roman middleweight class, Estonian Martin Klein and Finn Alfred "Alpo" Asikáinen battled it out for 11 hours and 40 minutes, until Klein finally pinned Asikáinen. Claes Johanson of Sweden, however, won the gold, by default, because Klein was too exhausted to compete in the final.

At the 1920 Games, Sweden's Carl Westergren earned the first of his three gold medals—a feat only two other wrestlers, Ivar Johansson, also from Sweden, and Soviet Aleksandr Medved, have equalled. Westergren earned his 1920 gold in the Greco-Roman middleweight division, but went on to earn the other two titles in different divisions, in 1924 and 1932.

The 1924 Paris Games witnessed a number of repeat medalists. In the Greco-Roman events, Finn Kaarlo "Kalle" Anttila won his second Olympic gold, this time in the featherweight division (his 1920 gold was in the freestyle lightweight division); in the lightweight division, Finn Oskar Friman, who had won the featherweight title in the previous Games, earned his second gold, and Carl Westergren moved up to gold in the Greco-Roman light heavyweight division. In the freestyle events, Finn Kustaa Pihlajamäki won the first of his three Olympic medals in the bantamweight division; later his brother, Hermanni, won the featherweight gold in the 1932 Games.

In 1928, the US managed a few titles in the freestyle events: Allie Morrison won the featherweight division, while Lloyd Appelton took second place in the welterweight division. In the Greco-Roman events, the US failed to medal, while Germany, Estonia, Hungary, Finland, Sweden, and even Egypt took home gold. Also that year Hungarian Lajos Keresztes turned in a gold medal match in the lightweight division, having taken up wrestling on his doctor's advice as a cure for "prolonged neurosis."

fact: US president Abraham Lincoln was known as a first-class wrestler.

Sweden's Ivar Johansson won a total of three gold medals, two of them at the 1932 Games: having won the freestyle middleweight division, he fasted and sweat it out in a sauna to be able to compete as a welterweight in the Greco-Roman competition. He lost eleven pounds, and gained a second gold medal. His third came in 1936, in the Greco-Roman middleweight division.

The only man to win a gold medal in both freestyle and Greco-Roman was heavyweight Kristjan Palusalu of Estonia in 1936, the year when American Frank Lewis won a gold medal in the welterweight division of the freestyle competition. In London in 1948, Turkey dominated, with a total of six gold medals in the two competitions, while Sweden continued to be a contender in the Greco-Roman events, winning five titles.

When the Turkish entry forms for the 1952 Games arrived late, the best athletes of their team were not allowed to compete, and Russian wrestlers captured most of the medals; Khalil Taha won a bronze medal for Lebanon that year. The Russians repeated their sweep definitively in Melbourne in 1956, where they took six gold, two silver and five bronze medals—even though their team did not include any World or Olympic champions. In fact, the Russians failed to place in the top three in only one event. One gold medal went to Hamit Kaplan of Turkey, in the freestyle heavyweight category; in 1960 he earned a silver medal in that event, and completed the set with a bronze in 1964.

The Turkish team swept seven gold medals at the 1960 Games. Turk Mustafa Dagistanli, who had won the freestyle bantamweight title in Melbourne, added a featherweight gold from Rome to his collection. Probably the most noteworthy performance, though, came from West Germany's Wilfried Dietrich, who took his second silver in freestyle wrestling and a gold in Greco-Roman in the super-heavyweight division; Dietrich was atypical of most wrestlers, who concentrate on one form or the other.

The 1964 Tokyo Games were dominated by the host country, whose sister sport of judo made Japanese athletes competitive in the lighter classes. The Japanese captured the most wrestling medals, earning five golds, three in freestyle and two in Greco-Roman. One of the freestyle medalists, Osamu Watanabe, a featherweight, won his 186th consecutive victory in taking the Olympic gold, and denied his opponents even a single point in any of his six Olympic matches. Also competing in Tokyo was Hungarian Greco-Roman featherweight, who, after a string of three silver medals, finally pinned down the gold in 1964.

fact: One of the referee's jobs is to make sure the wrestlers' fingernails are cut short.

The USSR primarily, and to some extent Turkey, dominated the 1968 Games, although other Eastern bloc countries put in their bids for medals. Hungarian Istvan "Pici" ("Tiny") Kozma successfully defended his heavyweight

Greco-Roman title, only to lose his life two years later in a car accident. Japan contributed three champions, including Shigero Nakata, the freestyle flyweight world champion, who managed an upset defeat of American Dick Sanders.

The USSR became a stronger force yet in the 1972 Games, taking a total of nine titles. Claiming his third gold, Soviet super-heavyweight freestyle wrestler Aleksandr Medved became the first to win wrestling gold medals in three consecutive Games. Also that year, Soviet heavyweight Ivan Yarygin managed to pin all of his opponents, a rare feat. Turkey was no longer a real contender, but the US regained its form, taking three freestyle titles: lightweight Dan Gable, welterweight Wayne Wells and light heavyweight Ben Peterson all won their divisions. Another American, Chris Taylor, earned the distinction of becoming the heaviest competitor ever in any Olympic event, tipping the scales somewhere between 401 and 419 pounds. He also won the freestyle super-heavyweight bronze.

Ben Peterson's brother, middleweight John Peterson, was the only US gold medalist at Montréal, although the US team did advance six of its 10 members to the finals. The Americans wound up with three silver medals, including one to Ben Peterson, and two bronzes. With some exceptions—such as Finland's Pertti Ukkola, Bulgaria's Hassan Issaev, South Korea's Yang Mo Yang, and Japan's Ijichiro Date and Yuki Takada—the Soviets continued to dominate gold-medaling performances in 1976. Mongolia claimed its only medal in the Games with a silver in the freestyle featherweight division captured by Zevegin Oydov.

fact: An influential turn-of-the-century wrestling champion, George Hackenschmidt, wrote several books, including a philosophical treatment of athletics titled *Men and Cosmic Antagonism to Mind and Spirit.*

1980 witnessed the first-ever "Greco" to win a Greco-Roman title at the Games; Greece's Stilianos Migiakis took the gold in the featherweight division. Other medalists included Romania, Hungary, Italy, and Bulgaria, although the Soviets outscored all others in their winnings. Bulgarian Valentin Angelov, who competed as a welterweight in the freestyle competition, won the gold by racking up five victories in a single day.

The 1984 Games were marked by a unique occurrence: two sets of brothers, Ed and Lou Banach and Dave and Mark Schultz—all Americans—won titles at the LA Games. The Greco-Roman competition, in the absence of most Eastern bloc countries, awarded medals far and wide: South Korea, Italy, Japan, West Germany, Yugoslavia, Finland, and Romania all took gold medals. The United States, typically weak in the Greco-Roman competition, took home two golds, thanks to Steven Fraser and Jeffrey Blatnick. Faring even better in the freestyle competition, the US earned seven gold medals, thanks to Robert

Weaver, Randy Lewis, the Schultz brothers, the Banach brothers, and Bruce Baumgartner.

In Seoul in 1988, the US managed two more golds in the freestyle competition—won by John Smith, with his signature single-leg takedown, and Kenneth Monday—although they failed to win a Greco-Roman title. Bruce Baumgartner, the previous Games' super heavyweight winner, placed second to Soviet David Gobedjichvili. Apart from the eight Soviet golds, the medals were again fairly widespread: in freestyle, Japan, South Korea, and Romania took gold medals, while in the Greco-Roman competition, Italy, Norway, Hungary, South Korea, Bulgaria, and Poland all pinned down golds.

Medalists

Wrestling, Freestyle — 48 kg

1988	1. Takashi Kobayashi, Japan
	2. Ivan Tzonov, Bulgaria
	3. Serguei Karamtchakov, Soviet Union
1984	1. Robert Weaver, USA
	2. Takashi Irie, Japan
	3. Gab-Do Son, Republic of Korea
1980	1. Claudio Pollio, Italy
	2. Se Hong Jang, Democratic People's Republic of Korea
	3. Sergei Kornilaev, Soviet Union
1976	1. Hassan Issaev, Bulgaria
	2. Roman Dmitriev, Soviet Union
	3. Akira Kudo, Japan
1972	1. Roman Dmitriev, Soviet Union
	2. Ognian Nikolov, Bulgaria
	3. Ebrahim Javadi, Iran
1906-	
1968	Not held
1904	1. Robert Curry, USA
	2. John Hein, USA
	3. Gustav Thiefenthaler, USA
1896-	
1900	Not held

Wrestling, Freestyle — 52 kg

1988	1. Mitsuru Sato, Japan
	2. Saban Trstena, Yugoslavia
	3. Vladimir Togouzov, Soviet Union
1984	1. Saban Trstena, Yugoslavia
	2. Jong-Kyu Kim, Republic of Korea
	3. Yuji Takada, Japan
1980	1. Anatoli Beloglazov, Soviet Union
	2. Wladyslaw Stecyk, Poland
	3. Nermedin Selimov, Bulgaria
1976	1. Yuji Takada, Japan
	2. Alexandr Ivanov, Soviet Union
	3. Hae Sup Jeon, Republic of Korea
1972	1. Kiyomi Kato, Japan
	2. Arsen Alkhverdiev, Soviet Union
	3. Gwong-Hyong Kim, Democratic People's Republic of Korea
1968	1. Shigeo Nakata, Japan
	2. Richard Sanders, USA

1964	3. Surenjav Sukhbaatar, Mongolia
	1. Yoshikatsu Yoshida, Japan
	2. Chang-sun Chang, Republic of Korea
	3. Ali-Akbar Haydari, Iran
1960	1. Ahmet Bilek, Turkey
	2. Masayuki Matsubara, Japan
	3. Ebrahim Saifpour, Iran
1956	1. Mirian Tsalkalamanidze, Soviet Union
	2. Mohamad-Ali Khojastehpour, Iran
	3. Huseyin Akbas, Turkey
1952	1. Hasan Gemici, Turkey
	2. Yushu Kitano, Japan
	3. Mahmoud Mollaghassemi, Iran
1948	1. Lennart Viitala, Finland
	2. Halit Balamir, Turkey
	3. Thure Johansson, Sweden
1906-	
1936	Not held
1904	1. George Mehnert, USA
	2. Gustave Bauers, USA
	3. William Nelson, USA
1896-	
1900	Not held

Wrestling, Freestyle — 57 kg

1988	1. Sergei Beloglazov, Soviet Union
	2. Askari Mohammadian, Iran
	3. Kyung-Sun Noh, South Korea
1984	1. Hideaki Tomiyama, Japan
	2. Barry Davis, USA
	3. Evi Kon Kim, Republic of Korea
1980	1. Sergei Beloglazov, Soviet Union
	2. Ho Pyong Li, Democratic People's Republic of Korea
	3. Dugarsuren Ouinbold, Mongolia
1976	1. Vladimir Umin, Soviet Union
	2. Hans-Dieter Bruechert, East Germany
	3. Masao Arai, Japan
1972	1. Hideaki Yanagida, Japan
	2. Richard Sanders, USA
	3. Laszlo Klinga, Hungary
1968	1. Yojiro Uetake, Japan
	2. Donald Behm, USA
	3. Abutaleb Talebi, Iran
1964	1. Yojiro Uetake, Japan

593

2. Huseyin Akbas, Turkey
3. Aydyn Ibragimov, Soviet Union
1960 1. Terrence McCann, USA
2. Nedschet Zalev, Bulgaria
3. Tadeusz Trojanowski, Poland
1956 1. Mustafa Dagistanli, Turkey
2. Mohamad Yaghoubi, Iran
3. Mikhail Chachov, Soviet Union
1952 1. Shohachi Ishii, Japan
2. Raschid Mamedbekov, Soviet Union
3. Kha-Shaba Jadav, India
1948 1. Nasuh Akar, Turkey
2. Gerald Leeman, USA
3. Charles Kouyos, France
1936 1. Odon Zombori, Hungary
2. Ross Flood, USA
3. Johannes Herbert, Germany
1932 1. Robert Pearce, USA
2. Odon Zombori, Hungary
3. Aatos Jaskori, Finland
1928 1. Kaarlo Makinen, Finland
2. Edmond Spapen, Belgium
3. James Trifunov, Canada
1924 1. Kustaa Pihlajamaki, Finland
2. Kaarlo Makinen, Finland
3. Bryant Hines, USA
**1912-
1920** **Not held**
1908 1. George Mehnert, USA
2. William Press, Great Britain
3. Aubert Cote, Canada
1906 **Not held**
1904 1. Isaac Niflot, USA
2. August Wester, USA
3. Z. B. Strebler, USA
**1896-
1900** **Not held**

Wrestling, Freestyle — 62 kg

1988 1. John Smith, USA
2. Stepan Sarkissian, Soviet Union
3. Simeon Chterev, Bulgaria
1984 1. Randy Lewis, USA
2. Kosei Akaishi, Japan
3. Jung-Keun Lee, Republic of Korea
1980 1. Magomedgasan Abushev, Soviet Union
2. Mikho Dukov, Bulgaria
3. Georges Hajiioannidis, Greece
1976 1. Yang Mo Yang, Republic of Korea
2. Zevegin Oydov, Mongolia
3. Gene Davis, USA
1972 1. Sagalav Abdulbekov, Soviet Union
2. Vehbi Akdag, Turkey
3. Ivan Krastev, Bulgaria
1968 1. Masaaki Kaneko, Japan
2. Enyu Todorov, Bulgaria
3. Shamseddin Seyed-Abassy, Iran
1964 1. Osamu Watanabe, Japan
2. Stantcho Ivanov, Bulgaria
3. Nodar Khokhashvili, Soviet Union
1960 1. Mustafa Dagistanli, Turkey
2. Stantcho Ivanov, Bulgaria
3. Vladimir Rubashvili, Soviet Union
1956 1. Shozo Sasahara, Japan
2. Joseph Mewis, Belgium
3. Erkki Penttila, Finland
1952 1. Bayram Sit, Turkey
2. Nasser Guivehchi, Iran
3. Josiah Henson, USA
1948 1. Gazanfer Bilge, Turkey

2. Ivar Sjolin, Sweden
3. Adolf Muller, Switzerland
1936 1. Kustaa Pihlajamaki, Finland
2. Francis Millard, USA
3. Gosta Jonsson, Sweden
1932 1. Hermanni Pihlajamaki, Finland
2. Edgar Nemir, USA
3. Einar Karlsson, Sweden
1928 1. Allie Morrison, USA
2. Kustaa Pihlajamaki, Finland
3. Hans Minder, Switzerland
1924 1. Robin Reed, USA
2. Chester Newton, USA
3. Katsutoshi Naito, Japan
1920 1. Charles E. Ackerly, USA
2. Samuel Gerson, USA
3. P. W. Bernard, Great Britain
1912 **Not held**
1908 1. George Dole, USA
2. James Slim, Great Britain
3. William McKie, Great Britain
1906 **Not held**
1904 1. Benjamin Bradshaw, USA
2. Theodore McLear, USA
3. Charles Clapper, USA
**1896-
1900** **Not held**

Wrestling, Freestyle — 68 kg

1988 1. Arsen Fadzaev, Soviet Union
2. Jang-Soon Park South Korea
3. Nate Carr, USA
1984 1. In-Tak Youh, Republic of Korea
2. Andrew Rein, USA
3. Jukka Rauhala, Finland
1980 1. Saipulla Absaidov, Soviet Union
2. Ivan Yankov, Bulgaria
3. Saban Sejdi, Yugoslavia
1976 1. Pavel Pinegin, Soviet Union
2. Lloyd Keaser, USA
3. Yasaburo Sugawara, Japan
1972 1. Dan Gable, USA
2. Kikuo Wada, Japan
3. Ruslan Ashuraliyev, Soviet Union
1968 1. Abdollah Movahed Ardabili, Iran
2. Enyu Waltschev, Bulgaria
3. Sereeter Danzandarjaa, Mongolia
1964 1. Enyu Waltschev, Bulgaria
2. Klaus-Jurgen Rost, West Germany
3. Iwao Horiuchi, Japan
1960 1. Shelby Wilson, USA
2. Vladimir Sinyavsky, Soviet Union
3. Enyu Dimov, Bulgaria
1956 1. Emamali Habibi, Iran
2. Shigeru Kasahara, Japan
3. Alimbeg Bestayev, Soviet Union
1952 1. Olle Anderberg, Sweden
2. J. Thomas Evans, USA
3. Djahanbakte Tovfighe, Iran
1948 1. Celal Atik, Turkey
2. Gosta Frandfors-Jonsson, Sweden
3. Hermann Baumann, Switzerland
1936 1. Karoly Karpati, Hungary
2. Wolfgang Ehrl, Germany
3. Hermanni Pihlajamaki, Finland
1932 1. Charles Pacome, France
2. Karoly Karpati, Hungary
3. Gustaf Klaren, Sweden
1928 1. Osvald Kapp, Estonia
2. Charles Pacome, France

3. Eino Leino, Finland
1924 1. Russell Vis, USA
2. Volmari Vikstrom, Finland
3. Arvo Haavisto, Finland
1920 1. Kalle Anttila, Finland
2. Gottfrid Svensson, Sweden
3. Peter Wright, Great Britain
1912 Not held
1908 1. George de Relwyskow, Great Britain
2. William Wood, Great Britain
3. Albert Gingell, Great Britain
1906 Not held
1904 1. Otto Roehm, USA
2. R. Tesing, USA
3. Albert Zirkel, USA
1896-
1900 Not held

Wrestling, Freestyle — 74 kg

1988 1. Kenneth Monday, USA
2. Adlan Varaev, Soviet Union
3. Rakhmad Sofiadi, Bulgaria
1984 1. David Schultz, USA
2. Martin Knosp, West Germany
3. Saban Sejdi, Yugoslavia
1980 1. Valentin Raitchev, Bulgaria
2. Jamtsying Davaajav, Mongolia
3. Dan Karabin, Czechoslovakia
1976 1. Ijichiro Date, Japan
2. Mansour Barzegar, Iran
3. Stanley Dziedzic, USA
1972 1. Wayne Wells, USA
2. Jan Karlsson, Sweden
3. Adolf Seger, West Germany
1968 1. Mahmut Atalay, Turkey
2. Daniel Robin, France
3. Dagvasuren Purev, Mongolia
1964 1. Ismail Ogan, Turkey
2. Guliko Sagaradze, Soviet Union
3. Mohamad-Ali Sanatkaran, Iran
1960 1. Douglas Blubaugh, USA
2. Ismail Ogan, Turkey
3. Muhammed Bashir, Pakistan
1956 1. Mitsuo Ikeda, Japan
2. Ibrahim Zengin, Turkey
3. Vakhtang Balavadze, Soviet Union
1952 1. William Smith, USA
2. Per Berlin, Sweden
3. Abdullah Modjtabavi, Iran
1948 1. Yasar Dogu, Turkey
2. Richard Garrard, Australia
3. Leland Merrill, USA
1936 1. Frank Lewis, USA
2. Ture Andersson, Sweden
3. Joseph Schleimer, Canada
1932 1. Jack Van Bebber, USA
2. Daniel MacDonald, Canada
3. Eino Leino, Finland
1928 1. Arvo Haavisto, Finland
2. Lloyd Appleton, USA
3. Maurice Letchford, Canada
1924 1. Hermann Gehri, Switzerland
2. Eino Leino, Finland
3. Otto Muller, Switzerland
1906-
1920 Not held
1904 1. Charles Erickson, USA
2. William Beckman, USA
3. Jerry Winholtz, USA

1896-
1900 Not held

Wrestling, Freestyle — 82 kg

1988 1. Myung-Woo Han, South Korea
2. Necmi Gencalp, Turkey
3. Josef Lohyna, Czechoslovakia
1984 1. Mark Schultz, USA
2. Hideyuki Nagashima, Japan
3. Chris Rinke, Canada
1980 1. Ismail Abilov, Bulgaria
2. Magomedhan Aratsilov, Soviet Union
3. Istvan Kovacs, Hungary
1976 1. John Peterson, USA
2. Viktor Novoyilov, Soviet Union
3. Adolf Seger, West Germany
1972 1. Levan Tediashvili, Soviet Union
2. John Peterson, USA
3. Vasile Iorga, Romania
1968 1. Boris Gurevitch, Soviet Union
2. Munkbat Jigjid, Mongolia
3. Prodan Gardschev, Bulgaria
1964 1. Prodan Gardschev, Bulgaria
2. Hasan Gungor, Turkey
3. Daniel Brand, USA
1960 1. Hasan Gungor, Turkey
2. Georgi Skhirtladze, Soviet Union
3. Hans Antonsson, Sweden
1956 1. Nikola Stantchev, Bulgaria
2. Daniel Hodge, USA
3. Georgi Skhirtladze, Soviet Union
1952 1. David Tsimakuridze, Soviet Union
2. Gholam-Reza Takhti, Iran
3. Gyorgy Gurics, Hungary
1948 1. Glen Brand, USA
2. Adil Candemir, Turkey
3. Erik Linden, Sweden
1936 1. Emile Poilve, France
2. Richard Voliva, USA
3. Ahmet Kirecci, Turkey
1932 1. Ivar Johansson, Sweden
2. Kyosti Luukko, Finland
3. Jozsef Tunyogi, Hungary
1928 1. Ernst Kyburz, Switzerland
2. Donald P. Stockton, Canada
3. Samuel Rabin, Great Britain
1924 1. Firtz Hagmann, Switzerland
2. Pierre Ollivier, Belgium
3. Vilho Pekkala, Finland
1920 1. Eino Leino, Finland
2. Vaino Penttala, Finland
3. Charles Johnson, USA
1912 Not held
1908 1. Stanley Bacon, Great Britain
2. George de Relwyskow, Great Britain
3. Frederick Beck, Great Britain
1896-
1906 Not held

Wrestling, Freestyle — 90 kg

1988 1. Makharbek Khadartsev, Soviet Union
2. Akira Ota, Japan
3. Tae-Woo Kim, South Korea
1984 1. Ed Banach, USA
2. Akira Ohta, Japan
3. Noel Loban, Great Britain
1980 1. Sanasar Oganesyan, Soviet Union
2. Uwe Neupert, East Germany

Wrestling

3. Aleksander Cichon, Poland

1976
1. Levan Tediashvili, Soviet Union
2. Ben Peterson, USA
3. Stelica Morcov, Romania

1972
1. Ben Peterson, USA
2. Gennady Strakhov, Soviet Union
3. Karoly Bajko, Hungary

1968
1. Ahmet Ayik, Turkey
2. Schota Lomidze, Soviet Union
3. Jozsef Csatari, Hungary

1964
1. Aleksandr Medved, Soviet Union
2. Ahmet Ayik, Turkey
3. Said Mustafov, Bulgaria

1960
1. Ismet Atli, Turkey
2. Gholam-Reza Takhti, Iran
3. Anatoli Albul, Soviet Union

1956
1. Gholam-Reza Takhti, Iran
2. Boris Kulayev, Soviet Union
3. Peter Blair, USA

1952
1. Wiking Palm, Sweden
2. Henry Wittenberg, USA
3. Adil Atan, Turkey

1948
1. Henry Wittenberg, USA
2. Fritz Stockli, Switzerland
3. Bengt Fahlkvist, Sweden

1936
1. Knut Fridell, Sweden
2. August Neo, Estonia
3. Erich Siebert, Germany

1932
1. Peter Mehringer, USA
2. Thure Sjostedt, Sweden
3. Eddie Scarf, Australia

1928
1. Thure Sjostedt, Sweden
2. Arnold Bogli, Switzerland
3. Henri Lefebre, France

1924
1. John Spellman, USA
2. Rudolf Svensson, Sweden
3. Charles Courant, Switzerland

1920
1. Anders Larsson, Sweden
2. Charles Courant, Switzerland
3. Walter Maurer, USA

1896-
1912
Not held

Wrestling, Freestyle — 100 kg

1988
1. Vasile Puscasu, Romania
2. Leri Khabelov, Soviet Union
3. Bill Scherr, USA

1984
1. Lou Banach, USA
2. Joseph Atiyeh, Syria
3. Vasile Puscasu, Romania

1980
1. Ilya Mate, Soviet Union
2. Slavcho Chervenkov, Bulgaria
3. Julius Strnisko, Czechoslovakia

1976
1. Ivan Yarygin, Soviet Union
2. Russell Hellickson, USA
3. Dimo Kostov, Bulgaria

1972
1. Ivan Yarygin, Soviet Union
2. Khorloo Baianmunkh, Mongolia
3. Jozsef Csatari, Hungary

1968
1. Aleksandr Medved, Soviet Union
2. Osman Duraliev, Bulgaria
3. Wilfried Dietrich, West Germany

1964
1. Aleksandr Ivanitsky, Soviet Union
2. Lyutvi Ahmedov, Bulgaria
3. Hamit Kaplan, Turkey

1960
1. Wilfried Dietrich, West Germany
2. Hamit Kaplan, Turkey
3. Savkus Dzarassov, Soviet Union

1956
1. Hamit Kaplan, Turkey
2. Hussein Mechmedov, Bulgaria

3. Taisto Kangasniemi, Finland

1952
1. Arsen Mekokischvili, Soviet Union
2. Bertil Antonsson, Sweden
3. Kenneth Richmond, Great Britain

1948
1. Gyula Bobis, Hungary
2. Bertil Antonsson, Sweden
3. Joseph Armstrong, Australia

1936
1. Kristjan Palusalu, Estonia
2. Josef Klapuch, Czechoslovakia
3. Hjalmar Nystrom, Finland

1932
1. Johan Richtoff, Sweden
2. John Riley, USA
3. Nikolaus Hirschl, Austria

1928
1. Johan Richtoff, Sweden
2. Aukusti Sihvola, Finland
3. Edmond Dame, France

1924
1. Harry Steele, USA
2. Henri Wenli, Switzerland
3. Andrew McDonald, Great Britain

1920
1. Robert Roth, Switzerland
2. Nathan Pendleton, USA
3. Frederick Meyer, USA
3. Ernst Nilsson, Sweden

1912
Not held

1908
1. George C. O'Kelly, Great
Britain/Ireland
2. Jacob Gundersen, Norway
3. Edward Barrett, Great Britain/Ireland

1906
Not held

1904
1. B. Hansen, USA
2. Frank Kungler, USA
3. F. Charles Warmbold, USA

1896-
1900
Not held

Wrestling, Freestyle — 130 kg

1988
1. David Gobedjichvili, Soviet Union
2. Bruce Baumgartner, USA
3. Andreas Schroeder, East Germany

1984
1. Bruce Baumgartner, USA
2. Bob Moll, Canada
3. Ayhan Taskin, Turkey

1980
1. Soslan Andiev, Soviet Union
2. Jozsef Balla, Hungary
3. Adam Sandurski, Poland

1976
1. Soslan Andiev, Soviet Union
2. Jozsef Balla, Hungary
3. Ladislau Simon, Romania

1972
1. Aleksandr Medved, Soviet Union
2. Osman Duraliev, Bulgaria
3. Chris Taylor, USA

1896-
1968
Not held

Wrestling, Greco-Roman — 48 kg

1988
1. Vincenzo Maenza, Italy
2. Andrzej Glab, Poland
3. Bratan Tzenov, Bulgaria

1984
1. Vincenzo Maenza, Italy
2. Markus Scherer, West Germany
3. Ikuzo Saito, Japan

1980
1. Zaksylik Ushkempirov, Soviet Union
2. Constantin Alexandru, Romania
3. Ferenc Seres, Hungary

1976
1. Aleksei Shumakov, Soviet Union
2. Gheorghe Berceanu, Romania
3. Stefan Angelov, Bulgaria

1972	1. Gheorghe Berceanu, Romania
	2. Rahim Aliabadi, Iran
	3. Stefan Angelov, Bulgaria
1896-	
1968	**Not held**

Wrestling, Greco-Roman — 52 kg

1988	1. Jon Ronningen, Norway
	2. Atsuji Miyahara, Japan
	3. Jae-Suk Lee, South Korea
1984	1. Atsuji Miyahara, Japan
	2. Daniel Aceves, Mexico
	3. Dae-Du Bang, Republic of Korea
1980	1. Vakhtang Blagidze, Soviet Union
	2. Lajos Racz, Hungary
	3. Mladen Mladenov, Bulgaria
1976	1. Vitali Konstantinov, Soviet Union
	2. Nicu Ginga, Romania
	3. Koichiro Hirayama, Japan
1972	1. Petar Kirov, Bulgaria
	2. Koichiro Hirayama, Japan
	3. Giuseppe Bognanni, Italy
1968	1. Petar Kirov, Bulgaria
	2. Vladimir Bakulin, Soviet Union
	3. Miroslav Zeman, Czechoslovakia
1964	1. Tsutomu Hanahara, Japan
	2. Angel Keresov, Bulgaria
	3. Dumitru Pirvulescu, Romania
1960	1. Dumitru Pirvulescu, Romania
	2. Osman Sayed, United Arab Republic
	3. Mohamed Paziraye, Iran
1956	1. Nikolai Solovyov, Soviet Union
	2. Ignazio Fabra, Italy
	3. Dursun Ali Egribas, Turkey
1952	1. Boris Gurevitch, Soviet Union
	2. Ignazio Fabra, Italy
	3. Leo Honkala, Finland
1948	1. Pietro Lombardi, Italy
	2. Kenan Olcay, Turkey
	3. Reino Kangasmaki, Finland
1896-	
1936	**Not held**

Wrestling, Greco-Roman — 57 kg

1988	1. Andras Sike, Hungary
	2. Stoyan Balov, Bulgaria
	3. Charalambos Holidis, Greece
1984	1. Pasquale Passarelli, West Germany
	2. Masaki Eto, Japan
	3. Charalambos Holidis, Greece
1980	1. Shamil Serikov, Soviet Union
	2. Jozef Lipien, Poland
	3. Benni Ljungbeck, Poland
1976	1. Pertti Ukkola, Finland
	2. Ivan Frgic, Yugoslavia
	3. Farhat Mustafin, Soviet Union
1972	1. Rustem Kazakov, Soviet Union
	2. Hans-Jurgen Veil, West Germany
	3. Risto Bjorlin, Finland
1968	1. Janos Varga, Hungary
	2. Ion Baciu, Romania
	3. Ivan Kochergin, Soviet Union
1964	1. Masamitsu Ichiguchi, Japan
	2. Vladlen Trostyansky, Soviet Union
	3. Ion Cernea, Romania

1960	1. Oleg Karavayev, Soviet Union
	2. Ion Cernea, Romania
	3. Petrow Dinko, Bulgaria
1956	1. Konstantin Vyrupayev, Soviet Union
	2. Edvin Vesterby, Sweden
	3. Francise Horvat, Romania
1952	1. Imre Hodos, Hungary
	2. Zakaria Chihab, Lebanon
	3. Artem Teryan, Soviet Union
1948	1. Kurt Pettersen, Sweden
	2. Ali Mahmoud Hassan, Egypt
	3. Halil Kaya, Turkey
1936	1. Marton Lorincz, Hungary
	2. Egon Svensson, Sweden
	3. Jakob Brendel, Germany
1932	1. Jakob Brendel, Germany
	2. Marcello Nizzola, Italy
	3. Louis Francois, France
1928	1. Kurt Leucht, Germany
	2. Jindrich Maudr, Czechoslovakia
	3. Giovanni Gozzi, Italy
1924	1. Eduard Putsep, Estonia
	2. Anselm Ahlfors, Finland
	3. Vaino Ikonen, Finland
1896-	
1920	**Not held**

Wrestling, Greco-Roman — 62 kg

1988	1. Kamander Madjidov, Soviet Union
	2. Jivko Vanguelov, Bulgaria
	3. Dae-Hyun An, South Korea
1984	1. Weon-Kee Kim, Republic of Korea
	2. Kentolle Johansson, Sweden
	3. Hugo Dietsche, Switzerland
1980	1. Stilianos Migiakis, Greece
	2. Istvan Toth, Hungary
	3. Boris Kramorenko, Soviet Union
1976	1. Kazimierz Lipien, Poland
	2. Nelson Davidian, Soviet Union
	3. Laszlo Reczi, Hungary
1972	1. Georgi Markow, Bulgaria
	2. Heinz-Helmut Wehling, East Germany
	3. Kazimierz Lipien, Poland
1968	1. Roman Rurua, Soviet Union
	2. Hideo Fujimoto, Japan
	3. Simeon Popescu, Romania
1964	1. Imre Polyak, Hungary
	2. Roman Rurua, Soviet Union
	3. Branislav Martinovic, Yugoslavia
1960	1. Muzahir Sille, Turkey
	2. Imre Polyak, Hungary
	3. Konstantin Vyrupayev, Soviet Union
1956	1. Rauno Makinen, Finland
	2. Imre Polyak, Hungary
	3. Roman Dzneladze, Soviet Union
1952	1. Jakov Punkin, Soviet Union
	2. Imre Polyak, Hungary
	3. Abdel Rashed, Egypt
1948	1. Mehmet Oktav, Turkey
	2. Olle Anderberg, Sweden
	3. Ferenc Toth, Hungary
1936	1. Yasar Erkan, Turkey
	2. Aarne Reini, Finland
	3. Einar Karlsson, Sweden
1932	1. Giovanni Gozzi, Italy
	2. Wolfgang Ehrl, Germany
	3. Lauri Koskela, Finland
1928	1. Voldemar Vali, Estonia

2. Erik Malmberg, Sweden
3. Gerolomo Quaglia, Italy
1924 1. Kalle Anttila, Finland
2. Aleksanteri Toivola, Finland
3. Erik Malmberg, Sweden
1920 1. Oskari Friman, Finland
2. Heikki Kahkonen, Finland
3. Fritiof Svensson, Sweden
1912 1. Kaarlo Koskelo, Finland
2. Georg Gerstacker, Germany
3. Otto Lasanen, Finland
1896-
1908 **Not held**

Wrestling, Greco-Roman — 68 kg

1988 1. Levon Djoulfalakian, Soviet Union
2. Sung-Moon Kim, South Korea
3. Tapio Sipila, Finland
1984 1. Vlado Lisjak, Yugoslavia
2. Tapio Sipila, Finland
3. James Martinez, USA
1980 1. Stefan Rusu, Romania
2. Andrzej Supron, Poland
3. Lars-Erik Skiold, Sweden
1976 1. Suren Nalbandyan, Soviet Union
2. Stefan Rusu, Romania
3. Heinz-Helmut Wehling, East Germany
1972 1. Schamil Khisamutdinov, Soviet Union
2. Stojan Apostolov, Bulgaria
3. Gian-Matteo Ranzi, Italy
1968 1. Munji Mumemura, Japan
2. Stevan Horvat, Yugoslavia
3. Petros Galaktopoulos, Greece
1964 1. Kazim Ayvaz, Turkey
2. Valeriu Bularca, Romania
3. David Gvantseladze, Soviet Union
1960 1. Avtandil Koridze, Soviet Union
2. Branislav Martinovic, Yugoslavia
3. Gustav Freij, Sweden
1956 1. Kyosti Lehtonen, Finland
2. Riza Dogan, Turkey
3. Gyula Toth, Hungary
1952 1. Schasam Safin, Soviet Union
2. Gustav Freij, Sweden
3. Mikulas Athanasov, Czechoslovakia
1948 1. Gustav Freij, Sweden
2. Aage Eriksen, Norway
3. Karoly Ferencz, Hungary
1936 1. Lauri Koskela, Finland
2. Josef Herda, Czechoslovakia
3. Voldemar Vali, Estonia
1932 1. Erik Malmberg, Sweden
2. Abraham Kurland, Denmark
3. Eduard Sperling, Germany
1928 1. Lajos Keresztes, Hungary
2. Eduard Sperling, Germany
3. Edvard Westerlund, Finland
1924 1. Oskari Friman, Finland
2. Lajos Keresztes, Hungary
3. Kalle Westerlund, Finland
1920 1. Eemil Vare, Finland
2. Taavi Tamminen, Finland
3. Frithjof Andersen, Norway
1912 1. Eemil Vare, Finland
2. Gustaf Malmstrom, Sweden
3. Edvin Matiason, Sweden
1908 1. Enrico Porro, Italy
2. Nikolai Orlov, Russia

3. Arvid Linden, Finland
1906 1. Rudolf Watzl, Austria
2. Karl Karlsen, Denmark
3. Ferenc Holuban, Hungary
1896-
1904 **Not held**

Wrestling, Greco-Roman — 74 kg

1988 1. Young-Nam Kim, South Korea
2. Daoulet Tourlykhanov, Soviet Union
3. Josef Tracz, Poland
1984 1. Jouko Salomaki, Finland
2. Roger Tallroth, Sweden
3. Stefan Rusu, Romania
1980 1. Ferenc Kocsis, Hungary
2. Anatoli Bykov, Soviet Union
3. Mikko Huhtala, Finland
1976 1. Anatoli Bykov, Soviet Union
2. Vitezslav Macha, Czechoslovakia
3. Karl-Heinz Helbing, West Germany
1972 1. Vitezslav Macha, Czechoslovakia
2. Petros Galaktopoulos, Greece
3. Jan Karlsson, Sweden
1968 1. Rudolf Vesper, East Germany
2. Daniel Robin, France
3. Karoly Bajko, Hungary
1964 1. Anatoli Kolesov, Soviet Union
2. Kiril Petkov Todorov, Bulgaria
3. Bertil Nystrom, Sweden
1960 1. Mithat Bayrak, Turkey
2. Gunter Maritschnigg, West Germany
3. Rene Schiermeyer, France
1956 1. Mithat Bayrak, Turkey
2. Vladimir Maneyev, Soviet Union
3. Per Berlin, Sweden
1952 1. Miklos Szilvasi, Hungary
2. Gosta Andersson, Sweden
3. Khalil Taha, Lebanon
1948 1. Gosta Andersson, Sweden
2. Miklos Szilvasi, Hungary
3. Henrik Hansen, Denmark
1936 1. Rudolf Svedberg, Sweden
2. Fritz Schafer, Germany
3. Eino Virtanen, Finland
1932 1. Ivar Johansson, Sweden
2. Vaino Kajander, Finland
3. Ercole Gallegati, Italy
1896-
1928 **Not held**

Wrestling, Greco-Roman — 82 kg

1988 1. Mikhail Mamiachvili, Soviet Union
2. Tibor Komaromi, Hungary
3. Sang-Kyu Kim, South Korea
1984 1. Ion Draica, Romania
2. Dimitrios Thanopoulos, Greece
3. Soren Claeson, Sweden
1980 1. Gennady Korban, Soviet Union
2. Jan Dolgowicz, Poland
3. Pavel Pavlov, Bulgaria
1976 1. Momir Petkovic, Yugoslavia
2. Vladimir Cheboksarov, Soviet Union
3. Ivan Kolev, Bulgaria
1972 1. Csaba Hegedus, Hungary
2. Anatoli Nazarenko, Soviet Union

	3. Milan Nenadic, Yugoslavia
1968	1. Lothar Metz, East Germany
	2. Valentin Olenik, Soviet Union
	3. Branislav Simic, Yugoslavia
1964	1. Branislav Simic, Yugoslavia
	2. Jiri Kormanik, Czechoslovakia
	3. Lothar Metz, East Germany
1960	1. Dimiter Dobrev, Bulgaria
	2. Lothar Metz, East Germany
	3. Ion Taranu, Romania
1956	1. Givi Kartoziya, Soviet Union
	2. Dimiter Dobrev, Bulgaria
	3. Rune Jansson, Sweden
1952	1. Axel Gronberg, Sweden
	2. Kalervo Rauhala, Finland
	3. Nikolai Byelov, Soviet Union
1948	1. Axel Gronberg, Sweden
	2. Muhlis Tayfur, Turkey
	3. Ercole Gallegati, Italy
1936	1. Ivar Johansson, Sweden
	2. Ludwig Schweickert, Germany
	3. Jozsef Palotas, Hungary
1932	1. Vaino Kokkinen, Finland
	2. Jean Foldeak, Germany
	3. Axel Cadier, Sweden
1928	1. Vaino Kokkinen, Finland
	2. Laszlo Papp, Hungary
	3. Albert Kusnets, Estonia
1924	1. Edvard Westerlund, Finland
	2. Artur Lindfors, Finland
	3. Roman Steinberg, Estonia
1920	1. Carl Westergren, Sweden
	2. Artur Lindfors, Finland
	3. Matti Perttila, Finland
1912	1. Claes Johanson, Sweden
	2. Martin Klein, Russia
	3. Alfred Asikainen, Finland
1908	1. Frithiof Martensson, Sweden
	2. Mauritz Andersson, Sweden
	3. Anders Andersen, Denmark
1906	1. Verner Weckman, Finland
	2. Rudolf Lindmayer, Austria
	3. Robert Behrens, Denmark
1896-	
1904	**Not held**

Wrestling, Greco-Roman — 90 kg

1988	1. Atanas Komchev, Bulgaria
	2. Harri Koskela, Finland
	3. Vladimir Popov, Soviet Union
1984	1. Steven Fraser, USA
	2. Ilie Matei, Romania
	3. Frank Andersson, Sweden
1980	1. Norbert Noevenyi, Hungary
	2. Igor Kanygin, Soviet Union
	3. Petre Dicu, Romania
1976	1. Valeri Rezantsev, Soviet Union
	2. Stoyan Nikolov, Bulgaria
	3. Czeslaw Kwiecinski, Poland
1972	1. Valeri Rezantsev, Soviet Union
	2. Josip Corak, Yugoslavia
	3. Czeslaw Kwiecinski, Poland
1968	1. Bojan Radev, Bulgaria
	2. Nikolai Yakovenko, Soviet Union
	3. Nicolae Martinescu, Romania
1964	1. Bojan Radev, Bulgaria
	2. Per Svensson, Sweden
	3. Heinz Kiehl, West Germany

1960	1. Tevfik Kis, Turkey
	2. Krali Bimbalov, Bulgaria
	3. Givi Kartoziya, Soviet Union
1956	1. Valentin Nikolayev, Soviet Union
	2. Petko Sirakov, Bulgaria
	3. Karl-Erik Nilsson, Sweden
1952	1. Kaelpo Grondahl, Finland
	2. Chalva Chikhladze, Soviet Union
	3. Karl-Erik Nilsson, Sweden
1948	1. Karl-Erik Nilsson, Sweden
	2. Kaelpo Grondahl, Finland
	3. Ibrahim Orabi, Egypt
1936	1. Axel Cadier, Sweden
	2. Edwins Bietags, Latvia
	3. August Neo, Estonia
1932	1. Rudolf Svensson, Sweden
	2. Onni Pellinen, Finland
	3. Mario Gruppioni, Italy
1928	1. Ibrahim Moustafa, Egypt
	2. Adolf Rieger, Germany
	3. Onni Pellinen, Finland
1924	1. Carl Westergren, Sweden
	2. Rudolf Svensson, Sweden
	3. Onni Pellinen, Finland
1920	1. Claes Johanson, Sweden
	2. Edil Rosenqvist, Finland
	3. Johannes Eriksen, Denmark
1912	2. Anders Ahlgren, Sweden
	2. Ivar Bohling, Finland
	3. Bela Varga, Hungary
1908	1. Verner Weckman, Finland
	2. Yrjo Saarela, Finland
	3. Carl Jensen, Denmark
1896-	
1906	**Not held**

Wrestling, Greco-Roman — 100 kg

1988	1. Andrzej Wronski, Poland
	2. Gerhard Himmel, West Germany
	3. Dennis Koslowski, USA
1984	1. Vasile Andrei, Romania
	2. Greg Gibson, USA
	3. Jozef Tertelje, Yugoslavia
1980	1. Georgi Raikov, Bulgaria
	2. Roman Bierla, Poland
	3. Vasile Andrei, Romania
1976	1. Nikolai Bolboshin, Soviet Union
	2. Kamen Goranov, Bulgaria
	3. Andrzej Skrzydlewski, Poland
1972	1. Nicolae Martinescu, Romania
	2. Nikolai Iakovenko, Soviet Union
	3. Ferenc Kiss, Hungary
1968	1. Istvan Kozma, Hungary
	2. Anatoli Roshin, Soviet Union
	3. Petr Kment, Czechoslovakia
1964	1. Istvan Kozma, Hungary
	2. Anatoli Roshin, Soviet Union
	3. Wilfried Dietrich, West Germany
1960	1. Ivan Bogdan, Soviet Union
	2. Wilfried Dietrich, West Germany
	3. Bohumil Kubat, Czechoslovakia
1956	1. Anatoli Parfenov, Soviet Union
	2. Wilfried Dietrich, West Germany
	3. Adelmo Bulgarelli, Italy
1952	1. Johannes Kotkas, Soviet Union
	2. Josef Ruzicka, Czechoslovakia
	3. Tauno Kovanen, Finland
1948	1. Ahmet Kirecci, Turkey

599

2. Tor Nilsson, Sweden
3. Guido Fantoni, Italy
1936　1. Kristjan Palusalu, Estonia
2. John Nyman, Sweden
3. Kurt Hornfischer, Germany
1932　1. Carl Westergren, Sweden
2. Josef Urban, Czechoslovakia
3. Nikolaus Hirschl, Austria
1928　1. Rudolf Svensson, Sweden
2. Hjalmar Nystrom, Finland
3. Georg Gehring, Germany
1924　1. Henri Deglane, France
2. Edil Rosenqvist, Finland
3. Rajmund Bado, Hungary
1920　1. Adolf Lindfors, Finland
2. Poul Hansen, Denmark
3. Marti Nieminen, Finland
1912　1. Yrjo Saarela, Finland
2. John Olin, Finland
3. Soren M. Jensen, Denmark
1908　1. Richard Weisz, Hungary
2. Aleksandr Petrov, Russia
3. Soren M. Jensen, Denmark
1906　1. Soren M. Jensen, Denmark
2. Henri Baur, Austria
3. Marcel Dubois, Belgium

1900-
1904　**Not held**
1896　1. Carl Schuhmann, Germany
2. Georgios Tsitas, Greece
3. Stephanos Christopoulos, Greece

Wrestling, Greco-Roman — 130 kg

1988　1. Alexandre Kareline, Soviet Union
2. Ranguel Guerovski, Bulgaria
3. Tomas Johansson, Sweden
1984　1. Jeffrey Blatnick, USA
2. Refik Memisevic, Yugoslavia
3. Victor Dolipshi, Romania
1980　1. Aleksandr Kolchinsky, Soviet Union
2. Aleksandr Tomov, Bulgaria
3. Hassan Bchara, Lebanon
1976　1. Aleksandr Kolchinsky, Soviet Union
2. Aleksandr Tomov, Bulgaria
3. Roman Codreanu, Romania
1972　1. Anatoli Roshin, Soviet Union
2. Aleksandr Tomov, Bulgaria
3. Victor Dolipshi, Romania
1896-
1968　**Not held**

600

YACHTING

WARM-UP

The sailing of boats has been a preferred mode of water travel ever since people got tired of rowing, sculling, paddling, or punting their boats wherever they needed to go. The Dutch—maybe the first to tire—were particularly adept at the art of sailing.

By the 17th century they had colonized parts of the Americas, southern Africa, and the East Indies. Plenty of goods needed shipping to and from the colonies, and these overseas cargoes were vulnerable to piracy. To protect their cargo ships, the Dutch developed fast, agile sailing vessels called *jaghtschips*; the *jaght* part of the name means "to chase, hunt, or pursue"; the *schip* part just has an extra "c" to infuriate Anglophones. These *jaghtschips* proved to be excellent vehicles in which to run down pirates and also, as it turned out, very fun to sail. They were fast and easy to handle, and soon the aristocrats (who cornered the market on fun in those days) were sailing *jaghtschips* for sport.

In 1660 England's King Charles I lost his government to Oliver Cromwell and was beheaded in the process. His son fled to Holland, head intact, and it was there that he was introduced to the *jaghtschip*, probably because he needed a little fun in his life at that time. When he returned home to England as the reigning monarch, Charles II, he brought with him one of these boats, graciously given to him by the East India Company (schmoozing knows no era). The new sport caught on around the British Empire, and the English adapted the craft's name as yacht (which isn't a great improvement, frankly).

The first organized sailing club was the Water Club of the Harbour of Cork, established in Ireland in 1720. Yachting spread to the New World where, in 1811, the first American club, the Knickerbocker Boat Club, was formed on Long Island.

In 1851 the first international yachting event took place with the running of the Hundred Guineas Cup race, a 60-mile circuit around the Isle of Wight. The brand-new New York Yacht Club sent the 110-ton schooner *America* to sail across the ocean and represent them in the race. The Americans not only competed, they triumphed. They duly brought home their trophy, renamed it the *America*'s Cup and proceeded to defend it for the next 132 years. In 1983 *Australia II* defeated the American yacht *Liberty* and sailed away with the cup, breaking the longest win streak in sports history.

601

Yachting has been an Olympic sport since the 1896 Games in Athens, although in that Olympiad the yacht racing events were all canceled due to foul weather. At the start of the century the classes of boats sailed at Olympic Games and other international competitions were meter classes. In this system, officials rated boats with an elaborate set of rules and formulae based on length, breadth, and sail area, in order to place them into categories bearing names such as 8-meter, 10-meter, etc.

What's important to realize is that an 8-meter boat, for instance, is *not* eight meters long, wide, tall, or deep. Rather, its various pertinent dimensions, taken together and arranged according to a formula, give it the 8-meter rating, and it can race against other boats accorded the 8-meter rating. The problem that arose at the turn of the century in Olympic yachting was that not all the entered countries were using the same method of rating boat classes. Obviously this could lead to severe inequities, since boat designs from one country might be limited more stringently than those from another.

In 1904 (an Olympiad with no yachting events, incidentally) Britain and France agreed (amazingly!) on a rating system called the International Rule of Rating. Universal acceptance was not forthcoming, however, and in 1906 the International Yacht Racing Union was formed. This group, comprised of several European countries, produced the "International Rule of 1906," which became the standard for the 1908 Games.

Over the years many alterations have been made to the list of boat classes raced in the Olympics. In 1908 a 15-meter event was offered, but no one entered it; a 15-meter boat would be at least 75 feet long, and an amateur crew to race such a boat must have been difficult to assemble, the idle rich notwithstanding. That year also marked the one-time-only appearance of a motorboat in Olympic competition, a very temporary bout of insanity.

At the 1920 Antwerp Games, 12-foot and 18-foot dinghy classes were added, beginning a trend toward smaller boats with smaller crews. Another trend moved away from the meter classes to the so-called "one-design" classes, in which each boat is built from the same design, with tight restrictions on modifications, so that boats are virtually identical; this way the sailing skills of the crew are what's being tested in a race. Two one-design classes, the Olympiajolle and the Finn, were created especially for Olympic competition.

SPECTATORS' GUIDE

In sailing, an old cliché states that the shortest distance between two points is a "Z." What this tepid witticism refers to is the sailor's practice of **tacking** in a zig-zag pattern in order to travel in a direction opposite to the wind. Primitive sailing rigs couldn't sail upwind (opposite the direction of the wind) at all. The early sails were simply big pieces of cloth, like a bedspread billowing on the clothesline or a rain poncho suspended between canoe paddles. These sails would simply catch the breeze and push the boat downwind. If the wind was blowing the same direction that early sailors wanted to go, everyone could take it easy and let the wind carry the boat. Otherwise, it was time to get the oars or paddles back out, or else wait for the wind to change.

In modern times, however, this inconvenience is hardly acceptable. A recreational sailor needs to be able to get back to his or her starting place (i.e., where the car is parked), and can't wait for the wind to change; and no sailor wants to motor any great distance (providing motors were invented). With the development of modern sail design, sailing in an upwind direction is possible, and this is accomplished through **tacking**.

The main type of sail on a modern sailboat is usually of triangular configuration. One vertical spar, the **mast**, is mounted on the bottom of the boat somewhere forward of the boat's midpoint. The horizontal spar, or **boom**, is attached perpendicular to the mast, just above the point where the mast enters the deck of the boat. The sail is attached to this framework of spars, the mast and boom.

The key to sailing against the wind is the cut of the sail, which allows it to bag out a bit in the forward area, creating an airfoil shape reminiscent of the profile of an airplane wing. The force generated by air rushing around this curved surface pulls the boat forward. Now, so that sailing won't be too easy for those aristocrats to master, there are limits. A boat cannot aim directly into the wind and hope to move at all. In fact, the closest it can come to sailing into the wind is about 45 degrees, a **point** of sailing known as **beating**. So, if your destination is dead into the wind, what you must do is set a course 45 degrees off the wind's direction on one side, then turn, or **tack**, to sail 45 degrees off the wind's direction on the other side. Thus the Z-shaped path.

To help the boat keep from sliding sideways during this routine, some form of **centerboard** is used. The centerboard extends below the boat's **hull** on a longitudinal plane (from bow to stern) like a fin. It can take the form of a retractable centerboard, which can be pulled up out of the water, or a fixed **keel**, which also serves to add stability by means of **ballast**, or extra weight.

Points of sailing in addition to beating include **running**, which is sailing directly with the wind, and **reaching**, which generally accounts for every arrangement between the two extremes of beating and running.

In competitive sailing, such as the Olympic yachting events, courses are devised that require a crew to use all the points of sailing. The course is in the form of a circuit composed of several segments, or **legs**. The terminal point of each leg is defined by a **buoy** or **mark**. In sailing the course, the boat must round the marks in sequence, but the precise route followed is left up to the skipper. Many of the strategic decisions made in yacht racing involve choosing the best route to reach each mark. On an upwind leg, for example, beating as close to the wind direction as possible may seem expeditious, but higher speed may be achieved by sailing "off the wind" somewhat and reaching instead.

Courses for the Olympics are laid out in varying lengths; the faster classes of boats sail the longer courses. An average course length is about eleven miles. The courses are each composed of six legs. The first leg is upwind, followed by two reaching legs, another upwind leg, a run, and a final upwind leg. Some of the boat classes are allowed to add to their rig large balloon-like sails, called **spinnakers**, that are used during the downwind legs. This presents quite a colorful display to the spectator.

One of the most interesting aspects of yacht racing is the start of the race, or, rather, that portion just prior to the start. As the beginning of the race approaches, visual and audible warnings are given at five-minute intervals. In the vicinity of the starting line, boats maneuver for position. At the moment the starting gun sounds, each crew wants to be as close to the line as possible, without going over it (sort of like "The Price Is Right"). A boat over the line at the gun is disqualified. Rules concerning right-of-way add to the excitement in the pre-race jockeying.

One race is sailed each day in each class. The better a crew finishes, the fewer the points received. Point totals for all the races are added together, dropping the worst race, to determine final standings.

Seven one-design classes are raced in Olympic competition. The **Finn** is a 14' 6" inch centerboard boat with a single-sail **cat rig** sailed by a single crew member. The **470** is a 15' 6" inch centerboard **sloop rigged** (two sails) boat sailed by a crew of two. The **Flying Dutchman** is a 19' 10" inch sloop with a centerboard sailed by two crew. The **Star** and the **Soling** are both fixed-keel sloops. Star measures 22' 7" in length and carries two crew members. Soling is the largest Olympic boat class with the largest crew, at 26' 9" and three crew members.

In addition to these relatively conventional designs, Olympic competition is held for a two-person, 20' **catamaran** (two-hulled boat) called **Tornado**, and a **sailboard** (upon which the sailor stands like a surfboard) called **Windglider.**

BALLAST: extra weight carried for stability; usually lodged in the fixed **keel**.

BEAT: point of sailing most directly upwind or into the wind (about 45 degrees from wind direction); also considered a **close reach**.

BOOM: horizontal pole or spar that the bottom of the sail attaches to.

CAT RIG: sail plan composed of a single sail.

CENTERBOARD: fin-shaped protrusion under the hull that prevents the boat from sliding sideways; unlike a fixed **keel**, a centerboard can be pulled out of the water.

GENOA: in a sloop-rigged boat, the large triangular forward sail (larger than a **jib**, but used in the same way).

JIB: in a sloop-rigged boat, the smaller triangular forward sail (smaller than a **genoa**, but used in the same way).

KEEL: a fixed, fin-shaped protrusion on the bottom of the hull that prevents the boat's sideways slippage; also contains **ballast** (weight) to enhance stability.

LEG: a segment of the yachting race course.

MARK: buoy that defines the endpoint of a **leg** of a race; racers must "round the mark."

MAST: vertical spar or pole that the front edge of the sail attaches to.

REACH: any of the points of sailing between the extremes of **beat** and **run**.

RUDDER: vertical board hinged to the back of the boat that turns the craft.

RUN: point of sailing in which the boat sails directly downwind or with the wind.

SLOOP RIG: sail plan composed of two sails: a mainsail and a **jib** or **genoa**.

TACK: to change direction relative to the wind direction (e.g., changing from having the wind on your right to having the wind on your left; also the term for the technique of sailing zig-zags to travel upwind.

SPINNAKER: large, billowing sail that can be used in place of or with a **jib** or **genoa**; used on downwind points of sailing only.

TILLER: stick attached to the rudder used by the skipper (played by Alan Hale, Jr.) to control steering.

HOPEFULS

Olympic host country Spain has seven Olympic sailing medals, more than in all the other sports combined, and expects to add to that total when the sailing begins at Barcelona. In a summer 1991 Olympic Practice Regatta at the site of the 1992 Olympic Games, Spain garnered the greatest number of medals. Look for 1988 gold medalist José Doreste to sail in the Finn Class, and his brother, 1980 gold medalist Luis Doreste, to skipper a men's 470 Class yacht.

New Zealand will be tough to beat, though, especially if two-time Windgliding gold medalist Bruce Kendall sails again, and Great Britain's Star Class gold medalist Michael McIntyre has maintained his high performance in international competitions through 1991.

The USA—which finished second behind Spain in medals won at the Olympic Practice Regatta—boasts an especially well-rounded sailing team. They dominated the Star Class event at the practice regatta, with Ed Adams and Tom Olson taking the gold, and 1988 Olympic silver medalists Mark Reynolds and Hal Haenel finishing second. Kevin Mahaney skippered a silver medal-winning Soling team, and Courtenay Becker won the bronze in the new Europe Dinghy Class.

The addition of that class to the Olympic Games in 1992 has fueled Elizabeth Kratzig's hope for Olympic competition. In 1991, 17-year-old Kratzig became the first woman to win the coveted Smythe Trophy in the 18-year history of the US Junior Rolex Championships, which happened to feature the Europe dinghy—Kratzig's specialty—in its latest competition. The USA's best hope, though, may be its best female sailor, J. J. Isler, who was also the highest ranking woman in world match race standings in 1991. She will skipper one Women's 470 team, and Jodi Swanson will skipper another.

Schedule

The tentative yachting schedule is as follows:

Monday, July 27
First race

Tuesday, July 28
Second race

Wednesday, July 29
Third race

Thursday, July 30
Fourth race

Friday, July 31
Fifth race

Saturday, August 1
Sixth race

Sunday, August 2
Seventh race

Monday, August 3
Eighth race

Tuesday, August 4
Ninth race

606

HIGHLIGHTS

Although scheduled to be held in the Bay of Salmis in 1896, the first Olympic regattas were held at Meulan and Le Havre, with six nations participating, as part of the 1900 Paris Games. After the sport's eight-year Olympic hiatus, five nations competed in the London Games, but the winners in every class were British. Frances Clytie Rivett-Carnac, who won the seven-meter class with her husband, was the first woman to win in an event not restricted to women or mixed pairs in any sport. Also that year, the Olympic program featured two motorboating events, which were subsequently deep-sixed from the Games.

Four sailing events were held in 1912, the year when four Norwegian brothers—Henrik, Jan, Kristian, and Ole Östervold—won gold medals in the 12-meter class. By 1920 the total number of events had risen to 13, with a complicated scoring system that combined all the races for all the boats of each country. Norway won with 11 yachts sailing in 27 races. Sweden took two classes, the 30- and 40-meter classes; the crew of the larger boat included the Swedish designer Tore Holm.

Nineteen countries took part in the yachting events in Paris in 1924, when the competition was trimmed to three categories. The Dinghy class was won by the Belgians, while Norway sailed away with two medals in the meter classes: Eugen Lunde, whose son, grandson, and daughter-in-law medaled in the 1952 and 1960 Games, sailed the winning Norwegian six-meter in the Paris regatta, while the father-son crew of the two August Ringvolds sailed to victory in the eight-meter event.

The 1928 Olympic regatta hosted a number of celebrities. Twenty-three countries participated in three classes, and the Crown Prince of Norway—soon to be known as King Olav V—won the gold for the six-meter class in *Norna*, while his compatriot, Henrik Robert, won his second silver medal in the 12-foot Dinghy. The well-known French yachtswoman, Virginie Hériot, also made her appearance in the Amsterdam regatta, in a yacht chosen from her fleet named *L'Ailée VI*.

Only eleven countries entered the LA Games, where Tore Holm won his second gold medal, this time in the six-meter. The French captured the single-handed Dinghy, while gold in the Star class, appearing for the first time, was taken by the US. The host country also managed to keep the eight-meter gold at home. The number of participating countries climbed back to twenty-six in the Berlin Games, where the Kieler Förde was the site of the Olympic races. Twenty-five boats participated in the special class of the Olympiajolle, by far the most popular class of 1936; the Netherlands won that class, while the host country took the Star, Great Britain the six-meter, and Italy the eight-meter.

Twenty-three countries participated in the post-war regatta, which was held at Torbay, on the south coast of England. Denmark's Paul Elvstrom won the first of four consecutive one-design titles—from 1948 to 1960—making him the first man to hold on to a title through four quadrennia—in any sport. Also that year, Norwegian Magnus Konow matched the longest span of Olympic participation when he competed in the six-meter events four decades after he first competed in the eight-meter class of 1908, and Great Britain's Durward Knowles took part in the first of what would be a record of seven Olympic Games.

Rickard Sarby, a Swedish hairdresser, submitted the winning Firefly single-hander in the 1952 Games, and Sarby's Finn remained the Olympic single-hander in subsequent Games. Having come in fourth at Torbay, Sarby earned a bronze in the Firefly at the Helsinki Games. A total of 29 countries participated: Norwegian Thor Thorvladsen captured his second gold in the Dragon, and Italy won the gold in the Star. American Herman Whiton won his second gold in the six-meter, and his compatriot, Dr. Britton Chance—sailing the only American 5.5-meter of the day—took home the gold as well.

In 1956, 28 countries competed with a total of 71 boats, not least of which was the royally pedigreed *Bluebottle*, owned by Queen Elizabeth II and Prince Philip, and skippered by the Royal Navy's Commander Graham Mann. While the *Bluebottle* took the bronze for the Dragon, Sweden's Folke Bohlin won on a tie breaker with Denmark's Ole Bernsten in that class. New Zealand took the 12-meter and the US claimed gold in the Star, while Paul Elvstrom went on to his third gold medal, in the Finn class.

The Russians took their first yachting gold medal at Naples in 1960, in the Star class, albeit in an American boat with American sails. The US took the 5.5-meter gold, while the Dragon gold this time went to the Crown Prince Constantine of the Hellens, who would later become the King of Greece. Norwegian Peder Lunde, Jr.—part of the famous Lunde sailing clan—took the inaugural Flying Dutchman gold, while Paul Elvstorm won yet another gold in the single-handed Dinghy.

At Enoshima, in 1964, Denmark's Ole Berntsen this time succeeded in capturing the Dragon gold; the Flying Dutchman went to New Zealand, while the Bahamas captured the Star. Although East and West Germany entered a combined team, the IYRU authorized a West German helmsman, Willi Kuhweide, who took the Finn gold for Germany.

In Acapulco in 1968, 123 boats from 41 countries competed. The Soviets medaled again, this time in the Finn class. Great Britain's Flying Dutchman, *Super . . . docious*, helmed by Rodney Pattison, finished first in every race except one. Pattison not only won the Flying Dutchman, but set Olympic records as well; their record-setting boat is now in the Britain's National Maritime Museum in Greenwich, England.

In 1972, when the Soling and Tempest classes were introduced, 42 countries competed with 165 boats in six classes. Bud Melges, Bill Allen, and Bill Bensten won the gold medal for the US in the Soling class, while Glen Foster and Peter Dean earned a silver in the Tempest; the crew of Don Cohan, Charles Horter, and John Marshall took the bronze in the Dragon class. Soviet Valentin

Mankin won his second gold in the Finn class, Australia won the Star and the Dragon, while Serg Maury won the gold for France in the Finn class. Great Britain's Rodney Pattisson won his second Flying Dutchman gold in *Superdoso*, and Paul Elvstrom, who had attempted to become the first man to win gold medals at five different Games, finished only 13th overall in the Soling class.

The Danish Soling team won by such a narrow margin in 1976 that another eight seconds would have put them out of the running for medals. The US team of John Kolius, Walter Glasgow, and Richard Hoepfner came in second, while the German Democratic Republic took third. The US also took a silver in the Tornado, and a bronze in the now discontinued Tempest class, with a crew of Dennis Conner and Conn Findlay.

At the age of 41, Valentin Mankin captured his third gold medal for the Soviets in the Star class in 1980, when the host country won an additional silver and bronze. Brazil took two golds at Moscow, in the Tornado and 470 classes, while Spain's victory in the Flying Dutchman class was its lone gold in the 1980 Games. Denmark, in the Soling class, and Finland, in the Finn class, were the other gold medalist nations. Also in 1980, a yachtsman competed from Botswana, a country so arid that it calls its money by the Botswanian word for "rain."

All 13 members of the US team won either gold or silver medals at the 1984 Games: US skippers captured three golds and four silvers in seven classes of boats. The most "weathered" sailor of 1984 was Denmark's Paul Elvstrom, at 59, whose fourth and last Olympic gold had come in 1960; his daughter Trine served as crew, flying on the boat-stabilizing trapeze of the Tornado catamaran class; the boat came in fourth. Also that year, Canadians and New Zealanders won three medals each. In the debut appearance of windgliding at the Games, the Netherlands won the gold medal while Randall Scott Steele of the US took the silver; Bruce Kendall of New Zealand came in third.

1988 marked the inauguration of women's yachting events at the Games, and the team of Allison Jolly and Lynne Jewell won the women's 470 class for the US; Sweden and the Soviet Union came in second and third; a French team won the men's 470. New Zealand's Bruce Kendall this time took first place in windgliding's second appearance at the Games, Spain took the Finn class gold— while the Virgin Islands took the silver—Denmark won the Flying Dutchman, East Germany the Soling, and Great Britain won the Star class, in which the US took silver. France captured the Tornado class, while New Zealand and Brazil placed second and third, respectively.

Dennis Conner

Some sports fans know Dennis Conner as the first American in 132 years to lose the *America's* Cup in 1987, then reclaim it three years later.

Others know him as a man who is simply obsessed with winning—at any and all costs. "I think I'm abnormal, yes," Conner confessed to *The New York Times* in September, 1990.

Few know him as an Olympian. But bad boy Dennis Conner, 49, won a bronze medal for the United States during the 1976 Montréal Olympics, competing in the Tempest small-boat class, an event that Conner has characterized as "'the America's Cup of small-boat racing."

Conner describes himself in his book, *No Excuse To Lose*, as a chubby, clumsy kid with a "bit of an inferiority complex," who hung out around the San Diego Yacht Club, a half block—five doors— from his house, "the way some kids hang around the local pool parlor."

The son of a commercial fisherman and factory worker, Conner had a paper route for the *San Diego Union* and a *TV Guide* route and was constantly doing boat chores for the club's sailors in exchange for rides.

He didn't so much develop a passion for sailing as he did a single-minded drive to succeed. "Sailing was one of the few things that I could do really well," Conner wrote in his book, "and since it was important for me to excel at something, I kept at it."

He told *Time* magazine in 1987: "I don't like to sail. I like to compete. I guess I don't *dislike* it, but my sailing is just the bottom line, like adding up the final score in bridge. My real interest is in the tremendous game of life."

He wrote in his book: "It's almost as though I'm addicted to the competition."

At Kingston, Ontario, in 1976, site of the small boat Olympic events, Conner and crewmate Conn Findlay were leading by almost four minutes at a stage in the fifth—and pivotal—of the seven races. Wind shifts and a flat calm dropped them to ninth and out of serious contention for a gold medal, the "one Olympic medal," he said heading into the race, "that really counts."

Conner and Findlay's bad luck was described by one racing expert as a "whim of the weather, something no one can predict. The wind just lightened up—he got shut out."

After the race, Conner, ever the competitor, said: "Winning the bronze medal was a lot better than winning no medal at all, but losing the chance at the gold because of that terrible fifth race was depressing."

Described as emotional, often less than articulate, and lacking in charisma—though highly intelligent and amazingly retentive— Conner was depicted by sailing competitors in *American Baby* magazine as someone with "an ability to judge time and distance with mechanical accuracy, a skill which is uncanny," and as a person "able to concentrate [a] highly technical mind for long periods on a single goal, to the exclusion of almost everything else."

No surprises there. Conner, who runs a wholesale and retail carpeting and drapery business in San Diego, postponed his wedding day twice because of sailboat races.

"Let me tell you how ambitious Dennis was," Conner's mother, Pamela told *The New York Times*. "He would go [to the service station at the corner] and take the discarded oil cans ... and he would drain the oil into a jar. He'd sell the oil back to the guys at the yacht club."

During the last year he's been competing *against* the Olympics. In trying to raise $27 million in corporate pledges for his May 1992 America's Cup defense in San Diego, he's bucked up against fundraisers trying to woo some of the same sponsors—and money— for the Barcelona Games. —*E.K.*

Medalists

Yachting — Men's 470

1988 1. France, 34.70, Thierry Peponnet, Luc Pillot
2. Soviet Union, 46.00, Tynou Tyniste, Toomas Tyniste
3. USA, 51.00, John Shadden, Charlie McKee

1984 1. Spain, 33.70, Jose Luis Doreste, Roberto Molina
2. USA, 43.00, Stephen Benjamin, H. Christopher Steinfeld
3. France, 49.40, Thierry Peponnet, Luc Pillot

1980 1. Brazil, 36.4, Marcos Pinto Rizzo Soares, Eduardo Henrique Penido
2. East Germany, 38.7, Jorn Borowski, Egbert Swensson
3. Finland, 39.7, Jouko Lindgren, Georg Tallberg

1976 1. West Germany, 42.40, Frank Huebner, Harro Bode
2. Spain, 49.70, Antonio Gorostegui, Pedro Luis Millet
3. Australia, 57.00, Ian Brown, Ian Ruff

Yachting — Women's 470

1988 1. USA, 26.70, Allison Jolly, Lynne Jewell
2. Sweden, 40.00, Marit Soderstrom, Birgitta Bengtsson
3. Soviet Union, 45.40, Larissa Moskalenko, Irina Tchounikhovskai

Yachting — Finn

1988 1. Jose Luis Doreste, Spain, 38.10
2. Peter Holmerg, Virgin Islands, 40.40
3. John Cutler, New Zealand, 45.00

1984 1. Russell Coutts, New Zealand, 34.70
2. John Bertrand, USA, 37.00
3. Terry Neilson, Canada, 37.70

1980 1. Esko Rechardt, Finland, 36.7
2. Wolfgang Mayrhofer, Austria, 46.7
3. Andrei Balashov, Soviet Union, 47.4

1976 1. Jochen Schumann, East Germany, 35.40
2. Andrei Balashov, Soviet Union, 39.70
3. John Bertrand, Australia, 46.40

1972 1. Serge Maury, France, 58.0
2. Ilias Hatzipavlis, Greece, 71.0
3. Viktor Potapov, Soviet Union, 74.7

1968 1. Valentin Mankin, Soviet Union, 11.7
2. Hubert Raudaschl, Austria, 53.4
3. Fabio Albarelli, Italy, 55.1

1964 1. Wilhelm Kuhweide, West Germany, 7638
2. Peter Barrett, USA, 6373
3. Henning Wind, Denmark, 6190

1960 1. Paul Elvstrom, Denmark, 8171
2. Aleksandr Chuchelov, Soviet Union, 6520
3. Andre Nelis, Belgium, 5934

1956 1. Paul Elvstrom, Denmark, 7509
2. Andre Nelis, Belgium, 6254
3. John Marvin, USA, 5953

1952 1. Paul Elvstrom, Denmark, 8209
2. Charles Currey, Great Britain, 5449
3. Rickard Sarby, Sweden 5051

1948 1. Paul Elvstrom, Denmark, 5543
2. Ralph Evans, USA, 5408
3. Jacobus H. de Jong, Netherlands, 5204

1936 1. Daniel M. J. Kagchelland, Netherlands, 163
2. Werner Krogmann, Germany, 150
3. Peter M. Scott, Great Britain, 131

1932 1. Jacques Lebrun, France, 87
2. Adriaan L. J. Maas, Netherlands, 85
3. Santiago Amat Cansino, Spain, 76

1928 1. Sven Thorell, Sweden
2. Henrik Robert, Norway
3. Bertil Broman, Finland

1924 1. Leon Huybrechts, Belgium, 2
2. Henrik Robert, Norway, 7
3. Hans Dittmar, Finland, 8

1896-1920 **Not held**

Yachting — Flying Dutchman

1988 1. Denmark, 31.40, Jorgen Bojsen-Moller, Christian Gronborg
2. Norway, 37.40, Olepetter Pollen, Erik Bjorkum
3. Canada, 48.40, Frank McLaughlin, John Millen

1984 1. USA, 19.70, Jonathan McKee, William Carl Buchan
2. Canada, 22.70, Terry McLaughlin, Evert Bastet
3. Great Britain, 48.70, Jonathan Richards, Peter Allam

1980 1. Spain, 30.0, Alesandro Abascal, Miguel Noguer
2. Ireland, 30.0, David Wilkins, James Wilkinson
3. Hungary, 45.7, Szabolcs Detre, Zsolt Detre

1976 1. West Germany, 34.70, Jorg Diesch, Eckart Diesch
2. Great Britain, 51.70, Rodney Pattison, Julian Brooke Houghton
3. Brazil, 52.10, Reinaldo Conrad, Peter Ficker

1972 1. Great Britain, 22.7, Rodney Pattison, Christopher Davies
2. France, 40.7, Yves Pajot, Marc Pajot
3. West Germany, 51.1, Ullrich Libor, Peter Naumann

1968 1. Great Britain, 3.0 Rodney Pattison, Iain S. MacDonald-Smith
2. West Germany, 43.7, Ullrich Libor, Peter Naumann
3. Brazil, 48.4, Reinaldo Conrad, Burkhard Cordes

1964 1. New Zealand, 6255, Helmer Pedersen, Earle Wells
2. Great Britain, 5556, Franklyn Musto, Arthur Morgan
3. USA, 5158, Harry Melges, William Bentsen

1960 1. Norway, 6774, Peder Lunde Jr., Bjorn Bergvall
2. Denmark, 5991, Hans Fogh, Ole Erik Petersen
3. West Germany, 5882, Rolf Mulka, Ingo von Bredow, Achim Kadelbach

1896-1956 Not held

Yachting — Division II Sailboard (Windgliding)

1988 1. Bruce Kendall, New Zealand, 35.40
2. Jan D. Boersma, Netherlands Antilles, 42.70
3. Michael Gebhardt, USA, 48.00

1984 1. Stephan Van Den Berg, Netherlands, 27.70
2. Randall Scott Steele, USA, 46.00
3. Bruce Kendall, New Zealand, 46.40

Yachting — Soling

1988 1. East Germany, 11.70, Jochen Schuemann, Thomas Flach, Bernd Jackel
2. USA, 14.00, John Kostecki, William Baylis, Robert Billingham
3. Denmark, 52.70, Jesper Bank, Jesper Mathiasen, Steen Secher

1984 1. USA, 33.70, Robert Haines Jr., Edward Trevelyan, Roderick Davis
2. Brazil, 43.40, Torben Grael, Daniel Adler, Ronaldo Senfft
3. Canada, 49.70, Hans Fogh, John Kerr, Steve Calder

1980 1. Denmark, 23.0, Paul R. H. Jensen, Valdemar Bandolowski, Erik Hansen
2. Soviet Union, 30.4, Boris Budnikov, Aleksandr Budnikov, Nikolai Poliakov
3. Greece, 31.1, Anastassios Boudouris, Anastassios Gavrilis, Aristidis Rapanakis

1976 1. Denmark, 46.70, Paul R. H. Jensen, Valdemar Bandolowski, Erik Hansen
2. USA, 47.40, John Kolius, Walter Glasgow, Richard Hoepfner

3. East Germany, 47.40, Dieter Below, Michael Zachries, Olaf Engelhardt

1972 1. USA, 8.7, Harry Melges, William Bentsen, William Allen
2. Sweden, 31.7, Stig Wennerstrom, Lennart Roslund, Bo Knape, Stefan Krook
3. Canada, 47.1, David Miller, John Ekels, Paul Cote

1896-1968 Not held

Yachting — Star

1988 1. Great Britain, 45.70, Michael McIntyre, Bryn Vaile
2. USA, 48.00, Mark Reynolds, Hal Haenal
3. Brazil, 50.00, Torben Grael, Nelson Falcao

1984 1. USA, 29.70, William E. Buchan, Stephen Erikson
2. West Germany, 41.40, Joachim Griese, Michael Marcour
3. Italy, 43.50, Giorgio Gorla, Alfio Peraboni

1980 1. Soviet Union, 24.7, Valentin Mankin, Aleksandr Muzychenko
2. Austria, 31.7, Hubert Raudaschl, Karl Ferstl
3. Italy, 36.1, Giorgio Gorla, Alfio Peraboni

1976 Not held

1972 1. Australia, 28.1, David Forbes, John Anderson
2. Sweden, 44.0, Pelle Pettersson, Stellan Westerdahl
3. West Germany, 44.4, Wilhelm Kuhweide, Karsten Meyer

1968 1. USA, 14.4, Lowell North, Peter Barrett
2. Norway, 43.7, Peder Lunde, Per Olav Wiken
3. Italy, 44.7, Franco Cavallo, Camilo Gargano

1964 1. Bahamas, 5664, Durward Knowles, C. Cecil Cooke
2. USA, 5585, Richard Stearns, Lynn Williams
3. Sweden, 5527, Pelle Pettersson, Holger Sundstrom

1960 1. Soviet Union, 7619, Timir Pinegin, Fyodor Shutkov
2. Portugal, 6665, Jose Quina, Mario Quina
3. USA, 6269, William Parks, Robert Halperin

1956 1. USA, 5876, Herbert Williams, Lawrence Low
2. Italy, 5649, Agostino Straulino, Nicolo Rode
3. Bahamas, 5223, Durward Knowles, Sloan Farrington

1952 1. Italy, 7635, Agostino Straulino, Nicolo Rode
2. USA, 7126, John Reid, John Price
3. Portugal, 4903, Joaquim De Mascarenhas Fiuza, Francisco Rebelo De Andrade

1948 1. USA, 5828, Hilary Smart, Paul Smart
2. Cuba, 4949, Carlos De Cardenas Culmell, Carlos De Cardenas, Jr.

612

3. Netherlands, 4731, Adriaan Maas, Edward Sutterheim

1936 1. Germany, 80, Peter Bischoff, Hans-Joachim Weise
2. Sweden, 64, Arvid Laurin, Uno Wallentin
3. Netherlands, 63, Willem de Vries-Lentsch, Adriaan Maas

1932 1. USA, 46, Gilbert Gray, Andrew Libano
2. Great Britain, 35, Colin Ratsey, Peter Jaffe
3. Sweden, 28, Gunnar Asther, Danile Sunden-Cullberg

1896-1928 Not held

Yachting — Tornado

1988 1. France, 16.00, Jean-Yves Le Deroff, Nicolas Henard
2. New Zealand, 35.40, Christopher Timms, Rex Sellers
3. Brazil, 40.10, Lars Grael, Clinio Freitas

1984 1. New Zealand, Rex Sellers, Christopher Timms
2. USA, Randy Smyth, Jay Glaser
3. Australia, Chris Cairns, John Anderson

1980 1. Brazil, 21.4, Alexandre Welter, Lars Sigurd Bjorkstrom
2. Denmark, 30.4, Peter Due, Per Kjergard
3. Sweden, 33.7, Goran Marstrom, Jorgen Ragnarsson

1976 1. Great Britain, 18.00, Reginald White, John Osborn
2. USA, 36.00, David McFaull, Michael Rothwell
3. West Germany, 37.70, Jorg Spengler, Jorg Schmall

Yachting — Tempest

1976 1. Sweden, 14.0, John Albrechtson, Ingvar Hansson
2. Soviet Union, 30.4, Valentin Mankin, Vladislav Akimenko
3. USA, 32.7, Dennis Conner, Conn Findlay

1972 1. Soviet Union, 28.1, Valentin Mankin, Vitali Dyrdyra
2. Great Britain, 34.4, Alan Warren, David Hunt
3. USA, 47.7, Glen Foster, Peter Dean

1896-1968 Not held

Yachting

613

Photographs and illustrations appearing in *Olympics Factbook* were received by the following sources: photograph of Terry Schroeder: courtesy of United States Water Polo; photo of Erika Saloumiae: courtesy of K. A. Hugelier; all other photographs: AP/Wide World Photos